APA Handbook of

Forensic
Psychology

APA Handbooks in Psychology® Series

APA Handbook of Industrial and Organizational Psychology—three volumes
  Sheldon Zedeck, Editor-in-Chief

APA Handbook of Ethics in Psychology—two volumes
  Samuel J. Knapp, Editor-in-Chief

APA Educational Psychology Handbook—three volumes
  Karen R. Harris, Steve Graham, and Tim Urdan, Editors-in-Chief

APA Handbook of Research Methods in Psychology—three volumes
  Harris Cooper, Editor-in-Chief

APA Addiction Syndrome Handbook—two volumes
  Howard J. Shaffer, Editor-in-Chief

APA Handbook of Counseling Psychology—two volumes
  Nadya A. Fouad, Editor-in-Chief

APA Handbook of Behavior Analysis—two volumes
  Gregory J. Madden, Editor-in-Chief

APA Handbook of Psychology, Religion, and Spirituality—two volumes
  Kenneth I. Pargament, Editor-in-Chief

APA Handbook of Testing and Assessment in Psychology—three volumes
  Kurt F. Geisinger, Editor-in-Chief

APA Handbook of Multicultural Psychology—two volumes
  Frederick T. L. Leong, Editor-in-Chief

APA Handbook of Sexuality and Psychology—two volumes
  Deborah L. Tolman and Lisa M. Diamond, Editors-in-Chief

APA Handbook of Personality and Social Psychology—four volumes
  Mario Mikulincer and Phillip R. Shaver, Editors-in-Chief

APA Handbook of Career Intervention—two volumes
  Paul J. Hartung, Mark L. Savickas, and W. Bruce Walsh, Editors-in-Chief

APA Handbook of Forensic Psychology—two volumes
  Brian L. Cutler and Patricia A. Zapf, Editors-in-Chief

APA Handbooks in Psychology

APA Handbook of
Forensic Psychology

VOLUME 1

Individual and Situational Influences in
Criminal and Civil Contexts

Brian L. Cutler and Patricia A. Zapf, *Editors-in-Chief*

American Psychological Association • Washington, DC

Published by
American Psychological Association
750 First Street, NE
Washington, DC 20002-4242
www.apa.org

To order
APA Order Department
P.O. Box 92984
Washington, DC 20090-2984
Tel: (800) 374-2721; Direct: (202) 336-5510
Fax: (202) 336-5502; TDD/TTY: (202) 336-6123
Online: www.apa.org/books/
E-mail: order@apa.org

In the U.K., Europe, Africa, and the Middle East, copies may be ordered from
American Psychological Association
3 Henrietta Street
Covent Garden, London
WC2E 8LU England

AMERICAN PSYCHOLOGICAL ASSOCIATION STAFF
Gary R. VandenBos, *Publisher*
Julia Frank-McNeil, *Senior Director, APA Books*
Theodore J. Baroody, *Director, Reference, APA Books*
Patricia D. Mathis, *Reference Editorial Manager, APA Books*
Lisa T. Corry, *Project Editor, APA Books*

Typeset in Berkeley by Cenveo Publisher Services, Columbia, MD

Printer: Maple Press, York, PA
Cover Designer: Naylor Design, Washington, DC

Library of Congress Cataloging-in-Publication Data

APA handbook of forensic psychology / Brian L. Cutler and Patricia A. Zapf,
Editors-in-Chief.
     pages   cm. — (APA handbooks in psychology)
  Includes bibliographical references and index.
  ISBN 978-1-4338-1793-9 — ISBN 1-4338-1793-4
  1. Forensic psychology—Handbooks, manuals, etc. I. Cutler, Brian L.,
editor of compilation. II. Zapf, Patricia A., 1971– editor of compilation.
  RA1148.A63 2014
  614′.1—dc23
                      2014014393

British Library Cataloguing-in-Publication Data
A CIP record is available from the British Library.

Printed in the United States of America
First Edition

http://dx.doi.org/10.1037/14461-000

Contents

Editorial Board

About the Editors-in-Chief

Brian L. Cutler, PhD, earned a doctorate degree in social psychology from the University of Wisconsin–Madison in 1987. He served on the faculties of Florida International University and the University of North Carolina at Charlotte. He currently serves as professor and associate dean of the Faculty of Social Sciences and Humanities at the University of Ontario Institute of Technology. Dr. Cutler's primary area of research is forensic psychology. He is the editor of *Reform of Eyewitness Identification Procedures, Conviction of the Innocent: Lessons From Psychological Research, Expert Testimony on the Psychology of Eyewitness Identification*, and the *Encyclopedia of Psychology and Law*. He is also the author or coauthor of four books; 25 chapters in edited volumes; and 67 articles in peer-reviewed psychology, social psychology, psychology-law, and law journals. Dr. Cutler has taught undergraduate and graduate courses in introductory psychology, social psychology, psychology-law, research methods, professional writing, and professional development. He has trained undergraduate, masters, and doctoral students in psychology-law research. He has also served as a mentor to junior faculty members, providing professional development guidance and advice. Dr. Cutler served as editor-in-chief of *Law and Human Behavior*, the journal of the American Psychology-Law Society, from 2005 to 2011. He also served as president-elect, president, and immediate past president of the American Psychology-Law Society from 2011 to 2013. He has taught continuing legal education courses on psychology-law topics to attorneys in the United States and has served as a consultant and expert witness in cases involving eyewitness identification and false confessions in the United States and Canada.

Patricia A. Zapf, PhD, earned a doctorate degree in clinical forensic psychology from Simon Fraser University in Canada and is currently a professor in the Department of Psychology at John Jay College of Criminal Justice, The City University of New York. She was recently elected president of the American Psychology-Law Society, and she is the editor of the American Psychology-Law Society book series and the associate editor of *Law and Human Behavior*. Dr. Zapf is the author of eight books and manuals and more than 85 articles and chapters, mainly on the assessment and conceptualization of criminal competencies. She was appointed Fellow of the American Psychological Association and Distinguished Member of the American Psychology-Law Society in 2006 for outstanding contributions to the field of law and psychology for her work in competency evaluation. In addition to her academic endeavors, Dr. Zapf serves as a consultant to various criminal justice and policy organizations and has a private practice in forensic assessment. She has conducted more than 2,500 forensic evaluations in the United States and Canada and has served as an expert witness in a number of cases, including the competency hearing of Jose Padilla. Dr. Zapf is the author of *Best Practices in Forensic Mental Health Assessment: Evaluation of Competence to Stand Trial*; editor of *Forensic Assessments in Criminal and Civil Law: A Handbook for Lawyers*; and associate editor of the *Encyclopedia of Psychology and Law*. She served on the National Judicial College's Mental Competency: Best Practices Model panel of experts and travels throughout the United States and internationally to train legal and mental health professionals on best practices in forensic evaluation.

Contributors

Marc J. Ackerman, PhD, Wisconsin School of Professional Psychology, Milwaukee

Sara C. Appleby, PhD, Department of Psychology, John Jay College of Criminal Justice, The City University of New York

Leslie Ashburn-Nardo, PhD, Department of Psychology, Indiana University–Purdue University at Indianapolis

Craig Bennell, PhD, Department of Psychology, Carleton University, Ottawa, Ontario, Canada

Eve M. Brank, JD, PhD, Department of Psychology, University of Nebraska–Lincoln

Shelley L. Brown, PhD, Department of Psychology, Carleton University, Ottawa, Ontario, Canada

Sonja P. Brubacher, PhD, Department of Psychology, Central Michigan University, Mt. Pleasant

Erin Crites, MA, Department of Criminology, Law and Society, George Mason University, Fairfax, VA

Keith R. Cruise, PhD, MLS, Department of Psychology, Fordham University, New York, NY

Jennie Davis, MS, Department of Psychology, Drexel University, Philadelphia, PA

David DeMatteo, JD, PhD, ABPP, Department of Psychology and School of Law, Drexel University, Philadelphia, PA

Jason J. Dickinson, PhD, Robert D. McCormick Center for Child Advocacy and Policy, Montclair State University, Montclair, NJ

Kevin S. Douglas, LLB, PhD, Department of Psychology, Simon Fraser University, Burnaby, British Columbia, Canada

Eric Y. Drogin, JD, PhD, ABPP, Harvard Medical School, Department of Psychiatry, Beth Israel Deaconess Medical Center, Boston, MA

John F. Edens, PhD, Department of Psychology, Texas A&M University, College Station

Helen M. Farrell, MD, Harvard Medical Faculty Physicians, Beth Israel Deaconess Medical Center, Boston, MA

Chelsea E. Fiduccia, Doctoral Candidate, Department of Psychology, University of North Texas, Denton

Sarah Filone, MA, Department of Psychology, Drexel University, Philadelphia, PA

Melodie Foellmi, Doctoral Candidate, Department of Psychology, Fordham University, New York, NY

Erika Fountain, **Doctoral Candidate**, Department of Psychology, Georgetown University, Washington, DC

Shannon Gottschall, **Doctoral Candidate**, Department of Psychology, Carleton University, Ottawa, Ontario, Canada

Jonathan W. Gould, **PhD, ABPP**, Charlotte Psychotherapy and Consultation Group PLLC, Charlotte, NC

Duncan Greig, **MA**, Department of Psychology, Simon Fraser University, Burnaby, British Columbia, Canada, and British Columbia Mental Health and Substance Use Services, Provincial Health Services Authority, Port Coquitlam, British Columbia, Canada

Jennifer Groscup, **JD, PhD**, Department of Psychology, Scripps College, Claremont, CA

Thomas J. Guilmette, **PhD, ABPP-CN**, Department of Psychology, Providence College, Providence, RI; and Department of Psychiatry and Human Behavior, Alpert Medical School of Brown University, Providence, RI

Laura S. Guy, **PhD**, Department of Psychiatry, University of Massachusetts Medical School, Worcester ProActive ReSolutions Inc., Vancouver, British Columbia, Canada

Leigh D. Hagan, **PhD, ABPP**, Department of Psychiatry and Behavioral Sciences, Eastern Virginia Medical School, Norfolk

John Hamel, **LCSW**, John Hamel and Associates, San Rafael, CA

Craig Haney, **PhD**, Department of Psychology, University of California, Santa Cruz

Stephen D. Hart, **PhD**, Department of Psychology, Simon Fraser University, Burnaby, British Columbia; and Faculty of Psychology, University of Bergen, Norway

Kirk Heilbrun, **PhD**, Department of Psychology, Drexel University, Philadelphia, PA

Larry Heuer, **PhD**, Department of Psychology, Barnard College, Columbia University, New York, NY

Holly Hinz, **Doctoral Candidate**, Department of Psychology, Fordham University, New York, NY

Jacqueline Howe, **Doctoral Candidate**, Department of Psychology, Fordham University, New York, NY

Jennifer S. Hunt, **PhD**, Department of Psychology, Buffalo State, State University of New York

Saul M. Kassin, **PhD**, Department of Psychology, John Jay College of Criminal Justice, The City University of New York

Michael Keesler, **JD, PhD**, Department of Psychology, Drexel University, Philadelphia, PA

Shannon E. Kelley, **Doctoral Candidate**, Department of Psychology, Texas A&M University, College Station

Drew A. Kingston, **PhD**, Royal Ottawa Health Care Group, Brockville, Ontario, Canada

Margaret Bull Kovera, **PhD**, Department of Psychology, John Jay College of Criminal Justice, The City University of New York

Jeff Kukucka, **MA**, Department of Psychology, John Jay College of Criminal Justice, The City University of New York

Casey D. LaDuke, **Doctoral Candidate**, Department of Psychology, Drexel University, Philadelphia, PA

Lora M. Levett, **PhD**, Department of Sociology and Criminology & Law, University of Florida, Gainesville

Mona Lynch, **PhD**, Department of Criminology, Law and Society, University of California, Irvine

Douglas Mossman, MD, Department of Psychiatry and Behavioral Neuroscience, University of Cincinnati, Cincinnati, OH

Megan Murphy, JD, Doctoral Candidate, Department of Psychology and School of Law, Drexel University, Philadelphia, PA

Daniel C. Murrie, PhD, Institute of Law, Psychiatry, and Public Policy, University of Virginia, and Department of Psychiatry and Neurobehavioral Sciences, University of Virginia School of Medicine, Charlottesville, VA

Tonia L. Nicholls, PhD, Department of Psychiatry, University of British Columbia, Vancouver, British Columbia, Canada; Department of Psychology, Simon Fraser University, Burnaby, British Columbia, Canada; and British Columbia Mental Health and Substance Use Services, Provincial Health Services Authority, Port Coquitlam, British Columbia, Canada

Natalia L. Nikolova, PhD, Department of Psychology, Simon Fraser University, Burnaby, British Columbia, Canada

Ira K. Packer, PhD, ABPP, University of Massachusetts Medical School, Worcester, MA

Jennifer T. Perillo, PhD, Department of Psychological Sciences, Winston-Salem State University, Winston-Salem, NC

Lisa Drago Piechowski, PhD, ABPP, American School of Professional Psychology, Argosy University, Washington, DC

Ashley Pierson, Doctoral Candidate, Department of Psychology, Fordham University, New York, NY

Debra Ann Poole, PhD, Department of Psychology, Central Michigan University, Mt. Pleasant

Courtney Porter, MA, Department of Criminology, Law and Society, George Mason University, Fairfax, VA

Louise Porter, PhD, ARC Centre of Excellence in Policing and Security, Griffith University, Mt. Gravatt, Australia

Richard Rogers, PhD, ABPP, Department of Psychology, University of North Texas, Denton

Barry Rosenfeld, PhD, ABPP, Department of Psychology, Fordham University, New York, NY

R. Barry Ruback, JD, PhD, Department of Sociology and Criminology, Pennsylvania State University, University Park

Michael C. Seto, PhD, Royal Ottawa Health Care Group, Brockville, Ontario, Canada

Diane Sivasubramaniam, PhD, Department of Psychological Sciences, Swinburne University of Technology, Hawthorn, Australia

Katherine A. Sliter, PhD, Department of Psychology, Indiana University–Purdue University at Indianapolis

Brent Snook, PhD, Department of Psychology, Memorial University of Newfoundland, St. John's, Newfoundland, Canada

Nancy K. Steblay, PhD, Department of Psychology, Augsburg College, Minneapolis, MN

Skye Stephens, Doctoral Candidate, Department of Psychology, Ryerson University, Toronto, Ontario, Canada

Margaret S. Stockdale, PhD, Department of Psychology, Indiana University–Purdue University at Indianapolis

Heidi Strohmaier, MS, Department of Psychology, Drexel University, Philadelphia, PA

Faye S. Taxman, PhD, Department of Criminology, Law and Society, George Mason University, Fairfax, VA

Paul J. Taylor, PhD, Department of Psychology, Lancaster University, Lancaster, England; and Department of Psychology of Conflict, Risk, and Safety, University of Twente, Enschede, the Netherlands

Sarah Vidal, Doctoral Candidate, Department of Psychology, Georgetown University, Washington, DC

Jill Viglione, Doctoral Candidate, Department of Criminology, Law and Society, George Mason University, Fairfax, VA

Aldert Vrij, PhD, Department of Psychology, University of Portsmouth, Portsmouth, England

Joanna Weill, Doctoral Candidate, Department of Psychology, University of California, Santa Cruz

Jennifer L. Woolard, PhD, Department of Psychology, Georgetown University, Washington, DC

Lindsey E. Wylie, MA, JD, Department of Psychology, University of Nebraska–Lincoln

Heather Zelle, JD, PhD, Institute of Law, Psychiatry, and Public Policy, University of Virginia, Charlottesville

Series Preface

The *APA Handbook of Forensic Psychology* is the 14th publication to be released in the American Psychological Association's *APA Handbooks in Psychology®* series, instituted in 2010. The series primarily comprises two-, three-, and four-volume sets focused on core subfields, but several single-volume handbooks on highly focused content areas and emerging subfields will also be released in coming years. A complete listing of the series titles to date can be found on p. ii.

Each publication in the series is primarily formulated to address the reference interests and needs of researchers, clinicians, and practitioners in psychology. Each also addresses the needs of graduate students for well-organized and highly detailed supplementary texts, whether to "fill in" their own specialty areas or to acquire solid familiarity with other specialties and emerging trends across the breadth of psychology. Many of the sets additionally bear strong interest for professionals in pertinent complementary fields (i.e., depending on content area), be they corporate executives and human resources personnel; psychiatrists; doctors and other health personnel; teachers and school administrators; cultural diversity and pastoral counselors; legal professionals; and so forth.

Under the direction of small and select editorial boards consisting of top scholars in the field, with chapters authored by both senior and rising researchers and practitioners, each reference set commits to a steady focus on best science and best practice. Coverage converges on what is currently known in the particular topical area (including basic historical reviews) and the identification of the most pertinent sources of information in both the core and evolving literature. Volumes and chapters alike pinpoint practical issues; probe unresolved and controversial topics; and highlight future theoretical, research, and practice trends. The editors provide guidance to the "dialogue" among chapters through internal cross-referencing that demonstrates a robust integration of topics. The user is thus offered a clear understanding of the complex interrelationships within each field.

With the imprimatur of the largest scientific and professional organization representing psychology in the United States and the largest association of psychologists in the world, and with content edited and authored by some of its most respected members, the *APA Handbooks in Psychology* series is an indispensable and authoritative reference resource to turn to for researchers, instructors, practitioners, and field leaders alike.

Gary R. VandenBos
APA Publisher

Introduction: The Definition, Breadth, and Importance of Forensic Psychology

Forensic psychology denotes the application of the science and practice of psychology to law and legal systems. The science of forensic psychology applies basic psychological theory and research methods from diverse psychological perspectives to address issues of relevance to law, legal practice, and law-related policy. Some academic programs use the name forensic psychology to refer to the more narrow application of clinical psychology to the legal setting, but contemporarily, forensic psychology is broadly defined with respect to psychological perspectives. The diverse psychological approaches to forensic psychology influence both the research and practice of forensic psychologists.

For example, *clinical* psychological approaches advance our understanding of the relation between psychological disorders, symptoms, and criminal behavior and the extent to which psychological evaluations can help determine a person's risk of dangerousness or recidivism. In practice, clinical psychologists may conduct forensic psychological evaluations that are relevant to criminal and civil litigation, addressing such issues as competence (e.g., to stand trial, to fulfill responsibilities as a parent or guardian), or they may become involved in psychological treatment in forensic settings, such as juvenile detention centers and prisons. The *cognitive* psychological approach has improved our understanding of the workings of eyewitness memory. In practice, cognitive psychologists assist police departments and commissions with developing guidelines for improving the techniques that are used to interview eyewitnesses and conduct eyewitness identification tests and may serve as expert witnesses on the psychology of eyewitness memory. The *developmental* psychological approach has improved our knowledge of children's abilities and limitations in court proceedings, such as their ability to recall details of their interactions with adults accurately, their ability to tell the difference between true and fabricated details, and their susceptibility to social influence. In practice, developmental psychologists are involved in developing protocols for interviewing children in criminal investigations and developing accommodations associated with children's testimony in court. The *social* psychological approach has led to advances in our understanding of the functioning of juries and of social influence in criminal investigations (e.g., suspect interrogations, eyewitness identification procedures). In practice, social psychologists work with police departments and commissions to improve investigative procedures and may work as trial consultants, assisting attorneys with preparing for trial and selecting juries, or as expert witnesses, testifying on the psychology of interrogation and false confession or eyewitness identification. The *biological–psychological* approach (or neuropsychological approach) has contributed to our understanding of the physiological and neuropsychological correlates of deception in criminal contexts and the contribution of neuropsychological disorders to deviant behavior and criminal competencies. In practice, biological psychologists may serve as consultants or expert witnesses in cases involving the polygraph. Psychologists with clinical neuropsychology training may conduct neuropsychological assessments in order to provide information that is used in competency evaluations. The *industrial–organizational* approach has sharpened our understanding of workplace issues that have legal implications, such as employment discrimination and sexual harassment. In practice, industrial–organizational psychologists may be involved in personnel selection and training, may help employers develop effective policies and procedures addressing legal issues, and may serve as consultants and expert witnesses in civil cases involving discrimination and harassment.

The breadth of psychological approaches to forensic psychology is evident in other sources as well. Contemporary forensic psychological textbooks have chapters representing the diverse approaches. For example, the table of contents of Roesch, Zapf, and Hart's (2009) *Forensic Psychology and the Law* has chapters representing clinical (e.g., Forensic Assessment in Criminal Domains), cognitive (e.g., Eyewitness Identification), developmental (e.g., Juveniles and Legal Decision Making), and social (e.g., Juries and Legal Decision Making) approaches. Neuropsychological and industrial–organizational approaches are also represented in various chapters (e.g., Forensic Assessment and Police Psychology, respectively). The breadth of approaches is likewise recognized in the American Psychological Association's (APA's) *Specialty Guidelines for Forensic Psychologists*:

> For the purposes of these *Guidelines*, forensic psychology refers to professional practice by any psychologist working within any sub-discipline of psychology (e.g., clinical, developmental, social, cognitive) when applying the scientific, technical, or specialized knowledge of psychology to the law to assist in addressing legal, contractual, and administrative matters. Application of the *Guidelines* does not depend on the practitioner's typical areas of practice or expertise, but rather on the service provided in the case at hand. These *Guidelines* apply in all matters in which psychologists provide expertise to judicial, administrative, and educational systems including, but not limited to, examining or treating persons in anticipation of or subsequent to legal, contractual, administrative, proceedings; offering expert opinion about psychological issues in the form of *amicus* briefs or testimony to judicial, legislative or administrative bodies; acting in an adjudicative capacity; serving as a trial consultant or otherwise offering expertise to attorneys, the courts, or others; conducting research in connection with, or in the anticipation of, litigation; or involvement in educational activities of a forensic nature. (APA, 2011)

Our vision for this handbook is to consolidate and advance knowledge about the scientific foundations and practical application of psychology to law, the practice of law, and law-related policy. Drawing on contemporary psychological research and practice, we provide a thorough, up-to-date, and far-reaching reference on forensic psychological issues that are important to researchers, practitioners, and students in psychology, other social sciences and practice disciplines, and law.

Forensic psychology has become a highly important area of psychology. Psychological knowledge is now regularly used in trial, appellate, and supreme court cases at state and federal levels and is used to craft law on relevant topics. Psychologists routinely provide testimony about criminal defendants, litigants, and psychological issues in trial courts. Psychological knowledge even finds its way into amicus briefs that are submitted to appellate and supreme courts. For example, since 1962, the APA has submitted more than 200 amicus briefs on topics such as abortion, child abuse, child custody, competency, death penalty, duty to warn, expert witnesses, eyewitness identification, false confession, insanity defense, juvenile sentencing, the rights of mentally ill, residential treatment, sexual harassment, and the validity of psychological tests. Forensic psychology is now a common course in undergraduate programs, and there are masters and doctoral programs that focus on forensic psychology training.

There are also several professional organizations that represent forensic psychology. These organizations include the American Psychology-Law Society (APA Division 41) and the American Academy of Forensic Psychology, as well as professional organizations in Europe and elsewhere. Forensic psychology is also well represented in publications. Several scientific and legal journals are entirely devoted to forensic psychology research and practice. These journals include *Law and Human Behavior*; *Psychology, Public Policy, and Law*; *Behavioral Sciences and the Law*; *Legal and Criminological Psychology*; *Psychology, Crime & Law*; and the *Journal of Forensic Psychology Practice*. These journals are cited frequently in the pages of this handbook.

In sum, forensic psychology is a vital and thriving subfield of psychology. Forensic psychology has also captured the public's attention, as evidenced by its popularity in contemporary television shows (e.g., *CSI, Law and Order, Lie to Me, Criminal Minds*); movies (e.g., *One Flew Over the Cuckoo's Nest, The Silence of the Lambs, Black Swan*); and books, both fiction (e.g., *Runaway Jury*), and nonfiction (e.g., *Without Conscience: The Disturbing World of the Psychopaths Among Us*; *Mind Hunter: Inside the FBI's Elite Serial Crime Unit*).

CONTENTS AND FORMAT

This handbook is divided into two volumes, each of which is divided into three sections, containing entries on contemporary science and practice issues that together comprehensively represent the field of modern forensic psychology. The first volume represents individual and situational influences in criminal and civil contexts. The first section of Volume 1, "Forensic Evaluation and Treatment in Criminal Cases," showcases the application of clinical psychological science to criminal cases. This section contains the following chapters: Foundational Aspects of Forensic Mental Health Assessment, Forensic Assessment Instruments, Risk Assessment and Communication, Legal Insanity and *Mens Rea* Defenses, Criminal Competencies, Mental Health Treatment of Criminal Offenders, and Capital Case Considerations. This section is the heart of clinical forensic psychology within the criminal context because it addresses core topics in which clinical forensic psychologists have conducted research for years and have made valuable contributions to legal practice and policy.

The second section of Volume 1, "Individual and Situational Predictors of Criminal Behavior," articulates theories of criminal behavior and the roles of risk factors and context on criminal behavior among specific offender groups. The chapters in this section include Criminal Behavior, Psychopathy, Substance Use and Crime, Sexual Offending, and Intimate Partner Violence. These chapters articulate the interplay between individual and situational factors in crime and offending.

The third section of Volume 1, "Applications of Forensic Psychology in Civil Cases," highlights the application of clinical psychological science to various aspects of the civil justice system. The chapters in this section include Child Custody and Access, Personal Injury and Other Tort Matters, Employment Discrimination, and Civil Competencies. These chapters describe the contributions of clinical science to the evaluation of individuals who have been injured by the negligence or misconduct of others or who are involved in family court or guardianship matters as well as in employment settings.

The second volume of the handbook represents the state of the field with respect to criminal investigation, adjudication, and sentencing outcomes. The first section of Volume 2, "Victim and Offender Groups," describes issues that are relevant to specific groups of individuals. The chapters in this section include Children as Witnesses, Juvenile Offenders, Elders and the Justice System, Female Offenders, and Race in the Justice System. These chapters provide in-depth reviews of the justice-related challenges facing specific subpopulations, children, elderly, and members of minority groups in the various capacities in which they may be involved in the legal system (e.g., victims, witnesses, defendants).

The second section of Volume 2, "Criminal Investigations and Jury Trials," addresses the role of forensic psychology in modern investigation and trial procedures. The chapters in this section include Investigative Psychology, Eyewitness Memory, Deception Detection, Confessions, Jury Decision Making, Media and the Law, and Procedural Justice. These chapters examine how cognitive and social psychological research have been used to enhance our understanding of the quality of evidence and the effectiveness of techniques that are used to obtain evidence (e.g., the accuracy of eyewitness testimony and how various line-up techniques affect eyewitness identification accuracy).

The final section of Volume 2, "Sentencing and Incarceration," addresses the forensic psychological issues that are involved in postconviction outcomes. The chapters in this section are Probation and Parole, Sentencing, Prison Overcrowding, Community Corrections, and The Death Penalty. These chapters focus on the impact of various courts and detention environments on the recidivism, health, and well-being of sentenced individuals.

In sum, we have selected a comprehensive set of chapters that represent the core of contemporary forensic psychology and the diverse psychological approaches to our exciting and growing subdiscipline of psychology. In doing so, we aim to articulate the foundational science and implications of forensic psychology for law, legal practice, and law-related policy. Science and practice issues are a focus in each chapter.

In order to enhance the cohesiveness of the handbook's chapters and to ensure that each chapter addresses the core topics of interest, we adopted a common set of first-level headings:

I. Importance of the Problem
II. Relevant Psychological Theory and Principles
III. Research Review
IV. Practice and Policy Issues
V. Summary and Conclusions

In selecting these headings, we sought to strike a balance between obtaining the afore-mentioned benefits of a common heading structure and minimizing the constraints that may reduce the informativeness of the chapters. This system of headings was chosen because each chapter contains important content under each heading and because the headings serve as a familiar and standard guide for our readers. Each chapter addresses at least one important contemporary societal problem that is addressed in forensic psychology, and each chapter topic draws on theory from one or more core areas of psychology. Each chapter has a rich set of empirical research from which to draw in a research review and addresses a topic that has relevance for the practice of psychology, policy, and/or law. Authors have exercised their flexibility to add more structure through content-specific second- and third-level headings.

The "Importance of the Problem" section serves to explain why the chapter topic represents a vital and contemporary social problem. The authors draw on combinations of vivid anecdotes, prevalence statistics, noteworthy criminal or civil cases, legal decisions, laws, and law- and policymaking to demonstrate importance. The "Relevant Psychological Theory and Principles" section serves to highlight the fundamental scientific psychological perspectives on the problem, drawing from the core areas of clinical, cognitive, developmental, social, and biological psychology. In the "Research Review" section, the authors provide an up-to-date, comprehensive review of the empirical research on the topic, citing conclusions from meta-analyses and other such authoritative works. They address such issues as research methodology, methodological limitations, generally accepted conclusions, conclusions for which there is mixed or little support, commonly held views that are not supported by the research, gaps in our understanding, and directions for future research. In the "Practice and Policy Issues" section, the authors explain how the chapter topic is addressed in the modern practice of forensic psychology, in courts, and/or in the formation of policy and law. The authors address such issues as how a topic is dealt with in practice/policy and the practitioners (e.g., qualifications, professions). Last, the "Summary and Conclusions" section reiterates the main points of the chapters in a succinct, "take-home" message format.

The second feature that is used to enhance the cohesiveness of these volumes is cross-referencing of the chapters. There is naturally some overlap of chapters, as the topics are distinct but not mutually exclusive. The authors and editors have made efforts to draw readers' attention to relevant content in other chapters through cross-references.

The field of forensic psychology is becoming increasingly important and is being recognized more often in psychological, legal, and legislative circles. The science and practice of forensic psychology provides a wealth of opportunity to aspiring students and researchers because the field is relatively young, fascinating, and fluid. Forensic psychologists have demonstrable impact on law, practice, and policy. This handbook will serve as a catalyst to advance the field and inform professionals about the workings and contributions of forensic psychology.

CONTRIBUTORS

Our selection of chapter authors represents the diversity of forensic psychology researchers and practitioners. Many of our authors are university professors with active research agendas. Some of these university professors also actively practice forensic psychology. Other authors are full-time practicing psychologists. Our practicing psychologists include licensed clinical psychologists who perform forensic evaluations in legal settings or offer psychological treatment to forensic populations. Others are nonclinical psychologists who offer some combination of research services, consultation, and expert psychological testimony. The combination of research and consulting provides numerous benefits to the field of forensic psychology. Psychologists provide valuable services throughout the legal sectors, as explained in our chapters, and the legal environments in which psychologists practice contribute significantly to our research agendas. The practice experiences open our eyes to new research questions and sometimes provide an environment—including unique forensic populations—in which we conduct our research.

The field of forensic psychology has always been—and continues to be—a friendly, nurturing environment for graduate students and early career psychologist researchers and practitioners. Their voices are well represented at forensic psychology conferences and in forensic psychology publications. This handbook is no exception. Although many of our authors are well-established and internationally recognized scholars and practitioners, many others are graduate students and early career psychologists who are being mentored by their more established and experienced advisors and colleagues. We are proud to represent all of these voices in the pages of this handbook, for there is no better way to ensure the continuity and prosperity of our exciting field than to nurture the younger generations of researchers and practitioners and include them in setting the directions of forensic psychology.

AUDIENCE

This handbook should be useful to a variety of readers. Experienced researchers and practitioners, early career psychologists, and graduate students who are already steeped in forensic psychology or who aspire to pursue careers in forensic psychology will benefit from up-to-date reviews of the many key forensic psychology topics that are covered in this handbook. Legal practitioners such as lawyers and judges who see the application of psychology in their legal work may use this handbook to gain a more in-depth understanding of the psychological foundations for the issues they face, the resolved and unresolved research questions, and the various ways in which psychology can be applied to their profession.

ACKNOWLEDGMENTS

We express our highest appreciation to one another, to the many authors and coauthors who are represented in the chapters, and to the APA reference team for efforts to bring this volume from concept to publication. We are fortunate to have colleagues across the board who are highly competent, giving of their time and expertise, and driven to educate the above-noted audiences about forensic psychology. We thank our university colleagues who support our scholarly and educational agendas, which include the publication of this handbook. We thank our family members who granted us the time needed (including the overtime needed) to complete this work.

Brian L. Cutler and Patricia A. Zapf
Editors-in-Chief

References

American Psychological Association. (2011). *Specialty guidelines for forensic psychologists*. Retrieved from http://www.apa.org/practice/guidelines/forensic-psychology.aspx

Roesch, R., Zapf, P. A., & Hart, S. D. (2009). *Forensic psychology and the law*. New York, NY: Wiley.

PART I

FORENSIC EVALUATION AND TREATMENT IN CRIMINAL CASES

CHAPTER 1

FOUNDATIONAL ASPECTS OF FORENSIC MENTAL HEALTH ASSESSMENT

Kirk Heilbrun and Casey D. LaDuke

This chapter addresses the nature and importance of forensic mental health assessment (FMHA), beginning with definitional considerations and applications. It discusses the important sources of authority relevant to forensic assessment—law, ethics, science, and practice—and considers the components of each domain that are broadly applicable to forensic assessment. The chapter concludes with a discussion of the implications of this information for FMHA policy and practice.

We do not focus on any specific form of assessment in this chapter. Domains including criminal responsibility (see Chapter 4, this volume), criminal competencies (see Chapter 5, this volume), capital evaluations (see Chapter 7, this volume), child custody (see Chapter 13, this volume), personal injury (see Chapter 14, this volume), and civil competencies (see Chapter 16, this volume) are addressed in chapters later in this volume. Rather, this chapter is the first in a two-step process employed in this volume and elsewhere (e.g., Grisso, 2003; Melton, Petrila, Poythress, & Slobogin, 2007; Roesch & Zapf, 2013) to describe forensic assessment: initial consideration of broad foundational aspects followed by a more specific description of particular kinds of assessment divided according to legal question.

IMPORTANCE OF THE PROBLEM

Evaluations for legal decision makers provided by mental health professionals have evolved considerably in the last three decades. These evaluations (a) constitute one of the most important services

provided in forensic psychology and forensic psychiatry, (b) are recognized in different ways by relevant law and policy, (c) are supported by a large and growing body of research (see, e.g., Grisso, 2003; Heilbrun, 2001; Heilbrun, Grisso, & Goldstein, 2009; Melton et al., 2007), and (d) can be critically analyzed through the lens of evidence-based practice.

The process of conducting mental health evaluations for legal decision makers and attorneys has variously been termed forensic assessment, forensic psychological assessment, and forensic psychiatric assessment. We prefer the term *forensic mental health assessment* because it reflects the reality that such evaluations may be conducted by individuals from different disciplines (e.g., psychology, psychiatry, social work). However, using the term FMHA raises several important questions: "What is meant by *forensic*?" "What does the term *mental health* imply regarding the nature of FMHA?" "What makes FMHA different from general mental health assessment as a practice and a subspecialty?" In this section, we add to the discussion of these questions presented elsewhere (Heilbrun, Grisso, & Goldstein, 2009; Heilbrun, Grisso, Goldstein, & LaDuke, 2012).

The term *forensic* is often used to refer to the context involving legal proceedings, with forensic mental health assessments accordingly referring to those that are used in legal proceedings. But this description is not as straightforward as it might seem. First, it might be that the modifier forensic means that any assessment conducted by a mental health professional could be a forensic assessment as long as it is used in a legal forum. This first

http://dx.doi.org/10.1037/14461-001
APA Handbook of Forensic Psychology: Vol. 1. Individual and Situational Influences in Criminal and Civil Contexts,
B. L. Cutler and P. A. Zapf (Editors-in-Chief)

definition is problematic because it mixes accidental clinical by-products with assessments that are deliberately designed for legal applicability. For example, if a clinical psychologist assesses a patient as part of a standard course of clinical treatment, and the clinician is later subpoenaed to describe that assessment in a legal proceeding involving the patient, this definition might include that particular assessment within the FMHA domain. Many researchers would argue, however, that an assessment must be performed with the intention of being used in a legal proceeding in order to meet this definition. Including intentionality in the definition means that FMHA is "an evaluation that is performed . . . as part of the legal decision-making process, for the purpose of assisting the [legal] decision-maker or one of the litigants in using relevant clinical and scientific data" (Heilbrun, 2001, p. 3). An assessment is forensic not because its results become evidence in a court, but because the assessment was undertaken specifically in order to produce evidence that would be used in a legal context. We will use this second definition of FMHA, which requires that an assessment be conducted for the purpose of application in legal contexts and with the anticipation that it will be used this way in order to be termed forensic.

Despite the use of *mental health* to distinguish this kind of assessment from other types of evaluations that are conducted for legal purposes (e.g., pathology, chemistry, accounting), it does not mean that FMHA focuses only on mental health disorders. There are a variety of motivations, skills, and behavioral propensities that are also relevant in the legal decisions involving questions addressed by FMHA (Melton et al., 2007). Finally, the term *assessment* is intended to make it clear that FMHA methodology is anchored in the scientific and clinical methods of the mental health profession. These methods include objective observation, measurement informed by validated tests and specialized tools, and the support of theory and empirical research when interpreting data. There has been a trend in mental health assessment toward the use of methods designed to (a) obtain specific information, (b) reduce examiner bias through specialized measures, and (c) use relevant research on mental states or behaviors related to the examiner's inferences (Heilbrun, Grisso, &

Goldstein, 2009). These influences are even more prominent in FMHA because of both the importance of the legal decision and the absence of opportunity to correct evaluator errors following the decision that the FMHA informs.

The inclusion of the intention of assisting legal decision makers among the definitional criteria for FMHA has several important implications for individuals conducting these assessments. A primary question at the beginning of any FMHA involves the specific legal question(s) facing the court. FMHAs are conducted in a variety of cases with a variety of legal questions, including the criminal justice system (e.g., competency to stand trial, capital sentencing), the civil justice system (e.g., civil commitment, personal injury, child custody), and the juvenile justice system (e.g., transfer between juvenile and criminal courts, adjudication and placement decisions). Further, FMHAs involve the appraisal of mental states, motivations, and behaviors during past events (e.g., criminal responsibility); deficits in current relevant capacities (e.g., competencies in criminal and delinquency proceedings); and predictions of future behavior and mental states (e.g., sentencing; Heilbrun, Grisso, & Goldstein, 2009). There is a body of law relevant to these legal questions, and the evaluator must be aware of both the legal questions and the relevant law in planning, conducting, and describing the evaluation. Knowing the relevant law allows the evaluator to identify the kind of information that is relevant to that legal question and to develop an assessment procedure designed specifically to obtain that information: The legal issues therefore shape the *referral question* in FMHA.

There is also an important distinction between the nature of the referral question in forensic practice as contrasted with most questions that are addressed in the clinical practice role. The forensic referral question is posed to help inform a legal decision maker or help an attorney make an argument about a legal decision. Its focus is on whether an individual has certain functional abilities—capacities or behavioral skills—that would allow that person to satisfy the specified legal test. By contrast, a clinical assessment is focused on appraising a patient's clinical needs and formulating intervention recommendations that are in his or her best interest. There is certainly a degree of overlap between the substances of each kind of evaluation: Many kinds of forensic evaluation, for example, call for an appraisal of an individual's current clinical condition, including symptoms, strengths and weaknesses, and, possibly, diagnosis. But even such similar content is distinguished by the primary purpose for which it is obtained: informing legal decision making (in a forensic context) versus informing treatment planning (in a clinical context).

This distinction has important implications for individuals who perform FMHA. First, the forensic clinician must translate legal constructs involving relevant abilities and conditions into constructs that can be appraised by mental health professionals. Second, the relationship between examiner and examinee differs in forensic versus clinical contexts. General clinical assessments are performed in the context of a treatment or consulting relationship that is guided by the best interests of the patient; the forensic assessment calls for a primary allegiance to the legal process and its decision makers, not to the examinee. Third, this distinction has differential implications for the communication of assessment results. Clinical assessments typically are performed to inform patients, families, and other clinicians, whereas forensic assessments are primarily used by legal professionals (judges and lawyers) and other nonclinicians (e.g., jurors). Results must therefore be conveyed differently, both because they focus on different questions and because knowledge about mental health on the part of individuals using these results cannot be assumed.

RELEVANT PSYCHOLOGICAL THEORY AND PRINCIPLES

There are four broad domains of authority that are relevant to FMHA: law, ethics, science, and practice (Heilbrun, 2001; Heilbrun, Grisso, & Goldstein, 2009; Heilbrun, Kelley, Koller, Lane, & Peterson, 2013). The law provides the question that the court will address in the case and for which the FMHA is requested. Relevant law also may describe the functional–legal capacities associated with the legal question and help to guide the process and shape the form of the evaluator's conclusions. Ethical standards

provide the basis for ethical guidance in forensic practice and include standards that are either broadly applicable to specific disciplines (e.g., ethical principles of psychologists; American Psychological Association [APA], 2010a; principles of medical ethics with annotations especially applicable to psychiatry; American Psychiatric Association, 2010) or more specifically applicable to FMHA (e.g., specialty guidelines for forensic psychologists; APA, 2011b; ethical guidelines for the practice of forensic psychiatry; American Academy of Psychiatry and the Law [AAPL], 2005). Science provides the empirical research that is important to support the sources of information, interpretation of data, and reasoning to conclusions. Science also offers the principles of parsimony and falsifiability, so evaluators who form hypotheses as part of FMHA and interpret them parsimoniously in light of observed findings are using the process of scientific inquiry. Finally, there is a body of literature focused on practice, which is not clearly legal, ethical, or scientific, but that nevertheless provides important guidance for many aspects of mental health assessments that are conducted in legal contexts. In this section, we discuss the literature that either provides important guidance in one of these areas or integrates multiple sources of FMHA authority.

The *Best Practices for Forensic Mental Health Assessments* series published by Oxford University Press describes both the foundations of FMHA (Heilbrun, Grisso, & Goldstein, 2009) and the more specific assessment procedures considered by legal questions. Each book in this series describes the relevant law, ethics, science, and practice associated with a specific form of FMHA. Despite the substantial progress in FMHA during the last two decades that has made it possible to do a best practices series, there is some inconsistency in the advances that have occurred in different FMHA areas. In some areas, there has been relatively little research, resulting in limited progress in the development of a specialized measure (which in turn must incorporate the empirical evidence necessary for the development of such a measure); in other areas, there has been so much research that the field now enjoys the luxury of having numerous validated specialized measures available. It is hoped that future research will more fully address types of FMHA that do not presently have a validated specialized measure, such as juvenile competence to stand trial and child custody.

Relevant Law

Several aspects of law are particularly important in FMHA. The statutes, case law, and administrative code contained within this area help to define the assessment process, the reporting of results and conclusions, and subsequent testimony. The law also defines who can be an expert, what is admissible as expert evidence, and how FMHA is practiced within and across states (see Ewing, 2003).

Legal authority and the focus of FMHA.   Legal and psychological constructs are not synonymous and are sometimes quite distinct. Accordingly, the forensic clinician must have a reasonable understanding of the components of the legal question associated with the evaluation. These components, which have been called "functional legal capacities" (Grisso, 2003), describe the knowledge, skills, and capacities that a litigant must have in order to satisfy the broader legal test. Functional legal capacities are also better defined than, more clearly psychological in nature than, and without the substantial discretionary component associated with the legal question. For example, FMHA focusing on an individual's competence to stand trial that is limited to clinical information (e.g., symptoms, diagnosis) rarely provides an adequate basis for the court's decision about the individual's capacities to understand the legal circumstances and assist counsel in his or her defense against criminal charges. By contrast, focusing on both clinical symptoms and functional legal capacities to understand and assist provides a good deal of useful information to the decision maker on the issue of trial competence.

Deciding who is an expert.   The determination by a court that an individual meets the criteria to be designated an *expert witness* provides special status to the mental health professional; this status must be conferred before expert testimony can be provided. This special status allows the designated expert to render an opinion, using his or her own observations and data, on a question that is before the court. The expert can go beyond the role of *fact witness*, which is limited to testifying about what

has been seen or heard directly. In *Jenkins v. United States* (1962), the court held that expert status is not simply a function of one's professional discipline. Rather, expert status is to be determined by a broader set of criteria, including knowledge, skills, training, or education, which reflects expertise that could be helpful to the court. The *Jenkins* criteria have subsequently been incorporated into Rule 702 of the Federal Rules of Evidence (FRE 702):

> If scientific, technical, or other specialized knowledge will assist the trier of fact to understand the evidence or to determine a fact in issue, a witness qualified as an expert by knowledge, skill, experience, training, or education, may testify thereto in the form of an opinion or otherwise, if (1) the testimony is based upon sufficient facts or data, (2) the testimony is the product of reliable principles and methods, and (3) the witness has applied the principles and methods reliably to the facts of the case.

Determining admissibility of expert testimony on a particular legal question.   There is no generic expertise in FMHA. The range of legal questions and associated needs for expertise is far too broad to assume that because one is an expert in a single form of FMHA (e.g., competence to stand trial) that he or she will necessarily be qualified as an expert in another quite different form (e.g., child custody evaluation). The expert must therefore have the specialized knowledge, skills, experience, training, or education associated with the specific legal question before the court.

In addition to qualifying as an expert, the evaluator offering testimony must also be prepared to describe the basis for the testimony and the methods used in obtaining the information about which he or she is testifying. The evaluator must be confident that he or she would qualify as an expert and that the procedures used in the evaluation would meet the legal standard for admissibility before accepting a referral. There have been two major legal standards for the admissibility of expert evidence. Each will be described in turn.

The earlier standard was described in *Frye v. United States* (1923), in which the court held that the criterion for admissibility was whether the foundation on which the expert evidence is based is "sufficiently established to have gained general acceptance in the particular field in which it belongs" (p. 10). The *Frye* standard was incorporated into federal and state jurisdictions and still serves as the prevailing standard in some state jurisdictions. A second standard was established in *Daubert v. Merrell Dow Pharmaceuticals, Inc.* (1993), when the U.S. Supreme Court held that the standard described in the FRE would be used in federal jurisdictions. The Court reasoned that the *Frye* criterion was overly narrow, so although the FRE criteria (often termed the "*Daubert* criteria" since this decision) does include *Frye's* "general acceptance" test, it also includes considerations such as whether the testimony would be likely to assist the trier of fact and whether the evidence was based on a process that was scientifically respectable (i.e., testable, tested, subject to peer review, published, having a known or potentially known error rate, and having existing standards controlling its functioning). *Daubert* is now the expert admissibility standard in the federal and many state jurisdictions. Given the more expansive standard described in *Daubert*, the court using this standard must go beyond determining merely whether the approaches used by an expert are generally accepted in the field and consider the additional criteria in the attempt to gauge the scientific foundation supporting the expert's methods. Further, this decision by the trial court cannot be overturned by an appellate court except in rare cases involving the abuse of judicial discretion (*General Electric Co. v. Joiner*, 1997).

Limits on expert testimony: Third-party information and the ultimate legal issue. There are two limitations regarding expert testimony in the context of FMHA: the use of third-party information as a source of data and whether experts can testify to the ultimate legal issue (the question of law that is before the court).

FMHA differs from clinical evaluations in the extent to which litigants may be motivated to distort information that is provided to the evaluator. The management of this potential bias is handled in several ways, including (a) observing the internal consistency of individuals' accounts, (b) using response-style scales on standard psychological tests, and (c) using specialized measures that have been constructed to detect the underreporting or overreporting of symptoms and deficits. In addition to these approaches, the evaluator can gather third-party information (records and interviews of third parties). Third-party information is a potentially powerful source of information with several advantages: (a) It can increase the overall accuracy of the data and resulting opinions; (b) it offers a commonsense appeal that is much easier to understand than are the results of scales or specialized inventories; (c) it enhances the face validity of the evaluation and testimony; (d) it provides evidence against which factual errors in self-reports can be checked; and (e) it consequently functions as an important *third leg* of the three-legged FMHA methodology stool, which includes self-report and formalized psychological, medical, or specialized testing as the other two legs (Heilbrun, Warren, & Picarello, 2003; Otto, Slobogin, & Greenberg, 2007).

The expert using such third-party information is using indirect sources. This is hearsay under the law of evidence and would not be permitted as the basis for testimony by a fact witness. However, part of the expert role includes an important distinction with respect to hearsay and, by extension, the use of third-party information. The FRE permit the use and admissibility of third-party information under some circumstances: "If of a type reasonably relied upon by experts in the particular field in forming opinions or inferences upon the subject, the facts or data need not be admissible in evidence in order for the opinion or inference to be admitted" (FRE 703). This is a crucial distinction, as the use of third-party information is clearly something that is "reasonably relied upon by experts" in FMHA in conducting evaluations (Melton et al., 2007).

The second limitation regarding expert testimony is less clear, as the law is not consistent across jurisdictions on the question of direct testimony on the ultimate legal issue. In some jurisdictions on some issues, ultimate-issue testimony is prohibited (see, e.g., Tenn. Code Ann., 1995; FRE 704(b)); in other jurisdictions, it is required (e.g., Mich. Stat.

Ann., 1954; see also *United States v. Davis*, 1988; *United States v. Kristiansen*, 1990; *United States v. Salamanca*, 1993). There are both practical as well as theoretical considerations involved in the expression of such an opinion. For example, an expert report from a staff member at a federal medical center or state forensic hospital conveying the opinion that a hospitalized defendant appeared to have regained trial competence that did not answer this question directly would create considerable confusion in individuals responsible for the transportation, community incarceration, and legal proceedings against the defendant—and probably result in continued hospitalization. Unless ultimate-issue testimony is explicitly barred until jurisdiction-specific evidence law, it remains within the discretion of the court to require it, allow it, allow it with qualifications, or limit it.

The legal constraints on ultimate-issue testimony, limited though they are, have perhaps developed in part through recognition of the debate within forensic psychiatry and forensic psychology on this topic. There remains a wide variety of positions on this issue, ranging from favoring such testimony as desired by and useful to the court without being unduly harmful (Rogers & Ewing, 2003; Rogers & Shuman, 2000) to recommending its exclusion because of the potential to mix clinical and scientific considerations with community values, and hence to invade the province of the decision maker (Heilbrun, 2001; Melton et al., 2007; Morse, 1999; Tillbrook, Mumley, & Grisso, 2003). This remains an unresolved debate. However, individuals choosing (or required) to address the ultimate legal issue as part of FMHA should at least be mindful of this range of opinions and take steps to minimize any potentially adverse impact of the ultimate opinions. Such steps might include (a) directly stating in the report and in testimony that the evaluator recognizes that the court is responsible for the legal decision in this matter, and the ultimate opinion expressed in the report or testimony is hence the clinical opinion of the evaluator; and (b) writing a thorough and detailed report describing all methods, findings, and the reasoning relating the findings to the opinions.

Legal regulation of FMHA practice. Licensing laws regulate the practice of FMHA. Jurisdictions establish their own licensing requirements, which restrict the professional activities of mental health professionals to activities designated by those requirements. Requirements for licensure typically include training (having attained a certain degree in a given discipline) and supervised experience (the amount varies across jurisdictions but is often one full-time postdoctoral year for psychologists), along with satisfactorily passing a national and state-level examination. Licensure signifies the satisfaction of generic educational, experiential, and knowledge requirements, but not specialty expertise. Some jurisdictions (e.g., Massachusetts, Michigan, and Missouri) also provide specialty certification for certain kinds of FMHA, and others (e.g., Florida and Virginia) offer continuing education that evaluators must attend in order to maintain approval for conducting FMHA in that jurisdiction. More advanced specialty certification is offered by various boards, the oldest and most respected of which is the American Board of Professional Psychology.

Ethics

Formal sources of ethical guidance differ across disciplines, and they also differ in their specific application to FMHA. In this section, we discuss the relevant ethical guidelines for both psychology and psychiatry.

APA's *Ethical Principles of Psychologists and Code of Conduct* (*Ethics Code*; 2010a) is a broad document, applicable to all psychologists, that contains both aspirational principles and enforceable code. The principles provide broad guidance in professional decision making and behavior, but it is the various sections of code that specify the particular acts to be avoided. This often means that a circumstance that is encountered in a highly specialized context such as forensic assessment will not be covered very well by the principles, and perhaps not at all within the code. But, the ethical demand within specialty practice is that professional behavior be at least consistent with the broader ethics code, even if the code does not cover the behavior very specifically.

Often, the distinctions between ethical considerations more broadly applicable for FMHA (described by the *Ethics Code*; APA, 2010a) and ethical considerations specifically applicable for FMHA revolve around the question of who the client is. This distinction has been recognized for many years and encompasses the question of who is owed the duty conferred by "client" status. In FMHA, the primary client is typically the court and/or the referring attorney rather than the individual being evaluated. The distinction further considers the nature of the professional relationship, the nature of privilege, and the competence of the expert (Appelbaum, 1997; Appelbaum & Gutheil, 2007; Goldstein, 2003; Greenberg & Shuman, 1997; Rosner, 2003; Weissman & DeBow, 2003).

The ethical guidelines more specifically applicable for forensic psychology are the *Specialty Guidelines for Forensic Psychologists* (*Specialty Guidelines*; Committee on Ethical Guidelines for Forensic Psychologists, 1991) and the recently adopted revision, *Specialty Guidelines for Forensic Psychology* (*Revised Specialty Guidelines*; APA, 2011b). These guideliens provide much more specific information for individuals who are involved in FMHA. They are also aspirational—meaning that they are not enforceable in the same way as the *Ethics Code*, and also that they describe professional behavior that might not be achievable in every case but to which the forensic practitioner should aspire. In addition to the *Revised Specialty Guidelines*, APA provides other guidelines in even more specific forensic evaluation areas such as child custody assessments (APA, 2010b) and child protection (APA, 2011a).

The book *Principles of Medical Ethics With Annotation Especially Applicable to Psychiatry* (American Psychiatric Association, 2010), provides ethical standards for all psychiatrists. Similar to the APA *Ethics Code* (2010a), however, its applicability to forensic psychiatry is limited. The more specific ethical document applicable to forensic psychiatry is the *Ethical Guidelines for the Practice of Forensic Psychiatry* (AAPL, 2005). These guidelines address the domains of (a) confidentiality, (b) consent, (c) honesty and striving for objectivity, and (d) qualifications of examiners.

Codes of ethics and specialized forensic guidelines have some influence on regulating FMHA practice. Their violation does not result in administrative law sanctions in the same way that a licensure violation could. However, a violation of ethical standards as determined by APA can result not only in penalties up to and including expulsion from APA, but also in notification to the licensing board in the individual's jurisdiction of practice, which can result in legal sanctions. In addition, ethics codes help to define the appropriate standard of practice, and as such, may be considered by licensure boards or courts in malpractice litigation. Indeed, at least one jurisdiction (Pennsylvania) has incorporated the APA *Ethics Code* (2010a) into its own administrative law standards for the practice of psychology; as a result, any violation of the criteria described in the *Ethics Code* can have the immediate effect of being adjudicated a violation of licensure law.

Science and Practice

Both the science and practice literatures are important sources of authority for FMHA. Science will be discussed later in the Relevant Reviews section, and practice will be discussed in the Practice and Policy Issues section.

Principles of FMHA

Other scholars (Heilbrun, 2001; Heilbrun, Grisso, & Goldstein, 2009; Heilbrun et al., 2012) have described the principles, guidelines, and maxims for FMHA that provide theoretical contributions to a best practice standard. These have included both broad principles and more specific guidelines that may be derived from them. Psycholegal scholars have taken two different approaches to describing FMHA. The first approach identified a specific kind of FMHA—as defined by the legal question—and discussed the relevant law, ethics, science, and practice (see, e.g., Grisso, 2003; Melton et al., 2007; Weiner & Hess, 2005). The second approach assumes that all kinds of FMHA have a common foundation, seeks to identify the elements of that foundation, and then discusses different kinds of evaluations in light of those common elements (for a description of models that apply in FMHA, see, e.g., Grisso, 2003; Morse, 1978). Several scholars have also taken an approach that combines these two approaches, both discussing foundational aspects of FMHA and describing specific kinds (see, e.g., Melton et al., 2007; Simon & Gold, 2004). Heilbrun (2001) initially focused on broad principles but then subsequently sought to apply them to specific kinds of FMHA (Heilbrun, DeMatteo, & Marczyk, 2004; Heilbrun,

Marczyk, & DeMatteo, 2002; Heilbrun, Marczyk, et al., 2003; Heilbrun et al., 2005).

The broad, foundational principles of FMHA have most recently been described and updated to reflect developments in the field (Heilbrun, Grisso, & Goldstein, 2009). These principles are listed in Exhibit 1.1 and are discussed in detail elsewhere (Heilbrun, 2001; Heilbrun, Grisso, & Goldstein, 2009; Heilbrun et al., 2012).

Exhibit 1.1
Principles of Forensic Mental Health Assessment: An Integration

---

GENERALLY

1. Be aware of the important differences between clinical and forensic domains.
2. Obtain appropriate education, training, and experience in one's area of forensic specialization.
3. Be familiar with the relevant legal, ethical, scientific, and practice literatures pertaining to FMHA.
4. Be guided by honesty and striving for impartiality, actively disclosing the limitations on as well as the support for one's opinions.
5. Control potential evaluator bias in general through monitoring case selection, continuing education, and consultation with knowledgeable colleagues.
6. Be familiar with specific aspects of the legal system, particularly communication, discovery, deposition, and testimony.
7. Do not become adversarial, but present and defend your opinions effectively.

IN SPECIFIC CASES
Preparation

8. Identify relevant forensic issues.
9. Accept referrals only within area of expertise.
10. Decline the referral when evaluator impartiality is unlikely.
11. Clarify the evaluator's role with the attorney.
12. Clarify financial arrangements.
13. Obtain appropriate authorization.
14. Avoid playing the dual roles of therapist and forensic evaluator.
15. Determine the particular role to be played within forensic assessment if the referral is accepted.
16. Select the most appropriate model to guide data gathering, interpretation, and communication.

Data Collection

17. Use multiple sources of information for each area being assessed. Review the available background information and actively seek important missing elements.
18. Use relevance and reliability (validity) as guides for seeking information and selecting data sources.
19. Obtain relevant historical information.
20. Assess clinical characteristics in relevant, reliable, and valid ways.
21. Assess legally relevant behavior.
22. Ensure that conditions for evaluation are quiet, private, and distraction-free.
23. Provide appropriate notification of purpose and/or obtain appropriate authorization before beginning.
24. Determine whether the individual understands the purpose of the evaluation and the associated limits on confidentiality.

Data Interpretation

25. Use third party information in assessing response style.
26. Use testing when indicated in assessing response style.
27. Use case-specific (idiographic) evidence in assessing clinical condition, functional abilities, and causal connection.
28. Use nomothetic evidence is assessing clinical condition, functional abilities, and causal connection.
29. Use scientific reasoning in assessing causal connection between clinical condition and functional abilities.
30. Carefully consider whether to answer the ultimate legal question. If it is answered, it should be in the context of a thorough evaluation clearly describing data and reasoning, and with the clear recognition that this question is in the domain of the legal decision-maker.
31. Describe findings and limits so that they need change little under cross examination.

Written Communication

32. Attribute information to sources.
33. Use plain language; avoid technical jargon.
34. Write report in sections, according to model and procedures.

Testimony

35. Base testimony on the results of the properly performed FMHA.
36. Prepare.
37. Communicate effectively.
38. Control the message. Strive to obtain, retain, and regain control over the meaning and impact of what is presented in expert testimony.

Note. From *Foundations of Forensic Mental Health Assessment* (pp. 135–137), by K. Heilbrun, T. Grisso, and A. Goldstein, 2009, New York, NY: Oxford University Press. Copyright 2009 by Oxford University Press, USA. Reprinted with permission.

RESEARCH REVIEW

Human behavior is complex and multidetermined. Our legal system, however, provides a framework for decision making in which options are usually dichotomous and mutually exclusive (e.g., sane vs. insane, civilly committed vs. not committed, liable vs. not liable). In the behavioral sciences, such legal constructs have no equivalent. The terms have no clinical meaning; by their dichotomous nature, they also draw a "bright line," resulting in mutually exclusive categorization. The application of science to FMHA—including designing, conducting, interpreting, and communicating research that is relevant to legal decision making—is affected by this differential emphasis in various ways, including (among others) categorization (law) versus continuous measurement (science) and individually referenced (law) versus other referenced (science). One area of compromise has been the focus on functional–legal capacities (which are somewhat amenable to research measurement) rather than on ultimate legal question categorization (which includes a healthy component of what the law would consider judicial discretion and what behavioral science would call *error variance*).

Theoretical Models and FMHA

It has been recommended that (a) FMHA be guided by relevant statutes and case law associated with the referral question, (b) objective measures (such as psychological tests and forensic assessment instruments) be used in conducting evaluations, and

(c) evaluations include information from multiple sources (Goldstein, 2003, 2007; Grisso, 2003; Heilbrun, 2001; Heilbrun et al., 2002, 2003; Heilbrun, Marczyk, DeMatteo, & Mack-Allen, 2007; Melton et al., 2007; Otto et al., 2007). For more than 25 years, the model described in *Evaluating Competencies* (Grisso, 1986, 2003) has been used to guide and structure FMHA. The model underscores the importance of identifying and understanding the legal competency construct (determined by statutory and case law definitions relevant to the legal referral question) and expressing this construct largely in terms of its functional–legal capacities. The model stresses the importance of using empirical data rather than relying primarily or exclusively on observations and clinical impressions. An important FMHA question is the extent to which the evaluee's functional abilities are consistent with those required by the legal question.

Relevant Reviews

A recent valuable addition to the literature regarding FMHA discussed the science associated with FMHA and ther psychology–law areas (Skeem, Douglas, & Lilienfeld, 2009). Contributors to this book reviewed the supporting scientific evidence on various topics and drew conclusions about whether different kinds of activities were *scientifically supported, scientifically controversial*, or *scientifically unsupported*. Reviews were conducted in the assessment of psychological injuries (Koch, Nader, & Haring, 2009), child custody evaluations (O'Donohue,

Beitz, & Tolle, 2009), competence to stand trial (Poythress & Zapf, 2009), and violence risk assessment (Heilbrun, Douglas, & Yasuhara, 2009). The conclusions drawn in each area will be described briefly.

Koch et al. (2009) discussed the forensic assessment of psychological injuries and described the following uses as scientifically supported:

- Psychological evaluation of current mental health functioning as long as it includes cautions regarding response style in litigating samples and the limits of current assessment of such response style;
- Descriptions of reports of past functioning provided by claimants and collateral interviewees, again accompanied by caveats pertaining to limits of this task; and
- Use of well-validated measures of symptom overendorsement, applied to opinions about claimants' response style during the present assessment and not necessarily to a larger conclusion regarding malingering.

Koch et al. (2009) described one scientifically untested or controversial use: conclusions regarding the impact of psychological injury on particular areas of future disability (e.g., capacity to perform some but not other work tasks, precise estimates about the duration of functional incapacity in certain domains). The authors also concluded that there are certain scientifically unsupported procedures that have been used in this kind of FMHA:

- Definitive conclusions that current incapacity was caused by the legally contested adverse event;
- Definitive descriptions of past psychological functioning derived from current psychological testing;
- Conclusions that an individual is malingering without strong evidence of intentionality; and
- Prognoses about future psychological functioning or disability made using mental health variables alone.

The next kind of FMHA discussed in the book by Skeem et al. (2009) was child custody evaluation. In this chapter, O'Donohue et al. (2009) described the following procedures as scientifically supported:

- Conclusions about current psychological or psychiatric functioning of children, including special needs, mental health functioning, and problems that can be addressed through planned intervention; and
- Research evidence on the impact of divorce on children.

The major use cited as untested or controversial involved predictions about children's functioning in the future using tests or measures with sound psychometric properties for present assessment. Finally, predictions about custody arrangements in the best interests of children using specialized measures that have not been validated for making such predictions were described as scientifically unsupported (O'Donohue et al., 2009).

On the topic of competence to stand trial, Poythress and Zapf (2009) described the scientifically supported procedures as follows:

- Incorporating the results of idiographic assessment measures (assessing the individual's functioning relative to his or her own potential and prior performance);
- Incorporating the results of nomothetic assessment measures (assessing the individual's functioning relative to known groups); and
- Using either or both in describing the competence-related abilities of the individual being evaluated.

One scientifically untested or controversial use was identified: relying solely on data from idiographic assessment (without incorporating nomothetic assessment results) in drawing conclusions regarding the defendant's competence-relevant capacities (Poythress & Zapf, 2009). Several areas of scientifically unsupported use were described for FMHA in this area:

- Combining clinical ratings from different idiographic items or scales and interpreting these scores as meaningfully relevant to trial competence;
- Using nomothetic measures, without case-specific idiographic inquiry, as the only basis for conclusions relevant to trial competence; and

■ Combining scores on nomothetic measures toward a dichotomous conclusion regarding trial competence.

Heilbrun, Douglas, and Yasuhara (2009) provided the chapter on violence risk assessment. Unlike the previous three topics, risk assessment is not associated with a single legal question. Rather, it is associated with a number of different kinds of FMHA (e.g., civil commitment, sentencing, capital sentencing, juvenile commitment) as an important included element. Scientifically supported uses of risk assessment procedures were described by Heilbrun, Douglas, and Yasuhara as follows:

■ Conclusions that individuals scoring higher on validated risk assessment instruments are at greater risk for violence;
■ Actuarial prediction strategies applied to groups, obtained using large derivation and validation samples, citing mean probability, and specifying margin of error;
■ Use of extreme risk categories as both more informative and less affected by the possibility of overlapping 95% confidence intervals; and
■ Indication that applying group-based data to a small number of cases (or an individual case) will result in wider confidence intervals than when such data are applied to a larger number of cases.

Two untested or controversial uses were identified by Heilbrun, Douglas, and Yasuhara (2009):

■ Actuarial prediction strategies with appropriately large derivation and validation samples and correctly citing mean probability but not specifying margin of error and its increased uncertainty when applied to single cases; and
■ Assumption of the existence of reliable, known probability estimates (robust across samples) even at the group level.

Finally, three scientifically unsupported uses of violence risk assessment were noted by Heilbrun, Douglas, and Yasuhara (2009):

■ Actuarial prediction strategies that were developed without the requisite large derivation and validation samples;

■ Application of actuarial prediction approaches to populations without empirical foundation (via either the derivation or validation samples) for doing so; and
■ Drawing of conclusions about the probability of an individual's future violence without providing applicable confidence intervals associated with the prediction measure and caution about less certainty in the individual case.

Several conclusions about the scientific support for FMHA follow from these reviews. These can be discussed in terms of both available scientific data and the use of scientific thinking to guide the conceptualization, data gathering, interpretation, and reasoning associated with FMHA.

The first conclusion involves the value of specialized forensic assessment measures. In order to develop such a measure properly, there must be supporting empirical evidence. Such evidence may be gathered as part of the derivation and validation of the specialized instrument; it may also be obtained by reviewing the literature to determine whether other investigators have gathered such data. Finally, other investigators conduct research independently once specialized measures are published in peer-reviewed journals. This use of specialized measures has been one of the most direct and effective ways of linking the process of FMHA with the supporting empirical evidence. When there is an available specialized measure for a given FMHA topic, the evaluator should incorporate that measure into the assessment unless there is a good reason not to.

The second conclusion refers to the value of multiple sources of information. Common sources include self-report, idiographic self-report, and nomothetic standardized testing, as well as collateral sources such as records and third-party interviews.

The third conclusion cautions against drawing conclusions with insufficient support. There are numerous ways in which this can be done: using tests or measures to address questions they are not designed to address, or using them with a population for which there is no validation evidence; applying a single source of information to reach a conclusion without support from other sources; or combining or even altering existing tests or measures without evidence regarding how successfully this can be done. The approach of careful and thorough investigation followed by conservative and evidence-based interpretation of results can be seen clearly as an antidote for errors of this kind.

The final conclusion involves communication that is appropriately cautious. It is often the case that some important information is missing or cannot be gathered. Likewise, the available sources may provide inconsistent evidence on some of the questions being addressed by the evaluator. When confidence and strength of conclusions are indicated by the data, then this should be reflected in the way in which the findings are communicated. When cautions are warranted for various reasons, it is equally appropriate to ensure that they accompany the conclusions provided as part of the FMHA.

Judging by the research base cited in the various books in the Oxford best practices series, there is inconsistency in the amount and quality of research that has been conducted on the different forms of FMHA. Some areas (e.g., juvenile competence to stand trial) have not been sufficiently researched to yield a specialized assessment measure, whereas others (e.g., risk assessment) have been the subject of intensive research, with multiple specialty measures as a result. Additional research in the next decade will hopefully be conducted and distributed so as to facilitate a stronger research base in the areas of child custody, juvenile competence to stand trial, and mental state at the time of offense. It also would be helpful if the range of best practice guidelines developed by national organizations (e.g., APA, American Psychology-Law Society) were expanded to more explicitly link the supporting research base in each area with the recommended procedures and limitations for practitioners.

PRACTICE AND POLICY ISSUES

Another source of authority in FMHA is the professional literature, including guidance provided by the profession's primary organizations and centers of training. Professional organizations help to define the requirements for specialization. The growth in professional organizations that focus on law and mental health, such as the American Psychology-Law Society,

the American Board of Forensic Psychology, and the American Academy of Psychiatry and Law, has contributed greatly to the development and dissemination of forensic research, scientific knowledge, ethics, and practice expertise. Formal practice guidelines provided by professional organizations are important in helping to define a standard of practice generally (Heilbrun, DeMatteo, Marczyk, & Goldstein, 2008; Otto & Heilbrun, 2002; Wettstein, 2005) and, in particular, forensic specialty areas (American Academy of Child and Adolescent Psychiatry, 1997a, 1997b, 1997c, 1998, 1999; APA, 1994, 1999, 2002, 2005; Association of Family and Conciliation Courts, 2006; Giorgi-Guarnieri et al., 2002; Mossman et al., 2007; Packer & Grisso, 2011; Society for Industrial and Organizational Psychology, 2003). The disciplines of both psychiatry and psychology have been actively involved in developing descriptions of good practice for various aspects of FMHA.

Likewise, the training literature contributes to defining the nature of practice for FMHA. Training in FMHA occurs at different levels (Bersoff et al., 1997; Marczyk, DeMatteo, Kutinsky, & Heilbrun, 2008; Otto, Heilbrun, & Grisso, 1990; Rosner, 1983). In psychology, some colleges and universities offer training in forensic psychology through master-level degrees (MA or MS), doctoral training (typically as a forensic concentration or minor in clinical or counseling psychology programs), or joint degrees in law and psychology (PhD/JD, PsyD/JD, JD/MA, PhD/MLS (see http://www.ap-ls.org/education/GraduatePrograms.php for a current listing of programs). Psychiatrists pursuing forensic specialization must first obtain a year (or more) of accredited forensic fellowship training following the completion of residency. There are a number of forensic fellowships available in the United States (see http://www.aapl.org/fellow.php).

Presently, psychologists are not required to complete a specialty postdoctoral fellowship in order to become a forensic specialist, although there has been movement toward increasing the availability of postdoctoral fellowship training. Such fellowships can now be accredited by APA (2009, section C-11[b]), and formal specialty training in FMHA for individuals who have completed a doctorate in psychology is increasingly occurring at the fellowship level (typically 1–2 years of training; see Packer & Borum, 2003, for a sample curriculum) or as the result of participating in continuing education programs taught by specialists in particular areas of forensic research or practice.

Board certification is often cited as an indication of specialized competence in forensic psychology and psychiatry. The American Board of Professional Psychology (ABPP) is the oldest and most rigorous of the organizations offering board certification in psychology. ABPP confers board certification in forensic psychology on individuals who meet the credentialing requirements of the American Board of Forensic Psychology, which is one member of ABPP. Those attaining ABPP forensic board certification must (a) possess an earned doctoral degree from an APA-approved program (or one that meets APA criteria), (b) maintain an active license as a psychologist, (c) have completed a minimum of 100 hr of APA-approved continuing education and face-to-face supervision in forensic psychology, and (d) obtain 1,000 hr of experience in forensic psychology over a 5-year period (or satisfy [c] and [d] with an approved postdoctoral year in a forensic psychology training program). When these criteria are met, candidates must then pass a written examination, submit practice samples to be approved for an oral examination, and pass a 3-hr oral examination.

The process of forensic specialization in psychiatry includes board certification through the American Board of Psychiatry and Neurology, with added qualifications for certification in the subspecialty of forensic psychiatry. Applicants are required to have completed an approved 1-year fellowship in forensic psychiatry and must first become board certified from the American Board of Psychiatry and Neurology in general psychiatry. Successful candidates are also examined in areas that include the legal regulation of psychiatry, criminal law, civil law, methodology, risk assessment, diagnosis and treatment, and forensic psychiatry practice. AAPL provides a 3-day intensive training course for individuals who are seeking forensic board certification in psychiatry.

To the extent that training, knowledge, and supervised experience can enhance the level of performance in conducting FMHA, it is reasonable to assume that specialty training is useful in helping individuals to provide more relevant, accurate, and impartial forensic evaluations. To our knowledge, this has not yet been tested through empirical research.

SUMMARY AND CONCLUSIONS

In this chapter, we discussed FMHA broadly, without focusing on a particular kind of forensic assessment. More specific topics will be discussed in subsequent chapters of this book. In reviewing the nature of FMHA and the associated law, ethics, science, and practice, it seems clear that FMHA is a well-defined professional activity that is supported to a large extent by these various sources of authority. Nevertheless, it is equally clear that further progress in FMHA, particularly in this era of evidence-based practice, will be contingent on the extent to which high-quality empirical research data can guide, support, and evaluate practice in this area. Toward this end, we see three particular priorities for further progress in the field: the development of further practice guidelines, the development of additional specialty measures, and the conduct of additional research on the value of specialty training at various levels.

One of the most helpful ways of linking forensic practice with foundational research is through the development of practice guidelines, particularly when these guidelines are promulgated by a forensic specialty organization. AAPL has been quite successful in developing such guidelines. Organized psychology has not yet provided such practice guidelines, at least across the range of topics addressed by AAPL, although psychology does offer guidelines in the areas of child custody evaluations and child protection evaluations. The Oxford best practices series does address the needed range of topics, but it is healthier for a profession to offer such guidelines through a process for which the major specialty organization is primarily responsible—and for which members and consumers can provide input. Accordingly, our first recommendation is that the American Psychology-Law Society undertakes the development of practice guidelines that focus on a comprehensive range of topics across FMHA.

Related to the first recommendation, it is quite clear that forensic specialty measures (when properly developed) provide perhaps the most direct link between FMHA and the foundational science. There are a number of FMHA areas for which high-quality specialty measures exist. There are also areas in which no such measure has yet been developed, or the existing measures are not well designed and supported through empirical derivation and validation. Developing specialty measures in these areas would immediately improve the uniformity of evaluations across various topics. One of the recommendations that will be made with increasing frequency in years to come will involve the use of a specialized measure as part of FMHA. To implement this recommendation consistently, such specialty measures must be available for each form of FMHA.

Finally, it will be important to devote more empirical attention to our current models of specialty training. Current training opportunities do not allow for the training of a sufficient number of forensic specialists to meet the demand for all of the forms of FMHA that will be requested over the next decade. It is reasonable to assume that much FMHA will be conducted by individuals who (in the terms of the Villanova Conference; Bersoff et al., 1997) are proficient in certain aspects of FMHA. The most effective ways to train specialists and proficient clinicians in forensic assessment have largely gone unresearched. If the shrinking public resources provided in the last decade are any indication of the level of support that will be available in years to come, it will be crucial to invest such limited resources in the most cost and time efficient ways to yield maximal returns in FMHA performance.

References

American Academy of Child and Adolescent Psychiatry. (1997a). Practice parameters for child custody evaluation. *Journal of the American Academy of Child and Adolescent Psychiatry, 36,* 57S–68S.

American Academy of Child and Adolescent Psychiatry. (1997b). Practice parameters for the assessment and treatment of children and adolescents with conduct disorder. *Journal of the American Academy of Child and Adolescent Psychiatry, 36,* 122S–139S.

American Academy of Child and Adolescent Psychiatry. (1997c). Practice parameters for the forensic evaluation of children and adolescents who may have been physically or sexually abused. *Journal of the American Academy of Child and Adolescent Psychiatry, 36,* 37S–56S.

American Academy of Child and Adolescent Psychiatry. (1998). Practice parameters for the assessment and treatment of children and adolescents with post-traumatic stress disorder. *Journal of the American Academy of Child and Adolescent Psychiatry, 37,* 997–1001.

American Academy of Child and Adolescent Psychiatry. (1999). Practice parameters for the assessment and treatment of children and adolescents who are sexually abusive of others. *Journal of the American Academy of Child and Adolescent Psychiatry, 38,* 55S–76S.

American Academy of Psychiatry and the Law. (2005). *Ethical guidelines for the practice of forensic psychiatry.* Retrieved from http://www.aapl.org/pdf/ethicsgdlns.pdf

American Psychiatric Association. (2010). *The principles of medical ethics with annotations especially applicable to psychiatry.* Retrieved from http://www.psychiatry.org/practice/ethics/resources-standards

American Psychological Association. (1994). Guidelines for child custody evaluations in divorce proceedings. *American Psychologist, 49,* 677–680. doi:10.1037/0003-066X.49.7.677

American Psychological Association. (1999). Guidelines for psychological evaluations in child protection matters. *American Psychologist, 54,* 586–593. doi:10.1037/0003-066X.54.8.586

American Psychological Association. (2002). *Guidelines on multicultural education, training, research practice, and organizational change for psychologists.* Washington, DC: Author.

American Psychological Association. (2005). *Guidelines on effective behavioral treatment for persons with mental retardation and developmental disabilities: A resolution by APA Division 33.* Retrieved from http://www.apa.org/divisions/div33/effectivetreatment.html

American Psychological Association. (2009). *Guidelines and principles for accreditation of programs in professional psychology.* Retrieved from http://www.apa.org/ed/accreditation/index.aspx

American Psychological Association. (2010a). *Ethical principles of psychologists and code of conduct (2002, Amended June 1, 2010).* Retrieved from http://www.apa.org/ethics/code/index.aspx

American Psychological Association. (2010b). Guidelines for child custody evaluations in family law proceedings. *American Psychologist, 65,* 863–867. doi:10.1037/a0021250

American Psychological Association. (2011a). *Guidelines for psychological evaluations in child protection matters*. Retrieved from http://www.apa.org/practice/guidelines/child-protection.pdf

American Psychological Association. (2011b). *Specialty guidelines for forensic psychologists*. Retrieved from http://www.apa.org/practice/guidelines/forensic-psychology.aspx

Appelbaum, P., & Gutheil, T. (2007). *Clinical handbook of psychiatry and the law* (4th ed.). Baltimore, MD: Lippincott Williams & Wilkins.

Appelbaum, P. S. (1997). A theory of ethics for forensic psychiatry. *Journal of the American Academy of Psychiatry and the Law, 25*, 233–247.

Association of Family and Conciliation Courts. (2006). *Model standards of practice for child custody evaluation*. Milwaukee, WI: Author.

Bersoff, D., Goodman-Delahunty, J., Grisso, T., Hans, V., Poythress, N., & Roesch, R. (1997). Training in law and psychology: Models from the Villanova conference. *American Psychologist, 52*, 1301–1310. doi:10.1037/0003-066X.52.12.1301

Committee on Ethical Guidelines for Forensic Psychologists. (1991). Specialty guidelines for forensic psychologists. *Law and Human Behavior, 15*, 655–665.

Daubert v. Merrell Dow Pharmaceuticals, 509 U.S. 579 (1993).

Ewing, C. P. (2003). Expert testimony: Law and practice. In A. M. Goldstein (Ed.), *Handbook of psychology: Vol. 11. Forensic psychology* (pp. 55–68). Hoboken, NJ: Wiley.

Fed. R. Ev. 702.

Fed. R. Ev. 703.

Fed. R. Ev. 704(b).

Frye v. United States, 293 F. 1013 (D.C. Cir. 1923).

General Electric Company et al. v. Joiner et ux., 522 U.S. 136 (1997).

Giorgi-Guarnieri, D., Janofsky, J., Keram, E., Lawsky, S., Merideth, P., Mossman, D., . . . Zonana, H. (2002). AAPL practice guideline for forensic psychiatric evaluation of defendants raising the insanity defense. *Journal of the American Academy of Psychiatry and the Law, 30*(2, suppl.), S3–S40.

Goldstein, A. M. (Ed.). (2003). *Handbook of psychology: Vol. 11. Forensic psychology*. Hoboken, NJ: Wiley.

Goldstein, A. M. (Ed.). (2007). *Forensic psychology: Emerging topics and expanding roles*. Hoboken, NJ: Wiley.

Greenberg, S. A., & Shuman, D. W. (1997). Irreconcilable conflict between therapeutic and forensic roles. *Professional Psychology: Research and Practice, 28*, 50–57. doi:10.1037/0735-7028.28.1.50

Grisso, T. (1986). *Evaluating competencies: Forensic assessments and instruments*. New York, NY: Plenum. doi:10.1007/978-1-4899-5046-8

Grisso, T. (2003). *Evaluating competencies: Forensic assessments and instruments* (2nd ed.). New York, NY: Kluwer Academic/Plenum.

Heilbrun, K. (2001). *Principles of forensic mental health assessment*. New York, NY: Kluwer Academic/Plenum.

Heilbrun, K., DeMatteo, D., & Marczyk, G. (2004). Pragmatic psychology, forensic mental health assessment, and the case of Thomas Jefferson: Applying principles to promote quality. *Psychology, Public Policy, and Law, 10*, 31–70. doi:10.1037/1076-8971.10.1-2.31

Heilbrun, K., DeMatteo, D., Marczyk, G., Finello, C., Smith, R., & Mack-Allen, J. (2005). Applying principles of forensic mental health assessment to capital sentencing. *Widener Law Review, 11*, 93–118.

Heilbrun, K., DeMatteo, D., Marczyk, G., & Goldstein, A. M. (2008). Standards of practice and care in forensic mental health assessment: Legal, professional, and principles-based considerations. *Psychology, Public Policy, and Law, 14*, 1–26. doi:10.1037/1076-8971.14.1.1

Heilbrun, K., Douglas, K., & Yasuhara, K. (2009). Violence risk assessment: Core controversies. In J. Skeem, K. Douglas, & S. Lilienfeld (Eds.), *Psychological science in the courtroom: Controversies and consensus* (pp. 333–357). New York, NY: Guilford Press.

Heilbrun, K., Grisso, T., & Goldstein, A. (2009). *Foundations of forensic mental health assessment*. New York, NY: Oxford University Press.

Heilbrun, K., Grisso, T., Goldstein, A. M., & LaDuke, C. (2012). Foundations of forensic mental health assessment. In R. Roesch & P. Zapf (Eds.), *Forensic assessments in criminal and civil law: A handbook for lawyers* (pp. 1–15). New York, NY: Oxford University Press.

Heilbrun, K., Kelley, S. M., Koller, J. P., Lane, C., & Peterson, L. (2013). The role of university-based forensic clinics. *International Journal of Law and Psychiatry, 36*, 195–200. doi:10.1016/j.ijlp.2013.04.019

Heilbrun, K., Marczyk, G., & DeMatteo, D. (2002). *Forensic mental health assessment: A casebook*. New York, NY: Oxford University Press.

Heilbrun, K., Marczyk, G., DeMatteo, D., & Mack-Allen, J. (2007). A principles-based approach to forensic mental health assessment: Utility and update. In A. M. Goldstein (Ed.), *Forensic psychology: Emerging topics and expanding roles* (pp. 45–72). Hoboken, NJ: Wiley.

Heilbrun, K., Marczyk, G., DeMatteo, D., Zillmer, E., Harris, J., & Jennings, T. (2003). Principles of forensic mental health assessment: Implications for neuropsychological assessment in forensic contexts. *Assessment, 10*, 329–343. doi:10.1177/1073191103258591

Heilbrun, K., Warren, J., & Picarello, K. (2003). Third party information in forensic assessment. In A. M. Goldstein (Ed.), *Handbook of psychology: Vol. 11. Forensic psychology* (pp. 69–86). Hoboken, NJ: Wiley. doi:10.1002/0471264385.wei1105

Jenkins v. United States, 307 F.2d 637 (U.S. App. D.C., 1962).

Koch, W., Nader, R., & Haring, M. (2009). The science and pseudoscience of assessing psychological injuries. In J. Skeem, K. Douglas, & S. Lilienfeld (Eds.), *Psychological science in the courtroom: Consensus and controversy* (pp. 263–283). New York, NY: Guilford Press.

Marczyk, G., DeMatteo, D., Kutinsky, J., & Heilbrun, K. (2008). Training in forensic assessment and intervention: Implications for principles-based models. In R. Jackson (Ed.), *Learning forensic assessment* (pp. 3–31). New York, NY: Routledge/Taylor & Francis Group.

Melton, G., Petrila, J., Poythress, N., & Slobogin, C. (2007). *Psychological evaluations for the courts: A handbook for mental health professionals and lawyers* (3rd ed.). New York, NY: Guilford Press.

Michigan Statute Annotated § 28.1043, 20a(6)(c) (1954).

Morse, S. (1978). Law and mental health professionals: The limits of expertise. *Professional Psychology, 9*, 389–399. doi:10.1037/0735-7028.9.3.389

Morse, S. J. (1999). Crazy reasons. *Journal of Contemporary Legal Issues, 10*, 189–226.

Mossman, D., Noffsinger, S., Ash, P., Frierson, R., Gerbasi, J., Hackett, M., . . . Zonana, H. (2007). AAPL practice guideline for the forensic psychiatric evaluation of competence to stand trial. *Journal of the American Academy of Psychiatry and the Law, 35*, S3–S72.

O'Donohue, W., Beitz, K., & Tolle, L. (2009). Controversies in child custody evaluations. In J. Skeem, K. Douglas, & S. Lilienfeld (Eds.), *Psychological science in the courtroom: Consensus and controversy* (pp. 284–308). New York, NY: Guilford Press.

Otto, R., Heilbrun, K., & Grisso, T. (1990). Training and credentialing in forensic psychology. *Behavioral Sciences and the Law, 8*, 217–231. doi:10.1002/bsl.2370080305

Otto, R. K., & Heilbrun, K. (2002). The practice of forensic psychology: A look toward the future in light of the past. *American Psychologist, 57*, 5–18. doi:10.1037/0003-066X.57.1.5

Otto, R. K., Slobogin, C., & Greenberg, S. A. (2007). Legal and ethical issues in accessing and utilizing third-party information. In A. M. Goldstein (Ed.), *Forensic psychology: Emerging topics and expanding roles* (pp. 190–208). Hoboken, NJ: Wiley.

Packer, I., & Borum, R. (2003). Forensic training and practice. In A. M. Goldstein (Ed.), *Handbook of psychology: Vol. 11. Forensic psychology* (pp. 21–32). Hoboken, NJ: Wiley. doi:10.1002/0471264385.wei1102

Packer, I., & Grisso, T. (2011). *Specialty competencies in forensic psychology*. New York, NY: Oxford University Press.

Poythress, N., & Zapf, P. (2009). Controversies in evaluating competence to stand trial. In J. Skeem, K. Douglas, & S. Lilienfeld (Eds.), *Psychological science in the courtroom: Consensus and controversy* (pp. 309–329). New York, NY: Guilford Press.

Roesch, R., & Zapf, P. (Eds.). (2013). *Forensic assessments in criminal and civil law: A handbook for lawyers*. New York, NY: Oxford University Press.

Rogers, R., & Ewing, C. P. (2003). The prohibition of ultimate opinions: A misguided enterprise. *Journal of Forensic Psychology Practice, 3*, 65–75.

Rogers, R., & Shuman, D. (2000). *Conducting insanity evaluations* (2nd ed.). New York, NY: Guilford Press.

Rosner, R. (1983). Education and training in forensic psychiatry. *Psychiatric Clinics of North America, 6*, 585–595.

Rosner, R. (Ed.). (2003). *Principles and practice of forensic psychiatry* (2nd ed.). New York, NY: Oxford University Press.

Simon, R., & Gold, L. (Eds.). (2004). *Textbook of forensic psychiatry*. Washington, DC: American Psychiatric Publishing.

Skeem, J., Douglas, K., & Lilienfeld, S. (Eds.). (2009). *Psychological science in the courtroom: Controversies and consensus*. New York, NY: Guilford Press.

Society for Industrial and Organizational Psychology. (2003). *Validation and use of personnel selection procedures* (4th ed.). Bowling Green, OH: Author.

Tennessee Code Annotated § 39-11-501 (1995).

Tillbrook, C., Mumley, D., & Grisso, T. (2003). Avoiding expert opinions on the ultimate legal question: The case for integrity. *Journal of Forensic Psychology Practice, 3*, 77–87. doi:10.1300/J158v03n03_05

United States v. Davis, 714 F. Supp. 853 (1988).

United States v. Kristiansen, 901 F.2d 1463 (1990).

United States v. Salamanca, 990 F.2d 629 (D.C. Cir.1993).

Weiner, I., & Hess, A. (Eds.). (2005). *The handbook of forensic psychology* (3rd ed.). New York, NY: Wiley.

Weissman, H., & DeBow, D. (2003). Ethical principles and professional competencies. In A. M. Goldstein (Ed.), *Handbook of psychology: Vol. 11. Forensic psychology* (pp. 33–54). Hoboken, NJ: Wiley. doi:10.1002/0471264385.wei1103

Wettstein, R. M. (2005). Quality and quality improvement in forensic mental health evaluations. *Journal of the American Academy of Psychiatry and the Law, 33*, 158–175.

CHAPTER 2

FORENSIC ASSESSMENT INSTRUMENTS

Richard Rogers and Chelsea E. Fiduccia

In the last half-century, the field of forensic psychology has grown exponentially in its rigor and sophistication, fueled substantially by the development and validation of forensic assessment instruments (FAIs). Today, these highly specialized tools are routinely used when considering legal standards within forensic evaluations. This chapter begins with a historical overview regarding the development of FAIs and forensically relevant instruments (FRIs), with considerable emphasis on the interplay between empirical rigor and legal standards. Next, we address both psychological and legal standards for the development and evaluation of FAIs and FRIs. In considering research on FAIs and FRIs, we identify three distinct levels of complexity that may be found in a given legal standard and how that affects the development and validation of measures. Finally, we discuss issues related to the practical application of FAIs and FRIs, including relevant ethical standards, time perspectives, and incremental accuracy.

IMPORTANCE OF THE PROBLEM

Prior to the 1970s, forensic assessments routinely used traditional clinical methods that were regularly applied to legal issues without any rigorous analysis of their theoretical underpinnings or empirical support. Ames Robey (1965) authored a seminal article recommending that forensic psychiatry advance beyond traditional practices and begin to systematically apply clearly defined criteria to legal constructs. As a result of his efforts, a straightforward checklist was produced for evaluating an individual's competency to stand trial. Although lacking by today's standards for test development and validation, Robey's work clearly delineated the beginning of a new era in forensic assessments.

Saleem Shah became the driving force in the empirically based development of forensic assessments. As capably summarized by Grisso (1995), mental health disciplines "should strive to *develop reliable and valid methods to measure what the law wanted to know* that was of a psychological or psychiatric nature" (p. 26). In his pivotal role as director of the National Institute of Mental Health Center for Studies of Crime and Delinquency, Shah spurred the development of the first standardized methods for assessing an individual's competency to stand trial, conducting *Miranda* assessments, and assessing violence risk. At their core, these advances sought to critically examine the relevant psycholegal constructs and systematically approach their empirical validation.

More recently, Rogers and Shuman (2005) outlined three broad and overlapping phases in the development of forensic psychology and related disciplines. First, *clinical tradition* represents the pre-Robey era in its customary usage of clinical tools without any research-based applications to specific psycholegal issues. Second, Melton, Petrila, Poythress, and Slobogin (1987) promoted the *legal–clinical* model, with its emphasis on case law and legal theory in framing the issues relevant to forensic practice. Importantly, this model provides a legally informed conceptual basis for conducting

http://dx.doi.org/10.1037/14461-002
APA Handbook of Forensic Psychology: Vol. 1. Individual and Situational Influences in Criminal and Civil Contexts,
B. L. Cutler and P. A. Zapf (Editors-in-Chief)

forensic assessments and structuring their conclusions. In general, specialized forensic measures are given relatively less weight even in the book's most recent revision (Melton, Petrila, Poythress, & Slobogin, 2007). For the third phase of development, Grisso (1986, 2003) pursued groundbreaking work—paying homage to Shah (Grisso, 1995)—that balanced the legal framework with rigorous research that prominently features FAIs. This third phase is described as the *legal–empirical–forensic* model (Rogers & Shuman, 2005).

Each element of the legal–empirical–forensic model underscores the importance and centrality of FAIs to forensic psychology and allied disciplines. The legal framework is critically important in conceptualizing a legal standard (e.g., competency to stand trial) and outlining its broad parameters. However, U.S. Supreme Court and other appellate decisions often use language that is open to interpretation, even among jurists and other legal scholars. Therefore, experts in mental health and law are needed to operationalize the legal standard and, when feasible, relate this standard to established psychological constructs. Without this first element, the content and construct validity of forensic assessment measures are jeopardized. Empirical validation relies on sound psychometric practices in the development of test items; the construction of relevant scales; and the painstaking analysis of reliability, validity, and generalizability. Finally, the skillful application of specialized measures demands forensic expertise. Given the complex, open-textured constructs associated with psycholegal issues (Roesch & Golding, 1980), FAIs—no matter how well validated—require an integrative expertise in combining their standardized data with highly relevant, case-specific information.

Classification of Forensic Measures

As a critically important distinction, forensic measures are classified by their relevance to legal standards as either FAIs or FRIs. Heilbrun, Rogers, and Otto (2002) defined FAIs as those psychological measures that focus on a specific legal standard and the measurement of its key components. In contrast, FRIs examine clinical constructs that are relevant to legal standards without attempting—directly or indirectly—to assess any legal construct. Although this chapter is entitled "Forensic Assessment Instruments," its analyses are sometimes broadened to embrace FRIs because of their importance—conceptually and empirically—to sophisticated forensic appraisals. Both types of measures are frequently used within the legal–empirical–forensic framework.

Within the criminal–forensic domain, FAIs are best exemplified by a constellation of measures that are intended to assess an individual's competency to stand trial based on the *Dusky* standard. In *Dusky v. United States* (1960), the Supreme Court propounded the competency standard in a single sentence with virtually no explanatory material: "The test must be whether he has sufficient present ability to consult with his lawyer with a reasonable degree of rational understanding—and whether he has a rational as well as factual understanding of the proceedings against him" (p. 789). Despite its seeming simplicity, researchers and scholars have differed on whether the *Dusky* standard is best conceptualized as two or three components (Rogers, Grandjean, Tillbrook, Vitacco, & Sewell, 2001). Competency measures will be used to illustrate key conceptual and psychometric issues in the Relevant Psychological Theory and Principles section.

Importance of Specialized Forensic Measures

The importance of FAIs and FRIs is highlighted by their extensive coverage in this handbook. Most chapters in Part I are informed by FAIs, and many chapters feature FAIs as essential components for the forensic assessment of a particular legal standard. As an exception, several chapters in this volume (i.e., Chapters 9 and 11) have relatively little coverage of FAIs. This de-emphasis simply reflects a lack of empirical development of FAIs for these legal standards. In some instances, the clear operationalization of legal standards can pose a formidable challenge, which stands in the way of FAI development. We hold that FAIs should constitute a central role in all domains of clinical forensic practice. Simply put, FAIs provide both standardization and science to the practice of forensic psychology and psychiatry.

FRIs also play a central role in forensic assessments and interventions. Malingering and other response styles must be considered for virtually all forensic determinations, whether they involve specific legal standards or they focus on less formal aspects of forensic decision making. For example, personal injury evaluations rely on the accuracy of clinical data at both pre-injury and postinjury assessment. More specifically, exaggerated adjustment at pre-injury or exaggerated impairment at postinjury may, when undetected, affect the accuracy and credibility of forensic conclusions. The detection of response styles is occasionally embedded within an FAI. An example involves the Atypical Presentation scales on the Evaluation of Competency to Stand Trial—Revised (ECST–R; Rogers, Tillbrook, & Sewell, 2004), which are used to screen for feigning and provide ancillary data regarding feigned incompetency. However, response styles are more frequently assessed via stand-alone FRIs.

Beyond response styles, risk assessments have generated a plethora of FRIs, ranging from highly sophisticated measures to simple actuarial scales that are devoid of psychological constructs. Recently, Singh and Fazel (2010) identified a total of 120 risk assessment measures; these same authors (Singh, Grann, & Fazel, 2011) subsequently evaluated nine commonly used risk assessment measures with mixed success for the two main test designs (i.e., structured clinical judgment and actuarial). Risk assessments and their research designs are discussed in detail in Chapter 3 of this volume (see also Douglas, Skeem, & Nicholson, 2011)

In summary, FAIs and FRIs form a complementary approach for conducting scientifically grounded forensic evaluations. They bring science to forensic practice via their standardization of the methodology in terms of both the clinical inquiries and the examinee responses. This standardization allows the accuracy of measurement to be rigorously examined via scale homogeneity and reliability. The validation of these measures typically involves construct validity, addressing both convergent and discriminant validity. Regarding the latter, the sine qua non standard for FAIs and FRIs is their accuracy at differentiating relevant criterion groups, such as genuine posttraumatic stress disorder from feigned posttraumatic stress disorder, or recidivism from nonrecidivism.

RELEVANT PSYCHOLOGICAL THEORY AND PRINCIPLES

Grisso (1986, 2003) provided an elegant model for the development and validation of FAIs; his work is featured as the centerpiece for this important section. From a legal perspective, FAIs will be critically examined via the *Daubert* (*Daubert v. Merrell Dow Pharmaceuticals, Inc.*, 1993) criteria for admissibility. Although Grisso's primary focus addressed FAIs, much of this analysis can be similarly applied to FRIs.

Grisso's Model of FAI Development and Validation

Rather than covering each of Grisso's (1986, 2003) components, this analysis examines those elements of greatest concern in the development and validation of FAIs. The greatest emphasis is placed on defining and operationalizing legal standards.

Defining the legal standard. Grisso's (2003) functional component addressed the specific capacities that are needed for an operationally defined legal competence: "*Reviews of law* typically involve comprehensive analysis of relevant statutes, case law, proposed legal standards, and legal commentary (e.g., law review journals)" (p. 462). In our estimation, the law (statutes and case law) constitutes the core consideration, with proposals and commentaries providing ancillary information. In many instances, however, case law mostly addresses the Constitutional minima.[1] As a recent example in *Florida v. Powell* (2010), the Supreme Court readily acknowledged that the particular *Miranda* warning that was administered to Powell was less than ideal yet was still adequate to convey his rights. Therefore, we strongly endorse Grisso's subsequent idea of surveying legal experts (e.g., judges and attorneys) with relevant professional experiences and developing a consensus.

We are largely in agreement with Grisso's (2003) functional component and simply wish to add several possible refinements. In our recent development of

---

[1]Important exceptions do occur. For instance, competency to stand trial in Hawaii (see *State v. Soares*, 1996) provides detailed criteria, including the abilities to maintain a consistent defense, to testify, and to identify witnesses' misstatements.

Miranda measures (Rogers, Sewell, Drogin, & Fiduccia, 2012), we found that legal experts often lack the clinical knowledge to bridge the two disciplines (e.g., criminal law and forensic psychology). The simple solution was to use dually trained experts (JDs and PhDs) who could appreciate both the open-textured constructs (Roesch & Golding, 1980) of legal standards as well as the need to clearly identify and operationalize representative elements of this standard. In fact, Grisso (2003) suggested that mental health professionals who have acquired the "special knowledge of the functional abilities and behaviors that are relevant for the legal competence question" (p. 26) are uniquely poised to describe the relationship between legal and clinical constructs. These experts can help us to define best practices standards that can augment the typically minimal criteria that are generally found in appellate cases.

Rather than rely on simple categorical agreements to reach a consensus (Grisso, 2003), we recommend the use of prototypical analysis to standardize the ratings used in developing a consensus. With prototypical analysis, the importance of each variable can be quantified in relationship to the legal construct. As a specific example, the ECST–R includes only those items within each domain of competency to stand trial with prototypical ratings ≥5.40 on a 7-point scale; the overall average of 6.10 fell between *very representative* (6) and *extremely representative* (7). Thus, the use of legal experts combined with prototypical analyses can provide highly relevant, easily quantified data as an initial step in operationalizing the legal standard.

Measure development and the legal standard.
Grisso (2003) outlined general principles of FAI measure development but eschewed specific models for constructing test items and assessing the item–examinee match. Regarding item construction, FAIs must clearly represent each of the relevant constructs, which typically are prongs of the legal standard. We recommend that FAI developers obtain input from dually trained experts and systematically create a substantial pool of potential items based on appellate decisions, law reviews, and forensic

research. This essential step to measure development (Clark & Watson, 1995) allows for extensive item refinement for legal prongs based on their conceptual relevance and empirically tested discriminability. As a simple example, one prong of the *Dusky* standard for competency to stand trial requires that the defendant have a rational ability to consult with counsel. Using the Georgia Court Competency Test (GCCT; Wildman et al., 1979) as an early FAI example, the question is raised whether rational abilities to communicate with counsel can be fully captured by three GCCT items that address the lawyer's name, contact information, and one inquiry about how the examinee can assist counsel. As illustrated by the GCCT and other early competency measures, a highly systematic approach to item generation is required that provides a broad coverage of relevant capacities. Rational abilities to communicate with counsel (see Rogers & Shuman, 2005) may include reasoning and concomitant decisions about (a) the relevant information to share with counsel; (b) the basic capacities to communicate with counsel; (c) autonomous decision making; and (d) the ability to rationally discuss defense strategies, such as the cross-examination of adverse witnesses.

Going beyond Grisso's (2003) guidelines, we suggest that the item–examinee match is critically relevant to FAI measure refinement. To further standardize assessment responses, some FAIs provide simulation instructions that ask examinees to assume that they are the same person but in entirely different circumstances, such as a fictitious crime or the hypothetical friend of a pretrial defendant. The key issue is whether the examinee is able to identify with the simulated scenario and its hypothetical details. For instance, are younger criminal defendants familiar with billiards and pool halls[2] in our increasing world of web-based connectivity? For FAI measures using hypothetical suppositions, research is obligated to test the item–examinee match as a partial test of its ecological validity. Borrowing simulation research on response styles (Rogers & Gillard, 2011), realistic scenarios can be developed and tested for targeted populations (e.g., pretrial defendants).

---

[2]This example is taken from the MacArthur Competence Assessment Tool—Criminal Adjudication (MacCAT–CA; Poythress et al., 1999); 16 of the 22 items address a hypothetical scenario involving a pool hall.

Grisso (2003)—also within the realm of ecological validity and his interactive component—stressed that the development of FAIs should consider jurisdictional variabilities in legally relevant statements. He specifically cited differences in *Miranda* warnings and phrases as special challenges to FAI development. His concern is completely warranted given the heterogeneity of *Miranda* warnings with hundreds of different versions for both general (i.e., all ages; Rogers, Hazelwood, Sewell, Harrison, & Shuman, 2008) and juvenile (Rogers, Blackwood, et al., 2012) warnings. FAI developers of *Miranda* measures are confronted with a serious quandary when faced with such heterogeneity; they can adopt either standardized (Goldstein, Zelle, & Grisso, 2012) or case-specific (e.g., the Miranda Comprehension Template; Rogers, 2012) approaches. The standardized (i.e., nomothetic) approach involves adoption of a single, uniformly applied *Miranda* warning. This option may create interpretation issues: "What is the level of similarity/dissimilarity between the tested warning and the actual warning used in the evaluated case?" Alternatively, a case-specific (i.e., idiographic) approach uses that actual *Miranda* warning and tailors its administration (e.g., oral vs. written) to the examinee's advisement. For the case-specific approach, ecological validity is partially preserved, but systematic comparisons to other pretrial defendants are severely limited.[3] In cases where jurisdiction-specific information is critical to the legal construct (e.g., the knowing waiver of *Miranda* rights), some combination of standardized and case-specific approaches will likely be useful.

Reliability and validity of FAI measures. Grisso (2003) underscored a critical point that reliability of the FAI must be established for the relevant forensic population. According to Grisso (2003), "Reliability coefficients based on the administration of a FAI to college sophomores cannot be trusted to provide estimates of measurement error that are meaningful for the use of an instrument in pretrial examinations of criminal defendants or parents seeking custody of a child" (p. 56). We agree with Grisso's recommendation and suggest that all FAIs

need to be evaluated on this metric. For instance, we believe that the recently released Inventory of Legal Knowledge (Otto, Musick, & Sherrod, 2010) needs to be updated. Although intended for use exclusively with criminal defendants, its internal consistency is derived only from community adults, whereas its test–retest reliability relies solely on college students. The need for test validation with relevant samples parallels the importance of item–examinee match.

For criterion-related validity, Grisso (2003) appropriately cautioned about the limitations of legal outcomes and clinical opinions and their uses as a *gold standard*. Grisso is entirely correct that a method with unknown reliability (e.g., a verdict) cannot be equated with a gold standard. Instead, one imprecise measure can be used to assist in refining and validating a new measure; this process is sometimes referred to as a *bootstrapping procedure* (Rogers, 2001).

Response styles and FAI measures. Grisso (2003) emphasized the importance of examining response styles and their effects on the valid interpretation of FAIs. In keeping with his point, it would be advantageous to test the effects of defensiveness (i.e., the denial and minimization of psychological symptoms) and feigning on all FAIs. Some FAIs with face validity and close-ended questions may be much more susceptible to intentional distortion than others in either denying an individual's abilities or emphasizing an impairment. A pseudoexample would be the following: "Did voices tell you to commit the crime?" With minimal effort, an examinee could affirm the feigned command hallucinations. In contrast, measures requiring open-ended responses increase the cognitive load on examinees, which may negatively affect their ability to dissimulate (Rogers, Boals, & Drogin, 2011).

Simulated adjustment is a possible motivation for certain FAI administrations where something may be potentially gained from intentionally appearing unimpaired (e.g., parenting capacity in child custody proceedings and preemployment assessments of police officers). Simulated adjustment may take several related forms, such as defensiveness and social desirability (i.e., overplaying positive personal attributes). In addition, stigmatization may play a

---

[3]As a sole exception, the "right to silence" component is nearly universal.

role with defensiveness, with a certain proportion of examinees being motivated not to appear "crazy".

Conclusory opinions based on FAI measures. Grisso (2003) was concerned that FAI conclusory opinions, expressed as either statements or cut scores, may step into the province of the judge and jury in rendering a "moral or social judgment" (p. 38). However, he readily acknowledged the possibility that "in actual practice these features of FAIs do little harm" (p. 473). The merits of conclusory opinions have been vigorously debated, with arguments both attacking them (e.g., Melton et al., 1987; Melton, Petrila, Poythress, & Slobogin, 1997) and defending them (Rogers & Ewing, 1989, 2003). The use of criterion groups (e.g., likely competent vs. likely incompetent defendants) is a critical component of FAI test validation. The crucial issue is whether a particular FAI can reliably differentiate between relevant criterion groups. Despite their general opposition to conclusory opinions, Slobogin, Melton, and Showalter (1984) illustrated the centrality of conclusory opinions in their validation of an FAI screen, the Mental State at the Time of the Offense Screening Evaluation.[4]

Grisso (2003) expressed concerns about the use of FAI cut scores in actual forensic practice to discriminate between criterion groups in order to automatically classify examinees according to a legal standard. This problem appears to be associated with overreliance on a single score and the lack of consideration of additional case-specific information. Moreover, classification issues may involve not only explicit conclusions by forensic evaluators, but in their absence, subjective inferences by triers of fact, such as judges. To minimize unnecessary subjectivity, quantification and cut scores are essential elements of psychometric measures in general and FAIs in particular.

Without cut scores (or other methods of systematic quantification and classification), we assert that interpretive statements would be meaningless exercises in subjectivity and futility. Without some form of quantification and systematic discrimination, forensic psychologists could endlessly spar from a

dimensional perspective over how much of "some" is "enough" to provide particular interpretations. As subsequently discussed, the absence of cut scores would also be germane to the *Daubert* framework. Without clearly delineated classifications, error rates cannot be ascertained.

Applicability of the *Daubert* Framework to FAIs

For this section, we use the *Daubert* criteria to provide a general framework for the evaluation of FAIs and intentionally avoid any detailed analysis regarding the admissibility of particular measures. According to *Daubert*, four components may be considered in evaluating the admissibility of expert evidence: (a) falsifiability, (b) peer review and publication, (c) known or potential rate of error, and (d) general acceptance. This discussion focuses on (a) and (c), which are the most difficult for judges to understand (Gatowski et al., 2001)

The U.S. Supreme Court in *Daubert* affirmed that "the criterion of the scientific status of a theory is its falsifiability, or refutability, or testability" (p. 593). For example, can any measure or combination of measures capture the "best interests of the child" as required for child custody cases in many jurisdictions? As illustrated by Rotgers and Barrett (1996), the Ackerman–Schoendorf Parent Evaluation of Custody Test (ASPECT; Ackerman & Schoendorf, 1992) falls far short of measuring good parenting, a "construct that has resisted attempts at adequate scientific definition" (p. 471). The ASPECT lacks testability due to (a) an inadequately defined construct, (b) its lack of congruence with this construct, and (c) the formidable array of scale combinations that militate against acceptable validation.

More recently, the *Daubert* component of testability was applied to the Malingered Neurocognitive Dysfunction (MND; Slick, Sherman, & Iverson, 1999) model, which is widely used in the validation of FRI measures for feigned cognitive impairment. The MND uses an innumerable array of possible variables in examining any discrepancies for all combinations of test data, observations, collateral data, past history, and brain functioning. As observed by Rogers, Bender, and Johnson (2011),

---

[4]Interestingly, Melton et al. (1997) touted this measure for rendering a conclusory opinion, affirming that it "may be able to detect the *obviously insane* [emphasis added] individual for whom a more comprehensive evaluation is unnecessary" (p.235). After a questioning of its merits (Rogers & Ewing, 2003), this FAI screen was entirely omitted from the most recent edition of the book (Melton et al., 2007).

"For MND, the virtually unlimited set of idiosyncratic variables (e.g., hundreds of variables in medical and psychiatric records alone) makes this model untestable and, therefore unverifiable" (p. 153). Thus, measures and their underlying models can fail to meet the *Daubert* criteria due to their sheer complexity.[5]

The U.S. Supreme Court in *Daubert* (1993) also held that courts "should consider the known or potential rate of error" (p. 594) associated with a scientific technique. As mentioned previously, some classification or categorization must occur before an error rate can be established. Single or multiple cut scores are very commonly found with FRIs, such as those used by feigning measures. For example, the Structured Inventory of Malingered Symptomatology (Widows & Smith, 2005) uses a total cut score to identify a high frequency of atypical symptoms, "raising the suspicion of malingering" (p. 15). In contrast, the Structured Interview of Reported Symptoms, Second Edition (SIRS–2; Rogers, Sewell, & Gillard, 2010) uses multiple steps for identifying likely feigning and likely genuine groups.

FAIs vary substantially in their use of cut scores for the classification of legally relevant abilities. For example, the first-generation competency measures used single cut scores with varying success (Nicholson, Robertson, Johnson, & Jensen, 1988) for classifying defendants as likely competent (e.g., GCCT ≥ 70) or likely incompetent (e.g., GCCT < 70). However, such early efforts failed on conceptual grounds: Using just a total score, it is possible to exceed the cut score yet have very limited abilities on one of *Dusky*'s three prongs.

The two second-generation competency measures—the MacArthur Competence Assessment Tool—Criminal Adjudication (MacCAT–CA; Poythress et al., 1999) and ECST–R—based their categorizations on individual *Dusky* prongs. For instance, the MacCAT–CA has established scores for *clinically significant impairment*, with percentile ranks for presumed competent and presumed incompetent groups. For example, a score of 4 on the Reasoning measure (i.e., the assist counsel prong) was found for 0.8% of presumed competent

but 13.3% of presumed incompetent defendants (Poythress et al., 1999; see Table 5). If this score were due to "limited intellectual functioning," Poythress et al. (1999) affirm that it "may constitute a legitimate basis for a finding of incompetence" (p. 21). For the ECST–R, the Consult-with-Counsel scale is interpreted as extreme impairment for T scores between 80 and 89 for nonfeigning defendants. At this level, pretrial defendants typically evidence severe deficits in their ability to communicate rationally with counsel. However, forensic evaluators are instructed to consider case-specific abilities in making their determinations of competency.

The ECST–R addresses error rates via standard errors of measurement (SEM) that are considered at three levels of certitude beyond simple preponderance: *probable* (1.00 SEM above the cut score; error rate ≤ 15.9%), *very probable* (1.65 SEM above the cut score; error rate ≤ 5.0%), and *definite* (2.06 SEM above the cut score; error rate ≤ 2.0%). For the MacCAT–CA, we recommend a similar process using the weighted *SD* and estimates of interrater reliability to address error rates. For example, the SEM for the Understanding measure remains small (i.e., 1.13) because of the high interrater reliability (Intraclass correlation coefficient [ICC] = .90; weighted *SD* = 3.57). As with the ECST–R, the SEM can be applied to different levels of certitude, thereby documenting estimated error rates for the *Daubert* standard.

An important but often overlooked component of *Daubert* error rates requires that standardized administration be used. As stated in *Daubert* (1993), error rates are based on the "existence and maintenance of standards controlling the technique's operation" (p. 594). Without such standardization, variability would be introduced into the use of the scientific technique that would obviously affect, and likely increase, its error rates. An unfortunately common example in forensic assessments is the use of an FRI with an idiosyncratic translation into a different language. Such ad hoc translations typically violate professional ethics, the standards of the test translation and adaptation guidelines of the

---

[5]Interestingly, the MND (Slick et al., 1999) also fails the testability criterion of *Daubert* by making impermissible assumptions that confuse a potential incentive (e.g., unwarranted financial gain) with a proven motivation (e.g., the presence of the incentive proves the motivation to malinger).

International Test Commission (see Hambleton, 2001), and copyright law. In addition, such translations violate the test's validation and militate against the accurate use of this message. As an egregious example, one author (RR) consulted on an idiosyncratic translation of the SIRS (Rogers, Bagby, & Dickens, 1992); more than half (57.0%) of the Kinyarwanda translation was inaccurate. Beyond the pervasive problems with linguistic equivalence, no research is available on this translated version, including any data on its utility estimates in general and error rates in particular.

RESEARCH REVIEW

This section provides a general overview and conceptualization of research knowledge as applied to FAIs and FRIs. Subsequent sections will focus more closely on the research status of individual measures and their clinical applicability to forensic practice. The section begins with a review regarding the scope of forensic measures.

Scope of Forensic Measures

Heilbrun et al. (2002; see Table 4.1) summarized the 20th-century research on forensic measures. For the 1960s and 1970s, such research efforts were focused entirely on an individual's competency to stand trial. This focus broadened substantially during the 1980s. Criminal forensic measures included Grisso's (1998) *Miranda* instruments and criminal responsibility (Rogers, 1984), whereas initial scales to evaluate child custody were developed in the civil domain. Work on malingering was initiated in the 1980s, with a proliferation of feigning measures being developed in the next decade. In the 1990s, forensic measures were developed for competency to stand trial, response styles, psychopathy, and risk assessment.

The development and validation of forensic measures has continued unabated since Heilbrun et al. (2002). Criminal forensic issues include (a) the second generation of *Miranda* measures (i.e., the Miranda Rights Comprehension Instruments [MRCI; Goldstein et al., 2012] and Standardized Assessment of Miranda Abilities [SAMA; Rogers et al., 2012], to be discussed later in this chapter), (b) juvenile waivers

to adult court (Salekin, 2004), (c) competency to stand trial with an embedded feigning screen (ECST–R), (d) feigned incompetency and legal knowledge (Otto et al., 2010), and (e) initial checklist on competency to be executed (Zapf, Boccaccini, & Brodsky, 2003). As previously noted, this period also included a marked upsurge in risk assessment measures (Singh & Fazel, 2010) intended mostly for criminal forensic settings.

Extending beyond the criminal forensic domain, forensic measures continue to be developed for the assessment of response styles, especially as they relate to feigned mental disorders and feigned cognitive impairment. However, we were unable to find FAIs or FRIs developed in the last decade to address common civil issues such as personal injury and child custody.

Legal Standards and the Complexity of FAI Assessments

Forensic evaluations in the criminal domain vary markedly in their complexity, ranging from clear, easily operationalized legal standards to their intricate counterparts with seemingly innumerable variations. The simple–complex dimension exerts multiple effects on the development and validation of forensic measures. Legal standards can be conceptualized with at least three levels of increasing complexity and ambiguity. Using the criminal–forensic domain for the purposes of illustration, Table 2.1 exemplifies how legal standards can range from highly focused with several related constructs to broad conceptualizations entailing innumerable variations.

At least within the United States, the legal standard for competency to stand trial is an exemplary model of simplicity and uniformity. As noted previously, the U.S. Supreme Court established the *Dusky* standard in 1960 in its one-page decision. After more than five decades, forensic researchers have considerable confidence that the *Dusky* criteria are enduring. As summarized, both second-generation competency measures (i.e., MacCAT–CA and ECST–R) agree on its three specific prongs, although they are operationalized very differently (Rogers & Johansson-Love, 2009). Even with competency to stand trial, greater complexity can be introduced. For example, the American Bar

TABLE 2.1

The Complexity of Legal Standard With Sample Forensic Measures From the Criminal Domain

Complexity	Legal issue	Sample measure[a]	Framework (e.g., standardization and case-specific information)
Single focus with some variations	Competency to stand trial: All jurisdictions rely on the *Dusky* standard, which requires both factual knowledge and rational abilities. Some jurisdictions have adopted extra components, such as the *Drope* component.	CAST–MR	The CAST–MR focuses on two standardized scales—Basic Legal Concepts and Skills to Assist Defense—that ask general questions and provide three multiple-choice responses. For the second scale, examinees are asked hypothetical questions (e.g., "What if . . . ?" and "Let's pretend . . ."). The third scale, Understanding Case Events, is entirely case specific about the offense being evaluated.
		MacCAT–CA	The MacCAT–CA concentrates on standardization and deemphasizes case-specific information. It includes (a) factual understanding, (b) relevant information to share with counsel in a hypothetical case, and (c) the defendant's case-specific views and reasoning as it applied to his or her upcoming trial.
		ECST–R	The ECST–R emphasizes the standardization of case-specific information regarding the defendant's factual and rational understanding as well as the ability to consult with his or her counsel. It also provides an opportunity to supplement standardized ratings with additional case-specific information. Finally, it performs a forensically relevant instrument (FRI) function in informing forensic evaluators regarding the possibility of feigned incompetence.
		CAI	The CAI strongly emphasizes case-specific information. Although sample questions are provided, forensic evaluators are free to use their own inquiries and integration of data. Only the ratings of broad categories are standardized.
Cluster of legal standards with closely related constructs	Most states and federal jurisdictions have retained some test of criminal responsibility, although the components vary in coverage. All current standards include cognitive impairment; several also address volitional impairment.	R–CRAS	Similar to the CAI, the R–CRAS strongly emphasizes case-specific information. It provides detailed ratings related to the components of the American Law Institute standard with relatively little data about other standards. Only the ratings and decision model are standardized.
Broad array of related constructs	The validity of *Miranda* waivers is premised on accurate knowledge of *Miranda* rights. However, hundreds of highly varied *Miranda* warnings present a formidable challenge to forensic assessment instruments. Moreover, these determinations are highly complex and must take into account the *totality of circumstances*.	MRCI	Like the MacCAT–CA, the MRCI concentrates on standardization and deemphasizes case-specific information. It addresses *Miranda* vocabulary, the recall and subsequent recognition of a particular *Miranda* warning, and vignette-based decisions about an examinee's perceptions and hypothetical decisions regarding *Miranda* advisements and interrogation. [check]
		SAMA	Three SAMA measures focus solely on standardization; they emphasize *Miranda* vocabulary, *Miranda* misconceptions, and acquiescence as it relates to police custody and interrogation. In contrast, the remaining two measures emphasize case-specific information. Examinees are tested on their ability to recall a particular *Miranda* warning; scoring is only provided for common components. Their reasoning as applied to their own waiver decision is also considered, but the concomitant ratings are only considered individually and are not compiled into subscales.

(Continued)

TABLE 2.1 (CONTINUED)		
Sexually violent predator (SVP) standards share several commonalities but can include highly diverse diagnoses and different approaches to volitional issues.	SORAG	The SORAG is an FRI that is designed to evaluate sexual recidivism. As an actuarial measure, it strongly emphasizes standardization, although case-specific information (e.g., age of the victims) is included in its ratings.
	RRASOR	The RRASOR is a very brief FRI that strongly emphasizes standardization. It considers the background of the examinee and the pattern of past offenses. The RRASOR does not include any clinical variables.

Note. CAST–MR = Competence Assessment for Standing Trial for Defendants With Mental Retardation; MacCAT–CA = MacArthur Competence Assessment Tool–Criminal Adjudication; ECST–R = Evaluation of Competency to Stand Trial—Revised; CAI = Competency to Stand Trial Assessment Instrument; R–CRAS = Rogers Criminal Responsibility Assessment Scales; MRCI = Miranda Rights Comprehension Instruments; SAMA = Standardized Assessment of Miranda Abilities; SORAG = Sex Offense Risk Appraisal Guide (Quinsey, Harris, Rice, & Cormier, 1998); RRASOR = Rapid Risk Assessment of Sexual Offense (Hanson, 1997).
[a]Measures, unless specifically noted in the Framework, are forensic assessment instruments.

Association (1989) cited *Drope v. Missouri* (1974) in recommending an additional component,[6] requiring that defendants be able to "otherwise assist with [their] defense" (p. 170). Adopted by some jurisdictions, this component greatly increases the complexity of the competency determinations. Developers of forensic measures can easily envision dozens of viable possibilities that are linked to evidence gathering, cross-examination of adverse witnesses, and the development of defense strategies. Predictably, none of the first- or second-generation competency measures attempted to tackle this highly complex and case-specific component.

Competency measures vary in their standardization of constructs and their correspondence to the *Dusky* criteria. For example, the Competence Assessment for Standing Trial for Defendants With Mental Retardation (CAST–MR; Everington & Luckasson, 1992) focuses on standardization, rather than case-specific information, for two scales—Basic Legal Constructs and Skills to Assist Defense. In order to achieve uniformity, questions for the latter scale are hypothetical and likely do not apply to most criminal cases. In contrast, the third scale (Understanding Case Events) focuses entirely on case-specific information. Differences between the MacCAT–CA and ECST–R were previously

addressed. As a very different model, the Competency to Stand Trial Assessment Instrument (CAI; McGarry & Curran, 1973) focuses entirely on case-specific information and makes no attempt to develop scales or compare examinees to any normative data. Interestingly, Grisso (2003) included the CAI "primarily for its historical value" (p. 122), but "revised" CAI versions (e.g., Riley, 1998) that lack any systematic validation continue to be used.

The second level of FAI complexity involves a cluster of legal standards that include closely related constructs. This second level is best exemplified by insanity standards. Currently used insanity standards always contain a cognitive component but vary on the inclusion of a volitional component. Focusing on the cognitive component, very high agreement was found across insanity standards, including the American Law Institute (ALI), the M'Naghten rule (1843), and the American Psychiatric Association proposal (Wettstein, Mulvey, & Rogers, 1991). On this point, the Rogers Criminal Responsibility Assessment Scales (R–CRAS; Rogers, 1984) were validated for the ALI standard. However, subsequent research indicated that the discriminability of R–CRAS is similarly high for the M'Naghten standard (Rogers, Seman, & Clark, 1986). The R–CRAS focuses entirely on case-specific

---

[6]As observed by Rogers et al. (2001), the *Drope v. Missouri* (1974) decision contains only a passing reference to the phrase "assist in preparing his defense" (p. 505) and explicitly affirms the *Dusky v. United States* (1960) standard.

information, which is integrated from a variety of sources. Despite the integration of data from multiple sources, the majority of R–CRAS individual ratings (17 of 23, or 73.9%) evidence adequate to good test–retest reliabilities ($rs > .50$) after an interval averaging 2.8 weeks. Independent classifications of the ALI decision model evidenced high agreement for the components (85 to 100%) and the final classification (97%; kappa = .94). At this second level of complexity, FAIs can provide reliable and useful information to forensic evaluators.

The third level of complexity for legal standards involves a broad array of constructs that often include innumerable variations. We selected two legal standards as examples: (a) *Miranda* waivers currently involve two FAIs (i.e., MRCI and SAMA), and (b) sexually violent predator (SVP) standards often rely on FRIs that are designed to assess specific types of risk.

Assessments regarding the validity of *Miranda* waivers must consider examinees' *Miranda* comprehension and reasoning. Research (Rogers et al., 2008) has identified hundreds of general *Miranda* warnings with remarkably different lengths (i.e., 49–547 words) and reading levels (i.e., Grade 2 to higher than a college education). Additional barriers to the understanding of *Miranda* rights include serious misconceptions about these rights and permissible police practices (Rogers, Rogstad, et al., 2010). Finally, *Miranda* determinations are based on the *totality of circumstances*; in other words, they must take into account all common and unique factors that could affect the validity of the *Miranda* waivers.

This third level of complexity limits the ability of FAIs to grapple with the legal standards. Although taking very different approaches, both the MRCI and the SAMA assess an individual's basic abilities (e.g., vocabulary and knowledge) coupled with reasoning in order to provide valuable data about the examinee's *Miranda* abilities. In light of these complexities, neither measure attempts to operationalize either the knowing or intelligent prongs of *Miranda* waivers.

Legal standards for SVPs epitomize complexity and ambiguity. As described by Rogers and Shuman (2005), SVP standards typically include sexually

harmful behavior, although even this criterion varies both in terms of severity and in terms of evidence (e.g., conviction, charge, or other proof). The requisite clinical condition often includes *mental abnormality*, which is an undefined term that is completely open to interpretation. As the U.S. Supreme Court specified in *Kansas v. Crane* (2002), the prediction of future sexually harmful behavior must be linked to a "serious difficulty in controlling behavior" that is differentiated "from the dangerous but typical recidivist" (p. 413). Because all recidivists and SVP candidates control most of their criminal behavior,[7] the distinction between uncontrolled and uncontrollable behavior can range from a philosophical debate to extreme reductionism, with the lack of desire to control behavior being facilely equated with uncontrollability.

Available risk assessment measures fail to evaluate the SVP standards or most of their components. As summarized by Rogers and Jackson (2005), risk assessment measures fail to measure the prerequisite condition (e.g., mental abnormalities and disorders) and the causal nexus (e.g., lack of volition for past and future crimes). Thus, SVP standards—because of their complexity and ambiguity—have not been operationalized or empirically tested as forensic measures.

PRACTICE AND POLICY ISSUES

Forensic psychologists are informed by professional ethics and specialty guidelines regarding the parameters of professional practice. Because specific FAIs and FRIs will be discussed in subsequent chapters (see Chapters 3, 4, 5, 10, 12, 13, and 15, this volume), this section will focus on several general principles that should inform forensic assessments and subsequent reports.

FAIs have a substantial advantage over many general psychological measures in their clear specification of scope and validation. Regarding ethical standards, forensic evaluators are generally able to "use assessment techniques, interviews, tests or instruments in a manner and for purposes that are appropriate in light of the research" (American

[7]Sex offenders in the community have dozens of opportunities each day to commit harmful sexual conduct but typically inhibit their behavior for a multitude of reasons, including the fear of apprehension.

Psychological Association [APA], 2010, Standard 9.02, para. 1). Although the second component of 9.02 appears to invite subjectivity (i.e., "or evidence of the usefulness and proper application of the techniques"; para. 1), its application appears limited to techniques and not formally validated measures.

The second theme in APA (2010) ethical standards for psychological assessments involves explicit cautions regarding limitations in test validation and conclusions. Forensic psychologists are required to "indicate any significant limitations of their interpretations" (Standard 9.06, para. 1) and to describe "limitations of test results and interpretation" (Standard 9.02, para. 2) when applied to populations, and presumably referral issues, that extend beyond the scope of the measure's validation. Research is lacking on how often forensic psychologists explicitly describe both the strengths and weaknesses of FAIs as they apply to a particular case and their conclusions.

Forensic specialty guidelines were recently revised by the American Psychology-Law Society (AP–LS) and were officially adopted by the APA Council of Representatives (APA, 2013). The AP–LS guidelines affirm the importance of testing measures, including FAIs and FRIs, within a forensic context. When such research has not been conducted, forensic psychologists are asked "to describe the strengths and limitations of any test results and explain the extrapolation of these data to the forensic context" (APA, 2013, Standard 10.02, p. 15). Thus, both the process of extrapolation and concomitant limitations are provided. In addition, forensic psychologists should select measures based on their relevance to psycholegal factors (APA, 2013, Standard 10.01), seek multiple sources of data (APA, 2013, Standard 9.03), and actively test rival hypotheses (APA, 2013, Standard 9.01).

Although the primary audience for this book is forensic psychologists, readers should be aware of other professional standards for forensic practice. In particular, the American Academy of Psychiatry and the Law (AAPL) has been proactive in developing professional practice guidelines that provide (a) detailed summaries of forensic issues and (b) extensive descriptions of assessment methods and reports. Specific forensic issues include the insanity defense

(Giorgi-Guarnieri et al., 2002), competency to stand trial (Mossman et al., 2007), and psychiatric disability (Gold et al., 2008).

Time Perspective

Forensic measures must consider closely two time parameters (a) the time framework for the legal standard and (b) the stability of the relevant clinical constructs. Legal standards vary remarkably in their time framework. Some standards focus on the current time—such as civil commitment and competency to stand trial—although the latter issue may also include prospective estimates regarding restorability. Other issues, such as the insanity defense, are retrospective in nature. The forensic challenge is to assemble adequate information from multiple sources about an atypical and often very infrequent event (e.g., murder during a psychotic episode). Retrospective assessments differ fundamentally from prospective evaluations in that the atypical/infrequent event has occurred, and rival hypotheses are being critically examined. In contrast, prospective evaluations, such as SVP determinations, involve the prediction of events, which may or may not be rare. For FAIs, the critical question is whether the test development and validation takes into account the extended time perspective.

The other time parameter entails the stability of the clinical constructs. For example, traditional beliefs about the stability of personality disorders have been assailed. In a study by Gunderson et al. (2011), most of the patients who had been diagnosed with borderline and other personality disorders achieved remissions during a 10-year follow-up. For risk assessments, psychopathy is often considered a highly stable clinical construct. When considering the Psychopathy Checklist—Revised (PCL–R; Hare, 2003), for example, studies are very limited on its test–retest reliability, with data only available on chronic methadone users (Vitacco & Neumann, 2008). Inspection of these data (see Rutherford, Cacciola, Alterman, McKay, & Cook, 1999) raises major concerns about their forensic applicability: (a) sampling of mostly veterans with substance abuse histories, (b) use of a nonstandardized cut score of ≥25 for psychopathy, (c) a modest ICC of .48 for male participants, and (d) a doubling of female psychopaths after a 24-month follow-up.

Incremental Accuracy

Forensic practice is sometimes based more on tradition than on a rigorous testing of incremental validity and incremental accuracy. Staying with psychopathy as an example, Walters (2012) asked a simple question regarding incremental validity: "Would the PCL–R better predict general and violent recidivism than six easily accessed questions about offense history?" Walters (2012) found no incremental validity for the PCL–R once age and offense history were considered.

Rogers and Rogstad (2010) approached the issue of incremental accuracy from a different perspective. They asked whether a difference in the predictive abilities for the Psychopathy Checklist: Screening Version (PCL:SV; Hart, Cox, & Hare, 1995) and antisocial personality disorder (APD) could simply reflect disparities in cut scores given that the PCL measures are set much higher (i.e., ≥75% of the total score for psychopathy) than the APD measures (i.e., <50% of the *DSM–III–R* and *DSM–IV* criteria). Two findings are thought provoking: First, the much-touted asymmetrical relationship between psychopathy and the APD was severely attenuated. Second, when placed on an even playing field, the APD slightly outperformed the PCL:SV in terms of overall classification rates. Using psychopathy as simply one example, forensic evaluators must carefully consider whether clinical constructs add incremental validity and concomitant accuracy.

SUMMARY AND CONCLUSIONS

Progress toward the development and validation of FAIs and FRIs has been remarkably uneven, with several important advances being counterbalanced by widespread disregard for other critically important legal standards. Most FAIs are confined to the criminal domain, with the majority focused on a single issue: competency to stand trial. Early efforts in the civil domain have generally not been sustained with rigorous empirical research. FRIs have focused largely on malingering and psychopathy.

The greatest disappointment in the development of forensic measures has been the total neglect of legal standards related to the courtroom process. For example, an FAI could be developed to assess *death-qualified* jurors. Straightforward questions— such as putting aside one's own views of the death penalty—are obviously vulnerable to social desirability, including the desire to look fair and impartial. At present, opinions regarding the death penalty are typically viewed in categorical terms without any systematic consideration for their underlying influences (e.g., religious beliefs and faith in the fairness of the criminal justice system). As an important corollary, the construct of conviction proneness among death-qualified jurors needs systematic examination for each venireperson (Butler & Moran, 2007).

Two models were presented in this chapter for evaluating the use of FAIs: Grisso's (2003) conceptualization and the *Daubert* criteria. These models represent important starting points, informing research and forensic practice. The helpfulness of forensic measures varies directly with the clarity and simplicity of the legal standard. When both are present, FAIs can provide useful and highly relevant material as it applies to a particular case. When neither is available, then important themes or content areas can be effectively addressed. Although not attempting to capture the full legal standard, the FAI findings can still be germane to particular conclusions.

In closing, professional practice is informed by APA ethics and specialty guidelines, and by other professional guidelines. When using FAIs and FRIs, forensic evaluators must closely consider the validation and its applicability to the legal standard. Forensic measures are likely to be effective if they (a) successfully address the time framework for both legal standards and clinical constructs and (b) substantively contribute to forensic conclusions in terms of incremental validity and accuracy.

References

Ackerman, M. G., & Schoendorf, K. (1992). *Ackerman-Schoendorf Parent Evaluation of Custody Test*. Los Angeles, CA: Western Psychological Services.

American Bar Association. (1989). *ABA criminal justice mental health standards*. Washington, DC: Author.

American Psychological Association. (2010). *Ethical principles of psychologists and code of conduct (2002, Aemended June 1, 2010)*. Retrieved from http://www.apa.org/ethics/code/index.aspx

American Psychological Association. (2013). Specialty guidelines for forensic psychology. *American Psychologist, 68*, 7–19. doi:10.1037/a0029889

Butler, B., & Moran, G. (2007). The role of death qualification and need for cognition in venirepersons' evaluations of expert scientific testimony in capital trials. *Behavioral Sciences and the Law, 25*, 561–571. doi:10.1002/bsl.758

Clark, L., & Watson, D. (1995). Constructing validity: Basic issues in objective scale development. *Psychological Assessment, 7*, 309–319. doi:10.1037/1040-3590.7.3.309

Daubert v. Merrell Dow Pharmaceuticals, Inc., 509 U.S. 579 (1993).

Douglas, K. S., Skeem, J. L., & Nicholson, E. (2011). Research methods in violence risk assessment. In B. Rosenfeld & S. D. Penrod (Eds.), *Research methods in forensic psychology* (pp. 325–346). New York, NY: Wiley.

Drope v. Missouri, 420 U.S. 162 (1974).

Dusky v. United States, 362 U.S. 402 (1960).

Everington, C., & Luckasson, R. (1992). *Manual for Competence Assessment for Standing Trial for Defendants with Mental Retardation: CAST–MR*. Worthington, OH: IDS.

Florida v. Powell, 130 S. Ct. 1195 (2010).

Gatowski, S. I., Dobbin, S. A., Richardson, J. T., Ginsburg, G. P., Merlino, M. L., & Dahir, V. (2001). Asking the gatekeepers: A national survey of judges on judging expert evidence in a post-Daubert world. *Law and Human Behavior, 25*, 433–458. doi:10.1023/A:1012899030937

Giorgi-Guarnieri, D., Janofsky, J., Keram, E., Lawsky, S., Merideth, P., Mossman, D., . . . Zonana, H. (2002). AAPL practice guideline for forensic psychiatric evaluation of defendants raising the insanity defense. *Journal of the American Academy of Psychiatry and the Law, 30*(2, suppl.), S3–S40.

Gold, L. H., Anfang, S., Drukteinis, A., Metzner, J., Price, M., Wall, B., . . . Zonana, H. (2008). AAPL practice guideline for the forensic evaluation of psychiatric disability. *Journal of the American Academy of Psychiatry and the Law, 36*(4, suppl.), S3–S50.

Goldstein, N. E. S., Zelle, H., & Grisso, T. (2012). *The Miranda Rights Comprehension Instruments*. Sarasota, FL: Professional Resource Press.

Grisso, T. (1986). *Evaluating competencies: Forensic assessments and instruments*. New York, NY: Plenum. doi:10.1007/978-1-4899-5046-8

Grisso, T. (1995). Saleem Shah's contributions to forensic clinical assessment. *Law and Human Behavior, 19*, 25–30. doi:10.1007/BF01499068

Grisso, T. (1998). *Instruments for assessing understanding and appreciation of Miranda rights*. Sarasota, FL: Professional Resource Press.

Grisso, T. (2003). *Evaluating competencies: Forensic assessments and instruments* (2nd ed.). New York, NY: Kluwer Academic/Plenum.

Gunderson, J. G., Stout, R., McGlashan, T., Shea, M., Morey, L., Grilo, C., . . . Skodol, A. (2011). Ten-year course of borderline personality disorder: Psychopathology and function from the Collaborative Longitudinal Personality Disorders study. *Archives of General Psychiatry, 68*, 827–837. doi:10.1001/archgenpsychiatry.2011.37

Hambleton, R. K. (2001). The next generation of the ITC test translation and adaptation guidelines. *European Journal of Psychological Assessment, 17*, 164–172. doi:10.1027//1015-5759.17.3.164

Hanson, R. K. (1997). *The development of a brief actuarial risk scale for sexual offense recidivism*. Ottawa, Ontario, Canada: Department of the Solicitor General.

Hare, R. D. (2003). *Manual for the Hare Psychopathy Checklist—Revised* (2nd ed.). Toronto, Ontario, Canada: Multi-Health Systems.

Hart, S. D., Cox D. N., & Hare, R. D. (1995). *Manual for the Hare Psychopathy Checklist: Screening version*. Toronto, Ontario, Canada: Multi-Health Systems.

Heilbrun, K., Rogers, R., & Otto, R. K. (2002). Forensic assessment: Current status and future directions. In J. R. P. Ogloff (Ed.), *Taking psychology and law into the twenty-first century* (pp. 120–146). New York, NY: Kluwer Academic/Plenum.

Kansas v. Crane, 534 U.S. 407 (2002).

McGarry, A. L., & Curran, W. J. (1973). *Competency to stand trial and mental illness*. Rockville, MD: National Institute of Mental Health.

Melton, G. B., Petrila, J., Poythress, N. G., & Slobogin, C. (1987). *Psychological evaluations for the courts: A handbook for mental health professionals and lawyers*. New York, NY: Guilford Press.

Melton, G. B., Petrila, J., Poythress, N. G., & Slobogin, C. (1997). *Psychological evaluations for the courts: A handbook for mental health professionals and lawyers* (2nd ed.). New York, NY: Guilford Press.

Melton, G. B., Petrila, J., Poythress, N. G., & Slobogin, C. (2007). *Psychological evaluations for the courts: A handbook for mental health professionals and lawyers* (3rd ed.). New York, NY: Guilford Press.

M'Naghten, 8 Eng. Rep. 718 (1843).

Mossman, D., Noffsinger, S., Ash, P., Frierson, R., Gerbasi, J., Hackett, M., . . . Zonana, H. (2007). AAPL practice guideline for the forensic psychiatric evaluation of competence to stand trial. *Journal of the American Academy of Psychiatry and the Law, 35* (4, suppl.), S3–S72.

Nicholson, R. A., Robertson, H. C., Johnson, W. G., & Jensen, G. (1988). A comparison of instruments for assessing competency to stand trial. *Law and Human Behavior, 12,* 313–321. doi:10.1007/BF01044387

Otto, R. K., Musick, J. E., & Sherrod, C. B. (2010). *Inventory of Legal Knowledge: Professional manual.* Lutz, FL: Psychological Assessment Resources.

Poythress, N. G., Nicholson, R., Otto, R. K., Edens, J. F., Bonnie, R. J., Monahan, J., & Hoge, S. K. (1999). *Professional manual for the MacArthur Competence Assessment Tool—Criminal Adjudication.* Lutz, FL: Psychological Assessment Resources.

Quinsey, V. L., Harris, G. T., Rice, M. E., & Cormier, C. A. (1998). *Violent offenders: Appraising and managing risk.* Washington, DC: American Psychological Association. doi:10.1037/10304-000

Riley, J. A. (1998). *Assessment of trial competency: Use of the Revised Competency Assessment Instrument; Handbook.* Unpublished manuscript, Atascadero State Hospital, Atascardero, CA.

Robey, A. (1965). Criteria for competency to stand trial: A checklist for psychiatrists. *American Journal of Psychiatry, 122,* 616–623.

Roesch, R., & Golding, S. L. (1980). *Competency to stand trial.* Champaign: University of Illinois Press.

Rogers, R. (1984). *Rogers Criminal Responsibility Assessment Scales (R–CRAS) and test manual.* Lutz, FL: Psychological Assessment Resources.

Rogers, R. (2001). *Handbook of diagnostic and structured interviewing.* New York, NY: Guilford Press.

Rogers, R. (2012). *Miranda Comprehension Template (MCT) record form.* Lutz, FL: Psychological Assessment Resources.

Rogers, R., Bagby, R. M., & Dickens, S. E. (1992). *Structured Interview of Reported Symptoms (SIRS) and professional manual.* Lutz, FL: Psychological Assessment Resources.

Rogers, R., Bender, S. D., & Johnson, S. F. (2011). A critical analysis of the MND criteria for feigned cognitive impairment: Implications for forensic practice and research. *Psychological Injury and Law, 4,* 147–156. doi:10.1007/s12207-011-9107-2

Rogers, R., Blackwood, H. L., Fiduccia, C. E., Steadham, J. A., Drogin, E. Y., & Rogstad, J. E. (2012). Juvenile Miranda warnings: Perfunctory rituals or procedural safeguards? *Criminal Justice and Behavior, 39* 229–249. doi:10.1177/0093854811431934

Rogers, R., Boals, A., & Drogin, E. Y. (2011). Applying cognitive models of deception to national security investigations: Considerations of psychological research, law, and ethical practice. *Journal of Psychiatry and Law, 39,* 339–364.

Rogers, R., & Ewing, C. (1989). Ultimate opinion proscriptions: A cosmetic fix and a plea for empiricism. *Law and Human Behavior, 13,* 357–374. doi:10.1007/BF01056408

Rogers, R., & Ewing, C. (2003). The prohibition of ultimate opinions: A misguided enterprise. *Journal of Forensic Psychology Practice, 3,* 65–75. doi:10.1300/J158v03n03_04

Rogers, R., & Gillard, N. D. (2011). Research methods for the assessment of malingering. In B. Rosenfeld & S. D. Penrod (Eds.), *Research methods in forensic psychology* (pp. 174–188). New York, NY: Wiley.

Rogers, R., Grandjean, N. R., Tillbrook, C. E., Vitacco, M. J., & Sewell, K. W. (2001). Recent interview-based measures of competency to stand trial: A critical review augmented with research data. *Behavioral Sciences and the Law, 19,* 503–518. doi:10.1002/bsl.458

Rogers, R., Hazelwood, L. L., Sewell, K. W., Harrison, K. S., & Shuman, D. W. (2008). The language of Miranda warnings in American jurisdictions: A replication and vocabulary analysis. *Law and Human Behavior, 32,* 124–136. doi:10.1007/s10979-007-9091-y

Rogers, R., & Jackson, R. L. (2005). Sexually violent predators: The risky enterprise of risk assessment. *Journal of the American Academy of Psychiatry and the Law, 33,* 523–528.

Rogers, R., & Johansson-Love, J. (2009). Evaluating competency to stand trial with evidence-based practice. *Journal of the American Academy of Psychiatry and the Law, 37,* 450–460.

Rogers, R., & Rogstad, J. E. (2010). Psychopathy and APD in non-forensic patients: Improved predictions or disparities in cut scores? *Journal of Psychopathology and Behavioral Assessment, 32,* 353–362. doi:10.1007/s10862-009-9175-8

Rogers, R., Rogstad, J. E., Gillard, N. D., Drogin, E. Y., Blackwood, H. L., & Shuman, D. W. (2010). "Everyone knows their Miranda rights:" Implicit assumptions and countervailing evidence. *Psychology, Public Policy, and Law, 16,* 300–318. doi:10.1037/a0019316

Rogers, R., Seman, W., & Clark, C. R. (1986). Assessment of criminal responsibility: Initial validation of the R–CRAS with the M'Naghten and GBMI standards.

International Journal of Law and Psychiatry, 9, 67–75. doi:10.1016/0160-2527(86)90017-8

Rogers, R., Sewell, K. W., Drogin, E. Y., & Fiduccia, C. E. (2012). *Standardized Assessment of Miranda Abilities (SAMA) professional manual.* Lutz, FL: Psychological Assessment Resources.

Rogers, R., Sewell, K. W., & Gillard, N. D. (2010). *Structured Interview of Reported Symptoms* (2nd ed.). Lutz, FL: Psychological Assessment Resources.

Rogers, R., & Shuman, D. W. (2005). *Fundamentals of forensic practice: Mental health and criminal law.* New York, NY: Springer.

Rogers, R., Tillbrook, C. E., & Sewell, K. W. (2004). *Evaluation of Competency to Stand Trial—Revised professional manual.* Lutz, FL: Psychological Assessment Resources.

Rotgers, F., & Barrett, D. (1996). *Daubert v. Merrell Dow* and expert testimony by clinical psychologists: Implications and recommendations for practice. *Professional Psychology: Research and Practice, 27,* 467–474. doi:10.1037/0735-7028.27.5.467

Rutherford, M., Cacciola, J. S., Alterman, A. I., McKay, J. R., & Cook, T. G. (1999). The 2-year test–retest reliability of the Psychopathy Checklist—Revised in methadone patients. *Assessment, 6,* 285–292. doi:10.1177/107319119900600308

Salekin, R. T. (2004). *Risk–Sophistication–Treatment Inventory (RSTI).* Lutz, FL: Psychological Assessment Resources.

Singh, J. P., & Fazel, S. (2010). Forensic risk assessment: A metareview. *Criminal Justice and Behavior, 37,* 965–988. doi:10.1177/0093854810374274

Singh, J. P., Grann, M., & Fazel, S. (2011). A comparative study of violence risk assessment tools: A systematic review and metaregression analysis of 68 studies involving 25,980 participants. *Clinical Psychology Review, 31,* 499–513. doi:10.1016/j.cpr.2010.11.009

Slick, D. J., Sherman, E. S., & Iverson, G. L. (1999). Diagnostic criteria for malingered neurocognitive dysfunction: Proposed standards for clinical practice and research. *Clinical Neuropsychologist, 13,* 545–561. doi:10.1076/1385-4046(199911)13:04;1-Y; FT545

Slobogin, C., Melton, G. B., & Showalter, C. R. (1984). The feasibility of a brief evaluation of mental state at the time of the offense. *Law and Human Behavior, 8,* 305–320. doi:10.1007/BF01044698

State v. Soares, 81 Hawai'i 332, 916 P.2d 1233 (App. 1996).

Vitacco, M. J., & Neumann, C. S. (2008). The clinical assessment of psychopathy. In R. L. Jackson (Ed.), *Learning forensic assessment* (pp. 129–152). Mahwah, NJ: Erlbaum.

Walters, G. D. (2012). Psychopathy and crime: Testing the incremental validity of PCL–R-measured psychopathy as a predictor of general and violent recidivism. *Law and Human Behavior, 36,* 404–412. doi:10.1037/h0093928

Wettstein, R. M., Mulvey, E., & Rogers, R. (1991). Insanity defense standards: A prospective comparison. *American Journal of Psychiatry, 148,* 21–27.

Widows, M., & Smith, G. P. (2005). *Structured Inventory of Malingered Symptomatology (SIMS) professional manual.* Lutz, FL: Psychological Assessment Resources.

Wildman, R., Batchelor, E., Thompson, L., Nelson, F., Moore, J., Patteson, M., & deLaosa, M. (1979). *The Georgia Court Competency Test.* Unpublished manuscript, Forensic Services Division, Central State Hospital, Milledgeville, GA.

Zapf, P. A., Boccaccini, M. T., & Brodsky, S. L. (2003). Assessment of competency for execution: Professional guidelines and an evaluation checklist. *Behavioral Sciences and the Law, 21,* 103–120. doi:10.1002/bsl.491

CHAPTER 3

RISK ASSESSMENT AND COMMUNICATION

Laura S. Guy, Kevin S. Douglas, and Stephen D. Hart

Individuals in various professional roles such as mental health clinicians, police and other law enforcement officers, probation officers, human resources personnel, and teachers perform the task of assessing and managing an individual's risk of violence to others regularly across diverse settings. Moreover, more formal violence risk assessments are required in many legal and quasilegal situations, such as civil commitment, bail determination, juvenile transfer and decertification, and release decision making (e.g., from hospitals, correctional facilities, etc.). In addition to the more obvious areas such as criminal, civil, and family law, violence risk assessment also is required in workers compensation law, immigration law, freedom of information/privacy law, and national security efforts (Lyon, Hart, & Webster, 2001; Melton, Petrila, Poythress, & Slobogin, 2007; Shah, 1978).

Interpersonal violence is among the leading causes of death worldwide. In the United States, for example, homicide was among the top five causes of death among people 1 to 44 years of age in 2009, the most recent year for which statistics are available (Heron, 2012). As such, a well-conducted violence risk assessment that leads to the implementation of risk management strategies literally has the potential to save lives. Of course, because violence risk assessments implicate critical social values and legal rights, such as protection of the public and individual civil liberties, the costs associated with errors in these evaluations are serious

(see Schopp, 1996). Individuals who are assessed incorrectly as being at high risk for violence may face involuntary civil commitment, mandated outpatient treatment, forced administration of medication, and loss of a host of civil liberties (Canadian Charter of Rights and Freedoms, 1982; *Lyons v. the Queen*, 1987; see also Monahan et al., 2001). Individuals who are assessed incorrectly as not being at risk for violence, and hence are permitted to retain their freedom, may violate others' civil rights and legally protected interests to be free from injury by others. In light of the serious consequences that violence risk assessment may influence, the importance of performing such evaluations according to the highest standard of clinical practice is self-evident.

Within a fairly short amount of time—only a few decades—the field of what has come to be known as violence risk assessment has transformed dramatically (Hanson, 2005; Monahan, 1996; Monahan & Steadman, 2001; Steadman, 2000). The small number of studies that were conducted on the topic by the early 1980s suggested that clinicians' ability to assess an individual's risk for violence accurately was unremarkable. Reinterpretation of the literature conducted by the late 1980s using different analytic approaches indicated comparatively higher levels of predictive accuracy (Mossman, 1994), and the development of new risk assessment technologies has advanced the field even further.

This chapter contains ideas first published in Douglas, Hart, Groscup, and Litwack (2013).

http://dx.doi.org/10.1037/14461-003
APA Handbook of Forensic Psychology: Vol. 1. Individual and Situational Influences in Criminal and Civil Contexts,
B. L. Cutler and P. A. Zapf (Editors-in-Chief)

IMPORTANCE OF THE PROBLEM

The expanding role of violence risk assessment in the practice of clinical psychology and psychiatry over the past several decades has resulted in part from a series of developments in the legal arena in the United States and Canada as well as many other countries around the world (see Douglas, Macfarlane, & Webster, 1996; Lyon et al., 2001; McNiel, 1998; Melton et al., 2007). For example, in the United States, whereas the basis for involuntary hospitalization was once "need for treatment," this criterion was replaced in the 1960s by "dangerousness to others." In the 1972 case, *Lessard v. Schmidt*, "dangerousness" was introduced into civil commitment statutes as a basis for commitment in the United States. Also during the 1970s, the practice of imposing tort liability on clinicians who negligently failed to protect potential victims was established (*Tarasoff v. Regents of the University of California*, 1976). During the following decade, in the 1980s, many states enacted statutes authorizing involuntary treatment in the community for otherwise "dangerous" patients. In the 1990s, risk assessments of violence were mandated explicitly in the Americans With Disabilities Act (1990), which protects the employment rights of people with disabilities unless those disabilities result in an employee posing a "direct threat" of violence to coworkers or customers.

In Canada, the federal government introduced two legislative measures during the 1940s to deal with chronic and dangerous offenders. The Habitual Offender Act was enacted in 1947, and the Criminal Sexual Psychopath Act was proclaimed the following year. These two initiatives laid the groundwork for the dangerous offender legislation, which became law in 1977 (Part XXIV, Criminal Code; see Lyon et al., 2001). Twenty years later, in 1997, Bill C-55 was enacted, which included significant amendments to Part XXIV of the Criminal Code and was designed to deliver more severe sanctions to repeat and violent offenders. One of the Act's provisions was the creation of the long-term offender designation. This designation is given to offenders who have been convicted of a serious personal injury offence (as defined by the Criminal Code) and who are judged as being likely to re-offend.

The long-term offender legislation was developed primarily to address concerns that additional attention needed to be given to serious sexual and violent offenders who fell short of meeting criteria under the dangerous offender legislation. Similar sorts of laws, known as sexual psychopath or sexually violent predator (SVP) statutes, were created in the United States (see Witt & Conroy, 2009).

Cases in Canada (*Re Moore and the Queen*, 1984) and the United States (*Barefoot v. Estelle*, 1983; *Kansas v. Hendricks*, 1997; *Schall v. Martin*, 1984) have legitimized the role of mental health professionals (and in some cases, their reliance on clinical predictions of violence) as violence risk assessors. Although legal developments extended the practice of violence risk assessment into new domains, perhaps the most obvious context in which changes have occurred is involuntary civil commitment. We explore this topic in some detail next.

Civil Commitment

Until the early 1970s, commitment historically was conceptualized as an exercise of the state's *parens patriae* authority. One of the first cases to note this explicitly was *In re Oakes* (1845), in which the Supreme Judicial Court of Massachusetts held that involuntary treatment is justified not only by the dangerousness of a person, but also for the detainee's own welfare. During this early era, decisions about commitment tended to be made solely by medical professionals, statutes tended to be vaguely worded, and commitment procedures tended to be informal in that patients had little to no input and did not have the right to counsel. By 1970, 31 states provided for hospitalization based simply on certification of a physician that the person had a mental illness and needed treatment (see Lareau, 2012; Melton et al., 2007).

A key legal case on point here is that decided by a federal district court in *Lessard v. Schmidt* (1972). After a reported suicide attempt in 1971, police picked up Alberta Lessard, who was diagnosed with paranoid schizophrenia, and a judge committed her for treatment because she was deemed to be mentally ill and "a proper subject for custody and treatment" (p. 1078). With the help of Milwaukee Legal

Services, Lessard brought a class action suit on behalf of all adults who had been held on the basis of Wisconsin's involuntary civil commitment statutes. The suit challenged the grounds on which Wisconsin committed mentally ill individuals as being overly vague and also asserted that the procedures used were inappropriate.

The three-judge court in *Lessard v. Schmidt* ruled that the patient had the right to many of the same protections that were available to suspects in criminal proceedings (e.g., effective and timely notice of the "charges" against her, mandatory notice of right to a jury trial, a right to appointed counsel). The court also held that in order to avoid violating constitutional due process protections, the standard of persuasion must shift from a "preponderance of evidence" to that of "beyond a reasonable doubt." With respect to the "dangerousness to others" prong, the court held that there must be evidence of a recent overt act, attempt, or threat to do substantial harm to another person.

A few years later, in *Addington v. Texas* (1979), the Supreme Court unanimously ruled that the Constitution only required proof by the "clear and convincing" standard of persuasion in the civil commitment context (i.e., "preponderance of evidence" was too lenient a standard and "beyond a reasonable doubt" was not necessary, as in criminal cases) and reiterated the right of the state to commit individuals under police power as well as *parens patriae*. In domino-effect style in the wake of *Lessard v. Schmidt*, other states began tightening or eradicating the *parens patriae* grounds for commitment, swinging the pendulum toward a police power model. As such, *Lessard v. Schmidt* was critical for transforming mental health law and ushering in the practice of violence risk assessment to many domains of clinical practice.

Thereafter, under Chief Justice Berger, the U.S. Supreme Court issued a series of decisions that signalled a less "legalistic" approach to violence risk assessment was constitutionally permissible. In *O'Connor v. Donaldson* (1975), the Supreme Court reinforced the critical role that dangerousness played in civil commitment proceedings. Kenneth Donaldson was hospitalized after a traumatic event at the age of 43 and then resumed life with his

family. Approximately a decade later, he was visiting his parents in Florida and, while there, reported believing that his neighbor in Philadelphia might be poisoning his food. Concerned, Donaldson's father petitioned the court for a commitment hearing. Following an evaluation, Donaldson was civilly committed (without legal representation) to Florida's state mental health system. In the hospital, he was housed with reportedly dangerous criminals on a ward that was understaffed (e.g., there was one physician—an obstetrician—for more than 1,000 patients). No mental health professionals were available.

Throughout his 15-year period of commitment, Donaldson repeatedly sought his freedom and denied that he was ever mentally ill. He filed a lawsuit against the hospital and staff members claiming that he had been held against his will and that his constitutional rights had been violated. The U.S. Supreme Court held that the mere fact of mental illness alone could not justify a state's action of involuntarily committing a person and holding him or her indefinitely. More specifically, the Court held that

> A finding of "mental illness" alone cannot justify a State's locking a person up against his will and keeping him indefinitely in simple custodial confinement. . . . In short, a state cannot constitutionally confine without more a nondangerous individual who is capable of surviving safely in freedom by himself or with the help of willing and responsible family members or friends. (*O'Connor v. Donaldson*, 1975, p. 563)

This case is important legally because it set a minimum constitutional standard for civil commitment. It is important from practice and policy perspectives because it prohibits states from confining people who are judged to be not at risk for engaging in violence and who can survive or function in the community with the support of family or friends.

Mental illness remained a key component of the criteria required for civil commitment. This was emphasized by the U.S. Supreme Court in *Foucha v.*

Louisiana (1992). In this case, an individual who no longer suffered from the mental illness that served as a basis for his original commitment following an adjudication of not guilty by reason of insanity (NGRI) remained involuntarily confined on the justification that he was potentially dangerous. The Supreme Court held that potential dangerousness was not a justification to retain a person found NGRI if no mental illness was present. As such, the ruling required that states maintain a uniform standard for both involuntarily committed insanity acquittees and civilly committed individuals.

Relevance of Violence Risk Assessment in Other Legal Contexts

There are some narrow circumstances, however, under which dangerousness to others (or oneself) is not required for involuntary admission to a psychiatric hospital. In *Vitek v. Jones* (1980), the U.S. Supreme Court clarified the legal procedures to which prison inmates are entitled when the state seeks to transfer an inmate to a psychiatric hospital. The Supreme Court held that it was sufficient that the inmate have a serious mental illness and be in need of treatment that is unavailable in prison, but that she or he does not need to be judged at risk for engaging in dangerous behavior to others (or oneself). In effect, the Court provided for more protections than the state of Nebraska had been providing, but still fewer protections than those required for civil commitment in the community.

Violence risk also is at issue in release decision making with respect to parole from hospitalization in correctional settings. In the landmark case of *Baxstrom v. Harold* (1966), Baxstrom had been transferred to a psychiatric hospital that was located in a prison during his sentence. The director of the prison hospital filed a petition to retain him, and an informal hearing occurred during which Baxstrom was without counsel. When Baxstrom's sentence expired, legal custody shifted to New York's Department of Mental Health, but Baxstrom remained at the same prison hospital, where his commitment was for an indefinite length of time. The Supreme Court held that Baxstrom was denied equal protection of the laws by the statutory procedure under which a person may be civilly committed at the expiration of his penal sentence without the jury review that is available to all other persons who are civilly committed in the state. Of importance to the present discussion, the Supreme Court also held that Baxstrom was denied equal protection by his commitment to a hospital that was managed by the department of corrections after his prison term expired without a judicial determination "that he is dangerously mentally ill," similar to other civil committees. *Baxstrom v. Harold* holds significance not only because it occurred at the outset of the legal reforms in civil commitment, but also because it clarified that inmates whose prison sentences were expiring had to be afforded the same procedures as others in the community when instituting civil commitment.

Admissibility of Violence Risk Assessments

Historically, a fissure existed between practice recommendations offered by professional organizations and the highest court in the United States regarding the appropriateness of admitting evidence from violence risk assessments. In the first case of relevance that was decided by the U.S. Supreme Court, *Barefoot v. Estelle*, at issue was the admissibility in a death penalty case in Texas of clinical opinions given by two psychiatrists who had been hired by the prosecution who answered hypothetical questions regarding the defendant's future dangerousness and the likelihood that he would present a continuing threat to society. The American Psychiatric Association submitted an amicus curiae brief (1982) in support of the defendant's position that such testimony should be inadmissible and urged curtailment of psychiatric testimony regarding his future dangerousness and a prohibition of such testimony based on hypothetical data. The American Psychiatric Association also asserted that clinicians' predictions of violence were so unreliable that they should be barred from capital sentencing cases. Not persuaded, the Supreme Court, in a 6–3 vote, refused to exclude violence testimony from capital sentencing cases and held that there was no merit to the petitioner's argument that psychiatrists, individually or as a group, were incompetent to predict with an acceptable degree of reliability that a particular criminal would commit other crimes in the future, and so represent a danger to the community. The Court reasoned that the trial process could protect defendants from potential error in predictions of future violence.

The Supreme Court's logic appears to be enduring, and, remarkably, there has been an absence of conflict among the federal appellate and state courts regarding the admissibility of expert witness testimony based on unstructured clinical methods. For example, in 2011, the Supreme Court denied a petition for certiorari arising from a death penalty case, *Coble v. State of Texas* (2010), which centered on the reliability of expert testimony on the risk of "future dangerousness." Granting certiorari would have required the Supreme Court to reexamine their holding in *Barefoot v. Estelle*. The American Psychological Association (APA) submitted an amicus curiae brief for *Coble* (2011; as well as one in 2007 for the earlier Texas death penalty case of *United States v. Fields*, 2007).

The year following the U.S. Supreme Court's decision in *Barefoot v. Estelle*, it decided *Schall v. Martin*. This case, which involved a juvenile, upheld a New York statute that authorized pretrial detention without probable cause that there was a serious risk that the adolescent would commit a new crime (essentially, the preventive detention of juveniles). Among the Supreme Court's ruling was the assertion that there was "nothing inherently unattainable about a prediction of future criminal conduct" (p. 278). Again addressing the role of risk for violence using preventive detention, in *United States v. Salerno* (1987), the Supreme Court also permitted federal courts, under the Bail Reform Act of 1984, to detain an arrestee prior to trial if the government could prove that the individual was potentially dangerous to others in the community.

Little has changed during the past two decades with respect to the U.S. Supreme Court's willingness to promote or condone the practice of violence risk assessment. For example, in its 5–4 decision in *Kansas v. Hendricks*, the Supreme Court set forth procedures for the indefinite civil commitment of prisoners who are convicted of sex offenses who the state deems dangerous due to a mental abnormality. The Supreme Court also held that civil commitment

that occurred following detention in this context did not violate the Constitution's double jeopardy prohibition or the ban on *ex post facto* law because Kansas' Act did not establish criminal proceedings, meaning that the involuntary confinement was not considered punishment.

Although the Court's finding that preventive long-term confinement of individuals with a mental disorder is justified if one assumes that aspects of their behavior cannot be prevented, upholding the Act was seen as a major expansion of traditional civil commitment, which historically had involved short-term commitment based on imminent risk for physical harm due typically to serious mental illness (prototypically viewed as an acute and treatable condition associated with cognitive and volitional impairment). Commitment as an SVP, in contrast, may be unlimited in term (i.e., with annual or biennial review, rather than review after hours, days, or months), may be based not just on imminent risk but also on long-term risk (i.e., over the rest of the person's life, not just in the coming days and weeks), may take into account acts that may not involve significant physical injury (e.g., sexual communication or interference, including acts perpetrated without actual, attempted, or threatened physical harm or even with the assent of victims), and may have as the triggering event mental health conditions that may be chronic or even untreatable in nature and be associated only with emotional or volitional impairment (i.e., and not cognitive impairment). Moreover, the Supreme Court made clear that for constitutional purposes, the definition of mental disorder within the context of SVP civil commitment can be broad, and states can decide that definition. A few years later, the Supreme Court upheld its decision in *Kansas v. Crane* (2002), which held that people who are diagnosed with exhibitionism and antisocial personality disorder are eligible for civil commitment in the SVP context.

The Supreme Court's clear rejection of the constitutional challenges raised to violence risk assessment has been reinforced by developments in tort law. In the landmark case of *Tarasoff v. Regents of the University of California*, the California Supreme Court held that psychotherapists who know of or should know of their patient's likelihood of inflicting injury on identifiable third parties have an obligation to take reasonable steps to protect the foreseeable victim from that danger. Numerous states subsequently endorsed similar laws addressing the issue of duty to protect, and many have expanded this duty to include nonidentifiable victims. Based on the *Tarasoff* ruling, the U.S. District Court of Nebraska held in *Lipari v. Sears Roebuck* (1980) that therapists have a duty to detain dangerous people if they are a threat to the public. In that case, Mr. Cribbs, who had a history of involuntary psychiatric treatment provided by the Veterans Affairs (VA) administration, bought a shotgun at a Sears department store. One month later, he left an outpatient VA program against medical advice. Thirty days later, he shot and killed Mr. Lipari and wounded Mrs. Lipari at a club in Omaha. Mrs. Lipari sued Sears and the VA, and Sears sued the VA.

The U.S. Supreme Court also has made decisions that reinforce the necessity of providing informed consent when the possibility of a clinician testifying about an examinee's risk for violence is raised. In *Estelle v. Smith* (1981), the Supreme Court ruled on a Texas death penalty case regarding the use of a psychiatric examination to determine the defendant's competency to stand trial in order to predict his future dangerousness. In that case, the Court held that the Fifth Amendment's privilege against self-incrimination applied to pretrial psychiatric examinations by a prosecution psychiatrist who later testified regarding the defendant's future dangerousness without having warned the defendant that such evidence could be used against him. The Court reasoned that although a defendant has no generalized constitutional right to remain silent at a psychiatric examination regarding the issues of sanity or competency, full *Miranda* warnings must be given with respect to testimony concerning future dangerousness in that context.

Other Legal Cases of Direct Relevance to Clinical Practice

Case law often is inconsistent with the ethical practice espoused in the APA's *Ethical Principles of Psychologists and Code of Conduct* (APA, 2010) and the *Specialty Guidelines for Forensic Psychology* (APA, 2013). *Jablonski v. United States* (1983) is a landmark case in which the 9th Circuit Court of Appeals held that, among other things, a mental health professional's duty to predict dangerousness includes consulting a patient's prior records. In that case, Mr. Jablonski threatened to kill Ms. Kimball, whom he was dating, as well her mother (Ms. Pahls). After one incident that culminated in a threat toward her mother, Kimball took Jablonski to a VA hospital where the doctor conducted a risk assessment but did not consult Jablonski's prior records (which documented a history of violent behavior). The doctor concluded that Jablonski was not a danger to himself or others and released him. The doctor recommended that Kimball leave Jablonski but did not warn her about his risk for violence. Following Jablonski's release to the community, he killed Kimball. The Court held that the VA doctor's failure to obtain Jablonski's medical records constituted negligence given that the records contained information that would have influenced the doctor's opinion about Jablonski's risk for violence and that could have led to an intervention to protect Kimball, who was the foreseeable victim.

The constitutionality of automatic commitment upon a finding of NGRI was addressed in *Jones v. United States* (1983). The Court held that statutes providing for automatic commitment on a finding of NGRI were permissible because it was reasonable to presume that a defendant who has been adjudicated NGRI is both mentally ill and dangerous, thereby reaffirming assumptions about the mental illness and dangerousness of acquittees. The Court held that any criminal act by a defendant "certainly indicates dangerousness," despite the fact that, in this case, the defendant had been adjudicated NGRI for attempted shoplifting. That is, the Court established that a verdict of NGRI is sufficiently probative of mental illness and dangerousness to justify commitment of the acquittee for the purposes of treatment and the protection of society, and that proof of insanity by only a preponderance of the evidence adheres with the procedures that are required to satisfy due process.

One issue that was not addressed in *Jones v. United States* was whether an insanity acquittee must be released if either the mental illness or dangerousness no longer apply. In *Foucha v. Louisiana*, which addressed the substantive requirements for continued commitment of NGRI acquitees, it was held that dangerousness alone is insufficient to justify an individual's continued commitment. Although both mental illness and dangerousness are required elements to maintain a person's commitment status, as is the case in the civil commitment context, the typical nexus is absent in that the dangerousness does not have to be a result of the mental illness. The requirement for demonstrating both mental illness and dangerousness for civil commitment was challenged again in a case described earlier, *Kansas v. Hendricks*. In that case, the Supreme Court held that the state need only show that individuals have a "mental abnormality" that makes them "dangerous beyond their control" (p. 346), even if they are not treatable.

Substance abuse—independent of mental illness—also can be a substantive ground for civil commitment. In approximately two-thirds of U.S. states, statutes exist that allow for the involuntary civil commitment of individuals who are at risk for harming others (or oneself) on account of substance use. All such statutes require some degree of proof of chronic or habitual lack of self-control as a result of substance abuse; for some statutes, the definitions regarding dangerousness are broader compared to those that are most often required for general commitment.

Despite acknowledging significant limitations in the accuracy of violence risk assessments based on (unstructured) clinical methods, courts admit testimony about violence risk assessments routinely (see, e.g., *United States v. Scheffer*, 1998). Since *Daubert v. Merrell Dow Pharmaceuticals, Inc.* (1993), there have been no challenges heard by the U.S. Supreme Court on the admissibility of violence risk assessment testimony.

Although the preceding review only scratches the surface of the relevant law, it is clear that violence risk assessment is an important or even key element of decision making with respect to many legal issues. From a practical perspective, the major question is: How is one to assess violence risk?

RELEVANT PSYCHOLOGICAL THEORY AND PRINCIPLES

In this section, we review the three major approaches to risk assessment and examine their objectives, strengths, and weaknesses. Generally, approaches can be dichotomized into unstructured and structured methodologies. The two structured approaches are the actuarial and structured professional judgment (SPJ) models.

Unstructured Clinical Judgment Approach

Unstructured clinical judgment is based on professional experience and opinion. Using this approach, evaluators exercise complete discretion regarding which risk factors they consider and the way in which they amalgamate that information. Perhaps the most often quoted phrase describing this approach is from Grove and Meehl (1996), who asserted that clinical prediction is an "informal, 'in the head,' impressionistic, subjective conclusion, reached (somehow) by a human clinical judge" (p. 294). This approach offers the advantage of being well suited to promote case conceptualization and formulation as well as the development of individualized risk management plans. However, given the lack of structure inherent in this approach, one of its key limitations is that evaluators could fail to consider empirically supported risk factors, or, on the other hand, could rely on risk factors that are not associated with violence.

As a direct consequence of the absence of structure, two forms of inconsistency are likely to be characteristic of the unstructured approach: inconsistency across raters within cases and inconsistency within raters across cases. Such inconsistencies result in judgments about violence risk that are, generally, of inferior reliability and validity. The absence of structure also results in a lack of transparency about the process that was followed, including the factors that were considered, during the course of conducting the violence risk assessment. An inability to lend itself to review by others renders the unstructured clinical approach highly problematic from both ethical and legal perspectives.

Actuarial Approach

At the opposite end of the spectrum from the unstructured clinical approach is the actuarial approach to violence risk assessment (see Otto & Douglas, 2010, for a review of the instruments with the most empirical support). Again quoting from Grove and Meehl (1996), the actuarial approach is seen as "a formal method [that uses] an equation, a formula, a graph, or an actuarial table to arrive at a probability, or expected value, of some outcome" (p. 294). Risk factors are identified through various statistical procedures and are selected based on the strength of their association with violence in a particular construction sample; this is known as an *empirical item selection approach*. Risk factors also may be assigned weights (again, using one of several possible methods). The hallmark, or defining feature, of the actuarial model of prediction is the derivation and use of reproducible, unvarying rules for amalgamating predictive factors. Because it uses a routinized procedure for selecting and weighting risk factors, the actuarial approach should possess good reliability. In turn, one should expect relatively better predictive validity from an actuarial approach than from an unstructured one. Actuarial methods also are characterized by transparency, meaning that decisions are reviewable and accountable.

The actuarial approach also has several serious disadvantages or flaws. The predictive ability of an actuarial model is statistically optimized by taking advantage of chance associations in the initial or development sample from which the factors were selected (Dawes, Faust, & Meehl, 1989). As such, the risk factors may not generalize or perform as well when they are applied to different samples (Gottfredson & Gottfredson, 1988). This is especially problematic when the risk factors were selected on the basis of a single data set (i.e., in the absence of cross-validation or calibration), as is true for tests such as the Violence Risk Appraisal Guide (VRAG; Quinsey, Harris, Rice, & Cormier, 1998, 2006) and the Sex Offender Risk Assessment Guide (SORAG; Quinsey et al., 1998, 2006), Static–99 and its progeny (Hanson & Thornton, 2000; Phenix, Helmus, & Hanson, 2012), and the

Classification of Violence Risk (COVR; Monahan et al., 2005). Meta-analytic evidence from the violence risk assessment literature supports this well-known and expected statistical phenomenon. Blair, Marcus, and Boccaccini (2008) studied the *shrinkage* of predictive validities for the VRAG, SORAG, and Static–99—that originally were estimated solely on the basis of their respective construction or derivation samples—when they were used on new samples (i.e., cross-validation or calibration samples). Substantial shrinkage was observed for all three instruments. For instance, the VRAG's correlation with violent recidivism in the development sample was 0.44 versus 0.30 in cross-validation samples. Moreover, shrinkage was greatest when independent researchers conducted the cross-validation research (i.e., people other than those who developed the measures).

In addition to shrinkage in terms of overall predictive validity, evidence of instability in the estimates of the probability of violent recidivism that were made using actuarial tests were also found by Mills, Jones, and Kroner (2005). For example, the predicted probabilities of recidivism estimated using the VRAG and the Level of Service Inventory—Revised (LSI–R; Andrews & Bonta, 1995) did not match the observed probabilities in a cross-validation sample of 209 offenders (Mills et al., 2005). There was even evidence of *probability reversals* with respect to relative risk estimates for some measures. For example, for the VRAG, some groups of test scores (called "bins") that were expected to yield higher recidivism rates than other groups in fact had lower recidivism rates and vice versa.

Many actuarial models assign weights to risk factors of varying magnitude, assuming that weights that are optimized for a specific risk factor will be equally applicable to all individuals in the derivation sample, as well as all individuals from different samples with whom the instrument subsequently is used. Despite the apparent precision that one might infer from a complicated weighting scheme, some research (Grann & Långström, 2007) has indicated that more complex weighting procedures are associated with larger decreases in predictive accuracy when the measure is subjected to cross-validation relative to more straightforward schemes in which all of the risk factors are given equal weight.

Another issue related to the lack of precision of such statistical models is the larger issue of whether these estimates of probability of risk—which are *group*-based estimates—can be applied to a specific *individual* within that group. Hart and colleagues (Hart & Cooke, 2013; Hart, Michie, & Cooke, 2007b) demonstrated that confidence intervals (CIs) at the individual level for the VRAG and Static–99 were so broad (in some cases encompassing nearly the entire possible range of the interval) as to render individual-level prediction meaningless. Although some commentators questioned the points raised by Hart et al. (2007b) on logical or statistical grounds (e.g., Hanson & Howard, 2010; Harris & Rice, 2007; Mossman & Selke, 2007), the same commentators also agreed that it may not be possible or meaningful to make individual estimates of violence risk using actuarial tests (e.g., Hart, Michie, & Cooke, 2007a).

As this brief review makes clear, sample dependence is a crippling problem for actuarial models of violence risk assessment because the estimated probabilities may change when the measure is used in different samples. Decisions made at various steps in the development of an actuarial tool affect the subsequent performance of the tool in other samples. Examples of items that should be considered in the process include the initial selection of the larger group of risk factors from which the factors that appear on the measure are selected, length of follow-up, sample size, nature of the sample composition, and issues related to the way in which both risk factors and violence are defined and measured.

Problems related to the content of actuarial risk assessment instruments stemming from the use of a single sample or a few samples to select the factors (i.e., the serious problem of sample dependence) are noteworthy. A critical issue is that risk factors can only be selected for inclusion in an actuarial risk assessment tool if they were among the group of variables that were considered in the initial or derivation study. Unless all potential empirically supported risk factors were included in analyses driving the selection of the risk factors, it is possible that key risk factors could be omitted from the tool (e.g., the Static–99 tool for the risk of sexual violence excludes sexual deviation; the VRAG omits variables such as treatment noncompliance and anger; both tests exclude violent ideation, intent, and threats).

In addition to potentially omitting risk factors that have strong empirical support in the broad violence literature, actuarial models typically ignore low base rate factors and potentially vital case-specific information. Relatedly, selecting risk factors because of their observed predictive power in a particular sample may lead to the inclusion of risk factors that may be objectionable on legal or ethical grounds (e.g., gender, race). In addition to presuming that the particular group of risk factors selected will be predictive in different samples, actuarial models also postulate that any weights that are applied to risk factors will work equally well or in the same way for all people in the derivation sample as well as all people in subsequent samples with which the tool is used.

Using actuarial models for real-world clinical decision making is problematic if any of the conditions under which the measure was developed do not align with the conditions of clinical or legal relevance. For example, an actuarial tool that omits major mental illness as a risk factor (or that treats it as a protective or buffering factor, as in the case of the VRAG and COVR) is irrelevant for risk assessments that are completed to inform triers of fact in civil commitment proceedings, in which the risk observed must be causally related to the presence of a mental disorder (e.g., Hart, 2003). As another example, evaluators may be most concerned about assessing an individual's risk for imminent violence, but the algorithms that are used in most actuarial models involve lengthy follow-up periods. The use of actuarial models for clinical decision making also is difficult because most actuarial tools tend to exclude dynamic risk factors and therefore are unable to capture changes in risk over time (Douglas & Skeem, 2005), thus limiting their utility for informing violence prevention, intervention, and risk management (Dvoskin & Heilbrun, 2001; Hart, 1998).

Structured Professional Judgment Approach

The development of the structured professional judgment (SPJ) approach to violence risk assessment dates back to the mid-1990s (for early examples of SPJ instruments, see Kropp, Hart, Webster, & Eaves, 1994, 1995; Webster, Douglas, Eaves, & Hart, 1997; Webster, Eaves, Douglas, & Wintrup, 1995; for more general discussions, see Douglas, Cox, & Webster, 1999; Douglas & Kropp, 2002; Hanson, 1998; Hart, 2001). The impetus for developing this approach sprung in part from a motivation to rectify the weaknesses of the unstructured clinical and actuarial approaches. At the same time, however, the SPJ model aims to retain many strengths of the clinical approach—such as its relevance to intervention, risk management, and individual case formulation—as well as a key strength of the actuarial approach—its emphasis on developing and maintaining a strong empirical foundation for the decision-making model and individual instruments. In addition, because SPJ instruments are intentionally developed to be transparent, they may facilitate the objective evaluation of the adequacy of risk assessments in the course of routine quality assurance or critical incident reviews. Not including translations, 23 SPJ instruments have been developed for use with children, adolescents, and adults for assessing risk for general and specific forms of violence.[1]

Applying a degree of structure to the assessment process is another feature of the SPJ model that was retained from the actuarial model. Whereas in the actuarial model, all aspects of the assessment are structured, the SPJ model is less rigidly structured.

More specifically, the SPJ model provides guidance concerning the types of information that should be gathered; the standard set of risk factors to be considered by all evaluators for any case for a given type of concern about a given form of violence (e.g., stalking, group-based violence, sexual violence); operational definitions of risk factors; instructions for rating risk factors; guidance for making final judgments of low, moderate, or high risk based on the presence and relevance of factors and degree of intervention required; and facilitation of steps relevant to risk management activities. The ways in which evaluators benefit from such structure are described in the following paragraphs. In particular, because SPJ assessments are more systematic, reliability or agreement between evaluators is improved.

Lying at the heart of all SPJ instruments is a set of core risk factors (typically between 10 and 30) that should be considered, at a minimum, in all violence risk assessments, according to a review of the scientific, theoretical, and professional literatures. The literature review, although detailed, is also broad in that it was conducted across numerous samples and contexts. In the SPJ approach, comprehensiveness, rather than brevity or economy, is valued. The risk factors selected for inclusion in SPJ instruments have robust empirical associations with the type of violence of interest. This approach to item selection, known as *logical* or *rational* item selection, aims to minimize the likelihood of

---

[1]Two SPJ instruments are available for use with children to assess the risk of general violence: the Early Assessment Risk List for Boys (EARL–20B, Version 2; Augimeri, Koegl, Webster, & Levene, 2001) and the Early Assessment Risk List for Girls (EARL–21G, Version 2; Augimeri et al., 2001). The Structured Assessment of Violence Risk in Youth (SAVRY; Borum et al., 2006) assesses the risk for general violence among adolescents. The Short-Term Assessment of Risk and Treatability (START:AV; Viljoen, Nicholls, Cruise, Desmarais, & Webster, 2014) is a recently developed instrument that targets the same population. The Estimate of Risk of Adolescent Sexual Offense Recidivism, Version 2.0 (ERASOR; Worling & Curwen, 2001) is intended to assess the risk for sexual violence among adolescents. For use with adults, the Historical–Clinical–Risk Management—20 (HCR–20^{V3}; Douglas, Hart, Webster, & Belfrage, 2013; Webster et al., 1997) is the best validated instrument for the risk for general violence. Adaptations of the HCR–20 include the History, Current Behaviour & Future—30 (HKT–30; Werkgroep Pilotstudy Risicotaxatie Forensische Psychiatrie, 2002) for use in the Netherlands and the Structured Clinical Judgment: Risk (SCJ: Risk; Hogue & Allen, 2006) for use in the United Kingdom. The Short-Term Assessment of Risk and Treatability (START; Webster, Martin, Brink, Nicholls, & Desmarais, 2009) also is available for assessing an individual's risk for general violence. Instruments for assessing the risk for specific forms of violence among adults include the Spousal Assault Risk Assessment Guide (SARA; Kropp, Hart, Webster, & Eaves, 1994, 1995), Brief Spousal Assault Form for the Evaluation of Risk (B-SAFER; Kropp, Hart, & Belfrage, 2005, 2010), Stalking Assessment and Management Guidelines (SAM; Kropp, Hart, & Lyon, 2008), Stalking Risk Profile (SRP; MacKenzie et al., 2009), Risk for Sexual Violence Protocol (RSVP; Hart et al., 2003), Sexual Violence Risk—20 (SVR–20; Boer, Hart, Kropp, & Webster, 1997), Child Abuse Risk Evaluation (CARE; Agar, 2003), Workplace Assessment of Violence Risk (WAVR-21 Version 2; White & Meloy, 2010), Workplace Risk Assessment—20 (WRA–20; H. Bloom, Eisen, Pollock, & Webster, 2000), and Employee Risk Assessment—20 (ERA–20; H. Bloom, Eisen, & Webster, 2001). Additional SPJ instruments are available in draft version: the PATRIARCH (Kropp, Belfrage, & Hart, 2013) for honor-based violence, the Multilevel Guidelines (MLG; Cook, Hart, & Kropp, 2013) for group-based violence, the Elder Abuse Risk Assessment (EARA; Storey, Hart, & Kropp, in press) for violence against elderly persons, and the Structured Outcome Assessment and Community Risk Monitoring (SORM; Grann, 2001). Finally, there are two instruments intended for use with another SPJ instrument, typically the HCR–20^{V3}: The Structured Assessment of Protective Factors (SAPROF; de Vogel, de Ruiter, Bouman, & de Vries Robbé, 2012) and the Female Additional Manual (FAM; de Vogel, de Vries Robbé, van Kalmthout, & Place, 2011).

excluding important risk factors and including irrelevant factors. Because of this, the content coverage (of the risk factors) on SPJ measures is comprehensive, rendering these measures more generalizable across samples and settings compared with actuarial instruments. All SPJ instruments include dynamic risk factors that, as emphasized earlier, are necessary to engage in treatment and risk management planning and to monitor risk over time. Risk judgments therefore have an "expiry date" or "shelf life" and must be updated as necessary. The SPJ model provides guidance to evaluators regarding the time frame for conducting reassessments. Because items are not statistically derived from single samples in the SPJ approach, the model avoids being sample dependent and hence is generalizable across settings.

Descriptions of the SPJ assessment procedure have become increasingly detailed and precise. According to the most recent explications (e.g., Douglas, Hart, Webster, & Belfrage, 2013; Hart et al., 2003; Kropp, Hart, & Lyon, 2008), comprehensive SPJ evaluations contain several steps. First, evaluators gather the requisite information, drawing on multiple sources. Next, they consider the *presence* of the core set of risk factors (as identified in the guidelines being used) that have empirical support at the *nomothetic* (group-based) level, rating each risk factor according to whether it is *definitely present*, *partially/possibly present*, or *absent*. Third, evaluators judge the individual *relevance* for the risk of violence of each item at the *idiographic* (individual) level. In so doing, evaluators are expected to weight each item depending on the specific circumstances of the given case.

Next, evaluators engage in individual case formulation and then scenario planning. Finally, they communicate their judgments about different facets of risk and the steps they recommend for preventing or reducing that risk. In communicating their judgments about risk, evaluators using the SPJ model do not use numeric score cutoffs to categorize people. Similarly, they do not use numeric probability or frequency estimates of future risk for violence. Rather, SPJ approaches encourage evaluators to categorize individuals as being at low, moderate, or high risk depending on their perceived level of risk

and the corresponding degree of intervention required to diminish this risk. Judgments of high risk are reserved for evaluees who are considered to be high priority for receiving risk management or reduction interventions, without which the evaluator is confident that the evaluee would engage in violent behavior.

RESEARCH REVIEW

For decades, there has been vigorous commentary in the research and professional literature regarding the alleged superiority of the actuarial risk assessment approach in general as well as with respect to violence risk assessment specifically (e.g., de Groot, 1961; Gottfredson & Moriarty, 2006; Sarbin, 1943). Although some researchers have recommended that unstructured clinical judgment be supplanted completely by statistical devices (e.g., Grove & Meehl, 1996; Harris, Rice, & Cormier, 2002; Quinsey et al., 2006), other researchers have regarded such a strategy as a recommendation that is both professionally irresponsible and lacking empirical support (see Hart et al., 2003; Litwack, 2001; Skeem et al., 2005). In this section, we review the broad empirical literature examining approaches to violence risk assessment.

Empirical Evaluation of Approaches to Violence Risk Assessment

At least two meta-analyses focusing on the relative performance of decisions made using clinical and actuarial methods have been completed, both of which are cited frequently in support of the view that actuarial methods are superior to clinical methods. The first is the scholarly dissemination by Grove, Zald, Lebow, Snitz, and Nelson (2000). Grove et al. sampled from the general decision-making literature and quantitatively synthesized the outcomes of 136 instances in which direct comparisons between actuarial and clinical approaches were reported in the same study. In order to make these comparisons, Grove et al. transformed the findings from each study into a common metric, or effect size (ES). In their scheme, positive ES values indicated instances in which the mechanical or actuarial approach performed better than the clinical approach, and negative ES values indicated the reverse. Values between –0.1 and 0.1 indicated that the two approaches to violence risk assessment performed relatively equally. Grove et al. (2000) reported, "Using this categorization scheme, we found about half of the studies ($N = 63$; 47%) notably favor mechanical prediction, with as many ($N = 65$) yielding equal performance. In contrast, only eight studies (6%) notably favor clinical prediction" (p. 21).

Data presented by Grove et al. (2000) indicated that the smallest and largest ESs coded were –0.30 (i.e., clinical prediction superior) and 0.73 (mechanical prediction superior), respectively. Grove et al. noted that a 0.1 ES difference corresponds with roughly a 9%–10% difference in hit rates, meaning that, for every 0.1 increase, a corresponding 10% increase in predictive accuracy would be observed. A few points are worthy of emphasis. First, of the 63 studies that favored a mechanical approach, only 15 had a larger ES than the largest ES associated with clinical superiority (and many of these were larger by only a very small increment). Stated another way, there was a relatively small magnitude of increments in accuracy or hit rate for the comparisons in which the mechanical approach outperformed the clinical approach. The average standardized mean difference for actuarial prediction relative to clinical prediction was $d = .12$, which would be considered small in magnitude (Cohen, 1988).

Of more direct relevance to the field of violence risk assessment is the fact that the majority of the studies in this meta-analysis involved comparisons between actuarial and clinical approaches for decisions or diagnoses about *present-state* issues (e.g., comparing human vs. automated interpretation of X-rays for diagnosing lung cancer) and not predictions or prognoses *about the future* (Grove et al., 2000). In addition, of the 136 studies in the meta-analysis, eight examined general criminality (e.g., parole success, criminal behavior), and only two focused specifically on violence. In all 10 of these studies, the mechanical approach outperformed the clinical approach. Importantly, however, these 10 studies

were conducted between 1952 and 1988; therefore, the clinical approach studied was of the unstructured variant, which research unequivocally has shown to be of limited value in assessing an individual's risk for violence. Taken together, the findings from Grove et al.'s (2000) meta-analysis of the decision-making literature have no relevance to discussions about the comparative performance of actuarial and SPJ approaches to violence risk assessment.

A more recent meta-analysis that also is cited regularly in the violence risk assessment literature to support the alleged superiority of the actuarial approach is the study by Ægisdóttir et al. (2006). In this quantitative synthesis, the authors coded 92 ESs regarding judgment accuracy from 67 studies in which a direct comparison was reported between predictions that were made by mental health practitioners (including graduate students) and an actuarial approach regarding some type of a psychological or a mental health diagnosis, prognosis, or the like. Aggregating across four studies (completed between 1976 and 1996) in which the prediction was for future criminality or violence, Ægisdóttir et al. reported a small mean weighted standardized ES of $d = .17$ in favor of the actuarial approach. In two studies, the algorithm used in the actuarial approach was not cross validated; therefore, the ES in favor of the actuarial approach was almost certainly larger than what would be expected in subsequent evaluations. Finally, similar to Grove et al.'s (2000) meta-analysis, the clinical approaches for assessing violence risk that Ægisdóttir et al. studied consisted of unstructured approaches.

Given the serious consequences that may result from violence risk assessments both to the individual being evaluated and to society, it is vital to direct empirical scrutiny on recommendations that have been made by some researchers that the actuarial approach be the only approach used when conducting these assessments (Quinsey et al., 2006). As the research reviewed in the next section demonstrates, such recommendations are without merit and are indeed potentially harmful and unfair to evaluees in forensic and other clinical settings.

Research on Specific Violence Risk Assessment Instruments

Decades of research have yielded important evidence regarding which specific factors demonstrate robust empirical associations with antisocial behavior, including violence. In fact, a sufficiently large number of studies has been completed to warrant quantitative syntheses of risk factors among specific types of samples, including mentally disordered offenders (Bonta, Blais, & Wilson, 2013; Bonta, Law, & Hanson, 1998), sexual offenders (Hanson & Morton-Bourgon, 2005, 2009), stalkers (Rosenfeld, 2004), prisoners (Gendreau, Goggin, & Law, 1997), adult offenders (Gendreau, Little, & Goggin, 1996), juveniles (Cottle, Lee, & Heilbrun, 2001; Heilbrun, Lee, & Cottle, 2005), and delinquent girls (Hubbard & Pratt, 2002). Having progressed to a state in the scientific literature where researchers can reasonably identify the major risk factors for various types of crime and violence, efforts began to shift to the development of instruments for assessing the risk of violence to others. Literally hundreds of measures have been developed to assess an individual's risk for future violence, and meaningful research has informed the development of several formal risk assessment instruments (see Chapter 2, this volume). In the next section, we summarize results of meta-analyses that have evaluated the predictive validity of these, and other, measures.

Summary of Major Qualitative and Quantitative Syntheses of Violence Risk Assessment Research

Literally hundreds of primary research studies evaluating the predictive accuracy of various risk assessment instruments and methodologies have been completed, and an astoundingly sizable number of measures that purportedly assess an individual's risk for violence to others have been developed. In fact, a comprehensive review of the literature (both published and unpublished) that has accrued over the past five decades indicated the existence of at least 457 brief and more comprehensive measures (L. S. Guy, 2008). Given this magnitude of empirical output, researchers have applied meta-analytic methods to synthesize these data. Some meta-analyses have focused on specific types of offenses or offenders (e.g., sexual offenders), whereas others have evaluated the comparative performance of risk assessment instruments and/or approaches across all available sample types. We first describe findings from meta-analyses of specific samples and then turn our attention to meta-analyses of more heterogeneous samples.

Meta-analyses of specific sample types. We present the findings from meta-analyses examining specific samples, including offenders with mental disorders, sexual offenders, and offenders engaging in intimate partner violence.

Mentally disordered offenders. Among the earliest efforts of examining specific samples was a meta-analysis on predictors of violence among mentally disordered offenders (Bonta et al., 1998). Bonta et al. (1998) reported on 64 prospective studies and in a subsample of them compared objective risk assessments (which included study-specific actuarial models that were not cross-validated and excluded the major contemporary instruments that are used today) to unstructured clinical judgments of violence risk (based on a smaller subset of studies). Bonta and colleagues found that among that sample of mentally disordered offenders, actuarial approaches ($Zr = .27$) had a stronger association with violent recidivism than did (unstructured) clinical judgments ($Zr = .09$). More recently, Bonta et al. (2013) synthesized research on types of variables that were associated with criminal behaviors. The authors concluded that, apart from indices of antisocial personality disorder or psychopathy, mental health or clinical variables were not associated with recidivism, with the bulk of predictive power attributable to other types of static and dynamic risk factors.

Sexual offenders. Focusing on 45,398 sexual offenders across 118 samples, Hanson and Morton-Bourgon (2009) coded ESs for *any, violent,* and *sexual* recidivism risk made using unstructured clinical judgment, actuarial, and SPJ approaches. They found that actuarial approaches had superior predictive accuracy compared with unstructured clinical approaches for all outcomes evaluated, whereas SPJ instruments performed on average less accurately than actuarial tools but more accurately than unstructured clinical approaches (although one SPJ instrument, the Sexual Violence Risk—20 [SVR–20; Boer, Hart, Kropp, & Webster, 1997], yielded the highest ESs of all predictors according to some analyses). Across all types of instruments, risk judgments were most accurate when they were used to predict the type of recidivism for which they were designed. In part because of the specificity of the sample studied (i.e., offenders released following an index sexual offense), few studies using SPJ instruments were included. That limitation, coupled with the presence of significant variability in the results of that subset of studies, strongly indicates that conclusions regarding the relative accuracy of the SPJ and other assessment approaches should not be made based on Hanson and Morton-Bourgon's meta-analysis.

Also focusing on an individual's risk for sexual violence, but in young offenders, Viljoen, Mordell, and Beneteau (2012) evaluated the predictive accuracy of four instruments: the Juvenile Sex Offender Assessment Protocol—II (J–SOAP–II; Prentky & Righthand, 2003), the Estimate of Risk of Adolescent Sexual Offense Recidivism (ERA-SOR; Worling & Curwen, 2001), the Juvenile Sexual Offense Recidivism Risk Assessment Tool—II (JSORRAT–II; Epperson, Ralston, Fowers, DeWitt, & Gore, 2006), and the Static–99. Reporting on 33 studies sampling 6,196 male adolescents who had committed a sexual offense, Viljoen et al. found no significant differences between the measures for the prediction of sexual recidivism. The authors observed weighted correlations ranging from .12 to .20 and area under the curve (AUC) values ranging from .64 to .67; in some cases, significant heterogeneity across ESs was observed.

Intimate partner violence offenders. In a meta-analysis that focused on the validity of risk assessments for intimate partner violence, Hanson, Helmus, and Bourgon (2007) compared risk assessments that were made using various approaches coded from 18 nonredundant samples that were based on four approaches: spousal assault scales, other risk scales, SPJ, and victim judgment. The four approaches performed similarly (and were

not significantly different from one another) with respect to predictions for spousal assault recidivism.

Meta-analyses of nonspecific sample types. At least nine meta-analyses with more heterogeneous sample compositions, among adolescents and adults, comparing various approaches to risk assessment have been completed. We review each of these in turn. Focusing first on the three syntheses of the adolescent literature, Schwalbe (2007) reported on the predictive validity of 28 risk assessment instruments from 33 samples. Many of the instruments studied were brief and would be described more appropriately as risk *screening* rather than risk *assessment* instruments. The risk assessment measure with the most ESs ($k = 11$), the Youth Level of Service/Case Management Inventory (YLS/CMI; Hoge & Andrews, 2002), had a mean AUC value of .64 (95% CI [.51, .78]). The Psychopathy Checklist—Revised: Youth Version (PCL:YV; Forth, Kosson, & Hare, 2003; $k = 3$), which was developed to measure a specific constellation of maladaptive personality traits but is often used within the context of violence risk assessments, had a mean AUC value of .70 (95% CI [.49, .90]). The following year, Schwalbe (2008) again reported on the YLS/CMI but used a sample that contained fewer studies and presented results as a function of gender. Predictive accuracy was comparable across genders (mean weighted correlations of .32 and .40 for boys and girls, respectively) and was on par with ESs that Schwalbe reported in 2007.

In another meta-analysis of violence risk assessment of young offenders, Olver, Stockdale, and Wormith (2009) summarized 44 studies in which the YLS/CMI, Structured Assessment of Violence Risk in Youth (SAVRY; Borum, Bartel, & Forth, 2006), or PCL:YV was studied. All three measures significantly predicted general, nonviolent, and violent recidivism, yielding ESs of moderate magnitude. Across all three measures, mean weighted correlations ranged from $r = .28$ to .32 for general recidivism, $r = .16$ to .38 for nonviolent recidivism, and $r = .25$ to .30 for violent recidivism. Substantially weaker predictive accuracy was observed for sexual recidivism (which is not surprising given that none of the measures was developed to assess risk for this particular outcome). Between-measure performance was negligible. Excluding sexual recidivism, weighted correlations for each instrument ranged as follows: SAVRY, .30 to .38; YLS/CMI, .26 to .32; and PCL:YV, .16 to .28. Only two studies evaluated the two risk assessment measures (YCL/CMI and SAVRY) in the same sample, which is a methodological strength. Across the 179 youth from these two samples, the mean weighted correlation for the YLS/CMI was .28 (95% CI [.13, .43]), whereas for the SAVRY it was substantially higher, at .44 (95% CI [.29, .59]).

There were six meta-analyses that focused primarily on adult offenders. Campbell, French, and Gendreau (2009) were the first group to publish on the predictive validity of various self-report, actuarial, and structured clinical risk protocols. They reported on 88 studies conducted between 1980 and 2006. To be included in their meta-analysis, studies had to be prospective in nature and sample adults who were offenders or forensic psychiatric patients. The main outcome of analysis was general recidivism, although the authors examined nonsexual violence in a subset of analyses. The researchers compared the predictive accuracy for several instruments: Historical–Clinical–Risk Management—20, Version 2 (HCR–20; Webster et al., 1997); Psychopathy Checklist—Revised (PCL–R; Hare, 1991, 2003); Statistical Information on Recidivism (SIR; Nuffield, 1982); VRAG; and measures from the Level of Service family of instruments (i.e., the original Level of Supervision Inventory [LSI; Andrews, 1982] and its revisions, the LSI–R and the Level of Service/Case Management Inventory [LS/CMI; Andrews, Bonta, & Wormith, 2004]). ESs (Zr) for institutional violence ranged from .08 to .28 and for violent recidivism from .22 to .32. Tools that contained dynamic risk factors produced relatively larger ESs for violent recidivism. Campbell et al. (2009) concluded that "no one measure stood out as the most effective for predicting violent recidivism" (p. 580). Although SPJ tools were included in the analyses, the authors did not evaluate the performance of the tools as they were intended to be used in clinical practice (i.e., summary risk ratings [SRRs] were not included). As such, although

highly informative in many respects, Campbell et al.'s findings are limited in terms of their ability to evaluate fully the performance of the SPJ approach to violence risk assessment.

Investigating the narrow research question regarding the comparative predictive validity of the HCR–20 and PCL–R among samples in which both instruments were included, L. S. Guy, Douglas, and Hendry (2010) identified 34 samples for quantitative synthesis. The instruments for the most part had comparable performance (AUCs = .69 for both measures). However, the predictive power of the HCR–20 was not attributable to the PCL–R: When the psychopathy item was removed from the HCR–20, the instrument's AUC value essentially was the same (AUC = .71). Analyzing seven raw data sets, L. S. Guy et al. conducted multivariate analyses of the PCL–R and HCR–20 (with the psychopathy item removed). They observed the HCR–20 to add unique, incremental validity beyond the PCL–R, whereas the converse was not true. Using meta-analytic logistic regression, with both instruments included in the analysis, for every 1-point increase on the HCR–20, the probability of detecting violence increased 23%, whereas for every 1-point increase on the PCL–R, the probability of detecting violence decreased by 1%.

Yang, Wong, and Coid (2010) evaluated the predictive accuracy of nine measures across 28 samples: PCL–R/SV, LSI, Offender Group Reconviction Scale (OGRS; Copas & Marshall, 1998), Risk Matrix 2000 for Violence (RM2000V; Thornton, 2007), VRAG, HCR–20, General Statistical Information on Recidivism (GSIR; Nuffield, 1982), LSI–R, and the Violence Risk Scale (VRS; S. Wong & Gordon, 2000). The authors coded studies in which more than one risk measure was evaluated in the same sample and only considered studies that were disseminated between 1999 and 2008. Yang et al. observed most instruments to have moderate predictive validity, with few between-measure differences. The majority (approximately 85%) of the difference between ESs was attributable to methodological and sample characteristics (e.g., gender, age, length of follow-up, type of outcome). ESs for risk assessment instruments that were observed in a statistical model in which many variables that related to methodological differences between the studies were controlled for statistically (e.g., data structure, country of study, participants' sex and mean age, follow-up time to the outcome, etc.) ranged from .65 (for several of the measures) to .71 for the HCR–20 and the OGRS. Only the OGRS (when applied to men) and the HCR–20 were found to predict significantly better than the PCL–R; all other instruments predicted better than chance at about a medium level of efficacy (AUC values ranged from .65 to .70).

Singh, Grann, and Fazel (2011) also evaluated nine instruments (HCR–20, LSI–R, PCL–R, SARA, SAVRY, SORAG, Static–99, SVR–20 [Boer et al., 1997], and VRAG), drawing on 88 samples that were disseminated between 1995 and 2008. Studies were included in the meta-analysis if classification data in a 2 × 2 table with the outcomes of the risk predictions were published or were obtainable from the authors of the primary studies. Given those criteria, instrument-specific analyses typically were based on fewer than 10 ESs (and never more than 12). Median AUC values for the instruments for various outcomes ranged from .66 for the PCL–R to .78 for the SVR–20. The authors concluded that instruments designed to predict violence fared better than those designed to predict general recidivism. Although the range of median AUC values for most of the instruments was small, and median values tended to be in the low approximately .70s, the authors argued, based on an analytic approach in which the instruments were coded into predictive "bins" of low versus high risk, that substantial differences in the predictive accuracy of the measures existed (in contrast to findings from most other meta-analyses). The authors also examined potential moderator variables, most of which were not statistically significant, including gender, country, setting, and ethnicity.

Fazel, Singh, Doll, and Grann (2012) reported on 24,847 participants from 68 independent studies. They also studied nine instruments that are often used in violence risk assessments (LSI–R, VRAG, Static–99, SORAG, PCL–R, SVR–20, HCR–20, SARA, and SAVRY). Inclusion criteria were somewhat restrictive in that the studies had to report rates of

true positives, false positives, true negatives, and false negatives at a given cutoff score for the outcome that the instrument was designed to predict (or such information needed to be provided by the authors of the primary studies). Hence, Fazel et al.'s sample represents a subset of the predictive validity studies that are available for these instruments. The focus of the meta-analysis was not an investigation of the comparative performance of specific measures, but the instrument-level analyses that were performed indicated that the instruments that were designed to assess an individual's risk for violence (e.g., HCR–20, VRAG, SAVRY, and SARA) had superior predictive validity compared with the instruments that were designed or used for general criminality (e.g., LSI–R, LS/CMI), with odds ratios of 6.1 versus 2.84, respectively. Gender, ethnicity, age, type of instrument (developed to assess risk for violence, sexual violence, or any general offending), temporal design, assessment setting, location of offending outcome, length of follow-up, sample size, and publication status were not associated with statistically significant differences in the instrument's predictive validity.

Fazel et al.'s (2012) analyses indicated that the median AUC values were of the same general magnitude as those reported in other meta-analyses: .66 (interquartile range: .58–.67) for general offending, .72 (interquartile range: .68–.78) for violent offending, and .74 (interquartile range: .66–.77) for sexual offending. Based on analyses of positive and negative predictive values, the number needed to detain (i.e., the number of people estimated to be at risk who would need to be detained in order to prevent one incident of subsequent offending), and the number safely discharged (i.e., an indicator that was developed by the authors to estimate the number of people thought to be at low risk who could be discharged into the community before a single act of offending occurred), Fazel et al. concluded that the accuracy of risk assessment instruments was lower than what previous research had suggested. Consistent with common sense and practice guidelines about the use and application of psychological instruments, Fazel et al. concluded that the instruments on their own are insufficient for individual clinical decision making, reinforcing best practice standards that people—not instruments—make recommendations in the course of conducting a risk assessment.

Apart from Singh et al.'s (2011) meta-analysis (and also to some degree the synthesis by Hanson and Morton-Bourgon, 2009), the meta-analyses reviewed thus far focused on the numeric sum of SPJ instruments' item ratings, which is not how SPJ instruments are intended to be used in clinical practice. As noted by others (e.g., Douglas, 2001; Heilbrun, 1992, 2001), according to the test standards that were jointly derived and adopted in 1999 by the American Educational Research Association, APA, and the National Council on Measurement in Education, the empirical evaluation of psychological measures should correspond to their intended clinical use(s).

A meta-analysis that made a concerted effort to do just this was L. S. Guy's (2008) evaluation of all available research on the predictive validity of SPJ instruments that were available at that time. Data about the predictive validity for a variety of outcomes and potential moderating variables from 113 SPJ disseminations were coded. ESs for unstructured clinical judgment and actuarial approaches also were coded when available. Consistent with previous research, Guy found that unstructured approaches were significantly less strongly related to violence than were structured approaches (either actuarial or SPJ). More specifically, across all available instruments and ESs, SPJ SSRs produced larger ESs (AUC = .68) than actuarial instruments (AUC = .62). For unstructured predictions, the ESs were on average smaller (AUC = .59). Based on one composite ES per study, SPJ SRRs (AUC = .69) and actuarial instruments (.67) both had stronger associations with the outcome than did unstructured predictions (AUC = .58). In direct comparisons, SRRs and actuarial predictions produced very similar ESs that did not differ significantly. In addition, ESs did not differ as a function of gender, geographic location (Europe vs. North America), age (adult vs. adolescent), setting (civil, forensic, correctional, mixed/other), setting (institution vs. community), interview status (file only vs. file plus interview), or allegiance (whether instruments' authors conducted the research).

In a series of more focused analyses investigating the comparative predictive accuracy of the numeric use of SPJ instruments versus SRRs, L. S. Guy (2008) observed that SRRs consistently had stronger associations with violence. Consistent with subsequent meta-analytic work (Fazel et al., 2012; Singh et al., 2011), ESs were larger when there was a match between the type of outcome that an SPJ instrument was designed to assess and that particular outcome (e.g., HCR–20 SRRs were more strongly related to outcomes when they focused on violence—especially physical violence—as opposed to nonviolent or general criminality).

In our opinion, the meta-analytic evidence overwhelmingly indicates that claims (e.g., Quinsey et al., 1998, 2006) that clinically based estimates of violence risk, even when they are structured and anchored by research findings, are inappropriate for use in clinical practice are baseless. Since L. S. Guy's (2008) meta-analytic survey of the SPJ literature, numerous SPJ studies have been published that provide further support for this conclusion. In the following section, we review the studies that have evaluated the SRRs of low, moderate, and high risk used in the SPJ approach, paying particular attention to comparisons between the SRRs and the numeric (actuarial) use of such instruments or to actuarial instruments.

Research on the Structured Professional Judgment Model of Violence Risk Assessment

Among the 100+ research evaluations of SPJ instruments that have been conducted, there are at least 34 published studies in which the association between SRRs and violence has been investigated. This subset of studies has broad geographic representation, with data collected in 11 countries: Canada, Denmark, Finland, the Netherlands, Norway, Portugal, Serbia, Spain, Sweden, the United Kingdom, and the United States. The 34 studies evaluated SPJ instruments that had been developed for use with children, adolescents, and adults: Early Assessment Risk List for Boys (EARL–20B; Augimeri, Koegl, Webster, & Levene, 2001), Early Assessment Risk List for Girls (EARL–21G; Levene et al., 2001), ERASOR, HCR–20, Structured

Assessment of Protective Factors for Violence Risk (SAPROF; de Vogel, de Ruiter, Bouman, & de Vries Robbé, 2012), SARA, SAVRY, Short-Term Assessment of Risk and Treatability (START; Webster, Martin, Brink, Nicholls, & Desmarais, 2009), START: Adolescent Version (START:AV; Viljoen et al., 2014), and SVR–20. When unpublished disseminations are considered, the number of studies reporting on the predictive validity of the SRR of an SPJ instrument rises to almost 100.

What is the association between the SRR and violence?   Thirty of the 34 studies (88%) were significantly predictive of violence. In the other four studies (Braithwaite, Charette, Crocker, & Reyes, 2010; Schaap, Lammers, & de Vogel, 2009; Sjöstedt & Långström, 2002; Viljoen et al., 2008), the SRR did not have a statistically significant association with violence. Braithewaite et al. (2010) reported on only 34 individuals. Schaap et al. (2009) also reported on a small sample ($N = 45$) who were evaluated using both the PCL–R and HCR–20 and found that none of the many indices studied (i.e., total scores, subscale scores, and SRRs) was associated with either general or violent recidivism. Sjöstedt and Långström (2002) studied three actuarial instruments in addition to one SPJ measure and also reported that none of the four measures was associated with violence. Finally, Viljoen et al. (2008) found that the SRR was not associated with violence, but the numeric use of the SPJ instrument was. Taken together, the pattern of findings from these 34 studies in which the SRR was evaluated indicates that the SRR is associated with violence across geographic locations and specific instruments.

Do SRRs add incrementally to the prediction of violence over and above the numerical (or actuarial) use of the instrument, or of a PCL measure, an actuarial measure, or unstructured clinical prediction?   Researchers typically answer questions of this sort by using multivariate regression analyses in which the comparison index is entered in the first step of the model and the SRR is entered in the second step. If the addition of the SRR in step two adds in a statistically significant manner to the predictive

power of the multivariate model, then evidence for incremental validity is present. Seventeen of the published studies found evidence of predictive validity of the SRR investigated in this question; incremental validity was observed in most (15, or 88%) of these studies.

The studies in which evidence of incremental predictive validity of the SRRs relative to the numeric use of the SPJ instrument was found are heterogeneous with respect to the types of samples that were examined and include offenders with mental disorders (de Vogel & de Ruiter, 2005), civil psychiatric inpatients (Arbach-Lucioni, Andres-Pueyo, Pomarol-Clotet, & Gomar-Sones, 2011), forensic patients (Desmarais, Nicholls, Wilson, & Brink, 2012; Douglas, Ogloff, & Hart, 2003; Pedersen, Rasmussen, & Elsass, 2010; van den Brink, Hooijschuur, van Os, Savenije, & Wiersma, 2010), domestic violence offenders (Kropp & Hart, 2000), adult criminal offenders who had been released from prison (Douglas, Yeomans, & Boer, 2005) or were on probation or parole (Neves, Goncalves, & Palma-Oliveira, 2011). and young offenders (Dolan & Rennie, 2008; Enebrink, Långström, & Gumpert, 2006; Lodewijks, de Ruiter, & Doreleijers, 2008; Lodewijks, Doreleijers, & de Ruiter, 2008). In all of the studies in which incremental validity of the SRR over numeric use of the instrument was not observed, the samples consisted of young offenders (Schmidt, Campbell, & Houlding, 2011; Viljoen et al., 2012; Vincent, Chapman, & Cook, 2011). In addition to these primary studies, meta-analyses have been used to investigate this issue. Focusing on studies of the SARA (Kropp et al., 1995), Hanson and Morton-Bourgon (2009) compared the ESs of violence risk based on the SRR (two studies) or the sum of item ratings (five studies). The accuracy when SARA items were summed ($d = .43$, 95% CI [.32, .53]) appeared somewhat higher than when structured professional judgment was used ($d = .35$, 95% CI [.15, .55]), although this difference was not large, the CIs overlapped, and the number of studies was small.

Investigators also have studied whether the SRR adds predictive validity relative to non-SPJ instruments that are used frequently for assessing an individual's risk for violence. More specifically, there is evidence of incremental validity for the HCR–20

SRR over the PCL–R for violence among criminal offenders and for forensic patients (de Vogel & de Ruiter, 2005; Douglas et al., 2003, 2005), for the START SRR over the PCL:SV (Desmarais, Nicholls, et al., 2012), and for the SAVRY SRR over the PCL:YV (Dolan & Rennie, 2008). In addition, the SAVRY SRR was demonstrated to have incremental validity beyond unstructured clinical predictions (Lodewijks, Doreleijers, & de Ruiter, 2008), and the HCR–20 SRR and the VRAG were both shown to account for unique variance in predicting violence (Douglas et al., 2005).

Taken together, the empirical findings provide strong support for the SPJ model. First, one can conclude on the basis of the scientific evidence that SPJ SRRs are at least as or more accurate than actuarial instruments, unstructured clinical prediction, and the PCL family of instruments. Second, research conducted to date also indicates that professionals are able to make structured judgments about the risk of violence to others using SPJ instruments that are at least as accurate—and often more accurate—than when such instruments are used in numeric form (i.e., by summing item scores). Of course, the predictive accuracy of the SRRs and numeric applications would be expected to be, at a minimum, comparable because, in general, the more risk factors that are present for a given individual, the higher his or her risk might be. At the same time, however, it would be inappropriate to interpret the comparable performance of the numeric and SRR indices as a reason to discontinue the use of SRRs. Among other reasons, such ratings are critical for situations in which one or a few risk factors are deemed to be disproportionately important to an examinee's risk for violence; this is information that would be lost were item scores simply to be summed. In the next section, we begin by considering some of the issues that would be important to consider when selecting a model of violence risk assessment to use.

PRACTICE AND POLICY ISSUES

The evidence from meta-analyses and key primary studies reviewed thus far clearly indicates that there is no definitive advantage—in terms of predictive accuracy—for either actuarial or structured clinical approaches to assessing an individual's risk for violence. As such, claims that have been made by researchers to the contrary (e.g., Quinsey et al., 2006; Rice, Harris, & Hilton, 2010) are unjustifiable. Given no clear advantage for either approach as far as predictive validity is concerned, factors other than predictive accuracy indices should shape practitioners' decisions regarding which risk assessment strategy or approach to follow. Lavoie, Guy, and Douglas (2009) described five characteristics or principles that a defensible risk assessment procedure would embody, and that therefore would be important to consider when selecting an instrument for clinical practice.

First, according to Lavoie et al. (2009), a risk assessment scheme should include relevant scientifically supported risk factors. Decades of empirical efforts have generated critical research findings regarding the specific factors that are most reliably and robustly associated with antisocial behavior, including violence. Moreover, in addition to including appropriate risk factors, the risk assessment instrument should include clear definitions, descriptions, or rating guidelines for the various factors. Semantic precision of this sort is important in order to promote interrater reliability and remind users of the empirical association between violence and the risk factors included in the scheme.

Second, the instrument ought to have comprehensive coverage of violence risk factors. Instruments that do not contain most of the identified risk factors may yield inappropriately low or high estimates of risk status if potentially important and pertinent risk factors exist for a case and were not considered.

Third, a good violence risk assessment instrument should facilitate risk management planning and execution. In order to be positioned to do so, an instrument must contain dynamic violence risk factors that represent targets for treatment specifically or intervention more generally (Douglas & Skeem, 2005). Such risk factors also must be criminogenic (i.e., changing the degree to which a factor is present for a given individual will result in an attendant change in the individual's level of risk for violence; see, generally, Andrews & Bonta, 2006).

Fourth, a clear and logical method of communicating opinions and recommendations regarding risk and risk management activities should be part of the instrument or assessment model. The instrument should guide the evaluator to offer categorical, descriptive risk statements tied to the estimated risk level and to the associated intensity of management anticipated to reduce risk. An alternative approach followed by actuarial instruments—providing numerical or probabilistic estimates of risk based on the presence of risk factors—is highly problematic (see limitations associated with actuarial measures, earlier; and see the Risk Communication section later). Moreover, because specific prescriptive actions are not aligned with numerical or probabilistic estimates, an opportunity to reduce risk is not available.

Finally, in light of the potentially serious (including fatal) consequences that are associated with violence risk assessments, the decision-making process should be completely transparent and available for review by relevant stakeholders. Transparency in the risk assessment process entails a clear statement of risk factors included, scoring rules or rating guidelines used, and principles followed to integrate risk factors into a final risk decision. Naive users may be swayed by well-marketed risk measures that are commercially available but that fail to meet these minimum standards of transparency, which is a potential ethical problem and may also jeopardize the admissibility of expert evidence that is based on the instruments. For example, some instruments may be vulnerable to criticism that they lack transparency because they are scored using proprietary algorithms that are undisclosed to evaluators; such instruments include the Structured Interview for Violence Risk Assessment (SIVRA-35; http://nabita.org/resources/sivra-35/), the MOSAIC family of instruments (http://www.mosaicmethod.com), and the Correctional Offender Management Profiling for Alternative Sanctions (COMPAS; Northpointe Institute for Public Management, 1996).

An additional consideration for a defensible risk assessment procedure relates to the relevance of the instrument for addressing the specific psycholegal question. For example, within the context of civil commitment proceedings, by law there must be a causal nexus between an individual's risk for violence to others and the presence of a mental disorder. Therefore, risk assessment instruments that either omit mental disorder from their core risk factors (such as the LSI family of instruments) or include it as a protective factor and so purport that mental disorder reduces the risk for violence to others (such as the VRAG) are fundamentally useless and are inappropriate for assessing an individual's risk for violence to others in order to inform decision making about civil commitment suitability.

Finally, if one endorses the view that risk prediction is relatively meaningless in the absence of efforts to prevent, reduce, and manage risk, and considering the principles offered by Lavoie et al. (2009), the approach to violence risk assessment espoused by the SPJ model is a defensible decision-making framework. Indeed, international practice guidelines support the use of the SPJ approach. For example, after conducting a thorough review regarding the extent to which instruments that were developed to assess violent, sexual, and general recidivism have been empirically validated, the standards and guidelines published by Scotland's Risk Management Authority (RMA) arrived at the following conclusion:

> When conducting a detailed risk assessment for any offender, the use of tools based upon static assessment items—actuarial tools—is permissible only when it forms part of a structured professional assessment; identifying risk and protective factors specific to the individual; and formulating risk in an analytical manner. This is due to the limitations of actuarial tools in the crucial tasks of both identifying risk and protective factors specific to the individual and also guiding practitioners in the formulation of risk leading to tailored risk management plans. (RMA, 2007, p. 7)

Similarly, in a document that presents practice guidelines for the assessment and management of risk to self and others in mental health services that was prepared for England's National Mental Health

Risk Management Programme (Department of Health, 2007), Best Practice point 10 reads, "Where suitable tools are available, risk management should be based on assessment using the structured clinical judgement approach" (p. 18; see p. 20 for a detailed explanation of this point).

Moreover, in addition to the many reasons for adhering to the SPJ approach that are directly relevant to clinical practice, there also is a legal impetus. As noted by Kropp and Hart (2004):[2]

> The Supreme Court of Canada, in considering a wide range of cases related to violence and violence risk over many decades, has consistently held that the application of discretion by criminal justice and mental health professionals (e.g., police and corrections officers, prosecutors and judges, parole and review boards, psychiatrists and psychologists) is both necessary and appropriate. (p. 17)

Conducting Comprehensive Clinical Risk Assessments

There are few circumstances in which it is both legally justifiable and clinically feasible to conduct comprehensive violence risk assessments for every person who is referred for one. It is more common that evaluators themselves play some role in determining which of the people referred for a comprehensive violence risk assessment will actually undergo one or which will be assessed soonest. This process is variously referred to as selection, sorting, prioritization, screening, and triage.

Regardless of what one calls it, the selection process is important. Good selection decisions protect public safety while saving scarce resources, protect the rights and freedoms of people who are referred for assessment, and reduce evaluators' exposure to liability. In contrast, bad selection decisions may put people in danger, waste time and money, lead to the unnecessary detention of evaluees or invasion of their privacy, and result in complaints or even

lawsuits against evaluators and the agencies that hire them.

Selection decisions address two separate but related issues. The first concerns whether there are reasonable grounds, according to relevant law, to conclude that the person may pose a risk for violence. The decision concerns the evidence that the person poses a risk, not the nature of the risk posed. The law itself sets out what may constitute "reasonable grounds" in terms of the type, extent, or reliability of evidence. For example, consider the case of an employer who refers an employee for a comprehensive violence risk assessment under occupational health and safety law. The employer's grounds for concern are that (a) coworkers complained that the employee has been talking about his religious beliefs in a way that other people find odd and uncomfortable, and (b) the employee admitted in private conversations with some coworkers that he saw a counselor in the past. The evaluator should consider whether odd beliefs and a history of receiving mental health services constitute bona fide evidence that would justify a comprehensive violence risk assessment in light of occupational health and safety law, as well as in light of employment and human rights law more generally.

The second issue addressed by selection is the seriousness of the risk that the person may pose. Even when there are reasonable grounds to believe that a person poses a risk for violence, the law may require that risk to be of a certain type (e.g., with respect to the nature, seriousness, or imminence of the potential violence). And even when comprehensive violence risk assessments are authorized or required by law, it may be impossible to accept all referrals, to begin them all right away, or to complete them all quickly enough to guide immediate decisions regarding risk management. This means that evaluators must sort through referrals in order to determine which cases will be assessed, which will be accorded high priority, or which will require management strategies to be implemented even while the assessment is being conducted.

---

[2]Kropp and Hart (2004) provided several relevant legal citations: Canadian Foundation for Children, Youth and the Law v. Canada (Attorney General), 1 S.C.R. 76, (2004); Penetanguishene Mental Health Centre v. Ontario (Attorney General), 1 S.C.R. 498, (2004); R. v. Johnson, 2 S.C.R. 357, (2003); Smith v. Jones, 1 S.C.R. 455, (1999).

The various approaches to selection that are used by evaluators can be divided into three categories. We call the first approach *tracking* or *surveillance*. It involves systematically monitoring people who have been or may be referred for a comprehensive violence risk assessment. Cases are flagged for (immediate) assessment if monitoring detects the presence of specific risk factors or specific forms of violence. Tracking tends to be used by institutions or large agencies with good information management systems and procedures that allow for routine data collection and analysis. A good example of a tracking tool is the Brøset Violence Checklist (BVC; Almvik & Woods, 1999). The BVC is used to track cases in inpatient mental health settings. Nursing staff completes the BVC for all patients in a ward or unit on a shift-by-shift basis. Nurses check for the presence of six factors: confused, irritable, boisterous, physically threatening, verbally threatening, and attacking objects. Cases in which two or more factors are present are escalated; that is, these cases are flagged as being high risk and are prioritized for special assessment and management.

The tracking approach to selection has two major limitations. First, it is obviously reactive in nature. Cases are escalated only after the risk has escalated to the point that violence is imminent or after it has already occurred. This may hamper prevention efforts. Second, tracking typically can monitor only a very small number of risk factors, which means that it has a seriously limited ability to detect cases in which risk is high or escalating. Put simply, tracking is a very weak form of risk assessment.

The second approach to selection we call *screening*. Screening involves an abbreviated risk assessment that consists of a small number of items, typically historical in nature, that can be easily coded from records. Decisions to refer an individual for a comprehensive violence risk assessment are based on the outcome of the abbreviated risk assessment. This approach tends to be used by mental health or criminal justice agencies that have a large number of cases. Screening often uses actuarial risk assessment instruments, such as the Domestic Violence Screening Inventory (DVSI; Williams & Houghton, 2004). The DVSI is a 12-item actuarial instrument that was developed to screen people who have been charged

with or convicted of offenses related to intimate partner violence. Ratings on individual items are summed, and cases that exceed a cutoff are referred for specialized assessment and supervision.

The screening approach to selection has an advantage over tracking in that screening is proactive in nature: Screening does not wait until violence occurs before a case is flagged. However, due to the small number of risk factors considered, screening shares with tracking the limitation that it is a weak form of risk assessment. It is questionable logic to base decisions about who should get a "proper" risk assessment (i.e., an individualized assessment that considers the totality of circumstances) on the findings of a "quick-and-dirty" risk assessment (i.e., a statistical profile that is based on restricted historical information). There is one exception to this general rule: Screening tests make perfect sense if they are known to yield very specific, asymmetric patterns of predictive errors with respect to a gold standard. For example, a screening test may be very useful to "screen in" cases that require further assessment if it has near perfect sensitivity (i.e., flags virtually all cases that would be deemed high risk by a comprehensive assessment), even if it has much lower specificity (i.e., also flags cases that would be deemed low risk by a comprehensive assessment). Unfortunately, there are no screening tools that yield an asymmetric pattern of errors of the sort that would make them useful.

The third approach to selection we call *triage*. Triage involves sorting cases into a small number of categories (typically three or four) based on markers of seriousness rather than on detection of the outcome itself or on risk for the outcome. The markers of seriousness are selected rationally based on their direct relevance for a particular decision-making context. They are also combined rationally, often using a logic tree or flow chart. This approach, although used frequently in some areas of medicine, is not commonly used with respect to violence risk. There are, however, some noteworthy exceptions. For example, Watt and Hart (2013) developed a triage tool for use by police officers who are investigating alleged intimate partner violence in order to determine which cases should be referred for comprehensive risk assessment. The triage tool requires police to consider primary warning signs of case seriousness. These include the alleged perpetrator's history of (a) actual or attempted violence, (b) violent threats or intent, or (c) violent ideation. Police then consider secondary warning signs, which include the alleged perpetrator's history of (a) personal crisis, (b) interpersonal crisis, (c) mental health problems, or (d) other special considerations. Finally, police consider whether any of the primary and secondary warning signs are recent, serious, or escalating. Based on which warning signs are present, as well as whether they are recent, serious, or escalating, cases are sorted into one of three categories: *positive*, resulting in such things as referral for comprehensive risk assessment, assignment as case prioritization, and implementation of interim management strategies; *possible*, resulting in such outcomes as referral for clarification of information, a second opinion, monitoring, or a comprehensive assessment at low priority (i.e., if and when resources permit); or *negative*, resulting in no referral for a comprehensive assessment or delivery of routine services. Similar to screening, triage is proactive in nature. Unlike tracking or screening, the justification for triage is logical rather than predictive or statistical and so is not vulnerable to criticisms of using an inferior risk assessment to make decisions about who should receive a superior one.

Comprehensive Clinical Assessment: Step-by-Step

Descriptions of and instructions about the practice of conducting violence risk assessments have been written about for decades (Kozol, Boucher, & Garofalo, 1972; Litwack & Schlesinger, 1999; Litwack, Zapf, Groscup, & Hart, 2006; Monahan, 1981; Scott, 1977; Tardiff, 1996). Two distinct phases characterize such assessments. The goals of the first phase involve understanding the examinee's potential for violence (via analysis of risk and protective factors) and exploring various facets about the particular hazard that the person might pose. For example,

what type of violence is of concern (sexual aggression, stalking, etc.)? Who are the potential targets or victims (intimate partner, workplace colleague, etc.)? What are the possible reasons or motivations related to violence perpetration? What kinds of situational or contextual variables would be expected to be present in order for the violence to occur? This first phase involving what might happen in the future typically is referred to as *prediction*.[3]

The goal of the second phase of the assessment is to mitigate the risk of violence occurring by developing an individualized plan for intervention. This phase typically is referred to as *risk management*. Management entails understanding which of a broad array of factors (related to the evaluee as well as situational or contextual factors, such as likely living situation) could minimize or potentiate the individual's risk of violence.

Although there is consensus in the field that the goals of the two phases clearly differ, divergent perspectives exist regarding whether they can be conducted independently. Some researchers (Heilbrun, 1997; Quinsey et al., 2006) have argued in favor of the view that evaluators should first complete the prediction phase and then proceed with the management phase only if it is relevant to the particular legal context. Other researchers (Hart, Douglas, & Webster, 2001) have argued in favor of an opposite view and assert that a bidirectional or recursive relation exists between the two phases of prediction and management. From this perspective, good prediction is seen as being impossible to accomplish without systematic consideration of the evaluee's possible future living situations and interventions. On the flip side, good management is viewed as being impossible without systematic consideration of the individual's potential for violence. The two phases are seen as being interrelated in that judgments made at one phase affect judgments that are made at the other phase, actually changing the nature of the information that would be relevant for each phase. Because the prediction phase is viewed

---

[3]We use the term *prediction* in this sense to describe activities that are undertaken in order to understand one's potential for violence and appreciate what could occur in the future, and differentiate the term from *probabilistic* prediction, which putatively involves making precise, quantitative, probabilistic estimates of violence.

as being contingent on the management phase, in this framework, prediction is understood not to be legally relevant without the consideration of management.

Completing a violence risk assessment by relying solely on actuarial risk assessment instruments restricts the scope of the evaluation to only the prediction phase. Should practitioners wish to engage in a comprehensive assessment of an individual's risk for future violence, they would need to follow an approach that provides structure for that activity. The SPJ approach is the only empirically supported model for conducting comprehensive violence risk assessments. In the remainder of this section, we describe the framework underlying the administration of one SPJ instrument. Depending on the particular instrument and the setting in which it is intended to be used, relatively more or fewer steps are included as part of the instrument's administration.

In the next section, we describe the seven steps involved in the administration of the newest SPJ guidelines, Version 3 of the Historical–Clinical–Risk Management—20 (HCR–20^{V3}; Douglas, Hart, Webster, & Belfrage, 2013; also see Exhibit 3.1). We choose to do so because the HCR–20^{V3} includes the most comprehensive framework and absolute number of steps of all of the SPJ instruments (having been modeled closely after the framework of the Risk for Sexual Violence Protocol [RSVP]; Hart et al., 2003). We describe the general administration steps of the HCR–20^{V3} but do not focus on administration of the instrument specifically. Administration involves seven steps that fall into three broad categories: identifying facts, making meaning of those facts, and taking action. We turn now to describing the distinct steps within each of these categories.

Identifying facts. This category involves the first two steps in the overall administration procedure. In Step 1, evaluators gather and document basic case information. The reliability and validity of evaluators' judgments are tied directly to the quantity and quality of the information that is reviewed. With respect to quantity, evaluators should try to gather all of the information that is necessary to reach opinions regarding risk for the particular case. Thoroughness, persistence, and relentless

---

Exhibit 3.1
HCR–20^{V3}'s Violence Risk Factors

Historical scale (history of problems with . . .)
H1. Violence
    a. as a child (12 and under)
    b. as an adolescent (13–17)
    c. as an adult (18 and over)
H2. Other antisocial behavior
    a. as a child (12 and under)
    b. as an adolescent (13–17)
    c. as an adult (18 and over)
H3. Relationships
    a. intimate
    b. nonintimate
H4. Employment
H5. Substance use
H6. Major mental disorder
    a. psychotic disorder
    b. major mood disorder
    c. other major mental disorders
H7. Personality disorder
    a. antisocial, psychopathic, and dissocial
    b. other personality disorders
H8. Traumatic experiences
    a. victimization/trauma
    b. adverse childrearing experiences
H9. Violent attitudes
H10. Treatment or supervision response

Clinical scale (recent problems with . . .)
C1. Insight
    a. mental disorder
    b. violence risk
    c. need for treatment
C2. Violent ideation or intent
C3. Symptoms of major mental disorder
    a. psychotic disorder
    b. major mood disorder
    c. other major mental disorders
C4. Instability
    a. affective
    b. behavioral
    c. cognitive
C5. Treatment or supervision response
    a. compliance
    b. responsiveness

Risk management scale (future problems with . . .)
R1. Professional services and plans
R2. Living situation
R3. Personal support
R4. Treatment or supervision response
    a. compliance
    b. responsiveness
R5. Stress or coping

Note. Data from Douglas, Hart, Webster, and Belfrage (2013).

fact checking are essential. Consistent with good forensic practice generally, evaluators should gather information from multiple sources about multiple issues or topics. It is neither feasible nor required to gather and consider all of the information that is available in a given case. Evaluators should consider (and communicate) how limited information or the absence of a critical source or type of information might have impacted the evaluation. We recommend that evaluators balance comprehensiveness with efficiency by focusing on information that is directly relevant to the assessment task, not redundant with information that has already been gathered, and is provided by reliable sources. Regarding the latter point, evaluators will need to assess the credibility of the sources of information on which they relied and attempt to reconcile any contradictory information.

The specific information gathered will vary according to the nature of the risks being assessed and the specifics of the case. For example, if an evaluee has a history of a major mental disorder, it would be important to develop a good understanding of the nature of his or her symptoms across time, compliance with and response to any interventions, and insight related to the need for treatment as well as whether (and, if so, in what ways) the symptoms were related to the perpetration of violence.

For all cases, sources of information typically will include interviews with and direct observation of the evaluee, interviews with victims of, or witnesses to, past violence or review of their documented accounts, interviews with collateral informants (e.g., family members, friends, coworkers), and review of collateral records. Examples of such records include criminal histories from relevant agencies, police reports, statements by the evaluee, and statements by victims and witnesses concerning past violence; prosecution and court files; daily logs or other records from institutional and community corrections; presentence or predisposition reports; mental health and medical treatment records, including results of any psychometric or psychodiagnostic tests and assessment measures; assessment and treatment reports by civil and forensic mental health consultants; daily logs from outpatient and inpatient treatment facilities; and school, employment, and military records.

In all cases, information about the evaluee's history of violence always should be obtained. If there is such a history, it often is helpful to construct a timeline of violent incidents in order to look for patterns (e.g., a clear trajectory or triggering events). For each major incident, the evaluator should attempt to determine the key people involved (e.g., perpetrators, victims, witnesses), what happened and why (i.e., intentions, actions, motivations), where and when the incident occurred (e.g., physical and social context), and the evaluee's reactions (e.g., thoughts and feelings before, during, and after the incident).

In the next step within this category, Step 2 of the overall administration procedure, evaluators identify the presence of a core set of defined factors and any additional case-specific factors. The purpose of making presence ratings is to ensure that the evaluator has considered all of the relevant information about each factor and has formed opinions regarding the evaluee's problems in those domains that can facilitate subsequent decision making and communication about violence risks. In other words, judging whether a risk factor is present is a means to an end, not an end in itself.

The items included in any SPJ tool represent risk factors whose validity is supported by systematic review of the scientific and professional literature and which have established validity for the particular kind of violence of concern. Having an a priori defined set of core risk factors is intended to prevent evaluators from considering or giving too much weight to risk factors of little or questionable validity and, conversely, from giving insufficient weight to risk factors with established validity. Regular consideration of the core risk factors for every case also is intended to prevent evaluators from using an implicit framework in which they might not be entirely conscious or self-aware of what they did or did not consider as risk factors.

Although the core list of risk factors is intended to be reasonably thorough or comprehensive, it is not exhaustive. Evaluators using any SPJ instrument are encouraged to identify rare or case-specific risk factors that are not captured among the prespecified list that is available in the instrument, but only if they are able to provide a compelling clinical or logical rationale for doing so. These caveats are intended to help the evaluator avoid including risk factors that are unlikely to be associated with violence.

The presence of risk factors on most SPJ instruments is rated using a three-level response format that reflects the certainty of the evaluator's opinion: *Y* (information indicates that the factor is present), *P* (information indicates that the factor is possibly or partially present), and *N* (information indicates that the factor is not present or does not apply). In rare circumstances, evaluators may omit a rating if no reliable information exists by which to judge the presence of the factor.

Making meaning. This category contains three steps (i.e., Steps 3 through 5 of the overall administration procedure). In Step 3, evaluators assess the relevance of the factors for the specific individual. Whereas Step 2 involved identifying the extent to which an evaluee possessed risk factors that are relevant in general or on average according to the scientific and professional literature (i.e., at a nomothetic level), in Step 3, the evaluator applies information about risk factors in an idiographic manner for the case at hand. Ratings are made for each item using a three-level scale (e.g., *yes, possibly, no*; or *high, moderate, low*) after presence ratings for all items are made. Relevance ratings are intended to capture the extent to which a risk factor is critical to the evaluator's formulation of what caused the evaluee to perpetrate violence and how best to prevent future violence through the development of risk management strategies.

A risk factor may be judged as being relevant for an evaluee if it played a key contribution to past violence, is likely to influence the evaluee's decision to act violently in the future, is likely to impair the evaluee's capacity to use nonviolent problem-solving techniques or to engage in nonviolent or nonconfrontational interpersonal relations, or is deemed to be critical to include in the risk management plan.

In Step 4, evaluators integrate case information through formulation (Hart, Sturmey, Logan, & McMurran, 2011). This step furthers what was begun in Step 3 because it involves evaluators

actively integrating the individual risk factors into a conceptually meaningful framework in order to explain the evaluee's violence. Formulation of violence risk should be guided by theory, and the SPJ approach typically uses decision theory (Hart & Logan, 2011). Decision theory may be considered a version of the psychology of criminal conduct or the general personality and cognitive social learning perspective (Andrews & Bonta, 2006), but tailored specifically to violence. Psychology of criminal conduct and general personality and cognitive social learning are well-established theories of criminal behavior.

With few exceptions, all people think before they commit violence: they choose (a) the person(s) against whom they will commit violence, (b) when they will commit the violence, and (c) what kinds of violence they will commit. As such, in decision theory, violence is viewed as a purposive behavior that is intended to achieve one or more goals (i.e., a choice). The decision to engage in violence may be a bad decision or a decision that is made badly (e.g., it may be made quickly, based on poor information, and with little care or attention), but it nevertheless is a decision. Within this framework, people are assumed to proceed through a four-step thought process before engaging in violence (Hart & Logan, 2011). In the first step, an individual becomes aware that violence is a possible course of action and, rather than dismissing that notion, the individual entertains it as a possible course of action in the given situation. In the next step, the individual evaluates the possible positive consequences of violence and determines that violence might result in reward or benefit (i.e., she or he perceives that violence might pay off). In the third step, the individual evaluates the possible negative consequences of violence and determines that the costs are acceptable (i.e., perceived benefits outweigh perceived costs). In the final step, the individual evaluates his or her options for committing violence and determines that it is feasible.

Working within the framework of decision theory, evaluators who are completing comprehensive violence risk assessments must understand how and why an evaluee decided to engage in violence in the past, as well as why she or he decided not to engage in violence. In understanding how and why a person engaged or did not engage in violence, the evaluator will consider the various factors that impinged on or influenced the evaluee's decision making, and also understand what interventions, events, and occurrences might encourage the evaluee's decisions to act prosocially and discourage the decision to act nonviolently. Viewed from this perspective, then, risk factors are things that influence an individual's decision making. They can exert influence in several ways. For example, risk factors can motivate, disinhibit, or destabilize decisions. *Motivators* increase the perceived rewards or benefits of violence, *disinhibitors* decrease the perceived costs or negative consequences of violence, and *destabilizers* generally disturb or disorganize people's ability to monitor and control their decision making.

As part of engaging in risk formulation, evaluators would consider the extent to which risk factors (individually or as a combination of certain risk factors) act as motivators, disinhibitors, or destabilizers. Formulation activities also could involve evaluators constructing a hierarchy of relevant risk factors; in most cases, several risk factors stand out as more important than others. Evaluators also should think about which risk factors appear to covary or cluster together for the evaluee. Often, such clusters have a common root cause, and it should be possible to trace the origins of a number of risk factors to a single anteceding risk factor that acts as a root cause. Finally, in some cases, risk factors may serve as portals or gateways to a risk process, and evaluators should consider this possibility when engaging in formulation.

In the third activity of this category, evaluators complete Step 4 of the overall administration procedure: identifying and describing the most likely scenarios of future violence. A scenario is a story about violence that the examinee might perpetrate. In this step, the evaluator speculates about what might happen in the future. Such speculation is done in an informed way, in light of the factors that were identified as being present and relevant in Steps 2 and 3, and how they are integrated through formulation in Step 4.

Developing scenarios requires evaluators to consider what kinds of violence the examinee might

perpetrate, for which motivations, against which victims, with what kinds of consequences, and at which times. A scenario is not a prediction about what *will* happen but rather is a general forecast or speculation about what reasonably *could* happen given the evaluator's general knowledge and experience and the specifics of the particular case. Although the number of possible scenarios that could be constructed is virtually infinite, typically, in any given case, only a few scenarios should seem reasonable, credible, or plausible given what is known about fact and theory (e.g., Chermack & van der Merwe, 2003). Still other scenarios will be dismissed, or "pruned", because they will be perceived as implausible (e.g., Pomerol, 2001).

A very large literature base on the general management strategy known as *scenario planning* exists across numerous professional disciplines. This strategy has been used for more than 50 years in fields such as business, health care, and the military (Ringland, 1998; van der Heijden, 1997). The SPJ approach to developing scenarios of violence was derived from this more general management strategy. Scenario planning has been described as being "a process of positing several informed, plausible and imagined alternative future environments in which decisions about the future may be played out, for the purpose of changing current thinking, improving decision making, enhancing human and organization learning and improving performance" (Chermack & Lynham, 2002, p. 366). Scenario planning is most appropriate for situations of complexity and unbounded uncertainty (e.g., van der Heijden, 1994), which we believe to be an apt characterization of the state of affairs in which violence risk assessments often are conducted.

The SPJ approach to developing scenarios of violence encourages evaluators to consider four broad scenarios of violence. First, in a repeat, *flat trajectory, linear projection*, or *point projection* scenario, the evaluator considers a scenario in which the examinee commits violence similar to his or her most recent act. Second, in a *best case* or *optimistic* scenario, the evaluator considers a scenario in which the trajectory of violence decreases, and the examinee commits a less serious act or even chooses to desist altogether. In a *worst case* or *doom* scenario, the evaluator considers a scenario in which the trajectory increases, and the examinee commits a more serious, and perhaps even life-threatening, act of violence. Finally, the evaluator considers a *twist* or *sideways trajectory* scenario in which the nature of violence changes or evolves, such as with respect to the motivation for the incident or the manner of victim selection. Multiple scenarios could be developed within each of these four broad categories. For each scenario, the evaluator then develops a detailed description in terms of the nature, severity, imminence, frequency or duration, and likelihood of violence. Finally, the evaluator "prunes away" the scenarios that seem implausible based on theory, research, experience, and case facts. Typically, three to five general scenarios will be sufficient to capture the range of plausible outcomes in a given case. The scenarios developed will directly guide the development of risk management plans. Such plans will only be adequate if they address every major plausible scenario of future violence. We turn next to this penultimate step in the SPJ administration procedure.

Taking action. In Step 6 of the SPJ administration procedure, the evaluator recommends risk management strategies. The strategies recommended are related directly to the activities that are completed at each of the preceding steps. That is, consistent with general principles of scenario planning, evaluators develop case management plans based on plausible scenarios of violence, which in turn were based on the presence and relevance of risk factors. Using an SPJ approach, evaluators typically structure the development of risk management plans by considering four general categories of strategies: monitoring/surveillance, supervision/control, treatment/assessment, and, when relevant, victim safety planning (e.g., Hart et al., 2001, 2003; Kropp et al., 2008). Within each general category of strategies, evaluators identify specific strategies and then translate these into more detailed plans by considering tactics and logistics. Risk management plans should comport with the risk–need–responsivity (RNR) model of risk management (Andrews, 2012; Andrews & Bonta, 2010). As noted earlier,

meta-analytic research demonstrates that there is a positive association between general and violent recidivism reduction and adherence to these principles (see Andrews, 2012).

Finally, in Step 7 of the overall administration procedure, evaluators document their judgments about an individual's risk, assigning ratings of low, moderate, or high risk. Evaluators are encouraged to make judgments regarding an individual's overall risk for violence, risk for serious physical harm, and risk for imminent violence, as well as indication of other risks that the examinee may pose, any immediate actions taken or required, and critical dates or triggers for case review. The SRR regarding an individual's overall risk for violence is reflective of the degree of effort or intervention that the evaluator judges will be required to prevent the person from committing violence. Ratings regarding the risk of serious physical harm and imminent violence reflect the severity and imminence of violence, respectively, that the evaluee might commit.

In the course of completing a comprehensive violence risk assessment, an evaluator may learn information that causes him or her to know or have good reason to suspect that the evaluee may pose other types of risk, such as for specialized forms of violence (e.g., sexual violence, potentially lethal violence against oneself) or other harmful activities (e.g., suicide-related behavior; nonsuicidal self-harm). In making summary ratings about these other risks, evaluators are communicating the presence of risks that should be the focus of a further, separate evaluation (because, for example, risk factors for violence overlap partially but are inadequate for an assessment of suicide risk).

No numbers or putative probabilistic estimates are required to complete a comprehensive evaluation of an individual's risk for violence (and, in fact, they may be misleading or harmful). In the SPJ approach, evaluators use their discretion to consider, decide, and explain the relevance or meaningfulness of any factors that are present with respect to the risks posed and management of those risks. In this final step, evaluators should limit and qualify their opinions based on the quantity and quality of case information that was reviewed in Step 1.

Risk Communication and Report Writing

Considering the magnitude of empirical work that has accumulated on risk factors and approaches for assessing risk of violence, comparatively little research has been conducted on approaches for communicating one's opinions or findings from the risk assessment (for commentary about the nature of such communications and the potential complexities it entails, see Grisso & Tomkins, 1996; Litwack, 1997; Monahan & Steadman, 2006; Schopp, 1996). As described earlier, communication about risk in the SPJ model typically includes a categorical estimate regarding the likelihood of a particular form of violence (low, moderate, or high risk), information about other aspects of risk (e.g., nature of violence, likely target, potential for weapon use, possible severity of harm, etc.), and concrete recommendations regarding steps that can be taken to manage risk or prevent violence. In contrast, risk communication following an assessment using an actuarial approach may include the presentation of specific probabilities (e.g., "Mrs. Smith has an 83% likelihood of violence" or "Mrs. Smith's score is similar to the scores obtained by people in the group who, on average, were 83% likely to be violent") or frequencies (e.g., "Mrs. Smith has an 8 out of 10 chance of engaging in violence").

Some research on the impact of using various approaches to communicating actuarially based risk estimates is available. For example, in a survey of members of the American Academy of Psychiatry and the Law (Slovic, Monahan, & MacGregor, 2000), the use of frequency scales was associated with lower estimates of risk likelihood compared with the use of probability scales. However, when the risk level was held constant, the frequency format (e.g., 10 out of 100) was associated with higher perceptions of risk than the probability scale format (e.g., 10%). Risk communication using a frequency format led to perceptions of higher risk than when communication was made using a probability format.

In a more recent study, Scurich and John (2011) investigated two aspects of risk communication: (a) probabilistic statements about varying levels of risk and (b) the format in which risk probabilities were framed (i.e., probability of violence occurring vs. probability of violence not occurring). Using a mock juror paradigm, 303 undergraduates read case examples of the COVR (adapted from Monahan, 2008) and made decisions about civil commitment. The authors observed that when actuarial risk estimates were framed in terms of the probability of violence occurring, mock decisions were likely to be in support of commitment, but when risk estimates were described as the probability of violence not occurring, decisions not to commit were more likely.

In one of the field's most authoritative treatises, Melton et al. (2007) recommended that opinions about an individual's risk for violence be communicated using relative risk terms of a categorical nature, consistent with the SPJ model. Moreover, several research studies have shown that individuals from various professions prefer risk estimates to be communicated using a categorical rather than numerical framework. For example, Kwartner, Lyons, and Boccaccini (2006) surveyed 116 judges to investigate their preferences for probability, frequency, and categorical formats of communication. The authors observed a preference in this sample for categorical estimates of risk (e.g., high risk) versus probabilistic (e.g., 83%) and frequency (e.g., 83 out of 100) risk estimates, and they reported that a combination of categorical and numerical messages was perceived as being most useful. Regardless of the way in which risk was communicated, judges in the high-risk condition were more likely than those in the low-risk condition to rate the risk message as probative.

Consistent with principles espoused by the SPJ model, judges (Dolores & Redding, 2009) as well as professionals with expertise in violence risk (Heilbrun et al., 2004) prefer or are more influenced by communication that describes the specific risk factors of relevance to the evaluee and denotes the specific interventions recommended to reduce and manage risk over time (Heilbrun, O'Neill, Strohman, Bowman, & Philipson, 2000). Results of actuarial risk assessment tools were not intended to facilitate the development of this type of information, and so it perhaps is not surprising that judges tend to be unconvinced by actuarial results (Redding, Floyd, & Hawk, 2001). A preference for communication to include information about risk management strategies also has been observed among practicing clinicians (Heilbrun, Philipson, Berman, & Warren, 1999). Although proponents of the actuarial model have argued that categorical estimates of risk are problematic because forensic clinicians disagree regarding how to interpret nonnumerical terms (e.g., Hilton, Carter, Harris, & Sharpe, 2008), a clear pattern of research findings has shown that good to excellent levels of interrater agreement have been observed among professionals, including forensic clinicians, for SRRs using SPJ instruments (i.e., categorical risk estimates).

In addition to experimental or pseudo-experimental studies, there also has been some investigation of risk communication as it actually occurs "in the field". For example, studying the way in which communication about an individual's risk for future crime appeared in written reports that were authored by 142 forensic clinicians, Grann and Pallvik (2002) observed that in most cases (86%), a judgment about risk was communicated when the risk was perceived to be high. Researchers made judgments regarding the degree to which the risk communication was explained or elaborated. Grann and Pallvik observed that risk communication was well elaborated in 21/122 reports, moderately elaborated in 53/122, poorly or very poorly elaborated in 43/122, and not elaborated in 5/122. The level of elaboration had a strong association with the clinical diagnosis, the type of professional group to which the evaluator belonged, and the clinic where the evaluation occurred. Fortunately, recent research has demonstrated that training on assessing risk for violence generally, as well as how to document findings resulting from such assessments, improves communication about an individual's risk for violence. In the next section, we review this research and also discuss more broadly the factors that influence the use of violence risk assessment in the field.

How Can Violence Risk Assessment Improve Clinical Practice and Outcomes?

Although the use of risk assessment instruments is known to occur in many settings both domestically and abroad, and despite the strong empirical foundation for many of these measures, such instruments in general have not been incorporated into standard clinical practice. Challenges to translating scientific knowledge about risk assessment into clinical practice are multifaceted. Elbogen (2002) discussed how a lack of knowledge by professionals regarding violence risk assessment instruments limits their use in practice. Another obstacle involves deficits in the resources that are required to administer the instruments (e.g., Steadman et al., 2000). Appropriate and well-founded concerns regarding the validity of certain measures within various populations also have been cited as posing a barrier to their implementation (e.g., Otto, 2000).

Packer (2001) surveyed the state forensic director of each of the 50 United States and the District of Columbia in order to assess the extent to which various violence risk assessment tools are used in public sector forensic practice, as well as reasons for their lack of use. The response rate was 64%. Reasons for not using a formal measure included the instruments not being validated with the particular population, instruments being too time consuming, lack of staff training in the use of an instrument, lack of awareness of such instruments, cost, and unavailability of criminal background data (an essential element to using most tools). Packer concluded that many impediments to the use of structured instruments can be ameliorated easily (e.g., the need to train administrators how to implement and staff members how to use the instruments properly), but that concerns regarding validity issues require additional discussion and research.

Clearly, research is warranted to learn more about implementation strategies that would best support the successful integration of violence risk assessment by individual users or on a larger, agency-wide level. Implementation refers to a specified set of activities that are intended to put into practice an activity or program (see Fixsen, Naoom, Blase, Friedman, & Wallace, 2005). Evaluations of intervention efforts can include an analysis of intervention-level outcomes and of implementation-level outcomes (Fixsen et al., 2005). *Intervention-level* outcomes could include indicators such as changes in recidivism rates, changes in dispositions and placements (e.g., in cases of release decision making, whether an individual, because of his or her risk level, is placed in a secure setting or community placement), and changes in service usage and completion following recommendations to participate in particular interventions. *Implementation-level* outcomes include indicators such as the perceptions of staff and administrators regarding the feasibility and usefulness of the risk assessment tool, changes in staff knowledge regarding risk factors, changes in staff attitudes regarding rehabilitation and punitiveness, and changes in the rates of risk-level classification.

Serious deficiencies exist in the process of translating the field's substantial knowledge about violence risk assessment from the "bench" of the research lab to the "bedside" of practice in the field. Even if professionals receive good training on empirically validated risk assessment instruments, there is no guarantee that the measures will be applied in practice to inform judgments about an individual's risk and risk management activities. For example, some research suggests that frontline workers undervalue and underuse findings from risk assessment instruments to inform case management strategies. Approximately $1^1/_2$ years following implementation of the LSI–R in a correctional facility, only 42% of staff used findings from their LSI–R assessment to develop reentry case plans, and most staff surveyed did not believe that the LSI–R was appropriate for the offenders with whom they worked (Haas & DeTardo-Bora, 2009; also see Shook & Saari, 2007, for similar findings regarding lack of uptake of risk assessment instruments across four states following adoption in juvenile court and probation settings). Moreover, risk assessment instruments are unlikely to cause any positive changes in practice and individuals' outcomes if staff are not trained how to use the measure for their case management or if their work environment does not support or encourage appropriate use of the instrument (see Haas, Hamilton, & Hanley, 2006, describing use of the LSI–R in an offender reentry initiative).

Research is persuasive in highlighting the importance of attending to implementation issues (see Nonstad & Webster, 2011). For example, Flores,

Lowenkamp, Holsinger, and Latessa (2006) investigated the association between the predictive validity of the LSI–R (the risk assessment measure that had been implemented in that agency) and implementation variables. The researchers examined two measures of implementation integrity: participation in formal training activities (such as attendance at a training workshop and completion of practice cases) and length of time that the agency had been using the LSI–R. Among the evaluators who had formal training on the LSI–R, the correlation between LSI–R scores and reoffending was .21 (95% CI [.16, .26]), which is a statistically significant finding ($n = 1,635$ offenders), whereas among the untrained evaluators, the correlation was negligible and was not statistically significant, at .08 (95% CI [−.02, .18]). Predictive validity of the LSI–R was significantly greater when the instrument had been part of routine clinical practice for more than 3 years ($r = .25$, 95% CI [.19, .30]; $n = 1,109$) compared with fewer than 3 years ($r = .14$, 95% CI [.08, 20]; $n = 921$). In a more recent study, significant reductions in recidivism were observed for youth who were on the caseloads of probation officers who received intensive training in RNR case management principles, compared to youth who were on the caseloads of probation officers who did not receive the training (Bonta et al., 2011).

Additional research on implementation of empirically supported violence risk assessment and management activities is beginning to accrue. Likely because the primary goal of the SPJ model is violence reduction and prevention, most studies that have been published on the potential impact of risk assessment on risk management and reduction activities have focused on SPJ instruments (e.g., Dernevik, Grann, & Johansson, 2002). Crocker et al. (2011) described findings from a longitudinal prospective mixed-method (qualitative and quantitative) implementation evaluation of the START. Focusing on implementation outcomes, Crocker et al. reported that among frontline users of the instruments in a civil psychiatric hospital, 79% reported experiencing no difficulties in completing the Risk Formulation section, whereas 14% reported some difficulties (e.g., need for clarification around the concept of "risk"). The authors concluded that the START was well integrated into clinical and administrative activities.

Vojt, Thomson, and Marshall (2013) examined prospectively the predictive validity of the HCR–20 after it had been implemented into routine clinical practice in a forensic psychiatric hospital (also see Vojt, Slesser, Marshall, & Thomson, 2011). Coupled with implementation of the HCR–20 was the introduction of new care and treatment documentation, which reflected five key risk management domains and activities that primarily were informed by the HCR–20: intervention, treatment, supervision, monitoring, and victim safety planning. Risk assessment and management plans were completed at clinical team meetings. Vojt et al. reported on the 109 male inpatients who consented to participate in the study. Participants were followed up for an average of 31.0 months (SD = 8.3) in the hospital or the setting to which they were discharged during the study period. There was no statistically significant association between any of the HCR–20 indices studied (i.e., scale and total "scores" only; SRRs were not completed in routine practice at the time data were collected) and any (n = 46) or minor (n = 43) incidents in either the hospital or community, even when time at risk was taken into account. Although the HCR–20 predicted serious incidents (AUC = .86; 95% CI [.76, .96]), the base rate was extremely low (only three people had this outcome).

Noting the major discrepancy between their findings and the bulk of the scientific literature that shows evidence of good predictive validity for the HCR–20 (Douglas et al., 2014), Vojt et al. (2013) compared their findings with the results of a study of the HCR–20 (Thomson, Davidson, Brett, Steele, & Darjee, 2008) that was completed at the same hospital and in which the outcomes studied were operationalized in the same manner. Significant methodological differences exist between these two studies: The earlier study had a different research design (pseudoprospective) and a longer follow-up period (8–10 years), and researchers (rather than clinicians) completed the HCR–20. Nevertheless, Vojt et al. highlighted that whereas Thomson et al. (2008) observed a mean of 11.4 incidents, the rate was much lower in Vojt et al.'s implementation study (mean of 5.0 incidents).

The authors indicated that although it was possible that the HCR–20 simply lacked predictive validity in this inpatient setting when it was completed by clinicians, it was more likely that the decreased rate of incidents coupled with the study's low predictive power "may indicate that the HCR–20 when systematically implemented into clinical practice guides effective risk management as intended" (Vojt et al., 2013, p. 382).

Investigators in Denmark reached similar conclusions about the HCR–20's ability to affect risk reduction in a forensic psychiatric hospital (Pedersen, Ramussen, & Elass, 2012) after studying a cohort of primarily male patients who were discharged during a 2-year period (N = 81). Treating clinicians rated the HCR–20 as part of the clinical routine on the unit. Although AUC values for violent recidivism of the "scores" for the HCR–20 total (AUC = .68, 95% CI [.52, .84]) and historical scale (AUC = .66, 95% CI [.52, .80]) were statistically significant, the AUC for the SRR for that outcome was only .56. Statistically significant AUC values were observed for all numerical indices of the HCR–20 (ranging .66 to .70), but the AUC for the clinically salient SRR was not statistically significant (AUC = .64). Pedersen et al. (2012) concluded that although "the somewhat low predictive accuracy of the HCR–20 violence risk assessment scheme could possibly be related to clinical intervention and management efforts, . . . it does not necessarily indicate poor predictive accuracy of the HCR–20 but rather that knowledge of risk status and intensive risk management can reduce violence risk" (p. 742).

Using a prospective design, Belfrage et al. (2012) examined the SARA as used in routine practice by police in Sweden. The researchers investigated the nature of the association between officers' ratings of an individual's risk for intimate partner violence and their recommendations regarding intervention. The predictive validity of the SARA over a follow-up of 18 months also was examined. There was a positive association between risk level and management recommendations, such that the higher the risk, the more intensive were the officers' risk management recommendations. SARA ratings also were associated with subsequent contacts with police. Risk management mediated the association between risk level and this form of recidivism, in that among high-risk cases, high levels of intervention were associated with *decreased* recidivism compared with low levels of interventions (28% vs. 37%); in low-risk cases, however, high levels of intervention were associated with *increased* recidivism compared with low levels of intervention (21% vs. 12%).

Studying an instrument that was adapted from the SARA for use by police, Belfrage and Strand (2012) studied the impact on case management practices that was associated with use of the Brief Spousal Assault Form for the Evaluation of Risk (B-SAFER; Kropp, Hart, & Belfrage, 2005, 2010) among police officers in Sweden. Researchers coded the protective actions that police officers initiated following the B-SAFER assessments of 216 male alleged perpetrators of intimate partner violence toward 216 female victims. Protective actions were dichotomized as *low* interventions if they were required to be taken by the Swedish police law (i.e., conducting a file search regarding access to weapons, criminality history, etc.; contacting social authorities if children were involved; and contacting an advocate or shelter/safe house). *High* interventions included employing an alarm package (e.g., a cell phone with GPS connected to the National Swedish Alarm Centre) and initiating a no-contact order or protective living. Alleged perpetrators were followed up on average for 28 months (range 28–48 months). In general, there was a positive association between B-SAFER SRRs and intervention level, such that the higher the risk (whether for imminent violence or severe/fatal violence), the higher the level of intervention, and vice versa. The majority of all police resources were directed toward the high-risk cases, and consequently police engaged in very little, if any, intervention efforts for the remaining cases that were not assessed as high risk. Across all but one risk category, high rates of recidivism were observed: among the highest risk group, which received the most intensive intervention and management efforts, recidivism was significantly lower.

Storey, Kropp, Hart, Belfrage, and Strand (2014) also examined the B-SAFER as used by Swedish police officers when assessing and managing intimate partner violence. Consistent with the findings from Belfrage and Strand (2012), Storey et al.

observed risk and the intensity of management efforts to be positively related. Of note, management recommendations were associated with decreased recidivism among high-risk perpetrators but increased recidivism among low-risk perpetrators.

Working in a juvenile probation context, Vincent, Guy, Gershenson, and McCabe (2012) evaluated the impact of implementing the SAVRY at the postadjudication/predisposition point of case processing in probation offices. Using a pre–post quasi-experimental study, Vincent et al. studied 247 youth who had been adjudicated in the office during the year prior to SAVRY implementation and 217 youth who were adjudicated after full implementation of the SAVRY. Implementation procedures were extensive and included staff training on how to conduct the risk assessment, revision of office policies to include the risk assessment process, quality assurance, and development of a sound model for use of the assessment in decision making (see Vincent, Guy, & Grisso, 2012). Overall, analyses of intervention-level outcomes provided evidence that more appropriate resource allocation occurred wherein service referral *dosage* was matched to risk level, without a significant increase in reoffending. Following implementation, placement rates were reduced by 50%; the use of maximum levels of supervision dropped by almost 30%; and the use of community services decreased except for high-risk youth, but only after the SAVRY was properly implemented. Implementation-level outcomes (e.g., changes in staff attitudes about risk and reoffending, beliefs regarding case management decision making, etc.) also were studied (see Vincent, Paiva-Salisbury, Cook, Guy, & Perrault, 2012).

Studying the actuarial use (i.e., summing items to yield a total score) of a version of the LSI that was adapted for use in Saskatchewan (LSI–SK; Luong & Wormith, 2011), researchers evaluated the degree to which supervision and case management strategies were guided by the instrument. There was a strong association between LSI–SK risk level and youth probationers' assigned supervision level (e.g., low-risk youth were given minimum levels of supervision). There also was good correspondence generally between youth's needs as identified by the probation officer and the LSI–SK. However, officers tended to overidentify some need areas and overrefer youth to services for those need areas (e.g., only 13% of youth scored medium or high risk on the education/employment scale, but 81% were assigned an educational intervention).

In a pre–post evaluation of the degree to which implementation of a locally developed standardized risk assessment measure affected case management practices, Young, Moline, Farrell, and Bierie (2006) reported that average adherence to the policy for administering the instrument was only 55%. With respect to decisions about placements and service referrals, the use of risk assessments increased the weight that probation officers placed on some dynamic risk factors. However, data pertaining to changes in the overall percentage of service referrals or placements as a result of implementing the new instrument were not reported.

Other studies have examined the feasibility of completing instruments in real-world settings. Many such studies have described results of use of the START measures in different practice settings: Nicholls, Petersen, Brink, and Webster (2011) and Doyle, Lewis, and Brisbane (2008) reported on the use of the START in forensic psychiatric hospitals; Desmarais, Van Dorn, Telford, Petrila, and Coffey (2012) described the use of the START in a mental health diversion program; and Desmarais, Sellers, et al. (2012) presented findings from a pilot implementation of the START:AV in juvenile correctional facilities.

All of the research studies reviewed in this section have focused on the evaluation of comprehensive risk assessment instruments. However, positive results also have been observed following implementation of the BVC. Abderhalden et al. (2008) presented results of a cluster randomized controlled trial of the implementation of the BVC in acute civil psychiatric admission wards. On wards where the BVC was implemented as part of routine clinical practice during intake procedures together with mandatory use of risk prevention and management activities, incidence rates of aggression decreased substantially. However, negligible changes in rates of aggression occurred on wards where such implementation activities did not occur. More specifically,

the decline in the rate of severe aggressive events (operationalized as a score of ≥9 on the Staff Observation Aggression Scale—Revised; Nijman et al., 1999) on the units where the BVC was implemented (relative risk = 0.59, 95% CI [0.41, 83]) was significantly larger than the decline in the other units (relative risk = 0.85, 95% CI [0.64, 1.13]).

As noted at the outset of this chapter, violence risk assessments are expected or mandated for completion under a diverse array of circumstances. Despite that, surveys of psychiatrists (Schwartz & Park, 1999) and psychologists (J. Guy, Brown, & Poelstra, 1990) have suggested that practitioners may receive minimal formal training in conducting such assessments or have limited knowledge about violence risk factors (L. Wong, Morgan, Wilkie, & Barbaree, 2012). Not only is training on general principles related to violence risk assessment important, but so too is training on the specific instruments that one plans to use to structure such evaluations. Formal training, completion of practice cases, and group discussion or individual feedback are all important ways in which instrument users can increase their accuracy in using the instruments (i.e., increasing interrater agreement). Completing and applying a violence risk assessment instrument properly is a matter of professional practice and ethics—especially given the high-stakes decisions that are made on the basis of these assessments—as well as because research has demonstrated that stronger interrater reliability is associated with greater predictive validity of an instrument for predicting future violent behavior (e.g., McNiel, Lam, & Binder, 2000).

During the past few years, several empirical evaluations of violence risk assessment training workshops have been conducted. Studying skill acquisition among police officers who attended a training workshop on the Ontario Domestic Assault Risk Assessment (ODARA; Hilton, Harris, Rice, Eke, & Lowe-Wetmore, 2007), the authors compared officers' abilities to score the tool for a complex intimate partner violence case before and after ODARA training. Officers made significantly fewer errors following training.

McNiel, Chamberlain, Hall, Fordwood, and Binder (2008) compared trainees in psychiatry and psychology who participated in a 5-hr, systematic training program in evidence-based violence risk assessment (with a focus on the HCR–20) with similar trainees who did not receive such training. Coding clinical documentation in response to case vignettes, the researchers examined changes in risk assessment skill associated with the receipt of training. Practitioners who participated in the training were better able to identify risk and protective factors for violence, produced documentation of higher quality, and increased their knowledge about and ability to assess and manage an individual's risk for violence. Improvements in the quality of clinical documentation following structured training are especially noteworthy and of importance for clinical policy and practice in light of some evidence that particular patient and institutional variables may affect the content or quality of clinical documentation (Elbogen, Tomkins, Pothuloori, & Scalora, 2003).

A similarly positive finding was reported by Reynolds and Miles (2009), who evaluated practitioners at a forensic psychiatric facility in the United Kingdom who attended a 1-day workshop that included a didactic component, group discussions, and case examples. Following the initial training, attendees completed an HCR–20 under the supervision of the trainer. Three months later, they attended a booster session during which another case was completed, and they practiced skills for formulation and developing management plans. The quality of the HCR–20 assessments that were completed several months following participation in the workshop ($N = 68$) was evaluated. Reynolds and Miles observed a large increase in the overall quality of the risk assessments (Cohen's $d = 1.85$); improvements were particularly salient with respect to risk management planning.

Storey, Gibas, Reeves, and Hart (2011) investigated the degree to which participation in an 8-day training course affected criminal justice professionals' knowledge about violence risk assessment concepts, violence risk assessment skills, and attitudes regarding competence at assessing violence risk. The workshop consisted of approximately 54 contact hr across 8 days and covered numerous topics: principles of violence risk assessment and management,

key symptoms of mental disorder and the association between mental disorder and violence, assessment of threats, report writing and expert testimony, and the assessment of risk using SPJ instruments for specific forms of violence (e.g., general violence, sexual violence, intimate partner violence, stalking, child abuse and neglect, group violence, and school and workplace violence). Using a pre–post design, Storey et al. observed significant improvements on measures of knowledge about risk assessment (30% increase in correct responses, Cohen's $d = 1.27$), skills in the analysis of risk of violence (identification of risk factors, risk level, and management strategies) based on a practice vignette, and perceived confidence in conducting violence risk assessments.

McNiel, Hung, Cramer, Hall, and Binder (2011) recently developed a structured measure for assessing competency in violence risk assessment and management: the Competency Assessment Instrument for Violence (CAI–V). Preliminary evidence of the tool's internal consistency, concurrent validity, and interrater reliability was favorable (McNiel et al., 2011). As such, the CAI–V represents a promising structure to provide feedback and supervision within the context of evaluating skill development in this practice domain.

Training in violence risk assessment should include instruction and supervised practice in general assessment activities, didactics about violence and treatments to reduce the risk of violence, and so on. Although likely not part of traditional training activities, we believe that training in violence risk assessment also ought to include teaching about current controversies in the field, with an aim toward debunking or correcting commonly held misassumptions.

Persistent Myths Regarding Violence Risk Assessment

We now turn our attention to some of the more problematic myths that we perceive as being relevant to the field at present. In our view, these common myths are demonstrably untrue assertions that continue to be perpetuated in the literature. The persistence of these myths is due in part to a disregard and misinterpretation of the research literature, either unintentional or willful—something that Andrews and Wormith (1989) referred to as "knowledge destruction" (p. 289).

Myth #1: Violence cannot be predicted, and violence risk assessment is not useful. Decades of research have shown that structured, validated approaches to assessing an individual's risk of violence have on average moderate levels of predictive accuracy for various types of violence, whereas unstructured clinical approaches have no association with violence (e.g., Bonta et al., 1998; L. S. Guy, 2008; Hanson & Morton-Bourgon, 2009). Research has also shown that significant reductions in recidivism are achieved by following the RNR model (e.g., Andrews & Bonta, 2010) wherein (a) more intensive services are given to higher versus lower risk individuals, (b) interventions target dynamic risk factors of relevance for a given individual's risk of violence, and (c) treatment recommendations take into account any particular person or situation factors that may affect a person's ability to benefit from intervention. Despite this, objections persist regarding the involvement of mental health professionals.

For example, Ryan, Nielssen, Paton, and Large (2010) asserted that "risk assessment is a fundamentally flawed method of harm reduction and specifically argue against using risk assessment to categorize patients as high or low risk" (p. 398). Concerned about the impacts of misclassifying individuals as being a low, moderate, or high risk (i.e., false-positive and false-negative errors), Ryan et al. (2010) concluded that "the process of risk assessment itself consumes limited healthcare resources, further reducing clinicians' time available for actual patient care" (p. 401). In a more recent article, Nielssen (2013) made the assumption that the "large number of false negatives . . . (in violence risk assessment) means that the diversion of resources due to incorrect predictions would probably result in greater net harm than the harms prevented by identifying people for increased supervision and care" (p. 1199). These authors failed to consider the accruing evidence indicating that providing intervention to individuals who pose a low risk for reoffending can have the iatrogenic effect of increasing risk. For

example, in a 20-year longitudinal study of low-income youth in Montreal (Gatti, Tremblay, & Vitaro, 2009), youth who received even a minor treatment or intervention (e.g., community service) were still twice as likely to be arrested as adults than were youth with the same behavior problems who remained outside the system. Being placed on probation was associated with a 14-fold increase of adult arrest compared with similar peers who did not receive this form of intensive intervention.

Myth #2: Mental disorder is irrelevant to violence risk assessment. After conducting a recent meta-analysis of 96 unique samples (Bonta et al., 2013) in which they investigated the predictive validity of the "central eight" risk factors (see Andrews & Bonta, 2010) among mentally disordered offenders (MDO) and clinical/psychopathological factors, Bonta et al. (2013) concluded: "From both a risk prediction and a recidivism reduction perspective, symptoms of mental illness do not appear to play a major role. The reasons for this finding may be many but one possible explanation is that the factors that are a focus in the clinical model are inappropriate for the risk assessment and treatment of MDOs" (p. 5). The authors further explained,

> Although there are certainly cases when a crime is committed during a psychotic state, the presence of psychosis cannot be viewed as a useful predictor of recidivism. The reasons for this may be because psychosis is transitory (as in the finding of NGRI, which was also not predictive of recidivism) and amenable to treatment. These results leave us to conclude that major mental illnesses are unreliable predictors of general and violent recidivism. (Bonta et al., 2013, p. 14)

Discussing their findings, Bonta et al. (2013) completely ignored a substantial body of empirical evidence that leads to a different conclusion. For example, in a large-scale meta-analysis that aggregated findings on the association between psychosis and violence from 166 independent data sets

(Douglas, Guy, & Hart, 2009), psychosis was significantly associated with an approximately 49% to 68% increase in the odds of violence relative to the odds of violence in the absence of psychosis, representing a small, but reliable, ES. Importantly, several methodological variables moderated the association. Consistent with the meta-analytic findings that were reported by Fazel and Yu (2011), odds ratios were higher when individuals with psychosis were compared to persons without mental disorder (*Mdn* = 3.68) than when they were compared with individuals with other mental disorders (*Mdn* = 1.51). However, odds ratios were significantly greater than chance for both comparisons. Further demonstrating the importance of identifying the comparison group when estimating the relation between psychosis and violence, Douglas et al. (2009) found that psychosis had a stronger effect when it was compared with internalizing disorders (e.g., nonpsychotic mood disorders, anxiety disorders; *Mdn* = 2.15) than when it was compared with externalizing disorders (e.g., Cluster B personality disorders, substance-related disorders; *Mdn* = 0.85).

The results from Bonta et al. (2013) are not surprising but strongly reinforce the importance of viewing one's findings within the context of the field more broadly, rather than from a silo comprising only a subset of the population. As Douglas et al. (2009) discussed,

> Posing the question, "Are individuals with psychosis more likely to be violent than individuals without psychosis?" is sort of like asking whether 10-year olds are tall. Compared with toddlers, they certainly are. Compared with adults, they are decidedly short. And so it is with psychosis: Compared with individuals with no mental disorders, people with psychosis seem to be at a substantially elevated risk for violence. (p. 696)

Rather than eschewing *in toto* the predictive validity of mental disorders other than personality disorders, other researchers (e. g., Ghaziuddin, 2013) have asserted that specific kinds of mental disorders are not associated with violence, such as neurodevelopmental disorders (e.g., intellectual disability, autism spectrum

disorder). Research evidence, again, indicates otherwise. For example, in Bonta et al.'s (2013) meta-analysis, intellectual impairment was associated with an increased risk for general recidivism (*d* = .26 after removal of one outlier). Other researchers also have reported evidence of a moderate association between intelligence and crime (e.g., Cullen, Gendreau, Jarjoura, & Wright, 1997; Gendreau et al., 1996; Glueck & Glueck, 1950).

There is relatively little research on the relation between pervasive developmental disorders and violence (for a review, see Bjørkly, 2009). Available evidence suggests an association. For example, in a retrospective, longitudinal, register-based study that was conducted in Sweden, the histories of violent offending were examined among 422 individuals who had been hospitalized with autistic disorder or Asperger syndrome during 1988–2000 (Långström, Grann, Ruchkin, Sjöstedt, & Fazel, 2009). Violent individuals were more likely to be diagnosed with Asperger syndrome than with autistic disorder (adjusted OR = 5.82, 95% CI [2.56, 13.22]).

In sum, in our opinion, concluding that mental illness is irrelevant to violence risk assessment is reckless. Although we agree with other researchers (e.g., Skeem, Manchak, & Peterson, 2011) that the treatment for mental disorders should neither be an automatic nor the only intervention recommended to manage risk for violence among individuals with mental disorder, it certainly is an important management strategy in many cases.

Myth #3: Violence risk assessments are not equally valid for women and men. Citing research showing an increased prevalence of certain historical, contextual, and clinical variables among women compared with men—such as sexual abuse victimization and other forms of trauma, child care and other parenting issues, poverty, mental health problems, and dysfunctional relationships—increasingly greater attention is being paid to the discussion regarding the need to develop a gender-informed approach to violence risk assessment (e.g., B. Bloom, Owen, & Covington, 2003; Wright, Van Voorhis, Salisbury, & Bauman, 2012; see also Volume 2, Chapter 4, this handbook). When these and other potential risk factors have been examined, however, and the totality of the empirical literature is considered, the evidence indicates that the primary risk factors that are associated with violence perpetration among boys and men are the same factors that are associated with violent behavior among girls and women, respectively. That is, the same risk factors tend to be associated with the perpetration of violence in both males and females, even though there may be some gender differences in the ES of risk factors with respect to the prediction or postdiction of various types of violence (see, e.g., the epidemiological study by Magdol et al., 1997; also see manuals of risk assessment instruments such as the SAVRY [Borum et al., 2006], the EARL–20B for boys [Augimeri et al., 2001], and the EARL–21G for girls [Levene et al., 2001]).

So, should violence risk assessments be conducted differently for women and men? We believe so, in part. Because of the sample-dependent nature of actuarial instruments, it is very possible that different risk factors may be better candidates for inclusion on a particular actuarial tool, or that risk factors may be weighted differently, as a function of gender. As such, violence risk assessments *using an actuarial approach* might require different statistical models for women and men.

This is not the case for violence risk assessments that are conducted using an SPJ approach. In contrast to the way in which items tend to be selected for inclusion on actuarial measures, items on SPJ instruments are selected based on the robustness of their association with violence in research studies that have been conducted across a wide array of samples, settings, and countries. For this reason, the risk factors that are included on SPJ instruments are expected to generalize to diverse groups of people, including women. Indeed, in a meta-analysis of the SPJ literature, L. S. Guy (2008) investigated but found no statistically significant moderating effect of gender on predictive validity. However, a trend toward significance was observed whereby ESs appeared to be greater among samples comprising only women (AUCw = .78, based on 10 studies) than only men (AUCw = .68, based on 60 studies). That is, if any gender difference truly does exist, it appears that the predictive accuracy of SPJ instruments is even greater for women than men.

Similarly, results of many meta-analyses have indicated that both SPJ and actuarial risk assessment instruments have comparable levels of predictive validity among women and men (L. S. Guy, 2008; Olver et al., 2009; Schwalbe, 2007, 2008; Singh et al., 2011; Smith, Cullen, & Latessa, 2009; Walters, 2006).

Nonetheless, gender is an important consideration that should not be ignored in violence risk assessment and management. For example, there is ample evidence that the *nature* of the violence and the *context* in which violence is committed differ between women and men (e.g., Robbins, Monahan, & Silver, 2003; Strand & Belfrage, 2001; Teasdale, Silver, & Monahan, 2006). To offer just a few examples, whereas men tend to engage in more overt acts of violence, violence committed by women more often is likely to be covert and to occur within the contexts of relationships. Differences also exist with respect to the types of offenses for which men and women tend to be arrested. For example, women are less likely than men to be arrested and convicted for sexual violence. Women also tend to be less likely than men to use weapons (Greenfeld & Snell, 1999).

Given its flexibility, the SPJ model is especially well suited to take into account any specific issues that are related to gender (as would be the case for other facets of diversity, such as culture, race, ethnicity, disability, etc.). As is always the case for the assessment of violence risk within the SPJ framework, the evaluator is required to consider the manifestation and relevance of each risk factor for the specific person being evaluated. As such, should a female evaluee have a history that is characterized by a stereotypically gendered pathway to crime and violence that included, for example, chronic sexual abuse during childhood and intimate partner violence victimization as a young adult, maladaptive personality traits, poor work history, deficient social support, and substance use problems, the evaluator would consider the relevance of such factors when formulating an individual theory for the woman about her history of engaging in violence and also draw on the relevance of these risk factors when thinking about scenarios that could lead to improved, worsened, or different outcomes related to the perpetration of violence in the future. In addition, a hallmark of the SPJ model is its emphasis on considering the presence and relevance of case-specific risk factors that are unique to the particular evaluee. At this step of the SPJ assessment process, risk factors observed perhaps more frequently among women could be included as long as a strong justification could be made regarding their relevance to offending or expectation regarding response to intervention or other risk management activities for the particular woman being evaluated.

Despite evidence indicating that SPJ instruments are equally useful across genders, there are two SPJ instruments in which gender explicitly is identified as having influenced the process of risk factor selection. The EARL–21G, for use with girls, has two unique items (Caregiver-Daughter Interaction and Sexual Development) that are not included on the version of the instrument that was developed for assessing boys, the EARL–20B. Almost all of the items on the EARL measures are exactly the same; the content of the manuals differs in only limited respects. The Female Additional Manual (FAM; de Vogel, de Vries Robbé, van Kalmthout, & Place, 2011) was developed for concurrent use with the HCR–20/HCR–20^{V3} among women. The FAM contains nine putative risk factors as well as supplementary or adapted ratings guidelines for five HCR–20/HCR–20^{V3} items. Peer-reviewed, published research on these measures is forthcoming.

Finally, regarding the issue of intervention, we contend that it may be appropriate under many circumstances to consider gender as a potential responsivity variable that could affect recommendations regarding the way in which treatment should be delivered or the types of intervention strategies that are used in a given case. However, gender-specific approaches to assessing violence risk, including routine use of a different core set of risk factors than that which is used with men, is not supported at present by available research.

Myth #4: Actuarial instruments are superior to SPJ instruments for assessing the risk of violence.

The substantial body of research reviewed here indicates clearly that, overall, well-validated actuarial and SPJ instruments as a group are on par with one another in terms of their predictive validity for violence to others. The evidence reviewed here also details the serious conceptual and analytic problems associated with actuarially derived risk estimates and their inability to facilitate risk reduction. As such, it is our opinion that it would be scientifically irresponsible at this stage in the field's knowledge development to assert the superiority of actuarial tools.

Myth #5: Risk assessments are fatally flawed because they do not consider protective factors.

The importance of considering protective factors when assessing and managing an individual's risk of violence is well established (e.g., Hart, 2008; Rogers, 2000). In contrast to the hundreds if not thousands of research studies that have been aimed at identifying and evaluating risk factors, relatively little work on putative protective factors has been completed, and empirical efforts regarding protective factors have focused mainly on child and adolescent populations (see Farrington, Loeber, & Ttofi, 2012). Complicating the field's interest in advancing the research agenda on protective factors is a lack of consensus regarding the basic definition and operational parameters of protective factors.

At least three conceptually distinct models have been proposed to explain how a protective factor may affect a change in risk state (i.e., mediation, moderator, or buffer) and main effect models. Regardless of the technical definition, there appears to be consensus in the professional literature on risk assessment that protective factors are variables that may reduce the influence of risk factors (e.g., personal support may help buffer against some of the risk-enhancing characteristics of acute or chronic stress). But, how precisely they should be defined and how they interact with risk factors largely is unknown. For example, are they the opposite pole of risk factors or are they distinct from them? Are protective factors relevant only when risk factors are present or in their absence?

Although there certainly is a clear role for protective factors, also known as strengths, in the SPJ framework that was developed to manage risk and prevent violence, only three SPJ instruments explicitly require evaluators to make formal ratings regarding such strengths. The SAVRY was the first SPJ instrument to specifically include protective factors. Of the instrument's 30 items are six factors that together comprise the Protective scale. Describing this scale, the SAVRY's authors (Borum et al., 2006) noted:

> While the absence of a risk factor may, in some sense, be considered "protective," and used accordingly in a risk appraisal, the factors contained in this section of the SAVRY are all positive protective factors (those that are notable for their presence, not their absence), as opposed to negative protective factors (those notable for the absence of a risk factor). (p. 9)

In contrast to the SAVRY's approach for including *freestanding* protective factors, the START and the START:AV present a series of items for which the evaluator offers separate ratings regarding the extent to which an item represents a strength and vulnerability for the individual (although in the initial version of the START, evaluators used a continuous 6-point scale, with extreme scores indicating either a considerable strength or a substantial risk; possible total scores therefore ranged from 0 to 120). Some evaluations of the START have demonstrated that total strength scores added incrementally to the validity of the vulnerability scores when assessing inpatient aggression in forensic psychiatric patients (Desmarais, Nicholls, et al., 2012), but other studies have not (Wilson, Desmarais, Nicholls, & Brink, 2010). In one study (Chu, Thomas, Ogloff, & Daffern, 2011), total strength score was associated positively with violence.

The SAPROF, notable for its inclusion of only putative protective factors, is intended for use in combination with the HCR–20/HCR–20^{V3} or related structured risk assessment instruments (de Vogel et al., 2012). The SAPROF consists of two static and 17 dynamic factors that are organized into Internal, Motivational, and External factors and are rated on a three-level scale. Evaluators make a Final Protection Judgment (FPJ) using a three-level categorical scheme of *low, moderate,* and *high.* Evaluators combine clinically (in their head; i.e., not by way of an actuarial device) the FPJ with the SRR from the SPJ risk assessment instrument in order to identify an overall integrated final risk judgment. Research on the SAPROF is accruing, with some evidence that final risk judgments about an individual's risk for violence to others have stronger predictive validity compared to use of either the SAPROF or HCR–20 alone (Abidin et al., 2013; de Vries Robbé, de Vogel, & de Spa, 2011).

Most SPJ instruments do not require the evaluator to make formal ratings regarding strength or protective factors. Yet, there are many ways in which the assessment of clinically relevant strengths, consistent with recommendations by the American Psychological Association Presidential Task Force on Evidence-Based Practice (2006), are included as key parts of the SPJ model. First, somewhat analogous to considering whether an individual could have both strengths and vulnerabilities regarding a single variable or factor (practice consistent with the use of the START), evaluators using any of the SPJ instruments routinely should consider the extent to which there is evidence for or against an item. In addition, when using any SPJ instrument, every time a factor is judged to be *absent* or *partially/possibly present,* the evaluator should look for potentially important strengths, resources, and vulnerabilities in that area. Protective factors play an important role during the formulation stage of the SPJ model via the last step in Weerasekera's (1996) "Four P" model (see Douglas, Hart, Webster, & Belfrage, 2013, p. 55). According to the Four P model, clinicians should consider *predisposing, precipitating, perpetuating,* and *protective factors* (also see de Vogel et al., 2012). In addition, and critically, protective factors are considered routinely during scenario planning activities and when developing risk management plans (see Douglas, Hart, Webster, & Belfrage, 2013, pp. 56–61).

SUMMARY AND CONCLUSIONS

Considering the state of the field of violence risk assessment when Monahan (1981) published his insights and observations just more than three decades ago, remarkable advances have been made.

Nevertheless, many discoveries remain ahead of us. Justifiable concerns continue to be raised about the relative infancy of the state of the field and implications of the existing research on violence risk assessment. Dvoskin, Skeem, Novaco, and Douglas (2011) are persuasive in their observations that criminological and psychological science has much to offer in service of making all stages of the process that may be involved in violence risk assessment in various settings to be a better experience with improved outcomes for all of the major stakeholders involved. Moreover, the highest courts in the country historically have expected and almost certainly will continue to demand expert witness opinion on violence risk assessment. For these reasons, as well as the potential to contribute to public safety and the safeguarding of civil liberties, continued attention to resolving (as best as possible) existing debates and investigating important questions is paramount.

As the empirical base on violence risk assessment and communication continues to deepen and widen, it will be critical to persist in efforts to engage in knowledge translation. That so much has been written about clinically rich approaches to this important assessment task—for example, drawing on research regarding formulation and scenario planning informed by diverse literatures—and that several well-validated violence risk assessment instruments have been developed and tested, it is disheartening to know that most professionals continue to use unstructured assessment approaches. Moreover, when risk assessment measures are used, it is very common for large organizations and criminal justice agencies in institutions and the community to use locally developed measures that consist mainly of static risk factors, thereby preventing them from being of service to risk management efforts. Many such tools often have never been empirically validated.

If one takes the perspective, as we do, that the primary goal of violence risk assessment is the reduction of risk and prevention of violence, the importance of shifting policy and empirical efforts to focus on developing and testing treatments and other interventions that work in the field, not just in controlled research studies, is self-evident.

Continued research regarding the dynamic aspects of the violence risk assessment process need to occur in concert with evaluations of intervention strategies. The field remains in the early stages of investigating the questions related to how change in risk potential occurs over time, the nature of such change, and how quickly such change can be expected to occur and under what conditions. Clearly, answers to these questions are of the utmost importance for policy and clinical practice. Douglas and Skeem (2005) provided a highly informative conceptual and theoretical framework to structure this next critical frontier that the field must tackle.

In closing, we echo our call for continued work in the translation and dissemination of the science of violence risk assessment into the field where such evaluations occur regularly and as a matter of law. Such efforts should be broad and should reach beyond mental health professionals to include professionals from diverse settings—police, probation officers, social workers, human resource personnel, etc.—who are engaged directly and routinely in this legal and clinical task.

References

Abderhalden, C., Needham, I., Dassen, T. Halfens, R., Haug, H.-J., & Fischer, J. E. (2008). Structured risk assessment and violence in acute psychiatric wards: Randomised controlled trial. *British Journal of Psychiatry, 193*, 44–50.

Abidin, Z., Davoren, M., Naughton, L., Gibbons, O., Nulty, A., & Kennedy, H. G. (2013). Susceptibility (risk and protective) factors for in-patient violence and self-harm: Prospective study of structured professional judgement instruments START and SAPROF, DUNDRUM–3, and DUNDRUM–4 in forensic mental health services. *BMC Psychiatry, 13*(197). doi:10.1186/1471-244X-13-197

Addington v. Texas, 441 U.S. 418 (1979).

Ægisdóttir, S., White, M. J., Spengler, P. M., Maugherman, A. S., Anderson, L. A., Cook, R. S., . . . Rush, J. D. (2006). The meta-analysis of clinical judgment project: Fifty-six years of accumulated research on clinical versus statistical prediction. *Counseling Psychologist, 34*, 341–382.

Agar, S. (2003). *The development of general risk assessment guidelines for physical child abuse and neglect.* (Unpublished doctoral dissertation). Simon Fraser University, Burnaby, British Columbia, Canada.

Almvik, R., & Woods, P. (1999). Predicting inpatient violence using the Brøset Violence Checklist (BVC). *International Journal of Psychiatric Nursing Research, 4,* 498–505.

American Educational Research Association, American Psychological Association, & National Council on Measurement in Education. (1999). *Standards for educational and psychological testing.* Washington, DC: American Psychological Association.

American Psychological Association. (2006). APA Presidential Task Force on Evidence-Based Practice. *American Psychologist, 61,* 271–285.

American Psychological Association. (2010). *Ethical principles of psychologists and code of conduct (2002, Amended June 1, 2010).* Retrieved from http://www.apa.org/ethics/code/index.aspx

American Psychological Association. (2013). Specialty guidelines for forensic psychology. *American Psychologist, 68,* 7–19.

Americans With Disabilities Act of 1990 (ADA), 42 U.S.C. §§ 12101–12213 (2000).

Andrews, D. A. (1982). *The Level of Supervision Inventory (LSI): The first follow-up.* Toronto, Ontario, Canada: Ontario Ministry of Correctional Services.

Andrews, D. A. (2012). The risk-need-responsivity (RNR) model of correctional assessment and treatment. In J. A. Dvoskin, J. L. Skeem, R. W. Novaco, & K. S. Douglas (Eds.), *Using social science to reduce violent offending* (pp. 127–156). New York, NY: Oxford University Press.

Andrews, D. A., & Bonta, J. (1995). *Level of Service Inventory—Revised.* Toronto, Ontario, Canada: Multi-Health Systems.

Andrews, D. A., & Bonta, J. (2006). *The psychology of criminal conduct* (4th ed.). Cincinnati, OH: Anderson.

Andrews, D. A., & Bonta, J. (2010). Rehabilitating criminal justice policy and practice. *Psychology, Public Policy, and Law, 16,* 39–55.

Andrews, D. A., Bonta, J., & Wormith, S. J. (2004). *The Level of Service/Case Management Inventory (LS/CMI).* Toronto, Ontario, Canada: Multi-Health Systems.

Andrews, D. A., & Wormith, J. S. (1989). Personality and crime: Knowledge destruction and construction in criminology. *Justice Quarterly, 6,* 289–309.

Arbach-Lucioni, K., Andres-Pueyo, A., Pomarol-Clotet, E., & Gomar-Sones, J. (2011). Predicting violence in psychiatric inpatients: A prospective study with the HCR–20 violence risk assessment scheme. *Journal of Forensic Psychiatry and Psychology, 22,* 203–222. doi:10.1080/14789949.2010.530290

Augimeri, L. K., Koegl, C. J., Webster, C. D., & Levene, K. S. (2001). *Early Assessment Risk Lists for Boys: Version 2.* Toronto, Ontario, Canada: Earlscourt Child and Family Centre.

Bail Reform Act of 1984, 18 U.S.C. §§ 3141–3150, 3156 (1984).

Barefoot v. Estelle, 463 U.S. 880 (1983).

Baxstrom v. Harold, 383 U.S. 107 (1966).

Belfrage, H., & Strand, S. (2012). Measuring the outcome of structured spousal violence risk assessments using the B-SAFER: Risk in relation to recidivism and intervention. *Behavioral Sciences and the Law, 30,* 420–430. doi:10.1002/bsl.2019

Belfrage, H., Strand, S., Storey, J. E., Gibas, A. L., Kropp, P. R., & Hart, S. D. (2012). Assessment and management of risk for intimate partner violence by police officers using the Spousal Assault Risk Assessment Guide. *Law and Human Behavior, 36,* 60–67. doi:10.1037/h0093948

Bill C-55: An Act to Amend the Criminal Code (High Risk Offenders), the Corrections and Conditional Release Act, the Criminal Records Act, the Prisons and Reformatories Act, and the Department of the Solicitor General Act, S.C. 1997, c. 17.

Bjørkly, S. (2009). Risk and dynamics of violence in Asperger's syndrome: A systematic review of the literature. *Aggression and Violent Behavior, 14,* 306–312. doi:10.1016/j.avb.2009.04.003

Blair, P. R., Marcus, D. K., & Boccaccini, M. T. (2008). Is there an allegiance effect for assessment instruments? Actuarial risk assessment as an exemplar. *Clinical Psychology: Science and Practice, 15,* 346–360. doi:10.1111/j.1468-2850.2008.00147.x

Bloom, B., Owen, B., & Covington, S. (2003). *Gender-responsive strategies: Research, practice and guiding principles for women offenders.* Washington, DC: National Institute of Corrections.

Bloom, H., Eisen, R. S., Pollock, M., & Webster, C. D. (2000). *The Workplace Risk Assessment (WRA–20).* Toronto, Ontario, Canada: Workplace Calm.

Bloom, H., Eisen, R. S., & Webster, C. D. (2001). *The Employee Risk Assessment (ERA–20).* Toronto, Ontario, Canada: Workplace Calm.

Boer, D. P., Hart, S. D., Kropp, P. R., & Webster, C. D. (1997). *Sexual Violence Risk—20.* Burnaby, British Columbia, Canada: Simon Fraser University and British Columbia Forensic Psychiatric Services Commission.

Bonta, J., Blais, J., & Wilson, H. A. (2013). *The prediction of risk for mentally disordered offenders: A quantitative synthesis.* Ottawa, Ontario, Canada: Public Safety Canada.

Bonta, J., Bourgon, G., Rugge, T., Scott, T., Yessine, A. K., Gutierrez, & Li, J. (2011). An experimental demonstration of training probation officers in evidence-based community supervision. *Criminal Justice and Behavior, 38,* 1127–1148.

Bonta, J., Law, M., & Hanson, K. (1998). The prediction of criminal and violent recidivism among mentally disordered offenders: A meta-analysis. *Psychological Bulletin, 123*, 123–142.

Borum, R., Bartel, P., & Forth, A. (2006). *Structured Assessment of Violence Risk in Youth (SAVRY)*. Odessa, FL: Psychological Assessment Resources.

Braithwaite, E., Charette, Y., Crocker, A. G., & Reyes, A. (2010). The predictive validity of clinical ratings of the Short-Term Assessment of Risk and Treatability (START). *International Journal of Forensic Mental Health, 9*, 271–281. doi:10.1080/14999013.2010.534378

Brief for the American Psychological Association as Amicus Curiae, Barefoot v. Estelle, 463 U.S. 880 (1983).

Brief for the American Psychological Association as Amicus Curiae, Coble v. State of Tcxas, 330 S.W.3d 253 (2010).

Brief or the American Psychological Association as Amicus Curiae, United States v. Fields, 483 F.3d 313 (2007).

Campbell, M. A., French, S., & Gendreau, P. (2009). The prediction of violence in adult offenders: A meta-analytic comparison of instruments and methods of assessment. *Criminal Justice and Behavior, 36*, 567–590. doi:10.1177/0093854809333610

Canadian Charter of Rights and Freedoms, s 2, Part I of the *Constitution Act*, 1982, being Schedule B to the *Canada Act 1982* (UK), 1982, c 11.

Canadian Foundation for Children, Youth and the Law v. Canada (Attorney General), 1 S.C.R. 76 (2009).

Chermack, T. J., & Lynham, S. A. (2002). Definitions and outcome variables of resource planning. *Human Resource Development Review, 1*, 366–383. doi:10.1177/1534484302013006

Chermack, T. J., & van der Merwe, L. (2003). The role of constructivist learning in scenario planning. *Futures, 35*, 445–460. doi:10.1016/S0016-3287(02)00091-5

Chu, C., Thomas, S. M., Ogloff, J. P., & Daffern, M. (2011). The predictive validity of the Short-Term Assessment of Risk and Treatability (START) in a secure forensic hospital: Risk factors and strengths. *International Journal of Forensic Mental Health, 10*, 337–345. doi:10.1080/14999013.2011.629715

Coble v. State of Texas, 330 S.W.3d 253 (Tex. Crim. App., 2010).

Cohen, J. (1988). *Statistical power analysis for the behavioral sciences*. New York, NY: Erlbaum.

Cook, A. N., Hart, S. D., & Kropp, P. R. (2013). *Multilevel Guidelines (MLG) for the assessment and management of group-based violence*. Vancouver, British Columbia, Canada: ProActive ReSolutions.

Copas, J., & Marshall, P. (1998). The Offender Group Reconviction Scale: A statistical reconviction score for use by probation officers. *Applied Statistics, 47*, 159–171.

Cottle, C. C., Lee, R. J., & Heilbrun, K. (2001). The prediction of criminal recidivism in juveniles: A meta-analysis. *Criminal Justice and Behavior, 28*, 367–394.

Criminal Sexual Psychopath Act: An Act to Amend the Criminal Code, S.C. 1948, c. 39, s. 43.

Crocker, A. G., Braithwaite, E., Laferrière, D., Gagnon, D., Venegas, C., & Jenkins, T. (2011). START changing practice: Implementing a risk assessment and management tool in a civil psychiatric setting. *International Journal of Forensic Mental Health, 10*, 13–28. doi:10.1080/14999013.2011.553146

Cullen, F. T., Gendreau, P., Jarjoura, G. R., & Wright, J. P. (1997). Crime and the bell curve: Lessons from intelligent criminology. *Crime and Delinquency, 43*, 387–411

Daubert v. Merrell Dow Pharmaceuticals, Inc., 113 S. Ct. 2786 (1993).

Dawes, R. M., Faust, D., & Meehl, P. E. (1989). Clinical versus actuarial judgment. *Science, 243*, 1668–1674.

de Groot, A. D. (1961). Via clinical to statistical prediction. *Acta Psychologica, 18*, 274–284.

Department of Health. (2007). *Best practice in managing risk: Principles and evidence for best practice in the assessment and management of risk to self and others in mental health services*. London, England: Author.

Dernevik, M., Grann, M., & Johansson, S. (2002). Violent behaviour in forensic psychiatric patients: Risk assessment and different risk-management levels using the HCR–20. *Psychology, Crime & Law, 8*, 93–111.

Desmarais, S. L., Nicholls, T., Wilson, C. M., & Brink, J. (2012). Reliability and validity of the Short-Term Assessment of Risk and Treatability (START) in assessing risk for inpatient aggression. *Psychological Assessment, 24*, 685–700. doi:10.1037/a0026668

Desmarais, S. L., Sellers, B. G., Viljoen, J. L., Cruise, K. R., Nicholls, T. L., & Dvoskin, J. A. (2012). Pilot implementation and preliminary evaluation of START:AV assessments in secure juvenile correctional facilities. *International Journal of Forensic Mental Health, 11*, 150–164. doi:10.1080/14999013.2012.737405

Desmarais, S. L., Van Dorn, R., Telford, R. P., Petrila, J., & Coffey, T. (2012). Characteristics of START assessments completed in mental health jail diversion programs. *Behavioral Sciences and the Law, 30*, 448–469. doi:10.1002/bsl.2022

de Vogel, V., & de Ruiter, C. (2005). The HCR–20 in personality disordered female offenders: A comparison with a matched sample of males. *Clinical Psychology and Psychotherapy, 12*, 226–240.

de Vogel, V., de Ruiter, C., Bouman, Y., & de Vries Robbé, M. (2012). *SAPROF. Guidelines for the assessment of protective factors for violence risk* (2nd ed.). Utrecht, the Netherlands: Forum Educatief.

de Vogel, V., de Ruiter, C., van Beek, D., & Mead, G. (2004). Predictive validity of the SVR–20 and Static–99 in a Dutch sample of treated sex offenders. *Law and Human Behavior, 28,* 235–251.

de Vogel, V., de Vries Robbé, M., van Kalmthout, W., & Place, C. (2011). *FAM. Female Additional Manual: Additional guidelines to the HCR–20 for assessing risk for violence in women.* Utrecht, Holland: Forum Educatief.

de Vries Robbé, M., de Vogel, V., & de Spa, E. (2011). Protective factors for violence risk in forensic psychiatric patients: A retrospective validation study of the SAPROF. *International Journal of Forensic Mental Health, 10,* 178–186.

Dolan, M. C., & Rennie, C. E. (2008). The Structured Assessment of Violence Risk in Youth as a predictor of recidivism in a United Kingdom cohort of adolescent offenders with conduct disorder. *Psychological Assessment, 20,* 35–46. doi:10.1037/1040-3590.20.1.35

Dolores, J. C., & Redding, R. E. (2009). The effects of different forms of risk communication on judicial decision making. *International Journal of Forensic Mental Health, 8,* 142–146.

Douglas, K. S. (2001). *Making structured clinical decisions about violence risk: Reliability and validity of the HCR–20 violence risk assessment scheme* (Unpublished doctoral dissertation). Simon Fraser University, Burnaby, British Columbia, Canada.

Douglas, K. S., Cox, D. N., & Webster, C. D. (1999). Violence risk assessment: Science and practice. *Legal and Criminological Psychology, 4,* 149–184. doi:10.1348/135532599167824

Douglas, K. S., Guy, L. S., & Hart, S. D. (2009). Psychosis as a risk factor for violence to others: A meta-analysis. *Psychological Bulletin, 135,* 679–706. doi:10.1037/a0016311

Douglas, K. S., Hart, S. D., Groscup, J. L., & Litwack, T. R. (2013). Assessing violence risk. In I. B. Weiner & R. K. Otto (Eds.), *The handbook of forensic psychology* (4th ed., pp. 385–441). New York, NY: Wiley.

Douglas, K. S., Hart, S. D., Webster, C. D., & Belfrage, H. (2013). *HCR–20 (Version 3): Assessing risk of violence—User guide.* Burnaby, British Columbia, Canada: Mental Health, Law, and Policy Institute, Simon Fraser University.

Douglas, K. S., & Kropp, P. R. (2002). A prevention-based paradigm for violence risk assessment: Clinical and research applications. *Criminal Justice and Behavior, 29,* 617–658. doi:10.1177/009385402236735

Douglas, K. S., Macfarlane, E., & Webster, C. D. (1996). Predicting dangerousness in the contemporary Canadian mental health and criminal justice systems. *Canada's Mental Health, 43,* 4–11.

Douglas, K. S., Ogloff, J. R. P., & Hart, S. D. (2003). Evaluation of a model of violence risk assessment among forensic psychiatric patients. *Psychiatric Services, 54,* 1372–1379.

Douglas, K. S., Shaffer, C., Blanchard, A., Guy, L. S., Reeves, K., & Weir, J. (2014). *HCR–20 violence risk assessment scheme: Overview and annotated bibliography.* Retrieved from http://kdouglas.files.wordpress.com/2014/01/HCR–20-annotated-bibliography-version-12-january-20142.pdf

Douglas, K. S., & Skeem, J. L. (2005). Violence risk assessment: Getting specific about being dynamic. *Psychology, Public Policy, and Law, 11,* 347–383.

Douglas, K. S., Yeomans, M., & Boer, D. P. (2005). Comparative validity analysis of multiple measures of violence risk in a sample of criminal offenders. *Criminal Justice and Behavior, 32,* 479–510.

Doyle, M., Lewis, G., & Brisbane, M. (2008). Implementing the Short-Term Assessment of Risk and Treatability (START) in a forensic mental health service. *Psychiatric Bulletin, 32,* 406–408.

Dvoskin, J., Skeem, J. S., Novaco, R., & Douglas, K. S. (Eds.). (2011). *Using social science to reduce crime.* New York, NY: Oxford University Press.

Dvoskin, J. A., & Heilbrun, K. (2001). Risk assessment and release decision-making: Toward resolving the great debate. *Journal of the American Academy of Psychiatry and the Law, 29,* 6–10.

Elbogen, E. B. (2002). The process of violence risk assessment: A review of descriptive research. *Aggression and Violent Behavior, 7,* 591–604.

Elbogen, E. B., Tomkins, A. J., Pothuloori, A. P., & Scalora, M. J. (2003). Documentation of violence risk information in psychiatric hospital patient charts: An empirical examination. *Journal of the American Academy of Psychiatry and the Law, 31,* 58–64.

Enebrink, P., Långström, N., & Gumpert, C. H. (2006). Predicting aggressive and disruptive behavior in referred 6- to 12-year-old boys: Predictive validation of the EARL–20B risk/needs checklist. *Assessment, 13,* 356–367. doi:10.1177/1073191106290649

Epperson, D. L., Ralston, C. A., Fowers, D., DeWitt, J., & Gore, K. S. (2006). Actuarial risk assessment with juveniles who offend sexually: Development of the Juvenile Sexual Offense Recidivism Risk Assessment Tool—II (JSORRAT–II). In D. Prescott (Ed.), *Risk assessment of youth who have sexually abused: Theory, controversy, and emerging strategies* (pp. 118–169). Oklahoma City, OK: Woods N Barnes.

Estelle v. Smith 451 U.S. 454 (1981).

Farrington, D.P., Loeber, R., & Ttofi, M.M. (2012). Risk and protective factors for offending. In B. C. Welsh & D. P. Farrington (Eds.), *The Oxford handbook of crime prevention* (pp. 46–69). Oxford, England: Oxford University Press.

Fazel, S., Singh, J. P., Doll, H., & Grann, M. (2012). Use of risk assessment instruments to predict violence and antisocial behaviour in 73 samples involving 24,827 people: Systematic review and meta-analysis. *BMJ, 345,* e4692. doi:10.1136/bmj.e4692

Fazel, S., & Yu, R. (2011). Psychotic disorders and repeat offending: Systematic review and meta-analysis. *Schizophrenia Bulletin, 37,* 800–810. doi:10.1093/schbul/sbp135

Fixsen, D. L., Naoom, S. F., Blase, K. A., Friedman, R. M., & Wallace, F. (2005). *Implementation research: A synthesis of the literature* (FMHI Publication No. 231). Tampa: University of South Florida, Louis de la Parte Florida Mental Health Institute, The National Implementation Research Network.

Flores, A. W., Lowenkamp, C. T., Holsinger, A. M., & Latessa, E. J. (2006). Predicting outcome with the Level of Service Inventory—Revised: The importance of implementation integrity. *Journal of Criminal Justice, 34,* 523–529. doi:10.1016/j.jcrimjus.2006.09.007

Forth, A. E., Kosson, D. S., & Hare, R. D. (2003). *The Hare Psychopathy Checklist—Revised: Youth Version.* Toronto, Ontario, Canada: Multi-Health Systems.

Foucha v. Louisiana 504 U.S. 71 (1992).

Gatti, U., Tremblay, R. E., & Vitaro, F. (2009). Iatrogenic effect of juvenile justice. *Journal of Child Psychology and Psychiatry, 50,* 991–998. doi:10.1111/j.1469-7610.2008.02057.x

Gendreau, P., Goggin, C. E., & Law, M. A. (1997). Predicting prison misconducts. *Criminal Justice and Behavior, 24,* 414–431.

Gendreau, P., Little, T., & Goggin, C. (1996). A meta-analysis of the predictors of adult offender recidivism: What works. *Criminology, 34,* 575–607.

Ghaziuddin, M. (2013). Violent behavior in autism spectrum disorder: Is it a fact, or fiction? *Current Psychiatry, 12*(10), 22–32.

Glueck, S., & Glueck, A. (1950). *Unraveling juvenile justice.* Cambridge, MA: Harvard University Press.

Gottfredson, S. D., & Gottfredson, D. M. (1988). Violence prediction methods: Statistical and clinical strategies. *Violence and Victims, 3,* 303–324.

Gottfredson, S. D., & Moriarty, L. J. (2006). Clinical versus actuarial judgments in criminal justice decisions: Should one replace the other? *Federal Probation, 70,* 15–18.

Grann, M. (2001). *Structured Outcome Assessment and Community Risk Monitoring.* Stockholm, Sweden: Centre for Violence Prevention, Karolinska Institute.

Grann, M., & Långström, N. (2007). Actuarial assessment of violence risk: To weigh or not to weigh? *Criminal Justice and Behavior, 34,* 22–36. doi:10.1177/0093854806290250

Grann, M., & Pallvik, A. (2002). An empirical investigation of written risk communication in forensic psychiatric evaluations. *Psychology, Crime & Law, 8,* 113–130. doi:10.1080/10683160208401812

Greenfeld, L., & Snell, T. C. (1999). *Women offenders* (Bureau of Justice Statistics Special Report). Washington, DC: Bureau of Justice Statistics. Retrieved from http://www.bjs.gov/content/pub/pdf/wo.pdf

Grisso, T., & Tomkins, A. J. (1996). Communicating violence risk assessments. *American Psychologist, 51,* 928–930.

Grove, W. M., & Meehl, P. E. (1996). Comparative efficiency of informal (subjective, impressionistic) and formal (mechanical, algorithmic) prediction procedures: The clinical–statistical controversy. *Psychology, Public Policy, and Law, 2,* 293–323.

Grove, W. M., Zald, D. H., Lebow, B. S., Snitz, B. E., & Nelson, C. (2000). Clinical versus mechanical prediction: A meta-analysis. *Psychological Assessment, 12,* 19–30.

Guy, J., Brown, C., & Poelstra, P. (1990). Who gets attacked? A national survey of patient violence directed at psychologists in clinical practice. *Professional Psychology: Research and Practice, 21,* 493–495. doi:10.1037/0735-7028.21.6.493

Guy, L. S. (2008). *Performance indicators of the structured professional judgement approach for assessing risk for violence to others: A meta-analytic survey* (Unpublished doctoral dissertation). Simon Fraser University, Burnaby, British Columbia, Canada.

Guy, L. S., Douglas, K. S., & Hendry, M. (2010). The role of psychopathic personality disorder in violence risk assessments using the HCR–20. *Journal of Personality Disorders, 24,* 551–580. doi:10.1521/pedi.2010.24.5.551

Haas, S. M., & DeTardo-Bora, K. A. (2009, Spring). Inmate reentry and the utility of the LSI-R in case planning. *Corrections Compendium.* Retrieved from http://www.jrsa.org/pubs/forum/full-articles/inmate-reentry.pdf

Haas, S. M., Hamilton, C. A., & Hanley, D. (2006). *Implementation of the West Virginia Offender Reentry Initiative: An examination of staff attitudes and the application of the LSI–R.* Charleston, WV: Mountain State Criminal Justice Research Services. Retrieved from http://www.ojp.usdoj.gov/BJA/evaluation/psi_rp/wv-implementation.pdf

Habitual Offender Act: An Act to Amend the Criminal Code, S.C. 1947, c. 55.

Hanson, R. K. (1998). What do we know about sex offender risk assessment? *Psychology, Public Policy, and Law, 4*, 50–72.

Hanson, R. K. (2005). Twenty years of progress in violence risk assessment. *Journal of Interpersonal Violence, 20*, 212–217.

Hanson, R. K., Helmus, L., & Bourgon, G. (2007). *The validity of risk assessments for intimate partner violence: A meta-analysis.* Report submitted to Public Safety Canada, Ottawa, Ontario, Canada.

Hanson, R. K., & Howard, P. D. (2010). Individual confidence intervals do not inform decision-makers about the accuracy of risk assessment evaluations. *Law and Human Behavior, 34*, 275–281. doi:10.1007/s10979-010-9227-3

Hanson, R. K., & Morton-Bourgon, K. (2005). The characteristics of persistent sexual offenders: A meta-analysis of recidivism studies. *Journal of Consulting and Clinical Psychology, 73*, 1154–1163.

Hanson, R. K., & Morton-Bourgon, K. E. (2009). The accuracy of recidivism risk assessments for sexual offenders: A meta-analysis of 118 prediction studies. *Psychological Assessment, 21*, 1–21. doi:10.1037/a0014421

Hanson, R. K., & Thornton, D. (1999). *Static 99: Improving actuarial risk assessments for sex offenders.* Ottawa, Ontario, Canada: Department of the Solicitor General of Canada.

Hanson, R. K., & Thornton, D. (2000). Improving risk assessments for sex offenders: A comparison of three actuarial scales. *Law and Human Behavior, 24*, 119–136. doi:10.1023/A:1005482921333

Hare, R. (1991). *The Hare Psychopathy Checklist—Revised.* Toronto, Ontario, Canada: Multi-Health Systems.

Hare, R. D. (2003). *The Revised Psychopathy Checklist.* Toronto, Ontario, Canada: Multi-Health Systems.

Harris, G. T., & Rice, M. E. (2007). Characterizing the value of actuarial violence risk assessments. *Criminal Justice and Behavior, 34*, 1638–1658. doi:10.1177/0093854807307029

Harris, G. T., Rice, M. E., & Cormier, C. A. (2002). Prospective replication of the Violence Risk Appraisal Guide in predicting violent recidivism among forensic patients. *Law and Human Behavior, 26*, 377–394.

Hart, S. D. (1998). The role of psychopathy in assessing risk for violence: Conceptual and methodological issues. *Legal and Criminological Psychology, 3*, 121–137. doi:10.1111/j.2044-8333.1998.tb00354.x

Hart, S. D. (2001). Assessing and managing violence risk. In K. Douglas, C. Webster, S. Hart, D. Eaves, & J. Ogloff (Eds.), *HCR–20 violence risk management companion guide* (pp. 13–25). Burnaby, British Columbia, Canada: Mental Health, Law, and Policy Institute, Simon Fraser University.

Hart, S. D. (2003). Actuarial risk assessment: Commentary on Berlin et al. *Sexual Abuse: A Journal of Research and Treatment, 15*, 383–388. doi:10.1023/A:1025012530682

Hart, S. D. (2008). Preventing violence: The role of risk assessment and management. In A. C. Baldry & F. W. Winkel (Eds.), *Intimate partner violence prevention and intervention: The risk assessment and management approach* (pp. 7–18). Hauppauge, NY: Nova Science.

Hart, S. D., & Cooke, D. J. (2013). Another look at the (im-)precision of individual risk estimates made using actuarial risk assessment instruments. *Behavioral Sciences and the Law, 31*, 81–102. doi:10.1002/bsl.2049

Hart, S. D., Douglas, K. S., & Webster, C. D. (2001). Risk management using the HCR–20: A general overview focusing on historical factors. In K. S. Douglas, C. D. Webster, S. D. Hart, D. Eaves, & J. R. P. Ogloff (Eds.), *HCR–20 violence risk management companion guide* (pp. 27–40). Burnaby, British Columbia, Canada: Mental Health, Law, and Policy Institute, Simon Fraser University.

Hart, S. D., Kropp, P. R., Laws, D. R., Klaver, J., Logan, C., & Watt, K. A. (2003). *The Risk for Sexual Violence Protocol (RSVP): Structured professional guidelines for assessing risk of sexual violence.* Burnaby, British Columbia, Canada: Mental Health, Law, and Policy Institute, Simon Fraser University.

Hart, S. D., & Logan, C. (2011). Formulation of violence risk using evidence-based assessments: The structured professional judgment approach. In P. Sturmey & M. McMurran (Eds.), *Forensic case formulation* (pp. 83–106). Chichester, England: Wiley-Blackwell.

Hart, S. D., Michie, C., & Cooke, D. J. (2007a). Authors' reply: Margins of error for individual risk estimates: Large, unknown, or incalculable [Letter]. *British Journal of Psychiatry, 191*, 561–562. doi:10.1192/bjp.191.6.561a

Hart, S. D., Michie, C., & Cooke, D. J. (2007b). Precision of actuarial risk assessment instruments: Evaluating the "margins of error" of group v. individual predictions of violence. *British Journal of Psychiatry, 190*, S60–S65. doi:10.1192/bjp.190.5.s60

Hart, S. D., Sturmey, P., Logan, C., & McMurran, M. (2011). Forensic case formulation. *International Journal of Forensic Mental Health, 10*, 118–126. doi:10.1080/14999013.2011.577137

Heilbrun, K. (1992). The role of psychological testing in forensic assessment. *Law and Human Behavior, 16*, 257–272. doi:10.1007/BF01044769

Heilbrun, K. (1997). Prediction versus management models relevant to risk assessment: The importance of legal decision-making context. *Law and Human Behavior, 21*, 347–359.

Heilbrun, K., Lee, R., & Cottle, C. C. (2005). Risk factors and intervention outcomes: Meta-analyses of juvenile offending. In K. Heilbrun, N. E. S. Goldstein, & R. E. Redding (Eds.), *Juvenile delinquency: Prevention, assessment, and intervention* (pp. 111–133). New York, NY: Oxford University Press.

Heilbrun, K., O'Neill, M. L., Stevens, T. N., Strohman, L. K., Bowman, Q., & Lo, Y.-W. (2004). Assessing normative approaches to communicating violence risk: A national survey of psychologists. *Behavioral Sciences and the Law*, 22, 187–196.

Heilbrun, K., O'Neill, M. L., Strohman, L. K., Bowman, Q., & Philipson, J. (2000). Expert approaches to communicating violence risk. *Law and Human Behavior*, 24, 137–148.

Heilbrun, K., Philipson, J., Berman, L., & Warren, J. (1999). Risk communication: Clinicians' reported approaches and perceived values. *Journal of the Academy of Psychiatry and Law*, 27, 397–406.

Heilbrun, K. S. (2001). *Principles of forensic mental health assessment*. New York, NY: Kluwer Academic/Plenum.

Heron, M. (2012). Deaths: Leading causes for 2009. *National Vital Statistics Reports*, 61(7), 1–95. Retrieved from http://www.cdc.gov/nchs/data/nvsr/nvsr61/nvsr61_07.pdf

Hilton, N. Z., Carter, A. M., Harris, G. T., & Sharpe, A. J. (2008). Does using nonnumerical terms to describe risk aid violence risk communication? Clinician agreement and decision making. *Journal of Interpersonal Violence*, 23, 171–188.

Hilton, N. Z., Harris, G. T., Rice, M. E., Eke, A. W., & Lowe-Wetmore, T. (2007). Training front-line users in the Ontario Domestic Assault Risk Assessment (ODARA), a tool for police domestic investigations. *Canadian Journal of Police and Security Services*, 5, 1–5.

Hoge, R. D., & Andrews, D. A. (2002). *Youth Level of Service/Case Management Inventory: User's manual*. Toronto, Ontario, Canada: Multi-Health Systems.

Hogue, T. E., & Allen, C. (2006). *Structured Clinical Judgement: Risk: Multidisciplinary assessment of risk—A system for structuring clinical judgements of risk related to high security hospital needs*. Unpublished manuscript, Rampton Secure Hospital, Rampton, Nottinghamshire, England.

Hubbard, D. J., & Pratt, T. C. (2002). A meta-analysis of the predictors of delinquency among girls. *Journal of Offender Rehabilitation*, 34, 1–13.

In re Oakes, 8 Law Rep. 123 (Mass. 1845).

Jablonski v. United States 712 F.2d 391 (1983).

Jones v. United States, 463 U.S. 354 (1983).

Kansas v. Crane, 534 U.S. 407 (2002).

Kansas v. Hendricks, 521 US 346 (1997).

Kozol, H. L., Boucher, R. J., & Garofalo, R. F. (1972). The diagnosis and treatment of dangerousness. *Crime and Delinquency*, 18, 371–392. doi:10.1177/001112877201800407

Kropp, P. R., Belfrage, H., & Hart, S. D. (2013). *Assessment of risk for honour-based violence (PATRIARCH): User manual*. Vancouver, British Columbia, Canada: ProActive ReSolutions.

Kropp, P. R., & Hart, S. D. (2000). The Spousal Assault Risk Assessment (SARA) Guide: Reliability and validity in adult male offenders. *Law and Human Behavior*, 24, 101–118.

Kropp, P. R., & Hart, S. D. (2004). *The development of the Brief Spousal Assault Form for the Evaluation of Risk (B–SAFER): A tool for criminal justice professionals*. Ottawa, Ontario, Canada: Department of Justice Canada.

Kropp, P. R., Hart, S. D., & Belfrage, H. (2005). *Brief Spousal Assault Form for the Evaluation of Risk (B–SAFER): User manual*. Vancouver, British Columbia, Canada: ProActive ReSolutions.

Kropp, P. R., Hart, S. D., & Belfrage, H. (2010). *Brief Spousal Assault Form for the Evaluation of Risk (B–SAFER), version 2: User manual*. Vancouver, British Columbia, Canada: ProActive ReSolutions.

Kropp, P. R., Hart, S. D., & Lyon, D. R. (2008). *The Stalking Assessment and Management Guidelines (SAM): User manual*. Vancouver, British Columbia, Canada: ProActive ReSolutions.

Kropp, P. R., Hart, S. D., Webster, C. D., & Eaves, D. (1994). *Manual for the Spousal Assault Risk Assessment Guide*. Vancouver, British Columbia, Canada: British Columbia Institute on Family Violence.

Kropp, P. R., Hart, S. D., Webster, C. D., & Eaves, D. (1995). *Manual for the Spousal Assault Risk Assessment Guide* (2nd ed.). Vancouver, British Columbia, Canada: British Columbia Institute on Family Violence.

Kwartner, P. P., Lyons, P. M., &, Boccaccini, M. T. (2006). Judges' risk communication preferences in risk for future violence cases. *International Journal of Forensic Mental Health*, 5, 185–194.

Långström, N., Grann, M., Ruchkin, V., Sjöstedt, G., & Fazel, S. (2009). Risk factors for violent offending in autism spectrum disorder: A national study of hospitalized individuals. *Journal of Interpersonal Violence*, 24, 1358–1370.

Lareau, C. (2012). Civil commitment and involuntary hospitalization of the mentally ill. In R. K. Otto (Ed.), *Comprehensive handbook of psychology: Vol. 11. Forensic psychology* (2nd ed., pp. 308–331). Hoboken, NJ: Wiley.

Lavoie, J. A. A., Guy, L. A., & Douglas, K. S. (2009). Violence risk assessment: Principles and models bridging prediction to management. In J. Ireland (Ed.), *Violent and sexual offenders: Assessment, treatment and management* (pp. 3–19). London, England: Willan.

Lessard v. Schmidt, 349 F. Supp. 1078 (E.D. Wis. 1972).

Levene, K. S., Augimeri, L. K.. Pepler, D. J., Walsh, M. M., Koegl, C. J., & Webster, C. D. (2001). *Early Assessment Risk List for Girls: EARL–21G, Version 1, Consultation Edition.* Toronto, Ontario, Canada: Earlscourt Child and Family Centre.

Lipari v. Sears Roebuck 497 F.Supp. 185 (1980).

Litwack, T. R. (1997). Communications regarding risk. *American Psychologist, 52*, 1245. doi:10.1037/0003-066X.52.11.1245.a

Litwack, T. R. (2001). Actuarial versus clinical assessments of dangerousness. *Psychology, Public Policy, and Law, 7,* 409–443.

Litwack, T. R., & Schlesinger, L. B. (1999). Dangerousness risk assessments: Research, legal, and clinical considerations. In A. K. Hess & I. B. Weiner (Eds.), *The handbook of forensic psychology* (2nd ed., pp. 171–217). New York, NY: Wiley.

Litwack, T. R., Zapf, P. A., Groscup, J. L., & Hart, S. D. (2006). Violence risk assessment: Research, legal, and clinical considerations. In I. B. Weiner & A. K. Hess (Eds.), *The handbook of forensic psychology* (3rd ed., pp. 487–533). Hoboken, NJ: Wiley.

Lodewijks, H. P. B., de Ruiter, C., & Doreleijers, T. A. H. (2008). Gender differences in violent outcome and risk assessment in adolescent offenders after residential treatment. *International Journal of Forensic Mental Health, 7,* 133–146. doi:10.1080/14999013.2008.9914410

Lodewijks, H. P. B., Doreleijers, T. A. H., & de Ruiter, C. (2008). SAVRY risk assessment in relation to sentencing and subsequent recidivism in a Dutch sample of violent juvenile offenders. *Criminal Justice and Behavior, 35,* 696–709. doi:10.1177/0093854808316146

Luong, D., & Wormith, J. S. (2011). Applying risk/need assessment to probation practice and its impact on the recidivism of young offenders. *Criminal Justice and Behavior, 38,* 1177–1199. doi:10.1177/0093854811421596

Lyon, D. R., Hart, S. D., & Webster, C. D. (2001). Violence and risk assessment. In R. A. Schuller & J. R. P. Ogloff (Eds.), *Introduction to psychology and law: Canadian perspectives* (pp. 314–350). Toronto, Ontario, Canada: University of Toronto Press.

Lyons v. the Queen, 37 C.C.C. (3d) 1 at 47 (S.C.C.) (1987).

MacKenzie, R. D., McEwan, T. E., Pathé, M. T., James, D. V., Ogloff, J. R. P., & Mullen, P. E. (2009). *The Stalking Risk Profile: Guidelines for the assessment and management of stalkers.* Elwood, Australia: Centre for Forensic Behavioural Science, School of Psychology and Psychiatry, Monash University.

Magdol, L., Moffitt, T. E., Caspi, A., Newman, D. L., Fagan, J., & Silva, P. A. (1997). Gender differences in partner violence in a birth cohort of 21-year-olds: Bridging the gap between clinical and epidemiological approaches. *Journal of Consulting and Clinical Psychology, 65,* 68–78.

McNiel, D. E. (1998). Empirically based clinical evaluation and management of the potentially violent patient. In P. M. Kleespies (Ed.), *Emergencies in mental health practice: Evaluation and management.* (pp. 95–116). New York, NY: Guilford Press.

McNiel, D. E., Chamberlain, J., Hall, S., Fordwood, S., & Binder, R. L. (2008). Impact of clinical training on violence risk assessment. *American Journal of Psychiatry, 165,* 195–200.

McNiel, D. E., Hung, E. K., Cramer, R. J., Hall, S. E., & Binder, R. L. (2011). An approach to evaluating competency in assessment and management of violence risk. *Psychiatric Services, 62,* 90–92.

McNiel, D. E., Lam, J. N., & Binder R. L. (2000). Relevance of interrater agreement to violence risk assessment. *Journal of Consulting and Clinical Psychology. 68,* 1111–1115.

Melton, G. B., Petrila, J., Poythress, N. G., & Slobogin, C. (2007). *Psychological evaluations for the courts: A handbook for mental health professionals and lawyers* (3rd ed.). New York, NY: Guilford Press.

Mills, J. F., Jones, M. N., & Kroner, D. G. (2005). An examination of the generalizability of the LSI–R and VRAG probability bins. *Criminal Justice and Behavior, 32,* 565–585. doi:10.1177/0093854805278417

Monahan, J. (1981). *Predicting violent behavior: An assessment of clinical techniques.* Beverly Hills, CA: Sage. doi:10.1037/e664392007-001

Monahan, J. (1996). Violence prediction: The last 20 years and the next 20 years. *Criminal Justice and Behavior, 23,* 107–120.

Monahan, J. (2008). Structured risk assessment of violence. In R. Simon & K. Tardiff (Eds.), *Textbook of violence assessment and management* (pp. 17–33). Washington, DC: American Psychiatric Association.

Monahan, J., Steadman, H., Appelbaum, P., Grisso, T., Mulvey, E., Roth, L., . . . Silver, E. (2005). *Classification of Violence Risk: Professional manual.* Lutz, FL: Psychological Assessment Resources.

Monahan, J., & Steadman, H. J. (2001). Violence risk assessment: A quarter century of research. In L. E. Frost & R. J. Bonnie (Eds.), *The evolution of mental health law* (pp. 195–211). Washington, DC: American Psychological Association.

Monahan, J., & Steadman, H. J. (2006). Violent storms and violent people: How meteorology can inform risk communication in mental health law. *American Psychologist, 51*, 931–938.

Monahan, J., Steadman, H. J., Silver, E., Applebaum, P. S., Robbins, P. C., Mulvey, E. P., . . . Banks, S. (2001). *Rethinking risk assessment: The MacArthur study of mental disorder and violence.* New York, NY: Oxford University Press.

Mossman, D. (1994). Assessing predictors of violence: Being accurate about accuracy. *Journal of Consulting and Clinical Psychology, 62*, 783–792. doi: 10.1037/0022-006x.62.4.783

Mossman, D., & Selke, T. M. (2007). Avoiding errors about "margins of error." *British Journal of Psychiatry, 191*, 561. doi:10.1192/bjp.191.6.561

Neves, A. C., Goncalves, R. A., & Palma-Oliveira, J. M. (2011). Assessing risk for violent and general recidivism: A study of the HCR–20 and the PCL–R with a non-clinical sample of Portuguese offenders. *International Journal of Forensic Mental Health, 10*, 137–149. doi:10.1080/14999013.2011.577290

Nicholls, T. L., Petersen, K., Brink, J., & Webster, C. (2011). A clinical risk profile of forensic psychiatric patients: Treatment team STARTs in a Canadian service. *International Journal of Forensic Mental Health, 10*, 187–199. doi:10.1080/14999013.2011.600234

Nielssen, O. (2013). Scientific and ethical problems with risk assessment in clinical practice. *Australian and New Zealand Journal of Psychiatry, 47*, 1198–1199. doi:10.1177/0004867413498278

Nijman, H. L., Muris, P., Merckelbach, H. L. G. J., Palmstierna, T., Wistedt, B., Vos, A. M., . . . Allertz, W. (1999). The Staff Observation Aggression Scale—Revised (SOAS–R). *Aggressive Behavior, 25*, 197–209.

Nonstad, K., & Webster, C. D. (2011). How to fail in the implementation of a risk assessment scheme or any other new procedure in your organization. *American Journal of Orthopsychiatry, 81*, 94–99.

Northpointe Institute for Public Management. (1996). COMPAS [Computer software]. Traverse City, MI: Author.

Nuffield, J. (1982). *Parole decision-making in Canada: Research towards decision guidelines.* Ottawa, Ontario, Canada: Supply and Services Canada.

O'Connor v. Donaldson, 422 U.S. 563 (1975).

Olver, M., Stockdale, K., & Wormith, J. (2009). Risk assessment with young offenders: A meta-analysis of three assessment measures. *Criminal Justice and Behavior, 36*, 329–353. doi:10.1177/0093854809331457

Otto, R. K. (2000). Assessing and managing violence risk in outpatient settings. *Journal of Clinical Psychology, 56*, 1239–1262.

Otto, R. K., & Douglas, K. S. (2010). *Handbook of violence risk assessment.* New York, NY: Taylor & Francis.

Packer, I. K. (2001, March). *Use of violence risk assessment instruments: A national survey.* Paper proposal submitted to the annual conference of the American Psychology-Law Society, Austin, TX.

Pedersen, L., Rasmussen, K., & Elsass, P. (2010). Risk assessment: The value of structured professional judgments. *International Journal of Forensic Mental Health, 9*, 74–81. doi:10.1080/14999013.2010.499556

Pedersen, L., Rasmussen, K., & Elsass, P. (2012). HCR–20 violence risk assessments as a guide for treating and managing violence risk in a forensic psychiatric setting. *Psychology, Crime & Law, 18*, 733–743.

Penetanguishene Mental Health Centre v. Ontario (Attorney General), 1 S.C.R. 498 (2004).

Phenix, A., Helmus, L., & Hanson, R. K. (2012). *Static–99R and Static–2002R evaluator's workbook.* Retrieved from http://www.static99.org./pdfdocs/Static–99RandStatic-2002R_Evaluators Workbook2012-07-26.pdf

Pomerol, J.-C. (2001). Scenario development and practical decision making under uncertainty. *Decision Support Systems, 31*, 197–204.

Prentky, R., & Righthand, S. (2003). *Juvenile Sex Offender Assessment Protocol–II (J–SOAP–II) manual.* Washington, DC: Office of Juvenile Justice and Delinquency Prevention.

Quinsey, V., Harris, G., Rice, M., & Cormier, C. (1998). *Violent offenders: Appraising and managing risk.* Washington, DC: American Psychological Association. doi:10.1037/10304-000

Quinsey, V., Harris, G., Rice, M., & Cormier, C. (2006). *Violent offenders: Appraising and managing risk* (2nd ed.). Washington, DC: American Psychological Association.

Redding, R. E., Floyd, M. Y., & Hawk, G. L. (2001). What judges and lawyers think about the testimony of mental health experts: A survey of the courts and bar. *Behavioural Sciences and the Law, 19*, 583–594.

Re Moore and the Queen, 10 C.C.C. (3d) 306 (Ont C.A. 1984).

R. v. Johnson, 2 S.C.R. 357 (2003).

Reynolds, K., & Miles, H. L. (2009). The effect of training on the quality of HCR–20 violence risk assessments in forensic secure services. *Journal of Forensic Psychiatry and Psychology, 20*, 473–480.

Rice, M. E., Harris, G. T., & Hilton, N. Z. (2010). The Violence Risk Appraisal Guide and Sex Offender Risk Appraisal Guide for violence risk assessment and the Ontario Domestic Assault Risk Assessment and Domestic Violence Risk Appraisal Guide for wife assault risk assessment. In R. Otto & K. Douglas (Eds.), *Handbook of violence risk assessment tools* (pp. 99–120). Oxford, England: Routledge/Taylor & Francis.

Ringland, G. (1998). *Scenario planning: Managing for the future*. Chichester, England: Wiley.

Risk Management Authority Scotland. (2007). *Risk management authority standards and guidelines: Risk management of offenders subject to an order for lifelong restriction*. Retrieved from http://www.rmascotland.gov.uk/files/5813/7114/3816/riskManagementGuidelines.pdf

Robbins, P. C., Monahan, J., & Silver, E. (2003). Mental disorder, violence, and gender. *Law and Human Behavior, 27*, 561–571. doi:10.1023/B:LAHU.0000004886.13268.f2

Rogers, R. (2000). The uncritical acceptance of risk assessment in forensic practice. *Law and Human Behavior, 24*, 595–605. doi:10.1023/A:1005575113507

Rosenfeld, B. (2004). Violence risk factors in stalking and obsessional harassment: A review and preliminary meta-analysis. *Criminal Justice and Behavior, 31*, 9–36.

Ryan, C., Nielssen, O., Paton, M., & Large, M. (2010). Clinical decision in psychiatry should not be based on risk assessment. *Australasian Psychiatry, 18*, 398–403.

Sarbin, T. (1943). A contribution to the study of actuarial and individual methods of prediction. *American Journal of Sociology, 48*, 593–602.

Schaap, G., Lammers, S., & de Vogel, V. (2009). Risk assessment in female forensic psychiatric patients: A quasi-prospective study into the validity of the HCR–20 and PCL–R. *Journal of Forensic Psychiatry and Psychology, 20*, 354–365. doi:10.1080/14789940802542873

Schall v. Martin, 467 US 253 (1984).

Schmidt, F., Campbell, M. A., & Houlding, C. (2011). Comparative analyses of the YLS/CMI, SAVRY, and PCL:YV in adolescent offenders: A 10-year follow-up into adulthood. *Youth Violence and Juvenile Justice, 9*, 23–42. doi:10.1177/1541204010371793

Schopp, R. F. (1996). Communicating risk assessments: Accuracy, efficacy, and responsibility. *American Psychologist, 51*, 939–944. doi:10.1037/0003-066X.51.9.939

Schwalbe, C. S. (2007). Risk assessment for juvenile justice: A meta-analysis. *Law and Human Behavior, 31*, 449–462.

Schwalbe, C. S. (2008). A meta-analysis of juvenile justice risk assessment instruments: Predictive validity by gender. *Criminal Justice and Behavior, 35*, 1367–1381.

Schwartz, T. L., & Park, T. L. (1999). Assaults by patients on psychiatric residents: A survey and training recommendations. *Psychiatric Services, 50*, 381–383.

Scott, P. D. (1977). Assessing dangerousness in criminals. *British Journal of Psychiatry, 131*, 127–142. doi:10.1192/bjp.131.2.127

Scurich, N., & John, R. S. (2011). The effect of framing actuarial risk probabilities on involuntary civil commitment decisions. *Law and Human Behavior, 35*, 83–91. doi:10.1007/s10979-010-9218-4

Shah, S. A. (1978). Dangerousness: A paradigm for exploring some issues in law and psychology. *American Psychologist, 33*, 224–238. doi:10.1037/0003-066X.33.3.224

Shook, J. J., & Sarri, R. C. (2007). Structured decision making in juvenile justice: Judges' and probation officers' perceptions and use. *Children and Youth Services Review, 29*, 1335–1351. doi:10.1016/j.childyouth.2007.05.008

Singh, J. P., Grann, M., & Fazel, S. (2011). A comparative study of violence risk assessment tools: A systematic review and metaregression analysis of 68 studies involving 25,980 participants. *Clinical Psychology Review, 31*, 499–513. doi:10.1016/j.cpr.2010.11.009

Sjösted, G., & Långström, N. (2002). Assessment of risk for criminal recidivism among rapists: A comparison of four different measures. *Psychology, Crime & Law, 8*, 25–40.

Skeem, J., Schubert, C., Stowman, S., Beeson, S., Mulvey, E., Gardner, W., & Lidz, C. (2005). Gender and risk assessment accuracy: Underestimating women's violence potential. *Law and Human Behavior, 29*, 173–186.

Skeem, J. L., Manchak, S., & Peterson, J. K. (2011). Correctional policy for offenders with mental illness: Creating a new paradigm for recidivism reduction. *Law and Human Behavior, 35*, 110–126.

Slovic, P., Monahan, J., & MacGregor, D. G. (2000). Violence risk assessment and risk communication: The effects of using actual cases, providing instruction, and employing probability versus frequency formats. *Law and Human Behavior, 24*, 271–296.

Smith, P., Cullen, F. T., & Latessa, E. J. (2009). Can 14,737 women be wrong? A meta-analysis of the LSI–R and recidivism for female offenders. *Criminology and Public Policy, 8*, 183–208.

Smith v. Jones, 1 S.C.R. 455 (1999).

Steadman, H. J. (2000). From dangerousness to risk assessment of community violence: Taking stock at the turn of the century. *Journal of the American Academy of Psychiatry and the Law, 28*, 265–271.

Steadman, H. J., Silver, E., Monahan, J., Appelbaum, P. S., Robbins, P. C., Mulvey, E. P., . . . Banks, S. (2000). A classification tree approach to the development of actuarial violence risk assessment tools. *Law and Human Behavior, 24*, 83–100.

Storey, J., Gibas, A. L., Reeves, K. A., & Hart, S. D. (2011). Evaluation of a violence risk (threat) assessment training program for police and other criminal justice professionals. *Criminal Justice and Behavior, 38,* 554–564.

Storey, J., Kropp, P. R., Hart, D. S., Belfrage, H., & Strand, S. (2014). Assessment and management of risk for intimate partner violence by police officers using the Brief Spousal Assault Form for the Evaluation of Risk (B-SAFER). *Criminal Justice and Behavior, 41,* 256–271.

Storey, J. E., Hart, S. D., & Kropp, P. R. (in press). *Elder Abuse Risk Assessment (EARA): User manual.* Vancouver, British Columbia, Canada: ProActive ReSolutions.

Strand, S., & Belfrage, H. (2001). Comparison of HCR–20 scores in violent mentally disordered men and women: Gender differences and similarities. *Psychology, Crime & Law, 7,* 71–79.

Tarasoff v. Regents of University of California 17 Cal. 3d 425 (1976)

Tardiff, K. (1996). *Concise guide to assessment and management of violent patients* (2nd ed.). Washington, DC: American Psychiatric Press.

Teasdale, B., Silver, E., & Monahan, J. (2006). Gender, threat/control override delusions, and violence. *Law and Human Behavior, 30,* 649–658. doi:10.1007/s10979-006-9044-x

Thomson, L. D. G., Davidson, M., Brett, C., Steele, J., & Darjee, R. (2008). Risk assessment in forensic patients with schizophrenia: The predictive validity of actuarial scales and symptom severity for offending and violence over 8–10 years. *International Journal of Forensic Mental Health, 7,* 173–189. doi:10.1080/14999013.2008.9914413

Thornton, D. (2007). *Scoring guide for Risk Matrix 2000.9/SVC.* Retrieved from http://www.cfcp.bham.ac.uk/Extras/SCORING%20GUIDE%20FOR%20RISK%20MATRIX%202000.9-%20SVC%20-%20(ver.%20Feb%202007).pdf

United States v. Fields, 483 F.3d 313 (5th Cir., 2007).

United States v. Salerno, 481 U.S. 739 (1987).

United States v. Scheffer, 523 U.S. 303 (1998).

van den Brink, R. H. S., Hooijschuur, A., van Os, T. W. D. P., Savenije, W., & Wiersma, D. (2010). Routine violence risk assessment in community forensic mental healthcare. *Behavioral Sciences and the Law, 28,* 396–410.

van der Heijden, K. (1994). Probabilistic planning and scenario planning. In G. Wright & P. Ayton (Eds.), *Subjective probability* (pp. 549–572). Chichester, England: Wiley.

van der Heijden, K. (1997). *Scenarios: The art of strategic conversation.* New York, NY: Wiley.

Viljoen, J. L., Beneteau, J. L., Gulbransen, E., Brodersen, E., Desmarais, S. L., Nicholls, T., & Cruise, K. (2012). Assessment of multiple risk outcomes, strengths, and change with the START:AV: A short-term prospective study with adolescent offenders. *International Journal of Forensic Mental Health, 11,* 165–180. doi:10.1080/14999013.2012.737407

Viljoen, J. L., Nicholls, T. L., Cruise, K. R., Desmarais, S. L., & Webster, C. D. (2014). *Short-Term Assessment of Risk and Treatability: Adolescent Version (START:AV)—User guide.* Burnaby, British Columbia, Canada: Mental Health, Law, and Policy Institute.

Viljoen, J. L., Mordell, S., & Beneteau, J. L. (2012). Prediction of adolescent sexual reoffending: A meta-analysis of the J–SOAP–II, ERASOR, J–SORRAT–II, and Static–99. *Law and Human Behavior, 36,* 423–438. doi:10.1037/h0093938

Viljoen, J. L., Scalora, M., Cuadra, L., Bader, S., Chavez, V., Ullman, D., & Lawrence, L. (2008). Assessing risk for violence in adolescents who have sexually offended: A comparison of the J–SOAP–II, J–SORRAT–II, and SAVRY. *Criminal Justice and Behavior, 35,* 5–23.

Vincent, G. M., Chapman, J., & Cook, N. (2011). Predictive validity of the SAVRY, racial differences, and the contribution of needs factors. *Criminal Justice and Behavior, 38,* 42–62. doi:10.1177/0093854810386000

Vincent, G. M., Guy, L. S., Gershenson, B. G., & McCabe, P. (2012). Does risk assessment make a difference? Results of implementing the SAVRY in juvenile probation. *Behavioral Sciences and the Law, 30,* 384–405. doi:10.1002/bsl.2014

Vincent, G. M., Guy, L. S., & Grisso, T. (2012). *Risk assessment in juvenile justice: A guidebook for implementation.* Retrieved from http://modelsforchange.net/publications/346

Vincent, G. M., Paiva-Salisbury, M. L., Cook, N. E., Guy, L. S., & Perrault, R. T. (2012). Impact of risk/needs assessment on juvenile probation officers' decision making: Importance of implementation. *Psychology, Public Policy, and Law, 18,* 549–576. doi:10.1037/a0027186

Vitek v. Jones. 445 U.S 480, 100 S.Ct. 1254 (1980).

Vojt, G., Slesser, M., Marshall, L., & Thomson, L. D. G. (2011). The clinical reality of implementing formal risk assessment and management measures within high secure forensic care. *Medicine, Science, and the Law, 51,* 220–227. doi:10.1258/msl.2011.010149

Vojt, G., Thomson, L. D. G., & Marshall, L. A. (2013). The predictive validity of the HCR–20 following clinical implementation: Does it work in practice? *Journal of Forensic Psychiatry and Psychology, 24,* 371–385.

Walters, G. (2006). Risk-appraisal versus self-report in the prediction of criminal justice outcomes: A meta-analysis. *Criminal Justice and Behavior, 33,* 279–304.

Watt, K. A., & Hart, S. D. (2013, June). *Violence triaging.* Paper presented at the annual meeting of the International Association of Forensic Mental Health Services, Maastricht, the Netherlands.

Webster, C. D., Douglas, K., Eaves, D., & Hart, S. (1997). *HCR–20: Assessing risk for violence* (version 2). Burnaby, British Columbia, Canada: Simon Fraser University.

Webster, C. D., Eaves, D., Douglas, K. S., & Wintrup, A. (1995). *The HCR–20 scheme: The assessment of dangerousness and risk.* Burnaby, British Columbia, Canada: Mental Health, Law, and Policy Institute, and Forensic Psychiatric Services Commission of British Columbia.

Webster, C. D., Martin, M. L., Brink, J., Nicholls, T. L., & Desmarais, S. L. (2009). *Manual for the Short-Term Assessment of Risk and Treatability (START;* version 1.1). Coquitlam, British Columbia, Canada: British Columbia Mental Health and Addiction Services.

Weerasekera, P. (1996). *Multiperspective case formulation: A step towards treatment integration.* Malabar, FL: Krieger.

Werkgroep Pilotstudy Risicotaxatie Forensische Psychiatrie. (2002). *Bevindingen van een landelijke pilotstudy naar de HKT-30* [Findings of the nationwide pilot study of HKT-30]. The Hague, the Netherlands: Ministerie van Justitie.

White, S. G., & Meloy, J. R. (2010). *WAVR-21: A structured professional guide for the Workplace Assessment of Violence Risk* (2nd ed.). San Diego, CA: Specialized Training Services.

Williams, K. R., & Houghton, A. B. (2004). Assessing the risk of domestic violence reoffending: A validation study. *Law and Human Behavior, 28,* 437–455. doi:10.1023/B:LAHU.0000039334.59297.f0

Wilson, C. M., Desmarais, S. L., Nicholls, T. L., & Brink, J. (2010). The role of client strengths in assessments of risk using the Short-Term Assessment of Risk and Treatability (START). *International Journal of Forensic Mental Health, 9,* 282–293. doi:10.1080/14999013.2010. 534694

Witt, P. H., & Conroy, M. A. (2009). *Evaluation of sexually violent predators.* New York, NY: Oxford University Press.

Wong, L., Morgan, A., Wilkie, T., & Barbaree, H. (2012). Quality of resident violence risk assessments in psychiatric emergency settings. *Canadian Journal of Psychiatry, 57,* 375–380.

Wong, S., & Gordon, A. (2000). *Manual for the Violence Risk Scale.* Saskatoon, Saskatchewan, Canada: University of Saskatchewan.

Worling, J. R., & Curwen, T. (2001). *Estimate of Risk of Adolescent Sexual Offense Recidivism (ERASOR) Version 2.0.* Toronto, Ontario, Canada: SAFE-T Program, Thistletown Regional Centre, Ontario Ministry of Community and Social Services.

Wright, E., Van Voorhis, P., Salisbury, E., & Bauman, A. (2012). Gender responsive lessons learned and policy implications for women in prison: A review. *Criminal Justice and Behavior, 30,* 1612–1632.

Yang, M., Wong, S. C. P., & Coid, J. (2010). The efficacy of violence prediction: A meta-analytic comparison of nine risk assessment tools. *Psychological Bulletin, 136,* 740–767. doi:10.1037/a0020473

Young, D., Moline, K., Farrell, J., & Bierie, D. (2006). Best implementation practices: Disseminating new assessment technologies in a juvenile justice agency. *Crime and Delinquency, 52,* 135–158. doi:10.1177/0011128705281752

CHAPTER 4

LEGAL INSANITY AND *MENS REA* DEFENSES

Ira K. Packer

This chapter focuses on the legal and clinical issues related to determinations of criminal responsibility (CR). It begins with an analysis of the legal standards and then addresses the applicability of relevant clinical analyses to these standards. The insanity defense and the oft-misunderstood legal concept of "diminished capacity" are also discussed.

IMPORTANCE OF THE PROBLEM

In order to be found legally culpable, not only must an individual have committed an act that is prohibited by law (*actus reus*, which is Latin for *bad act*), but he or she also must have had the requisite mental state (*mens rea*, which means *guilty mind*). Even if the individual clearly committed the act, the legal significance of the act may hinge on his or her intentions, understanding, or motivation. For example, if a man shoots and kills an intruder in his home who was threatening him with a knife, he may very well be considered not guilty as a result of self-defense. The situation becomes much more complex when the behavior would not otherwise be justified, but rather an "excuse" defense is raised. For instance, if the man shot the victim as a result of delusional beliefs, issues may be raised as to whether he (a) fully understood what he was doing, (b) was able to think rationally, or (c) acted in an intentional manner. In such cases, the relevant factors are often related to issues of a disturbed mental state. There is significant controversy regarding setting the criteria for determining when someone may be excused for committing an *actus reus* due to a

mental disorder or mental illness. This chapter will begin with a discussion of the development of the legal bases for mental-state defenses and will then focus on the application of clinical expertise to the legal standards.

The decision to excuse a defendant from CR is a legal and moral one. As will be discussed in the following sections, such decisions can be informed by scientific knowledge of human behavior and psychology, but *insanity* is a legal term, not a clinical condition or term. The courts have reinforced this notion; in the case of *Bigby v. State* (1994), the court stated explicitly that "the issue of insanity is not strictly medical; it also invokes both legal and ethical considerations. Otherwise the issue of sanity would be decided in the hospitals and not the courtrooms" (p. 877). Thus, courts and legislatures determine the standards and criteria to be used for an insanity defense, and these standards differ across jurisdictions (Packer, 2009). Indeed, four states have abolished the insanity defense (i.e., Idaho, Kansas, Montana, and Utah), and the U.S. Supreme Court has never ruled whether this is constitutional or not. Furthermore, once the legal definition has been established, "ultimately the issue of insanity at the time of the offense excusing criminal responsibility lies in the province of the jury, not only as to the credibility of the witnesses and the weight of the evidence, but also as to the limits of the defense itself" (*Graham v. State*, 1978, p. 949). Thus, the disciplines of psychology and psychiatry can provide expertise to aid in the development of legal standards (as will be discussed below relative

http://dx.doi.org/10.1037/14461-004
APA Handbook of Forensic Psychology: Vol. 1. Individual and Situational Influences in Criminal and Civil Contexts,
B. L. Cutler and P. A. Zapf (Editors-in-Chief)

to the American Law Institute's [ALI's] 1985 standard) and can aid trial judges and juries in understanding a particular defendant's mental state, but the ultimate decision to excuse the defendant from CR will be made on moral and legal grounds.

RELEVANT PSYCHOLOGICAL THEORY AND PRINCIPLES

Although the current standards used in the United States are embedded within the context of the American legal system, the concept that certain individuals, due to disturbed mental states, should not be held responsible for their actions is more universal. This concept has been documented as far back as the Hebrew *Mishna* (almost 2,000 years ago). In the Middle Ages, under Anglo-Saxon law, individuals who were considered to be *lunatics* were similarly excused from responsibility. In 18th-century England, in the case of *Rex v. Arnold*, (1724), the following standard was adopted: "A man must be *totally deprived* [emphasis added] of his understanding and memory, and doth not know what he is doing, no more than an *infant, brute, or a wild beast* [emphasis added]." This standard has become known as the *wild beast test*. As is evident from the terms used in these early standards, there were no clear criteria offered, which reflects the limited knowledge of human psychology that was available at the time. Since that time, various standards for determining an individual's responsibility for a crime have evolved, as described in the following paragraphs.

M'Naghten Standard

The modern underpinning for the insanity defense standard prevalent in most U.S. jurisdictions stems from the case of Daniel M'Naghten in England in 1843 (M'Naghten case, 1843). M'Naghten shot and killed Edward Drummond, the private secretary of the Tory Prime Minister, Sir Robert Peel, under the mistaken impression that Drummond was the prime minister. M'Naghten's defense was that he was laboring under a delusion that the Tories were his enemies and thus he should not be held legally responsible for his actions. He indeed was acquitted by reason of insanity, which resulted in public

outrage at what was considered a lenient verdict (although the result of his acquittal was that he was confined to institutions for the criminally insane until his death 22 years later). In response to the unpopular verdict, the House of Lords held hearings on the issue of the insanity defense and then crafted a new insanity defense standard for England, which has become known as the *M'Naghten standard*:

> To establish a defense on the ground of insanity, it must be proved that, at the time of the committing of the act, the party accused was laboring under such a defect of reason, from disease of the mind, as not to know the nature and quality of the act he was doing or if he did know it, that he did not know he was doing what was wrong. (M'Naghten case, 1843)

This standard is often referred to as the *right–wrong test* and was subsequently adopted in many jurisdictions in the United States. In the 20th century, in response to advances in scientific and clinical understanding of human behavior, concerns were raised that the standard was too narrow. Specifically, a major criticism was that it focused only on cognitive capacities (*knowing*) and failed to consider the impact of impairments in emotional capacities and volitional control (e.g., Goldstein, 1967). Some jurisdictions attempted to address the volitional prong by adding another criterion to the M'Naghten standard: that a defendant could also be found insane if, due to mental disease, he or she acted in response to an "irresistible impulse." However, there was no clear guidance given regarding how to distinguish between an impulse that *could* not be resisted versus an impulse that *was* not resisted.

Product Test

One federal court responded to concerns about the insanity standards by adopting a wholly different approach (*Durham v. United States*, 1954). In 1954, in an opinion written by Judge David Bazelon, the Federal Court of Appeals for the District of Columbia adopted the *product standard*. The *Durham* court departed from the previous approaches by eschewing any specific standards regarding cognitive or volitional abilities, focusing instead on whether the criminal behavior was deemed to be the "product of mental disease or mental defect" (pp. 874–875). The rationale offered for this divergent approach was twofold: The court noted that the existing standards were "antiquated" in light of advances in the science of human behavior and changing community standards, and the court was concerned that those standards forced psychiatrists to focus on legal criteria rather than provide the courts with their expertise on the nature of psychiatric disorders.[1] *Durham*'s language was intended to give the forensic expert more leeway in providing the courts with relevant mental health testimony.

The expectations of the *Durham* court were not borne out in practice. One problem was that the standard did not provide clear criteria about what constituted a mental disease or defect from a legal perspective, thus resulting in a lack of consistency from the psychiatric community. Recognizing this problem, the same court defined the relevant mental disorder as referring to "any abnormal condition of the mind which substantially affects mental or emotional processes and substantially impairs behavior controls" (*McDonald v. United States*, 1962, p. 851). Reflecting on this definition, the court noted that "while the *McDonald* standard of mental disease was not without an attribute of circularity, it was useful in the administration of justice because it made plain that clinical and legal definitions of mental disease were distinct" (*United States v. Brawner*, 1972, p. 978).

This change did not address the more basic problem posed by the *Durham* standard: the lack of guidelines to aid in determining whether a particular criminal behavior was the *product* of the symptoms of a mental illness. Specifically, evidence that a defendant suffered from a mental illness at the time of the offense did not necessarily mean that the particular criminal behavior was the result of the mental illness. Individuals who experience symptoms of mental illness nonetheless act rationally most of the time. Furthermore, even when the behavior could be related to the mental illness,

there was no guidance about how to assess the role of the mental illness relative to other factors. The Court attempted to address this issue in the case of *Carter v. United States* (1957) by adopting the concept of legal causation known as "but for" (i.e., the "act would not have been committed if the person had not been suffering from the disease" [p. 234]).

Despite these attempts to narrow the criteria for an insanity defense, difficulties persisted in obtaining agreement among experts about whether the behavior was indeed a product of mental illness in any given case. In addition, commentators raised issues about the appropriateness of the formulation, arguing that it was too broad. Most notably, in the commentary accompanying the ALI's (1985) Model Penal Code (MPC), the following hypothetical case was offered. A man delusionally believes that he will inherit a large sum of money if a wealthy relative dies. He therefore kills this relative for the purpose of inheriting the funds. He would not have committed the act *but for* his delusional belief about the relative. However, he has full knowledge and appreciation that killing for this purpose is wrong. Using the product test, this defendant would be found not guilty by reason of insanity (NGRI), although holding this person "legally unresponsible on the ground that the mental disorder was an antecedent but for which the criminal conduct would not have occurred would seem simply unprincipled" (ALI, 1985, p. 173).

Recognizing these difficulties, the D.C. Circuit Court abandoned its experiment with the *Durham* standard and instead adopted the ALI's standard (described below) for its jurisdiction (*United States v. Brawner*, 1972). In reversing its previous rulings, the court commented:

> There is, indeed, irony in a situation under which the *Durham* rule, which was adopted in large part to permit experts to testify in their own terms concerning matters within their domain which the jury should know, resulted in testimony by the experts in terms not their own

---

[1]In 1954, only psychiatrists were recognized as expert witnesses in such cases; this practice was overturned in the landmark case of *Jenkins v. United States* (1962), in which psychologists were recognized as experts in the diagnosis of mental disorders.

to reflect unexpressed judgments in a domain that is properly not theirs but the jury's. The irony is heightened when the jurymen, instructed under the esoteric "product" standard, are influenced significantly by "product" testimony of expert witnesses really reflecting ethical and legal judgments rather than a conclusion within the witnesses' particular expertise. (p. 983)

American Law Institute's Model Penal Code

In 1962, ALI proposed an MPC that included a standard for the insanity defense (hereafter referred to as the *ALI standard*). ALI published both its recommendations and annotated and lengthy discussions about its process. ALI considered not only legal and moral considerations, but also input from the mental health community, including lengthy comments from Manfred Guttmacher, a leading forensic psychiatrist. The proposed language indicated that a defendant would be found not guilty by reason of insanity if "as a result of mental illness or mental defect he lacked substantial capacity either to appreciate the criminality [wrongfulness] of his conduct or to conform his conduct to the requirements of the law" (ALI, 1985, p. 163). It should be noted that this standard is disjunctive: A defendant will be considered insane if impairment exists in either the ability to appreciate wrongfulness (i.e., cognitive prong) or in the ability to conform conduct (i.e., volitional prong).

In developing this standard, there was an explicit recognition that "a sense of understanding broader than mere cognition and a reference to volitional capacity should be achieved directly in the formulation of the defense" (ALI, 1985, p. 168). In amending the M'Naghten language, ALI adopted the terms *appreciate* and *wrongfulness*. The term "appreciate" was used in order to broaden the conceptualization beyond intellectual knowledge and consider the actor's awareness of the significance of the act. The use of the term "wrongfulness" connotes the defendant's appreciation that the act would have been considered morally wrong by the community, not

simply that it is legally prohibited or criminal (e.g., Fingarette, 1972).

The developers of the ALI standard acknowledged that it would be rare for this distinction between wrongfulness and criminality to matter significantly. There are a few types of cases, though, in which this distinction is relevant. For example, Hans Schmidt (*New York v. Schmidt*, 1915) acknowledged killing a woman in response to what he believed was the voice of God commanding him to offer a sacrifice. He knew that it was against the law to kill, but he believed that it was morally justified because he was responding to God's authority. Schmidt was convicted following the trial judge's instruction to the jury that it should consider whether Schmidt understood that the act was against the law. The appellate court overturned the verdict and ruled that the relevant standard should be Schmidt's understanding of the moral wrongfulness. Judge Benjamin Cardozo, writing for the majority, stated that using the narrower definition of legal wrongfulness would

rob the rule of all relation to the mental health and true capacity of the criminal. The interpretation placed upon the statute by the trial judge may be tested by its consequences. A mother kills her infant child to whom she has been devotedly attached. She knows the nature and quality of the act; she knows that the law condemns it; but she is inspired by an insane delusion that God has appeared to her and ordained the sacrifice. It seems a mockery to say that, within the meaning of the statute, she knows that the act is wrong. . . . We find nothing either in the history of the rule, or in its reason and purpose, or in judicial exposition of its meaning, to justify a conclusion so abhorrent. (*New York v. Schmidt*, 1915, p. 949)

This interpretation is not uniformly accepted in jurisdictions using only the M'Naghten standard. For example, the Iowa Supreme Court (*State v. Hamann*, 1979) ruled that the appropriate standard was whether the defendant understood that the act was illegal. Its reasoning was that "impossible uncertainty over the so-called general mores renders the appreciation of morality a tool unfit for the task of measuring insanity" (p. 183). However, this is a minority position, as most jurisdictions have adopted the definition of moral wrongfulness. Again, these contrasting rulings highlight the fact that ultimately, insanity is a legal, not a clinical, matter.

It is noteworthy that issues have also been raised about the terms used in the M'Naghten standard. In the case of *Clark v. Arizona* (2006), the U.S. Supreme Court addressed the issue of the significance of the term "nature and quality" of the act. Arizona had (a) modified the M'Naghten standard to include only the criterion that the defendant did not know that the act was wrong and (b) eliminated the language about not knowing the nature and quality of the act. The Supreme Court first ruled that no minimum standard was constitutionally required, and therefore Arizona was within its rights to change the language. The Court went on to provide an interesting discussion of the standard, pointing out that the nature and quality prong would be subsumed under the wrongfulness prong. The Court stated that if indeed a defendant did not know the nature and quality of the act, then this would necessarily mean that he or she could not perceive that it was wrong. Thus, such a defendant would be found legally insane under the wrongfulness standard and would not be harmed by exclusion of the nature and quality prong. The Supreme Court thus concluded that this prong added nothing substantive beyond the wrongfulness criterion.

The ALI standard also contains language regarding the volitional prong ("ability to conform conduct"). Importantly, the standard includes language focusing on a lack of "substantial capacity" (as opposed to a total lack of capacity implied in the previous term "irresistible impulse"), recognizing that there is a continuum of such capacity, and that even severely impaired individuals maintain some limited capacity. The volitional prong has remained the most controversial element of the ALI standard, particularly after John Hinckley was acquitted by reason of insanity in 1983 for shooting both President Ronald Reagan and James Brady, his press secretary. Following that unpopular verdict (similar to the M'Naghten case), there was both a

public outcry and legislative attempts to modify the insanity defense. There was a perception (although no clear evidence) that the jury acquitted Hinckley primarily due to the volitional prong. As a result, the federal standards for insanity were revised to specifically exclude the volitional prong and were incorporated into the Insanity Defense Reform Act of 1984 (IDRA, 1984). Both the American Psychiatric Association (1983) and the American Bar Association (1983) supported this change, arguing that the volitional prong was not amenable to reliable assessment by mental health professionals. The American Psychiatric Association's (1983) position included the observation that "the line between an irresistible impulse and an impulse not resisted is probably no sharper than that between twilight and dusk" (p. 685).

Opposition to the inclusion of the volitional prong has included not only these pragmatic concerns, but also conceptual and philosophical objections. Morse (1994) put forth the argument that although the individual may describe the experience as feeling "compelled" to act, an alternative formulation would be that the individual is faced with difficult choices between conflicting options (i.e., the pressure from the impulse to commit the wrongful act and the competing pressure to avoid the negative consequences of the act). Morse suggested that the relevant issue should be the irrationality of the thinking rather than perceived choice.

Perhaps the disorder that could be conceptualized as most impacting primarily the volitional prong would be mania (Giorgi-Guarnieri et al., 2002; Vitacco & Packer, 2004). The racing thoughts and highly energized behavior that occur in individuals with a severe manic condition (*Diagnostic and Statistical Manual of Mental Disorders*, 5th edition; American Psychiatric Association, 2013) could impact the individual's ability to reflect on his or her behavior, consider alternatives, and choose how to respond in a given situation. Nonetheless, there are degrees of severity of mania, and it is often difficult to assess retrospectively the degree of mania at the time of the alleged offense. Thus, even for this disorder, the relation of the symptoms experienced to the standard of substantial impairment in volitional capacity may be unclear. It therefore should not be surprising that as of 2012, only 16 states still include the volitional prong as part of their insanity defense. Furthermore, empirical data confirm that evaluators less often rely on the volitional prong. For instance, Warren, Murrie, Chauhan, Dietz, and Morris (2004) reviewed more than 5,000 insanity evaluations in Virginia over a 10-year period and found that only 9% of those recommended as insane were deemed by evaluators to meet just the volitional prong (as opposed to 44% who met only the cognitive prong and 47% deemed to meet both the volitional and cognitive prongs).

Despite these concerns about the viability of the volitional prong, evaluators in those jurisdictions that still include it are faced with the challenge of obtaining information relevant to this criterion. Rogers (1987) proposed what he called "representative criteria," identifying areas of inquiry that would be useful to consider regarding the individual's capacity for control at the time of the alleged offense. He included five criteria: (a) capacity to make choices, (b) capacity for delay, (c) regard for apprehension, (d) foreseeability and avoidability, and (e) result of a mental disorder. These criteria are discussed in more detail by Packer (2009). These are not additive or quantifiable criteria; rather, they are areas of inquiry that can be used to operationalize the issue of volition. In practice, it is easier to establish that an individual demonstrated volitional control (for instance, by evidence that he or she chose the time and circumstances to act criminally or took clear precautions to avoid apprehension). When the data suggest that these factors were not present, the evaluator is still faced with the difficulty of assessing whether the defendant *did not* exercise control or whether the defendant was impaired in his or her *ability* to conform the conduct.

Antisocial Personality Disorder and Psychopathy

In the ALI (1985) standard, there is a clear statement that the terms "mental disease" and "mental defect" do not include "an abnormality manifested only by repeated criminal or otherwise antisocial conduct" (p. 163). This caveat is included in other standards as well. Using modern nomenclature, this exception would clearly apply to individuals who have been diagnosed with antisocial personality disorder. But, does it apply to the concept of psychopathy as well? The annotated discussion in the ALI MPC indicates that the intent was to exclude psychopathy. Part of the rationale was concern that professional differences about whether psychopathy is indeed a mental illness would create confusion for the courts. This was aptly demonstrated in the case of *In re Rosenfield* (1957). On a Friday, a psychiatrist from St. Elizabeth's Hospital testified that the defendant was not mentally ill because he was diagnosed with sociopathy (an alternative term for psychopathy). However, during the weekend, staff members at the hospital met and determined that as a matter of policy, from that point on, they would consider sociopathy or psychopathy to be a mental disease, and therefore the testimony was reversed. This case was derisively referred to in the *Durham* (1954) decision as the "weekend flip flop case" (p. 978). This example again demonstrates the legal system's limited willingness to defer to clinical definitions when they are applied to the insanity defense.

It is interesting, in this context, to consider the implications for CR issues of recent advances in the understanding of psychopathy. Studies using functional magnetic resonance imaging have implicated the paralimbic system of the brain (e.g., Kiehl, 2006) in psychopathy. There is also evidence of genetic deficits in the neurotransmitter monoamine oxidase A, or MAOA (e.g., Caspi et al., 2002), which have been associated with violent and antisocial behaviors. Although some attempts have been made to introduce this type of evidence in criminal trials (e.g., *Mobley v. State*, 1995), the state of the science is such that application in individual cases is premature (e.g., G. Miller, 2012). The findings are based on group differences, and thus a claim that any given individual committed a violent act due to a genetic predisposition is unwarranted. There are also conceptual problems with such explanations. As several commentators have noted, there is no rational basis for attributing less culpability to an individual whose behavior can be related to biological mechanisms than to one whose behavior can be attributed to environmental causes (e.g., G. Miller, 2012).

Two recent studies have looked at the impact on triers of fact of introducing genetic or physiological evidence as mitigation. Monterosso, Royzman, and Schwartz (2005) presented vignettes to college students and suburban residents and found that these subjects were more willing to attribute causality to physiological explanations of behavior as opposed to experiential explanations (e.g., that the defendant had been physically abused as a child). Aspinwall, Brown, and Tabery (2012), using vignettes with a sample of 181 U.S. trial court judges, found that the judges gave lesser sentences to defendants identified as psychopaths when they were told that psychopathy was caused by a "biomechanism" (i.e., a biological mechanism, including lower levels of MAOA) than when no biomechanism explanation was offered. These two studies highlight the problems identified earlier: Even though biological explanations do not provide a rational basis for lesser culpability, triers of fact are likely to be swayed more by them.

Morse (2008) provided a comprehensive analysis of the arguments for and against the inclusion of psychopathy as a basis for legal insanity. He summarized the argument for considering psychopaths to not be responsible for their behavior as follows: "The psychopath is not responsive to moral reasons, even if they are responsive to other reasons. Consequently, they do not have the capacity for moral rationality, at least when their behavior implicates moral concerns, and thus they are not responsible" (p. 208). Nonetheless, Morse acknowledged that current law does not recognize psychopathy as excusing CR because psychopaths do possess many rational capacities, including an understanding that society considers their behaviors wrongful and subject to punishment. Furthermore, psychopaths do not experience a loss of self-control in the sense of experiencing their impulses as overwhelming. Morse also pointed out the practical obstacles to including psychopaths in the class of excused mentally ill offenders, such as increased resources to provide inpatient psychiatric hospitalization and the lack of current treatment modalities to treat psychopathy. Another practical concern, not cited by Morse, is that if psychopaths

were considered insane, they would be hospitalized alongside other insanity acquittees, who are among the most severely mentally ill individuals. This would create significant risks for this very vulnerable population.

Role of Substance Use

A position that is consistent across jurisdictions is that voluntary intoxication does not constitute a basis for an insanity defense. As with other aspects of the insanity defense, the basis for this caveat is a legal/moral one, not necessarily a clinical one. Thus, even if an individual is so intoxicated as to be severely impaired in his or her ability to appreciate wrongfulness or conform conduct, the legal system does not recognize this as a valid excuse. *Kane v. United States* (1968), for example, expressed the rationale for this caveat by noting that impairing mental disorders are "brought about by circumstances beyond the control of the actor" (p. 735), whereas intoxication is a result of purposeful behavior on the part of the actor. Courts do not credit, for the purposes of the insanity defense, the type of volitional impairment associated with addiction.

Despite this caveat, courts have recognized other situations in which the impairing mental state was related to substance abuse. These include

- Long-term sequelae of substance use (such as dementia);
- Substance-induced psychotic disorders that persist after the period of intoxication has passed;
- Idiosyncratic and unexpected reactions to substances; and
- Sequelae of cessation of substance abuse (e.g., delirium tremens, or DTs).

Fixed insanity. In referring to the first category of long-term sequelae, courts have used the term *fixed insanity* (e.g., *People v. Conrad*, 1986; *People v. Lim Dum Dong*, 1938; *Porreca v. State*, 1981). Most courts have recognized the qualitative distinction between an acutely intoxicated condition and a chronic disorder that was brought about by substance use when the actor was not using substances at the time of the crime. It should be noted, though, that although this is the majority position, at least one court (e.g., *Bieber v. People*, 1993) has not accepted this distinction.

Settled insanity.   The term *settled insanity* has been used to refer to the category of individuals whose psychotic symptoms continue long after the acute intoxication has worn off. The case of *People v. Kelly* (1973) elucidates this issue. Valerie Kelly was convicted of assault with a deadly weapon for attacking her mother with kitchen knives. Testimony at Kelly's trial revealed that she was acutely psychotic and delusional at the time of the incident, as she was experiencing auditory hallucinations and believed that her parents were going to kill her. However, although the judge agreed that Kelly did not understand that her behavior was wrong due to these symptoms, she was nonetheless convicted based on reasoning that her psychotic state had been brought about by her voluntary drug intoxication. Specifically, in the months preceding the assault, Kelly had ingested LSD and mescaline, between 50–100 times, although she was not directly under the influence of either on the day of the assault. The California Supreme Court overturned the verdict, recognizing that the psychotic state was a "settled one"—that is, it may have been initiated by substance use but persisted significantly beyond the period of intoxication. This concept has been adopted by courts in other jurisdictions as well (e.g., *Parker v. State*, 1969).

The language of the *Parker* court is instructive:

> If a person drinks intoxicating liquor and is sane both prior to drinking and after the influences of the intoxicant has worn off, but is insane by the applicable test while under the influence of the intoxicant, he comes under the first category [i.e., will not qualify for the insanity defense]. If he is insane whether or not he is directly under the influence of an intoxicant, even though that insanity was caused by voluntary drinking, he comes under the second category [i.e., can be considered insane]. (p. 388)

Idiosyncratic or pathological intoxication.   The third category of substance abuse relates to idiosyncratic or pathological reaction to alcohol (or other substances). For example, an individual whose mental state becomes impaired in response to a small amount of alcohol that would not be anticipated to cause such a severe reaction would fall under this category. This term is defined in the ALI (1985) standard as "intoxication grossly excessive in degree, given the amount of intoxicant, to which the actor does not know he is susceptible" (p. 366). In the case of *Kane v. United States* (1968), a federal court of appeals focused on the issue of the defendant's knowledge of his susceptibility. The *Kane* court noted that as there was evidence that the defendant was aware of both his lower tolerance for alcohol and the likely impact this would have on his behavior, he would not qualify for the insanity defense. Using this logic, it is likely that when a defendant genuinely experiences a pathological and unanticipated reaction to low levels of alcohol, he or she would likely be able to rely on the impaired mental state as a component of the insanity defense. However, this defense would most likely only be available the first time the defendant has the experience; it would be less tenable to argue that further occurrences were *unanticipated* because the individual already had knowledge of his or her susceptibility.

Withdrawal effects.   A similar analysis, in most jurisdictions, would likely apply to individuals who are experiencing delirium in response to withdrawal from alcohol or other substances (such as anxiolytics or sedative drugs). DTs can result in disorientation, hallucinations, and a loss of reality testing, which could impair an individual's cognitive and volitional capacities related to some criminal offenses (such as violent behavior in response to feeling acutely threatened). This level of impairment may be considered not an effect of intoxication, but an effect of the cessation of intoxication, and thus not be subject to exclusion from the insanity defense. Furthermore, unlike acute effects of inebriation, symptoms of delirium are not an anticipated consequence of substance use. However, as with pathological intoxication, an individual who has had repeated episodes of delirium associated with withdrawal is not as likely to prevail with an insanity defense because he or she would likely have an expectation of such effects (e.g., *People v. Toner*, 1922).

Diminished Capacity or *Mens Rea* Defense

The insanity defense, as noted, is an affirmative defense (i.e., there is a presumption of sanity unless the defense raises insanity as an issue), and if successful, provides a complete defense (i.e., the defendant is found not guilty). By contrast, *diminished capacity* (also referred to as a *mens rea*[2] defense) is a partial defense, referring to a situation in which the defendant does not have the required intent element. Specifically, this defense is used only in crimes that are considered "specific intent" crimes as opposed to "general intent" crimes. For example, assault and battery is considered a general intent crime, but assault and battery with intent to kill is considered a specific intent crime. First-degree murder typically requires the specific intent element of premeditation, as opposed to manslaughter, which does not. If a defendant prevails with such a defense (i.e., successfully rebutting the intent element), he or she will usually be convicted of a lesser offense (e.g., manslaughter). Furthermore, there is no special disposition for these defendants, so they are not subject to psychiatric hospitalization or conditional release.

The earlier-cited case of *Clark v. Arizona* (2006) provides a good example of both the issues involved in diminished capacity defenses and some of the controversy regarding the admissibility of evidence. Eric Clark was driving his truck and blaring loud music in the middle of the night. When a police officer came to investigate, Clark shot him and then left the scene. Clark was charged with first-degree murder under an Arizona statute that requires that the defendant "intentionally or knowingly" kill a law enforcement officer. Clark's defense was that he was under the delusional belief that aliens had infiltrated the town, were impersonating government officials, and were trying to kill him. As a result, Clark's lawyers argued that he did not intend to kill a police

officer but rather believed that he was killing an alien. Based on these claims (which were supported by both the defense and prosecution experts), Clark put forth an insanity defense, although the judge (it was a bench trial) ruled that despite Clark's disorder (schizophrenia, paranoid type), the evidence did not indicate that he was so impaired as to have been unaware that his actions were wrong. Clark then proceeded to present a diminished capacity defense, arguing that he should not be convicted of first-degree murder because he lacked the requisite intent of killing a law enforcement officer. Under Arizona law, Clark was able to call mental health experts to provide evidence relative to the insanity defense, but they could not address the issue of diminished capacity. Rather, only lay witnesses could be called relative to that issue. Clark was convicted of first-degree murder and later appealed to the U.S. Supreme Court.

In a rather controversial ruling, the Supreme Court upheld the constitutionality of the Arizona system, which limited the use of expert testimony in diminished capacity cases. Although recognizing that most other states allow such testimony, the Court upheld Arizona's right to limit expert testimony in this matter on the grounds that expert testimony about a defendant's *capacity* to form the required intent could be confusing to the jury. The Court also noted that unlike the insanity defense (which could result in hospitalization), there was no such provision for a defendant who prevailed with diminished capacity, and therefore a state would have an interest in being more restrictive concerning the latter.

The Supreme Court's focus on testimony regarding capacity to form the requisite intent highlights an important distinction between whether the individual had the capacity to form the intent versus whether he or she actually did form the intent. Both Morse (1979) and Clark (1999) discussed the difficulty for forensic evaluators to identify circumstances under which an individual *could not* form the requisite intent due to a mental disorder or intoxication. Even a paranoid defendant who would qualify for the insanity defense on the grounds that

---

[2]Unfortunately, although the term *mens rea* in this context is used to refer to a specific defense, focused on lack of requisite intent, it is also used, as noted above, to refer to the more general concept of *guilty mind* required for conviction.

he killed a stranger because he thought this man was part of a conspiracy to kill him would nevertheless be considered to have formed the intent to kill. In the *Clark* case, if expert testimony had been permitted, the experts could have testified that Clark's claim that he did not intend to kill a police officer was consistent with his paranoid delusions, and the trier of fact would then decide if he indeed formed the intent. Similar formulations would be relevant when the claim is that intent was not formed due to intoxication. Clark (1999) presents an example of a defendant who was intoxicated and who shot at a police officer through a locked door. Although the defendant claimed that he did not intentionally shoot (i.e., that it was an accident), there would be no basis for a forensic psychologist to opine that he was incapable of forming the intent.

There has also been controversy around this defense due to confusion between diminished capacity and diminished responsibility. The latter term does not focus on intent, but rather suggests a lower level of responsibility, suggesting a "mini" insanity defense. California pioneered this latter development in another example of a well-intentioned but ultimately misguided attempt to broaden the application of psychological expertise to the legal justice system. Bernard Diamond, a well-respected forensic psychiatrist, was in the forefront of this effort, reacting to the narrowness of the M'Naghten standard. His intention was to allow more nuanced and sophisticated testimony about the relationship between various forms of psychopathology and criminal behavior (Diamond, 1961). Indeed, the California Supreme Court expanded the applicability of diminished capacity over a series of cases (e.g., *People v. Gorshen*, 1959; *People v. Poddar*, 1974; *People v. Wolff*, 1964). For instance, even in cases where there was clear evidence that the defendant had planned the homicide, the court ruled that premeditation also required that the defendant be able to "maturely and meaningfully reflect" on the enormity of the planned act (*People v. Wolff*, 1964).

In the case of *People v. Poddar* (1974), where the defendant had not only planned the act but also had conveyed his intentions to his therapist in advance,[3] the court ruled that he could not be convicted of first-degree murder unless the state could prove that Poddar was both "aware of his duty to act within the law and was not incapable of so doing" (Clark, 1999, p. 361).

This broad interpretation of the diminished capacity defense was criticized on conceptual grounds (e.g., Dix, 1971; Morse, 1979) but, as often happens, the final nail in the coffin for California's expansion of the defense resulted from a highly publicized and unpopular case. Dan White shot and killed San Francisco Mayor George Moscone and Harvey Milk, a well-known advocate for gay rights. Despite evidence of premeditation, White used the diminished capacity defense (based on a claim of depression) to successfully rebut a first-degree murder charge and was instead convicted of manslaughter. The resulting public uproar over this outcome ultimately resulted in California's statutes being amended to more narrowly define the mental-state elements required for homicide.[4] In addition, California adopted a "diminished actuality" standard (California Penal Code § 28, 2012), which means that the defendant can present evidence that he or she did not in fact form the requisite intent, which is an element of the crime charged, rather than claim a lack of capacity to do so (Weinstock, Leong, & Silva, 1996).

There is significant variability across jurisdictions regarding diminished capacity: Some states do not recognize it as a defense, some limit it only to homicide cases, and some do not allow evidence of intoxication to be used to negate specific intent. The revision of the federal standards for CR (IDRA, 1984) included a provision that other than the insanity defense, "mental disease or defect does not otherwise constitute a defense" (IDRA, 1984). This provision was interpreted by some courts to mean that diminished capacity could not be used in

---

[3]Poddar is the individual who killed Tatiana Tarasoff, and his disclosure to the therapist created the precedent of therapists having a *duty to protect* (*Tarasoff v. Board of Regents*, 1976).

[4]One of the defense experts commented on White's binging on junk food as one of the contributors to his mental state. This was picked up by the media and was ridiculed as the "Twinkie defense." However, there is no evidence that this particular statement impacted the verdict.

federal courts. However, appeals courts (e.g., *United States v. Cameron*, 1990; *United States v. Frisbee*, 1985; *United States v. Pohlot*, 1987) confirmed that defendants in federal courts could continue to present evidence that they did not have the requisite intent due to either a mental disorder or intoxication. The rationale behind these rulings was that the burden is on the prosecution to prove all elements of a crime, including intent. Thus, if the prosecution could not prove intent, the defendant could not be convicted of that particular offense.

These rulings regarding diminished capacity apply only to federal jurisdictions. Montana's statute explicitly prohibits evidence of intoxication from being used to negate intent. The rationale is similar to the exclusion of intoxication from the insanity defense—that a defendant should not be able to benefit legally from a mental condition caused by voluntary intoxication. This statute was reviewed by the U.S. Supreme Court in the case of *Montana v. Egelhoff* (1996). Egelhoff was charged with two counts of homicide for shooting two victims. The statute required that the state prove that he had acted "knowingly and purposely." Egelhoff attempted to argue that he was too intoxicated (he had a blood alcohol level of .36 an hour after the shootings) to have caused the victims' deaths knowingly and purposely; however, he was not permitted to provide such evidence under Montana law. Egelhoff was convicted and appealed to the U.S. Supreme Court, which ultimately upheld the Montana statute. Although the Montana law was declared constitutional, most other jurisdictions did not follow suit. These states recognize that if the requisite intent were not formed, it is irrelevant whether it was a function of intoxication because it is a basic element of the crime that the prosecution must prove.

Even in these jurisdictions, forensic evaluators have a narrow role to play in applying information about intoxication to the issue of intent. For instance, individuals who experience blackouts during periods of intoxication are unable to remember what transpired during that period; however, this does not mean that they did not act intentionally.

Indeed, one feature of a blackout is that other people describe the individual as engaging in purposeful and intentional behaviors while intoxicated. One of the effects of alcohol is to disrupt memory consolidation so that the person does not remember the next day what he or she did. Nevertheless, a lack of memory does not imply a lack of intent.

RESEARCH REVIEW

Several studies have addressed the reliability of CR evaluations. Stock and Poythress (1979) reported on simultaneous interviews that were conducted by pairs of psychologists in the same facility in Michigan. In that small sample, there was a very high rate of agreement (97%) between the evaluations. Fukunaga, Pasewark, Hawkins, and Gudeman (1981) used a sample of 335 defendants in Hawaii, each evaluated independently by two psychiatrists, and also reported a high rate of agreement (92%). In that system, however, the psychiatrists were able to confer prior to offering their opinions, so the data do not indicate their independent agreement. Similarly, Phillips, Wolf, and Coons (1988), in a sample of 66 cases in Alaska, reported a 76% rate of agreement, although those opinions were also not independent of each other. Raifman (1979), in a larger study of 214 cases in Arizona, found a 64% rate of agreement between pairs of psychiatrists. In that sample, one of the psychiatrists was chosen by the defense and the other by the prosecution. It should be noted that the first three studies were in jurisdictions using the ALI standard, and the last used the M'Naghten standard.

More recently, Gowensmith, Murrie, and Boccaccini (2012) examined a large sample (165 cases, 483 reports) in Hawaii. The examiners were psychologists and psychiatrists who offered independent opinions using the ALI standard. In that state, three independent evaluators are appointed for each case and, unlike the situation in the Fukunaga et al. (1981) study, do not confer among themselves prior to issuing their report. In this recent study, the three evaluators reached unanimous agreement in 55%–61% of the cases.[5] In this sample, the base rate of

[5]The authors reported rates of agreement using different formulas. The 61% agreement figure includes those cases in which two of the evaluators agreed and the third did not give an opinion. The lower rate of 55% counted those cases as disagreements.

recommendations across all evaluators for a finding of insanity was 36%. Therefore, by chance, one would expect only 5% of cases to result in unanimous agreement that the defendant was insane and 26% unanimous agreement that the defendant was sane. The actual numbers were 17% unanimity about insanity (an odds ratio of more than 3) and 38% unanimity about sanity (an odds ratio of almost 1.5).

The results of this last study (Gowensmith et al., 2012), which had a large sample size of independent evaluators, provides useful information about reliability and also raises questions for future research. It is noteworthy that the rate of agreement was highest in cases in which there was agreement about the presence of a psychotic disorder or when the defendant had been psychiatrically hospitalized shortly before the offense. The rate of agreement was lowest when the defendant was intoxicated (alcohol or drugs) at the time of the alleged offense. Thus, several different factors that could impact the reliability of CR evaluations are worth considering for future research.

- *Diagnostic disagreement:* Given the data on the high proportion of insanity acquittees with a psychotic diagnosis, the extent of agreement on the presence/absence of a psychotic disorder is likely to have a significant impact on the evaluator's decision (and indeed, there was less disagreement in the Gowensmith et al. [2012] study when all agreed on the presence of psychosis). Is the rate of agreement on psychosis lower in CR evaluations than in clinical settings?
- *Adversarial allegiance:* In the Gowensmith et al. (2012) study, all of the evaluators were court appointed. Are the rates of agreement lower when evaluators are retained independently by the defense and prosecution rather than by the court? Data from sex offender evaluations (Murrie et al., 2009) suggest that *adversarial allegiance* (i.e., bias toward the side retaining the evaluator) impacts certain types of clinical assessments (particularly psychopathy). However, there are no clear data on whether this also applies in CR evaluations.
- *Nature of the disagreement:* Given that insanity is a legal, not a clinical, concept, we would expect

a lack of unanimity to occur even when evaluators come to the same diagnostic formulation. For instance, in the context of a delusional belief, how *substantially* impaired was the defendant's capacity to appreciate the wrongfulness of the conduct? If evaluators were to disagree on the threshold but clearly delineate their opinions, this lack of agreement would not be concerning. The finding by Gowensmith et al. (2012) that disagreement was highest in cases involving intoxication is relevant to this issue. As discussed earlier, distinguishing the relative contributions of substance abuse and mental illness can be murky from a legal perspective. In addition, it is also one of the most difficult clinical tasks associated with a CR evaluation (e.g., Packer, 2009). Thus, it would be helpful to conduct more fine-grained analyses about the nature of the disagreements found.

Who Is Found Legally Insane?

Public perceptions about the insanity defense tend to be inaccurate. For instance, there is a misconception that the insanity defense is frequently used and often successful (e.g., Appelbaum, 1982; Steadman et al., 1993). In reality, a reasonable estimate is that no more than 1% of felony defendants raise the insanity defense and, when it is raised, it is successful only approximately 25% of the time (Melton, Petrila, Poythress, & Slobogin, 2007). Furthermore, defendants who are acquitted by reason of insanity may end up spending more time committed to an institution than if they had been convicted (e.g., Steadman et al., 1993). This is illustrated clearly by the case of *Jones v. United States* (1983). Jones was found NGRI for the crime of larceny (specifically, stealing a jacket from a department store). Although the larceny occurred in 1975 and the maximum sentence he would have served if convicted would have been 1 year, 8 years later Jones was still committed to a psychiatric hospital. He appealed, arguing that he should not have been subject to a commitment period that exceeded the maximum sentence he could have served. However, the U.S. Supreme Court upheld his continued hospitalization on the grounds that there is no relationship between the sentence for the crime (for the purposes of retribution, deterrence, and/or rehabilitation) and the length of hospitalization (for the purpose of treatment and protection of the individual and society).

Furthermore, even after release from a hospital, an insanity acquittee may be subject to prolonged periods of monitoring in the community and can be easily rehospitalized. In many jurisdictions, insanity acquittees are subject to what is known as *conditional release*; that is, their continued freedom from hospitalization can be made dependent on certain conditions (such as abstinence from using substances, compliance with treatment), and they are subject to being recommitted at a lower threshold than is required for civil commitment. Indeed, data from jurisdictions with conditional release (e.g., Wiederanders, Bromley, & Choate, 1997) indicate that individuals who are conditionally released are more likely to be rehospitalized than to be reincarcerated.

A number of studies have examined the diagnostic distribution of individuals who have been recommended (or adjudicated) as insane. In a study of 50 defendants who were found NGRI of homicide in Michigan, compared with a randomly selected (within-gender) group of homicide defendants evaluated for sanity but convicted, Packer (1987) found that 82% of the acquittees had a diagnosis of a psychotic disorder versus only 14% of the convictees. Callahan, Steadman, McGreevy, and Robbins (1991) collected data across eight states and found that 84% of insanity acquittees had been diagnosed with a major mental illness (i.e., schizophrenia, other psychotic disorder, or an affective disorder). In a study of 1,710 federal defendants, Cochrane, Grisso, and Frederick (2001) found that those with a diagnosis of psychosis had the highest likelihood of being adjudicated NGRI. A study in Virginia (Warren et al., 2004) found that 65% of defendants recommended as NGRI had received a diagnosis of psychosis (as contrasted with only 26% of those recommended as sane).

Taken together, these studies indicate that most defendants who are found to be NGRI are diagnosed with a psychotic disorder. This is consistent with the recommendation of the American Psychiatric Association (1983) that, for the purpose of the insanity defense, the requisite mental *disease* should be limited to "only those severely abnormal mental conditions that grossly and demonstrably impair a person's perception or understanding of reality" (p. 685). However, it is also important to recognize that the presence of a psychotic disorder is not sufficient for a finding of insanity. Although the majority of insanity acquittees have been diagnosed with a psychotic disorder, this does not mean that the majority of individuals with a psychotic disorder are recommended as insane. For instance, in the Cochrane et al. (2001) study, 60% of individuals with a psychotic disorder were recommended as criminally responsible. This is consistent with the basic principle that insanity is ultimately a legal decision, not a clinical diagnosis. Further, the Cochrane et al. study offers a strong rebuttal to misconceptions that the insanity defense is used broadly and exploited. (It should be noted that although most insanity acquittals are based on mental illness, individuals who are diagnosed with mental retardation could also qualify for the defense based on meeting criteria for "mental defect.")

Attempts to modify policies affecting the insanity defense have met with mixed success. As stated earlier, the case that most significantly affected both public opinion and policy involved John Hinckley. Following Hinckley's acquittal by reason of insanity, many jurisdictions amended their laws, policies, and procedures regarding the insanity defense. Steadman et al. (1993) studied reforms in five states and found that (a) adjudication reform (i.e., changing the insanity defense standard, eliminating the volitional prong) had little impact on either the rate that insanity defenses were raised or their success (in California); (b) changing the burden of proof (i.e., instead of requiring the state to prove that the defendant was sane, the defendant was required to prove that he or she was insane) appeared to decrease the rate of insanity defenses being raised (in New York and Georgia); and (c) abolishing the insanity defense (in Montana) resulted in a significant increase in the number of defendants adjudicated as incompetent to stand trial, many of whose charges were dismissed or deferred. In other words, some severely mentally ill individuals were still diverted from the criminal justice system, but through the mechanism of incompetence to stand trial rather than through an insanity acquittal.

Quality of CR Reports

There is a limited literature concerning the quality of CR reports. Heilbrun and Collins (1995) reviewed a sample of 277 reports from Florida, which included both competence to stand trial and CR, in both hospital and community settings. They found that

- a majority of the reports in the community failed to note that the defendant had been informed about the purpose of the interview;
- fewer than half of the reports included collateral sources of information; and
- only approximately half of the reports articulated how the results obtained related directly to the legal prong of the insanity standard.

A subsequent study in Florida (Otto, Barnes, & Jacobson, 1996) found that only 10% of CR reports included data from third-party sources. In a large study in Virginia (5,171 reports over a 10-year period), Warren et al. (2004) found that in the majority of cases, evaluators offered opinions about sanity without having adequate data (including, in some cases, failure to obtain a police report, witness statements, or the defendant's criminal record). By contrast, in a study of the results of a quality improvement project in Massachusetts in which 102 CR reports were reviewed blindly by a panel of three experienced forensic evaluators, Packer and Leavitt (1998) found that 80% were rated as having obtained sufficient data to address the CR issue. Perhaps more significantly, given the studies noted here, as well as data from studies on competence to stand trial (e.g., Nicholson & Norwood, 2000; Skeem & Golding, 1998), 72% of the CR reports were rated as having provided clear reasoning for the conclusions offered. It is noteworthy that these more positive findings occurred in a jurisdiction with the most intensive training program for forensic psychologists and psychiatrists who provide CR evaluations in the public sector (Fein et al., 1991; Frost, deCamara, & Earl, 2006).

PRACTICE AND POLICY ISSUES

In addition to differences across jurisdictions concerning the standard to be used for the insanity defense, there are also differences in the burden and standards of proof. Some jurisdictions place the burden of proving sanity on the prosecution, with the standard ranging from *preponderance of the evidence* (least stringent) to *beyond a reasonable doubt* (most stringent). Other jurisdictions place the burden on the defendant to prove that he or she was insane by preponderance of the evidence or *clear and convincing evidence* (an intermediate standard). It is important for evaluators to keep in mind that their role is not to address these legal standards; rather, the forensic clinician can convey the strength of the data and conclusions and leave it up to the trier of fact to decide whether this meets the legal burden.

Appointment or Retention as a Forensic Evaluator

A forensic psychologist can become involved in a CR case either through appointment by the court or by being retained by one of the parties involved (i.e., prosecution or defense). Depending on the source of the referral and the jurisdiction involved, there can be differences in terms of how, and with whom, the evaluator communicates with the parties. In court-ordered evaluations, some jurisdictions provide for the report to be sent only to the court; others require that the report be shared with all parties. The forensic evaluator must be aware at the outset of the case what the procedures are in the particular jurisdiction. These procedures determine what the evaluator informs the defendant of prior to beginning the evaluation and also might limit communications. The reason for this heightened concern is that CR evaluations require a detailed inquiry of the defendant's version of the alleged offense, which typically contains much incriminating information. Premature release of such information to the prosecutor can jeopardize the defendant's constitutional rights (e.g., Fifth Amendment right against self-incrimination). Although there are legal protections preventing the prosecution from introducing the defendant's statements to the evaluator as evidence of guilt (except for the purposes of proving the requisite mental state), there is a risk that the prosecutor may be able to use the information in a secondary manner to generate other evidence. Thus, evaluators must take special care in communicating with the prosecution consistent with the local laws and policies.

Even when the evaluator is retained directly by the defense, the issue of discovery will depend on the jurisdiction. For instance, in the case of *Edney v. Smith* (1976), an appellate court ruled that the prosecution could subpoena an expert who had been retained by the defense (who had arrived at an opinion that the defendant did not meet the insanity standard). The *Edney* court recognized that this impinged on the ability of the defense to obtain a confidential expert opinion but nonetheless decided that this was superseded by "the strong counterbalancing interest of the State in accurate fact-finding by its courts" (p. 1054). By contrast, the court in *United States v. Alvarez* (1975) recognized the importance of preserving the defendant's rights and ruled that the prosecution could not have access to or call the defense witness to testify. Thus, because laws differ across jurisdictions, it is incumbent on the forensic evaluator to be knowledgeable about the applicable laws in his or her jurisdiction.

Forensic evaluators in CR cases should also be aware of how the referral source could potentially impact their impartiality. Zusman and Simon (1983) described the process of *forensic identification* by which evaluators come to identify with the interest of the party that retained them. Murrie et al. (2009) found evidence of differences in evaluations attributable to *adversarial allegiance* (i.e., ratings of evaluees were significantly affected by the side that retained the evaluator). Although these articles focused on personal injury and sex offender commitment cases, respectively, the principles identified apply to CR evaluations as well. Forensic clinicians who are aware of the potential bias of forensic identification are more likely to be able to counteract the bias. For example, Rogers and Shuman (2000) recommended that forensic evaluators in CR cases refrain from discussing their initial impressions of the case with the retaining attorney until they have

completed a thorough evaluation (in order to minimize subtle or overt pressure from the attorney).

Avoiding Conflicts of Interest

When possible, forensic psychologists should avoid accepting a referral for a defendant with whom they have had a previous treatment relationship. Greenberg and Shuman (1997) elucidated the significant differences between the roles of therapist and forensic evaluator, which can create significant conflict. The *Specialty Guidelines for Forensic Psychology* (American Psychological Association [APA], 2013) include a statement that "providing forensic and therapeutic psychological services to the same individual or closely related individuals involves multiple relationships that may impair objectivity and/or cause exploitation or other harm" (p. 11). Nonetheless, the guidelines include the recognition that in some cases (e.g., in very small communities), there may be overriding considerations that necessitate such dual roles and, in those circumstances, the psychologist should "seek to minimize the potential negative effects of this circumstance" (p. 11).

Another type of dual role arises when a forensic psychologist is asked by an attorney to serve both as an evaluator and as a consultant. These roles impose contradictory expectations and role boundaries. The forensic evaluator is expected to be neutral and impartial in arriving at an opinion about the CR issue, whereas a consultant is typically hired to work on behalf of the retaining attorney, and thus is not impartial. Therefore, psychologists should avoid being retained in a dual role. After completing an impartial evaluation, an evaluator may then change roles and become a consultant; however, reversing that process is problematic as it likely interferes with the psychologist's requirement to provide an objective evaluation.

Third-Party Sources of Information

In order to conduct a thorough CR evaluation, it is important to rely on multiple sources of data, including official records as well as information obtained from third-party sources (e.g., Heilbrun, Warren, & Picarello, 2003; Packer, 2009). Typically, the evaluator will have access to a police report of the alleged offense. It is advisable to obtain as much detailed information on the event as possible, including statements made by the defendant to the police as well as witness statements. Records of previous treatment (inpatient and outpatient) are often very helpful in developing a picture of the defendant's mental health history. The forensic psychologist's ability to obtain such information will differ by jurisdiction. Some states require the defendant to authorize release of such privileged records; others allow for the records to be released as part of the order for the CR evaluation.

Third-party sources, also referred to as *collateral informants*, may include family members, friends, or others who can describe the defendant's functioning over time. The defendant's consent is typically not required to contact such sources. When contacting these individuals, the forensic evaluator should clearly explain the purpose of the interview and clarify that any information provided can be used in the report and in testimony. It is not appropriate to have the informant provide information off the record. This would create an ethical problem as the information could influence the evaluator's conclusions but would not be disclosed to the attorneys, and thus would not be subject to discovery and cross-examination.

In addition to these sources, it is often helpful to obtain information directly from individuals who observed the defendant close in time to the alleged offense, including witnesses and police officers. It is best to contact these individuals through the attorneys or the court. Victims and witnesses may be made uncomfortable when they are contacted by an evaluator whom they do not know. It is therefore advisable to arrange for such interviews through either the retaining attorney or the prosecutor's office (if court ordered). Many prosecutors' offices have victim–witness units that can be helpful in arranging for an interview.

Forensic evaluators should be aware of some of the issues related to the admissibility of information that is obtained from third-party sources. None of the issues described below should deter the evaluator from fully pursuing these sources; however, awareness of potential limitations on the admissibility of such information can aid the evaluator in finding additional corroborations. Rule 703 of the Federal Rules of Evidence (703; state rules of evidence are similar), for example, provides that

> [t]he facts or data in the particular case upon which an expert bases an opinion or inference may be those perceived by or made known to the expert at or before the hearing. If of a type reasonably relied upon by experts in the particular field in forming opinions or inferences upon the subject, the facts or data need not be admissible in evidence in order for the opinion or inference to be admitted. Facts or data that are otherwise inadmissible shall not be disclosed to the jury by the proponent of the opinion or inference unless the court determines that their probative value in assisting the jury to evaluate the expert's opinion substantially outweighs their prejudicial effect.

This rule allows more leeway for experts to testify about information that has been obtained from other sources that are typically and reasonably relied on in the field of psychology. These include both psychological and psychiatric records as well as information obtained from collateral sources. However, it may be up to the judge in a particular case to rule whether the information is otherwise considered prejudicial to the defendant and thus cannot be admitted. The case of *People v. Goldstein* (2005) provides a good example of this balancing of interests. In this case, a third-party source informed the psychiatrist that the victim was similar in appearance to another woman who had previously teased the defendant. The psychiatrist took this into account in terms of arriving at an opinion regarding Goldstein's motives and mental state. The defense argued that this uncorroborated information was too prejudicial (as the jury may have credited this information as factual) and, on appeal, the court ruled that the information should not have been admitted. This case highlights that the decision about admissibility may be made after the fact by the court, and that forensic evaluators are often not in a position to know ahead of time whether certain information will be admitted. The implication is not that forensic evaluators should be deterred from seeking collateral sources whenever relevant; rather, they should be thoughtful about whether they can find further corroboration if there is a question about admissibility. This can sometimes be accomplished by asking the defendant directly. For example, if the defendant confirms a collateral informant's report of an incident that is not otherwise recorded, the problem is avoided. If the defendant denies the incident, then further corroboration from other sources would likely be required. This problem can also be remedied by the attorneys involved; if they call the third party to testify as a fact witness, then the information will be admitted and can be relied on by the evaluator.

Conducting the CR Evaluation

At the initiation of the evaluation, the forensic evaluator must inform the defendant of the purpose of the evaluation, the evaluator's role, and the limits on confidentiality and privilege. The term *privilege* refers to the legal principle that certain communications from an individual cannot be used as evidence in court. Typically, statements made to a treating psychologist cannot be revealed, with limited exceptions. However, statements made to a forensic evaluator, once the defendant has been informed of the exception, are usually admissible. It is important that the defendant understand that he or she is not speaking to a treating professional, whose role is therapeutic, but rather to an objective forensic evaluator. Thus, it is important both from a legal perspective as well as from a professional ethical perspective to fully inform the individual of the evaluator's role prior to proceeding with the interview (APA, 2010, § 9.03; APA, 2013, § 6.03).

It is particularly important in CR evaluations for the evaluator to inform the defendant of his or her role because the evaluation involves detailed inquiry into the specifics of the alleged offense, which can provide incriminating information. Although this information is not admissible as evidence to establish guilt (other than for a mental state element), statements made by the defendant may lead the prosecutor to other evidence (known legally as "fruits of the statement") that could negatively impact the defendant. Thus, it is necessary not only

to provide this explanation to the defendant, but also to assess his or her understanding of it. If the defendant does not understand the explanation, given the high stakes involved, the best practice is to contact the attorney or court for guidance (Packer, 2009).

Presence of Defense Attorney During CR Evaluations

Defense attorneys may request that they be allowed to sit in on the CR evaluation. This allows them to observe directly the questions asked by the evaluator and the defendant's responses. However, the presence of the attorney could interfere with the evaluation, particularly if the defendant is looking for the attorney to provide cues or guidance about how to respond. The American Bar Association's (2012) Criminal Justice Standards section on mental health recommends that it is up to the forensic evaluator to decide whether to allow the defense attorney to be present, although it is never acceptable to allow the prosecutor to sit in.

The issue of having the defense attorney present during a CR evaluation has been addressed by a number of courts. The majority position is that the defendant does not have a right to have an attorney present during a CR evaluation. However, as these courts have not prohibited such a practice, they leave the decision up to the discretion of the trial judge (e.g., *Commonwealth v. Baldwin*, 1997; *People v. Larsen*, 1977). Because the evaluation is considered a *critical stage* of the process, some courts have ruled that the defendant does have a right to attorney presence (e.g., *Houston v. State*, 1979; *Lee v. County Court of Erie County*, 1971).

In those cases in which an attorney is present, the forensic evaluator should take precautions to avoid interference with the evaluation. Such precautions include attending to the seating arrangements such that the attorney is not within the line of sight of the defendant and informing the attorney not to speak or communicate with the client during the evaluation. A less intrusive approach is to audiotape or videotape the evaluation (the American Bar Association, 2012, specifically recommends this approach for all CR evaluations that are conducted on behalf of the prosecution, although again there is no clear judicial consensus). However, even when taping an interview, care should be taken to avoid recording any psychological testing, which could compromise test security (APA, 2010, § 9.11).

Style of Interviewing

The CR interview requires a different approach than a standard clinical assessment. In addition to specific areas of inquiry, there are differences in the style of the interactions (e.g., Greenberg & Shuman, 1997; Heilbrun, Grisso, & Goldstein, 2008). As the purpose of the CR evaluation is to arrive at an objective assessment, the forensic evaluator should treat the defendant's account as simply one source of data that requires corroboration. The defendant's self-report may be accurate but also could reflect unconscious or conscious (i.e., attempts to present as either more or less pathological) distortions. This critical attitude requires the evaluator, at times, to confront the evaluee about conflicting data. This does not mean that the evaluator should adopt an adversarial tone; rather, what is required is a clear, firm, yet respectful approach to explaining that there are inconsistencies, either internal ones between different statements the evaluee has given or external ones between the individual's accounts and collateral data (Packer & Grisso, 2011). In addition, given the high percentage of racial, ethnic, and cultural minorities in the criminal justice system, forensic evaluators must be cognizant of how these different backgrounds may affect both the presentation of symptoms as well as attitude toward the evaluator (e.g., Gaines, 1995; Tseng, Matthews, & Elwyn, 2004).

Elements of the CR Evaluation

There is widespread agreement about the essential elements required in a CR evaluation (Borum & Grisso, 1995; Giorgi-Guarnieri et al., 2002; Packer, 2009). These include relevant aspects of the defendant's history, mental status, and account of the alleged offense. The following sections provide a brief synopsis of these essential elements.

History. These include standard elements of history taking used in clinical assessments (see Exhibit 4.1),

---

> **Exhibit 4.1**
> **Historical Information Relevant to Criminal Responsibility Evaluations**
>
> - Family and developmental history
> - Educational history
> - Social history
> - Employment history
> - Mental health history
> - Medical history
> - Religious history (in some cases)
> - Substance use history
> - Criminal history

---

with specialized focus on areas that are particularly relevant to CR issues. The latter include

- *Criminal history:* A careful review of previous criminal history (including arrests, convictions, and previous insanity acquittals) is helpful in placing the defendant's behavior in context. For instance: Is the current alleged offense out of character for this individual? If the defendant has a prior criminal history, have the charges occurred in the context of acute mental illness or substance abuse? This information should be obtained both from direct inquiry of the evaluee as well as by review of criminal history records available (known as a *rap sheet*). Formal records typically contain only the name of the charge and the disposition; therefore, information about the specifics of the crimes should be obtained directly from the defendant and collateral informants.
- *Substance abuse history:* Although information about substance use is a standard part of a clinical assessment, a more focused inquiry is required for CR issues due to the legal implications of such use for mental-state defenses (see earlier discussion). This may include
  - whether the defendant was intoxicated at the time of the alleged offense;
  - last use of substances prior to the alleged offense;
  - relationship of substance abuse to symptoms of mental illness (i.e., Does the defendant

experience symptoms of mental illness independent of substance use? Do the symptoms emerge only when the defendant is intoxicated? Are the symptoms present but exacerbated by substance use?);

- whether there was evidence of withdrawal symptoms around the time of the alleged offense; and

- access to any toxicology tests performed close in time to the alleged offense.

Mental status. A standard mental status evaluation is considered an essential component of CR evaluations (e.g., Borum & Grisso, 1995); however, CR evaluations often take place many weeks or months after the time of the alleged offense. Thus, the forensic evaluator should be cautious about extrapolating from information that was obtained about mental functioning at the time of the interview to the mental state at the time of the alleged offense. Nonetheless, the mental status examination can provide insight into longstanding symptoms as well as the individual's current understanding of any symptoms that have remitted (e.g., when a defendant describes previously held delusions but now is able to express insight into their irrationality).

Defendant's account of the alleged offense. Perhaps the core unique element of a CR evaluation is the questioning of the defendant about his or her account of the alleged offense. This involves obtaining not only a detailed account of what the defendant did but also of his or her thoughts and emotions around that time. This is a retrospective evaluation, meaning that the evaluator must construct a formulation regarding the defendant's mental state at some point in the past, based on the individual's current description, integrated with other sources of information. In doing so, it is important for the evaluator to conduct the interview in a manner that minimizes leading questions and maintains the distinction between current thoughts and feelings from those present at the time of the alleged offense. When asked to reflect on reasons and motivations for past behaviors, individuals tend to reconstruct based on their current understanding (e.g., Nisbett & Wilson, 1977). This problem can be compounded when the defendant's

mental state at the time of the evaluation is significantly different than what it was at the time of the alleged offense (which frequently occurs for defendants who were acutely mentally ill but have since been treated, or individuals who were intoxicated at the time of the incident but are sober during the evaluation).

In recognition of these issues, the evaluator should be cognizant of the need to ask questions that focus on the defendant's thoughts, feelings, and behaviors *at the time of the alleged offense.* Thus, asking questions such as "Why did you enter the building?" is less helpful than reframing as "What were you thinking when you entered the building?" The evaluator should also begin this part of the evaluation by using an open-ended approach, asking the defendant to provide his or her own description of the relevant time period. Only after obtaining such an account should the evaluator ask very specific questions regarding the defendant's symptoms, thoughts regarding wrongfulness, and questions relative to the ability to control behavior. It is also helpful to have the defendant begin the narrative by providing the relevant context. This may include information about his or her functioning in the days or weeks prior to the alleged offense as well as information about the defendant's relationship with the victim (if relevant). It is also frequently important to obtain a timeline of the defendant's use of medications as well as alcohol and drugs around the time of the alleged offense.

The level of detail involved in this inquiry exceeds what is usually obtained in clinical settings. The forensic evaluator has to ask very specific, probing questions—a *microanalysis.* For example, if a defendant reports that she shot the victim twice, the evaluator may need to ask her exactly what transpired in between the two shots, what she was thinking, and how she was feeling. The style of questioning will likely need to be tailored to the individual situation because some crimes involve very disturbing and difficult elements (e.g., sex offenses, crimes with high degrees of violence).

Once the defendant has provided an account of the incident, more focused questions relative to the legal standard are usually required. For the cognitive prong, this includes questions about the defendant's thoughts at the time regarding whether he or she understood and appreciated the illegality and wrongfulness of the act. When a defendant reports thinking at the time that the behavior was legally or morally justified, additional probing is required. The evaluator needs to obtain adequate data to allow for a full assessment of whether and how the defendant's symptoms at the time interfered with (or did not) his or her appreciation of wrongfulness. Evaluators need to be sensitive not just to the possibility of overreporting of symptoms and dysfunction (malingering), but also to the possibility of underreporting (dissimulation).

As discussed above, assessment of the volitional prong is particularly difficult. The representative criteria recommended by Rogers (1987) can help in the formulation of relevant questions such as the following:

- Did the defendant consider other options besides the course of action chosen? If so, what were the reasons for rejecting those alternatives?
- How long before committing the alleged offense did the defendant decide to act? What were the reasons for delaying before acting?
- Did the defendant take steps to avoid detection (either in preparation for the act or afterward)?

These are not only questions that the evaluator should ask the defendant; rather, they are also questions that can be informed by behavioral evidence (e.g., if the defendant put on a ski mask to avoid identification or hid behind a door and waited to steal an item until there was no one around). Furthermore, the data need to be considered holistically; that is, information about any one of these components must be understood in context. For example, a defendant may describe choosing between alternatives but nonetheless describe a circumstance under which he felt compelled to act in order to prevent a dire consequence that was rooted in a delusion.

A common technique that purportedly addresses the volitional prong is known as the *policeman at the elbow* test (i.e., asking the defendant whether he or she would have committed the act if a police officer had been present).

The implication is that if the defendant could have resisted committing the act in the presence of the police, then he or she maintained volitional control. Although this question may be useful for generating additional data, it should be used and interpreted very cautiously (Packer, 2009). The most significant limitation of this question is that it presents a hypothetical situation and requires the individual to answer in the present what he or she *would* have done at some point in the past (as opposed to asking what he or she actually did). The validity of such a reconstruction, in terms of assessing the individual's mental state at the time of the incident, is limited. This problem is exacerbated when the defendant is in a different mental state at the time of the interview relative to the time of the crime. The defendant's ability in such circumstances to accurately consider how he or she might have reacted in the past, in a different mental state, may be very limited.

This critique does not mean that the policeman at the elbow test should not be used. It can be very helpful if it leads to an inquiry into whether, at the time of the incident, the defendant had considered the possibility of apprehension. The focus would then be on what the defendant was thinking at the time rather than on what he or she now thinks would have happened. It is also important to understand that some defendants may not be deterred by police presence for reasons unrelated to mental illness, and indeed some crimes involve attacks on police. In those situations, further inquiry would be needed into the defendant's rationale at the time for continuing with the behavior even in the presence of the police officer.

Use of Psychological Tests

Surveys of forensic evaluators have indicated that the use of psychological testing in CR evaluations is common but is not required in all cases. Borum and Grisso (1996) surveyed a group of forensic psychologists and found that 57% reported using tests almost always (i.e., >80% of the time) in CR evaluations, and 11% reported frequent use (41%–80%). The authors concluded that the use of testing is the norm and that "psychologists ought to be held accountable to explain why they have *not* used psychological testing" (p. 471) in a CR case in which testing was not employed.

In that same study (Borum & Grisso, 1996), the psychologists who reported using tests at least occasionally were asked to identify which instruments they used most often. The two tests that were reported as used most frequently were the Minnesota Multiphasic Personality Inventory—2nd edition (MMPI–2; Butcher et al., 2001) and the Wechsler Adult Intelligence Scale—3rd edition (WAIS–III; Wechsler, 1997) (Borum & Grisso, 1995). A little less than one-third of the respondents reported using the Rorschach (Exner, 2001) in CR cases. Lally (2003) surveyed all psychologists who were listed as diplomates in forensic psychology by the American Board of Professional Psychology. Rather than ask which tests they used, he framed the question in terms of whether they thought a test was *recommended, acceptable*, or *unacceptable* for use in CR evaluations. Sixty-four psychologists responded to the survey. Similar to the Borum and Grisso (1995) results, the only tests recommended for CR evaluations by more than half of the respondents were the MMPI–2 and the WAIS–III. However, the following tests were also considered acceptable by more than half of those surveyed: Personality Assessment Inventory (PAI; Morey, 1991); Millon Clinical Multiaxial Inventory—III (Millon, 1994); Stanford–Binet Revised (Thorndike, Hagen, & Sattler, 1986); Rogers Criminal Responsibility Assessment Scales (RCRAS; Rogers, 1984); and neuropsychological batteries (Halstead–Reitan and Luria–Nebraska). More than half of the respondents indicated that projective drawings (Thematic Apperception Test; Murray, 1943) and sentence completion were unacceptable. Lally categorized the Rorschach test as "equivocal–unacceptable" because the responses were split between psychologists considering it unacceptable and psychologists who found it acceptable.

In reviewing these data, it is important to consider changes over time. For instance, in the 1995 study by Borum and Grisso, the PAI was not cited as a test that are used by most evaluators. By 2003, the respondents in Lally's study rated the PAI as acceptable. In a 2006 study of forensic psychologists that focused on test use across forensic evaluations (not limited to CR evaluations), Archer, Buffington-Vollum, Stredny, and Handel (2006) found that the MMPI–2 and the PAI were the most frequently cited inventories, and the WAIS–III was the most widely cited intelligence test. Packer (2009) noted that the PAI is a newer instrument than the MMPI, and that data on its use in forensic settings are relatively recent (e.g., Morey, Warner, & Hopwood, 2007). Similarly, the restructured version of the MMPI is too new to have been included in the published studies. Thus, forensic psychologists should be guided in their use of these tests by advances in the literature regarding the reliability and validity of newer instruments.

Use of the Rorschach in CR cases. There is no consensus within the fields of forensic psychology and psychiatry regarding the use of the Rorschach for CR evaluations. Weiner (2007) cited evidence that the Rorschach has been accepted by courts for a variety of forensic evaluations, and he provided data regarding its utility, including in CR cases. However, other researchers have raised concerns about the Rorschach's reliability and validity (e.g., Lilienfeld, Wood, & Garb, 2000) as well as its acceptability in court proceedings (Grove, Barden, Garb, & Lilienfeld, 2002) per legal standards established for admissibility of tests and methodologies (*Daubert v. Merrell Dow Pharmaceuticals, Inc.*, 1993). Nevertheless, even these critics agree that there is good evidence of the validity of the Rorschach for the specific purpose of detecting thought disorder. Thus, when there are questions about whether a particular defendant, who may otherwise be quite guarded, is indeed experiencing a thought disorder (such as schizophrenia), the Rorschach could be helpful in addressing this issue (Packer, 2009). In this circumstance, the test is not being used to address legal insanity per se but rather as one source of information relative to the issue of whether the defendant meets the threshold criterion for being considered to have a mental illness that is legally relevant.

Symptom validity tests. Given the importance of verifying defendants' self-reports in forensic evaluations, forensic evaluators should use standardized tests to assess the validity of reported symptoms.

Although test results should be integrated with a thorough clinical assessment, the validity of unstructured clinical interviews as the sole method for detecting malingering has not been supported (e.g., Melton et al., 2007; Ogloff, 1990). There are validity scales embedded in standardized clinical instruments (such as the MMPI–2, PAI) that address both the exaggeration and minimization of symptoms; however, employment of tests designed specifically to assess symptom validity "should be considered the standard of practice whenever there is a basis for suspecting overreporting of symptoms" (Packer, 2009, p. 120) in CR evaluations.

In the Archer et al. (2006) study, the tests most often cited by forensic psychologists for the assessment of malingering were the Structured Interview of Reported Symptoms (SIRS; Rogers, Bagby, & Dickens, 1992) for assessing psychiatric symptoms[6] and the Test of Memory Malingering (TOMM; Tombaugh, 1996) and the Validity Indicator Profile (VIP; Frederick, 1997) for assessing cognitive symptoms. As noted above, other instruments may become more widely used over time (e.g., screening instruments such as the Structured Inventory of Malingered Symptomatology [SIMS; Smith & Burger, 1997] and the Miller—Forensic Assessment of Symptoms Test [M–FAST; H. A. Miller, 2001]), and forensic evaluators should stay updated on the burgeoning literature in the field.

Rogers Criminal Responsibility Assessment Scales. In addition to these clinical tests, the other instrument cited by forensic psychologists for use in CR evaluations, as noted above, is the RCRAS. This is a *forensic assessment instrument* because it directly addresses the psycholegal issue. Although in the Borum and Grisso study (1995), only a minority of forensic psychologists (approximately one third) reported ever using the RCRAS, the vast majority of respondents (94%) in the Lally (2003) study rated it as acceptable. Thus, although experienced forensic psychologists have assessed the RCRAS as a valid measurement tool, it is rarely used. This discrepancy is likely a result of the nature of the instrument. The RCRAS consists of 25 data variables that the evaluator rates on a scale of 1–5 or 1–6, depending on the item. The evaluator then scores five summary scales relevant to the definitions of legal insanity (i.e., M'Naghten or ALI). Although the RCRAS has both good reliability (e.g., Rogers & Shuman, 2000) and internal validity (Borum, 2003), it does not provide a quantitative measurement. Rather, it serves as "an organizing model or template" (Rogers & Shuman, 2000, p. 238). Thus, the RCRAS may be of utility to less experienced clinicians as an "aid to guide an evaluator regarding which issues to address and a framework for integrating the data into an analysis relevant to the legal criteria" (Packer, 2009, p. 75).

Guidelines for Choosing Psychological Tests

In addition to empirical data about the acceptability of specific instruments, forensic evaluators can also be guided by principles for the use of tests in forensic settings, and CR evaluations in particular (e.g., Heilbrun, 1992; Heilbrun et al., 2008; Packer, 2009). In choosing whether or not to use tests, and the particular tests to use, the forensic evaluator should first consider what information derived from the test could be relevant to the issue of CR. Psychological tests (other than the RCRAS) do not directly address the psycholegal issue and cannot specifically address the defendant's mental state at the time of the alleged offense. Therefore, the tests chosen should provide some information about the presence/absence of a severe psychiatric disorder that could impact the defendant's capacities relevant to the legal standard.

As the standards for the admissibility of tests in forensic settings are higher than those in clinical settings (*Daubert v. Merrell Dow*, 1993; *Frye v. United States*, 1923; *Kumho Tire v. Carmichael*, 1999), forensic evaluators should carefully consider the reliability and validity of any new tests that are developed. Any test employed should have a published manual that includes data about its reliability, standard error of measurement, and evidence of peer review (*Daubert v. Merrell Dow*, 1993). In addition,

---

[6]More recently, the second edition of the SIRS, called the SIRS–2 (Rogers, Sewell, & Gillard, 2010), has been developed.

psychologists should ensure that all tests have been validated on a population that is relevant to the individual evaluee (including gender, race, ethnicity, and age).

Communicating Results of CR Evaluations

The standards for report writing and testimony for CR evaluations follow the guidelines for all forensic mental health evaluations (e.g., Bank & Packer, 2007; Heilbrun, 2001; Packer & Grisso, 2011). Among the major principles are that the data and interpretations should be distinguishable, that the forensic evaluator should not omit data that do not support the conclusions reached, and that the rationale for opinions offered should be clearly articulated based on the data presented. Exhibit 4.2 offers a guideline for the organization of CR reports based on models in the literature (Giorgi-Guarnieri et al., 2002; Heilbrun, 2001; Knoll & Resnick, 2008; Melton et al., 2007; Rogers & Shuman, 2000). This is not a required or recommended format, but rather is an example of how data and conclusions can be organized for a CR report.

An important issue that arises in both report writing and expert testimony is the extent to which

---

Exhibit 4.2

Template for Criminal Responsibility Report

- Identifying information (e.g., name, age, court, charges)
- Sources of information
- Notification of purpose of interview and limits of privilege
- Citation of legal standard
- History
- Mental status
- Results of psychological testing
- Official (police) version of the alleged offense
- Defendant's version of the alleged offense
- Third-party information related to alleged offense (e.g., victim, witnesses)
- Conclusions/opinion

Note. From *Evaluation of Criminal Responsibility* (p. 142), by I. K. Packer, 2009, New York, NY: Oxford University Press. Copyright 2009 by Oxford University Press. Adapted with permission.

---

the forensic evaluator should offer an opinion on the ultimate legal issue (such as whether or not the defendant meets the criteria for legal insanity). The arguments for and against offering such opinions are not unique to CR evaluations and have been discussed in detail elsewhere (e.g., Heilbrun, 2001; Packer & Grisso, 2011; Rogers & Ewing, 1989, 2003; Tillbrook, Mumley, & Grisso, 2003). The *Specialty Guidelines for Forensic Psychology* (APA, 2013) do not directly address this issue but rather include the statement that "in their communications, forensic practitioners strive to distinguish observations, inferences, and conclusions. Forensic practitioners are encouraged to explain the relationship between their expert opinions and the legal issues and facts of the case at hand" (p. 16). This is consistent with the standards for forensic psychiatry, as the issue is not included in the American Academy of Psychiatry and the Law (AAPL) *Ethics Guidelines for the Practice of Forensic Psychiatry* (AAPL, 2005), and the AAPL practice guidelines for the insanity defense includes a statement that "there is nothing to prevent its [ultimate issue opinion] inclusion in a report" (Giorgi-Guarnieri et al., 2002, p. S30).

In addition to the issue of professional standards, there are also legal considerations. Some state jurisdictions include language specifically requiring that the forensic evaluator address whether the defendant meets the criteria for legal insanity. By contrast, the rules in federal court single out mental health testimony on mental state at the time of the alleged offense as the exception to experts being allowed to address the ultimate legal issue (Federal Rules of Evidence, 704).

The differences of perspective on this issue relate to whether or not a forensic evaluator *should* offer an ultimate opinion as to whether a particular defendant meets the criteria for legal insanity or diminished capacity. However, there is consensus, captured in the *Specialty Guidelines for Forensic Psychology* (APA, 2013) language quoted earlier, that forensic evaluators should not offer opinions that go beyond the relevant data. Thus, there will be cases in which the evaluator *cannot* offer such an opinion because the data are unclear or there is inadequate guidance regarding the legal standard.

This can occur when crucial data are missing (e.g., hospital records from very close to the time of the alleged offense), there are contradictory factual data that cannot be resolved (e.g., the defendant's version and the victim's version are so divergent that they suggest alternate explanations), the defendant cannot or will not provide relevant information about his or her mental status at the time of the alleged offense, or the law in the jurisdiction is unclear relative to the particular case (e.g., lack of clarity regarding whether an understanding of legal or moral wrongfulness is required or whether the particular state recognizes settled insanity brought about by substance use). In these circumstances, professional standards require that the evaluator appropriately clarify the limits of the data and explain why he or she cannot offer a more definitive opinion.

SUMMARY AND CONCLUSIONS

The decision to excuse a particular individual from CR for a prohibited act is a complex one that ultimately is determined by a judge or jury. The review of the legal history of mental-state defenses in U.S. jurisdictions demonstrates that advances in the knowledge of human psychology have informed the standards adopted. However, the legal system tends to be conservative and is unlikely to significantly alter standards until new advances in the mental health field are firmly established and can lead to practical consequences.

The most significant role played by forensic evaluators is to apply their expertise in individual cases to aid the trier of fact in determining whether or not the defendant met the legal criteria for legal insanity or another *mens rea* defense. Although the ultimate decision will be up to the judge or jury, a well-trained forensic evaluator can provide specialized expertise about the relevance of the defendant's mental functioning to the legal issues. Over the last several decades, the fields of forensic psychology and forensic psychiatry have developed methodologies and standards that allow practitioners who become familiar with both the professional literature and the relevant case law to provide a valuable service when issues of CR are raised at trial.

References

American Academy of Psychiatry and the Law. (2005). *Ethics guidelines for the practice of forensic psychiatry.* Retrieved from http://www.aapl.org/pdf/ethicsgdlns.pdf

American Bar Association. (1983). The insanity defense. *Mental and Physical Disability Law Reporter, 7,* 136–141.

American Bar Association. (2012). *Criminal justice standards.* Retrieved from http://www.americanbar.org/groups/criminal_justice/standards.html

American Law Institute. (1985). *Model penal code and annotations.* Washington, DC: Author.

American Psychiatric Association. (1983). APA statement on the insanity defense. *American Journal of Psychiatry, 140,* 681–688.

American Psychiatric Association. (2013). *Diagnostic and statistical manual of mental disorders* (5th ed.). Washington, DC: Author.

American Psychological Association. (2010). *Ethical principles of psychologists and code of conduct (2002, Amended June 1, 2010).* Retrieved from http://www.apa.org/ethics/code/index.aspx

American Psychological Association. (2013). Specialty guidelines for forensic psychology. *American Psychologist, 68,* 7–19. doi:10.1037/a0029889

Appelbaum, P. S. (1982). The insanity defense: New calls for reform. *Hospital and Community Psychiatry, 33,* 13–14.

Archer, R. P., Buffington-Vollum, J., Stredny, R. V., & Handel, R. W. (2006). A survey of psychological test use patterns among forensic psychologists. *Journal of Personality Assessment, 87,* 84–94. doi:10.1207/s15327752jpa8701_07

Aspinwall, L. G., Brown, T. R., & Tabery, J. (2012). The double-edged sword: Does biomechanism increase or decrease judges' sentencing of psychopaths? *Science, 337,* 846–849. doi:10.1126/science.1219569

Bank, S. C., & Packer, I. K. (2007). Expert witness testimony: Law, ethics, and practice. In A. M. Goldstein (Ed.), *Forensic psychology: Emerging topics and expanding roles* (pp. 421–455). Hoboken, NJ: Wiley.

Bieber v. People, 856 P.2d 811 (1993).

Bigby v. State, 892 S.W.2d 864 (1994).

Borum, R. (2003). Criminal responsibility. In T. Grisso (Ed.), *Evaluating competencies: Forensic assessments and instruments* (2nd ed., pp. 193–227). New York, NY: Kluwer Academic/Plenum.

Borum, R., & Grisso, T. (1995). Psychological test use in criminal forensic evaluations. *Professional Psychology: Research and Practice, 26,* 465–473. doi:10.1037/0735-7028.26.5.465

Borum, R., & Grisso, T. (1996). Establishing standards for criminal forensic reports: An empirical analysis. *Bulletin of the American Academy of Psychiatry and the Law, 24,* 297–317.

Butcher, J. N., Graham, J. R., Ben-Porath, Y. S., Tellegen, A., Dahlstrom, W. G., & Kaemmer, B. (2001). *Minnesota Multiphasic Personality Inventory—2 (MMPI–2): Manual for administration and scoring* (Rev. ed.). Minneapolis: University of Minnesota Press.

California Penal Code § 28 (2012).

Callahan, L. A., Steadman, H. J., McGreevy, M. A., & Robbins, P. C. (1991). The volume and characteristics of insanity defense pleas: An eight-state study. *Bulletin of the American Academy of Psychiatry and the Law, 19,* 331–338.

Carter v. United States, 102 U.S. App. D.C. 227 (1957).

Caspi, A., McClay, J., Moffitt, T. E., Mill, J., Martin, J., Craig, I. W., . . . Poulton, R. (2002). Role of genotype in the cycle of violence in maltreated children. *Science, 297,* 851–854. doi:10.1126/science.1072290

Clark, C. R. (1999). Specific intent and diminished capacity. In A. K. Hess & I. B. Weiner (Eds.), *The handbook of forensic psychology* (2nd ed., pp. 350–378). Hoboken, NJ: Wiley.

Clark v. Arizona, 126 S. Ct. 2709 (2006).

Cochrane, R. E., Grisso, T., & Frederick, R. I. (2001). The relationship between criminal charges, diagnoses, and psycholegal opinions among federal pretrial defendants. *Behavioral Sciences and the Law, 19,* 565–582. doi:10.1002/bsl.454

Commonwealth v. Baldwin, 686 N.E.2d 1001 (1997).

Daubert v. Merrell Dow Pharmaceuticals, Inc., 509 U.S. 579 (1993).

Diamond, B. (1961). Criminal responsibility of the mentally ill. *Stanford Law Review, 14,* 59–86. doi:10.2307/1226566

Dix, G. E. (1971). Psychological abnormality as a factor in grading criminal liability: Diminished capacity, diminished responsibility and the like. *Journal of Criminal Law, Criminology, and Police Science, 62,* 313–334. doi:10.2307/1142172

Durham v. United States, 214 F.2d 862 (1954).

Edney v. Smith, 425 F. Supp. 1038 (1976).

Exner, J. E., Jr. (2001). *A Rorschach workbook for the Comprehensive System.* Asheville, NC: Rorschach Workshops.

Fed. R. Ev. 703.

Fed. R. Ev. 704.

Fein, R. A., Appelbaum, K., Barnum, R., Baxter, P., Grisso, T., & Leavitt, N. (1991). The designated forensic professional program: A state government–university partnership to improve forensic mental health services. *Journal of Mental Health Administration, 18,* 223–230. doi:10.1007/BF02518593

Fingarette, H. (1972). *The meaning of criminal insanity.* Los Angeles: University of California Press.

Frederick, R. (1997). *The Validity Indicator Profile.* Minneapolis, MN: National Computer Systems.

Frost, L. E., deCamara, R. L., & Earl, T. R. (2006). Training, certification, and regulation of forensic evaluators. *Journal of Forensic Psychology Practice, 6,* 77–91. doi:10.1300/J158v06n02_06

Frye v. United States, 293 F. 1013 (1923).

Fukunaga, K. K., Pasewark, R. A., Hawkins, M., & Gudeman, H. (1981). Insanity plea: Interexaminer agreement and concordance of psychiatric opinion and court verdict. *Law and Human Behavior, 5,* 325–328. doi:10.1007/BF01044947

Gaines, A. D. (1995). Culture-specific delusions: Sense and nonsense in cultural context. *Psychiatric Clinics of North America, 18,* 281–301.

Giorgi-Guarnieri, D., Janofsky, J., Keram, E., Lawsky, S., Merideth, P., Mossman, D., . . . Zonana, H. V. (2002). Practice guideline: Forensic psychiatric evaluation of defendants raising the insanity defense. *Journal of the American Academy of Psychiatry and the Law, 30,* S3–S40.

Goldstein, A. S. (1967). *The insanity defense.* New Haven, CT: Yale University Press.

Gowensmith, W. N., Murrie, D. C., & Boccaccini, M. T. (2012). How reliable are forensic evaluations of legal sanity? *Law and Human Behavior, 37,* 98–106. doi:10.1037/lhb0000001

Graham v. State, 566 S.W.2d 941 (1978).

Greenberg, S. A., & Shuman, D. W. (1997). Irreconcilable conflict between therapeutic and forensic roles. *Professional Psychology: Research and Practice, 28,* 50–57. doi:10.1037/0735-7028.28.1.50

Grove, W. M., Barden, R. C., Garb, H. N., & Lilienfeld, S. O. (2002). Failure of Rorschach-Comprehensive-System-based testimony to be admissible under the Daubert-Joiner-Kumho standard. *Psychology, Public Policy, and Law, 8,* 216–234. doi:10.1037/1076-8971.8.2.216

Heilbrun, K. (1992). The role of psychological testing in forensic assessment. *Law and Human Behavior, 16,* 257–272. doi:10.1007/BF01044769

Heilbrun, K. (2001). *Principles of forensic mental health assessment.* New York, NY: Kluwer Academic/Plenum.

Heilbrun, K., & Collins, S. (1995). Evaluations of trial competency and mental state at the time of offense: Report characteristics. *Professional Psychology: Research and Practice, 26,* 61–67. doi:10.1037/0735-7028.26.1.61

Heilbrun, K., Grisso, T., & Goldstein, A. (2008). *Foundations of forensic mental health assessment.* New York, NY: Oxford University Press.

Heilbrun, K., Warren, J., & Picarello, K. (2003). Use of third-party information in forensic assessment. In A. M. Goldstein (Ed.), *Handbook of psychology: Vol. 11. Forensic psychology* (pp. 69–86). Hoboken, NJ: Wiley.

Houston v. State, 602 P.2d 784 (1979).

In re Rosenfield, 157 F. Supp. 18 (1957).

Insanity Defense Reform Act of 1984, 18 U.S.C. § 17 (1984).

Jenkins v. United States, 307 F2d. 637 (1962).

Jones v. United States, 463 U.S. 354 (1983).

Kane v. United States, 399 F.2d 730 (1968).

Kiehl, K. A. (2006). A cognitive neuroscience perspective on psychopathy: Evidence for paralimbic system dysfunction. *Psychiatry Research, 142,* 107–128. doi:10.1016/j.psychres.2005.09.013

Knoll, J. L., & Resnick, P. J. (2008). Insanity defense evaluations: Towards a model of evidence-based practice. *Brief Treatment and Crisis Intervention, 8,* 92–110. doi:10.1093/brief-treatment/mhm024

Kumho Tire v. Carmichael, 526 U.S. 137 (1999).

Lally, S. J. (2003). What tests are acceptable for use in forensic evaluations: A study of experts. *Professional Psychology: Research and Practice, 34,* 491–498. doi:10.1037/0735-7028.34.5.491

Lee v. County Court of Erie County, 267 N.E.2d 452 (1971).

Lilienfeld, S. O., Wood, J. M., & Garb, H. N. (2000). The scientific status of projective techniques. *Psychological Science in the Public Interest, 1,* 27–66.

McDonald v. United States, 312 F.2d 347 (1962).

Melton, G. B., Petrila, J., Poythress, N. G., & Slobogin, C. (2007). *Psychological evaluations for the courts: A handbook for mental health professionals and lawyers* (3rd ed.). New York, NY: Guilford Press.

Miller, G. (2012). Science and the courts: In mock case, biological evidence reduces sentences. *Science, 337,* 788. doi:10.1126/science.337.6096.788

Miller, H. A. (2001). *Miller—Forensic Assessment of Symptoms Test (M–FAST): Professional manual.* Odessa, FL: Psychological Assessment Resources.

Millon, T. (1994). *Manual for the Millon Clinical Multiaxial Inventory (MCMI–III).* Minneapolis, MN: National Computer Systems.

M'Naghten case, 8 English Reporter 718 (1843).

Mobley v. State, 463 S.E.2d 166 (1995).

Montana v. Egelhoff, 518 U.S. 37 (1996)

Monterosso, J., Royzman, E. B., & Schwartz, B. (2005). Explaining away responsibility: Effects of scientific explanation on perceived culpability. *Ethics and Behavior, 15,* 139–158. doi:10.1207/s15327019eb1502_4

Morey, L. C. (1991). *Personality Assessment Inventory: Professional manual.* Odessa, FL: Psychological Assessment Resources.

Morey, L. C., Warner, M. B., & Hopwood, C. J. (2007). The Personality Assessment Inventory: Issues in legal and forensic settings. In A. M. Goldstein (Ed.), *Forensic psychology: Emerging topics and expanding roles* (pp. 97–126). Hoboken, NJ: Wiley.

Morse, S. J. (1979). Diminished capacity: A moral and legal conundrum. *International Journal of Law and Psychiatry, 2,* 271–298. doi:10.1016/0160-2527(79)90009-8

Morse, S. J. (1994). Causation, compulsion, and involuntariness. *Bulletin of the American Academy of Psychiatry and the Law, 22,* 159–180.

Morse, S. J. (2008). Psychopathy and criminal responsibility. *Neuroethics, 1,* 205–212. doi:10.1007/s12152-008-9021-9

Murray, H. A. (1943). *Thematic Apperception Test manual.* Cambridge, MA: Harvard University Press.

Murrie, D. C., Boccaccini, M. T., Turner, D. B., Meeks, M., Woods, C., & Tussey, C. (2009). Rater (dis)agreement on risk assessment measures in sexually violent predator proceedings: Evidence of adversarial allegiance in forensic evaluation? *Psychology, Public Policy, and Law, 15,* 19–53. doi:10.1037/a0014897

New York v. Schmidt, 110 N.E. 945 (1915).

Nicholson, R. A., & Norwood, S. (2000). The quality of forensic psychological assessments, reports, and testimony: Acknowledging the gap between promise and practice. *Law and Human Behavior, 24,* 9–44. doi:10.1023/A:1005422702678

Nisbett, R. E., & Wilson, T. D. (1977). Telling more than we can know: Verbal reports on mental processes. *Psychological Review, 84,* 231–259. doi:10.1037/0033-295X.84.3.231

Ogloff, J. R. (1990). The admissibility of expert testimony regarding malingering and deception. *Behavioral Sciences and the Law, 8,* 27–43. doi:10.1002/bsl.2370080105

Otto, R. K., Barnes, G., & Jacobson, K. (1996, March). *The content and quality of criminal forensic evaluations in Florida.* Paper presented at the American Psychology-Law Society Conference, Hilton Head, SC.

Packer, I. K. (1987). Homicide and the insanity defense: A comparison of sane and insane murderers.

Behavioral Sciences and the Law, 5, 25–35. doi:10.1002/bsl.2370050104

Packer, I. K. (2009). *Evaluation of criminal responsibility.* New York, NY: Oxford University Press.

Packer, I. K., & Grisso, T. (2011). *Specialty competencies in forensic psychology.* New York, NY: Oxford University Press.

Packer, I. K., & Leavitt, N. (1998, March). *Designing and implementing a quality assurance process for forensic evaluations.* Paper presented at American Psychology-Law Society Conference, Redondo Beach, CA.

Parker v. State, 254 A.2d 381 (1969).

People v. Conrad, 385 N.W.2d 277 (1986).

People v. Goldstein, 843 N.E.2d 727 (2005).

People v. Gorshen, 336 P.2d 492 (1959).

People v. Kelly, 516 P.2d 875 (1973).

People v. Larsen, 361 N.E.2d 713 (1977).

People v. Lim Dum Dong, 78 P.2d 1026 (1938).

People v. Poddar, 518 P.2d 342 (1974).

People v. Toner, 187 N.W. 386 (1922).

People v. Wolff, 394P.2d 1308 (1964).

Phillips, M. R., Wolf, A. S., & Coons, D. J. (1988). Psychiatry and the criminal justice system: Testing the myths. *American Journal of Psychiatry, 145,* 605–610.

Porreca v. State, 433 A2d 1204 (1981).

Raifman, L. (1979, March). *Interjudge reliability of psychiatrists' evaluations of criminal defendants' competency to stand trial and legal insanity.* Paper presented at the American Psychology-Law Society Conference, Baltimore, MD.

Rex v. Arnold, 16 How. St. Tr. 695 (1724).

Rogers, R. (1984). *Rogers Criminal Responsibility Assessment Scales (RCRAS) and test manual.* Odessa, FL: Psychological Assessment Resources.

Rogers, R. (1987). The APA position on the insanity defense: Empiricism vs. emotionalism. *American Psychologist, 42,* 840–848. doi:10.1037/0003-066X.42.9.840

Rogers, R., Bagby, R. M., & Dickens, S. E. (1992). *Structured Interview of Reported Symptoms (SIRS) and professional manual.* Odessa, FL: Psychological Assessment Resources.

Rogers, R., & Ewing, C. P. (1989). Proscribing ultimate opinions: A quick and cosmetic fix. *Law and Human Behavior, 13,* 357–374. doi:10.1007/BF01056408

Rogers, R., & Ewing, C. P. (2003). The prohibition of ultimate opinions: A misguided enterprise. *Journal of*

Forensic Psychology Practice, 3, 65–75. doi:10.1300/J158v03n03_04

Rogers, R., Sewell, K. W., & Gillard, N. D. (2010). *Structured Interview of Reported Symptoms, 2nd edition: Professional manual.* Lutz, FL: Psychological Assessment Resources.

Rogers, R., & Shuman, D. W. (2000). *Conducting insanity evaluations* (2nd ed.). New York, NY: Guilford Press.

Skeem, J., & Golding, S. (1998). Community examiners' evaluations of competence to stand trial: Common problems and suggestions for improvement. *Professional Psychology: Research and Practice, 29,* 357–367. doi:10.1037/0735-7028.29.4.357

Smith, G. P., & Burger, G. K. (1997). Detection of malingering: Validation of the Structured Inventory of Malingered Symptomatology (SIMS). *Journal of the American Academy of Psychiatry and the Law, 25,* 183–189.

State v. Hamann, 285 N.W.2d 180 (1979).

Steadman, H. J., McGreevy, M. A., Morrissey, J. P., Callahan, L. A., Clark Robbins, P., & Cirincione, C. (1993). *Before and after Hinckley: Evaluating insanity defense reform.* New York, NY: Guilford Press.

Stock, H., & Poythress, N. G. (1979, September). *Psychologists' opinions on competency and sanity: How reliable?* Paper presented at the annual meeting of the American Psychological Association, New York, NY.

Tarasoff v. Board of Regents, 551 P.2d 334 (1976).

Thorndike, R. L., Hagen, E. P., & Sattler, J. M. (1986). *The Stanford–Binet Intelligence Scale, 4th edition: Technical manual.* Chicago, IL: Riverside.

Tillbrook, C., Mumley, D., & Grisso, T. (2003). Avoiding expert opinions on the ultimate legal question: The case for integrity. *Journal of Forensic Psychology Practice, 3,* 77–87. doi:10.1300/J158v03n03_05

Tombaugh, T. N. (1996). *TOMM: The Test of Memory Malingering.* North Tonawanda, NY: Multi-Health Systems.

Tseng, W. S., Matthews, D., & Elwyn, T. S. (2004). *Cultural competence in forensic mental health.* New York, NY: Brunner-Routledge.

United States v. Alvarez, 519 F.2d 1036 (1975).

United States v. Brawner, 471 F.2d 969 (1972).

United States v. Cameron, 907 F.2d 1051 (1990).

United States v. Frisbee, 623 F. supp. 1217 (1985).

United States v. Pohlot, 827 F.2d 889 (1987).

Vitacco, M. J., & Packer, I. K. (2004). Mania and insanity: An analysis of legal standards and recommendations for clinical practice. *Journal of Forensic Psychology Practice, 4,* 83–95. doi:10.1300/J158v04n03_06

Warren, J. I., Murrie, D. C., Chauhan, P., Dietz, P. E., & Morris, J. (2004). Opinion formation in evaluating sanity at the time of the offense: An examination of 5175 pre-trial evaluations. *Behavioral Sciences and the Law*, 22, 171–186. doi:10.1002/bsl.559

Wechsler, D. (1997). *Wechsler Adult Intelligence Scale* (3rd ed.). San Antonio, TX: Psychological Corporation.

Weiner, I. B. (2007). Rorschach assessment in forensic cases. In A. M. Goldstein (Ed.), *Forensic psychology: Emerging topics and expanding roles* (pp. 127–153). Hoboken, NJ: Wiley.

Weinstock, R., Leong, G. B., & Silva, J. A. (1996). California's diminished capacity defense: Evolution and transformation. *Bulletin of the American Academy of Psychiatry and the Law*, 24, 347–366.

Wiederanders, M. R., Bromley, D. L., & Choate, P. A. (1997). Forensic conditional release programs and outcomes in three states. *International Journal of Law and Psychiatry*, 20, 249–257. doi:10.1016/S0160-2527(97)00006-X

Zusman, J., & Simon, J. (1983). Differences in repeated psychiatric examinations of litigants to a lawsuit. *American Journal of Psychiatry*, 140, 1300–1304.

CHAPTER 5

CRIMINAL COMPETENCIES

Daniel C. Murrie and Heather Zelle

Competence, in the context of criminal justice proceedings, refers to a defendant's capacity to meaningfully participate and make decisions during the criminal justice process. Competence is relevant at any stage of the process, from a defendant's first words to arresting officers, through that defendant's decision about pleas, until—in the gravest of cases—the moment of execution. Because questions about competence can be raised at any point in criminal justice proceedings, this chapter describes *criminal competencies*, and many scholars use broad terms such as *adjudicative competence* (see Bonnie, 1992) or *competence to proceed*, to cover the span from arrest to verdict to sentencing. Nevertheless, this chapter focuses primarily on the defendant's capacities that comprise his or her *competence to stand trial* because this is, by far, the most commonly adjudicated competence (Melton, Petrila, Poythress, & Slobogin, 2007), and far more scholarly research literature addresses this particular competence. Authorities estimate that at least 60,000 defendants—approximately 5% of all felony defendants—are evaluated for trial competence each year in the United States, making trial competence assessments the most common form of criminal forensic mental health assessment (Bonnie & Grisso, 2000; Poythress, Bonnie, Monahan, Otto, & Hoge, 2002). Most practicing clinical forensic psychologists evaluate trial competence on a routine basis. Indeed, evaluating, adjudicating, and restoring competence consumes most of the financial resources that jurisdictions devote to forensic mental health services (Golding, 1992).

This chapter also addresses defendants' capacity to waive their *Miranda* rights, that is, defendants' capacity to knowingly, intelligently, and voluntarily waive their Fifth Amendment rights to silence and counsel during custodial interrogation. *Miranda* waivers have received increasing scholarly attention in recent years (e.g., A. M. Goldstein & Goldstein, 2010; N. E. S. Goldstein, Goldstein, Zelle, & Oberlander Condie, 2012) and appear to be the competence next most often examined after competence to stand trial. Finally, we give only brief attention to another criminal competence—competence for execution (CFE)—which is in proportion to its less frequent attention in legal proceedings and clinical practice.

IMPORTANCE OF THE PROBLEM

A core principle in modern criminal law is that every defendant has the right to a fair trial. But, for a trial to be truly fair, the defendant must be able to comprehend the trial process and be able to attempt some form of defense. Defendants must understand the charges against them; they must be able to meaningfully understand the proceedings to determine their guilt; and they must be able to help defend themselves during those proceedings, whether by arguing innocence or pursuing a favorable sentence. In short, defendants must have a basic level of *competence* in order for the justice system to have fair and dignified proceedings.

The principle that a defendant must be competent in order to face adjudication has deep roots in

http://dx.doi.org/10.1037/14461-005
APA Handbook of Forensic Psychology: Vol. 1. Individual and Situational Influences in Criminal and Civil Contexts,
B. L. Cutler and P. A. Zapf (Editors-in-Chief)

English common law (see William Blackstone's *Commentaries on the Laws of England*, 1769/1979, and *King v. Frith*, 1790). Some accounts suggest that the principle arose even earlier, in an era when defendants were not guaranteed a right to defense counsel but were expected to present their own defense (Grisso, 2003; Zapf & Roesch, 2009). When a defendant refused to enter a plea, the court was then left to determine whether he or she was "mute by malice" or "mute by visitation of God" (e.g., deaf, mute, or suffering psychiatric illness). Defendants determined to be the former were usually tortured, with heavy stones placed on their chests until they pled. But, the latter were spared this process, reflecting even then a recognition that some defendants may not have the capacity to face the weight of legal proceedings against them (Melton et al., 2007).

U.S. law was built on English common law, so U.S. courts quickly acknowledged the problem of incompetent defendants as American jurisprudence developed. For example, a trial court found the man who attempted to assassinate President Andrew Jackson not fit to stand trial (*United States v. Lawrence*, 1835), and a court of appeals concluded that subjecting "an insane person" to trial violated due process (*Youtsey v. United States*, 1899).

The U.S. Supreme Court established the formal standard for competence to stand trial in *Dusky v. United States* (1960), when it held that

> It is not enough for the district judge to find "the defendant [is] oriented to time and place and [has] some recollection of events," but that the "test must be whether he has sufficient present ability to consult with his lawyer with a reasonable degree of rational understanding—and whether he has a rational as well as factual understanding of the proceedings against him." (p. 402)

This brief opinion is typically viewed as the Court interpreting the constitutional right to due process to require that defendants have a minimal level of competence. Subsequently, all state statutes and case law have modeled their discussion of competence on this *Dusky* language. Three decades after *Dusky*, the Supreme Court concluded that the same standard for trial competence should apply to waiving counsel and pleading guilty (*Godinez v. Moran*, 1993).[1]

The principle of competence per se is hardly controversial, and authorities have detailed strong rationales for prohibiting the prosecution of incompetent defendants. For example, Bonnie (1992) emphasized dignity, reliability, and autonomy:

- *Dignity*: Proceeding with trial and punishment against a defendant who lacks a rudimentary understanding of the nature and purpose of proceedings, or a moral understanding of wrongdoing and punishment, offends the "moral dignity" (Bonnie, 1992, p. 295) of the justice process.
- *Reliability*: Proceeding with trial against a defendant who cannot recognize or communicate relevant information to counsel increases the chance of an erroneous verdict. This is not only unfair to the defendant but also undermines society's interest in reliable, or accurate, court decisions.
- *Autonomy*: Our justice system prioritizes defendant self-determination by requiring that the defendant, not counsel, make those certain key decisions—such as how to plead—that affect the defendant more than anyone else. But proceeding with trial against a defendant who lacks decisional competence undermines this core value of defendant autonomy.

Other authorities have offered similar rationales for a competence doctrine (e.g., Group for the Advancement of Psychiatry, 1974; Melton et al., 2007).

Thus, the values and rationale underlying a competence requirement are well established. But, these values and rationale direct attention to the problem of incompetence because *some portion of criminal defendants are impaired in ways that may render them incompetent to participate in their*

---

[1]Although the *Godinez* decision has been understood as holding that the same competence standard applies to any actions that a defendant may take (i.e., waiving counsel and pleading guilty), a more recent case has modified this understanding. In *Indiana v. Edwards* (2008), the U.S. Supreme Court considered the unusual case of a mentally ill defendant who not only waived counsel but represented himself at trial (rather than simply pleading guilty, as in *Godinez*). The Court decided that the state could indeed limit this defendant's right to represent himself, even though he met the *Dusky* standard for trial competence, because self-representation in trial requires greater capacities. Thus, the recent *Edwards* decision suggests that the standard for competence may indeed vary in at least some circumstances.

criminal justice proceedings. Criminal defendants are disproportionately likely to suffer from mental illness and intellectual disabilities compared to the general population (Teplin, 1990, 1994). For example, recent estimates have suggested that 15% of male and 31% of female jail inmates have a *serious* mental disorder (Steadman, Osher, Robbins, Case, & Samuels, 2009). More generally, according to the Bureau of Justice Statistics (James & Glaze, 2006), 74% of jail inmates have had a recent "mental health problem." Conservative estimates suggest that 900,000 persons with serious mental illness are admitted annually to U.S. jails, usually as pretrial detainees (Steadman, Scott, Osher, Agnese, & Robbins, 2005). Within the juvenile justice system, rates of mental disorder are similarly high; more than 60% of youth in juvenile detention met the criteria for at least one psychiatric disorder (Teplin, Abram, McClelland, Dulcan, & Mericle, 2002), and approximately 50% met the criteria for at least two disorders (Abram, Teplin, McClelland, & Dulcan, 2003). Of course, the presence or formal diagnosis of a mental disorder does not by itself render a defendant incompetent. But, depending on the disorder, the defendant, and the legal context, certain symptoms of the mental disorder may grossly interfere with the basic capacities necessary for competence.

Given the prevalence and severity of mental disorders among individuals involved with the criminal justice system, it is inevitable that some defendants lack the basic abilities necessary to participate meaningfully in the proceedings that determine their fate. Even if only a small proportion of mental disorders manifest in symptoms that are severe enough to interfere with a defendant's basic legal capacities, the sheer volume of defendants with a mental disorder ensures that many defendants will be incompetent to progress through certain stages of legal proceedings. Thus, in a meaningful portion of cases, defendants' fundamental rights are jeopardized, which is a problem that requires the attention of psychologists and other mental health professionals involved in the justice system.

Questions of competence arise as early as pre-arrest interactions with police officers during custodial interrogation. At this time, a suspect has certain rights, so his or her capacities to comprehend his or her circumstances and make decisions become legally relevant. *Miranda* warnings were intended to provide useful information to suspects who might be unversed in their rights (*Miranda v. Arizona*, 1966), but research suggests that the vast majority of suspects waive their rights and provide statements to police (e.g., Kassin et al., 2007). Rogers and colleagues demonstrated the widespread misconceptions that defendants, and even the general population, hold about *Miranda* warnings (e.g., Rogers, 2011; Rogers, Rogstad, et al., 2010). Moreover, evidence that vulnerable groups, such as individuals with intellectual deficits and/or mental illness, are disproportionately represented in the criminal justice system raises concerns about suspects waiving their rights even though they may lack the capacity to do so.

After suspects proceed beyond the police interview and formally become criminal defendants, concerns about their competence become more acute. Defense attorneys have reported concerns about defendants' trial competence in up to 15% of their cases (Hoge, Bonnie, Poythress, & Monahan, 1992; Poythress et al., 2002). However, for strategic reasons (e.g., to avoid delays or hospitalization), attorneys sometimes decline to pursue a formal competence evaluation even when they doubt a client's competence. In other instances, attorneys may simply fail to recognize the deficits (such as well-disguised symptoms of intellectual disability) that may render a defendant incompetent.

Similar competence concerns arise in juvenile court.[2] After youth in delinquency hearings became entitled to many of the same rights and procedures as adult defendants (*Kent v. United States*, 1966; *In re Gault*, 1967), states began to recognize that youths' due process rights required that they be competent in order to be adjudicated in juvenile court. In practice, attorneys raised the issue more often after the juvenile justice reforms of the 1990s, which left

---

[2] Nevertheless, this chapter does not specifically address adjudicative competence among juveniles, which requires a detailed understanding of adolescent development. See Grisso (2013) or Kruh and Grisso (2009) for excellent coverage of adjudicative competence among juveniles.

youths facing more serious sanctions in juvenile court.

Whether in juvenile court or criminal court, the issue of competence can be raised at any point before or during trial (*Drope v. Missouri*, 1975). Indeed, it must be raised by court personnel (i.e., defense counsel, prosecutor, or judge) when they have a legitimate doubt about a defendant's competence (*Pate v. Robinson*, 1966). Thus, each particular stage of a defendant's proceedings—such as the decision to enter a plea, to stand trial, or to proceed *pro se*—may prompt questions about the defendant's competence, even if such questions did not arise at earlier stages of the proceedings. Even at the last stage of the most severe sentence, the court may ask for an evaluation of *the last competency* (Brodsky, Zapf, & Boccaccini, 2001; Zapf, Boccaccini, & Brodsky, 2003)—competence for execution (CFE).

RELEVANT PSYCHOLOGICAL THEORY AND PRINCIPLES

At the most obvious level, psychological theory is relevant to the criminal competencies because *in*competence is always attributable to psychological problems, broadly defined. Nearly every jurisdiction requires that a finding of incompetence must be based on a mental disorder ("a mental disease or defect," in many statutes). Mere ignorance of the law or inexperience with the justice system is never a basis for incompetence.

Incompetence Must Be Based on Mental Disorder

Though not explicitly mentioned in the brief *Dusky* decision, almost all jurisdictions hold, whether through statute or case law, that mental disorder is a *necessary* condition for any kind of incompetence. But, mental disorder alone is never a *sufficient* condition for a finding of incompetence (e.g., *Feguer v. United States*, 1962; *Swisher v. United States*, 1965; *United States v. Adams*, 1969; *Wieter v. Settle*, 1961). Rather, the symptoms of a mental disorder must interfere with a defendant's relevant, practical abilities in a way that leaves that defendant unable to meaningfully participate in the adjudicative process.

What psychological conditions tend to be most relevant to competence determinations? There is no diagnosis—and no particular symptom pattern—that ensures a finding of incompetence. Indeed, studies suggest that most of the defendants in any particular diagnostic group are found competent (e.g., Pirelli, Gottdiener, & Zapf, 2011; Warren et al., 2006). But, studies also suggest that the two general conditions most often underlying incompetence findings are psychosis and cognitive impairments.

Psychosis. Psychosis itself is neither a specific mental disorder nor a formal diagnosis. Rather, the term refers to particular symptoms that may be associated with several different disorders or other conditions, such as substance intoxication or certain medical conditions. Psychosis refers broadly to a severe impairment in an individual's ability to distinguish reality from that which is not real. More specifically, it typically denotes a group of severe symptoms including hallucinations (false sensory experiences such as seeing sights or hearing sounds that do not exist in reality), delusions (fixed, false beliefs that persist despite clear evidence to the contrary), and/or grossly disorganized behavior. There are countless ways that psychosis might interfere with adjudicative competence; in severe cases, a psychotic defendant may be too paranoid, disorganized, or agitated to cooperate with counsel or understand proceedings at even a minimal level. But, less severe cases could also preclude adjudicative competence; for example, if a defendant's psychosis is limited to a delusional belief that his attorney is part of an international conspiracy against him, this narrow delusion may preclude the defendant from working productively with his attorney.

Despite the disruptive nature of psychotic symptoms, a diagnosis of a psychotic disorder does not guarantee a finding of incompetence. In a recent meta-analysis, defendants who had been diagnosed with psychotic disorders (e.g., schizophrenia) were approximately eight times more likely to be found incompetent compared to defendants without such a diagnosis. Nevertheless, the majority of defendants who had been diagnosed with a psychotic disorder were still found competent (Pirelli et al., 2011).

Cognitive impairment. The term cognitive impairment, like psychosis, refers to a variety of deficits that may result from a variety of mental disorders or medical conditions. Perhaps most common among incompetent defendants are cognitive impairments due to intellectual disability (formerly called mental retardation) or developmental disabilities that leave the defendant with well below–average intellectual skills. Of course, low intelligence alone does not render a defendant incompetent, and clinicians performing competence evaluations find that most of the defendants they diagnose with intellectual disability are, nonetheless, competent to stand trial (Cochrane, Grisso, & Frederick, 2001; Warren et al., 2006). But, depending on the circumstances, severe intellectual impairments could preclude a defendant from understanding proceedings at even a rudimentary level or making basic legal decisions in an autonomous manner.

Of course, psychosis and cognitive impairments are not the only psychological deficits or conditions that could lead to incompetence. But, they are the conditions that most often correspond with incompetence (Pirelli et al., 2011). The reason that no particular condition or set of symptoms always renders a defendant incompetent is because competence always depends on the exact functional deficits that these symptoms cause as related to the exact functional demands of the particular legal context.

Competence Is Functional and Contextual

Competence is a legal construct that has no single, easily identifiable psychological correlate. In fact, any legal competence is an "open-textured" (Golding, 2008; Meehl, 1970) construct in the sense that competence may vary across contexts, is subject to a variety of operational definitions, and can probably never be adequately captured by one fixed set of facts (Grisso, 2003). Even examining a single, specific legal competence, such as competence to stand trial, underscores the open-textured nature of the concept.

Recall that the brief *Dusky* decision (1960) conveyed only that the defendant must have sufficient present ability to consult with his or her lawyer with a reasonable degree of rational

understanding and a rational and factual understanding of proceedings against him or her. Despite the brevity of the Court's opinion, its wording carries implications that are crucial to defining and assessing a defendant's trial competence (see Kruh & Grisso, 2009; Zapf & Roesch, 2009). First, *sufficient* ability implies that the defendant need not have a sophisticated, perfect, or wholly unimpaired ability to work with defense counsel, merely an adequate one. In the same way, the defendant needs only a *reasonable degree* of rational understanding. This "suggests that the test [of competence] as applied to a particular case is a flexible one" (Melton et al., 2007, p. 128). The term *reasonable* implies that it be adequate *for the situation at hand.*

This emphasis on sufficient, reasonable abilities underscores what may be the most important principle underlying the assessment of trial competence or any other legal competence: Competence is both *functional* and *contextual.* Grisso (2003) clearly described the functional and contextual nature of legal competencies when he explained:

> Legal competence constructs focus on person–context interactions. A legal competence question does not merely ask the degree of functional ability or deficit that a person manifests. It asks further, "Does this person's level of ability meet the demands of the specific situation with which the person will be . . . faced?" Defined more formally, a decision about legal competence is in part a statement about the *congruency or incongruency between (a) the extent of a person's functional ability and (b) the degree of performance demand that is made by the specific instance of the context in that case.* Thus an interaction between individual's ability and situational demand, not an absolute level of ability, is of special significance for legal competence decisions. . . . The individual's level of ability will be important to consider, yet the fact finder can assess its significance only when it is weighed against the demands

of the individual's specific situation. (pp. 32–33)

This emphasis on function and context underlies any discussion of competence. Recall that the forensic evaluation of competence involves the intersection of two fields. Although the field of psychology typically takes a nomothetic (group-based) approach, the legal field typically takes an idiographic (individualized) approach. Competence is not framed as an absolute standard in which an individual is compared against the general population because the legal field reviews on a case-by-case basis in order to allow for individualized application of general rules to each particular defendant's case. Practically speaking, this principle means that any question about competence will require individualized consideration of the defendant and the defendant's unique case. Also practically speaking, this means that no assessment instrument or checklist, however well designed, can by itself answer the question of competence for all defendants in all contexts. It is crucial to remember this foundational principle—that competence is open textured and context dependent—before considering the specific abilities that are relevant in most evaluations of competence.

Competence Requires Certain Basic Abilities

An evaluation of any legal competence is an evaluation of whether the defendant's threshold condition (a mental disorder) has caused functional impairments that interfere with the basic skills or abilities that are essential to a particular legal task in the context of the defendant's unique case. What are those basic skills or abilities? Scholars have identified several broad abilities that are particularly relevant to most legal competencies. Such abilities may be thought of as psycholegal *variables* and are theory based by nature. That is, these abilities are derived through theoretical examination of legal standards and practices in order to identify what is apparently required of defendants and then translate those requirements into measurable psychological variables. Perhaps most broadly, Appelbaum and Grisso (1988) identified four abilities that tend to comprise any legal competence. The abilities do not necessarily

make up a single definition of competence and, depending on the context, a competence standard might require just one of the abilities, all four abilities, or a combination of some of the abilities. But, these four aspects are basic components of most legal competencies.

- *Understanding relevant information*: This concept refers to being able to comprehend information that is relevant to decision making. It is the ability that is most often explicitly identified because of the basic need to understand information before one can genuinely decide to accept or reject that information.
- *Appreciating the situation and its consequences*: This concept builds on the first and speaks to the need for a person to grasp what information means *in his or her own case*.
- *Manipulating information rationally*: This concept refers to the ability to use logical thinking (reasoning) to weigh the risks and benefits of options when making a decision.
- *Communicating choices*: This concept refers to the basic ability to convey a choice as evidence of one's ability to make decisions. It often is not formally assessed because it is generally accepted as a self-evident indication of whether someone can make decisions independently.

These four basic abilities were originally derived through theoretical consideration of patients' competence to make medical treatment decisions (Appelbaum & Grisso, 1988), but they are also relevant to understanding any legal competence. Subsequently, several scholars (e.g., Bonnie, 1992; Cruise & Rogers, 1998; Grisso, 2003; Rogers, Tillbrook, & Sewell, 2004) worked to apply the broad abilities that are necessary for legal competence generally to the more specific context of competence to stand trial (see Kruh & Grisso, 2009; Zapf & Roesch, 2009, for reviews). Despite some differences in organization and emphasis, almost all of their analyses have in common the following five capacities:

- *Understanding*: Defendants must have a factual understanding of the legal proceedings, including the adversarial arrangements and procedures in court as well as the roles of key court personnel (i.e., judge, defense attorney, prosecuting attorney). Understanding also involves the case at hand because defendants must know the charges and the range of possible penalties they are facing as well as the plea options and basic rights to which they are entitled. Understanding is a foundational ability in that a defendant's understanding of his or her legal situation is a prerequisite for appreciating, reasoning, and making rational decisions about that legal situation.

- *Appreciating*: A defendant must not only be able to understand certain information on a factual level, but he or she must also be able to rationally abstract that information to apply it to his or her case and grasp the important implications. Whereas *understanding* involves only recognizing or identifying certain facts, *appreciation* involves the defendant's beliefs underlying those facts. Are the defendant's beliefs grossly distorted or unrealistic due to psychopathology? Or are the defendant's beliefs accurate enough that he or she can proceed through adjudication in a rational manner that conforms to the reality of the situation? Is the defendant's appreciation of his or her situation grossly concrete and simplistic due to cognitive limitations? Or can the defendant reasonably appraise the evidence against him or her and anticipate the likely outcomes of legal proceedings? Appreciation involves a reality-based, logical grasp of the relevant facts.
- *Reasoning*: A defendant must not only appreciate the legally relevant information, but he or she must also be able to perform a closely related task of manipulating and weighing that information to make reasonable—though not necessarily impeccable—decisions (Zapf & Roesch, 2009). Can the defendant use a logical process to identify and evaluate the information that is most relevant to the case and then use a logical process to weigh that information and choose a reasonable course of action? Reasoning need not be sophisticated, but it should be rational and logical. Competent reasoning is self-interested, as the client considers the relevant information and approaches decisions with his or her best interests in mind.

- *Assisting*: With adequate understanding, appreciation, and reasoning, a defendant should be capable and motivated enough to assist counsel in mounting a vigorous defense (or be able to make a reasonable decision not to pursue a defense). Assisting counsel will entail communicating with counsel to provide information that is relevant to the case and opinions regarding legal strategy. In cases that proceed to trial, assisting includes behaving appropriately in the courtroom; following courtroom proceedings as they occur; providing counsel with relevant input as the trial develops; and, if the defendant chooses to testify, doing so appropriately.
- *Decision Making*: Finally, competent defendants must be able to make decisions. That is, they must consider alternatives and make crucial legal decisions such as whether to accept a plea agreement or proceed to trial, which plea to enter, and which steps to take (e.g., testifying, calling witnesses) at trial. Although rational decision making will certainly require careful consideration of guidance from counsel, certain key decisions are reserved solely for the defendant. Thus, the ability to make decisions in a rational, reality-based manner is usually considered a core capacity for competence to stand trial.

Of the five core abilities listed here, decision making is the least clearly addressed in the *Dusky* standard, so it has tended to receive less focus than the other abilities. Nonetheless, Bonnie (1992) proposed that adjudicative competence involved (a) a foundational competence necessary to assist counsel and (b) a somewhat more demanding decisional competence. He argued for an additional, more context-specific, decisional competence because defendants who have only basic abilities (e.g., understanding one's charges, appreciating one's situation, skills needed to assist) may not be competent to make some of the specific decisions necessary for certain steps of adjudication.

The U.S. Supreme Court's ruling in *Godinez v. Moran* (1993) addressed decision making directly; however, its final holding effectively undermined decision making as a requisite for adjudicative competence. The *Godinez* decision discussed at length the ways in which defendants make decisions during the adjudicative process.[3] In doing so, it appeared to make clear that a defendant's decision-making skills are indeed a part of the *Dusky* standard. Nonetheless, the Court ruled that the standard for a defendant to perform any number of tasks during adjudication (i.e., to plead guilty, to stand trial, to waive counsel and proceed *pro se*) should be considered the same as the general standard for competence to stand trial. So, there is little chance for legal proceedings to address competence in the way Bonnie (1992) proposed. However, because of the Court's dicta recognizing decision making, authorities tend to include it as a component of other key abilities. For example, Grisso (2003) described decision making as an implied aspect of a defendant's rational understanding.

Distinction for *Miranda* Waiver

Technically, the idea of *competence* to waive the *Miranda* rights is inaccurate because case law has not developed in the same fashion as for adjudicative competence. That is, a court ruling on a *Miranda* waiver challenge is concerned with whether the *waiver* was valid or invalid, and not with whether the *defendant* was competent or incompetent. The term competence has often been used in reference to *Miranda* waivers; however, because of the difference in focus, it is more accurate to discuss a defendant's *capacity* to waive his or her *Miranda* rights. The *Dusky* standard does not apply to *Miranda* waiver questions because they are not questions of competence to stand trial. Rather, the constitutional rights waiver standard of *knowing, intelligent, and voluntary* applies in such cases (*Miranda v. Arizona*, 1966). Voluntariness, in the police interview context, has been defined through case law as freedom from coercion, particularly police coercion (e.g., *Brown v. Mississippi*, 1936; *Spano v. New York*, 1959). The knowing and intelligent components of the standard have been equated by scholars to understanding and appreciation in the Appelbaum and Grisso (1988) model of necessary abilities for legal decision making (A.M. Goldstein & Goldstein, 2010).

RESEARCH REVIEW

A review of the research on the three primary types of criminal competencies is presented in this section. We begin with the research on an individual's capacity to waive *Miranda*, then present the research on competency to stand trial, and end with a brief review of the research regarding CFE.

Research Addressing Capacity to Waive Miranda

Research on understanding and appreciating *Miranda* rights (or *Miranda* rights comprehension) addresses the prevalence of waivers, the correlates and predictors of *Miranda* rights comprehension, and the legal standard for rights waivers. There are differences between adjudicative competence research and *Miranda* rights research due to the particular nature of *Miranda* rights comprehension as a capacity that is concerned with waiving limited pretrial rights. (See A. M. Goldstein & Goldstein, 2010, and N. E. S. Goldstein, Goldstein, et al., 2012, for more detailed overviews.)

Frequency of *Miranda* waivers and *Miranda* waiver challenges. Relatively little research has been conducted examining the occurrence of *Miranda* waivers and waiver challenges. Although it is unclear how (in)frequently attorneys may challenge the admissibility of inculpatory statements by challenging the validity of a *Miranda* waiver, the rate is likely low given the low referral rates that have been found for adjudicative competence. Research shows high rates of *Miranda* rights waivers by suspects, however, and that most suspects offer inculpatory statements to police (see Volume 2, Chapter 9, this handbook for more details about confessions). Approximately 80% of adult suspects waive their *Miranda* rights (Cassell & Hayman, 1996; Kassin et al., 2007; Leo, 1996), and juveniles waive their rights at even higher rates (Ferguson & Douglas, 1970; Grisso & Pomicter, 1977; Viljoen, Klaver, & Roesch, 2005). Early studies showed that more than 90% of juveniles waived their *Miranda* rights (Ferguson & Douglas, 1970; Grisso & Pomicter,

---

[3]Writing for the majority, Justice Thomas explained that "*all* criminal defendants—not merely those who plead guilty—may be required to make important decisions once criminal proceedings have been initiated. And while the decision to plead guilty is undeniably a profound one, it is no more complicated than the sum total of decisions that a defendant may be called upon to make during the course of a trial" (*Godinez v. Moran*, 1993, p. 398).

1977), and that only approximately 7% of juveniles refused to talk with police, whereas the rest provided statements varying in their amount of admission or denial (Grisso & Pomicter, 1977). A more recent study found that only approximately 13% of juveniles questioned about an offense reported that they asserted the right to silence, whereas 55% reported confessing and 31% reported talking to police but denying involvement (Viljoen et al., 2005). Similarly, only 10% of juveniles requested a lawyer, and less than 1% had a lawyer present during interrogation (Viljoen et al., 2005).

High rates of *Miranda* rights waivers are also likely for other vulnerable populations. Rogers and Shuman (2005) calculated a conservative estimate of suspects with mental retardation in custodial interrogation settings, determining that more than 400,000 such suspects waive their *Miranda* rights each year. A conservative estimate of suspects with mental illness in custodial interrogation settings is even higher, suggesting that approximately 695,000 such suspects waive their *Miranda* rights each year (Rogers, Harrison, Hazelwood, & Sewell, 2007).

Despite high rates of waivers, research suggests that *Miranda* waivers are not challenged very often. Direct studies of *Miranda* challenges are not available, but related research addressing the impact of motions to suppress inculpatory statements is informative. Such research has shown that cases are rarely lost on the basis of suppression motions (Cassell, 1996), that *Miranda*-based suppression motions are successful less than 1% of the time (Cassell, 1996), that only one case out of 10,500 was won by the defense on the basis of an excluded confession (Nardulli, 1983, 1987), and that appeals based on *Miranda* challenges rarely result in overturned convictions (Davies, 1982; Guy & Huckabee, 1988). Although such studies focused on the impact of *Miranda*-related motions in *defeating convictions*, they suggest the limited use of *Miranda* motions overall. In addition, they appear congruent with findings by Leo (2001a, 2001b), who reviewed several studies and determined that the provision of *Miranda* rights has not burdened police during

interrogation and has had limited impact on individuals' waiver and confession rates.

Totality of circumstances factors. When considering the validity of a suspect's *Miranda* rights waiver, judges are guided by a general legal standard called the *totality of circumstances* approach. Under the totality of circumstances approach, the validity of a *Miranda* waiver cannot be predicated on a single factor but must be based on a consideration of several relevant factors in a case. As with competence to stand trial, the capacity to waive *Miranda* rights is a functional and contextual matter because the analysis is based on an individual's abilities and characteristics in the particular circumstances of his or her case. Totality of circumstances factors are typically categorized as suspect related (e.g., defendant age and intelligence) or situation related (e.g., length and setting of interrogation). Awareness of the totality of circumstances approach is helpful for organizing research, and the following sections review research on several of the most often considered factors.[4]

Suspect-related factors. Across many decades and several studies, age and intelligence have consistently been identified as primary correlates of *Miranda* rights comprehension. The foundational research in the area, conducted by Grisso in the 1970s and 1980s, determined that juveniles ages 12 or younger generally demonstrated inadequate understanding of *Miranda* and that juveniles ages 13 to 15 demonstrated variable understanding. Older adolescents demonstrated variable comprehension as well and, ultimately, age was shown to be a better predictor of comprehension when it was combined with IQ (Grisso, 1981). More recent research has supported the varied difficulty in comprehending *Miranda* rights demonstrated by juveniles (e.g., Abramovitch, Peterson-Badali, & Rohan, 1995; Colwell et al., 2005; N. E. S. Goldstein, Zelle, & Grisso, 2012; Otto & Goldstein, 2005; Viljoen & Roesch, 2005; see also Chapter 12, this volume on juvenile offenders).

Comprehension of *Miranda* rights appears to plateau around ages 14 to 16, and adults demonstrate

---

[4]Research has largely focused on examining correlates and predictors of the two "cognitive" requirements for *Miranda* waiver (knowing and intelligent) because Supreme Court case law has limited causes for finding a waiver involuntary to police activities that are unduly coercive. Accordingly, the following subsections review research that is mostly concerned with examining the understanding and appreciation of *Miranda* warnings.

generally better comprehension that is more consistent across ages (Everington & Fulero, 1999; Grisso, 1981). Overall, it appears that "differences among adults in understanding of *Miranda* warnings are related primarily to differences among them in general intellectual functioning" (Grisso, 1981, p. 101).

Given the clear trends in *Miranda* comprehension by age, research has begun to examine how known cognitive, psychosocial, and neurological developmental trends may underlie age-related *Miranda* comprehension deficits. For example, abstract and logical thinking abilities develop during adolescence (Baird & Fugelsang, 2004), as does sustained attention (McKay, Halperin, Schwartz, & Sharma, 1994) and reasoning (Klaczynski, 2001). One *Miranda*-specific study found that improvements in cognitive functioning played a role in age-related differences in *Miranda* comprehension (Viljoen & Roesch, 2005). Similarly, research has demonstrated that psychosocial maturity is related to legal decision making by adolescents—for example, younger adolescents are less able to recognize long-term consequences and are more likely to comply with authority figures (Grisso et al., 2003)—and is also related to *Miranda* comprehension (Colwell et al., 2005; Grisso et al., 2003).

The second primary suspect-related totality of circumstances factor considered by judges is intelligence, and research has consistently associated IQ with *Miranda* understanding and appreciation abilities (Colwell et al., 2005; N. E. S. Goldstein, Condie, Kalbeitzer, Osman, & Geier, 2003; N. E. S. Goldstein, Zelle, & Grisso, 2012; Grisso, 1981; Otto & Goldstein, 2005; Viljoen & Roesch, 2005). In particular, verbal intelligence is strongly associated with *Miranda* comprehension (Colwell et al., 2005; N. E. S. Goldstein, Zelle, & Grisso, 2012; Viljoen & Roesch, 2005). As noted earlier, IQ appears to interact with age when examining juveniles, especially those with lower IQs (Colwell et al., 2005; Grisso, 1981; Viljoen & Roesch, 2005). In contrast, intelligence alone appears to be the foremost predictor of *Miranda* comprehension in adults (Grisso, 1981). Intellectual impairment rising to the level of mental retardation is particularly salient because individuals with such deficits have consistently been shown

to have inadequate comprehension of *Miranda* warnings (e.g., Clare & Gudjonsson, 1991; Cloud, Shepherd, Barkoff, & Shur, 2002; Everington & Fulero, 1999; Fulero & Everington, 1995; O'Connell, Garmoe, & Goldstein, 2005). Past research has also examined the relationship between a defendant's history of special education and *Miranda* comprehension, but it appears to be an inconsistent predictor of comprehension (e.g., N. E. S. Goldstein et al., 2003; Riggs Romaine, Zelle, Wolbransky, Zelechoski, & Goldstein, 2008), probably because individuals can be placed in special education for a wide variety of reasons, each of which may or may not be related to *Miranda* comprehension.

More specific skills such as academic abilities, as opposed to a broad categorization like special education history, have shown promise in recent research. Reading and listening skills are relevant to *Miranda* because the warnings may be delivered orally, in written format, or both, and the vocabulary and syntax of the *Miranda* warnings in many jurisdictions is above reading levels that may be expected of suspects with cognitive deficits (Fulero & Everington, 1995). One study found that academic achievement was a strong predictor of *Miranda* comprehension, even when controlling for the primary predictors of age and IQ (Zelle et al., 2008). In particular, juveniles with reading abilities that are at or below the fourth-grade level performed significantly worse on measures of *Miranda* comprehension than their peers with higher reading abilities. Rogers, Rogstad, et al. (2010), however, found only modest correlations between scores on a measure of *Miranda* rights misconceptions and those on measures of reading and listening comprehension. Nevertheless, it is clear that *Miranda* warnings vary widely in their reading comprehension level, as one study of 560 *Miranda* warnings included warnings ranging from Grade 2.8 to postgraduate level (Rogers, Harrison, Shuman, Sewell, & Hazelwood, 2007). Even more recently, research has extended to examine the *listenability* of *Miranda* warnings (Eastwood & Snook, 2012) because most warnings (67%) are delivered orally (Kassin et al., 2007), and attempts to reduce reading complexity have not yielded substantial improvements in *Miranda* comprehension (e.g., Eastwood, Snook, & Chaulk, 2010). Initial results suggest that helpful listenability alterations to *Miranda* warnings include explanatory components, instructions about the waiver process, and the listing of information into discrete rights (Eastwood & Snook, 2012).

The presence of mental illness, especially psychotic symptoms, also appears to be relevant to *Miranda* comprehension. In particular, adults with psychotic symptoms demonstrated poorer *Miranda* comprehension than adults without psychotic symptoms (Cooper & Zapf, 2008; Olley, 1998) and, even more specifically, individuals with schizophrenia performed more poorly than those with other psychotic disorders (Viljoen, Roesch, & Zapf, 2002). More generally, adult psychiatric inpatients demonstrated similar *Miranda* misunderstandings as juveniles and individuals with intellectual impairment (Cooper & Zapf, 2008).

The presence of other psychiatric symptoms, such as depressive symptoms and anxiety, has not demonstrated a significant relationship with *Miranda* comprehension (e.g., Olubadewo, 2008; Viljoen & Roesch, 2005). Symptoms of attention-deficit/hyperactivity disorder, in contrast, were associated with a greater likelihood of juveniles waiving the right to counsel (Viljoen et al., 2005) and poorer *Miranda* comprehension in adults (Viljoen & Roesch, 2005). Only one study examined the direct relationship between general substance use and *Miranda* comprehension, finding that self-reported drug and alcohol use was related to *Miranda* comprehension deficits in juveniles (Olubadewo, 2008). Generally, intoxication is associated with relevant considerations such as reduced inhibition, attention, and reasoning (e.g., Fromme, Katz, & D'Amico, 1997), and is likely to affect *Miranda* comprehension in many cases because many youth (Ferguson & Douglas, 1970; Viljoen et al., 2005) and adults (Sigurdsson & Gudjonsson, 1994) have reported being under the influence of drugs or alcohol during interrogation.

Finally, personality characteristics have not been investigated in the context of *Miranda* comprehension, with the exception of factors such as suggestibility and compliance. Although suggestibility has traditionally been presumed to be associated with behaviors during interrogation, more recent research has implied that suggestibility may not be a key factor in the context of *Miranda* comprehension and decision making (Rogers, Harrison, Rogstad, LaFortune, & Hazelwood, 2010). A stronger relationship may exist between compliance and *Miranda* capacities, as adult defendants who scored higher on a measure of compliance tended to perform more poorly on measures of *Miranda* comprehension and reasoning (Rogers, Rogstad, et al., 2010). This research raises interesting challenges to the intuitive links between increased suggestibility, voluntariness, and vulnerable suspects in interrogation settings. It may be that suggestibility is less relevant to the initial consideration of waiving *Miranda* rights than it is to later interactions between suspects and police that may lead to inculpatory statements. (Suggestibility and false confessions are discussed in more detail in Volume 2, Chapter 9, this handbook.) Rather, the related construct of compliance, or the tendency toward obedience that may lead to decisions to cooperate with authority figures (i.e., waive one's rights and talk with police), may be the more relevant consideration. Further research is needed in this area (Rogers, Rogstad, et al., 2010).

Courts have long cited experience with the criminal justice system as a consideration when making *Miranda* waiver validity assessments, yet research generally has not supported criminal justice experience as a significant predictor of *Miranda* comprehension (Cooper & Zapf, 2008; N. E. S. Goldstein et al., 2003; Grisso, 1981; Rogers, Rogstad, et al., 2010; Viljoen & Roesch, 2005). Interestingly, one study showed that the history of contact with attorneys is associated with better *Miranda* comprehension for juveniles, including younger juveniles and those with low IQ scores (Viljoen & Roesch, 2005). It is widely assumed that suspects (and the general population) know the *Miranda* rights because of repeated exposure via popular media (Nguyen, 2000; Rogers, 2008, 2011; Rogers, Rogstad, et al., 2010). Research has shown this presumption to be false, however, as defendants and college students alike have demonstrated several misconceptions about the *Miranda* rights (Rogers, 2011; Rogers, Rogstad, et al., 2010).

Finally, background characteristics such as race and socioeconomic status (SES) have been investigated as moderators of *Miranda* comprehension with mixed results. It is highly likely, however, that a complex relationship exists between race/ethnicity and *Miranda* comprehension due to shared correlates such as SES and level and quality of an individual's education. Moreover, when controlling for the two primary predictors of age and IQ, there appears to be no relationship between racial/ethnic identity and *Miranda* comprehension (Everington & Fulero, 1999; N. E. S. Goldstein et al., 2003). Regarding other social variables, one study found that low-SES juveniles were less likely than high-SES juveniles to assert their rights to silence and counsel (Viljoen et al., 2005), and another study found that they demonstrated poor *Miranda* comprehension (Viljoen & Roesch, 2005).

Situation-related factors. For the most part, the relationship between the characteristics of the interrogation, such as the setting and the length of questioning, and *Miranda* comprehension has not been directly examined. Nevertheless, there are several areas of related research that underscore the relevance of situation-related factors and how they may interfere with an individual's understanding, appreciation, and voluntariness. For example, lengthy interrogations can cause stress and persuade suspects to talk in order to end the unpleasant experience. In fact, recent research has examined the effect of experimentally induced stress on individuals' *Miranda* comprehension and reasoning using mock-crime paradigms and found that even short periods of stress induced through accusations and interrogation-type techniques negatively impact individuals' comprehension and reasoning (Rogers, Gillard, Wooley, & Fiduccia, 2011; Scherr & Madon, 2012). Other considerations that are likely to accompany long interrogation sessions, such as sleep deprivation, have been shown to impact cognitive skills that would be relevant for suspects in custodial interrogation (e.g., Harrison & Horne, 1996; McCarthy & Waters, 1997; Williams, Lubin, & Goodnow, 1959).

The delivery method of a *Miranda* warning may also be an important factor in cases. Beyond whether the warning was administered orally or in written format, factors such as the length and complexity of the warning, how understanding was checked by police, how the warning was introduced (e.g., as a mere formality), and when and how many times the warning was provided are potentially relevant (Grisso, 1986; Oberlander & Goldstein, 2001). Additional research directly examining the impact of warning delivery method is needed, particularly because the wide variability across jurisdictions may mean that some defendants are placed at greater (dis)advantage than others simply due to regional practices.

In the case of juveniles, a jurisdiction may require that a parent or other "interested adult" be present during interrogation as a mechanism to protect the juveniles' rights. Whether required or not, the presence of an interested adult has not been well supported by research, which demonstrated that parents provided little advice to children (Grisso & Pomicter, 1977), and when they did offer advice, the majority (60%) advised waiving the rights to silence and counsel (Grisso & Ring, 1979). More recently, Viljoen et al. (2005) demonstrated that parental presence remains of mixed value: Of juveniles who knew their parents' opinion, more than half (56%) stated that their parents wanted them to "tell the truth," whereas 11% stated that their parents wanted them to deny the offense. None of the juveniles surveyed reported that their parents had advised them to remain silent.

Waiver decision making. Whether a suspect sufficiently comprehends the *Miranda* rights is separate from the suspect's decision to either invoke or waive his or her rights. As Kassin et al. (2010) noted, there is likely to be a range among suspects who do comprehend the rights as to how well they are able to decide about waiving or invoking their rights. Therefore, research has examined what factors may be associated with *Miranda* waiver decision making, especially among adolescents. Generally, suspects who are less able to consider long-term consequences are more likely to make a waiver decision based on the immediate negative consequences (Kassin et al., 2010). Research suggests a tie between *Miranda* comprehension and decision making, as would be expected. For example, one vignette-based study found that 90% of adolescents who could understand a waiver form indicated that they would not sign the waiver, whereas 65% of adolescents who could not understand the form said that they would sign the waiver (Abramovitch, Higgins-Biss, & Biss, 1993). Similar results were obtained in a more recent study by Viljoen et al. (2005), who found that adolescents with poor legal abilities (i.e., poor understanding and appreciation of the rights) were more likely to waive their right to counsel, and that poor legal ability was a better predictor of rights waiver than broader cognitive abilities.

Other potential influences on *Miranda* decision making include suggestibility and psychotic symptoms. Although intuitively appealing, the relationship between suggestibility and *Miranda* comprehension and decision making is not all that strong. One recent study determined that suggestibility was not significantly related to *Miranda* reasoning (Rogers, Harrison, et al., 2010), instead suggesting that the related concept of compliance (i.e., intentional obedience to authority) was significantly related to *Miranda* reasoning. Specifically, participants who were high in compliance were less able to consider the long-term benefits of invoking the rights (Rogers, Harrison, et al., 2010). These results join the mixed findings from previous studies that have shown differing patterns of relationship between suggestibility and comprehension (McLachlan, Roesch, & Douglas, 2011), appearing to imply that suggestibility is not as relevant a factor for decision making (Rogers, Harrison, et al., 2010).

Finally, research has supported a limited, yet important, role of psychotic symptoms in *Miranda* decision making. Although some results have indicated that psychotic symptoms among defendants in the general population "play a minimal overall role in assessing impaired *Miranda* reasoning" (Rogers, Blackwood, Fiduccia, Drogin, & Sewell, 2011, as cited in Rogers, 2011, p. 734), there is evidence that active psychotic symptoms have a notable impact on *Miranda* reasoning among hospitalized defendants (Rogers, Harrison, Hazelwood, & Sewell, 2007). Overall, less research has examined factors relevant to *Miranda* waiver decision making than *Miranda* rights comprehension, and additional study is needed in this area because of the consequential nature of deciding to waive one's rights and talk with police.

Assessment methods. Given the relationship between factors like IQ and *Miranda* comprehension noted earlier, the assessment of an individual's capacity to waive his or her *Miranda* rights may involve general instruments that are designed to measure relevant capacities, such as intelligence and language comprehension. In addition, specialized forensic assessment instruments that were designed specifically to assess *Miranda*-related capacities are available.

The first of these tools is Grisso's Instruments for Assessing Understanding and Appreciation of *Miranda* Rights, which is a standardized set of four measures that were initially designed for research purposes in the 1970s and were widely adopted for clinical use since then (Grisso, 1998). The instruments were recently revised to broaden their applicability and provide updated normative data. The *Miranda* Rights Comprehension Instruments (MRCI; N. E. S. Goldstein, Zelle, & Grisso, 2012) include revised versions of the original four measures: the Comprehension of *Miranda* Rights—II (an assessment of *Miranda* understanding that asks examinees to paraphrase each warning), the Comprehension of *Miranda* Rights—Recognition—II (an assessment of *Miranda* understanding that uses preconstructed sentences that examinees must identify as having the same or different meaning as each warning), the Function of Rights in Interrogation (an assessment of *Miranda* appreciation of three relevant domains: the nature of interrogation, the right to silence, and the right to counsel), and the Comprehension of *Miranda* Vocabulary—II (an assessment of understanding of vocabulary that is common to many *Miranda* warnings). The MRCI include normative data from two samples of 21st-century juvenile and nonjuvenile youth, and an overview of their development and psychometrics can be found in N. E. S. Goldstein et al., (2011). Updated normative data for adults will be available in 2014.

A second set of measures was recently published as the Standardized Assessment of *Miranda* Abilities (SAMA; Rogers, Sewell, Drogin, & Fiduccia, 2012). The SAMA are the result of a program of development studies with adult defendants, and details of their development can be found in Rogers et al. (2009) and Rogers, Harrison, Hazelwood, and Sewell (2007). Like the MRCI, the SAMA contain independent measures that each aim to assess related elements of an individual's *Miranda* capacities. The *Miranda* Quiz uses true or false questions to assess whether examinees hold certain common misconceptions, and the *Miranda* Vocabulary Scale is a vocabulary measure of relevant terms. The *Miranda* Comprehension Template allows an evaluator to assess an examinee's understanding of the *Miranda* warning given in his or her jurisdiction by having the examinee paraphrase the warning. The *Miranda* Acquiescence Questionnaire assesses the examinee's level of acquiescence, and the *Miranda* Reasoning Measure assesses the examinee's thinking and reasoning around his or her *Miranda* waiver decision.

Remediation.   Efforts to improve an individual's legal knowledge as compared to efforts to develop measures of legal abilities are relatively young, and examination of *Miranda*-related learning is even less studied than the restoration/remediation of adjudicative competence. To date, there appears to be only one program that was developed specifically to address the remediation of understanding and appreciation of *Miranda* rights (Kalbeitzer, 2008; Strachan, 2008), which focused on adolescents. Ultimately, *Miranda*-specific instruction improved individuals' understanding and appreciation in the short term, whereas cognitive maturation appeared to account for improvements in the long term, and psychosocial capacities and legal judgment did not appear to be affected by instruction or maturation (Kalbeitzer, 2008; Strachan, 2008).

Research Addressing Adjudicative Competence

By all accounts, evaluations of an individual's adjudicative competence are the most common type of forensic mental health evaluation (Melton et al., 2007). Widely cited estimates suggest that 4%–8% of all felony defendants are referred for competence evaluation, and attorneys may have concerns about competence in as many as 15% of all cases (Hoge et al., 1992; LaFortune & Nicholson, 1995; Poythress et al., 2002). But, these estimates are based on small surveys from a few jurisdictions, so the actual rates of referral probably vary more. Indeed, there are no available wide-scale data on the rates of, and reasons for, competence referrals. Some early data suggest that attorneys may have requested many competence evaluations erroneously (simply due to misunderstanding the relevant legal concepts; Roesch & Golding, 1980; Rosenberg & McGarry, 1972) or strategically (e.g., to delay trial; Melton et al., 2007), although these incorrect referrals are probably less common currently. The available data do suggest a *sliding scale* approach to competence referral, wherein attorneys are more likely to request evaluations when defendants face more serious charges (Berman & Osborne, 1987; Hoge et al., 1992). This finding certainly appears congruent with most legal and clinical guidance, which suggests that forensic evaluators should expect a defendant to demonstrate greater capacities when he or she is facing more serious charges or proceedings (e.g., American Bar Association [ABA], 1989).

Rates and correlates of incompetence.   Of those defendants who are referred for formal evaluation, clinicians find approximately one in five incompetent to stand trial (IST).[5] In a large meta-analysis of 68 studies that were published between 1967 and 2008, the base rate of IST was 27.5% (Pirelli et al., 2011). Of course, IST rates vary greatly across samples and jurisdictions, ranging from 7% to 70% in the meta-analysis. Large, jurisdiction-wide studies tend to reveal IST rates around 20%. For example, in the largest single study of competence evaluations—reviewing 8,000 cases over a 12-year period—clinicians opined that 19% of the Virginia defendants they evaluated were IST (Warren et al., 2006). Similarly, clinicians found 19% of Alabama defendants IST (Cooper & Zapf, 2003) and 18% of federal defendants IST (Cochrane et al., 2001). Clinicians found slightly higher rates of IST

---

[5]Far more research has examined competence "findings" at the stage when clinicians offer an opinion on competence than at the later stage when a judge renders a formal decision about competence. In other words, researchers more often examine clinicians' opinions than judges' rulings. But, because the court so often follows clinician opinions about competence (e.g., Hart & Hare, 1992; Zapf et al., 2004), the rates of incompetence are probably similar whether clinician opinion or judicial disposition is measured.

among Hawaii defendants (25% in Gowensmith, Murrie, & Boccaccini, 2012) and much higher rates among a small sample of Utah defendants (53% in Skeem, Golding, Cohn, & Berge, 1998), but most statewide samples appear to reveal IST rates around the 18%–25% range.

What factors influence a clinician's opinion about a defendant's competence to stand trial? Psychosis, not surprisingly, appears to be the characteristic that is most strongly associated with incompetence. In a comprehensive meta-analysis (Pirelli et al., 2011), defendants who were diagnosed with a psychotic disorder were approximately eight times more likely to be found IST than those without a psychotic diagnosis (see Nicholson & Kugler, 1991, for similar, but earlier findings). The presence of a psychotic disorder was also the strongest predictor of IST in most large, single-site studies (e.g., Cochrane et al., 2001; Cooper & Zapf, 2003; Warren et al., 2006). But, these findings do not indicate that evaluators simply equate psychosis with incompetence. In most studies, even the majority of defendants who were diagnosed with a psychotic disorder were opined competent to stand trial (CST).

Cognitive disorders (a broad category including mental retardation, brain damage, and other conditions that impair cognition) tend to be the second condition most strongly associated with IST (e.g., Cochrane et al., 2001; Warren et al., 2006). Again, despite this apparent relationship, most defendants with mental retardation or other forms of cognitive disorder are still opined CST. For example, 70% of Virginia defendants who were diagnosed with mental retardation or learning disorders were still opined competent (Warren et al., 2006). Indeed, not all studies have found an association between mental retardation and IST (Nicholson & Kugler, 1991).

Of course, research depends largely on the data that are easy to obtain and code, so many studies examine broad diagnostic categories, and fewer studies examine the more precise symptoms and behaviors that relate to incompetence. However, these more focused studies are crucial because incompetence is attributable to specific psychological symptoms interfering with specific legal capacities, not simply a clinical diagnosis. Indeed, specific

symptoms, rather than diagnoses, are better predictors of an individual's IST. In their detailed study, Rosenfeld and Wall (1998) found that incompetent defendants were significantly higher on clinicians' ratings of thought disorder, delusional beliefs, paranoia, disorientation, and hallucinations, but not necessarily depressive symptoms or estimated intellectual functioning. The MacArthur study of adjudicative competence revealed that "conceptual disorganization" (as measured by the scale of this name on the Brief Psychiatric Rating Scale [Overall & Gorham, 1962]) was the symptom that was most clearly associated with impaired competence across all diagnostic groups (Hoge, Poythress, et al., 1997). Likewise, Viljoen, Zapf, and Roesch (2004) found that conceptual disorganization was associated with impairments on another measure of trial competence.

These detailed studies are helpful in shedding light on the types of symptoms that are most commonly associated with findings of incompetence. However, because competence is such an individualized question regarding the match between a particular defendant and a particular legal context, it remains unlikely—and undesirable—that clinicians will ever rely on a research-generated list of symptoms to perfectly *predict* an individual's incompetence.

Nevertheless, psychiatric variables appear to be the strongest correlates of incompetence (Pirelli et al., 2011)—a finding that is hardly surprising but is certainly reassuring. Only severe psychiatric symptoms (those typically associated with psychosis or profound cognitive disorders) would be sufficient to interfere with the simple capacities that a defendant must demonstrate for trial competence. But, research often reveals that social and demographic factors correspond with findings of incompetence, presumably due to their covariation with serious mental illness. For example, compared to defendants who were evaluated and found competent, defendants found IST "were slightly older (35 years old vs. 31.8), predominantly non-White (52.3 vs. 43.1%), had a higher unemployment rate (70.8 vs. 58.2%) and a greater percentage were unmarried (84 vs. 77.3%)" (Pirelli et al., 2011, p. 15), according to the largest meta-analysis. Of these common demographic factors, unemployment tends to be the one that is most strongly associated with findings of incompetence (Cooper & Zapf, 2003; Pirelli et al., 2011). Of course, any demographic differences between those defendants found IST versus CST are more striking when we consider that even the broader population of defendants who are *referred* for evaluation tend to be "marginalized individuals with extensive criminal and mental health histories" (Zapf & Roesch, 2009, p. 50).

Validity, reliability and quality of competence evaluations.　Can clinicians reach valid, or accurate, conclusions about a defendant's trial competence? This simple research question has been remarkably difficult to answer. As Zapf and Roesch (2006, 2009) emphasized, there is no gold standard or clear criterion by which to gauge the accuracy of a competence opinion. Judicial opinions cannot serve as the criterion because they are not independent of clinician opinion; indeed, they tend to closely follow the clinicians' opinions (e.g., Zapf, Hubbard, Cooper, Wheeles, & Ronan, 2004). Another criterion might involve opinions from a *blue ribbon panel* of experts (Golding, Roesch, & Schreiber, 1984), but this is more a test of reliability (described below) than validity. The ideal validity study might arrange a provisional trial in which researchers document a defendant's competence-relevant abilities and behavior and a judge renders an independent decision about his or her competence (Zapf & Roesch, 2006, 2009). But, this ideal study has never been conducted, probably due to the tremendous practical challenges.

One recent attempt to study validity used mathematical models to infer validity from reliability (Mossman, 2008; Mossman et al., 2010). Mossman et al. (2010) arranged for experienced forensic evaluators to review written competence reports and offer competence opinions on a graded scale (rather than dichotomous competent/incompetent opinions). Using sophisticated techniques to analyze these ratings, the authors concluded that "experts' intrinsic ability to discriminate between competent and incompetent defendants is high (but not perfect)" (Mossman et al., 2010, pp. 411–412).

Relative to validity research, more research has addressed *reliability*, which is certainly a prerequisite for validity. Authorities have suggested that evaluations of trial competence may be the most *reliable* types of forensic evaluations (Melton et al., 2007; Zapf & Roesch, 2009). That is, it seems reasonable to expect different evaluators to reach the same conclusions about the same defendant. After all, competence evaluations involve a narrow focus on a defendant's *present* abilities for a circumscribed task (i.e., understanding and participating in proceedings), as opposed to the more complex retrospective inferences necessary for evaluations of legal sanity (see Chapter 4, this volume for a discussion of criminal responsibility). Consistent with this expectation, some studies have reported excellent reliability in evaluations of trial competence. In a study by Rogers and Johansson-Love (2009), when trained raters scored structured competence measures (usually based on the same interview), rates of agreement ranged from good to excellent, albeit with stronger agreement for overall competent/incompetent status than for individual scales of the instruments (e.g., Golding et al., 1984; Roesch & Golding, 1980). These instrument-focused reliability studies are important, but they probably reveal more about the instruments than about the evaluators or the competence construct itself.

Fewer reliability studies have examined clinicians in practice, but the first two such studies revealed excellent agreement among clinicians who offered opinions about whether or not a particular defendant was CST (R. L. Goldstein & Stone, 1977; Poythress & Stock, 1980). However, clinicians in these early studies appear to have worked and trained together in the same setting. Even scholars who are optimistic about the reliability of competence evaluations acknowledge that reliability may be weaker among independent clinicians from different institutions or "evaluation centers" (Melton et al., 2007, p. 144). Evidence of weaker reliability emerged in a national survey of 273 board-certified forensic psychologists and psychiatrists who responded to two brief vignettes describing defendants who had been referred for competence evaluations (G. Morris, Haroun, &

Naimark, 2004a, 2004b); clinicians offered an over-all competence opinion for each of the two vignettes in light of three different competence standards. Overall, rater agreement was remarkably poor; the participants were evenly divided (49.2% vs. 50.8%) regarding the defendant's competence in one vignette. Researchers lamented the results and concluded that "the defendant's fate depends only upon who performed the evaluation" (G. Morris et al., 2004b, p. 216). But, because several aspects of the study methodology seemed particularly conducive to eliciting poor rater agreement (e.g., brief vignettes with limited detail describing ambiguous cases), these results should not be used to characterize wide-scale practice.

In a study that better reflects wide-scale practice, Skeem et al. (1998) reviewed 100 competence reports—two evaluations for each of 50 defendants—from a sample of 18 Utah clinicians. Evaluators demonstrated fair agreement (82%) regarding whether a defendant was competent or incompetent but poorer agreement (approximately 25% on average) regarding whether a defendant was impaired on specific psycholegal skills necessary for trial competence. Indeed, evaluator agreement fell below 10% regarding almost half of these skills (Skeem et al., 1998).

In the largest available study of *field reliability* or agreement among forensic evaluators in routine practice, researchers reviewed 216 cases from Hawaii (Gowensmith et al., 2012). Hawaii is uniquely suited for reliability studies because the state requires three separate evaluations from independent clinicians for each felony defendant who is referred for CST evaluation. In 71% of the initial CST evaluations, all of the evaluators agreed about a defendant's competence or incompetence. Agreement was somewhat lower (61%) in reevaluations of defendants who were originally found incompetent and were sent for restoration services. Overall, the results reflected moderate agreement among independent evaluators. Reliability was significantly better than chance but clearly weaker than the reliability reported in small studies in which cooperating clinicians conducted the same interviews or used the same instruments. The disagreement among the trios of Hawaii evaluators (29% in

Gowensmith et al., 2012) and the pairs of Utah evaluators (18% in Skeem et al., 1998) seems to suggest that approximately 20%–30% of CST cases in the field result in divergent opinions among independent evaluators. So, overall, a fair view of the research suggests that the reliability of competence evaluations is not as poor as "flipping coins in the courtroom" (G. Morris et al., 2004b, p. 216), but reliability remains less than perfect.

Some unreliability is certainly due to difficult cases. Although the legal determination regarding competence is dichotomous (i.e., competent or not competent), it seems reasonable to think of the capacities underlying trial competence as dimensional; in other words, some defendants are *more competent* and others are *less competent*. If these capacities are dimensional, we might not be surprised to find some disagreement among reasonable clinicians regarding cases that fall toward the midpoint of this continuum (Murrie, Boccaccini, Zapf, Warren, & Henderson, 2008). But, clinicians themselves may also differ in terms of where they draw the threshold for competence versus incompetence. If this were the case, we might expect different clinicians to differ in the rates at which they *find* incompetence among the same population of defendants. Therefore, in order to examine whether individual clinicians vary in terms of how often they find defendants IST, researchers studied 60 practicing clinicians who conducted a combined total of more than 7,000 evaluations. The rates of IST findings varied considerably—from 0% to 62%—across evaluators, suggesting that individual evaluators may differ in terms of how they define, conceptualize, and opine competence (Murrie et al., 2008).

Although researchers can rarely observe actual evaluator practices in an attempt to understand the reasons for differences or unreliability, they can study one end product of evaluator practice—the written report of a competence evaluation. Several studies across different locations have examined the quality of forensic evaluation reports and have found that "the practice of forensic psychological assessment falls far short of its promise" (Nicholson & Norwood, 2000, p. 40). For example, after reviewing 100 CST reports from Utah, Skeem and colleagues (Skeem & Golding, 1998; Skeem et al.,

1998) reported that evaluators often provided reasonable clinical information but failed to detail the reasoning underlying their psycholegal opinions. Many of the evaluators also failed to explicitly address many of the specific capacities related to trial competence.

Disposition of competence cases.   Of course, questions about competence are ultimately legal decisions, not clinical decisions. After evaluators form opinions, the courts must render formal decisions about the defendants' adjudicative competence. But, in the vast majority of cases, research suggests that the courts agree with the forensic evaluator. In the Hawaii study that examined multiple evaluations, judges followed the *majority opinion* among evaluators in most cases (93% of initial competence evaluations and 77% of reevaluations that followed restoration efforts; Gowensmith et al., 2012). When judges did decide against the majority opinion, they more often did so by finding the defendant incompetent than competent, reflecting a conservative approach. Of course, judges do not typically consider multiple opinions in routine cases. More often, they receive only one opinion and tend to follow—or at least agree with—that single opinion. One study reported a 99.6% agreement rate between forensic evaluator opinions and Alabama court dispositions (Zapf et al., 2004), and other studies reported at least 90% agreement (e.g., Cruise & Rogers, 1998; Hart & Hare, 1992).

"Restoration" to competence.   For the minority of defendants who are found IST (usually approximately 20% of the defendants referred for evaluation), the courts typically order remediation efforts to "restore" competence (as described in the later Practice and Policy Issues section). Fortunately, most defendants make significant progress toward competence. Indeed, most defendants who are originally found incompetent attain competence within 6 months, and the vast majority does so within 1 year (e.g., D. Morris & DeYoung, 2012; D. Morris & Parker, 2008; Nicholson & McNulty, 1992). Overall, at least 80%–90% of IST defendants with mental illness are eventually restored (or trained) to competence (Pinals, 2005; Samuel & Michaels, 2011).

Generally, a few factors appear to be associated with competence restoration. For example, younger age, diagnoses of mood disorder or nonpsychotic disorders, and more serious criminal charges are associated with successful competence restoration. Those defendants least likely to be restored to competence tend to be older, have more prior hospitalizations or incompetence findings, carry diagnoses of mental retardation or comorbid mental retardation and serious psychiatric illness, and face less serious charges (e.g., Colwell & Gianesini, 2011; D. Morris & Parker, 2008; Mossman, 2007; Zapf & Roesch, 2011). Similar to most research on competence evaluation, most research on competence restoration tends to rely on diagnoses and/or demographic factors that are easily coded from case files. When conducting archival research, this is probably a practical necessity, but studying broad diagnostic categories and the dichotomous competent versus incompetent status is only indirectly relevant to the more nuanced assessments that clinicians must make about a defendant's trial competence. More precise research on the defendant's specific *symptoms* and specific *functional capacities* that are amenable to restoration would be more helpful for clinicians in the field (Zapf & Roesch, 2011).

A few early studies described specific programming for competence restoration (Brown, 1992; Davis, 1985; Pendleton, 1980), and a few studies have more formally studied specific programming among small samples of defendants. For example, Siegel and Elwork (1990) compared a group of defendants who received an experimental intervention (court-related education via videotape, courtroom models, and verbal instruction) to a control group who received standard group treatment addressing psychiatric issues and found that many more of the defendants in the competence-specific experimental intervention were restored to competence.

Bertman et al. (2003) also used a control group comparison to study competence restoration programming. The control condition involved the hospital's default 4-times-per-week educational group addressing legal rights. The experimental groups involved two different strategies for competence restoration: supplemental legal-rights education and supplemental "deficit-focused" individual education addressing deficits specific to trial competence. Both experimental interventions led to better performance and faster improvement on posttests that involved competence assessment instruments. However, the experimental intervention groups were similarly effective (i.e., neither was clearly superior to the other), leaving it unclear whether it was the nature of the interventions or simply the additional patient contacts that were responsible for the improvement. Practically speaking, the authors concluded that the *group* supplemental legal-rights education appeared more feasible than the *individualized* deficit-focused intervention.

Of course, much of the success in interventions for defendants who are incompetent due to psychosis is probably due to concurrent treatment by psychiatric medication. Concurrent medication for defendants who are incompetent due to mental retardation is probably less common and less effective. So, restoration programs for defendants with mental retardation have appeared less successful than those for defendants with psychosis.[6] In one of the better studies of mentally retarded defendants in a competence restoration program, only 18% were restored to competence (Anderson & Hewitt, 2002). Nevertheless, one of the most rigorous and well-developed restoration programs in the literature addressed mentally retarded defendants (Wall, Krupp, & Guilmette, 2003). Wall and Christopher (2012) reported that Rhode Island's restoration program using the "Slater method"—a comprehensive approach that involved extensive education to the defendant and guidance to attorneys—resulted in a 61% rate of restoration to competence compared to 17% with traditional treatment alone.

Research Addressing Competence for Execution

Because CFE evaluations are so rare, there has been remarkably little empirical research on this type of criminal competence. The vast majority of scholarship on these evaluations have debated the ethics of

performing them at all (e.g., Appelbaum, 1986; Bonnie, 1990; Brodsky, 1990; Brodsky, Zapf, & Boccaccini, 2001, 2005; Ewing, 1987; Radelet & Barnard, 1986) or proposed procedures for performing them appropriately (e.g., Brodsky, Zapf, & Boccaccini, 2001, 2005; Cunningham & Goldstein, 2003; Heilbrun & McClaren, 1988; Small & Otto, 1991). The very limited *empirical* literature tends to be descriptive. For example, Young and colleagues (Young, Boccaccini, Conroy, & Lawson, 2007; Young, Boccaccini, Lawson, & Conroy, 2008) described the practices and perspectives of 16 Texas clinicians who performed CFE evaluations. A few other studies simply surveyed clinician attitudes regarding CFE (Deitchman, Kennedy, & Beckham, 1991; Leong, Silva, Weinstock, & Ganzini, 2000; Pirelli & Zapf, 2008). Currently, the field lacks even basic research on the frequency and outcomes of these evaluations, although anecdotal evidence suggests that they are quite rare.

PRACTICE AND POLICY ISSUES

This section discusses practice and policy issues regarding criminal competencies. We begin by discussing general practices regarding the evaluation of criminal competencies and then discuss issues relevant to each of the three primary types of criminal competencies that are discussed throughout this chapter.

General Practices Regarding the Evaluation of Criminal Competencies

As with any forensic evaluation, practice for evaluating criminal competencies is guided by general field standards that consider the unique requirements produced by the intersection of law and psychology. Several sources provide clinical guidance for evaluating criminal competencies and preparing evaluation reports (e.g., Golding, 2008; Kruh & Grisso, 2009; Mossman et al., 2007; National Judicial College [NJC], 2011; Zapf & Roesch, 2009). In addition, authorities in forensic psychology and psychiatry have prepared ethical/practice guidelines that

---

[6]For incompetent defendants with mental retardation, *restoration* is probably a misnomer because they may have never had the trial-related skills that clinicians are attempting to "restore." More appropriate terms might be competence training or competence *attainment* (e.g., Schouten, 2003; Wall et al., 2003).

address considerations specific to forensic work (e.g., American Psychological Association [APA], 2013; Mossman et al., 2007). Although there is some minor variability among this guidance, the series of steps described in the following sections is common across most sources and is generally consistent with best practices (see Chapter 1, this volume for additional guidance concerning forensic assessment).[7]

Evaluator qualifications.　The appointed evaluator should be a licensed psychologist or psychiatrist with ample training in forensic evaluation, particularly criminal competence evaluations (e.g., ABA Criminal Justice Mental Health Standard [hereinafter ABA Standard] 7-3.10; 1989). Evaluating criminal competence requires training and experience beyond that typical of general clinical practice. Generally, this involves a doctoral degree in psychology or a medical specialization in psychiatry, followed by specialized training—whether a formal fellowship or extensive continuing education—in forensic evaluation, including evaluations of adjudicative competence. Several states specifically identify training and continuing education requirements that evaluators must meet in order to be eligible to perform court-ordered evaluations of criminal competence (e.g., Raising Question of Competency, 1982; *United States v. Miller*, 2005). But, even absent specific state requirements, psychologists who agree to evaluate an individual's competence have an ethical duty to demonstrate competence specific to the evaluations and the case at hand (APA, 2013).

The clinician who evaluates a defendant's competence should *not* be the same clinician who provides treatment services to the defendant (e.g., APA, 2013; NJC, 2011). This ethical guideline is typically easy to follow in systems that rely on private, outpatient forensic evaluations. It may be more challenging to follow in hospital systems that provide inpatient evaluations. Yet, even inpatient settings can arrange services so that one clinician performs *only* the evaluation role, and other clinicians provide only treatment roles, for any given defendant.

Evaluation preparation.　As with any forensic evaluation, an evaluation of criminal competence requires that the evaluator prepare by clarifying the referral question and gathering the case facts. For example, the question of trial competence is well defined (i.e., all state statutes closely follow the *Dusky* criteria), but clarifying the referral question is crucial because attorneys may use the term *competency* generically, sometimes confusing competence to stand trial with capacity to waive *Miranda*, or even with mental state at the time of the offense. It is also crucial to inquire about the factors that prompted the referral; these may be historical factors such as a history of psychiatric hospitalization or special education, or more recent factors such as problems communicating with defense counsel. This data gathering usually requires a conversation with the referral source (often defense counsel, but sometimes the court or prosecutor). Some evaluators also rely on a standard referral form that queries basic case information and the reason for referral (see Kruh & Grisso, 2009; Melton et al., 2007; Zapf & Roesch, 2009, for examples).

Even when defense counsel is not the referral source, a conversation with defense counsel is usually necessary to (a) ensure that counsel is aware of the pending evaluation, (b) gather information about the defendant's interaction with counsel up to this point (after all, adjudicative competence requires the ability to assist counsel, and an attorney may have educated his or her client about *Miranda* since the interrogation), and (c) gather information about the tasks likely facing the defendant during the proceedings (again, adjudicative competence is contextual, requiring the functional abilities necessary for a specific case). Of course, regardless of who requested the evaluation, all conversations with the defense counsel should remain neutral, and evaluators should be cautious about any attempts to sway the course or outcome of the evaluation. Defense counsel is a crucial source of information but not a collaborator in the evaluation.

---

[7]This series of steps serves as a descriptive summary of the typical evaluation process; it is not intended to serve as stand-alone guidance, nor is it sufficient instruction for performing a criminal competence evaluation. Clinicians who anticipate performing *Miranda* comprehension or adjudicative competence evaluations should study more comprehensive guides (e.g., A. M. Goldstein & Goldstein, 2010; Kruh & Grisso, 2009; Zapf & Roesch, 2009) and engage in more formal instruction.

Preparation for evaluation also requires proper authorization. For court-ordered evaluations, authorization is simply the formal court order. For ex parte evaluations (i.e., those arranged by defense counsel, without initial court involvement), authorization involves the written request (a form of consent) from counsel and eventually involves informed consent by the defendant.

Finally, as with other forms of forensic evaluation, preparation for evaluations of criminal competencies involves gathering records. At a minimum, evaluators should gather arrest reports, indictments, and other details of the pending charges. These are crucial in order to gauge whether the defendant accurately understands the charges; they can also help illuminate how accurately the defendant can relay the circumstances surrounding those charges. Often, it is important to gather historical records that might detail the defendant's psychiatric illness (e.g., records from prior psychiatric hospitalizations) or intellectual disability (e.g., records from special education services or disability evaluations).

Evaluation process.   After a careful review of the records, conversation with defense counsel, and other preparation, the evaluator can proceed to interview the defendant. As with other forensic evaluations, an interview must begin with a clear notification to the defendant, describing the purpose of the evaluation, reasons for evaluation, who requested the evaluation and who will receive evaluation reports, and limits on confidentiality (see Zapf & Roesch, 2009, for a sample notification). For court-ordered evaluations, formal *consent* by the defendant is not necessary because the court has ordered the evaluation performed regardless of defendant preferences (furthermore, defendants whose criminal competencies are in question may not be competent to provide genuine informed consent). Nevertheless, the evaluator has a duty to help the defendant understand the evaluation purpose and context to the extent possible. For ex parte evaluations, formal consent by the defendant *is* necessary (if the defendant appears unable to provide meaningful consent, consent from defense counsel may be sufficient).

Background information and history are usually a necessary part of any interview in a forensic

evaluation, although the depth and breadth of the background discussion will vary depending on the defendant and the case context. For any defendant, it is necessary to review a general social history, including information about adaptive behaviors and day-to-day functioning. This process is useful in providing content (e.g., defendant's history of relationships and *real-world* functioning) as well as process (e.g., samples of how well the defendant can communicate relevant information and converse collaboratively). Generally, the discussion of a defendant's background—in the interview and in the eventual report—should be proportional to its potential relevance to the referral question. For example, a defendant who might be incompetent due to intellectual limitations will warrant detailed attention to his or her educational background, whereas a defendant who might be incompetent due to psychiatric illness will warrant much more attention to his or her mental health history.

Clinical status, including current mental status, is a second focus of any interview in a forensic evaluation. This portion of the interview may appear similar to interviews in other clinical contexts, in that the evaluator attempts to thoroughly assess the individual's current mental status and identify any active psychiatric symptoms. The evaluator will gather enough information about the defendant's historical and current symptoms to assign a diagnosis, if warranted (particularly after comparing interview content to collateral sources of information). But again, even in this portion of the interview, the attention given to symptoms should be proportional to their relevance to the criminal competence at issue. For example, certain disorders or diagnoses rarely bear on adjudicative competence (e.g., most personality disorders, paraphilias, etc.) and therefore usually warrant much less attention. Other conditions (e.g., psychosis, intellectual disability, certain developmental disorders) are quite likely to bear on adjudicative competence and require meticulous exploration of the condition's course and symptoms. But in contrast to traditional clinical interviews, in which the goal is primarily to assign the appropriate diagnosis, the goal of a clinical interview in a criminal competence evaluation is to identify specific symptoms that may interfere with the defendant's criminal competence and to understand the scenarios under which they are mostly likely to interfere.

Psychological testing. Psychological testing is not a required component of a criminal competence evaluation, but appropriate assessment instruments can enhance an evaluation. Appropriate testing may include one or both of the following strategies:

- *General psychological testing* is occasionally appropriate when such testing can help illuminate or clarify the deficits underlying an individual's incompetence. Perhaps the most common example involves a defendant who is apparently incompetent due to intellectual disability, prompting an evaluator to administer intelligence or neuropsychological testing in order to better describe and quantify the specific intellectual deficits underlying the defendant's inability to perform certain competence-related tasks. Another example might involve a defendant who is incompetent due to a combination of symptoms related to mood and thought disorder, prompting the evaluator to administer psychological testing that might help clarify the diagnosis that best summarizes these symptoms. Note that in both examples, the general psychological testing performed an illustrative or clarifying function but was not the basis of the actual opinion about competence. Finally, another instance of applying general psychological testing (or a forensically relevant instrument) might occur when an evaluator is concerned that a defendant's apparent deficits are actually feigned deficits. The evaluator might administer a broad psychological test that has validity scales, or even an instrument specifically designed to measure malingering, to help determine whether a defendant's reported symptoms are exaggerated or feigned.
- *Forensic assessment instruments*, in contrast, are probably used more often in evaluations of adjudicative competence (see Chapter 2, this volume for additional discussion of forensic assessment instruments). These instruments were developed to guide evaluators through an evaluation of *Miranda* comprehension or trial competence in a structured, standardized manner, ensuring that

they address the relevant conceptual information and thereby enhance reliability across evaluators and evaluations.

The evaluation report. In the vast majority of cases, the evaluation report is the crucial end product of the evaluation. Although some ex parte evaluations will not end in a report, nearly all court-ordered evaluations do, and most of these do not require expert testimony. Thus, in most cases, the report may be the only evidence of the evaluation that the court or attorneys receive. Therefore, the goal of the report is to carefully document the assessment procedures, the data obtained, the evaluator's analysis of that data, and the resulting conclusions. Although the report culminates in the evaluator's opinion regarding the defendant's competence, the report should so clearly detail the underlying procedures, information, and analysis that readers can reach their own well-informed conclusion.

Specific Practices Regarding *Miranda*

Challenges to *Miranda* waivers are relatively rare, due at least in part to the limited scope of *Miranda*'s application to the criminal justice process. Typical practices regarding *Miranda* that may be followed in a jurisdiction include the following.

- First, the relevance of *Miranda* must be determined. *Miranda* is relevant only to individuals who are taken into custody and questioned regarding a crime. Whether a situation rises to the level of custodial interrogation requiring application of *Miranda* is assessed by courts via the objective *reasonable person* standard (*Yarborough v. Alvarado*, 2004), which examines the circumstances of the situation to determine if a reasonable person would have felt free to end the questioning and leave (*Thompson v. Keohane*, 1995). In circumstances that do not meet this standard (e.g., police ask questions of a potential suspect at the person's home), *Miranda* is not required and thus no *Miranda* waiver exists to be challenged.
- Variation in procedures exists across jurisdictions; however, suspects are generally assumed to be capable of waiving their *Miranda* rights.

In the majority of cases where *Miranda* is at issue, a *Miranda* waiver challenge will be raised pretrial by the defense in order to request the suppression of inculpatory statements made by the defendant. A pretrial hearing may be held that could include testimony to establish the circumstances of the interrogation and the defendant's apparent comprehension of the *Miranda* warnings.

- The prosecution has the burden of proof to establish that the knowing, intelligent, and voluntary standard was met, although the burden varies across jurisdictions, with some states requiring preponderance of the evidence (e.g., *Colorado v. Al-Yousif*, 2002; *Maine v. Coombs*, 1998; *United States v. Miller*, 2005) and others requiring beyond a reasonable doubt (*Massachusetts v. Jackson*, 2000).

- The judge then enters a ruling on the validity of the waiver. If the waiver is deemed valid, then inculpatory statements are admissible at trial; if the waiver is deemed invalid, then statements made by the defendant are suppressed. In many jurisdictions, if a defendant's waiver is found valid, the defense may still challenge the trustworthiness of any statements that are subsequently admitted during trial (A. M. Goldstein & Goldstein, 2010).

Evaluator practices: Recommended *Miranda* evaluation process. The current section provides only a brief overview of the relevant practice recommendations, supplementing those covered in the General Practices section above, for evaluating an individual's capacity to waive his or her *Miranda* rights. These recommendations are derived from DeClue (2005, 2010); Frumkin (2000, 2010); A. M. Goldstein and Goldstein (2010); N. E. S. Goldstein, Zelle, and Grisso (2012); Grisso (1981, 1998); and Oberlander and Goldstein (2001). Readers preparing to conduct a *Miranda* evaluation should look to those sources for more detailed coverage.

- An evaluation includes not only measurement of the specific legal capacity at issue, but also broader psychological considerations that are relevant to the issue (e.g., intellectual functioning), as well as the larger context of the individual (e.g., relevant historical data). Thus, evaluation of an individual's capacity to waive his or her *Miranda* rights entails record review and a general clinical interview in order to gather relevant data regarding areas such as the defendant's development, social history, academic and work history, medical and mental health history, and criminal history.

- A record that is particularly important in *Miranda* waiver cases, if available, is a copy of the *Miranda* warning that is given in the defendant's jurisdiction. Information about the delivery method, reading level, and language is important to understanding whether a particular defendant may or may not have comprehended the warnings. Similarly, if an audio or video recording of the interrogation is available, it should be reviewed to assess how the warnings were actually delivered and the defendant's apparent comprehension.

- The clinical interview may also yield information about potential collateral sources of information and the defendant's view of the interrogation circumstances. Under best practice standards, collateral sources are particularly important in conducting forensic evaluations because information obtained from defendants must be corroborated (A. M. Goldstein, 2003, 2007; Grisso, 2003; Heilbrun, Warren, & Picarello, 2003; Melton et al., 2007).

Evaluator practices: Relevant instruments for *Miranda* evaluations. The relevant records and instruments used in the evaluation of *Miranda* rights comprehension can vary because of the wide variety of potentially relevant factors under the totality of circumstances standard.

- In some cases, an assessment of an individual's broader abilities, such as his or her intellectual functioning or reading comprehension, may be relevant; however, in many cases, administration of an intellectual battery is unnecessary. Therefore, there is no one fixed *assessment battery* for *Miranda* evaluations; instead, evaluators must carefully select appropriate instruments and assessment approaches based on hypotheses developed from initial record reviews and the referral circumstances. Ultimately, evaluators should pick relevant, reliable, and valid instruments because any conclusions about the defendant should be based on reliable data that demonstrate consistency across the various sources of information (A. M. Goldstein & Goldstein, 2010; Heilbrun, Grisso, & Goldstein, 2009).

- The two sets of instruments that were developed specifically to assess *Miranda* comprehension, the MRCI and the SAMA, were described in the Research section. The use of such instruments is strongly recommended for *Miranda* waiver evaluations because of the specific nature of the material and the fact that such instruments allow for standardized assessment and comparison to normative data for this narrow psycholegal question. Surveys of practitioners have shown that the majority recommends using instruments that are designed to measure *Miranda* comprehension in addition to other relevant measures, such as intelligence tests (Lally, 2003; Ryba, Brodsky, & Shlosberg, 2007). In addition to these tools, clinicians performing *Miranda* evaluations should consider several chapters, models, and protocols that detail the relevant steps from referral through expert testimony (e.g., DeClue, 2010; Frumkin, 2010; A. M. Goldstein & Goldstein, 2010, chapters 4–7).

Specific Practices Regarding Adjudicative Competence

Authorities have provided guidelines, or best practices, for courts that are handling questions of adjudicative competence (ABA, 1989; NJC, 2011). Of course, not every court follows these practices in every case, but a common flow of events, consistent with good practices, would involve the following sequence.

- First, when defense counsel (or, less commonly, the court or the prosecution) raises a question about an individual's competence, the court holds a hearing to determine whether there is a reasonable basis to refer the defendant for

formal evaluation. Authorities recommend that the court conduct a colloquy with the defendant and confirm that apparent incompetence is not due solely to nonmental-health factors such as brief intoxication or cultural differences (NJC, 2011). But, because the court has a duty to order an evaluation when there is any *reasonable* basis for concerns about the defendant's competence (*Drope v. Missouri*, 1975; *Pate v. Robinson*, 1966), the bar for ordering an evaluation is relatively low.

- Next, if the court finds reason to believe that an individual's competence may be at issue, the court appoints an independent evaluator (e.g., ABA Standard 7-4.4(a), 1989). Ideally, use of an independent evaluator reduces the likelihood that opposing sides will order their own, competing evaluations. Yet, even authorities who recommend "neutral" evaluators also recommend that each party have the *option* of retaining a second evaluation if they are not satisfied with the court-appointed evaluation (NJC, 2011). When appointing an evaluator, the court should also establish a deadline to receive the evaluation report, typically within 1 month of ordering the evaluation (e.g., ABA Standard 7-4.4(c)). Generally, resolving the competence question quickly is fairest to the defendant and most congruent with the goals of the justice system (*Drope v. Missouri*, 1975; *Jackson v. Indiana*, 1972).

- Generally, the court should order the competence evaluation to be performed in the least restrictive setting possible, considering the defendant's safety risk and treatment needs (Miller, 2003; NJC, 2011). Although historically, most evaluations tended to take place in psychiatric hospitals, this tends to be the option that is most expensive, time consuming, and disruptive to the defendant (Melton et al., 2007; Melton, Weithorn, & Slobogin, 1985). Community-based evaluations (whether based in jail or outpatient clinics) can be just as accurate while better stewarding scarce resources and better protecting defendants' rights and interests (Melton et al., 1985).

- Upon completion of the evaluation, the evaluator should submit the evaluation report to defense counsel and the court (NJC, 2011; see also ABA Standards 7-3.7 to 7-3.8, 1989). Some state statutes require that the report also be sent to the prosecution. Of these, some (e.g., Raising Question of Competency, 1982; *United States v. Miller*, 2005) explicitly prohibit the evaluator from including information about the defendant's account of the offense in the report. In states without similar prohibitions, the NJC (2011) recommends that the judge review the competence report *in camera* to ensure that the report does not include defendant statements about the offense or trial strategy before providing the report to the prosecution.

■ A formal hearing on the defendant's competence should follow receipt of the report if the defense requests such a hearing or if the conclusions of the report are otherwise contested (NJC, 2011). Any hearing required should be scheduled shortly after receipt of the report, because opinions in the report become less relevant over time; competence is a dynamic issue that changes with time and circumstances (ABA Standards 7-4.7 to 7-4.8, 1989). The defendant should be present at that hearing (unless significant safety concerns preclude this; ABA Standard 4.8, 1989), and the court should conduct an independent colloquy with the defendant in order to inform the court's opinion on competence. It may also be necessary for the evaluator(s) to testify regarding his or her competence findings (ABA Standards 7-3.9 and 7-3.11, 1989). The burden of proving incompetence rests on the party asserting incompetence (*Medina v. California*, 1992), which is usually the defense, and they must prove incompetence by a preponderance of the evidence (*Cooper v. Oklahoma*, 1996).

Practices regarding competence restoration. If, after the procedures detailed above, the court finds the defendant CST, then the adjudication process simply proceeds. If, however, the court find the defendant IST, the court orders some form of restoration services.

■ Best practice dictates that courts refer a defendant for competence restoration services in the least restrictive setting, considering safety and treatment needs (ABA Standards 7-4.9 to 7-4.10, 1989; NJC, 2011). For defendants who do not have a severe psychiatric illness that requires inpatient treatment, the appropriate location for restoration is often the jail or the community. States increasingly allow, and even encourage, *outpatient* restoration, whether in community clinics or jails (Frost & Gowensmith, 2010), because doing so tends to save scarce resources and better protect defendants' rights and interests (Kapoor, 2011; Miller, 2003). Practically, however, even states that allow or recommend outpatient restoration may fail to provide it consistently, particularly outside urban jurisdictions. So in many situations, inpatient restoration, albeit more lengthy and expensive, remains the default.

■ Authorities recommend that initial court orders commit a defendant to restoration treatment for no more than 3–4 months (e.g., NJC, 2011). Certainly, defendants should not be ordered into restoration treatment for a period longer than the sentence they would have served if they were convicted of their charges (see, generally, *Jackson v. Indiana*, 1972). Regardless of length, though, restoration treatment providers should keep the court notified of the defendant's progress toward restoration (ABA Standard 7-4.11, 1989). As detailed earlier, research suggests that most defendants can be restored to competence within 3–6 months (Pinals, 2005).

■ Treatment providers should determine the best regimen for restoring an individual's competence. Because most defendants who have been deemed IST, suffer psychiatric illness, the primary treatment modality is usually psychiatric medication. However, as detailed in the research review presented earlier, psychoeducational groups are often provided as an adjunct to medication, or even as the primary form of intervention for defendants who have only intellectual disabilities. Regardless of modality, it is important that treatment providers ensure continuity of treatment (particularly medication) across settings so that "restored" defendants do not decompensate and become incompetent again before returning to court due to changes in medication or monitoring (NJC, 2011).

- In many instances, defendants voluntarily take the medication that is recommended as part of their restoration treatment plan. In some instances when defendants refuse medication, however, involuntary medication is permissible in order to restore competence. In short, the U.S. Supreme Court has held that involuntary medication is appropriate *only* if the treatment is (a) medically appropriate, (b) unlikely to have side effects that may undermine the fairness of legal proceedings, and (c) necessary to further important government interests. Furthermore, involuntary medication is permissible only if restoration is not feasible via less intrusive alternatives (*Sell v. United States*, 2003).

Evaluator practices: Recommended adjudicative competence evaluation process. Beyond the general practices relevant for criminal competence evaluations (described earlier), particular areas of focus for adjudicative competence include the following.

- *Competence-specific interview content* is the crux of the interview in a competence evaluation. During this portion of the interview, the evaluator asks the defendant about criminal proceedings, generally, and the defendant's case, specifically. For example, evaluators often begin by asking the defendant about the typical process for court proceedings (e.g., plea, trial, sentencing) and the roles of key courtroom personnel (i.e., judge, prosecutor, defense counsel, jury). This discussion should extend beyond basic facts and definitions to gauge important conceptual issues, such as the adversarial nature of the proceedings and the defendant's basic legal rights. A defendant need not know this material perfectly from the start, but in order to be considered CST, the defendant should demonstrate the *capacity* to learn and retain this material when instructed.
- Beyond asking about the generalities of legal proceedings, evaluators should ask about the defendant's particular case, including the specific charges, potential penalties, and viable plea options. The evaluator should also explore the defendant's opinions and expectations regarding his or her defense counsel and trial outcome.[8] Consistent with the *Dusky* standard, the evaluator seeks to gauge not only whether the defendant's understanding is factually correct, but also whether it is rational and reasonable or is impaired by the symptoms identified in the clinical interview. The evaluator also inquires about the circumstances of the offense—not to assess the defendant's guilt or mental state at the time of the alleged offense (indeed, it is inappropriate to address these issues in competence reports or testimony), but solely to determine whether the defendant is capable of providing relevant information to defense counsel.

- An important but sometimes overlooked aspect of the competence interview involves exploring the defendant's expectations, reasoning, and judgment about the pending case. The evaluator must gather enough information to determine whether the defendant's decision making in the case at hand is generally rational or whether it is impaired by a mental disorder.

- Reports of adjudicative competence evaluations should be tightly focused and carefully written. Generally, some background information is necessary to provide a context for understanding the defendant's functioning, but reports should not detail the types of personal information that are irrelevant to the legal question. Furthermore, evaluators should not reveal in competence reports the defendant's version of the alleged offense, the defendant's legal strategy, or the content of the defendant's communication with counsel. Evaluators must be able to address a defendant's capacities related to competence (e.g., whether he can describe a coherent version of events surrounding his alleged offense, whether he can communicate constructively with counsel, etc.) without disclosing substantive details that would compromise the defendant's

---

[8]In some cases, it is helpful to go further and actually observe the defendant interact with counsel as the two prepare for the case. Perhaps for logistical reasons, this rarely occurs in routine practice, except in some of the most serious cases (e.g., capital sentencing). But, obviously, one aspect of competence is the ability to work constructively with defense counsel. Although this can often be inferred from a defendant's interaction with an evaluator during the interview, there is no substitute for actually observing defendant/counsel interactions, particularly in complicated or ambiguous cases.

confidentiality or other legal rights. Although a few state statutes specifically direct evaluators to exclude such sensitive information from reports (e.g., Raising Question of Competency, 1982; *United States v. Miller*, 2005), many do not, making it particularly important that evaluators are attuned to their ethical duty to avoid compromising a defendant's rights.[9]

■ Finally, adjudicative competence reports often conclude with additional recommendations. For example, many jurisdictions require that when an evaluator opines that a defendant is IST, the evaluator offer guidance for restoration services (e.g., inpatient vs. outpatient). Even when an evaluator finds a defendant CST, the evaluator may offer suggestions to counsel or the court for working constructively with the defendant in order to maximize his or her understanding or participation.

Evaluator practices: Relevant adjudicative competence instruments or guides.   Over the past few decades, authorities have developed a variety of instruments or guides to assist in trial competence evaluations. No instrument is sufficient to replace a full evaluation, but a well-developed instrument may supplement an evaluation, and a well-developed guide may be useful for organizing an evaluation. Furthermore, instruments provide more structure to the examination and ensure that certain content is addressed, which may improve reliability across evaluators. Although the following list does not address every competence instrument developed—and it cannot replace a thorough literature review—it briefly summarizes the most commonly used competence assessment instruments in roughly chronological order (from the oldest to the most recently developed).

■ *The Competency Screening Test* (Lipsitt, Lelos, & McGarry, 1971) is a 22-item sentence-completion test in which defendants answer questions based on case scenarios. The Competency Screening Test was developed as a screening measure to efficiently distinguish between defendants who are clearly competent versus those who require further comprehensive evaluation with the Competency to Stand Trial Assessment Instrument (Laboratory of Community Psychiatry, 1973; McGarry & Curran, 1973). Although a reasonable instrument at the time it was developed, the Competency Screening Test is subject to some criticism (see Melton et al., 2007; Zapf & Roesch, 2009) and is not frequently used today.

■ *The Competence to Stand Trial Assessment Instrument* was developed as a semistructured interview to help evaluators assess 13 functions that the authors considered relevant for trial competence, based on a review of the legal literature. Each function is scored on a 5-point scale, quantifying the degree of impairment. However, the instrument does not include detailed rules for administration or overall scoring (i.e., translating item scores into an overall score of judgment about competence), nor are scores linked to any normative sample. Historically, the instrument has been fairly popular. It has probably been used more as a general guide to structure interviews than as a formal test, though even this has been a valuable contribution in earlier eras where other guidance on forensic evaluation was less readily available.

■ *The Interdisciplinary Fitness Interview* (IFI; Golding et al., 1984) was designed as an interview to assess both legal and clinical issues. *Ideally*, it is conducted jointly by both a clinician and an attorney. Addressing three broad areas (i.e., legal issues, psychopathological issues, and overall evaluation), the IFI attempts to facilitate an evaluation that is specific to the defendant's individual case (based on attorney input), consistent with the functional and contextual nature of competence.

■ *The Interdisciplinary Fitness Interview—Revised* (IFI–R; Golding, 1993) is a more recent version of the IFI and reflects an additional decade of case law and professional literature addressing trial competence. The measure addresses 31

---

[9]Although this issue arises most often in written reports of competence evaluations, it is just as applicable to expert testimony about adjudicative competence and documentation produced during competence restoration services.

psycholegal abilities across 11 broad domains. As with the earlier version, the IFI–R may be a helpful guide to facilitate a thorough interview, with the strength of including attorney input. However, there has been little formal empirical research addressing the instrument.

- *The Fitness Interview Test* (FIT; Roesch, Webster, & Eaves, 1984) and *Fitness Interview Test—Revised* (FIT–R; Roesch, Zapf, & Eaves, 2006; Roesch, Zapf, Eaves, & Webster, 1998) are also interview guides. They were developed in the Canadian justice system, though the FIT–R has been revised to be relevant in the United States as well. Using a semistructured interview format, the examiner scores the defendant using a 3-point rating scale across 16 brief sections that comprise three broad domains: (a) factual knowledge of criminal procedure, (b) understanding the possible consequences of proceedings and appreciating personal involvement in these proceedings, and (c) communicating with counsel and participating in one's defense. Generally, the instrument has been well researched, demonstrating good psychometric properties (Viljoen et al., 2002) and strong potential as a screening instrument to identify defendants who warrant a more comprehensive evaluation (Zapf, Roesch, & Viljoen, 2001).

- *The MacArthur Competence Assessment Tool—Criminal Adjudication* (MacCAT–CA; Hoge, Bonnie, Poythress, & Monahan, 1999; Poythress et al., 1999) was derived from a broader research instrument, the MacArthur Structured Assessment of the Competencies of Criminal Defendants (Hoge, Bonnie, Poythress, Monahan, & Eisenberg, 1997), which was used during the extensive work by the MacArthur Foundation's Research Network on Mental Health and the Law. Unlike most other measures, the MacCAT–CA is based on a vignette about a fictional crime, which the evaluator reads to the defendant. The defendant then responds to 22 questions addressing his or her understanding, reasoning, and appreciation of the crime. Both understanding and reasoning are assessed with respect to the case vignette, whereas appreciation is assessed by inquiring about the defendant's

own charges and situation. Scores can be compared to normative data from three groups of defendants, including jail inmates, jail inmates receiving mental health services, and incompetent defendants in a psychiatric hospital. Overall, the instrument is psychometrically strong and is well supported by research (e.g., Otto et al., 1998). But, like most instruments, the authors stress that it is a tool to be used in conjunction with other evaluation procedures, not a replacement for a comprehensive evaluation of adjudicative competence.

- *The Evaluation of Competency to Stand Trial—Revised* (ECST–R; Rogers et al., 2004) was designed to assess a defendant's competence, closely tracking the *Dusky* criteria, but also the defendant's response style, particularly the possibility of feigned incompetence. Eighteen items comprise four different content scales: Factual Understanding of Courtroom Proceedings, Rational Understanding of Courtroom Proceedings, Consulting With Counsel, and Overall Rational Ability. An additional 28 items comprise five Atypical Presentation (response style) scales. The instrument is interview based but includes structured and semistructured components.

Specific Practices Regarding Competence for Execution

Questions about CFE can be raised by any party (i.e., the state, defense, or court), though in practice, it is almost always the defense who raises the issue. When courts consider CFE, they attempt to address the substantive standards provided in the key U.S. Supreme Court decisions that addressed CFE (i.e., *Ford v. Wainwright*, 1986; *Panetti v. Quarterman*, 2007).

In the *Ford* decision, the Court concluded that the Eighth Amendment's prohibition of cruel and unusual punishment should prohibit the execution of incompetent offenders, primarily because such executions would offend humanity and would fail to serve the traditional goals of punishment (i.e., deterrence and retribution). Although the Court's plurality decision offered very little guidance as to when an offender would be considered incompetent, an influential concurring opinion from Justice Powell provided more guidance. Powell suggested that the Eighth Amendment should prohibit the "execution only of those who are unaware of the punishment they are about to suffer and why they are to suffer it" (*Ford v. Wainwright*, 1986, p. 422). Thus, his proposed standard required that the offender have a factual understanding of the capital proceedings and that the test for competency should be whether the offender understands the nature, pendency, and purpose of the looming execution. After *Ford*, most of the courts that addressed the CFE issue adopted similar rationale and criteria for excluding incompetent offenders from capital punishment (see e.g., DeMatteo, Murrie, Anumba, & Keesler, 2011; Otto, 2009; Reisner, Slobogin, & Rai, 2004). Practically, courts considered only whether an offender had a factual awareness of his or her impending execution and the reasons for it.

More than two decades later, in *Panetti v. Quarterman* (2007), the Supreme Court more specifically addressed whether the Eighth Amendment permits the execution of an offender who has a *factual* awareness, but apparently lacks a *rational* understanding, of the reasons for execution. Panetti's attorneys conceded that he had a sufficient factual awareness of the reasons for his execution (he was facing execution for murdering two people), but they argued that he lacked an adequate rational understanding (due to significant mental illness, Panetti held a delusional belief that he was also being executed as a form of religious persecution). By a narrow vote, the Supreme Court concluded that the factual understanding standard articulated by Justice Powell in *Ford* was not sufficient. Rather, a prisoner must have a factual understanding of the offense, the impending execution, and the state's reason for the execution, and also a rational understanding of the connection between the offense and the impending execution. Explaining its decision, the Court emphasized that an offender's mental illness could undermine the retributive and deterrent purposes of the death penalty (see DeMatteo et al., 2011).

By holding that CFE require both a factual and rational understanding of the reasons for the impending execution, the *Panetti* decision provided more specific guidance than *Ford*. However, the Supreme Court again declined to offer a detailed, explicit standard for courts to use when determining whether an offender is competent for execution. Writing for the majority, Justice Kennedy stated that the factual record was not sufficient to permit the Court to define a specific standard for CFE. The Court also recognized that defining "rational understanding" could be difficult. Thus, states and courts will likely continue to engage in some degree of interpretation when implementing the *Panetti* decision.

Recommended evaluation process. Despite the rarity of CFE evaluations, they share many similarities with evaluations of other criminal competencies. After all, they are essentially a question of whether an inmate has the functional capacities necessary for a specific task (i.e., facing execution with adequate understanding and appreciation), so many of the initial considerations that apply to any evaluation of a criminal competency (described earlier) apply to CFE evaluations. The considerations specific to CFE evaluations generally involve a focus on the defendant's understanding of his or her impending death.

As with any evaluation, CFE evaluations should begin with a broad review of relevant records (e.g., Heilbrun et al., 2009; Heilbrun & McClaren, 1988; Small & Otto, 1991). But, the most relevant records are likely those that address the inmate's psychological functioning on death row, in the period following his or her death sentence and approaching his or her impending execution. Thus, crucial collaterals include the inmate's legal counsel (i.e., original defense counsel, but also any habeas counsel), prison staff who have routine contact with the inmate, prison mental health staff, and any family who have contact with the inmate. These, and similar collateral sources, are usually in the best position to describe the defendant's current statements or reactions to the pending execution. As always, obtaining information from multiple sources can help the evaluator to assess the inmate's response style (e.g., truthful responding vs. exaggeration/ minimization of deficits) in the subsequent clinical interview.

The clinical interview is likely the most important component of a CFE evaluation. Although the evaluator will be well informed about the defendant's psychiatric history after reviewing historical records, CFE is a question of *present* abilities, so focusing on the inmate's *current* psychological functioning is essential. Conducting the evaluation over the course of more than one meeting may help an evaluator better gauge the nuances and stability of an inmate's symptoms (Heilbrun & McClaren, 1988).

Again, the focus of the clinical interview in a CFE evaluation is on *assessing the degree to which the offender understands his or her pending execution and the reasons for the execution*. Specifically, the inmate must have both a factual and a rational understanding of the issue.

Otto (2009) recently provided guidance to help evaluators explore four broad categories of symptoms that may impede an inmate's rational and factual understanding of his or her impending execution. First, Otto noted that *impaired thought content*, such as grandiose delusions, paranoid delusions, and religious delusions, might hamper an inmate's understanding and appreciation of his or her death sentence. Second, *impaired thought process or form* can hamper the capacities necessary for competence. For example, disordered thinking, including tangential thinking or circumstantial thinking, could affect an offender's understanding or appreciation of the death sentence. The psychotic symptoms that cause impaired thought content or impaired thought process are not uncommon among death row inmates (e.g., Cunningham & Vigen, 2002). Although psychotic symptoms do not necessarily render a defendant incompetent for execution, evaluators should certainly screen for them carefully and explore them in depth if they are present. Third, *cognitive impairment*, including deficits in memory, attention/concentration, orientation, executive functioning, and intellectual functioning, could lead to a finding of incompetence for execution. Finally, Otto noted that severe *mood disorders* might affect an offender's ability to understand or appreciate the death sentence. Thus, evaluators should carefully explore these four broad categories of symptoms and examine their relation to the inmate's perceptions of his pending execution in detail.

Evaluator practices: Relevant CFE instruments or guides. Despite the rarity of CFE evaluations, a few checklists and measures have been developed to assist evaluators in conducting them. Presumably, instruments developed for use in CFE evaluations may help evaluators to assess the relevant criteria in a more structured and easy-to-replicate manner. However, one important limitation of all existing measures is that they were developed prior to the Supreme Court's ruling in *Panetti*. Thus, they fit imperfectly, or at least incompletely, with our current understanding of the CFE standard in that they tend to focus more on factual understanding and give less focus to rational understanding.

Ebert (2001) offered a checklist of 12 items, with eight focused on functional legal abilities and four more clinical in nature that could be rated on a 6-point Likert-type scale. However, Ebert did not provide information for determining how the level of incapacity is determined or how the item ratings can be combined for making an overall determination of CFE (Zapf, 2008). Moreover, Ebert did not provide sample questions for all items or data about the measure's psychometric properties.

Zapf et al. (2003) developed the Interview Checklist for Evaluations of Competency for Execution, not so much as a formal measure, but rather "to serve as an aide memoire to assist professionals" (p. 115) with the clinical interview in CFE evaluations. They developed the checklist after reviewing the literature on criminal competencies, reviewing relevant case law, and consulting with professionals who conduct CFE evaluations. The checklist is divided into four sections that assess an offender's (a) understanding of the reasons for punishment, (b) understanding of the punishment, (c) appreciation and reasoning, and (d) ability to assist the attorney. Although developed before the *Panetti* decision, the guide directs evaluators to assess the offender's appreciation and reasoning beyond a superficial factual understanding.

The most recently developed CFE guide is the Competency for Execution Research Rating Scales (CERRS; Ackerson, Brodsky, & Zapf, 2005). Ackerson and colleagues developed the CERRS after surveying 113 judges with authority to give death penalty sentences about issues they considered important when determining CFE. The CERRS has four sections: understanding and appreciating punishment, understanding and appreciating death, capacity to work with counsel, and relevant clinical information. Each item is scored on a 5-point Likert-type scale (from *severe incapacity* to *no incapacity*) following item descriptions in the instrument manual.

Policy

For each of the criminal competencies we have discussed in this chapter, certain broad policy issues—such as standards for each competency as defined by the U.S. Supreme Court and typical procedures for litigating each competence—have already been addressed. Thus, this section addresses only a few recent policy developments, and a few areas in which policy is unsettled, creating ongoing challenges to the criminal justice system.

Recent policy regarding *Miranda*. The protections afforded by *Miranda v. Arizona* (1966) were soon extended to juveniles in *Kent v. United States* (1966) and *In re Gault* (1967), which established the application of the Fifth and Fourteenth Amendment-based protections to delinquency proceedings. In *Fare v. Michael C.* (1979), the Court made it clear that the *Miranda* requirements applied to the custodial interrogation of juveniles. In *J. D. B. v. North Carolina* (2011), the Court highlighted the critical importance of adolescent age when considering whether a custodial interrogation occurred under the reasonable person standard.

The attention to such differences in adolescents has led to ancillary case law and legislation that is meant to protect this group. For example, in *Gallegos v. Colorado* (1962), the Supreme Court held that the impact of adolescent immaturity during interrogation might be assuaged by having a lawyer, adult relative, or friend present. State court holdings since then have applied and further refined this idea, leading to the *interested adult* standard that calls for the presence of a relevant, presumably helpful adult (e.g., *Massachusetts v. Guyton*, 1989; *Massachusetts v. MacNeill*, 1987).

The availability, and even required presence, of an interested adult appears to be helpful policy, but

as noted in the research section earlier, there is little evidence to support the presumed beneficial impact of an interested adult. Research suggests that parent–adolescent consultations often do not provide the protection assumed because the adult either does not offer advice, miscommunicates with the adolescent, or advises a youth to cooperate with police and "tell the truth" (Grisso & Ring, 1979; Viljoen et al., 2005).

Several studies have demonstrated the wide variability in reading level of jurisdictions' *Miranda* warnings (e.g., Kahn, Zapf, & Cooper, 2006; Rogers, Harrison, Shuman, et al., 2007; Rogers, Hazelwood, Sewell, Harrison, & Shuman, 2008), with some warnings requiring as low as a 2.8 grade reading ability and others requiring as high as a postgraduate-level reading ability. Rogers and colleagues (Rogers, Harrison, Shuman, et al., 2007; Rogers, Hazelwood, Sewell, Harrison, & Shuman, 2008) analyzed 122 juvenile-specific warnings. Although such versions were presumably created to simplify the warnings and make them more understandable, findings suggested that juvenile warnings were on average 60 words longer than standard warnings, still required reading abilities higher than many juveniles likely have, and contained vocabulary very much like that in standard warnings intended for adult suspects (Rogers, Hazelwood, Sewell, Shuman, & Blackwood, 2008).

Varying waiver standard across states. In *Miranda v. Arizona* (1966), the Supreme Court clearly stated that it did not intend to prescribe a specific phrasing to be afforded to suspects, leading to wide variability across jurisdictions. Similarly, the Court indicated that the knowing, intelligent, and voluntary standard would apply to *Miranda* waivers, but it did not further define the standard in the custodial interrogation context. In particular, the cognitive *knowing and intelligent* components were left open to interpretation, whereas the Court's precedent concerning coerced confessions in the decades preceding *Miranda* outlined the general definition of *voluntary*. Later Supreme Court cases suggested a distinction between knowing and intelligent (e.g., *Brady v. United States*, 1970; *Fare v. Michael C.*, 1979), and in *Moran v. Burbine* (1986), the Court noted that a suspect must be aware of both the nature and consequences of a *Miranda* waiver. The standard remains largely open to interpretation, however, leading to variation among states as to what is required for a valid *Miranda* waiver. Many states require that a suspect meet two requirements: (a) understanding of the basic factual elements of the rights, and (b) appreciation of the consequences of a waiver (e.g., *Arkansas v. Bell*, 1997; *In re Patrick W.*, 1978; *Pennsylvania v. DeJesus*, 2001; *Tennessee v. Stephenson*, 1994). Other states, however, have case law explicitly requiring only a basic understanding of the *Miranda* rights (e.g., *Illinois v. Bernasco*, 1990; *Michigan v. Daoud*, 2000). Yet other states appear to use an intermediate approach that requires understanding of some consequences (e.g., *Colorado v. Al-Yousif*, 2002; *New Hampshire v. Bushey*, 1982). A recent survey of state court judges suggested that the majority of judges distinguish between knowing and intelligent (Zelle, 2012). It appears that, while recognizing the need to maintain flexibility in legal standards so they can be applied on a case-by-case basis, there is reason to develop a "floor" threshold for what the knowing and intelligent standard requires. Without such a clarification, the variation across states likely leads to inconsistent and unfair application across defendants—especially given the great weight that inculpatory statements carry in criminal cases. Further research and policy discussion in this area are needed.

Recent Supreme Court changes to Miranda doctrine. The Supreme Court has revisited *Miranda* to clarify several areas of its application, especially in recent years. Some cases have resulted in protecting and extending *Miranda*, but many have circumscribed *Miranda*'s application and made it more difficult to invoke. An understanding of the changes to *Miranda* doctrine is important for both practice and research, as psycholegal constructs and policy questions are relevant to the evolution of police, court, and clinical practices. Several of the more prominent cases are reviewed very briefly here.

In *Colorado v. Connelly* (1986), the Court made clear that a *Miranda* waiver will be considered voluntary unless it is the result of coercive *police* activity. In *Connelly*, the suspect was mentally ill and had confessed to a murder after being told to do so by a command hallucination. In 2000, the Supreme Court upheld *Miranda* against a legislative attempt to limit its applicability in federal criminal law cases (*Dickerson v. United States*, 2000). In *Missouri v. Seibert* (2004), the Supreme Court held that police may not use a *question-first* interrogation in which they question a suspect until they obtain a confession, then *Mirandize* the suspect, then question the suspect again in order to obtain an admissible confession.

In just the last few years, the Supreme Court has paid additional attention to *Miranda*. In *Maryland v. Shatzer* (2010), the Court defined the length of time for which a rights invocation lasts before a suspect must again clearly reinvoke his or her rights. In a previous case, the Court had extended a suspect's invocation of his or her right to counsel to subsequent interrogations; however, in *Shatzer*, the Court held that a *Miranda* invocation will be automatically extended for only 14 days, not indefinitely. The Court also spoke to the mechanics of rights invocation in *Berghuis v. Thompkins* (2010), where it held that an invocation of the right to silence (as with an invocation of the right to counsel) must be made explicitly by a suspect, and that remaining silent alone will not constitute a rights invocation. In the same opinion, the Court made clear that rights waivers can be made implicitly, placing the onus on suspects to speak up in order to assert their rights.

In contrast to the recent cases that increased the threshold for *Miranda* applicability in adult cases, the Court in *J. D. B. v. North Carolina* (2011) appeared to strengthen the applicability of *Miranda* in juvenile cases. In *J. D. B.*, the Court made clear that age is a relevant factor that should be considered when using the reasonable person standard to assess whether a juvenile suspect would have felt that he or she was in custody. That is, the Court noted that younger individuals were more likely to feel unable to end an interview and leave, thus lowering the bar for an interview to constitute interrogation and require application of the *Miranda* warnings. Overall, though, the Supreme Court seems to be slowly eroding its *Miranda* precedent, and scholars have suggested that recent cases seriously jeopardize its status (e.g., Weisselberg, 2008; Weisselberg & Bibas, 2010).

Policy regarding adjudicative competence. As detailed earlier in this chapter, the criminal justice system has well-established policies and procedures for raising and adjudicating the relatively common question of CST. Policies are less well developed and less uniform, however, after the adjudication process, when defendants are sent for restoration services.

Competence restoration efforts are commonplace; Mossman (2007) estimated that defendants who are referred for competence restoration occupy at least one-ninth of U.S. psychiatric hospital beds, which is approximately 4,000 patients on any given day. This rate may still be rising, as forensic patients increasingly account for state psychiatric hospital admissions.

As described in the Research and Practice sections of this chapter, defendants who have been deemed IST are ordered to undergo competence restoration efforts *before* they are adjudicated. As a result, they may be held in a secure facility, such as a forensic psychiatric hospital, without having been convicted of a crime, and often without having met the criteria for civil commitment. Historically, this arrangement left many defendants spending more time in the hospital for restoration efforts than they could have served in prison had they been convicted of their charges (e.g., Laben, Kashgarian, Nessa, & Spencer, 1977; McGarry, 1971). The U.S. Supreme Court addressed this dilemma directly when they considered the case of Theon Jackson, who was an illiterate, mute, and deaf man who allegedly stole $9.00 worth of property (*Jackson v. Indiana*, 1972). Because experts testified that Jackson was virtually certain to never become competent, defense counsel argued that Jackson's commitment for competence restoration was, in effect, a life sentence to a psychiatric facility. The Court agreed and ruled that a defendant who is found IST cannot be held beyond "the reasonable period of time necessary to determine whether there is a substantial probability that he will attain [trial competence] in the foreseeable future" (*Jackson v. Indiana*, 1972, p. 738). Since *Jackson*, defendants may still be hospitalized with the goal of restoring trial competence, but commitment cannot be based *indefinitely* on restoration efforts, and ongoing commitment must be justified by ongoing progress toward restoring competence (see also ABA Standard 7-4.13, 1989).

Since the *Jackson* decision, many state statutes (e.g., Raising Question of Competency, 1982; *United States v. Miller*, 2005), hospital policies, and courtroom judges require clinicians to make predictions about restoration by opining whether an incompetent defendant is ever likely to gain competence or by estimating the time and services necessary to regain competence. Historically, however, most authorities have concluded that clinicians are not particularly skilled at making predictions about an individual's restorability (e.g., Hubbard, Zapf, & Ronan, 2003; Nicholson, Barnard, Robbins, & Hankins, 1994; Pinals, 2005; Roesch & Golding, 1980; Samuel & Michaels, 2011; Zapf & Roesch, 2011; cf. Mossman, 2007). One clear challenge to accurate prediction is "the base rate" problem: Because most defendants are restored to competence, clinicians may appear reasonably accurate by predicting that all defendants are restorable, but they have trouble identifying the small minority of patients who are not restorable (Pinals, 2005; Zapf & Roesch, 2011).

Recently, Mossman (2007) suggested a much more optimistic perspective on the potential for clinicians to accurately predict competence restoration. After studying an Ohio sample, Mossman found that a lower likelihood of restoration was associated with having a misdemeanor charge; a longer cumulative length of stay; older age; and diagnoses of mental retardation, schizophrenia, and schizoaffective disorder. He concluded that

> these findings provide scientific support for testimony that two types of incompetent evaluees have well-below-average probabilities of being restored: chronically psychotic defendants with histories of lengthy inpatient hospitalizations and defendants whose incompetence stems from irremediable cognitive disorders (such as mental retardation). Nonetheless, courts may still deem low probabilities of success to be "substantial" enough to warrant attempts at restoration. (p. 34)

In short, clinicians may be able to identify, with reasonable success, the defendants who are most likely to remain unrestorably incompetent. But, because so few defendants are unrestorably incompetent, and restoration efforts are so often successful, courts may still err on the side of caution and encourage at least an initial attempt to restore almost any incompetent defendant.

Finally, although clinicians and research usually treat restorability as an attribute of the defendant, it seems reasonable to think that restorability may depend, at least in part, on the type of restoration services that a defendant receives. Despite the widespread provision of restoration services, however, research about restoration program elements and efficacy is remarkably sparse. Surveys have revealed that most restoration takes place inpatient, at state psychiatric hospitals, and the primary means of restoration is psychiatric medication (GAINS Center, 2007; Miller, 2003; Pinals, 2005). These informal surveys also suggest that a majority of large facilities provide some sort of didactic or psychoeducational intervention, and a substantial minority have some sort of written manual or curricula (Mueller, unpublished survey, as cited in Pinals, 2005). Thus, competence restoration increasingly involves two processes: traditional psychiatric treatment of the underlying mental disorder alongside didactic education regarding legal concepts and the trial process (Noffsinger, 2001).

Other than this minimal overview from informal surveys, our field knows surprisingly little about where, how, and how effectively competence restoration services are delivered. States increasingly allow, or even encourage, outpatient restoration in community clinics or jails (Frost & Gowensmith, 2010). This approach is almost certainly preferable for defendants who do not require inpatient psychiatric hospitalization (see Kapoor, 2011; Miller, 2003) because outpatient approaches are likely far less expensive and better protect defendants' rights and interests (particularly defendants who are in the community on bond, rather than pending trial in jail). Practically, however, even states that allow or recommend outpatient restoration may fail to provide it consistently, particularly outside urban jurisdictions. Furthermore, we know of few well-established policies or practice guidelines for delivering outpatient restoration services. Thus, developing and disseminating policy for competence

restoration—particularly on an outpatient basis—remains one of the primary policy tasks related to adjudicative competence.

SUMMARY AND CONCLUSIONS

Studying and evaluating the criminal competencies is a core task of forensic psychology research and practice. Regarding adjudicative competence, the field has well-established practices from the level of policy (i.e., raising and adjudicating the issue) to the level of clinical practice (i.e., assessing competence to stand trial among individual defendants). Yet even for this commonly examined competence, the field has more work to do, particularly in terms of predicting and improving the restorability of some defendants to competence and establishing best practices for competence restoration services.

Regarding the less common criminal competencies—such as waiving *Miranda* rights or facing execution—the efforts to define and evaluate competence are much more recent and less well established. Questions about the capacity to waive *Miranda* rights are relevant to so many defendants that the field will likely give increasing attention to raising and examining these questions and further developing clinical procedures to do so. CFE questions, though they involve only the slightest fraction of defendants, will also likely receive continued attention given the grave significance of these questions. Despite differences across the criminal competencies, all require a case-specific consideration of whether a particular defendant manifests the particular psycholegal capacities necessary for a particular case context. Thus, all will continue to require careful study and evaluation by forensic psychologists.

References

Abram, K. M., Teplin, L. A., McClelland, G. M., & Dulcan, M. K. (2003). Comorbid psychiatric disorders in youth detention. *Archives of General Psychiatry, 60,* 1097–1108. doi:10.1001/archpsyc.60.11.1097

Abramovitch, R., Higgins-Biss, K. L., & Biss, S. R. (1993). Young persons' comprehension of waivers in criminal proceedings. *Canadian Journal of Criminology, 35,* 309–322.

Abramovitch, R., Peterson-Badali, M., & Rohan, M. (1995). Young people's understanding and assertion of their rights to silence and legal counsel. *Canadian Journal of Criminology, 37*, 1–18.

Ackerson, K. S., Brodsky, S. L., & Zapf, P. A. (2005). Judges' and psychologists' assessments of legal and clinical factors in competence for execution. *Psychology, Public Policy, and Law, 11*, 164–193. doi:10.1037/1076-8971.11.1.164

American Bar Association. (1989). *American Bar Association criminal justice mental health standards.* Washington, DC: Author.

American Psychological Association. (2013). Specialty guidelines for forensic psychology. *American Psychologist, 68*, 7–19. doi:10.1037/a0029889

Anderson, S. D., & Hewitt, J. (2002). The effect of competency restoration training on defendants with mental retardation found not competent to proceed. *Law and Human Behavior, 26*, 343–351. doi:10.1023/A:1015328505884

Appelbaum, P. S. (1986). Competence to be executed: Another conundrum for mental health professionals. *Hospital and Community Psychiatry, 37*, 682–684.

Appelbaum, P. S., & Grisso, T. (1988). Assessing patients' capacities to consent to treatment. *New England Journal of Medicine, 319*, 1635–1638. doi:10.1056/NEJM198812223192504

Arkansas v. Bell, 948 S.W.2d (Ark. 1997).

Baird, A. A., & Fugelsang, J. A. (2004). The emergence of consequential thought: Evidence from neuroscience. *Philosophical Transactions of the Royal Society: B, 359*, 1797–1804. doi:10.1098/rstb.2004.1549

Berghuis v. Thompkins, 130 S.Ct. 2250 (2010).

Berman, L. M., & Osborne, Y. H. (1987). Attorney's referrals for competency to stand trial evaluations: Comparisons of referred and nonreferred clients. *Behavioral Sciences and the Law, 5*, 373–380. doi:10.1002/bsl.2370050310

Bertman, L. J., Thompson, J. W., Jr., Waters, W. F., Estupinan-Kane, L., Martin, J. A., & Russell, L. (2003). Effect of an individualized treatment protocol on restoration of competency in pretrial forensic inpatients. *Journal of the American Academy of Psychiatry and the Law, 31*, 27–35.

Blackstone, W. (1979). *Commentaries on the laws of England: Vol. 4. Of public wrongs.* Chicago, IL: University of Chicago Press. (Original work published 1769)

Bonnie, R. J. (1990). Dilemmas in administering the death penalty: Conscientious abstention, professional ethics, and the needs of the legal system. *Law and Human Behavior, 14*, 67–90. doi:10.1007/BF01055790

Bonnie, R. J. (1992). The competence of criminal defendants: A theoretical reformulation. *Behavioral Sciences and the Law, 10*, 291–316. doi:10.1002/bsl.2370100303

Bonnie, R. J., & Grisso, T. (2000). Adjudicative competence and youthful offenders. In T. Grisso & R. G. Schwartz (Eds.), *Youth on trial: A developmental perspective on juvenile justice* (pp. 73–103). Chicago, IL: University of Chicago Press.

Brady v. United States, 397 U.S. 742 (1970).

Brodsky, S. (1990). Professional ethics and professional morality in the assessment of competence for execution: A response to Bonnie. *Law and Human Behavior, 14*, 91–97. doi:10.1007/BF01055791

Brodsky, S. L., Zapf, P. A., & Boccaccini, M. T. (2001). The last competency: An examination of legal, ethical, and professional ambiguities regarding evaluations of competence for execution. *Journal of Forensic Psychology Practice, 1*, 1–25. doi:10.1300/J158v01n02_01

Brodsky, S. L., Zapf, P. A., & Boccaccini, M. T. (2005). Competency for execution assessments: Ethical continuities and professional tasks. *Journal of Forensic Psychology Practice, 5*, 65–74. doi:10.1300/J158v05n04_04

Brown, D. R. (1992). A didactic group program for persons found unfit to stand trial. *Hospital and Community Psychiatry, 43*, 732–733.

Brown v. Mississippi, 297 U.S. 278 (1936).

Cassell, P. G. (1996). *Miranda*'s social costs: An empirical reassessment. *Northwestern University Law Review, 90*, 387–499.

Cassell, P. G., & Hayman, B. S. (1996). Police interrogation in the 1990s: An empirical study of the effects of *Miranda. UCLA Law Review, 43*, 839–931.

Clare, I., & Gudjonsson, G. H. (1991). Recall and understanding of the caution and rights in police detention among persons of average intellectual ability and persons with a mild mental handicap. *Issues in Criminological and Legal Psychology, 1*, 34–42.

Cloud, M., Shepherd, G. B., Barkoff, A. N., & Shur, J. V. (2002). Words without meaning: The Constitution, confessions, and mentally retarded suspects. *University of Chicago Law Review, 69*, 495–624. doi:10.2307/1600500

Cochrane, R. E., Grisso, T., & Frederick, R. I. (2001). The relationship between criminal charges, diagnoses, and psycholegal opinions among federal pretrial defendants. *Behavioral Sciences and the Law, 19*, 565–582. doi:10.1002/bsl.454

Colorado v. Al-Yousif, 49 P.3d 1165 (Colo. 2002).

Colorado v. Connelly, 479 U.S. 157 (1986).

Colwell, L. H., Cruise, K. R., Guy, L. S., McCoy, W. K., Fernandez, K., & Ross, H. H. (2005). The influence of psychosocial maturity on male juvenile offenders' comprehension and understanding of the *Miranda* warning. *Journal of the American Academy of Psychiatry and the Law, 33*, 444–454.

Colwell, L. H., & Gianesini, J. (2011). Demographic, criminogenic, and psychiatric factors that predict competency restoration. *Journal of the American Academy of Psychiatry and the Law, 39*, 297–306.

Cooper v. Oklahoma, 517 U.S. 348 (1996).

Cooper, V. G., & Zapf, P. A. (2003). Predictor variables in competency to stand trial decisions. *Law and Human Behavior, 27*, 423–436. doi:10.1023/A:1024089117535

Cooper, V. G., & Zapf, P. A. (2008). Psychiatric patients' comprehension of *Miranda* rights. *Law and Human Behavior, 32*, 390–405. doi:10.1007/s10979-007-9099-3

Cruise, K. R., & Rogers, R. (1998). An analysis of competency to stand trial: An integration of case law and clinical knowledge. *Behavioral Sciences and the Law, 16*, 35–50. doi:10.1002/(SICI)1099-0798(199824)16:1<35::AID-BSL292>3.0.CO;2-4

Cunningham, M. D., & Goldstein, A. M. (2003). Sentencing determinations in death penalty cases. In I. B. Weiner (Series Ed.), *Handbook of psychology: Vol. 11. Forensic psychology* (pp. 407–436). Hoboken, NJ: Wiley.

Cunningham, M. D., & Vigen, M. P. (2002). Death row inmate characteristics, adjustment, and confinement: A critical review of the literature. *Behavioral Sciences and the Law, 20*, 191–210. doi:10.1002/bsl.473

Davies, T. Y. (1982). Affirmed: A study of criminal appeals and decision-making norms in a California court of appeal. *American Bar Foundation Research Journal, 7*, 543–648. doi:10.1111/j.1747-4469.1982.tb00467.x

Davis, D. L. (1985). Treatment planning for the patient who is incompetent to stand trial. *Hospital and Community Psychiatry, 36*, 268–271.

DeClue, G. (2005). *Interrogations and disputed confessions: A manual for forensic psychological practice.* Sarasota, FL: Professional Resource Press.

DeClue, G. (2010). Oral *Miranda* warnings: A checklist and a model presentation. In G. D. Lassiter & C. A. Meissner (Eds.), *Police interrogations and false confessions: Current research, practice, and policy recommendations* (pp. 179–190). Washington, DC: American Psychological Association. doi:10.1037/12085-011

Deitchman, M. A., Kennedy, W. A., & Beckham, J. C. (1991). Self-selection factors in the participation of mental health professionals in competency for execution evaluations. *Law and Human Behavior, 15*, 287–303. doi:10.1007/BF01061714

DeMatteo, D., Murrie, D. C., Anumba, N., & Keesler, M. (2011). *Forensic mental health assessments in death penalty cases.* New York, NY: Oxford University Press. doi:10.1093/acprof:oso/9780195385809.001.0001

Dickerson v. United States, 530 U.S. 428 (2000).

Drope v. Missouri, 420 U.S. 162 (1975).

Dusky v. United States, 362 U.S. 402 (1960).

Eastwood, J., & Snook, B. (2012). The effect of listenability factors on the comprehension of police cautions. *Law and Human Behavior, 36*, 177–183. doi:10.1037/h0093955

Eastwood, J., Snook, B., & Chaulk, S. J. (2010). Measuring reading complexity and listening comprehension of Canadian police cautions. *Criminal Justice and Behavior, 37*, 453–471. doi:10.1177/0093854810362053

Ebert, B. (2001). Competency to be executed: A proposed instrument to evaluate an inmate's level of competency in light of the Eighth Amendment prohibition against the execution of the presently insane. *Law and Psychology Review, 25*, 29–57.

Everington, C., & Fulero, S. M. (1999). Competence to confess: Measuring understanding and suggestibility of defendants with mental retardation. *Mental Retardation, 37*, 212–220. doi:10.1352/0047-6765(1999)037<0212:CTCMUA>2.0.CO;2

Ewing, C. P. (1987). Diagnosing and treating "insanity" on death row: Legal and ethical perspectives. *Behavioral Sciences and the Law, 5*, 175–185. doi:10.1002/bsl.2370050209

Fare v. Michael C., 442 U.S. 707 (1979).

Feguer v. United States, 302 F.2d 214 (8th Cir. 1962).

Ferguson, A. B., & Douglas, A. C. (1970). A study of juvenile waiver. *San Diego Law Review, 7*, 39–54.

Ford v. Wainwright, 477 U.S. 399 (1986).

Fromme, K., Katz, E., & D'Amico, E. (1997). Effects of alcohol intoxication on the perceived consequences of risk taking. *Experimental and Clinical Psychopharmacology, 5*, 14–23. doi:10.1037/1064-1297.5.1.14

Frost, L., & Gowensmith, W. N. (2010, March). *National models of community-based restoration of juveniles and adults.* Paper presented at the meeting of the American Psychology-Law Society, Vancouver, British Columbia, Canada.

Frumkin, I. B. (2000). Competency to waive *Miranda* rights: Clinical and legal issues. *Mental and Physical Disability Law Reporter, 24*, 326–331.

Frumkin, I. B. (2010). Evaluations of competency to waive *Miranda* rights and coerced or false confessions: Common pitfalls in expert testimony. In

G. D. Lassiter & C. A. Meissner (Eds.), *Police interrogations and false confessions: Current research, practice, and policy recommendations* (pp. 191–209). Washington, DC: American Psychological Association. doi:10.1037/12085-012

Fulero, S. M., & Everington, C. (1995). Assessing competency to waive *Miranda* rights in defendants with mental retardation. *Law and Human Behavior, 19,* 533–543. doi:10.1007/BF01499342

GAINS Center. (2007). *Quick fixes for effectively dealing with persons found incompetent to stand trial.* Retrieved from http://gainscenter.samhsa.gov/topical_resources/integrating_services.asp

Gallegos v. Colorado, 370 U.S. 49 (1962).

Godinez v. Moran, 509 U.S. 389 (1993).

Golding, S. L. (1992). Studies of incompetent defendants: Research and social policy implications. *Forensic Reports, 5,* 77–83.

Golding, S. L. (1993). *Interdisciplinary Fitness Interview—Revised: A training manual.* Unpublished monograph, Utah Division of Mental Health.

Golding, S. L. (2008). Evaluations of adult adjudicative competency. In R. Jackson (Ed.), *Learning forensic assessment* (pp. 75–108). New York, NY: Routledge/Taylor & Francis Group.

Golding, S. L., Roesch, R., & Schreiber, J. (1984). Assessment and conceptualization of competency to stand trial: Preliminary data on the Interdisciplinary Fitness Interview. *Law and Human Behavior, 8,* 321–334. doi:10.1007/BF01044699

Goldstein, A. M. (2003). Overview of forensic psychology. In I. B. Weiner (Series Ed.), *Handbook of psychology: Vol. 11. Forensic psychology* (pp. 3–15). Hoboken, NJ: Wiley.

Goldstein, A. M. (2007). Forensic psychology: Toward a standard of care. In A. M. Goldstein (Ed.), *Forensic psychology: Emerging topics and expanding roles* (pp. 3–41). Hoboken, NJ: Wiley.

Goldstein, A. M., & Goldstein, N. E. S. (2010). Evaluating capacity to waive *Miranda* rights. New York, NY: Oxford University Press.

Goldstein, N. E. S., Condie, L. O., Kalbeitzer, R., Osman, D., & Geier, J. L. (2003). Juvenile offenders' *Miranda* rights comprehension and self-reported likelihood of offering false confessions. *Assessment, 10,* 359–369. doi:10.1177/1073191103259535

Goldstein, N. E. S., Goldstein, A. M., Zelle, H., & Oberlander Condie, L. (2012). Capacity to waive *Miranda* rights and the assessment of susceptibility to police coercion. In I. B. Weiner (Series Ed.), *Handbook of psychology: Vol. 11. Forensic psychology* (2nd ed., pp. 381–411). New York, NY: Wiley.

Goldstein, N. E. S., Riggs Romaine, C. L., Zelle, H., Kalbeitzer, R., Mesiarik, C., & Wolbransky, M.

(2011). Psychometric properties of the *Miranda* Rights Comprehension Instruments with a juvenile justice sample. *Assessment, 18,* 428–441. doi:10.1177/1073191111400280

Goldstein, N. E. S., Zelle, H., & Grisso, T. (2012). *The Miranda Rights Comprehension Instruments manual.* Sarasota, FL: Professional Resource Press.

Goldstein, R. L., & Stone, M. (1977). When doctors disagree: Differing views on competency. *Bulletin of the American Academy of Psychiatry and the Law, 5,* 90–97.

Gowensmith, W. N., Murrie, D. C., & Boccaccini, M. T. (2012). Field reliability of competence to stand trial opinions: How often do evaluations agree, and what do judges decide when evaluators disagree? *Law and Human Behavior, 36,* 130–139. doi:10.1037/h0093958

Grisso, J. T., & Pomicter, C. (1977). Interrogation of juveniles: An empirical study of procedures, safeguards, and rights waivers. *Law and Human Behavior, 1,* 321–342. doi:10.1007/BF01048593

Grisso, T. (1981). *Juveniles' waiver of rights: Legal and psychological competence.* New York, NY: Plenum Press. doi:10.1007/978-1-4684-3815-4

Grisso, T. (1986). *Evaluating competencies: Forensic assessments and instruments.* New York, NY: Plenum Press. doi:10.1007/978-1-4899-5046-8

Grisso, T. (1998). *Assessing understanding and appreciation of Miranda rights: Manual and materials.* Sarasota, FL: Professional Resource Press.

Grisso, T. (2003). *Evaluating competencies: Forensic assessments and instruments* (2nd ed.). New York, NY: Kluwer Academic/Plenum.

Grisso, T. (2013). *Forensic evaluation of juveniles* (2nd ed.). Sarasota, FL: Professional Resource Press.

Grisso, T., & Ring, M. (1979). Parents' attitudes toward juveniles' rights in interrogation. *Criminal Justice and Behavior, 6,* 211–226. doi:10.1177/009385487900600301

Grisso, T., Steinberg, L., Woolard, J., Cauffman, E., Scott, E., Graham, S., . . . Schwartz, R. (2003). Juveniles' competence to stand trial: A comparison of adolescents' and adults' capacities as trial defendants. *Law and Human Behavior, 27,* 333–363. doi:10.1023/A:1024065015717

Group for the Advancement of Psychiatry. (1974). *Misuse of psychiatry in the criminal courts: Competency to stand trial.* New York, NY: Committee on Psychiatry and the Law.

Guy, K. L., & Huckabee, R. G. (1988). Going free on a technicality: Another look at the effect of the *Miranda* decision on the criminal justice process. *Criminal Justice Research Bulletin, 4,* 1–3.

Harrison, Y., & Horne, J. A. (1996). Performance on a complex frontal lobe oriented task with "real-world" significance is impaired following sleep loss. *Journal of Sleep Research, 5,* 87.

Hart, S. D., & Hare, R. D. (1992). Predicting fitness to stand trial: The relative power of demographic, criminal, and clinical variables. *Forensic Reports, 5,* 53–65.

Heilbrun, K., Grisso, T., & Goldstein, A. M. (2009). *Foundations of forensic mental health assessment.* New York, NY: Oxford University Press.

Heilbrun, K., Warren, J., & Picarello, K. (2003). Third party information in forensic assessment. In I. B. Weiner (Series Ed.), *Handbook of psychology: Vol. 11. Forensic psychology* (pp. 69–86). Hoboken, NJ: Wiley.

Heilbrun, K. S., & McClaren, H. A. (1988). Assessment of competency for execution: A guide for mental health professionals. *Bulletin of the American Academy of Psychiatry and the Law, 16,* 205–216.

Hoge, S. K., Bonnie, R. J., Poythress, N., & Monahan, J. (1992). Attorney–client decision-making in criminal cases: Client competence and participation as perceived by their attorneys. *Behavioral Sciences and the Law, 10,* 385–394. doi:10.1002/bsl.2370100308

Hoge, S. K., Bonnie, R. J., Poythress, N., & Monahan, J. (1999). *The MacArthur Competence Assessment Tool—Criminal Adjudication.* Odessa, FL: Psychological Assessment Resources.

Hoge, S. K., Bonnie, R. J., Poythress, N., Monahan, J., & Eisenberg, M. (1997). The MacArthur Adjudicative Competence Study: Development and validation of a research instrument. *Law and Human Behavior, 21,* 141–179.

Hoge, S. K., Poythress, N., Bonnie, R. J., Monahan, J., Eisenberg, M., & Feucht-Haviar, T. (1997). The MacArthur Adjudicative Competence Study: Diagnosis, psychopathology, and adjudicative competence-related abilities. *Behavioral Sciences and the Law, 15,* 329–345. doi:10.1002/(SICI)1099-0798(199722/06)15:3<329::AID-BSL276>3.0.CO;2-Z

Hubbard, K. L., Zapf, P. A., & Ronan, K. A. (2003). Competency restoration: An examination of the differences between defendants predicted restorable and not restorable to competency. *Law and Human Behavior, 27,* 127–139. doi:10.1023/A:1022566328781

Illinois v. Bernasco, 562 N.E.2d 958 (Ill. 1990).

In re Gault, 387 U.S. 1 (1967)

In re Patrick W., 84 Cal.App.3d 520 (Cal. App. 1978).

Indiana v. Edwards, 554 U.S. 164 (2008).

Jackson v. Indiana, 406 U.S. 715 (1972).

James, D. J., & Glaze, L. E. (2006). *Mental health problems of prison and jail inmates* (Bureau of Justice Statistics Special Report NCJ 213600). Washington, DC: U.S. Department of Justice.

J. D. B. v. North Carolina, 131 S. Ct. 2394 (2011).

Kahn, R., Zapf, P. A., & Cooper, V. G. (2006). Readability of *Miranda* warnings and waivers: Implications for evaluating *Miranda* comprehension. *Law and Psychology Review, 30,* 119–142.

Kalbeitzer, R. (2008). *Evaluating legal learning: The effects of time and development on adolescents' understanding of legal rights* (Doctoral dissertation). Retrieved from http://dspace.library.drexel.edu

Kapoor, R. (2011). Commentary: Jail-based competency restoration. *Journal of the American Academy of Psychiatry and the Law, 39,* 311–315.

Kassin, S. M., Drizin, S. A., Grisso, T., Gudjonsson, G. H., Leo, R. A., & Redlich, A. D. (2010). Police-induced confessions: Risk factors and recommendations. *Law and Human Behavior, 34,* 3–38. doi:10.1007/s10979-009-9188-6

Kassin, S. M., Leo, R. A., Meissner, C. A., Richman, K. D., Colwell, L. H., Leach, A., & La Fon, D. (2007). Police interviewing and interrogation: A self-report survey of police practices and beliefs. *Law and Human Behavior, 31,* 381–400. doi:10.1007/s10979-006-9073-5

Kent v. United States, 383 U.S. 541 (1966).

King v. Frith, 22 How. St. Tr. 307 (1790).

Klaczynski, P. A. (2001). Analytic and heuristic processing influences on adolescent reasoning and decision-making. *Child Development, 72,* 844–861. doi:10.1111/1467-8624.00319

Kruh, I., & Grisso, T. (2009). *Evaluation of juveniles' competence to stand trial.* New York, NY: Oxford University Press.

Laben, J. K., Kashgarian, M., Nessa, D. B., & Spencer, L. D. (1977). Reform from the inside: Mental health center evaluations and competence to stand trial. *Journal of Community Psychology, 5,* 52–62. doi:10.1002/1520-6629(197701)5:1<52::AID-JCOP2290050109>3.0.CO;2-L

Laboratory of Community Psychiatry. (1973). *Competency to stand trial and mental illness.* (DHEW Publication No. ADM77-103). Rockville, MD: Department of Health, Education, and Welfare.

LaFortune, K. A., & Nicholson, R. A. (1995). How adequate are Oklahoma's mental health evaluations for determining competency in criminal proceedings? The Bench and the Bar respond. *Journal of Psychiatry and Law, 23,* 231–262.

Lally, S. J. (2003). What tests are acceptable for use in forensic evaluations? A survey of experts.

Professional Psychology: Research and Practice, 34, 491–498. doi:10.1037/0735-7028.34.5.491

Leo, R. A. (1996). Inside the interrogation room. *Journal of Criminal Law and Criminology, 86,* 266–303. doi:10.2307/1144028

Leo, R. A. (2001a). False confessions: Causes, consequences, and solutions. In S. D. Westervelt & J. A. Humphrey (Eds.), *Wrongly convicted: Perspectives on failed justice* (pp. 36–54). New Brunswick, NJ: Rutgers University Press.

Leo, R. A. (2001b). Questioning the relevance of *Miranda* in the twenty-first century. *Michigan Law Review, 99,* 1000–1029. doi:10.2307/1290525

Leong, G. B., Silva, J. A., Weinstock, R., & Ganzini, L. (2000). Survey of forensic psychiatrists on evaluation and treatment of prisoners on death row. *Journal of the American Academy of Psychiatry and the Law, 28,* 427–432.

Lipsitt, P. D., Lelos, D., & McGarry, A. L. (1971). Competency for trial: A screening instrument. *American Journal of Psychiatry, 128,* 105–109.

Maine v. Coombs, 704 A.2d 387 (Me. 1998).

Maryland v. Shatzer, 559 U.S. 98 (2010).

Massachusetts v. Guyton, 541 N.E.2d 1006 (Mass. 1989).

Massachusetts v. Jackson, 731 N.E.2d 1066 (Mass. 2000).

Massachusetts v. MacNeill, 502 N.E.2d 938 (Mass. 1987).

McCarthy, M. E., & Waters, W. F. (1997). Decreased attentional responsibility during sleep deprivation: Orienting response latency, amplitude, and habituation. *Sleep: Journal of Sleep Research and Sleep Medicine, 20,* 115–123.

McGarry, A. L. (1971). The fate of psychotic offenders returned for trial. *American Journal of Psychiatry, 127,* 1181–1184.

McGarry, A. L., & Curran, W. J. (1973). *Competency to stand trial and mental illness.* Rockville, MD: National Institute of Mental Health.

McKay, K. E., Halperin, J. M., Schwartz, S. T., & Sharma, V. (1994). Developmental analysis of three aspects of information processing: Sustained attention, selective attention, and response organization. *Developmental Neuropsychology, 10,* 121–132. doi:10.1080/87565649409540572

McLachlan, K., Roesch, R., & Douglas, K. S. (2011). Examining the role of interrogation suggestibility in Miranda rights comprehension in adolescents. *Law and Human Behavior, 35,* 165–177. doi:10.1007/s10979-009-9198-4

Medina v. California, 505 U.S. 437 (1992).

Meehl, P. (1970). Some methodological reflections on the difficulties of psychoanalytic research. In M. Radner & S. Winokur (Eds.), *Minnesota studies in the philosophy of science* (Vol. 4, pp. 403–416). Minneapolis: University of Minnesota Press.

Melton, G. B., Petrila, J., Poythress, N. G., & Slobogin, C. (2007). *Psychological evaluations for the courts: A handbook for mental health professionals and lawyers* (3rd ed.). New York, NY: Guilford Press.

Melton, G. B., Weithorn, L. A., & Slobogin, C. (1985). *Community mental health centers and the courts: An evaluation of community-based forensic services.* Lincoln: University of Nebraska Press.

Michigan v. Daoud, 614 N.W.2d 152 (Mich. 2000).

Miller, R. D. (2003). Hospitalization of criminal defendants for evaluation of competence to stand trial or for restoration of competence: Clinical and legal issues. *Behavioral Sciences and the Law, 21,* 369–391. doi:10.1002/bsl.546

Miranda v. Arizona, 384 U.S. 436 (1966).

Missouri v. Seibert, 542 U.S. 600 (2004).

Moran v. Burbine, 465 U.S. 412 (1986).

Morris, D. R., & DeYoung, N. J. (2012). Psycholegal abilities and restoration of competence to stand trial. *Behavioral Sciences and the Law, 30,* 710–728. doi:10.1002/bsl.2040

Morris, D. R., & Parker, G. F. (2008). *Jackson's* Indiana: State hospital competence restoration in Indiana. *Journal of the American Academy of Psychiatry and the Law, 36,* 522–534.

Morris, G. H., Haroun, A. M., & Naimark, D. (2004a). Assessing competency competently: Toward a rational standard for competency-to-stand-trial assessments. *Journal of the American Academy of Psychiatry and the Law, 32,* 231–245.

Morris, G. H., Haroun, A. M., & Naimark, D. (2004b). Health Law in the Criminal Justice System Symposium: Competency to stand trial on trial. *Houston Journal of Health Law and Policy, 4,* 193–238.

Mossman, D. (2007). Predicting restorability of incompetent criminal defendants. *Journal of the American Academy of Psychiatry and the Law, 35,* 34–43.

Mossman, D. (2008). Conceptualizing and characterizing accuracy in assessments of competence to stand trial. *Journal of the American Academy of Psychiatry and the Law, 36,* 340–351.

Mossman, D., Bowen, M. D., Vanness, D. J., Bienenfeld, D., Correll, T., Kay, J., . . . Lehrer, D. S. (2010). Quantifying the accuracy of forensic examiners in the absence of a "gold standard." *Law and Human Behavior, 34,* 402–417. doi:10.1007/s10979-009-9197-5

Mossman, D., Noffsinger, S. G., Ash, P., Frierson, R. L., Gerbasi, J., Hackett, M., . . . Zonana, H. V. (2007). AAPL practice guideline for the forensic psychiatric evaluation of competence to stand trial. *Journal of the American Academy of Psychiatry and the Law, 35,* S3–S72.

Murrie, D. C., Boccaccini, M. T., Zapf, P. A., Warren, J. I., & Henderson, C. E. (2008). Clinician variation in findings of competence to stand trial. *Psychology, Public Policy, and Law, 14,* 177–193. doi:10.1037/a0013578

Nardulli, P. F. (1983). The societal costs of the exclusionary rule: An empirical assessment. *American Bar Foundation Research Journal, 8,* 585–609. doi:10.1111/j.1747-4469.1983.tb00886.x

Nardulli, P. F. (1987). The societal costs of the exclusionary rule revisited. *University of Illinois Law Review, 2,* 223–239.

National Judicial College. (2011). *Mental competency: Best practices model.* Retrieved from http://www.mentalcompetency.org/model/model-sec-I.html

New Hampshire v. Bushey, 453 A.2d 1265 (N.H. 1982).

Nguyen, A. (2000). The assault on *Miranda. American Prospect, 13,* 58–62.

Nicholson, R. A., Barnard, G. W., Robbins, L., & Hankins, G. (1994). Predicting treatment outcome for incompetent defendants. *Bulletin of the American Academy of Psychiatry and the Law, 22,* 367–377.

Nicholson, R. A., & Kugler, K. E. (1991). Competent and incompetent criminal defendants: A quantitative review of comparative research. *Psychological Bulletin, 109,* 355–370. doi:10.1037/0033-2909.109.3.355

Nicholson, R. A., & McNulty, J. L. (1992). Outcome of hospitalization for defendants found incompetent to stand trial. *Behavioral Sciences and the Law, 10,* 371–383. doi:10.1002/bsl.2370100307

Nicholson, R. A., & Norwood, S. (2000). The quality of forensic psychological assessments, reports, and testimony: Acknowledging the gap between promise and practice. *Law and Human Behavior, 24,* 9–44. doi:10.1023/A:1005422702678

Noffsinger, S. G. (2001). Restoration to competency practice guidelines. *International Journal of Offender Therapy and Comparative Criminology, 45,* 356–362. doi:10.1177/0306624X01453007

Oberlander, L. B., & Goldstein, N. E. (2001). A review and update on the practice of evaluating *Miranda* comprehension. *Behavioral Sciences and the Law, 19,* 453–471. doi:10.1002/bsl.453

O'Connell, M. J., Garmoe, W., & Goldstein, N. E. S. (2005). *Miranda* comprehension in adults with mental retardation and the effects of feedback style on suggestibility. *Law and Human Behavior, 29,* 359–369. doi:10.1007/s10979-005-2965-y

Olley, M. C. (1998). *The utility of the test of charter comprehension for ensuring the protection of accuseds' rights at the time of arrest* (Unpublished doctoral dissertation). Simon Fraser University, Burnaby, British Columbia, Canada.

Olubadewo, O. B. (2008). *The relationship between mental health symptoms and comprehension of Miranda rights in male juvenile offenders* (Doctoral dissertation). Retrieved from http://idea.library.drexel.edu

Otto, R. K. (2009). Meaningful consideration of competence to be executed. In R. F. Schopp, R. L. Wierner, B. H. Bornstein, & S. L. Willborn (Eds.), *Mental disorder and criminal law: Responsibility, punishment, and competence* (pp. 191–204). New York, NY: Springer. doi:10.1007/978-0-387-84845-7_9

Otto, R. K., & Goldstein, A. M. (2005). Juveniles' competence to confess and competency to participate in the juvenile justice process. In K. Heilbrun, N. E. S. Goldstein, & R. E. Redding (Eds.), *Juvenile delinquency: Prevention, assessment, and intervention* (pp. 179–208). New York, NY: Oxford University Press.

Otto, R. K., Poythress, N. G., Nicholson, R. A., Edens, J. F., Monahan, J., Bonnie, R. J., . . . Eisenberg, M. (1998). Psychometric properties of the MacArthur Competence Assessment Tool—Criminal Adjudication (MacCAT–CA). *Psychological Assessment, 10,* 435–443. doi:10.1037/1040-3590.10.4.435

Overall, J. E., & Gorham, D. R. (1962). The Brief Psychiatric Rating Scale. *Psychological Reports, 10,* 799–812. doi:10.2466/pr0.1962.10.3.799

Panetti v. Quarterman, 551 U.S. 930 (2007).

Pate v. Robinson, 383 U.S. 375 (1966).

Pendleton, L. (1980). Treatment of persons found incompetent to stand trial. *American Journal of Psychiatry, 137,* 1098–1100.

Pennsylvania v. DeJesus, 787 A.2d 394 (Pa. 2001).

Pinals, D. A. (2005). Where two roads meet: Restoration of competence to stand trial from a clinical perspective. *New England Journal on Criminal and Civil Confinement, 31,* 81–108.

Pirelli, G., Gottdiener, W. H., & Zapf, P. A. (2011). A meta-analytic review of comparative competency to stand trial research. *Psychology, Public Policy, and Law, 17,* 1–53. doi:10.1037/a0021713

Pirelli, G., & Zapf, P. A. (2008). An investigation of psychologists' practices and attitudes toward participation in capital evaluations. *Journal of Forensic Psychology Practice, 8,* 39–66. doi:10.1080/15228930801947294

Poythress, N. G., Bonnie, R. J., Monahan, J., Otto, R., & Hoge, S. K. (2002). *Adjudicative competence:*

The MacArthur studies. New York, NY: Kluwer Academic/Plenum. doi:10.1007/978-1-4419-8493-7

Poythress, N. G., Nicholson, R. A., Otto, R. K., Edens, J. F., Bonnie, R. J., Monahan, J., & Hoge, S. K. (1999). *The MacArthur Competence Assessment Tool—Criminal Adjudication*. Odessa, FL: Psychological Assessment Resources.

Poythress, N. G., & Stock, H. V. (1980). Competency to stand trial: A historical review and some new data. *Journal of Psychiatry and Law, 8*, 131–146.

Radelet, M. L., & Barnard, G. W. (1986). Ethics and the psychiatric determination of competency to be executed. *Bulletin of the American Academy of Psychiatry and the Law, 14*, 37–53.

Raising question of competency to stand trial or plead; Evaluation and determination of competency, Virgina Code Ann. § 19.2-169.1 (1982).

Reisner, R., Slobogin, C., & Rai, A. (2004). *Law and the mental health system: Civil and criminal aspects* (4th ed.). St. Paul, MN: Thomson/West.

Riggs Romaine, C. L., Zelle, H., Wolbransky, M., Zelechoski, A. D., & Goldstein, N. E. S. (2008, August). *Juveniles' Miranda rights comprehension: Comparing understanding in two states*. Poster presented at the annual conference of the American Psychological Association, Boston, MA.

Roesch, R., & Golding, S. L. (1980). *Competency to stand trial*. Urbana: University of Illinois Press.

Roesch, R., Webster, C. D., & Eaves, D. (1984). *The Fitness Interview Test: A method for examining fitness to stand trial*. Toronto, Ontario, Canada: Research Report of the Centre of Criminology, University of Toronto.

Roesch, R., Zapf, P. A., & Eaves, D. (2006). *Fitness Interview Test: A structured interview for assessing competency to stand trial*. Sarasota, FL: Professional Resource Press.

Roesch, R. Zapf, P. A., Eaves, D., & Webster, C. D. (1998). *Fitness Interview Test* (rev. ed.). Burnaby, British Columbia, Canada: Mental Health, Law, and Policy Institute, Simon Fraser University.

Rogers, R. (2008). A little knowledge is a dangerous thing: Emerging *Miranda* research and professional roles for psychologists. *American Psychologist, 63*, 776–787. doi:10.1037/0003-066X.63.8.776

Rogers, R. (2011). Getting it wrong about *Miranda* rights: False beliefs, impaired reasoning, and professional neglect. *American Psychologist, 66*, 728–736. doi:10.1037/a0024988

Rogers, R., Gillard, N. D., Wooley, C. N., & Fiduccia, C. E. (2011). Decrements in *Miranda* abilities: An investigation of situational effects via a mock-crime paradigm. *Law and Human Behavior, 35*, 392–401. doi:10.1007/s10979-010-9248-y

Rogers, R., Harrison, K. S., Hazelwood, L. L., & Sewell, K. W. (2007). Knowing and intelligent: A study of *Miranda* warnings in mentally disordered defendants. *Law and Human Behavior, 31*, 401–418. doi:10.1007/s10979-006-9070-8

Rogers, R., Harrison, K. S., Rogstad, J. E., LaFortune, K. A., & Hazelwood, L. L. (2010). The role of suggestibility in determinations of *Miranda* abilities: A study of the Gudjonsson Suggestibility Scales. *Law and Human Behavior, 34*, 66–78. doi:10.1007/s10979-009-9186-8

Rogers, R., Harrison, K. S., Shuman, D. W., Sewell, K. W., & Hazelwood, L. L. (2007). An analysis of *Miranda* warnings and waivers: Comprehension and coverage. *Law and Human Behavior, 31*, 177–192. doi:10.1007/s10979-006-9054-8

Rogers, R., Hazelwood, L. L., Sewell, K. W., Blackwood, H. L., Rogstad, J. E., & Harrison, K. S. (2009). Development and initial validation of the Miranda Vocabulary Scale. *Law and Human Behavior, 33*, 381–392. doi:10.1007/s10979-008-9159-3

Rogers, R., Hazelwood, L. L., Sewell, K. W., Harrison, K. S., & Shuman, D. W. (2008). The language of *Miranda* warnings in American jurisdictions: A replication and vocabulary analysis. *Law and Human Behavior, 32*, 124–136. doi:10.1007/s10979-007-9091-y

Rogers, R., Hazelwood, L. L., Sewell, K. W., Shuman, D. W., & Blackwood, H. L. (2008). The comprehensibility and content of juvenile *Miranda* warnings. *Psychology, Public Policy, and Law, 14*, 63–87. doi:10.1037/a0013102

Rogers, R., & Johansson-Love, J. (2009). Evaluating competency to stand trial with evidence-based practice. *Journal of the American Academy of Psychiatry and the Law, 37*, 450–460.

Rogers, R., Rogstad, J. E., Gillard, N. D., Drogin, E. Y., Blackwood, H. L., & Shuman, D. W. (2010). "Everyone knows their *Miranda* rights": Implicit assumptions and countervailing evidence. *Psychology, Public Policy, and Law, 16*, 300–318. doi:10.1037/a0019316

Rogers, R., Sewell, K. W., Drogin, E. Y., & Fiduccia, C. E. (2012). *Standardized Assessment of Miranda Abilities*. Lutz, FL: Psychological Assessment Resources.

Rogers, R., & Shuman, D. (2005). *Fundamentals of forensic practice: Mental health and criminal law*. New York, NY: Springer.

Rogers, R., Tillbrook, C. E., & Sewell, K. W. (2004). *Evaluation of Competency to Stand Trial—Revised (ECST–R)*. Odessa, FL: Psychological Assessment Resources.

Rosenberg, A. H., & McGarry, A. L. (1972). Competency for trial: The making of an expert. *American Journal of Psychiatry, 128*, 1092–1096.

Rosenfeld, B., & Wall, A. (1998). Psychopathology and competence to stand trial. *Criminal Justice and Behavior, 25*, 443–462. doi:10.1177/0093854898025004003

Ryba, N. L., Brodsky, S. L., & Shlosberg, A. (2007). Evaluations of capacity to waive *Miranda* rights: A survey of practitioners' use of the Grisso instruments. *Assessment, 14*, 300–309. doi:10.1177/1073191110730284

Samuel, S. E., & Michaels, T. J. (2011). Competency restoration. In E. Y. Drogin, F. M. Dattilio, R. L. Sadoff, & T. G. Gutheil (Eds.), *Handbook of forensic assessment: Psychological and psychiatric perspectives* (pp. 79–96). Hoboken, NJ: Wiley. doi:10.1002/9781118093399.ch4

Scherr, K. C., & Madon, S. (2012). You have the right to understand: The deleterious effect of stress on suspects' ability to comprehend *Miranda*. *Law and Human Behavior, 36*, 275–282. doi:10.1037/h0093972

Schouten, R. (2003). Commentary: Training for competence: Form or substance? *Journal of the American Academy of Psychiatry and the Law, 31*, 202–204.

Sell v. United States, 539 U.S. 166 (2003).

Siegel, A. M., & Elwork, A. (1990). Treating incompetence to stand trial. *Law and Human Behavior, 14*, 57–65. doi:10.1007/BF01055789

Sigurdsson, J. F., & Gudjonsson, G. H. (1994). Alcohol and drug intoxication during police interrogation and the reasons why suspects confess to the police. *Addiction, 89*, 985–997. doi:10.1111/j.1360-0443.1994.tb03358.x

Skeem, J. L., & Golding, S. L. (1998). Community examiners' evaluations of competence to stand trial: Common problems and suggestions for improvement. *Professional Psychology: Research and Practice, 29*, 357–367. doi:10.1037/0735-7028.29.4.357

Skeem, J. L., Golding, S. L., Cohn, N. B., & Berge, G. (1998). Logic and reliability of evaluations of competence to stand trial. *Law and Human Behavior, 22*, 519–547. doi:10.1023/A:1025787429972

Small, M. A., & Otto, R. K. (1991). Evaluations of competency to be executed: Legal contours and implications for assessment. *Criminal Justice and Behavior, 18*, 146–158. doi:10.1177/0093854891018002003

Spano v. New York, 360 U.S. 315 (1959).

Steadman, H. J., Osher, F. C., Robbins, P. C., Case, B., & Samuels, S. (2009). Prevalence of serious mental illness among jail inmates. *Psychiatric Services, 60*, 761–765. doi:10.1176/appi.ps.60.6.761

Steadman, H. J., Scott, J. E., Osher, F. C., Agnese, T. K., & Robbins, P. C. (2005). Validation of the Brief Jail Mental Health Screen. *Psychiatric Services, 56*, 816–822. doi:10.1176/appi.ps.56.7.816

Strachan, M. K. (2008). *The development of a theory-based, Miranda rights educational curriculum: Are there cognitive developmental limitations to legal learning?* (Doctoral dissertation). Retrieved from http://dspace.library.drexel.edu

Swisher v. United States, 237 F.Supp. 921 (W.D.Mo. 1965).

Tennessee v. Stephenson, 878 S.W.2d 530 (Tenn., 1994).

Teplin, L. A. (1990). The prevalence of severe mental disorder among urban male detainees: Comparison with the epidemiologic catchment area program. *American Journal of Public Health, 80*, 663–669. doi:10.2105/AJPH.80.6.663

Teplin, L. A. (1994). Psychiatric and substance abuse disorders among male urban jail detainees. *American Journal of Public Health, 84*, 290–293. doi:10.2105/AJPH.84.2.290

Teplin, L. A., Abram, K. M., McClelland, G. M., Dulcan, M. K., & Mericle, A. A. (2002). Psychiatric disorders in youth and juvenile detention. *Archives of General Psychiatry, 59*, 1133–1143. doi:10.1001/archpsyc.59.12.1133

Thompson v. Keohane, 516 U.S. 99 (1995).

United States v. Adams, 297 F.Supp. 596 (S.D.N.Y. 1969).

United States v. Lawrence, 26 F. Cas. 886 (C.C.D.C. 1835).

United States v. Miller, 328 F.Supp.2d 350 (N.D.N.Y. 2005).

Viljoen, J. L., Klaver, J., & Roesch, R. (2005). Legal decisions of preadolescent and adolescent defendants: Predictors of confessions, pleas, communication with attorneys, and appeals. *Law and Human Behavior, 29*, 253–277. doi:10.1007/s10979-005-3613-2

Viljoen, J. L., & Roesch, R. (2005). Competence to waive interrogation rights and adjudicative competence in adolescent defendants: Cognitive development, attorney contact, and psychological symptoms. *Law and Human Behavior, 29*, 723–742. doi:10.1007/s10979-005-7978-y

Viljoen, J. L., Roesch, R., & Zapf, P. A. (2002). An examination of the relationship between competency to stand trial, competency to waive interrogation rights, and psychopathology. *Law and Human Behavior, 26*, 481–506. doi:10.1023/A:1020299804821

Viljoen, J. L., Zapf, P. A., & Roesch, R. (2004). Diagnosis, current symptomatology, and the ability to stand trial. *Journal of Forensic Psychology Practice, 3*, 23–37. doi:10.1300/J158v03n04_02

Wall, B. W., & Christopher, P. P. (2012). A training program for defendants with intellectual disabilities who are found incompetent to stand trial. *Journal of the American Academy of Psychiatry and the Law, 40*, 366–373.

Wall, B. W., Krupp, B. H., & Guilmette, T. (2003). Restoration of competency to stand trial: A training program for persons with mental retardation. *Journal of the American Academy of Psychiatry and the Law, 31*, 189–201.

Warren, J. I., Murrie, D. C., Stejskal, W., Collwell, L. H., Morris, J., Chauhan, P., & Deitz, P. (2006). Opinion formation in evaluating the adjudicative competence and restorability of criminal defendants: A review of 8,000 evaluations. *Behavioral Sciences and the Law, 24*, 113–132. doi:10.1002/bsl.699

Weisselberg, C. D. (2008). Mourning *Miranda*. *California Law Review, 96*, 1519–1601.

Weisselberg, C. D., & Bibas, S. (2010). The right to remain silent. *University of Pennsylvania Law Review, 159*, 69–93.

Wieter v. Settle, 193 F.Supp. 318 (W.D.Mo. 1961).

Williams, H. L., Lubin, A., & Goodnow, J. J. (1959). Impaired performance with acute sleep loss. *Psychological Monographs: General and Applied, 73*, 1–26. doi:10.1037/h0093749

Yarborough v. Alvarado, 541 U.S. 652 (2004).

Young, B., Boccaccini, M. T., Conroy, M. A., & Lawson, K. (2007). Four practical and conceptual assessment issues that evaluators should address in capital case mental retardation evaluations. *Professional Psychology: Research and Practice, 38*, 169–178. doi:10.1037/0735-7028.38.2.169

Young, B. A., Boccaccini, M. T., Lawson, K., & Conroy, M. A. (2008). Competence-for-execution evaluation practices in Texas: Findings from a semi-structured interview with experienced evaluators. *Journal of Forensic Psychology Practice, 8*, 280–292. doi:10.1080/15228930802282022

Youtsey v. United States, 97 F. 937 (6th Cir. 1899).

Zapf, P. A. (2008). Competency for execution. In R. Jackson (Ed.), *Learning forensic assessment* (pp. 239–261). New York, NY: Routledge/Taylor & Francis Group.

Zapf, P. A., Boccaccini, M. T., & Brodsky, S. L. (2003). Assessment of competency for execution: Professional guidelines and an evaluation checklist. *Behavioral Sciences and the Law, 21*, 103–120. doi:10.1002/bsl.491

Zapf, P. A., Hubbard, K. L., Cooper, V. G., Wheeles, M. C., & Ronan, K. A. (2004). Have the courts abdicated their responsibility for determination of competency to stand trial to clinicians? *Journal of Forensic Psychology Practice, 4*, 27–44. doi:10.1300/J158v04n01_02

Zapf, P. A., & Roesch, R. (2006). Competency to stand trial: A guide for evaluators. In I. B. Weiner & A. K. Hess (Eds.), *The handbook of forensic psychology* (3rd ed., pp. 305–331). Hoboken, NJ: Wiley.

Zapf, P. A., & Roesch, R. (2009). *Best practices in forensic mental health assessment: Evaluation of competence to stand trial*. New York, NY: Oxford University Press.

Zapf, P. A., & Roesch, R. (2011). Future directions in the restoration of competence to stand trial. *Current Directions in Psychological Science, 20*, 43–47. doi:10.1177/0963721410396798

Zapf, P. A., Roesch, R., & Viljoen, J. L. (2001). Assessing fitness to stand trial: The utility of the Fitness Interview Test (revised edition). *Canadian Journal of Psychiatry, 46*, 426–432.

Zelle, H. (2012). *Judges' treatment of the knowing and intelligent requirements for Miranda waivers* (Doctoral dissertation). Retrieved from http://dspace.lirbary.drexel.edu

Zelle, H., Riggs Romaine, C. L., Serico, J. M., Wolbransky, M., Osman, D. A., Taormina, S., & Goldstein, N. E. S. (2008, August). *Adolescents' Miranda rights comprehension: The impact of verbal expressive abilities*. Poster presented at the annual conference of the American Psychological Association, Boston, MA.

CHAPTER 6

MENTAL HEALTH TREATMENT OF CRIMINAL OFFENDERS

Barry Rosenfeld, Jacqueline Howe, Ashley Pierson, and Melodie Foellmi

Despite the obvious importance of reducing crime and violence, criminal offenders have received surprisingly little attention from the mental health community. Relatively few mental health interventions have been specifically developed to target criminal offenders generally, or the cognitions, emotions, and impulses that are thought to underlie criminal behaviors. Fewer still have been empirically evaluated. This state of relative neglect has no doubt arisen from multiple sources, including the greater emphasis that is placed on punishment, incapacitation, and deterrence by the criminal justice system as well as the all too frequent lack of motivation to seek treatment on the part of offenders. Thus, although some forms of mental health treatment are available in virtually every correctional facility in the United States (as well as in most developed nations), the extent to which empirically supported, or even empirically grounded, interventions have been developed and systematically assessed—beyond those specifically geared toward substance abuse— pales in comparison to more *typical* forms of mental health treatment such as that for depression, anxiety, or schizophrenia. Nevertheless, the last two decades have witnessed a growing interest on the part of mental health researchers to identify effective interventions for this long-neglected population that creates so many challenges for contemporary society. This chapter attempts to provide a broad overview of this literature.

This chapter begins with an overview of the problems that are posed by *untreated* criminal offenders, including the frequency (and social costs) of recidivism (reoffense), followed by a brief summary of the research and the methodological issues that complicate this area of study. The bulk of this chapter consists of a comprehensive review of the published literature, including both general treatment approaches that have been adapted to offender populations (e.g., cognitive–behavioral interventions geared to the needs of criminal offenders) as well as those interventions that have been developed specifically to target particular elements of criminal offending (e.g., criminal cognitions, anger management). Following this overview is a review of the literature on the treatment of psychopathy, given the importance of this construct for both the criminal justice and forensic mental health communities as well as the frequent, but seemingly erroneous, assumption that psychopaths are simply untreatable. Finally, the chapter concludes with a summary and clinical practice recommendations.

Although the intent of this chapter is to provide a broad review of the offender treatment literature, there are several overlapping but more specialized topics that have been deliberately omitted from this review. These topics include the (a) treatment of juveniles who are involved in the criminal justice system (see Volume 2, Chapter 2, this handbook); (b) treatment of sexual deviance and sex offenders (see Chapter 11, this volume); (c) treatment of substance abuse within criminal justice settings (see Chapter 10, this volume); and (d) treatment of domestic violence (often termed interpersonal violence), including stalking, spousal assault, and child abuse (see Chapter 12, this volume). Although clearly relevant to the overarching goals of this chapter, these topics represent specialized areas of investigation and warrant a more focused and in-depth review than can realistically be accomplished

http://dx.doi.org/10.1037/14461-006
APA Handbook of Forensic Psychology: Vol. 1. Individual and Situational Influences in Criminal and Civil Contexts,
B. L. Cutler and P. A. Zapf (Editors-in-Chief)

in this chapter. The interested reader is advised to consult other chapters in this volume that address these issues.

IMPORTANCE OF THE PROBLEM

The impetus for developing mental health treatments for criminal offenders comes primarily from two fronts: the overrepresentation of severely mentally ill individuals in criminal justice settings and the perception that even those offenders without an obvious form of mental illness may change their antisocial behaviors with adequate intervention. The former problem, the overrepresentation of severe mental illness among incarcerated offenders, has been well established and is largely undisputed, although discrepancies certainly exist regarding the magnitude of the problem and optimal solutions. However, the high rate of mental illness among criminal offenders, although important, is not the focus of this chapter. Although many barriers, both legal and pragmatic, impact the ease with which mentally ill offenders are identified and treated within the criminal justice system, the actual treatments for severe mental illness (many, but not all, of which are pharmacological) are often the same, regardless of whether the individual is incarcerated or at liberty.

Treatment of criminality, on the other hand, has long been a focus for mental health professionals. Early approaches to the treatment of criminal offenders were largely a function of the treating clinician's theoretical orientation and were broadly focused on *rehabilitation* of the offender (Hollin, 2002). Not surprisingly, these early treatment efforts were rarely successful. In his seminal meta-analysis of 231 empirical studies of prison rehabilitative programs, Martinson (1974) concluded that "with few and isolated exceptions, the rehabilitative efforts that have been reported so far have had no appreciable effect on recidivism" (p. 25). In fact, the discouraging conclusions of Martinson and his colleagues (e.g., Lipton, Martinson, & Wilks, 1975) led many mental health professionals, correctional settings, and policy makers to abandon efforts to rehabilitate criminal offenders altogether. However, other professionals used

Martinson's conclusions as an impetus to renew, and even enhance, their efforts at identifying the critical and potentially changeable aspects of criminal behavior. The literature that emerged in the decade following Martinson's widely publicized review has painted a more optimistic picture, as evidenced by Gendreau and Ross's (1987) conclusion that "successful rehabilitation of offenders had been accomplished, and continued to be accomplished quite well" (p. 350).

Although research scholars have never lost interest in studying the impact of correctional policies on criminal behavior, policy changes have typically lagged far behind the scientific advances in offender treatment. For example, the U.S. Supreme Court, in *Mistretta v. United States* (1989), upheld federal sentencing guidelines that all but eliminated rehabilitation as a goal of criminal sentencing. Writing for the majority, Justice Blackmun cited the Senate Report on the 1984 sentencing law as stating that "the efforts of the criminal justice system to achieve rehabilitation of offenders had failed" (p. 361). This conclusion, like the 1984 Sentencing Reform Act that spurred the case, was rooted in Martinson's (1974) seminal paper, which had been widely disseminated and had become, by then, generally accepted as the state of the science.

Despite the pessimistic outlook on offender rehabilitation that characterized the 1970s and 1980s, researchers and mental health clinicians continued to push forward in identifying potentially beneficial interventions. Indeed, the past two decades have witnessed a growing acknowledgment that some forms of treatment might work for some offenders. This acknowledgment, coupled with the increased attention that was paid to distinct offender subgroups (e.g., those with substance abuse disorders or who commit sexual offenses), has led to a marked resurgence of interest and even some increases in the public funding that is available for offender treatment, both in the United States and elsewhere (e.g., Crighton & Towl, 2008). One key element of this second generation of offender rehabilitation efforts has been the far greater focus on matching particular characteristics of the offender and the recommended treatment. This approach, and the research it has given rise to, forms a substantial portion of the literature review that is summarized in this chapter.

RELEVANT PSYCHOLOGICAL THEORY AND PRINCIPLES

The idea of targeting treatments to those offenders who are most likely to benefit from them, an approach that we refer to as the *second generation* of offender treatment, forms the heart and soul of the risk–need–responsivity (RNR) model (Andrews, Bonta, & Hoge, 1990). Indeed, despite variations in the specific techniques that are used to target criminogenic needs, the RNR approach has rapidly emerged as the dominant theoretical model underlying virtually all offender treatment interventions for the past two decades (e.g., Blanchette & Brown, 2006; Ward, Mesler, & Yates, 2007). The principles of the RNR model involve identifying and targeting the criminogenic variables that are most salient for each individual offender. Although many specific approaches have been developed to address offender needs, the interventions applied in RNR-based approaches have typically been derived from social learning theory (Bandura, 1977) and are best characterized as being cognitive–behavioral in their approach (Andrews & Bonta, 2003).

The three elements of the RNR model require, respectively, determining the appropriate level of intervention needed (the *risk* principle), identifying the specific elements of an offender's psychological profile that require treatment (the *need* principle), and selecting interventions that are best suited to modifying the identified needs (the *responsivity* principle). Thus, the risk principle dictates that the services provided should correspond to the level of risk posed by an individual; those offenders at the greatest risk for reoffending require the most intensive services (e.g., ranging from no treatment needed to inpatient or residential treatment for those at extreme levels of risk). The need principle requires an initial and ongoing assessment of an offender's personality characteristics, behaviors, and criminogenic attitudes in order to determine the appropriate targets for intervention. In addition to being directly linked to the offender's criminal behavior, the needs identified should be changeable,

or dynamic, if they are to be amenable to intervention. Finally, the responsivity principle encompasses both general and specific elements of responsivity. General responsivity involves the use of treatment techniques that have been derived from social learning and cognitive–behavioral theories that explain the mechanisms influencing behavior. As will be described in more detail later in this chapter, offender rehabilitation approaches based on cognitive–behavioral therapy (CBT) have typically demonstrated the strongest treatment effects in the extant literature, regardless of the characteristics of the offender that are targeted. Specific responsivity requires tailoring the intervention to the forensic context in general, as well as identifying unique characteristics of the offender that require treatment. Accordingly, in developing the most appropriate treatment services for a specific individual, treatment providers following this principle would take into account the individual offender's strengths, learning style, personality, motivation, and biosocial (e.g., gender, race, culture) characteristics. In short, the objective of the responsivity principle is to maximize the offender's potential for treatment gains from the chosen rehabilitative intervention(s), which is accomplished by providing a CBT-based treatment that is tailored to the individual's background, learning style, motivation, abilities, and strengths.

As evident from this discussion of the RNR model, CBT is a central element of virtually all contemporary approaches to offender treatment. Within this overarching framework, however, interventions for criminal offenders can be divided into two broad categories of approaches: those that apply or modify traditional CBT-based interventions to the needs of an offender population, and those that were developed specifically to address criminogenic variables that have been identified through past research and theoretical developments. These interventions, and the research supporting each, are described in the following pages. Finally, given the importance of psychopathy in the context of criminal offending generally, and the controversy surrounding the treatment of psychopathy in particular, we review this treatment literature independently from more general interventions that have been described in the offender treatment literature. We would note, of course, that some psychopathic offenders are no doubt included in almost any offender treatment study, but because the focus of these studies is rarely on psychopathy per se, the impact of this construct on treatment outcome is infrequently addressed in the more general treatment literature.

Andrews, Zinger, et al. (1990) identified a number of critical elements that should be included in a treatment program in order for the program to be appropriate for correctional settings. They found that 65.2% of the offender treatment studies included in their literature review met these criteria and were considered at least somewhat appropriate; conversely, many programs did not meet any of their criteria and were deemed inappropriate. In addition to relying on cognitive–behavioral principles, Andrews, Zinger, et al. identified programs as being appropriate if they were intensive, included structured programming, and/or specifically targeted criminogenic needs. Interpreting this literature, however, is complicated by the tremendous heterogeneity that exists across individual research studies. For example, although the interventions the authors reviewed averaged approximately 6 months in length, the treatment ranged from 1.5 weeks to 78 weeks of intended intervention. Likewise, follow-up intervals also varied widely, ranging from 2 to 260 weeks. The most common methodology used in offender treatment studies was the pretest–posttest design, without inclusion of any type of control or comparison group. Although some studies included a control or comparison group, and occasionally even randomly assigned offenders to a treatment arm, such rigor is uncommon in the offender treatment literature.

Based on their meta-analysis of correctional treatment programs, F. T. Cullen and Gendreau (2000) highlighted the importance of specifically addressing dynamic risk factors that directly influence an individual's criminal behavior. They identified known predictors of renewed criminal behavior, including control deficits, criminogenic attitudes, and affiliation with other offenders. In addition, Cullen and Gendreau emphasized the importance of ensuring that treatment implementation adheres to a specified theory. Regardless of whether the intervention uses a manualized or principle-based approach

to treatment, failure to adhere to the theory underlying an intervention appears to reduce the likelihood of finding a significant treatment effect. Unfortunately, published studies have rarely addressed treatment integrity or treatment adherence in offender treatment outcome research (Perepletchikova & Kazdin, 2005). Despite these caveats and limitations, an ever-growing body of research has focused on both broad and narrow interventions for criminal offenders, including offenders both with and without identified mental disorders.

A primary focus of offender treatments, particularly as conceptualized by the RNR model, is identifiable treatment targets (i.e., the need principle). Among offenders who suffer from a major mental disorder, treatment needs are largely identical to what would be found in nonforensic psychiatric settings. Likewise, a number of unique offender subgroups exist in which treatment needs are well defined and distinct (e.g., substance abuse, sexual deviance). However, for a large segment of the offender population, the primary needs that are identified are criminogenic attitudes and behaviors or a general tendency toward aggression. Both of these domains represent dynamic risk factors that directly increase the likelihood of renewed criminal offending (i.e., recidivism). The following section begins with a discussion of critical methodological issues that are relevant to treatment outcome research and follows with a review of the relevant published literature.

RESEARCH REVIEW

An essential prerequisite to interpreting the published literature on the treatment of criminal offenders is an understanding of the techniques that are used to evaluate treatment outcome more generally. Unfortunately, much of the offender treatment literature has been plagued by methodological problems that limit the conclusiveness of many published clinical trials. In fact, the prototypical approach to evaluating treatment effectiveness, the randomized clinical trial (RCT), has rarely been applied to offender treatment settings. There are many practical reasons for this apparent neglect, such as the ethical challenges inherent in conducting true experimental research in forensic or criminal justice settings. Thus, much of the published literature has relied on open trials in which an intervention group is compared on relevant study measures that are administered before and after treatment (i.e., a pretest–posttest design). When a comparison group is employed, studies often rely on treatment-as-usual (TAU) or an untreated comparison sample rather than a true control group. Unfortunately, without randomization (which is all too rare in the offender treatment literature), disentangling treatment effects from sample biases is often more challenging than the investigators acknowledge. This, and other relevant considerations in interpreting the published literature, is reviewed in the following paragraphs and provides a backdrop for interpreting the literature review that follows.

Although this section delineates a number of weaknesses that pervade the offender treatment literature, it seems appropriate to begin by addressing one of the noteworthy strengths in the published studies: the reliance on clearly articulated—and often manualized—clinical interventions. Many treatment outcome studies in the general psychology literature are subject to the criticism of an insufficiently detailed treatment program. However, the offender treatment literature, particularly over the past 20 years, has been notable for its frequent reliance on well-documented treatment approaches that are grounded in a plausible underlying theory. Although adherence to established treatment manuals is certainly more variable (e.g., many studies simply ignore this issue altogether, and few do more than describe the training and supervision of study clinicians), and few published studies document treatment adherence, the *replicability* of clinical interventions stands as a noteworthy strength of the research literature addressing offender treatment outcome.

On the other hand, there is wide variability in how offender treatment studies conceptualize treatment outcome. This is, of course, a particularly thorny issue, particularly for treatment studies that are based in criminal justice settings. One obvious choice of outcome variable is reoffense, whether specific to a particular type of offense that has been targeted (e.g., interpersonal violence, sexual assault, etc.) or a more general measure (i.e., any rearrest or

reconviction). However, even within this narrow band of outcome variables, the decision as to whether to focus on rearrest or reconviction is an important one because reconviction often underestimates the true rate of reoffending (because many offenders are not caught). The discrepancy between rearrest and reconviction may be heightened when researchers focus on a specific type of offense, as offenders may plea bargain to a lesser charge (or even a dismissal of charges) that obscures the actual recidivism rate.

A second issue with the focus on recidivism is the dichotomous nature of this outcome; reoffenses are either present or absent. Thus, treatment effects must be demonstrated through a reduced frequency of reoffending in the study sample—a difference that is often modest and may necessitate large sample sizes in order to be demonstrated reliably (i.e., statistically). Of course, many other complications exist when relying on reoffense as the primary or sole measure of treatment success, including the need for extended follow-up periods, particularly for low-frequency behaviors. In fact, many treatment studies of incarcerated samples offer little or no opportunity for any reoffense to occur if the treated individuals have not yet been released from prison. Given these many challenges, it is not surprising that researchers have often sought alternative indicators of treatment success, such as self-report measures that address relevant psychological constructs (e.g., anger, aggression, empathy).

Unfortunately, many issues also arise when researchers rely on self-report measures to assess treatment outcome, including, but not limited to, an individual's accuracy in responding. Inaccurate responding need not be solely attributable to deliberate distortion (although the risk of distortion in criminal justice samples is certainly high), but can also include a lack of insight or, as is true of virtually all samples, socially desirable responding. In fact, we have observed a particularly challenging phenomenon in our offender treatment studies, with high levels of defensiveness and social desirability in self-report measures that are collected prior to treatment (i.e., the baseline assessment) and lower levels of defensiveness at follow-up assessments. Whether a function of treatment (i.e., improving insight) or trust in the researchers (i.e., greater willingness to disclose problems), this pattern can result in seemingly counterintuitive outcomes, giving the appearance of worsening problems after treatment whereas no such worsening might occur for untreated individuals. In short, although often appealing because of the desire to study and quantify constructs that are directly relevant to the treatment targets, reliance on self-report measures is fraught with challenges in criminal justice settings and often bears little relationship to whether an individual's treatment outcome is *successful*.

Although the challenges associated with measuring dependent variables for offender treatment studies are relatively obvious, there are also many challenges associated with the measurement of independent variables and potentially relevant covariates. For example, although nonrandom assignment often creates havoc for the interpretation of treatment effects (because treated and untreated groups can differ on multiple variables), the inclusion of propensity scores as a covariate can help minimize these confounds by adjusting for the group differences. In addition, although infrequently used in offender treatment, the application of intent-to-treat analyses and mixed models that include multiple data points can often provide a much more rigorous index of treatment effects. Such approaches, however, are rare in offender treatment studies where samples of convenience, nonrandom assignment, and high rates of attrition are common. Given these constraints, it is perhaps surprising that as many consistent findings have emerged from this literature as the following review would suggest.

Another problem that confounds the interpretation of offender treatment research is the high rate of attrition that is frequently observed. Attrition rates typically range from 20% to 50% in the general psychotherapy literature and are only slightly lower in offender treatment settings, in part because treatment is often mandated by the court or a probation officer. Olver, Stockdale, and Wormith (2011), in their review of the variables that predict attrition in offender settings, identified a number of variables that corresponded to greater or lower rates of attrition. Among the many variables associated with treatment completion in their meta-analysis were a

diagnosis of borderline and/or antisocial personality disorder; psychopathy; a history of substance abuse; and a range of attitudinal or personality characteristics such as anger, impulsivity, criminal thinking, lack of treatment engagement, negative attitude toward treatment, perceived lack of motivation to change, and denial. These findings led Olver et al. to conclude that offenders who drop out of treatment are typically at higher risk (pretreatment) than those who complete treatment, suggesting that studies focusing only on treatment completers likely overestimate the effectiveness of a treatment outcome study. However, the authors noted that the association between attrition and recidivism was modest and was even smaller for violent reoffense ($r = .20$ for general recidivism and $r = .10$ for violent recidivism).

A final set of methodological concerns pertains to the inclusion criteria for determining who constitutes a study case. Although not unique to offender treatment, criminal justice settings pose frequent problems for researchers who are seeking to use rigorous experimental designs. For both pragmatic as well as ethical reasons, researchers may not be able to randomly assign offenders to different treatments, particularly if one option is a no-treatment control arm. Imagine the potential problems posed by randomly assigning a potentially violent offender who has been deemed in need of mental health treatment to an inactive treatment condition. Thus, researchers are often forced to rely on quasi-experimental designs in which treated offenders are compared to an untreated, but likely not identical, comparison sample. Although statistical methods exist for minimizing the influence of nonrandom assignment (e.g., propensity scores), these techniques cannot eliminate the biases that are inherent in nonrandom assignment.

A related problem pertains to the motivation to genuinely participate in treatment. In many settings, offenders are coerced to participate, whether explicitly (e.g., court ordered to attend treatment) or implicitly (e.g., in anticipation that completing treatment will result in a reduced sentence). Thus, the genuineness of a treatment program participants' motivation is often questionable, which can diminish the seeming effectiveness of treatment were it conducted only with individuals who were genuinely motivated to change. Of course, a number of other methodological challenges exist in conducting offender treatment and have been described in detail elsewhere (Rosenfeld, Byers, & Galietta, 2011), but this brief summary highlights many of the issues that plague the literature that is described in the next section.

The Early History of Offender Treatment

The history of interventions designed to reduce criminal behavior is not a flattering one. Although mental health professionals began working in criminal justice settings during the early part of the 20th century, few psychiatrists or psychologists were employed by prisons, and those who were typically had a broad goal: *curing* offenders of their criminality (Morris & Rothman, 1995). Although the treatment of criminal offenders was not widespread until the 1970s, the increased availability of mental health treatment corresponded to the emergence of *rehabilitative* approaches to reduce offending. Indeed, in the 1970s, the rehabilitation model began to supplant the purely punitive approach that had predominated the criminal justice system. The emergence of mental health treatment in criminal justice settings reflected the growing optimism that psychology, drawing largely on developments in behavior modification, can change problem behaviors such as law breaking. Although many of these interventions began in and were limited to custodial settings (e.g., prison), the emergence of court-ordered treatments extended the application of offender treatments to many community settings. In fact, much of the published literature focuses on offenders who are living in the community, and these programs encompass the lion's share of current offender mental health services. These settings are sometimes referred to as *diversion* programs, when treatment is offered in lieu of incarceration, but also includes postrelease treatment programs for parolees or probationers.

In an effort to synthesize the ever-growing offender rehabilitation literature, the last few decades have witnessed an unusually large number of meta-analyses. One focal point in this metaresearch has been an attempt to identify overarching patterns in the treatment literature that might help identify characteristics or treatment elements that are associated with greater (or lesser) success in treatment outcomes. A conclusion of much of this literature has been that interventions relying on CBT principles have typically generated stronger results than those based on other approaches (Lösel, 1995; Pearson, Lipton, Cleland, & Yee, 2002; Wilson, Bouffard, & MacKenzie, 2005). For example, a series of studies by Lipsey and colleagues (Lipsey, Chapman, & Landenberger, 2001; Lipsey & Landenberger, 2005) found that the improvement for CBT-based offender treatment programs, when compared to other, non-CBT treatment programs, was substantial, with recidivism rates typically falling between one-half and one-fourth lower than those observed for offenders who had been treated with other (or no) treatment approaches.

The principles of CBT assume that an individual's thoughts affect his or her behaviors. Through treatment, offenders are taught to monitor and alter their thought processes with the assumption that these changes in thought processes will ultimately result in changes in behavior (Dobson & Block, 1988). Hence, CBT programs aim to help individuals become aware of the thought processes that lead to their maladaptive behaviors. Among the many specific deficiencies targeted by forensic CBT programs, the most common include impulse control, critical reasoning abilities, moral reasoning, cognitive style, and general social skills. Although each CBT program has its own unique theoretical justification and corresponding specific treatment targets, the overarching goal of these cognitive–behavioral interventions is to modify the criminogenic thinking and behavior of offenders using cognitive and/or behavioral or learning techniques. Based on these meta-analytic findings, researchers have developed a framework on which to construct a new generation of CBT intervention for offenders. These *brand-name* CBT interventions have become the cornerstone of most offender treatment programs (Wormith et al., 2007) and are frequently implemented in correctional and community settings worldwide.

Mahoney and Lyddon (1988) distinguished between two types of CBT-based programs for criminal offender rehabilitation: those that operate under the belief that offenders have dysfunctional information processing skills (e.g., Reasoning and Rehabilitation [R&R]; Ross & Fabiano, 1985) and those that operate under the belief that offenders have a lower level of moral development (e.g., Moral Reconation Therapy [MRT]; Little & Robinson, 1988). The former strive to enhance offenders' cognitive processing skills, whereas the latter seek to increase offenders' weak moral reasoning abilities. Some interventions combine aspects of both cognitive skills enhancement and moral education into one packaged program (e.g., Aggression Replacement Training [ART]; Goldstein, Glick, & Gibbs, 1986); others place emphasis on some combination of cognitive restructuring, increasing coping skills, or developing problem-solving abilities (Mahoney & Arnkoff, 1978). Most of these programs involve highly structured interventions that are detailed in treatment manuals and are delivered primarily in group settings, as individual treatment is often impractical in correctional settings, where resources are typically scarce (Wilson et al., 2005). The most widely used and well-studied interventions are discussed in more detail in the following subsections.

Reasoning and Rehabilitation. The R&R program (Ross & Fabiano, 1985) is one of the most widely used CBT programs for offenders and has been implemented in a wide range of correctional settings. Drawing on social learning theory (Bandura, 1977), the R&R program is predicated on the assumption that offenders have not been provided sufficient opportunity to learn critical cognitive skills (e.g., problem identification, alternative solution generation, means-end thinking, anticipation of consequences of actions, perspective taking) that most people acquire during the course of their development. This assumption is bolstered by research indicating that many offenders have developmental delays in the acquisition of the cognitive skills necessary for adaptive social functioning (Ross & Fabiano, 1980). Therefore, the main emphasis of the R&R program is on teaching offenders these cognitive skills so that when they are released back into the community, they will be less likely to reoffend because of their newly acquired skills. Specifically, the R&R program attempts to

modify impulsive, egocentric, illogical, and rigid thinking by teaching social skills, problem solving, and critical thinking through adaptations of structured learning therapy, values education, assertiveness training, and negotiation skills training. The program consists of thirty-eight 2-hr group sessions that are delivered over the course of 8 to 12 weeks and includes audiovisual presentations, games, group discussion, and role-playing (Porporino & Robinson, 1995). The program is intended to be delivered by a wide range of professionals, including probation officers, in order to enable the integration of R&R into probation supervision.

In one of the initial studies to test the utility of the R&R program, Ross, Fabiano, and Ewles (1988) found that high-risk male probationers who had been randomly assigned to receive R&R as a component of their probation were less likely to reoffend than were probationers who received a life skills training intervention and a third group who received only probation. Specifically, Ross et al. found that 69.5% of probationers in the probation-only group reoffended compared to 47.5% of probationers who received life skills training and only 18.1% of those assigned to the R&R group. However, these promising results should be evaluated in the context of the study's small sample size ($N = 62$) and the absence of any statistical tests. There were also a number of methodological limitations that should be considered when interpreting the results of this study. First, the R&R program was delivered by the same probation officers who provided both the life skills training and the regular probation supervision; thus, probation officers were clearly not "blind" to the probationers' treatment condition. Second, the researchers provided no information about the participants' attendance or treatment dose. They described the attendance of participants in the life skills group as "sporadic," but it is unclear whether there were significant differences in attendance rates across the three conditions. If probationers in the R&R group did in fact attend more sessions, it could be that the lower recidivism rates in that group were attributable to the amount of time the probationers spent in a rehabilitative context rather than to the content of those sessions. Furthermore, the researchers did not specify who was included in the final recidivism rates—whether it was an intent-to-treat analysis or only those participants who successfully completed the program. Despite problems with this study, several subsequent studies have demonstrated evidence for the effectiveness of the R&R program and its variants (e.g., Porporino & Robinson, 1995; Robinson, 1995, 1996; Robinson, Grossman, & Porporino, 1991).

In one such study, Wilkinson (2005) found that although offenders who were assigned to the R&R program were no less likely to be reconvicted after 2 years than was a comparison group who received alternative sentences, attending the R&R program was associated with a 17% reduction in custody at reconviction, indicating that perhaps the R&R group had committed less serious offenses. In addition, offenders who completed the R&R program were less likely to be reconvicted and only half as likely to be sentenced to custody at reconviction compared to offenders who did not complete the program and those in the comparison group. It is important to note that the comparison group in this study included individuals who were sentenced to prison, which raises the issue of how much opportunity these individuals actually had to reoffend. Moreover, other research teams have not found that R&R leads to lower rates of reoffense (e.g., Knott, 1995; Porporino & Robinson, 1995). For example, Raynor and Vanstone (1996) evaluated the Straight Thinking on Probation program, which is a variant of R&R, and found that although reconviction rates after 1 year were lower for the study group, differences disappeared after a second year of follow-up, suggesting that the benefits of R&R may be short lived.

More recently, S. Young et al. (2013) described the application of a modified version of R&R with a sample of offenders with an antisocial and/or borderline personality disorder who were diagnosed with a comorbid attention deficit/hyperactivity disorder (ADHD). The authors found significantly greater improvements in anger and impulsivity among the 16 individuals who had been treated with R&R compared to those who received TAU ($n = 15$), but found no change in a number of other outcome variables. Despite the pilot nature of this study, the authors concluded that their modification of R&R "is feasible with severely

personality-disordered patients in a high-secure unit setting and effective in improving social problem solving ability, reducing antisocial attitudes, reducing reactivity and anger problems, reducing ADHD symptoms, and increasing behavioral control and emotional stability" (p. 604).

Two meta-analyses synthesizing outcome studies have concluded that the R&R program reduced recidivism by approximately 14% (Tong & Farrington, 2006, 2008). The mean effect size was slightly larger for programs that were implemented in community settings (1.22, $p = .02$) rather than institutional settings (1.15, $p = .06$). In addition, the low-risk offenders (1.18, $p = $ n.s.) appeared to benefit more from the program than did high-risk offenders (1.12, $p = .011$), perhaps because high-risk offenders have a greater likelihood of dropping out of the program. The researchers noted that this finding, which contradicts the premise underlying the RNR model, is interesting in light of the fact that the program was developed for high-risk offenders (Tong & Farrington, 2008). The meta-analysis provided support for the R&R program's effectiveness in Canada, the United Kingdom, and the United States, with the highest effect sizes being found in Canadian settings, where the program was originally developed.

A number of studies have also examined the mechanism of change by which R&R presumably impacts an individual's offending behaviors. The typical methodology involves comparing pre- and posttreatment scores on measures of criminogenic cognitions, attitudes, and related behaviors. These studies have typically demonstrated improvements in an individual's impulsivity, self-control, awareness of the consequences of actions, problem solving, and perspective taking (McGuire, Broomfield, Robinson, & Rowson, 1995; Porporino, Fabiano, & Robinson, 1991; Robinson et al., 1991; Wettermann, Schläfke, & Fegert, 2012). However, improved recidivism has not always corresponded to changes in these measures. A study conducted by Wilkinson (2005) found that offenders who were reconvicted reported more self-control and a lesser likelihood of reoffending when compared to their pretreatment scores. In contrast, those who did not reoffend reported, on average, less self-control and a greater likelihood of reoffending compared to their pretreatment scores. These paradoxical findings raise questions as to the actual mechanism by which R&R effects change. Given the range of interventions that have been studied in offender populations, there may be a general factor underlying many of the CBT interventions that have been developed for offender populations.

Moral Reconation Therapy. The underpinnings of MRT (Little & Robinson, 1988), drawn from Kohlberg's (1971) and Piaget's (1964) theories of moral and cognitive development (respectively), propose that criminal behavior is a consequence of insufficient moral reasoning skills (Arbuthnot & Gordon, 1988). The MRT program attempts to increase moral reasoning by confronting an individual's thoughts and behaviors, often using moral dilemmas as the starting point for group discussions. Another element of this intervention includes teaching delayed gratification and the value of evaluating whether the ends justify the means. Because of the emphasis on developing a more moral lifestyle, offenders are encouraged to sever relationships with antisocial peers who may hinder their moral development.

The MRT program consists of 12 to 16 sessions (or *steps*) in which offenders meet twice weekly in groups of 10 to 15 for approximately 90 min. Group members are also provided with workbooks that include exercises and tasks that they must complete (Little & Robinson, 1988). The program can be delivered within correctional institutions or after conditional release (i.e., while on probation or parole). The developers of MRT published several studies of offenders who received MRT, with follow-up time periods ranging from 1 to 7 years, typically finding that participation in MRT corresponded to lower rates of recidivism (Little, Robinson, & Burnette, 1989, 1990, 1991a, 1991b, 1993a, 1993b; Little, Robinson, Burnette, & Swan, 1995). However, critics have cited a lack of random assignment and a failure to control for extraneous variables as significant methodological limitations in these early studies, casting doubt on the validity and generalizability of the initial findings (Allen, MacKenzie, & Hickman, 2001; Armstrong, 2003).

A number of studies have sought to improve on the initial MRT development studies, some of which have also demonstrated reduced recidivism rates for individuals who participated in MRT either during incarceration or while living in the community on probation. For example, Burnett (1997) found that 1 year after release into the community, a sample of offenders who had received MRT within the department of corrections had a 10% rate of rearrest, but none had been reincarcerated. However, in a matched control group that had not received MRT, 20% had been rearrested and 10% had been reincarcerated. Although the results suggest that MRT led to a significant (50%) reduction in recidivism, the difference in recidivism rates between groups was not statistically significant, in part because of the small sample size, consisting of only 30 individuals. Moreover, the control group, although matched to the treatment group on some demographic variables, was not matched on other, potentially relevant variables.

Similarly, Godwin, Stone, and Hambrock (1995) found that male offenders who participated in MRT while they were housed in a Florida detention center were significantly less likely to be reincarcerated than was a comparison group of offenders who had been released from the same institution but had not received MRT. In the treatment group, 11.2% of the offenders who participated in MRT had been reincarcerated within 1 year of release compared to 29.7% of the offenders in the comparison group. Although the rates of reoffense rose after a second year of follow-up, the difference in recidivism rates remained significant; 29.7% of those who had received MRT had been reincarcerated compared to 37.3% of those in the comparison group. However, the methodology in this study has also been criticized because the researchers did not employ random assignment or identify a matched comparison group, and the treatment and comparison groups were significantly different from one another prior to receiving the intervention (Allen et al., 2001). Thus, offenders who received MRT may have been more motivated and less treatment resistant than the typical offender, resulting in lower rates of reoffense regardless of whether they had received any formal mental health intervention.

Similar concerns plagued a study by Krueger (1997), who also compared individuals who had received MRT prior to being released from an Ohio jail to individuals who had been released from the same jail during the same time period but did not receive MRT. Although the same methodological limitations that characterized Godwin et al. (1995) applied to this study (e.g., failure to use random assignment or matching), the researchers followed the participants for an extended period of time. After 5 years, Krueger found that the rearrest rate for offenders who participated in MRT was only 11% compared to 51% in the comparison group of untreated offenders.

Taken as a whole, the MRT literature provides consistent support for the efficacy of this program in reducing recidivism. However, none of the studies described here reflected true RCT designs nor provided any meaningful statistical control for potentially important differences between individuals who received MRT and those who did not (i.e., the comparison group). Moreover, none of the studies compared offenders completing MRT to those receiving other types of mental health interventions, whether they were developed specifically to reduce recidivism among criminal offenders or were a more general mental health treatment. Such studies are clearly needed in order to more realistically appraise the extent to which MRT provides unique benefits for the treatment and rehabilitation of criminal offenders, as well as to evaluate the developmental theory that underlies this intervention.

Aggression Replacement Training. ART (Glick & Gibbs, 2011; Glick & Goldstein, 1987; Goldstein, Glick, & Gibbs, 1998) is another CBT-based intervention that is widely used in a range of criminal justice settings across North America and Europe (Hatcher et al., 2008). Although ART was originally developed for aggressive youths, it has been adapted for adult offenders with considerable success (Barto Lynch, 1995; Hatcher et al., 2008; Sugg, 2000). The ART approach represents a hybrid model, incorporating some of the cognitive skills used in the R&R model with the moral reasoning aspect of MRT into a multimodal psychoeducational intervention (Gundersen & Svartdal, 2009). The ART program

is grounded in the belief that aggressive behavior can be traced back to both external (e.g., parents, peers, media) and internal (e.g., deficits in interpersonal and social skills, low levels of anger control, primitive moral reasoning, and a propensity toward impulsivity) factors. Thus, the program features three coordinated components that seek to reduce the impact of these factors: structured learning training, anger control training, and moral education.

The *structured learning training* represents the behavioral component of ART and seeks to teach offenders how to replace antisocial behavior with positive alternatives using modeling techniques and role-playing. *Anger control training* addresses the affective deficits that are common in offenders and focuses on teaching individuals how to identify personal triggers for anger and the likely consequences of aggression. Finally, the *moral education* component of ART uses group discussion of moral dilemmas and decision making to increase the offender's level of moral reasoning and decrease his or her concrete and egocentric thinking (Hatcher et al., 2008). The ART program can vary in length but is typically 10 weeks long and is administered in a group format, with roughly three sessions per week (one session devoted to each of the three components weekly).

Early studies of the ART program were conducted in a secure facility for young offenders. Male delinquents who completed the program showed significantly less acting-out behaviors following treatment compared to an untreated control group. When the control group was later provided with ART, they also showed a significant reduction in the number and intensity of acting-out behaviors (Glick & Goldstein, 1987). Since that time, the utility of ART has been supported in a wide range of populations (see Goldstein, 2004, for a review), including gang members (Goldstein, Glick, Carthan, & Blancero, 1994), adolescents who had been diagnosed with conduct disorder (Coleman, Pfeiffer, & Oakland, 1991), forensic psychiatric patients (Hornsfeld, Van Dam Beggen, Leenaars, & Jonkers, 2004), and offenders with learning disabilities (Curilla, 1990). For example, Sugg (2000) found that at 1-year follow-up, 20.4% of ART program completers had been reconvicted compared to 34.5% in a control group. However, the two groups were not matched on relevant variables.

Hatcher et al. (2008) used a quasi-experimental design and a one-to-one matching procedure in studying 53 individuals who had been convicted of violent offenses who were ordered to attend ART as a condition of their release. These individuals were compared to a matched sample of 53 offenders who were also released into the community but were not required to participate in ART. After a follow-up period of 10 months, the participants who had been assigned to ART showed a 13.3% reduction in the rate of reconviction compared to the control group. When offenders who did not complete the program were excluded from the analysis, the reduction in reconviction attributable to ART increased to 15.1%. On the other hand, offenders who were assigned to treatment but did not complete the program were more likely to reoffend than the matched comparison sample. Based on this finding, the authors acknowledged that the low reconviction rate for treatment program completers may be attributable to greater motivation in this subgroup such that regardless of the type of intervention, treatment program completers would have reoffended at lower rates than the comparison group. In addition to decreasing recidivism rates, the ART program has been shown to be effective at increasing an individual's interpersonal skills and prosocial behavior (Barto Lynch, 1995; Goldstein, Glick, Irwin, Pask-McCartney, & Rubama, 1989).

Thinking for a Change. In collaboration with the U.S. Department of Justice's National Institute of Corrections, Bush, Glick, and Taymans (1997) developed the Thinking for a Change (TFC) program, which has been implemented in numerous correctional facilities and community-based treatment settings over the last 15 years (Stem, 2011). The TFC program draws on cognitive restructuring and skill development programs in an effort to induce prosocial change in the lifestyles of criminal offenders. The philosophy of the TFC program is that offenders' thoughts (cognitions) drive both their feelings and actions and, as such, offenders can change their emotions and behaviors by learning more effective ways of thinking. This goal is accomplished, in theory, by encouraging offenders to identify thought patterns that lead to risky or problem behaviors, and then to

generate new, more adaptive thought patterns. The generation of new, more adaptive thought patterns is accomplished through the three interrelated components of the program: cognitive restructuring, social skills training, and problem-solving skill development. In the *cognitive restructuring* element of the TFC program, offenders are taught how to recognize their thought patterns, understand the feelings of others and themselves, respond appropriately to anger, and deal with accusations against them. In the *social skills* training component, offenders are taught how to listen actively, how to ask questions so as to receive information that is critical to their own needs, and how to give feedback when conversing with others. In the *problem-solving* skill development element, offenders are shown how to describe one's problems, how to set goals, and how to examine one's choices and the consequences of those choices. In the treatment sessions, clients observe group leaders model different forms of prosocial behavior and then role-play their newly learned skills. Clients are given homework that is intended to further the acquisition of these skills, such as using *thinking reports* in which they are asked to describe a situation and list all of the thoughts, feelings, and beliefs they had in that situation.

TFC is a manualized treatment that is delivered in a group format. The treatment manual includes scripts that group leaders can follow as well as examples of handouts and homework that may be distributed to group members during sessions. Groups typically consist of eight to 12 members and two staff facilitators. The course typically consists of 22 sessions, with one to three sessions per week, but often includes an additional 10 sessions to further develop the offenders' skills.

A handful of studies have evaluated the effectiveness of the TFC program at changing criminogenic cognitions and reducing recidivism. Golden (2002) conducted one of the first studies to evaluate the effectiveness of TFC in a probation setting. This study found that although probationers who participated in the TFC program demonstrated an improvement in their interpersonal and problem-solving skills compared to a comparison group of untreated probationers, there was no difference between groups in the rate of reoffense. Golden, Gatchel, and Cahill (2006) found stronger results for the TFC program in their study, as individuals who had completed the program as a condition of probation had 33% fewer probation violations and showed greater improvement in problem-solving skills compared to a group who did not participate in the program. Although these results are promising, the researchers only monitored participants for 1 year following treatment, and program dropouts were excluded from the analyses, possibly creating a selection bias.

Lowenkamp, Hubbard, Makarios, and Latessa (2009) improved on this methodology by evaluating TFC in a real-world setting and extending the follow-up period to an average of 2 years. Participants in the treatment group, who had been sentenced to probation following a felony conviction, were referred to, and attended, at least one session of TFC in a community-based setting. The comparison group included individuals who had been sentenced to probation during the same period but had not been referred to TFC. Of those in the treatment group, 23% reoffended during the follow-up period as compared to 36% of the comparison group—a difference that was statistically significant. Although this study represents an improvement on the limited published research in this area, there was still no random assignment to treatment (vs. no treatment). Moreover, the length of follow-up varied across participants: Some participants were followed for only a 6-month period, and others were followed for a great deal longer, with the average being 2 years.

Most recently, Stem (2011) examined an incarcerated population that participated in TFC. Unlike in previous studies, this study found no relationship between treatment program participation and any of the primary outcome variables—prison misconduct, a reduction in criminal thinking, readiness for change, or an increase in problem-solving abilities—compared to a comparison group. In sum, although the TFC program has become increasingly popular in correctional and community-based settings, empirical support for its benefits is still limited, and considerable variability exists across studies.

The evidence base reviewed in this subsection, although generating considerable enthusiasm among researchers and correctional mental health professionals, has raised nearly as many questions as it has answered. Among the most pressing questions has been the search for unifying themes that cut across this literature. The approach taken for addressing this goal has typically been through meta-analysis.

A comparison of major treatment approaches. Among the most widely cited analyses of offender treatment approaches are those that have been conducted by Lipsey and colleagues (Lipsey et al., 2001; Lipsey & Landenberger, 2005). These authors identified a number of program characteristics that were associated with lower recidivism rates, including the presence of an individual treatment component (as opposed to purely group-based interventions), greater frequency of sessions and more treatment sessions overall, and lower rates of attrition. They also found stronger reductions in recidivism for programs incorporating anger management, cognitive restructuring, and interpersonal problem solving into their treatment approach; programs focusing more heavily on behavior change fared more poorly. These findings are particularly noteworthy in light of the growing number of brand-name interventions that use one or more of these treatment elements. Despite the appearance of a consensus as to which treatment elements are most effective, a review of 13 meta-analyses of CBT-based research (Lösel, 1995) concluded that the evidence base remains underdeveloped, and there is limited agreement between reviews as to which treatment elements are responsible for the reduced rates of recidivism that have been frequently observed.

Despite the seeming superiority of CBT-based interventions for offender treatment, there is less consensus about whether some of the leading treatment approaches are more effective than others. One meta-analysis of 20 studies that focused on group-based CBT programs suggested that R&R programs might be less effective than other CBT programs. The mean effect size of R&R programs was .16 as compared to .33 for MRT programs and .49 for other CBT programs (Wilson et al., 2005). However, closer examination of these studies revealed that the R&R programs that showed modest positive effects were based on large-scale evaluations, whereas several of the MRT studies that were responsible for the large overall effect size lacked scientific rigor (Allen et al., 2001). Other meta-analyses (e.g., Landenberger & Lipsey, 2005; Lipsey & Landenberger, 2005; Lösel, 1995; Polaschek & Collie, 2004) have not found one CBT approach to be superior to others in terms of reducing recidivism rates.

The role of anger in CBT-based interventions for offenders. A particularly important issue in offender treatment pertains to anger management. The majority of CBT-based interventions for offenders include a focus on anger management, either as a major component of the treatment (e.g., ART, TFC) or as the primary focus. This focus is supported by numerous studies demonstrating that anger is a significant predictor of offending behavior, and of violent behavior in particular. Moreover, anger is a frequently encountered emotion when treating individuals who are involved in the criminal justice system, though rarely is it the root cause of most criminal behavior. Therefore, programs that focus exclusively or excessively on anger management may not be effective in treating many of the offenders for whom anger is not a central concern (Howells et al., 2005).

Nevertheless, a wide range of anger management programs has emerged in the past three decades, and many of these interventions have occasionally generated some optimism. Several meta-analytic reviews of this literature have suggested that anger management programs generate modest treatment effect (e.g., Beck & Fernandez, 1998; Del Vecchio & O'Leary, 2004), but this literature is fraught with problems, thereby limiting any conclusions of its clinical utility. DiGiuseppe and Tafrate (2003) found that although providing anger management treatment is more effective than leaving offenders untreated, there is little evidence to support the claim that it is more effective than other types of interventions.

Other concerns with regard to anger management include the lack of motivation that often complicates all offender treatments and the tendency of many programs to cram too much content into a limited amount of time (Watt & Howells, 1999). Many anger management interventions also provide little opportunity for offenders to practice the skills that are taught, resulting in a more *classroom* approach. Other elements of anger management programs appear more effective, such as relaxation training and desensitization (Howells et al., 2005), but these elements may be better incorporated into more holistic interventions that conceptualize anger as one aspect of a more general heightened emotional responsivity.

Traditional Mental Health Treatment Approaches Used With Criminal Offenders

In addition to the treatment approaches that have been designed specifically for rehabilitating criminal offenders, a number of more traditional mental health interventions have been applied to this population. As noted earlier, the history of mental health treatments applied to criminal justice settings has not been noted for its successes, as evidenced by the largely unsuccessful applications of psychoanalysis and psychosurgery. However, the growing popularity of CBT-based interventions and the availability of the RNR model as a mechanism for targeting treatments has led to a growing enthusiasm regarding the potential benefits of traditional mental health approaches. Some of the more widely used interventions are described in this section.

Motivational interviewing. Motivational interviewing (MI; Miller & Rollnick, 1991, 2002) has become increasingly popular in offender treatment settings because of its strong linkage to the RNR model and to the responsivity element of the model in particular. Encompassed in the responsivity principle is the need for a program's content to match the learning styles and characteristics of those individuals who are enrolled in the program. Not surprisingly, treatments are rarely effective when a program does not motivate offenders to engage in treatment and change their behavior (McMurran, 2009), and research has consistently shown that offenders who fail to complete a treatment program reoffend even more frequently than those who do not receive any treatment at all (McMurran & Theodosi, 2007). Therefore, treatment programs that fail to engage offenders will be unlikely to reduce recidivism rates and will waste resources that might be better used with offenders who are more motivated.

In the context of offender treatment, MI focuses squarely on the individual's readiness for change and commitment to transforming his or her life. The primary objectives of MI in this context involve increasing an offender's problem acceptance and recognition, highlighting the benefits of change, and helping him or her reach a decision to change while continuing to support self-efficacy. The intervention can be delivered in groups or on an individual basis, in a single session or through a series of sessions. A number of offender rehabilitation settings use MI as a preprogram intervention (Chambers, Eccleston, Day, Ward, & Howells, 2008; McMurran, 2009; Ward, Day, Howells, & Birgden, 2004), typically to prepare clients for an intensive treatment program that will follow. In many settings, probation officers are encouraged to use MI techniques in their day-to-day interactions with offenders because they can be effective in dealing with resistance and building stronger relationships in their clients (Clark, Walters, Gingerich, & Meltzer, 2006; Walters, Clark, Gingerich, & Meltzer, 2007).

Offending-focused MI approaches are highly varied, ranging from freestanding interventions to complementary approaches that are used in conjunction with psychoeducational or CBT programs. One subpopulation where MI has been used most often is with offenders whose crimes are related to drug and alcohol use. For example, Harper and Hardy (2000) described the use of MI in a probation setting with offenders who had a history of substance abuse problems. The authors trained a group of probation officers in the use of MI and compared outcomes from the first six individuals who were treated with this approach to a comparable group of offenders who were monitored by probation officers who had no such training. Although this study suffered from numerous methodological flaws, including a sample size that precluded a statistical comparison of differential treatment effects, the data suggest some areas in which MI appeared to lead to greater change than TAU, such as the offenders' perception of crime as worthwhile and self-perception of drug/alcohol problems.

Relatively little research has systematically examined the benefits of MI in terms of criminal justice outcomes, but a handful of studies have applied this approach to the treatment of prison inmates. For example, Anstiss, Polaschek, and Wilson (2011) used a quasi-experimental design to compare 58 men who participated in a brief (four session) MI intervention to a matched sample of offenders housed in a facility in which this treatment was not available. The authors found a significantly greater change in readiness to change, based on the stages of change model (Prochaska & Velicer, 1997) underlying MI, among those who attended MI. More importantly, this improvement corresponded to a significantly and substantially lower rate of reoffense following release from the facility among those offenders who participated in the MI intervention compared to those who received TAU. Moreover, the authors found little evidence that completion of criminogenic programs (typically R&R) had an impact on reoffense after controlling for the impact of MI. In fact, outcomes were worse for those offenders who completed MI and then went on to complete another criminogenic program. Of course, the quasi-experimental design, which included only those patients referred to MI who agreed to participate in the program, limits the conclusiveness of this study.

Despite the limitations inherent in this and other treatment studies, McMurran (2009) concluded, on the basis of a review of this emerging literature, that MI offered a number of clinical benefits for offenders who are treated with this approach. She identified a rise in retention in treatment, an increase in motivation to change, and reduced rates of reoffending as the primary benefits of MI. However, of the 19 studies McMurran reviewed, 15 focused on offenders who were identified as having drug- or alcohol-related problems. Moreover, only 10 of the studies McMurran reviewed were identified as RCTs, raising questions as to the rigor of the investigations. Nevertheless, MI appears to show some promise as a useful technique for enhancing treatment engagement, whether in isolation or as an adjunct to traditional criminal justice and mental health interventions.

Dialectical Behavior Therapy. Another treatment approach that has become increasingly popular in recent years is Dialectical Behavior Therapy (DBT; Linehan, 1993), which was originally developed for the treatment of self-injury in women with borderline personality disorder (BPD). A growing number of publications have described the adaptation of DBT to forensic settings, typically targeting anger, aggression, and impulsivity. However, these interventions have also, at times, directly targeted criminogenic patterns in offenders' thought processes and decision making. Unfortunately, these adaptations have not, to date, applied rigorous methodologies to assess the intervention's effectiveness (e.g., Berzins & Trestman, 2004; Rosenfeld et al., 2007), but the lack of strong empirical support does not appear to have diminished the enthusiasm of practitioners.

One of the few studies to systematically assess treatment outcome for offenders who were treated with DBT was published by Rosenfeld et al. (2007), who described the application of DBT to a small sample of stalking offenders. Not surprisingly, the authors found that stalking offenders who completed DBT were significantly less likely to reoffend during the follow-up period compared to those who had terminated treatment prematurely. Rosenfeld et al. also found a significantly lower rate of reoffense among all stalking offenders who had initiated treatment (regardless of whether they completed treatment) compared to published recidivism data for stalking offenders. Although the authors acknowledged that the pilot nature of the study precluded strong conclusions, they nevertheless emphasized the potential utility of DBT for this subgroup of offenders.

More recently, a study by van den Bosch, Hysaj, and Jacobs (2012) offered similar enthusiasm for the potential utility of DBT, albeit with even more limited data. These authors investigated the effectiveness of DBT in an outpatient treatment setting with a sample of criminal offenders who had been diagnosed with BPD. The authors compared treatment outcomes (completion vs. premature termination) in 29 offenders with BPD to a comparison sample of women with BPD who had no legal system involvement but were seeking voluntary treatment. Although the authors found comparable rates of treatment completion in the forensic and nonforensic samples, and few differences in patient characteristics, their methodology precluded a comparison of whether DBT decreased the likelihood of future criminal behavior. Nevertheless, the authors concluded that "it is possible to provide DBT in a forensic setting as the patients are not dissimilar, whether the patient is court mandated or not. The findings also indicate that the clinical and etiological differences between forensic BPD patients and borderline patients from general mental health settings are relatively small" (van den Bosch et al., 2012, p. 314).

A number of other publications have described the application of DBT, but typically with even less empirical rigor. For example, McCann, Ball and Ivanoff (2000) conducted a quasi-experimental study comparing DBT to TAU in a sample of male forensic psychiatric patients, most of whom had been convicted of a violent crime. However, rather than focusing on a range of offenders, the authors limited their sample to individuals who had been diagnosed with BPD and/or an antisocial personality disorder (APD). Participants in the DBT group reportedly displayed significantly more adaptive coping skills compared to the TAU sample and had greater reductions in depressed and hostile mood, paranoia, psychotic behaviors, and maladaptive interpersonal coping styles. However, the inpatient setting for this study precluded an analysis of whether treatment impacted an individual's reoffending behavior, and the authors did not analyze institutional misconduct.

Evershed et al. (2003) incorporated institutional behavior problems into their 18-month study comparing eight male forensic patients with nine patients receiving TAU in a high-security hospital in England. These authors tailored their DBT intervention to address violent behavior, ideation, and urges and emotions as well as treatment-interfering behaviors. They observed decreased violence in both the treated and untreated groups but noted that violent acts committed by the group treated with DBT appeared to be less severe than those committed by TAU participants. However, the authors also acknowledged that their treatment groups "were not equivalent at intake, were not contemporaneous and the comparison group was not offered a comparable level of therapeutic contact" (Evershed et al., 2003, p. 210). Because of these (and other) limitations, any conclusions that can be drawn from this study are extremely limited.

Trupin, Stewart, Beach, and Boesky (2002) adapted DBT to the treatment of incarcerated juvenile offenders, also focusing on violence, oppositional defiance, and victimizing behaviors. They compared juveniles housed on three units: a mental health cottage where DBT was implemented, a general population cottage where DBT was initiated, and a third general population unit receiving TAU. Although the nonequivalence of treatment groups and staff training significantly limits the interpretation of their findings, Trupin et al. observed significant reductions in serious problem behaviors among those youths who were treated with DBT who had exhibited the most severe behavioral problems prior to DBT treatment.

In sum, although a growing literature has emerged to support the applicability of DBT for a wide range of criminal offenders, this literature has been limited by methodological shortcomings that hinder any strong conclusions as to its utility. Moreover, most of these studies have adapted DBT to target narrow populations or behavioral problems rather than providing a more general and inclusive offender treatment focus. Nevertheless, this literature should generate some cautious optimism regarding the potential for DBT as a useful approach for the treatment of some of the most difficult behavioral problems exhibited by criminal offenders.

Other mental health interventions used in correctional settings. Several structured CBT-based interventions have integrated spirituality into more traditional psychological interventions in order to motivate offenders to change their behavior. Since 2002, the Federal Bureau of Prisons has offered a pilot faith-based residential program, the Life Connections Program (LCP), to offenders who are seeking (voluntarily) behavioral change. This 18-month program has operated in five U.S. prisons and is considered compatible with multiple religious practices. However, limited evidence has emerged to support its effectiveness, even with a voluntary

population. One study analyzing the impact of LCP reported that program completion was associated with increased scripture reading, perception of self-worth, and degree of desire for community integration; however, no significant relationship with recidivism rates was reported (Hall, 2003). Other programs, such as the InnerChange Freedom Initiative (IFI), which is operated by Texas prisons, have reported an impact on recidivism but used quasi-experimental designs that compared treatment program completers to dropouts (e.g., Camp, Klein-Safran, Kwon, Dagget, & Joseph, 2006).

A number of studies have also described the British program for treating dangerous and severe personality disorders (DSPD), which typically relies on combinations of CBT, DBT, and behavioral therapy. Because of the predominance of psychopathy in this classification, the research addressing the DSPD program is described in the next section, which focuses on the treatment of psychopathy and APD.

In short, although a substantial evidence base has emerged in support of many name-brand criminogenic interventions, the evidence to support the applicability of more traditional mental health interventions has been far more limited. Although potentially useful, these interventions have typically been tailored to specific populations and have rarely been the subject of systematic research, let alone RCT. However, one population that mental health interventions have more often targeted is antisocial and psychopathic offenders. Because of the controversy surrounding this topic, we review this literature separately in the following pages.

Treatment of Antisocial and Psychopathic Offenders

Given the tremendous overlap between current conceptualizations of APD and criminal behavior, one might argue that offender treatment is little more than treatment for APD. However, clinicians have long distinguished *psychopaths* from the larger population of criminal offenders (with or without APD) as representing a particularly problematic subgroup of offenders. Although the distinction between APD and psychopathy did not emerge until the 1980s, following publication of the *Diagnostic and Statistical Manual, Third Edition* (American Psychiatric

Association, 1980), important distinctions have emerged since that time, in part based on Hare's publication of the Psychopathy Checklist (Hare, 1980). The diagnosis of APD relies primarily on a history of criminal behavior, whereas psychopathy encompasses a broad range of affective deficits, interpersonal relationship difficulties, and behavioral problems (e.g., impulsivity, irresponsibility). Moreover, the empirical literature published over the past three decades has largely been premised on the distinction between these two disorders, consistently demonstrating elevated rates of recidivism and violent behavior among those persons who have been identified as psychopathic. Likewise, whether warranted or not, clinicians have also typically equated psychopathy with a resistance to mental health treatments that far exceeds the "nothing works" attitude that many health care providers have toward criminal offenders more generally. This section presents an overview of treatment efforts specifically geared toward psychopathic offenders in order to disentangle clinical lore from empirical reality. It should be noted, however, that many studies have collapsed psychopathy and APD into a single entity, focusing more broadly on the pathological personality characteristics that are present in criminal offenders. Thus, although some of the research discussed in this section focuses squarely on psychopathy, other studies focus more broadly on offenders with personality disorders. Despite potentially important differences, this literature is reviewed in the following sections.

In addition to the more general methodological issues noted earlier in this chapter, there are a number of additional confounds that are specific to the assessment of treatment success in offenders with psychopathy and/or APD. Among the most obvious of these issues is accuracy in the diagnosis. Whereas studies of psychopathy have, in recent years, been relatively consistent in their reliance on the Psychopathy Checklist—Revised (PCL–R; Hare, 1991), studies focusing on APD have been far more variable, at times relying on medical chart diagnoses or other unreliable techniques to define groups. Very few studies have distinguished between offenders who meet the criteria for APD and/or psychopathy, and fewer still have compared outcomes for offenders with and without the disorders. Ironically, some studies control for psychopathy and antisocial personality characteristics as if they were "noise" rather than systematically examining the impact of these personality characteristics on treatment outcome (e.g., A. E. Cullen et al., 2012)

Another important challenge faced by research on the treatability of psychopathy and APD is the question of outcome measures. As evident from the preceding information in this chapter, much of the research on offender treatment more generally has focused on reducing recidivism as the primary (or sole) outcome measure. However, if the research in question is focused on the treatment of APD or psychopathy, one might expect to see reductions in antisocial or psychopathic traits. This is, of course, further complicated by reliance on the PCL–R because this scale is intended to tap lifetime behavioral patterns, not short-term changes. A more recently developed scale to measure psychopathy, the Comprehensive Assessment of Psychopathic Personality (CAPP; Cooke, Hart, Logan, & Michie, 2011), is specifically intended to address this shortcoming in the design of the PCL–R but has not yet gained widespread use. To date, few research studies have attempted to demonstrate changes in psychopathic personality traits, and none has used the CAPP.

The origins of therapeutic pessimism. The treatment of individuals with psychopathic personality disorders has, it seems, a far longer history than general offender treatment programming, with early studies dating back to the 1920s (Salekin, 2002). Early treatment approaches were primarily grounded in psychoanalytic theory, which perceived psychopathy and APD to be the result of unresolved conflicts from early life. Although most of the literature addressing the utility of psychoanalytic techniques to reduce psychopathy consists of case studies, Salekin's (2002) meta-analysis (described in more detail below) estimated that psychoanalytic treatments had a success rate of approximately 59%. This rate was somewhat, but not substantially, lower than the rate found for other treatment approaches. However, the objectivity of these case reports and the absence of any controlled research addressing the utility of psychoanalysis for the treatment of APD and/or psychopathy raises serious doubts about the effectiveness of this approach to treatment. Despite the absence of empirical support, some researchers continue to promote the application of psychoanalytic treatment approaches to psychopathic offenders (e.g., Gullhaugen & Nottestad, 2012).

As the field of psychiatry began to rely more heavily on medical interventions than on psychotherapy, the application of then-novel treatments such as electroconvulsive therapy (ECT, also known as shock therapy) and psychosurgery (prefrontal lobotomy) began to be applied to the treatment of individuals who were identified as psychopathic. Indeed, psychosurgical interventions were used to treat a range of behavioral problems, including criminality, kleptomania, and sexual perversions, in addition to psychopathy more generally (Poppen, 1948). The theoretical justification for psychosurgery as a response to criminal behavior was rooted in the theory that a biological diathesis existed for delinquent behavior, and that the biological underpinnings of crime could be altered (Nassi & Abramowitz, 1976). Early anecdotal reports described occasional successes from surgical interventions, with case reports describing reductions in criminogenic attitudes and impulses, particularly aggression and sexual deviance (e.g., Banay & Davidoff, 1942; Koskoff & Goldhurst, 1968). However, systematic investigations of treatment outcome were far more disappointing, typically indicating no evidence of clinical improvement and unacceptably high rates of serious side effects, even including fatalities (e.g., Darling, 1945; Kolb, 1949). Within two decades, this practice had largely ended, in part due to the emergence of psychotropic medications and in part because of ethical concerns (Rada, 1978; Usematsu, 1970).

Not surprisingly, particularly given the limited evidence for successful treatment of the psychopathic personality, mental health clinicians and criminal justice scholars have typically expressed skepticism regarding the efficacy of traditional mental health treatments for the treatment of psychopathic individuals. Perhaps the most widely cited description of the mental heath field's assessment of the prognosis for psychopaths was published by Hervey Cleckley, in his seminal work, *The Mask of Sanity* (1941/1988). This volume, which

has been regularly reprinted for more than 70 years, has heavily influenced the modern conceptualization of psychopathy and is often cited in support of the conclusion that psychopathic individuals cannot be treated, in part due to their inability to form an emotional bond with the treating therapist. Cleckley wrote:

> Over a period of many years I have remained discouraged about the effect of treatment on the psychopathy. Having regularly failed in my own efforts to help such patients alter their fundamental pattern of inadequacy and antisocial activity, I had hoped for a while that treatment by others would be more successful. I have had the opportunity to see patients of this sort who were treated by psychoanalysis, by psychoanalytically oriented psychotherapy, by group and by milieu therapy, and by many other variations of dynamic method. I have seen some patients who were treated for years. I have also known cases in which not only the patient but various members of his family were given prolonged psychotherapy. None of these measures impressed me as achieving successful results. The psychopaths continued to behave as they had in the past. . . . Therapeutic failure in all such patients observed leads me to feel that we do not at present have any kind of psychotherapy that can be relied upon to change the psychopath fundamentally. (pp. 438–439)

Although Cleckley's (1941/1988) opinion, like those of other researchers, was based on clinical experience and theory rather than empirical data, the accepted course of action in order to limit the damages caused by psychopathic offenders has typically been incarceration or commitment to an institution rather than mental health treatment.

The perception of psychopaths as untreatable culminated in a widely cited study by Rice, Harris, and Cormier (1992) that examined the effects of a prison-based therapeutic community in a sample of psychopathic and nonpsychopathic offenders. This article demonstrated elevated rates of reoffense among violent psychopaths following treatment compared to untreated psychopaths, whereas improvement (lower rates of reoffense) was found for nonpsychopaths who were participating in treatment. However, the treatment modality investigated in this study, which was a variation on the therapeutic community approach, was far from the typical CBT-based intervention. The program was described as highly coercive and poorly supervised and included treatment elements that would be considered questionable, if not unethical, such as nude encounter groups, feeding through tubes in the walls, and the administration of psychoactive drugs (including lysergic acid diethylamide, or LSD) to increase their anxiety. Thus, although this study has frequently been cited in support of the argument that treatment should not be provided to psychopaths, the basis for this opinion is clearly questionable. In fact, it is surprising that any conclusions regarding the treatability of psychopaths would be drawn from this study.

Despite the obvious methodological limitations of the early psychopathy treatment literature, a number of more recent, more rigorous studies have generated similarly unenthusiastic conclusions. These studies have used therapeutic communities, anger management interventions, and social skills training to treat psychopathic offenders (Hare, Clark, Grann, & Thornton, 2000; Ogloff, Wong, & Greenwood, 1990) and have typically reported poor outcomes. In short, the conclusions drawn from these early studies of psychopathy treatment are that psychopathic offenders (a) appear to have less motivation for treatment than the typical offender, (b) are more likely to drop out of treatment prematurely, (c) show less clinical improvement when they do engage in treatment, and (d) are more likely to behave violently or to reoffend following treatment as compared with nonpsychopathic offenders (Polaschek & Daly, 2013). Several authors also hypothesized that psychopathic offenders used treatment to manipulate others and become more effective predators (e.g., Hare et al., 2000).

A turning point in the psychopathy treatment literature occurred in 2002, when Skeem, Monahan, and Mulvey published their analysis of treatment outcomes for a sample of 267 psychopathic or potentially psychopathic psychiatric patients and compared these individuals to 604 nonpsychopathic civil psychiatric patients. Using data from the MacArthur Violence Risk Assessment Study (a large-scale study of violence risk in civil psychiatric patients by Monahan et al., 2001), Skeem et al. analyzed posttreatment violence as a function of psychopathy status and treatment intensity. In this study, participants were interviewed on admission to a psychiatric hospital and were then reinterviewed five times, at 10-week intervals, over the following year. During these follow-up interviews, patients self-reported if they had attended any treatment since the last interview and, if so, what type and how many sessions.

Skeem et al. (2002) found a significant relationship between the number of treatment sessions attended and the likelihood of violence during the subsequent follow-up period for psychopathic individuals. Psychopathic individuals who had attended fewer than seven treatment sessions were 3.6 times more likely to behave violently in the follow-up period compared to psychopathic individuals who had attended seven or more sessions, even after controlling for selection bias. Because small doses of treatment (<7 sessions) did not improve outcomes for psychopathic patients, the authors concluded that a more substantial dose of treatment was necessary to achieve treatment gains. However, this study did not focus on psychopathic criminal offenders (although many likely had criminal justice histories) but rather addressed the treatability of psychopaths who suffered from a major mental disorder. Thus, these findings may present a distorted picture of the treatability of psychopathic criminal offenders.

Whereas Skeem et al. (2002) focused on the quantity of treatment received, Salekin's (2002) meta-analysis focused on which types of treatment seemed most effective for psychopaths. Salekin incorporated data from 42 studies that had been published between 1940 and 1996, all of which focused on the treatment of psychopathy. These studies ranged from small case studies to larger, more systematic studies with samples as large as 1,300. A variety of treatment approaches was included in this analysis, and outcome variables ranged from personality characteristics (e.g., degree of psychopathy, impulsivity, hostility) to interpersonal and behavioral outcomes (e.g., criminal conduct, quality of relationships with others, increased emotional range). Salekin reported effect sizes ranging from 0.22 to 1.00 for treated psychopathic subjects, whereas the effect size for control groups (i.e., nonpsychopaths) was 0.20. However, some treatment approaches (e.g., ECT, psychoanalytic therapies, therapeutic communities, and a subset of CBT) resulted in no better improvements in the group of psychopaths than in the control group. Across studies, CBT approaches demonstrated the most consistently positive effects, with a success rate of 62%. Eclectic therapies (which usually included CBT but were supplemented with other types of interventions) had somewhat higher rates of success (68%). Interestingly, one study combined antidepressant medication with CBT and generated a 100% success rate. These findings led Salekin to conclude that further research is required regarding the appropriateness of medication for the treatment of psychopathy. Despite the mixed results from Salekin's review, the past decade has witnessed a resurgence of interest in developing and investigating mental health treatment programs for antisocial and psychopathic offenders, many of which have generated considerable enthusiasm.

In a more recent meta-analysis using stricter inclusion criteria than past reviews, Salekin, Worley, and Grimes (2010) analyzed 13 treatment studies that focused squarely on psychopathic offenders, eight of which focused on adults and five on adolescents. Salekin et al. included only studies that measured psychopathy using versions of the Psychopathy Checklist (PCL–R, PCL: Screening Version [Hart, Cox, & Hare, 1995], or PCL:YV [Forth, Kosson, & Hare, 2003]) and focused on treatment outcomes specific to psychopathy. Even among these 13 studies, all of which used a rigorous methodology, the authors found mixed results, with some studies showing treatment gains and others showing a negative association between treatment and psychopathic traits (i.e., psychopaths were less likely to respond to treatment). Salekin et al. concluded that, on average, adult psychopathic offenders in the included studies showed a moderate to poor response to treatment. However, there was some ambiguity about how *poor* treatment response

was defined: in some cases, poor represented *no discernible response to treatment*, whereas in other studies, poor represented *a lesser degree of treatment response* compared to a nonpsychopathic sample. The latter would be consistent with empirical evidence that psychopathic offenders have a slower response to treatment and need greater doses of treatment in order to make clinically significant gains (Skeem, Polaschek, & Manchak, 2009).

Although this chapter focuses on the treatment of adult offenders, it is important to note that treatment efforts with adolescent offenders exhibiting psychopathic traits have demonstrated stronger effects than those with adult offenders. In their review, Salekin et al. (2010) found stronger treatment effects for studies of psychopathic young offenders. Such findings stress the importance of early intervention and demonstrate the greater responsiveness of personality in childhood and adolescence. The following section describes some of the more recent studies addressing the treatability of antisocial and psychopathic offenders.

Somewhat less optimistic conclusions were reached by Gibbon et al. (2010) in their Cochrane review of research studies addressing the treatment of APD. Because of the strict methodological requirements for inclusion in a Cochrane review, the authors only identified 11 published studies that met the requirements for inclusion, and even fewer analyzed reoffense or posttreatment violence. Although Gibbon et al. observed stronger results for programs that included CBT and/or MI, the authors concluded that "there is insufficient trial evidence to justify using any psychological intervention for adults with [APD]" (p. 2).

Recent advances in the treatment of psychopathy and APD. A growing literature has applied *modern* or integrative treatment approaches to the treatment of psychopathy and/or APD, although the evidence base to support these is still quite limited. One of the few RCTs focusing on the treatment of offenders with personality disorders was published by Davidson et al. (2009), who studied the utility of CBT for offenders living in the community who were diagnosed with APD. All participants acknowledged a history of violent behavior within the preceding 6 months. These researchers randomly assigned 52 prison inmates with APD to either CBT ($n = 25$) or TAU ($n = 27$), with the CBT intervention consisting of either fifteen 1-hr sessions over a 6-month period or 30 sessions over the course of 1 year. Although no explanation was provided for why offenders received differing numbers of CBT sessions, nor was the nature of the TAU condition described, the authors acknowledged that the CBT intervention was implemented by well-trained and experienced therapists whereas TAU was typically provided by correctional staff. Despite these differences in the nature and intensity of treatment, Davidson et al. reported that offenders in both conditions demonstrated a reduction in verbal and physical aggression following treatment, indicating that CBT was effective but no more so than other approaches that are routinely used in the correctional system.

Wong and Hare (2005) described a CBT-based program that was grounded in the RNR model. They proposed using cognitive–behavioral strategies to encourage psychopathic offenders to take responsibility for their behavior and to identify needs and wants rather than trying to create empathy or develop a conscience. In their model, the therapist examines the needs and wants of each offender and identifies the link to past problematic behavior in order to teach clients more prosocial ways to obtain what they want. The authors emphasized the importance of maintaining a high degree of structure and oversight in such a program, in part by involving highly trained personnel and administrators. Wong, Witte, Gordon, Gu, and Lewis (2006) evaluated this approach with 34 psychopathic offenders and found that treatment reduced reoffense severity, although it did not seem to reduce the recidivism rate.

In a subsequent study, Wong, Gordon, Gu, Lewis, and Olver (2012) described results from a sample of 150 violent, psychopathic offenders who were treated using an intervention that closely resembles the model described in the previous paragraph. The authors found reductions in risk levels, as measured by the Violence Risk Scale (VRS; Wong & Gordon, 2006), for individuals who received treatment, even when these individuals were highly psychopathic. When Wong et al.

categorized offenders into four groups based on the extent of change in perceived risk (i.e., *low change, moderate–low change, moderate–high change,* and *high change*), a linear association was found between change in risk and likelihood of recidivism following release into the community. Specifically, more than 50% of the participants in the low-change group were identified as having committed a violent reoffense compared to only 23% of those in the high-change group. However, the authors also described another set of analyses comparing 32 high-risk psychopathic offenders who were treated with their CBT-based intervention to a matched (on race and age at first conviction) sample of psychopathic offenders who received TAU (e.g., anger management, stress management). Wong et al. found no difference in any of their 11 measures of recidivism, including time to reconviction, number of reconvictions, and number of violent reconvictions. However, they also found that treated offenders received shorter sentences than those in the comparison sample. Wong et al. interpreted these findings as being supportive of their two-component theory of psychopathy treatment, with the first component focusing on enhancing treatment motivation and reducing treatment interfering behaviors and the second component focusing on addressing criminogenic needs. Although preliminary, these studies provide cautious optimism that a subset of psychopathic offenders can demonstrate clinically meaningful benefits using CBT techniques.

In an ongoing study, Bernstein et al. (2012) described a multicenter RCT using schema therapy to treat forensic patients in several Dutch hospitals for the criminally insane and/or mentally ill offenders. Schema therapy (J. E. Young, Klosko, & Weishaar, 2003) is an integrative treatment that draws on CBT, psychoanalysis, Gestalt therapy, and attachment theory in order to help change longstanding patterns of thinking about the world, oneself, and others (i.e., schemas). Although Bernstein et al.'s study sample included individuals with a range of "cluster B" personality disorders, 60% of the sample met the criteria for APD and 30% had PCL–R scores of 30 or higher. In the first wave of data analysis, 30 patients were randomly assigned to 3 years of either schema therapy or TAU, which varied by hospital but most often involved some type of CBT. In their preliminary results, Bernstein et al. found that schema therapy was associated with lower recidivism rates and higher rates of supervised release compared to TAU, though these differences were not statistically significant, which was likely due to the small sample size. Further, in this preliminary analysis, Bernstein et al. did not analyze treatment outcomes for those patients with APD or psychopathy as compared with other Cluster B disorders.

The dangerous and severe personality disorders program. In 1999, the United Kingdom implemented the DSPD program in order to refine and evaluate treatment of the most challenging criminal offenders, many (but not all) of whom would be labeled as psychopathic (Duggan, 2011). In the 12 years it was in existence, the DSPD treated many of the most dangerous and refractory offenders in the United Kingdom, with treatment units established in two prisons and two secure hospitals. In order to qualify for this treatment program, the offender had to be identified as posing a significant risk of violent behavior and having a severe personality disorder based on a PCL–R score greater than 30 (indicative of psychopathy), a PCL–R score of 25 to 30 along with a diagnosis of a personality disorder other than APD, or meeting criteria for two separate personality disorders (Duggan, 2011).

Despite the initial enthusiasm that this program generated, evidence of its success has been modest at best. For example, in one study analyzing whether treatment impacted the *symptoms* of psychopathy, Draycott, Askari, and Kirkpatrick (2011) analyzed changes in perceived dominance and warmth (based on staff ratings) in 34 male psychopathic patients who were treated in the DSPD unit of a high-security hospital. They found a different pattern of change based on the individual's level of psychopathy, with highly psychopathic patients exhibiting more dominance following treatment and less psychopathic patients exhibiting less dominance and more warmth. Although limited, these results suggest that the most psychopathic patients may have responded poorly to this treatment setting.

Similarly limited evidence has been provided in support of the Chromis program, which is one of the prison-based treatment programs for DSPD offenders. This program integrates elements of MI, schema therapy, and more traditional CBT to address behavioral problems in psychopathic offenders (Atkinson & Tew, 2012). Although a series of case studies described substantial improvement in a handful of program participants, the representativeness of these participants and the genuineness of the perceived improvement are far from clear (Tew, Dixon, Harkins, & Bennett, 2012).

One of the few studies to provide systematic outcome data from the DSPD program was published by Tyrer et al. (2009), who described a randomized comparison of two subgroups of offenders that had participated in the program. The authors compared offenders who received an in-depth evaluation within 2 weeks of admission to the program to another set of offenders who were assessed at least 6 months after referral to the program (roughly analogous to a wait-list control group). Further confounding this methodology was the authors' acknowledgment of problems in the execution of this unusual design, which led to blurred boundaries between the two groups. Moreover, Tyrer et al.'s description of the sample suggested that many of the participants did not meet all of the identified criteria outlined for the DSPD. Given these methodological problems, it is not surprising that no significant differences in treatment outcome were observed between the two groups. In fact, the authors noted that the offenders' aggression actually increased during the course of the study, and this deterioration (worsening aggression) was particularly striking for those offenders with the most serious personality disorders. Tyrer et al. concluded that their results provided no support for the DSPD program. Unfortunately, the problems in executing this study and with the DSPD program more generally raise questions about the extent to which this program fulfilled its intended goals. The DSPD program was decommissioned in 2011, in large part due to the perception of ineffectiveness in achieving its stated mission (to successfully treat refractory offenders with personality disorders).

Novel approaches to treating antisocial and psychopathic offenders. A number of authors have proposed interventions for psychopathy and APD but without providing any systematic examination of the program's effectiveness. Such recommendations might appear suspect given the checkered history of past efforts to treat psychopathy efforts. Nevertheless, many of these recommendations are grounded in theoretically sound justifications and may, over time, prove fruitful.

One such proposed treatment approach, presumably in response to research suggesting that psychopaths actually fare worse with treatment than without, was proposed by Harris and Rice (2006). These authors suggested that the best strategy for treating violent psychopathic offenders is long-term institutionalization with a strictly regulated token economy to modify problematic behavior. This program was designed to explicitly reinforce behavior that is contrary to psychopathy, such as delaying gratification, being truthful, and being cooperative. Punishment occurs when the individual engages in psychopathic behavior, such as lying, acting impulsively, committing a crime, or acting aggressively. The idea behind such a program is that psychopathic offenders are only truly motivated to act in ways that will lead to immediate gratification; therefore, psychopathic behaviors must be shaped with contingencies that are of consequence. Harris and Rice specified that the program should be open ended rather than time limited, and that this should be made clear to the participants. In addition, in order to avoid lying and manipulation of staff by inmates, the consequences should be based only on observed behaviors, not on inmate reports of their own thoughts, feelings, or behaviors. Harris and Rice conceded that applying the structure and principles they proposed to a noncustodial setting would be challenging and offered no evidence of either feasibility or success for this approach.

Another treatment approach with rapidly growing popularity for criminal offenders in general, and antisocial/psychopathic offenders in particular, is DBT (Linehan, 1993). Using a model that was developed for the treatment of court-ordered probationers, Galietta, Rosenfeld, and colleagues (Galietta, Fineran, Fava, & Rosenfeld, 2010; Galietta & Rosenfeld, 2012) described an adaptation of DBT that was designed to target the unique problems that are common to antisocial and psychopathic offenders. These authors provided a theoretical justification for their use of DBT, with particular emphasis on issues such as emotion regulation (or, in the case of psychopaths, overregulation) and impulsivity. However, Galietta and colleagues have not published any systematic outcome data to support the effectiveness of DBT in this population. Instead, they simply described anecdotal observations regarding the potential utility of DBT for this population, along with a single case study describing its application. Clearly, more research is needed to evaluate the utility of DBT for psychopathic offenders.

Patrick, Drislane, and Strickland (2012) also outlined an untested treatment program that targets the three main features of Patrick and colleagues' triarchic conceptualization of psychopathy: boldness, disinhibition, and meanness. Drawing heavily from neuropsychology and biofeedback techniques, this three-part treatment approach includes a specific intervention to target each facet of psychopathy identified in the model. To address *boldness* (the term they use to describe the overconfidence, lack of reactivity to stressful situations, and social effectiveness that characterizes many psychopathic individuals), Patrick et al. suggested using functional magnetic resonance imaging and skin conductance biofeedback to increase an individual's reactivity to stimuli. The idea behind this technique is to draw the individual's attention to small changes in affect, particularly anxiety, in order to increase the fear response and to integrate that reactivity into psychopaths' decision making about their behavior. In order to target disinhibition, Patrick et al. suggested providing psychopaths with explicit feedback on their performance so as to compensate for the lack of negative emotion they experience when they have committed an error. Using biofeedback, it may also be possible to measure neural activity associated with negative responses to errors and to reinforce these appropriate reactions. Finally, to counter meanness, Patrick et al. recommended training psychopathic individuals to attend to cues of sadness and fear in others and to objectively measure their reactivity in order to ensure that the pain and emotion centers in their brains are truly activated. Of course, this innovative treatment approach has not yet been empirically tested—or even piloted—and might present significant challenges in implementation due to both equipment costs and the need for well-trained and knowledgeable clinicians in order to correctly implement the complex procedures.

In sum, the past 15 years have witnessed a resurgence of interest in developing and systematically evaluating treatments for criminal offenders with psychopathy and APD. Although the existing research base is clearly still limited, and very few studies have used a true RCT approach, the rapid growth of this literature bodes well for the future of offender treatment.

PRACTICE AND POLICY ISSUES

More then four decades have passed since Martinson's (1974) discouraging literature review appeared to slam the door on society's efforts to rehabilitate criminal offenders. But, rather than give up on the important goal and move on to more fruitful or less challenging endeavors, mental health professionals have continued to make advances in developing, refining, and evaluating interventions to reduce criminal and violent behaviors. Much of this research has been guided by the RNR model, which has provided a useful framework for conceptualizing offender treatment programming. At present, although no single theory or intervention approach has emerged to dominate the field of forensic psychology, a number of programs have demonstrated moderate levels of success. These include both name-brand interventions targeting specific criminogenic variables as well as more traditional mental health treatment approaches that are tailored to the unique needs of offenders. There appears little doubt that mental health interventions have the potential to facilitate change in even the most refractory criminal offenders, including those with psychopathic personality styles who have long been assumed to be untreatable.

Given the apparent benefits of some types of mental health or behavioral interventions for some subgroups of offenders, a number of next steps seems obvious. Most importantly, determining which interventions are best for what type of offenders and under which particular circumstances represents a crucial gap in the existing literature. Much

like the practice at the time of Martinson's (1974) review, many practitioners continue to use a "one size fits all" approach to offender treatment, simply applying the intervention they prefer in a wide range of scenarios and/or offenders. This approach represents a marked difference from the eclectic approach to mental health intervention that is taken by most clinicians practicing in the community, where a range of intervention strategies might be selected depending on the specific problems presented by a given patient. Although little systematic research has supported the effectiveness of this type of problem-focused treatment planning in general mental health practice, such research is clearly needed to help advance the provision of offender treatment. Particularly in settings where resources are chronically scarce, the assumption that all offenders would (or could) benefit from a particular type of intervention seems hopelessly naive. It appears quite likely that stronger treatment effects will emerge once more effective mechanisms for triaging offenders into the most appropriate interventions become possible. However, this step requires considerable research analyzing potential mediating influences on treatment outcome, which has been lacking to date.

Another critical need in order to advance the science of offender treatment is the development of reliable and valid outcome measures. At present, most treatment programs rely on recidivism, institutional misconduct, or responses on self-report questionnaires. A critical concern, particularly in the literature focusing on psychopathic and antisocial offenders, is whether clinicians can reliably gauge improvement in the clients they treat. Such assessments are especially critical in release decision making, whether in the context of sentencing, parole, or postincarceration mandated treatment (e.g., for sexually violent predators). Clearly, further research is needed regarding the appropriateness of changing recidivism from a simple dichotomous outcome into a more complex variable, such as might be reflected with a *harm reduction* model (i.e., conceptualizing less frequent or serious offending as improvement). Likewise, the development of behavioral indicators of potentially important outcomes, such as anger or impulsivity, has the potential to move treatment programming beyond the all-too-frequent reliance on the self-report measures that are known to be of questionable validity. These important questions have received surprisingly little attention in the treatment outcome literature.

The limitations of our current knowledge notwithstanding, this review certainly contradicts the traditional wisdom that offender treatment programs are ineffective and highlights a number of areas in which tremendous progress has been made. This progress should, in theory, justify continued, and perhaps enhanced, efforts at developing and implementing many of the programs that have demonstrated some success. Clearly, no absolute threshold exists for identifying how large a treatment effect is needed in order to justify the expenditures involved in implementing offender treatment programs. Balancing the social and financial gains from reduced recidivism versus the expenses involved in providing effective treatment programs is not simply economic but includes both community- and individual-level outcomes (e.g., enhanced quality of life for community members through reduced offending). Nevertheless, when possible, such cost–benefit analyses may help justify the institutional commitment necessary to promote offender treatment programs.

Despite the advances in conceptualizing and implementing offender treatment over the past decades, there remain a number of areas in which further research is needed. Among the most glaring is the need for systematic research (e.g., RCTs) that analyzes specific treatment programs and compares the benefits of the different programs and approaches that have been promoted. Only with a research literature consisting of rigorous, well-designed studies can we begin to identify guidelines for the selection of interventions that are based on offender characteristics and determine which of the many available programs are most deserving of taxpayer support. Of course, such investigations require a genuine commitment to investigating offender treatment programs on the part of funding agencies, which has typically been lacking in the United States as well as in many developed countries. As the present review demonstrates, few published studies have used RCTs with

sufficient power to test treatment group differences, or even large-scale studies that use rigorous methodologies (e.g., intent-to-treat analyses, propensity scores for quasi-experimental designs, monitoring of treatment fidelity). Such designs are crucial in order to reliably identify offender characteristics that mediate treatment outcome. In the absence of such systematic research, offender treatment programs, when available, will likely continue to reflect the idiosyncratic decision making of the clinicians and/ or administrators who are responsible for selecting and implementing these interventions, and the utility of these interventions will remain variable. Without systematic evidence of such systematic evidence of a program's utility, the perceptions of the lay public and policy makers will be guided by the occasional, high-profile treatment failure rather than the modest treatment benefits that might be accrued by a larger number of offender/participants.

SUMMARY AND CONCLUSIONS

Nearly 40 years ago, mental health and criminal justice professionals sounded the death knell on offender treatment programs. Since that time, substantial advances have been made in a wide range of areas, fueled by both the development of the RNR model as well as the growing application of cognitive–behavioral and integrative treatment approaches. Although considerable variability in the research findings exists both within and across different intervention approaches, the available evidence suggests that effective treatments do exist, and that even those offenders who seem most refractory (e.g., psychopaths) can benefit from treatment. Of course, this conclusion does not mean that all offenders will be effectively treated because motivation and compliance remain no less critical in offender treatment than in any other mental health intervention. However, the potential utility of treatment programming certainly justifies continued research, both to further refine interventions and improve treatment outcomes as well as to help guide clinical treatment decisions regarding which interventions are best for what types of offenders. A societal commitment to reducing criminal offending would seem to justify an ever greater emphasis on offender treatment.

References

Allen, L. C., MacKenzie, D. L., & Hickman, L. J. (2001). The effectiveness of cognitive behavioral treatment for adult offenders: A methodological, quality-based review. *International Journal of Offender Therapy and Comparative Criminology, 45*, 498–514. doi:10.1177/0306624X01454009

American Psychiatric Association. (1980). *Diagnostic and statistical manual of mental disorders* (3rd ed.). Washington, DC: Author.

Andrews, D., Bonta, J., & Hoge, R. (1990). Classification for effective rehabilitation: Rediscovering psychology. *Criminal Justice and Behavior, 17*, 19–52. doi:10.1177/0093854890017001004

Andrews, D. A., & Bonta, J. (2003). *The psychology of criminal conduct* (3rd ed.). Cincinnati, OH: Anderson.

Andrews, D. A., Zinger, I., Hoge, R. D., Bonta, J., Gendreau, P., & Cullen, F. T. (1990). Does correctional treatment work? A clinically relevant and psychologically informed meta-analysis. *Criminology, 28*, 369–404. doi:10.1111/j.1745-9125.1990.tb01330.x

Anstiss, B., Polaschek, D. L., & Wilson, M. (2011). A brief motivational interviewing intervention with prisoners: When you lead a horse to water, can it drink for itself? *Psychology, Crime & Law, 17*, 689–710. doi:10.1080/10683160903524325

Arbuthnot, J., & Gordon, D. A. (1988). Crime and cognition: Community applications of sociomoral reasoning development. *Criminal Justice and Behavior, 15*, 379–393. doi:10.1177/0093854888015003009

Armstrong, T. A. (2003). The effect of moral reconation therapy on the recidivism of youthful offenders: A randomized experiment. *Criminal Justice and Behavior, 30*, 668–687. doi:10.1177/0093854803256452

Atkinson, R., & Tew, J. (2012). Working with psychopathic offenders: Lessons from the Chromis program. *International Journal of Forensic Mental Health, 11*, 299–311. doi:10.1080/14999013.2012.746758

Banay, R. S., & Davidoff, L. (1942). Apparent recovery of a sex psychopath after lobotomy. *Journal of Criminal Psychopathology, 4*, 59–66.

Bandura, A. (1977). Self-efficacy: Toward a unifying theory of behavioral change. *Psychological Review, 84*, 191–215. doi:10.1037/0033-295X.84.2.191

Barto Lynch, J. (1995). The use of aggression replacement training with adult offenders: A program for violent and aggressive inmates. *Dissertation Abstracts International: Section B. Sciences and Engineering, 56*(4), 2314.

Beck, A. T., & Fernandez, E. (1998). Cognitive–behavioral therapy in the treatment of anger: A meta-analysis. *Cognitive Therapy and Research, 22*, 63–74. doi:10.1023/A:1018763902991

Bernstein, D. P., Nijman, H. L. I., Karos, K., Keulen-de Vos, M., de Vogel, V., Lucker, T. P., & Arntz, A. (2012). Schema therapy for forensic patients with personality disorder: Design and preliminary findings of a multicenter randomized clinical trial in the Netherlands. *International Journal of Forensic Mental Health, 11*, 312–324. doi:10.1080/14999013.2012.746757

Berzins, L. G., & Trestman, R. L. (2004). Development and implementation of dialectical behavior therapy in forensic settings. *International Journal of Forensic Mental Health, 3*, 93–103.

Blanchette, K., & Brown, S. L. (2006). Gender-informed correctional practice: Integrating gender-neutral and gender-specific/responsive paradigms. *Women, Girls, and Criminal Justice, 7*(4), 49–64.

Burnett, W. L. (1997). Treating post-incarcerated offenders with moral reconation therapy: A one-year recidivism study. *Cognitive–Behavioral Treatment Review, 6*, 2.

Bush, J., Glick, B., & Taymans, J. (1997). *Thinking for a change: Integrated cognitive behavior change program.* Washington, DC: U.S. Department of Justice.

Camp, S. D., Klein-Safran, J., Kwon, O., Dagget, D. M., & Joseph, V. (2006). An exploration into participation in a faith-based prison program. *Criminology and Public Policy, 5*, 529–550. doi:10.1111/j.1745-9133.2006.00387.x

Chambers, J. C., Eccleston, L., Day, A., Ward, T., & Howells, K. (2008). Treatment readiness in violent offenders: The influence of cognitive factors on engagement in violence programs. *Aggression and Violent Behavior, 13*, 276–284. doi:10.1016/j.avb.2008.04.003

Clark, M. D., Walters, S., Gingerich, R., & Meltzer, M. (2006). Motivational interviewing for probation officers: Tipping the balance toward change. *Federal Probation, 70*, 38–44.

Cleckley, H. (1988). *The mask of sanity.* St. Louis, MO: Mosby. (Original work published 1941)

Coleman, M., Pfeiffer, S., & Oakland, T. (1991). *Aggression replacement training with behavioral disordered offenders.* Unpublished manuscript, University of Texas, Austin.

Cooke, D. J., Hart, S. D., Logan, C., & Michie, C. (2011). Explicating the construct of psychopathy: Development and validation of a conceptual model, the Comprehensive Assessment of Psychopathic Personality (CAPP). *International Journal of Forensic Mental Health, 11*, 242–252. doi:10.1080/14999013.2012.746759

Crighton, D. A., & Towl, G. T. (2008). *Psychology in prisons* (2nd ed.). Oxford, England: Blackwell. doi:10.1002/9781444301724

Cullen, A. E., Clarke, A. Y., Kuipers, E., Hodgins, S., Dean, K., & Fahy, T. (2012). A multisite randomized trial of a cognitive skills program for male mentally disordered offenders: Violence and antisocial behavior outcomes. *Journal of Consulting and Clinical Psychology, 80,* 1114–1120. doi:10.1037/a0030291

Cullen, F. T., & Gendreau, P. (2000). Assessing correctional rehabilitation: Policy, practice and prospects. *Criminal Justice, 3,* 109–175.

Curilla, V. L. (1990). *Aggression replacement training in the community for adult learning disabled offenders.* Unpublished manuscript, University of Washington, Seattle.

Darling, H. F. (1945). Shock therapy in psychopathic personality. *Journal of Nervous and Mental Disease, 101,* 247–250. doi:10.1097/00005053-194503000-00006

Davidson, K. M., Tyrer, P., Tata, P., Cooke, D., Gumley, A., Ford, I., . . . Crawford, M. J. (2009). Cognitive behaviour therapy for violent men with antisocial personality disorder in the community: An exploratory randomized controlled trial. *Psychological Medicine, 39,* 569–577. doi:10.1017/S0033291708004066

Del Vecchio, T., & O'Leary, K. D. (2004). Effectiveness of anger treatments for specific anger problems: A meta-analytic review. *Clinical Psychology Review, 24,* 15–34. doi:10.1016/j.cpr.2003.09.006

DiGiuseppe, R., & Tafrate, R. C. (2003). Anger treatments for adults: A meta-analytic review. *Clinical Psychology: Science and Practice, 10,* 70–84. doi:10.1093/clipsy.10.1.70

Dobson, K. S., & Block, L. (1988). Historical and philosophical bases of the cognitive–behavioral therapies. In K. S. Dobson (Ed.), *Handbook of cognitive–behavioral therapies* (pp. 3–38). New York, NY: Guilford Press.

Draycott, S., Askari, R., & Kirkpatrick, T. (2011). Patterns and changes in psychopathic interpersonal behaviour in forensic inpatient treatment. *Personality and Mental Health, 5,* 200–208. doi:10.1002/pmh.171

Duggan, C. (2011). Dangerous and severe personality disorder. *British Journal of Psychiatry, 198,* 431–433. doi:10.1192/bjp.bp.110.083048

Evershed, S., Tennant, A., Boomer, D., Rees, A., Barkham, M., & Watson, A. (2003). Practice-based outcomes of dialectical behavior therapy (DBT) targeting anger and violence, with male forensic patients: A pragmatic and non-contemporaneous comparison. *Criminal Behaviour and Mental Health, 13,* 198–213. doi:10.1002/cbm.542

Forth, A. E., Kosson, D., & Hare, R. D. (2003). *The Hare PCL: Youth Version.* Toronto, Ontario, Canada: Multi-Health Systems.

Galietta, M., Fineran, V., Fava, J., & Rosenfeld, B. (2010). Antisocial and psychopathic individuals. In D. McKay, J. S. Abramowitz, & S. Taylor (Eds.), *Cognitive–behavioral therapy for refractory cases: Turning failure into success* (pp. 385–405). Washington, DC: American Psychological Association. doi:10.1037/12070-018

Galietta, M., & Rosenfeld, B. (2012). Adapting dialectical behavior therapy (DBT) for the treatment of psychopathy. *International Journal of Forensic Mental Health, 11,* 325–335. doi:10.1080/14999013.2012.746762

Gendreau, P., & Ross, R. R. (1987). Revivification of rehabilitation: Evidence from the 1980s. *Justice Quarterly, 4,* 349–407. doi:10.1080/07418828700089411

Gibbon, S., Duggan, C., Stoffers, J., Huband, J., Vollm, B. A., Ferriter, M., & Lieb, K. (2010). Psychological interventions for antisocial personality disorder. *Cochrane Database of Systematic Reviews, 6,* Art. No. CD007668

Glick, B., & Gibbs, J. C. (2011). *Aggression replacement training: A comprehensive intervention for aggressive youth* (3rd ed. rev. and exp.). Champaign, IL: Research Press.

Glick, B., & Goldstein, A. P. (1987). Aggression replacement training. *Journal of Counseling and Development, 65,* 356–362. doi:10.1002/j.1556-6676.1987.tb00730.x

Godwin, G., Stone, S., & Hambrock, K. (1995). Recidivism study: Lake County, Florida detention center. *Cognitive–Behavioral Treatment Review, 4,* 6.

Golden, L. (2002). *Evaluation of the efficacy of a cognitive behavioral program for offenders on probation: Thinking for a change.* Dallas: University of Texas Southwestern Medical Center.

Golden, L., Gatchel, R. J., & Cahill, M. (2006). Evaluating the effectiveness of the National Institute of Corrections' 'Thinking for a Change' program among probationers. *Journal of Offender Rehabilitation, 43,* 55–73. doi:10.1300/J076v43n02_03

Goldstein, A. P. (2004). Evaluations of effectiveness. In A. P. Goldstein, R. Nensen, B. Daleflod, & M. Kalt (Eds.), *New perspectives on aggression replacement training* (pp. 230–244). Chichester, England: Wiley. doi:10.1002/0470030380

Goldstein, A. P., Glick, B., Carthan, M., & Blancero, D. (1994). *The prosocial gang: Implementing aggression replacement training.* Thousand Oaks, CA: Sage.

Goldstein, A. P., Glick, B., & Gibbs, J. (1986). *Aggression replacement training: A comprehensive intervention for aggressive youth.* Champaign, IL: Research Press.

Goldstein, A. P., Glick, B., & Gibbs, J. C. (1998). *Aggression replacement training: A comprehensive intervention for aggressive youth* (2nd ed.). Champaign, IL: Research Press.

Goldstein, A. P., Glick, B., Irwin, M., Pask-McCartney, C., & Rubama, I. (1989). *Reducing delinquency: Intervention in the community*. Elmsford, NY: Pergamon Press.

Gullhaugen, A. S., & Nottestad, J. A. (2012). Testing theoretical models for future clinical practice in the treatment of psychopathy. *Journal of Forensic Psychiatry and Psychology, 23*, 635–653. doi:10.1080/14789949.2012.729390

Gundersen, K., & Svartdal, F. (2009). Aggression replacement training: Decreasing behaviour problems by increasing social competence. In C. Cefai & P. Cooper (Eds.), *Promoting emotional education: Engaging children and young people with social, emotional and behavioural difficulties* (pp. 161–168). London, England: Jessica Kingsley.

Hall, S. T. (2003). Faith-based cognitive programs in corrections. *Corrections Today, 65*, 108–113.

Hare, R. D. (1980). A research scale for the assessment of psychopathy in criminal populations. *Personality and Individual Differences, 1*, 111–119. doi:10.1016/0191-8869(80)90028-8

Hare, R. D. (1991). *The Hare Psychopathy Checklist—Revised*. Toronto, Ontario, Canada: Multi-Health Systems.

Hare, R. D., Clark, D., Grann, M., & Thornton, D. (2000). Psychopathy and the validity of the PCL–R: An international perspective. *Behavioral Sciences and the Law, 18*, 623–645. doi:10.1002/1099-0798(200010)18:5<623::AID-BSL409>3.0.CO;2-W

Harper, R., & Hardy, S. (2000). Research note: An evaluation of motivational interviewing as a method of intervention with clients in a probation setting. *British Journal of Social Work, 30*, 393–400. doi:10.1093/bjsw/30.3.393

Harris, G. T., & Rice, M. E. (2006). Treatment of psychopathy: A review of empirical findings. In C. J. Patrick (Ed.), *Handbook of psychopathy* (pp. 555–572). New York, NY: Guilford Press.

Hart, S. D., Cox, D. N., & Hare, R. D. (1995). *Manual for the Psychopathy Checklist: Screening Version (PCL:SV)*. Toronto, Ontario, Canada: Multi-Health Systems.

Hatcher, R. M., Palmer, E. J., McGuire, J., Hounsome, J. C., Bilby, C. L., & Hollin, C. R. (2008). Aggression replacement training with adult male offenders within community settings: A reconviction analysis. *Journal of Forensic Psychiatry and Psychology, 19*, 517–532. doi:10.1080/14789940801936407

Hollin, C. R. (2002). Risk–needs assessment and the allocation to offender programmes. In J. McGuire (Ed.), *Offender rehabilitation and treatment: Effective programmes and policies to reduce reoffending* (pp. 309–332). Chichester, England: Wiley.

Hornsfeld, R., Van Dam Beggen, R., Leenaars, E., & Jonkers, P. (2004). Aggression control therapy for forensic psychiatric patients with violent offenses: Development and application. *Dutch Journal of Psychotherapy, 30*, 22–38.

Howells, K., Day, A., Williamson, P., Bubner, S., Jauncey, S., Parker, A., & Heseltine, K. (2005). Brief anger management programs with offenders: Outcomes and predictors of change. *Journal of Forensic Psychiatry and Psychology, 16*, 296–311. doi:10.1080/14789940500096099

Knott, C. (1995). The STOP programme: Reasoning and rehabilitation in a British setting. In J. McGuire (Ed.), *What works: Reducing reoffending—Guidelines from research and practice* (pp. 115–126). New York, NY: Wiley.

Kohlberg, L. (1971). *Stages of moral development*. Retrieved from http://www.xenodochy.org/ex/lists/moraldev.html

Kolb, L. C. (1949). An evaluation of lobotomy and its potentialities for future research in psychiatry and the basic sciences. *Journal of Nervous and Mental Disease, 110*, 112–148. doi:10.1097/00005053-194911020-00002

Koskoff, Y. D., & Goldhurst, R. (1968). *The dark side of the house*. New York, NY: Dial Press.

Krueger, S. (1997). Five-year recidivism study of MRT(r)-treated offenders in a county jail. *Cognitive–Behavioral Treatment Review, 6*, 3.

Landenberger, N. A., & Lipsey, M. W. (2005). The positive effects of cognitive–behavioral programs for offenders: A meta-analysis of factors associated with effective treatment. *Journal of Experimental Criminology, 1*, 451–476. doi:10.1007/s11292-005-3541-7

Linehan, M. M. (1993). *Cognitive behavioral treatment of borderline personality disorder*. New York, NY: Guilford Press.

Lipsey, M. W., Chapman, G. L., & Landenberger, N. A. (2001). Cognitive–behavioral programs for offenders. *Annals of the American Academy of Political and Social Science, 578*, 144–157. doi:10.1177/0002716201578001009

Lipsey, M. W., & Landenberger, N. A. (2005). Cognitive–behavioral interventions: A meta-analysis of randomized controlled studies. In B. C. Welsh & D. P. Farrington (Eds.), *Preventing crime: What works for children, offenders, victims, and places* (pp. 57–72). New York, NY: Springer.

Lipton, D. S., Martinson, R., & Wilks, J. (1975). *The effectiveness of correctional treatment: A survey of treatment evaluation studies*. New York, NY: Praeger.

Little, G. L., & Robinson, K. D. (1988). Moral reconation therapy: A systematic step-by-step treatment system for treatment resistance clients. *Psychological Reports, 62*, 135–151. doi:10.2466/pr0.1988.62.1.135

Little, G. L., Robinson, K. D., & Burnette, K. D. (1989). Treating drunk drivers with moral reconation therapy: A one-year recidivism report. *Psychological Reports, 64*, 960–962. doi:10.2466/pr0.1989.64.3.960

Little, G. L., Robinson, K. D., & Burnette, K. D. (1990). Treating drunk drivers with moral reconation therapy: A two-year recidivism study. *Psychological Reports, 66*, 1379–1387. doi:10.2466/PR0.66.3.1379-1387

Little, G. L., Robinson, K. D., & Burnette, K. D. (1991a). Treating drug offenders with moral reconation therapy: A three-year recidivism report. *Psychological Reports, 69*, 1151–1154. doi:10.2466/pr0.1991.69.3f.1151

Little, G. L., Robinson, K. D., & Burnette, K. D. (1991b). Treating drunk drivers with moral reconation therapy: A three-year report. *Psychological Reports, 69*, 953–954. doi:10.2466/pr0.1991.69.3.953

Little, G. L., Robinson, K. D., & Burnette, K. D. (1993a). Cognitive behavioral treatment of felony drug offenders: A five-year recidivism report. *Psychological Reports, 73*, 1089–1090. doi:10.2466/pr0.1993.73.3f.1089

Little, G. L., Robinson, K. D., & Burnette, K. D. (1993b). 42-month alcohol treatment data: Multiple DWI offenders treated with MRT show lower recidivism rates. *Cognitive–Behavioral Treatment Review, 2*, 5.

Little, G. L., Robinson, K. D., Burnette, K. D., & Swan, S. (1995). Seven-year recidivism of felony offenders treated with MRT. *Cognitive–Behavioral Treatment Review, 4*, 498–514.

Lösel, F. (1995). The efficacy of correctional treatment: A review and synthesis of metaevaluations. In J. McGuire (Ed.), *What works: Reducing reoffending: Guidelines from research and practice* (pp. 79–111). Oxford, England: Wiley.

Lowenkamp, C. T., Hubbard, D., Makarios, M. D., & Latessa, E. J. (2009). A quasi-experimental evaluation of thinking for a change: A 'real-world' application. *Criminal Justice and Behavior, 36*, 137–146. doi:10.1177/0093854808328230

Mahoney, M. J., & Arnkoff, D. B. (1978). Cognitive and self-control therapies. In S. L. Garfield & A. E. Bergin (Eds.), *Handbook of psychotherapy and behavior change: An empirical analysis* (pp. 698–722). New York, NY: Wiley.

Mahoney, M. J., & Lyddon, W. J. (1988). Recent developments in cognitive approaches to counseling and psychotherapy. *Counseling Psychologist, 16*, 190–234. doi:10.1177/0011000088162001

Martinson, R. (1974). What works? Questions and answers about prison reform. *Public Interest, 3*, 22–54.

McCann, R., Ball, E. M., & Ivanoff, A. (2000). DBT with an inpatient forensic population: The CMHIP forensic model. *Cognitive and Behavioral Practice, 7*, 447–456. doi:10.1016/S1077-7229(00)80056-5

McGuire, J., Broomfield, D., Robinson, C., & Rowson, B. (1995). Short-term effects on probation programs: An evaluative study. *International Journal of Offender Therapy and Comparative Criminology, 39*, 23–42. doi:10.1177/0306624X9503900104

McMurran, M. (2009). Motivational interviewing with offenders: A systematic review. *Legal and Criminological Psychology, 14*, 83–100. doi:10.1348/135532508X278326

McMurran, M., & Theodosi, E. (2007). Is treatment non-completion associated with increased reconviction over no treatment? *Psychology, Crime & Law, 13*, 333–343. doi:10.1080/10683160601060374

Miller, W. R., & Rollnick, S. (1991). *Motivational interviewing: Preparing people to change addictive behavior.* New York, NY: Guilford Press.

Miller, W. R., & Rollnick, S. (2002). *Motivational interviewing: Preparing people to change addictive behavior* (2nd ed.). New York, NY: Guilford Press.

Mistretta v. United States, 488 U.S. 361 (1989).

Monahan, J., Steadman, H., Silver, E., Appelbaum, P., Robbins, P., Mulvey, E., . . . Banks, S. M. (2001). *Rethinking risk assessment: The MacArthur study of mental disorder and violence.* New York, NY: Oxford University Press.

Morris, N., & Rothman, D. J. (1995), *Oxford history of the prison.* New York, NY: Oxford University Press.

Nassi, A. J., & Abramowitz, S. I. (1976). From phrenology to psychosurgery and back again: Biological studies of criminality. *American Journal of Orthopsychiatry, 46*, 591–607. doi:10.1111/j.1939-0025.1976.tb00958.x

Ogloff, J. P., Wong, S., & Greenwood, A. (1990). Treating criminal psychopaths in a therapeutic community program. *Behavioral Sciences and the Law, 8*, 181–190. doi:10.1002/bsl.2370080210

Olver, M. E., Stockdale, K. C., & Wormith, J. (2011). A meta-analysis of predictors of offender treatment attrition and its relationship to recidivism. *Journal of Consulting and Clinical Psychology, 79*, 6–21. doi:10.1037/a0022200

Patrick, C. J., Drislane, L. E., & Strickland, C. (2012). Conceptualizing psychopathy in triarchic terms: Implications for treatment. *International Journal of Forensic Mental Health, 11*, 253–266. doi:10.1080/14999013.2012.746761

Pearson, F. S., Lipton, D. S., Cleland, C. M., & Yee, D. S. (2002). The effects of behavioral/cognitive–behavioral programs on recidivism. *Crime and*

Delinquency, 48, 476–496. doi:10.1177/0011128702048003006

Perepletchikova, F., & Kazdin, A. E. (2005). Treatment integrity and therapeutic change: Issues and research recommendations. *Clinical Psychology: Science and Practice, 12*, 365–383. doi:10.1093/clipsy.bpi045

Piaget, J. (1964). Part I: Cognitive development in children: Piaget development and learning. *Journal of Research in Science Teaching, 2*, 176–186.

Polaschek, D. L., & Collie, R. M. (2004). Rehabilitating serious violent adult offenders: An empirical and theoretical stocktake. *Psychology, Crime & Law, 10*, 321–334. doi:10.1080/10683160410001662807

Polaschek, D. L. L., & Daly, T. E. (2013). Treatment and psychopathy in forensic settings. *Aggression and Violent Behavior, 18*, 592–603. doi:10.1016/j.avb.2013.06.003

Poppen, J. L. (1948). Technic of prefrontal lobotomy. *Journal of Neurosurgery, 5*, 514–520.

Porporino, F. J., Fabiano, E. A., & Robinson, D. (1991). *Focusing on successful reintegration: Cognitive skills training for offenders, R-19*. Ottawa, Ontario, Canada: Correctional Service of Canada, Research and Statistics Branch.

Porporino, F. J., & Robinson, D. (1995). An evaluation of the Reasoning and Rehabilitation Program with Canadian federal offenders. In R. R. Ross & B. Ross (Eds.), *Thinking straight* (pp. 155–191). Ottawa, Ontario, Canada: Cognitive Centre.

Prochaska, J. O., & Velicer, W. F. (1997). The transtheoretical model of health behavior change. *American Journal of Health Promotion, 12*, 38–48. doi:10.4278/0890-1171-12.1.38

Rada, R. T. (1978). Legal aspects in treating rapists. *Criminal Justice and Behavior, 5*, 369–378. doi:10.1177/009385487800500408

Raynor, P., & Vanstone, M. (1996). Reasoning and rehabilitation in Britain: The results of the Straight Thinking on Probation (STOP) programme. *International Journal of Offender Therapy and Comparative Criminology, 40*, 272–284. doi:10.1177/0306624X96404003

Rice, M. E., Harris, G. T., & Cormier, C. A. (1992). An evaluation of a maximum security therapeutic community for psychopaths and other mentally disordered offenders. *Law and Human Behavior, 16*, 399–412. doi:10.1007/BF02352266

Robinson, D. (1995). *The impact of cognitive skills training on post-release recidivism among Canadian federal offenders* (Research Report No. R-41). Ottawa, Ontario, Canada: Correctional Service of Canada, Correctional Research and Development.

Robinson, D. (1996). Factors influencing the effectiveness of cognitive skills training. *FORUM on Corrections Research, 8*(3), 6–9.

Robinson, D., Grossman, M., & Porporino, F. (1991). *Effectiveness of the cognitive skills training program. From pilot project to national implementation* (Research Report No. B-07). Ottawa, Ontario, Canada: Correctional Services of Canada, Research and Statistics Branch.

Rosenfeld, B., Byers, K., & Galietta, M. (2011). Psychotherapy outcome research with forensic populations. In B. Rosenfeld & S. Penrod (Eds.), *Research methods in forensic psychology* (pp. 309–324). New York, NY: Wiley.

Rosenfeld, B., Galietta, M., Ivanoff, A., Garcia-Mansilla, A., Martinez, R., Fava, J., . . . Green, D. (2007). Dialectical behavior therapy for the treatment of stalking offenders. *International Journal of Forensic Mental Health, 6*, 95–103. doi:10.1080/14999013.2007.10471254

Ross, R., & Fabiano, E. (1980). *Time to think: Cognition and crime: Link and remediation*. Ottawa, Ontario, Canada: Ministry of the Solicitor General.

Ross, R., & Fabiano, E. (1985). *Time to think: A cognitive model of crime and delinquency prevention and rehabilitation*. Johnson City, TN: Academy of Arts and Sciences.

Ross, R., Fabiano, E., & Ewles, C. D. (1988). Reasoning and rehabilitation. *International Journal of Offender Therapy and Comparative Criminology, 32*, 29–35. doi:10.1177/0306624X8803200104

Salekin, R. T. (2002). Psychopathy and therapeutic pessimism: Clinical lore or clinical reality? *Clinical Psychology Review, 22*, 79–112. doi:10.1016/S0272-7358(01)00083-6

Salekin, R. T., Worley, C., & Grimes, R. D. (2010). Treatment of psychopathy: A review and brief introduction to the mental model approach for psychopathy. *Behavioral Sciences and the Law, 28*, 235–266. doi:10.1002/bsl.928

Sentencing Reform Act of 1984, 98 Stat. (1987).

Skeem, J. L., Monahan, J., & Mulvey, E. P. (2002). Psychopathy, treatment involvement, and subsequent violence among civil psychiatric patients. *Law and Human Behavior, 26*, 577–603. doi:0147-7307/02/1200-0577/1

Skeem, J. L., Polaschek, D. L. L., & Manchak, S. (2009). Appropriate treatment works, but how? Rehabilitating general, psychopathic, and high risk offenders. In J. L. Skeem, K. Douglas, & S. Lilienfeld (Eds.), *Psychological science in the courtroom: Controversies and consensus* (pp. 358–385). New York, NY: Guilford Press.

Stem, P. C. (2011). *An evaluation for a cognitive behavioral group program for offenders in a medium security prison setting: Thinking for a change* (Doctoral dissertation). Retrieved from ProQuest Dissertations and Theses database. (UMI No. 3455205)

Sugg, D. (2000). *Aggression replacement training: Research report*. Unpublished report prepared for the Correctional Services Accreditation Panel, London, England.

Tew, J., Dixon, L., Harkins, L., & Bennett, A. (2012). Investigating changes in anger and aggression in offendees with high levels of psychopathic traits attending the Chromis violence reduction programme. *Criminal Behaviour and Mental Health, 22*, 191–201. doi:10.1002/cbm.1832

Tong, L., & Farrington, D. P. (2006). How effective is the "Reasoning and Rehabilitation" programme in reducing reoffending? A meta-analysis of evaluations in four countries. *Psychology, Crime & Law, 12*, 3–24. doi:10.1080/10683160512331316253

Tong, L. S., & Farrington, D. P. (2008). Effectiveness of "Reasoning and Rehabilitation'" in reducing reoffending. *Psicothema, 20*, 20–28.

Trupin, E. W., Stewart, D. G., Beach, B., & Boesky, L. (2002). Effectiveness of dialectical behaviour therapy program for incarcerated female juvenile offenders. *Child and Adolescent Mental Health, 7*, 121–127. doi:10.1111/1475-3588.00022

Tyrer, P., Cooper, S., Rutter, D., Seivewright, H., Duggan, C., Maden, T., . . . Byford, S. (2009). The assessment of dangerousness and severe personality disorder: Lessons from a randomized controlled trial linked to qualitative analysis. *Journal of Forensic Psychiatry and Psychology, 20*, 132–146. doi:10.1080/14789940802236872

Usematsu, T. (1970). Some legal aspects of psychosurgical treatments—with particular reference to the removal of criminal tendencies. *Journal of Forensic Psychology, 1*, 4–10.

van den Bosch, L. M. C., Hysaj, M., & Jacobs, P. (2012). DBT in an outpatient forensic setting. *International Journal of Law and Psychiatry, 35*, 311–316. doi:10.1016/j.ijlp.2012.04.009

Walters, S. T., Clark, M. D., Gingerich, R., & Meltzer, M. (2007). *Motivating offenders to change: A guide for probation and parole*. Washington, DC: National Institute of Corrections.

Ward, T., Day, A., Howells, K., & Birgden, A. (2004). The multi-factor offender readiness model. *Aggression and Violent Behavior, 9*, 645–673. doi:10.1016/j.avb.2003.08.001

Ward, T., Mesler, J., & Yates, P. (2007). Reconstructing the risk–need–responsivity model: A theoretical elaboration and evaluation. *Aggression and Violent Behavior, 12*, 208–228. doi:10.1016/j.avb.2006.07.001

Watt, B. D., & Howells, K. (1999). Skills training for aggression control: Evaluation of an anger management programme for violent offenders. *Legal and Criminological Psychology, 4*, 285–300. doi:10.1348/135532599167914

Wettermann, A., Schläfke, D., & Fegert, J. M. (2012). The modification of criminogenic factors on addicted offenders. The effectiveness of the Reasoning and Rehabilitation Program. *International Journal of Law and Psychiatry, 35*, 202–206. doi:10.1111/j.1468-2311.2005.00356.x

Wilkinson, J. (2005). Evaluating evidence for the effectiveness of the Reasoning and Rehabilitation Programme. *Howard Journal of Criminal Justice, 44*, 70–85. doi:10.1111/j.1468-2311.2005.00356.x

Wilson, D. B., Bouffard, L., & MacKenzie, D. L. (2005). A quantitative review of structured, group-oriented, cognitive–behavioral programs for offenders. *Criminal Justice and Behavior, 32*, 172–204. doi:10.1177/0093854804272889

Wong, S. C. P., & Gordon, A. (2006). The validity and reliability of the Violence Risk Scale: A treatment friendly violence risk assessment scale. *Psychology, Public Policy, and Law, 12*, 279–309. doi:10.1037/1076-8971.12.3.279

Wong, S. C. P., Gordon, A., Gu, D., Lewis, K., & Olver, M. E. (2012). The effectiveness of violence reduction treatment for psychopathic offenders: Empirical evidence and a treatment model. *International Journal of Forensic Mental Health, 11*, 336–349. doi:10.1080/14999013.2012.746760

Wong, S. C. P., & Hare, R. D. (2005). *Guidelines for a psychopathy treatment program*. Toronto, Ontario, Canada: Multi-Health Systems.

Wong, S. C. P., Witte, T., Gordon, A., Gu, D., & Lewis, K. (2006, June). *Can a treatment program designed primarily for violent risk reduction reduce recidivism in psychopaths?* Paper presented at the Canadian Psychological Association Annual Conference, Calgary, Alberta, Canada.

Wormith, J., Althouse, R., Simpson, M., Reitzel, L. R., Fagan, T. J., & Morgan, R. D. (2007). The rehabilitation and reintegration of offenders: The current landscape and some future directions for correctional psychology. *Criminal Justice and Behavior, 34*, 879–892. doi:10.1177/0093854807301552

Young, J. E., Klosko, J. S., & Weishaar, M. (2003). *Schema therapy: A practitioner's guide*. New York, NY: Guilford Press.

Young, S., Hopkin, G., Perkins, D., Farr, C., Doidge, A., & Gudjonsson, G. (2013). A controlled trial of a cognitive skills program for personality-disordered offenders. *Journal of Attention Disorders, 17*, 598–607. doi:10.1177/1087054711430333

CHAPTER 7

CAPITAL CASE CONSIDERATIONS

David DeMatteo, Michael Keesler, Megan Murphy, and Heidi Strohmaier

Over the nearly 40 years since the United States reinstated the death penalty in *Gregg v. Georgia* (1976), the involvement of forensic mental health professionals in capital cases has increased considerably. Forensic mental health professionals now routinely conduct assessments at every stage of death penalty proceedings. Some types of evaluations have long been a common feature of death penalty cases, other types of evaluations are less frequently conducted, and still others were developed after recent decisions by the U.S. Supreme Court. Given the obvious importance of mental health evaluations that are conducted in capital cases, evaluators who are—or wish to become—involved in these types of cases must have a thorough understanding of the legal and clinical issues inherent in capital cases.

This chapter discusses the legal and clinical considerations that are most relevant for forensic mental health professionals who are involved in capital cases. We begin by reviewing death penalty jurisprudence, with a particular focus on relevant cases decided by the U.S. Supreme Court. Following this review of Supreme Court case law, we briefly address the various roles that may be assumed by forensic mental health professionals in capital cases. Next, we consider the role of punishment in the U.S. criminal justice system, followed by an examination of the risk and protective factors that are most relevant to criminal offending. Then, we summarize the empirical literature on the effectiveness of the death penalty, societal views about the death penalty, and assessments of future dangerousness in capital contexts. We then discuss several types of forensic mental

health assessments that can be conducted in capital cases, including *Atkins*-type evaluations (*Atkins v. Virginia*, 2002), competence for execution (CFE) evaluations, and capital sentencing evaluations. We conclude the chapter by summarizing key points and highlighting several areas for future research.

IMPORTANCE OF THE PROBLEM

The modern era of the death penalty began in 1972 with the U.S. Supreme Court's decision in *Furman v. Georgia* (1972). In a brief unsigned opinion, followed by separate opinions from each of the nine Justices, the Court held that death penalty statutes that left the sentencing decision to the unguided discretion of the judge or jury were unconstitutional. In the wake of *Furman*, many states rewrote their death penalty statutes, and the moratorium on capital punishment ended 4 years later when the Supreme Court decided *Gregg v. Georgia*. In *Gregg*, the Court held that the death penalty can be constitutional if it is not mandatory and if the relevant statute is adequate to guide and limit the sentencing jury in reaching an individualized sentencing decision. The result of *Gregg* and later Supreme Court decisions is a death penalty process in which the sentencing decision must be based on a specific consideration of the defendant's *moral*—rather than *legal*—culpability (Cunningham, 2010). To this end, sentencing juries are required to consider aggravating and mitigating factors relating to the defendant and the offense, and the capital sentencing schemes of all death penalty states generally

http://dx.doi.org/10.1037/14461-007
APA Handbook of Forensic Psychology: Vol. 1. Individual and Situational Influences in Criminal and Civil Contexts,
B. L. Cutler and P. A. Zapf (Editors-in-Chief)

reflect this process. In most jurisdictions, the jury must find at least one aggravating factor and find that any mitigating factors do not make the imposition of death inappropriate.

With more than 3,000 people on death row in the United States and numerous defendants being tried in capital proceedings, it is not uncommon for mental health professionals to be involved in capital cases (Cunningham, 2010). Because of the individualized sentencing focus required by *Gregg*, forensic mental health professionals may be asked to assist at various stages of the proceedings. For example, forensic mental health professionals may help the court determine whether a defendant is eligible for a death sentence (either pretrial or postsentencing) or help the jury make a more informed determination about the offender's moral culpability (and whether it justifies imposing a death sentence). These and other evaluations conducted at the various stages of death penalty proceedings differ considerably, and the various roles assumed by forensic mental health professionals determine the nature of their involvement.

Before discussing the various types of assessments that can be conducted in capital cases, it is necessary to describe the roles that may be filled by forensic mental health professionals. Broadly speaking, in capital cases, forensic mental health professionals can be retained either as nonobjective consultants or as objective experts. *Consultants* are hired by either the defense or prosecution to assist with a variety of tasks, including jury selection, witness preparation, trial strategy, and advising on mental health issues. Consultants are not expected to be objective and instead are hired to advocate for the retaining party. By contrast, *experts* remain objective and function to assist the legal decision maker in imposing a sentence. Typically, experts conduct evaluations of the offender on a variety of issues, although they may also serve as a *teaching witness* who presents empirical evidence to the court in an effort to enhance the court's understanding of clinical or social issues.

RELEVANT PSYCHOLOGICAL THEORY AND PRINCIPLES

The punishment of individuals who commit crimes is a fundamental feature of the U.S. criminal justice system. Punishments vary and can range from community service or fines to incarceration and death. The reasons for punishment also vary and, many times, are imposed on offenders to meet several punishment purposes. Scholars traditionally separate the justifications for punishment into two categories: utilitarian and nonutilitarian (Frase, 2005).

Utilitarian punishments are thought to have a use or serve a purpose, such as preventing future crime. According to this view, the benefits of punishment must outweigh the harm/costs of that punishment to the individual offender and/or society. Traditional utilitarian justifications for punishment include rehabilitation, incapacitation, specific deterrence, and general deterrence (Frase, 2005). The goal of *rehabilitation* is to provide the offender with the treatment, education, and skills needed to become a prosocial and contributing member of society. Rehabilitation is forward looking and assumes that offenders have identifiable and remediable problems that cause them to commit crimes. *Incapacitation*, on the other hand, prevents future offending by imprisoning offenders and thereby physically restricting their ability to commit crime. *Specific deterrence* discourages the individual offender from recidivating by instilling fear about receiving similar or more severe punishment in the future. *General deterrence* seeks to discourage society at large from committing similar crimes by instilling fear in potential offenders of receiving a similar punishment. In this way, criminal penalties communicate the standards of a community to its members and allow society to gauge the relative seriousness of a crime based on the seriousness of the punishment that is imposed on the defendant.

By contrast, *nonutilitarian* punishments focus on the principles of justice and fairness (Frase, 2005). *Retribution*, perhaps the most well-known nonutilitarian purpose of punishment, is the idea that offenders should pay for their crimes and receive the "just desserts" of their actions. The theory of retribution asserts that offenders should be punished in direct proportion to the blameworthiness of their criminal actions (Frase, 2005). Blameworthiness is determined by the nature and seriousness of the harm caused and the offender's degree of culpability in committing the crime (Frase,

2005). *Proportionality* and *uniformity* in sentencing are also said to be nonutilitarian purposes of punishment because they are viewed as ends in themselves.

Like criminal punishment more generally, commonly cited rationales for the death penalty are retribution, incapacitation, deterrence, and denunciation. Taking up retribution first, in *Gregg*, the Supreme Court stated that retribution is one of several acceptable bases for the death penalty, although several of the Justices expressed the belief that punishment based primarily on retribution was beneath the dignity of the law. Death penalty proponents argue that there is no valid substitute for the death penalty and that the law should place less value on the life of a convicted murderer and more value on the life of the victim; death penalty opponents argue that death is never a just punishment for a crime and that legally sanctioned killing is morally wrong (Radelet & Borg, 2000).

Incapacitation is another justification cited by death penalty advocates insofar as executing convicted murderers will prevent them from committing violent crimes in the future (Radelet & Borg, 2000). Supporters of the death penalty argue that the death penalty axiomatically satisfies the purpose of incapacitation better than any other criminal punishment, whereas opponents note that a life sentence incapacitates an offender just as well as the death penalty does (Radelet & Borg, 2000).

Another penological justification for the death penalty is general deterrence. Imposing the death penalty on one murderer is believed to deter other potential murderers for fear of receiving the death penalty themselves (Radelet & Borg, 2000). However, general deterrence theory in a death penalty context raises two important questions. First, does imposition of the death penalty actually deter potential murderers? Second, is the death penalty unnecessary to deter those other murderers because a lesser punishment could achieve the same objective? The empirical research surrounding the deterrent effect of the death penalty is discussed later in this chapter.

Finally, although not a traditional justification for punishment, denunciation plays a role in death penalty jurisprudence on both a societal and individual level. On a societal level, imposing the death penalty sends a message that society considers certain crimes so heinous that individuals who commit them should face death at the hands of the state. On an individual level, the decision to seek the death penalty in a particular case can demonstrate that society considers the crime against that specific victim to be a great loss. On the other hand, putting offenders to death can be seen as devaluing life.

Risk Factors and Protective Factors

The identification of risk and protective factors for criminal offending has been widely studied and has substantial empirical support. *Risk factors* are those factors that suggest an increased probability of offending, and they may be causally linked to offending behavior or simply correlated with it (Andrews & Bonta, 2003). *Protective factors* serve as a buffer between an individual and the offending behavior. Protective factors mitigate the effect of risk factors on offending behavior and therefore reduce the likelihood of future offending (Shader, 2001).

Both risk factors and protective factors are cumulative, such that the ability to predict criminal behavior increases (or decreases) with the number of factors present and with the number of different sources of information used (Andrews & Bonta, 2003). Additionally, risk and protective factors interact with one another and can have a synergistic effect when several factors are present. Finally, different risk and protective factors become salient at different life stages. For example, risk factors related to the family have the greatest influence when people are young, whereas community-related risk factors (e.g., delinquent peers) have a larger effect during adolescence (e.g., DeMatteo & Marczyk, 2005).

To date, research regarding the identification of risk factors has focused on two areas: factors associated with initial criminal behavior and factors associated with criminal recidivism. Broadly speaking, there are two types of risk factors: static and dynamic. *Static* factors are those factors that do not change over time, such as gender and criminal history. *Dynamic* factors, also known as criminogenic needs, are changeable over time and include things like social support networks, educational level, substance use, and employment (Andrews & Bonta, 2003).

Risk factors are an important consideration because identifying dynamic risk factors for treatment is an empirically supported way to reduce the likelihood that an offender will engage in future violent behavior (Andrews & Bonta, 2003). Dynamic factors can be further divided into stable and acute risk factors (Hanson & Harris, 2001). Both stable and acute risk factors are changeable over time, but stable factors are more resistant to change and include characteristics like having procriminal associates or having antisocial personality disorder. Acute factors, by contrast, are capable of rapid change over time and include things such as mood and cooperation with authorities (Hanson & Harris, 2001).

The "big eight." The most well-supported factors for criminal offending are the "big (or central) eight," risk factors that were identified by Andrews and Bonta (2003): antisocial attitudes, antisocial associates, antisocial behavior, antisocial personality, problems at home, problems at school/work, problems in leisure circumstances, and substance use. In addition to these risk factors, researchers have identified other risk factors linked to violent crime. An exhaustive review of all risk factors linked to violent crime is beyond the scope of this chapter, so we instead summarize several major risk factors by domain.

Biological factors. Several researchers have found a relationship between prenatal care, delivery complications, and criminal offending (e.g., Raine, Brennan, & Mednick, 1994). For example, maternal smoking during pregnancy is associated with conduct disorder and problem behaviors in childhood and adolescence (e.g., Wakschlag et al., 1997). The research is inconsistent, however, with some researchers finding no relationship among these variables (e.g., Farrington, 1997). Regarding psychological and behavioral characteristics, several researchers have suggested that hyperactivity, attention difficulties, impulsivity, and risk-taking behavior are risk factors for later violent behavior (Hawkins et al., 1998). Low verbal IQ and delayed language development are also risk factors for offending, even after controlling for race and socioeconomic status (Moffitt, Lynam, & Silva, 1994).

Familial factors. Familial risk factors related to offending behavior include poor parenting skills, large family size, home discord, parental conflict, child maltreatment, and antisocial parents (Wasserman & Seracini, 2001). Harsh and punitive discipline has also been linked to later violent offending (McCord, 1979). Some researchers have suggested a relationship between being raised in a single-parent household and juvenile delinquency (McCord, Widom, & Crowell, 2001), although other researchers have suggested that socioeconomic conditions may account for this apparent relationship (Crockett, Eggebeen, & Hawkins, 1993).

School/employment factors. Difficulties at school or with employment are empirically supported risk factors for offending. One study found that children with academic problems, poor commitment to school, and low educational goals during elementary and middle school are at an increased risk for delinquency (Herrenkohl, Hawkins, Chung, Hill, & Battin-Pearson, 2001). Additionally, suspension and expulsion have been linked to increased delinquent behavior (McCord et al., 2001).

Peer/community factors. There is a strong link between involvement in a delinquent peer group and delinquent behavior (e.g., Lipsey & Derzon, 1998), and some researchers have suggested that spending time with peers who disapprove of offending behavior may be a protective factor that reduces later violent offending (Elliott, 1994). The influence of peers on offending behavior appears to be greater when youth have little interaction with their parents (Steinberg, 1987). Living in a neighborhood with high levels of poverty and crime also increases the likelihood that adolescents will commit crimes (McCord et al., 2001), but the exact interaction between personal and environmental factors remains unclear.

Protective factors. Empirically supported protective factors include high IQ, intolerant attitudes toward deviance, guilt, trustworthiness, high accountability, a positive attitude, strong relationships and communication with family, commitment to school, high educational achievement, associations with nondelinquent peers, and residing in a neighborhood with low crime rates (see Howell, 2003). Other protective factors may include positive social orientation, perceived sanctions for transgressions, supportive relationship with parents, parental monitoring, and recognition for involvement in conventional activities (Shader, 2001). Many of the protective factors related to juvenile delinquency also apply to criminal offending later in life, although some appear to be specific to juveniles.

Capital Sentencing–Specific Considerations

Mitigating factors. In the sentencing phase of a capital trial, jurors are asked to weigh aggravating and mitigating factors when reaching a sentencing decision. In most jurisdictions, the prosecution must prove the existence of at least one aggravating factor before the death penalty can be imposed. Aggravating factors are used to justify the sentence of death, whereas mitigating factors are used to make the defendant appear less culpable. Examples of defendant-specific mitigating factors include whether the defendant is remorseful, has limited intellectual abilities, suffers from organic brain syndrome, was under the influence of drugs or alcohol at the time of the offense, was abused as a child, and has a mental health history.

Categorical exclusions. The U.S. Supreme Court has categorically excluded certain classes of offenders from the death penalty, and two such classes are relevant for this chapter. In *Atkins v. Virginia* (2002), the Supreme Court held that executing offenders who are mentally retarded violates the Eighth Amendment's ban on cruel and unusual punishment (U.S. Const. amend. VIII). In a 6–3 decision, the Court reasoned that the execution of people with mental retardation is inconsistent with the retributive and deterrent functions of the death penalty because of the diminished moral and legal culpability of such persons. The Supreme Court also prohibited executing offenders who were under age 18 at the time of the offense. In *Roper v. Simmons* (2005),

in a 5–4 decision, the Court held that the execution of juvenile offenders was excessive and therefore violated the Eighth Amendment. In its Eighth Amendment analysis in both cases, the Court relied on evolving standards of decency to determine that there was a national consensus against executing these categories of offenders.

Mental Illness and the Death Penalty

Since the decisions in *Atkins* and *Roper*, scholars have questioned whether executing capital defendants with serious mental illness should also be categorically prohibited. Arguably, the same reasoning about diminished culpability as it relates to mental retardation could apply to the execution of individuals who are seriously mentally ill. Although mental retardation and mental illness differ in key respects, the analysis regarding diminished culpability given in *Atkins* seems applicable to individuals with a serious mental illness.

The American Bar Association (ABA), American Psychological Association (APA), American Psychiatric Association, and National Alliance on Mental Illness have all adopted nearly identical policies regarding mental disability and the death penalty. All four policies assert that defendants should not be executed or sentenced to death if, at the time of the offense, they had significant limitations in their intellectual functioning and adaptive behavior or had a severe mental disorder that significantly impaired their capacity to (a) appreciate the nature, consequences, or wrongfulness of their conduct; (b) exercise rational judgment in relation to conduct; or (c) conform their conduct to the requirements of the law (ABA Section of Individual Rights and Responsibilities, 2006; American Psychiatric Association, 2004; APA, 2001; National Alliance on Mental Illness, 2009). The policies promulgated by these organizations also urge exemption from the death penalty for capital offenders whose onset of mental disorder or disability occurred after sentencing, arguing that these offenders may not be able to fully understand the nature of their punishment and may not be able to adequately communicate information and make rational decisions about the associated legal proceedings.

In addition to being repudiated by leading national mental health and legal organizations, executing the mentally ill is prohibited by several sources of international law. According to Amnesty International (2006), nearly every country in the world bans the execution of people with mental illness. A report from Amnesty International indicated that the international resolution, "United Nations Safeguards Guaranteeing Protection of the Rights of Those Facing the Death Penalty," which was adopted in 1984, prohibits the execution of offenders with mental illness. Additionally, this report urged governments that continue to impose death sentences on offenders with mental illness to bring their domestic legislation into conformity with international legal standards. Finally, in 2000, the United Nations Commission on Human Rights adopted a resolution urging all states that maintain the death penalty to not impose it on (or execute) a person who is suffering from any form of mental disorder (Amnesty International, 2006).

RESEARCH REVIEW

Effectiveness of the Death Penalty

A common argument in support of capital punishment is that it has a greater deterrent effect on murder than does a life sentence or lengthy incarceration (see Radelet & Borg, 2000). Presumably, according to this line of reasoning, potential murderers are deterred from committing murder because they view the threat of execution as being greater than the threat of imprisonment. Death penalty advocates often cite empirical research as supporting their assertion that capital punishment reduces homicide rates (see Radelet & Borg, 2000). Several of these oft-cited studies make lofty claims about the general deterrent effect of capital punishment, arguing that one execution saves as many as 18 lives (Dezhbakhsh, Rubin, & Shepherd, 2003), and that one commutation of a death sentence leads to four or five murders (Fagan, 2006). Other researchers have argued that the deterrent effect of executions is sufficiently powerful to influence irrational acts such as *heat-of-passion* murders (Shepherd, 2004) and even

to enhance the deterrent effect of lesser punishments (Liu, 2004).

However, other researchers caution against drawing broad conclusions based on deterrence studies. After reanalyzing data that had been previously used to support claims of the deterrent effect of capital sentencing, Donohue and Wolfers (2005) found that when the low base rate of executions was taken into account, it would be impossible to disentangle the potential deterrent effects of executions from the annual fluctuations in homicide rates. Similarly, researchers whose work has been widely cited as supporting the deterrent effect of capital punishment in Texas recently reanalyzed some of their data (Land, Teske, & Zheng, 2012; see Land, Teske, & Zheng, 2009; Siennick, 2012) and found that the previously observed short-term deterrent effect of capital punishment in Texas actually did not apply to felony homicides; rather, death-eligible felony homicides increased after an execution, and the observed reduction in nonfelony homicides was short lived. A potential explanation for these findings is that potential murderers are confused or uneducated about the death penalty. Unfortunately, we know little about potential murderers' comprehension of capital sentencing, which makes it challenging to draw conclusions about whether their perception of capital sentencing is accurate and whether it influences their behavior (Fagan, Geller, & Zimring, 2012).

There is little evidence to support the claim that capital punishment deters homicide. Most of the early studies from the 1970s that seemingly supported the deterrence hypothesis were later criticized and discredited (Radelet & Lacock, 2009), and recent studies supporting the deterrent effect have faced similar reproach. It is admittedly difficult to study the effects of capital sentencing on crime, but the weight of the evidence suggests that the death penalty does not reduce the rate of homicides. In fact, some studies have found that capital punishment increases homicide rates in some jurisdictions (e.g., Shepherd, 2005). Two years after the Supreme Court effectively reinstated the death penalty, the National Research Council (NRC) issued a statement concluding that the extant research provided no useful evidence on the deterrent effect of capital punishment (NRC, 1978). A more recent comprehensive review of data collected over the past three decades indicated that there is still insufficient data to conclude that capital punishment affects homicide rates (NRC, 2012).

Societal Views

Capital punishment has also been tried in the court of public opinion. Societal views about the death penalty have changed over the past few decades and reflect waning support for the deterrence hypothesis of capital punishment. A 1985 Gallup poll revealed that 62% of respondents believed that the death penalty deterred murder; by 2006, only 34% of respondents answered the same question affirmatively (J. M. Jones, 2006). A 1995 survey of police chiefs and sheriffs revealed that these criminal justice professionals generally shared public sentiment regarding the deterrent effect of executions, with two-thirds of respondents espousing the belief that the death penalty does not reduce the rate of homicides (D. W. Moore, 2004). Importantly, 88% of premier criminologists in the United States concluded that capital punishment does not deter homicide (Radelet & Lacock, 2009).

Public opinion polls paint a mixed picture of public support for capital punishment. Gallup's 2012 annual survey showed steady support for the death penalty, with 63% of Americans favoring it as a punishment for murder, which was a 2% increase from 2011 (Saad, 2013). Conversely, the 2012 American Values Survey revealed that more Americans supported life without parole (47%) than capital punishment (46%) as a penalty for murder (R. P. Jones, Cox, Navarro-Rivera, Dionne, & Galston, 2012). Notably, there are demographic divisions, with Caucasians, males, and Republicans showing greater support for capital sentencing than other groups (J. M. Jones, 2003). Interestingly, public support for capital punishment wanes considerably when alternative punishment options are presented (such as life imprisonment), suggesting that although many Americans may find capital punishment to be an *acceptable* form of punishment, they find other forms of punishment to be *preferable* (e.g., Bowers, Vandiver, & Dugan, 1994).

Assessments of Future Dangerousness

Questions about violence risk play an integral role in death penalty cases, so it is not surprising that many researchers have focused on this important topic. Of the 35 states that currently permit the death penalty, at least 21 states allow or require capital sentencing juries to consider a defendant's risk for future violence when deciding on an appropriate sentence (see DeMatteo, Murrie, Anumba, & Keesler, 2011). In many death penalty jurisdictions, consideration of a defendant's risk for future violence is a common component of capital sentencing proceedings, and research suggests that sentencing juries appear to focus a great deal on a defendant's likelihood of being violent in the future even if such a focus is not required in that jurisdiction (see, e.g., Blume, Garvey, & Johnson, 2000).

The focus on a defendant's risk for future violence stems from the Supreme Court's emphasis on *individualized sentencing* of capital defendants. In a series of cases that were decided after the death penalty was effectively reinstated by the Court in 1976 (see *Gregg v. Georgia*), the Court held that capital sentencing juries must particularize the sentence to the offender and offense (e.g., *Eddings v. Oklahoma*, 1982). This approach was viewed as a safeguard against the imposition of arbitrary and/or disproportionate punishment in capital cases. The Supreme Court has also specifically upheld capital sentencing schemes that require an assessment of a defendant's risk of future violence (e.g., *Jurek v. Texas*, 1976). Although the Court recognized in *Jurek* that assessing an individual's risk of future violence is difficult, it upheld the process as being an integral part of the sentencing determination. A few years later, in *Barefoot v. Estelle* (1983), the Court upheld the admissibility of psychiatric testimony addressing a capital defendant's risk of future violence.

It is important to note, however, that capital sentencing juries are typically deciding between a sentence of death or a sentence of life in prison without the possibility of parole; release to the community in the foreseeable future is not an option in the vast majority of capital cases. As such, assessments of a defendant's risk of future violence should focus on the risk of prison violence, not violence in the community (see Cunningham, 2008; Edens, Buffington-Vollum,

Keilen, Roskamp, & Anthony, 2005). Although some courts have recognized that violence risk assessments are specific to the prison context, other courts have not explicitly acknowledged the specific context.

Given the context of violence risk assessments, it is instructive to examine relevant research on base rates of violence in correctional contexts. Such an inquiry is particularly important because violence risk is a function of the individual and the context in which the individual is placed (see Conroy & Murrie, 2007). DeMatteo et al. (2011) recently provided a synthesis of the relevant research on the base rates of violence in correctional contexts.

- Rates of serious prison violence are no higher among murderers than among other types of offenders (Cunningham, Reidy, & Sorensen, 2008; Sorensen & Cunningham, 2010).
- Rates of prison violence are no higher among capital murderers who are sentenced to death than among capital murderers who are sentenced to life without parole (Cunningham, Reidy, & Sorensen, 2005).
- Rates of prison violence among capital murderers who are sentenced to life without parole are no higher than rates among inmates who are convicted of lesser degrees of murder (Sorensen & Wrinkle, 1996) or other inmates who are serving long-term sentences (Cunningham et al., 2008).
- Capital murderers who are eligible for parole in the distant future are less likely to commit violence than are capital murderers who are eligible for parole in the nearer future (Morris, Longmire, Buffington-Vollum, & Vollum, 2010).
- Most capital murderers are never sanctioned for physical violence in prison (Edens et al., 2005; Marquart, Ekland-Olson, & Sorensen, 1994).
- Rates of prison violence among capital offenders are low (<10%; Cunningham et al., 2008; Edens et al., 2005).
- Rates of prison homicide among capital murderers are low (<1%) and are no higher than those among noncapital inmates (e.g., Cunningham et al., 2008; Sorensen & Cunningham, 2009).

For forensic mental health professionals who conduct assessments of future violence in capital cases,

the starting point is recognizing that serious violence in prison settings is exceedingly rare. The assessment can then be individualized, which contributes to individualized sentencing, by considering empirically supported risk factors of prison violence. Researchers have identified several risk factors for prison violence, including younger age (Gendreau, Goggin, & Law, 1997), prior prison violence (Sorensen & Cunningham, 2009; Sorensen & Pilgrim, 2000), prior prison terms (Cunningham & Sorensen, 2006; Cunningham, Sorensen, & Reidy, 2005), failing to complete high school or obtain a general educational development (GED) certificate (Cunningham & Sorensen, 2006; Cunningham, Sorensen, & Reidy, 2005), and prison gang membership (Sorensen & Pilgrim, 2000). Consideration of relevant base rates and empirically supported risk factors for prison violence form the basis of a capital sentencing evaluation.

Methodological Limitations

Research on the deterrence hypothesis has faced considerable rebuttal over the years. Most studies that have examined the deterrent effect of capital sentencing fall into one of two categories. *Panel data* studies analyze sets of states over time, comparing homicide rates with the status of capital punishment and the frequency of executions, whereas *time-series* studies generally explore short-term changes in homicide frequency in a particular geographic region immediately following an execution. Both forms of research suffer from methodological flaws and reliance on unverifiable assumptions.

The NRC (2012) identified two flaws plaguing most research examining the deterrent effect of capital punishment. First, although most convicted murderers are not executed (even in states with capital punishment), existing studies do not account for noncapital alternative sanctions for homicide that are used by jurisdictions with capital punishment. This is unfortunate because it is imperative that the differential deterrent effect of execution over other possible sanctions be considered in order to determine whether capital punishment has a deterrent effect. In fact, research suggests that it is not the severity of punishment but rather the likelihood that it will be meted out that affects deterrence (von Hirsch, Bottoms, Burney, & Wikstrom, 1999).

Second, the NRC (2012) noted that most studies examining the deterrent effect of capital punishment fail to use complete and plausible models that capture potential murderers' conceptualization of and response to capital punishment as a potential consequence of homicide. Making a decision of whether to kill while weighing the objective risk of potential execution is a complex calculation that requires the consideration of many facts that are likely unknown to the potential murderer, such as the small percentage of individuals who are sentenced to death who have been executed and the large number of death sentences that are overturned. It is unlikely that such individuals would have sufficient understanding of the practical implementation of capital sentencing in order to compute an accurate calculation of execution risk. In actuality, a potential murderer's *perceived* risk of being executed likely varies substantially from his or her *objective* risk of being executed, but the direction and degree of this discrepancy are unknown. Making assumptions about deterrence based in part on such ambiguous information may lead to erroneous conclusions and ill-informed legislation and policy making.

Studies supporting the deterrent effect of capital punishment have raised other methodological concerns. Taking issue with the lack of scientific rigor and deficient peer review process that are in place to evaluate the integrity of research on capital punishment and deterrence, Fagan (2006) described several fundamental flaws afflicting a recent wave of studies supporting the deterrent effect of executions on homicide rates and purported antagonistic effect of pardons, commutations, and exonerations. Fagan argued that many researchers used inappropriate statistical analyses, erroneously drew causal connections between executions and homicide rates while ignoring potentially confounding variables, and statistically confounded homicide rates with death sentences. Moreover, Fagan asserted that several of the studies (a) were missing key data on important variables, (b) capitalized on extreme outliers and truncated time frames, and (c) neglected to consider the general effectiveness of the criminal justice system on reducing homicide rates.

Recently, researchers have made efforts to conduct studies that address these methodological

concerns. In one study, researchers analyzing state panel data using well-known econometric procedures found no deterrent effect of executions on homicide rates (Kovandzic, Vieraitis, & Boots, 2009). The researchers argued that their study was superior to other deterrence studies because it avoided common statistical problems and controlled for many potentially confounding variables (Kovandzic et al., 2009). Admittedly, it is challenging to conduct quality research on the deterrent effect of capital punishment. Randomized controlled trials, which are the gold standard of research in many fields, are rare in criminal justice settings, and it simply may not be possible to draw meaningful conclusions about the deterrent effect of capital sentencing based on observational studies. Because capital punishment is such a polarizing subject, however, people on both sides of the aisle often tout their beliefs as being well supported by the literature, despite limited empirical evidence.

There are many myths about capital punishment, which clouds the facts and hinders the dissemination of empirical evidence. Myths about capital punishment include beliefs that it is the most cost-effective solution to crime, vindicates victims' families, is widely supported by the public, and is reserved for the worst criminals. However, capital sentences are more expensive than life sentences, with estimates suggesting that they cost roughly eight times as much as life sentences (Gould & Greenman, 2010). Moreover, there are many examples of victims' families speaking out against capital punishment, and there is mixed evidence regarding whether the majority of U.S. citizens prefer the death penalty to other sanctions (e.g., Niven, 2002). Finally, rather than being reserved for the most reprehensible offenders, research suggests that death sentences may be influenced by extra-legal variables such as the defendant's or victim's demographics (e.g., Baldus, Pulaski, & Woodworth, 1983).

In light of the flaws in many studies examining capital sentencing, particularly those investigating its deterrent effect, the NRC (2012) offered recommendations for future research. Specifically, it proposed that future research examine potential murderers' perceptions of various murder sanctions and include comprehensive specification of capital and noncapital homicide sanctions. Moreover, the NRC recommended using methodology based on more credible and verifiable assumptions regarding the effect of capital punishment on the homicide rate. Ultimately, the quality of research on capital sentencing rests heavily on the types of questions that are asked. Future studies should continue to examine whether and how capital punishment affects homicide rates in the short and long term and whether the manner and frequency with which executions are carried out are important variables impacting crime.

PRACTICE AND POLICY ISSUES

Since its ruling in *Gregg v. Georgia*, the U.S. Supreme Court has consistently held that the death penalty is only appropriate in certain instances and with certain types of offenders. A litany of rulings since 1976 has helped to limit and guide legal decision makers in determining whether to impose a life sentence or death sentence. Cases like *Atkins* (prohibiting the execution of offenders with mental retardation) and *Roper* (prohibiting the execution of juvenile offenders) reflect the Supreme Court's emphasis on moral culpability in capital sentencing.

In addition to the issue of moral culpability, the Supreme Court has consistently held that the death penalty may not be imposed on individuals who are not competent to be executed (*Ford v. Wainwright*, 1986; *Panetti v. Quarterman*, 2007). The reasoning here has less to do with moral culpability but rather with the notion that it offends a collective sense of justice to execute someone who does not comprehend the reason for the ultimate punishment (*Ford v. Wainwright*). Additionally, scholars have acknowledged that traditional notions of sentencing and punishment (e.g., deterrence, retribution) are not served by such executions (Slobogin, Rai, & Reisner, 2009).

Guided by the aforementioned case law and relevant legal questions, forensic mental health professionals working in capital cases may conduct (a) *Atkins*-type evaluations to determine whether a capital defendant is intellectually disabled, (b) CFE evaluations to determine whether a defendant is competent to be executed, and (c) capital sentencing evaluations to identify historical or contextual factors that enhance or lessen an individual's moral culpability in the eyes of the sentencing jury. These evaluations will each be addressed in turn, but first a few principles to guide these evaluations should be highlighted.

Principles of Forensic Mental Health Assessment in Capital Cases

Although entire works have been devoted to principled forensic mental health assessment (e.g., Heilbrun, 2001; Heilbrun, Grisso, & Goldstein, 2009; Heilbrun, Marczyk, & DeMatteo, 2002), a few items are worth highlighting in the context of capital cases. At the outset, conducting a thorough evaluation is of paramount importance. Examinees in such evaluations are facing the ultimate penalty, which is irreversible once carried out, and there may not be any possibility of meaningful redress for evaluator error or misconduct. Thus, evaluators who are insufficiently trained, lack the necessary time, or cannot proceed without bias should avoid becoming involved in capital cases. Before becoming involved in capital cases, evaluators should be knowledgeable about relevant substantive and procedural law, including the procedural process and legal standards governing how the evaluation will be conducted and what it will address. Moreover, evaluators should have experience with complex clinical presentations, co-occurring mental health disorders, chronic substance use, and the possibility of malingering, all of which can be present in capital cases.

Prior to beginning the evaluation, the evaluator should obtain informed consent (if hired by an attorney) or provide a notification of purpose (if the evaluation is court ordered); notification of purpose involves relaying to the examinee the purpose of the evaluation, who requested the evaluation, what it will entail, potential outcomes, how the evaluation will be used, and limits on confidentiality. Throughout the evaluation, the evaluator should meet applicable standards of practice but also aspire to best practices (see APA, 2002, 2013).

In addition to obtaining data from the examinee (typically through interview and testing), the evaluator should consult relevant records and other third-party sources of information. This multimodal assessment aids in assessing an examinee's response style and the veracity of self-report. Individuals being evaluated in forensic contexts have incentives to engage in impression management by providing information (self-report, clinical presentation) that they think could tilt a legal disposition in their favor (Heilbrun, DeMatteo, Brooks Holliday, & LaDuke, 2014). To confirm self-report, the evaluator should seek information from a range of sources, including knowledgeable third parties (e.g., family, friends, significant others, coworkers, supervisors, correctional officers) and archival records (e.g., medical, mental health, educational, criminal justice, employment). There are also some measures that can help assess an examinee's response style, including the Structured Interview of Reported Symptoms (Rogers, Sewell, & Gillard, 2010), the Miller Forensic Assessment of Symptoms Test (Miller, 2001), and the Validity Indicator Profile (Frederick, 1997). Personality measures such as the Minnesota Multiphasic Personality Inventory—2 (Butcher, Dahlstrom, Graham, Tellegen, & Kaemmer, 1989) and the Personality Assessment Inventory (Morey, 1991) also contain validity indicators that can be used to help assess an examinee's response style.

After gathering the data, the evaluator communicates the information via a report and possibly testimony. An ongoing debate focuses on whether the evaluator should answer the ultimate legal question being decided by the court (e.g., "Yes, the defendant is competent to be executed"). Opponents of rendering ultimate-issue opinions contend that offering such opinions invades the province of the legal decision maker (e.g., Grisso, 2003), whereas proponents argue that answering the ultimate legal issue is expected by judges, attorneys, and jurors, and also leads to enhanced understanding of the evaluation results (e.g., Rogers & Shuman, 2000). Although no resolution to the debate appears imminent, the evaluator should be aware of its existence and the arguments on each side, including applicable state and/ or federal law.

Atkins-Type Evaluations

As noted earlier, in *Atkins v. Virginia* (2002), the U.S. Supreme Court held that executing offenders who are mentally retarded violates the Eighth Amendment's prohibition against cruel and unusual punishment. Although the *Atkins* decision appears straightforward, the Supreme Court left much undetermined. Among other things, the Court did not define mental retardation. Instead, the Court simply stated that each state's definition must be consistent with a "national consensus," and it charged each state with "developing appropriate ways to enforce the constitutional restriction" (*Atkins v. Virginia*, 2002, p. 317). The Court did, however, offer guidance in a footnote that referenced (not endorsed) definitions of mental retardation from the American Association on Intellectual and Developmental Disabilities (AAIDD, 2010) and the American Psychiatric Association (per the *Diagnostic and Statistical Manual of Mental Disorders, Fourth Edition, Text Revision; DSM–IV–TR;* American Psychiatric Association, 2000).

The *DSM–IV–TR* (American Psychiatric Association, 2000) defines mental retardation using three criteria: significantly subaverage intellectual functioning (which is an IQ score of approximately ≤70), concurrent deficits in adaptive functioning in two or more areas, and age of onset before age 18. The recently released *DSM–5* (American Psychiatric Association, 2013) defines intellectual disability as requiring deficits in intellectual functioning (IQ score of 65–75); deficits in adaptive functioning in conceptual, social, and practical domains; and onset during the developmental period. AAMR, which is now the American Association on Intellectual and Developmental Disabilities (AAIDD), defined mental retardation in 2010 using the same three elements as the *DSM–IV–TR*, but the IQ cutoff was 75 and adaptive functioning was defined differently.

Although not referenced by the Supreme Court in *Atkins*, it is worth noting that the APA has its own definition of mental retardation: APA defines mental retardation in terms of significant limitations in general intellectual functioning (i.e., IQ scores that are ≥2 *SD*s below the mean IQ score on a valid and comprehensive individual measure of intelligence), significant concurrent limitations in adaptive functioning, and age of onset prior to age 22 (Jacobson & Mulick, 1996).

Given the Court's lack of guidance in *Atkins*, it was unclear how states would respond in terms of both defining mental retardation and outlining a procedural framework. In the wake of *Atkins*, DeMatteo, Marczyk, and Pich (2007) conducted a state-by-state statutory survey and grouped states by their statutory definition of mental retardation. Results revealed that less than one-quarter of the states defined mental retardation using accepted clinical standards—*DSM–IV–TR* (American Psychiatric Association, 2000; 5 states), AAIDD (6 states), APA (1 state)—with the majority of states neglecting to mention all three elements or failing to operationally define the key elements. In addition to definitional differences, variations exist among states in their procedural framework for determining mental retardation (DeMatteo et al., 2007). These include when evaluations can be conducted (e.g., pretrial, after guilt, postsentencing), who can conduct them (e.g., MD, PhD), and how they should be conducted. Finally, there are variations among states regarding the burden of proof for mental retardation in terms of what burden must be satisfied, whether the burden rests on the defense or prosecution, and whether the ultimate finding of mental retardation is made by a judge or jury.

Conducting an *Atkins*-type evaluation. The first step in an *Atkins*-type evaluation is for the evaluator to ensure familiarity with the guiding law. In addition to checking sources that describe the relevant state laws (e.g., DeMatteo et al., 2011), the evaluator can check with the hiring attorney or ordering court. As described in the following paragraphs, there are several considerations relevant to the assessment of clinically defined mental retardation in relation to the three key elements: measurement of IQ, assessment of adaptive functioning, and age of onset.

All clinical definitions of mental retardation include an element relating to intellectual functioning, so a formal measurement of IQ is an indispensable component of an *Atkins*-type evaluation. Unfortunately, common legal reliance on IQ as a bright-line test of mental retardation (i.e., ≤70) does not align well with psychology's conceptualization of IQ measurement. Namely, psychologists recognize an inherent degree of measurement error in commonly used intelligence tests; the Wechsler (2008) and Stanford–Binet (Roid, 2003) measures of intelligence, for example, have a measurement error

of between three and five points (e.g., Koocher, 2003). Measurement error can arise from various sources, including administration, environment, condition of examinee, timing errors, and properties of the instrument. Thus, evaluators should recognize that the IQ yielded by intelligence testing is an IQ estimate *plus* measurement error.

The *DSM–5* (American Psychiatric Association, 2013) recognizes an upper limit measurement error of five points and provides that an IQ of 75 can support a diagnosis of mental retardation if the criteria for adaptive functioning and age of onset are met. Measurement error proves more problematic in states that define mental retardation without reference to such error. For example, there are cases in which a defendant seeking *Atkins* protection challenged an IQ score that was slightly greater than 70. In *Cherry v. Florida* (2007), the defendant reportedly had an IQ of 72. The state argued that this disqualified him from *Atkins* protection; the defense asserted that Cherry's IQ should be viewed as falling between 67 and 77 due to measurement error. The Supreme Court of Florida rejected the defense's argument and dismissed the *Atkins* claim because Cherry's IQ of 72 was over the statutory cutoff of 70. Although this is a sobering example, it contextualizes a good teaching point. In attempts to better align the legal bright-line approach with a more balanced approach, evaluators should consider reporting IQ with a confidence interval, which highlights that it is an IQ estimation rather than a perfect measurement. In a recent decision that supports the consideration of measurement error, the U.S. Supreme Court held that Florida's use of a strict IQ cutoff score of 70 was unconstitutional because, among other things, it failed to take account of measurement error (*Hall v. Florida*, 2014).

In calculating an IQ estimate, there are other issues of which evaluators should be aware. IQ is a human construct that is designed to capture the population's normally distributed intelligence (Wasserman & Tulsky, 2005). During test construction and norming, tests are adjusted until normally distributed patterns of performance emerge, at which point the mean performance is tethered to an IQ of 100. As time passes, though, the population gradually and systematically improves its performance, such that a random sample will no longer yield a mean IQ of 100 (Kamphaus, Winsor, Rowe, & Kim, 2005). Named for the researcher who identified this trend, the Flynn effect produces IQ estimates of increasing inflation since the most recent norming, ultimately making IQ test norms obsolete every 20 years or so (Flynn, 1998, 2006). Most sources report an increase in measured IQ of approximately .3 points each year between renormings (Flynn, 1984, 1999), with the previously mentioned Wechsler and Stanford–Binet measures changing at roughly uniform rates (Flynn, 2006).

The Flynn effect has clear implications for *Atkins*-type evaluations in light of courts' heavy reliance on IQ scores. We are unaware of any state statutes that specifically address the Flynn effect, though some case law has emerged as courts have adopted positions concerning it (see Flynn, 2006). The obvious practical solution may seem to be to lower an examinee's measured IQ by .3 points for each year since the test was last normed. Whereas some researchers support this approach (e.g., Kanaya, Scullin, & Ceci, 2003), others counter that adjusting IQ scores does not represent best practices (e.g., Hagan, Drogin, & Guilmette, 2008; R. B. Moore, 2006). Lacritz and Cullum (2003) noted that such simple algebra presumes that nomothetic data about populations can generalize to an individual, which is an error known as the *ecological fallacy*. There is no agreed-on solution for the Flynn effect, but it is important for evaluators to be aware of it.

Practice effects or *test–retest effects* occur when intelligence tests are administered in close temporal proximity, which yields inflated estimates of an individual's intellectual functioning (Lichtenberger & Kaufman, 2009). Death penalty jurisdictions vary regarding the number of assessments that are permissible within a given time frame. Some death penalty jurisdictions account for test–retest effects, some are silent on the issue, and others require multiple administrations by opposing sides despite contraindicating research (DeMatteo et al., 2011). According to the Wechsler Adult Intelligence Scale—Fourth Edition (Wechsler, 2008) technical and interpretive manual, the shortest test–retest time interval that will not produce practice effects is currently unknown. Of note, though, the technical

manual for the Wechsler Adult Intelligence Scale—Third Edition (Wechsler, 1997) cautions that the mean full-scale IQ score for adults between ages 30 and 54 increases by approximately 5 points if those adults retook the same test within 12 weeks of the initial administration. A difference of 5 points has clear implications for *Atkins*-type evaluations, especially in states where an IQ of less than 70 is the hallmark criterion. As such, an interval of at least 1 to 2 years between tests is advisable. In states that allow the prosecution to rebut a defense finding of mental retardation with its own evaluation, a particular danger of practice effects exists, setting the stage for conflicting measurements between defense and prosecution experts.

The *DSM–5* (American Psychiatric Association, 2013), AAIDD, and APA definitions of mental retardation require deficits in adaptive functioning. Although there are slight variations among the three criteria sets, they are generally comparable, and *adaptive functioning* refers to how well individuals meet the routine demands of life and whether they are able to do so at a level that is consistent with their age, social and cultural background, and living situation (DeMatteo et al., 2007). Deficits in adaptive functioning are typically clear in cases of moderate, severe, or profound mental retardation, but it becomes more difficult to identify adaptive functioning deficits in cases of mild mental retardation. When assessing adaptive functioning in capital cases, the evaluator should rely on multiple sources of information, including observation, interview, and collateral interviews. The evaluator should exercise caution when using standardized measures to assess deficits in adaptive functioning because existing measures have not been designed or normed for use with a correctional population (Brodsky & Galloway, 2003; Tassé, 2009). Additionally, although standardized measures may be more appropriate for pretrial inmates than for death row inmates, the jurisdiction may nonetheless demand the use of such measures (DeMatteo et al., 2011). In such an instance, the evaluator should be aware of this issue and be able to defend any heightened reliance on clinical judgment over the standardized measure.

A few other issues are worth highlighting regarding the assessment of an individual's adaptive functioning. The structure of a correctional facility can facilitate an offender's ability to meet the demands of daily living, which may give a false appearance that the offender has no substantial adaptive deficits. Also, due to the antisocial overtones of the environment, the definition of adaptive or normative behavior can be different from how adaptive is defined in the community (Brodsky & Galloway, 2003). Further, a debate exists about whether information relating to criminal behavior and incarcerated behavior provides evidence of adaptive behavior, with only certain courts and legislatures concluding that criminal behavior is relevant (see Blume, Johnson, & Seeds, 2009).

With any determination of adaptive functioning, there is an element of clinical judgment, but following best practices and arriving at well-supported conclusions places evaluators on stronger footing. In choosing standardized measures of adaptive functioning, it is important to pick those with good psychometric properties while acknowledging that they were not designed for an offender population. If an evaluator decides not to use standardized measures, the assessment should nonetheless use multimodal assessment and multiple sources of data (Heilbrun, 2001).

The final criterion for a diagnosis of mental retardation is age of onset, and there is variability among the three primary clinical definitions of intellectual disability. The *DSM–5* requires that the deficits be present during childhood and adolescence, AAIDD requires that the disorder manifest before age 18 years, and APA specifies a cutoff age of 22 years (American Psychiatric Association, 2013; DeMatteo et al., 2007). Despite the Supreme Court's language in *Atkins* that focuses on the reduced moral culpability of the intellectually impaired, individuals with acquired impairment (e.g., veterans with traumatic brain injury) are not protected by *Atkins* if the impairment occurred after the age cutoff. Although the Court's approach was likely intended to offer limited and specific protection, restricting *Atkins* protection to individuals with true mental retardation rather than those with exclusively intellectual and functional impairment reduces the likelihood of malingering. After all, feigning a diagnosis of mental retardation for *Atkins* protection would require

historical continuity dating to before the capital offense. Age of onset is typically determined by reviewing educational, mental health, and other records with information that is relevant to the defendant's intellectual and adaptive deficits. However, it should be noted that the age of onset requirement does not require that a formal diagnosis was ever made, nor does it require standardized test scores from that time period; there must simply be evidence that the disorder manifested prior to the age of onset cutoff (DeMatteo et al., 2011).

Presenting findings of an *Atkins*-type evaluation. As with other forensic mental health assessments, *Atkins*-type evaluations typically culminate with a report and possibly testimony (Heilbrun et al., 2002). An unusual aspect of an *Atkins*-type evaluation is that the evaluator is answering the ultimate legal issue. Although evaluators are often advised to avoid answering the ultimate legal issue (see, e.g., Heilbrun et al., 2009), the ultimate legal issue in an *Atkins*-type evaluation is the presence or absence of mental retardation, which must necessarily be addressed in the evaluation.

CFE Evaluations

The common law prohibition against executing incompetent defendants dates back several hundred years, but the first time the U.S. Supreme Court addressed the issue was in 1986 in *Ford v. Wainwright*, which held that the Eighth Amendment's prohibition against cruel and unusual punishment prohibited executing incompetent offenders. Unfortunately, the Court did not provide a legal standard for determining incompetence and (as in *Atkins*) charged each state with developing appropriate procedural safeguards to carry out its decision. However, in a concurring opinion in *Ford* (1986), Justice Powell stated that the Eighth Amendment should prohibit "execution of those who are unaware of the punishment they are about to suffer and why they are to suffer it" (p. 422). Most courts that addressed the issue after *Ford* adopted Justice Powell's standard (Otto, 2009).

More than 20 years later, in *Panetti v. Quarterman*, the Supreme Court addressed whether to extend the protection that was initially afforded by

Ford. Specifically, the Court examined whether the Eighth Amendment (U.S. Const. amend. VIII) permits execution of an offender who *has factual awareness* of the reasons for execution but, because of severe mental illness, *lacks rational understanding* about why the execution is taking place. The Court held that CFE requires both factual awareness and rational understanding of the reasoning. Although the Court specified the need for both factual and rational understanding in order for an offender to be competent for execution, it did not articulate what standard to apply. As a result, states have adopted differing frameworks, with some adding the additional requirement that a defendant be capable of assisting legal counsel (see DeMatteo et al., 2011).

The *Ford* and *Panetti* decisions have both philosophical and practical support. Philosophically, society recognizes that to execute an individual who cannot comprehend his or her execution is unjust and does not serve either deterrence or retribution (Slobogin et al., 2009). Practically, the common age of onset for severe and persistent mental illness—late adolescence and early adulthood—overlaps with the age range of many capital defendants (Costanzo & White, 1994). Additionally, mental health professionals have noted that the stress of years spent on death row can contribute to an individual's psychological deterioration (e.g., Haney, 2003).

Conducting a CFE evaluation. Brodsky, Zapf, and Boccaccini (2001) described CFE evaluations as "low demand, high impact evaluations" (p. 21). These evaluations are rarely conducted, so there is limited literature on best practices. Shortly after *Ford,* Heilbrun (1987) and Heilbrun and McClaren (1988) addressed the ethical considerations and clinical procedures in preadjudication versus postadjudication evaluation contexts. Small and Otto (1991) offered additional guidance, discussing specific evaluation techniques and placing less emphasis on testing and more on functional abilities. More recently, after *Panetti,* Zapf and colleagues identified guiding frameworks and professional standards for these evaluations (Zapf, 2008, 2009; Zapf, Boccaccini, & Brodsky, 2003). Most recently, DeMatteo et al. (2011) synthesized and distilled recommendations and guidelines based on the extant literature, and those major recommendations and guidelines are condensed here.

The hallmark of most forensic evaluations, the clinical interview, is the most critical component in CFE evaluations. Because competence is a present-focused legal question, assessing an examinee's current psychological function is a necessity (Heilbrun, 2001). The scope of the clinical interview should be guided by the legal standard, which means focusing on whether the examinee possesses a factual understanding of the offense, impending execution, and reason for the execution, *as well as* a rational understanding of the nexus between the offense and the execution (see *Panetti,* 2007). Whereas assessing factual understanding may be straightforward, assessing rational understanding is more amorphous. Otto (2009) provided some guidance, highlighting how impaired thought content, impaired thought process or form, cognitive impairment, or mood disorders can all affect an individual's rational understanding.

Despite the rarity of CFE evaluations, several instruments have been developed to assist evaluators, although these instruments have not been updated since *Panetti.* Ebert (2001) developed a checklist for CFE evaluations that assessed eight functional legal abilities and four clinical areas. Unfortunately, there are no psychometric data for Ebert's measure, and there is no indication for how information gleaned from this instrument should be used to determine post-*Panetti* competence. Two years later, Zapf et al. (2003) developed the Interview Checklist for Evaluations of Competency for Execution, which assesses an offender's (a) understanding of the reasons for punishment, (b) understanding of the punishment, (c) appreciation and reasoning, and (d) ability to assist the attorney. Zapf et al. deemed these four criteria to be representative of the legal criteria for CFE that are found in many states. Although this measure was developed before *Panetti,* Zapf et al. recognized the importance of assessing an offender's appreciation and reasoning abilities.

More recently, Ackerson, Brodsky, and Zapf (2005) developed the Competency for Execution Research Rating Scales (CERRS), which to our knowledge is the only instrument with empirical research support. The CERRS was developed following a survey of 113 judges with authority to impose a death sentence, and it assesses an individual's (a) understanding and appreciation of punishment, (b) understanding and appreciation of death, (c) capacity to work with counsel, and (d) relevant clinical information. Ackerson et al. then asked 90 forensic psychologists to assess CFE based on nine fictional vignettes. Of those 90 psychologists, 41 respondents used the CERRS, and those 41 appropriately weighed both legal and clinical factors when making their determinations (Ackerson et al., 2005).

Presenting findings of a CFE evaluation. The product of a CFE evaluation is typically a report with the possibility of testimony. Because of the charged nature of such evaluations, the expert is likely to come under scrutiny, so it is important that the evaluation and report reflect best practices (Heilbrun et al., 2002). In reporting or testifying on the findings of a CFE evaluation, there is concern about addressing the ultimate issue. In light of the debate described earlier in this chapter, DeMatteo et al. (2011) recommended that evaluators limit their conclusions to the functional legal capacities that will allow legal decision makers to reach an informed conclusion unless they are specifically instructed otherwise by the court.

Capital Sentencing Evaluations

As noted earlier, after a capital defendant is convicted, the next stage in the bifurcated capital case process is sentencing. During the sentencing phase, the prosecution seeks to prove aggravating factors that call for imposition of the death penalty, whereas the defense seeks to prove mitigating factors that make the imposition of the death penalty inappropriate. The U.S. Supreme Court has defined capital mitigation as "any aspect of a defendant's character or record, or any of the circumstances of the offense that the defendant proffered as a basis for a sentence less than death" (*Lockett v. Ohio*, 1978, p. 604). The Supreme Court later protected specific mitigating factors as being valid for consideration, including background (*Eddings v. Oklahoma*, 1982), pretrial incarcerated behavior (*Skipper v. South Carolina*,

1986), and mitigation that was not enumerated in the relevant sentencing statute (*Hitchcock v. Dugger*, 1987). In each case, though, the Court reiterated its principle from *Lockett* that mitigation was truly limited only by relevance to the defendant's case and the thoroughness of defense counsel.

Today, death penalty jurisprudence is fairly consistent across jurisdictions in the sense that mitigation evidence is broadly defined, so the task for forensic experts who are conducting capital sentencing evaluations is to identify factors that are potentially mitigating. Some guidance is provided by statute in the form of sample mitigating factors, such as the defendant's youth, limited history of criminality, minor role in the offense, impairment that affected his or her capacity to appreciate the offense, or impairment that limited his or her ability to conform behavior to the law. Some factors are straightforward and may not warrant input from forensic evaluators, whereas others may be especially suited to evaluation by a mental health expert. Also, most statutes contain a catch-all provision that covers any factor that the sentencer deems to be of mitigating value (DeMatteo et al., 2011).

Whereas *Atkins*-type and CFE evaluations address a circumscribed legal question, the scope of capital sentencing evaluations is the broadest of any evaluation that is undertaken by forensic mental health professionals. However, the scope of this type of evaluation is affected by the forensic mental health professional's role as either a consultant or an expert. A professional may be hired by the defense team as a partisan consultant to help present mitigating evidence, but these *mitigation specialists* do not render an objective expert opinion. The more often discussed scenario, and the one that will be described here, is that of an objective evaluator who, although hired by one party, nonetheless presents findings in an evenhanded and nonpartisan manner.

Objective evaluators tend to focus on mitigation because they have less to say about aggravating factors, which are typically issues of fact (e.g., the victim was a police officer, murder was committed while fleeing capture, murder was undertaken for pecuniary gain). As such, evaluators are more frequently asked to identify potentially mitigating factors, though it is up to the sentencer to determine whether those factors mitigate the crime and, if so, to what degree. However, as noted, the scope of the evaluation is quite broad.

With such a broad scope, a mitigation evaluation can be challenging. Rather than simply gathering mitigating data, which can be done effectively by a defense attorney or mitigation specialist, the evaluator should also synthesize the data and offer a scientifically supported perspective on how the data may be mitigating. The focus of capital sentencing is moral culpability, which is influenced by "the defendant's character or record" and the "circumstances of the offense" (*Lockett v. Ohio*, 1978, p. 604), so evaluators should focus on historical/developmental factors of the defendant and specific factors of the offense that may affect the defendant's perceived moral culpability.

Historical and developmental factors.
Cicchetti (2006) identified developmental psychopathology as focusing on the interplay among biological, psychological, social, and contextual influences that shape development. A lengthy discussion of historical and developmental factors is beyond the scope of this chapter, but a few major topic areas are worth noting. Much of developmental psychopathology highlights risk factors and protective factors, which were discussed earlier in this chapter. Also the subject of some research, *resilience* may mediate the relationship between risk and protective factors in producing ultimate outcomes, and essentially refers to one's capacity for adapting well despite adversity or trauma (Cicchetti, 2006; Rutter, 1987; Salekin, 2007). Individuals with resilience may become comparatively well-adjusted and prosocial members of society, despite a heavy balance of risk to protective factors.

In addition to examining the factors that may affect an individual's developmental trajectories, developmental psychopathology explores those trajectories themselves. *Equifinality* is the observation that, for any individual, multiple pathways may lead to the same outcome (Cicchetti & Rogosch, 1996). The counterpart to equifinality is *multifinality*, which recognizes that individuals following very similar pathways may nonetheless arrive at very different outcomes (Cicchetti, 2006). Combined with

moral culpability, equifinality and multifinality underscore capital sentencing. After all, many people with adverse life experiences do not go on to commit murder (multifinality), and although capital defendants found guilty of murder are diverse (equifinality), only some will be found deserving of the death penalty (morally culpable). A skilled expert may be able to highlight this dynamic for a capital jury in an attempt to place an individual defendant in the larger context of society.

Offense-specific factors and ultimate moral culpability.
In addition to developmental and historical factors, the circumstances surrounding the offense may prove mitigating by suggesting reduced moral culpability. Intuitively, moral culpability seems greater when a defendant has the information, capacities, influences, and experiences to consider multiple paths yet knowingly chooses a behavior that is illegal and morally reprehensible. By contrast, moral culpability is reduced when a defendant lacks the aforementioned resources or when his or her options are limited by the context of a situation (DeMatteo et al., 2011).

Using that as guidance, an examination of context-specific moral culpability requires attention to the internal and external forces that shaped the offender's behavior incident to the capital offense. An understanding of the defendant's internal state leading up to and during the offense may reveal mitigating information. Remember, though, that the evaluator is not providing a judgment about a defendant's moral culpability. In fact, such a determination is contraindicated by best practice standards in the field (see, e.g., Melton, Petrila, Poythress, & Slobogin, 2007).

This may be confusing for the evaluator and sentencer alike. After all, the evaluator's decision to present data questioning the defendant's moral culpability may convey that he or she views the data as doing precisely that. Additionally, a presentation of factors that may have contributed to the defendant's behavior may be viewed as deterministic or as suggesting that the defendant was lacking in free will to choose a different course or action. A philosophical discussion is beyond the scope of this chapter, but it is important to note that an emphasis on context-specific factors and issues of moral culpability only considers the psychological, social, and biological factors that influenced—not determined—a particular behavior.

Thus, the job for an expert is to show how historical or contextual factors may have contributed to an individual's opportunity for capital offending. The evaluator can explain the relationship between a defendant's cognitive impairment and his or her judgment, history of abuse and ultimate value system, and psychosocial maturity and impulse control. However, the analysis must be supported by data, and no such data support determinism in light of specific historical and contextual factors. To use a metaphor, such factors may have opened the door, but the defendant made the decision to pass through the door. Ultimately, the expert's goal is to equip jurors to make an informed decision about sentencing the defendant.

Performing a capital sentencing evaluation. The broad scope of a capital sentencing evaluation means that the evaluator must explore multiple domains (see Connell, 2003). The evaluator should seek to understand the defendant's multigenerational family history, which may reveal patterns of psychosocial dysfunction, a history of mental illness, or a history of general adversity. Additionally, the evaluator should attempt to construct a history of the offender's birth and early development. Premature birth, anoxic or hypoxic incidents during delivery, fetal alcohol syndrome, or delayed/missing developmental milestones are relevant factors in a capital sentencing evaluation. The evaluator should obtain a clear picture of the defendant's childhood and adolescence, including his or her medical and psychological history, academic performance, extracurricular interests and activities, social functioning, and vocational achievements or aspirations. The evaluator should also solicit a history of the individual's adulthood, regardless of whether there is a prior record of violence or crime. Lastly, as already mentioned, the evaluator should make sure to assess the internal and external forces that were acting on the defendant at the time of the capital offense.

Having identified the domains of information on which an evaluator should focus, the next step in a capital sentencing evaluation is to determine how data collection and synthesis should proceed. As discussed elsewhere, best practices suggest that the evaluator obtain data from multiple sources, including clinical interview, collateral interviews, collateral records, and testing (see Heilbrun et al., 2009). A few considerations regarding each of these sources of information in the capital context are worth highlighting.

Although the interview with the offender may seem like the most important component of any forensic mental health assessment, the interview may be less fruitful in a capital case. Because so much time is needed to conduct a thorough capital sentencing evaluation, the evaluation is typically conducted pretrial (i.e., before a decision of guilt has been rendered). As such, the evaluator may be faced with a defendant who still professes his or her innocence, which makes it challenging to gather information relating to the offense from the defendant.

In addition to interviewing the offender, the evaluator should conduct collateral interviews with people who know the defendant well. Collateral interviews are recommended in most forensic assessment contexts, but they are particularly valuable in capital sentencing evaluations because they can provide information that is potentially unavailable from the defendant. Family and caregivers may well prove to be better historians than the defendant for information pertaining to his or her birth, childhood, and early development. Collateral interviews can also be conducted with teachers, correctional officers, medical and mental health professionals, and a variety of other people who knew the defendant from various perspectives and at various times.

Historical records may be a valuable source of mitigating data because they may, for example, include detailed narratives that flesh out mitigating data in ways that examinees could not. Also, with examinees being subject to the frailties of memory and motivation to present information in a certain light, historical records can help fill in informational gaps. Criminal defendants may also be reluctant to admit information about which they are ashamed (e.g., sexual abuse), though such information could potentially have mitigating value.

Further, individuals may neglect to mention information that they think is irrelevant (e.g., history of special education) but that an evaluator recognizes as potentially mitigating information.

Although testing is a standard component of most forensic mental health assessments, its value should be critically weighed in capital sentencing evaluations, largely due to the nature of the legal–moral question of whether the defendant deserves the death penalty. Personality testing, for example, can offer little to help answer that question. As Heilbrun (2001) reminded evaluators, the criterion for deciding whether to use a test is whether the test offers data that are relevant to the legal question being addressed. Granted, personality testing may help assess an individual's response style or uncover psychiatric symptoms, but there are more pointed ways to uncover such data in a capital evaluation. Moreover, concerns have been raised that capital defendants may demonstrate clinical elevations on scales measuring antisocial personality, which is unremarkable as compared to other incarcerated individuals but is potentially prejudicial if it is presented to the legal decision maker (Cunningham, 2008, 2010). It is possible, though, that tests of neuropsychological or cognitive dysfunction may yield relevant data because evidence of a defendant's inability to weigh options, control impulsivity, and make good judgments can be relevant to capital sentencing decisions.

Presenting findings of a capital sentencing evaluation.   As with most forensic mental health assessments, capital sentencing evaluations typically yield a written report. In fact, many jurisdictions require that such a report be rendered as part of the evaluation (DeMatteo et al., 2011). The report should convey information relevant to the capital sentencing determination in an even-handed, objective, and accessible fashion. An objective evaluator is not a member of the legal team, and it is thus improper to exclude damaging information or frame information in a light that is most favorable to the hiring party. Also, because expert reports may be shared with opposing counsel—whether incident to rules of discovery or in negotiating a plea arrangement—it is important that the evaluator's methodology and conclusions be sound and defensible (Heilbrun, 2001).

In addition to written reports, experts often present their findings via testimony. The decision of whether to ask an expert to testify may turn on whether the evaluator has expertise that is worth sharing. In situations in which mitigating evidence of developmental psychopathology is present, the defense may be more likely to ask the evaluator to highlight the nexus between development and relevant outcomes. On the other hand, in situations in which mitigating evidence may be less clinical in nature (e.g., the defendant was a friendly neighbor, the defendant was always a hard worker), there may be less need for an expert to convey such information. Defense may instead opt for such information to come from sources who are emotionally invested in the defendant, hoping that they can better appeal to the sympathies of the jury. In any case, testimony, like the report, should be scientifically grounded and should convey information in an accessible manner.

SUMMARY AND CONCLUSIONS

The involvement of forensic mental health professionals in capital cases has increased considerably over the past several decades, and forensic experts may be involved at every stage of death penalty proceedings. Given the nature of death penalty cases, the considerations that are relevant in capital cases are often different from the considerations that are relevant to evaluations that are conducted in noncapital cases. As such, evaluators must possess sufficient legal, clinical, and forensic knowledge before becoming involved in capital cases. This chapter described the special expertise required of evaluators who work in capital cases in the context of *Atkins*-type, CFE, and capital sentencing evaluations.

This chapter also highlighted research relating to the deterrent effect of the death penalty, societal views on the death penalty (which may be relevant for the Supreme Court's Eighth Amendment analysis in capital cases), and jury decision making in capital cases. Conducting methodologically rigorous research in criminal justice settings is challenging, and it is even more difficult to conduct good research in death penalty contexts. Nevertheless, researchers have made great strides in some areas, such as jury decision making. Future research efforts should focus on developing and/or validating assessment measures that are or could be used in death penalty evaluations. For example, as discussed in this chapter, the assessment of adaptive functioning among incarcerated offenders, which is a central component of *Atkins*-type evaluations, is impeded because existing measures were not designed or normed for use with a correctional population. The validation or development of measures of adaptive functioning that could be used with offenders would allow evaluators to reach firmer diagnostic conclusions. Also, the continued development and empirical testing of measures that could be used in CFE evaluations would be of great benefit.

Evaluations in death penalty contexts are often among the most visible evaluations that are conducted, and the evaluator can expect heightened scrutiny on all aspects of his or her involvement in the case. As such, it is essential that forensic mental health professionals adhere to best practices when conducting evaluations in capital cases. The recommendations highlighted in this chapter, which were derived from a synthesis of the relevant practice literature, are offered to assist evaluators who work in capital cases.

References

Ackerson, K. S., Brodsky, S. L., & Zapf, P. A. (2005). Judges' and psychologists' assessments of legal and clinical factors in competence for execution. *Psychology, Public Policy, and Law, 11,* 164–193. doi:10.1037/1076-8971.11.1.164

American Association of Intellectual and Developmental Disabilities. (2010). *Definition of intellectual disability.* Retrieved from http://www.aamr.org/content_100.cfm?navID=21

American Bar Association Section of Individual Rights and Responsibilities. (2006). *Recommendation 122A.* Retrieved from http://www.abanet.org/media/docs/122A.pdf

American Psychiatric Association. (2000). *Diagnostic and statistical manual of mental disorders* (4th ed., text revision). Washington, DC: Author.

American Psychiatric Association. (2004). *Diminished responsibility in capital sentencing: Position statement.* Retrieved from http://www.psych.org/edu/other_res/lib_archives/archives/200406.pdf

American Psychiatric Association. (2013). *Diagnostic and statistical manual of mental disorders* (5th ed.). Washington, DC: Author.

American Psychological Association. (2001). *The death penalty in the United States.* Available at www.apa.org/pi/deathpenalty.html

American Psychological Association. (2002). Ethical principles of psychologists and code of conduct. *American Psychologist, 57,* 1060–1073. doi:10.1037/0003-066X.57.12.1060

American Psychological Association. (2013). Specialty guidelines for forensic psychology. *American Psychologist, 68,* 7–19. doi:10.1037/a0029889

Amnesty International. (2006). *The death penalty disregards mental illness.* Available at www.amnestyusa.org/abolish/mental_illness.html

Andrews, D. A., & Bonta, J. (2003). *The psychology of criminal conduct* (3rd ed.). Cincinnati, OH: Anderson.

Atkins v. Virginia, 536 U.S. 304 (2002).

Baldus, D. C., Pulaski, C., & Woodworth, G. (1983). Comparative review of death sentences: An empirical study of the Georgia experience. *Journal of Criminal Law and Criminology, 74,* 661–753. doi:10.2307/1143133

Barefoot v. Estelle, 463 U.S. 880 (1983).

Blume, J. H., Garvey, S. P., & Johnson, S. L. (2000). Future dangerousness in capital cases: Always at issue. *Cornell Law Review, 86,* 397–410.

Blume, J. H., Johnson, S. L., & Seeds, C. (2009). *Of Atkins and men: Deviations from clinical definitions of mental retardation in death penalty cases* (Cornell Law School Research Paper No. 09-001). Ithaca, NY: Cornell Law School. Retrieved from http://ssrn.com/abstract=1327303

Bowers, W., Vandiver, M., & Dugan, P. (1994). A new look at public opinion on capital punishment: What citizens and legislators prefer. *American Journal of Criminal Law, 22,* 77–150.

Brodsky, S., & Galloway, V. (2003). Ethical and professional demands for forensic mental health professionals in the post-*Atkins* era. *Ethics and Behavior, 13,* 3–9. doi:10.1207/S15327019EB1301_02

Brodsky, S. L., Zapf, P. A., & Boccaccini, M. T. (2001). The last competency: An examination of legal, ethical, and professional ambiguities regarding evaluations of competence for execution. *Journal of Forensic Psychology Practice, 1,* 1–25. doi:10.1300/J158v01n02_01

Butcher, J., Dahlstrom, W., Graham, J., Tellegen, A., & Kaemmer, B. (1989). *MMPI–2: Manual for administration and scoring.* Minneapolis: University of Minnesota Press.

Cherry v. Florida, 959 So.2d 702 (Fla. 2007).

Cicchetti, D. (2006). Development and psychopathology. In D. Cicchetti & D. J. Cohen (Eds.), *Developmental psychopathology* (2nd ed., pp. 1–23). Hoboken, NJ: Wiley.

Cicchetti, D., & Rogosch, F. A. (1996). Equifinality and multifinality in developmental psychopathology. *Development and Psychopathology, 8,* 597–600. doi:10.1017/S0954579400007318

Connell, M. A. (2003). A psychobiographical approach to the evaluation for sentence mitigation. *Journal of Psychiatry and Law, 31,* 319–354.

Conroy, M. A., & Murrie, D. C. (2007). *Forensic assessment of violence risk: A guide for risk assessment and risk management.* Hoboken, NJ: Wiley. doi:10.1002/9781118269671

Costanzo, M., & White, L. T. (1994). An overview of the death penalty and capital trials: History, current status, legal procedures, and cost. *Journal of Social Issues, 50,* 1–18. doi:10.1111/j.1540-4560.1994.tb02408.x

Crockett, L. J., Eggebeen, D. J., & Hawkins, A. J. (1993). Father's presence and young children's behavioral and cognitive adjustment. *Journal of Family Issues, 14,* 355–377. doi:10.1177/019251393014003002

Cunningham, M. D. (2008). Forensic psychology evaluations at capital sentencing. In R. Jackson (Ed.), *Learning forensic assessment* (pp. 211–238). New York, NY: Routledge/Taylor & Francis Group.

Cunningham, M. D. (2010). *Evaluation for capital sentencing.* New York, NY: Oxford University Press.

Cunningham, M. D., Reidy, T. J., & Sorensen, J. R. (2005). Is death row obsolete? A decade of mainstreaming death-sentenced inmates in Missouri. *Behavioral Sciences and the Law, 23,* 307–320. doi:10.1002/bsl.608

Cunningham, M. D., Reidy, T. J., & Sorensen, J. R. (2008). Assertions of "future dangerousness" at federal capital sentencing: Rates and correlates of subsequent prison misconduct and violence. *Law and Human Behavior, 32,* 46–63. doi:10.1007/s10979-007-9107-7

Cunningham, M. D., & Sorensen, J. R. (2006). Actuarial models for assessment of prison violence risk: Revisions and extensions of the Risk Assessment Scale for Prison (RASP). *Assessment, 13,* 253–265. doi:10.1177/1073191106287791

Cunningham, M. D., Sorensen, J. R., & Reidy, T. J. (2005). An actuarial model for assessment of prison violence risk among maximum security inmates. *Assessment, 12,* 40–49. doi:10.1177/1073191104272815

DeMatteo, D., & Marczyk, G. (2005). Risk factors, protective factors, and the prevention of antisocial behavior among juveniles. In K. Heilbrun, N. E. Sevin Goldstein, & R. E. Redding (Eds.), *Juvenile delinquency: Prevention, assessment, and intervention* (pp. 19–44). New York, NY: Oxford University Press.

DeMatteo, D., Marczyk, G., & Pich, M. (2007). A national survey of state legislation defining mental retardation: Implications for policy and practice after *Atkins. Behavioral Sciences and the Law, 25,* 781–802. doi:10.1002/bsl.777

DeMatteo, D., Murrie, D. C., Anumba, N. M., & Keesler, M. E. (2011). *Forensic mental health assessment in death penalty cases.* New York, NY: Oxford University Press. doi:10.1093/acprof:oso/9780195385809.001.0001

Dezhbakhsh, H., Rubin, P. H., & Shepherd, J. M. (2003). Does capital punishment have a deterrent effect? New evidence from postmoratorium panel data. *American Law and Economics Review, 5,* 344–376. doi:10.1093/aler/ahg021

Donohue, J. J., & Wolfers, J. (2005). Uses and abuses of empirical evidence in the death penalty debate. *Stanford Law Review, 58,* 791–845.

Ebert, B. (2001). Competency to be executed: A proposed instrument to evaluate an inmate's level of competency in light of the Eighth Amendment prohibition against the execution of the presently insane. *Law and Psychology Review, 25,* 29–57.

Eddings v. Oklahoma, 455 U.S. 104 (1982).

Edens, J. F., Buffington-Vollum, J. K., Keilen, A., Roskamp, P., & Anthony, C. (2005). Predictions of future dangerousness in capital murder trials: Is it time to "disinvent the wheel"? *Law and Human Behavior, 29,* 55–86. doi:10.1007/s10979-005-1399-x

Elliott, D. S. (1994). Serious violent offenders: Onset, developmental course, and termination—The American Society of Criminology 1993 presidential address. *Criminology, 32,* 1–21. doi:10.1111/j.1745-9125.1994.tb01144.x

Fagan, J. (2006). Death and deterrence redux: Science, law, and causal reasoning on capital punishment. *Ohio State Journal of Criminal Law, 4,* 255–320.

Fagan, J., Geller, A., & Zimring, F. E. (2012). The Texas deterrence muddle. *Criminology and Public Policy, 11,* 579–591. doi:10.1111/j.1745-9133.2012.00832.x

Farrington, D. P. (1997). Early prediction of violent and non-violent youthful offending. *European Journal on Criminal Policy and Research, 5,* 51–66. doi:10.1007/BF02677607

Flynn, J. R. (1984). The mean IQ of Americans: Massive gains 1932 to 1978. *Psychological Bulletin, 95*, 29–51. doi:10.1037/0033-2909.95.1.29

Flynn, J. R. (1998). WAIS–III and WISC–III gains in the United States from 1972 to 1995: How to compensate for obsolete norms. *Perceptual and Motor Skills, 86*, 1231–1239. doi:10.2466/pms.1998.86.3c.1231

Flynn, J. R. (1999). Searching for justice: The discovery of IQ gains over time. *American Psychologist, 54*, 5–20. doi:10.1037/0003-066X.54.1.5

Flynn, J. R. (2006). Tethering the elephant: Capital cases, IQ, and the Flynn effect. *Psychology, Public Policy, and Law, 12*, 170–189. doi:10.1037/1076-8971.12.2.170

Ford v. Wainwright, 477 U.S. 399 (1986).

Frase, R. S. (2005). Punishment purposes. *Stanford Law Review, 58*, 67–81.

Frederick, R. (1997). *Validity Indicator Profile manual*. Minnetonka, MN: NSC Assessments.

Furman v. Georgia, 408 U.S. 238 (1972).

Gendreau, P., Goggin, C., & Law, M. A. (1997). Predicting prison misconduct. *Criminal Justice and Behavior, 24*, 414–431. doi:10.1177/0093854897024004002

Gould, J., & Greenman, L. (2010). *Update on cost, quality, and availability of defense representation in federal death penalty cases*. Retrieved from http://www.uscourts.gov/FederalCourts/AppointmentOfCounsel/Publications/UpdateFederalDeathPenaltyCases.aspx

Gregg v. Georgia, 428 U.S. 153 (1976).

Grisso, T. (2003). Advances in assessments for legal competencies. In T. Grisso (Ed.), *Evaluating competencies: Forensic assessments and instruments* (2nd ed., pp. 1–20). New York, NY: Kluwer Academic/Plenum.

Hagan, L. D., Drogin, E. Y., & Guilmette, T. J. (2008). Adjusting IQ scores for the Flynn effect: Consistent with the standard of practice? *Professional Psychology: Research and Practice, 39*, 619–625. doi:10.1037/a0012693

Hall v. Florida, No. 12-10882, slip op. (U.S. Supreme Court, May 27, 2014).

Haney, C. (2003). Mental health issues in long-term solitary and "supermax" confinement. *Crime and Delinquency, 49*, 124–156. doi:10.1177/0011128702239239

Hanson, R. K., & Harris, A. J. R. (2001). A structured approach to evaluating change among sexual offenders. *Sexual Abuse: Journal of Research and Treatment, 13*, 105–122.

Hawkins, J. D., Herrenkohl, T. L., Farrington, D. P., Brewer, D., Catalano, R. F., & Harachi, T. W. (1998). A review of predictors of youth violence. In R. Loeber & D. P. Farrington (Eds.), *Serious and violent juvenile offenders: Risk factors and successful interventions* (pp. 106–146). Thousand Oaks, CA: Sage.

Heilbrun, K. (2001). *Principles of forensic mental health assessment*. New York, NY: Kluwer Academic/Plenum.

Heilbrun, K., DeMatteo, D., Brooks Holliday, S., & LaDuke, C. (Eds.). (2014). *Forensic mental health assessment: A casebook* (2nd ed.). New York, NY: Oxford University Press.

Heilbrun, K., Grisso, T., & Goldstein, A. M. (2009). *Foundations of forensic mental health assessment*. New York, NY: Oxford University Press.

Heilbrun, K., Marczyk, G., & DeMatteo, D. (2002). *Forensic mental health assessment: A casebook*. New York, NY: Oxford University Press.

Heilbrun, K. S. (1987). The assessment of competency for execution: An overview. *Behavioral Sciences and the Law, 5*, 383–396. doi:10.1002/bsl.2370050403

Heilbrun, K. S., & McClaren, H. A. (1988). Assessment of competency for execution: A guide for mental health professionals. *Bulletin of the American Academy of Psychiatry and the Law, 16*, 205–216.

Herrenkohl, T. L., Hawkins, J. D., Chung, I., Hill, K. G., & Battin-Pearson, S. (2001). School and community risk factors and interventions. In R. Loeber & D. P. Farrington (Eds.), *Child delinquents: Development, intervention, and service needs* (pp. 211–246). Thousand Oaks, CA: Sage.

Hitchcock v. Dugger, 481 U.S. 393 (1987).

Howell, J. C. (2003). *Preventing and reducing juvenile delinquency: A comprehensive framework*. Thousand Oaks, CA: Sage.

Jacobson, J. W., & Mulick, J. A. (Eds.). (1996). *Manual on diagnosis and professional practice in mental retardation*. Washington, DC: American Psychological Association. doi:10.1037/10203-000

Jones, J. M. (2003). *Understanding Americans' support for the death penalty*. Retrieved from http://www.gallup.com/poll/8557/understanding-americans-support-death-penalty.aspx

Jones, J. M. (2006). *Support for the death penalty 30 years after the Supreme Court ruling: Two in three currently support it*. Retrieved from http://www.gallup.com/poll/23548/support-death-penalty-years-after-supreme-court-ruling.aspx

Jones, R. P., Cox, D., Navarro-Rivera, J., Dionne, E. J., & Galston, G. A. (2012). *The 2012 American values survey*. Retrieved from http://publicreligion.org/site/wp-content/uploads/2012/10/AVS-2012-Pre-election-Report-for-Web.pdf

Jurek v. Texas, 428 U.S. 262 (1976).

Kamphaus, R. W., Winsor, A. P., Rowe, E. W., & Kim, S. (2005). A history of intelligence test interpretation. In D. P. Flanagan & P. L. Harrison (Eds.),

Contemporary intellectual assessment (pp. 23–38). New York, NY: Guilford Press.

Kanaya, T., Scullin, M. H., & Ceci, S. J. (2003). The Flynn effect and U.S. policies: The impact of rising IQ scores on American society via mental retardation diagnoses. *American Psychologist, 58*, 778–790. doi:10.1037/0003-066X.58.10.778

Koocher, G. (2003). IQ testing: A matter of life and death. *Ethics and Behavior, 13*, 1–2. doi:10.1207/S15327019EB1301_01

Kovandzic, T., Vieraitis, L., & Boots, D. P. (2009). Does the death penalty save lives? New evidence from state panel data, 1977 to 2006. *Criminology and Public Policy, 8*, 803–843. doi:10.1111/j.1745-9133.2009.00596.x

Lacritz, L. H., & Cullum, C. M. (2003). The WAIS–III and WMS–III: Practical issues and frequently asked questions. In D. S. Tulsky, D. H. Saklofske, G. J. Chelune, R. K. Heaton, R. J. Ivnik, R. Bornstein, . . . M. F. Ledbetter (Eds.), *Clinical interpretation of the WAIS–III and WMS–III* (pp. 491–532). Boston, MA: Elsevier. doi:10.1016/B978-012703570-3/50019-5

Land, K. C., Teske, R. H. C., & Zheng, H. (2009). The short-term effects of executions on homicides: Deterrence, displacement or both? *Criminology: An Interdisciplinary Journal, 47*, 1009–1043. doi:10.1111/j.1745-9125.2009.00168.x

Land, K. C., Teske, R. H. C., & Zheng, H. (2012). The differential short-term impacts of executions on felony and non-felony homicides. *Criminology and Public Policy, 11*, 541–563. doi:10.1111/j.1745-9133.2012.00834.x

Lichtenberger, E. O., & Kaufman, A. S. (2009). *Essentials of WAIS–IV assessment.* Hoboken, NJ: Wiley.

Lipsey, M. W., & Derzon, J. H. (1998). Predictors of violent or serious delinquency in adolescence and early adulthood: A synthesis of longitudinal research. In R. Loeber & D. P. Farrington (Eds.), *Serious and violent juvenile offenders: Risk factors and successful interventions* (pp. 86–105). Thousand Oaks, CA: Sage.

Liu, Z. (2004). Capital punishment and the deterrence hypothesis: Some new insights and empirical evidence. *Eastern Economic Journal, 30*, 237–258.

Lockett v. Ohio, 438 U.S. 586 (1978).

Marquart, J. W., Ekland-Olson, S., & Sorensen, J. R. (1994). *The rope, the chair, and the needle: Capital punishment in Texas, 1923–1990.* Austin: University of Texas Press.

McCord, J. (1979). Some child-rearing antecedents of criminal behavior in adult men. *Journal of Personality and Social Psychology, 37*, 1477–1486.

McCord, J., Widom, C. S., & Crowell, N. A. (Eds.). (2001). *Juvenile crime, juvenile justice.* Washington, DC: National Academy Press.

Melton, G. B., Petrila, J., Poythress, N. G., & Slobogin, C. (2007). *Psychological evaluation for the courts: A handbook for mental health professionals and lawyers* (3rd ed.). New York, NY: Guilford Press.

Miller, H. (2001). *Miller Forensic Assessment of Symptoms Test (M–FAST): Professional manual.* Odessa, FL: Psychological Assessment Resources.

Moffitt, T. E., Lynam, D., & Silva, P. A. (1994). Neuropsychological tests predict persistent male delinquency. *Criminology, 32*, 277–300. doi:10.1111/j.1745-9125.1994.tb01155.x

Moore, D. W. (2004). *Public divided between death penalty and life imprisonment without parole.* Retrieved from http://www.gallup.com/poll/11878/Public-Divided-Between-Death-Penalty-Life-Imprisonment-Without-Parole.aspx

Moore, R. B. (2006). Modification of individual's IQ scores is not accepted professional practice. *Psychology in Mental Retardation and Developmental Disabilities, 31*, 11–12.

Morey, L. (1991). *Personality Assessment Inventory professional manual.* Odessa, FL: Psychological Assessment Resources.

Morris, R. G., Longmire, D. R., Buffington-Vollum, J., & Vollum, S. (2010). Managing career inmates: Differential parole eligibility and institutional misconduct among capital inmates. *Criminal Justice and Behavior, 37*, 417–438. doi:10.1177/0093854810361672

National Alliance on Mental Illness. (2009). *Public policy platform of the National Alliance on Mental Illlness (NAMI), 10.8 Death Penalty.* Retrieved from http://www.nami.org/Template.cfm?Section=NAMI_Policy_Platform&Template=/ContentManagement/ContentDisplay.cfm&ContentID=41302

National Research Council. (1978). *Deterrence and incapacitation: Estimating the effects of criminal sanctions on crime rates.* Washington, DC: National Academy Press.

National Research Council. (2012). *Deterrence and the death penalty.* Washington, DC: National Academy Press.

Niven, D. (2002). Bolstering an illusory majority: The effects of the media's portrayal of death penalty support. *Social Science Quarterly, 83*, 671–689. doi:10.1111/1540-6237.00108

Otto, R. K. (2009). Meaningful consideration of competence to be executed. In R. F. Schopp, R. L. Wierner, B. H. Bornstein, & S. L. Willborn (Eds.), *Mental disorder and criminal law: Responsibility, punishment, and competence* (pp. 191–204). New York, NY: Springer. doi:10.1007/978-0-387-84845-7_9

Panetti v. Quarterman, 551 U.S. 930 (2007).

Radelet, M., & Lacock, T. (2009). Do executions lower homicide rates? The views of leading criminologists. *Journal of Criminal Law and Criminology*, *99*, 489–508.

Radelet, M. L., & Borg, M. J. (2000). The changing nature of death penalty debates. *Annual Review of Sociology*, *26*, 43–61. doi:10.1146/annurev.soc.26.1.43

Raine, A., Brennan, P., & Mednick, S. A. (1994). Birth complications combined with early maternal rejection at age 1 year predispose to violent crime at age 18 years. *Archives of General Psychiatry*, *51*, 984–988. doi:10.1001/archpsyc.1996.01830060090012

Rogers, R., Sewell, K. W., & Gillard, N. D. (2010). *Structured Interview of Reported Symptoms* (2nd ed.). Odessa, FL: Psychological Assessment Resources.

Rogers, R., & Shuman, D. (2000). *Conducting insanity evaluations* (2nd ed.). New York, NY: Guilford Press.

Roid, G. H. (2003). *Stanford–Binet Intelligence Scales, fifth edition: Technical manual*. Itsaca, IL: Riverside.

Roper v. Simmons, 542 U.S. 551 (2005).

Rutter, M. (1987). Psychosocial resilience and protective mechanisms. *American Journal of Orthopsychiatry*, *57*, 316–331. doi:10.1111/j.1939-0025.1987.tb03541.x

Saad, L. (2013). *U.S. death penalty support stable at 63%: Decade-long decline in support after 2001 seem mostly among democrats*. Retrieved from http://www.gallup.com/poll/159770/death-penalty-support-stable.aspx

Salekin, K. L. (2007). Capital mitigation from a developmental perspective: The importance of risk factors, protective factors, and the construct of resilience. In M. Costanzo, D. Krauss, & K. Pezdek (Eds.), *Expert psychological testimony for the courts* (pp. 149–176). Mahwah, NJ: Erlbaum.

Shader, M. (2001). *Risk factors for delinquency: An overview*. Retrieved from http://www.ncjrs.gov/pdffiles1/ojjdp/frd030127.pdf

Shepherd, J. M. (2004). Murders of passion, execution delays, and the deterrence of capital punishment. *Journal of Legal Studies*, *33*, 283–321. doi:10.1086/421571

Shepherd, J. M. (2005). Deterrence versus brutalization: Capital punishment's differing impacts among states. *Michigan Law Review*, *104*, 203–255.

Siennick, S. E. (2012). Deterrence and the death penalty: A new look at some recent findings. *Criminology and Public Policy*, *11*, 535–537. doi:10.1111/j.1745-9133.2012.00833.x

Skipper v. South Carolina, 476 U.S. 1 (1986).

Slobogin, C., Rai, A., & Reisner, R. (2009). *Law and the mental health system: Civil and criminal aspects* (5th ed.). St. Paul, MN: Thomson/West.

Small, M. A., & Otto, R. K. (1991). Evaluations of competency to be executed: Legal contours and implications for assessment. *Criminal Justice and Behavior*, *18*, 146–158. doi:10.1177/0093854891018002003

Sorensen, J. R., & Cunningham, M. D. (2009). Once a killer always a killer? Prison misconduct of former death-sentenced inmates in Arizona. *Journal of Psychiatry and Law*, *37*, 237–267.

Sorensen, J. R., & Cunningham, M. D. (2010). Conviction offense and prison violence: A comparative study of murderers and other offenders. *Crime and Delinquency*, *56*, 103–125. doi:10.1177/0011128707307175

Sorensen, J. R., & Pilgrim, R. L. (2000). An actuarial risk assessment of violence posed by capital murder defendants. *Journal of Criminal Law and Criminology*, *90*, 1251–1270. doi:10.2307/1144202

Sorensen, J. R., & Wrinkle, R. D. (1996). No hope for parole: Disciplinary infractions among death-sentenced and life-without-parole inmates. *Criminal Justice and Behavior*, *23*, 542–552. doi:10.1177/0093854896023004002

Steinberg, L. (1987). Single parents, stepparents, and the susceptibility of adolescents to antisocial peer pressure. *Child Development*, *58*, 269–275. doi:10.2307/1130307

Tassé, M. J. (2009). Adaptive behavior assessment and the diagnosis of mental retardation in capital cases. *Applied Neuropsychology*, *16*, 114–123. doi:10.1080/09084280902864451

U.S. Const. amend. VIII.

von Hirsch, A., Bottoms, A. E., Burney, E., & Wikstrom, P.-O. (1999). *Criminal deterrence and sentence severity: An analysis of recent research*. Oxford, England: Hart.

Wakschlag, L. S., Lahey, B. B., Loeber, R., Green, S. M., Gordon, R. A., & Leventhal, B. L. (1997). Maternal smoking during pregnancy and the risk of conduct disorder in boys. *Archives of General Psychiatry*, *54*, 670–676. doi:10.1001/archpsyc.1997.01830190098010

Wasserman, G. A., & Seracini, A. G. (2001). Family risk factors and interventions. In R. Loeber & D. P. Farrington (Eds.), *Child delinquents: Development, intervention, and service needs* (pp. 165–189). Thousand Oaks, CA: Sage.

Wasserman, J. D., & Tulsky, D. S. (2005). A history of intellectual assessment. In D. P. Flanagan & P. L. Harrison (Eds.), *Contemporary intellectual assessment* (pp. 3–22). New York, NY: Guilford Press.

Wechsler, D. (1997). *Wechsler Adult Intelligence Scale— Third edition: Administration and scoring manual.* San Antonio, TX: The Psychological Corporation.

Wechsler, D. (2008). *Wechsler Adult Intelligence Scale—Fourth edition: Technical and interpretive manual.* San Antonio, TX: The Psychological Corporation.

Zapf, P. A. (2008). Competency for execution. In R. Jackson (Ed.), *Learning forensic assessment* (pp. 239–261). New York, NY: Routledge/Taylor & Francis Group.

Zapf, P. A. (2009). Elucidating the contours of competency for execution: The implications of *Ford* and *Panetti* for the assessment of CFE. *Journal of Psychiatry and Law, 37,* 269–307.

Zapf, P. A., Boccaccini, M. T., & Brodsky, S. L. (2003). Assessment of competency for execution: Professional guidelines and an evaluation checklist. *Behavioral Sciences and the Law, 21,* 103–120. doi:10.1002/bsl.491

PART II

INDIVIDUAL AND SITUATIONAL PREDICTORS OF CRIMINAL BEHAVIOR

CHAPTER 8

CRIMINAL BEHAVIOR

Shelley L. Brown, Shannon Gottschall, and Craig Bennell

The Italian physician and psychiatrist Cesare Lombroso (1835–1909) was the first scholar to apply scientific methods to the study of crime, resulting in notable publications such as *L'Uomo Delinquente* (*Criminal Man*; Lombroso, 1876) and *La Donna Delinquente, la Prostitute, e la Donna Normale* (*Criminal Woman, the Prostitute, and the Normal Woman*; Lombroso & Ferrero, 1893). Despite intense criticism, Lombroso's voluminous work has, in part, catalyzed the emergence of countless theories of crime. In our view, the vast majority of post-Lombrosian criminological theories fall into one of five broad categories (a) evolutionary perspectives that underscore distal explanations; (b) biological explanations that emphasize genetics, neurochemistry, autonomic arousal, the brain, and even diet; (c) mainstream psychological and criminological theories that stress microlevel variables operating at the individual level, such as personality, and environmental factors, such as child-rearing practices, neighborhood, and peers; (d) critical criminological perspectives that stress macrolevel factors that function predominantly at the group level (e.g., race, class, sex, poverty); and (e) specialized theories of crime that focus either on specific groups of offenders such as women or on specific offending behaviors such as intimate partner violence or serial killing.

It is not possible to adequately cover each of these five overarching perspectives in one chapter. Given the focus of this handbook—forensic psychology—and this chapter in particular—criminal behavior—we instead concentrate on general theories of crime that

emphasize individual-level factors. Theories of this nature fall within evolution, biology, psychology, and mainstream criminology. Critical criminological perspectives emphasizing macrolevel factors such as race, sex, and poverty, as well as specialized theories of crime that target specific groups (e.g., women) or specific behaviors (sexual offending), are not covered. However, when we review and critique the extant research germane to each individual-level perspective, we do so through the lens of less psychologically orientated perspectives such as, for example, feminist criminology. Additionally, other chapters in this handbook are devoted to specialized offender groups (see Chapter 9, this volume for psychopathy; Chapter 11, this volume for sex offenders; Chapter 2, this volume for intimate partner violence; Volume 2, Chapter 12, this handbook for juvenile offenders; and Volume 2, Chapter 4, this handbook for female offenders).

Like all preceding chapters, this chapter is divided into five sections. Notably, in the theory section, we first describe the key tenets of each general perspective of crime—evolutionary, biological, psychodynamic, and learning perspectives. Next, we provide an overview of specific theories falling within each of these four broad paradigms. For example, first, within the evolutionary perspective, we elaborate on two specific evolutionary-based theories of crime: (a) why females commit less crime than males, and (b) why males perpetrate homicide against other males. Second, within biological accounts, we examine how genetics, neurochemistry, autonomic arousal, the brain, and other environmental factors that may trigger biological changes can enhance our understanding of how and when criminal conduct is most likely to occur. Third, four specific psychodynamic perspectives are described, including Freudian (1901, 1938) principles followed by more contemporary psychodynamic theories such as the Gluecks' collective works (Glueck & Glueck, 1950, 1968), Hirschi's (1969, 2002) social control theory, and Gottfredson and Hirschi's (1990) general theory of crime. Lastly, we describe learning theories that are grounded in both psychology and criminology; specifically, classical conditioning, operant conditioning, and social learning perspectives. After the relevant theoretical perspectives have been described, corresponding research evidence associated with each perspective is reviewed. Associated criticisms are also presented. Lastly, practical and policy issues along with a general summary are provided.

It is necessary to emphasize that although we present each theory independently, mutual exclusivity should not be assumed. Similarly, the theories should not always be viewed as competing perspectives. We hope that it will become evident throughout the chapter that most perspectives complement, rather than compete with, one another. For example, different theories may emphasize different causal factors or focus on different levels of explanation ranging from the distant past—our ancestral environment—to the immediate situation—opportunity. Despite this, one theory's emphasis on a particular level of explanation, or a specific causal factor for that matter, does not necessarily preclude the importance of another level of explanation or another causal factor(s). The challenge for theorists has been, and will continue be, theoretical integration between and within disciplines. Impressive attempts of this nature have been made (see Moffitt's explanation of adolescent limited offenders vs. life course persistent offenders, for example, as described in Volume 2, Chapter 2, this handbook).

IMPORTANCE OF THE PROBLEM

Official arrest statistics coupled with national victimization surveys continue to demonstrate that crime has steadily declined in virtually all categories over the last two to three decades (Snyder, 2011; Truman, 2011). Nonetheless, crime continues to impact a staggering number of Americans every single day. In 2010, Americans experienced approximately 18.7 million victimizations. These criminal victimizations included 3.8 million violent victimizations, 1.4 million serious violent victimizations (i.e., victim of rape or sexual assault, robbery, or aggravated assault), 14.8 million property victimizations, and 138,000 personal thefts (Truman, 2011). Notably, this translates into approximately 52,000 individual victimizations occurring daily in the United States.

Media and personal accounts abound detailing the harrowing effects that crime exacts on victims and society. The National Crime Victims Fund (NCVF), a nonprofit charity based in San Diego, California, has provided assistance and services to crime victims since 1982 (NCVF, 2012). The NCVF's website provides poignant anecdotal accounts demonstrating the devastating effects that crime exacts on its victims:

- A middle-aged man was found by two passers-by lying in a pool of blood next to the curb. He had no idea what had happened because he had been attacked from behind. With stab wounds to his back and arms, he is in critical condition with a lacerated kidney, a severed artery in his arm and other internal problems. He was the primary bread-winner for his family.
- An elderly gentleman was attacked by a transient who damaged his only mode of transportation—his bicycle.
- An 83-year old woman was attacked from behind by an unknown suspect, knocked to the ground and robbed. She borrowed money from friends to pay bills and does not have money for food for 8 days until she receives her social security check.
- A domestic violence victim is struggling to make ends meet with the loss of income. She and her 2 young children have moved in with a friend fleeing her abuser.
- A victim's ex-boyfriend went to her apartment and shot and killed her new boyfriend. He pointed

the gun at her and threatened to kill her. The police arrived and ultimately shot and killed the suspect. Victim is extremely traumatized and has been unable to work and is currently in danger of eviction and needs assistance with rent. (NCVF, 2012)

The costs of crime have also been monetized. Every time a crime occurs, tangible costs result. Criminal justice expenses abound, encompassing police, court, and correctional costs. Victims may require medical care and/or social/victim services. Consequently, ambulance expenses, emergency room fees, hospitalization expenses, and mental health costs ensue. Victims may also suffer from property loss and/or damage as well as lost wages. Increased costs will even impact members of society, for example, who may eventually experience increases in insurance premiums or food cost increases resulting from insurance fraud or repeated thefts from the local supermarket. Employers and the economy may endure productivity losses associated with absentee employees who were recently victimized by crime.

In addition to every imaginable tangible cost associated with crime, numerous intangible costs also exist. Individual victims may experience fear, pain, suffering, reduced quality of life, and ultimately, loss of life. Family members and close friends may also suffer emotionally alongside their victimized family member or friend. Friends and family of crime victims may also develop new fears and change their behaviors as a direct result of a crime that is experienced by a loved one. For example, the mother of a daughter who was recently raped near their home may no longer wish to run outside in a neighborhood that was once presumed safe. These particular crime costs are known as *intangible* or nonmonetary expenses associated with crime.

Although it may seem difficult if not impossible to assign a monetary value to these sorts of intangible costs, it has been done. For example, Miller, Cohen, and Wiersema (1996) painstakingly calculated the projected costs of crime to victims in 1993 dollars. In total, they estimated that crime personally costs crime victims 105 billion dollars annually.

When this amount factored in nonmonetary costs, the figure climbed to $450 billion dollars annually. Although Miller et al.'s estimates are 20 years old, they are still used today by prominent researchers who conduct cost–benefit analyses to examine if correctional treatment is worth the economic investment (e.g., Drake, Aos, & Miller, 2009).

In sum, anecdotal accounts and surface-level crime statistics readily illustrate that crime impacts a substantial number of individuals and families as well as society at large. In addition, economic-based research that quantifies both the tangible and intangible costs of crime has demonstrated that crime exacts an exceedingly high financial burden on individual victims, their families, and society. Thus, understanding why certain individuals engage or do not engage in crime is a mandatory first step toward the development of cost-effective crime reduction programs and policies.

RELEVANT PSYCHOLOGICAL THEORY AND PRINCIPLES

In this section, we discuss various perspectives on crime, including evolutionary, biological, psychodynamic, and learning perspectives. Within each broad perspective, we describe several specific theories that correspond to each perspective.

Forensic Evolutionary Theories

Genghis Khan (*c.* 1155—1227), a legendary Mongolian conqueror, created one of the most expansive empires in the world that eventually spanned from the Sea of Japan to Afghanistan to parts of Central Europe. His conquests exceeded those of Alexander the Great and Napoleon. Although praised for his military tactics and revered by his people, Genghis Khan is most remembered for his unparalleled savagery—using women and children as human shields during battle, mercilessly slaughtering countless enemies, brutally raping women, and torturing defiant tribal leaders. In addition to exercising extreme terror, violence, and sexual violence on his conquests, Khan and his army also kept multiple wives and concubines (Turnbull, 2004).

At this stage, it may seem perplexing that we have chosen to devote an entire paragraph to a legendary warrior who died almost 800 years ago. However, Genghis Khan exemplifies how evolutionary theory can operate in practice. A team of 23 researchers (Zerjal et al., 2003) from Europe and Asia studied the Y chromosome in 2,123 men living in Asia. Noteworthy, 8% of the sample possessed a near identical Y chromosome that was indicative of a common forefather—identified as Genghis Khan's paternal grandfather, or quite possibly Genghis Khan himself. Based on these findings, Zerjal et al. extrapolated that approximately 16 million men currently living between the Sea of Japan and Afghanistan also possess this particular Y chromosome. Thus, there are approximately 16 million men currently alive who are direct descents of Genghis Khan or his grandfather. Given that the average man who lived alongside Genghis Khan has approximately 20 living descents, it would seem that Khan's power and status, as well as his physical and sexual violence, ensured his genetic immortality. The notion that certain behaviors, thoughts, and emotions exhibited by our hunter/gatherer ancestors (in the case of Khan—power, status, military prowess, aggression) somehow increased the odds that a person's genes would be passed on from generation to generation to eventually become part of the human gene pool is at the heart of evolutionary psychology.

Evolutionary psychology would not exist without the seminal works of Charles Darwin. In 1859, Darwin published *On the Origins of Species*. Darwin's groundbreaking thesis was that all species have changed or evolved over thousands of years through the mechanism of natural selection. In brief, natural selection is the process by which genetically based traits (e.g., physical, emotional, cognitive, or biological) become part of the human gene pool. More specifically, natural selection occurs when traits that enhance the odds that an individual will live long enough to have children, who in turn will also live long enough to procreate, become part of the human gene pool as a function of genetic transmission from one generation to the next. Traits that did not increase the odds of having children, or their subsequent survival, clearly did not have the same opportunity to survive vis-à-vis genetic transmission. Hence, such traits would not be naturally selected for in the population, and they would eventually die

out. Darwin's seminal manuscript generated and continues to generate controversy among creationists who believe that God, and only God, created all species. However, Darwin's work has also catalyzed an explosion in evolutionary-based theory and research. In particular, the science of evolutionary psychology is a direct descendant of Darwin's original work.

Interest in evolutionary psychology has burgeoned considerably over the last 20 years, with scholars exploring a wide range of human behaviors through the lens of evolution, from understanding love (L. Campbell & Ellis, 2005) to understanding aggression (Duntley & Shackelford, 2008; Shackelford & Weekes-Shackelford, 2012). In brief, evolutionary psychology argues that contemporary cognitions, emotions, and behaviors are the result of thousands of years of evolution. More specifically, evolutionary theory posits that the human mind evolved in response to various environmental characteristics, also known as *selection pressures* or adaptive problems that are characteristic of our ancestral or hunter/gatherer environments. These selection pressures were about either (a) staying alive (i.e., securing protection from the elements, hunting for food, gathering food, avoiding predators), or (b) finding a sexual partner or mate. Individuals who managed to stay alive and find a sexual partner were more likely to procreate and pass their genetic material onto the next generation. Individuals who died prematurely because of an inability to survive the harsh conditions that were indicative of the hunter/gathering era, or who were unable to attract a mate, would not have children and hence would not transmit their genetic blueprint into the next generation. Herein lies the crux of evolutionary theory: Evolutionary psychologists posit that those traits or psychological mechanisms that ultimately enhanced reproductive success among our hunter/gatherer ancestors would be maintained in the gene pool. Importantly, traits that enhanced reproductive success—"the number of surviving descents who themselves go on to reproduce" (Cross & Campbell, 2012, p. 199)—in the ancestral environment are known as *successful adaptations*. Equally important, these successful adaptations that ultimately lead to reproductive success are located in our genes. Moreover, it is through genetic transmission, and only genetic transmission, that these successful adaptations (e.g., brute strength to fight off rival suitors, speed to outrun predators, ability to attract and secure sexual partners) are passed onto the next generation. Lastly, successful adaptations always start out as chance genetic mutations (Duntley & Shackelford, 2008; Tooby & Cosmides, 2005).

Scholars who examine crime, violence, and aggression using evolutionary-based paradigms belong to the discipline of *forensic evolutionary psychology*. Evolutionary concepts have been used to explain a vast array of criminal behaviors, from homicide (Daly & Wilson, 1988) to child maltreatment (Harris & Rice, 2012). Additionally, evolutionary accounts have been put forth to explain female-perpetrated crime (Cross & Campbell, 2012) as well as psychopathic behavior (Harris, Rice, & Lalumière, 2001). In essence, forensic evolutionary theorists argue that recurring conflicts and problems that typified the ancestral environment (e.g., finding food, securing protection from the elements, avoiding predators, finding a mate, protecting and providing for one's children) shaped the development of evolved psychological mechanisms that can manifest themselves in various forms of antisocial behavior under the right circumstances. More specifically, forensic evolutionary theorists hypothesize that ancestral selection pressures resulted in the development of evolved psychological mechanisms, not behaviors that can activate in the presence of certain environmental cues. Environmental cues that promote crimes of violence and theft, for example, could include resource scarcity (e.g., no/little food, poor shelter options) and mate scarcity (Buss, 2011; Little, Shackelford, & Weekes-Shackelford, 2012). Given that there are several evolutionary explanations devoted to explaining a myriad of specialized forms of violence and crime, we only address two specific ones: (a) why females engage in less crime, particularly less violent crime than males, and (b) why extrafamilial male-on-male homicide occurs.

An evolutionary account for why females commit less crime than males. It is a universally accepted fact that girls and women commit substantially less crime, particularly less serious and violent crime, than their male counterparts (Blanchette & Brown, 2006; Ellis, 1988; Greenfeld & Snell, 1999; Moffitt & Caspi, 2001). This finding pervades culture, time, research methodology, and disciplinary orientation. The scholarly contributions of Anne Campbell and her colleagues (A. Campbell, 2002; A. Campbell, Muncer, & Bibel, 2001) are among the richest evolutionary accounts of female aggression and crime.

In essence, Cross and Campbell (2012) argued that gender differences in parental investment and fear threshold ultimately explain why females commit less crime, particularly less violent crime, than their male counterparts. To elaborate, in the ancestral environment, an offspring's survival was heavily dependent on his or her mother just as it is today (see Sear & Mace, 2008). The death of a pregnant woman also resulted in the death of her unborn child. Similarly, a young infant's only source of nourishment during infancy would have been from his or her lactating mother. Thus, if a pregnant or nursing mother opted for risky resource acquisition strategies that were naturally associated with a high probability of serious injury or even death (e.g., direct physical confrontation of a potential female rival), she would have been risking not only her own life but that of her child as well. Hence, evolutionary theorists such as Campbell have argued that over hundreds of thousands of years, natural selection favored girls and women who not only adopted less risky strategies (e.g., indirect aggression against female rivals) to acquire resources but also invested heavily in keeping their children alive (i.e., demonstrated high parental investment). However, Cross and Campbell (2012) also underscored that when resources are scarce (e.g., poverty), girls and women will opt for more risky strategies, including overt aggression. Further, the authors posited that the evolved psychological mechanism that inhibits risk-taking behavior among girls and women is fear. Individual differences in fear thresholds explain why some impoverished females resort to crime and others do not. The authors argued that over hundreds of thousands of years of evolution, natural selection has favored girls and women who possess a lower fear threshold relative to males. This evolved lower fear threshold in girls and women, relative to boys and men, is the proximal psychological mechanism that is hypothesized to inhibit females from engaging in various risky behaviors such as theft and direct forms of serious aggression.

In contrast, Campbell and colleagues (e.g., A. Campbell et al., 2001; Cross & Campbell, 2012) postulated that a male's reproductive success was improved rather than diminished by engaging in risky behaviors and by exhibiting something that evolutionists refer to as *high mating effort*. In brief, mating effort refers to a constellation of behaviors that increase the odds of inseminating as many females as possible. In men, mating effort manifests itself in traits such as dominance, independence, strength, fearlessness, and physical prowess as well as risky behaviors such as fighting or a willingness to fight (Mishra & Lalumière, 2008; Trivers, 1972). Unlike a female's reproductive success, which was ultimately linked to how much parental investment she afforded her offspring, a male's reproductive success was linked to how much mating effort he expended (Trivers, 1972). Thus, it will come as no surprise that males' evolved proclivity for risky behaviors and high mating effort plays a significant role in evolutionary accounts of male-on-male homicide.

An evolutionary account for male-on-male homicide.   In the United States, male-on-male homicides accounted for approximately two-thirds of all homicides between 1980 and 2008 (Cooper & Smith, 2011). Most homicides occur between unemployed and unmarried men as the result of altercations stemming from arguments, insults, or rivalries between male acquaintances (Serin et al., 2011). Daly and Wilson (1988), two prominent evolutionary theorists, postulated that in a vast number of circumstances, male homicide perpetrators are responding to perceived threats or challenges to their reputation as credible fighters. Daly and Wilson argued that in an ancestral environment, a male's reputation was largely dependent on his ability to maintain a credible threat of violence, and establishing and maintaining one's reputation as a formidable rival was critically linked to a

male's reproductive success. First, one's reputation as a formidable rival prevented competitors from stealing one's life-sustaining resources (e.g., food, shelter, and mates), and thus by extension, it prolonged one's life, thereby increasing the likelihood that one's genetic blueprint would be transmitted to the next generation. Second, one's reputation also signaled desirability to prospective mates (e.g., not only can I provide food and shelter, but I can also ward off predators and keep you and your offspring safe). Thus, evolutionary theorists such as Daly and Wilson posited that males have evolved psychological mechanisms that enhance the likelihood that they will react to status threats with violence.

It is important to emphasize that Daly and Wilson's (1988) hypothesis explains general aggression between males; it does not explain homicide per se. Rather, Daly and Wilson argued that violence and aggression have been naturally selected for, and that homicide is simply a fatal by-product of violence. Noteworthy, Duntley and Buss (2008) presented an alternative argument, positing that homicide in and of itself has been naturally selected. Empirical evidence associated with evolutionary accounts of crime is presented in the Research Review section.

Biological Theories

Stephen Anthony Mobley grew up in a White, middle-class American family and was never abused or mistreated. Inexplicably, he became increasingly violent. At the age of 25, Mobley shot and killed the manager of a Domino's Pizza store and was subsequently executed by lethal injection on March 1, 2005. During Mobley's trial, his aunt testified that the last four generations of Mobley's family had evidenced extreme violence, aggression, and criminality (Conner, 1995). Interestingly, Mobley's defense team petitioned the court to fund genetic testing to ascertain if Mobley suffered from an enzyme-related monoamine oxidase (MAOA) disorder. The court rejected the petition on the grounds that the science linking the MAOA gene to aggression was simply too preliminary (*Mobley v. The State*, 1995).

Although certain disciplines, criminology in particular, have been reluctant to recognize biologically based theories of crime (Wright, Beaver, Vaughn, Boisvert, & Vaske, 2008), biologically based explanations of crime have continued to garner increasing support from the scholarly community (Anderson, 2007; Caspi et al., 2002). Similarly, the American legal system is starting to consider biology in criminal court cases. Unlike Mobley, Bradley Waldroup, a Tennessee murder defendant, had his sentence successfully reduced from homicide to manslaughter in 2009 based on the MAOA defense (Brooks-Crozier, 2011). Importantly, however, biological explanations of crime are far more encompassing than the MAOA gene. In sum, biological explanations of crime fall into one of six broad categories: (a) behavioral genetics; (b) molecular genetics; (c) neurochemistry; (d) psychophysiology; (e) the brain; and (f) environmental perspectives that underscore how certain environmental insults such as pregnancy/birth complications, environmental toxins, and even diet may increase one's propensity for violence and crime in general.

Behavioral genetics and crime. The first official empirical quest to establish a link between genetics and crime occurred in 1929 when a German researcher, Lange (1929/1931), compared the incarceration records of 13 pairs of identical twins (i.e., monozgotic, or MZ twins) with the records of 17 pairs of fraternal twins (i.e., dizygotic, or DZ twins). Whereas MZ twins share 100% of their DNA, DZ twins share only 50% of their DNA. Therefore, if a hereditary component to crime does in fact exist, MZ twins should evidence a higher concordance rate for imprisonment (i.e., the percentage of time that both pairs of MZ twin pairs end up in prison) in comparison to DZ twins who share only 50% of their DNA. Lange found striking evidence in support of a link between genetics and crime in that the incarceration concordance rate for the MZ twins was astoundingly high—77%. In stark contrast, the corresponding concordance rate for the DZ twins was only 12%.

The Lange (1929/1931) study suffered from staggering methodological flaws, most notable being that Lange already knew who had a prison record and who did not before he determined MZ versus DZ membership. Additionally, Lange determined MZ/DZ status based solely on pictures. Despite these limitations, Lange's study is one of the first examples of using behavioral genetics to test the gene–crime link. In sum, the field of behavioral genetics uses twin (as well as adoption) studies to tease out the extent to which genetics, as well as the environment, influences human behavior.

Every member of the human species shares 99% of the same DNA sequence. Thus, 99% of our collective genetic makeup is fixed, or not subject to vary from person to person. Further, this 99% accounts for our species' most basic similarities. Genetic abnormalities aside, we all have two arms, one heart, two lungs, a nervous system, and so forth (Plomin, Defries, McClearn, & McGuffin, 2001). Consequently, behavioral geneticists do not focus on the shared 99% but rather study the 1% that does vary from individual to individual. Given that this 1% is 100% identical among MZ twins and only 50% identical among DZ twins, it stands to reason that if there is a genetic component to behavior, and crime in particular, then MZ twins should evidence higher concordance rates relative to their less genetically identical DZ twin counterparts.

In the context of research that attempts to establish a link between genetics and crime, concordance rates are calculated as follows. First, the researcher tracks the number of times that both members of the twin pair evidence antisocial behavior. Next, this frequency count is converted into a concordance rate that represents the percentage of times that both twin pairs evidence antisocial behavior. It is up to the researcher to decide how antisocial behavior is operationalized (e.g., official criminal convictions, self-report, collateral reports). Concordance rates are calculated separately for MZ and DZ twins and are subsequently compared. Concordance rates are typically converted into correlation coefficients, which in turn are squared, thereby rendering a heritability coefficient. A *heritability coefficient* represents the proportion of variance in crime that can be attributed to genetics (Falconer, 1965). However, more complex statistical approaches such as biometric modeling are now being used to estimate heritability coefficients (Rhee & Waldman, 2002). Notably, some of these methods, particularly the statistical modeling methods, generate three variance estimates: (a) proportion of variance due to genetics, (b) proportion of variance due to shared environmental influences (i.e., aspects of the environment shared by all family members, for example, living in poverty), and (c) proportion of variance due to nonshared environmental influences (i.e., aspects of the environment not shared by all family members, for example, exposure to different peer groups, differential treatment by parents; Quinsey, Skilling, Lalumière & Craig, 2004). Meta-analytic research involving more than 100 twin and adoption studies has illustrated that 41% of the variance in antisocial behavior can be attributed to genetics, whereas 59% of the variance in antisocial behavior can be attributed to the environment (16% shared environment, and 43% nonshared environment; Rhee & Waldman, 2002). We will have more to say about behavioral genetics research in the Research Review section of this chapter.

Molecular genetics and crime. The field of behavioral genetics explores the extent to which genetics does or does not account for variation in human behavior. However, behavioral genetics does not and cannot identify the actual gene(s) that is involved. This is the domain of molecular genetics. *Molecular genetics* is a subdivision of biology that examines both the structure and function of genes (Anderson, 2007). Historically, researchers have focused on understanding the structure and function of 1.5% to 2.0% of the human genome, specifically, genes that are involved in coding proteins (ENCODE Project Consortium et al., 2012). Proteins are ultimately responsible for the phenotypic or outward/visible expression of our genotype.

Researchers have linked one variant of the MAOA gene to antisociality and aggression in humans (Caspi et al., 2002; McDermott, Tingley, Cowden, Frazzetto, & Johnson, 2009). In brief, the MAOA gene encodes the MAOA enzyme. In turn, the MAOA enzyme is responsible for metabolizing or breaking down brain neurotransmitters like serotonin, dopamine, and norepinephrine. These neurotransmitters regulate an individual's emotion, sleep, appetite, motivation, reward and punishment, and fight-or-flight response (Anderson, 2007). Two variants of the MAOA gene occur naturally in the population: a low-activity/short-allele version and a high-activity/long-allele version. The low-activity variant does not metabolize neurotransmitters as effectively as the high-activity variant does. Notably, it is the low-activity version that has been associated with aggression (Caspi et al., 2002). Ann Gibbon, a science writer, popularized the MAOA gene when she used the term *warrior gene* to describe the MAOA gene during a scientific conference (Gibbon, 2004). As we will see shortly, one of the strongest methodological studies involving the MAOA gene illustrated that the MAOA gene in and of itself does not elevate one's propensity toward crime and violence. Rather, it is the combined effect of the low-activity MAOA gene variant and childhood maltreatment that escalates one's risk for future violence and antisociality (Caspi et al., 2002).

Neurochemistry and crime. Another branch of science—neurochemistry—has focused on understanding how certain hormones such as testosterone and specific neurotransmitters such as serotonin play a role in aggression and crime. More than 50 different hormones regulate an individual's metabolism, growth, and development and influence behavior. Hormones are transported throughout our bodies via bodily fluids, usually the blood system, and are distributed from nine central glands that comprise the endocrine system (e.g., hypothalamus, thyroid, and gonads). Hormones act as chemical messengers that carry instructions to a target cell to perform functions such as deepen voice or enlarge breasts (N. A. Campbell, Reece, & Mitchell, 1999). One hormone in particular, testosterone, has been linked to aggression. Although testosterone exists in both genders, greater amounts of testosterone exist in males. Testosterone is largely responsible for the development of the primary (e.g., testis and prostate) and secondary (e.g., muscle mass, hair growth) reproductive tissues (Anderson, 2007).

Hormones act as chemical messengers within the endocrine system; neurotransmitters act as chemical messengers within the nervous system, operating specifically within the brain. In brief, neurotransmitters play a critical role in how the brain communicates with the rest of the human body. Fundamentally, neurotransmitters are responsible for the infinite number of thoughts, actions, and feelings that an average human experiences daily. For example, in order to pick up a pencil or put on one's shoes, millions of electrical signals must travel along nerve cells or neurons. However, gaps or synapses exist between neurons, and in order for the electrical message to pass between neurons, a bridge is required. Neurotransmitters are essentially the bridge that enables electrical messages to be transmitted. They do so by converting electrical impulses into chemical messages. This conversion process is also described as *reuptake* (N. A. Campbell et al., 1999). Although more than 100 neurotransmitters have been identified, three in particular have been linked to crime; namely, serotonin, dopamine, and norepinephrine. *Serotonin* is associated with mood regulation, impulsivity, and aggression, and *dopamine* is linked to pleasurable activities such as sex, love, and food. Notably, the dopamine pleasure center can be triggered artificially with illicit drugs such as alcohol and nicotine. *Norepinephrine* is responsible for instructing the body to react to short-term stress (Anderson, 2007; N. A. Campbell et al., 1999).

Psychophysiology and crime.   Perhaps one of the most influential psychophysiological theories of antisocial behavior and crime is Gray's (1987) arousal model. The field of psychophysiology explores how physiological responses such as heart rate and galvanic skin response (also known as electrodermal activity, or EDA) are linked to psychological constructs such as motivation, emotion, and learning. According to Gray, personality, learning, motivation, and emotions are regulated by two biological systems of autonomic arousal. One system is the *behavioral activation system* (BAS). It is described as a reward-seeking system that becomes activated in the presence of positive incentives and rewards. A BAS example would be something like, "If I beat up Sam for insulting me in front of my friends, I will feel better." In contrast, the other system is the *behavioral inhibition system* (BIS). The BIS is best thought of as a punishment avoidance system: It helps to inhibit behavior because of the threat of punishment. For example, a BIS response might be, "I won't give in to my sexual impulses to rape because I fear going to prison."

The BAS system is associated with impulsivity and sensation-seeking behavior, whereas the BIS system is associated with anxiety (Fowles, 1980; Gray, 1987; Raine, 1993).

Gray (1987) hypothesized that because of an underactive BIS system, antisocial individuals are more fearless, less anxious, and less responsive to aversive stimulus. This in turn translates into a low resting heart rate or low EDA. Gray also posited that antisocial individuals have overactive BASs that, in turn, translate into elevated levels of sensation-seeking and impulsive tendencies. These tendencies increase an individual's risk for antisocial behavior.

The brain and crime.   Phineas Gage (1823–1860) was known to friends and family as a kind, polite, responsible person up until a large iron rod was accidently driven completely through his frontal lobe during a blasting rock accident that occurred during construction of a railroad. Although Gage survived, he was no longer the same man. After the accident, he reportedly became irritable, profane, and violent. Gage's unfortunate accident was the first documented natural experiment directly linking the brain to antisocial behavior (Anderson, 2007).

Contemporary researchers study the brain's involvement in antisocial behavior using two distinct types of research—brain imaging and neuropsychology. Brain or neuro imaging research examines both the structure and function of the brain. Structural elements encompass factors such as reduced grey matter, tumors, and lesions and are studied using magnetic resonance imaging (MRI) and computed tomography (CT). In contrast, functional elements include factors such as blood flow and glucose metabolism and are studied using positron-emission tomography (PET) and single photon emission computed tomography (SPECT; Anderson, 2007; Raine, 1993).

Raine and Yang (2006) posited that structural and/or functional damage to the areas of the brain that are responsible for moral reasoning and emotional regulation yield an "antisocial tendency." This antisocial tendency manifests in various ways, from psychopathic tendencies and violence to general criminality. Raine and Yang identified the following four areas of the brain as being particularly important in the expression of antisocial behavior:

- The frontal lobe—associated with higher order cognitive functioning such as cognitive reasoning, planning, solid judgment, abstract and moral reasoning, and aggression regulation;
- The temporal lobe—includes the amygdala (regulates emotional and fear responses) and the hippocampus (involved in memory, learning, and emotional regulation);
- The parietal lobe—integrates sensory information linked to space and movement; and
- The cingulated gyrus—partially surrounds the corpus callosum, which links the left and right hemispheres of the brain.

Importantly, several of these structures—the amygdala, hippocampus, and cingulated gyrus—are part of the interconnected limbic system. The limbic system regulates the autonomic expression of emotion such as increases in heartbeat and respiration and trembling and sweating as well as basic survival instincts including sex, hunger, thirst, and the fight-or-flight response (Anderson, 2007; Raine & Yang, 2006).

Whereas brain imaging studies explore how structural and functional aspects of the brain may be linked to violence and antisocial tendencies, neuropsychology uses indirect means; namely, pencil/paper and motor skills tests. For example, following an accident with suspected brain injury, a neuropsychologist might administer a battery of questionnaires and motor skills tests to ascertain which part, if any, of the brain was injured during the accident.

Other biological considerations—Toxins and diet. It should be becoming apparent that the causes of crime do not lie with nature or nurture. Rather, nature and nurture interact in very complex ways, either heightening or reducing one's risk for engaging in antisocial behavior. Thus far, we have presented biological theories of crime that describe how one's biology (e.g., low-activity variant of the MAOA gene) can predispose individuals to be more sensitive to environmental risk factors (e.g., child maltreatment) associated with crime. However, we have not explored how the environment itself

may actually change biology in such a manner as to either increase or decrease one's criminal propensity. There is evidence to suggest that environmental risk factors such as improper diet, hypoglycemia (i.e., low blood sugar), and even environmental toxins such as lead can elevate one's risk for antisocial behavior. The research evidence associated with each biological perspective is presented in the Research Review section.

Psychodynamic Theories

Between 1888 and 1939, Sigmund Freud published 24 volumes detailing his perspectives on human personality, and in particular, the development and treatment of psychopathology (Freud, 1901, 1938). Freud is perhaps best known for being the forefather of psychoanalysis, which is a form of psychotherapy or talk therapy. During psychotherapy, Freud believed that letting patients engage in free association (i.e., verbalize random thoughts spontaneously in a relaxed setting) would allow them to retrieve suppressed unconscious memories and feelings. According to Freud, suppressed unconscious memories, feelings, or thoughts are ultimately the root causes of psychopathology. The actual analysis of these unconscious thoughts was called psychoanalysis (Freud, 1953). Thus, Freud's theory of personality is often referred to as *psychoanalytic or psychodynamic theory*.

Despite Freud's voluminous works, he expressed very few opinions about criminal behavior (see Freud, 1901, 1938). However, his views on antisocial behavior stem largely from the key tenets of his psychoanalytic theory of personality; namely, the id, ego, and super ego. Moreover, as we will see, Freud's basic personality tenets permeate contemporary psychodynamic theories discussed in this section; namely, the Gluecks' collective works (Glueck & Glueck, 1950, 1968), social control theory (Hirschi, 1969, 2002), and the general theory of crime (Gottfredson & Hirschi, 1990).

Freud's perspective on crime. According to Freud (1938), personality consists of three interconnected systems: the id, the ego, and the superego. The *id* is the basin for unconscious psychic energy that continually strives to satisfy basic survival needs such as hunger, thirst, and sex. Freud stipulated that the id is guided by the pleasure principle, meaning that it seeks immediate gratification, unconstrained by reality. The newborn baby exemplifies the id, demanding immediate attention and crying out when his or her needs are not immediately met. There is no recognition that external constraints exist in an outside world. Additionally, Freud postulated that humans are born with a fully intact id. In contrast, the *ego* gradually develops over time as the infant learns how to balance his or her internal needs with the demands of the outside world. The ego operates according to the reality principle. In essence, the reality principle dictates that the ego will attempt to meet the id's demands, albeit in realistic ways. The ego contains an individual's conscious thoughts, judgments, and memories. Lastly, the *superego* represents the moral imperative of personality. It represents the conscience and considers what one should do in an ideal world. Thus, the superego gives us our sense of right and wrong. The superego develops in response to the morals and values that society and parents impose on us. Given that the superego strives for perfection, it causes feelings of pride when we act in accordance with its ideals. Conversely, the superego causes feelings of guilt when our actions go against its moral imperative.

Psychoanalysts following in Freud's tradition have proposed three main pathways to crime. Interestingly, each pathway results from a poorly developed superego. In the first paradigm, crime is postulated to result due to an overdeveloped superego. This individual has been coined the *neurotic* criminal (Alexander, 1935; Blackburn, 1995). In essence, in a neurotic criminal, the overdeveloped superego results in pathological unconscious guilt. It is posited that the neurotic criminal commits crime to satiate the subconscious' desire for punishment. In contrast, a weak or underdeveloped superego leads to *psychopathic* tendencies (Millon, Simonsen, Davis, & Birket-Smith, 1998). In the absence of a well-developed superego, the primitive needs of the id remain unregulated. Hence, this individual is characterized as "egocentric, impulsive guiltless, and unempathic" (Blackburn, 1995, p. 114). The final criminal type results

from a *deviant*-developed superego. Unlike the neurotic and psychopathic criminals, with overdeveloped and underdeveloped superegos, respectively, the deviant criminal's superego has developed, albeit vis-à-vis identification with deviant role model(s), such as a criminal parent (Blackburn, 1995).

Freud influenced each of the forthcoming psychodynamic perspectives on crime in three important ways. First, contemporary psychodynamic theorists focus on explaining why individuals conform to societal rules (e.g., follow the superego) rather than on why they engage in crime (e.g., follow the id). Second, in the same way that Freud emphasized the unconscious, these theorists underscore inner drives and psychic mechanisms that lead people to engage in antisocial behavior. Third, each perspective delineates how parent(s) are the primary socialization agents through whom individuals develop criminal or prosocial tendencies.

Glueck and Glueck's perspective on crime. The Gluecks were a husband and wife research team who studied delinquency in the 1950s and 1960s. They conducted two seminal research studies and interpreted several of their findings through the lens of Freudian psychodynamic theory. The first cross-sectional research study compared 500 delinquent and 500 nondelinquent individuals who were matched on a number of key variables, including age, race, neighborhood, and intelligence (Glueck & Glueck, 1950). In the second study, the delinquent sample was followed up longitudinally (Glueck & Glueck, 1968). The Gluecks used an impressive array of measurement strategies and data sources to reach their conclusions. Consistent with psychodynamic perspectives, the Gluecks emphasized the importance of poor parenting (e.g., poor supervision, criminal role modeling) in the etiology of delinquency. Additionally, Freudian principles permeated the Glueck's work, as evidenced by statements such as, "the development of a mentally hygienic and properly oriented superego (conscience) must have been greatly hampered by the kind of parental ideals, attitudes, temperaments, and behavior found to play such a major role on the family stage of the delinquents" (Glueck & Glueck, 1950, p. 281).

Hirschi's control theory. Although Hirschi did not rely on Freudian thinking to the same extent as the Gluecks did (Andrews & Bonta, 2010), he did seek to answer a fundamentally psychodynamic question—"Why *don't* more people behave antisocially?"—rather than traditional theories of crime that ask "Why *do* people act antisocially?" Hirschi's original social control theory (or social bond theory) posited that the reason people do not commit crime or engage in antisocial activities is due to an individual's ties or bonds to society (Hirschi, 1969, 2002). More specifically, Hirschi presented four distinct types of social bonds: (a) *attachment* to conventional people and institutions—parents, friends and teachers—in the form of emotional bonds, respect, and love; (b) *commitment* or investment in achieving conventional goals such as getting an education and securing employment; (c) *involvement*, the degree to which individuals are actually engaged in conventional pursuits in various spheres such as education, employment, community, and leisure; and (d) *belief* in, and respect for, the law.

The linkages between Hirschi's (1969, 2002) social bonds and Freud's (1938) id-ego-superego triad are readily apparent. For example, it is not difficult to imagine how a weak or absent belief system mirrors the absence of a strong superego. Similarly, the notion of attachment to conventional others reflects the ego ideal. In addition, according to Hirschi, commitment—the time and energy devoted to the pursuit of conventional behaviors such as education, establishing a business, or a virtuous reputation—parallels ego functioning in many ways. Consistent with Freudian principles, Hirschi also emphasized the importance of parents during the socialization process.

Gottfredson and Hirschi's (1990) general theory of crime. In brief, the general theory of crime posits that self control coupled with opportunity is the primary causal agent that leads to crime and antisocial behavior in general. Gottfredson and Hirschi (1990) defined low self-control as having an enduring propensity to pursue short-term, immediate gratification at the expense of long-term consequences. Individuals with low self-control are defined as "impulsive, insensitive, physical (as opposed to mental), risk-taking, short-sighted, and non-verbal" (Gottfredson & Hirschi, 1990, p. 90). Thus, individuals who have low self-control will engage in criminal conduct or analogous behavior when given the opportunity to do so. Consistent with the psychodynamic tradition, the authors posited that individual differences in self-control emerge during childhood as a result of parental practices. Specifically, the authors suggested that poor parental supervision along with parental failure to identify and punish inappropriate behavior leads to low self-control.

Learning Theories

Unlike biological or psychodynamic perspectives on criminal behavior, learning theories locate the causes of criminal behavior, for the most part, in the environment. For example, the Columbine massacre in 1999, in which two teens murdered 13 people and wounded 24 others at a Colorado high school, led some to blame the effects of violent video games and the media. Such arguments are based on learning theories or the general idea that criminal behavior can be learned through such sources. Within the context of learning theory, learning may be defined as "a change in pre-existing behavior or mental processes that occurs as a result of experience" (Cassel & Bernstein, 2001, p. 85). Three types of learning theories have been applied to explanations of criminal behavior and are discussed in this subsection of the chapter: *classical conditioning*, or learning by association; *operant conditioning*, or learning through reinforcement and punishment; and *social learning*, or learning through models and observations. The subsection ends with a discussion of a theory that integrates each of these learning perspectives with elements of other theories, including the control theories that were discussed in the previous subsection.

Classical conditioning. Learning by association is achieved through practices of classical conditioning. The principles of classical conditioning were developed based on the famous experiments of Ivan

Pavlov in the early 1900s, in which Pavlov was able to condition dogs to salivate at the sound of a tone after repeatedly pairing that tone with food. The dogs learned to associate the tone (i.e., the conditioned stimulus, or CS) with the food (i.e., the unconditioned stimulus, or UCS), thereby producing salivation (i.e., the conditioned response, or CR, which was originally an unconditioned response, or UCR, to the food). Learning by association has also been demonstrated through experiments with human participants; in a classic example, a similar process was used to condition a young boy ("Little Albert") to fear a rat for which he had no previous fear (Watson & Rayner, 1920).

H. J. Eysenck (1977, 1996) used classical conditioning to explain criminal behavior. His biosocial theory of crime suggested that criminal behavior is produced by an interaction between biological and environmental factors. In particular, Eysenck believed that the functioning of one's nervous system affects one's ability to be conditioned by events in the environment and therefore, one's ability to develop a conscience. In his view, the conscience is essentially fear that is associated with particular acts because of a history of punishment for those acts; in other words, conscience is a conditioned fear response to thoughts of a particular act (the CS) because of the act's having been previously paired with unpleasant punishment experiences (the UCS). Criminal behavior then arises either from not being exposed to conditioning experiences that are meant to punish antisocial behavior or from having poor conditionability. Raine (1997) provided a good example of how conscience is developed in this theory.

> Taking the scenario of a small child stealing a cookie (CS) from the kitchen, punishment by the parent (scolding or physical punishment—UCS) elicits an unconditional response (UCR) whereby the child is upset and feels uncomfortable. After a number of similar "learning trials," the sight of the cookie (or even the thought of stealing the cookie) will elicit an uncomfortable feeling in the child (conditional response—CR) which acts to avert the child from enacting the "theft." Similar "conditioned emotional responses" developed relatively early in life in varying situations combine, in Eysenck's view, to represent what we call "conscience." In this analysis, socialized individuals develop a feeling of uneasiness at even contemplating a criminal act (robbery, assault) presumably because such thoughts elicit representations or "unconscious" memories of punishment early in life for milder but related misdemeanors (theft, behaving aggressively). (p. 124)

H. J. Eysenck (1977, 1996) theorized that three facets of personality are key to conditionability and, therefore, criminal behavior: extraversion, neuroticism, and psychoticism. Each facet exists on a continuum such that individuals can be high or low on each. Based on Eysenck's theory, an individual's personality is linked to one's baseline level of cortical arousal and the amount of stimulation needed to reach optimal levels of cortical arousal. Individuals high in extraversion (extraverts) have underaroused central nervous systems and are therefore outgoing and impulsive sensation-seekers, whereas individuals low in extraversion (introverts) are more cautious and reserved. Individuals who are neurotic (high on neuroticism) have very sensitive autonomic nervous systems and are emotionally reactive, whereas those who are low on neuroticism are emotionally stable. The biology behind the psychoticism dimension is not as well defined, but individuals who are high in psychoticism are cold, impulsive, and hostile compared to individuals who are low in psychoticism. Essentially, criminals are predicted to be extraverts (because of their poor conditionability and underdeveloped conscience), neurotics (because of their high emotionality and their reversion to automatic behaviors when in a highly emotional state), and psychotics (because of their callousness). Psychoticism in Eysenck's theory is defined more similarly to psychopathy rather than to the clinical definition of psychoticism (i.e., a break from reality).

Operant conditioning. The principles of operant conditioning are typically attributed to the work of Skinner (1938, 1953), but operant conditioning builds on Thorndike's (1898) law of effect. This law suggests that one is more likely to repeat an act that results in desirable outcomes and less likely to repeat an act that results in unpleasant outcomes. Expanding on this law, the principles of operant conditioning refer to these desirable and unpleasant outcomes that determine behavior as reinforcements and punishments, respectively; further, these reinforcements and punishments can be either positive (i.e., involving the addition of a stimulus) or negative (i.e., involving the removal of a stimulus). Thus, *positive reinforcement* increases the frequency of a behavior through the addition of something pleasant (e.g., money or food) and *negative reinforcement* increases the frequency of a behavior through the removal of something unpleasant (e.g., removing pain or discomfort). Similarly, *positive punishment* decreases the frequency of a behavior through the addition of something unpleasant (e.g., pain or discomfort), and *negative punishment* decreases the frequency of a behavior through the removal of something pleasant (e.g., removing money or food). According to these principles of operant conditioning, reinforcement, by definition, must result in increases in the frequency of a behavior, whereas punishment, by definition, must result in decreases in the frequency of a behavior. However, the particular stimulus involved in the reinforcement or punishment may differ depending on the situation or the person; in other words, what is reinforcing or punishing to one person in one situation may not have the same effect on the same person in another situation or another person in the same situation.

Jeffery (1965) applied the principles of operant conditioning to crime when building on Sutherland's (1939, 1947) differential association theory. Differential association theory is a sociological/criminological theory of crime that has nine propositions at its core:

1. Criminal behavior is learned.
2. Criminal behavior is learned in interaction with other persons in a process of communication.
3. The principal part of the learning of criminal

behavior occurs within intimate personal groups.
4. When criminal behavior is learned, the learning includes (a) techniques of committing the crime, which are sometimes very complicated, sometimes very simple; and (b) the specific direction of motives, drives, rationalizations, and attitudes.
5. The specific direction of motives and drives is learned from definitions of the legal codes as favorable or unfavorable.
6. A person becomes delinquent because of an excess of definitions favorable to violation of law over definitions unfavorable to violation of law.
7. Differential associations may vary in frequency, duration, priority, and intensity.
8. The process of learning criminal behavior by association with criminal and anti-criminal patterns involves all of the mechanisms that are involved in any other learning.
9. While criminal behavior is an expression of general needs and values, it is not explained by those general needs and values since non-criminal behavior is an expression of the same needs and values. (Sutherland, 1947, pp. 6–8)

Differential association theory did not detail the specific learning process involved (e.g., classical, operant conditioning; Sutherland & Cressey, 1974). Jeffery (1965) addressed this limitation by combining the theory with operant conditioning in his differential reinforcement theory. According to Jeffery,

> the theory of differential reinforcement states that a criminal act occurs in an environment in which in the past the actor has been reinforced for behaving in this manner, and the aversive consequences attached to the behavior have been of such a nature that they do not control or prevent the response. (p. 295)

In other words, whether one becomes involved in criminal behavior is determined by one's individual learning history in terms of reinforcement and punishment. Again, what is reinforcing or punishing in this learning history will differ between people and situations. For example, an individual's socioeconomic status may affect what is reinforcing or punishing; if one is from a disadvantaged minority group, incarceration may not be as effective a punishment for behavior than it would be for a member of a group that is more accustomed to privilege (Hollin, 1989).

Around the same time as Jeffery's (1965) work, Burgess and Akers (1966) developed differential association-reinforcement theory, which also combined differential association theory with operant conditioning to explain criminal behavior, although this theory did not receive much attention (however, Aker's later work was more widely recognized, as will be discussed later). Operant conditioning has been criticized for its neglect of the role of cognition in behavior (Hollin, 1989). Social learning theory addresses this criticism to a certain extent through its inclusion of more internal factors in the learning process.

Social learning.   Social learning theory is sometimes referred to as cognitive learning theory because of its incorporation of cognitive factors such as expectancies and perceptions in the learning process. Rotter's (1954) expectancy theory proposed that whether a given behavior will occur is influenced by one's expectancies regarding its outcome and one's perceptions of the value of that outcome. Bandura (1973, 1977; Bandura & Walters, 1963) specified that one can learn behaviors and their outcomes through observing others (especially others who one considers high-status models of behavior), as well as through having one's own behavior reinforced or punished in the environment. This allows for multiple types of reinforcement: reinforcement from the environment (external reinforcement), reinforcement from observing others' outcomes (vicarious reinforcement), and reinforcement from the self based on one's own standards (self-reinforcement). Bandura and colleagues demonstrated vicarious conditioning in a classic modeling experiment with an inflatable "Bobo doll" (Bandura, Ross, & Ross, 1963). Children acted aggressively toward the doll after observing an adult hitting the doll in a film; the effect was stronger when children had also observed the adult being rewarded for the aggressive behavior.

Akers (1973) drew on his earlier differential association-reinforcement theory with Burgess (i.e., Burgess & Akers, 1966), which was based on differential association theory and operant conditioning, and added elements of social learning theory to his explanation of criminal behavior. Akers (1990) described his theory as follows:

> As applied by Akers to crime and deviance, social learning is a behavioral approach to socialization which includes individuals' response to rewards and punishments in the current situation, the learned patterns of responses they bring to that situation, and the anticipated consequences of actions taken now and in the future in the initiation, continuation, and cessation of those actions. It is a "soft behaviorism" that allows for choice and cognitive processes. It views the individual's behavior as responding to and being conditioned by environmental feedback and consequences. It does not view the individual as unreasoning and only passively conditioned. (p. 666)

Akers (2009) described the four key concepts in his social learning theory of crime in detail: differential association, definitions, imitation, and differential reinforcement. *Differential association* is exposure to definitions that are favorable and unfavorable to prosocial or antisocial behavior. As in differential association theory, the associations can differ in priority, duration, frequency, and intensity such that earlier, longer, more frequent, and more intense/closer associations are most influential. *Definitions* are essentially the attitudes that one has toward given behaviors. Sources of these definitions include family, friends, figures and representations in the media, and so on. *Imitation* describes engaging in acts that are modeled by others, which is most critical when one initially learns a behavior. *Differential reinforcement* is more important to the continuation of behavior and refers to the balance of the benefits and costs associated with a given behavior. Reinforcement for a given behavior can include three types of rewards: social (rewards from others; e.g., approval), nonsocial (physical or material rewards; e.g., money), and self-reinforcement (rewards from oneself for one's own behavior; e.g., sense of pride).

Personal, interpersonal, and community-reinforcement theory. The personal, interpersonal, and community-reinforcement (PIC–R) theory (Andrews & Bonta, 2003, 2006, 2010) was developed specifically to explain criminal behavior. It integrates control and learning perspectives while giving attention to the strongest predictors of criminal behavior. Central to the PIC–R theory are the big four predictors of criminal behavior: antisocial attitudes, antisocial associates, antisocial personality, and a history of antisocial behavior. One can see the link between this theory and others in some of these predictors. For example, there are similarities between *antisocial attitudes* and the definitions that are central to Akers's (1973) social learning theory of crime. *Antisocial associates* are predicted to influence these attitudes and model behaviors, which is also consistent with social learning theory. Part of the *antisocial personality* relates to H. J. Eysenck's (1977) discussion of the link between personality and crime, in which individuals who are callous (i.e., high on psychoticism) and impulsive (i.e., high on extraversion) are more likely to engage in criminal behavior.

More generally, PIC–R (Andrews & Bonta, 2003, 2006, 2010) suggests that the balance of benefits and costs from a particular antisocial act will determine whether it is committed. There are four categories of factors that influence this balance and determine whether a crime is committed: personal (e.g., antisocial attitudes, personality), interpersonal (e.g., antisocial associates, family), community (e.g., neighborhood influences), and situational (e.g., opportunities, stressors). For example, the personal factors of antisocial attitudes and personality may influence whether one derives self-reinforcement from a criminal act. In addition, interpersonal factors such as antisocial associates may influence whether one receives social reinforcement for a criminal act.

The PIC–R is a very practical theory that is driven by evidence, which will become clear in the Research Review section of this chapter. It is meant to succinctly explain criminal behavior to the fullest extent possible by integrating multiple perspectives. All of this is with the goal of informing practice; hence, the development of the principles of effective correctional programs derived from the theory, which are described in the Practice and Policy Issues section of this chapter. Despite its being a newer theory, the PIC–R has influenced many current correctional practices (Ward, Melser, & Yates, 2007).

RESEARCH REVIEW

In this section, we provide a brief review of the empirical research that supports each of the theoretical perspectives that were discussed in the previous section.

Evolutionary Explanations

Researchers who study criminal behavior through the lens of evolutionary psychology use standard methodological approaches that are considered commonplace in psychology. These include paper/pencil questionnaires, experimental studies conducted in laboratories, aggregate crime statistics, and ethnographic approaches. Moreover, researchers study the attitudes, thoughts, and behaviors of living, breathing people but interpret the results within an evolutionary framework. Thus, evolutionary psychologists use psychological data that are proximally measured to test hypotheses about distal levels of explanations.

Recall that Anne Campbell and her evolutionary colleagues (e.g., A. Campbell, 2002; A. Campbell et al., 2001; Cross & Campbell, 2012) posited that greater parental investment resulting in an evolved lower fear threshold (or greater aversion to risk) among females relative to males explains the gender gap in crime, particularly overt forms of aggression. Additionally, A. Campbell (2002) argued that resource scarcity (e.g., poverty) is a necessary yet not sufficient precursor to female criminality. Individual differences in fear thresholds explain why some impoverished girls and women resort to crime and others do not.

If Campbell and colleagues' (e.g., A. Campbell, 2002; A. Campbell et al., 2001; Cross & Campbell, 2012) accounts are correct, the empirical evidence should illustrate at the very least that (a) poverty is indeed a strong risk predictor of crime among females; (b) in the general population, females should evidence a lower fear threshold relative to males; and (c) among incarcerated populations, females and males should evidence similar fear thresholds. In sum, although direct tests of Campbell's perspective are absent, indirect evidence supports Campbell's perspective. For example, in regard to poverty, feminist scholars strongly endorse the role that poverty plays in the etiology of crime among girls and women. For example, Hunnicutt and Broidy (2004) stated that "there is general agreement among scholars that the economic marginality of women is closely linked to female crime . . . it is one of the most pervasive explanations for female crime" (p. 132). Moreover, comprehensive reviews of the women offender literature underscore the importance of alleviating economic marginalization through the development of education and employment opportunities for women (Bloom, Owen, & Covington, 2003). Similarly, the quantitative evidence supports a strong correlation between aggregate crime statistics and aggregate poverty statistics among females (see Blanchette & Brown, 2006, for a review). In addition, a relatively recent study that was conducted at the person level illustrated that poverty predicted self-reported arrest rates in a small sample of female offenders ($N = 134$; Holtfreter, Reisig, & Morash, 2004). Similarly, Farrington and Painter (2004) illustrated that poverty (e.g., low social class, low family income, poor housing) predicted criminal behavior more strongly in a sample of sisters ($N = 519$) relative to their brothers ($N = 494$). Thus, there appears to be evidence that resource scarcity—operationalized in a variety of ways—plays a substantial role in female criminal conduct. However, the extent to which resource scarcity plays more of a role in the onset and maintenance of female-perpetrated crime relative to male-perpetrated crime requires further investigation. Similarly, the extent to which criminal versus noncriminal females differ in terms of fear threshold has not been investigated. Although prominent correctional scholars who have developed general theories of crime (e.g., Andrews & Bonta, 2010) do recognize the role that unemployment and poor education play in criminal offending, they tend to afford more importance to other factors, such as criminal

attitudes and antisocial associates. In addition, the role of systematic poverty is typically underemphasized by psychological theorists such as Andrews and Bonta (2010; see the PIC–R model discussed in the section on social learning theories).

There is also evidence to suggest that females in general are more risk averse (i.e., evidence higher fear thresholds) than males (Blackwell & Piquero, 2005; Lagrange & Silverman, 1999). The strongest evidence comes from a recent meta-analysis that was conducted by Cross, Copping, and Campbell (2011). These researchers examined sex differences in impulsivity and risk taking. Cross et al. summarized the results of 127 different studies involving approximately 23,000 males and 29,000 females. In sum, the researchers found no differences between the genders for measures of cognitive impulsivity ($d = 0.08$). However, they did find medium effect sizes that favored male risk-taking/sensation-seeking behavior in comparison to females. This result held regardless of whether questionnaire measures ($d = .41$) or behavioral indices ($d = .36$) were used. Interestingly, the meta-analytic results also showed that females are more sensitive to punishment than males ($d = -0.33$). Collectively, these findings provide support for evolutionary perspectives espousing fear threshold as a central causal variable accounting for gender differences in criminal conduct. However, more research comparing incarcerated samples to nonincarcerated samples (male and female) is required. Similarly, laboratory studies that examine how central constructs such as resource scarcity and fear ultimately lead to criminal conduct, particularly among female samples, requires exploration.

As seen thus far, evolutionary explanations posit that the reason that females engage in less crime, particularly less violent crime, than their male counterparts is essentially because of evolved sex differences in parental investment. In contrast, evolutionary accounts focusing on male crime and male-perpetrated violence underscore the role of mating effort. Recall that mating effort refers to a set of behaviors that enhance a male's chances of finding and attracting sexual partners, which in turn enhances his reproductive success. Such behaviors would include risky demonstrations of strength, physical prowess, or any demonstration that convinces a potential female mate that her own reproductive success would be enhanced by pairing up with said male (e.g., he can fend off predators, hunt successfully, protect me and my children from the elements). Mating effort behaviors would also include more direct actions that enhance reproductive success; namely, inseminating multiple partners. Recall that evolutionists argue that male-on-male aggression including homicide results largely from perceived threats to a male's reputation and status (e.g., his ability to fight, ward off potential predators, or provide for his offspring).

Daly and Wilson (1988) provided convincing evidence linking male-on-male aggression to behaviors that are associated with high mating effort. For example, they reported that approximately one in three young men were killed during male competition for resources and social status across a range of preindustrial societies. Additionally, these authors interpreted preexisting analyses of homicide studies through the lens of evolution, or more specifically, in accordance with what perhaps could be referred to as a *threatened reproductive value hypothesis*. One notable example includes Wolfgang's (1958) classic homicide study. Specifically, Wolfgang classified a large number of homicides as "altercations of relatively trivial origin; insult, curse, jostling, etc." (p. 125). Daly and Wilson also referenced various historical accounts (e.g., duels often led to status enhancement among prominent men in American history) and anthropological accounts that support the hypothesis that reputation threats lead to violence among men. For example, they provided this quote from a Dani tribesman from New Guinea: "A man without valor is kepu—a worthless man, a man-who-has-not-killed" (Matthiessen, 1962, as cited in Daly & Wilson, 1988, p. 313). Thus, although there is substantial anecdotal and correlational evidence in support of the threatened reproductive value hypothesis, creative research conducted in controlled laboratory settings would help establish the extent to which this particular proximal trigger is causally linked to aggression in males. Additionally, research that examines whether or not male and female offenders actually differ in what triggers threats to their respective reputations would also help elucidate the value of this particular perspective.

More generally, if evolutionary theorists are correct, examples of mating effort should be much higher among males than females in the general population. In fact, this does seem to be the case. Hyde (2005) conducted a landmark meta-analysis of 46 existing meta-analyses that examined sex differences across a wide range of attitudes and behaviors. Notably, large gender differences emerged in regard to attitudes toward casual sex and self-reported masturbation. Specifically, males evidenced more favorable attitudes toward casual sex ($d = .81$) and reported engaging in masturbation more frequently than females ($d = .96$). In a more recent meta-analysis, Petersen and Hyde (2010) examined sex differences across 30 specific sexual behaviors and attitudes. The meta-analysis was extremely comprehensive. It included 834 studies and 1,000,000 participants from 87 different countries. Interestingly, of the 30 different sexual behaviors and attitudes examined, 25 rendered either small or no sex differences whatsoever. However, noticeable sex differences did emerge in five domains: Men reported (a) masturbating more frequently ($d = .53$), (b) using pornography more often ($d = .63$), (c) having more casual sex ($d = .38$), (d) having more sexual partners ($d = .36$), and (e) exhibiting more casual attitudes toward sex ($d = .45$). Thus, collectively, the meta-analytic results are consistent with the notion that sex differences in mating effort do exist. Specifically, consistent with evolutionary predictions, males exhibit substantially more mating effort than females. However, more research that explicitly links mating effort to criminal conduct is required. Similarly, direct tests of Daly and Wilson's (1988) hypothesis that homicide is a by-product of aggression versus Duntley and Buss's (2008) position that homicide in and of itself has been naturally selected for requires investigation.

Evolutionary explanations for criminal behavior have been intensely criticized by some researchers (e.g., Belknap, 2007) and enthusiastically embraced by others (e.g., Quinsey et al., 2004). The most common criticisms levied against evolutionary perspectives include the legitimization of existing patriarchal structures and social injustices, biological determinism, and ideological incongruence (Belknap, 2001; Coyne, 2009; Fausto-Sterling, 1992). Belknap (2001) encapsulated the ideological incongruence perspective as evidenced by the following statement: "This perspective is . . . insulting to girls and women, viewing them as pathetic, needy competitors for male attention" (p. 57). Proponents of evolutionary perspectives invoke the naturalistic fallacy in response to the criticism that evolutionary accounts only further legitimize social injustices and existing patriarchal structures. In brief, the naturalistic fallacy refers to the faulty assumption that because something is based in evolution, it must be natural, and in turn, all things natural are fair and just.

Criticisms that are grounded in determinism purport that evolutionary accounts (and biology for that matter) are not useful because the past, specifically our ancestral past, cannot be changed. Thus, theories that rely heavily on ancestral heritage bear no importance on present-day behavior. Further, if our evolutionary history is indeed stored in our DNA, this information is unimportant because we cannot change our genes. Determinists also argue that evolutionary accounts ignore environmental influences (Serin et al., 2011). Evolutionists would rebut this, indicating that biological determinism is a myth, as evidenced by countless studies illustrating how genes interact with the environment, either increasing risk or providing additional buffers to environmental insults.

At this juncture, it is necessary to highlight two points that evolutionary theorists often raise. First, our existing evolved psychological adaptive mechanisms were useful in hunter and gatherer societies, that is, small tribal communities of less than 100. Thus, it does not logically follow that what kept one alive and one's children alive within a brutish ancestral environment will necessarily be adaptive in contemporary society (Serin et al., 2011). Second, evolved psychological mechanisms were not consciously selected. Our existing genome did not emerge because our ancestors thought, "I will do X, and then Y will happen." Rather, gradually, over hundreds of thousands of years, species learned to adapt to whatever environmental or selection pressures existed in their respective environmental niches. Organisms that adapted and hence were able to live long enough to propagate their genetic material were considered successful. Natural selection is an unconscious process that occurs at the level of the individual gene (Dawkins, 1976).

Biological Theories of Crime

Support for biological theories of crime comes from twin and adoption studies, molecular genetics research, psychophysiological research, research using brain imaging techniques, and neuropsychological studies.

Twin and adoption studies. Behavioral geneticists rely on twin and adoption studies to determine to what extent genetics and the environment play a role in criminal conduct. Recall that twin studies typically involve having a researcher(s) identify a sample of MZ twins and a sample of DZ twins, raised by their respective biological parents. The researcher(s) then compares the degree to which the DZ twin pairs both exhibit criminal behavior (i.e., the concordance rate) in comparison to the MZ twin pairs. Recall that MZ twins share 100% of their DNA in common, compared to DZ twins who share only 50%. Thus, if the MZ twins evidence higher concordance rates relative to the DZ twins (e.g., 0.70 vs. 0.40), this is taken as evidence in favor of a genetic contribution to crime.

Twin studies have typically been criticized for overestimating the genetic contribution to crime for several reasons. First, the parents of MZ twins are more likely to treat twins in a similar fashion (e.g., provide the same clothes, afford the same educational and extracurricular opportunities) in comparison to the parents of DZ twins (Anderson, 2007; Raine, 1993). Second, heritability coefficients for MZ twins may be artificially inflated given that MZ twins typically share one placenta versus DZ twins, who each have their own placenta. Thus, any observed commonalities between MZ twin pairs may be due to prenatal factors rather than genetic factors. Lastly, earlier twin studies (e.g., Lange, 1929/1931) have been criticized for using small samples and for being conducted within Nazi Germany, and hence were subject to political agendas (Anderson, 2007; Andrews & Bonta, 2010).

Adoption studies address many of the criticisms that have been levied against twin studies. The parent–offspring paradigm exemplifies how adoption studies have contributed to the nature/ nurture crime debate. In the parent–offspring paradigm, criminal behavior concordance rates are first calculated for the adoptive parents and the adoptees. Next, criminal behavior concordance rates are calculated for the biological parents and the adoptees. If the concordance rates are higher for the biological parent/biological child pairings versus the adoptive parent/adoptive child pairings, a genetic contribution to crime is inferred (Rhee & Waldman, 2002). As with twin studies, adoption studies are not without limitations. For example, adoptees tend to have higher rates of antisocial behavior relative to the general population. Additionally, the adopted offspring's environment tends to be more advantageous relative to the general population, which in turn reduces the extent to which crime is potentially due to shared environmental effects (see Rhee & Waldman, 2002).

To date, more than 100 twin and adoption studies have been conducted to study the extent to which an array of antisocial behaviors are based in genetics (Moffitt, 2005). Rhee and Waldman (2002) conducted one of the most comprehensive meta-analytic reviews of the literature. In sum, their meta-analytic review involved 55,525 participant pairs that included participants from 10 different adoption studies and 42 twin samples. Aggregating across all studies, the authors reported that the variance in antisocial behavior could be explained as follows: 0.41 was due to heritability, 0.16 to shared environment (factors experienced similarly by both twins; e.g., same neighborhood), and 0.43 to non-shared environment (factors experienced differently by both twins; e.g., different peer groups, being treated differently by parents). Interestingly, the authors also examined how a number of moderator variables influenced the results. Noteworthy moderators included (a) sex of the participants, (b) twin versus adoption studies, and (c) age of the participants. Interestingly, the heritability coefficient did not vary as a function of sex in the methodologically rigorous studies. In addition, the twin studies tended to generate higher heritability coefficients than the adoption studies did. Lastly, genetic effects seemed to increase with age, with genes exerting more influence during adulthood versus childhood.

Historically, behavioral geneticists have focused on additive effects; that is, how genes and environment impact criminal behavior as main effects. This wealth of research has demonstrated that both genetics and the environment contribute to criminal behavior. However, increasingly, researchers are focusing on understanding how genes and the environment interact to cause multiplicative effects. Specifically, the next generation of behavioral geneticists will be (and are currently) focusing on understanding how genes either exacerbate or protect individuals in the face of environmental stressors (Moffitt, 2005).

Molecular genetics research.   Recall that whereas the field of behavioral genetics informs the extent to which genetics plays a role in criminal conduct, molecular genetics has the potential to identify which genes may be involved. As described earlier, the role that the MAOA gene plays in aggression and antisocial behavior has garnered the most attention. Recall that the MAOA gene is an X-linked gene that encodes the MAOA enzyme. The MAOA enzyme metabolizes brain neurotransmitters, thereby rendering them inactive. Importantly, two variants of the MAOA gene exist in the general population—a low-activity version and a high-activity version. Notably, it is the low-activity version that research suggests is linked to antisocial behavior and aggression.

Caspi et al. (2002) conducted a seminal study examining how the MAOA gene and the environment may interact to produce various antisocial outcomes. More specifically, the authors examined whether or not the variant MAOA gene type would moderate the relationship between childhood maltreatment and four measures of antisocial behavior and personality: (a) conduct disorder, (b) violent convictions, (c) disposition toward violence, and (d) antisocial personality disorder. The researchers conducted the study using a birth cohort of 1,037 children (52% male) who had been born in Dunedin, New Zealand. The population cohort was followed up until age 26 and was assessed at regular intervals using a comprehensive battery of interviews and tests with both the participants and collateral sources. Three important findings emerged. First, there was no MAOA main effect. Specifically, participants who possessed the low-activity variant of the MAOA gene were just as likely as their high-activity MAOA counterparts to be diagnosed with conduct disorder, be convicted for violent crimes, display antisocial personality disorder symptoms, and have a disposition toward violence. In contrast, there was a main effect for childhood maltreatment. Namely, participants who experienced childhood maltreatment scored higher on a composite index of antisocial personality and behavior than did participants who did not experience maltreatment. The third, and most groundbreaking, result was the finding that MAOA gene type did in fact moderate the relationship between childhood maltreatment and all four indices of antisocial behavior and personality. Specifically, the researchers reported that when paired with childhood maltreatment, only the low-activity variant of the MAOA gene dramatically increased the odds of subsequent violent offending, conduct disorder diagnoses, and antisocial personality symptomology. No such effect was observed among the high-activity MAOA variant participants who experienced childhood maltreatment.

Since the work of Caspi et al. (2002), replications have been published, albeit using less methodologically rigorous designs (see Foley et al., 2004; Frazzetto et al., 2007). The impact of MAOA activity level on aggression has even been studied in the laboratory. McDermott et al. (2009) illustrated that male participants who possessed the low-activity MAOA gene were more likely to respond aggressively (operationalized as giving varying amounts of hot sauce to their opponent) under a high-provocation condition in comparison to their high-activity MAOA counterparts.

The MAOA gene research, particularly the McDermott et al. study (2009), has been criticized for methodological and ideological reasons. Methodologically, McDermott et al. have been criticized for overemphasizing the MAOA gene effect. For example, overall, the group with the low-activity MAOA gene was only slightly more likely to behave aggressively in comparison to the group with the high-activity MAOA gene (75% vs. 62%; Crampton & Parkin, 2007). Notably, the p value associated with this particular analysis did not reach statistical

significance: $p = .08$. In addition, it has been argued that, at the very least, MAOA research resurrects racial stereotypes; at the worst, it repackages the eugenics movement under the guise of science (Crampton & Parkin, 2007). In sum, more MAOA-based research is required. In particular, the extent to which MAOA findings will replicate cross-culturally requires investigation. For example, Widom and Brzustowicz (2006) reported that the so-called protective effect that is seemingly afforded to high-activity MAOA gene holders applies to Whites but not to non-Whites.

Psychophysiological research. Recall that Gray's (1987) arousal model hypothesized that because of an underactive BIS, antisocial individuals are more fearless, less anxious, and less responsive to aversive stimulus than social individuals. The theory also indicates that antisocial individuals have overactive BASs, which translates into elevated levels of sensation-seeking and impulsive tendencies that, in turn, increase the risk for antisocial behavior.

During the last 50 years, psychophysiological theories of antisocial behavior such as Gray's (1987) arousal model have been tested on an array of samples ranging from youth with conduct disorder to incarcerated offenders who have been designated as psychopathic. Empirical tests of Gray's arousal model typically involve measuring heart rate or EDA/galvanic skin response in response to various stimuli that are administered in a laboratory setting. EDA refers to how much electrical current passes between two points on the skin. Increases in heart rate and EDA are associated with emotional responses such as fear, anger, and anxiety (Lang, 1994). Thus, if Gray's model is correct, antisocial individuals should score lower on measures of heart rate and EDA under various circumstances.

Research conducted to date has compared measures of autonomic arousal (e.g., heart rate and EDA) between antisocial and non- or less antisocial individuals under three laboratory paradigms. The first paradigm involves comparing autonomic responses between the antisocial and nonantisocial or less antisocial group (e.g., psychopaths vs. nonpsychopaths) at rest. The second paradigm compares the autonomic responses of each group after the completion of a task (e.g., solving a math problem). In the final paradigm, autonomic responses are compared after the presentation of an adverse stimulus (e.g., electric shock, loud burst of noise). In a meta-analysis of the results of 95 studies that explored the extent to which measures of autonomic arousal differentiated aggressive from nonaggressive individuals, individuals with conduct disorder from those without conduct disorder, and psychopathic individuals from nonpsychopathic individuals, Lorber (2004) found that only one study (out of 17) reported moderate sized effects in the expected direction (i.e., Cohen's *d* = –.38). More specifically, aggressive individuals evidenced a moderately lower resting heart rate relative to their nonaggressive counterparts. In contrast, the remaining effects were relatively small or not always in the expected direction (*d* ranged between –.20 and +.20 for six effects and between +.19 and –.19 for 10 effects). It is important to note that Lorber's meta-analysis was based on cross-sectional data. Thus, the extent to which an underactive behavioral inhibition system, for example, precedes or follows antisocial conduct cannot be answered with the extant research. Although research is beginning to examine the extent to which measures of autonomic arousal can predict future criminal conduct, to date, the results have been mixed (Loeber, Pardini, Stouthamer-Loeber, & Raine, 2007; Ortiz & Raine, 2004).

Brain imaging and neuropsychological research. Recall from our earlier theoretical review that some scholars have argued that functional (e.g., blood flow, glucose metabolism) and structural (e.g., reduced grey matter size, tumors, lesions) damage to the brain may play an etiological role in criminal conduct (e.g., Raine & Yang, 2006). Similarly, researchers have hypothesized a link between antisocial conduct and deficits in executive functioning, that is, the part of the brain that deals with cognitive functioning such as future goal-oriented behavior, purposive attention, organizational skills, and inhibitory control (Morgan & Lilienfeld, 2000). Notably, executive functioning is predominately associated with the frontal lobe. Research in support of this

perspective comes from two domains: (a) brain imaging/neuroimaging studies and (b) neuropsychological studies. Brain imaging studies use MRI, CT, or PET to test brain function and structure directly. In contrast, neuropsychological studies examine executive functioning indirectly using self-report paper/pencil questionnaires.

Brain imaging studies are manifold. However, they typically involve comparing a small number of identified antisocial individuals (e.g., sex offenders, violent offenders, psychopaths) with a small number of nonantisocial individuals (e.g., nonsex offenders, nonviolent offender, nonpsychopaths). Earlier studies compared the brain structures/functions of antisocial versus nonantisocial individuals at rest (see Raine, 1993, for a review). More recently, researchers have begun to examine brain function while participants are engaged in a cognitive activity (e.g., examining emotionally charged pictures; see Birbaumer et al., 2005). These studies have been reviewed by several researchers (see Anderson, 2007; Raine & Yang, 2006). In brief, Raine and Yang's (2006) insightful review made the following conclusions: (a) Structural/functional damage to the prefrontal lobe is the most consistently replicated finding among offender samples; (b) a small but growing body of evidence has begun to link antisocial conduct to damage to the temporal lobe and the limbic system, namely, the amygdala and the hippocampus; (c) multiple, rather than a single, brain structures are linked to antisocial conduct; and (d) as the number of deficit brain structures/functions increases, so too does the likelihood of criminal conduct. It is important to highlight that this body of research has been criticized for relying on offender-only samples that are often small and highly unique (e.g., sexual or violent offenders). Thus, the extent to which brain abnormalities are true antecedents of crime, rather than consequences of crime, remains unknown.

Two narrative reviews that have examined the evidence linking executive functioning to aggression and antisocial behavior rendered inconclusive results (E. Kandel & Freed, 1989; Lilienfeld, 1992). However, a meta-analytic review by Morgan and Lilienfeld (2000) of 39 studies involving 4,589 participants that compared antisocial individuals with nonantisocial individuals showed a relatively strong effect in the expected direction (Cohen's $d = .62$) that was indicative of poor executive functioning being associated with antisocial behavior. Although impressive, the meta-analysis summarized cross-sectional findings, thereby making it impossible to make causal statements. Moreover, considerable variability was evident across studies.

Other biological considerations (pregnancy, birth complications, toxins, and diet). Reviews of the existing evidence (see Anderson, 2007; Raine, 1993) suggest that there is a correlation between hypoglycemia and antisocial behavior. In brief, hypoglycemia or low blood sugar is known to result in panic, irritability, nervousness, and aggression (Raine, 1993). Additionally, a series of large-scale studies conducted by Schoenthaler (e.g., Schoenthaler, 1983a, 1983b) appear to have demonstrated that healthy eating can reduce antisocial behavior among incarcerated adolescent offenders. Using primarily pre–post research designs (e.g., antisocial behavior is compared before and after the introduction of a daily diet characterized by lower sugar consumption), Schoenthaler (1983b) reported a decline in general disruptions (declined 42%) and assaults (declined 25%) among 3,000 incarcerated adolescent offenders during a 12-month follow-up in contrast to the previous 12 months. Interestingly, Gesch, Hammond, Hampson, Eves, and Crowder (2002), a group of researchers in the United Kingdom, conducted a similar double-blind, placebo-controlled study with a sample of 231 young adult prisoners. However, this time, the researchers administered nutritional supplements consisting of vitamins, minerals, and essential fatty acids to the treatment group, whereas the control group only received a placebo. Compared to the placebo group, the treatment group committed 26.3% fewer offences during the follow-up period.

An equally important area of research has pointed to the impact of neurotoxins on brain development. Needleman, Riess, Tobin, Biesecker, and Greenhouse (1996) examined how lead concentration levels in a sample of 212 male youth correlated with antisocial behavior at the age of 12. In short, Needleman et al. reported a strong correlation between lead concentration levels and measures of aggression and delinquency when the boys were approximately 11 years old. Interestingly, the association between lead concentration levels and aggression and delinquency remained even after several controls were incorporated (e.g., maternal intelligence, socioeconomic status, and quality of child rearing). The authors hypothesized that lead indirectly causes delinquency and aggression through two specific mediators that are known to predict delinquency: (a) poor educational performance and (b) attention deficits. They argued that not only do attentional deficit problems predict delinquency, but they also lead to poor educational performance that, in turn, contributes to delinquency.

Psychodynamic Theories

Although Freud's (1938, 1953) work forms the foundation for several contemporary perspectives in psychology, he has been nonetheless intensely criticized. However, given that Freud devoted little time to developing detailed theories of criminal conduct, it is difficult to critique what does not exist. Although Freud's three general criminal types—neurotic, psychopathic, and deviant—provide useful descriptions, they provide little information about the causes of crime or how to treat offenders effectively.

The research evidence in general does not support a neurotic criminal subtype (Andrews & Bonta, 2010; Serin et al., 2011). However, there is clear evidence that individuals who score high on contemporary measures of psychopathy are more likely to engage in crime, particularly violent forms of crime (see Chapter 9, this volume). Moreover, the role of deviant or criminal role models and criminal attitudes in the onset and maintenance of criminal conduct has garnered considerable support. In fact, criminal attitudes and criminal peers have been identified as two of the strongest predictors of criminal conduct alongside criminal history and a criminal personality (Andrews & Bonta, 2010).

Sampson and Laub (1995) criticized the Gluecks' (1950, 1968) research for being atheoretical. Moreover, other scholars have highlighted how the Gluecks failed to pay attention to other important crime predictors such as peers and school misconduct (Andrews & Bonta, 2010). The Gluecks have also been criticized for using weak statistics and minimizing the importance of causal ordering (Hirschi & Selvin, 1967; Robins & Hill, 1966). Nonetheless, the Gluecks' collective works are still considered classic among prominent contemporary correctional scholars (e.g., Andrews & Bonta, 2010). Moreover, as predicted by the Gluecks, contemporary studies have repeatedly demonstrated that parental ideals, attitudes, and temperament play a strong role in the onset and maintenance of criminal behavior (Andrews & Bonta, 2010; Loeber & Farrington, 2000; Moffitt, 1993). However, parental practices are only one of several factors that interact in complex ways to yield antisocial outcomes.

Hirschi (1969) tested social control theory in a classic study that was published in his book, *Causes of Delinquency*. Using a cross-sectional design, Hirschi gathered an array of data for 4,077 youth (3,605 males), some of whom were delinquent and some of whom were not. In brief, his findings supported the importance of the core elements of social control theory. Concomitantly, Hirschi's study also provided support for the key tenets of the Gluecks' work (1950, 1968) as well as Andrews and Bonta's (2010) PIC–R theory.

Notably, social control theory has been subject to much empirical testing in the field of criminology (Akers & Sellers, 2004). Nonetheless, it is not without criticism (Bureind & Bartusch, 2005). Recall that social control theory predicts that the probability of engaging in delinquency declines as one's attachment to convention (e.g., to peers, family, school) strengthens, irrespective of whether the subject of attachment is criminally oriented or not. However, both theory and research clearly indicate that it is attachment to prosocial influences, peers in particular, that strengthens conventional actions and attitudes. In turn, attachment to criminal-oriented peers is one of the strongest predictors of delinquency (Andrews & Bonta, 2010; Gendreau, Little, & Goggin, 1996).

Additionally, social control theory has been criticized for not attending to causal ordering. For example, some research has illustrated that delinquency can precede weak attachment to social bonds (Liska & Reed, 1985; Matsueda, 1989).

Moreover, the fact that age may moderate the extent to which bonds influence behaviors was not fully articulated by Hirschi (LaGrange & White, 1985). Lastly, Hirschi remained relatively silent on the extent to which his theory was similar and/or different for females as well as for different ethnicities and races (Blanchette & Brown, 2006). Importantly, there is research that suggests that the importance of certain social bonds does vary as a function of gender (Rosenbaum & Lasley, 1990).

Recall that Gottfredson and Hirschi's (1990) general theory of crime essentially posited that all crime committed by all individuals can be explained by two global factors: impulsivity and opportunity. Gottfredson and Hirschi presented a vast amount of correlational evidence in support of their perspective. Like social control theory, the general theory of crime has amassed considerable attention from other researchers (Goode, 2008). The evidence definitely supports a link between self control and crime, even across many different cultures (Vazsonyi, Pickering, Junger, & Hessing, 2001). Additionally, a comprehensive meta-analytic review that was conducted by Pratt and Cullen (2000) clearly illustrated that self-control is indeed a strong predictor of criminal behavior. However, it also demonstrated that self-control is not the only predictor (it only accounted for 19% of the variance of criminal behavior). As will be discussed shortly, social learning variables also accounted for a substantial portion of the variance.

Despite the available support, various criticisms have been levied against the general theory of crime. For example, Akers (1991) argued that the theory is tautological. More specifically, Akers took issue with Gottfredson and Hirschi's (1990) definition of poor self-control as the failure to refrain from crime—the very definition of the causes of crime is grounded in the concept of crime itself. Thus, it is difficult to disentangle the predictor and criterion, making the theory circular. Debate ensues as to whether or not the purported circularity of the theory has been resolved to the satisfaction of scholars (Grasmick, Tittle, Bursik, & Arneklev, 1993). The theory has also been criticized for its static assumptions. Specifically, Gottfredson and Hirschi stated that between-individual differences in self-control will persist throughout the life span. However, longitudinal research has shown that social bonds that are developed beyond childhood (e.g., a good marriage) can cause offenders to change course toward a life of convention (Lilly, Cullen, & Ball, 2006).

The final criticism of the general theory of crime focuses on opportunities to commit crime, which plays a central role in the general theory of crime. In essence, criticisms have focused on the failure of the theory to adequately flesh out whether self-control and criminal opportunities are related or independent (Schulz, 2006). As Goode (2008) underscored, it is a real possibility that individuals with low self-control may be more likely than individuals with high self-control to perceive criminal opportunities. Thus, perhaps there is a synergistic interaction at play here. Also, people with low-self control may be exposed to more opportunities for crime.

Learning Theories

Although specific results differ depending on the learning theory discussed, the results of decades of research seem to support learning theories of crime in general. Research examining the validity of classical conditioning principles, operant conditioning principles, and social learning variables in explaining criminal or antisocial behavior will be discussed in this subsection. Elements of each of these theories (along with other theories) are integrated in the PIC–R theory such that support for each of these theories can indirectly support the PIC–R. A discussion of research specific to the PIC–R will conclude this section.

Classical conditioning. Reviews of research on H. J. Eysenck's (1977, 1996) predicted link between antisocial personalities and poor conditionability have concluded that, generally speaking, the research supports the theory (Hare, 1978; Raine, 1997). Most of this research has measured conditionability, with skin conductance as the conditioned response (Raine, 1997). Eysenck's theory proposed two routes to criminal behavior: One is through poor conditionability and the other is through not being conditioned to engage in prosocial behavior. Research by Raine and Venables (1981) provided evidence for both of these routes:

Antisocial boys from lower class homes had good conditionability, whereas antisocial boys from upper-class homes had poor conditionability (and prosocial boys showed the opposite pattern). It must be noted, however, that these findings only support Eysenck's theory if one assumes that children in upper class homes were being conditioned to be prosocial and children in lower class homes were being conditioned to be antisocial. Raine and Venables admitted that there were limitations to using class as a proxy of prosocial/antisocial conditioning. Nonetheless, the research seems to support the link between conditionability (in this case, the ability to learn by association) and antisocial behavior.

In contrast, mixed findings have emerged regarding H. J. Eysenck's (1977, 1996) hypothesized link between antisocial behavior and three particular facets of personality: psychoticism, neuroticism, and extraversion (Bartol & Bartol, 2008; Hollin, 1989). Specifically, research supports a link between crime and Eysenck's psychoticism and neuroticism dimensions, but there is only weak evidence supporting a link between extraversion and crime (see Cale, 2006, for a meta-analysis). These weak findings appear to be due to the fact that extraversion is made up of both sociability and impulsivity, but only impulsivity appears to be related to criminal behavior (S. B. G. Eysenck & Eysenck, 1971). Thus, research that defines extraversion in terms of sociability has failed to find a strong relationship with criminal behavior (see Cale, 2006, for a meta-analysis).

Philosophical critiques of H. J. Eysenck's (1977, 1996) theory have also been made. For example, Eysenck's theory portrays learning as a passive process and neglects the role that cognition plays in the process of learning to become a criminal (Bartol & Bartol, 2008). Operant conditioning has been similarly criticized, but its version of learning is not as passive in that behavior is viewed as more goal oriented.

Operant conditioning. Jeffery's (1965) differential reinforcement theory and Burgess and Akers's (1966) differential association-reinforcement theory combined operant conditioning principles

(Skinner, 1938, 1953) with Sutherland's (1939, 1947) differential association theory. Research has generally supported differential association theory (e.g., Andrews, 1980) and therefore indirectly supports the theories of Jeffery and of Burgess and Akers. Moreover, research has demonstrated that antisocial attitudes (or definitions) and associating with antisocial peers are some of the strongest predictors of criminal behavior (e.g., Andrews & Bonta, 2006; Simourd & Andrews, 1994).

Research on the application of the principles of operant conditioning in criminal justice settings has indicated that certain conditions need to be in place in order for these principles to be effective. In his review of research on criminal justice sanctions as punishments that are used to reduce antisocial behavior, J. McGuire (2002) determined that these sanctions were the least effective in decreasing antisocial behavior. He suggested that the conditions needed for effective punishment were not present in the criminal justice system. These conditions included the punishment being unavoidable, immediate, and severe, and alternative behaviors being available. McGuire found the most effective methods of decreasing antisocial behavior to be interventions that were essentially consistent with the principles of effective correctional programs, which are associated with the personal, interpersonal, and community-reinforcement theory (Andrews & Bonta, 2003, 2006, 2010) and draw heavily on social learning theory. Social learning theories of crime also include principles of operant conditioning, so there is overlap among research supporting these theories. Research specific to social learning theory is discussed next.

Social learning. Akers's (1973, 2000) social learning theory of crime combined Sutherland's (1939, 1947) differential association theory, the principles of operant conditioning (Skinner, 1938, 1953), and elements of social learning theories of general behavior (Bandura, 1973; Bandura & Walters, 1963). As such, previously mentioned research supporting differential association theory also supports Akers's social learning theory of crime. In addition to J. McGuire's (2002) findings mentioned above, other research on offender treatment has demonstrated that interventions that are grounded in social learning theory are effective at reducing recidivism (e.g., Andrews & Bonta, 2006; Pearson, Lipton, Cleland, & Yee, 2002).

A recent meta-analysis of research on social learning theory generally found research to support the theory, and the authors concluded that social learning theory "deserves its status as one of the core perspectives in criminology" (Pratt et al., 2010, p. 790). Furthermore, reviews of research comparing social learning theory variables with variables from other theories have found social learning theory variables to have as strong or stronger associations with antisocial behavior (e.g., Akers, 2009; Pratt & Cullen, 2000). In regard to the temporal sequence of the theory, a review of the research suggests that there can be relationships in both directions such that interacting with antisocial peers can increase one's likelihood of behaving in an antisocial manner, and behaving in an antisocial manner can also increase one's likelihood of coming into contact with (and interacting with) additional antisocial peers (Akers, 2000).

Research has demonstrated social learning theory's applicability in diverse cultures and countries as well (D. B. Kandel & Adler, 1982; Kim, Kwak, & Yun, 2010; López, Redondo, & Martin, 1989). A large body of research supports social learning theory with male samples (e.g., Andrews & Bonta, 2003; Pratt & Cullen, 2000), and limited research with female samples also supports the theory (Alarid, Burton, & Cullen, 2000; Brown & Motiuk, 2005; Simons, Miller, & Aigner, 1980). Further, research suggests that observed sex differences in antisocial behavior (i.e., with males exhibiting more antisocial behavior) may be explained, at least in part, through sex differences in social learning theory variables such as antisocial attitudes and/or interactions with antisocial associates (Morash, 1986; Simons et al., 1980). Some research does suggest, however, that there may be sex differences in the type of antisocial peers that are most important to antisocial behavior. For example, Benda's (2005) longitudinal research demonstrated that having an antisocial partner was a strong predictor of female recidivism but had little to no relationship to male recidivism, and antisocial peers was a weaker (though significant) predictor for females than it was for males.

It is clear that social learning theory is generally well regarded in the correctional field and well supported by research. Given the PIC–R theory's heavy reliance on social learning variables, it may be surmised that research is generally supportive of the PIC–R as well; this research is discussed next.

PIC–R theory.   This integrative theory includes elements of both control and learning theories. Research supporting these theories therefore indirectly supports the PIC–R. Most research that directly involves the PIC–R encompasses evaluations of correctional applications of the theory, particularly interventions that comply with the principles of effective correctional programs associated with the theory; namely, the principles of risk, need, and responsivity. These principles respectively state that offender risk should determine treatment intensity (i.e., high-risk offenders should receive high-intensity treatment), that criminogenic needs should serve as treatment targets (i.e., factors empirically associated with criminal behavior should be targeted), and that treatment should follow a cognitive–behavioral model (general responsivity) and take into account the learning style and other characteristics of offenders (specific responsivity; Andrews, 2001). Various meta-analytic reviews of the treatment correctional literature support the risk, need, and general responsivity principles, thereby providing support for the PIC–R perspective (see Andrews & Bonta, 2010, for a review).

Meta-analyses and reviews of predictors of criminal behavior are also supportive of PIC–R variables (Brown & Motiuk, 2005; Gendreau et al., 1996). Most of this research has been completed with male offender samples, but research with female offender samples is also supportive of the principles of effective correctional programs derived from the PIC–R theory (Dowden & Andrews, 1999). However, research on ethnic minorities, particularly African Americans and Hispanics, has produced mixed results regarding the validity of the PIC–R for these groups (Andrews & Bonta, 2010).

The PIC–R has also been criticized for not clearly explaining the relationships among variables in the theory and how the variables (and the relationships between them) produce particular forms of criminal behavior (Ward et al., 2007). The PIC–R theory has also been criticized because of the weak link between the PIC–R and the principles of effective correctional programs (Ward et al., 2007). Some feminists have criticized social learning theory for not making gender a central consideration (e.g., Morash, 1999), but new formulations of the theory have begun to explore the role that social structures (including gender, race, class, etc.) play in the learning process (Akers, 2009). Similar to other learning theories, these social structural variables are not central to the PIC–R, although their potential role in determining which rewards/costs are relevant to a particular individual in a particular setting is acknowledged.

PRACTICE AND POLICY ISSUES

Each theoretical perspective has impacted practice and policy to varying degrees. For example, evolutionary accounts have not made their way into the courtrooms, nor have they influenced how treatment programs are designed and delivered to offenders. In fact, it is for these very reasons that evolutionary perspectives are often criticized. It is difficult for individuals to ascertain how events that transpired millions of years ago could have any bearing on contemporary thoughts, feelings, and behaviors. Additionally, evolutionary critics contend that Darwinian perspectives only serve to rationalize racial stereotypes and legitimize patriarchal structures.

Conversely, biological explanations of crime have not only stimulated considerable scholarly debate, but they have also impacted legal decision making in the courtroom. Recall that in *Mobley*, Mobley's defense team unsuccessfully petitioned the court to fund genetic testing to ascertain if Mobley possessed the low-activity variant of the MAOA gene—the warrior gene. However, almost 15 years after Mobley, Bradley Waldroup's sentence was reduced from homicide to manslaughter given that he possessed the low-activity variant of the MAOA gene (Brooks-Crozier, 2011). Whether or not the

Waldroup decision will hold up in future court decisions remains to be seen.

Biological theories of crime have additional implications from a prevention and treatment standpoint. Recently, Brooks-Crozier (2011) made a detailed argument in support of statewide genetic screening for the MAOA gene. This direct quote taken from Brooks-Crozier's article, which was published in the *Connecticut Law Review*, captures the essence of her arguments.

> This Note argues that Brunner and Caspi's research can and should be used to prevent violent crime and to preserve the sense of peace and safety that is the foundation of free, civilized societies. More specifically, the Note proposes that states add a screening test for the MAOA-low genotype to their newborn screening programs and that states then offer "Part C" early intervention services to families with children who test positive for the genotype. The screening test would allow states to target a population of children at risk of criminal behavior. The intervention services—family education and counseling, home visits, parent support groups, and psychological and social work services—would prevent those at-risk children from suffering the maltreatment that would cause them to later develop aggressive, antisocial behavior. This Note examines the constitutionality and policy implications of the proposed legislation, presents a rudimentary cost-benefit analysis of the legislation, and ultimately concludes that it would pass constitutional muster and be a cost-effective public policy. (p. 537)

Although Brooks-Crozier (2011) clearly embraces the role of genetics wholeheartedly, others have raised serious ethical concerns about the use of MAOA gene research. Crampton and Parkin (2007), for example, raised a number of concerns ranging from informed consent issues to the misuse of faulty science to bolster racial stereotypes in the context of the Māori aboriginal people of New Zealand. In 2005 and 2006, Lea, Hall, Green, and Chambers presented findings germane to MAOA research and the Māori aboriginal people of New Zealand at two conferences. The results garnered considerable media attention, and quotes such as the following were widely circulated and criticized.

> [The gene] goes a long way to explaining some of the problems Maori have. Obviously, this means they are going to be more aggressive and violent and more likely to get involved in risk-taking behavior like gambling. They're much more likely to binge drink than other groups which are more likely to moderate their drinking. (Lea et al., 2006)

Consequently, Lea and Chambers (2007) attempted to quell criticisms and provide additional context for their research in a subsequent publication. Thus, it is clear that issues and debates concerning MAOA research and its implications are far from resolved.

Although psychodynamic theories in and of themselves have not significantly influenced correctional treatment programs, the vast majority of learning perspectives, including more comprehensive perspectives (i.e., PIC–R) that integrate learning principles with one particular psychodynamic theory—social control—have had a profound impact on the way that correctional treatment programs are designed, implemented, and evaluated (see Andrews & Bonta, 2010, for a review).

The general premise of learning theories of crime is that criminal behavior is learned (by association, by reinforcement/punishment, by imitation, and so on). It follows then that such behavior can be unlearned or that alternative behaviors can subsequently be learned. The principles of classical conditioning have been applied in treatment programs for offenders. For example, some researchers have suggested that sexual deviancy is a conditioned response to early associations between deviant objects or experiences and sexual arousal (Laws & Marshall, 1990; R. J. McGuire, Carlisle, & Young, 1965; Storms, 1981). One way to address this conditioned sexual deviancy is through aversive conditioning. Laws (1995) identified two components of aversive conditioning.

> (a) A sexually deviant fantasy (recorded or verbalized by client or therapist) is temporarily paired with (b) some type of noxious event (description of adverse consequences) or agent (a bad smell), with the result that the behavior controlled by the fantasy (penile erection) is observed to decrease over repeated trials. (p. 162)

Like the principles of classical conditioning, the principles of operant conditioning have been applied in treatment programs for offenders as well, but can also be seen in other criminal justice policies. For example, *tough-on-crime* policies that involve harsh punishments designed to deter criminal behavior are often popular, "and in some jurisdictions are seen as the preferred if not the exclusive route to follow to address the problem of crime" (J. McGuire, 2002, p. 201). However, as discussed in the Research Review section of this chapter, these policies are the least effective at reducing criminal behavior, likely because the conditions necessary for these punishments to be effective are largely absent in the criminal justice system (J. McGuire, 2002).

The principles of operant conditioning have been more appropriately applied in treatment programs for offenders. For example, these principles are at work in token economies that are used to reinforce good behavior and punish bad behavior among offenders in treatment facilities. A token economy was used in Achievement Place, a group-home program for delinquent boys that was established in the 1960s (Phillips, 1968). The boys could earn points for good behavior (e.g., being punctual in school, being tidy) and lose points for bad behavior (e.g., fighting, being disruptive). These points then earned the boys privileges (e.g., staying up late) and goods (e.g., snacks, games).

Social learning theory applications in offender treatment also include reinforcement and punishment. The additional element of vicarious conditioning and observational learning would be important to interventions that are based on social learning theory as well. For example, Achievement Place's successor, the Teaching Family model, was established in the 1970s and used a token economy to provide reinforcement and punishment; in addition, *teaching parents* of delinquents living together in this program would teach the youth "social, academic, and prevocational skills" (Akers, 2000, p. 92). The youth also served as prosocial peers that reinforced each other's prosocial behavior.

The PIC–R has influenced many current correctional practices (Ward et al., 2007). The theory's inclusion of some of the strongest predictors of criminal behavior has improved risk assessment in the field. The Level of Service Inventory—Revised (LSI–R; Andrews & Bonta, 1995), which is based on risk factors formulated within PIC–R, is one of the strongest risk assessment tools available in corrections (e.g., Gendreau, Goggin, & Smith, 2002; Gendreau et al., 1996). The LSI–R and its revision, Level of Service/Case Management Inventory (Andrews, Bonta, & Wormith, 2004), assess adult offenders' risk for criminal behavior using 54 items relating to risks and needs, including those strongest variables from the PIC–R (e.g., antisocial associates, antisocial attitudes; see Chapters 1, 2, and 3, this volume for more research on forensic assessments, instruments, and risk assessment).

The principles of effective correctional programs associated with the PIC–R have also had a positive influence on the correctional field. As seen in the Research Review section of this chapter, adhering to the principles of risk, need, and responsivity are directly linked to program effectiveness. Recall that these principles respectively state that offender risk should determine treatment intensity (i.e., high-risk offenders should receive high-intensity treatment), that criminogenic needs should serve as treatment targets (i.e., factors empirically associated with criminal behavior should be targeted), and that treatment should follow a cognitive–behavioral model (general responsivity). As previously discussed in this chapter, the PIC–R has been criticized for not making clear the link between the theory and these principles. Some feminists have also criticized the principles for not giving greater attention to gender. For example, in its original form, the principles consider gender as a specific responsivity factor (suggesting that treatments should be tailored to the learning styles and needs of males and females), but Blanchette and Brown (2006) considered gender to be a general responsivity factor.

> A gender-informed responsivity principle states that in general, optimal treatment response will be achieved when treatment providers deliver structured behavioral interventions (grounded in feminist philosophies as well as social learning theory) in an empathic and empowering manner (strength-based model) while simultaneously adopting a firm but fair approach. (p. 126)

In the short time since it was developed, the PIC–R has made a significant contribution to correctional policies and practice and shows every sign of continuing to do so as it continues to grow and develop.

SUMMARY AND CONCLUSIONS

Crime statistics, victim stories, and cost–benefit analyses have demonstrated that crime has a staggering impact on a substantial number of individuals, their families, and society at large. Consequently, the development and empirical testing of theoretical perspectives about the causal mechanisms that ultimately lead to crime and its devastating consequences is a necessary first step toward the creation of cost-effective crime reduction programs and policies.

We reviewed several theories of crime, each of which was categorized under one of three broad perspectives: (a) evolutionary, (b) biological, or (c) mainstream psychological/criminological. Evolutionary psychology posits that when certain psychological mechanisms that were exhibited by our hunter/gatherer ancestors increased the odds that a person's genes would be passed on from generation to generation, these successful adaptations eventually became part of the human gene pool. In regard to criminal behavior, evolutionists argued that recurring conflicts that characterized the ancestral environment, such as finding food, avoiding

predators, finding a mate, and providing for one's children, catalyzed the development of evolved psychological mechanisms such as risky behaviors and fearlessness in men and fearfulness and parental investment in women. These evolved psychological mechanisms, in part, explain why some males are willing to respond to perceived attacks on their reputation with direct aggression whereas females are less willing to use direct aggression, but, alternatively, may resort to less direct forms of aggression.

Forensic evolutionary theories of crime are more developed relative to the corresponding evidence. At this stage, more direct tests of the theory are needed (e.g., "How does mating effort translate into criminal conduct and under what circumstances?"). Ironically, despite criticisms that evolutionary perspectives legitimize existing patriarchal structures, it is one of the few gender-neutral perspectives that has theorized in thoughtful ways about why females commit crime and why they do so less often than males (A. Campbell, 2002; N. A. Campbell et al., 1999; Cross & Campbell, 2012).

In the biology section, we discussed how behavioral genetics (i.e., twin and adoption studies), molecular genetics, neurochemistry, psychophysiology, and the brain can account for criminal conduct and, in particular, aggression, under certain circumstances. The field of behavioral genetics uses twin and adoption studies to study to what extent genetics and the environment can account for individual variations in criminal behavior. In sum, more than 100 twin and adoption studies have demonstrated that on average, 0.41 percent of the variance in criminal conduct is due to genetics, whereas 0.59 is due to the environment.

Molecular geneticists have linked an actual gene—MAOA—to antisociality and aggression in humans. Recall that both a high- and low-activity MAOA gene occurs naturally in the population. The low-activity variant does not metabolize the neurotransmitters (serotonin, dopamine, norepinephrine) that are responsible for the regulation of emotion, sleep, motivation, reward/punishment, and the fight-or-flight response as efficiently as the high-activity variant does. Not surprisingly, it is the low-activity variant that has been associated with crime and aggression. Importantly, however, possessing the low-activity MAOA variant does not increase one's risk of future aggression and criminal conduct; rather, the combined effect of maltreatment and the low-activity MAOA variant increase one's propensity toward antisociality and aggression. However, MAOA research requires replication.

We also discussed how researchers have examined the association between criminal conduct and hormones such as testosterone and neurotransmitters such as serotonin, dopamine, and norepinephrine. Researchers have also examined how indices of autonomic arousal such as a low heart rate and reduced galvanic skin response may be associated with criminal conduct. Brain imaging and neuropsychological researchers have also implicated structural and/or functional damage to areas of the brain that are responsible for moral reasoning and emotional regulation (e.g., the frontal lobe, components of the limbic system in particular). However, much of the research that has examined the extent to which functional or structural brain damage translates into crime, or how hormones such as testosterone or proxies of low stress/anxiety (e.g., autonomic arousal) impact crime, have been largely correlational, thus precluding statements of causality.

Psychodynamic perspectives on crime are grounded in Freudian principles. Freud himself had little to say about crime other than that poor parenting can lead to three criminal subtypes: (a) the psychopathic criminal with an underdeveloped superego, (b) the neurotic criminal with an overdeveloped superego, and (c) the deviant criminal with a deviant superego (Freud, 1938, 1953). However, contemporary psychodynamic theorists have incorporated some of Freud's ideas into their respective work. For example, like Freud, Glueck and Glueck (1950) emphasized how good parenting was a prerequisite for a well-developed superego. Similarly, Hirschi's (2002) control theory sought to understand why individuals do not engage in crime/break social norms and hence give in to the id's inner drives. In essence, Hirschi argued that it is our social bonds to conventional goals, people, and institutions and our belief in these systems that prevents widespread mayhem. In a similar Freudian vein, Gottfredson and Hirschi's general theory of crime (1990) posits that low self-control (an underdeveloped superego) coupled with opportunity are the primary crime-causing agents.

In the final section, we reviewed three classes of learning theories: (a) classical conditioning, or learning through association; (b) operant conditioning, or learning through reinforcement and punishment; and (c) social learning, or learning through models and observations. Although Sutherland (1939, 1947) first proposed that criminal behavior is learned through interactions with others—differential association theory—it was Jeffery (1965) and Burgess and Akers (1966) who posited that Sutherland's learning occurred through the mechanisms of operant conditioning. Eventually, Akers would elaborate further on his earlier work with Burgess, adding elements from social learning theory such as imitation and role modeling to the differential reinforcement theory of crime. Finally, Andrews and Bonta's (2010) PIC–R theory incorporated elements from Aker's differential reinforcement theory as well as Gottfredson and Hirschi's (1990) general theory of crime. Social control theory, and PIC–R in particular, have garnered considerable empirical support in the literature. However, more research is needed, particularly examining how these largely gender/race/ethnicity invariant theories generalize to different cultures and sexes.

In sum, criminal behavior, like any form of human behavior, will never be explained by one theory, one voice, or one discipline. Although not all explanations of criminal behavior are necessarily compatible, even the most unlikely candidates have more in common than one might believe. For example, evolutionary accounts emphasize learning from the ancestral environment at the group/species level. In a similar vein, social learning theories also emphasize learning, albeit from the immediate environment, and at the individual level. Nonetheless, both perspectives fundamentally argue that the environment plays a central role in shaping human behavior. Undoubtedly, the most exciting discoveries within the realm of criminal behavior stem from approaches that proactively integrate elements from seemingly divergent perspectives.

References

Akers, R. L. (1973). *Deviant behavior: A social learning approach*. Belmont, CA: Wadsworth.

Akers, R. L. (1990). Rational choice, deterrence, and social learning theory in criminology: The path not taken. *The Journal of Criminal Law & Criminology, 81*, 653–676. doi:10.2307/1143850

Akers, R. L. (1991). Self-control as a general theory of crime. *Journal of Quantitative Criminology, 7*, 201–211. doi:10.1007/BF01268629

Akers, R. L. (2000). *Criminological theories: Introduction, evaluation, and application* (3rd ed.). Los Angeles, CA: Roxbury.

Akers, R. L. (2009). *Social learning and social structure: A general theory of crime and deviance*. New Brunswick, NJ: Transaction.

Akers, R. L., & Sellers, C. S. (2004). *Criminological theories: Introduction, evaluation, and application* (4th ed.). Los Angeles, CA: Roxbury.

Alarid, L. F., Burton, V. S., & Cullen, F. T. (2000). Gender and crime among felony offenders: Assessing the generality of social control and differential association theories. *Journal of Research in Crime and Delinquency, 37*, 171–199. doi:10.1177/0022427800037002002

Alexander, F. (1935). *Roots of crime*. New York, NY: Knopf.

Anderson, G. S. (2007). *Biological influences on criminal behavior*. Boca Raton, FL: CRC Press.

Andrews, D. A. (1980). Some experimental investigations of the principles of differential association through deliberate manipulations of the structure of service systems. *American Sociological Review, 45*, 448–462. doi:10.2307/2095177

Andrews, D. A. (2001). Principles of effective correctional programs. In L. L. Motiuk & R. C. Serin (Eds.), *Compendium 2000 on effective correctional programming* (pp. 9–17). Ottawa, Ontario, Canada: Correctional Service Canada.

Andrews, D. A., & Bonta, J. (1995). *The Level of Service Inventory—Revised (LSI–R): User's manual*. Toronto, Ontario, Canada: Multi-Health Systems.

Andrews, D. A., & Bonta, J. (2003). *The psychology of criminal conduct* (3rd ed.). Cincinnati, OH: Anderson.

Andrews, D. A., & Bonta, J. (2006). *The psychology of criminal conduct* (4th ed.). Cincinnati, OH: Anderson.

Andrews, D. A., & Bonta, J. (2010). *The psychology of criminal conduct* (5th ed.). New Providence, NJ: LexisNexis Matthew Bender.

Andrews, D. A., Bonta, J., & Wormith, J. S. (2004). *The Level of Service/Case Management Inventory: An offender assessment system*. Toronto, Ontario, Canada: Multi-Health Systems.

Bandura, A. (1973). *Aggression: A social learning analysis*. Englewood Cliffs, NJ: Prentice-Hall.

Bandura, A. (1977). *Social learning theory*. Orrville, OH: Prentice-Hall.

Bandura, A., Ross, D., & Ross, S. A. (1963). Imitation of film-mediated aggressive models. *The Journal of Abnormal and Social Psychology, 66*, 3–11. doi:10.1037/h0048687

Bandura, A., & Walters, R. H. (1963). *Social learning and personality development*. New York, NY: Holt, Rinehart and Winston.

Bartol, C. R., & Bartol, A. M. (2008). *Criminal behavior: A psychosocial approach* (8th ed.). Upper Saddle River, NJ: Prentice-Hall.

Belknap, J. (2001). *The invisible woman: Gender, crime, and justice* (2nd ed.). Belmont, CA: Wadsworth.

Belknap, J. (2007). *The invisible woman: Gender, crime, and justice* (3rd ed.). Belmont, CA: Wadsworth.

Benda, B. B. (2005). Gender differences in life-course theory of recidivism: A survival analysis. *International Journal of Offender Therapy and Comparative Criminology, 49*, 325–342. doi:10.1177/0306624X04271194

Birbaumer, N., Veit, R., Lotze, M., Erb, M., Hermann, C., Grodd, W., & Flor, H. (2005). Deficient fear conditioning in psychopathy: A functional magnetic resonance imaging study. *Archives of General Psychiatry, 62*, 799–805. doi:10.1001/archpsyc.62.7.799

Blackburn, R. (1995). *The psychology of criminal conduct: Theory, research and practice*. Chichester, England: Wiley.

Blackwell, B. S., & Piquero, A. R. (2005). On the relationships between gender, power control, self-control and crime. *Journal of Criminal Justice, 33*, 1–17. doi:10.1016/j.jcrimjus.2004.10.001

Blanchette, K., & Brown, S. L. (2006). *The assessment and treatment of women offenders: An integrative perspective*. Chichester, England: Wiley. doi:10.1002/9780470713013

Bloom, B., Owen, B., & Covington, S. S. (2003). *Gender-responsive strategies for women offenders: Research, practice, and guiding principles for women offenders*. Retrieved from http://nicic.gov/Library/Files/018017.pdf

Brooks-Crozier, J. (2011). The nature and nurture of violence: Early intervention services for the families of MAOA-low children as a means to reduce violent crime and the costs of violent crime. *Connecticut Law Review, 44*, 531–573.

Brown, S. L., & Motiuk, L. L. (2005). *The dynamic factor identification and analysis (DFIA) component of the offender intake assessment (OIA) process: A meta-analytic, psychometric and consultative review* (Research Report R-164). Ottawa, Ontario, Canada: Research Branch, Correctional Service Canada.

Bureind, J. W., & Bartusch, D. J. (2005). *Juvenile delinquency: An integrated approach.* Thousand Oaks, CA: Jones and Bartlett.

Burgess, R., & Akers, R. L. (1966). A differential association-reinforcement theory of criminal behavior. *Social Problems, 14,* 128–147. doi:10.2307/798612

Buss, D. M. (2011). *Evolutionary psychology: The new science of the mind* (4th ed.). Boston, MA: Pearson.

Cale, E. M. (2006). A quantitative review of the relations between the "big 3" higher order personality dimensions and antisocial behavior. *Journal of Research in Personality, 40,* 250–284. doi:10.1016/j.jrp.2005.01.001

Campbell, A. (2002). *A mind of her own: The evolutionary psychology of women.* Oxford, England: Oxford University Press. doi:10.1093/acprof:oso/9780198504986.001.0001

Campbell, A., Muncer, S., & Bibel, D. (2001). Women and crime: An evolutionary approach. *Aggression and Violent Behavior, 6,* 481–497. doi:10.1016/S1359-1789(00)00019-7

Campbell, L., & Ellis, B. J. (2005). Commitment, love, and mate retention. In D. M. Buss (Ed.), *The handbook of evolutionary psychology* (pp. 419–446). Hoboken, NJ: Wiley.

Campbell, N. A., Reece, J. B., & Mitchell, L. G. (1999). *Biology* (5th ed.). Menlo Park, CA: Addison Wesley Longman.

Caspi, A., McClay, J., Moffitt, T. E., Mill, J., Martin, J., Craig, I. W., . . . Poulton, R. (2002). Role of genotype in the cycle of violence in maltreated children. *Science, 297,* 851–854. doi:10.1126/science.1072290

Cassel, E., & Bernstein, D. A. (2001). *Criminal behavior.* Boston, MA: Allyn & Bacon.

Conner, S. (1995, February 12). Do your genes make you a criminal? *The Independent.* Retrieved from http://www.independent.co.uk/news/uk/do-your-genes-make-you-a-criminal-1572714.html

Cooper, A., & Smith, E. L. (2011). *Homicide trends in the United States, 1980–2008, Annual rates for 2009 and 2010.* Washington, DC: U.S. Department of Justice, Office of Justice Programs, Bureau of Justice Statistics. Retrieved from http://bjs.ojp.usdoj.gov/content/pub/pdf/htus8008.pdf

Coyne, J. (2009). *Why evolution is true.* New York, NY: Viking Penguin.

Crampton, P., & Parkin, C. (2007). Warrior genes and risk-taking science. *Journal of the New Zealand Medical Association, 120*(1250). Retrieved from http://www.nzma.org.nz/journal/120-1250/2439

Cross, C., & Campbell, A. (2012). Women and aggression. In T. K. Shackelford & V. A. Weekes-Shackelford (Eds.), *The Oxford handbook of evolutionary perspectives on violence, homicide, and war* (pp. 197–217). Oxford, England: Oxford University Press.

Cross, C. P., Copping, L., & Campbell, A. (2011). Sex differences in impulsivity: A meta-analysis. *Psychological Bulletin, 137,* 97–130. doi:10.1037/a0021591

Daly, M., & Wilson, M. (1988). *Homicide.* New York, NY: Aldine De Gruyte.

Darwin, C. (1968). *The origins of species.* New York, NY: Penquin Books. (Original work published 1859)

Dawkins, R. (1976). *The selfish gene.* New York, NY: Oxford University Press.

Dowden, C., & Andrews, D. A. (1999). What works in young offender treatment: A meta-analysis. *Forum on Corrections Research, 11,* 21–24.

Drake, E. K., Aos, S., & Miller, M. G. (2009). Evidence-based public policy options to reduce crime and criminal justice costs: Implications in Washington State. *Victims & Offenders, 4,* 170–196. doi:10.1080/15564880802612615

Duntley, J. D., & Buss, D. M. (2008). The origins of homicide. In J. D. Duntley & T. K. Shackelford (Eds.), *Evolutionary forensic psychology: Darwinian foundations of crime and law* (pp. 41–64). Oxford, England: Oxford University Press. doi:10.1093/acprof:oso/9780195325188.003.0003

Duntley, J. D., & Shackelford, T. K. (Eds.). (2008). *Evolutionary forensic psychology: Darwinian foundations of crime and law.* Oxford, England: Oxford University Press. doi:10.1093/acprof:oso/9780195325188.001.0001

Ellis, L. (1988). The victimful–victimless crime distinction, and seven universal demographic correlates of victimful criminal behavior. *Personality and Individual Differences, 9,* 525–548. doi:10.1016/0191-8869(88)90151-1

ENCODE Project Consortium, Bernstein, B. E., Birney, E., Dunham, I., Green, E. D., Gunter, C., & Snyder, M. (2012). An integrated encyclopedia of DNA elements in the human genome. *Nature, 489,* 57–74. doi:10.1038/nature11247

Eysenck, H. J. (1977). *Crime and personality* (2nd ed.). London, England: Routledge.

Eysenck, H. J. (1996). Personality and crime: Where do we stand. *Psychology, Crime & Law, 2*, 143–152. doi:10.1080/10683169608409773

Eysenck, S. B. G., & Eysenck, H. J. (1971). Crime and personality: Item analysis of questionnaire responses. *British Journal of Criminology, 11*, 49–62.

Falconer, D. S. (1965). The inheritance of liability to certain diseases, estimated from the incidence among relatives. *Annals of Human Genetics, 29*, 51–76. doi:10.1111/j.1469-1809.1965.tb00500.x

Farrington, D. P., & Painter, K. A. (2004). *Gender differences in offending: Implications for risk-focused prevention.* Retrieved from http://www.homeoffice.gov.uk/rds/pdfs2/rdsolr0904.pdf

Fausto-Sterling, A. (1992). *Myths of gender: Biological theories about women and men* (2nd ed.). New York, NY: Basic Books.

Foley, D. L., Eaves, L. J., Wormley, B., Silberg, J. L., Maes, H. H., Kuhn, J., & Riley, B. (2004). Childhood adversity, monoamine oxidase: A genotype, and risk for conduct disorder. *Archives of General Psychiatry, 61*, 738–744. doi:10.1001/archpsyc.61.7.738

Fowles, D. C. (1980). The three arousal model: Implications of Gray's two-factor learning theory for heart rate, electrodermal activity, and psychopathy. *Psychophysiology, 17*, 87–104. doi:10.1111/j.1469-8986.1980.tb00117.x

Frazzetto, G., Lorenzo, G. D., Carola, V., Proietti, L., Sokolwska, E., Siracusano, A., . . . Troisi, A. (2007). Early trauma and increased risk for physical aggression during adulthood: The moderating role of MAOA genotype. *PLOS ONE, 5*, e486. doi:10.1371/journal.pone.0000486

Freud, S. (1901). *The psychopathology of everyday life.* New York, NY: Macmillan.

Freud, S. (1938). *The basic writings of Sigmund Freud.* New York, NY: Modern Library.

Freud, S. (1953). *A general introduction to psychoanalysis.* New York, NY: Permabooks.

Gendreau, P., Goggin, C., & Smith, P. (2002). Is the PCL–R really the "unparalleled" measure of offender risk?: A lesson in knowledge cumulation. *Criminal Justice and Behavior, 29*, 397–426. doi:10.1177/0093854802029004004

Gendreau, P., Little, T., & Goggin, C. (1996). A meta-analysis of predictors of adult offender recidivism: What works! *Criminology, 34*, 575–608. doi:10.1111/j.1745-9125.1996.tb01220.x

Gesch, C. B., Hammond, S. M., Hampson, S. E., Eves, A., & Crowder, M. J. (2002). Influence of supplementary vitamins, minerals, and essential fatty acids on the antisocial behavior of young adult prisoners: Randomized, placebo-controlled trial. *The British Journal of Psychiatry, 181*, 22–28. doi:10.1192/bjp.181.1.22

Gibbon, A. (2004). American Association of Physical Anthropologists meeting: Tracking the evolutionary history of a "warrior" gene. *Science, 304*, 818–819. Retrieved from http://www.sciencemag.org/cgi/content/summary/304/5672/818a

Glueck, S., & Glueck, E. (1950). *Unravelling juvenile delinquency.* Cambridge, MA: Harvard University Press.

Glueck, S., & Glueck, E. (1968). *Delinquents and non-delinquents in perspective.* Cambridge, MA: Harvard University Press. doi:10.4159/harvard.9780674188754

Goode, E. (Ed.). (2008). *Out of control: Assessing the general theory of crime.* Palo Alto, CA: Stanford University Press.

Gottfredson, M., & Hirschi, T. (1990). *A general theory of crime.* Palo Alto, CA: Stanford University Press.

Grasmick, H. G., Tittle, C. R., Bursik, R. J., & Arneklev, B. J. (1993). Testing the core empirical implications of Gotteredson and Hirschi's general theory of crime. *Journal of Research in Crime and Delinquency, 30*, 5–29. doi:10.1177/0022427893030001002

Gray, J. A. (1987). Perspectives on anxiety and impulsivity: A commentary. *Journal of Research in Personality, 21*, 493–509. doi:10.1016/0092-6566(87)90036-5

Greenfeld, L. A., & Snell, T. L. (1999). *Women offenders* (Special Report NCJ 175688). Washington, DC: Bureau of Justice Statistics, U.S. Department of Justice. Retrieved from http://www.ojp.usdoj.gov/bjs/abstract/wo.htm

Hare, R. D. (1978). Electrodermal and cardiovascular correlates of psychopathy. In R. D. Hare & D. Schalling (Eds.), *Psychopathic behavior: Approaches to research* (pp. 107–144). New York, NY: Wiley.

Harris, G. T., & Rice, M. E. (2012). Filicide and child maltreatment: Prospects for ultimate explanation. In T. K. Shackelford & V. A. Weekes-Shackelford (Eds.), *The Oxford handbook of evolutionary perspectives on violence, homicide, and war* (pp. 91–105). Oxford, England: Oxford University Press. doi:10.1093/oxfordhb/9780199738403.013.0006

Harris, G. T., Rice, M. E., & Lalumière, M. L. (2001). Criminal violence: The role of psychopathy, neurodevelopmental insults and antisocial parenting. *Criminal Justice and Behavior, 28*, 402–426. doi:10.1177/009385480102800402

Hirschi, T. (1969). *Causes of delinquency.* Berkeley: University of California Press.

Hirschi, T. (2002). *Causes of delinquency.* New Brunswick, NJ: Transaction.

Hirschi, T., & Selvin, H. C. (1967). *Delinquency research: An appraisal of analytic methods.* New York, NY: Free Press.

Hollin, C. R. (1989). *Psychology and crime: An introduction to criminological psychology.* London, England: Routledge. doi:10.4324/9780203329368

Holtfreter, K., Reisig, M. D., & Morash, M. (2004). Poverty, state capital, and recidivism among women offenders. *Criminology & Public Policy, 3,* 185–208. doi:10.1111/j.1745-9133.2004.tb00035.x

Hunnicutt, G., & Broidy, L. M. (2004). Liberation and economic marginalization: A reformulation and test of formerly competing models. *Journal of Research in Crime and Delinquency, 41,* 130–155. doi:10.1177/0022427803257306

Hyde, J. S. (2005). The gender similarities hypothesis. *American Psychologist, 60,* 581–592. doi:10.1037/0003-066X.60.6.581

Jeffery, C. R. (1965). Criminal behavior and learning theory. *Journal of Criminal Law, Criminology, & Police Science, 56,* 294–300. doi:10.2307/1141238

Kandel, D. B., & Adler, I. (1982). Socialization into marijuana use among French adolescents: A cross-cultural comparison with the United States. *Journal of Health and Social Behavior, 23,* 295–309. doi:10.2307/2136488

Kandel, E., & Freed, D. (1989). Frontal-lobe dysfunction and antisocial behavior. *Journal of Clinical Psychology, 45,* 404–413. doi:10.1002/1097-4679(198905)45:3<404::AID-JCLP2270450309>3.0.CO;2-G

Kim, E., Kwak, D., & Yun, M. (2010). Investigating the effects of peer association and parental influence on adolescent substance use: A study of adolescents in South Korea. *Journal of Criminal Justice, 38,* 17–24. doi:10.1016/j.jcrimjus.2009.11.003

LaGrange, R. L., & White, H. R. (1985). Age differences in delinquency: A test of theory. *Criminology, 23,* 19–45. doi:10.1111/j.1745-9125.1985.tb00324.x

Lagrange, T. C., & Silverman, R. A. (1999). Low self-control and opportunity: Testing the general theory of crime as an explanation for gender differences in delinquency. *Criminology, 37,* 41–72. doi:10.1111/j.1745-9125.1999.tb00479.x

Lang, P. J. (1994). The varieties of emotional experiences: A meditation on James-Lange theory. *Psychological Review, 101,* 211–221. doi:10.1037/0033-295X.101.2.211

Lange, J. (1931). *Crime as destiny.* London, England: Unwin. (Original work published 1929)

Laws, D. R. (1995). Verbal satiation: Notes on procedure, with speculations on its mechanism of effect. *Sexual Abuse: Journal of Research and Treatment, 7,* 155–166.

Laws, D. R., & Marshall, W. L. (1990). A conditioning theory of the etiology and maintenance of deviant sexual preference and behavior. In H. E. Barbaree, W. L. Marshall, & D. R. Laws (Eds.), *Handbook of sexual assault: Theories and treatment of the offender* (pp. 209–229). New York, NY: Plenum. doi:10.1007/978-1-4899-0915-2_13

Lea, R. A., & Chambers, G. (2007). Monoamine oxidase, addiction, and the "warrior" gene hypothesis. *Journal of the New Zealand Medical Association, 120.* Retrieved from http://www.nzma.org.nz/journal/120-1250/2441

Lea, R. A., Hall, D., Green, M., & Chambers, G. K. (2005, June). *Tracking the evolutionary history of the warrior gene in the South Pacific.* Paper presented at the Molecular Biology and Evolution Conference, Auckland, New Zealand.

Lea, R. A., Hall, D., Green, M., & Chambers, G. K. (2006, August). *Tracking the evolutionary history of the warrior gene in the South Pacific.* Paper presented at the International Congress of Human Genetics, Brisbane, Australia.

Lilienfeld, S. O. (1992). The association between antisocial personality and somatization disorders: A review and integration of theoretical models. *Clinical Psychology Review, 12,* 641–662. doi:10.1016/0272-7358(92)90136-V

Lilly, J. R., Cullen, F. T., & Ball, R. A. (2006). *Criminological theory: Context and consequences* (4th ed.). Thousand Oaks, CA: Sage.

Liska, A. E., & Reed, M. D. (1985). Ties to conventional institutions and delinquency: Estimating reciprocal effects. *American Sociological Review, 50,* 547–560. doi:10.2307/2095438

Little, J. R., Shackelford, T. K., & Weekes-Shackelford, V. A. (2012). Evolutionary perspectives on violence, homicide, and war. In T. K. Shackelford & V. A. Weekes-Shackelford (Eds.), *The Oxford handbook of evolutionary perspectives on violence, homicide, and war* (pp. 3–22). Oxford, England: Oxford University Press.

Loeber, R., & Farrington, D. P. (2000). Young children who commit crime: Epidemiology, developmental origins, risk factors, early interventions, and policy implications. *Development and Psychopathology, 12,* 737–762. doi:10.1017/S0954579400004107

Loeber, R., Pardini, D. A., Stouthamer-Loeber, M., & Raine, A. (2007). Do cognitive, physiological, and psychological risk and promotive factors predict desistance from delinquency in males? *Development and Psychopathology, 19,* 867–887. doi:10.1017/S0954579407000429

Lombroso, C. (1876). *L'Uomo delinquente* [Criminal man]. Milan, Italy: Hoepli.

Lombroso, C., & Ferrero, L. (1893). *La donna delinquente, la prostituta e la donna normale* [Criminal women, the prostitute, and the normal woman]. Turin, Italy: Roux.

López, J. M. O., Redondo, L. M., & Martin, A. L. (1989). Influence of family and peer group on the use of drugs by adolescents. *International Journal of the Addictions, 24*, 1065–1082.

Lorber, M. F. (2004). Psychophysiology of aggression, psychopathy, and conduct problems: A meta-analysis. *Psychological Bulletin, 130*, 531–552. doi:10.1037/0033-2909.130.4.531

Matsueda, R. L. (1989). The dynamics of moral beliefs and minor delinquency. *Social Forces, 68*, 428–457.

McDermott, R., Tingley, D., Cowden, J., Frazzetto, G., & Johnson, D. D. P. (2009). Monoamine oxidase A gene (MAOA) predicts behavioral aggression following provocation. *PNAS Proceedings of the National Academy of Sciences of the United States of America, 106*, 2118–2123. doi:10.1073/pnas.0808376106

McGuire, J. (2002). Criminal sanctions versus psychologically-based interventions with offenders: A comparative empirical analysis. *Psychology, Crime & Law, 8*, 183–208. doi:10.1080/10683160208415005

McGuire, R. J., Carlisle, J. M., & Young, B. G. (1965). Sexual deviation as conditioned behavior: A hypothesis. *Behaviour Research and Therapy, 3*, 185–190. doi:10.1016/0005-7967(64)90014-2

Miller, T. R., Cohen, M. A., & Wiersema, B. (1996). *Victim costs and consequences: A new look* (NCJ-155282). Washington, DC: National Institute of Justice. doi:10.1037/e557572010-001

Millon, T., Simonsen, E., Davis, R. D., & Birket-Smith, M. (1998). *Psychopathy: Antisocial, criminal, and violent behavior.* New York, NY: Guilford Press.

Mishra, S., & Lalumière, M. L. (2008). Risk-taking, antisocial behavior, and life histories. In J. D. Duntley & T. K. Shackelford (Eds.), *Evolutionary forensic psychology: Darwinian foundations of crime and law* (pp. 139–159). Oxford, England: Oxford University Press. doi:10.1093/acprof:oso/9780195325188.003.0008

Mobley v. The State, 265 Ga. 292, S94P1271 (1995).

Moffitt, T. E. (1993). Adolescence-limited and life-course-persistent antisocial behavior: A developmental taxonomy. *Psychological Review, 100*, 674–701. doi:10.1037/0033-295X.100.4.674

Moffitt, T. E. (2005). The new look of behavioral genetics in developmental psychopathology: Gene-environment interplay in antisocial behaviors. *Psychological Bulletin, 131*, 533–554. doi:10.1037/0033-2909.131.4.533

Moffitt, T. E., & Caspi, A. (2001). Childhood predictors differentiate life-course-persistent and adolescence-limited antisocial pathways among males and females. *Development and Psychopathology, 13*, 355–375. doi:10.1017/S0954579402001104

Morash, M. (1986). Gender, peer group experiences, and seriousness of delinquency. *Journal of Research in Crime and Delinquency, 23*, 43–67. doi:10.1177/0022427886023001004

Morash, M. (1999). A consideration of gender in relation to social learning and social structure: A general theory of crime and deviance. *Theoretical Criminology, 3*, 451–462. doi:10.1177/1362480699003004005

Morgan, A. B., & Lilienfeld, S. O. (2000). A meta-analytic review of the relation between antisocial behavior and neuropsychological measures of executive function. *Clinical Psychology Review, 20*, 113–136. doi:10.1016/S0272-7358(98)00096-8

National Crime Victims Fund. (2012). *Victims' stories.* Retrieved from http://www.crimevictimsfund.org/victims.html

Needleman, H. L., Riess, R. A., Tobin, M. J., Biesecker, G. E., & Greenhouse, J. B. (1996). Bone lead levels and delinquent behavior. *JAMA: Journal of the American Medical Association, 275*, 363–369. doi:10.1001/jama.1996.03530290033034

Ortiz, J., & Raine, A. (2004). Heart rate level and antisocial behavior in children and adolescents: A meta-analysis. *Journal of the American Academy of Child & Adolescent Psychiatry, 43*, 154–162. doi:10.1097/00004583-200402000-00010

Pearson, F. S., Lipton, D. S., Cleland, C. M., & Yee, D. S. (2002). The effects of behavioral/cognitive–behavioral programs on recidivism. *Crime & Delinquency, 48*, 476–496. doi:10.1177/0011128702048003006

Petersen, J. L., & Hyde, J. (2010). A meta-analytic review of research on gender differences in sexualities, 1992–2007. *Psychological Bulletin, 136*, 21–38. doi:10.1037/a0017504

Phillips, E. L. (1968). Achievement place: Token reinforcement procedures in a home-style rehabilitation setting for "pre-delinquent" boys. *Journal of Applied Behavior Analysis, 1*, 213–223. doi:10.1901/jaba.1968.1-213

Plomin, R., Defries, J. C., McClearn, G. E., & McGuffin, P. (2001). *Behavioral genetics* (4th ed.). New York, NY: Worth.

Pratt, T. C., & Cullen, F. T. (2000). The empirical status of Gottfredson and Hirschi's general theory of crime: A meta-analysis. *Criminology, 38*, 931–964. doi:10.1111/j.1745-9125.2000.tb00911.x

Pratt, T. C., Cullen, F. T., Sellers, C. S., Winfree, L. T., Madensen, T. D., Daigle, L. E., . . . Gau, J. M. (2010).

The empirical status of social learning theory: A meta-analysis. *Justice Quarterly, 27,* 765–802. doi:10.1080/07418820903379610

Quinsey, V. L., Skilling, T. A., Lalumière, M. L., & Craig, W. (2004). *Juvenile delinquency: Understanding the origins of individual differences.* Washington, DC: American Psychological Association. doi:10.1037/10623-000

Raine, A. (1993). *The psychopathology of crime: Criminal behavior as a clinical disorder.* San Diego, CA: Academic Press. doi:10.1016/B978-0-08-057148-5.50005-8

Raine, A. (1997). Crime, conditioning, and arousal. In H. Nyborg (Ed.), *The scientific study of human nature: Tribute to Hans J. Eysenck* (pp. 122–141). Oxford, England: Elsevier.

Raine, A., & Venables, P. H. (1981). Classical conditioning and socialization—A biosocial interaction? *Personality and Individual Differences, 2,* 273–283. doi:10.1016/0191-8869(81)90082-9

Raine, A., & Yang, Y. (2006). Neural foundations to moral reasoning and antisocial behavior. *Social Cognitive and Affective Neuroscience, 1,* 203–213. doi:10.1093/scan/nsl033

Rhee, S. H., & Waldman, I. D. (2002). Genetic and environmental influences on antisocial behavior: A meta-analysis of twin and adoption studies. *Psychological Bulletin, 128,* 490–529. doi:10.1037/0033-2909.128.3.490

Robins, L. N., & Hill, S. Y. (1966). Assessing the contribution of family structure, class and peer groups to juvenile delinquency. *The Journal of Criminal Law, Criminology, and Police Science, 57,* 325–334. doi:10.2307/1140730

Rosenbaum, J. L., & Lasley, J. R. (1990). School, community context, and delinquency: Rethinking the gender gap. *Justice Quarterly, 7,* 493–513. doi:10.1080/07418829000090701

Rotter, J. (1954). *Social learning and clinical psychology.* New York, NY: Prentice-Hall. doi:10.1037/10788-000

Sampson, R. J., & Laub, J. H. (1995). *Crime in the making: Pathways and turning points through life.* Cambridge, MA: Harvard University Press.

Schoenthaler, S. J. (1983a). The Los Angeles Probation Department diet-behavior program: An empirical analysis of six institutional settings. *International Journal of Biosocial Research, 10,* 88–98.

Schoenthaler, S. J. (1983b). The Northern California diet-behavior program: An empirical examination of 3,000 incarcerated juveniles in Stanislaus County Juvenile Hall. *International Journal of Biosocial Research, 5,* 99–106.

Schulz, S. (2006). *Beyond self-control: Analysis and critique of Gottfredson and Hirschi's general theory of crime.* Berlin, Germany: Duncker and Homblot.

Sear, R., & Mace, R. (2008). Who keeps children alive? A review of the effect of kin on child survival. *Evolution and Human Behavior, 29,* 1–18. doi:10.1016/j.evolhumbehav.2007.10.001

Serin, R., Forth, A., Brown, S. L., Nunes, K., Bennell, C., & Pozzulo, J. (2011). *Psychology of criminal behavior: A Canadian perspective.* Toronto, Ontario, Canada: Pearson Canada.

Shackelford, T. K., & Weekes-Shackelford, V. A. (Eds.). (2012). *The Oxford handbook of evolutionary perspectives on violence, homicide, and war.* Oxford, England: Oxford University Press. doi:10.1093/oxfordhb/9780199738403.001.0001

Simons, R. L., Miller, M. G., & Aigner, S. M. (1980). Contemporary theories of deviance and female delinquency: An empirical test. *Journal of Research in Crime and Delinquency, 17,* 42–57. doi:10.1177/002242788001700104

Simourd, L., & Andrews, D. A. (1994). Correlates of delinquency: A look at gender differences. *Forum on Corrections Research, 6,* 26–31.

Skinner, B. F. (1938). *The behavior of organisms.* New York, NY: Appleton Century Crofts.

Skinner, B. F. (1953). *Science and human behavior.* New York, NY: Macmillan.

Snyder, H. N. (2011). *Patterns and trends: Arrests in the United States, 1980–2009.* Washington, DC: U.S. Department of Justice, Office of Justice Programs, Bureau of Justice Statistics. Retrieved from http://bjs.ojp.usdoj.gov/content/pub/pdf/aus8009.pdf

Storms, M. D. (1981). A theory of erotic orientation development. *Psychological Review, 88,* 340–353. doi:10.1037/0033-295X.88.4.340

Sutherland, E. H. (1939). *Principles of criminology* (3rd ed.). Philadelphia, PA: Lippincott.

Sutherland, E. H. (1947). *Principles of criminology* (4th ed.). Philadelphia, PA: Lippincott.

Sutherland, E. H., & Cressey, D. R. (1974). *Criminology* (9th ed.). Philadelphia, PA: Lippincott.

Thorndike, E. L. (1898). Animal intelligence: An experimental study of the associative processes in animals. *The Psychological Review: Monograph Supplements, 2*(4), 1–109.

Tooby, J., & Cosmides, L. (2005). Conceptual foundations of evolutionary psychology. In D. M. Buss (Ed.), *The handbook of evolutionary psychology* (pp. 5–67). Hoboken, NJ: Wiley.

Trivers, R. L. (1972). Parental investment and sexual selection. In B. Campbell (Ed.), *Sexual selection and the descent of man 1871–1971* (pp. 136–179). Chicago, IL: Aldine.

Truman, J. L. (2011). *Criminal victimization, 2010: National Crime Victimization Survey*. Washington, DC: U.S. Department of Justice, Office of Justice Programs, Bureau of Justice Statistics. Retrieved from http://bjs.ojp.usdoj.gov/content/pub/pdf/cv10.pdf

Turnbull, S. R. (2003). *Genghis Khan and the Mongol conquests, 1190–1400*. Botley, England: Osprey.

Vazsonyi, A., Pickering, L., Junger, M., & Hessing, D. (2001). An empirical test of a general theory of crime: A four-nation comparative study of self-control and the prediction of deviance. *Journal of Research in Crime and Delinquency*, *38*, 91–131. doi:10.1177/0022427801038002001

Ward, T., Melser, J., & Yates, P. M. (2007). Reconstructing the risk–need–responsivity model: A theoretical elaboration and evaluation. *Aggression and Violent Behavior*, *12*, 208–228. doi:10.1016/j.avb.2006.07.001

Watson, J. B., & Rayner, R. (1920). Conditioned emotional reactions. *Journal of Experimental Psychology*, *3*, 1–14. doi:10.1037/h0069608

Widom, C. S., & Brzustowicz, L. M. (2006). MAOA and the "cycle of violence": Childhood abuse and neglect, MAOA genotype, and risk for violent and antisocial behavior. *Biological Psychiatry*, *60*, 684–689. doi:10.1016/j.biopsych.2006.03.039

Wolfgang, M. E. (1958). *Patterns in criminal homicide*. Philadelphia: University of Pennsylvania Press.

Wright, J. P., Beaver, M. D., Vaughn, M. G., Boisvert, D., & Vaske, J. (2008). The miseducation of criminologists. *Journal of Criminal Justice Education*, *19*, 325–338. doi:10.1080/10511250802476137

Zerjal, T., Xue, Y., Bertorelle, G., Wells, R. S. Bao, W., Zhu, S., . . . Tyler-Smith, C. (2003). The genetic legacy of the Mongols. *The American Journal of Human Genetics*, *72*, 717–721. doi:10.1086/367774

CHAPTER 9

PSYCHOPATHY

Kevin S. Douglas, Natalia L. Nikolova, Shannon E. Kelley, and John F. Edens

Few descriptive terms raise more concern and fear than the term *psychopath*. Indeed, when presented with the term psychopath, laypersons who are asked to think of associated descriptors often respond with words such as *evil* or *monster* (Helfgott, 1997). Professional interest in a psychopathy-like construct dates back centuries, if not further. Philippe Pinel (1806/1962) used the term *manie sans delire* ("mania without insanity") to describe violent and impulsive persons who seemingly had nothing wrong with them from a mental health perspective. This concept was reflected in Cleckley's (1941/1988) classic and influential book, *The Mask of Sanity*. The field of psychology is much further ahead, scientifically, compared to the days of Pinel, or even Cleckley. There have been thousands of articles and books published over the past several decades on modern conceptions of psychopathy and the somewhat closely related construct of antisocial personality disorder (APD).

Yet, "volumes of research" does not necessarily equate to consensus among scholars. There remain numerous fundamental issues in the study of psychopathy that contemporary scholars debate, despite some areas of relative agreement. After briefly distinguishing between psychopathy and APD, this chapter will focus on some of these areas of controversy. In order to spend a meaningful amount of space on each topic, we have opted not to review the burgeoning biological and neuroscientific literature on psychopathy, and instead refer readers to useful reviews of these topics (see Kiehl & Sinnot-Armstrong, 2013; Patrick, 2006; see also Hare, 2003).

Controversy remains in simply *defining* the core elements of the construct of psychopathy. For this reason, we will spend some time discussing recent theoretical and conceptual debates in the field in terms of the appropriate inclusion of *criminality* in the construct, as well as recent discussions about whether the psychological construct of *boldness* is or is not part of psychopathy. Because these theoretical concerns find their way into the measurement of psychopathy, we also will review the different approaches to the *measurement* of psychopathy.

Considerable discussion in the field of psychology continues regarding the extent to which psychopathy is associated with violent behavior, and, if so, the extent to which different components of psychopathy may be more or less predictive of violence and other forms of antisocial conduct. As such, we will review the rather substantial literature on the link between psychopathy and crime and violence, focusing on meta-analytic work. Closely related to this topic is the extent to which we can reduce crime and violence among psychopathic individuals through treatment (see also Chapter 6, this volume). Although clinical lore has often held that highly psychopathic individuals are resistant to treatment, or even that "treatment makes psychopaths worse," recent research suggests more promising outcomes.

As most research on psychopathy focuses on adult men, less is known about the viability of the construct among females and among youth. For that reason, we spend considerable space on psychopathy among women and whether and how to think of the construct of psychopathy among youth. In addition, most

http://dx.doi.org/10.1037/14461-009
APA Handbook of Forensic Psychology: Vol. 1. Individual and Situational Influences in Criminal and Civil Contexts,
B. L. Cutler and P. A. Zapf (Editors-in-Chief)

early research on psychopathy was conducted with Caucasian participants in Canada and later, in the United States. Psychopathy is now studied, and measures of psychopathy are applied, in numerous countries with people from a variety of ethnic and cultural backgrounds. Therefore, we will examine the construct and measurement of psychopathy in terms of ethnicity and culture. Finally, most of what is known about psychopathy has stemmed from research studies that have been carried out in well-controlled settings, with high premium placed on standardized data collection procedures. Recent evidence about how psychopathy is assessed and applied outside of research settings has raised some concern about its utility in the everyday world. For this reason, we will discuss this recent research on the use of psychopathy measures and descriptions in the "real world". We start with a brief discussion of the differences between psychopathy and APD and our decision to focus on the former rather than the latter in this chapter.

IMPORTANCE OF THE PROBLEM

At a very basic level, psychopathy and APD are two ways to attempt to describe the same phenomenon—a personality style or disorder that is harmful or damaging to others and to society. Cleckley (1941/1988) acknowledged this years ago in reference to the first and second versions of the *Diagnostic and Statistical Manual of Mental Disorders* (*DSM*; American Psychiatric Association, 1952, 1968). The American Psychiatric Association's view of this phenomenon is captured by its diagnostic criteria in the various *DSM* manuals that, since *DSM–III*, have been heavily loaded with childhood and adult indicators of antisocial behavior—largely as an attempt to improve the reliability of diagnostic criteria for this disorder. Scholars have proposed other models or constructs, variously captured under the term *psychopathy*.

Although diagnoses of APD are meaningful and give rise to expectations about associated behaviors (such as crime and other irresponsible behavior), many scholars have focused their efforts on understanding this personality construct through the lens of psychopathy instead. One of the reasons for this is that APD has little utility within prison settings

because the majority of offenders meet its diagnostic criteria (see Hare, 2003, for a review). Another reason is that APD, relative to psychopathy, underemphasizes personality and emotional aspects of the condition, choosing instead to focus on behavioral problems. Most modern conceptualizations and measurements of psychopathy, however, dating back to seminal theorists such as Cleckley (1941/1988), have included greater emphasis on interpersonal and affective deficits of psychopathy, such as shallow affect, superficial charm, lack of remorse or guilt, callousness, and inflated self-worth. For these reasons, this chapter will focus on psychopathy rather than APD.

APD is more closely associated with behavioral aspects of psychopathy than with its interpersonal or affective deficits. This association is reflected by stronger correlations between measures of APD and the Psychopathy Checklist—Revised (PCL–R; Hare, 2003) Factor 2 (often in the .70s), which focuses more on behavioral indicators (i.e., impulsivity and antisociality) than Factor 1 (often in the .30s or .40s), which focuses on interpersonal and affective deficits (see Hare, 2003, for a review). Similarly, the second factor of the Psychopathic Personality Inventory (PPI; Lilienfeld, 1990) and its revision (PPI–R; Lilienfeld & Widows, 2005), PPI–II (Self-Centered Impulsivity, or SCI), is more strongly related to APD (meta-analytic correlation of .53) than is the first factor, PPI–I (Fearless Dominance, or FD), with a meta-analytic correlation of .07 (J. D. Miller & Lynam, 2012).

These patterns of findings are also reflected in the associations between psychopathy and APD with normal personality constructs, as measured with the Five-Factor Model (FFM) of personality (Costa & McCrae, 1992a). Meta-analytic work indicates that measures of both psychopathy and APD share some common associations with FFM indices. For instance, they are both associated with low conscientiousness, warmth, and agreeableness and with higher levels of anger-hostility, impulsiveness, and excitement seeking (Decuyper, de Pauw, de Fruyt, de Bolle, & de Clercq, 2009). However, psychopathy is also associated with lower anxiety and is more strongly (inversely) associated with agreeableness, straightforwardness, compliance, and modesty.

As we will explain later, attempting to specify and measure the unique aspects of psychopathy vis-à-vis APD continues to be an important, and sometimes contentious, component of contemporary psychopathy scholarship. In the next section, we outline some of the current debates about the nature and contours of psychopathy. Then, we review commonly used measures of psychopathy.

RELEVANT PSYCHOLOGICAL THEORY AND PRINCIPLES

Most classic and contemporary conceptions of psychopathy include emphasis on its affective and interpersonal deficits. There is some general agreement among scholars that psychopathy includes affective deficits such as impoverished emotional experience and capacity as well as an overinflated view of the self. Interpersonally, traits such as manipulativeness, antagonism, deceitfulness, and superficial charm are commonly used to describe psychopathy. Quite often, these terms collectively are referred to as *primary psychopathy*. There is some debate in the field about whether certain constructs (such as an absence of anxiety and boldness or FD) should be included under the psychopathy construct, and, even if they should, whether contemporary measures of psychopathy capture them adequately.

Other traits that are commonly associated with the psychopathy construct include irresponsible, destructive, impulsive, and antisocial behavior (essentially, APD). Again, there is provenance to these concepts, as early theorists such as Karpman (1946, 1948) highlighted their importance. Typically, these manifestations of psychopathy collectively are referred to as *secondary psychopathy*. Again, there is debate about the extent to which antisocial (in particular, criminal) behavior should form part of the construct itself.

A good deal of empirical support exists for a distinction between primary and secondary elements of psychopathy. For instance, cluster-analytic work often shows that there are groups of people who tend to possess mainly primary characteristics and also groups of people who possess mainly secondary characteristics. Several cluster-analytic studies have reported groups of offenders who tend to be higher on interpersonal and affective traits and lower on indices of anxiety (or other internalizing indices) compared to groups who are lower on interpersonal and affective traits but higher on behavioral aspects as well as anxiety.

As one example, Poythress et al. (2010) used model-based clustering in a sample of 691 offenders who met the criteria for APD to test whether groups of primary and secondary psychopaths emerged. This study is likely the most comprehensive and large-scale cluster analysis of psychopathy using the PCL–R and other theoretically relevant variables. The authors predicted that secondary groups, in addition to being lower on interpersonal and affective indices of the PCL–R and higher on behavioral indices, would show a greater degree of both internalizing and externalizing psychopathology, impulsivity, institutional infractions, and criminal recidivism. Primary groups, in contrast, were hypothesized to show elevations on interpersonal and affective PCL–R deficits and higher levels of dominance and passive-avoidance errors.

Clustering variables included the three factors from Cooke and Michie's (2001) three-factor PCL–R model (reviewed in detail later, these focus on interpersonal, affective, and behavioral features but exclude some items specifically dealing with criminality), the Anxiety scale (ANX) from the Personality Assessment Inventory (PAI; Morey, 1991, 2007), the Harm Avoidance (HA) scale from the Multidimensional Personality Questionnaire (MPQ; Tellegen, in press) as an index of fearless temperament, the three Behavioral Activation Scales (BASs; Carver & White, 1994), and the Child Abuse and Trauma Scale (CATS; Sanders & Giolas, 1991) to identify participants whose psychopathic symptoms may have stemmed from abuse.

Results indicated five clusters, one of which was very small ($n = 12$) and was very high on an index of negative impression and hence was excluded. As shown in Figure 9.1, the four meaningful groups were called *primary sychopath*, *Karpman's secondary psychopath*, *APD (nonpsychopathic)*, and (unexpectedly) *fearful psychopath*. The primary psychopath group had higher PCL–R interpersonal and affective features than behavioral features, as well as

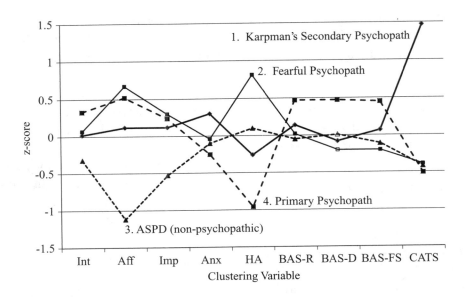

FIGURE 9.1. Cluster variable Z-score profiles for four emergent clusters. ASPD = Antisocial Personality Disorder; Int = interpersonal facet from the Psychopathy Checklist–Revised (PCL-R); Aff = affective facet from the PCL-R; Imp = impulsive lifestyle facet from the PCL-R; ANX = Anxiety scale from the Personality Assessment Inventory; HA = Harm Avoidance scale from the Multidimensional Personality Questionnaire; BAS-RR = Reward Responsiveness scale from the behavioral activation system scales; BAS-DR = Drive scale of the BAS scales; BAS-FS = Fun Seeking scale of the BAS scales; CATS = Child Abuse and Trauma Scale. From "Identifying Subtypes Among Offenders With Antisocial Personality Disorder: A Cluster-Analytic Study," by N. G. Poythress, J. F. Edens, J. L. Skeem, S. O. Lilienfeld, K. S. Douglas, P. J. Frick, C. J. Patrick, M. Epstein, and T. Wang, 2010. *Journal of Abnormal Psychology, 119*, p. 595. Copyright 2010 by the American Psychological Association.

relatively low ANX scores, very low HA scores, and average scores on the BAS indices. The Karpman secondary group had very high scores on the CATS scale, average scores on PCL–R interpersonal and affective deficits, somewhat higher PCL–R behavioral scores, average BAS scores, and high ANX scores. A nonpsychopathic group had low PCL–R indices and average scores on the other measures. The fearful psychopath group was unexpected and had average PCL–R interpersonal deficits, high affective deficits, and somewhat high behavioral deficits, as well as average ANX and BAS scores and very high HA scores (Poythress et al., 2010).

As predicted, the secondary group was higher than the primary group on external variables of internalizing and externalizing psychopathology as well as impulsivity. However, the primary group was not higher on dominance compared to the secondary group, although it was higher on passive-avoidance errors. Although the primary

group compared to the secondary group showed more unexcused absences from treatment and had lower counselor-rated treatment motivation, there were no differences in terms of disruptive behavior in treatment, skill mastery, or ratings of "treatment successes." There were also no differences between groups in terms of recidivism, although as predicted, the secondary group engaged in more institutional infractions (Poythress et al., 2010).

Although not all hypotheses were supported (Poythress et al., 2010), there was clear evidence for primary psychopathy, secondary psychopathy, and nonpsychopathic groups. These groups differed in meaningful ways not only on PCL–R profiles but also on other core theoretical indices (i.e., abuse history) and external validation variables (i.e., internalizing and externalizing indices). Other cluster-analytic studies, some using PCL measures and some using other psychopathy measures, have tended to find support for this basic distinction between primary and secondary variants of psychopathy (Hicks, Markon, Patrick, Krueger, & Newman, 2004; Skeem, Edens, Camp, & Colwell, 2004; Skeem, Johansson, Andershed, Kerr, & Louden, 2007; Swogger, Walsh, & Kosson, 2008; Vassileva, Kosson, Abramowitz, & Conrod, 2005; Vaughn, Edens, Howard, & Smith, 2009).

Despite this work on *subtypes* and *clusters*, it is important to emphasize that there does not appear to be a discrete discontinuity between *psychopath* and *nonpsychopath*. That is, people tend to vary along psychopathic dimensions. Those people who, for research purposes, fall into a primary or secondary cluster or subtype should be interpreted not as different in kind from others, but rather as different in degree from others. We discuss taxometric research on the construct of psychopathy next.

Is Psychopathy Dimensional or Taxonic?

An area of some debate over the past several years has focused on whether the underlying structure of psychopathy is dichotomous or dimensional: Are psychopaths a qualitatively discrete subgroup of individuals who are categorically different from "normal people" or is the concept of psychopathy continuously distributed throughout humankind? This "degree versus kind" debate has significant theoretical and etiological implications for the conceptualization of the disorder and also has significant practical implications for the applied use of psychopathy diagnoses in clinical–forensic contexts.

From a more conceptual perspective, evidence supporting the existence of psychopathy as a discrete entity would support the notion that (at least some) personality disorders are categorical in nature, consistent with the *DSM–5*'s retention of a categorical classification system (even though the *DSM* does not explicitly include a diagnosis of psychopathy per se; American Psychiatric Association, 2013). It would also suggest at least the plausibility of a relatively specific etiology that might result from one or relatively few hereditary or environmental factors (Meehl, 1977). Evidence of a dimensional model, in contrast, would be consistent with more recent conceptualizations of general personality and psychopathology and would converge with the *DSM–5* Personality Disorder Working Committee's (ultimately rejected) dimensional model of

personality disorders. A psychopathy dimension would also make relatively straightforward etiological models focusing on a single or specific cause of the disorder relatively less tenable.

From a more applied perspective, evidence of an underlying class of psychopaths would also have specific clinical implications in that it would suggest that assessment procedures should focus on quantifying the probability that an individual is a member of this discrete class. Evidence for dimensionality would suggest, however, that the goal of assessment should be a reliable and valid indication of where on the continuum of psychopathy an individual falls.

Evidence of an underlying discontinuity between psychopaths and nonpsychopaths would generally fit with the legal system's typical view of mental disorders (and legal statuses) as being categorical (see Marcus, Poythress, Edens, & Lilienfeld, 2010). For example, one either is or is not a "sexual psychopath" in terms of various civil commitment laws in several states in the United States—there is no middle ground or continuum of this status. Along these same lines, legal professionals (e.g., judges, attorneys, mental health expert witnesses) often describe psychopathy in categorical terms at the case level, frequently treating a score of at least 30 on the PCL–R (though in some instances, 25; DeMatteo et al., 2014) as being indicative of a discrete group of offenders who are categorically different from those with lower scores (Edens & Petrila, 2006). Evidence of a continuum of psychopathic traits would not preclude the establishment of legally meaningful groups for statutory purposes, but it would indicate that decision rules for placing people into such groups are not driven by any underlying discontinuity on the construct of interest.

Statistical procedures that are designed to identify whether latent, qualitatively distinct groups exist within a given sample have been in existence for decades. Over the course of his career, Paul Meehl (Meehl & Yonce, 1994, 1996; see also Meehl, 1995) developed a number of data-analytic approaches that are collectively referred to as *taxometric procedures* to address this question. An extended review of these is beyond the scope of this chapter, but an excellent overview of this approach is provided by Ruscio, Haslam, and Ruscio (2006). Summary information regarding the current taxometric status of personality and psychopathology constructs has been recently provided by Haslam, Holland, and Kuppens (2012).

Although early research studies suggested that numerous psychological constructs might be taxonic, quantitative reviews of the extant literature have suggested that relatively few constructs in the area of personality and psychopathology are likely to be underpinned by a latent taxon. Haslam et al. (2012), for example, reported that although early studies tended to identify taxa at a relatively high rate, more recent studies using the most advanced statistical procedures estimate that the true prevalence of taxonic findings across studies is only 14%. For studies that focused specifically on externalizing psychopathology, approximately 80% reported dimensional findings.

Although taxometric procedures have been in existence for several decades, the earliest published study applying them to the construct of psychopathy was not published until the mid-1990s (Harris, Rice, & Quinsey, 1994). Employing a relatively large sample of Canadian forensic psychiatric patients who had been scored on the PCL–R (based on file review data only), Harris et al. (1994) applied several taxometric procedures to their data and concluded that there was evidence to support the existence of a latent taxon underpinning the total score, with a base rate ranging from .42 to .44 across multiple analyses. In regard to the two factors of the PCL–R, results suggested that Factor 2 (but not Factor 1) scores appeared to be taxonic.

Since the publication of this study, numerous researchers have attempted to replicate the existence of a psychopathy taxon using a variety of assessment methods (e.g., PCL–R, PCL: Screening Version [PCL:SV; Hart, Cox, & Hare, 1995], PCL: Youth Version [PCL:YV; Forth, Kosson, & Hare, 2003], APD diagnoses, self-report psychopathy scales) and samples (e.g., adult prison inmates, substance abusers, juvenile delinquents, sex offenders). The results of these studies, however, have been rather uniformly consistent, with a dimensional underlying structure—not a categorical one. These findings, which echo the more general trend in the taxometric literature noted by Haslam et al. (2012) that early evidence of latent taxa do not replicate well in the

psychopathology field, suggest that the earlier studies may have suffered from serious statistical and methodological flaws (see Edens, Marcus, Lilienfeld, & Poythress, 2006, for an extended critique of the original Harris et al., 1994, analyses and conclusions). In fact, Haslam et al. noted that in the broader area of *antisociality*, the first seven studies examining this construct suggested the existence of a latent taxon, whereas the subsequent 17 studies that used more sophisticated statistical procedures demonstrated clearly dimensional results.

Collectively, this literature supports the argument that psychopaths differ in degree, not in kind, from nonpsychopaths, and that classification systems that create groups on this dimension are based on relatively arbitrary decision rules. We should state, however, that we do not intend to imply that arbitrary decision rules reflect practically meaningless categories, particularly for applied clinical–forensic purposes. It may very well be that clinically useful subgroups of psychopathic offenders can be identified that differ from each other in important ways (e.g., recidivism risk, responsiveness to particular types of rehabilitation efforts). But, such groups do not reflect an underlying discontinuity in terms of the latent concept that is tapped by the psychopathy assessment instruments themselves.

The results of these studies are consistent with dimensional models of personality disorder that were espoused for but were ultimately rejected by the *DSM–5* (American Psychiatric Association, 2013). Other than schizotypy, there is very little evidence to suggest that any personality disorders might actually represent discrete categories (Haslam et al., 2012). As such, it perhaps should not be surprising that psychopathic traits follow this same general pattern. The field of psychology might do well to move away from thinking about whether someone is or is not a psychopath and instead focus attention on where on the continuum of psychopathic traits someone falls.

In addition to relative agreement on the dimensionality of psychopathy, most scholars agree that some aspects of both primary and secondary psychopathy rightly belong under the larger construct of psychopathy. Disagreement exists in terms of how, exactly, elements of primary and secondary psychopathy should be defined (i.e., Is criminality part of the construct? Is boldness or fearless dominance?) as well as the best ways to measure such constructs. More recently, there has been spirited discussion of the very nature of the construct: Is it a coherent syndrome consisting of co-occurring symptoms from both the primary and secondary domains? Or, are there multiple, essentially unrelated symptom clusters that, when they coincide, form a cluster of symptoms that scholars simply call psychopathy? We explore these issues next.

The Criminal Behavior Debate

Hare (1991, 2003) has long argued that his model (and hence measure) of psychopathy was derived from Cleckley's (1941/1988) classic work. His Psychopathy Checklist (PCL; Hare, 1980), PCL–R, PCL:SV, and PCL:YV all include content reflecting interpersonal and affective deficits (grouped under Factor 1) as well as lifestyle and behavioral indices (grouped under Factor 2). Antisocial behavior is strongly represented throughout the rating criteria on the measures, as is overt criminal behavior (e.g., criminal versatility).

Skeem and Cooke (2010) issued a warning to the field that it was at risk of conflating the construct of psychopathy itself with its measurement through the PCL family of measures. There is little doubt that the PCL family of measures is the most heavily researched, and, as the first widely adopted measurement system on the market, it has been tremendously influential. Nonetheless, Skeem and Cooke argued that there might be limits to the PCL approach in terms of its content and how well it reflects theory. Specifically, following arguments made earlier by Cooke and Michie (2001) and by Cooke, Michie, Hart, and Clark (2004), Skeem and Cooke argued that the PCL family of measures overemphasizes criminality; underemphasizes constructs such as low anxiety, which is featured in classic accounts of psychopathy; and weighs antisociality as high as or higher than the affective deficits that are featured in foundational work by Cleckley (1941/1988), Karpman (1941), and others. In short, their argument was that criminal behavior is not part of the construct of psychopathy and that the PCL instruments overemphasize it.

The larger danger, Skeem and Cooke (2010) posited, is that the field has come to accept the PCL

instrument as the psychopathy construct itself. This, in turn, can stifle the investigation of the construct itself because its operationalization is frozen. It also gives rise to the implication that criminality is a core feature of psychopathy, and therefore that psychopaths always tend to be criminals. It thwarts attempts to understand to what extent psychopathy exists outside of the criminal justice system and that psychopathic individuals may harm others or society in less overtly criminal ways (i.e., such as sabotaging a person's reputation to gain advantage in business or lying about a colleague in order to gain advantage in the workplace).

There certainly is an advantage to the field in studying alternate conceptualizations and measurement approaches to psychopathy (Poythress & Petrila, 2010). Exposing multiple views and measures to the marketplace of ideas, and evaluating patterns of validities across different conceptualizations and measurement approaches, will doubtlessly lead to greater insights about psychopathy and likely to better agreement about its core features and correlates. The PCL family of instruments, as mentioned, has contributed a great deal to the field's understanding of psychopathy. However, more recent approaches and measures, which are reviewed in the following paragraphs, are also certainly adding to the scientific and theoretical understanding of psychopathy.

The "crime isn't central" to psychopathy position (Cooke & Michie, 2001; Cooke et al., 2004; Skeem & Cooke, 2010) has pragmatic, theoretical, and measurement implications. Most meta-analyses of the PCL family of measures have shown that it is the behavioral aspects (those for which ratings depend most heavily on past criminality) that are more strongly associated with future crime and violence. This (not terribly surprising) finding has implications for the applied use of the PCL measures for risk assessment. If the core affective and interpersonal features of psychopathy are not predictive of future violence and crime, then of what use is the PCL in informing risk assessments? We return to this topic later.

Hare and Neumann (2010) rebutted the arguments by Skeem and Cooke (2010). In their view, antisociality writ broadly is part of the construct, whereas criminality per se is not. Hare and Neumann also believed that Skeem and Cooke inaccurately depicted Hare's position on the role of criminality in psychopathy. They argued that all classic conceptualizations of psychopathy have included antisociality. The PCL measures, they argued, contain a good deal of reference to criminality because they were initially developed within prison settings, and they were developed within prison settings because there is a high concentration of psychopathy among inmates relative to members of the general population. Hare and Neumann also argued that a person could be rated under many of these items without reference to criminality, and that the PCL:SV removes much of the reliance on overt criminality. In their view, psychopathy is a unitary construct that is underpinned by features that are found on both "old" Factors 1 and 2.

Despite these arguments, it is certainly clear that the PCL–R, as a measure, includes a substantial amount of content about criminality and overt antisociality. More recent measures, such as the PPI and the PPI–R, which are reviewed in detail later, attempt to remove this reliance so as to facilitate the study of psychopathy without tying a substantial part of its operationalization to a pattern of overt criminal and antisocial acts (e.g., juvenile delinquency, failure on conditional release), which in many instances occur due to factors other than psychopathy (e.g., peer pressure, limited coping skills, extreme poverty, to name but a few possible causes of criminality). It is also clear that most foundational conceptualizations of psychopathy, such as the oft-cited Cleckleyan (1941/1988) description, do indeed consider antisociality to be a core component of psychopathy (though the behavioral indicators are thought to be directly caused by the underlying disorder). There does seem to be consensus that criminal behavior per se is not central to being psychopathic, although clearly there is spirited and at times acrimonious disagreement by scholars regarding each other's work and positions (Poythress & Petrila, 2010).

This debate has been accompanied by, and was to some extent triggered by, empirical work (factor- and cluster-analytic, item response theory [IRT]) on the PCL–R by Cooke and Michie (1997, 2001). Although factor analysis alone cannot inform us of the adequacy of a theory, it can inform us about how well certain manifest items (indicators) on an instrument fit underlying constructs. In the case of the PCL–R, and of relevance to arguments by Cooke and Michie (2001), Cooke et al. (2004), and later Skeem and Cooke (2010), the first major factor-analytic work conducted since the initial work produced a two-factor structure (Harpur, Hakstian, & Hare, 1988; Harpur, Hare, & Hakstian, 1989) by Cooke and Michie (2001) showed that better fit was achieved by dropping seven of the PCL–R's 20 items and reconfiguring the remaining items into three rather than two factors. Most of the items that were dropped were those that were loaded with criminality and overt antisocial behavior (i.e., criminal versatility, juvenile delinquency, revocation of conditional release). The "new" factors included an interpersonal factor (Factor 1, termed *Arrogant and Deceitful Interpersonal Style*), an affective factor (Factor 2, termed *Deficient Affective Experience*), and a lifestyle/behavioral factor (Factor 3, termed *Impulsive and Irresponsible Behavioral Style*). The items on new Factors 1 and 2 previously were captured on old Factor 1, which was just split into two. Factor 3 included elements of an unstable and irresponsible lifestyle. Gone were items that were heavily saturated with criminality.

Other researchers were quick to conduct their own factor analyses of the PCL–R, testing two-, three-, and four-factor models against one another. Some of these studies have provided further support for the three-factor model (Cooke, Michie, & Skeem, 2007; Morrissey et al., 2010; Walters, 2012; see Sevecke, Pukrop, Kosson, & Krischer, 2009, for the PCL:YV; see Skeem, Mulvey, & Grisso, 2003, for the PCL:SV), whereas others supported a four-factor model (Neumann, Hare, & Newman, 2007; see also Neumann, Hare, & Johansson, 2013; Olver, Neumann, Wong, & Hare, 2013) that essentially adds five of the seven items back into the mix in the form of an "Antisocial Behavior" factor, with the three factors identified by Cooke and Michie (2001) remaining as is. It is common in psychopathy parlance to refer to the new factors as *facets* in order to distinguish them from the factors under the old model (i.e., Factor 1, Factor 2). As Cooke et al. (2007) pointed out, some of the tests of the four-factor model have not compared it to the three-factor model, making claims about the relative adequacy of these models difficult. In Cooke et al.'s article, fit indices were strongest for a three-factor model, with the exception of a four-factor model that used a technique called *parceling* (which bundles items together and treats a summary index as the manifest indicator within factor-analytic analyses), which is a statistically questionable procedure to employ in factor analyses. For instance, Cooke et al. were able to find excellent fit indices for a four-factor model that intentionally placed items into the wrong parcel.

The "three versus four factor" debate seems to have subsided somewhat, supplanted perhaps by the debate that was described earlier regarding the role of criminal behavior in the construct of psychopathy and the debate that is described next on the relevance of boldness. Likely, it will take as much theory as data to come to a consensus in the field. In our view, it is clear that antisociality is an important element of psychopathy, from a theoretical perspective. However, this does not necessitate engagement in criminal behavior. There are numerous ways to harm others (i.e., betrayals in relationships, subterfuge in workplaces, economic decisions that harm others' livelihood), and only some of these are criminal.

The Boldness Debate

Not only has there been debate about the role of criminality in the construct of psychopathy, but there has also been more recent debate about the extent to which another concept—boldness or FD—should be considered part of the construct. Lilienfeld (1990) developed a model (and corresponding measure) of psychopathy that was relatively free from overt antisocial behavior and completely free of criminality. The measure is described more fully in a later section. In essence, in addition to including content that focuses on SCI and coldheartedness, the model and the measure also include content that is related to so-called FD. This construct refers to an interpersonal style that is characterized by fearlessness, being relatively immune to stress or anxiety, and being successful at negotiating social interactions to achieve desired goals. The construct also ostensibly taps quasi-adaptive features that theorists such as Cleckley (1941/1988) and Lykken (1995) stressed in their models of this disorder. According to this approach, high scores on both FD and SCI are indicative of psychopathy (Lilienfeld et al., 2012).

Based in many regards on earlier PPI research, Patrick, Fowles, and Krueger (2009) further developed a model and measure of psychopathy that they argued reflected classic theoretical accounts but also more recent empirical work in personality, genetics, and affective neuroscience. Their model, the triarchic conceptualization of psychopathy, includes three components. Two of these—meanness and disinhibition—are relatively uncontroversial. The former refers to the tendency to be callous, cruel, and predatory (similar to PCL–R Factor 1) and the latter to the tendency to be hostile, impulsive, and irresponsible (similar to PCL–R Factor 2). This model also includes boldness, which is generally isomorphic with Lilienfeld's (1990) FD construct. Boldness, for Patrick et al., refers to the tendency to be venturesome, socially dominant, poised, assured, and low in anxiety. In this model, the co-occurrence of boldness with either meanness or disinhibition forms psychopathy.

The triarchic model itself has not yet been subjected to a great deal of research, although research on Lilienfeld's (1990) model and measures has been accumulating quite quickly. Although we will discuss the measures in more detail in a later section, we will first address a debate that has recently arisen concerning the centrality, or lack thereof, of the boldness or FD construct. According to Patrick and colleagues (Patrick et al., 2009; Patrick, Venables, & Drislane, 2013), disinhibition reflects a prominent aspect of the externalizing spectrum of psychopathology, is closely linked with APD, and is well represented by Factor 2 of the PCL–R. Meanness, while also representing certain aspects of the externalizing spectrum, is temperamentally tied to trait fearlessness and phenotypically represents a ruthless and cruel exploitation of others. Combining boldness with either of these constructs could conceivably produce a phenotypic psychopath, though most of the research and theorizing has focused on the combinations of boldness and disinihibition and of meanness and disinhibition. As Patrick et al. (2013) stated, "It is the conjunction of boldness/FD and externalizing/SCI features that demarcates psychopathy from APD" (p. 81).

Two recent meta-analyses of Lilienfeld's measure (the PPI, PPI–R, and PPI–Short Form [PPI:SF]) raise important questions as to the role that self-reported boldness plays in psychopathy. These measures contain a superordinate scale to measure FD and another to measure SCI. A third construct, coldheartedness, is represented by a single subordinate scale.

In one meta-analysis, J. D. Miller and Lynam (2012) evaluated the construct validity for FD and SCI in terms of the patterns of associations that each had with external constructs across 61 samples. They concluded that there was strong convergent and divergent validity for SCI (and the total score) but not for FD. FD was moderately strongly related to features of positive adjustment, including positive emotionality, extraversion, openness, low neuroticism, and low negative emotionality, and was weakly related to indices of dysfunction or antisociality. SCI, on the other hand, was robustly associated with indices of antisociality, substance use, negative emotionality, impulsivity, and APD. Based on this, J. D. Miller and Lynam argued that there was strong evidence for SCI as a marker for elements of the psychopathy construct but little evidence that FD marked anything other than relatively good adjustment—"stable extraversion," as they termed it. From their perspective, at most, FD could be considered a nonnecessary "specifier" of a type of psychopathy. They asserted, however, that it could not be a core element of psychopathy due to its relative absence of any association with psychopathology or dysfunction.

In the other meta-analysis, Marcus, Fulton, and Edens (2013) came to generally similar conclusions regarding the nomological nets surrounding FD (and SCI) but interpreted their findings somewhat differently in relation to boldness (see also Marcus, Edens, & Fulton, 2013). In their meta-analysis, they reported that FD was more strongly associated with positive emotionality (and inversely associated with negative emotionality) than it was with extant measures of psychopathy (e.g., the PCL–R) or with low constraint. Marcus, Fulton, and Edens concluded that the role of FD/boldness was unclear in that it generally marks positive adjustment. In addition, they reported weak to nil correlations between FD and SCI. As such, the co-occurrence of FD/boldness with SCI or disinhibition would be coincidental. Although questioning the role of FD in traditional

models of psychopathy, these authors pointed out that the research has not yet thoroughly investigated whether FD and SCI (or meanness, or disinhibition) might interact to produce negative outcomes.

One interpretation of these meta-analyses is that FD/boldness (at least as operationalized by self-report) has relatively little to do with psychopathy per se, which is a position that was essentially endorsed by J. D. Miller and Lynam (2012). A number of counterarguments have been put forward to rebut this position, including an extensive critique of the J. D. Miller and Lynam meta-analysis by Lilienfeld et al. (2012). For example, the concept of boldness, though perhaps poorly encapsulated in many current psychopathy scales such as the PCL–R, plays a prominent role in seminal models of this disorder, particularly those that differentiate between primary and secondary subtypes and those that consider the possibility of *successful* or *subclinical psychopathy* (see, e.g., Karpman, 1946, 1948; Lykken, 1995). In their description of *corporate psychopaths*, for example, Babiak and Hare (2006) discussed these individuals' propensities for charm and interpersonal manipulation as "talents" and argued that these individuals can easily con unwary observers during employment interviews—despite being individuals who are relatively unlikely to obtain particularly high scores on the PCL–R.

Additionally, Lilienfeld et al. (2012) noted that FD does in fact correlate highly with some measures of psychopathy—including scales that were developed by the Lynam research group. Lynam et al. (2011) reported that FD scores correlated fairly highly ($r = .47$) with FFM psychopathy prototype scores. Similarly, S. R. Ross, Benning, Patrick, Thompson, and Thurston (2008) reported that FD scores correlated at $r = .50$ with this same FFM psychopathy prototype score in an earlier sample. As such, it appears that FD shares quite a bit of overlapping variance with the model of psychopathy that is specifically espoused by Lynam et al.

Along these same lines, a few recent studies have addressed whether characteristics of boldness are considered to be prototypical features of psychopathy. Edens, Clark, Smith, Cox, and Kelley (2013), for example, examined the extent to which laypersons and expert raters (i.e., forensic mental health professionals) rated boldness as important to their construals of psychopathy. In a sample of Swedish forensic mental health professionals, features of boldness were rated as very prototypical of this disorder, with social dominance being particularly germane to their conceptualizations of psychopathy. Laypersons in a separate sample of U.S. respondents also saw certain features of boldness as being characteristic of the prototypical psychopath, though they did not tend to associate being "emotionally stable" per se as being associated with this syndrome in the abstract (Sörman et al., 2014).

Lilienfeld et al. (2012) also criticized the argument that a personality construct must independently predict dysfunction in order to be considered a component of a broader disorder or syndrome, noting that few researchers would question the role of, for example, hypomanic symptoms (e.g., euphoria) in relation to bipolar disorder or expect that hypomania in isolation would predict adverse outcomes. That being said, to what extent is boldness actually seen as a positive personality characteristic by others? Most of the research examining this issue has focused on self-reported boldness traits (as assessed via FD), but a few recent studies have examined the issue in relation to how other persons (e.g., expert raters, laypersons) construe psychopathy. Edens, Clark, et al. (2013), for example, reported that community members attending jury duty who read a mock capital murder trial scenario saw characteristics of boldness (e.g., fearlessness, social dominance) as being strongly related to the PCL–R Factor 1 characteristics of psychopathy (e.g., remorselessness, lack of empathy). Their perceptions of boldness were also closely related to their perceptions that the defendant was a danger to society and the extent to which they viewed him as being evil (Edens, Clark, et al., 2013).

Noted earlier, Marcus, Fulton, and Edens (2013) highlighted the relative dearth of moderational studies examining potential interactive effects for self-reported FD and SCI as being an important limitation of the current body of literature. Since the publication of that article, however, research has been published suggesting that the combination of these two concepts may in fact predict various types of negative outcomes. For example, S. T. Smith,

Edens, and McDermott (2013) reported that the interaction between FD and SCI strongly predicted predatory violence in a sample of forensic inpatients. Similarly, Rock, Sellbom, Ben-Porath, and Salekin (2013) found that spousal abusers with high FD were highly narcissistic and rejected the idea that they required treatment and, particularly when coupled with SCI, were at increased risk of treatment failure. Among college students, the interaction between FD and SCI has been associated with risky sexual behavior (Kastner & Sellbom, 2012).

Although clearly more research is needed, and not all examinations of interaction effects have reported significant findings (e.g., S. T. Smith, Edens, & McDermott, 2011), the studies reviewed here do suggest that the combination of boldness and disinhibition may uniquely identify individuals who are likely to engage in various forms of dysfunctional behavior, even though FD in isolation may be associated with (self-reported) positive adjustment.

The relative lack of association between self-reported FD and SCI does raise questions regarding whether psychopathy is a coherent syndrome, at least as operationalized by self-report measures such as the PPI. Recently, Lilienfeld (2013) suggested that perhaps their findings (and those of Marcus, Fulton, & Edens, 2013) indicate that "psychopathy is not a classical syndrome" but is perhaps a "compound variable" (p. 85; see also Lilienfeld & Widows, 2005; Marcus, Edens, & Fulton, 2013). He went on to posit that psychopathy, instead of being a "genuine syndrome" could be an "interpersonal impact condition" (p. 85), meaning that it is not a condition consisting of covarying symptoms or even uncorrelated elements with a common etiology; it may simply reflect the copresence of different trait clusters with different etiologies that, when appearing together, make quite an impact on society. This issue promises to be an interesting field of study for some time to come. At the present time, it remains to be seen whether the accumulating research will support the inclusion of FD/boldness as a central element of psychopathy or merely a specifier—or even just a coincidental combination of characteristics. Despite that, there is certainly reason to continue the investigation along the lines that Marcus, Fulton, and Edens (2013) suggested (see also Blonigen, 2013).

RESEARCH REVIEW

In this section, we begin by reviewing common and emerging measurement instruments that can be used to measure an individual's psychopathic features. We then review various aspects of the research on psychopathy, including the relation between psychopathy and crime/violence, ethnicity, youth, gender, and treatment outcomes.

Measuring Psychopathy: Interview-Based Measures/Observer Ratings

PCL–R. The most commonly used measure of psychopathy is the PCL–R. PCL–R assessments are based on detailed semistructured interviews, which are completed by specifically trained raters, as well as on file and collateral information. The PCL–R adopts the four-factor operational model of psychopathy that was reviewed earlier. It consists of 20 items, each of which is scored on a 3-point scale ($0 = No$, $1 = Maybe$, and $2 = Yes$), and yields a score between 0 and 40. Based on recommendations in the original PCL–R manual (Hare, 1991), investigators would at times use cut scores to conduct extreme-group analyses. Specifically, a score of 30 and greater has been used to classify participants as psychopathic, and a score of 20 or less has been used to classify participants as nonpsychopathic.

The PCL–R has two primary derivatives: the PCL:SV and the PCL:YV, which are psychometrically, empirically, and conceptually similar to the PCL–R (Forth et al., 2003; Hare & Neumann, 2006). In terms of the psychometric properties of the PCL–R, original validation data included in the second edition of its manual (Hare, 2003) reveals high internal consistency and interrater reliability. Nevertheless, recent studies (reviewed in more detail in a later section) raise concerns about the PCL–R Factor 1 score, which has been found to have poor interrater reliability in several applied settings. Descriptive and validity data for different offender groups, as well as forensic psychiatric patients, are also available in the manual and are considered to be adequate.

Even though the PCL–R was designed strictly for the assessment of the clinical construct of psychopathy, its utility for assessing an individual's risk for recidivism and other applied purposes has been evaluated extensively. Although some studies show support for its utility in assessing the risk of recidivism (see Dolan & Doyle, 2000; Hare & Neumann, 2006; Olver et al., 2013), others have raised concerns or have shown that the PCL–R is outperformed by other measures in that regard (Gendreau, Goggin, & Smith, 2002; Guy, Douglas, & Hendry, 2010; Skeem & Cooke, 2010; Yang, Wong, & Coid, 2010). Similarly, the predictive validity of the PCL–R vis-à-vis crime and antisocial behavior has been examined in male and female samples, with some scholars showing support for it (e.g., M. A. Campbell, French, & Gendreau, 2009; Dolan & Völlm, 2009; Walters, 2003a, 2003b; Yang et al., 2010) and others raising questions in that respect (McKeown, 2010; Nicholls & Petrila, 2005; Strand & Belfrage, 2005).

When the PCL–R is disaggregated into its two factors, the prevailing literature indicates that Factor 2 (encompassing the antisocial and lifestyle facets) is a stronger predictor of recidivism and violence than Factor 1 (encompassing the interpersonal and affective facets; see Gonsalves, Scalora, & Huss, 2009; Kennealy, Skeem, Walters, & Camp, 2010; Olver et al., 2013; Walters, 2003a, 2003b). Further, with regard to the PCL–R's incremental validity, one recent study (Walters, Wilson, & Glover, 2011) revealed that when the antisocial and lifestyle facets were combined into a single factor, the PCL–R displayed incremental validity relative to the interpersonal and affective facets. In addition, the antisocial summed composite score predicted recidivism significantly better than did the summed composite score of the other three facets (i.e., interpersonal, affective, or lifestyle).

These findings are in line with two previous studies on general and violent recidivism (see Walters & Heilbrun, 2010; Walters, Knight, Grann, & Dahle, 2008). Nevertheless, in another study, the composite of the interpersonal, affective, and lifestyle facets failed to predict general and violent recidivism once age and criminal history were taken into account (Walters, 2011). All in all, although extensive support for the psychometric properties of the PCL–R exists, some contradictory findings have been reported recently. In addition, even though the

PCL–R was not originally developed as a risk assessment instrument, it has been used extensively in that capacity (DeMatteo & Edens, 2006). Yet, as alluded to earlier and discussed in more detail below, there appears to be a lack of agreement in the field in terms of its utility to assess an individual's risk for recidivism, which has raised questions and concerns in that regard.

Comprehensive Assessment of Psychopathic Personality: Institutional Rating Scale (CAPP–IRS).

The CAPP–IRS is a newer measure of psychopathy that was designed by Cooke, Hart, and Logan (2005). The CAPP–IRS focuses primarily on the symptoms and underlying personality traits of the psychopathy construct rather than on maladaptive patterns of behavior. The CAPP–IRS consists of a family of measures, including the Staff Rating Scale, the Lifetime version, and a prototype rating scale. The measures depict six domains of psychopathic symptomatology (see Figure 9.2): attachment, behavioral, cognitive, dominance, emotional, and self. They contain 33 items (each with three adjectival descriptors), and the severity of symptoms is scored on a 7-point scale, ranging from 0 = *not present* to 6 = *very severe*.

The primary difference between the Staff Rating Scale and the Life-Time version is the method of administration. The Life-Time version is to be administered by trained professionals, and ratings are based on an interview. The Staff Rating Scale, on the other hand, is intended for use by paraprofessionals at secure facilities (i.e., correctional staff members) and therefore imposes fewer demands for training prior to its use. Ratings of psychopathic symptoms are based on observations over a 6-month time frame during which the participant has been residing at the facility. Due to the fact that it covers six domains of psychopathy, the CAPP measures are optimized for use in a variety of settings—at secured treatment facilities as well as in the community—instead of being limited for use in a single setting. In addition, they are designed to assess not only the lifetime severity of an individual's symptoms but also changes in severity over discrete periods of time. For this reason, the CAPP–IRS can be useful when the temporal stability of symptom severity is of interest.

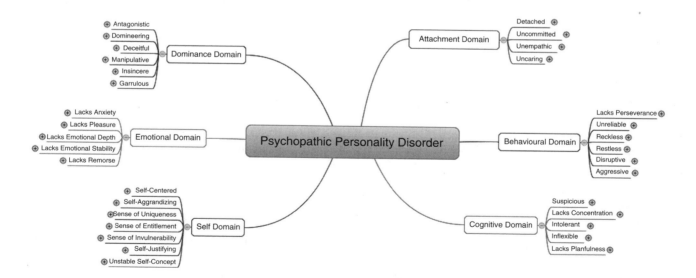

FIGURE 9.2. Conceptual model for the Comprehensive Assessment of Psychopathic Personality. From *Comprehensive Assessment of Psychopathic Personality—Institutional Rating Scale (CAPP–IRS)*, by D. J. Cooke, S. D. Hart, C. Logan, and C. Michie, 2004, unpublished manuscript. Reprinted with permission.

Considering the recent development of this measure, currently there are only a few published studies on the CAPP–IRS. Nevertheless, in combination with data from unpublished studies, there is preliminary support for what appear to be promising psychometric properties of the CAPP–IRS. Specifically, there is preliminary support for its high internal consistency and good-to-excellent interrater reliability (see Corrado, Watkinson, Hart, & Cohen, 2006; Corrado, Watkinson, Hart, Lussier, & Cohen, 2007; McCormick, Corrado, Hart, & Cohen, 2008). Preliminary support for the content and construct validity of the instrument and model have also been reported (see Cooke, Hart, Logan, & Kreis, 2009; Cooke, Logan, Kreis, & Hoff, 2009; Kreis & Cooke, 2011; Nikolova, 2009). Specifically, Kreis and Cooke (2011) found that the interpersonal domains of the CAPP (i.e., attachment, dominance, and self) were most salient of psychopathy, whereas the cognitive domain was the least salient. Further, there was support for the association between violence and some of the items on the CAPP–IRS (i.e., "suspicious" and "lack of emotional depth") as well as preliminary support for discriminant and convergent validity of the CAPP–IRS; namely, higher severity ratings of CAPP–IRS symptoms were given to patients with a diagnosis of a Cluster B personality disorder (see Corrado et al., 2006, 2007; McCormick et al., 2008; Strub, Kreis, & Hart, 2008; Watkinson, Corrado, Lussier, Hart, & Cohen, 2007). Finally, a recent study with forensic psychiatric patients in Denmark revealed support for the predictive accuracy of the CAPP–IRS in terms of violent recidivism, as well as for its concurrent validity with the PCL:SV in that regard (Pedersen, Kunz, Rasmussen, & Elsass, 2010).

Measuring Psychopathy: Self-Report Measures

Even though the PCL–R and the CAPP–IRS can be quite useful in clinical and research settings, there are practical limitations associated with their utility. The PCL–R and the Lifetime version of the CAPP–IRS, for example, are quite time and labor intensive and require a well-trained rater. The use of the Staff Rating version of the CAPP–IRS, which is less labor intensive, may be obstructed by other challenges such as limited time and resources for staff at correctional or treatment facilities who would need to complete the ratings. These issues limit the usefulness of these measures in applied settings, where a time-/resource-efficient assessment tool for psychopathy could be quite beneficial. As a result, there is an increased interest in alternative measures of psychopathy, such as self-reports, which would avoid the need for lengthy interviews and reviews of collateral information and would not impose additional demands on staff.

The idea of assessing psychopathy by using self-reports has been criticized by many. Lilienfeld and Fowler (2006) provided an excellent overview of the problems and pitfalls of self-report measures of psychopathy. First, considering that psychopathic individuals might lie quite frequently, it would be reasonable to suspect that they will not provide truthful information on self-report measures. Psychopathic individuals also often lack insight into their functioning and may be simply unaware of the extent of their psychological problems. Further, given their limited ability to experience certain emotional states, such as guilt or empathy, psychopathic individuals may not be able to accurately report the lack of such emotions. Alternatively, if they report experiencing emotions, their self-report may be confounded due to their lack of understanding of their true emotions (e.g., reporting feeling remorseful when in fact they regret being incarcerated). Another major criticism of self-report measures of psychopathy pertains to the fact that many of those instruments are saturated with items that assess negative emotionality, which lowers their discriminant validity (i.e., makes it difficult to distinguish psychopathy from other conditions).

Lilienfeld and Fowler (2006) also provided an overview of the advantages of self-report measures of psychopathy. First, self-reports may be particularly useful in providing information on an individual's subjective emotional states and traits. Even though psychopathic individuals are likely unreliable in reporting the lack of emotions such as guilt, empathy, and fear (as they may be simply unaware of this deficit), they may experience anger and alienation more frequently than those who do not show psychopathic features and may be capable of providing reliable accounts of such emotions. Self-reports are also quite economical. Often, self-reports are brief, are relatively easy to complete, and do not require specialized training to be administered.

Further, when response style indicators are incorporated in self-report measures, they can assess response styles systematically, which is not the case for interview-based measures. Assessing response styles is quite relevant when working with highly psychopathic individuals, given that engaging in pathological lying and being conning and manipulative are among the core characteristics of the disorder. In fact, a recent meta-analytic review of the literature on the associations between self-reported psychopathy and distorted response styles revealed support for the validity of self-report psychopathy measures, thus tapering concerns regarding positive response bias associated with self-report measures (Ray et al., 2012). Finally, interrater reliability is not applicable to self-reports because they are completed by respondents and require no judgment calls by interviewers or observers. This is particularly relevant to the topic of psychopathy because the assessment of psychopathy includes the evaluation of various affective and emotional states. This in turn requires significant clinical inference on the part of the interviewers, which is often quite challenging and could potentially negatively affect interrater reliability, as we review later in the chapter. As Lilienfeld and Fowler (2006) pointed out, "Because validity is limited by the square root of reliability (Meehl, 1986), the subjectivity inherent to interview-based measures will, *ceteris paribus*, constrain their validity" (pg. 108).

Some of the self-report measures that are used for the assessment of psychopathy (e.g., the Psychopathic Deviate scale of the Minnesota Multiphasic Personality Inventory—2 [MMPI–2; Butcher, Dahlstrom, Graham, Tellegen, & Kaemmer, 1989], and the Socialization scale of the California Psychological Inventory [CPI; Gough & Bradley, 1996]) have been found to exhibit low or modest intercorrelations, indicating that they are likely not measuring the same construct (Lilienfeld & Fowler, 2006). Another issue with the self-report assessment of psychopathy

pertains to the fact that due to method covariance (i.e., sole reliance on self-reports), the correlations between psychopathy questionnaires may be inflated. Finally, many of the measures that are most commonly used to assess psychopathy (i.e., Psychopathic Deviate scale of the MMPI–2, Socialization scale of the CPI, Antisocial scale of the Millon Clinical Multiaxial Inventory—II [MCMI–II; Millon, 1987], and Antisocial scale of the PAI) appear to primarily measure nonspecific behavioral deviance rather than core interpersonal or affective features of psychopathy, given that they relate preferentially to Factor 2 of the PCL–R (Lilienfeld & Fowler, 2006). In light of these limitations, the use of general measures of personality for the assessment of psychopathy, even though efficient, does not appear to be optimal. In response to these shortcomings, new self-report measures that have been designed specifically for the assessment of psychopathy, rather than general personality, have been developed. What follows is a brief overview of those measures.

Levenson Primary and Secondary Psychopathy Scales (LPSP). The LPSP (also referred to as the Levenson Self-Report Psychopathy scale) was developed by Levenson, Kiehl, and Fitzpatrick (1995) to capture psychopathic features in non-institutional samples. It contains 26 items that are scored on a 4-point Likert scale. The Primary and Secondary scales were designed to resemble the content of Factor 1 and Factor 2 of the PCL–R, respectively. Exploratory factor analyses that were conducted by the authors revealed a two-factor structure of the instrument, which has been supported via confirmatory factor analysis as well (Brinkley, Schmitt, Smith, & Neumann, 2001; Lynam, Whiteside, & Jones, 1999). Nevertheless, a more recent study of male correctional inmates, as well as male and female college students (Sellbom, 2011), which also implemented confirmatory factor analysis, revealed that the best fitting model for the measure was a three-factor model, which was initially proposed by Brinkley, Diamond, Magaletta, and Heigel (2008).

The LPSP has some promising psychometric properties, as evidenced by adequate internal consistencies for both scales. Similar to the two factors of the PCL–R, the two scales are moderately correlated, which is desired in terms of convergent validity but could also raise questions about discriminant validity. In addition, Sellbom (2011) showed support for the convergent and discriminant validity of the LPSP total and factor scores, with the exception of the Antisocial factor, which appeared to be too saturated with emotional distress. Further, positive correlations between the LPSP and self-report measures of sensation seeking, antisocial behavior, and passive avoidance errors have been reported (Levenson et al., 1995; Lynam et al., 1999). Nevertheless, the construct validity of the LPSP is questionable—the measure appears to be highly related to antisocial behavior rather than to the affective and interpersonal features of psychopathy (Lilienfeld & Hess, 2001; Lilienfeld, Skeem, & Poythress, 2004; Poythress et al., 2010; Wilson, Frick, & Clements, 1999). The LPSP was also found to have modest correlations with fearlessness and low empathy (Sellbom, 2011), and thus may not fully represent psychopathy. These findings highlight the need for future research and perhaps the need for potential revisions to the LPSP.

Self-Report Psychopathy Scale (SRP).   The SRP is a 29-item scale that was developed by Hare to resemble the factor structure of the PCL (see Hare, 1985). The original version of the measure correlated only modesty with the PCL and did not provide sufficient content coverage for some of the core personality characteristics of psychopathy (i.e., callousness, dishonesty, superficial charm). As a result, Hare, Harpur, and Hemphill (1989) developed a 60-item updated version of the instrument, the SRP–II. In this version, items are scored on a 5-point scale ranging from 1 = *False* to 5 = *True*. The SRP–II contains two factors resembling the factor structure of the PCL–R: The first factor captures personality and affective aspects of psychopathy, and the second one focuses on impulsivity and antisocial lifestyle. Confirmatory factor analysis revealed that the best fitting model for the measure was the original four-factor model that was proposed by Neal and Sellbom (2012). A 31-item abridged version of the instrument has been used in research settings (e.g., Paulhus & Williams, 2002; Salekin, Trobst, & Krioukova, 2001).

The internal consistency and construct validity of the SRP–II have been evaluated with various samples

and appear to be promising (see Derefinko & Lynam, 2006; Neal & Sellbom, 2012; Williams & Paulhus, 2004). There is support for the convergent validity of the SRP–II with respect to self-report measures of narcissism and social deviance as well as reversed conscientiousness, agreeableness, anxiety, and empathy (see Lilienfeld & Fowler, 2006; Rogers et al., 2002; Zágon & Jackson, 1994). Further, the total score of the SRP–II correlates positively with other self-report measures that are used to assess psychopathy (e.g., MMPI–2 Antisocial Practices content scale, PPI; see Paulhus & Williams, 2002). Promising criterion-related, convergent, and discriminant validity in terms of predicting scores on conceptually relevant external criteria (e.g., drug use, thrill seeking, aggression, irresponsibility, impulsiveness, fraud and theft, callous affect, as well as lack of dependability, honesty, empathy, emotional distress, negative emotionality, social avoidance, and shyness) have also been demonstrated (Neal & Sellbom, 2012). However, the discriminant validity of the SRP–II with respect to generalized criminality requires further clarification (see Lilienfeld & Fowler, 2006).

Finally, the SRP–II was further revised to its most recent version, the SPR–III (Paulhus, Neumann, & Hare, 2009). The authors of this version employed exploratory and confirmatory factor analyses in two different samples in order to predetermine that its factor structure adequately captures the four facets of psychopathy that were identified in the PCL–R (Williams, Paulhus, & Hare, 2007). Results revealed four distinct but uncorrelated factors, similar to those of the PCL–R, and the SRP–III exhibited appropriate construct validity with related personality measures (see also Mahmut, Menictas, Stevenson, & Homewood, 2011; Neal & Sellbom, 2012). Good convergent and discriminant validity for the instrument have also been reported in a community sample (Mahmut et al., 2011), and an acceptable level of internal consistency was obtained in a college sample (Neal & Sellbom, 2012).

PPI.   The PPI is the most widely validated self-report measure of psychopathy. It was originally developed by Lilienfeld (1990) to capture psychopathic traits in noncriminal samples. It contains 187 items that are scored on a 4-point Likert scale (i.e., 1 = *False* to 4 = *True*) and yields a total score representing global psychopathy as well as eight lower order facet scores: Social Potency, Fearlessness, Stress Immunity, Machiavellian Egocentricity, Impulsive Noncomformity, Blame Externalization, Carefree Nonplanfulness, and Coldheartedness. Three validity scales were also incorporated in the PPI in order to detect response styles (i.e., Positive Impression Management, Deviant Responding, and Careless or Random Responding).

Studies of the factor structure of the PPI subscales have revealed two factors: Factor 1, FD, includes Social Potency, Fearlessness, and Stress Immunity, and Factor 2 (initially labeled Impulsive Antisociality but subsequently changed to SCI; see Benning, Patrick, Hicks, Blonigen, & Krueger, 2003) includes Machiavellian Egocentricity, Impulsive Noncomformity, Blame Externalization, and Carefree Nonplanfulness. Of note, Coldheartedness did not load to either factor. Factor 1 and 2 of the PPI appear to be mainly orthogonal, which is different than the PCL–R, where the two factors are moderately correlated (Lilienfeld & Fowler, 2006; Marcus, Fulton, & Edens, 2013). This suggests that the PPI does not assess psychopathy as a unitary construct. Earlier, we reviewed two meta-analyses and some associated commentary concerning debates about the relevance of FD to psychopathy.

The psychometric properties of the PPI have been examined in multiple noncriminal samples, and there is support for its high internal consistency, test–retest reliability, and convergent validity with other measures of psychopathy and antisocial behavior or theoretically related concepts such as empathy, sensation seeking, and driving anger (see Lilienfeld, 1990; Lilienfeld & Andrews, 1996; Woltil, 2011). Further, there is evidence that the PPI can be useful in assessing APD as much as psychopathy, which raises questions about its discriminant validity from general measures of social deviancy (see Lilienfeld & Fowler, 2006). Despite that, there is support for the discriminant validity of the PPI from measures of depression, negative emotionality, and schizotypy (Benning et al., 2003; Blonigen, Carlson, Krueger, & Patrick, 2003; Lilienfeld & Andrews, 1996).

Further, results from a hierarchical multiple regression that was used to examine the incremental validity of the PPI revealed that the instrument captures variance in outcomes that was not shared with other measures of psychopathy or antisocial behavior (e.g., MMPI–2, Personality Diagnostic Questionnaire—Revised [Hyler & Rieder, 1988]; see Lilienfeld & Andrews, 1996). In addition, relative to the LPSP, the PPI has evidenced convergent and discriminant validity with regard to aggression and anxiety in a student sample (Falkenbach, Poythress, Falki, & Manchak, 2007).

Even though the PPI was developed for use with noncriminal populations, its psychometric properties have been examined with correctional samples. Results revealed negative associations with measures of empathy and positive associations with measures of aggression (Sandoval, Hancock, Poythress, Edens, & Lilienfeld, 2000). Further, meaningful associations between the PPI and some of the scales of the PAI, which are theoretically consistent with the conceptualization of psychopathy, have also been reported. Namely, the PPI correlated positively with the Antisocial, Aggression, Dominance, and Borderline scales of the PAI (Edens, Poythress, & Watkins, 2001). Positive correlations between the PPI and physical or nonaggressive disciplinary infractions were also reported in the same study. Furthermore, results from a study on the criterion-related validity and the relationship of the PPI with the BAS, Behavioral Inhibition Scale (BIS; Carver & White, 1994), and FFM of personality revealed that Factor 1 (i.e., FD) was related to low BIS, high BAS, expert prototype psychopathy scores, and primary psychopathy (S. R. Ross et al., 2008), and Factor 2 (i.e., Impulsive Antisociality or SCI) was associated with high BAS and other psychopathy measures. Further, high Extraversion and Openness and low Agreeableness and Neuroticism predicted Factor 1, whereas high Neuroticism and low Agreeableness and Conscientiousness predicted Factor 2.

Further, the association between the PPI and the PCL–R was examined in a sample of 50 male offenders, yielding moderately high correlations between the measures (Poythress, Edens, & Lilienfeld, 1998). Most importantly, the correlations were higher with Factor 1 ($r = .54$) than with Factor 2 ($r = .40$), which may suggest that the PPI is the first self-report measure to correlate substantially with the core characteristics of psychopathy, at least as measured by the PCL–R (Lilienfeld & Fowler, 2006). Of note, those findings were not replicated in a study that was conducted by Skeem and Lilienfeld (2004), where the associations with Factor 2 of the PCL–R were stronger than those of Factor 1. Similar results were reported by Malterer, Lilienfeld, Neumann, and Newman (2010), which raises questions regarding the convergent validity of the PPI factors with the PCL:SV. And, as we reviewed earlier, the FD scale tends to show rather low correlations with other measures of psychopathy.

The concurrent validity of the PPI relative to the PCL:SV and its associations with past violence were examined in a sample of insanity acquittees (Kruh et al., 2005). Results revealed significant correlations between the PPI total and several subscale scores (i.e., Social Potency, Machiavellian Egocentricity, and Impulse Noncomformity) and the total and factor scores of the PCL:SV, yielding support for the concurrent validity of the PPI in this sample. In the same study, the postdictive utility of the PPI was comparable to that of the PCL:SV with regard to past violence.

Poythress et al. (2010) compared the PPI and the LSRP relative to the PCL–R in a large sample of offenders. Results revealed better convergent and discriminant validity of the PPI and that the PPI had more consistent incremental validity in predicting PCL–R scores relative to the LPSP. The PPI's patterns of associations with measures of external criterion variables were also more similar to the patterns observed for the PCL–R. The concurrent and discriminant validity of the PPI were also examined in a male sample of maximum-security federal inmates (Rosner, 2004). Specifically, the PPI's relationship to corresponding scales on the PAI and the MCMI–III (Millon, 1994) was evaluated, and there was support for the convergent validity of the PPI as a measure of psychopathic personality features. Nevertheless, results were inconsistent with regard to its discriminant validity from measures of schizophrenia-spectrum disorder and mania.

The psychometric properties of the PPI have also been examined in female samples. In a female correctional sample, the PPI was negatively associated with the CPI Socialization scale and positively associated with the PAI Antisocial scale (Chapman, Gremore, & Farmer, 2003). These findings provide support for the convergent validity of the PPI. The findings are similar to those obtained from an undergraduate female sample (Hamburger, Lilienfeld, & Hogben, 1996). Berardino, Meloy, Sherman, and Jacobs (2005) found support for the concurrent and discriminant validity of the PPI in a sample of incarcerated women and concluded that the PPI assesses both the antisocial and interpersonal-affect facets of psychopathy.

As reviewed earlier, Marcus, Fulton, and Edens (2013) conducted a meta-analytic review of studies examining the theoretically important correlates of the two PPI factors. The authors found that each factor predicted distinct correlates, which were sometimes opposite from one another. Particularly, whereas SCI was highly correlated with PCL–R (Factor 2) and LSRP, FD was modestly correlated (at best) with PCL–R (Factor 1) and the Primary Psychopathy scale of the LPSP. In addition, whereas SCI was associated with measures of antisocial personality, FD was not. Instead, FD was correlated with positive traits and emotions, was negatively related with neuroticism, and was unrelated to constraint. Finally, results revealed that the FD factor was not highly correlated with most other measures of psychopathy, which raised questions regarding the role of FD in the conceptualization of psychopathy. Specifically, Marcus, Fulton, and Edens found that FD was not particularly maladaptive and that individuals who score high on FD are unlikely to appear especially pathological.

Similar findings were reported in another meta-analytic study that was reviewed earlier (J. D. Miller & Lynam, 2012). Specifically, the authors reported strong convergent associations between the SCI factor and other psychopathy measures (i.e., PCL/PCL–R, LSRP, and SRP) as well as expected correlations between SCI factor scores and theoretically important correlates (e.g., interpersonal antagonism, empathy, impulsivity, APD). Conversely, J. D. Miller and Lynam (2012) expressed skepticism that high scores on the FD factor alone could be used to identify individuals as psychopathic. Taken together, these findings raise the question of whether PPI-assessed psychopathy is a unitary construct or whether it is comprised of "relatively independent lower-order facets," as previously suggested by Lilienfeld and Widows (2005; see also Marcus, Edens, & Fulton, 2013).

Finally, the predictive validity of the PPI has been examined in correctional samples, and results provide support for the predictive utility of the instrument. Specifically, the PPI total and factor scores were predictive of the number of infractions, and Factor 1 was more strongly associated with non-aggressive misconduct, whereas Factor 2 was more strongly associated with aggressive misconduct (Edens, Poythress, Lilienfeld, & Patrick, 2008; Edens, Poythress, Lilienfeld, Patrick, & Test, 2008). Support for the predictive utility of the PPI was also evident in a sample of adult males who were seeking admission to an inpatient drug treatment facility (Abrams, 2005). Overall, its good psychometric properties suggest that the utility of the PPI in criminal justice settings is promising.

PPI:SF. An abbreviated version of the PPI, the PPI:SF, was created by Lilienfeld (1990, as cited in Lilienfeld & Hess, 2001). It contains 56 items derived from the original PPI that are scored on the same 4-point Likert scale. The items selected for the PPI:SF were the seven highest loading items within each subscale. Although there is not too much published research on the PPI:SF to date, its brevity and efficiency in research settings appear to be the primary benefits associated with its use (Kastner, Sellbom, & Lilienfeld, 2012). However, G. T. Smith, McCarthy, and Anderson (2000), warned against the potential for construct underrepresentation and possibly an atypical factor structure due to the way the measure was constructed. In fact, Wilson et al. (1999) found that Impulsive Nonconformity and Coldheartedness loaded on Factor 1, whereas all of the original subscales except Impulsive Nonconformity loaded on Factor 2. Further, the psychometric properties of the PPI:SF were evaluated against the full-length PPI in a college and a prison sample, and results revealed comparable discriminant validity for both instruments (Kastner et al., 2012). Nevertheless, the construct validity

and internal consistency of the PPI:SF were found to be lower than that of the PPI, and the PPI:SF also evidenced weaker correlations with conceptually relevant criteria (e.g., egocentricity, aggressiveness, and aggression). Concerns about the internal consistency of several of the PPI:SF subscales (e.g., Carefree Nonplanfulness, Impulsive Nonconformity, and Social Potency) were also raised by S. T. Smith, Edens, and McDermott (2011), who evaluated the measure in undergraduate, foster care, and juvenile justice samples. Yet, the expected associations of the PPI:SF scales and external correlates (e.g., egocentricity, hypochondriasis, deceptive practices, extraversion, depressive symptoms, hostility, etc.) were found to be generally consistent with prior studies evaluating the PPI. The authors concluded that their findings provide some evidence that the subscales that were combined to create Factor 1 and Factor 2 of the PPI:SF tap distinct constructs.

PPI–R. In 2005, the PPI was revised in order to lower its reading level and remove items with questionable psychometric properties or that were too culturally specific. The resulting PPI–R contains 154 items. Although some changes were made to the content of certain subscales (i.e., Stress Immunity), the structure is essentially identical to that of the PPI in terms of which subscales load on SCI and FD. The PPI–R produces a total score as well as eight content scores (i.e., Machiavellian Egocentricity, Social Influence, Coldheartedness, Carefree Nonplanfulness, Fearlessness, Blame Externalization, Rebellious Nonconformity, and Stress Immunity) and three factor scores (i.e., SCI, FD, and Coldheartedness, the latter of which is the same as the content score). This version of the instrument contains four validity scales: Virtuous Responding, Deviant Responding, and two Inconsistent Responding scales (i.e., a 15-item or a 40-item scale). Items are scored on a 4-point Likert scale (i.e., *False, Mostly False, Mostly True,* or *True*).

Two normative samples were used to validate the PPI–R: community/college ($N = 985$) and offender ($N = 154$). Results provide support for the reliability of the measure: internal consistency (i.e., alpha coefficients) for the total and content scores ranged from .78 and .92 in the community/college normative sample and from .71 and .84 in the offender normative sample. The mean alpha coefficients for the three factor scores were .87 for the community sample and .82 for the offender sample. Test–retest reliability based on an average of 19.9 days (ranging from 12 to 45) was .93 for the total score, .89 for the content scales, and .90 for the factor scores.

Support for the internal consistency of the PPI–R has also been demonstrated outside of the normative samples, with alpha coefficients being comparable or higher (e.g., Anestis, Caron, & Carbonell, 2011; Jones & Miller, 2012; Russell, 2005; Seibert, Miller, Few, Zeichner, & Lynam, 2011). Further, there is support for the discriminant and convergent validity of the instrument. Namely, the total, content, and factor scores of the PPI–R were found to be correlated to the LSRP, the SRP–II, the PAI, the NEO Five-Factor Inventory (Costa & McCrae, 1992c), the Activity Preference Questionnaire (APQ; Lykken, Tellegen, & Katzenmeyer, 1973), the Experiences of Close Relationships (ECR; Brennan, Clark, & Shaver, 1998), and the Multidimensional Personality Questionnaire (MPQ; Tellegen, in press; see also DeMauro & Leung, 2005; Lilienfeld & Widows, 2005; Uzieblo, Verschuere, Van den Bussche, & Crombez, 2010; Witt, Donnellan, Blonigen, Krueger, & Conger, 2009).

Finally, the construct validity of the PPI–R was examined in a sample of forensic psychiatric patients, and results revealed that the SCI factor predicted anger, hostility, impulsivity, drug abuse, overall psychiatric symptoms, and violence risk (Edens & McDermott, 2010). The FD factor predicted anger, depression, low anxiety, and alcohol abuse or dependence. Further, there was an association between impulsivity and the total score and SCI factor (Ray, Poythress, Weir, & Rickelm, 2009). FD, in contrast, appeared to be strongly associated with sensation seeking, weakly associated with a lack of premeditation, and negatively associated with a lack of perseverance.

Psychopathy, Crime, and Violence: Evidence From Meta-Analyses

Psychopathy has long been connected—rightly or wrongly—to an increased risk for crime and violence. We reviewed some of the evidence for this association briefly in the preceding section. As described earlier and endorsed by some (Skeem & Cooke, 2010), this putative link is central to some of the criticisms of the PCL–R and could be epiphenomenal. We review this area of research next. Given the sheer number of studies that have evaluated the link between psychopathy and crime or violence, we focus on meta-analytic studies. Most of these studies are based on the PCL–R, although some also include other measures. For single studies of other measures, we refer the reader to the previous section.

The first meta-analysis on contemporary measures of psychopathy vis-à-vis violence and crime was conducted by Salekin, Rogers, and Sewell (1996). Across 18 studies, they reported effect sizes ranging from moderate (Cohen's d of .55) to large (Cohen's d of .79) for general (violent or nonviolent) criminal recidivism or violent community, or institutional behavior, respectively. Some commentators (Gendreau et al., 2002; Hemphill, Hare, & Wong, 1998) criticized this meta-analysis because of its inclusion of retrospective and prospective studies as well as community and institutional outcomes. Other meta-analyses have focused more specifically on certain contexts (i.e., institutional vs. community) or designs, as reviewed in the following paragraphs.

Using a larger number of studies than Salekin et al. (1996), Hemphill, Hare, et al. (1998) reported moderate effect sizes (meta-analytic correlations of .23 to .27) between the PCL measures and violent and criminal recidivism in prospective studies. Factors 1 and 2 were shown to be comparably predictive of violent recidivism, whereas Factor 2 was more strongly predictive of general recidivism as compared to Factor 1. Subsequent meta-analyses have similarly reported moderate effect sizes between the PCL(–R) and general or violent recidivism (Gendreau et al., 2002; Walters, 2003a, 2003b). Walters (2003b) reported smaller effect sizes for Factor 1 with general (.15) and violent recidivism (.18) compared to Factor 2 (.32 and .26, respectively).

Douglas, Vincent, and Edens (2006) discussed the importance of studying the association between psychopathy and violence or crime as a function of important moderators, such as participant characteristics (e.g., age, gender, race, country of origin) or study design features (e.g., retrospective vs. prospective, setting, sample). They had also discussed the importance of testing the incremental validity of measures of psychopathy vis-à-vis risk assessment measures and other risk factors. Fortunately, several meta-analyses now exist that address these important issues.

For instance, Leistico, Salekin, DeCoster, and Rogers (2008) conducted a large-scale meta-analysis of 95 independent samples on the PCL family of measures and antisocial conduct (both institutional and community indices). They were also interested in studying numerous moderators. Analyses of PCL factors were based on subsamples of 54 (Factor 1) and 53 (Factor 2) studies. For the PCL total and Factor 2 scores, moderate effect sizes were reported (Median ds = .57 and .58, respectively), whereas the d for Factor 1 was statistically significantly lower (.38). There was significant heterogeneity for the total and both factors scores, so the authors pursued moderation analyses.

In moderation analyses, Leistico et al. (2008) reported that neither age, setting (institution or community), type of outcome (violent vs. nonviolent antisocial behavior), nor version of PCL (youth vs. adult versions) moderated the effect sizes. Hence, the authors collapsed across these features for subsequent moderation analyses. Several moderating effects were observed. Predictive strength, for example, was higher as a function of the following moderators: (a) Canadian and European samples compared to American samples (for total and Factor 2); (b) higher proportion of Caucasian participants in the sample (total and Factor 2); (c) higher proportion of females in the sample (total and Factor 1); (d) patients rather than offenders (Factor 2); (e) longer follow-up periods (Factor 2); (f) file only ratings as opposed to file plus interview (total and Factor 2 ratings); and (g) design, such that postdictive designs were associated with lower effect sizes for PCL total compared to predictive studies but higher for Factor 1.

Most of these comprehensive meta-analyses also observed considerable heterogeneity in effect sizes,

suggesting that the association between PCL(–R) psychopathy and crime and violence may be stronger or weaker depending on context or study features. Some meta-analyses focused on more specific contexts and age groups and also continued the investigation of the relative predictive strength of the two main components of the PCL family of measures. Most recently, there have been meta-analyses that have been able to compare the predictive strength of the PCL(–R) with various risk assessment instruments, and some meta-analyses that have been able to integrate other, newer measures of psychopathy. We review these more specific meta-analyses in the following subsections.

Juvenile-focused meta-analyses.   In a meta-analysis of 21 studies of the association between PCL measures and general and violent recidivism among juvenile offenders, Edens, Campbell, and Weir (2007) reported effect sizes similar to more general meta-analyses (r = .24 and .25 for general and violent recidivism, respectively). However, there was no significant association with sexual recidivism, and significant heterogeneity in effect sizes was reported. Samples consisting of fewer Caucasian participants and more females tended to produce lower effects sizes. Factor 2 produced somewhat larger effect sizes (.24, .25) than Factor 1 (.18, .19) for general and violent recidivism, respectively, although the confidence intervals overlapped. Edens and Campbell (2007) conducted a meta-analysis of 15 studies on the association between PCL measures and institutional misconduct among youth. Effect sizes (correlations) ranged from .24 to .28, although they were larger for published than nonpublished studies, and considerable heterogeneity was again observed.

Asscher et al. (2011) focused on the association between youth psychopathic traits and delinquency and violence. Their meta-analysis was able to add a large number of studies (published since 2005) relative to earlier meta-analyses (i.e., Edens et al., 2007), for a total of 60 independent samples from 53 studies that were published between 1990 and 2010. Asscher et al. included both self-reported and officially recorded nonviolent and violent criminality as well as multiple measures of psychopathic traits. They also investigated numerous moderators.

Overall, effect sizes (correlations) in Asscher et al.'s (2011) study were very consistent regardless of the type of outcome: Correlations ranged from .21 to .23 for self-reported delinquency, general recidivism, and official violent recidivism. These are small to moderate effect sizes. There were numerous significant moderators of effect sizes. The following (select) study features were associated with larger effect sizes for delinquency: rater (vs. self-report) measures, other (vs. self or official) report of delinquency, and female and mixed-gender (vs. male-only) samples. Similarly, there were moderators of the association between psychopathic traits and recidivism, with the following study features being associated with larger effect sizes: rater (vs. self) report of psychopathic traits, other (vs. self) report of recidivism, PCL measures (vs. other measures), Canadian (vs. American or European) samples, and published (vs. unpublished) studies. In addition, larger effect sizes were associated with more reliable measurement, with younger age of participants, and with a lower proportion of immigrants within samples. Similarly, for the analysis of violent recidivism, the following features were associated with larger effect sizes: other (vs. official) report of violent recidivism, published (vs. unpublished) studies, mixed gender (vs. male or female only), and more reliable measurement.

Several trends were evident from this meta-analysis (Asscher et al., 2011). Self-report measurement of both psychopathic traits and of outcomes tended to be associated with smaller effect sizes than did ratings of psychopathic traits by others (i.e., parents, teachers, professionals). There was also some evidence that PCL measures produced larger effects than other measures, although the authors surmised that this could stem from criterion contamination (i.e., some of the PCL measures' items require ratings of crime and other antisocial behavior, and some of the samples were cross-sectional). Not surprisingly, less reliable measurement was associated with smaller effect sizes. Further, there were moderating effects of gender such that all male samples tended to produce smaller effect sizes. It also appeared that the effects tended to be stronger in Canada and for nonimmigrants. It is not clear whether some of these

moderators were yoked with others. Regardless, these findings suggest that a *one-size-fits-all* interpretation of the association between psychopathic traits and crime or violence is not realistic, and that further investigation of putative moderators is necessary.

Institutional misconduct. Guy, Edens, Anthony, and Douglas (2005) focused their meta-analytic efforts on the association between PCL measures and institutional misconduct among adults. Across 38 independent samples, the effect sizes were quite variable, with overall effect sizes (r) between total, Factor 1 and Factor 2, and any institutional infractions being .29, .21, and .27, respectively. For physical violence, the effect sizes were smaller (.17, .14, and .15). Following observations in other meta-analyses that were reviewed earlier, the effect sizes were smaller in the United States compared to other countries. This held true for physical violence, with correlations between total scores and physical violence being .11 in U.S. prisons compared to .23 outside of the United States. It should be noted that these effect sizes were based on a small number of studies (five for the United States and four for non-United States), though subsequent publications examining this relationship continued to produce weak effect sizes (McDermott, Edens, Quanbeck, Busse, & Scott, 2008).

Psychopathy and sexual deviance. Several of the meta-analyses described here have distinguished between general criminality and violence and have also included sexual violence. Typically, the findings for sexual violence have been less strong than those for general crime or violence. A recent meta-analysis focused not only on the link between the PCL–R and sexual violence but also on the combination of PCL–R-measured psychopathy and sexual deviance in the prediction of future sexual violence (S. W. Hawes, Boccaccini, & Murrie, 2013). Across 20 studies, S. W. Hawes et al. (2013) reported a close to moderate effect size of $d = .40$ between the PCL–R and future sexual violence, surpassing an earlier meta-analysis (Hanson & Morton-Bourgon, 2005) that was based on fewer studies. Not surprisingly, Factor 2 ($d = .44$) and Facet 4 ($d = .40$) were most predictive, whereas effect sizes for Factor 1 and the other three facets were small or nil (.01 to .17). In a subset of six studies where sexual deviance was measured, the combination of high sexual deviance and high PCL–R score resulted in higher sexual recidivism rates than when this combination was not present.

Comparisons with risk instruments. A number of meta-analytic studies of PCL measures have been able to include risk assessment measures for comparative purposes. For instance, M. A. Campbell et al. (2009) evaluated the meta-analytic associations between several risk assessment measures (HCR–20 [Webster, Douglas, Eaves, & Hart, 1997], Violence Risk Appraisal Guide [Quinsey, Harris, Rice, & Cormier, 1998], Level of Service Instruments [LSI; Andrews, Bonta, & Wormith, 2010], Statistical Information on Recidivism [Bonta, Harman, Hann, & Cormier, 1996]), PCL measures, and both institutional and community violence across 88 studies that were carried out between 1980 and 2006. For institutional violence, although there was a wide range of effect sizes (average weighted *r*s from .14 to .28), confidence intervals overlapped; hence, the measures were not significantly different from one another. PCL(–R) did have a smaller association with violence (.14) than did the HCR–20 (.28) or LS measures (.24). The PCL:SV fared somewhat better (.22). The correlation for the VRAG was .15. It should be stressed that there were few studies for most of these instruments—only one had more than 10 studies used to calculate effect sizes. For community violence, the correlations ranged from .22 to .32, with the PCL(–R) being in the middle (.27) and not significantly different than the risk instruments.

Yang et al. (2010) evaluated the PCL measures vis-à-vis risk assessment instruments in an interesting manner: They used the PCL measures as a benchmark to test whether risk assessment instruments could improve on them. The authors focused on more recent literature, from 1999 to 2008. Most of the instruments, including the PCL and Factor 2, produced moderate effect sizes. Factor 1 was substantially weaker. Only two violence risk assessment instruments were able to significantly improve on the PCL–R's association with violence: the HCR–20 (based on 16 studies) and the Offender Group

Reconviction Scale (based on two studies; Copas & Marshall, 1998). Factor 1 was significantly weaker than the full PCL measures or Factor 2, and of all 16 measures evaluated, was the only one with a confidence interval that overlapped with 0.

In another comparative meta-analysis of various risk assessment measures and PCL measures based on 68 studies, Singh, Grann, and Fazel (2011) reported, based on a number of different analytic procedures, that the PCL–R produced the lowest predictive validity vis-à-vis violence. However, the distribution of effect sizes was relatively tight, with area under the curve (AUC) values ranging from .66 (PCL–R) to .78 (Sexual Violence Risk–20; Boer, Hart, Kropp, & Webster, 1997). Instruments that were designed to predict specifically violence (such as the Structured Assessment of Violence Risk in Youth [SAVRY; Borum, Bartel, & Forth, 2006], HCR–20, or VRAG) tended to outperform instruments that were designed to predict general criminality (LSI–R), and, as it turns out, PCL instruments, which were not designed to predict violence. In an overlapping meta-analysis of 73 studies, Fazel, Singh, Doll, and Grann (2012) reported that "built-to-purpose" violence risk assessment instruments such as the HCR–20, SAVRY, VRAG, and Spousal Assault Risk Assessment (Kropp, Hart, Webster, & Eaves, 1999) tend to predict violence more strongly than instruments for general criminality or PCL measures.

In a very focused meta-analysis, Guy et al. (2010) compared the HCR–20 and PCL–R in 34 samples that included both instruments. This permitted direct, head-to-head comparisons of the two instruments. Most past meta-analyses based their effect size estimates on different samples. That is, instrument X might be included in 10 of a meta-analysis's studies, whereas instrument Y might be included in only seven, and only some of these might be the same as the 10 that were used with instrument X. As such, study features can contaminate the comparison of effect sizes. Guy et al.'s meta-analysis included more direct HCR–20-PCL–R comparisons than any of the other meta-analyses.

Guy et al. (2010) reported that, at a bivariate level, the HCR–20 and PCL–R were equally predictive (AUCs = .69). The HCR–20 was not adversely affected when its psychopathy item was removed (AUC = .71). The authors were able to conduct multivariate analyses based on raw data from seven samples. In these analyses, in which the HCR–20 psychopathy item was removed, the HCR–20 added incrementally to the PCL–R, whereas the PCL–R did not add to the HCR–20. Specifically, with both instruments in the analysis, for every one-step increase on the HCR–20, the probability of a violent outcome increased 23%, whereas it decreased 1% for every one-step increase on the PCL–R.

Olver, Stockdale, and Wormith (2009) focused on three instruments that are used with young offenders: PCL:YV, SAVRY, and the Youth Level of Service/Case Management Inventory (YLS/CMI; Hoge & Andrews, 2002). Across 44 studies, the authors calculated effect sizes (r) for general, violent, and sexual recidivism. None of the instruments performed well for the prediction of sexual recidivism. Excluding sexual recidivism, the effect sizes were comparable and moderate in size for each instrument. For the SAVRY, the range was .30 to .38; for the YLS/CMI, it was .26 to .32; and for the PCL:YV, the range had a lower bottom and top end (.16–.28).

Most of the meta-analyses reviewed thus far have compared the two main factors on the PCL measures. Typically, Factor 2 has shown a stronger association with crime and violence than has Factor 1. One meta-analysis investigated not only the roles played by Factors 1 and 2, but whether these factors interact with each other to add incrementally to the use of the factors alone (Kennealy et al., 2010). Across 32 effect sizes, the short answer was no—there was no evidence for an interactive effect of the two factors. Further, consistent with other meta-analyses, effect sizes were stronger for Factor 2 ($d = .40$) than for Factor 1 ($d = .11$).

PPI. In J. D. Miller and Lynam's (2012) PPI meta-analysis, which was reviewed in some detail earlier, the authors investigated the association between the PPI(–R) and antisocial and aggressive behavior. Across 15 studies, FD had small correlations with antisocial behavior ($r = .12$) and aggression ($r = -.04$), whereas SCI was more strongly related to these indices ($rs = .36$ and .42, respectively). The PPI total score produced

moderate associations with these indices ($rs = .32$ and .33, respectively). These findings are similar to those reported for the PCL-based meta-analyses, in that the more behaviorally based aspect of the PPI(–R) was more strongly related to antisocial behavior and aggression than was its more personality-based aspect. It should be noted that this meta-analysis did not disaggregate studies according to whether they were predictive, postdictive, or concurrent. Many studies of the PPI(–R) and its association with antisocial behavior and aggression are postdictive or concurrent, which could inflate observed correlations.

Summary of meta-analyses. There are several notable themes that emerged from this review of meta-analyses. First, effect sizes for both violence and other crime are mainly in the moderate range, if not slightly smaller. Correlations in the mid 0s are common. Second, it appears that the behavioral and impulsivity features of PCL and other measures are more strongly (though still moderately) associated with violence and crime compared to the affective and interpersonal deficits of the PCL and other measures. In the next section, however, we review research on the association between Factor 1 and the nature of violence (in particular, instrumental violence), for which there appears to be a stronger link than for violence generally. Third, there is considerable heterogeneity in effect sizes, along with a substantial number of moderating variables. Although we cannot yet be certain which moderators will be robust in future analyses, two appear quite strong: U.S. studies and ethnic minority status are associated with lower effect sizes. Other moderators (e.g., gender, study design) will need to be investigated more thoroughly.

The fact that Factor 1 tends to be less strongly related to violence and crime than Factor 2 is of relevance to our earlier discussion of the theoretical and measurement debates surrounding the PCL–R. That is, if one subscribes to the position advocated by Cooke, Skeem, and others that elements of crime ought not to be included in the conceptual model of, or the measurement of, psychopathy, then the implication of meta-analyses is that the core features of the disorder are not terribly predictive of subsequent crime and violence. If, however, one subscribes to the other side of the debate, as advocated by Hare, Neumann, and others, then Factor 2 content, as core elements of psychopathy, is indeed of practical importance in terms of understanding future violence and criminality.

Incremental Validity of Psychopathy

Although many studies have evaluated the relationship between psychopathy and crime or violence, the incremental validity of psychopathy over and above other important risk factors such as demographic variables, criminal history, substance abuse, or mental disorders remains relatively underinvestigated. Some important findings have emerged, however, based on the available research. For instance, in their review of existing meta-analyses on psychopathy and criminal recidivism, Douglas et al. (2006) reported that there is support for the predictive incremental utility of psychopathy as measured by the PCL–R vis-à-vis crime and violence, and that appears to be the case even after controlling for factors such as substance abuse, criminal history, and demographics. Along the same lines, Hemphill, Hare, et al. (1998) and Hemphill, Templeman, Wong, and Hare (1998) reported that the PCL–R made significant contributions toward predicting recidivism not only beyond demographic characteristics and criminal history, but also beyond personality disorder diagnoses. Similar results were reported in a more recent meta-analysis that was conducted with male and female juvenile offenders, where psychopathy was found to be significantly associated with general and violent recidivism even after covariates of psychopathy were controlled for (Edens et al., 2007; Olver et al., 2009). That was also the case in a meta-analysis that was conducted with adults (M. A. Campbell et al., 2009).

The incremental validity of a number of psychopathy measures has also been examined. For instance, Jones and Miller (2012) examined the incremental validity of self- and informant reports of psychopathic traits that were assessed with three psychopathy measures (i.e., PPI–R, LSRP, FFM) in order to determine their utility in predicting externalizing behaviors such as substance abuse, antisocial behavior, gambling, and intimate partner

violence. The authors concluded that both self- and informant-reported psychopathy scores were related to externalizing behaviors and provided some degree of incremental validity. Specifically, Jones and Miller found that self-reported psychopathy scores were somewhat more useful than informant reports of psychopathy because they generally provided more unique information regarding externalizing behaviors, and in particular, substance abuse and gambling, whereas informant-reported psychopathy predicted intimate partner violence.

Nevertheless, in a study comparing the predictive incremental validity of the PCL:SV and a self-report measure assessing criminal thinking styles, the Psychological Inventory of Criminal Thinking Styles (PICTS; Walters, 1995), Walters (2009) found support for the incremental validity of the PICTS but not for the PCL:SV. Douglas, Epstein, and Poythress (2008) reported that none of three youth psychopathy measures demonstrated incremental validity above and beyond covariates such as past substance use and antisocial behavior. Further, Walters (2006) conducted a meta-analysis comparing the incremental predictive validity of risk appraisal instruments and self-report measures of various aspects of personality. Risk appraisal instruments included the PCL/PCL–R, VRAG, LSI–R, HCR–20, among others, and self-report measures included the NEO Personality Inventory—Revised (NEO–PI–R; Costa & McCrae, 1992b, 1992c), the Minnesota Multiphasic Personality Inventory (MMPI; Hathaway & McKinley, 1967), the Novaco Anger Scale (NAS; Novaco, 1994), and the PAI. Even though Walters (2006) found that risk appraisal measures have some advantage over self-reports in terms of predicting criminal justice outcomes, the two types of instruments performed comparably when institutional adjustment was used as the criterion (i.e., there was also support for the incremental predictive validity of both types of instruments). Of note, Walters (2006) pointed out that there was no clinically or statistically significant difference in mean effect sizes in studies contrasting the predictive utility of risk appraisal instruments with that of self-report measures reflecting criminal offending and antisocial behavior.

Taken together, these findings highlight the need for further research on this topic. Given the robust association between psychopathy and social deviance/criminality, it is reasonable to assume that measures of psychopathy should be preferred over general measures of personality when faced with the task of estimating an individual's risk for future offending. Nevertheless, thus far, there is not enough empirical support to make that assumption.

Regardless of whether features such as impulsivity and past antisociality are considered core features of psychopathy, it is clear that they elevate an individual's future risk for violence and crime to a moderate extent. The question then arises: Does treatment or intervention reduce the risk that is posed by offenders or patients who are high in such features? Another question that arises is: Of what relevance are Factor 1 traits for understanding an individual's risk for violence and crime? Are they irrelevant? Or, might they influence the expression of antisocial behavior when it does occur? That is, perhaps they can be better understood to influence the nature of and motivation for antisocial behavior more so than the risk thereof. We turn to these questions.

Treatment and Psychopathy

The first point to make is that there is now considerable evidence for the effect of correctional treatment and programming to reduce criminal behavior generally, and violent behavior specifically, among criminal offenders and psychiatric patients (for reviews, see Andrews, 2012; Douglas, Nicholls, & Brink, 2009). Interventions that subscribe to a risk–need–responsivity (RNR) approach have been shown to reduce recidivism risk by up to 40% (Andrews, 2012). At a very basic level, programs that target criminogenic needs (dynamic risk factors) and deliver a greater intensity of programming to higher as opposed to lower risk people are more likely to reduce crime and violence than programs that do not.

However, very little research has examined whether these findings apply to psychopathic offenders. Clinical lore has held that psychopathic individuals are not treatable, or, in fact, that treatment makes psychopaths worse. There is evidence that offenders who are high in psychopathic features pose problems within treatment programs in terms of breaking program rules, dropping out early, and misbehaving (Alterman, Rutherford, Cacciola,

McKay, & Boardman, 1998; Morrissey, Mooney, Hogue, Lindsay, & Taylor, 2007; Ogloff, Wong, & Greenwood, 1990). However, there is less evidence that the criminality and violence of psychopathic offenders cannot be reduced.

Evidence for the position that psychopathic offenders cannot benefit from treatment is often drawn from a study by Rice, Harris, and Cormier (1992). Rice et al. reviewed the criminal and violent outcomes of patients and offenders who had received treatment within a program that was developed and implemented in the 1960s in a forensic hospital in Ontario, Canada. The authors retroactively coded the PCL from patient files and then followed treatment participants after discharge. Rice et al. matched participants who had completed treatment with offenders who had not (on criminal history, age, and index offence) and reported that, at the end of 10 years, the treated high-psychopathy group was more likely to incur future violent offences (78%) than the untreated high-psychopathy group (55%). Similar findings were reported from a study in the United Kingdom by Hare, Clark, Grann, and Thornton (2000).

These two studies, particularly the former, have been widely cited as evidence that treatment makes psychopaths worse (Hare et al., 2000; Rice et al., 1992). However, these studies have also been criticized on both methodological and substantive grounds (see Skeem, Polaschek, & Manchak, 2009). Neither study used random assignment to treatment, and Rice et al. (1992) used only a few matching variables. Further, the treatment that was evaluated by Rice et al., which it should be noted was not designed or implemented by them, was highly unusual and did not subscribe to (and in fact predated) well-known RNR principles. For instance, treatment was compulsory and included the administration of lysergic acid diethylamide (LSD) and alcohol.

More recent evidence suggests that psychopathic offenders may indeed benefit from treatment and correctional programming. Salekin (2002) conducted a review and meta-analysis of 42 studies of the treatment–psychopathy issue. He adopted a wide approach in terms of defining psychopathy, such that many of the studies that were included in his review predated the existence of contemporary measurement procedures such as the PCL family of instruments. Nonetheless, he argued that, given the nascent state of the literature, a broad scope of analysis was warranted. Salekin concluded that there was, indeed, evidence for the effectiveness of treatment, particularly more intensive, longer term, multimodal therapies. Although encouraging, this review must be interpreted in light of its inclusion of studies that used suboptimal methodology and older measurement procedures of psychopathy.

However, a few recent studies using contemporary measures of psychopathy have been reported. Using data collected by the MacArthur study of mental disorder and violence (Monahan et al., 2001), Skeem, Monahan, and Mulvey (2002) revisited this controversial treatment–psychopathy issue among 871 civil psychiatric patients from the MacArthur data set. Of these, roughly 8.3% were classified on the PCL:SV as psychopathic, and 22.4% were classified as potentially psychopathic. Patients were followed for 1 year following discharge, and the number of treatment sessions that were recorded was used as an index of the *dose* of treatment that they received. The basic question was whether higher levels of psychopathy would moderate the effect of treatment in terms of violence reduction. That is, would those who were rated as possibly or highly psychopathic fare less well than nonpsychopathic patients? Skeem et al. also coded the dose of treatment so as to compare patients as a function of more versus less treatment. Although random assignment was not possible, the authors employed a fairly rigorous matching procedure called *propensity score analysis* to match, as well as could be, on variables (in this case, 16) that distinguish individuals who received more versus less treatment. Unfortunately, the data collected did not permit a description of the types of treatment encounters that patients had, just how many. The authors coded *low treatment dose* as zero to six sessions in the first 10 weeks following discharge and *high treatment dose* as seven or more sessions.

Skeem et al. (2002) reported that psychopathic traits did not moderate the effect of treatment on violence reduction, even after controlling for the 16 covariates. Psychopathic patients who received seven or more treatment sessions were roughly three times less likely to be violent in the 10 weeks following the initial community discharge period of 10 weeks (when the treatment was occurring) than psychopathic patients who received fewer than seven sessions. Roughly 23% of individuals in the low-treatment dose group were violent, compared to roughly 6% in the high-treatment dose group. A similar effect in an as-yet unpublished study of 381 offenders attending court-mandated substance abuse treatment was reported (Skeem, Douglas, Edens, Poythress, & Lilienfeld, 2005), as well as in a sample of young offenders (Caldwell, McCormick, Umstead, & Van Rybrock, 2007).

These findings hold some promise for the effectiveness of treatment on reducing the violence and crime of psychopathic offenders. Although it has yet to be tested formally, and therefore stands in need of verification, it is possible that the application of correctional and other treatment programs to psychopathic offenders and patients, if delivered at high doses, may reduce their risk for violence in the same manner as it does for nonpsychopathic persons. We encourage future research on this important topic, and especially using an RNR framework and treatment approaches (i.e., social learning, cognitive behavioral) that have been reported to be effective at reducing crime and violence (Andrews, 2012; Douglas et al., 2009).

Nature of Crime and Violence

As reviewed in the preceding section, evidence suggests that the behavioral features of psychopathy are more strongly related to crime and violence than are the interpersonal and affective features, although the latter remain predictive. However, there is some evidence to indicate that elements of primary psychopathy might influence the *nature* of violence, even if it does not raise the risk for the *occurrence* of violence to a substantial degree. Researchers have often evaluated whether the violence of individuals who are higher on primary psychopathy features is more likely to be instrumental in nature; that is, planned, premeditated, and in pursuit of some external goal.

Woodworth and Porter (2002), for instance, coded the instrumentality of 125 homicides that had been committed by Canadian offenders and reported that these were of a more instrumental nature among homicide offenders who scored high on the PCL–R. The correlation between PCL–R Factor 1 and instrumentality (.46) was higher than it was between Factor 2 and instrumentality (.31). More meaningfully, the partial correlation for Factor 1 remained significant and of meaningful size (.37) after partialling out Factor 2's variance, whereas the partial correlation for Factor 2 dropped to nonsignificance and small size (.09). Other researchers (Cornell et al., 1996; Porter & Woodworth, 2007) have also reported an association between instrumentality and the interpersonal and affective deficits of psychopathy. There is emerging evidence that the FD scale of the PPI(–R) is more strongly associated with proactive or instrumental violence than with reactive violence (Cima & Raine, 2009; Sellbom, Ben-Porath, Lilienfeld, Patrick, & Graham, 2005; Walsh, Swogger, & Kosson, 2009), and that FD and SCI interact to predict predatory aggression (S. T. Smith, Edens, & McDermott, 2011).

These findings suggest that greater attention should be paid to the nature and motivations for violence when studying the link between psychopathy and violence. It is understandable why there is relatively little research that does so compared to the totality of research on psychopathy and violence. Simply put, it is more difficult, methodologically, to study the nature of violence compared to the simple occurrence of violence. It requires an analysis of the context, function, goals, and motivations of violence and offenders and rarely can be discerned by reviewing official recidivism records. Nonetheless, it is a fair and reasonable statement to make that the affective and interpersonal characteristics of psychopathy may very well increase the risk for certain forms of violence, such as instrumental, planned, goal-based violence.

Thus far, we have discussed psychopathy and its measurement, presuming that it manifests similarly regardless of personal characteristics such as gender, ethnicity, or age. However, it is important not to simply assume that the construct and its measurement are invariant across these important dimensions. Measures of psychopathy are commonly applied to women, people from various ethnic backgrounds, and even to youth (not uncontroversially). As such, we examine these topics next. There has

been somewhat less large-scale research on psychopathy and gender, relative to ethnicity and youth, and hence, we will devote a considerable amount of space to it.

Psychopathy and Gender

Psychopathy shares similarities and commonalities with a number of personality and behavioral disorders for which gender differences have been reported (i.e., antisocial, histrionic, borderline, and narcissistic; Goldstein et al., 1996; Hartung & Widiger, 1998; Sprague, Javdani, Sadeh, Newman, & Verona, 2012; Verona & Carbonnell, 2000). In order to avoid pathologizing stereotypical gender traits, many personality inventories that are used to assess those disorders take gender into account during scoring by using gender-specific norms. This suggests that personality pathology varies across gender, and there is no reason to assume that the gender differences as reported in personality disorders such as antisocial, histrionic, borderline, and narcissistic, would not also be observed in psychopathy (Forouzan & Cooke, 2005).

Further, given that psychopathy is an important factor to comprehensive risk assessment for violence, it is reasonable to assume that when risk for violence among females is of concern, assessing psychopathy would be potentially relevant (Hare, 1991; Hart, 1998a, 1998b; Webster, 1999; Wynn, Hoiseth, & Pettersen, 2012). In reality, there are a number of facts in support of this argument. For instance, there is an increase in the number of adolescent girls (Odgers, Reppucci, & Moretti, 2005) and women (Weizmann-Henelius, Viemero, & Eronen, 2004) who get involved in the legal system (as cited in Nicholls & Petrila, 2005; see also Crime in America.net, 2010; Sentencing Project, 2007). Also, a large percentage of patients in civil (40%) and forensic (10%) hospitals are women (see Nicholls & Petrila, 2005), and higher rates of recidivism and institutional infractions were found among women with psychopathic traits (measured with the PCL–R) than among women without those traits (Hare et al., 2000). Similar trends have been reported for female offender samples (see Jackson & Richards, 2007). Finally, although the rates of perpetrating intimate partner violence appear to be comparable across gender, females have been found to be the most frequent perpetrators of child abuse (Brand & Fox, 2008; Dutton, 2006). In all of these settings, psychopathy is a potentially important risk factor for violence perpetrated by females, and it is therefore important to be studied (see Nicholls, Odgers, & Cooke, 2007; Nicholls & Petrila, 2005).

There have been numerous studies on psychopathy in women in recent years. Nevertheless, research on the topic has relied on the male conceptualization of psychopathy and has used instruments that were developed and validated on male samples (see Kreis & Cooke, 2011; Nicholls, Ogloff, Brink, & Spidel, 2005). This practice has raised concerns (see Forouzan & Cooke, 2005, Kreis & Cooke, 2011, Nicholls & Petrila, 2005) because it implies that the current male conceptualization of psychopathy and the available instruments are applicable across gender, yet, there is still no agreement as to whether or not that is the case.

Differences in symptoms and symptom severity. Going back to Cleckley's (1941/1988) conceptualization of psychopathy, highly psychopathic females exhibit personality traits that are similar to those of their male counterparts (e.g., truancy, pathological lying), yet, there is a difference in the degree and manifestation of these features. According to Kreis and Cooke (2011), who proposed a prototypical model of psychopathy among women, the female psychopath is likely to be more manipulative and emotionally unstable and may have a more unstable self-concept than a psychopathic man. At the same time, she may appear more empathic and anxious than her male counterparts and less aggressive, disruptive, self-centered, domineering, and self-aggrandizing. These characteristics paint an image that is quite different than that of men who exhibit psychopathy, as they are typically described as being more self-aggrandizing, domineering, disruptive, aggressive, and unempathic, with a strong sense of invulnerability and less anxiety.

Forouzan and Cooke (2005) pointed out that gender differences in psychopathy are also notable with regard to the degree of symptom severity as well as the meaning of particular behavioral indicators of the disorder. Specifically, the authors

indicated that interpersonal characteristics such as glibness, superficial charm, and grandiose self-worth among women are only apparent in extreme cases. In addition, the authors noted that indicators of psychopathy, such as promiscuous sexual behavior, might have different meaning for males versus females. Specifically, for females, it might be underpinned by a desire to exploit, and therefore could be used as a manipulation tactic to obtain financial, social, or narcissistic gain, and may be reflective of a parasitic or impersonal lifestyle. Conversely, for men, it may be underpinned by sensation seeking or may reflect mating effort.

Social norms may also affect how psychopathic traits are interpreted across gender. For instance, although financial dependency may be socially acceptable for females, it is looked down on for males, and it is considered to be parasitic (Forouzan & Cooke, 2005; Logan & Weizmann-Henelius, 2012). In addition, females with psychopathic traits may rely on different tactics than psychopathic males to achieve the same goals. For instance, given their lesser upper body strength, physical aggression is less likely to yield the same results for women as for men, and therefore women may resort to manipulation, flirtation, or coercion to reach their goals (Nicholls & Petrila, 2005). As a result of these differences, psychopathy among women may not be adequately captured by assessment instruments that are designed for men.

Even though the etiology of psychopathy is not fully understood, research thus far supports the notion that a number of factors (e.g., physiological, social, cultural, environmental, etc.) come into play in the shaping of gender differences in general and psychopathy in particular (see Kreis, 2009; Nicholls et al., 2007; Verona & Vitale, 2006, for a discussion). For instance, hormonal and neurochemical differences such as levels of androgens and dysregulated serotonin (5-HT) have been linked with differential prevalence of antisocial behavior and aggression across gender (Verona & Vitale, 2006). Specifically, abnormally high levels of androgens in girls seem o be linked to male-specific behavior during childhood (i.e., girls tend to be *tomboys*), which may be overridden by socialization and other developmental influences over time. In addition, male hormones have been linked to aggression and other types of antisocial behavior in both men and women, even though findings have not been entirely consistent (see Kreis, 2009; Nicholls et al., 2007; Verona & Vitale, 2006). Also, whereas lower levels of 5-HT have been associated with aggression and impulsivity in men (i.e., externalizing psychopathology), they have been linked with mood disorders such as anxiety and depression in women (i.e., internalizing psychopathology; Verona & Vitale, 2006).

Developmental socialization has also been highlighted as a reason for gender differences in the manifestation of psychopathy. For instance, assuming strong and dominant roles, as well as having high self-regard and mastery, is typically accepted and expected of men more so than of women (Nicholls et al., 2007; Perri & Lichtenwald, 2010). In a similar fashion, culture may influence the degree of gender differences in the expression of personality traits in general as well as psychopathy (Kreis, 2009; Nicholls et al., 2007). Specifically, cultural factors may play a role through modeling the manifestation of pathologies and by influencing the frequency of occurrence of psychopathology. Cultural factors may also be influential by determining specific patterns of coping with problems, which tend to differ across gender; by dictating whether specific conditions or behaviors are seen as pathological; and by shaping people's beliefs and reactions to different disorders (Kreis, 2009).

In addition, adverse backgrounds (i.e., being socially and economically marginalized and growing up in dysfunctional family environments) as well as childhood abuse and trauma have also been linked differentially with antisocial deviance and incarceration across gender, which in turn are linked with psychopathy (see Bottos, 2007; Verona & Vitale, 2006). Specifically, higher rates of abuse, and especially sexual abuse, have been recorded for incarcerated women. In addition, experiences of severe social and familial dysfunction, including childhood neglect and abuse, appear to be more strongly associated with antisocial deviance, substance abuse and dependence, and perpetration of intimate partner violence in women than in men. This suggests that early abuse experiences are linked to higher levels of externalizing maladjustment in women relative to men (see Verona & Vitale, 2006).

Some aspects of the differential manifestation of psychopathy across gender could be understood from a social dominance theory (Sidanius & Pratto, 1999) perspective, which postulates that "men have disproportionate social, political, and military power compared to women" (Pratto, Sidanius, & Levin, 2006, p. 273). This in fact is conceptualized as one of the primary reasons that men universally tend to exhibit higher levels of aggression and social dominance orientation (i.e., reflecting an individual's preference for hierarchy) in comparison to women (Pratto et al., 2006), which is of particular relevance to psychopathy.

Further, according to relational theory (Miller, 1976, as cited in Convington, 2007), men and women differ in their developmental goals in terms of reaching maturity. Specifically, men's goal is to become self-sufficient and autonomous; they achieve that through individuating and separating themselves from their caregivers until maturity is reached. Women, on the other hand, are primarily motivated by a sense of connection with others, which gives them a sense of self and self-worth. Thus, the guiding principle for growth in women is a sense of connection rather than separation (Convington, 2007), which is another possible explanation as to why there may be gender differences in the manifestation of psychopathy.

Differences in behavioral manifestation, clinical presentation, and comorbidity. Despite some mixed findings, it has been hypothesized that the behavioral manifestation of psychopathy varies across gender, where a more antisocial pattern has been noted among males and more of a histrionic pattern among females (Cloninger, 1978; Lilienfeld, Van Valkenburg, Larntz, & Akiskal, 1986; Marsee, Silverthorn, & Frick, 2005; see also Czar, Dahlen, Bullock, & Nicholson, 2011; Schmeelk, Sylvers, & Lilienfeld, 2008). Specifically, males tend to be more likely to express psychopathy through physical aggression or by engaging in conning behavior (Bobadilla, Wampler, & Taylor, 2012; Forouzan & Cooke, 2005; Logan & Weizmann-Henelius, 2012; Strand & Belfrage, 2005; Verona & Vitale, 2006). In contrast, females tend to be more likely to express psychopathy (though not exclusively) through relational aggression (i.e., behaviors intended to harm others' relationships such as back-stabbing, gossiping, rumor spreading, lying, deceitfulness, and lack of control), as females have been found to be significantly more relationally aggressive than males starting in childhood (see Bobadilla et al., 2012; Crick & Grotpeter, 1995; Logan, 2009; Logan & Weizmann-Henelius, 2012; Marsee et al., 2005).

It is important to highlight that results have been somewhat different in high-risk samples, where females have been found to be both relationally and physically aggressive, whereas males appeared to be more physically than relationally aggressive (Penney & Morretti, 2007; Stickle, Marini, & Thomas, 2012). Even so, these findings provide support for the notion that there are gender differences with regard to the type of aggression through which psychopathy is manifested, with relational aggression being more typical of females and physical aggression being more characteristic of males.

In addition, researchers have indicated that relative to their male counterparts, females tend to get involved in different types of violence (Robbins, Monahan, & Silver, 2003). Namely, female violence is most likely to be directed toward family members, and the magnitude of inflicted injuries is less serious. In addition, self-defense was identified as the primary reason for engaging in intimate partner violence among women (as opposed to retaliation among men), and their actions, though not exclusively, were found to be situationally motivated (J. M. Ross, 2011). Women also get arrested less frequently and for different crimes than men (Logan, 2009; Robbins et al., 2003; Skeem, Polaschek, Patrick, & Lilienfeld, 2011). Further, Goldstein et al. (1996) reported that relative to their male counterparts, women who are diagnosed with APD, which captures the behavioral aspects of psychopathy, were more likely to be irresponsible as parents, to be physically violent toward their children or partners, and to engage in prostitution. Such tendencies are often considered a violation of their societal role as females (e.g., shallow expression of nurturance, lack of selflessness; see Verona & Vitale, 2006). As a result of these gender differences, females' antisocial

behavior might be less likely to be reflected on official criminal records, and existing assessment instruments may not capture aggression demonstrated by them.

The differences in manifestation of psychopathy across gender are likely linked to the development and clinical presentation of the disorder. For instance, although early-onset antisocial behavior has been linked to psychopathy among males (e.g., Frick & Marsee, 2006; Salekin, 2006), the onset of antisocial behavioral patterns among females does not typically occur until adolescence, and as discussed earlier, the expression of antisocial behavior appears to vary across gender (e.g., Crick & Grotpeter, 1995). Despite the differences in the onset of conduct problems in males versus females, however, commonalities across gender have been reported in terms of poor impulse control and callous and unemotional interpersonal style (Silverthorn & Frick, 1999; Silverthorn, Frick, & Reynolds, 2001). Further, based on research on the clinical presentation of incarcerated women in general, it appears that they tend to experience a larger range of Axis I symptoms or disorders (e.g., somatization, anxiety) than incarcerated males, have lower rates of APD, and are most often diagnosed with borderline personality disorder (BPD; see Coolidge, Marle, Van Horn, & Segal, 2011; Verona & Vitale, 2006).

In terms of comorbidity with psychopathy, patterns among women are similar to those of men; namely, APD, other cluster B disorders (e.g., BPD or histrionic personality disorder), and substance use disorders are among the most commonly co-occurring disorders (for a review, see Verona & Vitale, 2006; Wynn et al., 2012; see also Taylor & Lang, 2006). This is true primarily in terms of the antisocial and lifestyle aspects of psychopathy as measured with the PCL–R. In contrast, internalizing behaviors and suicidality have more often been found to be negatively related to the affective–interpersonal aspects of psychopathy among women compared to men (see Verona & Vitale, 2006), even though findings among adolescent girls have not been entirely consistent (i.e., positive relations between suicidal behavior and the interpersonal aspect of psychopathy have been reported; see Sevecke,

Lehmkuhl, & Krischer, 2009). In addition, although PPI-assessed psychopathy in college men appears to be strongly correlated with APD, for college women, psychopathy was most strongly related to histrionic personality disorder (Hamburger et al., 1996). In fact, it has been suggested that psychopathy may be typically expressed in externalizing behaviors in males and as internalizing problems in women, although further research is needed to corroborate this hypothesis (Paris, 2007; Sevecke, Lehmkuhl, & Krischer, 2009; Skeem et al., 2011).

Results from studies examining the base rates of psychopathy, APD, and conduct disorder (CD) among women are also somewhat inconsistent. Although some studies using observer-based measures (e.g., PCL, PCL–R and PCL:SV) with correctional samples reported overlapping base rates for females and males (e.g., Louth, Hare, & Linden, 1998; Strachan, 1993; Strand & Belfrage, 2001; Tien, Lamb, Bond, Gillstrom, & Paris, 1993), others reported substantially lower base rates for females (Dolan & Völlm, 2009; Goldstein et al., 1996; Loucks, 1995; Neary, 1990; Nicholls et al., 2005; Salekin, Rogers, & Sewell, 1997; Vitale, Smith, Brinkley, & Newman, 2002; Warren et al., 2003). Further, findings from studies that were conducted with noninstitutionalized samples also differ: Although some reported higher mean PCL–R scores for males versus females (e.g., Forth, Brown, Hart, & Hare, 1996; Weiler & Widom, 1996), others found no gender difference in scores (e.g., Cooney, Kadden, & Litt, 1990; Stafford & Cornell, 2003).

Similar results have been reported by researchers who examined psychopathy across gender using studies based on self-reports (Hamburger et al., 1996; Lilienfeld & Hess, 2001; J. D. Miller, Watts, & Jones, 2011; Wilson et al., 1999; Zágon, & Jackson, 1994). With regard to the interpersonal-affective versus antisocial scales of psychopathy measures (i.e., PCL–R or PPI), larger gender differences in scores have been reported for the interpersonal-affective scales of those instruments (see Skeem et al., 2011; Vablais, 2007).

Differences in personality and behavioral correlates, and recidivism. Gender differences have also been reported with regard to the personality and behavioral correlates of psychopathy. Specifically, personality correlates such as experience of emotion, empathy, lack of attachment, self-control and socialization, interpersonal dominance, arrogance, calculation, and narcissism are relatively consistent across gender (e.g., Forth et al., 1996; Kreis, 2009; J. D. Miller et al., 2011; Patrick, 1994; Rutherford, Cacciola, Alterman, & McKay, 1996; Salekin, Rogers, Ustad, & Sewell, 1998; Strachan, 1993; Verona, Patrick, & Joiner, 2001; Vitale et al., 2002; Zágon & Jackson, 1994). Some exceptions have been noted by J. D. Miller et al. (2011), who found that the antisocial factor of psychopathy was correlated more strongly with impulse-related tendencies among males and with openness to experience among females. In addition, Kreis (2009) pointed out that women may present as less dominant and may engage in more impression management than their male counterparts.

Studies examining the behavioral correlates of psychopathy, however, have yielded more inconsistent results across gender: Poor treatment response, institutional adjustment, alcoholism, recidivism, and criminal behavior have been shown to be significantly related to high scores on the PCL–R and the PCL:YV in male samples, but results have been less consistent in female samples (e.g., Catchpole & Gretton, 2003; Hemphill, Hare, et al., 1998; Hemphill, Templeman, et al., 1998; Kreis, 2009; Nicholls et al., 2007; Richards, Casey, & Lucente, 2003; Salekin et al., 1997; Verona & Vitale, 2006; Walters, 2003a, 2003b; Wynn et al., 2012). Specifically, findings on the relationship between violence and psychopathy in women appear to be ambiguous: Some studies have reported a strong association between high scores on the PCL–R and previous violence, nonviolent criminality, arrests, or reoffending (e.g., Loucks & Zamble, 2000; Nicholls et al., 2005; Rutherford et al., 1996; Strachan, 1993; Vitale et al., 2002; Weiler & Widom, 1996), whereas others have reported poor to moderate associations between PCL–R scores and recidivism (e.g., Eisenbarth, Osterheider, Nedopil, & Stadtland, 2012; Salekin et al., 1998), or no significant associations between PCL–R scores and correctional officers' ratings of institutional infractions and future violence in female samples (e.g., Salekin et al., 1997). In addition, some studies found that PCL:YV scores were not predictive of future offending among adolescent females (Odgers et al., 2005; Vincent, Odgers, McCormick, & Corrado, 2008), and even though Odgers et al. (2005) reported that there was an association between deficient affective experiences and aggression, that effect was negated once victimization experiences were taken into account.

Further, as reviewed earlier, studies examining the relationship between psychopathy and recidivism in male samples, both Factor 1 and Factor 2 of the PCL–R, have been found to be associated with recidivism, although more strongly for Factor 2 than 1. Nevertheless, Salekin et al. (1998) reported a significant relationship only for Factor 1 and recidivism in a female sample. Similar results were reported in a study of detained adolescent girls, where Factor 1 of the PCL:YV was more discriminating of psychopathy than Factor 2, which had been shown in prior research as well (Schrum & Salekin, 2006). Along the same lines, in a study of violent female offenders, the affective deficits of psychopathy were found to improve the prediction of violent and nonviolent institutional infractions over general psychopathy scores on the PCL–R (Davis, 2010). Similarly, in a meta-analytic study, gender was found to be a significant moderator of PCL total and Factor 1 scores, which explained future antisocial conduct better when samples had more female participants (Leistico et al., 2008). Taken together, these findings potentially suggest a stronger association between recidivism and psychopathy in men relative to women; yet, this assumption requires further empirical validation.

Contextual factors related to the violence being committed were found to vary across gender as well. Specifically, men were more likely than women to engage in substance use and less likely to adhere to prescribed psychotropic medication prior to engaging in acts of violence (Robbins et al., 2003). Further, males were reported to show more anger, regardless of the context, whereas females tended to experience a wider range of negative effects such as anger, sadness, fear, or guilt more frequently and more intensely (see Forouzan & Cooke, 2005). As pointed out by Skeem et al. (2011), one possible explanation for such findings is reflected in the multifactorial threshold models (Cloninger,

Christiansen, Reich, & Gottesman, 1978), according to which, for biological reasons (i.e., lower testosterone) as well as social norms prohibiting against overaggression in females, a greater diathesis and associated traits are required for females to manifest psychopathy. Therefore, when psychopathy is detected among females with assessment measures that were designed for males, we might be dealing with individuals who have a particularly heightened predisposition for disinhibited behavior (Skeem et al., 2011).

Factor structure of commonly used psychopathy measures. The factor structure of PCL–R-assessed psychopathy across gender has also been examined in an attempt to determine if psychopathy measures are suitable for use across gender. Inconsistencies in the factor structure could be due to limitations of the original factor model or true gender differences in the structure of the instrument. So far, existing research has indicated that failure to replicate the factor structure of psychopathy across gender is primarily due to limitations of the original two-factor model. For example, Salekin et al. (1997) conducted an exploratory factor analysis of the PCL–R with a female sample and found that even though a two-factor model of psychopathy emerged, some of the PCL–R items loaded differentially on Factor 1 and Factor 2 for men and women. Gender differences in item loadings on the PCL–R were also reported by Dolan and Völlm (2009) based on a review of the existing literature, and by O'Connor (2003) based on confirmatory factor analyses that were conducted in female prison samples. Such differences in item loadings may be due to the fact that the instrument was developed in a specific sample and may not tap into the same construct in other samples, thus indicating the need for modification of the conceptualization of the structure of psychopathy for females (see Forouzan & Cooke, 2005).

Further, Sevecke, Pukrop, et al. (2009) used the PCL:YV in a sample of German adolescents and found satisfactory fit for the three-factor model for males, but none of the models (i.e., two-, three-, or four-factor) was satisfactory for females. Likewise, O'Connor (2003) did not find support for the goodness-of-fit of the two-factor model of psychopathy among females. Nevertheless, other authors have reported support for the three- or four-factor models of psychopathy across gender. For instance, Warren et al. (2003) examined the goodness of fit of the two-, three-, and four-factor model of psychopathy in a female sample and found that the best fit of the data was achieved with the three-factor model, although the four-factor presented a good fit as well. Similarly, Dolan and Völlm (2009), Strand and Belfrage (2005), and Weizmann-Henelius et al. (2010) showed support for the three-factor model of the PCL–R/PCL:SV in female populations. The goodness-of-fit of the data for the three-factor model using the PCL:SV was also confirmed using a mixed gender sample in a study by Skeem et al. (2003), who reported that their findings were invariant across gender.

Suitability of existing measures to assess psychopathy across gender. Even though studies have shown that there are some item differences and test functioning of the PCL–R across gender, some studies have suggested that the instrument is suited for use across gender (e.g., Bolt, Hare, Vitale, & Newman, 2004; Dolan & Völlm, 2009; Jackson & Richards, 2007). Nevertheless, claims regarding the equal suitability of psychopathy assessment instruments across gender were challenged by Forouzan and Cooke (2005). Specifically, the authors pointed out that such claims assume equivalence of the symptoms and characteristics of the disorder across gender, which may not be a valid assumption. In fact, Hare (1991) suggested that items on the PCL–R might need to be modified, as psychopathy might be "expressed" (p. 64) differently in females and thus may have limited utility in female samples (see also Salekin et al., 1997). Support for this hypothesis has been demonstrated in studies that found lower internal consistency for PCL–R items in female samples, as well as by scholars expressing concern about the generalizability of the PCL–R to women (see Kreis, 2009; Kreis & Cooke, 2011; Logan, 2009; Nicholls & Petrila, 2005; O'Connor, 2003). For instance, Salekin et al. (1998) found the classification accuracy of the PCL–R to be "moderate to poor" in a female sample where a cutoff score of 30

was used to classify inmates as psychopathic versus nonpsychopathic. Namely, 90% of the inmates who recidivated were classified as *nonpsychopathic*, and only 9% of those who recidivated were classified as *psychopathic*.

Further, there is a lack of consensus as to whether the raw scores of the PCL:SV reflect the same level of psychopathy across gender. As a result, some studies have used traditional cutoff scores on the PCL–R (i.e., score of 30), whereas others have lowered the score. This has led to significant variations of base rates in psychopathy among women across samples (see Jackson, Rogers, Neumann, & Lambert, 2002; Warren et al., 2003) as well as calls for further research and caution in interpreting the available literature (Falkenbach, 2008; Forouzan & Cooke, 2005; Logan, 2009).

Similar to the PCL–R, results from studies on the CAPP–IRS indicated that it might capture psychopathy in women, although some adjustments may be necessary (see Kreis & Cooke, 2008). Specifically, Kreis and Cooke (2011) reported support for the content validity of the CAPP–IRS across gender and suggested that at symptom and domain levels of the CAPP, psychopathic men and women share key similarities, but there are also important gender differences, which were likely a matter of degree. With regard to gender differences, men were rated as higher in the attachment, dominance, behavioral, and cognitive domains; and at the symptom level, "self-aggrandizing," "sense of invulnerability," "self-centered," "domineering," "reckless," "disruptive," "aggressive," "lacks anxiety," and "unempathic" were more relevant to psychopathy in men. As for women, symptoms such as "manipulative," "lacks emotional stability," and "unstable self-concept" were found to be more relevant to psychopathy. The authors concluded that although some symptoms or domains were found to be more prominent in psychopathic men versus psychopathic women (and vice versa), they were not specific to psychopathy in only one gender.

All in all, the literature suggests that gender differences should not be ignored in the assessment of psychopathy, and existing measures are likely to have at least some utility in assessing psychopathy in women, although some modification of the measures may be necessary to ensure assessment accuracy. Particular caution in the interpretation of findings is needed in areas where gender differences are likely to be detected. As noted earlier, gender differences may be expected in domains such as aggression, dominance, risk taking, interpersonal skills, and emotionality (Kreis, 2009; Kreis & Cooke, 2011). Gender differences in the manifestation of psychopathy would also be expected in those same domains from social dominance theory (i.e., aggression and dominance domains; Sidanius & Pratto, 1999) and relational theory perspectives (i.e., risk taking, interpersonal skills, and emotionality domains; Miller, 1976, as cited in Convington, 2007). Specifically, in consideration of their respective roles in the reproductive process, women, in comparison to men, would be expected to be less dominant and less risk taking. In addition, women would be less physically aggressive than men but rather relationally aggressive. Nevertheless, women would be capable of being on par with men with regard to physical aggression if need be or if they would personally gain from it. Further, women would have especially well-developed interpersonal skills and would typically use them as a primary manipulative or exploitive strategy. It is also likely that women would be less status seeking and overtly grandiose than men. Finally, differences in the emotional responses of men versus women would be expected in terms of intensity, frequency, and external expression of emotions, with a relatively higher degree for all among women, which they may use as a manipulative or exploitive tactic (see Kreis, 2009, for a discussion). As noted by Kreis (2009) given that the etiology of psychopathy is yet to be fully understood, the explanation offered in terms of expected gender differences is speculative in nature. Even so, the evolutionary psychological theory, social dominance theory, and relational theory provide a useful framework in understanding where to expect differences across gender.

It is important to recognize, however, that even though existing research on the assessment of psychopathy in women provides a good foundation of knowledge on the topic, the field is far from being unanimous. The lack of agreement extends not only to the utility of existing assessment instruments, but also to the theoretical conceptualization of the construct, as well as to findings regarding base rates and behavioral correlates of psychopathy among women. The issue becomes particularly complex as applied to female youth, about whom less is known in terms of psychopathy. These discrepancies dictate the need for further research.

Psychopathy and Ethnicity

Much of the research on psychopathy, in addition to being conducted with men, has been conducted with Caucasians. This was especially true in the early days of the development of the PCL measure, where most of the research was carried out with male, Caucasian, Canadian offenders. Although there has been a fair amount of research with women, studies have tended not to be large scale in terms of sample size. The field of psychopathy has benefitted from several large-scale investigations into its functioning across people from different cultural and ethnic groups. Despite this state of affairs, generally, we would argue that data are still relatively sparse in the United States concerning Hispanic individuals, and in the United States, Canada, and elsewhere concerning its functioning in Aboriginal populations.

Psychopathy, at its core, is personality. Personality, and personality disorders, can vary as a function of culture and socialization given that they are inherently situated within social and interpersonal contexts. This cultural facilitation model holds that socialization and social influences can encourage the expression of some interpersonal and behavioral features and suppress the expression of others (Weisz, Suwanlert, Chaiyasit, & Walter, 1987). In investigating the role of culture or ethnicity in psychopathy (or other constructs), it is important to focus not only on scale scores, but also on the latent constructs that underlie scale scores. Scale scores can vary for reasons that are unrelated to the construct or tests thereof, such as differing arrest or referral practices across countries or systematically different historical experiences across cultural groups. Despite this, even at the manifest level, meta-analytic work has indicated that African American and Caucasian scores on the PCL–R differed by only 0.7 points on the full-scale PCL–R (Skeem et al., 2004). Differences were even smaller for affective and interpersonal items compared to behavioral items, although the difference was small for the latter as well.

There have been several tests of the metric equivalence of the PCL–R across different ethnic groups using IRT. IRT allows for the testing of whether a given instrument measures an underlying construct in a similar manner across groups, regardless of whether these groups perform differently at the manifest level. Although relatively complex, essentially, IRT does this by testing whether items are equally responsive to the underlying trait and whether they are optimally responsive at the same or different level of the underlying trait across groups. For instance, a certain item might be very strongly indicative of the presence of high levels of psychopathy in one group but not in another. Another test of cross-cultural comparability stems from factor-analytic studies that test whether the factor structure of certain psychopathy instruments is comparable across ethnic groups. Such an analysis tests whether the latent structure of psychopathy, at least as defined by a given instrument, is the same or different across groups. There have been large-scale studies of cross-cultural performance of measures of psychopathy (especially the PCL–R) using both of these techniques.

Cooke, Michie, Hart, and Clark (2005) used confirmatory factor analysis (CFA) and IRT techniques to investigate the comparability of the PCL–R across large samples of North American (Canadian and American) and European offenders and forensic patients (from multiple non-United Kingdom countries). Using CFA, the authors reported that neither the two- nor four-factor model fit well, although the three-factor model did. However, a model that constrained parameters to be equal across North America and Europe fit significantly less well than a model that allowed parameters to vary unconstrained by continent. Nonetheless, the three-factor model did fit well in both North America and Europe, leading Cooke, Michie, et al. to conclude that there was no structural bias in PCL–R ratings. IRT analyses indicated that there was differential item functioning across continents. In particular, the discriminating power of items differed across groups. The end result was that, at similar levels of

the underlying trait, Europeans scored lower on the PCL–R than did North Americans. However, the difference was small. Interestingly, Cooke, Michie, et al. reported that the degree of bias was smallest (almost nonexistent) for the affective items of the PCL–R compared to those measuring interpersonal and lifestyle/behavioral symptoms. This led Cooke, Michie, et al. to conclude that the affective deficits of psychopathy might represent their "pan-cultural core." That is, affect-based deficits may be least affected by the sociocultural processes that can influence interpersonal and behavioral patterns. Cooke and Michie (1999) reported similar findings in a comparison of North American and U.K. participants (structural invariance; some metric inequivalence) with U.K. participants ultimately receiving lower scores at the same level of the underlying trait relative to North American participants, and least bias on affective features.

Cooke, Kosson, and Michie (2001) used CFA and IRT procedures to test both the structural and metric equivalence of the PCL–R across African American and Caucasian offenders. They reported that the three-factor model was invariant across race. IRT analyses indicated no presence of differential discriminating power of items across groups. However, there was some indication that certain items (all from the behavioral factor) tend to be rated as being present at lower levels of the trait across groups. Despite this, items did not do so consistently for one group or the other; there was essentially no pattern, and differences canceled out at the test level. Cooke et al. concluded that "items of the PCL–R appear to be similarly useful in diagnosing psychopaths of both ethnic groups" (p. 540).

In one of the few comparative studies of Aboriginal versus non-Aboriginal offenders, Olver et al. (2013) reported structural invariance of the PCL–R across Canadian Aboriginal and non-Aboriginal offenders. However, Olver et al. did not test whether the three-factor model fit the data and did not report IRT analyses. Vitacco, Neumann, and Jackson (2005) reported that both the three- and four-factor model fit the PCL:SV, and that fit was good for the four-factor model not only across race, but also across gender. They did not test the three-factor model on its own vis-à-vis race, although Skeem et al. (2003) had earlier reported that it fit well across Caucasian and African American patients. Similarly, Jones, Cauffman, Miller, and Mulvey (2006) reported that both the three- and four-factor models of the PCL:YV were invariant across race/ethnicity (African American, Caucasian, Hispanic) and gender in a sample of 1,354 adolescent offenders.

Based on the foregoing, the picture appears somewhat complex when it comes to the performance of psychopathy measures across different cultural or ethnic groups. First, it should be pointed out that most of the work used the PCL–R, so we would encourage similar investigations with other psychopathy instruments. There is fairly good evidence that there is factorial equivalence of the PCL–R and its derivatives across different ethnic and cultural groups, both within North America and between North America and Europe (Cooke, Michie, et al., 2005). IRT analyses suggest some minor item-level metric inequivalence across African American and European American offenders, although this likely cancels out at the scale level (Cooke & Michie, 1997). In terms of metric equivalence, comparing North American and European samples, it appears that the PCL–R does operate somewhat differently: Slightly lower scores in Europe index a comparable level of the underlying trait relative to somewhat higher scores in North America, and some items are more useful in North America compared to Europe.

An additional form of testing cross-group comparability is to test whether the pattern of validity findings is similar or different across groups. Using a subsample from the longitudinal Pittsburgh Youth Study (Loeber et al., 2001), Vachon, Lynam, Loeber, and Stouthamer-Loeber (2012) compared the nomological network of associated correlates of psychopathy (indexed with the PCL:SV) across 508 Caucasian and African American participants who were between 22 and 26 years of age. The authors essentially tested whether the correlations of the PCL:SV and a multitude of theoretically relevant external correlates were moderated by race. Of more than 100 moderator tests involving race, only three resulted in significant moderating effects. The authors concluded that "psychopathy behaves similarly across ethnic groups" (p. 268). There is also

evidence from this sample that the associations between measures of psychopathy taken roughly a decade apart are not moderated by race (Lynam, Loeber, & Stouthamer-Loeber, 2008). That is, the stability (which was not terribly high in this study, $rs = .15$ to $.33$) was the same, regardless of race.

However, some studies have reported differences in validity findings across different ethnic or cultural groups. Some of the meta-analyses reviewed earlier indicated that the association between PCL–R-measured psychopathy and crime or violence was lower within the United States compared to Canada or European studies. Other meta-analyses have reported slightly lower predictive effects for PCL–R psychopathy vis-à-vis crime or violence in samples with a higher proportion of minority participants (Singh et al., 2011). Some individual studies have reported poorer predictive effects among African American and Latino American offenders relative to Caucasian offenders (Walsh, 2013). Yet, in other studies, no such impact of race or ethnicity was observed, either in the United States (Vitacco et al., 2005, using the PCL:SV) or in Canada (Olver et al., 2013, using the PCL–R; Stockdale, Olver, & Wong, 2010, using the PCL:YV).

Some studies of other validity analyses have also reported ethnic differences. For instance, the association between the PCL:SV and impulsivity was reported to be moderated by race (Jackson, Neumann, & Vitacco, 2007). Kosson, Smith, and Newman (1990) similarly reported a difference between the PCL–impulsivity relationship between African American and Caucasian offenders in an early study of psychopathy and race using the 22-item PCL. Formal moderation analyses were not conducted. Passive avoidance learning errors have been found among Caucasians who are high in psychopathic features (Hiatt & Newman, 2006), but this effect was not reported in some African American samples (Thornquist & Zuckerman, 1995), although race also has been found not to moderate this deficit using the SRP (Epstein, Poythress, & Brandon, 2006). One cluster-analytic study with an African American sample identified some similar clusters, as have cluster-analytic studies using either mixed-ethnicity samples or Caucasian samples (i.e., primary, secondary, and nonpsychopathic groups), but also identified additional groups that were not found in other studies (Swogger et al., 2008). However, cluster-analytic studies are highly dependent on sample characteristics and methodology, so some differences across samples do not necessarily indicate race effects.

To some extent, it makes sense to expect minor fluctuations in how psychopathy is manifest, or how instruments perform, across groups defined in part by important social, cultural, and geographic dimensions. Comparing across single studies, however, risks making race difference conclusions that stem not from actual race differences, but rather from sampling or methodology differences across studies. IRT and CFA studies are more compelling, as are studies that compare within samples using a moderation framework, and meta-analyses.

At a basic level, it appears that psychopathy appears quite similar across dimensions of ethnicity and culture in terms of its basic structure, the performance of instruments, and its surrounding network of related constructs and behaviors. The association between the PCL–R and crime, violence, or institutional infractions may be smaller in U.S. versus non-U.S. samples, and slightly so in samples consisting of a greater proportion of minorities. Some items seem to perform somewhat differently in Europe than in North America, such that the disorder manifests at lower scores on the PCL–R in Europe relative to North America. Fundamentally, however, it does appear that the basic performance of the construct, particularly as measured by the PCL–R, is comparable across race, ethnicity, and culture. The extent to which this state of affairs applies to youth, as opposed to adults—a rather controversial subject—is tackled next.

Psychopathy and Youth

Few if any issues in the psychopathy field have been as controversial as the application of this construct to children and adolescents. Several early reviews (e.g., Edens, Skeem, Cruise, & Cauffman, 2001; Hart, Watt, & Vincent, 2002; Seagrave & Grisso, 2002; Steinberg, 2002; see also Edens & Vincent, 2008) raised a variety of concerns about the appropriateness of downward extensions of the adult psychopathy construct, given the fluidity of

personality among children; the normative and transient nature of certain psychopathic traits (e.g., impulsivity, egocentricity) among adolescents; and the significant potential for stigmatization, particularly in the legal system.

In a relatively short period of time, a voluminous research literature on psychopathic traits among youth has developed, focusing on several distinct (but overlapping) conceptualizations of the syndrome, etiological models, assessment instruments to operationalize the construct (described below), and correlates of psychopathic traits—to name but a few topics of research interest. In terms of the magnitude of this research base, as of September 6, 2013, use of the PsycINFO database to search the subject headings *psychopathic or psychopathy* and *child* or adolescen** (i.e., "su(psychopathic or psychopathy) AND su(child* or adolescen*))" resulted in the identification of more than 1,300 total citations—with, rather remarkably, more than 1,000 of these occurring since the year 2000. Collectively, this research literature has produced a number of important findings and suggests that there are significant parallels between the nomological nets surrounding this construct in adults and youth (for recent extensive reviews, see Pardini & Byrd, 2013; Salekin & Lynam, 2011; Vitacco & Salekin, 2013).

Although numerous instruments have been developed to assess psychopathic traits among children and adolescents, a large percentage of the burgeoning research literature has employed the PCL:YV or the Antisocial Process Screening Device (APSD; Frick & Hare, 2001). The PCL:YV is essentially a downward extension of the adult-focused PCL–R, with certain modifications to the 20 items and their scoring guidelines to account for developmental differences across adolescents and adults. Much like with the PCL–R, meta-analyses (reviewed above) indicated that the PCL:YV predicts various types of problematic behavior, including community recidivism (Edens et al., 2007) and institutional adjustment problems (Edens & Campbell, 2007), with small to moderate effect sizes typically reported. The bulk of predictive validity in these studies is attributable to Factor 2 of this instrument, which is also similar to the findings in the adult literature.

The APSD, though based originally on the item content of the PCL–R, differs in important ways from the PCL:YV. Scoring the PCL:YV involves the use of a trained rater who conducts an extensive psychosocial history interview and who also has access to adequate file data concerning the examinee. The APSD, on the other hand, typically is scored based on item ratings from parents, teachers, or a combination of the two—though self-report versions of the instrument have been used as well, particularly for adolescents. Correlations across raters have not been particularly high, though in general, measures of psychopathology across parents and teachers do not converge especially well (Frick & Hare, 2001).

The internal structure of the APSD has been the subject of considerable research, with studies over the years increasingly focusing primary interest on a six-item subscale labeled *Callous/Unemotional* (CU) traits (e.g., Frick, O'Brien, Wootton, & McBurnett, 1994). These traits seem to be particularly relevant in identifying a subgroup of youth who appear to be more prone to externalizing behaviors and at risk for numerous adverse outcomes, such as relatively poor treatment response (for an extended review, see Frick, Ray, Thornton, & Kahn, 2014).

Despite similar item content, the degree of convergence across the APSD and PCL:YV has been relatively poor (e.g., Dillard, Barker, Salekin, & Grimes, 2013), particularly in relation to subscales that ostensibly should be relatively strongly associated with each other (i.e., the APSD CU subscale and Factor 1 and Facet 2 of the PCL–R). This is generally true with adult measures of psychopathy as well, as there tend to be relatively weak correlations across scales—at least partly due to instrument method effects (i.e., self-report vs. expert rating scales; see Blonigen et al., 2010). That being said, given that these instruments seem to only partially tap the same underlying construct, it is important not to treat all psychopathy assessment devices as isomorphic or to assume that research findings based on one scale will replicate with another (see the later section on reliability as well).

Regardless of the general lack of convergence with the PCL:YV, the burgeoning APSD and related literature on CU traits culminated in the inclusion of a new specifier for the CD diagnosis in the recently released *DSM–5* (American Psychiatric Association, 2013) to identify youth "with limited prosocial emotions." Although various subtyping approaches to CD have existed in the iterations of the *DSM* system over the years, this specifier arguably is the most direct attempt to link CD to the psychopathy literature specifically, with *DSM–5* indicating that these characteristics "have often been labeled as callous and unemotional traits in research" (p. 471). The four individual traits comprising this specifier consist of "lack of remorse or guilt," "callous-lack of empathy," "unconcerned about performance," and "shallow or deficient affect" and the presence of at least two of them (over at least 12 months in multiple relationships and settings) is sufficient to trigger its application to the CD diagnosis. The *DSM–5* argues that these symptoms can be used to identify a subgroup of children with particularly severe behavior problems and that the "addition of the specifier will help specialize care and spur additional treatment and causal research" (American Psychiatric Association, 2012, p. 1).

Of course, it remains to be seen whether this specifier eventually does result in specialized care that leads to improved outcomes for youth with CD who have been identified as falling into this CU category. More generally, concerns about classifying children and adolescents with a stigmatizing label have been raised by numerous authors, and research reviewed later in this chapter suggests that psychopathic children are generally not going to be viewed in positive terms by society. But what do we actually know about the role and impact of psychopathy labels and diagnoses on youth in the real world at this time? Although relatively little research has focused on this topic, there have been some recent systematic attempts to examine how psychopathy is used "outside the lab," primarily in relation to the use of the PCL:YV in legal systems in North America. The focus on the PCL:YV appears to be primarily because it is the only psychopathy scale to have gained widespread acceptance for clinical/forensic use in applied settings.

Viljoen, McLachlan, and Vincent (2010) surveyed 215 primarily clinical and counseling psychologists (the majority of whom were members of the American Psychology-Law Society) who had extensive experience conducting forensic evaluations. Seventy-seven participants indicated that they conducted juvenile risk assessments, and typical purposes for the use of psychopathy assessments were for sentencing and disposition planning (general and sex offender-specific), juvenile transfer to adult courts, and diversion services. Roughly one-fourth of the respondents indicated that they used the PCL:YV in at least some of their cases, with self-report measures (e.g., Minnesota Multiphasic Personality Instrument—Adolescent; Butcher et al., 1992) being employed much more frequently. Interestingly, almost none (3%) of the participants reported that they used the label *psychopath* in their evaluations, although a higher percentage (29%) did indicate whether the juvenile had "characteristics associated with psychopathy" and referred to these traits as "psychopathy related." In contrast, 46% of the respondents reported that they had characteristics associated with psychopathy but did not refer to them explicitly as "psychopathy-related."

In a somewhat related vein of research, Viljoen, MacDougall, Gagnon, and Douglas (2010) conducted a comprehensive case law survey of the use of psychopathy in North American juvenile cases, identifying a total of 111 Canadian ($n = 71$) and U.S. ($n = 40$) cases. Generally similar to the results of Viljoen, McLachlan, and Vincent (2010), these authors found that psychopathy was primarily used in juvenile transfer cases as well as in cases involving sentencing and disposition planning. Cases noting psychopathy also were appearing with increasing frequency over the years, similar to the trend noted in the adult case law literature for the PCL–R (DeMatteo & Edens, 2006; DeMatteo et al., 2014).

The coding of these cases identified several interesting trends concerning the role of psychopathy evidence. For example, youth were judged to be difficult to treat specifically because of the presence of psychopathic traits in a significant percentage of cases (24% in Canada and 18% in the United States), and youth were judged to be "high risk" because of the presence of these traits in a smaller but still appreciable number of cases (16% in Canada and 13% in the United States). In contrast, determinations that youth were either "treatable" or

"low risk" due to the absence of psychopathic traits were much less common—consistent with claims in the adult literature that psychopathy primarily serves as a prosecution tool in most cases (DeMatteo et al., 2014). Judges specifically referred to psychopathy evidence in their final opinions relatively frequently (34% in Canadian and 23% in U.S. cases), suggesting that this evidence was given appreciable weight in their decision making. Unlike in the adult case law literature, challenges to the admissibility of psychopathy evidence in juvenile cases occurred somewhat frequently (24% of Canada and 20% of United States).

Collectively, these two studies (DeMatteo & Edens, 2006; DeMatteo et al., 2014) indicate that players in the legal system (e.g., judges, expert witnesses) seem relatively (and increasingly) receptive to the use of psychopathy evidence to inform decision making in cases with youthful offenders, particularly in relation to questions concerning risk assessment and rehabilitation potential. The specific term *psychopath* as applied to youth appears to be controversial and somewhat rare, but descriptions of *psychopathy-like* characteristics are relatively common. The extent to which the CU specifier for CD in the *DSM–5* (American Psychiatric Association, 2013) will accelerate the applied use of psychopathy-like traits in legal decision making for juvenile offenders is unclear, but it seems safe to assume that this trend will only increase in the foreseeable future.

Providing clinical–forensic opinions about psychopathy and future behavior is predicated on these assessments being based on reliable and valid measures of the disorder. A basic tenet of psychometric theory is that instruments cannot be valid measures of the underlying construct of interest unless they can reliably measure that construct. The reliability of psychopathy is a crucial topic that bears critical implications for a number of theoretical and practical issues. Theoretically, unreliable measures would make it impossible to test out conceptual models of any mental disorder because the constructs of interest are not adequately being operationalized. Practically, unreliable measures would make it impossible to have any confidence in claims that someone has a disorder actually being indicative of whether that person has that disorder (or that someone who scores "high" on a continuous measure actually has an elevated score on that continuum).

Of course, reliability is not really a dichotomous concept, and few if any psychological/psychiatric assessment instruments could be argued to be completely reliable or unreliable. An important consideration in this discussion is whether operationalizations of psychopathy are, essentially, reliable enough for the purpose for which they are being used. Reliable enough is itself a value judgment regarding how much error is tolerable in any given context. One could argue (e.g., Heilbrun, 1992) that the bar for reliability for psychopathy instruments should be much higher in applied settings (e.g., juvenile justice) if the consequences of error are much more significant than they are in research settings, in which even a relatively inexact assessment of a construct might still allow for meaningful inferences to be drawn about the relationship between, for example, child psychopathic traits and adolescent psychosocial functioning at the group (as opposed to individual) level.

Reliability itself is not a static property of an instrument but is instead a multifaceted psychometric concept that addresses psychopathy scales' internal consistency (i.e., Do they measure a coherent construct?), temporal stability (i.e., Do psychopathic children become psychopathic adolescents and do psychopathic adolescents turn into psychopathic adults?), and, in the case of diagnoses and rating scales, interrater reliability (i.e., Do independent examiners converge on their assessment of the presence/absence of psychopathic traits for the same examinee?). In terms of internal consistency, most published studies suggest that indicators such as Cronbach's alpha are at least adequate for research and clinical purposes for most of the commonly researched assessment instruments such as the PCL:YV and the APSD (Forth et al., 2003; Frick & Hare, 2001). Regarding temporal stability and interrater reliability, however, findings are much less straightforward.

In regard to temporal stability, despite the hundreds of studies that have examined the psychopathy construct among youth in the last 10–15 years, there is relatively limited longitudinal research addressing this topic—particularly in relation to the stability of the PCL:YV, which is the only scale that appears to be widely used in clinical and forensic settings at this time. Two of the most widely cited longitudinal studies (Frick, Kimonis, Dandreaux, & Farrell, 2003; Lynam, Caspi, Moffitt, Loeber, & Stouthamer-Loeber, 2007) provide interesting insights into temporal stability as it relates to research and clinical uses of these scales. In regard to the APSD, Frick et al. (2003) reported generally high 4-year stability for these ratings in a sample of high-risk youth—a finding that has replicated reasonably well in more recent studies (e.g., Barry, Barry, Deming, & Lochman, 2008). Occasionally overlooked in the results of this study, however, is evidence of significant regression toward the mean among the participants with the highest risk. That is, those who were the most psychopathic in terms of these ratings at time 1 were unlikely to obtain scores in that range at subsequent assessments. In fact, less than half of the individuals who were initially rated as high on CU traits were again rated as high over any of the subsequent follow-up periods.

More recently, in a large sample of twins, Viding, Fontaine, Oliver, and Plomin (2009) reported substantial instability in CU traits from 7 to 12 years of age, with trajectory group analyses suggesting that approximately 80% of those who were high on CU traits had substantial decreases in these features over time. Also, it should be noted that teacher reports of CU traits appear to be less stable over time than parental reports (for a review, see Pardini & Byrd, 2013). Although such results may stem from teachers having less extensive exposure to children over extended periods, one could counterargue that if CU traits truly are stable, then they should be relatively consistent across different (teacher) raters as well, and the stability of parental ratings perhaps suggests more about the parents' perceptions of the children than the children themselves.

Results of the Lynam et al. (2007) study are in some ways even more instructive than those of Frick et al. (2003), in that they involve the prediction of scores on a Hare measure (the PCL:SV) at the time of follow-up (age 24). Lynam et al. followed a relatively large sample ($n = 271$) of at-risk individuals and controls who participated in the Pittsburgh Youth Study who had been rated on a psychopathy measure at age 13. The correlation across these two measures for total scores was .31, indicating—at the aggregate level—a significant degree of temporal stability over a very extended time period. Correlations with Facet 1 and 2 scores were only .19 and .15, respectively. Such findings indicate that, for research purposes, there is clearly sufficient stability over time to warrant further investigation of such traits from childhood into adulthood. From a practical/applied perspective, however, what should be surmised about our ability to predict whether a child at 13 with a score of X on a psychopathy scale would be likely to be rated as psychopathic on an adult instrument such as the PCL:SV? We would argue that a correlation of .31 (or .15) is of limited clinical value if one attempts to predict that a high-scoring youth will in fact end up as a high-scoring adult, particularly given the results of Frick et al. (2003), who found that high scores tend to be particularly unstable over time—as did Viding et al. (2009). Clearly, youth who appear to be the most psychopathic at a relatively early age would be at relatively greater risk to continue down this developmental pathway, but nihilistic claims that, for example, such characteristics are immutable (Edens, 2006) ignores the growing literature on the instability of these "traits" over time.

Interrater reliability data for clinicians who use the new *DSM–5* "Limited Prosocial Emotions" CD specifier have yet to be published. Although based in large part on the CU scale of the APSD, there is relatively little reason to presume that results for that scale, which suggests at best moderate convergence across parent and teacher report, will generalize to the *DSM* specifier given that these diagnoses will be based on clinical assessments that will likely incorporate multiple sources of information. That being said, the generally weaker intraclass correlations (ICCs) for PCL–R/PCL:YV Factor 1 scores do not bode extremely well for examiners' ability to condense various sources of information (i.e., interview, collateral reports, file data) into highly reliable assessments of CU traits—which largely reflect Factor 1/Facet 2 characteristics from the PCL model of psychopathy. Interrater reliability generally is high for PCL:YV total scores (ICCs ranging from .82 to .98; see Andershed, Hodgins, & Tengström, 2007;

Cauffman, Kimonis, Dmitrieva, & Monahan, 2009; Das, de Ruiter, Doreleijers, & Hillege, 2009; Forth et al., 2003). The interrater reliability for factor scores, however, is more variable, ranging from a low of .43 to .86 in research studies (Forth et al., 2003; Skeem & Cauffman, 2003).

In regard to interrater reliability, it is worth reiterating that there are reasons to question whether statistics from published research reports necessarily generalize to applied settings, given the increasing number of studies being published suggesting that the PCL–R (Hare, 2003) is less reliable in field studies examining its stability across different raters (Edens et al., 2013). As such, concerns about the applied use of the PCL:YV are not obviated by the (relatively few) research reports indicating acceptable ICCs for the total score. To our knowledge, there have been no field reliability studies published of this instrument to date. Noted earlier, these concerns are even more pronounced for the *DSM–5* specifier, where very limited information exists concerning its likely reliability in the field.

Of course, even if psychopathy assessments are relatively stable across examiners and over time, it is important to consider whether scores on these scales are malleable in response to interventions. Although discussions of the potential treatment responsiveness of psychopathic individuals lean toward the nihilistic (Edens, 2006), it is worth noting that high-fidelity empirically based interventions do appear to reduce psychopathic features in youth (D. J. Hawes & Dadds, 2007; Kolko et al., 2009; Kolko & Pardini, 2010; McDonald, Dodson, Rosenfield, & Jouriles, 2011; cf. Manders, Deković, Asscher, van der Laan, & Prins, 2013). In addition, there is evidence that recidivism rates can be reduced if appropriate interventions are enacted with highly psychopathic youthful offenders. For example, Caldwell, Skeem, Salekin, and Van Rybroek (2006) reported that adolescent offenders who received treatment that was specifically designed to reduce antisocial behavior demonstrated fewer violent acts after release and recidivated at a slower rate than adolescents who received no treatment. Caldwell et al. (2007) reported that PCL:YV scores were unrelated to treatment outcomes or rearrest after release. As such, even if psychopathy scores were reasonably stable over time (and across examiners), one should not presume that an ostensibly intractable psychopathic youth at the young age of 14 cannot respond in a positive manner to empirically based intervention efforts.

PRACTICE AND POLICY ISSUES

Evidence regarding psychopathy has gained considerable traction in judicial proceedings and correctional systems, where the construct is frequently used to address an individual's risk of future dangerousness and to inform multiple types of civil and criminal legal decisions, including indefinite commitment and capital punishment (DeMatteo & Edens, 2006; DeMatteo et al., 2014; Edens & Cox, 2012; Viljoen, MacDougall, et al., 2010). Considering the tremendous potential ramifications of such evidence, several concerns have been raised regarding the appropriate use of PCL measures in "real-world" adversarial settings (Edens, Magyar, & Cox, 2013; Edens & Petrila, 2006; Edens, Skeem, & Kennealy, 2009; Zinger & Forth, 1998). Clearly, such concerns in principle could apply to any measure of psychopathy. However, it remains the case that the PCL family of measures are by far the measures of choice in applied settings.

One relatively recent controversy surrounding the transportability of psychopathy scales from research contexts to applied settings is the generalizability of published reliability statistics. Although PCL measures have demonstrated the capacity to be scored reliably in controlled research studies, reliability is a contextual rather than static psychometric property (Hunsley & Mash, 2007). Research and applied settings drastically differ in the privacy and confidentiality of information, voluntariness of assessment, and consequences of evaluation—all of which may be important moderators of self-disclosure and impression management. Furthermore, examiners who are retained by the prosecution or defense may face external pressures that compromise the detached objectivity that is typical of research settings, resulting in adversarial allegiance, if even unwittingly (T. W. Campbell, 2006). Such partisanship has been anecdotally observed among opposing experts providing highly discrepant PCL scores for criminal defendants (see Edens,

2006; Edens & Petrila, 2006; Edens & Vincent, 2008) and has more recently been documented empirically based on field studies of PCL–R scores introduced into evidence in criminal and civil cases and experimental studies that have randomly assigned raters to work for a particular side of a case (Murrie, Boccaccini, Guarnera, & Rufino, 2013).

In the first field study to document this effect, Murrie, Boccaccini, Johnson, and Janke (2008) examined the convergence of PCL–R total scores for the same individual from experts who were called by opposing sides sexually violent predator (SVP) civil commitment cases in Texas. Concordance between state-retained and defense-retained experts across 23 cases was substantially lower ($ICC_{1A} = .39$) than PCL–R interrater reliability statistics reported in controlled research settings (typically >.80). On average, state-retained expert ratings ($M = 26$, $SD = 8.48$) exceeded those of defense-retained experts ($M = 18$, $SD = 6.62$) by an alarming eight points. After expanding the initial sample of 23 cases to 35 in a subsequent report, Murrie et al. (2009) found similarly low agreement between opposing experts' ratings ($ICC_1 = .42$) and noted that 23% of the variability in these scores was attributable to the side of the case.

More recent research has extended the study of PCL–R field reliability to other jurisdictions (DeMatteo et al., 2014). Across 29 SVP cases from multiple states in which both prosecution- and defense-retained experts provided PCL–R scores, examiner agreement accounted for just more than one-half of the variability in scores ($ICC_{A,1} = .58$). Experts who were retained by the prosecution tended to report significantly higher PCL–R scores (by ~5 points, on average), which is a trend that was reflected in prosecution scores of 30 or greater in nearly half the cases, whereas defense-retained experts reached this benchmark less than 10% of the time ($\kappa = .29$). Less pronounced but still relatively low rater agreement was also observed between competing PCL–R scores that were presented by a small sample of Crown-retained and defense-retained experts in Canadian criminal cases ($ICC_{A,1} = .67$), with score differences (~3–4 points) displaying a clear trend toward adversarial allegiance (Lloyd, Clark, & Forth, 2010). Although earlier studies could conceivably be criticized for their narrow sampling (e.g., Texas SVP cases), these latter findings indicate that lower field reliability may be a systemic, rather than local, concern.

Although field studies are certainly informative, they cannot provide conclusive evidence about the mechanisms underlying observed discrepancies in opposing experts' scores. In addition to postretention allegiance effects, retaining entities may compromise objectivity through the selection of evaluators with favorable predispositions or by calling only those examiners with supportive assessment findings. To address these possibilities, Murrie et al. (2013) conducted an experiment in which 108 forensic psychologists and psychiatrists were randomly assigned to believe that they were working on a large-scale paid forensic consultation for either the prosecution or the defense. Evaluators who were led to believe that they had been retained by the prosecution tended to assign higher PCL–R scores than their defense-retained counterparts to the four identical offender cases, with mean differences reaching more than 3 points ($d = .85$). Furthermore, 13%–33% of the opposing evaluator pairs demonstrated prosecution score elevations that were greater than twice the standard error of measurement. The experimental nature of this evidence suggests that score differences are a product of adversarial allegiance rather than preexisting differences and are evident even in situations with minimal attorney contact and exclusively file-based opinions.

These findings raise an important question: Which of the two discrepant scores provides greater predictive utility? To address this issue, Boccaccini, Turner, Murrie, and Rufino (2012) examined the extent to which PCL–R total scores from state-retained and defense-retained experts predicted future misconduct among civilly committed sexual offenders ($n = 38$). An additional 32 cases in which multiple state-retained experts evaluated the same offender were examined for comparison purposes. Concordance rates for cases between opposing experts were low ($ICC_{A,1} = .43$ to $.52$), as were concordance rates for cases that had been evaluated by two state-retained experts ($ICC_{A,1} = .40$). However, scores from both state and defense experts

demonstrated moderate to strong prediction of future misconduct (AUCs in the .70 range), suggesting that opposing experts tend to at least rank order offenders in a consistent manner. Rather than one type of examiner exhibiting superior accuracy, it appears that scores from both sides harbor equivalent predictive validity but need to be interpreted on different metrics.

Poor field reliability for PCL scores may stem not only from potential partisanship but also from bias at the level of the individual examiner. Several researchers have suggested that reliability in applied contexts is unstable even between examiners who are retained by the same entity (e.g., Boccaccini, Turner, & Murrie, 2008; Boccaccini et al., 2012; C. S. Miller, Kimonis, Otto, Kline, & Wasserman, 2012; Sturup et al., 2013). In particular, Boccaccini, Turner, et al. (2008) found evidence of sizable *examiner effects*, that is, wide variation in the average PCL–R scores that were provided across state-retained examiners conducting civil commitment evaluations. For example, two of the more prolific SVP examiners differed by almost 10 points in the mean PCL–R scores that they provided. Far from the level of objectivity one would hope for in forensic evaluations, 34% of the variability in these PCL–R scores was attributable specifically to the expert who was conducting the evaluation.

Evaluations that were conducted by mental health professionals in Florida SVP proceedings demonstrated similar problems (C. S. Miller et al., 2012). Despite being retained by the same government agency, multiple evaluators who independently interviewed and rated the same offender within the same year exhibited low rater agreement for PCL–R scores ($ICC_1 = .60$). Within the 313 cases that were examined, evaluators for the same offender reported scores that differed by approximately 5 points on average, but reached a difference of 24 points in one instance. The influence of individual differences is also evident in naturalistic research on PCL–R reliability in some European jurisdictions (Sturup et al., 2013). Among Swedish forensic examination teams that were retained by an independent government authority to repeatedly assess inmates who had been sentenced to life imprisonment ($n = 27$), interrater reliability for total PCL–R scores was somewhat lower than research-based estimates ($ICC_{1,A} = .70$). Similar reliability estimates were observed for Factor 1 and 2 scores (.62 and .76, respectively, the latter of which comes closer to research-based estimates); however, much greater variability was observed at the level of individual items (.23 to .80). Clearly, poor field reliability is not an artifact of jurisdictional idiosyncrasies, nor is the issue limited to adversarial settings, although the Swedish data come closer to research-based estimates.

Again, these findings put forth the question of how "correct" the scores of disagreeing examiners are. The implications of individual differences for field validity are not as reassuring as those put forward by comparison studies of opposing experts. An analysis of PCL–R scores that were provided by forensic examiners for 333 male sexual offenders in the context of civil commitment screening revealed that, overall, the PCL–R scores failed to significantly predict sexually violent recidivism (A. K. Murrie, Boccaccini, Caperton, & Rufino, 2012). However, scores from some examiners tended to outperform scores from others, suggesting that the predictive validity that is claimed in controlled research studies may be attenuated by characteristics of the individual who administers the evaluation, particularly in relation to community recidivism. Despite this, it should be noted that this was but one study of applied validity.

What factors might explain these differences in PCL–R scores? One reasonable explanation for the observed variations is that examiners' perceptions of psychopathic traits in others are colored by their own personality; however, corresponding investigations have produced inconclusive findings. A. K. Miller, Rufino, Boccaccini, Jackson, and Murrie (2011) found that, even after training, some psychology graduate students and doctoral-level psychologists assigned consistently higher PCL scores across cases, which were associated with self-reports of Big Five personality characteristics (e.g., individuals lower in Agreeableness tended to provide higher scores on the Interpersonal facet). Although other researchers have reported relatively few associations between psychopathy and rater personality characteristics (e.g., Edens, Clark, et al., 2013), these conflicting results are based on jury panel member's responses rather than on trained raters scoring the PCL–R. More extensive and representative studies are needed to decipher these findings because the apparent discordance may reflect genuine differences in how rater personality influences perceptions of psychopathic traits in others across dissimilar contexts.

The role of subjective judgment in psychopathy assessment suggests that some PCL items, such as grandiosity or callousness, may be more conducive to bias or random error than others, such as those based on quantifiable behaviors. Indeed, Edens, Boccaccini, and Johnson (2010) examined the field reliability of the PCL–R separated out by its factor scores in a non-adversarial forensic context and found that, even after correction for potential range restriction, Factor 1 scores demonstrated drastically poorer agreement across examiners (corrected Pearson $r = .24$) relative to total (corrected Pearson $r = .78$) and Factor 2 (corrected Pearson $r = .76$) scores. Converging results from a much larger subsequent study by C. S. Miller et al. (2012) further indicated that agreement on the Affective ($ICC_{A,1} = .39$) and Interpersonal ($ICC_{A,1} = .48$) facets of the PCL–R presents a greater challenge than does agreement on the Lifestyle ($ICC_{A,1} = .56$) and Antisocial facets ($ICC_{A,1} = .69$). In parallel to interest in the influence of rater personality, additional findings from the archival data set that was analyzed by Edens et al. (2010) point to the role of the examinee's interpersonal style in relation to difficulties in converging on PCL–R scores. Johnson, Edens, and Boccaccini (2010) reported that across 19 offenders with two PCL–R scores, discrepancies between examiners on Factor 1 scores tended to recede when the examinees self-reported an interpersonal style of high warmth ($r = -.59$) and high dominance ($r = -.52$). Although high levels of warmth and dominance may assist examiners in judgments of superficiality and propensity for manipulation, the relative absence of such interpersonal characteristics could engender greater uncertainty. Moreover, Factor 1 traits may be more vulnerable to examiners' idiosyncratic thresholds or be expressed differently depending on examiners' interviewing styles.

These data cast serious doubt on the appropriateness of extrapolating estimates of interrater reliability and, to a lesser extent, predictive validity from research studies to applied legal contexts, especially adversarial settings where scores may be biased in a partisan direction. Because an unfortunately high proportion of variance in PCL scores (particularly affective and interpersonal traits) may be attributable to individual characteristics of the examiner as well, judicial and correctional systems should exercise caution when interpreting PCL–R scores for the purpose of legal decision making. Although this area of research clearly requires expansion and replication of findings, the observed consistency of low examiner agreement highlights the need to formulate and test solutions for improving reliability outside of the lab. For example, concern has been expressed regarding the extent to which PCL–R scores that are based solely on institutional file review are comparable to those that incorporate information from both file and interview sources (Rufino, Boccaccini, Hawes, & Murrie, 2012). Additionally, estimates of reliability from published research may also be overly optimistic for other psychopathy scales that are used in real-world contexts. For instance, motivations to create a positive impression have been shown to attenuate the predictive validity of self-report measures of psychopathy (Edens & Ruiz, 2006, see more generally Lilienfeld & Fowler, 2006).

Layperson Perceptions of Psychopaths

A relatively limited number of empirical investigations have addressed layperson perceptions of psychopathy and the perceived correlates of core psychopathic traits. Not surprisingly, laypersons generally judge the disorder as being socially undesirable, bearing few to no benefits to the self, and causing deleterious consequences for others (Rauthmann & Kolar, 2012). Social rejection of psychopathic individuals may be especially heightened given that the stigma of mental illness largely hinges on perceptions of personal responsibility, dangerousness, and rarity (Feldman & Crandall, 2007), which are qualities that reasonably map onto the disorder. Furthermore, individuals in the general population may have difficulty identifying psychopathy relative to other mental disorders, such as depression (Furnham, Daoud, & Swami, 2009), and

may tend to hold unsubstantiated beliefs about mental illness in general that can result in undue stigmatization (e.g., Jorm, 2000).

A cluster of studies have suggested that laypersons tend to think of psychopaths as relatively bright and socially assertive, but also monstrous, individuals who pose a threat of future violence (Edens, Clark, et al., 2013; Furnham et al., 2009; Helfgott, 1997; Rogers, Dion, & Lynett, 1992). For example, Rogers et al. (1992) analyzed prototypical ratings of a variety of criteria for psychopathy and *DSM* criteria for antisocial personality disorder that were gathered from a community sample of 250 Canadian adults. Four primary factors were derived from these prototypical ratings: impaired relationships and deception, aggressive behavior, nonviolent delinquency, and frequent sexual relationships. Participants rated items reflecting a lack of remorse, unlawful behavior, physical aggression, and lying as most prototypical among the adult criteria examined.

Subsequent studies extended this line of research in order to capture the attitudinal undertones of layperson beliefs. Surveying 353 residents of the Seattle metropolitan area, Helfgott (1997) compiled responses to numerous open- and close-ended questions about perceptions of psychopathy, such as what first came to mind when hearing the term psychopath. For this particular question, participants frequently made references to mental disorder (72% of responses), criminal behavior (23%), and, to a much lesser extent, evil (5%). Interestingly, participants who initially associated psychopathy with criminal behavior, rather than mental disorder, tended to hold more punitive views concerning how psychopathic offenders should be treated by the legal system. Additionally, when asked to consider a variety of descriptive terms that might characterize psychopaths, many respondents endorsed clearly contemptible descriptors, such as "evil" (66%), "monster" (64%), and "morally bankrupt" (49%), but also some quasi-adaptive terms, such as "genius" (34%).

More recently, in a factor analysis of a series of attitudinal statements concerning perceptions of the behavioral manifestations, etiology, and treatment of psychopathy as provided by 232 community members in Great Britain, Furnham et al. (2009) revealed three broad dimensions: criminality, demographic factors, and intelligence and social skill, the latter of which was most strongly endorsed as being prototypical of psychopaths. Specifically, participants viewed psychopaths as smarter, more socially adept, more prone to crime and violence, more likely to be male, and more likely to come from lower socioeconomic backgrounds relative to nonpsychopaths. Drawing from these findings, Edens et al. (2012) examined the correlates of perceived psychopathic traits among a sample of 285 community members who were attending jury duty. Ratings of core features of psychopathy of a hypothetical capital murder defendant, loosely based on PCL–R trait indicators, were strongly and independently predicted by ratings on measures of boldness (i.e. social dominance and fearlessness), intelligence, probability of future violence, and perceptions that he was "evil." The overall model explained more than one-third of the variance in Factor 1 ratings ($R^2 = .35$) and more than one-fourth of the variance in the separate Interpersonal and Affective subscales ($R^2 = .28$ and $.30$, respectively), although ratings of perceived intelligence failed to significantly predict Affective ratings. Finally, the model explained 22% of the variance in Lifestyle facet scores, with ratings of boldness, evilness, and dangerousness making unique contributions. Participants were also asked open-ended queries as to whom they tended to think of when they heard the term psychopath. Mirroring previous findings (Helfgott, 1997), the most common figures identified by participants as exemplars of psychopathy were famous serial or mass murderers, including Charles Manson (20%), Jeffrey Dahmer (14%), and Ted Bundy (11%). This category was followed by political figures (16%), such as Hitler and Stalin.

Layperson perceptions of boldness, social adeptness, and intelligence are particularly interesting with respect to the recent refocusing of theoretical attention (Patrick et al., 2009; see theories of psychopathy above) on ostensibly positive or quasi-adaptive characteristics that historically have been associated (though not without disagreement by some scholars) with psychopathy by seminal researchers such as Cleckley (1941/1988). However, the public's simultaneous perception of psychopaths as violent, amoral criminals suggests the potential for stigmatization and prejudicial reactions, particularly in legal proceedings.

Implications of Ascribing the Psychopathy Label and Psychopathic Traits

Recent research has begun to address the extent to which ascribing the label psychopath or psychopathic traits to an individual influences clinical and legal decision making (Edens et al., 2009; Rendell, Huss, & Jensen, 2010). Given the abundance of misconceptions surrounding the psychopathy construct (e.g., all psychopaths are violent and untreatable, Berg et al., 2013; Edens, 2006), the potential for prejudicial reactions to an individual's reported level of psychopathic traits warrants critical examination. In one of the first studies addressing this topic, Edens, Guy, and Fernandez (2003) had undergraduates ($n = 360$) read a newspaper account of a trial, including excerpts of testimony from various witnesses that manipulated the presence/absence of psychopathic traits as descriptors of the defendant. Regarding appropriate legal sanctions for the defendant, participants who were exposed to psychopathic trait descriptors were significantly more likely to support a sentence of death (36%) compared with participants who were exposed to nonpsychopathic trait descriptors (21%).

Murrie and colleagues subsequently undertook a series of studies examining the effects of diagnostic labels of psychopathy, psychopathic characterizations, and antisocial history on professional judgments of juvenile offenders. Collectively, these studies suggest that psychopathic traits, more so than the corresponding diagnostic label, have significant potential to elicit pessimistic and punitive attitudes. For example, Murrie, Cornell, and McCoy (2005) reported that juvenile probation officers ($n = 260$) rated hypothetical youth who were exhibiting psychopathic traits as more likely to recidivate into adulthood, regardless of antisocial history, whereas diagnostic labels (e.g., "meets criteria for psychopathy") had little effect. Using a similar vignette-based approach, Murrie, Boccaccini, McCoy, and Cornell (2007) reported that the presence of psychopathic traits significantly increased the likelihood that juvenile court judges ($n = 326$)

would consider a defendant as being at risk for future violence and criminal behavior in adulthood and decreased the likelihood of a deferred adjudication recommendation.

Rockett, Murrie, and Boccaccini (2007) extended this line of research to a sample of 109 clinicians who were working in the juvenile justice system. In this study, both psychopathic trait descriptors and a diagnostic label of psychopathy influenced clinicians' risk assessments. Clinicians assigned youth who were described as meeting the criteria for psychopathy and possessing a minimal history of antisocial behavior significantly greater risk ratings than they did youth who had a diagnosis of CD and minimal antisocial history. Youth with psychopathic personality characteristics were generally considered higher risk than youth without such traits.

Boccaccini, Murrie, Clark, and Cornell (2008) continued to examine the impact of the diagnostic criteria and label of psychopathy in a large sample of jury pool members (*n* = 891), yielding similar results. However, when the previously used diagnostic statement that the defendant "meets criteria for psychopathy" was modified to "is a psychopath," jurors were more likely to perceive him as dangerous and recommend harsher sanctions. This suggests that the underwhelming influence of diagnostic labels that was observed in earlier studies by Murrie and colleagues may have been more pronounced had the more widely recognized, and perhaps more connotative, term *psychopath* been used. Contemporary studies have generally replicated these results, noting that juvenile probation officers hold especially strict and pessimistic views toward psychopathic youth (Vidal & Skeem, 2007), and judges similarly perceived such offenders as being more dangerous and warranting longer sentences (Chauhan, Reppucci, & Burnette, 2007). Both psychopathic traits and a designation of psychopath may also influence judges' opinions about juvenile defendants' amenability to treatment and placement recommendations (Jones & Cauffman, 2008).

Supplementing research on the implications of psychopathy for youth who are involved in the juvenile justice system, several studies have systematically examined the influence of psychopathic traits for adult offenders, particularly in the context of capital sentencing and civil commitment. Two of these studies manipulated a capital defendant's mental health status (psychopathy, psychosis, or no disorder) and violence risk (low or high) in order to observe the effects on undergraduate mock jurors' sentencing decisions (Edens, Colwell, Desforges, & Fernandez, 2005; Edens, Desforges, Fernandez, & Palac, 2004). Participants rated the defendant who was described as psychopathic as posing a greater threat of future dangerousness regardless of the stated risk (Edens et al., 2004) and were decidedly more likely to support execution for this defendant (60%) compared to one who was described as psychotic (30%) or one who was described as nonmentally disordered (38%; Edens et al., 2005). Using a similar methodology, Cox, DeMatteo, and Foster (2010) conducted an experiment to specifically examine any incremental effects of the label psychopath beyond those due to descriptions of psychopathic traits per se. In this study, participants were presented with vignettes that described a prototypical psychopathic defendant and altered only the diagnostic label (psychopath vs. no diagnosis) and future dangerousness (high vs. low). Regardless of diagnostic label, defendants with a higher risk of future violence were more likely to receive a death sentence.

Corroborating this general pattern of findings are several experiments that investigated the role of psychopathy in SVP civil commitment decisions (Guy & Edens, 2003, 2006). In particular, perceptions of psychopathic traits in a hypothetical defendant predicted support for civil commitment independent of testimony content (although female undergraduates were also more likely to support civil commitment when they were exposed to testimony based on psychopathy assessment vs. clinical opinion or actuarial risk assessment testimony). Likewise, Edens, Davis, Fernandez Smith, and Guy (2013) reported that global ratings of a capital murder defendant's perceived level of psychopathy, particularly core affective and interpersonal traits, strongly predicted support of a death sentence among undergraduate mock jurors (AUC = .68). Naturalistic studies, too, reflect the appreciable influence of psychopathic traits on the decision making of various legal professionals and community jurors. For example, capital jurors retrospectively reported that death sentence deliberations involve consideration of defendant characteristics such as lack of remorse, grandiosity, and callousness (Sundby, 1998). Emphasis on such traits during prosecutor summations in capital sentence hearings also appears to affect trial outcomes (Costanzo & Peterson, 1994).

Empirical research on psychopathy primarily focuses on the criminal justice system, but implications of this disorder for the workplace have received both scholarly and popular media attention, largely stemming from anecdotal accounts of corporate "snakes" (Babiak & Hare, 2006). Perhaps encouraged by such sensationalization to believe that psychopathy is both ubiquitous and readily identifiable, laypersons demonstrate a rather liberal use of the label psychopath in describing unscrupulous employees. For example, Caponecchia, Sun, and Wyatt (2012) found that a high proportion of nonbullied employees endorsed an interpersonally problematic coworker as a psychopath (41.2%), although reports of behavioral criteria based on PCL–R indicators yielded more conservative estimates (13.4%). These perceptions of prevalence deviate markedly from current epidemiological estimates of psychopathy in the general population. The discrepancy between participants' classification of a coworker when using the psychopathy label versus behavioral criteria further indicates that public conceptualizations of the disorder may emphasize extreme manifestations of the disorder, perhaps because popular sources of information on this subject, namely, online media reports, overstate the relationship between workplace bullying and psychopathy while neglecting other salient diagnostic criteria. Little empirical evidence exists regarding the ramifications of attributing objectionable workplace behaviors to a stigmatizing personality pathology; however, the perpetuation of conflict, retaliatory victimization, and even defamation proceedings have been suggested as foreseeable risks (Caponecchia et al., 2012).

These results emphasize the pronounced negative attitudes and punitive responses that psychopathic personality traits may evoke across various settings and decision makers. However, an important distinction must be made between justifiable and undue prejudicial reactions to information about psychopathy for a given individual. At times, psychopathy assessments may provide valid information for accomplishing the goals of evaluation, such as when decisions draw on established empirical associations. The danger of stigmatization enters when evaluators and consumers of psychopathy test data make unsubstantiated assertions or accentuate factors that are irrelevant to the particular legal issue at hand. For example, heavy focus on interpersonal and affective traits holds the potential for undue prejudicial impact given that they are relatively more influential in formulating attitudes toward an individual but (a) are less predictive of future risk than are antisocial and lifestyle traits and (b) are comparatively less reliable in applied settings. Forensic evaluators and other legal professionals should exercise caution in using the term psychopath or otherwise discussing the diagnostic status of psychopathy and consider both scientific and ethical merits when weighing the probative value against the prejudicial impact of psychopathy scores.

One final note touches on the influx of neuroscientific and genetic evidence of psychopathy entering the courtroom (Eastman & Campbell, 2006). Although the discussed findings imply a uniformly prejudicial response to psychopathy indicators, biological explanations of the disorder conceivably may exert an attenuating influence in legal proceedings. Aspinwall, Brown, and Tabery (2012) presented 181 U.S. state trial judges with a hypothetical case involving a convicted defendant who had been diagnosed as psychopathic in which the presence/absence of expert testimony supporting a genetic and neurological contribution to the development of psychopathy was manipulated. Judges who were exposed to biological bases of behavior perceived psychopathy as less aggravating, were more likely to identify mitigating factors, and recommended significantly shorter sentences. However, increased mention of mitigating factors occurred alongside increased concern for the adverse implications of biological evidence, such as an inability to change and future dangerousness, demonstrating the "double-edged" nature of the evidence.

SUMMARY AND CONCLUSIONS

Psychopathy remains one of the most well-studied constructs in the fields of law and psychology, forensic mental health, personality, and criminal justice. Some of our basic knowledge about it has remained similar across centuries, harkening back to Pinel (1806/1962). Psychopathy continues to fascinate and scare the public. In this chapter, we reviewed a number of contemporary issues in the field of psychopathy that have important implications in terms of the very nature of the construct itself; differing approaches to its measurement; its association with crime and violence; its performance as a function of gender, ethnicity, and age; and how psychopathy plays out in the real world.

There seems to be fairly good agreement in the aforementioned fields about certain positions:

- There is likely both a primary and a secondary manifestation of psychopathy.
- Psychopathy is dimensional rather than taxonic.
- Psychopathy elevates the risk for crime and violence, although the extent to which this is so depends in part on one's conceptualization of the contours of the construct and preferred measurement model.
- Core affective and interpersonal features of psychopathy may be less strongly related to violence than the lifestyle and impulsive antisociality aspects of the disorder, although the former appear to be preferentially associated with certain types of violence (instrumental).
- The PCL–R's association with violence, crime, and institutional infractions appears to be somewhat lower in U.S. compared to non-U.S. samples, and in samples that contain a greater proportion of minorities.
- Although the PCL–R clearly has had the most research conducted on it, several self-report measures of psychopathy have been demonstrated to have a reasonable degree of construct validity.
- The PCL–R performs reasonably well across different ethnic and cultural groups in terms of structural equivalence and construct validity but shows some evidence of metric inequivalence between North America and Europe.
- There is promise that appropriate treatment, in sufficient doses, can reduce the crime and violence of psychopathic individuals.

There are also other areas that either seem to enjoy less consensus in the research that does exist and/or have not yet been subjected to enough research to draw firm conclusions:

- How the expression, manifestation, validity, and measurement of psychopathy among women differs from men, and what if any changes to its measurement and conceptualization there should be for women;
- The long-term stability of psychopathy from childhood through adulthood, and how the disorder first develops and manifests for youth;
- *A fortiori*, the expression, manifestation, validity, and measurement of psychopathy among subgroups defined by gender, age, and ethnicity (we know almost nothing about it in, say, female Hispanic youth, or in people from developing countries);
- The extent to which boldness or FD should be considered crucial, core elements of the construct, merely specifiers, or neither (essentially independent); and
- The extent to which psychopathy can be applied in an objective, reliable, and nonprejudicial manner within real-world, adversarial settings.

We would encourage research on these latter topics. Although not discussed in the present chapter, the extent to which neuroscience can help to address some of these issues (i.e., to understand etiologies of variants or subtypes of psychopathy) will remain an important focus. Psychopathy is here to stay and will continue to play an important role within criminal justice, judicial, and mental health settings. Its reach has expanded over the past few decades and will continue to do so. For that reason, there will remain a pressing need for both theoretical and empirical (basic and applied) work on psychopathy far into the future.

References

Abrams, A. (2005). *The relationship between Psychopathic Personality Inventory scores and dissimulation on two versions of the Addiction Severity Index* (Doctoral dissertation). Alliant International University, San Diego, CA.

Alterman, A. I., Rutherford, M., Cacciola, J., McKay, J., & Boardman, C. (1998). Prediction of 7 months methadone maintenance treatment response by four measures of antisociality. *Drug and Alcohol Dependence, 49*, 217–223. doi:10.1016/S0376-8716(98)00015-5

American Psychiatric Association. (1952). *Diagnostic and statistical manual of mental disorders*. Washington, DC: Author.

American Psychiatric Association. (1968). *Diagnostic and statistical manual of mental disorders* (2nd ed.). Washington, DC: Author.

American Psychiatric Association. (2012). *Conduct disorder*. Retrieved from http://www.dsm5.org/Documents/Conduct%20Disorder%20Factsheet%20Rev%209%206%2013.pdf

American Psychiatric Association. (2013). *Diagnostic and statistical manual of mental disorders* (5th ed.). Washington, DC: Author.

Andershed, H., Hodgins, S., & Tengström, A. (2007). Convergent validity of the Youth Psychopathic Traits Inventory (YPI): Association With the Psychopathy Checklist: Youth Version (PCL:YV). *Assessment, 14*, 144–154. doi:10.1177/1073191106298286

Andrews, D. A. (2012). The risk–need–responsivity (RNR) model of correctional assessment and treatment. In J. A. Dvoskin, J. L. Skeem, R. W. Novaco, & K. S. Douglas (Eds.), *Using social science to reduce violent offending* (pp. 127–156). New York, NY: Oxford University Press.

Andrews, D. A., Bonta, J., & Wormith, J. S. (2010). The Level of Service (LS) assessment of adults and older adolescents. In R. Otto & K. S. Douglas (Eds.), *Handbook of violence risk assessment* (pp. 199–225). New York, NY: Routledge.

Anestis, J. C., Caron, K. M., & Carbonell, J. L. (2011). Examining the impact of gender on the factor structure of the Psychopathic Personality Inventory—Revised. *Assessment, 18*, 340–349. doi:10.1177/1073191111403243

Aspinwall, L. G., Brown, T. R., & Tabery, J. (2012). The double-edged sword: Does biomechanism increase or decrease judges' sentencing of psychopaths? *Science, 337*, 846–849. doi:10.1126/science.1219569

Asscher, J. J., van Vugt, E. S., Stams, G. J. J. M., Deković, M., Eichelsheim, V. I., & Yousfi, S. (2011). The relationship between juvenile psychopathic traits, delinquency and (violent) recidivism: A meta-analysis. *Journal of Child Psychology and Psychiatry, 52*, 1134–1143. doi:10.1111/j.1469-7610.2011.02412.x

Babiak, P., & Hare, R. D. (2006). *Snakes in suits: When psychopaths go to work*. New York, NY: Harper Collins.

Barry, T. D., Barry, C. T., Deming, A. M., & Lochman, J. E. (2008). Stability of psychopathic characteristics in childhood—The influence of social relationships. *Criminal Justice and Behavior, 35*, 244–262. doi:10.1177/0093854807310508

Benning, S. D., Patrick, C. J., Hicks, B. M., Blonigen, D. M., & Krueger, R. F. (2003). Factor structure of the Psychopathic Personality Inventory: Validity and implications for clinical assessment. *Psychological Assessment, 15*, 340–350. doi:10.1037/1040-3590.15.3.340

Berardino, S. D., Meloy, J. R., Sherman, M., & Jacobs, D. (2005). Validation of the Psychopathic Personality Inventory on a female inmate sample. *Behavioral Sciences and the Law, 23*, 819–836. doi:10.1002/bsl.666

Berg, J. M., Smith, S. F., Watts, A. L., Ammirati, R., Green, S. E., & Lilienfeld, S. O. (2013). Misconceptions regarding psychopathic personality: Implications for clinical practice and research. *Neuropsychiatry, 3*, 63–74. doi:10.2217/npy.12.69

Blonigen, D. M. (2013). Is fearless dominance relevant to the construct of psychopathy? Reconciling the dual roles of theory and clinical utility. *Personality Disorders: Theory, Research, and Treatment, 4*, 87–88. doi:10.1037/a0027152

Blonigen, D. M., Carlson, S. R., Krueger, R. F., & Patrick, C. J. (2003). A twin study of self-reported psychopathic personality traits. *Personality and Individual Differences, 35*, 179–197. doi:10.1016/S0191-8869(02)00184-8

Blonigen, D. M., Patrick, C. J., Douglas, K. S., Poythress, N. G., Skeem, J. L., Lilienfeld, S. O., . . . Krueger, R. F. (2010). Multimethod assessment of psychopathy in relation to factors of internalizing and externalizing from the Personality Assessment Inventory: The impact of method variance and suppressor effects. *Psychological Assessment, 22*, 96–107. doi:10.1037/a0017240

Bobadilla, L., Wampler, M., & Taylor, J. (2012). Proactive and reactive aggression are associated with different physiological and personality profiles. *Journal of Social and Clinical Psychology, 31*, 458–487. doi:10.1521/jscp.2012.31.5.458

Boccaccini, M. T., Murrie, D. C., Clark, J., & Cornell, D. (2008). Describing, diagnosing and naming psychopathy: How do youth psychopathy labels influence jurors? *Behavioral Sciences and the Law, 26*, 487–510. doi:10.1002/bsl.821

Boccaccini, M. T., Turner, D. B., Murrie, D. C., & Rufino, K. A. (2012). Do PCL–R scores from state or defense experts best predict future misconduct among civilly committed sex offenders? *Law and Human Behavior, 36*, 159–169. doi:10.1037/h0093949

Boccaccini, M. T., Turner, D. T., & Murrie, D. C. (2008). Do some evaluators report consistently higher or lower scores on the PCL–R?: Findings from a state-wide sample of sexually violent predator evaluations. *Psychology, Public Policy, and Law, 14*, 262–283. doi:10.1037/a0014523

Boer, D. P., Hart, S. D., Kropp, P. R., & Webster, C. D. (1997). *Manual for the Sexual Violence Risk—20: Professional guidelines for assessing risk of sexual violence*. Vancouver, British Columbia, Canada: British Columbia Institute on Family Violence & Mental Health, Law, and Policy Institute, Simon Fraser University.

Bolt, D. M., Hare, R. D., Vitale, J. E., & Newman, J. P. (2004). A multigroup item response theory analysis of the Psychopathy Checklist—Revised. *Psychological Assessment, 16*, 155–168. doi:10.1037/1040-3590.16.2.155

Bonta, J., Harman, W. G., Hann, R. G., & Cormier, R. B. (1996). The prediction of recidivism among federally sentenced offenders: A re-validation of the SIR scale. *Canadian Journal of Criminology, 38*, 61–79.

Borum, R., Bartel, P., & Forth, A. (2006). *Manual for the Structured Assessment of Violence Risk in Youth (SAVRY)*. Odessa, FL: Psychological Assessment Resources.

Bottos, S. (2007). *Women and violence: Theory, risk, and treatment implications*. Retrieved from http://www.csc-scc.gc.ca/text/rsrch/reports/r198/r198-eng.shtml

Brand, G. L., & Fox, M. S. (2008). *Child abuse: A painful secret*. Retrieved from http://www.ianrpubs.unl.edu/live/g1309/build/g1309.pdf

Brennan, K. A., Clark, C. L., & Shaver, P. R. (1998). Self-report measurement of adult romantic attachment: An integrative overview. In J. A. Simpson & W. S. Rholes (Eds.), *Attachment theory and close relationships* (pp. 46–76). New York, NY: Guilford Press.

Brinkley, C. A., Diamond, P. M., Magaletta, P. R., & Heigel, C. P. (2008). Cross-validation of Levenson's psychopathy scale in a sample of federal female inmates. *Assessment, 15*, 464–482. doi:10.1177/1073191108319043

Brinkley, C. A., Schmitt, W. A., Smith, S. S., & Neumann, J. P. (2001). Construct validation of self-report psychopathy scale: Does Levenson's self-report psychopathy scale measure the same constructs as Hare's Psychopathy Checklist—Revised? *Personality and Individual Differences, 31*, 1021–1038. doi:10.1016/S0191-8869(00)00178-1

Butcher, J. N., Dahlstrom, W. G., Graham, J. R., Tellegen, A., & Kaemmer, B. (1989). *The Minnesota Multiphasic Personality Inventory—2 (MMPI–2): Manual for administration and scoring*. Minneapolis: University of Minnesota Press.

Butcher, J. N., Williams, C. L., Graham, J. R., Archer, R. P., Tellegen, A., Ben-Porath, Y. S., & Kaemmer, B. (1992). *MMPI–A (Minnesota Multiphasic Personality Instrument—Adolescent): Manual for administration, scoring, and interpretation*. Minneapolis: University of Minnesota Press.

Caldwell, M., Skeem, J., Salekin, R., & Van Rybroek, G. (2006). Treatment response of adolescent offenders with psychopathy features: A 2-year follow-up. *Criminal Justice and Behavior, 33*, 571–596. doi:10.1177/0093854806288176

Caldwell, M. F., McCormick, D. J., Umstead, D., & Van Rybroek, G. J. (2007). Evidence of treatment progress and therapeutic outcomes among adolescents with psychopathic features. *Criminal Justice and Behavior, 34*, 573–587. doi:10.1177/0093854806297511

Campbell, M. A., French, S., & Gendreau, P. (2009). The prediction of violence in adult offenders: A meta-analytic comparison of instruments and methods of assessment. *Criminal Justice and Behavior, 36*, 567–590. doi:10.1177/0093854809333610

Campbell, T. W. (2006). The validity of the Psychopathy Checklist—Revised in adversarial proceedings. *Journal of Forensic Psychology Practice, 6*, 43–53. doi:10.1300/J158v06n04_03

Caponecchia, C., Sun, A. Y., & Wyatt, A. (2012). 'Psychopaths' at work? Implications of lay persons' use of labels and behavioural criteria for psychopathy. *Journal of Business Ethics, 107*, 399–408. doi:10.1007/s10551-011-1049-9

Carver, C. S., & White, T. L. (1994). Behavioral inhibition, behavioral activation, and affective responses to impending reward and punishment: The BIS/BAS scales. *Journal of Personality and Social Psychology, 67*, 319–333. doi:10.1037/0022-3514.67.2.319

Catchpole, R. E. H., & Gretton, H. M. (2003). The predictive validity of risk assessment with violent young offenders: A 1-year examination of criminal outcome. *Criminal Justice and Behavior, 30*, 688–708. doi:10.1177/0093854803256455

Cauffman, E., Kimonis, E. R., Dmitrieva, J., & Monahan, K. C. (2009). A multimethod assessment of juvenile psychopathy: Comparing the predictive utility of the PCL:YV, YPI, and NEO PRI. *Psychological Assessment, 21*, 528–542. doi:10.1037/a0017367

Chapman, A. L., Gremore, T. M., & Farmer, R. F. (2003). Psychometric analysis of the Psychopathic Personality Inventory (PPI) with female inmates. *Journal of Personality Assessment, 80*, 164–172. doi:10.1207/S15327752JPA8002_05

Chauhan, P., Reppucci, N., & Burnette, M. (2007). Application and impact of the psychopathy label to juveniles. *International Journal of Forensic Mental Health, 6*, 3–14. doi:10.1080/14999013.2007.10471245

Cima, M., & Raine, A. (2009). Distinct characteristics of psychopathy relate to different subtypes of aggression. *Personality and Individual Differences, 47,* 835–840. doi:10.1016/j.paid.2009.06.031

Cleckley, H. M. (1988). *The mask of sanity.* Oxford, England: Mosby. (Original work published 1941)

Cloninger, C. R. (1978). The link between hysteria and sociopathy. In H. S. Akiskal & W. Webb (Eds.), *Psychiatric diagnosis: Explorations of biological predictors* (pp. 189–218). New York, NY: Spectrum.

Cloninger, C. R., Christiansen, K. Q., Reich, T., & Gottesman, I. I. (1978). Implications of sex differences in the prevalences of antisocial personality, alcoholism, and criminality for familial transmission. *Archives of General Psychiatry, 35,* 941–951. doi:10.1001/archpsyc.1978.01770320035002

Convington, S. (2007). The relational theory of women's psychological development: Implications for the criminal justice system. In R. T. Zaplin (Ed.), *Female offenders: Critical perspectives and effective interventions* (2nd ed., pp. 135–165). Sudbury, MA: Jones & Bartlett.

Cooke, D., Hart, S., & Logan, C. (2005). *Comprehensive Assessment of Psychopathic Personality Disorder: Institutional Rating Scale, Version 1.1.* Unpublished manuscript.

Cooke, D. J., Hart, S. D., Logan, C., & Kreis, M. K. F. (2009, June). *Recent developments in the use of the Comprehensive Assessment of Psychopathic Personality (CAPP).* Symposium conducted at the Ninth International Association of Forensic Mental Health Services, Edinburgh, Scotland.

Cooke, D. J., Kosson, D. S., & Michie, C. (2001). Psychopathy and ethnicity: Structural, item, and test generalizability of the Psychopathy Checklist—Revised (PCL–R) in Caucasian and African American participants. *Psychological Assessment, 13,* 531–542. doi:10.1037/1040-3590.13.4.531

Cooke, D. J., Logan, C., Kreis, M. K. F., & Hoff, H. A. (2009, September). *New developments and new findings with the Comprehensive Assessment of Psychopathic Personality.* Symposium conducted at the 19th European Association of Psychology and Law Conference, Sorrento, Italy.

Cooke, D. J., & Michie, C. (1997). An item response theory analysis of Hare's Psychopathy Checklist. *Psychological Assessment, 9,* 3–14. doi:10.1037/1040-3590.9.1.3

Cooke, D. J., & Michie, C. (1999). Psychopathy across cultures: North America and Scotland compared. *Journal of Abnormal Psychology, 108,* 58–68. doi:10.1037/0021-843X.108.1.58

Cooke, D. J., & Michie, C. (2001). Refining the construct of psychopathy: Towards a hierarchical model. *Psychological Assessment, 13,* 171–188. doi:10.1037/1040-3590.13.2.171

Cooke, D. J., Michie, C., Hart, S. D., & Clark, D. A. (2004). Reconstructing psychopathy: Clarifying the significance of antisocial and socially deviant behavior in the diagnosis of psychopathic personality disorder. *Journal of Personality Disorders, 18,* 337–357.

Cooke, D. J., Michie, C., Hart, S. D., & Clark, D. (2005). Searching for the pan-cultural core of psychopathic personality disorder. *Personality and Individual Differences, 39,* 283–295. doi:10.1016/j.paid.2005.01.004

Cooke, D. J., Michie, C., & Skeem, J. (2007). Understanding the structure of the Psychopathy Checklist—Revised: An exploration of methodological confusion. *British Journal of Psychiatry, 190*(Suppl. 49), S39–S50. doi:10.1192/bjp.190.5.s39

Coolidge, F. L., Marle, P. D., Van Horn, S. A., & Segal, D. L. (2011). Clinical syndromes, personality disorders, and neurocognitive differences in male and female inmates. *Behavioral Sciences and the Law, 29,* 741–751. doi:10.1002/bsl.997

Cooney, N. L., Kadden, R. M., & Litt, M. D. (1990). A comparison of methods for assessing sociopathy in male and female alcoholics. *Journal of Studies on Alcohol, 51,* 42–48.

Cooke, D. J., Hart, S. D., Logan, C., & Michle, C. (2004). *Comprehensive Assessment of Psychopathic Personality–Institutional Rating Scale (App–IRS).* Unpublished manuscript.

Copas, J., & Marshall, P. (1998). The Offender Group Reconviction Scale: The statistical reconviction score for use by probation officers. *Journal of the Royal Statistical Society: Series C. Applied Statistics, 47,* 159–171. doi:10.1111/1467-9876.00104

Cornell, D. G., Warren, J., Hawk, G., Stafford, E., Oram, G., & Pine, D. (1996). Psychopathy in instrumental and reactive violent offenders. *Journal of Consulting and Clinical Psychology, 64,* 783–790. doi:10.1037/0022-006X.64.4.783

Corrado, R. R., Watkinson, A. V., Hart, S. D., & Cohen, I. M. (2006, June). *Comprehensive Assessment of Psychopathic Personality Disorder: Initial results with a serious and violent youth sample.* Paper presented at the 6th annual conference of the International Association for Forensic Mental Health Society, Amsterdam, the Netherlands.

Corrado, R. R., Watkinson, A. V., Hart, S. D., Lussier, P., & Cohen, I. M. (2007, July). *The interrater reliability of the Comprehensive Assessment of Psychopathic Personality.* Paper presented at the International Congress of Psychology and Law, Adelaide, Australia.

Costa, P. T., Jr., & McCrae, R. R. (1992a). The Five-Factor Model of personality and its relevance to personality disorders. *Journal of Personality Disorders, 6,* 343–359. doi:10.1521/pedi.1992.6.4.343

Costa, P. T., Jr., & McCrae, R. R. (1992b). *NEO–PI–R professional manual.* Odessa, FL: Psychological Assessment Resources.

Costa, P. T., Jr., & McCrae, R. R. (1992c). *Revised NEO Personality Inventory (NEO–PI–R) and NEO Five-Factor Inventory (NEO–FFI) professional manual.* Odessa, FL: Psychological Assessment Resources.

Costanzo, M., & Peterson, J. (1994). Attorney persuasion in the capital penalty phase: A content analysis of closing arguments. *Journal of Social Issues, 50,* 125–147. doi:10.1111/j.1540-4560.1994.tb02413.x

Cox, J., DeMatteo, D. S., & Foster, E. E. (2010). The effect of the Psychopathy Checklist—Revised in capital cases: Mock jurors' responses to the label of psychopathy. *Behavioral Sciences and the Law, 28,* 878–891. doi:10.1002/bsl.958

Crick, N. R., & Grotpeter, J. K. (1995). Relational aggression, gender, and social–psychological adjustment. *Child Development, 66,* 710–722. doi:10.2307/1131945

Crime in America.net. (2010, March). *Female involvement in crime growing: Crime news.* Paper presented at the 34th annual meeting of the Academy of Criminal Justice Sciences, Louisville, KY. Retrieved from http://crimeinamerica.net/2010/03/15/female-involvement-in-crime-growing-crime-news

Czar, K. A., Dahlen, E. R., Bullock, E. E., & Nicholson, B. C. (2011). Psychopathic personality traits in relational aggression among young adults. *Aggressive Behavior, 37,* 207–214. doi:10.1002/ab.20381

Das, J., de Ruiter, C., Doreleijers, T., & Hillege, S. (2009). Reliability and construct validity of the Dutch Psychopathy Checklist: Youth Version: Findings from a sample of male adolescents in a juvenile justice treatment institution. *Assessment, 16,* 88–102. doi:10.1177/1073191108321999

Davis, C. (2010). The affective features of psychopathy in incarcerated women. *Dissertation Abstracts International: Section B. Sciences and Engineering, 71*(3), 2043.

Decuyper, M., de Pauw, S., de Fruyt, F., de Bolle, M., & de Clercq, B. J. (2009). A meta-analysis of psychopathy-, antisocial PD- and FFM associations. *European Journal of Personality, 23,* 531–565. doi:10.1002/per.729

DeMatteo, D., & Edens, J. F. (2006). The role and relevance of the Psychopathy Checklist—Revised in court: A case law survey of U.S. courts (1991–2004). *Psychology, Public Policy, and Law, 12,* 214–241. doi:10.1037/1076-8971.12.2.214

DeMatteo, D., Edens, J. F., Galloway, M., Cox, J., Toney Smith, S., & Formon, D. (2014). The role and reliability of the Psychopathy Checklist—Revised in U.S. sexually violent predator evaluations: A case law survey. *Law and Human Behavior, 38,* 248–255. doi:10.1037/lhb0000059

DeMauro, G. E., & Leung, S. A. (2005). Review of the Psychopathic Personality Inventory—Revised. In K. F. Geisinger, R. A. Spies, J. F. Carlson, & B. S. Plake (Eds.), *The 17th mental measurements yearbook* [Electronic version]. Retrieved from http://www.ebscohost.com/academic/mental-measurements-yearbook

Derefinko, K. J., & Lynam, D. R. (2006). Convergence and divergence among self-report psychopathy measures: A personality-based approach. *Journal of Personality Disorders, 20,* 261–280. doi:10.1521/pedi.2006.20.3.261

Dillard, C. L., Barker, E. D., Salekin, R. T., & Grimes, R. D. (2013). Psychopathy in adolescent offenders: An item response theory study of the Antisocial Process Screening Device—Self Report and the Psychopathy Checklist: Youth Version. *Personality Disorders: Theory, Research, and Treatment, 4,* 101–120. doi:10.1037/a0028439

Dolan, M., & Doyle, M. (2000). Violence risk prediction: Clinical and actuarial measures and the role of the Psychopathy Checklist. *British Journal of Psychiatry, 177* 303–311.

Dolan, M., & Völlm, B. (2009). Antisocial personality disorder and psychopathy in women: A literature review on the reliability and validity of assessment instruments. *International Journal of Law and Psychiatry, 32,* 2–9. doi:10.1016/j.ijlp.2008.11.002

Douglas, K., Vincent, G., & Edens, J. (2006). Risk for criminal recidivism: The role of psychopathy. In C. J. Patrick (Ed.), *Handbook of psychopathy* (pp. 533–554). New York, NY: Guilford Press.

Douglas, K. S., Epstein, M. E., & Poythress, N. G. (2008). Criminal recidivism among juvenile offenders: Evaluating the incremental and predictive validity of three measures of psychopathic features. *Law and Human Behavior, 32,* 423–438. doi:10.1007/s10979-007-9114-8

Douglas, K. S., Nicholls, T. L., & Brink, J. (2009). Reducing the risk of violence among persons with mental illness: A critical analysis of treatment approaches. In P. M. Kleespies (Ed.), *Behavioral emergencies: An evidence-based resource for evaluating and managing risk of suicide, violence, and victimization* (pp. 351–376). Washington, DC: American Psychological Association. doi:10.1037/11865-016

Dutton, D. G. (2006). Domestic abuse assessment in child custody disputes: Beware the domestic violence research paradigm. *Journal of Child Custody, 2,* 23–42. doi:10.1300/J190v02n04_02

Eastman, N., & Campbell, C. (2006). Neuroscience and legal determination of criminal responsibility. *Nature Reviews Neuroscience, 7,* 311–318. doi:10.1038/nrn1887

Edens, J. F. (2006). Unresolved controversies concerning psychopathy: Implications for clinical and forensic decision-making. *Professional Psychology: Research and Practice, 37,* 59–65. doi:10.1037/0735-7028.37.1.59

Edens, J. F., Boccaccini, M. T., & Johnson, D. W. (2010). Inter-rater reliability of the PCL–R total and factor scores among psychopathic sex offenders: Are personality features more prone to disagreement than behavioral features? *Behavioral Sciences and the Law, 28,* 106–119. doi:10.1002/bsl.918

Edens, J. F., & Campbell, J. S. (2007). Identifying youths at risk for institutional misconduct: A meta-analytic investigation of the Psychopathy Checklist measures. *Psychological Services, 4,* 13–27. doi:10.1037/1541-1559.4.1.13

Edens, J. F., Campbell, J. S., & Weir, J. M. (2007). Youth psychopathy and criminal recidivism: A meta-analysis of the Psychopathy Checklist measures. *Law and Human Behavior, 31,* 53–75. doi:10.1007/s10979-006-9019-y

Edens, J. F., Clark, J., Smith, S. T., Cox, J., & Kelley, S. E. (2013). Bold, smart, dangerous and evil: Perceived correlates of core psychopathic traits among jury panel members. *Personality and Mental Health, 7,* 143–153.

Edens, J. F., Colwell, L. H., Desforges, D. M., & Fernandez, K. (2005). The impact of mental health evidence on support for capital punishment: Are defendants labeled psychopathic considered more deserving of death? *Behavioral Sciences and the Law, 23,* 603–625. doi:10.1002/bsl.660

Edens, J. F., & Cox, J. (2012). Examining the prevalence, role and impact of evidence regarding antisocial personality, sociopathy and psychopathy in capital cases: A survey of defense team members. *Behavioral Sciences and the Law, 30,* 239–255. doi:10.1002/bsl.2009

Edens, J. F., Davis, K. M., Fernandez Smith, K., & Guy, L. S. (2013). No sympathy for the devil: Attributing psychopathic traits to capital murderers also predicts support for executing them. *Personality Disorders: Theory, Research, and Treatment, 4,* 175–181. doi:10.1037/a0026442

Edens, J. F., Desforges, D., Fernandez, K., & Palac, C. (2004). Effects of psychopathy and violence risk testimony on mock juror perceptions of dangerousness in a capital murder trial. *Psychology, Crime & Law, 10,* 393–412. doi:10.1080/10683160310001629274

Edens, J. F., Guy, L. S., & Fernandez, K. (2003). Psychopathic traits predict attitudes toward a juvenile capital murderer. *Behavioral Sciences and the Law, 21,* 807–828. doi:10.1002/bsl.567

Edens, J. F., Magyar, M. S., & Cox, J. (2013). Taking psychopathy measures "out of the lab" and into the legal system: Some practical concerns. In K. Kiehl & W. Sinnott-Armstrong (Eds.), *Handbook on psychopathy and law* (pp. 250–272). New York, NY: Oxford University Press.

Edens, J. F., Marcus, D. K., Lilienfeld, S. O., & Poythress, N. J. (2006). Psychopathic, not psychopath:

Taxometric evidence for the dimensional structure of psychopathy. *Journal of Abnormal Psychology, 115,* 131–144. doi:10.1037/0021-843X.115.1.131

Edens, J. F., & McDermott, B. E. (2010). Examining the construct validity of the Psychopathic Personality Inventory—Revised: Preferential correlates of fearless dominance and self-centered impulsivity. *Psychological Assessment, 22,* 32–42. doi:10.1037/a0018220

Edens, J. F., & Petrila, J. (2006). Legal and ethical issues in the assessment and treatment of psychopathy. In C. Patrick (Ed.), *Handbook of psychopathy* (pp. 573–588). New York, NY: Guilford Press.

Edens, J. F., Poythress, N. G., Lilienfeld, S. O., & Patrick, C. J. (2008). A prospective comparison of two measures of psychopathy in the prediction of institutional misconduct. *Behavioral Sciences and the Law, 26,* 529–541. doi:10.1002/bsl.823

Edens, J. F. Poythress, N. G., Lilienfeld, S. O., Patrick, C. J., & Test, A. (2008) Further evidence of the divergent correlates of the Psychopathic Personality Inventory factors: Prediction of institutional misconduct among male prisoners. *Psychological Assessment, 20,* 86–91. doi:10.1037/1040-3590.20.1.86

Edens, J. F., Poythress, N. G., & Watkins, M. M. (2001). Further validation of the Psychopathic Personality Inventory among offenders: Personality and behavioral correlates. *Journal of Personality Disorders, 15,* 403–415. doi:10.1521/pedi.15.5.403.19202

Edens, J. F., & Ruiz, M. A. (2006). On the validity of validity scales: The importance of defensive responding in the prediction of institutional misconduct. *Psychological Assessment, 18,* 220–224.

Edens, J. F., Skeem, J. L., Cruise, K. R., & Cauffman, E. (2001). Assessment of "juvenile psychopathy" and its association with violence: A critical review. *Behavioral Sciences and the Law, 19,* 53–80. doi:10.1002/bsl.425

Edens, J. F., Skeem, J. L., & Kennealy, P. (2009). The Psychopathy Checklist in the courtroom: Consensus and controversies. In J. L. Skeem, K. S. Douglas, & S. O. Lilienfeld (Eds.), *Psychological science in the courtroom: Consensus and controversy* (pp. 175–201). New York, NY: Guilford Press.

Edens, J. F., Smith, S. T., Clark, J., Kristiansson, M., Sörman, K., Svensson, O., & Howner, K. (2013, June). Layperson and expert perceptions of boldness and its relation to psychopathy. In L. Drislane & N. Venables (Chairs), *Clarifying the role of boldness/fearless dominance in the psychopathy construct.* Symposium presented at the biannual conference of the Society for the Scientific Study of Psychopathy, Washington, DC.

Edens, J. F., & Vincent, G. M. (2008). Juvenile psychopathy: A clinical construct in need of restraint? *Journal of Forensic Psychology Practice, 8,* 186–197. doi:10.1080/15228930801964042

Eisenbarth, H., Osterheider, M., Nedopil, N., & Stadtland, C. (2012). Recidivism in female offenders: PCL–R lifestyle factor and VRAG show predictive validity in a German sample. *Behavioral Sciences and the Law, 30,* 575–584. doi:10.1002/bsl.2013

Epstein, M. K., Poythress, N. G., & Brandon, K. O. (2006). The Self-Report Psychopathy Scale and passive avoidance learning: A validation study of race and gender effects. *Assessment, 13,* 197–207. doi:10.1177/1073191105284992

Falkenbach, D. (2008). Psychopathy and the assessment of violence in women. *Journal of Forensic Psychology Practice, 8,* 212–224. doi:10.1080/15228930801964125

Falkenbach, D., Poythress, N., Falki, M., & Manchak, S. (2007). Reliability and validity of two self-report measures of psychopathy. *Assessment, 14,* 341–350. doi:10.1177/1073191107305612

Fazel, S., Singh, J. P., Doll, H., & Grann, M. (2012). Use of risk assessment instruments to predict violence and antisocial behaviour in 73 samples involving 24,827 people: Systematic review and meta-analysis. *British Medical Journal, 345,* e4692. doi:10.1136/bmj.e4692

Feldman, D. B., & Crandall, C. S. (2007). Dimensions of mental illness stigma: What about mental illness causes social rejection? *Journal of Social and Clinical Psychology, 26,* 137–154. doi:10.1521/jscp.2007.26.2.137

Forouzan, E., & Cooke, D. J. (2005). Figuring out la femme fatale: Conceptual and assessment issues concerning psychopathy in females. *Behavioral Sciences and the Law, 23,* 765–778. doi:10.1002/bsl.669

Forth, A. E., Brown, S. L., Hart, S. D., & Hare, R. D. (1996). The assessment of psychopathy in male and female noncriminals: Reliability and validity. *Personality and Individual Differences, 20,* 531–543. doi:10.1016/0191-8869(95)00221-9

Forth, A. E., Kosson, D. S., & Hare, R. D. (2003). *The Psychopathy Checklist: Youth Version manual.* Toronto, Ontario, Canada: Multi-Health Systems.

Frick, P., & Hare, R. D. (2001). *Technical manual for the Antisocial Process Screening Device.* North Tonawanda, NY: Multi-Health Systems.

Frick, P. J., Kimonis, E. R., Dandreaux, D. M., & Farrell, J. M. (2003). The 4 year stability of psychopathic traits in non-referred youth. *Behavioral Sciences and the Law, 21,* 713–736. doi:10.1002/bsl.568

Frick, P. J., & Marsee, M. A. (2006). Psychopathy and developmental pathways to antisocial behavior in youth. In C. J. Patrick (Ed.), *Handbook of psychopathy* (pp. 353–374). New York, NY: Guilford Press.

Frick, P. J., O'Brien, B. S., Wootton, J. M., & McBurnett, K. (1994). Psychopathy and conduct problems in children. *Journal of Abnormal Psychology, 103,* 700–707. doi:10.1037/0021-843X.103.4.700

Frick, P. J., Ray, J. V., Thornton, L. C., & Kahn, R. E. (2014). Can callous-unemotional traits enhance the understanding, diagnosis, and treatment of serious conduct problems in children and adolescents? A comprehensive review. *Psychological Bulletin, 140,* 1–57. doi:10.1037/a0033076

Furnham, A., Daoud, Y., & Swami, V. (2009). "How to spot a psychopath:" Lay theories of psychopathy. *Social Psychiatry and Psychiatric Epidemiology, 44,* 464–472. doi:10.1007/s00127-008-0459-1

Gendreau, P., Goggin, C., & Smith, P. (2002). Is the PCL–R really the 'unparalleled' measure of offender risk? A lesson in knowledge cumulation. *Criminal Justice and Behavior, 29,* 397–426. doi:10.1177/0093854802029004004

Goldstein, R. B., Powers, S. I., McCusker, J., Mundt, J., Lewis, B. F., & Bigelow, C. (1996). Gender differences in the manifestation of antisocial personality disorder among residential drug abuse treatment clients. *Drug and Alcohol Dependence, 41,* 35–45. doi:10.1016/0376-8716(96)01222-7

Gonsalves, V. M., Scalora, M. J., & Huss, M. T. (2009). Prediction of recidivism using the Psychopathy Checklist—Revised and the Psychological Inventory of Criminal Thinking Styles within a forensic sample. *Criminal Justice and Behavior, 36,* 741–756. doi:10.1177/0093854809335688

Gough, H. G., & Bradley, P. (1996). *CPI manual* (3rd ed.). Palo Alto, CA: Consulting Psychologists Press.

Guy, L. S., Douglas, K. S., & Hendry, M. (2010). The role of psychopathic personality disorder in violence risk assessments using the HCR–20. *Journal of Personality Disorders, 24,* 551–580. doi:10.1521/pedi.2010.24.5.551

Guy, L. S., & Edens, J. F. (2003). Juror decision-making in a mock sexually violent predator trial: Gender differences in the impact of divergent types of expert testimony. *Behavioral Sciences and the Law, 21,* 215–237. doi:10.1002/bsl.529

Guy, L. S., & Edens, J. F. (2006). Gender differences in attitudes toward psychopathic sexual offenders. *Behavioral Sciences and the Law, 24,* 65–85. doi:10.1002/bsl.665

Guy, L. S., Edens, J. F., Anthony, C., & Douglas, K. S. (2005). Does psychopathy predict institutional misconduct among adults? A meta-analytic investigation. *Journal of Consulting and Clinical Psychology, 73,* 1056–1064. doi:10.1037/0022-006X.73.6.1056

Hamburger, M. E., Lilienfeld, S. O., & Hogben, M. (1996). Psychopathy, gender, and gender roles: Implications for antisocial and histrionic personality disorders. *Journal of Personality Disorders, 10,* 41–55. doi:10.1521/pedi.1996.10.1.41

Hanson, R. K., & Morton-Bourgon, K. (2005). The characteristics of persistent sexual offenders: A meta-analysis of recidivism studies. *Journal of Consulting and Clinical Psychology, 73,* 1154–1163. doi:10.1037/0022-006X.73.6.1154

Hare, R. D. (1980). A research scale for the assessment of psychopathy in criminal populations. *Personality and Individual Differences, 1,* 111–119. doi:10.1016/0191-8869(80)90028-8

Hare, R. D. (1985). A comparison of procedures for the assessment of psychopathy. *Journal of Consulting and Clinical Psychology, 53,* 7–16. doi:10.1037/0022-006X.53.1.7

Hare, R. D. (1991). *The Psychopathy Checklist—Revised.* Toronto, Ontario, Canada: Multi-Health Systems.

Hare, R. D. (2003). *Hare Psychopathy Checklist—Revised (PCL–R): Technical manual* (2nd ed.). Toronto, Ontario, Canada: Multi-Health Systems.

Hare, R. D., Clark, D., Grann, M., & Thornton, D. (2000). Psychopathy and the predictive validity of the PCL–R: An international perspective. *Behavioral Sciences and the Law, 18,* 623–645. doi:10.1002/1099-0798(200010)18:5<623::AID-BSL409>3.0.CO;2-W

Hare, R. D., Harpur, T. J., & Hemphill, J. F. (1989). *Scoring pamphlet for the Self-Report Psychopathy scale: SRP–II.* Unpublished manuscript, Simon Fraser University, Vancouver, British Columbia, Canada.

Hare, R. D., & Neumann, C. S. (2006). The PCL–R assessment of psychopathy: Development, structural properties, and new directions. In C. J. Patrick (Ed.), *Handbook of psychopathy* (pp. 58–90). New York, NY: Guilford Press.

Hare, R. D., & Neumann, C. S. (2010). The role of antisociality in the psychopathy construct: Comment on Skeem and Cooke (2010). *Psychological Assessment, 22,* 446–454. doi:10.1037/a0013635

Harpur, T. J., Hakstian, A., & Hare, R. D. (1988). Factor structure of the Psychopathy Checklist. *Journal of Consulting and Clinical Psychology, 56,* 741–747. doi:10.1037/0022-006X.56.5.741

Harpur, T. J., Hare, R. D., & Hakstian, A. R. (1989). Two-factor conceptualization of psychopathy. Construct validity and assessment implications. *Psychological Assessment: A Journal of Consulting and Clinical Psychology, 1,* 6–17. doi:10.1037/1040-3590.1.1.6

Harris, G. T., Rice, M. E., & Quinsey, V. L. (1994). Psychopathy as a taxon: Evidence that psychopaths are a discrete class. *Journal of Consulting and Clinical Psychology, 62,* 387–397. doi:10.1037/0022-006X.62.2.387

Hart, S., Cox, D., & Hare, R. D. (1995). *Manual for the Psychopathy Checklist: Screening Version (PCL:SV).* Toronto, Ontario, Canada: Multi-Health Systems.

Hart, S. D. (1998a). Psychopathy and risk for violence. In D. J. Cooke, A. E. Forth, & R. D. Hare (Eds.), *Psychopathy: Theory, research and implications for society* (pp. 355–373). Dordrecht, the Netherlands: Kluwer Academic. doi:10.1007/978-94-011-3965-6_15

Hart, S. D. (1998b). The role of psychopathy in assessing risk for violence: Conceptual and methodological issues. *Legal and Criminological Psychology, 3,* 121–137. doi:10.1111/j.2044-8333.1998.tb00354.x

Hart, S. D., Watt, K. A., & Vincent, G. M. (2002). Commentary on Seagrave and Grisso: Impressions of the state of the art. *Law and Human Behavior, 26,* 241–245. doi:10.1023/A:1014648227688

Hartung, C. M., & Widiger, T. A. (1998). Gender differences in the diagnosis of mental disorders: Conclusions and controversies of the *DSM–IV. Psychological Bulletin, 123,* 260–278. doi:10.1037/0033-2909.123.3.260

Haslam, N., Holland, E., & Kuppens, P. (2012). Categories versus dimensions in personality and psychopathology: A quantitative review of taxometric research. *Psychological Medicine, 42,* 903–920. doi:10.1017/S0033291711001966

Hathaway, S. R., & McKinley, J. C. (1967). *Minnesota Multiphasic Personality Inventory manual* (Rev. ed.). New York, NY: The Psychological Corporation.

Hawes, D. J., & Dadds, M. R. (2007). Stability and malleability of callous–unemotional traits during treatment for childhood conduct problems. *Journal of Clinical Child and Adolescent Psychology, 36,* 347–355. doi:10.1080/15374410701444298

Hawes, S. W., Boccaccini, M. T., & Murrie, D. C. (2013). Psychopathy and the combination of psychopathy and sexual deviance as predictors of sexual recidivism: Meta-analytic findings using the Psychopathy Checklist—Revised. *Psychological Assessment, 25,* 233–243. doi:10.1037/a0030391

Heilbrun, K. (1992). The role of psychological testing in forensic assessment. *Law and Human Behavior, 16,* 257–272. doi:10.1007/BF01044769

Helfgott, J. B. (1997, March). *The popular conception of the psychopath: Implications for criminal justice policy and practice.* Paper presented at the 34th annual meeting of the Academy of Criminal Justice Sciences, Louisville, KY.

Hemphill, J., Templeman, R., Wong, S., & Hare, R. D. (1998). Psychopathy and crime: Recidivism and criminal careers. In D. J. Cooke, A. E. Forth, & R. D. Hare (Eds.), *Psychopathy: Theory, research, and implications for society* (pp. 375–399). Boston, MA: Kluwer Academic/Plenum. doi:10.1007/978-94-011-3965-6_16

Hemphill, J. F., Hare, R. D., & Wong, S. (1998). Psychopathy and recidivism: A review. *Legal and Criminological Psychology, 3,* 141–172.

Hiatt, K. D., & Newman, J. P. (2006). Understanding psychopathy: The cognitive side. In C. J. Patrick (Ed.), *Handbook of psychopathy* (pp. 334–352). New York, NY: Guilford Press.

Hicks, B. M., Markon, K. E., Patrick, C. J., Krueger, R. F., & Newman, J. P. (2004). Identifying psychopathy subtypes on the basis of personality structure. *Psychological Assessment, 16*, 276–288. doi:10.1037/1040-3590.16.3.276

Hoge, R. D., & Andrews, D. A. (2002). *Youth Level of Service/Case Management Inventory: User's manual.* Toronto, Ontario, Canada: Multi-Health Systems.

Hunsley, J., & Mash, E. J. (2007). Evidence-based assessment. *Annual Review of Clinical Psychology, 3*, 29–51. doi:10.1146/annurev.clinpsy.3.022806.091419

Hyler, S. E., & Rieder, R. O. (1988). *The Personality Disorder Questionnaire—Revised.* New York, NY: New York State Psychiatric Institute.

Jackson, R., & Richards, H. (2007). Psychopathy in women: A valid construct with clear implications. In H. Herve & J. C. Yuille (Eds.), *The psychopath: Theory, research, and practice* (pp. 389–410). Mahwah, NJ: Erlbaum.

Jackson, R. L., Neumann, C. S., & Vitacco, M. J. (2007). Impulsivity, anger, and psychopathy: The moderating effect of ethnicity. *Journal of Personality Disorders, 21*, 289–304. doi:10.1521/pedi.2007.21.3.289

Jackson, R. L., Rogers, R., Neumann, C. S., & Lambert, P. L. (2002). Psychopathy in female offenders: An investigation of its underlying dimensions. *Criminal Justice and Behavior, 29*, 692–704. doi:10.1177/009385402237922

Johnson, D., Edens, J. F., & Boccaccini, M. T. (2010, March). *Unreliability of PCL–R Factor 1 among sexual offenders.* Paper presented at the annual meeting of the American Psychology-Law Society, Vancouver, British Columbia, Canada.

Jones, S., & Cauffman, E. (2008). Juvenile psychopathy and judicial decision making: An empirical analysis of an ethical dilemma. *Behavioral Sciences and the Law, 26*, 151–165. doi:10.1002/bsl.792

Jones, S., Cauffman, E., Miller, J. D., & Mulvey, E. (2006). Investigating different factor structures of the Psychopathy Checklist: Youth Version: Confirmatory factor analytic findings. *Psychological Assessment, 18*, 33–48. doi:10.1037/1040-3590.18.1.33

Jones, S., & Miller, J. D. (2012). Psychopathic traits and externalizing behaviors: A comparison of self- and informant reports in the statistical prediction of externalizing behaviors. *Psychological Assessment, 24*, 255–260. doi:10.1037/a0025264

Jorm, A. F. (2000). Mental health literacy: Public knowledge and beliefs about mental disorders. *British Journal of Psychiatry, 177*, 396–401. doi:10.1192/bjp.177.5.396

Karpman, B. (1941). On the need of separating psychopathy into two distinct clinical types: The symptomatic and the idiopathic. *Journal of Criminal Psychopathology, 3*, 112–137.

Karpman, B. (1946). Psychopathy in the scheme of human typology. *Journal of Nervous and Mental Disease, 103*, 276–288. doi:10.1097/00005053-194603000-00007

Karpman, B. (1948). The myth of psychopathic personality. *American Journal of Psychiatry, 104*, 523–534. doi:10.1176/appi.ajp.104.9.523

Kastner, R. M., & Sellbom, M. (2012). Hypersexuality in college students: The role of psychopathy. *Personality and Individual Differences, 53*, 644–649. doi:10.1016/j.paid.2012.05.005

Kastner, R. M., Sellbom, M., & Lilienfeld, S. O. (2012). A comparison of the psychometric properties of the Psychopathic Personality Inventory—Full length and short-form versions. *Psychological Assessment, 24*, 261–267. doi:10.1037/a0025832

Kennealy, P. J., Skeem, J. L., Walters, G. D., & Camp, J. (2010). Do core interpersonal and affective traits of PCL–R psychopathy interact with antisocial behavior and disinhibition to predict violence? *Psychological Assessment, 22*, 569–580. doi:10.1037/a0019618

Kiehl, K., & Sinnott-Armstrong, W. (Eds.). (2013). *Handbook on psychopathy and law.* New York, NY: Oxford University Press.

Kolko, D. J., Dorn, L. D., Bukstein, O. G., Pardini, D., Holden, E. A., & Hart, J. (2009). Community vs. clinic-based modular treatment of children with early-onset ODD or CD: A clinical trial with 3-year follow-up. *Journal of Abnormal Child Psychology, 37*, 591–609. doi:10.1007/s10802-009-9303-7

Kolko, D. J., & Pardini, D. A. (2010). ODD dimensions, ADHD, and callous–unemotional traits as predictors of treatment response in children with disruptive behavior disorders. *Journal of Abnormal Psychology, 119*, 713–725. doi:10.1037/a0020910

Kosson, D. S., Smith, S. S., & Newman, J. P. (1990). Evaluating the construct validity of psychopathy in Black and White male inmates: Three preliminary studies. *Journal of Abnormal Psychology, 99*, 250–259. doi:10.1037/0021-843X.99.3.250

Kreis, M. K. (2009). *Psychopathy in women: A multimethod exploration of the construct using the Comprehensive Assessment of Psychopathic Personality (CAPP).* (Doctoral dissertation). Retrieved from British Library EthOS. (No. 517968)

Kreis, M. K. F., & Cooke, D. J. (2008, July). *Capturing the psychopathic female: Piloting the CAPP–IRS with women offenders.* Paper presented at the 8th annual conference of the International Association for Forensic Mental Health Society, Vienna, Austria.

Kreis, M. K. F., & Cooke, D. J. (2011). Capturing the psychopathic female: A prototypicality analysis of the Comprehensive Assessment of Psychopathic Personality (CAPP) across gender. *Behavioral Sciences and the Law, 29*, 634–648. doi:10.1002/bsl.1003

Kropp, P. R., Hart, S. D., Webster, C. D., & Eaves, D. (1999). *Spousal Assault Risk Assessment guide user's manual.* Toronto, Ontario, Canada: Multi-Health Systems.

Kruh, I. P., Whittemore, K., Arnaut, G. L. Y., Manley, J., Gage, B., & Gagliardi, G. J. (2005). The concurrent validity of the Psychopathic Personality Inventory and its relative association with past violence in a sample of insanity acquittees. *International Journal of Forensic Mental Health, 4,* 135–145. doi:10.1080/14999013.2005.10471219

Leistico, A.-M. R., Salekin, R. T., DeCoster, J., & Rogers, R. (2008). A larger-scale meta-analysis relating the Hare measures of psychopathy to antisocial conduct. *Law and Human Behavior, 32,* 28–45. doi:10.1007/s10979-007-9096-6

Levenson, M. R., Kiehl, K. A., & Fitzpatrick, C. M. (1995). Assessing psychopathic attributes in a non-institutionalized population. *Journal of Personality and Social Psychology, 68,* 151–158. doi:10.1037/0022-3514.68.1.151

Lilienfeld, S. O. (1990). *Development and preliminary validation of a self-report measure of psychopathic personality* (Unpublished doctoral dissertation). University of Minnesota, Minneapolis.

Lilienfeld, S. O. (2013). Is psychopathy a syndrome? Comment on Marcus, Fulton and Edens (2011). *Personality Disorders: Theory, Research, and Treatment, 4,* 85–86.

Lilienfeld, S. O., & Andrews, B. P. (1996). Development and preliminary validation of a self-report measure of psychopathic personality traits in noncriminal populations. *Journal of Personality Assessment, 66,* 488–524. doi:10.1207/s15327752jpa6603_3

Lilienfeld, S. O., & Fowler, K. (2006). The self-report assessment of psychopathy: Problems, pitfalls, and promises. In C. J. Patrick (Ed.), *Handbook of psychopathy* (pp. 107–132). New York, NY: Guilford Press.

Lilienfeld, S. O., & Hess, T. (2001). Psychopathic personality traits and somatization: Sex differences and the mediating role of negative emotionality. *Journal of Psychopathology and Behavioral Assessment, 23,* 11–24. doi:10.1023/A:1011035306061

Lilienfeld, S. O., Patrick, C. J., Benning, S. D., Berg, J., Sellbom, M., & Edens, J. F. (2012). The role of fearless dominance in psychopathy: Confusions, controversies, and clarifications. *Personality Disorders: Theory, Research, and Treatment, 3,* 327–340.

Lilienfeld, S. O., Skeem, J. L., & Poythress, N. G. (2004, March). *Psychometric properties of self-report psychopathy measures.* Paper presented at the annual meeting of the American Psychology-Law Society, Scottsdale, AZ.

Lilienfeld, S. O., Van Valkenburg, C., Larntz, K., & Akiskal, H. S. (1986). The relationship of histrionic personality disorder to antisocial personality disorder and somatization disorders. *American Journal of Psychiatry, 143,* 718–722.

Lilienfeld, S. O., & Widows, M. R. (2005). *The Psychopathic Personality Inventory—Revised (PPI–R) professional manual.* Lutz, FL: Psychological Assessment Resources.

Lloyd, C. D., Clark, H. J., & Forth, A. E. (2010). Psychopathy, expert testimony and indeterminate sentences: Exploring the relationship between Psychopathy Checklist—Revised testimony and trial outcome in Canada. *Legal and Criminological Psychology, 15,* 323–339. doi:10.1348/135552509X468432

Loeber, R., Farrington, D. P., Stouthamer-Loeber, M., Moffitt, T. E., Caspi, A., & Lynam, D. (2001). Male mental health problems, psychopathy, and personality traits: Key findings from the first 14 years of the Pittsburgh Youth Study. *Clinical Child and Family Psychology Review, 4,* 273–297. doi:10.1023/A:1013574903810

Logan, C. (2009). Psychopathy in women: Conceptual issues, clinical presentation and management. *Neuropsychiatrie (Deisenhofen), 23*(Suppl. 1), 25–33.

Logan, C., & Weizmann-Henelius, G. (2012). Psychopathy in women: Presentation, assessment, and management. In H. Häkkänen-Nyholm & J.-O. Nyholm (Eds.), *Psychopathy and law: A practitioner's guide* (pp. 99–125). Chichester, England: Wiley. doi:10.1002/9781119944980.ch5

Loucks, A. D. (1995). *Criminal behavior, violent behavior, and prison maladjustment in federal female offenders* (Unpublished doctoral dissertation). Queen's University, Kingston, Ontario, Canada.

Loucks, A. D., & Zamble, E. (2000). Predictors of criminal behaviour and prison misconduct in serious female offenders. *Empirical and Applied Criminal Justice Review, 1,* 1–47.

Louth, S. M., Hare, R. D., & Linden, W. (1998). Psychopathy and alexithymia in female offenders. *Canadian Journal of Behavioural Science/Revue, 30,* 91–98. doi:10.1037/h0085809

Lykken, D. T. (1995). *The antisocial personalities.* Hillsdale, NJ: Erlbaum.

Lykken, D. T., Tellegen, A., & Katzenmeyer, C. G. (1973). *Manual for the Activity Preference Questionnaire.* Unpublished manuscript, University of Minnesota, Minneapolis.

Lynam, D. R., Caspi, A., Moffitt, T. E., Loeber, R., & Stouthamer-Loeber, M. (2007). Longitudinal evidence that psychopathy scores in early adolescence predict adult psychopathy. *Journal of Abnormal Psychology, 116,* 155–165. doi:10.1037/0021-843X.116.1.155

Lynam, D. R., Gaughan, E. T., Miller, J. D., Miller, D. J., Mullins-Sweatt, S., & Widiger, T. A. (2011). Assessing the basic traits associated with psychopathy: Development and validation of the Elemental Psychopathy Assessment. *Psychological Assessment, 23*, 108–124. doi:10.1037/a0021146

Lynam, D. R., Loeber, R., & Stouthamer-Loeber, M. (2008). The stability of psychopathy from adolescence into adulthood: The search for moderators. *Criminal Justice and Behavior, 35*, 228–243. doi:10.1177/0093854807310153

Lynam, D. R., Whiteside, S., & Jones, S. (1999). Self-reported psychopathy: A validation study. *Journal of Personality Assessment, 73*, 110–132. doi:10.1207/S15327752JPA730108

Mahmut, M. K., Menictas, C., Stevenson, R. J., & Homewood, J. (2011). Validating the factor structure of the Self-Report Psychopathy Scale in a community sample. *Psychological Assessment, 23*, 670–678. doi:10.1037/a0023090

Malterer, M. B., Lilienfeld, S. O., Neumann, C. S., & Newman, J. P. (2010). Concurrent validity of the Psychopathic Personality Inventory with offender and community samples. *Assessment, 17*, 3–15. doi:10.1177/1073191109349743

Manders, W. A., Deković, M., Asscher, J. J., van der Laan, P. H., & Prins, P. J. M. (2013). Psychopathy as predictor and moderator of multisystemic therapy outcomes among adolescents treated for antisocial behavior. *Journal of Abnormal Child Psychology, 41*, 1121–1132. doi:10.1007/s10802-013-9749-5

Marcus, D. K., Edens, J. F., & Fulton, J. J. (2013). Is it the inventory, the meta-analysis, or the construct? Reply to the comments on Marcus, Fulton, and Edens. *Personality Disorders: Theory, Research, and Treatment, 4*, 89–90. doi:10.1037/a0027219

Marcus, D. K., Fulton, J. J., & Edens, J. F. (2013). The two-factor model of psychopathic personality: Evidence from the Psychopathic Personality Inventory. *Personality Disorders: Theory, Research, and Treatment, 4*, 67–76. doi:10.1037/a0025282

Marcus, D. K., Poythress, N. G., Edens, J. F., & Lilienfeld, S. O. (2010). Adjudicative competence: Evidence that impairment in 'rational understanding' is taxonic. *Psychological Assessment, 22*, 716–722. doi:10.1037/a0020131

Marsee, M. A., Silverthorn, P., & Frick, P. J. (2005). The association of psychopathic traits with aggression and delinquency in non-referred boys and girls. *Behavioral Sciences and the Law, 23*, 803–817. doi:10.1002/bsl.662

McCormick, A. V., Corrado, R. R., Hart, S. D., & Cohen, I. M. (2008, July). *Interrater reliability and internal consistency reliability of the CAPP–IRS among incarcerated young offenders.* Paper presented at the 8th annual conference of the International Association for Forensic Mental Health Society, Vienna, Austria.

McDermott, B. E., Edens, J. F., Quanbeck, C. D., Busse, D., & Scott, C. L. (2008). Examining the role of static and dynamic risk factors in the prediction of inpatient violence: Variable- and person-focused analyses. *Law and Human Behavior, 32*, 325–338. doi:10.1007/s10979-007-9094-8

McDonald, R., Dodson, M. C., Rosenfield, D., & Jouriles, E. N. (2011). Effects of a parenting intervention on features of psychopathy in children. *Journal of Abnormal Child Psychology, 39*, 1013–1023. doi:10.1007/s10802-011-9512-8

McKeown, A. (2010). Female offenders: Assessment of risk in forensic settings. *Aggression and Violent Behavior, 15*, 422–429. doi:10.1016/j.avb.2010.07.004

Meehl, P. E. (1977). Specific etiology and other forms of strong influence: Some quantitative meanings. *Journal of Medicine and Philosophy, 2*, 33–53. doi:10.1093/jmp/2.1.33

Meehl, P. E. (1986). Causes and effects of my disturbing little book. *Journal of Personality Assessment, 50*, 370–375.

Meehl, P. E. (1995). Bootstraps taxometrics: Solving the classification problem in psychopathology. *American Psychologist, 50*, 266–275. doi:10.1037/0003-066X.50.4.266

Meehl, P. E., & Yonce, L. J. (1994). Taxometric analysis: I. Detecting taxonicity with two quantitative indicators using means above and below a sliding cut (MAMBAC procedure). *Psychological Reports, 74*, 1059–1274.

Meehl, P. E., & Yonce, L. J. (1996). Taxometric analysis: II. Detecting taxonicity using covariance of two quantitative indicators in successive intervals of a third indicator (MAXCOV procedure). *Psychological Reports, 78*, 1091–1227. doi:10.2466/pr0.1996.78.3c.1091

Miller, A. K., Rufino, K. A., Boccaccini, M. T., Jackson, R. L., & Murrie, D. C. (2011). On individual differences in person perception: Raters' personality traits relate to their Psychopathy Checklist—Revised scoring tendencies. *Assessment, 18*, 253–260. doi:10.1177/1073191111402460

Miller, C. S., Kimonis, E. R., Otto, R. K., Kline, S. M., & Wasserman, A. L. (2012). Reliability of risk assessment measures used in sexually violent predator proceedings. *Psychological Assessment, 24*, 944–953. doi:10.1037/a0028411

Miller, J. D., & Lynam, D. R. (2012). An examination of the Psychopathic Personality Inventory's nomological network: A meta-analytic review. *Personality Disorders: Theory, Research, and Treatment, 3*, 305–326. doi:10.1037/a0024567

Miller, J. D., Watts, A., & Jones, S. E. (2011). Does psychopathy manifest divergent relations with components of its nomological network depending on gender? *Personality and Individual Differences, 50,* 564–569. doi:10.1016/j.paid.2010.11.028

Millon, T. (1987). *Millon Clinical Multiaxial Inventory—II manual.* Minneapolis, MN: National Computer Systems.

Monahan, J., Steadman, H. J., Silver, E., Appelbaum, P. S., Robbins, P. C., Mulvey, E. P., . . . Banks, S. (2001). *Rethinking risk assessment: The MacArthur Study of Mental Disorder and Violence.* New York, NY: Oxford University Press.

Morey, L. C. (1991). *Personality Assessment Inventory: Professional manual.* Tampa, FL: Psychological Assessment Resources.

Morey, L. C. (2007). *Personality Assessment Inventory: Professional manual* (2nd ed.). Lutz, FL: Psychological Assessment Resources.

Morrissey, C., Cooke, D., Michie, C., Hollin, C., Hogue, T., Lindsay, W. R., & Taylor, J. (2010). Structural, item, and test generalizability of the Psychopathy Checklist—Revised to offenders with intellectual disabilities. *Assessment, 17,* 16–29. doi:10.1177/1073191109344052

Morrissey, C., Mooney, P., Hogue, T., Lindsay, W., & Taylor, J. (2007). Predictive validity of the PCL–R for offenders with intellectual disability in a high security hospital: Treatment progress. *Journal of Intellectual and Developmental Disability, 32,* 125–133. doi:10.1080/13668250701383116

Murrie, D. C., Boccaccini, M. T., Caperton, J., & Rufino, K. (2012). Field validity of the Psychopathy Checklist—Revised in sex offender risk assessment. *Psychological Assessment, 24,* 524–529. doi:10.1037/a0026015

Murrie, D. C., Boccaccini, M. T., Guarnera, L. A., & Rufino, K. (2013). Are forensic experts biased by the side that retained them? *Psychological Science, 24,* 1889–1897. doi:10.1177/0956797613481812

Murrie, D. C., Boccaccini, M., Johnson, J., & Janke, C. (2008). Does interrater (dis)agreement on Psychopathy Checklist scores in sexually violent predator trials suggest partisan allegiance in forensic evaluations? *Law and Human Behavior, 32,* 352–362. doi:10.1007/s10979-007-9097-5

Murrie, D. C., Boccaccini, M., McCoy, W., & Cornell, D. (2007). Diagnostic labeling in juvenile court: How do descriptions of psychopathy and conduct disorder influence judges? *Journal of Clinical Child and Adolescent Psychology, 36,* 228–241. doi:10.1080/15374410701279602

Murrie, D. C., Boccaccini, M., Turner, D., Meeks, M., Woods, C., & Tussey, C. (2009). Rater (dis)agreement on risk assessment measures in sexually violent predator proceedings: Evidence of adversarial allegiance in forensic evaluation? *Psychology, Public Policy, and Law, 15,* 19–53. doi:10.1037/a0014897

Murrie, D. C., Cornell, D. G., & McCoy, W. K. (2005). Psychopathy, conduct disorder and stigma: Does diagnostic labeling influence juvenile probation officer recommendations? *Law and Human Behavior, 29,* 323–342. doi:10.1007/s10979-005-2415-x

Neal, T. M. S., & Sellbom, M. (2012). Examining the factor structure of the Hare Self-Report Psychopathy Scale. *Journal of Personality Assessment, 94,* 244–253. doi:10.1080/00223891.2011.648294

Neary, A. (1990). *DSM–III and psychopathy checklist assessment of antisocial personality disorder in Black and White female felons* (Unpublished doctoral dissertation). University of Missouri, St. Louis.

Neumann, C. S., Hare, R. D., & Johansson, P. T. (2013). The Psychopathy Checklist—Revised (PCL–R), low anxiety, and fearlessness: A structural equation modeling analysis. *Personality Disorders: Theory, Research, and Treatment, 4,* 129–137.

Neumann, C. S., Hare, R. D., & Newman, J. P. (2007). The superordinate nature of the Psychopathy Checklist—Revised. *Journal of Personality Disorders, 21,* 102–117. doi:10.1521/pedi.2007.21.2.102

Nicholls, T. L., Odgers, C. L., & Cooke, D. J. (2007). Women and girls with psychopathic characteristics. In A. R. Felthous & H. Sass (Eds.), *International handbook on psychopathic disorders and the law* (Vol. 1, pp. 347–366). New York, NY: Wiley.

Nicholls, T. L., Ogloff, J. R., Brink, J., & Spidel, A. (2005). Psychopathy in women: A review of its clinical usefulness for assessing risk for aggression and criminality. *Behavioral Sciences and the Law, 23,* 779–802. doi:10.1002/bsl.678

Nicholls, T. L., & Petrila, J. (2005). Gender and psychopathy: An overview of important issues and introduction to the special issue. *Behavioral Sciences and the Law, 23,* 729–741. doi:10.1002/bsl.677

Nikolova, N. L. (2009). *Comprehensive Assessment of Psychopathic Personality Disorder—Institutional Rating Scale (CAPP–IRS)–validation* (Unpublished master's thesis). Simon Fraser University, Burnaby, British Columbia, Canada.

Novaco, R. (1994). Anger as a risk factor for violence among the mentally disordered. In J. Monahan & H. J. Steadman (Eds.), *Violence and mental disorder* (pp. 21–59). Chicago, IL: University of Chicago Press.

O'Connor, D. A. (2003). The female psychopath: Validity and factor structure of the revised Psychopathy Checklist (PCL–R) in women inmates. *Dissertation Abstracts International: Section B. Sciences and Engineering, 63*(12), 6101.

Odgers, C. L., Reppucci, N. D., & Moretti, M. M. (2005). Nipping psychopathy in the bud: An examination of the convergent, predictive, and theoretical utility of the PCL–YV among adolescent girls. *Behavioral Sciences and the Law, 23,* 743–763. doi:10.1002/bsl.664

Ogloff, J., Wong, S., & Greenwood, A. (1990). Treating criminal psychopaths in a therapeutic community program. *Behavioral Sciences and the Law*, 8, 181–190. doi:10.1002/bsl.2370080210

Olver, M. E., Neumann, C. S., Wong, S. P., & Hare, R. D. (2013). The structural and predictive properties of the Psychopathy Checklist—Revised in Canadian Aboriginal and non-Aboriginal offenders. *Psychological Assessment*, 25, 167–179. doi:10.1037/a0029840

Olver, M. E., Stockdale, K. C., & Wormith, J. S. (2009). Risk assessment with young offenders: A meta-analysis of three assessment measures. *Criminal Justice and Behavior*, 36, 329–353. doi:10.1177/0093854809331457

Pardini, D. A., & Byrd, A. L. (2013). Developmental conceptualizations of psychopathic features. In K. A. Kiehl & W. Sinnott-Armstrong (Eds.), *Handbook on psychopathy and law* (pp. 61–77). New York, NY: Oxford University Press.

Paris, J. (2007). An overview on gender, personality and mental health. *Personality and Mental Health*, 1, 14–20. doi:10.1002/pmh.1

Patrick, C. J. (1994). Emotion and psychopathy: Startling new insights. *Psychophysiology*, 31, 319–330. doi:10.1111/j.1469-8986.1994.tb02440.x

Patrick, C. J. (2006). Back to the future: Cleckley as a guide to the next generation of psychopathy research. In C. J. Patrick (Ed.), *Handbook of psychopathy* (pp. 605–617). New York, NY: Guilford Press.

Patrick, C. J., Fowles, D. C., & Krueger, R. F. (2009). Triarchic conceptualization of psychopathy: Developmental origins of disinhibition, boldness, and meanness. *Development and Psychopathology*, 21, 913–938. doi:10.1017/S0954579409000492

Patrick, C. J., Venables, N. C., & Drislane, L. E. (2013). The role of fearless dominance in differentiating psychopathy from antisocial personality disorder: Comment on Marcus, Fulton, and Edens. *Personality Disorders: Theory, Research, and Treatment*, 4, 80–82. doi:10.1037/a0027173

Paulhus, D. L., Neumann, C. S., & Hare, R. D. (2009). *Manual for the Self-Report Psychopathy Scale (SRP–III)*. Toronto, Ontario, Canada: Multi-Health Systems.

Paulhus, D. L., & Williams, K. M. (2002). The dark triad of personality: Narcissism, Machiavellianism, and psychopathy. *Journal of Research in Personality*, 36, 556–563. doi:10.1016/S0092-6566(02)00505-6

Pedersen, L., Kunz, C., Rasmussen, K., & Elsass, P. (2010). Psychopathy as a risk factor for violent recidivism: Investigating the Psychopathy Checklist Screening Version (PCL:SV) and the Comprehensive Assessment of Psychopathic Personality (CAPP) in a forensic psychiatric setting. *International Journal of Forensic Mental Health*, 9, 308–315. doi:10.1080/14999013.2010.526681

Penney, S. R., & Morretti, M. M. (2007). The relation of psychopathy to concurrent aggression and antisocial behavior in high-risk adolescent girls and boys. *Behavioral Sciences and the Law*, 25, 21–41. doi:10.1002/bsl.715

Perri, S. F., & Lichtenwald, T. G. (2010, Summer). The last frontier: Myths and the female psychopathic killer. *Forensic Examiner*, 50–67

Pinel, P. (1962). *A treatise on insanity* (D. Davis, trans.). New York, NY: Hafner. (Original work published 1806)

Porter, S., & Woodworth, M. (2007). 'I'm sorry I did it . . . but he started it': A comparison of the official and self-reported homicide descriptions of psychopaths and non-psychopaths. *Law and Human Behavior*, 31, 91–107. doi:10.1007/s10979-006-9033-0

Poythress, N. G., Edens, J. F., & Lilienfeld, S. O. (1998). Criterion-related validity of the Psychopathic Personality Inventory in a prison sample. *Psychological Assessment*, 10, 426–430. doi:10.1037/1040-3590.10.4.426

Poythress, N. G., Lilienfeld, S. O., Skeem, J. L., Douglas, K. S., Edens, J. F., Epstein, M., & Patrick, C. J. (2010). Using the PCL–R to help estimate the validity of two self-report measures of psychopathy with offenders. *Assessment*, 17, 206–219. doi:10.1177/1073191109351715

Poythress, N. G., & Petrila, J. (2010). PCL–R psychopathy: Threats to sue, peer review, and potential implications for science and law. A commentary. *International Journal of Forensic Mental Health*, 9, 3–10. doi:10.1080/14999013.2010.483346

Pratto, F., Sidanius, J., & Levin, S. (2006). Social dominance theory and the dynamics of intergroup relations: Taking stock and looking forward. *European Review of Social Psychology*, 17, 271–320. doi:10.1080/10463280601055772

Quinsey, V. L., Harris, G. T., Rice, M. R., & Cormier, C. A. (1998). *Violent offenders: Appraising and managing risk*. Washington, DC: American Psychological Association.

Rauthmann, J. F., & Kolar, G. P. (2012). How "dark" are the dark triad traits? Examining the perceived darkness of narcissism, Machiavellianism, and psychopathy. *Personality and Individual Differences*, 53, 884–889.

Ray, J. V., Hall, J., Rivera-Hudson, N., Poythress, N. G., Lilienfeld, S. O., & Morano, M. (2012, January 23). The relation between self-reported psychopathic traits and distorted response styles: A meta-analytic review. *Personality Disorders: Theory, Research, and Treatment*. Advance online publication. doi:10.1037/a0026482

Ray, J. V., Poythress, N. G., Weir, J. M., & Rickelm, A. (2009). Relationships between psychopathy and impulsivity in the domain of self-reported personality features. *Personality and Individual Differences, 46,* 83–87. doi:10.1016/j.paid.2008.09.005

Rendell, J. A., Huss, M. T., & Jensen, M. L. (2010). Expert testimony and the effects of a biological approach, psychopathy, and juror attitudes in cases of insanity. *Behavioral Sciences and the Law, 28,* 411–425. doi:10.1002/bsl.913

Rice, M., Harris, G., & Cormier, C. (1992). An evaluation of a maximum security therapeutic community for psychopaths and other mentally disordered offenders. *Law and Human Behavior, 16,* 399–412. doi:10.1007/BF02352266

Richards, H. J., Casey, J. O., & Lucente, S. W. (2003). Psychopathy and treatment response in incarcerated female substance users. *Criminal Justice and Behavior, 30,* 251–276. doi:10.1177/0093854802251010

Robbins, P. C., Monahan, J., & Silver, E. (2003). Mental disorders, violence, and gender. *Law and Human Behavior, 27,* 561–571. doi:10.1023/B:LAHU.0000004886.13268.f2

Rock, R. C., Sellbom, M., Ben-Porath, Y., & Salekin, R. T. (2013). Concurrent and predictive validity of psychopathy in a batterers' intervention sample. *Law and Human Behavior, 37,* 145–154. doi:10.1037/lhb0000006

Rockett, J. L., Murrie, D. C., & Boccaccini, M. (2007). Diagnostic labeling in juvenile justice settings: Do psychopathy and conduct disorder findings influence clinicians? *Psychological Services, 4,* 107–122. doi:10.1037/1541-1559.4.2.107

Rogers, R., Dion, K. L., & Lynett, E. (1992). Diagnostic validity of antisocial personality disorder. *Law and Human Behavior, 16,* 677–689. doi:10.1007/BF01884023

Rogers, R., Vitacco, M. J., Jackson, R. L., Martin, M., Collins, M., & Sewell, K. W. (2002). Faking psychopathy? An examination of response styles with antisocial youth. *Journal of Personality Assessment, 78,* 31–46.

Rosner, J. (2004). Concurrent validity of the Psychopathic Personality Inventory. *Dissertation Abstracts International: Section B. Sciences and Engineering, 65*(6), 3181.

Ross, J. M. (2011). Personality and situational correlates of self-reported reasons for partner violence among women versus men referred for batterers' intervention. *Behavioral Sciences and the Law, 29,* 711–727. doi:10.1002/bsl.1004

Ross, S. R., Benning, S. D., Patrick, C. J., Thompson, A., & Thurston, A. (2008). Factors of the Psychopathic Personality Inventory: Criterion-related validity and relationship to the BIS/BAS and Five-Factor Models of personality. *Assessment, 16,* 71–87. doi:10.1177/1073191108322207

Rufino, K. A., Boccaccini, M. T., Hawes, S. W., & Murrie, D. C. (2012). When experts disagreed, who was correct? A comparison of PCL–R scores from independent raters and opposing forensic experts. *Law and Human Behavior, 36,* 527–537. doi:10.1037/h0093988

Ruscio, J., Haslam, N., & Ruscio, A. M. (2006). *Introduction to the taxometric method: A practical guide.* Mahwah, NJ: Erlbaum.

Russell, L. A. (2005). Examination of the Psychopathic Personality Inventory—Revised and the psychopathy construct in a college sample. *Dissertation Abstracts International: Section B. Sciences and Engineering, 65*(8), 4303.

Rutherford, M. J., Cacciola, J. S., Alterman, A. I., & McKay, J. R. (1996). Reliability and validity of the Revised Psychopathy Checklist in women methadone patients. *Assessment, 3,* 145–156.

Salekin, R. T. (2002). Psychopathy and therapeutic pessimism: Clinical lore or clinical reality? *Clinical Psychology Review, 22,* 79–112. doi:10.1016/S0272-7358(01)00083-6

Salekin, R. T. (2006). Psychopathy in children and adolescents: Key issues in conceptualization and assessment. In C. J. Patrick (Ed.), *Handbook of psychopathy* (pp. 389–414). New York, NY: Guilford Press.

Salekin, R. T., & Lynam, D. R. (Eds.). (2011). *Handbook of child and adolescent psychopathy.* New York, NY: Guilford Press.

Salekin, R. T., Rogers, R., & Sewell, K. W. (1996). A review and meta-analysis of the Psychopathy Checklist and Psychopathy Checklist—Revised: Predictive validity of dangerousness. *Clinical Psychology: Science and Practice, 3,* 203–215. doi:10.1111/j.1468-2850.1996.tb00071.x

Salekin, R. T., Rogers, R., & Sewell, K. W. (1997). Construct validity of psychopathy in a female offender sample: A multitrait–multimethod evaluation. *Journal of Abnormal Psychology, 106,* 576–585. doi:10.1037/0021-843X.106.4.576

Salekin, R. T., Rogers, R., Ustad, K. L., & Sewell, K. W. (1998). Psychopathy and recidivism among female inmates. *Law and Human Behavior, 22,* 109–128. doi:10.1023/A:1025780806538

Salekin, R. T., Trobst, K. K., & Krioukova, M. (2001). Construct validity of psychopathy in a community sample: A nomological net approach. *Journal of Personality Disorders, 15,* 425–441. doi:10.1521/pedi.15.5.425.19196

Sanders, B., & Giolas, M. H. (1991). Dissociation and childhood trauma in psychologically disturbed adolescents. *American Journal of Psychiatry, 148,* 50–54.

Sandoval, A.-M. R., Hancock, D., Poythress, N., Edens, J. F., & Lilienfeld, S. (2000). Construct validity of the Psychopathic Personality Inventory in a correctional sample. *Journal of Personality Assessment, 74,* 262–281. doi:10.1207/S15327752JPA7402_7

Schmeelk, K. M., Sylvers, P., & Lilienfeld, S. O. (2008). Trait correlates of relational aggression in a nonclinical sample: DSM–IV personality disorders and psychopathy. *Journal of Personality Disorders, 22,* 269–283. doi:10.1521/pedi.2008.22.3.269

Schrum, C. L., & Salekin, R. T. (2006). Psychopathy in adolescent female offenders: An item response theory analysis of the Psychopathy Checklist: Youth Version. *Behavioral Sciences and the Law, 24,* 39–63. doi:10.1002/bsl.679

Seagrave, D., & Grisso, T. (2002). Adolescent development and the measurement of juvenile psychopathy. *Law and Human Behavior, 26,* 219–239. doi:10.1023/A:1014696110850

Seibert, L. A., Miller, J. D., Few, L. R., Zeichner, A., & Lynam, D. R. (2011). An examination of the structure of self-report psychopathy measures and their relations with general traits and externalizing behaviors. *Personality Disorders: Theory, Research, and Treatment, 2,* 193–208. doi:10.1037/a0019232

Sellbom, M. (2011). Elaborating on the construct validity of the Levenson Self-Report Psychopathy Scale in incarcerated and non-incarcerated samples. *Law and Human Behavior, 35,* 440–451. doi:10.1007/s10979-010-9249-x

Sellbom, M., Ben-Porath, Y. S., Lilienfeld, S. O., Patrick, C. J., & Graham, J. R. (2005). Assessing psychopathic personality traits with the MMPI–2. *Journal of Personality Assessment, 85,* 334–343. doi:10.1207/s15327752jpa8503_10

Sentencing Project. (2007). *Women in the criminal justice system: Briefing sheets.* Retrieved from http://www.sentencingproject.org/doc/publications/womenincj_total.pdf

Sevecke, K., Lehmkuhl, G., & Krischer, M. K. (2009). Examining relations between psychopathology and psychopathy dimensions among adolescent female and male offenders. *European Child and Adolescent Psychiatry, 18,* 85–95. doi:10.1007/s00787-008-0707-7

Sevecke, K., Pukrop, R., Kosson, D. S., & Krischer, M. K. (2009). Factor structure of the Hare Psychopathy Checklist: Youth Version in German female and male detainees and community adolescents. *Psychological Assessment, 21,* 45–56. doi:10.1037/a0015032

Sidanius, J., & Pratto, F. (1999). *Social dominance: An intergroup theory of social hierarchy and oppression.* New York, NY: Cambridge University Press. doi:10.1017/CBO9781139175043

Silverthorn, P., & Frick, P. J. (1999). Developmental pathways to antisocial behavior: The delayed onset pathway in girls. *Development and Psychopathology, 11,* 101–126. doi:10.1017/S0954579499001972

Silverthorn, P., Frick, P. J., & Reynolds, R. (2001). Timing of onset and correlates of severe problems in adjudicated girls and boys. *Journal of Psychopathology and Behavioral Assessment, 23,* 171–181. doi:10.1023/A:1010917304587

Singh, J. P., Grann, M., & Fazel, S. (2011). A comparative study of violence risk assessment tools: A systematic review and metaregression analysis of 68 studies involving 25,980 participants. *Clinical Psychology Review, 31,* 499–513. doi:10.1016/j.cpr.2010.11.009

Skeem, J., Douglas, K., Edens, J., Poythress, N., & Lilienfeld, S. (2005, March). Whether and how antisocial and psychopathic traits moderate the effect of substance abuse treatment. In N. Poythress (Chair), *Research in antisocial personality and psychopathy.* Symposium conducted at the annual conference of the American Psychology-Law Society, San Diego, CA.

Skeem, J., Johansson, P., Andershed, H., Kerr, M., & Louden, J. E. (2007). Two subtypes of psychopathic violent offenders that parallel primary and secondary variants. *Journal of Abnormal Psychology, 116,* 395–409. doi:10.1037/0021-843X.116.2.395

Skeem, J. L., & Cauffman, E. (2003). Views of the downward extension: Comparing the youth version of the Psychopathy Checklist with the Youth Psychopathic Traits Inventory. *Behavioral Sciences and the Law, 21,* 737–770. doi:10.1002/bsl.563

Skeem, J. L., & Cooke, D. J. (2010). Is criminal behavior a central component of psychopathy? Conceptual directions for resolving the debate. *Psychological Assessment, 22,* 433–445. doi:10.1037/a0008512

Skeem, J. L., Edens, J. F., Camp, J., & Colwell, L. H. (2004). Are there ethnic differences in levels of psychopathy? A meta-analysis. *Law and Human Behavior, 28,* 505–527. doi:10.1023/B:LAHU.0000046431.93095.d8

Skeem, J. L., & Lilienfeld, S. O. (2004, March). *Psychometric properties of self-report psychopathy measures.* Paper presented at the annual meeting of the American Psychology-Law Society, Scottsdale, AZ.

Skeem, J. L., Monahan, J., & Mulvey, E. (2002). Psychopathy, treatment involvement, and subsequent violence among civil psychiatric patients. *Law and Human Behavior, 26,* 577–603. doi:10.1023/A:1020993916404

Skeem, J. L., Mulvey, E. P., & Grisso, T. (2003). Applicability of traditional and revised models of psychopathy to the Psychopathy Checklist: Screening Version. *Psychological Assessment, 15,* 41–55. doi:10.1037/1040-3590.15.1.41

Skeem, J. L., Polaschek, D. L. L., & Manchak, S. (2009). Appropriate treatment works, but how? Rehabilitating general, psychopathic, and high risk offenders. In J. L. Skeem, K. S. Douglas, & S. O. Lilienfeld (Eds.), *Psychological science in the courtroom: Controversies and consensus* (pp. 358–384). New York, NY: Guilford Press.

Skeem, J. L., Polaschek, D. L. L., Patrick, C. J., & Lilienfeld, S. O. (2011). Psychopathic personality: Bridging the gap between scientific evidence and public policy. *Psychological Science in the Public Interest, 12,* 95–162. doi:10.1177/1529100611426706

Smith, G. T., McCarthy, D. M., & Anderson, K. G. (2000). On the sins of short-form development. *Psychological Assessment, 12,* 102–111. doi:10.1037/1040-3590.12.1.102

Smith, S. T., Edens, J. F., & McDermott, B. (2011, March). *Predicting specific types of inpatient aggression with the PPI–R.* Paper presented at the 4th International Congress on Psychology and Law, Miami, FL.

Smith, S. T., Edens, J. F., & McDermott, B. E. (2013). Fearless dominance and self-centered impulsivity interact to predict predatory aggression among forensic inpatients. *International Journal of Forensic Mental Health, 12,* 33–41. doi:10.1080/14999013.2012.760186

Sörman, K., Edens, J. F., Smith, S. T., Svensson, O., Howner, K., Kristiansson, M., & Fischer, H. (2014). Forensic mental health professionals' perceptions of psychopathy: A prototypicality analysis of the comprehensive assessment of psychopathic personality in Sweden. *Law and Human Behavior.* Advance online publication. doi:10.1037/lhb0000072

Sprague, J., Javdani, S., Sadeh, N., Newman, J. P., & Verona, E. (2012). Borderline personality disorder as a female phenotypic expression of psychopathy? *Personality Disorders: Theory, Research, and Treatment, 3,* 127–139. doi:10.1037/a0024134

Stafford, E., & Cornell, D. G. (2003). Psychopathy scores predict adolescent inpatient aggression. *Assessment, 10,* 102–112. doi:10.1177/1073191102250341

Steinberg, L. (2002). The juvenile psychopath: Fads, fictions, and facts. In *National Institute of Justice perspectives on crime and justice: 2001 lecture series* (Vol. 5, pp. 35–64). Washington, DC: U.S. Department of Justice.

Stickle, T. R., Marini, V. A., & Thomas, J. N. (2012). Gender differences in psychopathic traits, types, and correlates of aggression among adjudicated youth. *Journal of Abnormal Child Psychology, 40,* 513–525. doi:10.1007/s10802-011-9588-1

Stockdale, K. C., Olver, M. E., & Wong, S. P. (2010). The Psychopathy Checklist: Youth Version and adolescent and adult recidivism: Considerations with respect to gender, ethnicity, and age. *Psychological Assessment, 22,* 768–781. doi:10.1037/a0020044

Strachan, C. E. (1993). *The assessment of psychopathy in female offenders* (Unpublished doctoral dissertation). University of British Columbia, Vancouver, British Columbia, Canada.

Strand, S., & Belfrage, H. (2001). Comparison of HCR–20 scores in violent mentally disordered men and women: Gender differences and similarities. *Psychology, Crime & Law, 7,* 71–79. doi:10.1080/10683160108401784

Strand, S., & Belfrage, H. (2005). Gender differences in psychopathy in a Swedish offender sample. *Behavioral Sciences and the Law, 23,* 837–850. doi:10.1002/bsl.674

Strub, D. S., Kreis, M. K. F., & Hart, S. D. (2008, July). *A new approach to the assessment of psychopathy: Discriminant and convergent validity of the CAPP across personality disorder clusters.* Paper presented at the 8th annual conference of the International Association for Forensic Mental Health Society, Vienna, Austria.

Sturup, J., Edens, J. F., Sorman, K., Karlberg, D., Fredriksson, B., & Kristiansson, M. (2013). *Field reliability of the Psychopathy Checklist—Revised among life sentenced prisoners in Sweden.* Unpublished manuscript.

Sundby, S. E. (1998). The capital jury and absolution: The intersection of trial strategy, remorse, and the death penalty. *Cornell Law Review, 83,* 1557–1598.

Swogger, M. T., Walsh, Z., & Kosson, D. S. (2008). Psychopathy subtypes among African American county jail inmates. *Criminal Justice and Behavior, 35,* 1484–1499. doi:10.1177/0093854808324506

Taylor, J., & Lang, A. (2006). Psychopathy and substance use disorders. In C. J. Patrick (Ed.), *Handbook of psychopathy* (pp. 495–511). New York, NY: Guilford Press.

Tellegen, A. (in press). *Manual for the Multidimensional Personality Questionnaire.* Minneapolis: University of Minnesota Press.

Thornquist, M. H., & Zuckerman, M. (1995). Psychopathy, passive avoidance learning, and basic dimensions of personality. *Personality and Individual Differences, 19,* 525–534. doi:10.1016/0191-8869(95)00051-7

Tien, G., Lamb, D., Bond, L., Gillstrom, B., & Paris, F. (1993). *Report on the needs assessment of women at the Burnaby Correctional Centre for Women.* Burnaby, British Columbia, Canada: Institute of Family Violence.

Uzieblo, K., Verschuere, B., Van den Bussche, E., & Crombez, G. (2010). The validity of the Psychopathic Personality Inventory—Revised in a community sample. *Assessment, 17,* 334–346. doi:10.1177/1073191109356544

Vablais, C. M. (2007). Toward a new model of psychopathy in women: A qualitative analysis of the Psychopathy Checklist—Revised and the construct of psychopathy in female offenders. *Dissertation Abstracts International: Section B. Sciences and Engineering, 68*(2), 1323.

Vachon, D. D., Lynam, D. R., Loeber, R., & Stouthamer-Loeber, M. (2012). Generalizing the nomological network of psychopathy across populations differing on race and conviction status. *Journal of Abnormal Psychology, 121*, 263–269. doi:10.1037/a0024683

Vassileva, J., Kosson, D. S., Abramowitz, C., & Conrod, P. (2005). Psychopathy versus psychopathies in classifying criminal offenders. *Legal and Criminological Psychology, 10*, 27–43. doi:10.1348/135532504X15376

Vaughn, M. G., Edens, J. F., Howard, M. O., & Smith, S. T. (2009). An investigation of primary and secondary psychopathy in a statewide sample of incarcerated youth. *Youth Violence and Juvenile Justice, 7*, 172–188. doi:10.1177/1541204009333792

Verona, E., & Carbonell, J. L. (2000). Female violence and personality: Evidence for a pattern of overcontrolled hostility among one-time violent female offenders. *Criminal Justice and Behavior, 27*, 176–195. doi:10.1177/0093854800027002003

Verona, E., Patrick, C. J., & Joiner, T. T. (2001). Psychopathy, antisocial personality and suicide attempt history risk. *Journal of Abnormal Psychology, 110*, 462–470. doi:10.1037/0021-843X.110.3.462

Verona, E., & Vitale, J. (2006). Psychopathy in women: Assessment, manifestation and etiology. In C. J. Patrick (Ed.), *Handbook of psychopathy* (pp. 415–436). New York, NY: Guilford Press.

Vidal, S., & Skeem, J. L. (2007). Effect of psychopathy, abuse, and ethnicity on juvenile probation officers' decision-making and supervision strategies. *Law and Human Behavior, 31*, 479–498. doi:10.1007/s10979-006-9077-1

Viding, E., Fontaine, N. M., Oliver, B. R., & Plomin, R. (2009). Negative parental discipline, conduct problems and callous–unemotional traits: Monozygotic twin differences study. *British Journal of Psychiatry, 195*, 414–419. doi:10.1192/bjp.bp.108.061192

Viljoen, J. L., MacDougall, E. A., Gagnon, N. C., & Douglas, K. S. (2010). Psychopathy evidence in legal proceedings involving adolescent offenders. *Psychology, Public Policy, and Law, 16*, 254–283. doi:10.1037/a0019649

Viljoen, J. L., McLachlan, K., & Vincent, G. M. (2010). Assessing violence risk and psychopathy in juvenile and adult offenders: A survey of clinical practices. *Assessment, 17*, 377–395. doi:10.1177/1073191109359587

Vincent, G. M., Odgers, C., McCormick, A., & Corrado, R. (2008). The PCL:YV and recidivism in male and female juveniles: A follow-up into young adulthood. Psychopathy and risk taxation. *International Journal of Law and Psychiatry, 31*, 287–296. doi:10.1016/j.ijlp.2008.04.012

Vitacco, M. J., Neumann, C. S., & Jackson, R. L. (2005). Testing a four-factor model of psychopathy and its association with ethnicity, gender, intelligence, and violence. *Journal of Consulting and Clinical Psychology, 73*, 466–476. doi:10.1037/0022-006X.73.3.466

Vitacco, M. J., & Salekin, R. T. (2013). Adolescent psychopathy and the law. In K. A. Kiehl & W. Sinnott-Armstrong (Eds.), *Handbook on psychopathy and law* (pp. 78–89). New York, NY: Oxford University Press.

Vitale, J. E., Smith, S. S., Brinkley, C. A., & Newman, J. P. (2002). The reliability and validity of the Psychopathy Checklist—Revised in a sample of female offenders. *Criminal Justice and Behavior, 29*, 202–231. doi:10.1177/0093854802029002005

Walsh, Z. (2013). Psychopathy and criminal violence: The moderating effect of ethnicity. *Law and Human Behavior, 37*, 303–311. doi:10.1037/lhb0000017

Walsh, Z., Swogger, M. T., & Kosson, D. S. (2009). Psychopathy and instrumental violence: Facet level relationships. *Journal of Personality Disorders, 23*, 416–424. doi:10.1521/pedi.2009.23.4.416

Walters, G. D. (1995). The Psychological Inventory of Criminal Thinking Styles: Part I. Reliability and preliminary validity. *Criminal Justice and Behavior, 22*, 307–325. doi:10.1177/0093854895022003008

Walters, G. D. (2003a). Predicting criminal justice outcomes with the Psychopathy Checklist and Lifestyle Criminality Screening Form: A meta-analytic comparison. *Behavioral Sciences and the Law, 21*, 89–102. doi:10.1002/bsl.519

Walters, G. D. (2003b). Predicting institutional adjustment and recidivism with the Psychopathy Checklist factor scores: A meta-analysis. *Law and Human Behavior, 27*, 541–558. doi:10.1023/A:1025490207678

Walters, G. D. (2006). Risk-appraisal versus self-report in the prediction of criminal justice outcomes: A meta-analysis. *Criminal Justice and Behavior, 33*, 279–304. doi:10.1177/0093854805284409

Walters, G. D. (2009). The Psychological Inventory of Criminal Thinking Styles and Psychopathy Checklist: Screening Version as incrementally valid predictors of recidivism. *Law and Human Behavior, 33*, 497–505. doi:10.1007/s10979-008-9167-3

Walters, G. D. (2011). Psychopathy and crime: Testing the incremental validity of PCL–R-measured psychopathy as a predictor of general and violent recidivism. *Law and Human Behavior*. Advance online publication. doi:10.1037/h0093928

Walters, G. D. (2012). Psychopathy and crime: Testing the incremental validity of PCL–R-measured psychopathy as a predictor of general and violent recidivism. *Law and Human Behavior, 36*, 404–412. doi:10.1037/h0093928

Walters, G. D., & Heilbrun, K. (2010). Violence risk assessment and Facet 4 of the Psychopathy Checklist: Predicting institutional and community aggression in two forensic samples. *Assessment, 17*, 259–268. doi:10.1177/1073191109356685

Walters, G. D., Knight, R. A., Grann, M., & Dahle, K.-P. (2008). Incremental validity of the Psychopathy Checklist facet scores: Predicting release outcome in six samples. *Journal of Abnormal Psychology, 117*, 396–405. doi:10.1037/0021-843X.117.2.396

Walters, G. D., Wilson, N. J., & Glover, A. J. J. (2011). Predicting recidivism with the Psychopathy Checklist: Are factor score composites really necessary? *Psychological Assessment, 23*, 552–557. doi:10.1037/a0022483

Warren, J. I., Burnette, M. L., South, S. C., Preeti, C., Bale, R., Friend, R., & Van Patten, I. (2003). Psychopathy in women: Structural modeling and comorbidity. *International Journal of Law and Psychiatry, 26*, 223–242. doi:10.1016/S0160-2527(03)00034-7

Watkinson, A. V., Corrado, R. R., Lussier, P., Hart, S. D., & Cohen, I. M. (2007, July). *Comprehensive Assessment of Psychopathic Personality Disorder and the Psychopathy Checklist: Youth Version.* Paper presented at the 7th annual conference of the International Association for Forensic Mental Health Society, Montreal, Quebec, Canada.

Webster, C. D. (1999). *Risk assessment and risk management with women offenders.* Ottawa, Ontario, Canada: National Parole Board, Ottawa.

Webster, C. D., Douglas, K. S., Eaves, D., & Hart, S. D. (1997). *HCR–20: Assessing Risk for Violence (Version 2).* Burnaby, British Columbia, Canada: Mental Health, Law, and Policy Institute, Simon Fraser University.

Weiler, B. L., & Widom, C. S. (1996). Psychopathy and violent behavior in abused and neglected young adults. *Criminal Behaviour and Mental Health, 6*, 253–271. doi:10.1002/cbm.99

Weisz, J. R., Suwanlert, S., Chaiyasit, W., & Walter, B. R. (1987). Over-and undercontrolled referral problems among children and adolescents from Thailand and the United States: The Wat and Wai of cultural differences. *Journal of Consulting and Clinical Psychology, 55*, 719–726. doi:10.1037/0022-006X.55.5.719

Weizmann-Henelius, G., Putkonen, H., Grönroos, M., Lindberg, N., Eronen, M., & Häkkänen-Nyholm, H. (2010). Examination of psychopathy in female homicide offenders—Confirmatory factor analysis of the PCL–R. *International Journal of Law and Psychiatry, 33*, 177–183. doi:10.1016/j.ijlp.2010.03.008

Weizmann-Henelius, G., Viemero, V., & Eronen, M. (2004). Psychological risk markers in violent female behavior. *International Journal of Forensic Mental Health, 3*, 185–196. doi:10.1080/14999013.2004.10471206

Williams, K. M., & Paulhus, D. L. (2004). Factor structure of the Self-Report Psychopathy Scale (SRP–II) in non-forensic samples. *Personality and Individual Differences, 37*, 765–778. doi:10.1016/j.paid.2003.11.004

Williams, K. M., Paulhus, D. L., & Hare, R. D. (2007). Capturing the four-factor structure of psychopathy in college students via self-report. *Journal of Personality Assessment, 88*, 205–219. doi:10.1080/00223890701268074

Wilson, D. L., Frick, P. J., & Clements, C. B. (1999). Gender, somatization, and psychopathic traits in a college sample. *Journal of Psychopathology and Behavioral Assessment, 21*, 221–235. doi:10.1023/A:1022825415137

Witt, E. A., Donnellan, M. B., Blonigen, D. M., Krueger, R. F., & Conger, R. D. (2009). Assessment of fearless dominance and impulsive antisociality via normal personality measures: Convergent validity, criterion validity, and developmental change. *Journal of Personality Assessment, 91*, 265–276. doi:10.1080/00223890902794317

Woltil, J. M. (2011). Validity study of the Psychopathic Personality Inventory in a noncriminal population. *Dissertation Abstracts International: Section B. Sciences and Engineering, 72*(1), 562.

Woodworth, M., & Porter, S. (2002). In cold blood: Characteristics of criminal homicides as a function of psychopathy. *Journal of Abnormal Psychology, 111*, 436–445. doi:10.1037/0021-843X.111.3.436

Wynn, R., Hoiseth, M. H., & Pettersen, G. (2012). Psychopathy in women: Theoretical and clinical perspectives. *International. Journal of Women's Health, 4*, 257–263. doi:10.2147/IJWH.S25518

Yang, M., Wong, S. P., & Coid, J. (2010). The efficacy of violence prediction: A meta-analytic comparison of nine risk assessment tools. *Psychological Bulletin, 136*, 740–767. doi:10.1037/a0020473

Zágon, I., & Jackson, H. (1994). Construct validity of a psychopathy measure. *Personality and Individual Differences, 17*, 125–135. doi:10.1016/0191-8869(94)90269-0

Zinger, I., & Forth, A. (1998). Psychopathy and Canadian criminal proceedings: The potential for human rights abuses. *Canadian Journal of Criminology, 40*, 237–276.

CHAPTER 10

SUBSTANCE USE AND CRIME

David DeMatteo, Sarah Filone, and Jennie Davis

A great deal of research over the past few decades has firmly documented the relationship between substance use and criminal behavior. The rate of drug involvement among criminal offenders is so extensive that it is arguably a false dichotomy to talk about individuals who commit crimes and those who use substances as being separate populations. As such, substance use takes on increased relevance among a criminal justice population. For example, because research suggests that substance use is a robust risk factor for criminal behavior and recidivism, substance use is a relevant consideration when designing treatment plans for correctional and forensic populations. Furthermore, given the established link between substance use and crime, forensic mental health professionals often encounter substance use among the offenders they evaluate. In forensic assessment contexts, substance use may be relevant to several forensic issues, including assessments that are focused on some types of criminal competencies, mental state at the time of the offense, and sentencing. It is therefore imperative that forensic mental health professionals have a sufficient understanding of how substance use may relate to the legal issue being addressed.

This chapter discusses the relationship between substance use and crime, with a particular focus on how substance use is relevant for forensic mental health professionals. We begin by highlighting the prevalence of substance use, among both the general population and criminal offenders. Next, we review relevant psychological theories relating to the etiology of substance use, which suggest that substance

use is a complex and multidetermined phenomenon. Then, we summarize the voluminous empirical research literature on the relationship between substance use and crime, including research on various interventions and outcomes for substance users. We then discuss the relevance of substance use to forensic psychology, with a specific focus on how substance use may be relevant to an individual's competence, criminal responsibility, and sentencing. Finally, we conclude the chapter by summarizing key points and highlighting several areas for future research.

IMPORTANCE OF THE PROBLEM

Substance use is a significant public health concern in the United States. According to 2010 data from the National Survey on Drug Use and Health (NSDUH), which was sponsored by the Substance Abuse and Mental Health Services Administration (SAMHSA; 2011), 22.6 million Americans ages 12 or older were current users (past month) of illicit drugs. This represents roughly 9% of all Americans ages 12 or older and indicates that illicit drug use is continuing to increase. The 2010 SAMHSA data also indicated that drug use increased among adolescents and young adults, with 10.1% of youth ages 12 to 17 and 21.5% of young adults ages 18 to 25 reporting current drug use (past month; SAMHSA, 2011). In 2010, 3 million people ages 12 or older used an illicit drug for the first time within the past 12 months (SAMHSA, 2011). Finally, in 2010, 22.1 million Americans ages 12 or older met the diagnostic

http://dx.doi.org/10.1037/14461-010
APA Handbook of Forensic Psychology: Vol. 1. Individual and Situational Influences in Criminal and Civil Contexts,
B. L. Cutler and P. A. Zapf (Editors-in-Chief)

criteria for substance abuse or dependence in the 1 year prior to the NSDUH survey (SAMHSA, 2011).

Compared to the rate of drug use in the general population, the rate of drug use among criminal offenders is staggering. Substance users are disproportionally represented in the criminal justice system. Perhaps the most sobering statistic to illustrate this point is that more than 80% of U.S. criminal offenders meet a broad definition of substance involvement—meaning that they were arrested for a substance-related offense, were intoxicated at the time of the offense, committed the offense to support a drug habit, or have a history of serious substance use (National Center on Addiction and Substance Abuse, 2010). In addition, roughly half of all drug-involved criminal offenders satisfy the diagnostic criteria for substance abuse or dependence (Fazel, Bains, & Doll, 2006).

A closer look at the criminal justice population reveals the extent of drug involvement. Multisite studies have shown that large portions of adult arrestees—averaging more than 60%—tested positive for at least one illicit drug at the time of arrest (Office of National Drug Control Policy, 2012). Moreover, illicit drug use is implicated in 50% of violent crimes (National Institute of Justice [NIJ], 2000), 50% of domestic violence crimes (Center for Substance Abuse Treatment, 2000), 60%–80% of substantiated child abuse and neglect cases (Child Welfare League of America, 1990), 50%–75% of theft and property offenses (NIJ, 2000), and 75%–99% of prostitution and drug dealing/manufacturing offenses (NIJ, 2000).

Among prisoners who are released from incarceration, drug-using offenders have substantially higher rates of criminal recidivism and relapse to drug use than their nondrug-using counterparts. Without treatment, roughly 85% of drug-using offenders relapse to drug use within the first 6 to 12 months after release from incarceration (Beck & Shipley, 1989; Hanlon, Nurco, Bateman, & O'Grady, 1998), and that figure increases to 95% within 3 years of release (Martin, Butzin, Saum, & Inciardi, 1999). In addition, within 3 years of release, 68% of drug-using offenders are rearrested, 47% are reconvicted, and 25% are sentenced to prison for a new crime (Langan & Levin, 2002). Indeed, research

suggests that continued substance use is associated with a 200%–400% increase in the likelihood of recidivism (Bennett, Holloway, & Farrington, 2008).

The costs of substance use are considerable, reflecting the effects of drugs on crime, productivity, health, underemployment, and family stability. The Office of National Drug Control Policy (2011) estimated the total cost of illegal drug use in the United States at $193 billion in 2007, and that number has increased since then. This figure represents roughly $120 billion in lost productivity, $11 billion in health care costs (for drug treatment and drug-related medical consequences), and $61 billion in criminal justice costs (due to criminal investigation, prosecution, incarceration, and victim costs).

RELEVANT PSYCHOLOGICAL THEORIES AND PRINCIPLES

Substance use is a complex phenomenon, and like many complex phenomena, the etiology and maintenance of substance use are determined by multiple factors. Fortunately, over the past several decades, researchers in various disciplines have made great strides in identifying the causal and associated factors for substance use. The resulting literature is vast, complex, and difficult to synthesize. For example, the factors that contribute to the *initiation* of substance use often differ from the factors that contribute to the *maintenance* of substance use, and the factors that underlie substance use cut across several domains. In this section, we focus on the physiological, psychological, and social factors underlying substance use (see Chapter 8, this volume for a review of theories of crime and criminal behavior).

Biological Perspectives

Biological theories explain substance use etiology in terms of the brain's neuropsychological predisposition to addiction and the acute and chronic effects of drugs on the brain. Some risk factors for drug use appear to be inherited, but environmental factors also play a role. To that effect, numerous studies have identified differences in the brains of drug users and those of nondrug users. It is important, however, to distinguish between features that predate drug use and changes that result from drug use, as repeated administration of addictive substances strengthens the maladaptive neuronal links that develop in response to drug use. Because not every individual who is predisposed to substance use develops a substance use problem, researchers are still trying to determine to what extent nature and nurture interact.

The biopsychology of addiction. Many researchers believe that the reward circuit underlies drug addiction (Luscher & Bellone, 2008). The reward circuit involves several brain areas that are associated with learning, reinforcement, and the mediation of goal-directed behavior, including the nucleus accumbens, ventral tegmental area (VTA), prefrontal cortex, amygdala, basal ganglia, and possibly the hippocampus (Kalivas & Volkow, 2005). The nucleus accumbens in particular is considered the addiction center of the brain due to its involvement in motivation, its wealth of dopamine receptors, and the fact that many drugs increase dopamine levels in the nucleus accumbens (Dackis & O'Brien, 2001; Leshner & Koob, 1999).

Dopamine, the neurotransmitter that is associated with pleasure and positive reinforcement, is heavily implicated in the drug addiction literature because addictive drugs block the reuptake or stimulate the release of more dopamine into the reward circuitry, thereby prolonging its effects. The brain adapts to excess dopamine by producing less dopamine and/or reducing the number of dopamine receptors in the area (Kauer & Malenka, 2007). As a result, the drug's impact on the reward circuit is lessened, thereby reducing the user's ability to enjoy the drug (i.e., tolerance). The down regulation of dopamine receptors in the ventral striatum is associated with craving severity in chronic drug users, and repeated drug ingestion dysregulates glutaminergic projections to the nucleus accumbens, reducing the value of and physiological response to natural rewards, such as food, sex, and social interaction, and contributing to the compulsive drug-seeking behavior (Kalavis & Volkow, 2005).

Stress mechanisms also play a role in substance use, as stress hormones called glucocorticoids produce physiological effects and feed back into the reward circuitry. Exposure to stressors activates the hypothalamic-pituitary-adrenal (HPA) axis, which secretes glucocorticoids and triggers the release of dopamine in the VTA and nucleus accumbens. This sensitizes the reward system to the effects of substances, making the individual more responsive to the substance and priming the brain for addiction (Goeders, 2004; Sinha, 2008). The brain experiences a large influx of stress hormones during drug binges, but the HPA axis is reactivated during withdrawal, causing an uncomfortable state of heightened nervous system arousal that helps explain why exposure to stressors can trigger relapse (Koob & Kreek, 2007).

Physiological effects of substance use. Different substances have a variety of acute and long-term effects on physiological functioning. Substance use affects the central nervous system (CNS), producing changes in an individual's mood, awareness, perception, and sensation. Individual predispositions and pharmacokinetics also play a role in how a drug impacts the body. The addictive potential of a drug depends on the substance itself and individual vulnerability, but generally speaking, substances that produce more immediate, intense effects have greater abuse potential. Furthermore, certain drugs make other similar drugs more reinforcing, which helps to explain polysubstance use (e.g., Helzer & Pryzbeck, 1988).

CNS stimulants such as cocaine, nicotine, and amphetamine derivatives cause heightened alertness and energy, pleasant feelings, and euphoria. Stimulants prolong the rewarding effects of dopamine by blocking reuptake, reducing the number of dopamine receptors in the brain, and triggering the release of additional dopamine, thereby making stimulants positively reinforcing and highly addictive (Pihl, 2009). Cocaine, for example, blocks dopamine reuptake in the nucleus accumbens and reduces the inhibitory effects of gamma-aminobutyric acid (GABA), thereby allowing the release of more dopamine. Cocaine also causes serotonin dysregulation, which is associated with behavioral disinhibition and heightened sensitivity to stress and threats.

Amphetamines prolong the effects of norepinephrine by blocking its reuptake and stimulating the release of more norepinephrine (Luscher & Ungless, 2006). Once stimulant intoxication wears off, the user may feel depressed and crave another dose, with studies showing that rebound craving after cocaine administration exceeds the baseline level of craving (e.g., Dackis & O'Brien, 2001).

CNS depressants such as alcohol, anxiolytics (e.g., benzodiazepines, barbiturates), and other sedatives facilitate relaxation, relieve pain, and reduce anxiety. Depressants work by strengthening GABA's inhibitory effects. Alcohol decreases excitatory neurotransmission and thereby decreases overall physiological arousal, and heavy alcohol consumption further reduces GABA receptor density, contributing to tolerance, dependence, and withdrawal (Pihl, 2009). GABA dysregulation also indirectly stimulates dopamine release in the nucleus accumbens, VTA, and substantia nigra (Stacy, Ames, Wiers, & Krank, 2010), which helps explain alcohol's rewarding properties and addictive potential. Alcohol affects an individual's mood by decreasing serotonergic functioning (Pihl, 2009).

Opioids such as morphine, methadone, and heroin are also CNS depressants. There is an endogenous opioid system in the brain and opioid receptors throughout the body, and the body secretes endogenous opioids in order to achieve palliative results and possibly a slight euphoric high. Endogenous opioids are positively reinforcing and underlie rewards from natural stimuli. The brain is therefore primed for addiction to synthetic opioids that bind to endogenous opioid receptors. Opioids decrease the transmission of glutamate and GABA, which has the net effect of increasing the release of dopamine into the reward circuit (Cruz, Bajo, Scwheitzer, & Roberto, 2008; Luscher & Ungless, 2006). Opioids are highly addictive because their use results in the down regulation of opioid receptors in the brain and spinal cord, causing rapid development of tolerance to, dependence on, and withdrawal from the substances' analgesic effects.

Cannabis alters the physiological processes that are related to an individual's cognition, movement, appetite, and pain sensation. Cannabinoid receptors are abundant in the brain, particularly in the cerebellum, cortex, hippocampus, and striatum (Cruz et al., 2008). The active ingredient in cannabis, tetrahydrocanabinol, interacts with the opioid system, particularly cannabinoid receptors in the nucleus accumbens and VTA, to stimulate the release of dopamine, which produces analgesia, modulates stress, stimulates hunger, and has an overall rewarding effect. Although cannabis is the most commonly abused illicit drug in the Unites States (SAMHSA, 2011), research on its addictive potential has produced mixed findings. Cannabis does not seem to down regulate dopamine receptors in the brain like other addictive drugs.

Hallucinogens such as lysergic acid diethylamide (LSD) and psychedelic mushrooms produce distortions of visual, auditory, and tactile perception and can induce psychosis. They are often grouped together with dissociative anesthetics, such as phencyclidine (PCP) and ketamine (National Institute on Drug Abuse, 2001). Hallucinogens, being chemically similar to serotonin, have an affinity for serotonin receptors and thereby disrupt serotonergic functioning in the locus ceruleus (responsible for sensory signaling) and in brain areas that are involved with mood, cognition, and perception. Dissociative drugs stimulate glutamate release into the cortex, which is involved with perception and memory. Although these substances are widely abused, there is no clear consensus on their addictive properties (Luscher & Ungless, 2006).

3,4-methylenedioxy-N-methylamphetamine (MDMA, or Ecstasy) is a psychoactive drug with hallucinogenic and stimulant properties. MDMA blocks the reuptake of serotonin and releases more serotonin into the synapse, prolonging its effects and producing feelings of euphoria, energy, and distorted perceptions. MDMA also stimulates the release of norepinephrine, and its effects are further mediated by the dopaminergic system (Tancer & Johanson, 2003). Although these mechanisms are less studied, dopamine involvement likely contributes to MDMA's acute reinforcing effects. The addictive potential of MDMA is also due to the withdrawal following intoxication: The user may feel confused, anxious, and depressed; may have trouble sleeping; and may desire to use the drug again.

Nature versus nurture. The etiology of substance use is influenced by both genetic (e.g., metabolic, physiological, psychological) and environmental factors. To examine the independent influences of nature and nurture on the etiology of substance use, researchers have turned to twin and adoption studies.

Studies have shown that twin resemblances for substance use are high and are greater among monozygotic than dizygotic twins (Kendler, Karkowski, Neale, & Prescott, 2000; Prescott & Kendler, 1999). Kendler (2001) found that heritability estimates of sedative, stimulant, cocaine, and opiate use range from 60%–80%. Evidence from twin and adoption studies consistently supports the existence of moderate heritability for alcoholism among males, with genes accounting for 50%–60% of the liability (Kendler, Neale, Heath, Kessler, & Eaves, 1994; Prescott et al., 2005). Heritability of alcoholism among females is less clear: Some studies have indicated a significant genetic component (e.g., Kendler et al., 1994), whereas others have found heritability to be limited, with environmental factors being more influential (e.g., Prescott et al., 2005). In addition, having an alcoholic biological parent increases an individual's risk for alcoholism by roughly 2.5 times, regardless of whether the parent raised the child (Cloninger, Bohman, & Sigvardsson, 1981).

Other inherited behavioral, temperamental, and personality traits may serve as risk or protective factors for addiction. For example, some studies found a genetic link between drug dependency and antisocial behavior (e.g., Stallings et al., 2005), and other studies found that the traits of alienation, anger, interaction anxiety, and lower self-regulation reliably predict adolescent drug use (e.g., Quinn & Fromme, 2010). Further, several genes are involved in sensitivity to acute intoxication and alcohol withdrawal and can be protective against alcoholism (Hinckers et al., 2006; Pihl, 2009).

Although genes can predispose a person to develop drug addiction, environmental factors interact with inherited traits to increase an individual's vulnerability to drug addiction. Environmental influences such as culture, parenting, peers, schooling, socioeconomics, and individual experiences may be mediated by the class of a drug.

For example, a twin study by Fowler et al. (2007) found that genetic factors were more responsible for heavy substance use whereas environmental factors were more responsible for substance use initiation. Kendler et al.'s (2000) twin study found that familial–environmental factors accounted for cannabis and hallucinogen use more so than other drugs. Some adoption studies have shown that alcohol problems in the adoptive family increase an individual's risk for alcoholism (Cadoret, Troughton, & O'Gorman, 1987), suggesting that the behavior is learned. Another study found that harsh and inconsistent childhood discipline and low socioeconomic status were predictive of alcohol abuse among adults (Holmes & Robins, 1988).

Cognitive Perspectives

Cognitive impairments can contribute to the development of addiction and/or be the result of drug use. Several studies have suggested that cognitive deficiencies, expressed as impulsiveness, behavioral self-regulation problems, affect dysregulation, inadequate problem-solving skills, difficult temperament, and novelty-sensation seeking, can predispose or exacerbate addiction, as individuals may turn to substances to cope (e.g., Scheier, 2010). For example, individuals with cognitive deficits can be hyperreactive to stimuli, and using depressants will dampen their autonomic arousal (Peterson & Pihl, 1990). Substance use further negatively affects cognition by impairing an individual's inhibition and decision making. Disruption of the orbitofrontal cortex functions, the area of the brain that is associated with drive and compulsive behaviors, may cause a loss of the ability to evaluate drug rewards against harm, leading to further maladaptive cognitions (Volkow & Fowler, 2000).

Individuals at a higher risk for developing substance use have shown premorbid mild to moderate impairment in several areas of cognition, including executive functioning, behavioral and emotional control, abstraction, planning, problem solving, language, attention, memory, and learning (Peterson & Pihl, 1990; Sinha, 2008). Cognitive function and risk for substance use can be gauged in part by school performance, although this does not necessarily reflect an individual's intelligence; for example, in a study by Peterson and Pihl (1990), sons of male alcoholics showed an increased incidence of conduct disorder and hyperactivity. Similarly, Block, Erwin, and Ghoneim (2002) found that chronic drug abusers' childhood academic achievement scores were significantly lower than those of the control group of nonusers.

Polysubstance use makes it difficult to differentiate the cognitive effects of specific drugs. Cannabis users exhibit acute impairments in memory and attention but not mental flexibility (e.g., Ehrenreich et al., 1999; Yuille, Tollestrup, Marxsen, Porter, & Herve, 1998). Cocaine and methamphetamine users exhibit impaired visuospatial skills, decision making, memory, attention, and abstraction (e.g., Mittenberg & Motta, 1993). Ecstasy users show impaired selective memory, executive function, verbal fluency, general intelligence, and planning (e.g., Fox, Parrot, & Turner, 2001; Wareing, Fisk, & Murphy, 2000). Opioid use is associated with short-term impairments in memory, motor skills, attention, concentration, decision making, and response inhibition (e.g., Mintzer & Stitzer, 2002).

Cognitive impairments resulting from drug use can be long lasting and potentially irreversible, and not all drug users recover equally. For example, the cognitive recovery of users of stimulants is worse than that of users of alcohol, opioids, and/or polysubstances (Block et al., 2002; Verdejo-Garcia & Perez-Garcia, 2007). Chronic alcohol abuse can lead to thiamine deficiency and neurotoxicity, which causes long-term memory impairment known as Korsakoff's syndrome (van Amsterdam, Brunt, McMaster, & Niesink, 2012). Ecstasy users show significant long-term impairments in memory, but not in intelligence or attention (Thomasius et al., 2003). Research has yielded mixed findings regarding the long-term effects of opioid use, with some studies showing chronic deficits in executive functioning (Lyvers & Yakimoff, 2003) and other studies finding little permanent dysfunction (Pau, Lee, & Chan, 2002). Research has found little significant permanent damage from cannabis to cognitive functioning other than subtle selective memory impairment (I. Grant, Gonzalez, Carey, Natarajan, & Wolfson, 2003).

Developmental Perspectives

In utero exposure to substances can impact child development, but it is difficult to isolate the effects of drugs on fetal outcomes because other confounding variables associated with substance use, such as poor nutrition and psychological stress, can affect the pregnancy. Maternal use of alcohol, cocaine, nicotine, and marijuana, for example, have been linked to poor fetal outcomes and/or birth defects (e.g., Kandel, Wu, & Davies, 1994; Robins & Mills, 1993; Tate, Drapkin, & Brown, 2009).

The stage of life in which an individual initiates drug use is also related to behavior patterns and outcomes. The early onset of substance use is a significant predictor of a future substance use disorder (Scheier, 2010). Drinkers who initiate early are four times as likely to become dependent than those who start at a later age (B. Grant & Dawson, 1998). Additionally, women exhibit a particular vulnerability to drug problems, as evidenced by studies showing accelerated progression from substance use to abuse and dependence among females, which is a phenomenon that is referred to as *telescoping* (Haas & Peters, 2001).

Negative life events are associated with substance use, perhaps due to self-medicating (Moselhy, Fahmy, Mikhael, & El-Sheikh, 2012). Events associated with substance use include parental death, divorce, discrimination, childhood abuse, and violence victimization (Brent, Melhem, Donohoe, & Walker, 2009; Gibbons et al., 2012; Sinha, 2008; Widom, Weiler, & Cottler, 1999). Dawson, Grant, and Ruan (2005) found a significant correlation between negative past-year events and the frequency and quantity of an individual's alcohol consumption. Lifetime stress exposure has been shown to be positively associated with alcohol dependence in a way that suggests a cumulative impact of negative life events (Lloyd & Turner, 2008).

Substance use behaviors are maintained by long-term biochemical changes in the brain that help explain the progression from acute intoxication to tolerance, dependence, and withdrawal.

Neuroadaptations associated with chronic drug use include overactive glutaminergic pathways, altered autonomic responses to stress, and underactive dopamine and GABA systems. Repeated overstimulation of the reward system can lead to the long-term potentiation or long-term depression of synapses in the nucleus accumbens and down regulation of dopamine receptors in the VTA (Sinha, 2008). These changes in the dopamine and stress pathways contribute to the development of substance tolerance, dependence, and cravings (Sinha, 2007).

An individual abstaining from the substance to which he or she is addicted may experience withdrawal symptoms, which vary by substance. Unpleasant physiological symptoms of withdrawal are common among users of alcohol, opioids, sedatives, hypnotics, and anxiolytics but are less so among stimulant and cannabis users and are unlikely among hallucinogen users. Withdrawal from sedatives and alcohol can even be fatal. Unfortunately, relapse is common among substance users, and exposure to stress and/or drug-related cues can be powerful relapse triggers (Sinha, 2007). The severity of withdrawal symptoms and the presence of co-occurring psychopathology are also associated with relapse (Dodge, Sindelar, & Sinha, 2005).

Social Perspectives

Social context, including peers, family interactions, and social environments, has been shown to contribute to substance use. Expectancies of positive effects of substances learned from family, peers, and the media can predict substance use initiation, progression, and relapse (Smith, Goldman, Greenbaum, & Christiansen, 1995). The influence of peers on adolescents is particularly powerful and positively reinforcing (Shoal, Gudonis, Giancola, & Tarter, 2007). Studies have indicated that adolescents show increased alcohol consumption in the presence of other adolescents who are drinking (e.g., Curran, Stice, & Chassin, 1997). Epstein and Botvin (2002) found that greater peer involvement with substances and greater perceived peer acceptance of substance use are risk factors for adolescent substance involvement. Peer influence is also linked

to availability: Adolescents who associate with substance users have greater access to substances, which could lead to the adoption of values/beliefs that foster a substance use lifestyle and/or pressure to use substances (Tate et al., 2009).

Substance use behaviors are influenced not only by parental genes, but also by the familial environment. Parental influence can serve as a risk or protective factor: Although there is some evidence that children learn substance use behaviors from parental modeling (e.g., Biederman, Faraone, Monuteax, & Feighner, 2000), other evidence has indicated that children of alcohol-abusing parents are more likely to abstain from substances (Kendler et al., 1994). A strong parent–child relationship can be protective against substance use (Anderson & Henry, 1994), whereas low parental monitoring, poor parent–child communication, and low socioeconomic status are associated with increased risk (Jackson, Henriksen, & Dickinson, 1999). Studies suggest that the modeling of substance use occurs among siblings as well (Windle, 2000). In addition, researchers have theorized that an assortative mating effect exists, as supported by research showing correlations between spouses' alcohol use behaviors (Kendler et al., 1994).

Societal influences such as culture and religion influence substance use on a broader scale. For example, research has suggested that Native Americans use substances at a higher rate than non-Native Americans, which may be due to spiritual beliefs about intoxication and cultural conflicts between Native Americans and the larger society (Schinke, Tepavac, & Cole, 2000). On the other hand, the Muslim culture considers alcohol and drug use to be a social, legal, and religious taboo (AlMarri & Oei, 2009).

Clinical Perspectives

Clinicians rely on structured clinical interviews, assessment measures, and the recently released *Diagnostic and Statistical Manual of Mental Disorders, Fifth Edition* (DSM–5; American Psychiatric Association, 2013) to diagnose substance use disorders. Diagnoses can be difficult to make given vague diagnostic criteria and the high comorbidity between substance use and other psychological disorders (discussed later in the chapter).

The *DSM–5* (American Psychiatric Association, 2013) substance-related and addictive disorders category includes diagnoses for 10 distinct drug classes (e.g., alcohol, opioids, stimulants), although several classes share similar features. For *DSM–5* purposes, *substance* refers to any drug of abuse, medication (over-the-counter or prescription), or toxin. Diagnoses within this category are classified as either substance use disorders or substance-induced disorders.

Substance use disorders. Substance use disorder diagnoses reflect a pattern of persistent substance use despite associated negative consequences in an individual's life. The diagnoses range along a continuum on the basis of the number of symptoms (out of a possible 11) an individual displays. The presence of two or three symptoms indicates a mild substance use disorder, four or five symptoms reflect a moderate substance use disorder, and six or more symptoms suggest the presence of a severe substance use disorder. Clinicians diagnose substance use disorders for each specific substance an individual uses (e.g., alcohol use disorder, opioid use disorder), meaning that an individual could be diagnosed with several substance use disorders of varying severity. Diagnostic specifiers can be also be used to supply additional information, such as remission or maintenance therapy.

Substance-induced disorders. This category of *DSM–5* diagnoses classifies symptoms of substance intoxication, withdrawal, and other psychological disorders resulting from ingestion of a substance. Symptoms of substance intoxication vary greatly by the individual, substance, and a variety of other factors, but the essential features of the disorder are maladaptive behavioral or psychological changes that are directly due to a substance. Substance withdrawal requires the presence of maladaptive physiological and cognitive changes resulting from reduced substance use. Symptoms of withdrawal vary according to the substance and individual characteristics, but withdrawal symptoms are generally the opposite of the substance's intoxication symptoms. Individuals in withdrawal often experience intense cravings to readminister the substance to reduce withdrawal symptoms.

Because individuals may self-medicate with substances when they are experiencing psychological symptoms, it is not surprising that substance-related disorders are comorbid with many psychiatric disorders. When the psychological symptoms are a direct consequence of substance use, as opposed to merely being exacerbated by intoxication or withdrawal, a differential diagnosis of a substance-induced disorder is given. Such diagnoses include substance- or medication-induced psychotic disorder, substance- or medication-induced depressive disorder, and substance- or medication-induced anxiety disorder.

DSM–5 changes. The *DSM–5*'s conceptualization of substance use disorders represents a significant departure from its predecessor, the *Diagnostic and Statistical Manual of Mental Disorders, Fourth Edition, Text Revision* (*DSM–IV–TR*; American Psychiatric Association, 2000). The most notable alteration to substance-related diagnoses is the elimination of the distinction between abuse and dependence diagnoses. The *DSM–5* taxonomy replaces the previous categorical conceptualization of substance use with a more dynamic model, allowing clinicians to specify the severity of substance use disorders along a continuum. This change stems from empirical evidence suggesting that dependence and abuse criteria form a unidimensional structure (see American Psychiatric Association, 2012, for a review of this literature).

The name of the diagnostic category for substance use disorders also has been changed to include nonsubstance addictions (e.g., gambling), and disorders are now grouped by substance (e.g., alcohol-related disorders, opioid-related disorders) rather than by disorder (e.g., abuse, dependence). New *DSM–5* diagnoses include hallucinogen-related disorders, sedative- or hypnotic-related disorders, caffeine withdrawal (under caffeine-related disorders), cannabis withdrawal (under cannabis-related disorders), stimulant-related disorders, and gambling disorder. Other relevant criteria changes include the addition of a symptom reflecting craving or strong desire to use and the elimination of a polysubstance use diagnosis.

Alternative Conceptualizations of Substance Use

The considerations that led to the revision of diagnostic criteria in the *DSM–5* also led researchers to propose alternative conceptualizations of substance use disorders. Some researchers have argued that the *DSM–IV–TR* diagnostic criteria for substance abuse and dependence were so broad and generic that they did not provide clinically precise or meaningful information (Marlowe, DeMatteo, Patapis, & Festinger, 2012). The diagnostic criteria blurred the distinction between substance abuse and substance dependence such that an individual could have been diagnosed with substance dependence without exhibiting the features that are typically associated with addiction (e.g., withdrawal symptoms, compulsive use, cravings).

Lack of satisfaction with the *DSM* diagnostic criteria has led some researchers propose that the label *substance dependence* be reserved for those who suffer from severe withdrawal symptoms when they stop using a substance (Langenbucher et al., 2000) or who experience overwhelming cravings or compulsions to use drugs or alcohol (O'Brien, Childress, Ehrman, & Robbins, 1998). The argument is that anything short of substance dependence may constitute substance abuse or substance misuse, and that these latter conditions may be undeserving of a formal psychiatric diagnosis (Marlowe, 2010; Marlowe et al., 2012).

Comorbid Psychopathology

Substance use often co-occurs with other mental health disorders (B. R. Grant et al., 2004). Most explanations for these comorbidities hypothesize either a causal relationship (i.e., one condition causes the other, or the conditions influence each other) or that shared genetic and environmental predispositions underlie both (Tate et al., 2009). Regardless, co-occurring disorders complicate diagnosis (e.g., intoxication and withdrawal can mimic and/or exacerbate psychiatric symptoms) and treatment (e.g., drugs can interact with psychotropic medications and reduce treatment adherence; Tate et al., 2009), resulting in poorer treatment outcomes for individuals with comorbid disorders

(e.g., Dobkin, Chabot, Maliantovitch, & Craig, 1998).

Substance use disorders are highly comorbid with mood disorders; namely, depression and bipolar disorder. A large epidemiological study found that 20% of individuals with a mood disorder had at least one comorbid substance use disorder (B. R. Grant et al., 2004). Researchers have documented an increased risk of mood disorders among adolescents with substance use disorders (Roberts, Roberts, & Xing, 2007), and a history of substance dependence is associated with a more than four times greater risk of being diagnosed with a mood disorder (Hasin & Grant, 2002). Additionally, alcohol/substance use is associated with increased suicidality (Claassen et al., 2007). Bipolar disorders and substance use also often co-occur, but drug use can obfuscate or complicate symptomatology, contributing to treatment noncompliance, accelerated relapse, worsening depressive features, and increased suicide risk (Goldberg, 2001).

Given the relationship between stress and substance use, it is not surprising that anxiety disorders often co-occur with substance use disorders. When compared to controls, alcohol-dependent adults have significantly higher lifetime prevalence rates of agoraphobia, panic disorder, obsessive-compulsive disorder, and social phobia (Schuckit et al., 1997). Furthermore, certain anxiety disorders are associated with different drugs; for example, Conrad, Pihl, Stewart, and Dongier (2000) found that substance users with comorbid diagnoses of simple phobia, somatization disorder, and generalized anxiety disorder were more likely to be anxiolytic dependent, whereas substance users with comorbid diagnoses of panic disorder, agoraphobia, and social phobia were more likely to be opioid dependent. Among men with posttraumatic stress disorder, alcohol and substance use disorders are the most common comorbidities (Kessler, Sonnega, Bromet, Hughes, & Nelson, 1995).

Among individuals with schizophrenia, 40%–50% exhibit symptoms of substance use disorders (Blanchard, Brown, Horan, & Sherwood, 2000). Substance use among individuals with psychosis interferes with daily functioning; for example, these individuals have higher rates of homelessness and incarceration and poorer treatment outcomes compared to individuals with schizophrenia alone (e.g., Blanchard et al., 2000). Examining substance misuse among individuals with first-episode psychosis, Cantwell et al. (1999) found that substance users were more likely to be male and to have a younger age of onset of psychosis. In a study of individuals with comorbid schizophrenia and substance use disorders, Gut-Fayand et al. (2001) found that the onset of substance use was likely to occur after the first prodromal symptoms but before the first psychotic episode, suggesting that substance use was a maladaptive response to the symptoms.

Some psychological comorbidities are more common among particular genders or age groups. For example, depression predicts alcohol use among women, and women with substance use issues are more frequently diagnosed with co-occurring depression and anxiety disorders than men, whereas men with substance use issues are more frequently diagnosed with antisocial personality disorder than women (Tate et al., 2009). Co-occurring substance use and eating disorders are more prevalent among women, and research suggests that inhibition and impulsivity are involved (Wolfe & Maisto, 2000). Youth with alcohol use disorders have significantly higher rates of disorders that are typically diagnosed in childhood or adolescence, including conduct disorder, oppositional defiant disorder, and attention-deficit hyperactivity disorder (Ohlmeier et al., 2007). A diagnosis of conduct disorder greatly increases an individual's risk of early onset of substance use and predicts the transition to dependence (Elkins, McGue, & Iacono, 2007).

RESEARCH REVIEW

Over the past few decades, researchers have generated a great deal of research on the relationship between substance use and crime. As the link between substance use and criminal behavior became increasingly clear, researchers began asking more nuanced and specific questions about the relationship, which has increased our knowledge base considerably. There has also been an increase in research on interventions for substance users and drug-involved offenders, and the results of some of

these lines of research provide reason to be optimistic about the effects of these interventions.

Substance Use and Crime

Although the link between substance use and crime is well documented, the statistics alone do not capture the complicated nature of the relationship. Fortunately, researchers have amassed a sizeable literature on substance use as a predictor of criminal behavior (see Chapter 8, this volume for a review of theories of criminal behavior). In an early meta-analysis of recidivism predictors, Gendreau, Little, and Goggin (1996) examined 131 studies and found a modest correlation ($r = .10$) between substance abuse and reoffending. By comparison, several other dynamic risk factors, such as criminal companions ($r = .21$) and antisocial personality ($r = .18$), yielded stronger relationships to recidivism. A more recent meta-analysis by Dowden and Brown (2002) found an identical mean effect size ($r = .10$) for substance use and general recidivism and a slightly weaker relationship between substance use and violent recidivism ($r = .06$).

Researchers have also examined alcohol use and illegal drug use as separate risk factors. This distinction is important because although alcohol use and illegal drug use are highly correlated ($r = .39$ in one U.S. prison sample of $N = 18,313$), the relationship is not perfect (Andrews & Bonta, 2010). In addition, legal restrictions on alcohol are less stringent than those placed on illicit substances, so legal consequences arise only under specific circumstances (e.g., driving while intoxicated). By contrast, simply purchasing or possessing illicit substances can result in criminal justice system involvement. For this reason, we discuss alcohol use and illegal drug use separately whenever possible.

Correlation between alcohol use and crime. Alcohol use is prevalent in correctional samples, and both offenders and victims often report alcohol use at the time of an offense (Lipsey, Wilson, Cohen, & Derzon, 1997). A systematic literature review by Fazel et al. (2006) found an alcohol abuse/dependence prevalence of 18%–30% in male prisoners and 10%–24% in female prisoners. Empirical studies examining the relationship between alcohol use and crime typically either use data that are from correctional samples or experimentally manipulate the presence/amount of alcohol consumed by participants in order to observe its effect on behaviors related to criminal activity, so both categories of research will be discussed.

Correlational studies have the advantage of ecological validity, but they lack experimental control. Nevertheless, this type of study can help explain the link between alcohol use and crime. Most correlational studies have reported a small (mean effect sizes of .09 to .22) but consistent relationship between the two. In a meta-analysis, Lipsey et al. (1997) reviewed 44 studies that examined alcohol use and criminal activity and reported mean effect sizes for both acute and chronic alcohol use and violence (criminal and domestic). The largest mean effect size ($r = .22$) was reported for the domestic-chronic category (chronic alcohol use and domestic violence), followed by criminal-chronic ($r = 0.15$) and criminal-acute categories ($r = 0.10$).

With regard to reoffending, Dowden and Brown's (2002) meta-analysis of the predictive utility of substance use reported a modest mean effect size ($r = .12$) between alcohol use and recidivism. Interestingly, this relationship yielded a lower correlation than several other factors, including combined alcohol and drug use, drug use only, and parental substance use. Andrews and Bonta (2010) examined eight large correctional and community samples and reported a slightly lower mean effect size between alcohol use and recidivism ($r = .09$).

Experimental research on alcohol use and crime.

Experimental examinations of the alcohol–crime association most often employ competitive reaction time or the teacher/learner paradigm in order to gauge an individual's aggressiveness. In competitive reaction time studies, participants are led to believe that they are competing against another individual in a series of tasks. Each time the participant wins a task, he or she is allowed to shock the "loser" at an intensity of the participant's choosing; in reality, there is no other participant, and the wins/losses are manipulated by the experimenter. The presence and amount of alcohol are the independent variables, and the intensity

of the shock that is selected by participants is the dependent variable. In the teacher/learner paradigm, participants are told that they have been randomly selected to play the teacher in a study examining the effects of alcohol consumption on learning or memory. The learner role is played by a confederate. Each time the learner gives an incorrect answer, the teacher is given the choice of delivering either an "aggressive response" (e.g., shock or noxious noise) or a neutral response (e.g., a red light). In this type of study, alcohol is the independent variable, and the response selection is the dependent variable.

Several researchers have attempted to synthesize these lines of research. One of the earliest meta-analyses of alcohol use and experimental aggression reviewed 49 studies and reported an overall mean effect size of .54 for alcohol and aggression, with larger doses of alcohol associated with greater effect sizes ($r = .53$) than lower doses ($r = .35$; Ito, Miller, & Pollock, 1996). Lipsey et al. (1997) also conducted a meta-analysis of experimental alcohol-aggression studies and reported a mean effect size ($r = .54$) for comparisons between the aggression levels of participants who had consumed alcohol and those who had not. Thus, participants in the alcohol group scored, on average, roughly 1/2 *SD* higher on measures of aggression than those in the control group. For the competitive reaction time studies, individuals who had consumed alcohol administered a shock that was approximately one intensity step higher than those who had not consumed alcohol.

Although this evidence suggests a relationship between alcohol use and experimental aggression, researchers have noted that these studies are variable in their findings and that effect sizes may have been influenced by factors such as an individual's anxiety, frustration, self-focused attention, distraction, trait agreeableness, and trait aggressiveness (Ito et al., 1996; Lipsey et al., 1997; C. A. Miller, Parrott, & Giancola, 2009). In addition, these studies have limited ecological validity.

Illegal drug use and crime.

The use of illegal drugs is more closely associated with crime because the act of buying or possessing these substances is illegal in itself. A systematic literature review found a drug abuse/dependence prevalence of 10%–48% in male prisoners and 30%–60% in female prisoners (Fazel et al., 2006). Although the link between drug use and criminal behavior appears strong, questions remain regarding the nature and direction of the relationship. For example, it is possible that there is a bidirectional causal link between drug use and crime, but it is also possible that there is either an indirect link or no link at all (Bennett et al., 2008).

Two meta-analyses attempted to clarify the nature of the relationship between illicit drug use and crime. Dowden and Brown (2002) examined the association between illegal drug use and criminal recidivism and reported a mean effect size of .19 for general recidivism and .14 for violent recidivism. These mean effect sizes were stronger than those that were derived from alcohol use alone (.12 and .10, respectively). Bennett et al. (2008) conducted a meta-analysis examining the association between drug use and criminal activity. Based on a review of 30 studies, they reported that individuals who reported drug use were 2.79 times more likely to offend than individuals who did not report drug use. Examining several drugs individually, Bennett et al. found that the odds of offending were highest among individuals reporting the use of crack (six times greater than among noncrack users; odds ratio [OR] = 6.09), followed by heroin/opiate use (OR = 3.08) and cocaine use (OR = 2.56). The observed relationship was consistent across multiple types of offenses, including robbery, burglary, prostitution, and shoplifting.

For the sake of comparison in this chapter, Bennett et al.'s (2008) reported OR statistics were converted to Cohen's d (see Chinn, 2000, for formula), and then to Pearson's r. According to Cohen's (1992) guidelines, these calculations yielded a small to moderate mean effect size for any drug use ($r = .27$), a moderate to large effect size for crack ($r = .45$), a moderate effect size for heroin ($r = .30$), and a small to moderate effect size for cocaine ($r = .25$). Recall that meta-analytic reviews of the correlational literature regarding alcohol use and recidivism yielded mean effect sizes ranging from .09 to .22. Consequently, the literature seems to suggest that drug use (vs. alcohol use) is more strongly related to criminal activity.

Offenders with mental health issues. Bonta, Law, and Hanson (1998) conducted a meta-analysis of 64 studies that examined predictors of general and violent recidivism among offenders with mental disorders. Use of any substances yielded a slightly stronger mean effect size for general recidivism ($r = .11$) than for violent recidivism ($r = .08$). For general recidivism, the predictive validity of any drug use was attributable more to drug use ($r = .09$) than to alcohol use ($r = .06$). These findings suggest that the relationship between substance use and recidivism is comparable for individuals with and without additional mental health diagnoses.

Female offenders. Much of the substance use and crime literature has focused on male offenders, and few studies have examined the gender-specific relationship between substance use and recidivism (see Volume 2, Chapter 4, this handbook for a review of female offenders). Dowden and Brown's (2002) meta-analysis found that one variable differentiated between male and female offenders—the use of substances by a parent had a significant between-gender effect—whereby the mean effect size for female offenders ($r = .20$) was considerably larger than that for male offenders ($r = .09$). The finding that drug use was a more robust predictor of recidivism than alcohol use was consistent across genders.

Bennett et al.'s (2008) meta-analysis of the predicative validity of drug use included six studies that examined females separately from males. Of those six studies, three reported a positive significant relationship between drug use and crime among females and three reported no relationship. Two studies using the same methods to compare males to females found significantly greater effect sizes for females, suggesting a greater likelihood of offending among female drug users. Similar results were obtained by Andrews and Bonta (2010) in their study of the predictive utility of drug use in male and female samples: Drug use was more predictive of criminal activity in all five female samples compared to the male samples.

Treatment Outcomes for Substance Users and Drug-Involved Offenders

Given the high rates of drug use among both general and correctional populations, it is not surprising that a range of interventions have been developed. The literature is extensive, so we necessarily focus on broad findings from large-scale studies and systematic reviews (see Chapter 6, this volume for a review of more general issues associated with treatment in forensic settings).

Pharmacological treatment.   Medications that are used to treat alcohol dependence include disulfuram (Antabuse), naltrexone, and acomprosate. Antabuse, the first medication for the treatment of alcohol dependence that was approved by the U.S. Food and Drug Administration, works by interfering with the metabolism of alcohol, which leads to nausea and vomiting. The theory underlying the use of Antabuse is that the aversive symptoms will deter individuals from drinking. To be effective, Antabuse must be taken in daily doses, and studies suggest poor compliance (as low as 19%; Fuller et al., 1986). In a study of justice-involved individuals who were court ordered to take Antabuse, 33% admitted to intentionally not taking it (Mustard, May, & Phillips, 2006).

Naltrexone and acamprosate decrease an individual's cravings for alcohol and other drugs by interfering with pleasure receptors in the brain. Two meta-analyses compared the treatment efficacy of these drugs. Kranzler and Van Kirk (2001) examined all published placebo-controlled trials of naltrexone or acamprosate for the treatment of alcohol dependence and found that both yielded small but significant effects on drinking outcomes and/or treatment retention. Rösner, Leucht, Lehert, and Soyka (2008) examined 41 randomized control trials involving naltrexone or acamprosate and reported that acamprosate was more effective in maintaining abstinence, whereas naltrexone was more effective in preventing one drink from becoming a relapse.

Opioid maintenance.   Opioid maintenance therapy is typically a daily dose of an opiate, such as methadone, buprenorphine, or levo-alpha-acetylmethadol (LAAM), that aims to stabilize an individual's drug levels, reduce cravings, and increase the opportunity for behavioral interventions. This type of intervention has been studied extensively, and results consistently indicate that opioid maintenance is associated with reductions in illicit drug use, criminal activity, and human immunodeficiency virus (HIV)-risk behaviors (see Gossop, 2004). Farre, Mas, Torrens, Moreno, and Cami (2002) conducted a meta-analysis of randomized control trials for the three most common opiates used in maintenance therapy and concluded that high doses of methadone were most effective for treatment retention and the reduction of illicit drug use, particularly when compared with LAAM maintenance or low doses of buprenorphine. The literature regarding prison-based opioid maintenance is mixed. Although these programs may reduce drug use, evidence suggests that they are not effective at reducing recidivism; in fact, some studies found that opioid maintenance participants were more likely to reoffend than were controls (Mitchell, Wilson, & MacKenzie, 2007; Pearson & Lipton, 1999).

Cognitive–behavioral therapy (CBT).   Treatment outcomes for all forms of pharmacological interventions are considerably improved by adding concurrent behavioral therapy (e.g., Andrews & Bonta, 2010; Kranzler & Van Kirk, 2001). CBT seeks to restructure an individual's maladaptive thinking patterns in order to bring about behavioral change, and it has been used to treat substance use in both general and correctional populations. In correctional populations, CBT-based treatment programs include moral reconation therapy, reasoning and rehabilitation (R&R), relapse prevention, and various cognitive-restructuring programs (Andrews & Bonta, 2010; Wilson, Bouffard, & MacKenzie, 2005). As a whole, research suggests that these programs consistently yield small to moderate effect sizes (Magill & Ray, 2009). Recidivism reductions are associated with moral reconation therapy, R&R, and several cognitive-restructuring programs (Wilson et al., 2005). Several meta-analyses have found that CBT may be particularly effective for decreasing marijuana use (Dutra et al., 2008; Magill & Ray, 2009).

Relapse prevention (RP) is a CBT-based intervention that is designed to help individuals maintain abstinence by recognizing high-risk situations and triggers that previously led to substance use (Marlatt & Gordon, 1980). Research has found that RP improves an individual's psychosocial adjustment and reduces his or her use of alcohol, cigarettes, and illegal drugs, with the strongest effects associated with alcohol use ($r = .37$; Irvin, Bowers, Dunn, & Wang, 1999). Dutra et al. (2008) conducted a meta-analysis of psychosocial interventions for substance use and reported a moderate effect size for RP ($d = 0.32$; 95% confidence interval [CI] = [0.06, 0.56]). In addition, treatments involving RP strategies were associated with the highest posttreatment abstinence levels (39%) as compared to contingency management (31%) and CBT (27.1%; Dutra et al., 2008).

Motivational interviewing (MI). MI is a skill set/counseling style that seeks to engage clients in a nonthreatening therapeutic relationship, guide them through stages of change, and assist with the resolution of ambivalence toward treatment (W. R. Miller, 1983). MI is often used as a catalyst to engage clients in more formal substance use treatment, and it may be particularly useful for justice-involved individuals who are mandated to treatment (Andrews & Bonta, 2010).

Several meta-analyses have synthesized MI outcome data and consistently found it to be more effective than no treatment (effect sizes of $r = .13$ to $r = .25$) for substance use disorders and other problems necessitating behavioral change (Andrews & Bonta, 2010; Rubak, Sandbæk, Lauritzen, & Christensen, 2005). McMurran (2009) conducted a systematic review of MI outcomes for offender populations and found that MI can lead to improvements in treatment retention, heightened motivation to change, and reduced recidivism.

Corrections-specific treatment. Given the prevalence of substance use among correctional

populations, many substance use treatment models have been incorporated into criminal justice settings. Commonly used treatment modalities for offenders with substance use disorders include narcotic maintenance, boot camps, residential substance abuse treatment, group counseling, and therapeutic communities (TCs; Mitchell, Wilson, & MacKenzie, 2006).

TCs are a rigorous, highly structured treatment model in which offenders with substance use disorders are housed separately from other offenders (typically for 6–12 months) and are required to take part in intensive therapy. Behavioral expectations are emphasized and reinforced in an effort to foster self-mastery and responsibility. Corrections-based TCs have consistently been found to reduce drug relapse and recidivism among offenders with serious drug use issues, and several meta-analyses have found TCs to be among the most effective treatments for offenders with drug issues (Holloway, Bennett, & Farrington, 2006; McMurran, 2007; Mitchell et al., 2006, 2007; Pearson & Lipton, 1999).

Interestingly, some treatments that are used with offender populations may lead to iatrogenic effects. For example, although few studies have examined the *boot camp* model (highly structured militaristic programs in which participants are "scared straight"), researchers have consistently demonstrated that it is not effective at reducing recidivism or drug use and may in fact be associated with higher rates of drug use (Mitchell et al., 2007; Pearson & Lipton, 1999).

Drug courts. Drug courts are separate court dockets that provide judicially supervised drug abuse treatment and case management services to nonviolent, drug-involved offenders in lieu of prosecution or incarceration. Drug court judges receive regular updates regarding participants' treatment attendance and progress, and they mete out rewards or sanctions as needed. Completion of the program may be rewarded with noncustodial sentencing or record expungement. A large body of research has shown that drug courts reduce drug use and recidivism in a cost-effective manner (e.g., Belenko, DeMatteo, & Patapis,

2007; Bhati, Roman, & Chalfin, 2008; Huddleston & Marlowe, 2011; Mitchell, Wilson, Eggers, & MacKenzie, 2012).

Research Review: A Summary

Although research has consistently demonstrated the link between substance use and crime, the exact mechanism of this relationship is unknown. Causal claims regarding substance use and criminal behavior are difficult to support because many interrelated factors affect criminal behavior, and the experimental manipulation of substance use and/or intoxication levels presents obvious ethical concerns. Overall, the extant literature suggests that alcohol use and drug use increase an individual's chances of criminal activity, with drug use having a slightly larger effect size.

Several treatments effectively reduce substance use and criminal recidivism, but the lack of randomized control trials with correctional populations and the methodological problems of many studies make it difficult to draw firm conclusions regarding best practices for the treatment of substance use disorders. Weisburd, Lum, and Petrosino (2001) rated the methodological rigor of 308 evaluations of criminal justice interventions and reported that 73% were methodologically "weak" or "standard quasi-experiments," and only 24% were "rigorous quasi-experiments" or "randomized experiments." Despite these concerns, substantial evidence suggests that several treatments (e.g., pharmacological treatments, CBT-based interventions, TCs) are effective at reducing substance use and criminal behavior.

PRACTICE AND POLICY ISSUES

As previously noted, forensic mental health professionals frequently encounter substance use among the criminal offenders that they evaluate. In some contexts, an offender's substance use may be a primary focus of the evaluation; in other contexts, it may be a secondary consideration. The key task for forensic mental health professionals (and to some extent, the attorneys/courts that retain/appoint such professionals) is to determine whether substance use has relevance to the legal issue being addressed.

It is to this important question that we turn our attention. Because this chapter is focused on the relationship between substance use and crime, we will not discuss the relationship between substance use and civil liability (see Chapters 13, 14, 15, and 16, this volume for reviews of civil forensic issues). Instead, our attention will remain focused on whether substance use has relevance in specific types of criminal forensic contexts.

Competency

There are several points in the criminal adjudication process at which the law requires the accused to be competent (see Chapter 5, this volume for a more general review of criminal competencies). After the U.S. Supreme Court's decision in *Miranda v. Arizona* (1966), an offender cannot be subjected to custodial interrogation unless he or she understands and voluntarily waives certain constitutional rights (stemming mostly from the Fifth and Sixth Amendments [U.S. Const. amend. V; U.S. Const. amend. VI]). Further along in the criminal process, a defendant must be competent to waive his or her right to counsel (*Johnson v. Zerbst*, 1938) and competent to plead guilty (*Boykin v. Alabama*, 1969). The Supreme Court has also held that a defendant must be competent to stand trial (*Dusky v. United States*, 1960), competent to be sentenced (*Green v. United States*, 1961), and competent to be executed (*Ford v. Wainwright*, 1986; *Panetti v. Quarterman*, 2007; see also Chapter 7, this volume).

Although substance use could, in theory, have relevance to almost all types of competencies, it is less likely to be a relevant consideration when an individual is in a custodial setting and/or when the specific competency requires sustained functional capacity. For example, substance use is unlikely to have much relevance when evaluating a defendant for competence to stand trial, which in addition to requiring the defendant to understand the nature of the proceedings also requires the defendant to have a sustained capacity for assisting counsel. Substance use is also unlikely to be relevant when evaluating an offender for competence to be executed because these evaluations typically take place relatively close to the date of the execution, after the defendant has been incarcerated (which reduces access to drugs).

Therefore, of all of the criminal competencies, substance use has the most relevance for the competence to waive *Miranda* rights. In order to be competent to waive *Miranda* rights, U.S. courts require that a defendant have a basic understanding of his or her rights and waive those rights voluntarily, knowingly, and intelligently. The determination of competence relies on factors such as the defendant's cognitive abilities and previous legal experience.

For competence to waive *Miranda* rights, there is an important distinction between acute intoxication and dysfunction resulting from long-term substance use. As previously noted, multisite studies have revealed that large portions of adult arrestees—averaging more than 60% across sites—tested positive for at least one illicit drug at the time of arrest (Office of National Drug Control Policy, 2012). The effects of some drugs on an individual's cognitive abilities are well documented (and discussed earlier in this chapter), and it stands to reason that an arrestee's abilities to knowingly and intelligently waive his or her rights may be compromised if he or she is experiencing acute intoxication.

A separate but related issue is the long-term effects of substance use. Chronic substance use can result in long-term impairment, and the recovery of cognitive abilities on abstinence depends on several factors (e.g., length of prior use, type of drug). So even if an arrestee is not acutely intoxicated, he or she may have impairments due to long-term substance use. Several researchers have suggested that individuals with lower cognitive abilities have a poorer understanding of the *Miranda* warnings compared to adults of average intelligence (e.g., Everington & Fulero, 1999). Interestingly, however, the deficits associated with chronic drug use may not affect one's ability to knowingly and intelligently waive his or her *Miranda* rights. Viljoen, Roesch, and Zapf (2002) conducted a study in Canada comparing competence to waive interrogation warnings (and competence to stand trial) among defendants with a primary substance abuse disorder, psychotic disorder, affective disorder, or no mental illness. They found that the group with a substance abuse disorder outscored all of the other groups (including the controls) in their understanding of interrogation warnings, suggesting that the cognitive dysfunction resulting from chronic substance use may not impair an individual's understanding of *Miranda* rights as much as acute intoxication does (see Volume 2, Chapter 9, this handbook for a review of interrogations and confessions).

A real-world complication is that the evaluation for an individual's competence to waive his or her *Miranda* rights often takes place well after the individual has waived those rights, so the evaluator is tasked with reconstructing the individual's state of mind at the time that the *Miranda* rights were waived. The evaluator must rely on various sources of data, such as self-report, police reports, and interview records, in order to assess whether the offender waived his or her rights in a voluntary, knowing, and intelligent manner. If the offender was acutely intoxicated at the time of police questioning, the effects of such intoxication on the offender's cognitive abilities should be a focus of the evaluation. If the offender was not intoxicated but has a long history of substance use that may have resulted in cognitive impairment, the relationship between the impairment and the offender's ability to waive his or her *Miranda* rights should be a focus of the evaluation. In many ways, the cause of the cognitive impairment (e.g., long-term substance use, traumatic brain injury, or any other number of causes) is not particularly important; rather, the issue is how the impairment affected the offender's ability to waive his or her *Miranda* rights.

Criminal Responsibility

Compared to the relationship between substance use and competence, the question of whether substance use is relevant to an offender's criminal responsibility is much more involved (see Marlowe et al., 2012; Silberberg & Crosley, 2010; Yoshi-zuka & Perry, 2012; see Chapter 4, this volume for a review of more general issues associated with criminal responsibility). At the outset, several important legal distinctions must be drawn. First, criminal defenses may be based on *mens rea*, the requisite *mental state* for an offense, or on *actus reus*, the requisite *act* for an offense. Substance use may be relevant to both *mens rea* and *actus reus*, although there are only a few ways in which an offender's criminal responsibility can be reduced due to substance use. As will be discussed, whether substance use is given exculpatory effects depends in part on whether the resulting intoxication was voluntary, involuntary, or pathological. Another key distinction is between *general-intent crimes*, which require an intention to perform a proscribed act or closely related act (but not necessarily to cause the consequences), and *specific-intent crimes*, which require general intent plus deliberation (meaning the actor intended to engage in the act and cause the consequences). A third category of intent is *strict liability*, in which the individual's mental state is not relevant; the only relevant legal consideration is whether the offense was committed.

Voluntary intoxication.   Voluntary intoxication is self-induced intoxication by a nonaddicted individual. The general rule is that voluntary intoxication is not a sufficient basis for the insanity defense because intoxication does not constitute a mental disease or defect (Kermani & Casteneda, 1996), which is an element of all commonly used definitions of insanity. Many states statutorily preclude an insanity defense based on substance use, although a substantial minority of jurisdictions permit settled insanity to form the basis of an insanity defense. *Settled insanity*, a chronic organic condition resulting from long-term substance use, may be available as a defense if the condition was present for a substantial amount of time before and after the episode of intoxication, regardless of its permanence (Marlowe et al., 2012). Finally, an individual with a substance use problem could be found guilty but mentally ill in jurisdictions that offer that verdict. The guilty but mentally ill verdict provides a mechanism for imposing criminal responsibility on the defendant while recognizing that the defendant is in need of mental health treatment. As such, although substance use would not relieve the defendant of criminal responsibility, the judge or jury may view it as a sufficient basis for concluding that the defendant needs treatment.

Although voluntary substance use is rarely a sufficient basis for the insanity defense, it may support a diminished capacity defense (Yoshizuka & Perry, 2012), which holds that criminal responsibility should be reduced if the offender was unable to form the *mens rea* for the offense. The effect of intoxication would be to reduce the offender's culpability to a lesser offense that does not require specific intent. Not all jurisdictions permit evidence of intoxication to negate *mens rea* for specific-intent crimes, and some jurisdictions limit the diminished capacity defense to first-degree murder cases (Marlowe et al., 2012). The legal issue in diminished capacity cases is whether the offender had the requisite intent to commit the offense, and voluntary intoxication can negate such intent. Due in part to the U.S. Supreme Court's ruling in *Montana v. Egelhoff* (1996), which held that the U.S. Constitution does not forbid states from refusing to recognize voluntary intoxication as the basis of a criminal responsibility defense, several states have eliminated the voluntary intoxication defense.

Involuntary intoxication.   Involuntary intoxication is intoxication that results from coercion (i.e., being forced to ingest a substance) or innocent mistake (i.e., believing the substance was a nonintoxicating lawful substance, or experiencing unusual side effects). This type of intoxication requires that the offender was unaware that the substance was intoxicating, or that the drug was ingested under duress. Involuntary intoxication can form the basis for an insanity defense and, indeed, can be a complete defense against both general-intent and specific-intent crimes, but not strict liability crimes.

Pathological intoxication.   Pathological intoxication is intoxication that is grossly disproportionate to the type and dose of the substance that was ingested, and voluntariness is not relevant because the effect of the substance was so disproportionate that it could not have been foreseen. Pathological intoxication, albeit rare, can form the basis for an insanity defense and a complete defense to general-intent and specific-intent crimes, but several factors limit such a defense. For example, courts would likely be reluctant to recognize a pathological intoxication defense if the person had experienced unusual reactions to the same substance in the past, or in cases involving commonly used illicit drugs that are well known to have intoxicating properties (*Commonwealth v. Henry*, 1990; Marlowe et al., 2012). Pathological intoxication can form the basis of an automatism defense if the intoxication resulted in dissociation. In these contexts, the law may view the person as being unconscious of his or her actions and therefore not having engaged in the actus reus (see, e.g., *Fulcher v. State*, 1981) Again, though, the fact patterns that would support an automatism defense are rare. As Marlowe et al. (2012) stated, "Absent evidence of spasmodic or flailing motor activity, or of a rare somnambulant fugue state, it is difficult to envision a scenario that could support such a defense" (p. 638).

Sentencing

Finally, substance use can have an impact on the sentencing of criminal defendants after a conviction (see Volume 2, Chapter 14, this handbook for a review of sentencing). It is possible that the sentencing court may use the existence of a substance use problem to impose a harsher or more lenient sentence. For example, if a defendant refuses or fails to acknowledge his or her substance use problem and/or the need for substance use treatment, the court may see the defendant as a poor candidate for court-supervised outpatient treatment and instead impose a period of incarceration or some other harsher sentence. A sentencing jury, unless otherwise instructed, is typically free to view the offender's substance use as either aggravating or mitigating. Although some juries may view the decision to use a substance as influential in the commission of an offense and therefore impose a harsher sentence, some juries may view the offender's substance use problem as reducing culpability (see Volume 2, Chapter 10, this handbook for research on jury decision making).

The U.S. Sentencing Commission created the *Federal Sentencing Guidelines* in 1987 to establish uniformity in federal courts by narrowing the wide disparity in sentences that are imposed for similar criminal offenses that are committed by similar offenders. In 2005, the Supreme Court held that the *Sentencing Guidelines* were advisory rather than mandatory (*United States v. Booker*, 2005). As such, courts are permitted, but not required, to sentence defendants using the *Sentencing Guidelines*

(U.S.S.G., 2012). Section 5K2.13 of the *Sentencing Guidelines* provides for a downward departure from the Sentencing Guidelines based on diminished capacity; however, the *voluntary* use of intoxicating substances does not constitute "significantly reduced mental capacity" as defined by the *Sentencing Guidelines* and therefore is not a sufficient basis for a downward departure. The statute is silent on whether involuntary or pathological intoxication would qualify a defendant for a downward departure, and we could not find any case law addressing that issue. Individuals who use substances are not categorically disqualified from a downward departure on the basis of significantly reduced mental capacity; they are disqualified only if voluntary substance use caused their reduced mental capacity. Finally, at least one court held that evidence of postarrest abstinence is not an impermissible consideration when determining if a downward departure is warranted (*United States v. Benally*, 2000).

SUMMARY AND CONCLUSIONS

A large body of empirical evidence suggests that substance use and crime are inextricably linked, and it is therefore not surprising that forensic mental health professionals frequently encounter issues relating to substance use in the context of various forensic mental health assessments. As such, it is imperative that forensic mental health professionals understand the relationship between intoxication and certain legal issues they may be asked to address. As Marlowe et al. (2012) emphasized, when conducting an evaluation, forensic mental health professionals should consider factors relating to characteristics of both the substance and characteristics of the defendant.

As this chapter illustrates, different substances have markedly different effects on thinking and behavior, and it is important that an offender's *substance use* be defined more precisely. Forensic mental health professionals should understand the most common effects of commonly used substances and understand how those effects may relate to the legal issue being addressed. Some substances can impair the comprehension and retention of information and therefore make it difficult for an offender to understand his or her *Miranda* rights and make a knowing, intelligent, and voluntary waiver of those rights. Also, although the effects of most substances would likely not interfere with an individual's ability to form specific criminal intent, the effects may affect the formation of general intent, which has implications for an offender's mental state at the time of the offense. Finally, depending on the jurisdiction and context, an offender's substance use may be considered aggravating or mitigating during sentencing.

Characteristics relating to the offender also deserve consideration. An important factor when evaluating an intoxication defense is whether the intoxication was voluntary, involuntary, or pathological. Offenders with a long history of substance use may have a difficult time arguing that their intoxication was involuntary or pathological, and courts and juries are unlikely to be accepting of such a defense. By contrast, an offender with no discernible history of substance use who experiences an unusual or unexpected reaction to a substance may be in a good position to assert a viable intoxication defense.

Despite the close relationship between substance use and crime, there is reason to be optimistic about treatment options. In recent years, a number of interventions for drug-involved offenders have shown great promise in reducing drug use and criminal recidivism (Heilbrun et al., 2012). A variety of community-based alternatives, including diversion programs, drug courts, and reentry initiatives, have been developed to break the cycle of arrest, conviction, incarceration, release, and rearrest that has characterized the treatment of drug-involved offenders for many years (DeMatteo, LaDuke, Locklair, & Heilbrun, 2013). Although some interventions, such as drug courts, have a large amount of empirical support and exist in all 50 states, other interventions are just beginning to amass empirical support. As these interventions continue to gain empirical support, they will likely become staples of the criminal justice system's response to drug-involved offenders.

References

AlMarri, T. S., & Oei, T. P. (2009). Alcohol and substance use in the Arab Gulf region: A review. *International Journal of Psychology, 44,* 222–233. doi:10.1080/00207590801888752

American Psychiatric Association. (2000). *Diagnostic and statistical manual of mental disorders* (4th ed., text revision). Washington, DC: Author.

American Psychiatric Association. (2012). *Timeline: American Psychiatric Association DSM–5 development.* Retrieved from http://www.dsm5.org/about/Pages/Timeline.aspx

American Psychiatric Association. (2013). *Diagnostic and statistical manual of mental disorders* (5th ed.). Washington, DC: Author.

Anderson, A. R., & Henry, C. S. (1994). Family system characteristics and parental behaviors as predictors of adolescent substance use. *Adolescence, 29,* 405–420.

Andrews, D. A., & Bonta, J. (2010). *The psychology of criminal conduct* (5th ed.). New Providence, NJ: Anderson.

Beck, A. J., & Shipley, B. E. (1989). *Recidivism of prisoners released in 1983.* Washington, DC: Bureau of Justice Statistics, U.S. Department of Justice.

Belenko, S., DeMatteo, D., & Patapis, N. (2007). Drug courts. In D. W. Springer & A. R. Roberts (Eds.), *Handbook of forensic mental health with victims and offenders: Assessment, treatment, and research* (pp. 385–423). New York, NY: Springer.

Bennett, T., Holloway, K., & Farrington, D. (2008). The statistical association between drug misuse and crime: A meta-analysis. *Aggression and Violent Behavior, 13,* 107–118. doi:10.1016/j.bbr.2011.03.031.

Bhati, A., Roman, J. K., & Chalfin, A. (2008). *To treat or not to treat: Evidence on the prospects of expanding treatment to drug-involved offenders.* Washington, DC: Urban Institute.

Biederman, J., Faraone, S. V., Monuteax, M. C., & Feighner, J. A. (2000). Patterns of alcohol and drug use in adolescents can be predicted by parental substance use disorders. *Pediatrics, 106,* 792–797. doi:10.1542/peds.106.4.792

Blanchard, J. J., Brown, S. A., Horan, W. P., & Sherwood, A. R. (2000). Substance use disorders in schizophrenia: Review, integration, and a proposed model. *Clinical Psychology Review, 20,* 207–234. doi:10.1016/S0272-7358(99)00033-1

Block, R. I., Erwin, W. J., & Ghoneim, M. M. (2002). Chronic drug use and cognitive impairments. *Pharmacology, Biochemistry, and Behavior, 73,* 491–504. doi:10.1016/S0091-3057(02)00816-X

Bonta, J., Law, M. A., & Hanson, R. K. (1998). The prediction of criminal and violent recidivism among mentally disordered offenders: A meta-analysis. *Psychological Bulletin, 123,* 123–142. doi:10.1037/0033-2909.123.2.123

Boykin v. Alabama, 395 U.S. 238 (1969).

Brent, D., Melhem, N., Donohoe, M. B., & Walker, M. (2009). The incidence and course of depression in bereaved youth 21 months after the loss of a parent to suicide, accident, or sudden natural death. *American Journal of Psychiatry, 166*, 786–794. doi:10.1176/appi.ajp.2009.08081244

Cadoret, R. J., Troughton, E., & O'Gorman, T. W. (1987). Genetic and environmental factors in alcohol abuse and antisocial personality. *Journal of Studies on Alcohol, 48*, 1–8.

Cantwell, R., Brewin, J., Glazebrook, C., Dalkin, T., Fox, R., Medley, I., & Harrison, G. (1999). Prevalence of substance misuse in first-episode psychosis. *British Journal of Psychiatry, 174*, 150–153. doi:10.1192/bjp.174.2.150

Center for Substance Abuse Treatment. (2000). *Linking substance abuse treatment and domestic violence services: A guide for treatment providers* (TIP No. 25). Rockville, MD: U.S. Department of Health and Human Services.

Child Welfare League of America. (1990). *Crack and other addictions: Old realities and new challenges.* Washington, DC: Author.

Chinn, S. (2000). A simple method for converting an odds ratio to effect size for use in meta-analysis. *Statistics in Medicine, 19*, 3127–3131. doi:10.1002/1097-0258

Claassen, C. A., Trivedi, M. H., Rush, A. J., Husain, M. M., Zisook, S., Young, E., . . . Alpert, J. (2007). Clinical differences among depressed patients with and without a history of suicide attempts: Findings from the STAR*D trial. *Journal of Affective Disorders, 97*, 77–84. doi:10.1016/j.jad.2006.05.026

Cloninger, C. R., Bohman, M., & Sigvardsson, S. (1981). Inheritenace of alcohol abuse: Cross-fostering analysis of adopted men. *Archives of General Psychiatry, 38*, 861–868.

Cohen, J. (1992). A power primer. *Psychological Bulletin, 112*, 155–159. doi:0.1037/0033-2909.112.1.155

Commonwealth v. Henry, 569 A.2d 929 (Pa. 1990).

Conrad, P. J., Pihl, R. O., Stewart, S. H., & Dongier, M. (2000). Validation of a system of classifying female substance abusers on the basis of personality and motivational risk factors for substance abuse. Subtypes of female substance dependents. *Psychology of Addictive Behaviors, 14*, 243–256. doi:10.1037//0893-164X.14.3.243

Cruz, M. T., Bajo, M., Scwheitzer, P., & Roberto, M. (2008). Shared mechanisms of alcohol and other drugs. *Alcohol Research and Health, 31*, 137–147.

Curran, P. J., Stice, E., & Chassin, L. (1997). The relation between adolescent alcohol use and peer alcohol use: A longitudinal random coefficients model. *Journal of*

Consulting and Clinical Psychology, 65, 130–140. doi:10.1037/0022-006X.65.1.130

Dackis, C. A., & O'Brien, C. P. (2001). Cocaine dependence: A disease of the brain's reward centers. *Journal of Substance Abuse Treatment, 21*, 111–117. doi:10.1016/S0740-5472(01)00192-1

Dawson, D., Grant, B., & Ruan, W. (2005). The association between stress and drinking: Modifying effects of gender and vulnerability. *Alcohol, 40*, 453–460. doi:10.1093/alcalc/agh176

DeMatteo, D., LaDuke, C., Locklair, B. R., & Heilbrun, K. (2013). Community-based alternatives for justice-involved individuals with severe mental illness: Diversion, problem-solving courts, and reentry. *Journal of Criminal Justice, 41*, 64–71. doi:10.1016/j.jcrimjus.2012.09.002

Dobkin, P. L., Chabot, L., Maliantovitch, K., & Craig, W. (1998). Predictors of outcome in drug treatment of adolescent inpatients. *Psychological Reports, 83*, 175–186. doi:10.2466/PR0.83.5.175-186

Dodge, R., Sindelar, J., & Sinha, R. (2005). The role of depression symptoms in predicting drug abstinence in outpatient substance abuse treatment. *Journal of Substance Abuse Treatment, 28*, 189–196. doi:10.1016/j.jsat.2004.12.005

Dowden, C., & Brown, S. L. (2002). The role of substance abuse factors in predicting recidivism: A meta-analysis. *Psychology, Crime & Law, 8*, 243–264. doi:10.1080/1068316021000015781

Dusky v. United States, 362 U.S. 402 (1960).

Dutra, L., Stathopoulou, G., Basden, S. L., Leyro, T. M., Powers, M. B., & Otto, M. W. (2008). A meta-analytic review of psychosocial interventions for substance use disorders. *American Journal of Psychiatry, 165*, 179–187. doi:10.1176/appi.ajp.2007.06111851

Ehrenreich, H., Rinn, T., Kunert, H. J., Moeller, M. R., Poser, W., Schilling, L., . . . Hoehe, M. R. (1999). Specific attentional disfunction in adults following early start of cannabis use. *Psychopharmacology, 142*, 295–301. doi:10.1007/s002130050892

Elkins, I. J., McGue, M., & Iacono, W. G. (2007). Prospective effects of attention-deficit/hyperactivity disorder, conduct disorder, and sex on adolescent substance use and abuse. *Archives of General Psychiatry, 64*, 1145–1152. doi:10.1001/archpsyc.64.10.1145

Epstein, J. A., & Botvin, G. J. (2002). The moderating role of risk-taking tendency and refusal assertiveness on social influences in alcohol use among inner-city adolescents. *Journal of Studies on Alcohol, 63*, 456–459.

Everington, C., & Fulero, S. M. (1999). Competence to confess: Measuring understanding and suggestibility of defendants with mental retardation.

Mental Retardation, 37, 212–220. doi:10.1352/
0047-6765(1999)037<0212:CTCMUA>2.0.CO;2

Farre, M., Mas, A., Torrens, M., Moreno, V., & Cami,
J. (2002). Retention rate and illicit opioid use
during methadone maintenance interventions:
A meta-analysis. *Drug and Alcohol Dependence,
65,* 283–290. doi:10.1016/S0376-8716(01)00171-5

Fazel, S., Bains, P., & Doll, H. (2006). Substance abuse
and dependence in prisoners: A systematic
review. *Addiction, 101,* 181–191. doi:10.1111/
j.1360-0443.2006.01316

Ford v. Wainwright, 477 U.S. 399 (1986).

Fowler, T., Lifford, K., Shelton, K., Rice, F., Thapar,
A., Neale, M. C., . . . van den Bree, M. B. (2007).
Exploring the relationships between genetic and
environmental influences on initiation and progression of substance use. *Addiction, 101,* 413–422.
doi:10.1111/j.1360-0443.2006.01694.x

Fox, H. C., Parrot, A. C., & Turner, J. J. (2001).
Ecstasy use: Cognitive deficits related to dosage
rather than self-reported problematic use of the
drug. *Journal of Psychopharmacology, 15,* 273–281.
doi:10.1177/026988110101500406

Fulcher v. State, 633 P.2d 142 (Wyo. 1981).

Fuller, R. K., Branchey, L., Brightwell, D. R., Derman,
R. M., Emrick, C. D., Iber, F. L., . . . Shaw, S.
(1986). Disulfiram treatment of alcoholism: A
Veterans Administration cooperative study. *Journal
of American Medical Association, 256,* 1449–1455.
doi:10.1001/jama.1986.03380110055026

Gendreau, P., Little, T., & Goggin, C. (1996). A meta-
analysis of the predictors of adult offender recidivism: What works! *Criminology, 34,* 575–607.
doi:10.1111/j.1745-9125.1996.tb01220.x

Gibbons, F. X., O'Hara, R. E., Stock, M. L., Gerrard, M.,
Weng, C., & Wills, T. A. (2012). The erosive effects
of racism: Reduced self-control mediates the relation
between perceived racial discrimination and substance use in African American adolescents. *Journal
of Personality and Social Psychology, 102,* 1089–1104.
doi:10.1037/a0027404

Goeders, N. E. (2004). Stress, motivation, and drug addiction. *Current Directions in Psychological Science, 13,*
33–35. doi:10.1111/j.0963-7214.2004.01301009.x

Goldberg, J. F. (2001). Bipolar disorder with comorbid
substance abuse: Diagnosis, prognosis, and treatment. *Journal of Psychiatric Practice, 7,* 109–122.
doi:10.1097/00131746-200103000-00004

Gossop, M. (2004). *Drug addiction and its treatment.*
New York, NY: Oxford University Press.

Grant, B., & Dawson, D. (1998). Age at onset of drug
use and its association with *DSM–IV* drug abuse and

dependence. *Journal of Substance Abuse, 10,* 163–173.
doi:10.1016/S0899-3289(99)80131-X

Grant, B. R., Stinson, F. S., Dawson, D. A., Chou, S. P.,
Dufour, M. C., Compton, W., . . . Kaplan, K. (2004).
Prevalence and co-occurrence of substance use dis-
orders and independent mood and anxiety disorders:
Results from the National Epidemiologic Survey
on Alcohol and Related Conditions. *Archives of
General Psychiatry, 61,* 807–816. doi:10.1001/arch-
psyc.61.8.807

Grant, I., Gonzalez, R., Carey, C. L., Natarajan, L., &
Wolfson, T. (2003). Non-acute (residual) neurocognitive effects of cannabis use: A meta analytic review.
*Journal of the International Neuropsychological Society,
9,* 679–689. doi:10.1017/S1355617703950016

Green v. United States, 365 U.S. 301 (1961).

Gut-Fayand, A., Dervaux, A., Olie, J., Loo, H., Poirier, M., &
Krebs, M. (2001). Substance abuse and suicidal-
ity in schizophrenia: A common risk factor linked
to impulsivity. *Psychiatry Research, 102,* 65–72.
doi:10.1016/S0165-1781(01)00250-5

Haas, A. L., & Peters, R. H. (2001). Development of
substance abuse problems among drug-involved
offenders: Evidence for the telescoping effect. *Journal
of Substance Abuse, 12,* 241–253. doi:10.1016/
S0899-3289(00)00053-5

Hanlon, T. E., Nurco, D. N., Bateman, R. W., & O'Grady,
K. E. (1998). The response of drug abuser parolees to
a combination of treatment and intensive supervision. *Prison Journal, 78,* 31–44. doi:10.1177/
0032855598078001003

Hasin, D. S., & Grant, B. F. (2002). Major depression in
6050 former drinkers: Association with past alcohol dependence. *Archives of General Psychiatry, 59,*
794–800. doi:10.1001/archpsyc.59.9.794

Heilbrun, K., DeMatteo, D., Yasuhara, K., Brooks-
Holliday, S., Shah, S., King, C., . . . LaDuke, C. (2012).
Community-based alternatives for justice-involved
individuals with severe mental illness: Review of the
relevant research. *Criminal Justice and Behavior, 39,*
351–419. doi:10.1177/0093854811432421

Helzer, J. E., & Pryzbeck, T. R. (1988). The occurrence
of alcoholism with other psychiatric disorders in
the general population and its impact on treatment.
Journal of Studies in Alcohol, 49, 219–224.

Hinckers, A. S., Laucht, M., Schmidt, M. H., Mann, K. F.,
Schumann, G., Schuckit, M. A., & Heinz, A. (2006).
Low level of response to alcohol as associated with
serotonin transporter genotype and high alcohol
intake in adolescents. *Biological Psychiatry, 60,*
282–287. doi:10.1016/j.biopsych.2005.12.009

Holloway, K. R., Bennett, T. H., & Farrington, D. P.
(2006). The effectiveness of drug treatment programs

at reducing criminal behavior: A meta-analysis. *Psichothema, 18*, 620–629.

Holmes, S. J., & Robins, L. N. (1988). The role of parental disciplinary practices in the development of depression and alcoholism. *Psychiatry: Interpersonal and Biological Processes, 51*, 24–36.

Huddleston, C. W., & Marlowe, D. B. (2011). *Painting the current picture: A national report card on drug courts and other problem-solving court programs in the United States.* Alexandria, VA: National Drug Court Institute.

Irvin, J. E., Bowers, C. A., Dunn, M. E., & Wang, M. C. (1999). Efficacy of relapse prevention: A meta-analytic review. *Journal of Consulting and Clinical Psychology, 67*, 563–570. doi:10.1037/0022-006X.67.4.563

Ito, T. A., Miller, N., & Pollock, V. E. (1996). Alcohol and aggression: A meta-analysis on the moderating effects of inhibitory cues, triggering events, and self-focused attention. *Psychological Bulletin, 120*, 60–82. doi:10.1037/0033-2909.120.1.60

Jackson, C., Henriksen, L., & Dickinson, D. (1999). Alcohol-specific socialization, parenting behaviors, and alcohol use by children. *Journal of Studies on Alcohol, 60*, 362–367.

Johnson v. Zerbst, 304 U.S. 458 (1938).

Kalivas, P. W., & Volkow, N. D. (2005). The neural basis of addiction: A pathology of motivation and choice. *American Journal of Psychiatry, 162*, 1403–1413. doi:10.1176/appi.ajp.162.8.1403

Kandel, D. B., Wu, P., & Davies, M. (1994). Maternal smoking during pregnancy and smoking by adolescent daughters. *American Journal of Public Health, 84*, 1407–1413. doi:10.2105/AJPH.84.9.1407

Kauer, J. A., & Malenka, R. C. (2007). Synaptic plasticity and addiction. *Nature Reviews Neuroscience, 8*, 844–858. doi:10.1038/nrn2234

Kendler, K. S. (2001). Twin studies of psychiatric illness. *Archives of General Psychiatry, 58*, 1005–1014. doi:10.1001/archpsyc.58.11.1005

Kendler, K. S., Karkowski, L. M., Neale, M. C., & Prescott, C. A. (2000). Illicit psychoactive substance use, heavy use, abuse, and dependence in a US population-based sample of male twins. *Archives of General Psychiatry, 57*, 261–269. doi:10.1001/archpsyc.57.3.261

Kendler, K. S., Neale, M. C., Heath, A. C., Kessler, R. C., & Eaves, L. J. (1994). A twin-family study of alcoholism in women. *American Journal of Psychiatry, 151*, 707–715.

Kermani, E. J., & Casteneda, R. (1996). Psychoactive substance use in forensic psychiatry. *American Journal of Drug and Alcohol Abuse, 22*, 1–27.

Kessler, R. C., Sonnega, A., Bromet, E., Hughes, M., & Nelson, C. B. (1995). Posttraumatic stress disorder in the National Comorbidity Survey. *Archives of General Psychiatry, 52*, 1048–1060. doi:10.1001/archpsyc.1995.03950240066012

Koob, G., & Kreek, M. J. (2007). Stress, dysregulation of drug reward pathways, and the transition to drug dependence. *American Journal of Psychiatry, 164*, 1149–1159. doi:10.1176/appi.ajp.2007.05030503

Kranzler, H. R., & Van Kirk, J. (2001). Efficacy of naltrexone and acamprosate for alcoholism treatment: A meta-analysis. *Alcoholism: Clinical and Experimental Research, 25*, 1335–1341. doi:10.1111/j.1530-0277.2001.tb02356

Langan, P. A., & Levin, D. J. (2002). *Recidivism of prisoners released in 1994.* Washington, DC: U.S. Department of Justice, Bureau of Justice Statistics.

Langenbucher, J., Martin, C. S., Labouvie, E., Sanjuan, P. M., Bavly, L., & Pollock, N. K. (2000). Toward the *DSM–V*: The withdrawal-gate model versus the *DSM–IV* in the diagnosis of alcohol abuse and dependence. *Journal of Consulting and Clinical Psychology, 68*, 799–809.

Leshner, A. I., & Koob, G. F. (1999). Drugs of abuse and the brain. *Proceedings of the Association of American Physicians, 111*, 99–108. doi:10.1046/j.1525-1381.1999.09218.x

Lipsey, M. W., Wilson, D. B., Cohen, M. A., & Derzon, J. H. (1997). Is there a causal relationship between alcohol use and violence? A synthesis of evidence. In M. Galanter (Ed.), *Recent developments in alcoholism* (Vol. 13, pp. 245–282). New York, NY: Plenum Press.

Lloyd, D. A., & Turner, R. J. (2008). Cumulative lifetime adversities and alcohol dependence in adolescence and young adulthood. *Drug and Alcohol Dependence, 93*, 217–226. doi:10.1016/j.drugalcdep.2007.09.012

Luscher, C., & Bellone, C. (2008). Cocaine-evoked synaptic plasticity: A key to addiction? *Nature Neuroscience, 11*, 737–738. doi:10.1038/nn0708-737

Luscher, C., & Ungless, M. A. (2006). The mechanistic classification of addictive drugs. *PLoS Medicine, 3*, e437. doi:10.1371/journal.pmed.0030437.

Lyvers, M., & Yakimoff, M. (2003). Neuropsychological correlates of opioid dependence and withdrawal. *Addictive Behaviors, 28*, 605–611. doi:10.1016/S0306-4603(01)00253-2

Magill, M., & Ray, L. (2009). Cognitive–behavioral treatment with adult alcohol and illicit drug users: A meta-analysis of randomized control trials. *Journal of Studies on Alcohol and Drugs, 70*, 516–527.

Marlatt, G. A., & Gordon, J. R. (1980). Determinants of relapse: Implications for the maintenance of behavior change. In P. O. Davidson & S. M. Davidson (Eds.), *Behavioral medicine: Changing health life styles* (pp. 410–452). Elmsford, NY: Pergamon.

Marlowe, D. B. (2010). Evidence-based sentencing for drug offenders: An analysis of prognostic risks and criminogenic needs. *Chapman Journal of Criminal Justice, 1,* 167–201.

Marlowe, D. B., DeMatteo, D. S., Patapis, N. S., & Festinger, D. S. (2012). Substance use, abuse, and dependence. In D. Faust (Ed.), *Coping with psychiatric and psychological testimony* (6th ed., pp. 636–652). New York, NY: Oxford University Press.

Martin, S. S., Butzin, C. A., Saum, S. A., & Inciardi, J. A. (1999). Three-year outcomes of therapeutic community treatment for drug-involved offenders in Delaware. *Prison Journal, 79,* 294–320.

McMurran, M. (2007). What works in substance misuse treatments for offenders? *Criminal Behaviour and Mental Health, 17,* 225–233. doi:10.1002/cbm.662

McMurran, M. (2009). Motivational interviewing with offenders: A systematic review. *Legal and Criminological Psychology, 14,* 83–100. doi:10.1348/135532508X278326

Miller, C. A., Parrott, D. J., & Giancola, P. R. (2009). Agreeableness and alcohol-related aggression: The mediating effect of trait aggressivity. *Experimental and Clinical Psychopharmacology, 17,* 445–455. doi:10.1037/a0017727

Miller, W. R. (1983). Motivational interviewing with problem drinkers. *Behavioural Psychotherapy, 11,* 147–172. doi:10.1017/S0141347300006583

Mintzer, M. Z., & Stitzer, M. L. (2002). Cognitive impairment in methadone maintenance patients. *Drug and Alcohol Dependence, 67,* 41–51. doi:10.1016/S0376-8716(02)00013-3

Miranda v. Arizona, 384 U.S. 436 (1966).

Mitchell, O., Wilson, D. B., Eggers, A., & MacKenzie, D. L. (2012). Assessing the effects of drug courts on recidivism: A meta-analytic review of traditional and non-traditional drug courts. *Journal of Criminal Justice, 40,* 60–71. doi:10.1016/j.jcrimjus.2011.11.009

Mitchell, O., Wilson, D. B., & MacKenzie, D. L. (2006). *The effectiveness of incarceration-based drug treatment on criminal behavior.* Retrieved from http://www.campbellcollaboration.org/doc-pdf/Incarceration-BasedDrugTxSept06final.pdf

Mitchell, O., Wilson, D. B., & MacKenzie, D. L. (2007). Does incarceration-based drug treatment reduce recidivism? A meta-analytic synthesis of the research. *Journal of Experimental Criminology, 3,* 353–375. doi:10.1007/s11292-007-9040-2.

Mittenberg, W., & Motta, S. (1993). Effects of chronic cocaine abuse in memory and learning. *Archives of Clinical Neuropsychology, 8,* 477–483. doi:10.1016/0887-6177(93)90048-6

Montana v. Egelhoff, 518 U.S. 37 (1996).

Moselhy, H. F., Fahmy, E., Mikhael, V. S., & El-Sheikh, H. (2012). Emotional control in patients with opioid dependence syndrome and reported history of negative life events. *Addictive Disorders and Their Treatment, 11,* 93–100. doi:10.1097/ADT.0b013e3182273c4d

Mustard, S., May, D. C., & Phillips, D. W. (2006). Prevalence and predictors of cheating on Antabuse: Is Antabuse a cure or merely an obstacle? *American Journal of Criminal Justice, 31,* 51–63. doi:10.1007/BF02885684

National Center on Addiction and Substance Abuse. (2010). *Behind bars II: Substance abuse and America's prison population.* New York, NY: Author.

National Institute of Justice. (2000). *1999 annual report on drug use among adult and juvenile arrestees.* Washington, DC: U.S. Department of Justice.

National Institute on Drug Abuse. (2001). *Hallucinogens and dissociative drugs* (NIH Pub. No. 01-4209). Retrieved from http://www.drugabuse.gov/publications/research-reports/hallucinogens-dissociative-drugs

O'Brien, C. P., Childress, A. R., Ehrman, R., & Robbins, S. J. (1998). Conditioning factors in drug abuse: Can they explain compulsions? *Journal of Psychopharmacology, 12,* 15–22.

Office of National Drug Control Policy. (2011). *How illicit drug use affects business and the economy.* Washington, DC: Author.

Office of National Drug Control Policy. (2012). *2011 annual report: Arrestee drug abuse monitoring program II.* Washington, DC: Author.

Ohlmeier, M. D., Peters, K., Kordon, A., Seifert, J., Wildt, B. T., Wiese, B., . . . Schneider, U. (2007). Nicotine and alcohol dependence in patients with comorbid attention-deficit/hyperactivity disorder (ADHD). *Alcohol and Alcoholism, 42,* 539–543. doi:10.1093/alcalc/agm069

Panetti v. Quarterman, 551 U.S. 930 (2007).

Pau, W. H., Lee, M. C., & Chan, S. F. (2002). The impact of heroin on frontal executive functions. *Archives of Clinical Neuropsychology, 17,* 663–670. doi:10.1093/arclin/17.7.663

Pearson, F., & Lipton, D. (1999). A meta-analytic review of the effectiveness of corrections-based treatments for drug abuse. *Prison Journal, 79,* 384–410. doi:10.1177/0032885599079004003

Peterson, J. B., & Pihl, R. O. (1990). Information processing, neuropsychological function, and the inherited predisposition to alcoholism. *Neuropsychology Review, 1,* 343–369. doi:10.1007/BF01109029

Pihl, R. O. (2009). Substance abuse: Etiological considerations. In P. H. Blaney & T. Millon (Eds.),

Oxford textbook of psychopathology (pp. 253–279). New York, NY: Oxford University Press.

Prescott, C. A., Caldwell, C. B., Carey, G., Vogler, G. P., Trumbetta, S. L., & Gottesman, I. I. (2005). The Washington University twin study of alcoholism. *American Journal of Medical Genetics Part B (Neuropsychiatric Genetics), 134B*, 45–55. doi:10.1002/ajmg.b.30124

Prescott, C. A., & Kendler, K. S. (1999). Genetic and environmental contributions to alcohol abuse and dependence in a population-based sample of male twins. *American Journal of Psychiatry, 156*, 34–40.

Quinn, P. D., & Fromme, K. (2010). Self-regulation as a protective factor against risky drinking and sexual behavior. *Psychology of Addictive Behaviors, 24*, 376–385. doi:10.1037/a0018547

Roberts, R. E., Roberts, C. E., & Xing, Y. (2007). Comorbidity of substance use disorders and other psychiatric disorders among adolescents: Evidence from an epidemiologic survey. *Drug and Alcohol Dependence, 88S*, S4–S13. doi:10.1016/j.drugalcdep.2006.12.010

Robins, L., & Mills, J. L. (1993). Effects of in-utero exposure to street drugs. *American Journal of Public Health, 83*(Suppl.), 8–32.

Rösner, S., Leucht, S., Lehert, P., & Soyka, M. (2008). Acamprosate supports abstinence, naltrexone prevents excessive drinking: Evidence from a meta-analysis with unreported outcomes. *Journal of Psychopharmacology, 22*, 11–23. doi:10.1177/0269881107078308

Rubak, S., Sandbæk, A., Lauritzen, T., & Christensen, B. (2005). Motivational interviewing: A systematic review and meta-analysis. *British Journal of General Practice, 55*, 305–312.

Scheier, L. M. (2010) Social–cognitive models of drug use etiology. In L. M. Scheier (Ed.), *Handbook of drug use etiology: Theory, methods, and empirical findings* (pp. 93–112). Washington, DC: American Psychological Association.

Schinke, S. P., Tepavac, L., & Cole, K. C. (2000). Preventing substance use among Native American youth: Three-year results. *Addictive Behaviors, 25*, 387–397. doi:10.1016/S0306-4603(99)00071-4

Schuckit, M. A., Tipp, J. E., Bucholz, K. K., Nurnberger, J. I., Hesselbrock, V. M., Crowe, R. R., & Kramer, J. (1997). The life-time rates of three major mood disorders and four major anxiety disorders in alcoholics and controls. *Addiction, 92*, 1289–1304. doi:10.1111/j.1360-0443.1997.tb02848.x

Shoal, G. D., Gudonis, L. C., Giancola, P. R., & Tarter, R. E. (2007). Delinquency as a mediator of the relation between negative affectivity and adolescent alcohol use disorder. *Addictive Behaviors, 32*, 2747–2765. doi:10.1016/j.addbeh.2007.04.011

Silberberg, J. M., & Crosley, A. (2010). Forensic psychiatry, substance use and mental illness. In N. S. Miller (Ed.), *Principles of addictions and the law: Applications in forensic, mental health, and medical practice* (pp. 203–227). New York, NY: Elsevier.

Sinha, R. (2007). The role of stress in addiction relapse. *Current Psychiatry Reports, 9*, 388–395. doi:10.1007/s11920-007-0050-6

Sinha, R. (2008). Chronic stress, drug use, and vulnerability to addiction. *Annals of the New York Academy of Sciences, 1141*, 105–130. doi:10.1196/annals.1441.030

Smith, G. T., Goldman, M. S., Greenbaum, P. E., & Christiansen, B. A. (1995). Expectancy for social facilitation from drinking: The divergent paths of high-expectancy and low-expectancy adolescents. *Journal of Abnormal Psychology, 104*, 32–40. doi:10.1037/0021-843X.104.1.32

Stacy, A. W., Ames, S. L., Wiers, R. W., & Krank, M. D. (2010). Associative memory in appetitive behavior: Framework and relevance to epidemiology and prevention. In L. M. Scheier (Ed.), *Handbook of drug use etiology: Theory, methods, and empirical findings* (pp. 165–182). Washington, DC: American Psychological Association.

Stallings, M. C., Corley, R. P., Dennehey, B., Hewitt, J. K., Krauter, K. S., Lessem, J. M., . . . Crowley, T. J. (2005). A genome-wide search for quantitative trait loci that influence antisocial drug dependence in adolescence. *Archives of General Psychiatry, 62*, 1042–1051. doi:10.1001/archpsyc.62.9.1042

Substance Abuse and Mental Health Services Administration. (2011). *Results from the 2010 National Survey on Drug Use and Health: Summary of national findings* (NSDUH Series H-41, HHS Publication No. (SMA) 11-4658). Rockville, MD: Author.

Tancer, M., & Johanson, C. (2003). Reinforcing, subjective, and physiological effects of MDMA in humans: A comparison with d-amphetamine and mCPP. *Drug and Alcohol Dependence, 72*, 33–44. doi:10.1016/S0376-8716(03)00172-8

Tate, S. R., Drapkin, M. L., & Brown, S. A. (2009). Substance abuse: Diagnosis, comorbidity, and psychopathology. In P. H. Blaney & T. Millon (Eds.), *Oxford textbook of psychopathology* (pp. 280–297). New York, NY: Oxford University Press.

Thomasius, R., Petersen, K., Buchert, R., Andresen, B., Zapletalova, P., Wartberg, L., . . . Schmoldt, A. (2003). Mood, cognition and serotonin transporter availability in current and former ecstasy (MDMA) users. *Psychopharmacology (Berlin), 167*, 85–96.

United States v. Benally, 215 F.3d 1068 (10th Cir. 2000).

United States v. Booker, 543 U.S. 220 (2005).

U.S. Const. amend. V.

U.S. Const. amend. VI.

U.S.S.G. § 5K2.13 (2012).

van Amsterdam, J. G., Brunt, T. M., McMaster, M. T., & Niesink, R. J. (2012). Possible long-term effects of y-hydroxybutyric acid (GHB) due to neurotoxicity and overdose. *Neuroscience and Biobehavioral Reviews, 36,* 1217–1227. doi:10.1016/j.neubiorev.2012.02.002

Verdejo-Garcia, A., & Perez-Garcia, M. (2007). Profile of executive deficits in cocaine and heroin poly-substance user: Common and differential effects on separate executive components. *Psychopharmacology, 190,* 517–530. doi:10.1007/s00213-006-0632-8

Viljoen, J. L., Roesch, R., & Zapf, P. A. (2002). An examination of the relationship between competency to stand trial, competency to waive interrogation rights, and psychopathology. *Law and Human Behavior, 25,* 481–506.

Volkow, N. D., & Fowler, J. S. (2000). Addiction, a disease of compulsion and drive: Involvement of the orbitofrontal cortex. *Cerebral Cortex, 10,* 318–325. doi:10.1093/cercor/10.3.318

Wareing, M., Fisk, J. E., & Murphy, P. N. (2000). Working memory deficits in current and previous users of MDMA ("ecstasy"). *British Journal of Psychology, 91,* 181–188. doi:10.1348/000712600161772

Weisburd, D., Lum, C. M., & Petrosino, A. (2001). Does research design affect study outcomes in criminal justice? *Annals of the American Academy of Political and Social Science, 578,* 50–70. doi:10.1177/0002716201578001004

Widom, C. S., Weiler, B. L., & Cottler, L. B. (1999). Childhood victimization and drug abuse: A comparison of prospective and retrospective findings. *Journal of Consulting and Clinical Psychology, 67,* 867–880. doi:10.1037/0022-006X.67.6.867

Wilson, D. B., Bouffard, L. A., & MacKenzie, D. L. (2005). A quantitative review of structured, group-oriented cognitive–behavioral programs for offenders. *Criminal Justice and Behavior, 32,* 172–204. doi:10.1177/0093854804272889

Windle, M. (2000). Parental, sibling, and peer influences on adolescent substance use and alcohol problems. *Applied Developmental Science, 4,* 98–110. doi:10.1207/S1532480XADS0402_5

Wolfe, W. L., & Maisto, S. A. (2000). The relationship between eating disorders and substance use: Moving beyond co-prevalence research. *Clinical Psychology Review, 20,* 617–631. doi:10.1016/S0272-7358(99)00009-4

Yoshizuka, K. I., & Perry, P. J. (2012). The association between pharmacologic drug intoxication and forensic-specific intent. *Journal of Pharmacy Practice, 25,* 50–60. doi:10.1177/0897190011431147

Yuille, J. C., Tollestrup, P. A., Marxsen, D., Porter, S., & Herve, H. M. (1998). An exploration of the effects of marijuana on eyewitness memory. *International Journal of Law and Psychiatry, 21,* 117–128. doi:10.1016/S0160-2527(97)00027-7

CHAPTER 11

SEXUAL OFFENDING

Michael C. Seto, Drew A. Kingston, and Skye Stephens

In this chapter, we provide an introduction and overview of the empirical literature on sexual offending. The chapter begins with a description of major theoretical models that have been developed to explain the occurrence of sexual offending and highlights their common underpinnings. We then differentiate sexual offenders from other types of criminal offenders and discuss subgroups of sexual offenders who are distinguished by victim age or by the offender's relationship to the victim. Drawing from the research presented in this chapter, we examine the translation of our scientific knowledge about sexual offending to clinical practices via applications in sexual offender assessment, treatment, prevention, and public policy.

IMPORTANCE OF THE PROBLEM

Sexual offending occurs throughout the world, though its incidence varies as a result of sociocultural factors, reporting practices, and laws. Sexual offending encompasses a range of criminal sexual acts, including sexual assaults of older adolescents or adults, sexual contacts with children under the legally defined age of majority, noncontact sexual offenses involving exhibitionism or voyeurism, and engagement with illegal pornography (e.g., child pornography). In this chapter, we focus on the literature pertaining to contact sexual offenses. Readers should refer to Laws and O'Donohue (2008) for information on noncontact and online sexual offending.

Across jurisdictions and across time, perpetrators of contact sexual offenses are predominantly male, whereas victims are predominantly female. The majority of contact sexual offenses are committed against minors by an adult, typically by someone who is known to them (e.g., Brennan & Taylor-Butts, 2008). Although many victims are resilient, some suffer for many years, experiencing anxiety, depression, sexually transmitted diseases, unwanted pregnancy, or trauma after the sexual offense has taken place (Beitchman et al., 1992; Rind, Tromovitch, & Bauserman, 1998).

In Canada and the United States, national rates of reported sexual violence have been decreasing along with overall levels of violent crime since the early 1990s (Brennan & Taylor-Butts, 2008; Mishra & Lalumière, 2009; Truman, 2011). In the United States, Truman (2011) reported that the official incidence of rape and sexual assault decreased by 24% from 2001 to 2010. However, official data are underestimates of all offending because approximately two-thirds of sexual crimes are not reported to police or other authorities (Berzofsky, Krebs, Langton, & Smiley-McDonald, 2012). Self-reported victimization data, which include undetected sexual offenses, also suggest that the rate of sexual violence has been declining (e.g., Finkelhor & Jones, 2006; Mishra & Lalumière, 2009). The explanations for this decline are not fully understood but include more policing, longer sentences, decreased risk taking, and the demographic effects of legalized abortion (Mishra & Lalumière, 2009; Zimring, 2007).

http://dx.doi.org/10.1037/14461-011

APA Handbook of Forensic Psychology: Vol. 1. Individual and Situational Influences in Criminal and Civil Contexts,
B. L. Cutler and P. A. Zapf (Editors-in-Chief)

RELEVANT PSYCHOLOGICAL THEORY AND PRINCIPLES

Ward, Polaschek, and Beech (2006) provided an extensive discussion and critical review of major theories of sexual offending. More prominent models that have undergone some empirical testing are summarized in this section; not all models are described due to a lack of space. Some models attempt to explain all contact sexual offending; others were specifically developed to explain sexual offenses involving children or adults.

Precondition Model

Finkelhor (1984) suggested that there are four factors that can explain sexual offending against children. The first three factors represent motivations for committing sexual offenses, including feeling sexually aroused by children (pedophilia), having more affinity for children than adults (emotional congruence with children), and feeling unable to meet one's emotional and sexual needs in relationships with adults (blockage). The fourth factor represents the ways that an individual's inhibitions about sexual offending can be overcome (disinhibition), which can include alcohol or drug use, antisocial attitudes and beliefs (e.g., a belief that children are not harmed by sex with an adult), and impulsivity. Studies comparing sexual offenders with child victims to other offenders have found strong support for the importance of pedophilia and disinhibition in explaining sexual offending against children (see Seto, 2008). There is also some evidence for the role of emotional congruence for some offenders (e.g., Wilson, 1999). Emotional congruence with children predicts sexual recidivism, but only offenders with boy victims are significantly different from nonsexual offenders (McPhail, Hermann, & Nunes, 2011). Dreznick (2003) found that sexual offenders are lower in social skills than other offenders, which is consistent with blockage.

Marshall and Barbaree's (1990) Vulnerability Model

Marshall and Barbaree (1990) described a developmental model of sexual offending that integrates biological vulnerabilities and adverse early experiences (particularly child maltreatment) in the development of social skills deficits and self-regulation problems. These deficits can then impede the development of positive relationships with peers and increase the risk of sexual contact with children or the use of sexual coercion with peers. Sexual offenders are substantially more likely than other offenders to have histories of sexual abuse; they are also more likely to have experienced physical abuse, but the group difference is much smaller for physical abuse, suggesting that there is a specific link between sexual abuse and sexual offending (Jespersen, Lalumière, & Seto, 2009; Seto & Lalumière, 2010). Another meta-analysis demonstrated that adult sexual offenders have more social skills deficits than other offenders (Dreznick, 2003); however, this difference in social skills deficits was much smaller in comparisons of adolescent offender groups (Seto & Lalumière, 2010).

Confluence Model of Sexual Aggression

The confluence model of sexual aggression emerged in the 1990s as a theoretical model of sexual aggression toward women, combining both evolutionary and feminist psychological perspectives (Malamuth, Linz, Heavey, Barnes, & Acker, 1995; Malamuth, Sockloskie, Koss, & Tanaka, 1991). In the confluence model, men are at a greater risk of engaging in sexual aggression if they are high in both hostile masculinity and impersonal sex. *Hostile masculinity* involves distrust and hostility toward women and stereotypical beliefs about sex roles and sexuality. *Impersonal sex* involves a preference and pursuit of casual, impersonal sex over sexual relationships that involve some emotional commitment. Both hostile masculinity and impersonal sex can be the result of childhood maltreatment and/or other adverse early experiences. Both pathways are independently associated with a greater likelihood of sexual aggression, but the interaction (confluence) of the two pathways poses the greatest risk for sexual aggression toward women (Malamuth et al., 1991).

The confluence model has been supported in multiple cross-sectional studies, mostly using male college students (e.g., Abbey, Jacques-Tiura, & LeBreton, 2011; Wheeler, George, & Dahl, 2002). Malamuth et al. (1995) conducted a 10-year longitudinal follow-up study of college-age males and found support for the confluence model in its prediction of (a) sexual aggression over time, (b) other forms of aggression that are perpetrated against women (e.g., intimate partner violence), and (c) relationship difficulties. Most of the research on the confluence model has been conducted with college students, but there are some studies that have been conducted with convicted sexual offenders (e.g., Marshall & Moulden, 2001; Milner & Webster, 2005). Many elements of the confluence model (e.g., hostility toward women) have been identified as psychologically meaningful risk factors among sexual offenders (Mann, Hanson, & Thornton, 2010). A brief review of major risk factors is provided later in the Assessment of Risk section.

Self-Regulation Model

A qualitative analysis of sexual-offending processes suggested that offenders vary in the paths they take to offend, with some trying to avoid (unsuccessfully) opportunities to offend and others actively seeking out such opportunities (Ward & Hudson, 1998, 2000). The self-regulation model includes nine phases in the offense progression that are organized into four main pathways to sexual offending. Research in support of the self-regulation model is accumulating, including its ability to account for diverse offender and offense characteristics and validation of the phases of the model and its resultant four pathways (Kingston, 2010; Proulx, Perreault, & Ouimet, 1999; Webster, 2005). Offense goals and strategies are differentially associated with offender and offense characteristics, such as offense planning, victim type, and treatment-relevant factors (Bickley & Beech, 2002, 2003; Kingston, Yates, & Firestone, 2012).

According to the self-regulation model, offenders engage in goal-directed action (Ward & Hudson, 2000). Some offenders are motivated to sexually offend and thus have *approach* goals. In contrast, some offenders desire to avoid such situations and/ or circumstances and thus are guided by *avoidance* goals. Passive or active strategies are implemented in order to achieve the predominant goal selected by the individual. Offenders tend to take a predominant pathway toward their crimes. The *avoidant-passive pathway* is characterized by a desire to refrain from offending, but the individual lacks the necessary coping strategies to achieve this goal. Offenders in this pathway use passive or covert strategies (e.g., ignoring sexual thoughts) to abstain from offending and, as such, are representative of an underregulated style. The strategies employed are insufficient to prevent offending. Following the offense, the offender will experience negative affect (e.g., guilt, shame) given the failure to achieve the desired goal. The *avoidant-active pathway* is characterized by a misregulated self-regulatory style. Offenders in this pathway want to avoid committing a sexual offense and employ active strategies to suppress their motivation or opportunities to offend. This active strategy is counterproductive, however, because a sexual offense can still occur, and the coping strategy that is used might actually make things worse (e.g., drinking alcohol to suppress sexual thoughts may actually lead to more disinhibited behavior). Following the offense, the offender will experience negative affect (e.g., guilt, shame) due to his self-regulatory failure.[1]

The *approach-automatic pathway* to offending is characterized by an underregulated style and a desire to offend sexually (Ward & Hudson, 2000). It is automatic because the offending is often impulsive or, if planned, the planning is rudimentary and unsophisticated. Following the offense, the offender is likely to experience positive rather than negative affect (e.g., increased self-esteem) as his goal to sexually offend has been achieved. Finally, *the approach-explicit pathway* is characterized by intentional planning of the sexual offense along with explicit and considered strategies to achieve this goal. As such, this pathway represents an intact self-regulation style. The offender maintains positive mood throughout the offense process and likely experiences positive affect (e.g., elation) following the offense, as he has achieved his goal (Ward & Hudson, 2000; Yates & Kingston, 2005).

Integrated Theory of Sexual Offending

Ward et al. (2006) attempted to integrate existing explanations of sexual offending into a broad

---

[1]Because most of the research we review is on male sexual offending, we use masculine pronouns throughout this chapter.

framework that they described as the integrated theory of sexual offending. The integrated theory outlines biological, ecological, and neuropsychological domains that converge in a cumulative and synergistic fashion to increase the likelihood of sexual aggression. Important biological factors include neurodevelopmental perturbations, gender-linked vulnerabilities such as the tendency for males to engage in impersonal sexual activity, and paraphilic sexual interests (Lalumière, Harris, Quinsey, & Rice, 2005; Seto, 2008). Ecological factors, which include social circumstances, personal circumstances, and physical environments, can interact with existing vulnerabilities to influence an individual's risk of sexual offending through social learning.

Biological functioning and social learning have an influence on sexual offending through three neuropsychological systems: (a) the motivational/emotional system, (b) the action selection/control system, and (c) the perception and memory system. The first system influences the goals and values of the individual, the second system drives self-regulation and goal-directed behavior, and the third system represents the organization of cognitive schema and expectations about sex and sexual offending. Problems in these core neuropsychological systems are manifested as dynamic risk factors for sexual offending, including deviant sexual interests, impulsivity, interpersonal deficits, and antisocial attitudes and beliefs. Though comprehensive, the integrated theory has not undergone the same level of empirical testing as the other models we described.

RESEARCH REVIEW

In this section, we review two major lines of research on sexual offending. The first examines the extent to which sexual offenders comprise a distinct population that is separate from other offenders, and the second examines different typological distinctions that have been made among sexual offenders, including distinctions by victim age and relatedness.

Comparing Sexual and Nonsexual Offenders

A fundamental question about sexual offending is the extent to which sexual offenders are *generalists*, engaging in a variety of sexual and nonsexual crimes, or *specialists*, engaging (mostly) in sexual crimes (D. A. Harris, Mazerolle, & Knight, 2009; Lussier, Leclerc, & Proulx, 2005; Seto & Lalumière, 2010). For example, a generalist may break into a house and in this context discover a woman alone and opportunistically commit a sexual assault. Another example is when someone under the influence of alcohol or drugs encounters a vulnerable person and impulsively commits a sexual offense. In contrast, although they may sometimes commit other crimes, specialists mostly commit sexual offenses and are more likely to be motivated by sexual deviance (see next section). Generalists can be explained by extant forensic and criminological models of offending, whereas specialists require the inclusion of unique or distinctive factors.

Seto and Lalumière (2010) tested generalist versus specialist explanations for adolescent sexual offending by analyzing data from 59 studies that compared adolescent sexual offenders and other adolescent offenders. Data were available for a wide range of domains, including conduct problems, antisocial personality traits, criminal history, sexual experiences, sexual interests, social competence, and psychopathology. Adolescent sexual offenders were most distinguished from other adolescent offenders by their sexual interests, sexual abuse history, exposure to sexual violence, and early exposure to sex/pornography, suggesting that these aspects of sexual development are the most distinctive. Studies comparing adult sexual offenders to other adult offenders have also found evidence that many of these same factors are distinctive (Allen, D'Alessio, & Emmers-Sommer, 2000; Jespersen et al., 2009; Lalumière et al., 2005; Seto, 2008).

A comparable multidomain meta-analysis has not been conducted for adult sexual offenders, though meta-analyses are available for specific domains such as sexual interest in coercive sex or social skills deficits (Dreznick, 2003; Lalumière, Quinsey, Harris, Rice, & Trautrimas, 2003). There is good evidence for sexual deviance as a specific factor for adult sexual offenders; the evidence is stronger than it is for adolescent sexual offenders, where there is more wariness about using phallometry to assess sexual arousal. Rapists differ from other men in their sexual responses to depictions of coercive sex or nonsexual violence (Lalumière et al., 2005), and offenders with child victims differ from other men in their sexual responses to children (Seto, 2008). Sexual offenders with adult victims tend to be similar to nonsexual offenders on measures of antisociality, such as psychopathy, whereas sexual offenders with child victims tend to score lower on psychopathy, nonsexual offense history, and delinquency (e.g., D. A. Harris et al., 2009). This is especially true of sexual offenders who have related child victims (e.g., Seto, 2008).

Antisociality and Sexual Deviance

Risk factors that have been empirically related to sexual recidivism among identified sexual offenders can be classified as indicators of one of two major risk dimensions: antisociality and sexual deviance (Hanson & Bussière, 1998; Hanson & Morton-Bourgon, 2005). Indicators of *antisociality* are factors that have been identified in general offender research, including early conduct problems, juvenile delinquency, criminal history, and antisocial personality traits such as risk taking and callousness. Indicators of *sexual deviance* are specific to sexual offenders and include excessive sexual preoccupation, sexual arousal to children or sexual violence, and other paraphilic interests such as exhibitionism (i.e., exposure of genitals to unsuspecting strangers) or voyeurism (i.e., observing an unsuspecting stranger undressing or other private activity). Sexual offenders who are high in antisociality are at the greatest risk of nonsexual reoffending, whereas those who are high in sexual deviance are at the greatest risk of sexual reoffending (e.g., Hanson & Morton-Bourgon, 2005). Offenders who are high on both dimensions pose the greatest risk of serious recidivism (e.g., Seto, Harris, Rice, & Barbaree, 2004).

Some, but not all, paraphilias are important sexual motivations for sexual offending. *Paraphilias* are clinically defined as recurrent and persistent sexual thoughts, fantasies, urges, or behaviors that cause clinically significant distress or impairment (American Psychiatric Association, 2013). The most common paraphilias to consider for sexual offending are pedophilia, hebephilia, sexual sadism, exhibitionism, and voyeurism. Paraphilias themselves are not

illegal, but acting on those interests with a nonconsenting person is. To illustrate, having pedophilia is not illegal in the United States, though it is highly stigmatized, but accessing child pornography and having sexual contact with a child are serious criminal offenses. Paraphilias and sexual offending are not synonymous; some pedophiles have not committed sexual offenses (e.g., child pornography, sexual solicitation of minors, or sexual contact crimes), and many sexual offenders with child victims would not meet the diagnostic criteria for pedophilia (Seto, 2008).

It appears to be well accepted that a substantial proportion of sexual offenders against children (child molesters) are sexually deviant (Seto, 2008). However, it is still controversial to claim that a substantial (and similar) proportion of sexual offenders against adults (rapists) are sexually deviant, showing relatively greater sexual arousal to depictions of sexual violence than to consensual sex. This is despite robust evidence that rapists differ from nonrapists in their phallometric responses to stories varying in sexual violence and coercion cues (Lalumière et al., 2003). Part of this lack of consensus may come from politicization of the discourse about the rape and sexual assault of women, with some feminist writers arguing that rape is an act of aggression, power, and control rather than a sexual act (e.g., Brownmiller, 1975; Burt, 1980). Evidence that some men are sexually aroused by cues of nonconsent and/or violence contradicts the idea that rape is solely a violent crime rather than both a sexual and violent crime.

The lack of consensus regarding sexual offending against adults and being sexually deviant might also be attributable to a lack of clarity about what cues drive rapists' arousal. Studies typically present stories describing consensual sex, sexual assault (varying in the amount of coercion and violence involved), and, sometimes, nonsexual violence (Lalumière et al., 2003). Male rapists differ from nonrapists in their response to these scenarios, but it is unclear whether they are responding to cues of coercion or to cues of violence and injury. In other words, it is unclear whether rapists are sexual sadists who are aroused by cues of physical suffering or whether they would qualify for the proposed diagnosis of paraphilic coercive disorder (i.e., sexual arousal to cues of nonconsensual sexual activity) instead. Two recent studies suggested that rapists are responding most to coercion/nonconsent, whereas self-identified sadists respond more to physical violence/injury (G. T. Harris, Lalumière, Seto, Rice, & Chaplin, 2012; Seto, Lalumière, Harris, & Chivers, 2012).

There are fewer sexual response studies of adolescents, but these studies also suggest that adolescent sexual offenders with child victims differ from young adult comparison groups in their sexual responses to children (Robinson, Rouleau, & Madrigano, 1997; Seto, Lalumière, & Blanchard, 2000). Moreover, sexual arousal to children is significantly correlated with child victim characteristics, including having boy victims and multiple child victims (Seto, Murphy, Page, & Ennis, 2003). Whether adolescent sexual offenders differ in their response to depictions of sexual coercion or violence has not yet been demonstrated.

Major Types of Sexual Offenders

Like any other offender population, sexual offenders are heterogeneous, varying on demographic characteristics, criminal histories, mental health histories, motivations for offending, and risk of reoffending. An exception to this heterogeneity is gender; most (often 90%+) identified sexual offenders are male, showing a gender bias that is much greater than the gender bias for offending in general (see Seto, 2008). This bias is less extreme, however, when one looks at self-report victimization surveys, which suggest that some women perpetrate sexual offenses, predominantly against children, that are not reported to police and therefore do not manifest in clinical or criminal justice settings (Denov, 2003). Given the disparity in prevalence, research on female sexual offending is underdeveloped in comparison to the literature on males.

Distinction by victim age. In order to derive more homogeneous groups of sexual offenders, researchers and clinicians have classified sexual offenders in different ways. The most common distinction made is between offenders who victimize children (often called *child molesters*) and those who victimize adults (often called *rapists*), with a pattern of meaningful differences emerging between the two subgroups (e.g., D. A. Harris et al., 2009). In the literature, a distinction is sometimes made between prepubescent or pubescent children and postpubertal adolescents. Victim age is relevant because of laws pertaining to the age of consent for sex. Clinically, however, victim age is a proxy for the physical maturity of sexual victims. A person is guilty of committing a sexual offense against a minor if the victim is 8, 12, or 15 years of age (when age of consent is 16); however, the perpetrator might be engaging in pedophilic behavior if the 8-year-old victim is clearly prepubescent, in hebephilic behavior if the 12-year-old victim is showing some early signs of puberty, and in neither pedophilic nor hebephilic behavior if the 15-year-old victim looks sexually mature and could be confused with a young adult woman by a reasonable observer.

Victim age is not synonymous with sexual-age interests. A conservative estimate is that approximately 50%–60% of sexual offenders with child victims would meet the diagnostic criteria for pedophilia (Kingston, Firestone, Moulden, & Bradford, 2007; see Seto, 2008, for a review). Other offenders are motivated by reasons other than a persistent and recurrent sexual attraction to children. Similarly, there are individuals who would meet the diagnostic criteria for pedophilia who are not known to have ever committed sexual offenses against children.

Child molesters are more likely than rapists to be specialists, and rapists are more likely than child molesters to be generalists (e.g., Lussier et al., 2005). Rapists tend to start their criminal careers earlier than child molesters, commit more offenses as juveniles, and be younger when they start sexually offending (Baxter, Marshall, Barbaree, Davidson, & Malcolm, 1984; Lalumière et al., 2005). Compared to offenders against children, offenders against adults have higher psychopathy scores, are more likely to exhibit early school-behavior problems, and are more likely to engage in adolescent delinquency (D. A. Harris et al., 2009; Porter et al., 2000). Further, offenders against adults are more likely to reoffend than are offenders against children, especially for nonsexual crimes (e.g., D. A. Harris et al., 2009; Olver & Wong, 2006).

Child molesters are more likely to have been sexually abused themselves as children than rapists

(Jespersen et al., 2009; Seto & Lalumière, 2010) and are more likely to have social skills and problem-solving deficits (Nezu, Nezu, Dudek, Peacock, & Stoll, 2005). A meta-analysis that was conducted by Cantor, Blanchard, Robichaud, and Christensen (2005) demonstrated that child molesters scored lower on measures of intelligence than rapists did. In comparison to rapists, child molesters (a) were more likely to have committed offenses that did not involve penetration, (b) used less physical violence, (c) were less likely to have used a weapon, (d) had a higher number of victims, and (e) were more likely to be older at the index offense (Cohen, Frenda, Mojatabai, Katsavdakis, & Galynker, 2007).

Contrary to public perception, sexual assaults that are committed against unknown children are rare, whereas a notable proportion of sexual assaults that are committed against adults are by strangers (e.g., Cohen et al., 2007). The majority of sexual offenses are committed by perpetrators who know their victim, regardless of victim age (Brennan & Taylor-Butts, 2008). The younger the victim, the more likely it is that the offender is closely related to the victim; many victims of father- or brother-committed incest are below the age of 11, for example, whereas many extrafamilial child victims are between the ages of 11 and 13 (Finkelhor, 1994). In addition, the younger the victim, the more likely it is that the offender has male victims, that the offense occurred in the victim's residence, and that the offense involved touching rather than sexual penetration (Carlstedt et al., 2009; Levenson, Becker, & Morin, 2008).

There is also evidence suggesting that the distinction between offenders with child victims and those with peer or adult victims is also a meaningful distinction among adolescents. For example, Kemper and Kistner (2007) compared adolescent sexual offenders distinguished by victim age and found that the majority of them victimized children. Adolescents who sexually victimized peers or adults were more likely to have longer criminal histories compared to adolescents who victimized children; the former group was also more likely to have extrafamilial victims. Mixed offenders (both child and peer/adult victims) were more likely to have victims that were both related and unrelated to the perpetrator, to have committed more physically intrusive sexual

acts, and to have engaged in a greater variety of sexual acts during their offense. In our meta-analysis, we found that adolescents who sexually victimized children tended to be less antisocial than those who sexually victimized peers or adults, as indicated by measures of conduct problems, antisocial personality traits, or criminal history (Seto & Lalumière, 2010).

Some studies have compared offenders who victimize adolescents to those who victimize children or adults. As a group, the offenders with adolescent victims were intermediate between the child molesters and rapists in using violence or a weapon during the commission of the offense or in having a male victim (Cohen et al., 2007). Offenders with adolescent victims were more likely than child molesters and rapists to have stable marriages at the time of the offense and were more likely to have had children who were the same age as their victim(s) (Baxter et al., 1984; Kuznestov, Pierson, & Harry, 1992). Carlstedt et al. (2009) found that offenders with adolescent victims were twice as likely to have a diagnosed mood disorder (e.g., depression) than those with child or adult victims. Both offenders who victimized children and those who victimized adolescents had similar patterns of childhood sexual abuse (Worling, 1995).

Taken together, these findings suggest that offenders who victimize adolescents can be distinguished from child molesters and rapists. One complication is that offenders with adolescent victims are more likely than child molesters and rapists to have victims in other age groups as well (e.g., Guay, Proulx, Cusson, & Ouimet, 2001). This raises an important limitation of classification schemes that rely on victim age, as these assume that an offender with multiple victims will only have victims in one age category and will select victims in the same age category if he reoffends (see Laws, 1994; Robertiello & Terry, 2007). However, as noted earlier, there is a minority of mixed offenders who have victims in different age categories (Guay et al., 2001). Victim age polymorphic offenders appear to be at higher risk to reoffend than other sexual offenders (Kingston et al., 2012; Parent, Guay, & Knight, 2011).

Distinction by relatedness. Another useful way of distinguishing between types of sexual offenders is between individuals who offend against a family member, someone who is known to them (e.g., friend or acquaintance), or strangers. This distinction has been frequently discussed for sexual offending against children, with clinically and theoretically meaningful distinctions between incest offenders and extrafamilial offenders (Seto, 2008). For example, incest offenders are more likely than extrafamilial offenders to victimize girls, to engage in intercourse, and to score lower on measures of antisociality and sexual deviance (e.g., Seto, Lalumière, & Kuban, 1999). Incest offenders also tend to be at a lower risk to reoffend as compared to extrafamilial offenders (Firestone et al., 1999; Kingston, Firestone, Wexler, & Bradford, 2008). In one study with a 10-year follow-up period, 10% of incest offenders compared to 32% of extrafamilial offenders sexually recidivated (Olver & Wong, 2006).

Incest is rare among those who sexually victimize adults only. A more useful distinction for rapists is between those who victimize strangers and those who victimize someone who is known to them, such as an acquaintance, friend, or romantic partner. Criminal justice samples tend to contain more offenders with stranger victims, whereas self-report victimization and community studies indicate that spouses, boyfriends, friends, or acquaintances commit the large majority of sexual assaults against adult women; sexual assaults by strangers are uncommon. For example, in a study of college-age women, 27% reported being the victim of some form of sexual coercion, ranging from forced kissing to forced intercourse (Gross, Winslett, Roberts, & Gohm, 2006). Of those who had been sexually assaulted during college, the most likely perpetrators were boyfriends; only 2% of offenders were strangers. Sexual assaults by someone known to the victim are less likely to be reported than are sexual assaults by strangers (Koss, Dinero, Seibel, & Cox, 1988). Comparisons of known and stranger rapists suggests that known rapists are more likely to provide alcohol or other drugs and to use more verbal coercion, whereas stranger rapists are more likely to cause physical injuries (McCormick, Maric, Seto, & Barbaree, 1998). Sexual assaults of romantic partners tend to be associated with a history of prior physical and sexual violence, indicating a more general pattern of partner abuse (DeMaris, 1997).

The boundaries established between intrafamilial/known victims and extrafamilial/stranger victims are not always clear. Relationship polymorphism has been reported to be as high as 20% in samples of serial sexual offenders (Cann, Friendship, & Gozna, 2007; Guay et al., 2001; Sim & Proeve, 2010; Sjöstedt, Langstrom, Sturidsson, & Grann, 2004) and is more likely to occur among offenders with a higher number of victims (Lussier, Leclerc, Healey, & Proulx, 2007; Sim & Proeve, 2010). Relationship polymorphic offenders have higher levels of sexual recidivism when compared to incest-only or extrafamilial-only child molesters (Olver & Wong, 2006).

Other typologies. Clinicians and researchers have developed other typologies in an effort to derive more homogeneous offender groups. These typologies have included information about the offender's demographic characteristics, personality, and/or offending history. In particular, Knight and Prentky (1990) developed the Massachusetts Treatment Center rapist and child molester typologies. These typologies have been validated in subsequent studies but have not achieved much traction in clinical practice, in part because it is not obvious how a typological distinction (e.g., between *nonsexual* and *sexual* types of rapists; Barbaree, Seto, Serin, Amos, & Preston, 1994) can contribute to a better understanding of risk to reoffend or intervention strategy than can directly assessing variation in the underlying traits, such as sexual arousal to sexual coercion or antisocial personality. On the other hand, knowing that someone has a history of sexual offending against children means that the risk of further sexual offenses involving children is different than the risk for other sexual offenders, and child offense–specific factors, such as sexual arousal to children, emotional identification with children, or attitudes and beliefs that are supportive of adult–child sex, need to be addressed in treatment and supervision.

PRACTICE AND POLICY ISSUES

In this section, we cover a wide range of topics, including the assessment of an individual's risk to reoffend and other clinical concerns; treatment and prevention models; and special sexual offender–specific policies that have been implemented to address concerns about sexual offending.

Assessment of Risk to Reoffend and Related Issues

Sexual offender–specific risk appraisal tools to predict sexual or violent recidivism have proliferated in the past 20 years. The majority of validated measures are actuarial in nature, meaning that they statistically combine risk factors that uniquely contribute to the prediction of recidivism and provide probabilistic estimates of the likelihood of a new offense. Some risk measures are structured professional guides that include risk factors that are empirically related to recidivism and those that are considered to be clinically important. Risk assessors then make judgments about an individual's risk to reoffend after considering the list of factors, without probabilistic estimates. A meta-analysis of follow-up studies has suggested that actuarial measures produce the highest predictive accuracy, followed by structured professional judgment measures and then unstructured professional judgments (Hanson & Morton-Bourgon, 2009).

The Static–99 (Hanson & Thornton, 2000) is one of the most widely used sexual offender risk tools (Archer, Buffington-Vollum, Stredny, & Handel, 2006). The Static–99 provides an actuarial probability estimate based on 10 static (historical or unlikely to change) risk factors, including noncontact sexual offenses, previous violent offenses, and cohabitation with an intimate partner (A. J. R. Harris, Phenix, Hanson, & Thornton, 2003). The Static–99 has recently been revised (Static–99R; Helmus, Thornton, Hanson, & Babchishin, 2012) in order to incorporate updated age weights. The Static–2002 (Hanson & Thornton, 2003) was developed to further improve the Static–99R; it contains four new items: density of sexual offending, number of arrests for sexual offenses (juvenile and adult), supervision failure, and number of years in the community prior to index offense. Two items (ever lived with a partner and index nonsexual violence—any convictions) were also left out of the Static–2002. Although it is updated and has been found to be slightly more accurate in the prediction of sexual recidivism (Hanson, Helmus, & Thornton, 2010), the

Static–2002 has not yet gained the same level of popularity as the Static–99 or Static–99R.

The Sexual Violence Risk—20 (SVR–20; Boer, Hart, Kropp, & Webster, 1997), another widely used sexual offender–specific risk appraisal tool, is an example of a structured professional guide. It contains 20 items reflecting sexual offense history, psychosocial adjustment, and future planning. In addition to measures that were specifically designed to predict sexual recidivism, the Sexual Offender Risk Appraisal Guide (SORAG; Quinsey, Harris, Rice, & Cormier, 2006) is an actuarial measure that was designed to predict violent (including contact sexual) recidivism among sexual offenders. The SORAG was developed based on the items contained in the Violence Risk Appraisal Guide, with additional sex offense–specific items (e.g., any female sexual victims under the age of 14).

Given the variety of risk appraisal tools that exist, it can be difficult for clinicians to pick the most appropriate one to use in order to assess an individual's risk for sexual recidivism. Numerous studies have compared various risk assessment tools that were designed to predict sexual offender recidivism. Early studies found no statistically significant differences between the most commonly used measures (e.g., Barbaree, Seto, Langton, & Peacock, 2001). Langton et al. (2007) reported that each of the risk assessment measures they examined were predictive of sexual recidivism. Among these measures, the Static–2002 had the highest level of accuracy in the prediction of sexual recidivism. In a meta-analysis, Hanson and Morton-Bourgon (2009) found the largest effect size for the Minnesota Sex Offender Screening Tool—Revised (Epperson, Kaul, et al., 2005), followed by the Static–2002 and the Static–99. Seto (2005) found that the combination of multiple risk measures, which is a common practice, did not improve predictive accuracy in risk assessment with sexual offenders.

Given the heterogeneity of sexual offenders, risk tools might perform differently across different types of offenders. Parent et al. (2011) compared various risk assessments over a 15-year period while taking into account both the type of sexual recidivism (i.e., contact vs. noncontact) and the type of offender (e.g., rapists, child molesters, incest offenders, and mixed offenders). A wide range of measures that were designed to predict violent and sexual recidivism were compared. All but one measure predicted sexual recidivism with moderate to good predictive accuracy; the Static–99 had the highest accuracy in predicting sexual recidivism. None of the measures significantly predicted noncontact sexual recidivism. Furthermore, Parent et al. found that different instruments were better at predicting recidivism in different subgroups of offenders. Specifically, all but one of the measures was predictive of sexual recidivism in child molesters, but many measures were not predictive among rapists (see also Rettenberger, Matthes, Boer, & Eher, 2010). None of the measures was able to predict recidivism among mixed offenders (those with both child and adult victims), even though these offenders were the quickest to sexually reoffend. The subgroup of mixed offenders was small, however, and further research is needed.

Adolescent sexual offender measures. Several risk assessment tools have been designed for use with adolescent sexual offenders. The Juvenile Sexual offender Assessment Protocol—II (J–SOAP–II; Prentky & Righthand, 2003) is a 28-item measure that is organized into the following scales: Sexual Preoccupation, Impulsivity and Antisociality, Intervention, and Community Adjustment. The Juvenile Sexual Offense Recidivism Risk Assessment Tool—II (J–SORRAT–II; Epperson, Ralston, Fowers, & DeWitt, 2005) has 12 items, reflecting sexual offense history, nonsexual offending, sexual offending tactics, sexual and physical abuse histories, and school problems. The Estimate of Risk of Adolescent Sexual Offense Recidivism (ERASOR; Worling & Curwen, 2001) is a structured professional guide consisting of 25 items over five domains: sexual interests, attitudes, and behaviors; historical sexual assaults; psychosocial functioning; family/environmental functioning; and treatment (Worling & Curwen, 2001). As with the adult measures, there is substantial item overlap across adolescent tools because they draw from the same follow-up research (see Caldwell, 2002).

The development of risk measures for juvenile sexual offenders has been complicated by low base rates of sexual recidivism and relatively small

follow-up samples, both of which reduce statistical power to detect predictive relationships (Viljoen et al., 2008). Moreover, some jurisdictions maintain different databases for criminal charges and convictions involving juveniles versus adults, which can make it more difficult to systematically collect accurate follow-up data. Viljoen et al. (2008) compared the J–SOAP–II, J–SORRAT–II, and Structured Assessment of Violence Risk in Youth (SAVRY, designed to predict violent recidivism in adolescent sexual offenders; Borum, 2006) in a sample of adolescent sexual offenders who were followed for an average of 7 years. Only the J–SOAP–II Sexual Preoccupation scale predicted sexual aggression committed while the youth was still involved in treatment, whereas scales from both the J–SOAP–II and the SAVRY predicted new violence during treatment. The J–SOAP–II approached statistical significance in predicting violent (nonsexual) recidivism committed while the youth was still in treatment, and the SAVRY total score predicted serious nonsexual violence. However, none of the instruments was able to predict sexual recidivism committed after the youth had left the treatment program. Across the measures and outcomes, predictive accuracy was greatest for older (16 to 18 years) as compared to younger (12 to 15 years) youth. In a recent study, Worling, Bookalam, and Litteljohn (2012) found that total scores on the ERASOR predicted recidivism in a sample of 191 adolescent male sexual offenders who were followed for an average of 3.7 years.

Dynamic risk measures. Many of the instruments that are used in sexual offender risk assessment do not contain dynamic risk items, that is, items reflecting factors that can change over time. Actuarial measures contain static or historical risk factors such as criminal history (which cannot change) or psychopathy (which is very difficult to change, if it can be changed at all; see Chapter 9, this volume on psychopathy). Static and historical information is helpful in estimating an individual's long-term risk of sexual or violent reoffending, but it does not help identify the most important intervention targets that could be addressed in order to reduce or manage an offender's risk (Andrews & Bonta, 2010). Risk tools that do not contain dynamic items also cannot record changes in risk that are attributable to interventions (Olver & Wong, 2011).

More recently, risk measures such as the Stable 2007 and Acute 2007 have been designed to measure dynamic risk factors (Hanson, Harris, Scott, & Helmus, 2007). These two measures differentiate between *stable dynamic risk factors* (i.e., factors that are more enduring and slower to change over time, such as sexual preoccupation) and *acute dynamic risk factors* (i.e., factors that can change quickly over short periods of time, such as stress level or mood; Hanson & Harris, 2000). The Stable 2007 provides an assessment of 16 stable dynamic factors reflecting intimacy deficits, social influences, cooperation with supervision, general self-regulation, and sexual self-regulation. The Acute 2007 includes seven acute dynamic items that can be assessed at each meeting: substance abuse, negative mood, hostility, access to victims, collapse of social support, sexual preoccupation, and rejection of supervision. Both the Stable 2007 and Acute 2007 are useful in community supervision and can predict an individual's sexual recidivism (Hanson et al., 2007). Dynamic risk scores can be added to the Static–99 to increase its predictive accuracy (e.g., Eher, Matthes, Schilling, Haubner-MacLean, & Rettenberger, 2012).

Some critics have suggested that these dynamic risk measures are only potentially dynamic because of the way data are collected and analyzed (Mills, Kroner, & Morgan, 2007; Quinsey et al., 2006). To illustrate, showing that Stable 2007 scores that were collected at Time 1 can predict recidivism by Time 2 does not demonstrate that the Stable 2007 items are dynamic because they are being analyzed as if they were static risk factors that were collected at one time only. To be truly dynamic, it is necessary to show that changes in putatively dynamic items are associated with changes in recidivism likelihood. This criticism led to development of the Violence Risk Scale—Sexual Offender Version (VRS–SO; Wong, Olver, Nicholaichuk, & Gordon, 2003). The VRS–SO is a 24-item risk and case management tool that assesses seven static items and 17 dynamic risk items. Olver and Wong (2011) found that higher risk offenders who showed positive changes on dynamic risk items as a result of treatment participation had lower recidivism rates (24%) than higher

risk offenders who did not show these changes (36%). Moreover, higher risk offenders who showed a high level of positive change had a recidivism rate that approached those of lower risk offenders, with or without positive change. Brown, St. Amand, and Zamble (2009) and Chagigiorgis, Michel, Laprade, Ahmed, and Seto (2012) used study designs that could illustrate true dynamicity: Both studies used multiple assessments over a 1-year time period and demonstrated that changes in assessment scores predicted changes in the incidence of recidivism during the follow-up period. The role of dynamic risk factors in sexual offender risk assessment is an important area for future research (A. J. R. Harris & Hanson, 2010).

Readiness to change. The assessment of an individual's readiness to change is an important clinical consideration among sexual offenders. Motivation to change consists of affective, behavioral, and cognitive aspects that can vary throughout the course of treatment (Barrett, Wilson, & Long, 2003; Tierney & McCabe, 2002). It has been argued that a primary aim of sexual offender treatment should be to increase an offender's motivation to desist from sexual offending (Grubin & Thornton, 1994), as offenders who drop out of treatment or who demonstrate poor treatment behavior are at a higher risk to reoffend than those who successfully complete treatment (e.g., Hanson & Bussière, 1998). Although this increased risk may reflect static factors that are associated with an individual's risk to reoffend (such as psychopathy) and with treatment involvement, it is also possible that the factors underlying treatment dropout or poor participation are amenable to intervention themselves (Seto & Barbaree, 1999). Lower to moderate-risk offenders are more likely to maintain their motivation on release to the community in comparison to higher risk offenders (Stirpe, Wilson, & Long, 2001).

A number of models have been proposed to explain an individual's motivation for change; perhaps the most popular is the transtheoretical model of behavior change, also referred to as the stages of change model (Prochaska & DiClemente, 1982). This model postulates that individuals progress, but not necessarily in a linear fashion, through the following stages of readiness to change: precontemplation, contemplation, preparation, action, and maintenance. In the *precontemplation* stage, the offender is not considering any sort of meaningful behavior change. In the *contemplation* stage, the offender is starting to consider the steps he would need to take in order to make meaningful change, but he has not taken any steps to put this into action. In the *preparation* stage, the offender is taking steps to put his plan for behavior change into action, and he signals that behavior change is in the near future. In the *action* stage, the offender takes steps to ensure that the plan for change is put in action and attempts to modify his behavior. In the *maintenance* stage, the offender makes efforts to consolidate and maintain these changes.

Whether or not an offender participates in treatment is not sufficient to make a determination regarding his motivation, as offenders may participate in treatment for a number of reasons, such as increasing the chances of an early release where that is permitted (Tierney & McCabe, 2002). Thus, a number of measures have been designed to specifically assess treatment readiness among sexual offenders. One of the most widely used measures of readiness to change is the University of Rhode Island Change Assessment Scale (URICA: McConnaughy, DiClemente, & Prochaska, 1989; McConnaughy, Prochaska, & Velicer, 1983), which is designed to assess an individual's current stage of readiness to change. An example of an item on the URICA is: "I've been thinking that I might want to change something about myself." Polaschek, Anstiss, and Wilson (2010) found that the structure of the URICA questions were consistent with the stages of change model (with the exception of the preparation stage) and had good internal consistency. Furthermore, the URICA correlated with other measures, such as measures of treatment needs, as expected, suggesting concurrent validity.

Another measure that has been evaluated with sexual offenders is the Stages of Change Questionnaire, which is a 32-item measure that was adapted by Tierney and McCabe (2005) for use with sexual offenders (e.g., "As far as I am concerned, I don't have any sexual problems that need changing"). Tierney and McCabe evaluated this measure in a sample of child sexual offenders who were at different stages of treatment. The questionnaire demonstrated good internal consistency but only low to moderate test–retest reliability; encouragingly, it was not correlated with a scale of social desirability. Tierney and McCabe discussed how different interventions might be appropriate for offenders who are in different stages of change. For example, they highlighted that the majority of sexual offenders are in the precontemplation stage. As a result, it is most appropriate to use motivational enhancement strategies that are designed to help offenders move to the contemplation stage.

Assessment of antisociality. Antisociality can be assessed using a variety of different measures. The most powerful is the Psychopathy Checklist—Revised (Hare, 2003), which provides information about an individual's personality traits, affective style, and lifestyle that are associated with a greater risk of criminality and other antisocial behavior in the future. The Psychopathy Checklist score is part of the SORAG. Psychopathic sexual offenders might perform differently in treatment than nonpsychopathic sexual offenders. Seto and Barbaree (1999) found that sexual offenders who scored high in psychopathy and who showed the most positive changes in treatment behavior and ratings were more, rather than less, likely to reoffend (though this effect seemed to fade over time: Seto, 2003; Barbaree, 2005). Psychopathic sexual offenders who are also sexually deviant pose the greatest risk of sexual recidivism (Seto et al., 2004).

Each of the validated risk measures mentioned here incorporates criminal history in some way, typically distinguishing between nonsexual and sexual offending. Other areas worth assessing in this domain include offense-supportive attitudes and beliefs. Even though such measures are usually obvious, scores on general measures of offense-supportive attitudes and beliefs, such as the Criminal Sentiments Scale, still predict recidivism (Witte, Di Placido, Gu, & Wong, 2006). The picture is less clear with measures that are specific to sexual offending. Malamuth et al. (1995) demonstrated that negative attitudes about women predict sexual aggression among men recruited from the community, and Hanson and Morton-Bourgon (2005) demonstrated that the endorsement of views such as the idea that children are not harmed by sex with adults is associated with sexual recidivism among identified sexual offenders, whereas endorsement of generally antisocial attitudes and beliefs is associated with nonsexual recidivism. At the same time, Seto and Lalumière's (2010) meta-analysis of comparison studies found no significant difference between adolescent sexual offenders and other adolescent offenders on measures of general antisocial attitudes and beliefs or measures of specific attitudes and beliefs about women, children, or sex.

Assessment of sexual deviance. Various procedures have been developed to assess the sexual preference of sexual offenders (see Kalmus & Beech, 2005, for a review). Evaluators can employ subjective measures of sexual interest, psychophysiological measures of sexual arousal, or indirect measures that have been adapted from cognitive science paradigms (e.g., viewing time, reaction time). Self-reported sexual interest can be obtained via a clinical interview, whereby respondents are asked questions pertaining to their sexual thoughts, interests, and behaviors; however, interviews are subject to socially desirable responding, and many sexual offenders deny or minimize certain aspects of their sexual histories. One way to reduce the reluctance of individuals to disclose their sexual interests is to administer questionnaires. Several questionnaires have been designed specifically to assess offenders' sexual interest, including the Multiphasic Sex Inventories (Nichols & Molinder, 1984); the Clarke Sex History Questionnaire for Males—Revised (Langevin & Paitich, 2001); and the Multidimensional Inventory of Development, Sex, and Aggression (Knight & Sims-Knight, 2003).

Currently, the most widely used method of assessing the sexual interests of offenders is penile plethysmography, or *phallometry*. Phallometry involves the objective measurement of erectile changes in response to stimuli that vary on the dimension of interest, such as the age and sex of the individual(s) depicted or the level of coercion exhibited. Phallometry has been the subject of much research to evaluate both discriminative and predictive validity, and

evidence has consistently supported the clinical and research use of phallometry in the assessment of deviant sexual preference (Hanson & Bussiére, 1998; Lalumière et al., 2003; Seto, 2008).

Some researchers have questioned the utility of phallometry (Clegg & Fremouw, 2009; Marshall & Fernandez, 2000). For example, some research has demonstrated that some offenders are able to suppress penile responses during phallometric assessment (Howes, 1995) and that the procedure yields low response rates (O'Donohue & Letourneau, 1992). Other critics have pointed to various ethical concerns, such as the use of child imagery and the potential for such images to produce harmful effects (i.e., new content for sexual fantasies) among those assessed (Launay, 1999). Another criticism is the significant lack of standardization in the stimuli, procedures, and data analyses. Howes (1995) surveyed 48 phallometric laboratories in North America and found significant heterogeneity in the methodology used and that many labs were not using validated procedures. Standardization of phallometric stimuli and procedures is needed in order to facilitate comparisons and the consistent reporting of results; empirical guidance on optimal phallometric testing procedures is available (see Lalumière & Harris, 1998).

Indirect measures are less intrusive than phallometry, such as unobtrusively recorded viewing time while viewing images, where attractive images are viewed longer than unattractive images (e.g., Abel, Huffman, Warberg, & Holland, 1998). Other researchers have examined the potential utility of other indirect measures of sexual interest: These include versions of the Implicit Association Test, which involves measuring response latency during a computerized task in order to examine the strength of association between a semantic concept (e.g., child or adult) and an attribute (e.g., attractive or unattractive; Greenwald, McGhee, & Schwartz, 1998). Several research teams have administered the Implicit Association Test to sexual offenders. Nunes, Firestone, and Baldwin (2007) administered the Implicit Association Test to 27 child molesters and 29 nonsexual offenders and found that child molesters viewed children as more sexually attractive than did nonsexual offenders, and viewing children as more sexually attractive was associated with a greater estimated risk of sexual recidivism (see also Banse, Schmidt, & Clarbour, 2010; Gray, Brown, MacCulloch, Smith, & Snowden, 2005).

Treatment

The most common psychosocial treatment approach for adult sexual offenders is relapse prevention, which uses cognitive–behavioral techniques to develop offenders' self-regulation skills (McGrath, Cumming, Burchard, Zeoli, & Ellerby, 2009). The relapse prevention framework was adapted from the addictions field by treatment providers who saw parallels between the compulsive behavior that was exhibited by substance-dependent persons and the compulsive sexual behavior that was exhibited by some sexual offenders (Laws & Ward, 2011). Individuals who were motivated to refrain from committing sexual offenses resisted their urges or opportunities to offend, but eventually failed through a series of seemingly unimportant decisions and failures in responding to risky situations or triggers. For example, someone who was sexually attracted to children might not realize that he had changed his walking route from his workplace to his home so that he passed by a playground. After several weeks of walking this route, he might encounter a child at the playground. Instead of coping effectively with this situation, such as moving away and changing his route, the individual might begin to engage in sexual fantasies about the child while masturbating. He might then start to create more opportunities to go by the playground and subsequently sexually offend against a child when an opportunity arose.

Programs that describe their approach as relapse prevention can vary greatly in their format and content, but relapse prevention programs typically share common elements. These include the identification of high-risk situations and triggers, development of avoidance and coping strategies, and use of cognitive–behavioral techniques to interrupt the relapse process (Laws & Ward, 2011). Marques, Wiederanders, Day, Nelson, and van Ommeren (2005) conducted and published the only peer-reviewed randomized clinical trial (RCT) of a relapse prevention program, the Sexual Offender Treatment Evaluation Project, which was established in 1985 in

California. Incarcerated adult male offenders who volunteered for this project were randomly assigned to treatment or no-treatment conditions after being matched for age, criminal history, and victim age. Unfortunately, the final evaluation showed no statistically significant difference in recidivism for the treated offenders as compared to the no-treatment control volunteers and a third comparison group of offenders who refused treatment (Marques et al., 2005).

Even before these discouraging results, the relapse prevention approach to adult sexual offender treatment had been criticized for several assumptions (Kingston, 2010; Ward & Hudson, 1996). Most importantly, the relapse prevention model failed to account for the diversity in offending processes, focusing on individuals who were motivated to abstain from offending but failed to do so. The model did not account for offenders who were motivated to offend and who actively sought opportunities to commit sexual offenses.

Meta-analytic treatment outcome findings. There is heated debate about the efficacy of sexual offender treatment in reducing recidivism (see Marshall & Marshall, 2007; Seto et al., 2008). Resolution of this debate has been complicated by the difficulties in using RCTs to evaluate treatment, the need for large samples, and the need for long follow-up periods given the low levels of recidivism among sexual offenders (Lösel & Schmucker, 2005). Meta-analyses, which combine data across outcome studies, are helpful in this regard.

Hanson et al. (2002) conducted a meta-analysis of 43 studies containing a total of 9,454 sexual offenders and reported an overall encouraging result: With an average follow-up time of 4 years, sexual recidivism was 12% among the treated sexual offenders and 17% among the untreated sexual offenders. Incidental assignment studies (where it was not obvious what selection effects might explain why someone was placed in treatment vs. not) showed a significant difference in recidivism, but there was no difference between the treated and comparison groups in the small set of RCTs.

Lösel and Schmucker (2005) conducted a meta-analysis of 69 studies containing a total of 22,181 offenders, including many of the outcome studies that were examined by Hanson et al. (2002). Lösel and Schmucker found that offenders who received treatment were 37% less likely to sexually recidivate than offenders in comparison conditions. A similar pattern was found for violent recidivism (44% difference) and general recidivism (11% difference). Lösel and Schmucker found that biomedical interventions (e.g., surgical castration) produced larger effect sizes than psychosocial interventions. When psychosocial interventions were categorized according to treatment approach, only evaluations of behavior therapy and cognitive behavioral therapy produced significant effects; other types of psychosocial programs did not produce any group differences. Lösel and Schmucker stated that their results should be interpreted with caution due to the weak methodological quality of most of the included studies.

Finally, Reitzel and Carbonell (2006) conducted a meta-analysis of nine outcome studies involving adolescent sexual offenders. A significant difference in sexual recidivism was found when comparing treated adolescents (7.4%) with adolescents who were not treated or who were in comparison conditions (18.5%). The authors were cautious about drawing conclusions, however, because of methodological issues such as nonequivalent follow-up times and how treatment attrition was handled in the individual studies.

The Good Lives Model. The Good Lives Model (GLM; Ward & Gannon, 2006; Ward & Stewart, 2003) is a strengths-based treatment approach in which the overarching goal is to equip individuals with the necessary conditions and resources to achieve their life goals in socially acceptable and personally satisfying ways so that they can desist from further offending. The GLM posits that sexual offenders (like all human beings) seek a number of primary human goods: Primary human goods are actions, states of affairs, or experiences that are inherently beneficial and are sought for their own intrinsic value rather than as a means to an end. Instrumental or secondary goods represent concrete ways of securing these primary goods (see Yates, Kingston, & Ward, 2009, for a more detailed discussion). For example, the primary good of relatedness

might be achieved by being in a romantic relationship, whereas the primary good of excellence in play might be achieved through involvement in sports. Criminogenic needs exert their influence through secondary goods; for example, associating with antisocial peers can also achieve the primary good of relatedness.

Empirical support for the GLM is emerging (Laws & Ward, 2011). Most of the studies have examined the utility of incorporating GLM concepts, such as the consideration of approach as well as avoidance goals, in treatment (see Ward & Maruna, 2007). These programs produce lower attrition rates, greater staff satisfaction, and generally better offender engagement in treatment than non-GLM programs (Mann, Webster, Schofield, & Marshall, 2004; Ware & Bright, 2008). Recently, Marshall, Marshall, Serran, and O'Brien (2011) described their treatment approach with sexual offenders, which incorporates many GLM concepts, and reported that among 535 sexual offenders who were followed for approximately 8 years in the community, the sexual recidivism rate was 6% compared to what would be expected (24%) based on the offenders' actuarially estimated risk to reoffend.

The importance of RCTs. Treatment proponents point to these meta-analytic findings as support for the efficacy of sexual offender treatment programs that adopt cognitive–behavioral approaches. Skeptics, however, point out that the best designed studies do not show a difference between treatment and comparison groups, and that there are many alternative explanations for apparent treatment effects. This highlights the importance of conducting research on sexual offender treatment involving RCTs (see Seto et al., 2008). Unfortunately, there are many obstacles, and therefore objections, to the implementation of further RCTs in the adult sexual offending field (see Marshall & Marshall, 2007), even though RCTs are considered to be the gold standard for evaluating psychosocial or medical interventions (e.g., the Cochrane Collaboration [http://www.cochrane.org]; Campbell Collaboration [http://www.campbellcollaboration.org]). On the positive side, there are some encouraging results from clinical trials with adolescent sexual offenders (Borduin, Schaeffer, & Heiblum, 2009; Letourneau et al.,

2009), children with sexual behavior problems (Carpentier, Silovsky, & Chaffin, 2006), and offenders in general (Farrington & Welsh, 2005).

Multisystemic therapy. Multisystemic therapy is an intensive, family-based treatment that focuses on adolescents who are at high risk of out-of-home placements (e.g., residential treatment, incarceration) due to their antisocial and criminal behavior (Henggeler, Schoenwald, Borduin, Rowland, & Cunningham, 1998). Multisystemic therapy adopts a social ecological perspective where interventions address individual, parent, family, school, and community targets. Treatment is home based rather than office based, and therapists are available to the youth and their families outside of traditional office hours in order to reduce treatment dropout, which is a perennial problem in the treatment of juvenile delinquency. Multisystemic therapy is usually delivered over a 3- to 5-month period, with intensity decreasing over time as the youth's caregiver becomes more competent in managing his or her behavior (Schoenwald, Heiblum, Saldana, & Henggeler, 2008).

Multisystemic therapy is founded on nine treatment principles: (a) The primary goal of assessment is to understand how problems are related to the youth's systemic contexts; (b) treatment should identify and build on strengths of the individual and his or her systems; (c) treatment should increase responsible behavior and decrease irresponsible behavior by caregivers and other family members; (d) treatment should focus on clearly specified behaviors; (e) therapists understand that multiple systems may sustain these problems; (f) techniques used must be appropriate to the youth's developmental level; (g) family members need to put in a considerable amount of effort to achieve goals; (h) the effectiveness of the intervention is continuously evaluated; and (i) the intervention should aim to have long-term impact, which is accomplished by empowering caregivers to target needs across the different systemic contexts.

Multiple outcome studies have found that multisystemic therapy decreases the likelihood of out-of-home placement, criminal behavior, parental mental health symptoms, and substance use when compared to treatment-as-usual (TAU) or other comparison conditions (Henggeler et al., 1998; Ogden & Halliday-Boykins, 2004; Timmons-Mitchell, Bender, Kishna, & Mitchell, 2006). Multisystemic therapy can also improve the target youth's academic performance and relationship with his or her family and peers (Bourdin et al., 2009). Treatment gains from multisystemic therapy tend to be maintained over time, with one study finding significant differences in recidivism and total time incarcerated even 13 years after the conclusion of treatment (Schaeffer & Borduin, 2005).

There is some evidence in support of multisystemic therapy for adolescent sexual offenders. In a small RCT, Borduin et al. (2009) reported that, when compared to TAU, multisystemic therapy resulted in decreased sexual recidivism, as 8% of those in the therapy group and 46% of those in the TAU group recidivated. Further, there was a reduction in nonsexual offending and an 80% decrease in the number of days that were spent in secure custody in the multisystemic therapy group. Letourneau et al. (2009) compared multisystemic therapy and TAU in a sample of 127 adolescent sexual offenders. At 1-year follow-up, offenders in the multisystemic therapy condition exhibited significant decreases in substance use, externalizing behaviors, and problematic sexual behaviors, as well as a reduction in out-of-home placements. In summary, multisystemic therapy is a promising intervention for adolescent sexual offenders.

Circles of Support and Accountability. The Circles of Support and Accountability (COSA) program is a lay volunteer program that assists in the community reintegration of high-risk sexual offenders (Wilson, Cortoni, & McWhinnie, 2009). COSA began as a project by the Mennonite Central Committee of Ontario after two high-risk sexual offenders were released at the end of their sentences, without any parole supervision, and were subsequently supported by a team of community members who were led by a Mennonite pastor. COSA was designed for offenders who are released at the end of their prison sentences without any parole or probation supervision. A COSA circle involves the offender and four to six community members. The community members provide emotional and social support to the offender while monitoring his adjustment and behavior at the same time (Wilson & Prinzo, 2002). For example, volunteers might confront the ex-offender and intervene if he is engaging in problematic activities such as missing work. COSA can be an intensive program, involving daily meetings with a circle member in the first 2 or 3 months and a weekly meeting with all circle members. Once the offender has started to adjust to life in the community, circles meet less often; however, the circle is always available to the offender if needed. Given the demands of volunteering as a COSA member, circles are supported themselves by professionals who can consult as needed.

Initial COSA evaluation results are encouraging: Offenders who participated in COSA were less likely to reoffend than a matched group of high-risk offenders in the community. Wilson et al. (2009) found that COSA resulted in 83% less sexual recidivism, 73% less violent recidivism, and 71% less general criminal recidivism when compared to similar high-risk offenders. Any new sexual offenses that were committed by offenders tended to be less severe than their index offenses (Wilson, Picheca, & Prinzo, 2007a). Further, the COSA program has been viewed positively by offenders, circle volunteers, and professional consultants, with all participants emphasizing the important role that COSA can play (Wilson, Picheca, & Prinzo, 2007b).

Two caveats to the COSA program are that offenders volunteer to be part of COSA, and individuals who are willing to volunteer for this kind of supervision and support may differ in their risk to reoffend from individuals with similar criminal histories and other personal characteristics who refuse to participate. Also, COSA evaluations have been small and have only begun to involve random assignment to conditions (Duwe, 2013). Nonetheless, some initial outcome data suggest that a positive community reintegration effort can prevent sexual recidivism. It is worth noting here that both COSA and multisystemic therapy share a social ecological approach to intervention, where the focus is not only the individual, but his environments as well.

Sex drive reduction. Some sexual offenders, such as those with a paraphilia such as pedophilia and/

or high sex drive, may benefit from biomedical treatment to reduce their sex drive. Sex drive reduction can be accomplished through anti-androgen medications such as cyproterone acetate or leuprolide acetate. There is some evidence that biomedical interventions are effective in reducing sexual thoughts and behavior, including sexual recidivism, though this evidence mostly comes from nonrandomized clinical evaluations (see Lösel & Schmucker, 2005). The biggest challenge with this treatment approach is noncompliance with medication, which is further complicated by potentially serious side effects, including bone mineral density loss, changes in glucose and lipid metabolism, and mood disturbances (see Gooren, 2011). For this reason, some investigators have proposed the use of selective serotonin reuptake inhibitors (SSRIs), which are commonly used in the treatment of depression, for individuals who cannot take anti-androgens for medical reasons or who would refuse to take anti-androgens. SSRIs have an effect on serotoninergic brain systems, and a common side effect is reduced sexual interest. Although there are case reports and small, uncontrolled trials, no RCTs have been reported for this use (see Thibaut et al., 2010).

Prevention

Treatments are administered after sexual offenses have already taken place, with the primary goal of preventing future offenses among identified offenders. The following section describes prevention and early intervention efforts that are intended to prevent sexual offenses from occurring in the first place.

Stop It Now! Stop It Now! is a social marketing and outreach program that aims to educate individuals who are concerned about child sexual abuse, ranging from concerned caregivers or professionals to individuals who self-identify as pedophiles or hebephiles through a website (http://www.stopitnow. org); clinical directory service; and confidential, toll-free hotline number. The aim of the program is to provide information that can help prevent sexual offending against children before it occurs. Although evaluation data are not available, public education and outreach efforts are important given the number of individuals who are likely to be at risk for sexual offending relative to the resources that are available for the treatment of identified sexual offenders. Prevention is preferred over intervention after an offense has already occurred; however, due to stigma and anxiety about mandatory child abuse reporting laws in Canada and the United States, it is difficult for at-risk individuals to obtain professional help in managing their sexual behavior, often leaving these individuals isolated in the community, without any professional support.

Prevention Project Dunkelfeld.   The Prevention Project Dunkelfeld (in German, *dark field*) uses mainstream media to advertise assessment and treatment services for self-identified individuals who are concerned that they might act on their sexual interests in children (https://www.dont-offend.org). Most of the individuals who come forward have acted in the past, either by accessing child pornography or by having sexual contact with children, but a significant minority have been inactive in the previous 6 months, suggesting an opportunity to intervene in order to gain or maintain desistance from sexual offending (Beier et al., 2009; Neutze, Seto, Schaefer, Mundt, & Beier, 2011). The initially Berlin-based project has now expanded to other centers in Germany, and evaluation of this program continues.

The number of individuals seen so far as part of the Prevention Project Dunkelfeld demonstrates how difficult outreach can be in the current sociopolitical climate surrounding pedophilia and sexual offending: of initial project contacts with 1,415 individuals in a 5.5 year period (an average of approximately 280 persons a year), evaluations were completed on 622 men, and treatment was offered to 319 men (Beier et al., 2009). A serious and inherent limitation of all prevention approaches is that the highest risk individuals may be the least likely to seek self-help options. Nonetheless, the hope is that some individuals who might otherwise have committed sexual offenses do not so do as a result.

Public Policy
Given the heavy costs associated with sexual violence, efforts to reduce its occurrence have greatly affected public policies. A set of extraordinary sexual offender control measures has been implemented in the past 20 years in the United States, including post-incarceration civil commitment, sexual offender registration, community notification, and residency restrictions in the community. These measures are extraordinary because they have not been created in response to other types of offenders that the public might also be concerned about, including those who commit domestic assaults, organized crime members, and drug traffickers (though there are local efforts in some areas, e.g., physical child abuse registries).

Civil commitment.   Current civil commitment laws in the United States have their origins in the sexual psychopath laws of the early 20th century (for more detail, see Doren, 2002). Civil commitment involves the indeterminate incapacitation of sexual offenders deemed to be *sexually violent predators* who have a major mental disorder that leads them to be at an unacceptable level of risk to sexually reoffend (typically *more likely than not*, though specific legal language varies across states; see Doren, 2002, and Elwood, 2009, for reviews). The major mental disorder might be pedophilia, sexual sadism, or some other recognized psychiatric disorder. Research evaluating the effects of civil commitment is limited as a result of methodological constraints; in particular, many sexual offenders who are civilly committed have not yet been released. Levenson (2003) highlighted the heated debate among mental health professionals and legal scholars on the ethics of civil commitment.

Civil commitment is a form of preventive detention of individuals who are deemed to be at high risk of sexual reoffending. Similar policies have been enacted elsewhere; for example, in Canada, sexual offenders who are judged to be at unacceptably high risk of sexually or violently reoffending and who are unlikely to respond sufficiently and positively to treatment can be designated as *dangerous offenders*, which results in an indeterminate prison sentence at the time of sentencing. Many but not all dangerous offenders have a history of sexual offending (Trevethan, Crutcher, & Moore, 2002). As in the United States, few dangerous offenders are ever released from custody, so it is difficult to evaluate the impact of this policy on public safety.

There is research, however, on the reliability and validity of the decisions that are made in civil commitment and dangerous offenders proceedings. If these proceedings were reliable, then one would expect a strong relation between an individual's diagnosis, arrived at by independent mental health professionals, and appraisals of the individual's risk to reoffend (Kingston, Seto, Firestone, & Bradford, 2010). One would also expect committed or designated offenders to be at higher risk and have more clinical needs than individuals who are not committed or designated. Research on dangerous offenders in Canada suggests that they are similar to other high-risk offenders in terms of their demographic characteristics, criminal histories, and risk of violent recidivism (Bonta, Zinger, Harris, & Carrière, 1998; Zanatta, 1996). Other research suggests that diagnostic reliability is poor in civil commitment proceedings, especially when comparing prosecution and defense experts (Levenson, 2004; though see Packard & Levenson, 2006).

Sexual offender registration. Murphy, Fedoroff, and Martineau (2009) provided an in-depth examination of the history of sexual offender registries in Canada and contrasted them with sexual offender registries in the United States. The primary difference between the sexual offender registries in these two countries is with regard to who can access them. In the United States, sexual offender registries such as http://www.nsopw.gov/Core/Portal.aspx are accessible to any member of the public, whereas registries in Canada are only available to law enforcement agencies.

Researchers have not found sexual offender registries to have an effect on sexual recidivism. For example, Sandler, Freeman, and Socia (2008) evaluated the effectiveness of the sexual offender registration law in New York and found that it had no deterrence effect; sexual offending rates remained stable after its implementation. Moreover, failure to register is not associated with sexual recidivism (Duwe & Donnay, 2010; Zgoba & Levenson, 2012). This finding suggests that there is a meaningful distinction between two explanations for failure to register: Sometimes failure to register is evidence of irresponsible or reckless behavior, which would

mean that failure to register is associated with a broader tendency to not comply with conditions, and thus is likely to predict recidivism (Hanson et al., 2007; Quinsey et al., 2006); other times, failure to register is a result of disorganization or a lack of understanding of the registration requirements, and thus is not related to recidivism. The available evidence supports the latter explanation.

Residency restrictions. Residency restrictions prevent registered sexual offenders from living near places with denser distributions of potential victims, such as schools, day care centers, or public playgrounds for offenders with child victims, or from living with other registered sexual offenders. There is limited and mixed evidence that residency restrictions have an impact on recidivism. Tewksbury and Jennings (2010) found evidence that the number of registered sexual offenders was correlated with sexual-offending rates in a single Kentucky county. In contrast, Socia (2013) found no significant correlation between registered sexual offender clustering and sexual recidivism across 52 counties in upstate New York.

Policy Summary

The policies described in this section were implemented because of public fears that sexual offenders are dangerous and are highly likely to reoffend. Despite their broad scope and potential impact on offenders and their families, there have been few systematic evaluations of these policies, and the evidence that is available so far is discouraging. There is no clear evidence that these policies have the desired effect in reducing sexual offending. More research to inform evidence-based policies is needed.

SUMMARY AND CONCLUSIONS

Sexual offending differs from other forms of offending because of the sexual motivations for criminal behavior. An important theoretical question has been to what extent sexual offending can be understood using general delinquency and criminality models, rather than using special explanation models. The results of studies comparing sexual offenders with other offenders suggests that there are some differences, with sexual offenders scoring lower on antisociality factors (driven mostly by those who have offended against children) and higher on sexual deviance factors (driven more by offenders with child victims than those with peer/adult victims). This suggests that both general and specific factors are relevant in explaining adolescent or adult sexual offending. Recent research has suggested that indicators of atypical sexual development are particularly germane, including sexual abuse history, exposure to sexual violence in the family, early exposure to sex/pornography, and paraphilic sexual interests (Lalumière et al., 2005; Seto, 2008; Seto & Lalumière, 2010).

This theoretical understanding of sexual offending has a number of important implications for practice and policy. First, a robust finding in the follow-up literature is that sexual offenders who are high only in antisociality are more likely to nonsexually offend, whereas those who are high in sexual deviance are more likely to sexually reoffend (Hanson & Morton-Bourgon, 2005). The highest risk sexual offenders are high on both dimensions. Second, risk assessment measures that have been developed in the past 20 years to accurately predict which sexual offenders will reoffend contain items that reflect one or both of these dimensions. Risk measures that have been developed for general offenders that do not include items assessing sexual deviance do not perform as well as risk measures that have been customized for sexual offenders. Third, it is clinically important to assess both antisociality and sexual deviance. Some clinicians may pay too much attention to the sexual aspects of the individual's history and behavior, neglecting that there is a general criminal component, and other clinicians may pay too much attention to the antisocial aspects, neglecting the relevance of deviant sexuality. Finally, interventions that target both general and specific risk factors are the most likely to produce positive effects.

Risk Assessment

Given the importance of risk information for decision making about sexual offenders, especially in high-stakes decisions such as civil commitment in the United States or designation as a dangerous offender in Canada, it is not surprising that sexual offender risk assessment has advanced greatly in the past 20 years. A number of validated measures are available, with multiple independent cross-validations in different jurisdictions and time periods, using different methodologies and sources of data (see Hanson & Morton-Bourgon, 2009).

We may be reaching an asymptote in the accuracy of long-term risk estimation, however, because studies that have few missing data and high interrater reliability can produce highly accurate results (see Quinsey et al., 2006). It is remarkable that prediction can achieve these levels of accuracy given that the goal—predicting behavior up to 20 years in the future that an offender will try to hide—is so complex. The risk measures tend to produce similar results, likely as a result of drawing from the same empirical literature on risk factors and using similar methods of data collection and scoring. The next major advances in risk assessment are likely to come in how validated instruments are used, including how to select the best instrument for one's risk-related question, whether to use multiple measures, and how to communicate results to decision makers (Seto, 2005).

Treatment

As is true for other offender populations, there is a better scientific understanding of risk assessment and needs assessment than there is of intervention. Validated static and dynamic risk measures are available, and there are validated measures for assessing antisociality and sexual deviance. There are also measures of readiness to change but, as is the case with other self-report measures, there are problems with socially desirable responding. Antisociality can be inferred from collateral information about past conduct, and sexual deviance can be more objectively assessed using phallometric or indirect measures of sexual interest.

Although several meta-analyses have suggested that treated sexual offenders have lower sexual or violent recidivism rates than untreated sexual offenders, the lack of RCTs prevents strong conclusions on the impact of treatment (see Hanson et al., 2002; Lösel & Schmucker, 2005). There is an interminable debate about the ethics and feasibility of conducting strong evaluation studies, but the sexual offender treatment field will not make progress until this debate is resolved (Duwe, 2013). We note here that RCTs have been conducted for adolescent sexual offenders, comparing a general delinquency intervention to services-as-usual; for children with sexual behavior problems; and for offenders in general (Carpentier et al., 2006; Letourneau et al., 2009). Although long follow-ups would likely be required to detect any differences in sexual recidivism rates, even short-term evaluations comparing treatment to an alternative treatment would identify promising interventions that can affect dynamic risk targets.

The *what works* offender rehabilitation literature suggests that effective sexual offender treatment will be similar to other empirically supported offender treatments by adhering to the risk, need, and responsivity principles (Andrews & Bonta, 2010). The *risk* principle dictates that interventions are more effective when they are matched to offender risk, the *need* principle dictates that interventions that target criminogenic needs are more effective than interventions that target other clinical concerns, and the *responsivity* principle dictates that interventions are more effective when they are matched to the individual's learning style. Indeed, Hanson, Bourgon, Helmus, and Hodgson (2009) demonstrated that sexual offender treatment programs that conformed to these principles produced larger effect sizes than treatment programs that did not. Research on dynamic risk factors has identified the most important treatment targets, including noncompliance, self-regulation deficits, offense-supportive attitudes and beliefs, and dysfunctional relationships (Hanson et al., 2007). Treatments that focus on these targets are more likely to reduce recidivism than treatments that focus their resources on other factors such as self-esteem, sexual abuse history, or acceptance of responsibility.

Treatment resources are limited and should be allocated to those individuals who are at higher risk of sexual offending. Even then, the number of offenders often exceeds the number of treatment spots that are available. Many sexual offenders are not offered treatment, and even if treatment were demonstrated to be highly effective and powerful,

offenses have already occurred. The next major innovations in the response to sexual offending may lie in prevention, including outreach efforts for self-identified pedophiles and hebephiles (e.g., Prevention Project Dunkelfeld and Stop It Now!) and situational crime prevention efforts that include better lighting, walk-home services, and education about acquaintance rape.

References

Abbey, A., Jacques-Tiura, A. J., & LeBreton, J. M. (2011). Risk factors for sexual aggression in young men: An expansion of the confluence model. *Aggressive Behavior*, 37, 450–464. doi:10.1002/ab.20399

Abel, G. G., Huffman, J., Warberg, B., & Holland, C. L. (1998). Visual reaction time and plethysmography as measures of sexual interest in child molesters. *Sexual Abuse: A Journal of Research and Treatment*, 10, 81–95.

Allen, M., D'Alessio, D., & Emmers-Sommer, T. M. (2000). Reaction of criminal sexual offenders to pornography: A meta-analytic summary. In M. Roloff (Ed.), *Communication yearbook* 22 (pp. 139–169). Thousand Oaks, CA: Sage.

American Psychiatric Association. (2013). *Diagnostic and statistical manual of mental disorders* (5th ed.). Washington, DC: Author.

Andrews, D. R., & Bonta, J. (2010). Rehabiliting criminal justice policy and practice. *Psychology, Public Policy, and Law*, 16, 39–55. doi:10.1037/a0018362

Archer, R. P., Buffington-Vollum, J. K., Stredny, R. V., & Handel, R. W. (2006). A survey of psychological test use patterns among forensic psychologists. *Journal of Personality Assessment*, 87, 84–94. doi:10.1207/s15327752jpa8701_07

Banse, R., Schmidt, A. F., & Clarbour, J. (2010). Indirect measures of sexual interest in child sexual offenders: A multimethod approach. *Criminal Justice and Behavior*, 37, 319–335. doi:10.1177/0093854809357598

Barbaree, H. E. (2005). Psychopathy, treatment behavior, and recidivism: An extended follow-up of Seto and Barbaree. *Journal of Interpersonal Violence*, 20, 1115–1131. doi:10.1177/0886260505278262

Barbaree, H. E., Seto, M. C., Langton, C. M., & Peacock, E. J. (2001). Evaluating the predictive accuracy of six risk assessment instruments for adult sexual offenders. *Criminal Justice and Behavior*, 28, 490–521. doi:10.1177/009385480102800406

Barbaree, H. E., Seto, M. C., Serin, R. C., Amos, N. L., & Preston, D. L. (1994). Comparisons between sexual and nonsexual rapist subtypes: Sexual arousal to rape, offense precursors, and offense characteristics.

Criminal Justice and Behavior, 21, 95–114. doi:10.1177/0093854894021001007

Barrett, M., Wilson, R. J., & Long, C. (2003). Measuring motivation to change in sexual offenders from institutional intake to community treatment. *Sexual Abuse: A Journal of Research and Treatment, 15*, 269–283. doi:10.1177/107906320301500404

Baxter, D. J., Marshall, W. L., Barbaree, H. E., Davidson, P. R., & Malcolm, P. B. (1984). Deviant sexual behavior: Differentiating sexual offenders by criminal and personal history, psychometric measures and sexual response. *Criminal Justice and Behavior, 11*, 477–501. doi:10.1177/0093854884011004007

Beier, M., Neutze, J., Mundt, I. A., Ahlers, C. J., Goecker, D., Konrad, A., & Schaefer, G.A. (2009). Encouraging self-identified pedophiles and hebephiles to seek professional help: First results of the Berlin Prevention Project Dunkelfeld (PPD). *Child Abuse & Neglect: The International Journal, 33*, 545–549. doi:10.1016/j.chiabu.2009.04.002

Beitchman, J. H., Zucker, K. J., Hood, J. E., daCosta, G. A., Akman, D., & Cassavia, E. A. (1992). A review of the long-term effects of child sexual abuse. *Child Abuse & Neglect: The International Journal, 16*, 101–118. doi:10.1016/0145-2134(92)90011-F

Berzofsky, M., Krebs, C., Langton, L., & Smiley-McDonald, H. (2012). *Victimizations not reported to the police, 2006–2010* (Research Report No. NCJ 238536). Washington, DC: Bureau of Justice Statistics. Retrieved from http://bjs.gov/content/pub/pdf/vnrp0610.pdf

Bickley, J. A., & Beech, R. (2002). An empirical investigation of the Ward & Hudson self-regulation model of the sexual offense process with child abusers. *Journal of Interpersonal Violence, 17*, 371–393. doi:10.1177/0886260502017004002

Bickley, J. A., & Beech, R. (2003). Implications for treatment of sexual offenders of the Ward and Hudson model of relapse. *Sexual Abuse: A Journal of Research and Treatment, 15*, 121–134.

Boer, D. P., Hart, S. J., Kropp, P. R., & Webster, C. D. (1997). *Manual for the Sexual Violence Risk–20: Professional guidelines for assessing risk of sexual violence.* Vancouver, British Columbia, Canada: Institute Against Family Violence.

Bonta, J., Zinger, I., Harris, A., & Carrière, D. (1998). The dangerous offender provisions: Are they targeting the right offenders? *Canadian Journal of Criminology, 40*, 377–400.

Borduin, C. M., Schaeffer, C. M., & Heiblum, N. (2009). A randomized clinical trial of multisystemic therapy with juvenile sexual offenders: Effects on youth social ecology and criminal activity. *Journal of Consulting and Clinical Psychology, 77*, 26–37. doi:10.1037/a0013035

Borum, R. (2006). *Manual for the Structured Assessment of Violence Risk in Youth (SAVRY).* Odessa, FL: Psychological Assessment Resources.

Brennan, S., & Taylor-Butts, A. (2008). *Sexual assault in Canada: 2004 and 2007.* Ottawa, Ontario, Canada: Canadian Centre for Justice Statistics.

Brown, S. L., St. Amand, M. D., & Zamble, E. (2009). The dynamic prediction of criminal recidivism: A three-wave prospective study. *Law and Human Behavior, 33*, 25–45. doi:10.1007/s10979-008-9139-7

Brownmiller, S. (1975). *Against our will: Men, women, and rape.* New York, NY: Bantam.

Burt, M. R. (1980). Cultural myths and supports for rape. *Journal of Personality and Social Psychology, 38*, 217–230. doi:10.1037/0022-3514.38.2.217

Caldwell, M. F. (2002). What we do not know about juvenile sexual reoffense risk. *Child Maltreatment, 7*, 291–302. doi:10.1177/107755902237260

Cann, J., Friendship, C., & Gozna, L. (2007). Assessing crossover in a sample of sexual offenders with multiple victims. *Legal and Criminological Psychology, 12*, 149–163. doi:10.1348/135532506X112439

Cantor, J. M., Blanchard, R., Robichaud, L. K., & Christensen, B. K. (2005). Quantitative reanalysis of aggregate data on IQ in sexual offenders. *Psychological Bulletin, 131*, 555–568. doi:10.1037/0033-2909.131.4.555

Carlstedt, A., Nilsson, T., Hofvander, B., Brimse, A., Innala, S., & Anckarsater, H. (2009). Does victim age differentiate between perpetrators of sexual child abuse? A study of mental health, psychosocial circumstances, and crimes. *Sexual Abuse: A Journal of Research and Treatment, 21*, 442–454. doi:10.1177/1079063209346699

Carpentier, M. Y., Silovsky, J. F., & Chaffin, M. (2006). Randomized trial of treatment for children with sexual behavior problems: Ten-year follow-up. *Journal of Consulting and Clinical Psychology, 74*, 482–488. doi:10.1037/0022-006X.74.3.482

Chagigiorgis, H., Michel, S., Laprade, K., Ahmed, A. G., & Seto, M. C. (2012). *Assessing short-term, dynamic changes in risk: The predictive validity of the Brockville Risk Checklist.* Manuscript submitted for publication.

Clegg, C., & Fremouw, W. (2009). Phallometric assessments of rapists. A critical review of the research. *Aggression and Violent Behavior, 14*, 115–125. doi:10.1016/j.avb.2009.01.001

Cohen, L. J., Frenda, S., Mojatabai, R., Katsavdakis, R., & Galynker, I. (2007). Comparison of sexual offenders against children with sexual offenders and adolescents and adults: Data from the New York State sexual offender registry. *Journal of*

Psychiatric Practice, 13, 373–384. doi:10.1097/01. pra.0000300123.83945.76

DeMaris, A. (1997). Elevated sexual activity in violent marriages: Hypersexuality or sexual extortion? *Journal of Sex Research, 34,* 361–373. doi:10.1080/00224499709551904

Denov, M. S. (2003). The myth of innocence: Sexual scripts and the recognition of child sexual abuse by female perpetrators. *Journal of Sex Research, 40,* 303–314. doi:10.1080/00224490309552195

Doren, D. M. (2002). *Evaluating sexual offenders: A manual for civil commitments and beyond.* Thousand Oaks, CA: Sage.

Dreznick, M. T. (2003). Heterosocial competence of rapists and child molesters: A meta-analysis. *Journal of Sex Research, 40,* 170–178. doi:10.1080/00224490309552178

Duwe, G. (2013). Can Circles of Support and Accountability (COSA) work in the United States? Preliminary results from a randomized experiment in Minnesota. *Sexual Abuse: A Journal of Research and Treatment, 25,* 143–165. doi:10.1177/1079063212453942

Duwe, G., & Donnay, W. (2010). The effects of failure to register on sexual offender recidivism. *Criminal Justice and Behavior, 37,* 520–536. doi:10.1177/0093854810364106

Eher, R., Matthes, A., Schilling, F., Haubner-MacLean, T., & Rettenberger, M. (2012). Dynamic risk assessment in sexual offenders using STABLE-2000 and the STABLE-2007: An investigation of predictive and incremental validity. *Sexual Abuse: A Journal of Research and Treatment, 24,* 5–28. doi:10.1177/1079063211403164

Elwood, R. W. (2009). Mental disorder, predisposition, prediction, and ability to control: Evaluating sexual offenders for civil commitment. *Sexual Abuse: A Journal of Research and Treatment, 21,* 395–411. doi:10.1177/1079063209347723

Epperson, D. L., Kaul, J. D., Goldman, R., Huot, S. J., Hesselton, D., & Alexander, W. (2005). *Minnesota Sex Offender Screening Tool—Revised.* Retrieved from https://www.waspc.org/files.php?bfid=3739

Epperson, D. L., Ralston, C. A., Fowers, D., & DeWitt, J. (2005). *Development of a sexual offense recidivism risk assessment tool—II (JSORRAT–II).* Unpublished manuscript, University of Iowa, Ames.

Farrington, D., & Welsh, B. C. (2005). Randomized experiments in criminology: What have we learned in the last two decades? *Journal of Experimental Criminology, 1,* 9–38. doi:10.1007/s11292-004-6460-0

Finkelhor, D. (1984). *Child sexual abuse.* New York, NY: Free Press.

Finkelhor, D. (1994). The international epidemiology of child sexual abuse. *Child Abuse & Neglect, 18,* 409–417. doi:10.1016/0145-2134(94)90026-4

Finkelhor, D., & Jones, L. (2006). Why have child maltreatment and child victimization declined? *Journal of Social Issues, 62,* 685–716. doi:10.1111/j.1540-4560.2006.00483.x

Firestone, P., Bradford, J. M., McCoy, M., Greenberg, D. M., Larose, M. R., & Curry, S. (1999). Prediction of recidivism in incest offenders. *Journal of Interpersonal Violence, 14,* 511–531. doi:10.1177/088626099014005004

Gooren, L. J. (2011). Ethical and medical considerations of androgen deprivation treatment of sexual offenders. *The Journal of Clinical Endocrinology and Metabolism, 96,* 3628–3637. doi:10.1210/jc.2011-1540

Gray, N. S., Brown, A. S., MacCulloch, M. J., Smith, J., & Snowden, R. J. (2005). An implicit test of the associations between children and sex in pedophiles. *Journal of Abnormal Psychology, 114,* 304–308. doi:10.1037/0021-843X.114.2.304

Greenwald, A. G., McGhee, D. E., & Schwartz, J. L. K. (1998). Measuring individual differences in implicit cognition: The Implicit Association Test. *Journal of Personality and Social Psychology, 74,* 1464–1480. doi:10.1037/0022-3514.74.6.1464

Gross, A. M., Winslett, A., Roberts, M., & Gohm, C. L. (2006). An examination of sexual violence against college women. *Violence Against Women, 12,* 288–300. doi:10.1177/1077801205277358

Grubin, D., & Thornton, D. (1994). A national program for the assessment and treatment of sexual offenders in the English prison system. *Criminal Justice and Behavior, 21,* 55–71. doi:10.1177/0093854894021001005

Guay, J.-P., Proulx, J., Cusson, M., & Ouimet, M. (2001). Victim-choice polymorphia among serious sexual offenders. *Archives of Sexual Behavior, 30,* 521–533. doi:10.1023/A:1010291201588

Hanson, R. K., Bourgon, G., Helmus, L., & Hodgson, S. (2009). The principles of effective correctional treatment also apply to sexual offenders: A meta-analysis. *Criminal Justice and Behavior, 36,* 865–891. doi:10.1177/0093854809338545

Hanson, R. K., & Bussière, M. T. (1998). Predicting relapse: A meta-analysis of sexual offender recidivism studies. *Journal of Consulting and Clinical Psychology, 66,* 348–362. doi:10.1037/0022-006X.66.2.348

Hanson, R. K., Gordon, A., Harris, A. J. R., Marques, J. K., Murphy, W., Quinsey, V. L., & Seto, M. C. (2002). First report of the Collaborative Outcome Data Project on the effectiveness of treatment for sexual offenders. *Sexual Abuse: A Journal of Research and Treatment, 14,* 169–194.

Hanson, R. K., & Harris, A. (2000). Where should we intervene? Dynamic predictors of sexual offense recidivism. *Criminal Justice and Behavior, 27,* 6–35. doi:10.1177/0093854800027001002

Hanson, R. K., Harris, A. J. R., Scott, T. L., & Helmus, L. (2007). *Assessing the risk of sexual offenders on community supervision: The Dynamic Supervision Project* (User Report 2007-05). Ottawa, Ontario, Canada: Public Safety Canada.

Hanson, R. K., Helmus, L., & Thornton, D. (2010). Predicting recidivism amongst sexual offenders: A multisite study of Static–2002. *Law and Human Behavior, 34,* 198–211. doi:10.1007/s10979-009-9180-1

Hanson, R. K., & Morton-Bourgon, K. E. (2005). The characteristics of persistent sexual offenders: A meta-analysis of recidivism studies. *Journal of Consulting and Clinical Psychology, 73,* 1154–1163. doi:10.1037/0022-006X.73.6.1154

Hanson, R. K., & Morton-Bourgon, K. E. (2009). The accuracy of recidivism risk assessments for sexual offenders: A meta-analysis of 118 prediction studies. *Psychological Assessment, 21,* 1–21. doi:10.1037/a0014421

Hanson, R. K., & Thornton, D. (2000). Improving risk assessments for sexual offenders: A comparison of three actuarial scales. *Law and Human Behavior, 24,* 119–136. doi:10.1023/A:1005482921333

Hanson, R. K., & Thornton, D. (2003). *Notes on the development of Static–2002* (Corrections Research User Report 2003–01). Ottawa, Ontario, Canada: Department of the Solicitor General of Canada.

Hare, R. D. (2003). *The Psychopathy Checklist—Revised, technical manual* (2nd ed.). Toronto, Ontario, Canada: Multi-Health Systems.

Harris, A. J. R., & Hanson, R. K. (2010). Clinical, actuarial, and dynamis risk assessment of sexual offenders: Why do things keep changing? *Journal of Sexual Aggression, 16,* 296–310. doi:10.1080/13552600.2010.494772

Harris, A. J. R., Phenix, A., Hanson, R. K., & Thornton, D. (2003). *Static–99 coding rules: Revised 2003.* Ottawa, Ontario, Canada: Solicitor General Canada.

Harris, D. A., Mazerolle, P., & Knight, R. A. (2009). Understanding male sexual offending: A comparison of general and specialist theories. *Criminal Justice and Behavior, 36,* 1051–1069. doi:10.1177/0093854809342242

Harris, G. T., Lalumière, M. L., Seto, M. C., Rice, M. E., & Chaplin, T. C. (2012). Explaining the erectile responses of rapists to rape stories: The contributions of sexual activity, non-consent, and violence with injury. *Archives of Sexual Behavior, 41,* 221–229.

Helmus, L., Thornton, D., Hanson, R. K., & Babchishin, K. M. (2012). Improving the predictive accuracy of

Static–99 and Static–2002 with older sexual offenders: Revised age weights. *Sexual Abuse: A Journal of Research and Treatment, 24,* 64–101.

Henggeler, S. W. Schoenwald, S. K., Borduin, C. M., Rowland, M. D., & Cunningham, P. B. (1998). *Multisystemic treatment of antisocial behavior in children and adolescents.* New York, NY: Guilford Press.

Howes, R. J. (1995). A survey of plethysmographic assessment in North America. *Sexual Abuse: A Journal of Research and Treatment, 7,* 9–24.

Jespersen, A. F., Lalumière, M. L., & Seto, M. C. (2009). Sexual abuse history among adult sexual offenders and non-sexual offenders: A meta-analysis. *Child Abuse & Neglect, 33,* 179–192. doi:10.1016/j.chiabu.2008.07.004

Kalmus, E., & Beech, A. R. (2005). Forensic assessment of sexual interest: A review. *Aggression and Violent Behavior, 10,* 193–217. doi:10.1016/j.avb.2003.12.002

Kemper, T. S., & Kistner, J. A. (2007). Offense history and recidivism in three victim-age-based groups of juvenile sexual offenders. *Sexual Abuse: A Journal of Research and Treatment, 19,* 409–424. doi:10.1177/107906320701900406

Kingston, D. A. (2010). *The offence progression in sexual offenders: An examination of the self-regulation model of the offence process* (Unpublished doctoral dissertation). University of Ottawa, Ottawa, Ontario, Canada.

Kingston, D. A., Firestone, P., Moulden, H. M., & Bradford, J. M. (2007). The utility of the diagnosis of pedophilia. A comparison of various classification procedures. *Archives of Sexual Behavior, 36,* 423–436. doi:10.1007/s10508-006-9091-x

Kingston, D. A., Firestone, P., Wexler, A., & Bradford, J. M. (2008). Factors associated with recidivism among intrafamilial child molesters. *Journal of Sexual Aggression, 14,* 3–18. doi:10.1080/13552600802074924

Kingston, D. A., Seto, M. C., Firestone, P., & Bradford, J. M. (2010). Comparing indicators of sexual sadism as predictors of recidivism among sexual offenders. *Journal of Consulting and Clinical Psychology, 78,* 574–584. doi:10.1037/a0019734

Kingston, D. A., Yates, P. M., & Firestone, P. (2012). The self-regulation model of sexual offending: Relationship to risk and need. *Law and Human Behavior, 36,* 215–224. doi:10.1037/h0093960

Knight, R. A., & Prentky, R. A. (1990). Classifying sexual offenders: The development and corroboration of taxonomic models. In W. L. Marshall, D. R. Laws, & H. E. Barbaree (Eds.), *Handbook of sexual assault: Issues, theories, and treatment of the offender* (pp. 23–52). New York, NY: Plenum. doi:10.1007/978-1-4899-0915-2_3

Knight, R. A., & Sims-Knight, J. E. (2003). The developmental antecedents of sexual coercion against women: Testing alternative hypotheses with structural equation modeling. *Annals of the New York Academy of Sciences, 989*, 72–85. doi:10.1111/j.1749-6632.2003.tb07294.x

Koss, M. P., Dinero, T. E., Seibel, C. A., & Cox, S. L. (1988). Stranger and acquaintance rape: Are there differences in the victim's experience? *Psychology of Women Quarterly, 12*, 1–24. doi:10.1111/j.1471-6402.1988.tb00924.x

Kuznestov, A., Pierson, T. A., & Harry, B. (1992). Victim age as a basis for profiling sexual offenders. *Federal Probation, 56*, 34–38.

Lalumière, M. L., & Harris, G. T. (1998). Common questions regarding the use of phallometric testing with sexual offenders. *Sexual Abuse: A Journal of Research and Treatment, 10*, 227–237.

Lalumière, M. L., Harris, G. T., Quinsey, V. L., & Rice, M. E. (2005). *The causes of rape: Understanding individual differences in male propensity for sexual aggression.* Washington, DC: American Psychological Association. doi:10.1037/10961-000

Lalumière, M. L., Quinsey, V. L., Harris, G. T., Rice, M. E., & Trautrimas, C. (2003). Are rapists differentially aroused by coercive sex in phallometric assessments? *Annals of the New York Academy of Sciences, 989*, 211–224. doi:10.1111/j.1749-6632.2003.tb07307.x

Langevin, R., & Paitich, D. (2001). *Clarke Sex History Questionnaire for Males—Revised (SHQ–R).* Toronto, Ontario, Canada: Multi-Health Systems.

Langton, C. M., Barbaree, H. E., Seto, M. C., Peacock, E. J., Harkins, L., & Hansen, K. T. (2007). Actuarial assessment of risk for reoffense among adult sexual offenders: Evaluating the predictive accuracy of the Static–2002 and five other instruments. *Criminal Justice and Behavior, 34*, 37–59. doi:10.1177/0093854806291157

Launay, G. (1999). The phallometric assessment of sexual offenders: An update. *Criminal Behaviour and Mental Health, 9*, 254–274. doi:10.1002/cbm.317

Laws, D. R. (1994). How dangerous are rapists to children? *Journal of Sexual Aggression, 1*, 1–14. doi:10.1080/13552609408413238

Laws, D. R., & O'Donohue, W. T. (Eds.). (2008). *Sexual deviance: Theory, assessment, and treatment* (2nd ed.). New York, NY: Guilford Press.

Laws, D. R., & Ward, T. (2011). *Desistance from sexual offending: Alternatives to throwing away the keys.* New York, NY: Guilford Press.

Letourneau, E. J., Henggeler, S. W., Borduin, C. M., Schewe, P. A., McCart, M. R., Chapman, J. E., & Saldana, L. (2009). Multisystemic therapy for juvenile sexual offenders: 1-year results from a randomized

effectiveness trial. *Journal of Family Psychology, 23*, 89–102. doi:10.1037/a0014352

Levenson, J. S. (2003). Policy interventions designed to combat sexual violence: Community notification and civil commitment. *Journal of Child Sexual Abuse, 12*, 17–52. doi:10.1300/J070v12n03_02

Levenson, J. S. (2004). Reliability of sexually violent predator civil commitment criteria in Florida. *Law and Human Behavior, 28*, 357–368. doi:10.1023/B:LAHU.0000039330.22347.ad

Levenson, J. S., Becker, J., & Morin, J. W. (2008). The relationship between victim age and gender crossover among sexual offenders. *Sexual Abuse: A Journal of Research and Treatment, 20*, 43–60. doi:10.1177/1079063208314819

Lösel, F., & Schmucker, M. (2005). The effectiveness of treatment for sexual offenders: A comprehensive meta-analysis. *Journal of Experimental Criminology, 1*, 117–146. doi:10.1007/s11292-004-6466-7

Lussier, P., Leclerc, B., Healey, J., & Proulx, J. (2007). Generality of deviance and predation: Crime-switching and specialization patterns in persistent sexual offenders. In M. Delisi & P. J. Conis (Eds.), *Violent offenders: Theory, public policy, and practice* (pp. 97–118). Boston, MA: Jones and Bartlett.

Lussier, P., Leclerc, B., & Proulx, J. (2005). The generality of criminal behavior: A confirmatory factor analysis of the criminal activity of sexual offenders in adulthood. *Journal of Criminal Justice, 33*, 177–189. doi:10.1016/j.jcrimjus.2004.12.009

Malamuth, N. M., Linz, D., Heavey, C. L., Barnes, G., & Acker, M. (1995). Using the confluence model of sexual aggression to predict men's conflict with women: A 10-year follow-up study. *Journal of Personality and Social Psychology, 69*, 353–369. doi:10.1037/0022-3514.69.2.353

Malamuth, N. M., Sockloskie, R. J., Koss, M. P., & Tanaka, J. S. (1991). Characteristics of aggressors against women: Testing a model using a national sample of college students. *Journal of Consulting and Clinical Psychology, 59*, 670–681. doi:10.1037/0022-006X.59.5.670

Mann, R. E., Hanson, R. K., & Thornton, D. (2010). Assessing risk for sexual recidivism: Some proposals on the nature of psychologically meaningful risk factors. *Sexual Abuse: A Journal of Research and Treatment, 22*, 191–217. doi:10.1177/1079063210366039

Mann, R. E., Webster, S. D., Schofield, C., & Marshall, W. L. (2004). Approach versus avoidance goals in relapse prevention with sexual offenders. *Sexual Abuse: A Journal of Research and Treatment, 16*, 65–75. doi:10.1023/B:SEBU.0000006285.73534.57

Marques, J. K., Wiederanders, M., Day, D. M., Nelson, C., & van Ommeren, A. (2005). Effects of a relapse prevention program on sexual recidivism: Final results from California's Sexual offender Treatment Evaluation Project (SOTEP). *Sexual Abuse: A Journal of Research and Treatment, 17,* 79–107.

Marshall, W. L., & Barbaree, H. E. (1990). An integrated theory of the etiology of sexual offending. In W. L. Marshall, D. R. Laws, & H. E. Barbaree (Eds.), *Handbook of sexual assault: Issues, theories, and treatment of the offender* (pp. 257–275). New York, NY: Plenum. doi:10.1007/978-1-4899-0915-2_15

Marshall, W. L., & Fernandez, Y. M. (2000). Phallometric testing with sexual offenders: Limits to its value. *Clinical Psychology Review, 20,* 807–822. doi:10.1016/S0272-7358(99)00013-6

Marshall, W. L., & Marshall, L. E. (2007). The utility of the random controlled trial for evaluating sexual offender treatment: The gold standard or an inappropriate strategy? *Sexual Abuse: A Journal of Research and Treatment, 19,* 175–191.

Marshall, W. L., Marshall, L. E., Serran, G. A., & O'Brien, M. D. (2011). *Rehabilitating sexual offenders: A strength-based approach.* Washington, DC: American Psychological Association. doi:10.1037/12310-000

Marshall, W. L., & Moulden, H. (2001). Hostility toward women and victim empathy in rapists. *Sexual Abuse: A Journal of Research and Treatment, 13,* 249–255.

McConnaughy, E. A., DiClemente, C. C., & Prochaska, J. O. (1989). Stages of change in psychotherapy: A follow-up report. *Psychotherapy, 26,* 494–503. doi:10.1037/h0085468

McConnaughy, E. A., Prochaska, J. O., & Velicer, W. E. (1983). Stages of change in psychotherapy: Measurement and sample profiles. *Psychotherapy, 20,* 368–375. doi:10.1037/h0090198

McCormick, J. S., Maric, A., Seto, M. C., & Barbaree, H. E. (1998). Victim–offender relationship predicts sentence length in rapists. *Journal of Interpersonal Violence, 13,* 413–420. doi:10.1177/088626098013003007

McGrath, R. J., Cumming, G. F., Burchard, B. L., Zeoli, S., & Ellerby, L. (2009). *Current practices and emerging trends in sexual abuser management: The Safer Society 2009 North American Survey.* Brandon, VT: Safer Society Press.

McPhail, I. V., Hermann, C. A., & Nunes, K. L. (2011, November). *Emotional congruence with children: A meta-analytic review.* Paper presented at the 30th annual conference of the Association for the Treatment of Sexual Abusers, Toronto, Ontario, Canada.

Mills, J. F., Kroner, D. G., & Morgan, R. D. (2007). *Clinician's guide to violence risk assessment.* New York, NY: Guilford Press.

Milner, R. J., & Webster, S. D. (2005). Identifying schemas in child molesters, rapists, and violent offenders.

Sexual Abuse: A Journal of Research and Treatment, 17, 425–439. doi:10.1007/s11194-005-8053-5

Mishra, S., & Lalumière, M. L. (2009). Is the crime drop of the 1990s in Canada and the USA associated with a general decline in risky and health-related behaviors? *Social Science & Medicine, 68,* 39–48. doi:10.1016/j.socscimed.2008.09.060

Murphy, L., Fedoroff, J. P., & Martineau, M. (2009). Canada's sexual offender registries: Background, implementation, and social policy considerations. *The Canadian Journal of Human Sexuality, 18,* 61–72.

Neutze, J., Seto, M. C., Schaefer, G. A., Mundt, I. A., & Beier, K. M. (2011). Predictors of child pornography offenses and child sexual abuse in a community sample of pedophiles and hebephiles. *Sexual Abuse: A Journal of Research and Treatment, 23,* 212–242. doi:10.1177/1079063210382043

Nezu, C. M., Nezu, A. M., Dudek, J. A., Peacock, M. A., & Stoll, J. G. (2005). Social problem-solving correlates of sexual deviancy and aggression among adult child molesters. *Journal of Sexual Aggression, 11,* 27–36. doi:10.1080/13552600512331329540

Nichols, H. R., & Molinder, I. (1984). *Multiphasic Sex Inventories.* Tacoma, WA: Nichols and Molinder Assessments, Inc.

Nunes, K. L., Firestone, P., & Baldwin, M. W. (2007). Indirect assessment of cognitions of child sexual abusers with the Implicit Association Test. *Criminal Justice and Behavior, 34,* 454–475. doi:10.1177/0093854806291703

O'Donohue, W., & Letourneau, E. (1992). The psychometric properties of the penile tumescence assessment of child molesters. *Journal of Psychopathology and Behavioral Assessment, 14,* 123–174. doi:10.1007/BF00965172

Ogden, T., & Halliday-Boykins, C. A. (2004). Multisystemic treatment of antisocial adolescents in Norway: Replication of clinical outcomes outside of the US. *Child and Adolescent Mental Health, 9,* 77–83. doi:10.1111/j.1475-3588.2004.00085.x

Olver, M. E., & Wong, S. C. P. (2006). Psychopathy, sexual deviance, and recidivism among sexual offenders. *Sexual Abuse: A Journal of Research and Treatment, 18,* 65–82. doi:10.1177/107906320601800105

Olver, M. E., & Wong, S. C. P. (2011). A comparison of static and dynamic assessment of sexual offender risk and need in a treatment context. *Criminal Justice and Behavior, 38,* 113–126. doi:10.1177/0093854810389534

Packard, R., & Levenson, J. (2006). Revisiting the reliability of diagnostic decisions in sexual offender civil commitment. *Sexual Offender Treatment, 1.* Retrieved from http://www.sexual-offender-treatment.org/50.html

Parent, G., Guay, J. P., & Knight, R. A. (2011). An assessment of long-term risk of recidivism by adult sexual offenders: One size doesn't fit all. *Criminal Justice and Behavior, 38*, 188–209. doi:10.1177/0093854810388238

Polaschek, D. L. L., Anstiss, B., & Wilson, M. (2010). The assessment of offending-related stage of change in offenders: Psychometric validation of the URICA with male prisoners. *Psychology, Crime & Law, 16*, 305–325. doi:10.1080/10683160802698766

Porter, S., Fairweather, D., Drugge, J., Herve, H., Brit, A., & Boer, D. (2000). Profiles of psychopathy in incarcerated sexual offenders. *Criminal Justice and Behavior, 27*, 216–233. doi:10.1177/0093854800027002005

Prentky, R., & Righthand, S. (2003). *Juvenile Sexual offender Assessment Protocol—II (J–SOAP–II) manual* (Report No. NCJ 202316). Washington, DC: Office of Juvenile Justice and Delinquency Prevention. Retrieved from http://www.ncjrs.gov/pdffiles1/ojjdp/202316.pdf

Prochaska, J. O., & DiClemente, C. C. (1982). Transtheoretical therapy: Toward a more integrative model of change. *Psychotherapy, 19*, 276–288. doi:10.1037/h0088437

Proulx, J., Perreault, C., & Ouimet, M. (1999). Pathways in the offending process of extra-familial sexual child molesters. *Sexual Abuse: A Journal of Research and Treatment, 11*, 117–129.

Quinsey, V. L., Harris, G. T., Rice, M. E., & Cormier, C. A. (2006). *Violent offenders: Appraising and managing risk* (2nd ed.). Washington, DC: American Psychological Association. doi:10.1037/11367-000

Reitzel, L. R., & Carbonell, J. L. (2006). The effectiveness of sexual offender treatment for juveniles as measured by recidivism: A meta-analysis. *Sexual Abuse: A Journal of Research and Treatment, 18*, 401–421.

Rettenberger, M., Matthes, A., Boer, D. P., & Eher, R. (2010). Prospective actuarial risk assessment: A comparison of five risk assessment instruments in different sexual offender subtypes. *International Journal of Offender Therapy and Comparative Criminology, 54*, 169–186. doi:10.1177/0306624X08328755

Rind, B., Tromovitch, P., & Bauserman, R. (1998). A meta-analytic examination of assumed properties of child sexual abuse using college samples. *Psychological Bulletin, 124*, 22–53. doi:10.1037/0033-2909.124.1.22

Robertiello, G., & Terry, K. J. (2007). Can we profile sexual offenders? A review of sexual offender typologies. *Aggression and Violent Behavior, 12*, 508–518. doi:10.1016/j.avb.2007.02.010

Robinson, M.-C., Rouleau, J.-L., & Madrigano, G. (1997). Validation de la pléthysmographie pénienne comme mesure psychophysiologique des intérêts sexuels des agresseurs adolescents [Validation of penile plethysmography as a psychophysiological measure of the sexual interests of adolescent sexual offenders]. *Revue Québécoise de Psychologie, 18*, 111–124.

Sandler, J. C., Freeman, N. J., & Socia, K. M. (2008). Does a watched pot boil? A time-series analysis of New York State's sexual offender registration and notification law. *Psychology, Public Policy, and Law, 14*, 284–302. doi:10.1037/a0013881

Schaeffer, C. M., & Borduin, C. M. (2005). Long-term follow-up to a randomized clinical trial of multisystemic therapy with serious and violent juvenile offenders. *Journal of Consulting and Clinical Psychology, 73*, 445–453. doi:10.1037/0022-006X.73.3.445

Schoenwald, S. K., Heiblum, N., Saldana, L., & Henggeler, S. W. (2008). The international implementation of multisystemic therapy. *Evaluation & the Health Professions, 31*, 211–225. doi:10.1177/0163278708315925

Seto, M. C. (2003). Interpreting the treatment performance of sexual offenders. In A. Matravers (Ed.), Managing sexual offenders in the community: Contexts, challenges, and responses, *Cambridge Criminal Justice Series* (pp. 125–143). London, England: Willan.

Seto, M. C. (2005). Is more better? Combining actuarial risk scales to predict recidivism among adult sexual offenders. *Psychological Assessment, 17*, 156–167. doi:10.1037/1040-3590.17.2.156

Seto, M. C. (2008). *Pedophilia and sexual offending against children: Theory, assessment, and intervention.* Washington, DC: American Psychological Association. doi:10.1037/11639-000

Seto, M. C., & Barbaree, H. E. (1999). Psychopathy, treatment behavior, and sexual offender recidivism. *Journal of Interpersonal Violence, 14*, 1235–1248. doi:10.1177/088626099014012001

Seto, M. C., Harris, G. T., Rice, M. E., & Barbaree, H. E. (2004). The Screening Scale for Pedophilic Interests and recidivism among adult sexual offenders with child victims. *Archives of Sexual Behavior, 33*, 455–466. doi:10.1023/B:ASEB.0000037426.55935.9c

Seto, M. C., & Lalumière, M. L. (2010). What is so special about male adolescent sexual offending? A review and test of explanations using meta-analysis. *Psychological Bulletin, 136*, 526–575. doi:10.1037/a0019700

Seto, M. C., Lalumière, M. L., & Blanchard, R. (2000). The discriminative validity of a phallometric test for pedophilic interests among adolescent sexual offenders against children. *Psychological Assessment, 12*, 319–327. doi:10.1037/1040-3590.12.3.319

Seto, M. C., Lalumière, M. L., Harris, G. T., & Chivers, M. L. (2012). The sexual responses of sexual sadists. *Journal of Abnormal Psychology, 121*, 739–753. doi:10.1037/a0028714

Seto, M. C., Lalumière, M. L., & Kuban, M. (1999). The sexual preferences of incest offenders. *Journal of Abnormal Psychology, 108,* 267–272. doi:10.1037/0021-843X.108.2.267

Seto, M. C., Marques, J. K., Harris, G. T., Chaffin, M., Lalumière, M. L., Miner, M. H., . . . Quinsey, V. L. (2008). Good science and progress in sexual offender treatment are intertwined: A response to Marshall and Marshall (2007). *Sexual Abuse: A Journal of Research and Treatment, 20,* 247–255. doi:10.1177/1079063208317733

Seto, M. C., Murphy, W. D., Page, J., & Ennis, L. (2003). Detecting anomalous sexual interests among juvenile sexual offenders. *Annals of the New York Academy of Sciences, 989,* 118–130. doi:10.1111/j.1749-6632.2003.tb07298.x

Sim, D. J., & Proeve, M. (2010). Crossover and stability of victim type in child molesters. *Legal and Criminological Psychology, 15,* 401–413. doi:10.1348/135532509X473869

Sjöstedt, G., Langstrom, N., Sturidsson, K., & Grann, M. (2004). Stability of modus operandi in sexual offending. *Criminal Justice and Behavior, 31,* 609–623. doi:10.1177/0093854804267094

Socia, K. M. (2013). Too close for comfort: Registered sexual offender spatial clustering and recidivistic sex crime rates. *Sexual Abuse: A Journal of Research and Treatment, 25,* 531–556.

Stirpe, T. S., Wilson, R. J., & Long, C. (2001). Goal attainment scaling with sexual offenders: A measure of clinical impact at posttreatment and at community follow-up. *Sexual Abuse: A Journal of Research and Treatment, 13,* 65–77.

Tewksbury, R., & Jennings, W. G. (2010). Assessing the impact of sexual offender registration and community notification on sexual offending trajectories. *Criminal Justice and Behavior, 37,* 570–582. doi:10.1177/0093854810363570

Thibaut, F., De La Barra, F., Gordon, H., Cosyns, P., Bradford, J. M. W., & WFSBP Task Force on Sexual Disorders. (2010). The World Federation of Societies of Biological Psychiatry (WFSBP) guidelines for the biological treatment of paraphilias. *The World Journal of Biological Psychiatry, 11,* 604–655. doi:10.3109/15622971003671628

Tierney, D. W., & McCabe, M. P. (2002). Motivation for behavior change among sexual offenders: A review of the literature. *Clinical Psychology Review, 22,* 113–129. doi:10.1016/S0272-7358(01)00084-8

Tierney, D. W., & McCabe, M. P. (2005). The utility of the trans-theoretical model of behavior change in the treatment of sexual offenders. *Sexual Abuse: A Journal of Research and Treatment, 17,* 153–170. doi:10.1177/107906320501700206

Timmons-Mitchell, J., Bender, M. B., Kishna, M. A., & Mitchell, C. C. (2006). An independent effectiveness trial of multisystemic therapy with juvenile justice youth. *Journal of Clinical Child and Adolescent Psychology, 35,* 227–236. doi:10.1207/s15374424jccp3502_6

Trevethan, S., Crutcher, N., & Moore, J.-P. (2002). *A profile of federal offenders designated as dangerous offenders or serving long-term supervision orders.* Retrieved from http://www.csc-scc.gc.ca/text/rsrch/reports/r125/r125-eng.shtml

Truman, J. L. (2011). *National crime victimization survey: Criminal victimization, 2010.* Washington, DC: U.S. Department of Justice.

Viljoen, J. L., Scalora, M., Cuadra, L., Bader, S., Chavez, V., Ullman, D., & Lawrence, L. (2008). Assessing risk for violence in adolescents who have sexually offended: A comparison of the J–SOAP–II, J–SORRAT–II, and SAVRY. *Criminal Justice and Behavior, 35,* 5–23. doi:10.1177/0093854807307521

Ward, T., & Gannon, T. (2006). Rehabilitation, etiology, and self-regulation: The good lives model of sexual offender treatment. *Aggression and Violent Behavior, 11,* 77–94. doi:10.1016/j.avb.2005.06.001

Ward, T., & Hudson, S. M. (1996). Relapse prevention: A critical analysis. *Sexual Abuse: A Journal of Research and Treatment, 8,* 177–200.

Ward, T., & Hudson, S. M. (1998). The construction and development of theory in the sexual offending area: A metatheoretical framework. *Sexual Abuse: A Journal of Research and Treatment, 10,* 47–63.

Ward, T., & Hudson, S. M. (2000). A self-regulation model of relapse prevention. In D. R. Laws, S. M. Hudson, & T. Ward (Eds.), *Remaking relapse prevention with sexual offenders: A sourcebook* (pp. 79–101). New York, NY: Sage.

Ward, T., & Maruna, S. (2007). *Rehabilitation: Beyond the risk assessment paradigm.* London, England: Routledge.

Ward, T., Polaschek, D., & Beech, A. R. (2006). *Theories of sexual offending.* Chicester, England: Wiley.

Ward, T., & Stewart, C. A. (2003). The treatment of sexual offenders: Risk management and good lives. *Professional Psychology: Research and Practice, 34,* 353–360. doi:10.1037/0735-7028.34.4.353

Ware, J., & Bright, D. (2008). Evolution of a treatment program: Recent changes to NSW custody based intensive treatment (CUBIT). *Psychiatry, Psychology and Law, 15,* 340–349. doi:10.1080/13218710802014543

Webster, S. D. (2005). Pathways to sexual offense recidivism following treatment: An examination of the Ward and Hudson self-regulation model of relapse. *Journal of Interpersonal Violence, 20,* 1175–1196. doi:10.1177/0886260505278532

Wheeler, J. G., George, W. H., & Dahl, B. J. (2002). Sexually aggressive college males: Empathy as a moderator in the "confluence model" of sexual aggression. *Personality and Individual Differences, 33,* 759–775. doi:10.1016/S0191-8869(01)00190-8

Wilson, R. J. (1999). Emotional congruence in sexual offenders against children. *Sexual Abuse: A Journal of Research and Treatment, 11,* 33–47.

Wilson, R. J., Cortoni, F., & McWhinnie, A. J. (2009). Circles of Support & Accountability: A Canadian national replication of outcome findings. *Sexual Abuse: A Journal of Research and Treatment, 21,* 412–430. doi:10.1177/1079063209347724

Wilson, R. J., Picheca, J. E., & Prinzo, M. (2007a). Evaluating the effectiveness of professionally facilitated volunteerism in the community-based management of high-risk sexual offenders: Part 1—A comparison of recidivism rates. *The Howard Journal of Criminal Justice, 46,* 327–337. doi:10.1111/j.1468-2311.2007.00480.x

Wilson, R. J., Picheca, J. E., & Prinzo, M. (2007b). Evaluating the effectiveness of professionally facilitated volunteerism in the community-based management of high-risk sexual offenders: Part 2—Effects on participants and stakeholders. *The Howard Journal of Criminal Justice, 46,* 289–302. doi:10.1111/j.1468-2311.2007.00475.x

Wilson, R. J., & Prinzo, M. (2002). Circles of support: A restorative justice initiative. *Journal of Psychology & Human Sexuality, 13,* 59–77. doi:10.1300/J056v13n03_05

Witte, T. D., Di Placido, C., Gu, D., & Wong, S. C. P. (2006). Investigation of the validity and reliability of the Criminal Sentiments Scale in a sample of treated sexual offenders. *Sexual Abuse: A Journal of Research and Treatment, 18,* 249–258.

Wong, S., Olver, M. E., Nicholaichuk, T. P., & Gordon, A. (2003). *The Violence Risk Scale: Sexual Offender version (VRS–SO).* Saskatoon, Saskatchewan, Canada: Regional Psychiatric Centre and University of Saskatchewan.

Worling, J. R. (1995). Sexual abuse histories of adolescent male sexual offenders: Diffferences on the basis of the age and gender of their victims. *Journal of Abnormal Psychology, 104,* 610–613. doi:10.1037/0021-843X.104.4.610

Worling, J. R., Bookalam, D., & Litteljohn, A. (2012). Prospective validity of the Estimate of Risk of Adolescent Sexual Offense Recidivism (ERASOR). *Sexual Abuse: A Journal of Research and Treatment, 24,* 203–223

Worling, J. R., & Curwen, T. (2001). Estimate of Risk of Adolescent Sexual Offense Recidivism (Version 2.0: The "ERASOR"). In M. C. Calder (Ed.), *Juveniles and children who sexually abuse: Frameworks for assessment* (pp. 372–397). Dorset, England: Russell House.

Yates, P. M., & Kingston, D. A. (2005). Pathways to sexual offending. In B. K. Schwartz & H. R. Cellini (Eds.), *The sexual offender* (Vol. 5, pp. 1–15). Kingston, NJ: Civic Research Institute.

Yates, P. M., Kingston, D. A., & Ward, T. (2009). *The self-regulation model of the offense and re-offense process: Vol. 3. A guide to assessment and treatment planning using the integrated good lives/self-regulation model of sexual offending.* Victoria, British Columbia, Canada: Pacific Psychological Assessment Corporation.

Zanatta, R. G. (1996). *Risk of violent recidivism: A comparison of dangerous and nondangerous offenders* (Unpublished master's thesis). Simon Fraser University, Vancouver, British Columbia, Canada.

Zgoba, K. M., & Levenson, J. S. (2012). Failure to register as a predictor of sex offense recidivism: The big bad wolf or a red herring? *Sexual Abuse: A Journal of Research and Treatment, 24,* 328–349. doi:10.1177/1079063211421019

Zimring, F. E. (2007). *The great American crime decline.* New York, NY: Oxford University Press.

CHAPTER 12

INTIMATE PARTNER VIOLENCE

Tonia L. Nicholls and John Hamel

Intimate partner violence (IPV) was first widely recognized as a major societal problem in the 1970s. Despite more than 40 years of research and substantial gains in acknowledging that violence between romantic partners is a legitimate crime, there remains considerable controversy in the IPV field and areas requiring further research and advancement in practice. In some cases, it appears that practice and policy have largely failed to keep pace with research developments.

There is general consensus that the prevalence of IPV is high (e.g., 10%–30% of the general population perpetrate IPV annually), and there is also longstanding acknowledgment of wide-ranging and serious negative effects of IPV for the individual, the family, and society alike (e.g., physical health, mental health, financial burdens). Controversy continues within the literature, however, with regard to basic operationalizations (e.g., who constitutes a valid IPV victim) and measurement (e.g., how to contextualize IPV), and these issues have important implications for research and practice. Despite more than 200 studies demonstrating the reciprocal nature of much of IPV (~50%), and the relatively equivalent rates of IPV perpetration and victimization among men and women in developed nations, this knowledge has been very slow to infiltrate the largely feminist-informed prevention and treatment approaches to IPV that predominate most of North America and other industrialized nations. This perspective counters that data with the assertion that IPV is a gendered problem; that is, it is a reflection of patriarchy and should be considered entirely in the context of a form of violence against women.

At the nexus of these issues is a flourishing theoretical debate about the etiology of IPV. There are two distinct and widely divided camps that generally adhere to gendered (i.e., IPV reflects women's inferior status in society, patriarchy) versus nongendered perspectives (i.e., IPV reflects motivations and risk factors that are similar to other forms of crime and violence). Closely related to this theoretical divide is a longstanding debate with regard to the extent to which female IPV perpetrators and male victims present a real and substantial concern that warrants research, funding, treatment, and/or interventions by social services or law enforcement agencies.

The present chapter adopts a gender-inclusive perspective; a view that maintains that both genders perpetrate IPV, are victimized in IPV encounters, and are negatively affected by these encounters. This perspective also recognizes that each gender experiences different effects of IPV (e.g., women tend to suffer worse physical injuries); yet maintains that holding both genders accountable for IPV (see Tjaden & Thoennes, 2000) is important for identifying appropriate interventions (Dutton & Nicholls, 2005; Hamel, 2005, 2014; Hamel & Nicholls, 2007). Theories that reflect patriarchy and an understanding of violence against women and women's historically subservient societal position, as well as theories that reflect general violence risk predictors and protective factors, provide an essential foundation for understanding IPV and can contribute to enhancing the field's capacity to prevent and treat this malicious health problem. In particular, some (but not all) research on the global front has

http://dx.doi.org/10.1037/14461-012
APA Handbook of Forensic Psychology: Vol. 1. Individual and Situational Influences in Criminal and Civil Contexts,
B. L. Cutler and P. A. Zapf (Editors-in-Chief)

demonstrated that IPV does correspond with gender inequities in nations that are characterized by less industrial development, women's lower social status, and traditional gender roles. However, there is also a vast and methodologically sophisticated bank of data from developed nations (primarily the United States) that, with the exception of injuries and homicide, largely reveals considerable gender equity in IPV perpetration and victimization. This research has firmly and irrevocably changed the face of who should be considered to constitute the likely victim/perpetrator of IPV. As such, we attend to literature reflecting IPV in heterosexual and homosexual relationships and, when there is sufficient and rigorous research data to warrant it, we have endeavored to include direct reference to research that covers the importance and implications of IPV for both men and women. Similarly, we explore the extent to which IPV and child abuse overlap and the implications of those experiences for children when they occur in isolation and in combination.

Our review of the IPV research reveals a rich and broad empirical basis on which to inform practice and policy. The sheer prevalence and pervasiveness of the problem is only magnified by the extent to which IPV cuts across demographic (e.g., age, ethnicity, socioeconomic), gender, and sexual boundaries; it is a testament to the need for broad-based IPV prevention and intervention efforts. Many topics have reached a virtual saturation point (e.g., prevalence research consistently demonstrates that IPV remains a pressing public health problem), whereas other topics are hampered by insufficient research and methodological limitations (e.g., effective treatment for perpetrators). The vast majority of research available on IPV comes from the United States, and there is considerable variability in the methodological strengths and limitations of studies, often limiting our capacity to draw firm conclusions.

The advancement of the IPV field has been marred somewhat by a lack of clarity in the definition and operationalization of associated terms (e.g., domestic violence, spouse assault, dating abuse) and the discrepancy between definitions that are used in academic versus legal circles. The World Health Organization's (WHO's) groundbreaking *World Report on Violence and Health* (Krug, Dahlberg, Mercy, Zwi, & Lozano, 2002) defined violence as "the intentional use of physical force or power, threatened or actual, against oneself, another person, or against a group or community, that either results in or has a high likelihood of resulting in injury, death, psychological harm, maldevelopment or deprivation" (p. 5). Gelles and Straus (1999), two of the world's foremost authorities on diverse forms of violence in the family, defined violence as an act that is carried out with the intention, or perceived intention, of causing physical pain or injury to another person. Violence, according to these experts, is relatively synonymous with the term *physical aggression* that is used in social psychology (Bandura, 1973). In comparison, the concept of *spousal assault* which is often used in this field, is a legal term and therefore is somewhat distinct from the definitions of physical aggression or violence. Moreover, what is classified as criminal violence depends on what is included in a nation's criminal code. According to these definitions of violence, physical aggression such as slapping, hitting, kicking, beating, and choking an intimate partner would be classified as IPV in most westernized nations.

Increasingly, there also has been an expansion of the standards of humane conduct in interpersonal relationships to extend to other noxious behaviors such as financial abuse, emotional or psychological abuse, and verbal aggression, as well as domineering and controlling behaviors. The WHO (2006), for instance, defined IPV much more broadly than the definitions of violence mentioned previously: "any behaviour within an intimate relationship that causes physical, psychological or sexual harm to those in the relationship" (p. 1). Similarly, the American Psychological Association (APA) Intimate Partner Abuse and Relationship Violence Working Group (2002) concluded that relationship violence includes physical, sexual, psychological abuse, and stalking that is committed by one partner against the other in a relationship. We concur with the determination that the definition explicitly excludes elder abuse and child abuse, which are important, related, but separate public health issues (see Volume 2, Chapter 3, this handbook).

The APA Working Group went on to assert that "although relationship violence affects both genders, women are victimized more often and sustain more injuries. For this reason, relationship violence is sometimes viewed within the scope of the field of violence against women" (APA Intimate Partner Abuse and Relationship Violence Working Group, 2002, p. 8). In contrast, as a reflection of insurmountable research evidence, "Most state domestic violence legislation has defined violence as an individual act, usually a physical assault or threat of physical harm intended to cause physical harm" (Buzawa & Buzawa, 2002a, p. 16) *without specific reference to the gender/ sex of the parties.* Consistent with Buzawa and Buzawa (2002a), we will adopt a gender-inclusive perspective of IPV (Hamel & Nicholls, 2007). The research that is explored in detail in this chapter documents the prevalence and implications of abuse in a variety of intimate relationships and considers female and male perpetration and victimization in both homosexual and heterosexual relationships to be equally valid considerations. Our definition of IPV reflects the field's move away from terms such as *domestic violence* or *spousal abuse*, which implied that IPV occurred solely or primarily in married couples when, in fact, as will be demonstrated, there is a preponderance of IPV in cohabitating relationships, separated couples, and dating relationships.

As this chapter demonstrates, what gets included in a definition of violence, abuse, or crime shifts and changes depending on the characteristics of the perpetrator and the victim and the nature of the relationship between the parties, as well as with time and context. Straus (1991) described this phenomenon with reference to normative ambiguity or a lack of clear standards regarding what is normative behavior. He asserted that the public, researchers, and policy makers are "far from unanimous" about what constitutes violence/crime in the family (Straus, 1991, p. 21). According to this perspective, there is a lack of consensus regarding answers to the following questions:

- What should be defined as IPV?
- What is criminal violence?
- What is minor violence (e.g., slapping, pushing)?
- What is severe violence (e.g., kicking, punching)?

Most readers would likely agree that slapping your partner or child would not be perceived in the same way as slapping the stranger sitting next to you on the bus, or your boss! But, is it? A reluctance to view minor violence in the family as a criminal assault has inhibited research and policy links between family and nonfamily violence. As we will show, psychological abuse can have severe and long-lasting implications for the health and well-being of victims that often are described as comparable or in excess to those resulting from physical abuse (see Carney & Barner, 2012; Straus, 1999a). IPV has been defined as "any actual, attempted, or threatened physical harm perpetrated by a man or woman against someone with whom he or she has, or has had, an intimate, sexual relationship" (Kropp, Hart, Webster, & Eaves, 2008, p. 1). Kropp et al.'s (2008) definition reflects attention to legal criteria and the need for a focus on physical assaults and threats from a violence risk assessment perspective (see Chapter 3, this volume). For present purposes, we will adopt a more inclusive definition that captures the full range of noxious behaviors that are found in abusive relationships, including financial, emotional, psychological, and verbal abuse and intimidation. Dixon and Graham-Kevan (2011) recently adopted the following useful definition of IPV: "any form of aggression and/or controlling behaviors used against a current or past intimate partner of any gender or relationship status" (p. 1145).

IMPORTANCE OF THE PROBLEM

From an early age, we are taught about *stranger danger*. Children are warned to be suspicious and cautious of people who they and their parents do not know. In contrast, traditionally, children have been admonished not to question adults in positions of authority (e.g., teachers, babysitters, grandparents). The cruel irony is that the greatest danger of personal attacks is often presented by people we know, and commonly, these violent events occur in one's own home (MacDonell, 2012). A generation of research has demonstrated that perpetrators of interpersonal crime and violence are more likely to be loved ones and family members than strangers (Gelles & Straus, 1988). Based on their pioneering research in the first National Family Violence Survey (NFVS) in 1975, Straus, Gelles, and Steinmetz (1981/2006) concluded that violence in the family is virtually ubiquitous. Gelles and Straus's (1988) research led them to conclude that "you are more likely to be physically assaulted, beaten, and killed in your own home at the hands of a loved one than anyplace else, or by anyone else in our society" (p. 18; also see Campbell, Glass, Sharps, Laughon, & Bloom, 2007).

Prevalence and Incidence

Prevalence estimates from the general population are useful for demonstrating the scope of a problem; they also provide "a benchmark for understanding and interpreting clinical prevalences" (Knickerbocker, Heyman, Slep, Jouriles, & McDonald, 2007, p. 36). Gelles and Straus (1999) completed two national studies in the 1970s and 1980s reflecting the first efforts to measure the incidence of IPV in a large and representative sample of American families. Data for the 1975 survey were collected by in-person interview and the 1985 survey was conducted over the phone. Straus and Gelles (1999) noted that the telephone survey offered more anonymity and had a greater response rate. Specifically, Straus and Gelles (1999) reported that the 1985 survey had an 85% completion rate, whereas the 1975 survey had a 65% completion rate. According to their landmark research, the risk of diverse forms of violence in the family was unexpectedly common. Both the first study, which involved a household survey of 2,143 individuals, and the second, which was a telephone survey of 6,002 individuals, focused on spousal and parent–child violence and psychological abuse (Straus & Gelles, 1999). In the 1975 study, on average, one wife or child in 21 was found to have a chance of being physically abused from three to four times per year (Straus & Gelles, 1999). The authors were shocked to see dramatic reductions in violence in the 10 years that passed between the two surveys: Reports of severe wife beating declined 27% from 38 incidents per 1,000 women in 1975 to 30 incidents per 1,000 women in 1985; reports of severe violence toward husbands remained essentially unchanged in the 10-year period (46 per 1,000 men in 1975 vs. 44 per 1,000 men in 1985; Straus & Gelles, 1999).

The primary goal of IPV prevalence estimates is to provide an estimation of the proportion of people in a given population at a given point in time who have

---

Exhibit 12.1 The Early Response to Intimate Partner Violence

On June 10, 1983, Charles Thurman Sr. went to the home where his wife, Tracy, and son Charles Jr. were staying with friends, in Torrington, Connecticut. Thurman demanded to speak to his twenty-one-year-old wife. After calling police, as she had done multiple times before, Tracy went outside to speak with her husband and attempted to calm him down, hoping to prevent another episode of violence. When a police officer arrived about 25 minutes later, he found Tracy on the ground, stabbed thirteen times. Charles Sr. dropped a bloody knife, kicked his estranged wife in the head, and dashed into the house. He came out of the house carrying his son, dropped the boy on his unconscious mother, and yelled that he had killed the boy's "***ing mother." Again he kicked the prostrate Tracy in the head. Three more officers arrived, and Charles continued to wander around the yard yelling and screaming before he was finally arrested. Following the assault, Tracy Thurman was in a coma for eight days, hospitalized for several months, and remains scarred and partially paralyzed. Charles Sr. was convicted of assault and received a fifteen-year prison term.

Her story likely would only have made the local news had Tracy not brought a civil suit in district court against the city of Torrington, twenty-nine police officers, and three police chiefs. Tracy argued that the police failed to provide her with equal protection as guaranteed by the Fourteenth Amendment of the U.S. Constitution. She maintained that the police treated her numerous requests for help differently because her assailant was her husband. Her second argument was that the police had been negligent in failing to protect her from assault by her estranged husband. On June 25, 1985, a jury awarded Tracy Thurman $2.3 million in compensatory damages against twenty-four police officers. The jury held that the police officers in Torrington had acted negligently in failing to protect Tracy and Charles Thurman, Jr., from the violent acts of Charles Thurman Sr. Three years to the day after Tracy Thurman was stabbed and kicked into unconsciousness, Connecticut Governor William A. O'Neill signed into law a family violence bill that, among other provisions, requires police officers to arrest offenders in cases of probable domestic assault, regardless of whether the victim is willing to sign a complaint. Thus, Connecticut joined seven other states that had initiated what is commonly referred to as 'mandatory arrest' for domestic violence.

Note. Data from Gelles and Straus (1988); *Thurman v. City of Torrington* (1984).

experienced IPV. Such statistics are useful to agencies that are charged with policing and with planning for the provision of health care and other services such as shelters. From an academic standpoint, it is imperative to be an educated and critical consumer, as some previous reports of prevalence rates have contributed to misinformation due to data limitations, sample characteristics, and the lack of a standard methodology. Crime victimization estimates often report substantially lower rates of IPV than victimization and self-report surveys due to the likelihood that only the most serious assaults are reported to the police (for a review, see Nicholls & Dutton, 2001). In the 1975 and 1985 surveys by Straus and colleagues (Straus & Gelles, 1999), the annual assault rates reported were approximately 16 times higher than those reported in the National Violence Against Women Surveys (NVAWS; Straus, 1999a; Tjaden & Thoennes, 2000;). It was for this reason that Straus and colleagues avoided using the *crime victim* label of the earlier uniform crime report studies that routinely found extremely low reported rates of IPV (Federal Bureau of Investigation, n.d.). Personal safety or crime contexts in interviews typically elicit responses only from those who were physically injured (see Dutton & Nicholls, 2005).

The 1975 and 1985 NFVS (Straus & Gelles, 1999) found that an intimate partner physically assaulted 11% to 12% of married/cohabiting women annually and 12% of married/cohabiting men. In addition, a total of 4% of women reported being severely assaulted. In comparison, in their sample of 8,000 men and 8,000 women, the NVAWS (Tjaden & Thoennes, 1998) concluded that 22.1% of women and 7.4% of men reported any physical assault by an intimate partner across the lifetime, and 1.3% of women and 0.9% of men reported a physical assault by a partner in the previous 12 months. The NVAWS provided essential information about violence that is perpetrated against women in the United States; however, it was presented to respondents as a study of *victimization of women* and, as such, contained filters or demand characteristics that would make men less

likely to report their own victimization (see Archer, 2000; Straus, 1999a). More recently, a study of data from the 2010 National Intimate Partner and Sexual Violence Survey (NISVS; Black et al., 2011), perhaps free of the demand characteristics of a study that was labeled "Violence Against Women," reported nearly identical 12-month prevalence rates of physical IPV: 4.0% of women ($n = 4,741,000$) and 4.7% of men ($n = 5,365,000$). The lifetime prevalence of intimate partner physical victimization was also much more comparable than is typically reported in crime surveys or criminal justice statistics: 32.9% of women ($n = 39,167,000$) and 28.2% of men ($n = 31,893,000$). In contrast, the latest national crime victimization survey that was conducted by the U.S. Department of Justice (Catalano, 2012) reported rates of 5.9 per 1,000 for females and 1.1 per 1,000 for males. The low overall rates, and much higher proportion of female-to-male victims (84% vs. 16%), can be attributed to the nature of the survey, which looked at crime in general and is less reliable than surveys that use the Conflict Tactics Scale (CTS and CTS-2; Straus, 1990; Straus, Hamby, Boney-McCoy, & Sugarman, 1996; for a fuller discussion, see Straus, 1999a).

According to victimization survey data from Canada, approximately 7% of women (653,000) and 6% of men (546,000) ages 15 years or older who were currently or had previously been in a married or common-law relationship reported having experienced IPV in the 5 years prior to the 2004 General Social Survey (Statistics Canada, 2004).[1] Self-reported IPV victimization rates remained highly consistent between 2004 and 2009, at 6% (Statistics Canada, 2011). Women, however, reported a higher rate of multiple victimizations than did men, at 57% and 40%, respectively. According to police data, in 2010, there were more than 102,500 victims of IPV in Canada (a rate of 363 per 100,000 population); the estimate includes spousal and dating violence among individuals ages 15 years and older (Sinha, 2012). Police data continue to reflect a higher risk of IPV for women than men. In 2010, women had a rate that was nearly four times higher than that of men

---

[1]The Canadian General Social Survey examines victimization and is considered a complement to police-reported data in that it helps to explore the large amount of crime that goes unreported to police. This *dark figure* may be particularly relevant to IPV given it typically occurs in the privacy of the home and is more likely to go unreported to authorities.

(574 per 100,000 vs. 147 per 100,000). This elevated rate for women was evident for both spousal relationships and dating relationships.

Who hits whom?   For the past several years, Martin Fiebert has maintained an annotated bibliography of IPV that to date examines 286 scholarly investigations—221 empirical studies and 65 reviews and/or analyses—and reflects an aggregate sample size that exceeds 371,600 individuals (Fiebert, 2010). His overall conclusion from three related publications has consistently been that there is considerable symmetry in the perpetration and victimization reports of men and women (Fiebert, 2010).

More recently, a systematic review (Desmarais, Reeves, Nicholls, Telford, & Fiebert, 2012a; see Table 12.1) examined the prevalence of male and female physical violence *victimization* in heterosexual relationships using data that were extracted from 249 articles that had been published between 2000 and 2010. The majority of the studies had been conducted in the United States (85.5%, $k = 213$), and nearly half used the CTS or some variation of the measure to operationalize and measure IPV. Overall, the review suggested that physical violence victimization in heterosexual relationships remains common (22.4%); however, the prevalence rates ranged widely (0%–99%; lifetime: 33.6%; past year: 19.2%). The findings add to a growing body of literature documenting gender symmetry in the prevalence of male and female physical IPV victimization rates: 1 in 4 women (23.1%) and 1 in 5 men (19.3%); lifetime: female rate: 35.8%; male rate: 21.7%; past year:

female rate: 18.8%; male rate: 19.8%. Desmarais et al. (2012a) concluded that future research should be focused on increasingly standardizing measurement and rigorous designs. The results, which are consistent with many prior studies, suggest that methodological differences rather than sex may be the most important source of variability in estimates of IPV prevalence rates.

The same team also published a systematic review of the prevalence of physical violence *perpetration* in heterosexual relationships over the same 10-year time period using the same search strategies (Desmarais, Reeves, Nicholls, Telford, & Fiebert, 2012b). A total of 111 articles were examined, again reporting on primarily U.S. studies (85.5%, $k = 95$). There was a total of 272 rates of physical IPV perpetration reported in the articles. Twenty-five articles reported 34 rates of male perpetration, 14 articles reported 24 rates of female perpetration, and 72 articles reported 214 rates for both male and female partners. As with the victimization studies, the CTS was the most commonly used means of operationalizing and measuring physical IPV (CTS = 73%, $k = 81$) in studies reporting rates of perpetration. Far fewer studies reported lifetime (18 reported 32 rates) versus past-year (64 reported 175 rates) perpetration.

The findings for IPV perpetration (see Table 12.2) largely mirrored the results that were found in the victimization review. Overall, Desmarais et al. (2012b) reported a rate of physical IPV victimization at nearly one-fourth of all participants (24.8%). The prevalence rates again ranged widely (1.0%–68.9%) but were quite consistent across the time frames

---

TABLE 12.1

Prevalence of Physical Violence: Rates of Female and Male Victimization in Heterosexual Relationships

Sample	Overall	Women	Men
Population-based	16.7	17.6	14.6
Community	24.3	24.4	22.1
University or college	27.1	27.2	26.7
Middle/high school	18.7	18.1	19.5
Clinical	23.9	24.5	16.6
Justice or legal	31.6	31.1	49.0[a]

Note. Data from Desmarais et al. (2012a).

[a]Only one study contributed to this estimate.

TABLE 12.2

Prevalence of Physical Violence: Rates of Female and Male Perpetration in Heterosexual Relationships

Sample	Overall	Women	Men
Population-based	21.1	24.1	18.0
Community	25.9	29.7	22.4
University or college	23.9	27.5	20.0
Middle/high school	22.0	27.9	16.2
Clinical	35.7	41.7	32.9

Note. Data from Desmarais et al. (2012b).

reported: lifetime: 24.2%; past year: 25.6%; current or most recent partner: 22.9%. To summarize, 1 in 3.5 women (28.3%) and 1 in 5.0 men (21.6%) reported perpetrating physical IPV. According to studies reporting lifetime rates, 31.5% of women and 18.4% of men perpetrated physical IPV against their heterosexual partners. When examining studies that provided rates of physical IPV from the past year, the review again revealed that the rate of female-perpetrated physical IPV against male partners was higher (28.7%) than the rate of male-perpetrated physical IPV against female partners (22.3%). Findings underscore the need for interventions that acknowledge the use of violence by both sexes and the mutuality of abuse in many relationships.

Who hits first?   The NFVS (Stets & Straus, 1990) included data on a subset of 825 American respondents who reported experiencing at least one or more IPV assaults. The NFVS showed that "one-half (49%) of the couples reported reciprocal violence, one-fourth (23%) reported husband-only violence, and one-fourth we or more IPV assaults" (see Figure 12.1). More recently, Langhinrichsen-Rohling, Misra, Selwyn, and

Rohling's (2012) systematic review of the literature on bidirectional versus unidirectional IPV demonstrated that according to 50 studies, bidirectional violence is the most common IPV pattern. The authors concluded their review by suggesting that women play a larger role in the occurrence of IPV than was previously thought (Langhinrichsen-Rohling, Misra, et al., 2012). Specifically, they found that 57.9% of the abuse reported in studies was bidirectional, 28.3% was female-perpetrated unidirectional, and 13.8% was male-perpetrated unidirectional.

Considerable research now demonstrates that contrary to popular opinion about IPV, female-only partner violence exceeds male-only partner violence in adults and in youth (Straus & Ramirez, 2007; Whitaker, Haileyesus, Swahn, & Saltzman, 2007). For instance, a survey by the U.S. Centers for Disease Control and Prevention reported that among young adults, more than 50% of all partner aggression was mutual, and more than 71% of the instigators of nonreciprocal partner violence were female (Whitaker et al., 2007). Whitaker et al. (2007) analyzed data from the 2001 National Study on Adolescent Health in order to examine if relationships with

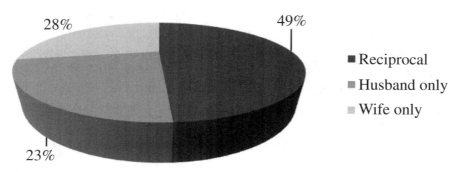

FIGURE 12.1.   Reciprocal abuse is the most common form of IPV. Data from Stets and Straus (1990).

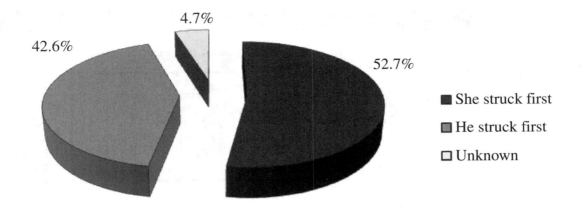

FIGURE 12.2. Prevalence of who hits first as reported by gender. Data from Stets and Straus (1990).

reciprocal violence had more frequent episodes of violence than nonreciprocally abusive relationships and whether or not they resulted in more severe injury. The authors found that of the more than 11,000 (*N* = 11,370) young adults ages 18–28 years old (mean age 22 years) who were included in the analysis, 24.8% of men and 28.8% of women reported ever being victimized by an intimate partner, and 17.3% of men and 35.5% of women reported perpetrating IPV violence. The participants reported having had almost 19,000 relationships in the past 5 years (*N* = 18,761); of these, 23.9% were abusive. Of the relationships with IPV, 50.3% included nonreciprocal violence (53.1% of men and 48.5% of women reported nonreciprocal violence in the relationship); women were the perpetrators in 70.7% of these relationships. Both women and men reported that women perpetrated the violence more often.

To summarize, large sample data sets have repeatedly shown that bilateral violence (i.e., both partners engage in aggression of a similar severity) is the most common form of IPV (Anderson, 2002; Capaldi & Owen, 2001; Gelles & Straus, 1988; Kessler, Molnar, Feurer, & Appelbaum, 2001; McCarroll, Ursano, Fan, & Newby, 2004; Medeiros & Straus, 2007; Moffitt, Caspi, Rutter, & Silva, 2001; Stets & Straus, 1989; Straus et al., 1981/2006; Whitaker et al., 2007; Williams & Frieze, 2005). Research also suggests

that women are just as likely as men to strike the first blow (see Figure 12.2), and that women (24%) are more likely than men to strike back in retaliation (15%; Stets & Straus, 1990).

Who hits hardest? As demonstrated in the Thurman case (see Exhibit 12.1), violence between intimate partners is often severe and may even result in death. According to Gordon (2000; see Figure 12.3), a relatively large proportion of the population engages in infrequent, nonsevere acts, if any, whereas a small proportion of the population engage in serious incidents and does so with considerable frequency.[2]

Based on the NISVS data, Black et al. (2011) reported that among victims of IPV approximately 1 in 4 women (24.3%) and 1 in 7 men (13.8%) have experienced severe physical IPV at some point in their lifetime (e.g., hit with a fist or something hard, beaten, slammed against something; see Figure 12.4). Straus's (2011) meta-analytic review of 91 empirical studies compared rates of "clinical-level" IPV that were perpetrated by men and women. *Clinical-level* IPV was defined as severe assaults such as punching, choking, and attacks with objects or physical acts resulting in injury. Results revealed slightly higher rates of perpetration by women than by men: The median percentage of clinical-level IPV that was perpetrated by women was 7.0% and by men was 5.0%. However, consistent with the general

[2]It is noteworthy that this finding holds across diverse forms of antisocial behavior (e.g., inpatient aggression, juvenile delinquency, general crime, IPV, child abuse, and drug use).

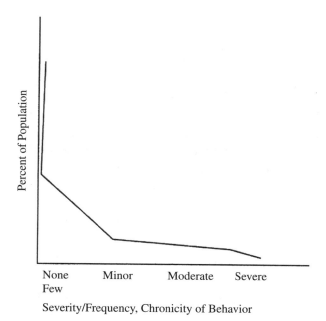

FIGURE 12.3. Distribution of aggressive behavior. From "Definitional Issues in Violence Against Women: Surveillance and Research From a Violence Research Perspective," by M. Gordon, 2000, *Violence Against Women, 6*, p. 753. Copyright 2000 Sage Publications, Inc. Reprinted with permission.

consensus in the field, Straus concluded that when the perpetrator of IPV is a man, the risk of injury is higher: The median percentage of individuals who injured a partner was double for men (14%) as compared to women (7%). In the 21 studies comparing the rates of severe assault or injury in agency samples—that is, studies of samples in which there was an intervention by social service or law enforcement—the median prevalence for male-perpetrated IPV was 63% and for female-perpetrated IPV was 48%.

In sum, despite evidence of reciprocity in many aspects of IPV, women are more likely than men to be severely injured or killed (Gelles & Straus, 1988; Straus, 2009, p. 246). Studies found these gender differences to be small, though, particularly in dating couples. Some research suggests that men generate only moderately more injuries than women (Straus, 2004; Whitaker et al., 2007), but as violence escalates, there appear to be greater gender differences in the use of violence in self-defense. However, as we will discuss later in the chapter, self-defense is a relatively uncommon motivation for IPV (Straus, 2009).

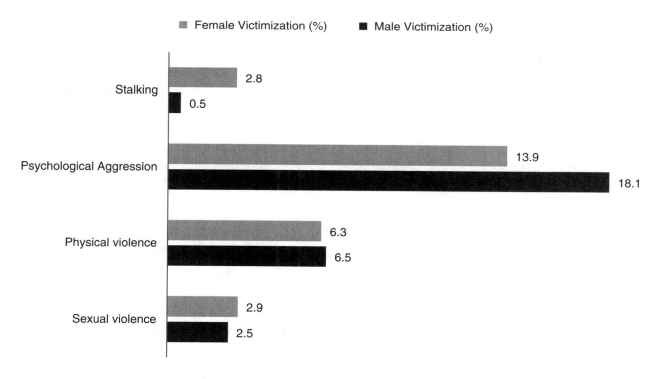

FIGURE 12.4. U.S. National Intimate Partner and Sexual Violence Survey: Summary of the 12-month prevalence rates for men and women across four forms of IPV. Data from Black et al. (2011).

Same-Sex Relationships

Despite initially being recognized in the late 1980s/early 1990s, there has been considerable resistance to examining women's violence in any IPV context, including lesbian relationships (Irwin, 2008). Irwin (2008) noted that there have been several studies, including a small number of relatively large investigations, of IPV in relevant samples. Wide variations in the rates of abuse between lesbian partners have been found, ranging between 17.0% (Loulan, 1987, as cited in Turell, 2000) and 73.0% (45.0% for physical aggression; Lie, Schilit, Bush, Montagne, & Reyes, 1991). There are several limitations that prevent the prevalence of IPV in same-sex relationships from being estimated accurately. Using data obtained in the NVAWS, Tjaden, Thoennes, and Allison (1999) replicated other studies in some respects and challenged prior findings in other respects. Consistent with prior findings, Tjaden et al. reported that men with same-sex partners reported double the rate of rape and physical assault (15.4%) than men with opposite-sex cohabiting partners reported (7.7%). However, in contrast to prior research and contrary to widely held views that abuse rates in homosexual relationships generally exceed abuse rates in heterosexual relationships, Tjaden et al. found that 11.4% of women with same-sex partners reported rape and/or physical assault by a female partner, which is substantially less than the 20.3% who reported that the same acts had been perpetrated against them by a male partner. As Tjaden et al. urged, the results of the research need to be replicated and considered cautiously. That being said, Tjaden et al. found disproportionate rates of forcible rape as minors and adults; physical assault in childhood; and physical assaults in adulthood by all categories of perpetrators, including intimate partners, thereby shining a light on the importance of exploring and better understanding what might account for the disproportionate rates of violence that are suffered by gay and lesbian men and women over the life course.

Seelau and Seelau (2005) reported that there were fewer than 30 IPV studies involving lesbian, gay, bisexual, and transsexual (LGBT) individuals. These authors concluded that to date, the prevalence and nature of abuse in gay relationships, including

rates of emotional abuse and control (Merrill & Wolfe, 2000), appears to be quite comparable to that reported by heterosexual partners (Seelau & Seelau, 2005; e.g., Island & Letellier, 1991; Renzetti, 1989, 1992; Turell, 2000; Waldner-Haugrud, Gratch, & Magruder, 1997). Seelau and Seelau also pointed to evidence that the recurrence and escalation of violence patterns in gay relationships largely mirror the patterns that are found in the larger IPV literature (Brand & Kidd, 1986; Renzetti, 1992; Waldner-Haugrud et al., 1997). Despite the importance of documenting the prevalence and incidence of IPV in lesbian and gay relationships, experts note that progress in this area has been challenging due to inconsistent operational definitions, sampling (e.g., nonrandom, self-selected, and opportunistic sampling methods), and variable data collection (Irwin, 2004). Renzetti (1989, 1992), for instance, cautioned that as long as there is a stigma associated with being gay or lesbian, it will be difficult to firmly establish prevalence rates in these types of relationships. Using exploratory analyses following from their systematic review of the literature, Langhinrichsen-Rohling, Misra, et al. (2012) concluded that the extent to which IPV was found to be bidirectional in heterosexual versus homosexual individuals did not differ.

Implications

A substantial body of research has examined the implications of IPV; largely, this research has studied the effects that are experienced by women who suffer abuse at the hands of their male partners. As such, our discussion here will focus on female victims of male perpetrators. Researchers and policy makers have reported on diverse outcomes for women who experience IPV, including financial and health costs for the individual and society alike, physical effects, mental health effects, and risk-taking behaviors.

IPV is widely acknowledged as a serious human rights violation that affects millions worldwide. Recognizing the pervasive nature of IPV, researchers have increasingly begun to examine the associated implications; however, relatively few attempts have been made to estimate the degree of injury and monetary costs of IPV (Gelles & Straus, 1999). There is, however, general agreement that any calculations are likely to be vast underestimates. Moreover, studies that are intended to synthesize national costs are largely from developed nations, which limits the generalizability of the conclusions.

Economic costs.   The 1994 Violence Against Women Act in the United States "has resulted in an estimated net benefit of $16.4 billion, including $14.8 billion in averted victim's costs. A separate analysis showed that providing shelters for victims of domestic violence resulted in a benefit to cost ratio between 6.8 and 18.4" (Waters et al., 2004, p. xi). In 1995, it was estimated that sexual and physical violence against women cost Canadians more than $1.5 billion in health, housing, workplace, and other long-term effects (Day, 1995). The partial estimated annual cost of IPV in Canada is believed to be in excess of $4.2 billion annually (Day, 1995; Greaves, Hankivsky, & Kingston-Riechers, 1995). A more recent Justice Canada study put the price for IPV at $2.6 billion for violence against men and $4.8 billion for violence against women (Zhang, Hoddenbagh, McDonald, & Scrim, 2012). In the United Kingdom, it is estimated that IPV costs £23 billion per year, of which £17 billion is attributed to the pain and suffering of victims. Additionally, £2.7 billion is from lost and reduced workdays (Walby, 2004).

In the United States, the National Center for Injury Prevention and Control (2003) estimated the costs of intimate partner rape, physical assault, and stalking to exceed $5.8 billion each year. That estimate reflected nearly $4.1 billion for direct medical and mental health care services, $0.9 billion in lost productivity from paid work and household chores for victims of nonfatal IPV, and $0.9 billion in lifetime earnings lost for victims of IPV homicide. The largest proportion of the cost reportedly was derived from physical assault victimization because that type of IPV is the most prevalent. In addition, the largest component of IPV-related costs was health care, which accounts for more than two-thirds of the total associated expenditure (National Center for Injury Prevention and Control, 2003).

A recent review demonstrated that IPV-victimized women had lower rates of educational accomplishments and were more likely to miss work or be unemployed than women without a history of IPV (Lawrence, Orengo-Aguayo, Langer, & Brock, 2012). Lawrence et al. (2012) also found that the women who were experiencing IPV were less able to manage day-to-day household responsibilities and child care. As the WHO succinctly stated, "Interpersonal violence is expensive" (Water et al., 2004, p. X). Importantly, the financial burden is shared by the public, private/group insurance, and victims, alike. For instance, the National Center for Injury Prevention and Control (2003) concluded that physical assault victims paid 28.6% of their medical costs out of pocket, whereas 48.3% of the costs was covered by private or group insurance, 11.0% by Medicaid, and just 6.1% by other public sources.

Physical health.   Alhabib, Nur, and Jones (2010) surmised that violence against women has been identified as a major public health and human rights issue (Joachim, 2000). Among young women (15–44 years), it has been estimated that IPV alone accounts for between 5% and 20% of healthy years of life lost (WHO, 1997). "Worldwide, domestic violence is as serious a cause of death and incapacity among women aged 15–49 years as cancer, and a greater cause of ill health than traffic accidents and malaria combined" (World Bank, 1993, cited in Alhabib et al., 2010, p. 370). Ill effects of IPV for women's physical well-being include acute injury, chronic illnesses, and risk behaviors that are known to be moderators for reduced physical health (e.g., substance misuse, unsafe sex). A recent review (Lawrence et al., 2012) demonstrated that compared to men

> physically victimized women were more likely to suffer from longstanding illnesses and chronic diseases, to suffer physical injuries including potentially lethal injuries (e.g., burns, broken bones, gunshot or knife wounds, facial injuries, concussions, losses of consciousness, traumatic brain injury), to visit emergency rooms, and to be seen by physicians compared to women who were not victimized. (p. 409)

Information from the NVAWS (Tjaden & Thoennes, 2000) indicated that of the estimated 4.8 million intimate partner rapes and physical assaults that are perpetrated against women annually in the United States, approximately 2 million will result in an injury to the victim, and 552,192 will result in some type of medical treatment to the victim (i.e., 59.1% required an emergency room visit, 16.7% resulted in an overnight stay). Wu, Huff, and Bhandari (2010) reviewed studies that observed physical injury as a result of IPV in women presenting at the emergency room for treatment. The overall goal was to gain information that could aid health care providers to identify victims of IPV. In that study, women presenting with more than one injury were approximately 15 times more likely to be IPV victims than another type of patient (Wu et al., 2010). The median number of injuries that victims of IPV presented with also was greater than that presented by other emergency room patients. Whereas IPV victims had a median of three injuries, non-IPV victims had a median of one injury ($p < .001$). Finally, Lawrence et al. (2012) completed a comprehensive review of the consequences of IPV and concluded that "the most striking finding is the consistent and strong correlation between physical victimization and poorer physical health outcomes" (p. 408).

Whitaker et al.'s (2007) examination of data from the 2001 National Study on Adolescent Health demonstrated that relationships with reciprocal violence resulted in more injury than did relationships with nonreciprocal violence. Similar to past studies, men were more likely to have caused injuries when perpetrating violence than women. Men who were in relationships with reciprocal violence were reportedly injured more often (25.2%) than women who were in relationships with nonreciprocal violence (20.0%; Whitaker et al., 2007).

Based on a meta-analytic review of 82 studies, Archer (2000) concluded that men were more likely than women to inflict an injury ($d = 0.15$), and overall, 62% of those who were injured by a partner were women. Archer noted that the majority of those injured were women, but the values of 0.62 and 0.65 indicated that a substantial minority of men was also injured by a partner. Straus's (2011) meta-analytic review of 91 empirical studies included a comparison of men's and women's perpetration of severe assault or injury in agency samples (i.e., studies of samples in which there was an intervention by social service or law enforcement agencies). The median prevalence for male-perpetrated severe assault or injury was 63%; for female-perpetrated severe assault or injury, it was 48%. In sum, women suffer more injuries and are more likely to require hospital care than men. It is not, however, the case that women's use of violence toward men that is severe enough to cause physical injury is negligible or nonexistent (see Exhibit 12.2; cf. Pagelow, 1984). Of particular importance from a policy and practice perspective, research suggests that reciprocal violence in romantic relationships results in as much as 4.4 times more injury than nonreciprocal violence in romantic relationships (Whitaker et al., 2007).

Intimate partner homicide. A consistently supported gender difference in partner violence by men and women is that attacks by men cause more fear and injury, including more deaths (Straus, 2009). Intimate partner homicide (IPH) data reveal findings that are highly similar to the research findings regarding physical injuries: Women are nine times as likely to be killed by an intimate partner (husband, boyfriend, same-sex partner, or ex-partner) than by a stranger (Campbell et al., 2007). IPHs are usually preceded by IPV against the female partner (65%–70% of male-perpetrated IPH; 75% of

---

Exhibit 12.2 Women Commit Serious Violence

77-year-old "Black Widow" Millie Weeks, AKA Melissa Friedrich

- **1991**: convicted of drugging and running over her then husband who she said was abusing her—she served 2 yrs of a 6 yr sentence for manslaughter.
- **2000**: married a Florida man—he fell ill/died in 2002—money disappeared from his bank account.
- **2002**: within weeks met a man online, arrested by Florida police and spent 5 years in prison after drugs were found in his body and his money was stolen.
- **2012**: charged with attempted murder, arrested in Cape Breton, Nova Scotia after her current husband was hospitalized, days after their wedding.

Note. Data from Besant (2012).

female-perpetrated IPH). In Felson and Messner's (1998) analysis of 2,000 IPHs, self-defense, which is defined as protecting oneself from bodily harm, accounted for 9.6% of the female-perpetrated killings but only 0.5% of the male-perpetrated ones. A definition that included retaliation to previous physical attacks yielded rates of 46.2% for women and 11.1% for men.

When demographics are taken into account, unemployment is a major risk factor for intimate partner femicide (Campbell et al., 2007; see also Chapter 3, this volume). Other important risk factors for female victims include gun access, estrangement, previous death threats, nonfatal strangulation, and the presence of stepchildren residing in the home (Campbell et al., 2007; Campbell, Webster, & Glass, 2009). It is a promising reflection of hard-won efforts to improve the safety and well-being of families who are coping with IPV to find that multiple reports reveal significant decreases in IPH in North America (e.g., Campbell et al., 2007; Catalano, 2007; Sinha, 2012). For instance, Sinha (2012) concluded that IPH rates for both dating partners and spouses in Canada are consistent with general homicide rates and show a consistent decline over the past 20 years. Specifically, the rates in 2010 were half the 1991 rates and 20% less than a decade previous. The decline is largely a reflection of reduced female IPH victims (dropped from 10.5 per million in 1991 to 4.4 per million in 2010); the rate for men has fluctuated much more and dropped less (30%; Sinha, 2012). There is also evidence to suggest that IPH among dating couples has remained relatively stable (Catalano, 2007).

Women's sexual and reproductive health. Perhaps less commonly considered than other adverse outcomes of IPV, the implications of IPV for female victim's sexual and reproductive health is substantial. A systematic review by Coker (2007) included 51 articles that addressed the effects that physical IPV can have on women's sexual health. The review discussed diverse sexual and reproductive health implications in relation to physical IPV, including sexual risk-taking behaviors, sexually transmitted infections, unplanned pregnancy, pelvic pain, and sexual satisfaction. Findings across the studies were generally quite consistent. Eight of 10 studies

reporting relevant data found a significant difference in the risk-taking behaviors of IPV victims and their partners compared to those of nonvictims. Specifically, seven of nine studies that examined IPV and condom use found that IPV victims used condoms less consistently or had partners who refused to use them more often than nonvictims. In addition, female victims of IPV were (a) more likely to report a greater number of sexual partners, (b) less likely to be monogamous, and (c) more likely to have non-monogamous partners. A total of 17 of 23 studies in the Coker review demonstrated a significant relationship between lifetime, current, or recent IPV and vaginal infections or urinary tract infections. Nine of 10 studies reported an association between pelvic and abdominal pain and IPV. Other similar findings of note include positive associations between painful menses, vaginal bleeding, painful intercourse, and IPV (Coker, 2007). Sexual dissatisfaction was also associated with male and female IPV victimization. Taft, Watson, and Lee (2004) sampled more than 14,500 women and found a significant association between both IPV victimization and pregnancy and IPV victimization and miscarriage. Victims of physical or sexual IPV have been found to be more likely to report having had more miscarriages and abortions than other women (Coker, 2007; WHO, 2005).

Mental health. Considerable research has examined the mental health of women who have been the victims of IPV; in contrast, there is a need for further exploration into the psychological consequences of IPV for male victims (of both female and male perpetrators). Lawrence et al. (2012) completed a comprehensive review of 122 empirical studies and 10 review articles that were published between 1989 and 2012 in English peer-reviewed journals that examined the consequences of physical and/ or psychological IPV. The authors concluded that women who experienced physical IPV present with decreased psychological well-being and increased rates of depression, anxiety, posttraumatic stress disorder (PTSD), and alcohol or other substance abuse problems. Overall, the impact is greater on female compared to male victims. Suicidal ideation and attempts, depression and anxiety, as well as memory and other cognitive impairments were also common among victims of physical IPV. Lawrence et al. further found that compared to nonvictimized women, women who reported being physically victimized by romantic partners were more likely to report higher than average levels of stress and more medication use (e.g., painkillers and tranquilizers) as well as more frequent visits to mental health professionals. Of particular interest, the review found evidence that psychological victimization has consequences for an IPV victim's mental health (including depression, PTSD, alcohol use) that are comparable to the consequences following from physical victimization. Psychological victimization is reflected in elevated rates of depression, PTSD, and alcohol use at least as strongly as physical victimization, and the link is evident even after controlling for physical victimization. With regard to male victims, Lawrence et al. concluded that there is insufficient research to draw firm conclusions, and the extant literature has yielded conflicting findings.

Summary

Abuse between intimate partners remains a serious public health concern that affects thousands of men and women annually. It is well documented that physical violence that is perpetrated by women against their male partners is less likely to result in physical injury than physical violence that is perpetrated by men against their female partners (Straus, 2004), and women suffer higher rates of serious injury than men (Black et al., 2011; Crowell & Burgess, 1996); however, the physical, psychological, and financial effects resulting from women's perpetration of physical IPV are neither infrequent nor inconsequential (e.g., Coker et al., 2002; Reid et al., 2008; Rennison, 2003; Zhang et al., 2012). In fact, when mild or moderate physical assaults are compared, there is little evidence of gender disparity in injuries (Lawrence et al., 2012). The NISVS (Black et al., 2011) found that 81% of women and 35% of men who experienced rape, physical violence, or stalking by an intimate partner reported at least one impact related to the IPV experiences, such as fear, concern for safety, injury, or having missed at least 1 day of work or school. Research clearly demonstrates that although women are injured more than men in IPV, men are far from immune to IPV.

RELEVANT PSYCHOLOGICAL THEORY AND PRINCIPLES

Theoretical development is essential in order to advance our understanding of the causal pathways that lead to IPV and to develop evidence-based and effective prevention and intervention models. Two primary and opposing schools of thought exist to account for IPV. According to the *gendered perspective* of IPV, violence that is committed by men and women in intimate relationships is distinct, and IPV has an etiology that distinguishes it from other forms of violence and criminal offending (Browne, 1987; R. E. Dobash & Dobash, 1979; for discussions, see Dutton, 2006; Felson, 2002, 2006; Felson & Lane, 2010; Hamel, 2005; Straus, 2004). This is in contrast with the *violence perspective* of IPV, which emphasizes similarities in the etiologies of violence against intimate partners and violence that is perpetrated against other victims and in other contexts (Felson, 2006; Felson & Lane, 2010). According to the violence perspective, the motivation for IPV is not dissimilar from the motivation for other types of violence. To account for the contrasting data that are evident from the two major streams of thought, Johnson (1995) proposed a third prominent perspective of IPV, asserting that there are two distinct categories of IPV: patriarchal terrorism and common couple violence, also known as *controlling coercive violence* and *situational couple violence*, respectively (Kelly & Johnson, 2008).

Gendered Perspective

Several scholars (Browne, 1987; R. E. Dobash & Dobash, 1979) have described IPV as a direct extension of patriarchy and women's "rightful" place as oppressed victims as a reflection of women's secondary status in the societal order. Abuse that is perpetrated against intimate partners is viewed as an expression of patriarchy in the form of men's gender-based domination of women (see R. E. Dobash & Dobash, 1979; R. P. Dobash & Dobash, 1995; Walker, 1984). Advocates of this perspective assert that male dominance and female subordination resulting from patriarchy are the direct causes of IPV, as opposed to one in a constellation of risk factors (Dixon & Graham-Kevan, 2011). Proponents of this perspective claim that "men who assault their wives are actually living up to cultural prescriptions that are cherished in Western society—aggressiveness, male dominance and female subordination and they are using physical force as a means to enforce that dominance" (R. E. Dobash & Dobash, 1979, p. 24). Bograd (1988) similarly noted that "feminists seek to understand why men in general use physical force against their partners and what functions this serves in a given historical context" (p. 13). As such, men are presumed to be the predominant perpetrators of IPV, and to the extent that women are involved in perpetrating relationship violence at all, it is considered to be largely a reflection of self-defense or a preemptive strike to instigate imminent violence on the part of their partner. R. P. Dobash and Dobash (2004) asserted that "professionals who work with male abusers . . . find that violence women direct at male partners usually, though not always, occurs in a context of ongoing violence and aggression by men directed at women" (p. 328; for an extensive critique, see Dutton & Nicholls, 2005).

The research literature supporting the gendered perspective draws largely from selected samples such as women in shelters and emergency rooms. This is highly important research about these subgroups; however, using the data to generalize to the general population is known as suffering from what is known as the *clinical fallacy* (Straus & Gelles, 1999). Importantly, some cross-cultural research does demonstrate that the victimization of women exceeds that of men in countries typified by less gender equality (Archer, 2006). Such findings suggest that as women have increasingly equal participation in economic and political operation in a nation, there is an inverse effect on violence against women (Archer, 2006), offering evidence for the role of patriarchy and gender equality in IPV (see the later discussion of IPV worldwide).

Although largely unsupported by the available literature and generally viewed as fundamentally flawed, the gendered perspective dominates in the print media (Sellers, Desmarais, & Tirotti, in press) and the public at large (Sorenson & Taylor, 2005). Perhaps not surprisingly, it remains the dominant point of view on the official websites of the National Coalition Against Domestic Violence, its state

subsidiaries, and related organizations that were funded as part of the Violence Against Women Act, as reflected in the preponderance of false facts that have been found in its information pages by Hines (2014). False or misleading information about IPV, based in a gendered perspective, has also been found on the website of the American Bar Association (Dutton, Corvo, & Hamel, 2009). National surveys have also revealed a high level of incorrect gendered assumptions among clinical psychologists (Follingstad, DeHart, & Green, 2004) and professionals who are working with IPV (Hamel, Desmarais, Nicholls, Malley-Morrison, & Aaronson, 2009).

Critics of the gendered perspective (Dixon & Graham-Kevan, 2011; Dutton & Nicholls, 2005; Hamel & Nicholls, 2007; Straus, 2010) maintain that this theory largely lacks empirical support given the considerable evidence base for gender symmetry in much of IPV, a lack of support for feminist-informed interventions such as the Duluth model (Babcock, Green, & Robie, 2004; Corvo, Dutton, & Chen, 2008), and little evidence to demonstrate that there are widely held beliefs that it is acceptable for men to strike women in Western nations. For instance, just 2% of North American males agree that it is permissible to "hit your wife to keep her in line" (Simon et al., 2001). Moreover, research suggests that less than 10% of North American marriages are male dominant (Coleman & Straus, 1986). Contemporary North American society is among the most gender egalitarian of societies both geographically and historically (Archer, 2006). In fact, in North America, most IPV is bilateral even when it is matched for the level of severity (Stets & Straus, 1989; Whitaker et al., 2007), and just 6% of couples who are violent demonstrate a "wife-battering" pattern (i.e., severe male violence and no female violence; Stets & Straus, 1989).

Scholars advocating for a gender-inclusive perspective maintain that although an important minority of women suffer systematic, repetitive, and severe IPV, the rate is much lower than what would be hypothesized according to the traditional patriarchal theory of IPV (Dutton & Nicholls, 2005; Stets & Straus, 1989). These same scholars acknowledge that severe female-perpetrated abuse occurs in the context of relationships with nonviolent male victims

(Dutton & Nicholls, 2005; Stets & Straus, 1989). In conclusion, rigorous evidence from meta-analyses (Archer, 2000, 2002; Stith, Smith, Penn, Ward, & Tritt, 2004) and systematic reviews (e.g., Carney & Barner, 2012; Desmarais et al., 2012a, 2012b) generally contradicts a narrow patriarchal perspective (for reviews, see Dutton & Nicholls, 2005; Straus, 2010). As Dixon and Graham-Kevan (2011) concluded, "such gendered approaches to policy are not informed by findings from methodological sound empirical research" (p. 1152).

Violence Perspective

In contrast to the gendered perspective, advocates of the violence perspective consider patriarchal oppression and gender inequalities a relevant but insufficient explanation for IPV. According to this view, IPV is not specific to men and cannot be explained on the basis of gender or gender roles alone (Dutton & Nicholls, 2005). Advocates of a gender-inclusive perspective (Buttell & Starr, 2013; Dixon, Archer, & Graham-Kevan, 2012; Dutton & Nicholls, 2005; Hamel & Nicholls, 2007; Lehmann & Simmons, 2009) maintain that the same barriers to healthy relationships, and the same risk factors that underlie general violence (e.g., substance misuse, poor coping strategies, low frustration tolerance, hostile [mis]attributions, personality dysfunction, antisocial role models and peers), also are found among IPV perpetrators (see Chapters 3 and 9, this volume).

Capaldi, Knoble, Shortt, and Kim (2012) examined IPV from an interactional perspective, which takes into account the experiences (e.g., upbringing) and characteristics (e.g., mental health problems) of both partners (also see Whitaker, Murphy, Eckhardt, Hodges, & Cowart, 2013). Men and women who inflict IPV have been found to be similar to other offenders in terms of their prior criminal records, alcohol and drug use, and experiences of abuse. Longitudinal research has demonstrated that in both men and women, abusive and violent behaviors develop early; remain as aggressive traits; and are not, as the patriarchy paradigm portrays, survival-based reactions to male violence (Capaldi et al., 2012; Moffitt et al., 2001; Serbin et al., 2004).

Supporters of the violence perspective point to large bodies of research demonstrating that men and women commit IPV at similar rates and severity levels and for similar reasons (Follingstad, Wright, Lloyd, & Sebastian, 1991; Langhinrichsen-Rohling, McCullars, & Misra, 2012; Langhinrichsen-Rohling, Misra, et al., 2012). The most commonly reported proximate motivations for the use of violence among both men and women are coercion, anger, and as a means of punishing misbehavior by their partner (Cascardi & Vivian, 1995; Follingstad et al., 1991; Kernsmith, 2005; Langhinrichsen-Rohling, McCullars, & Misra, 2012; Stets & Hammons, 2002). Follingstad, Bradley, Helff, and Laughlin (2002) reported that anxious attachment and angry temperament predicted dating violence in both sexes. Moreover, abuse types and prevalence rates in gay and lesbian relationships are similar to those in heterosexual relationships (Lie et al., 1991; Seelau & Seelau, 2005).

The violence perspective maintains that the etiologies of IPV largely mirror those that account for other forms of societal violence and draws on other large bodies of relevant theory and research. According to social learning theory, for instance (see Bandura, 1971; Mihalic & Elliott, 1997), family violence is considered to be a reflection of children growing up in dysfunctional families wherein violence is considered to be a viable option and healthy conflict resolution, coping, and communication strategies are less common. Similarly, proponents of family systems/power theory (see Straus, 1976; Straus et al., 1981/2006) and family violence theories (including systems theory, ecological theory, exchange/social control theory, resource theory, and the subculture-of-violence theory) consider IPV to be an expression of conflict within the family that can best be understood by examining the social structures that contribute to the use of violence.

Recent Theoretical Development— Patriarchal Terrorism and Common Couple Violence

As a means of addressing the divide between these two theoretical camps, Johnson (1995, 2008) asserted that there are two unique categories of IPV: patriarchal terrorism (also known as controlling–coercive violence) and common couple violence.

The first involves a pattern of more serious physical violence as well as emotional abuse, and the intent is to dominate and control the partner; the latter reflects families who experience occasional violent outbursts in the context of mutually escalated conflict. Johnson's typology was an attempt to build on prior theoretical advancements, including, for instance, Walker's (1979) three-phase cycle and male-batterer typologies such as the one proposed by Holzworth-Munroe and Stuart (1994), which identifies abusive men as family only (violence is minor and only occurs in the home), dysphoric borderline (more serious violence but perpetrator does not have a criminal history), and generally violent/antisocial (serious violence and a criminal history).

Because it takes into account the behavior of both partners, Johnson's (1995, 2008) scheme has become quite popular among scholars and is widely cited; however, it has three major limitations. First, Johnson asserted that intimate terrorism is almost exclusively perpetrated by men, whereas large population surveys in Canada and the United States have reported fairly comparable rates across gender (Felson & Outlaw, 2007; Laroche, 2005). Second, the categories in Johnson's scheme have been found to be poorly defined and to overlap greatly, and that includes the additional categories of violent resistance and mutual violence control, representing self-defensive responses by women and mutual intimate terrorism, respectively (Langhinrichsen-Rohling, Huss, & Ramsey, 2000; Simpson, Doss, Wheeler, & Christensen, 2007). Finally, Johnson's scheme does not satisfactorily account for the multitude of dynamics that are inherent in abusive interactions, including the role of fear, reinforcement contingencies, and attachment styles (Hamel, 2012). Clearly, there is a need for better typologies, but even more valuable would be more of the direct observation laboratory research that John Gottman and others conducted in the 1990s (see Dutton, 2006, for an excellent review).

RESEARCH REVIEW

In this section, we explore the research literature from several key areas: IPV on a global scale, risk factors for IPV and co-occurring child abuse, and the motivation for men's and women's IPV. With the exception of the subsection on victim safety plans, the empirical data presented in this section are drawn heavily from a series of extensive literature reviews that were recently published in the journal *Partner Abuse*; the reviews are collectively known as the Partner Abuse State of Knowledge Project (PASK).[3]

IPV on a Global Scale

Compared to the research on IPV that is available in the United States, there is considerably less English-language research from the rest of the world. The WHO sponsored a systematic review of world-wide evidence on the relevance of IPV (Alhabib et al., 2010). The authors stratified by quality scores and reported that there was considerable variability in their quality. The majority of the studies were from North America (41%) followed by Europe (20%), and 56% were population based. In their examination of 48 population surveys from around the world, Alhabib et al. (2010) discovered that 10% to 69% of women reported being assaulted by an intimate male partner at some point in their lives. The proportion of women who had been assaulted by a male partner in the previous 12 months varied considerably, from a low in developed Western nations (≤3% among women in Australia, Canada, and the United States) to substantially higher rates in places like Nicaragua (27% of women who have ever had an ongoing sexual partnership), the Republic of Korea (38% of currently married women), and Palestinian women in the West Bank and Gaza Strip (52% that are currently married). For many of these women, physical assault was not an isolated event but was part of a continuing pattern of abusive behavior.

In their review of IPV outside of the industrialized English-speaking world, Esquivel-Santovena, Lambert,

---

[3] The PASK project, which was conducted by 41 scholars at 20 universities and research institutes, reviews all of the quantitative studies on IPV that were published from 1990 to 2012 and includes 17 manuscripts that were published in five consecutive issues of *Partner Abuse* from April 2012 to April 2013. Summaries of 1,700+ articles are available for free at http://www.springerpub.com/pa.

and Hamel (2013) located 162 peer-reviewed or government-sponsored studies in 83 countries in Asia and Oceania, the Middle East, Africa, Latin America, the Caribbean, and Europe (not including the United Kingdom). The total number of locales sampled exceeded 200. Most of the studies reported on only female perpetration and/or male perpetration (i.e., as opposed to reporting both male perpetration and female perpetration in the same study) for physical, psychological, and sexual IPV. The rates of IPV in most of the countries, with the exception of much of Europe, were higher than those found in the United States. There were 69 studies from 49 countries that included rates for male victimization or female perpetration. Of these, 40 drew from dating, student, or adolescent samples (including many from the International Dating Violence Survey; Straus, 2008), and 29 were based on large population, community, or clinical samples. Across all 69 studies, there was a total of 93 direct comparisons across gender for physical IPV. The rates of physical IPV were symmetrical (comparable across gender or higher for females) in 65 of those comparisons, or 69.9%. A total of 59 direct comparisons across gender were made for psychological IPV, including controlling behaviors and dominance. These rates were symmetrical in 55 comparisons (93.2%). Finally, Esquivel-Santovena et al. reported 19 direct comparisons for sexual IPV, and these rates were symmetrical in eight comparisons (42.1%). For any IPV, there were 10 direct comparisons across gender, with symmetry found in 50% of those comparisons.

Esquivel-Santovena et al. (2013) also examined physical and psychological IPV as reported among large population, community, and clinical samples. Gender symmetry was found in 14 countries: Philippines, Thailand, Botswana, Kenya, Mozambique, Namibia, Swaziland, Zimbabwe, Jordan, Barbados, Chile, Jamaica, Trinidad/Tobago, and Russia. Gender asymmetry (i.e., disproportionate percentage of female victims/male perpetrators) was found in the six countries of South Korea, Lesotho, Malawi, Nigeria, Uganda, and Zambia. Both symmetry and asymmetry were found in seven countries: China, Pakistan, South Africa, Israel, Brazil, Portugal, and Ukraine.

At an international level, many studies of IPV provided information on prevalence rates only; others reported on the impact of IPV on victims, and on risk factors, but these studies were limited almost entirely to female-only samples. In comparison to research from the United States, the Esquivel-Santovena et al. (2013) review found few studies that provided information on the context of partner violence (e.g., who initiates, motives, and extent of self-defense). In those studies that did provide information, the consequences reported for female victims included physical injuries and other physical ailments, mental health symptoms (e.g., PTSD, depression), lower productivity, and higher risk for HIV infection. Among the most frequently cited contributing factors to IPV were the victim's low education level, perpetrator's alcohol abuse, victim's younger age, victim's low income, living in a rural versus urban location, being married at a young age, low socioeconomic status, childhood victimization (i.e., being physically victimized or witnessing parental aggression), and perpetrator's low education level.

There is some evidence that social factors are relevant to IPV worldwide. A sweeping, multicountry study by the WHO found higher rates of female IPV victimization in less industrialized countries and in rural compared to urban areas (Garcia-Moreno, Jansen, Ellsberg, Heise, & Watts, 2006). A meta-analytical review by Archer (2006) similarly found a strong correlation between female IPV victimization and women's lower social status, societal approval of a husband slapping his wife, and traditional attitudes about gender roles, as well as a generally low degree of individual rights. Findings from Straus' (2008) International Dating Violence Survey provided some support for these findings, with higher rates of violent men from more patriarchal nations (e.g., Iran) reporting high scores on a dominance scale in comparison to men from more equalitarian nations. However, Straus also found that dominance scores for women were actually higher than those for men in the majority of the 32 countries sampled, with dominance predicting IPV for both men and women.

The Esquivel-Santovena et al. (2013) review yielded somewhat different results. A regression analysis indicated that a country's level of human development (as measured by the United Nations Human Development Index) was not a significant predictor of male or female physical partner abuse perpetration. In addition, a nation's gender-inequality level, as measured by the United Nations Gender Inequality Index, failed to predict both male- and female-perpetrated physical IPV in studies that were conducted with general population or community samples (Esquivel-Santovena et al., 2013). In sum, research suggests that variables beyond gender inequities alone appear to be important o consider in IPV.

Risk Factors for IPV

A recent literature review by Capaldi et al. (2012) analyzed 228 studies of IPV risk factors. Most were published after 1996, and 170 used adult samples and 58 used adolescent samples. Capaldi et al. limited their search to countries in the industrialized English-speaking world. Studies that were not based on representative community or clinical samples and did not have a control group were excluded. Based on previous research, the authors conceptualized IPV as behaviors within a dyadic process that are influenced by the behaviors and developmental history of each partner, as well as contextual factors. Possible risk factors were divided into three broad categories: (a) *contextual characteristics* such as demographic, community, and school context; (b) *developmental characteristics/behaviors*, including family-of-origin exposure to abuse, peer associations, psychological/behavioral factors (e.g., conduct problems, hostility, personality disorders, depression, substance abuse), and cognitive factors (e.g., hostile, pro-violent beliefs); and (c) *relationship influences* and interactional patterns.

The demographic risk factors that were found to be predictive of IPV in the Capaldi et al. (2012) review included young age, low income, unemployment, and minority group membership. Married couples were at lower risk for IPV than dating couples; however, women who had been married but then separated were found to be the most at risk for IPV victimization. High levels of acculturation stress were also found to be predictive of IPV, as were financial and work-related stressors. Studies of community factors, such as high levels of crime, other neighborhood problems, and poor quality schools, yielded ambiguous results. Capaldi et al.

found low to moderate correlations between childhood and family-of-origin exposure to abuse and IPV, and these were mediated by subsequent problems in development, including substance abuse and antisocial tendencies. Involvement with peers who engage in negative activities, such as drug use, was correlated with teen dating violence. Conduct disorder in childhood and adolescence, as well as antisocial personality in adulthood, both predicted IPV among dating, cohabiting, and married adults. Capaldi et al. concluded that depending on the particular study, results from longitudinal research indicate that the presence of negative emotionality (e.g., anxiety, anger, hostility) among youth is predictive of adult IPV for both male and female perpetrators. A weak association was found between alcohol abuse and IPV generally; however, this association was much stronger for female-perpetrated IPV, and drug abuse was more predictive of IPV than alcohol abuse was. The correlation between IPV and depression was also weak, but again, it was strongest for women. Among relationship factors, low relationship satisfaction and high levels of conflict between partners were predictive of IPV. Finally, with few exceptions, IPV risk factors were roughly the same across gender (Capaldi et al., 2012).

Implications of IPV and Child Abuse: Is There a "Double Whammy?"

MacDonell (2012) examined 73 original research studies and literature reviews on the effects of child maltreatment and of witnessing interparental violence. The authors concluded:

> We draw the following eight implications for intervention and policy from this work.
>
> 1. Prevention and intervention programs should work on amelioration of proven risk factors (particularly malleable factors)—as identified in this review—rather than untested or less robust factors, to prevent and reduce IPV.
> 2. Efforts to increase public awareness that risk factors apply to men and women and that reducing risk for both sexes may ultimately reduce IPV.

3. More awareness for women that internalizing and alcohol use may be risk factors for them.

4. More awareness is needed of risk contexts (e.g., higher risk related to relationship separation).

5. More awareness of drug use as a risk factor to address in prevention and treatment.

6. As IPV is associated with deviant peer association, conduct problems, and substance use, prevention and treatment programs addressing these issues for adolescents and young adults should consider adding an IPV prevention component. This would be a cost effective way of addressing IPV prevention.

7. As couple conflict and dissatisfaction are very predictive proximal risk factors, increasing problem-solving and interaction skills and reducing negative behaviors are important targets of prevention and intervention.

8. As IPV emerges in dating couples, prevention programs should start early, and both prevention and intervention programs should be targeted particularly to the higher-risk ages of the teens and twenties. (Capaldi et al., 2012, p. 267)

Considerably fewer studies reported on the combined effects of both child maltreatment and witnessing interparental IPV, in which one type of abuse is a risk factor for the other, and the available data yielded contradictory findings. These effects have been examined in several cross-sectional studies, most of them based on studies using the Child Behavior Checklist (CBCL; Achenbach & Edelbrock, 1983) or the Youth Self-Report (YSR; Achenbach & Edelbrock, 1987). In comparison to children who have only witnessed interparental violence, those who had experienced both forms of abuse were significantly more likely to exhibit symptoms of trauma and dissociation, to suffer from depression, and to have difficulties with attention problems (Kaslow & Thompson, 2008). Kaslow and Thompson (2008) also found that children who suffer direct abuse as victims themselves are more likely to engage in delinquent and aggressive behaviors and to have a generally lower sense of well-being. In some studies, the impact of both types of abuse, also known as the "double-whammy" effect (Hughes, Parkinson, & Vargo, 1989), was significantly greater than the impact of having witnessed interparental violence only, for internalizing problems (e.g., depression, anxiety; O'Keefe, 1996) and externalizing problems (e.g., aggression; Kernic et al., 2003; O'Keefe, 1996). Other cross-sectional studies using the CBCL and other measures have failed to find such an effect on depression, intellectual functioning, aggression and attitudes approving of violence, and other behavior problems such as running away (e.g., Carlson, 1991; Huth-Bocks, Levendosky, & Semel, 2001).

Sternberg, Lamb, Guterman, and Abbott (2006) determined that when tested initially at a young age, children who both witnessed IPV and experienced child abuse were significantly more likely to exhibit internalizing and externalizing symptoms than children who had only witnessed IPV. However, only the internalizing symptoms retained their significance when the children were retested in adolescence. A possible reason that was offered by the researchers is that abuse has a much greater impact on small children, who are highly impressionable and vulnerable, and that by adolescence, some children have learned to adapt to their circumstances. Conceivably, as children, we have much less autonomy and control over our environment and our circumstances, whereas by the time we reach adolescence, the importance of the immediate family is reduced, and considerably more time and value is placed on our relationships with others. Although adolescents may continue to experience psychological distress, they may be better able to cope and therefore less likely to exhibit overt problems. Sternberg et al. also found boys to be more significantly impacted than girls. Another longitudinal study, this one of cases that were investigated by Child Protective Services (English, Marshall, & Stewart, 2003), did not find significant direct effects of combined child abuse and witnessed parental IPV but did find evidence of indirect effects: In homes where children were exposed to IPV, parental well-being and overall family functioning were negatively impacted.

Motivation for IPV

Physical assault prevalence rates by themselves provide only limited information about the nature of partner violence. A clearer understanding of the problem requires a more nuanced consideration of the context, including motives, in order to more completely understand what might drive an individual to assault his or her partner. In their systematic review of the literature, Langhinrichsen-Rohling, McCullars, and Misra (2012) coded the various motives that were reported in each of the 74 studies that met their inclusion criteria into seven broad categories: (a) power/control, (b) self-defense, (c) expression of negative emotion (e.g., anger), (d) communication difficulties, (e) retaliation, (f) jealousy, and (g) other. Studies that considered the most frequent motivations for perpetration as reported by men and women often involved similar motives—primarily to get back at a partner for emotionally hurting them, because of stress or jealousy, to express anger and other feelings that they could not put into words or communicate, and to get their partner's attention. Eight studies directly compared men and women on the power/control motive. Of these, three reported no significant gender differences, one showed mixed findings, one found that women were more motivated to perpetrate violence as a means to exercise power and control than were men, and three found that men were more motivated than women by a desire to exert power/control over their partner; however, overall gender differences were weak.

Of the 10 articles that were identified in the Langhinrichsen-Rohling, McCullars, and Misra (2012) review as containing gender-specific statistical analyses on self-defense, five indicated that women were significantly more likely than men to report self-defense as a motive for perpetration, and four did not find statistically significant gender differences. Although only one article reported that men were more likely to report this motive than women (Shorey, Meltzer, & Cornelius, 2010), Langhinrichsen-Rohling, McCullars, and Misra pointed out that it might be particularly difficult for men to admit to perpetrating violence in self-defense because this admission implies vulnerability. Indeed, self-reports are inherently limited, and none of the studies in the Langhinrichsen-Rohling, McCullars, and Misra review used a measure of social desirability. On the other hand, there are a handful of studies in which respondents were asked directly about who

initiates the violence, or, when both partners have been violent, who throws the "first blow" in the relationship. Among dating surveys (DeMaris, 1992; Henton, Cate, Koval, Lloyd, & Christopher, 1983; LeJeune & Follette, 1994) and large population surveys (Fergusson, Horwood, & Ridder, 2005; Kwong, Bartholomew, & Dutton, 1999; Morse, 1995; Williams & Frieze, 2005), violence initiation rates were comparable across gender. Research with samples of men who were arrested for domestic violence found that the female partners initiate violence between 33% and 40% of the time (Gondolf, 1996; Shupe, Stacey, & Hazlewood, 1987). Also worth noting were the lack of differentiation in the Langhinrichsen-Rohling, McCullars, and Misra (2012) review between self-defense and retaliation as motivators, and the fact that across studies, self-defense was endorsed by only a minority of respondents, both male and female. For nonperpetrator samples, the rates of self-defense reported by men ranged from 0% to 21%; for women, the range was 5% to 35%. The highest rates of reported self-defense motives (50% for men, 65.4% for women) came from samples of perpetrators, who may have reasons to overestimate this motive.

Findings related to jealousy as a motive for IPV were found in only a few correlational studies (Langhinrichsen-Rohling, McCullars, & Misra, 2012). A Spanish study (Fernández-Fuertes & Fuertes, 2010) found jealousy to be correlated with partner violence perpetration for both men and women, whereas Bookwala, Frieze, Smith, and Ryan (1992) reported jealousy to be significantly associated with expressed violence by women, but not by men. Another study, this one by O'Leary, Smith Slep, and O'Leary (2007), combined dominance and jealousy and found that this construct correlated significantly with men's as well as women's violence. Given that this motive has been linked with an insecure attachment style in romantic relationships, it might be that individuals who are in less secure and stable relationships are more susceptible to IPV because they are unsure of the commitment and fidelity of their partner. Still, in light of the small number of papers that have been summarized on this topic, findings should be considered preliminary.

None of the studies reported that anger/retaliation was significantly more of a motive for men's than women's IPV; instead, two articles indicated that anger was more likely to be a motive for women's violence as compared to men's. However, the authors cautioned against making firm conclusions about gender differences related to the anger motive because many authors measured this motive in conjunction with something else (e.g., jealousy, retaliation). Furthermore, it may be more culturally sanctioned for women to admit to perpetrating violence as a result of jealousy related to their partner's infidelity than to admit to committing violence as a power and control strategy (Langhinrichsen-Rohling, McCullars, & Misra, 2012).

PRACTICE AND POLICY ISSUES

Prevention: Primary and Secondary

A public health approach to IPV cannot be based strictly on arrest and prosecution but should include a prevention component to stop abuse before it begins. Prevention efforts must take into account the complexity of partner violence. Because IPV is manifested in various forms (i.e., physical, emotional, sexual) and in varying degrees of severity, the behaviors that are going to be targeted for prevention must be clearly identified. It is equally important to determine when IPV begins in order to know at what point and with whom to intervene. Although intimate partnerships are not acknowledged to exist prior to adolescence, antisocial and aggressive behaviors in pre-adolescence (e.g., bullying) have been found to predict IPV in adolescence and adulthood (Capaldi et al., 2012). In fact, research has established that a large proportion of IPV begins in adolescence, with one recent national survey finding that approximately 25% of adolescents, both girls and boys, experience IPV prior to adulthood (Whitaker et al., 2007). Therefore, prevention efforts should ideally target individuals not only in this age group, but perhaps also among school-age children.

In their review of the literature, Whitaker et al. (2013) examined 61 published articles, with an emphasis on primary prevention for high-risk individuals, although studies on IPV intervention were included if they did not select for known samples of perpetrators and/or victims. Of the 19 summarized studies, 15 used experimental designs, and the others either used control groups or tested two versions of the same intervention. All of the studies incorporated a curriculum-based intervention that had the primary goal of lowering rates of IPV. Schools provided the setting for two thirds of the interventions; the rest were conducted in a variety of community settings. Of the five most methodologically sound school-based studies, only one, the SafeDates program, found a clear-cut positive outcome on IPV behavior (Foshee et al., 2005). The SafeDates program features a 7.5-hr curriculum, play and poster activities for the participants, teacher training, and a number of activities that are conducted in the community. The program was initially tested in 14 North Carolina schools: Approximately half of the schools used the SafeDates intervention, and the other half were assigned to a comparison program. Participants were subsequently evaluated at 1-year, 2-year, and 4-year follow-ups. The SafeDates program was found to significantly reduce psychological, mild physical, and sexual abuse perpetration and victimization up to the 4-year follow-up assessment (Whitaker et al., 2013).

The programs that were evaluated in all five of the most methodologically sound community-based studies were deemed to be effective in changing relationship behaviors and reducing IPV (Whitaker et al., 2013). Among them were interventions targeting young couples, especially those using a behavioral and cognitive–behavioral treatment (CBT) approach (e.g., Hahlweg & Markman, 1988). The Youth Relationship Project (Wolfe et al., 2003), an 18-week intervention that includes a curriculum as well as community-based activities, targeted families in which the parents had been investigated by Child Protective Services for child abuse. A sample of 158 adolescents was randomly assigned to either the program or a control group, and their progress was measured at an 18-month postintervention follow-up. A reduction was found in physical abuse perpetration, especially for the girls, and in physical abuse victimization, which was stronger among the boys. With respect to threats and other forms of emotional abuse, the intervention resulted in a reduction of both perpetration and victimization, primarily for the girls.

Whitaker et al. (2013) concluded that, regardless of the setting in which the interventions are conducted,

> [t]here is increasing evidence that teen IPV can be conceptualized as a risk behavior that emerges in adolescence along with other risk behaviors such as smoking, substance abuse, risky sexual behavior, and violence and delinquency. Correlations between IPV perpetration and other risk behaviors are generally substantial. Also, as noted above, factors such as conduct problems and poor parenting behaviors have been shown to be predictive of IPV in longitudinal studies. These are precisely the same predictors of peer violence, substance use, and risky sexual behavior, suggesting that IPV shares causal roots with those behaviors, and that it may be addressed using similar interventions. (p. 189)

Tertiary Prevention: Victim Empowerment and Safety Planning

Victims of *coercive–controlling violence* or *battering* often incur serious physical and psychological consequences, with attempted suicide rates of approximately 25% that are directly attributable to the abuse (Geffner & Pagelow, 1990) and a very high risk of being killed on, or after, leaving the abuser (Wilson & Daly, 1992). These victims, mostly women but quite often men, are typically overwhelmed with stress and thus often make poor decisions in times of crisis. Psychotherapists and others who are in a position to help IPV victims should understand that victims cannot be expected to overcome their fears and take the steps needed to protect themselves unless they are convinced that the advocate has their best interests in mind. This requires the building of trust and a therapeutic alliance.

Prior to a more focused risk assessment (Nicholls, Pritchard, Reeves, & Hilterman, 2013; see also Chapter 3, this volume), the helper is advised to spend the first hour gathering the victim's history and helping the victim to feel as comfortable as possible. "Active listening without giving interpretations of behavior," advises Walker (2009), "validates the woman's experiences and reassure that you will not label her 'crazy' as both she and her partner have feared" (p. 378). With this approach, the client is more likely to disclose the abuse over the next hour (Walker, 2009).

According to Walker (2009), therapists are often squeamish about asking for details about the violence, or may be overly concerned about the victim's ability to discuss them. Research by Tetterton and Farnsworth (2011) indicated that elderly women in particular are reluctant to admit to having been battered. Once some basic level of trust with the victim is established, helpers are advised to ask direct questions about the client's abuse experiences, including the amount of contact the victim has with the abuser and, if separated, the amount of contact the abuser has with the children. With assistance, victims often are able to identify cues of an impending battering incident, even if they are not able to verbalize this initially. An early cue may be the victim's subjective appraisal of anxiety or an observed change in the abuser's facial expression (e.g., having a "nobody home" look in his eyes).

The helper is further advised to have a firm understanding of the cycles of abuse and diverse typologies of abusers, against which the victim and treatment provider can compare the index abuse experiences. The most well-known violence cycle, the three-phase cycle that was first proposed by Walker (1983, 2009), essentially involves a male batterer with traits of borderline personality disorder, but it can be applied to female batterers as well (Hamel, 2005). Victims should also be informed about the features of antisocial and psychopathic battering, in which there may be only one phase (the acute battering incident), as well as the various manifestations of bilateral violence, which is characterized by mutual, rapidly escalating cycles of conflict (Hamel, 2012). Furthermore, abuse over time can take a variety of forms, from short-term minor forms of abuse to chronic, predictable, and severe violence (Roberts, 2006).

Although often useful, actuarial risk assessment instruments such as the Danger Assessment (Campbell, 1986; Campbell et al., 2009), which was created specifically for clinics and advocates who work with battered women (Campbell et al., 2003), have their limitations (Nicholls et al., 2013; see also Chapter 3, this volume). A study that was conducted by Connor-Smith, Henning, Moore, and Holdford (2011) found that the Danger Assessment provides only a static account of risk, whereas "IPV survivors can draw on a rich knowledge of the frequency, severity, and context of problem behaviors. In addition, IPV survivors can attend to changes in perpetrator behavior or contextual factors that may influence risk for repeat violence" (p. 2520).

The safety plan. Because many IPV victims will not return to therapy after their initial visit, the helper should provide a basic safety plan for the victim at the earliest opportunity. This is particularly crucial when a victim has been treated at a hospital emergency department or a crisis center rather than a therapist's office (Niolon et al., 2009). When possible, follow-ups by phone can significantly increase the likelihood that a victim will implement the plan and feel safer (Kendall et al., 2009).

Victims who are unsure about staying with or leaving the abuser can be encouraged to make pro and con lists (Cook, 2009). Because "practitioners and advocates cannot assume that all abused women have the same priorities and needs in safety planning" (Glass, Eden, Bloom, & Perrin, 2010, p. 1959; see also Nicholls, Hilterman, & Tengrstrom, 2010), helpers may want to avail themselves of such tools as the Decision Making in Abusive Relationships Interview (Nicholls et al., 2010) a risk-needs assessment to help abused women and their advocates evaluate the woman's circumstances objectively and triage women ino appropriate services. Similarly, the Domestic Violence Survivor Assessment, which was developed to assist the helper conduct a systematic review of the major issues that are faced by abuse victims (Dienemann, Campbell, Landenburger, & Curry, 2002). The computerized program that was developed by Glass et al. (2010) can also help in safety planning. After using the computerized decision aid, most of the women with children placed the highest priority on making sure their children were safe and locating the resources necessary to provide for their families.

Goodkind, Sullivan, and Bybee (2004) reported on a study of 160 abused women from various clinics in an urban area and the strategies they used to keep safe. According to the participants, the most common strategy was trying to talk to the abuser about his violence (94%); 92% of the women had contacted the police, 90% avoided the abuser when necessary, and 89% tried or threatened to end the relationship. Approximately 83% said that they had fought back physically, and 48% used or threatened to use a weapon to protect themselves. None of the strategies was consistently useful; however, two strategies were found to enhance the women's feeling of safety: contacting a shelter or other victim services agency. Consistent with our earlier discussion of mutual IPV (e.g., results in higher rates of injury), fighting back physically was the strategy that was most likely to make things worse overall, although it did make the situation better for approximately one-fourth of the women. Indeed, other research suggests that women who confront the abuser and seek help early in the relationship experience less abuse, and these women credit themselves for staying safe (Follingstad, Hause, Rutledge, & Polek, 1992). One recent study of battered women found that they experience less violence when they either stay or permanently leave the relationship as opposed to going in and out of it (Bell, Goodman, & Dutton, 2007).

Even so, helpers are advised to remain open minded and accept their limitations (Davies, Lyon, & Monti-Cantania, 1998):

> Because of the combination of abuse (of the woman as well as the children); individual resources; timing; partner's behavior; other features of the relationship; reaction of friends, family and helping agencies; and the other factors known to play a role for at least some women varies so much, it is probably most helpful simply to know the broad features that support many women in making the best decisions for the safety of themselves and their children. (p. 79)

In the context of an abusive relationship, perhaps no decision is as important as whether to remain in the relationship or to leave. Regardless, victims need to be told that staying in the relationship does not mean acceptance of the violence; similarly, leaving will not necessarily make the person safe. For victims who intend to remain in an abusive relationship,

Davies et al. (1998) recommended that they find ways to protect themselves as best they can, including taking a self-defense class, building a support system, seeking professional counseling and/or maintaining contact with a shelter or other victim service agency, and striving to achieve some measure of financial independence (e.g., find a job, siphon off money given by the abuser for household expenses).

Male IPV victimization.   Among the strategies discussed in the previous paragraph, staying in contact with a shelter or other victim advocacy organization is a far less viable option for male victims than it is for female victims; men are often turned away from shelters, told they are lying, and referred instead to perpetrator programs (Douglas & Hines, 2011). Even though men generally are reluctant to seek professional psychotherapy, this may be a much more viable option for those who have been abused (Celi, 2011; Cook, 1997). In therapy, victims who obtain support and learn cognitive strategies such as reframing the way they perceive themselves and their situation are better able to cope and maintain self-respect (Zink, Jacobson, Pabst, Regan, & Fisher, 2006).

Because men are socially conditioned to be independent and to avoid appearing weak (Hamel, 2007), the Australian psychologist Elizabeth Celi (2011) works with her clients' strengths in order to help them reestablish control of their lives. She does so in several ways, such as teaching clients to develop a detached observer attitude in order to gain greater control over their emotions, which is highly useful when one is faced with a barrage of verbal abuse. One technique to empower abused men involves having the men put themselves in what she calls the "coach's box," which is a mental space in which they may more effectively use their reasoning abilities, take time to think through ways to keep safe, and revise their options or "game plan" as needed. Another technique to empower abused men is to help them reconnect with who they were prior to the abuse (e.g., their values, aspirations).

Before a safety plan is implemented, it is beneficial if it is first rehearsed, step-by-step, so that it becomes "an automatic and familiar response in crisis, in much the way of routine fire drills when you went to school" (Walker, 2009, p. 382). Appendix 12.1 provides a basic safety plan (from Hamel, 2005) to which additional information can be added such as local legal, counseling, and other resources as well as advice on filing for divorce and custody of children, getting an emergency order of protection, and asking the court to separate the victim's assets from the abuser's assets (Davies et al., 1998). For men, these latter steps can easily backfire because the judicial system tends to minimize the problem of male IPV victimization, as discussed in the next sections of this chapter. Cook (2009) advised men who intend to involve law enforcement or the courts to first consult an attorney, preferably one who is familiar with men's issues and the characteristics and biases of local judges and district attorneys.

Tertiary Prevention: Protection Orders

Domestic violence protection orders (POs), also known as restraining orders (ROs), are court injunctions that are issued on behalf of victims with the intent to stop further violence, sexual assault, and continued harassment, including stalking. Once a PO is issued, the perpetrator is legally compelled to stay away from the victim or risk incarceration (Buzawa & Buzawa, 2002b). A number of POs are available, which can be issued from either the civil or criminal courts. For immediate relief, a victim can file for a temporary restraining order (TRO); more permanent orders may also be obtained if the court determines that the threat is likely to persist. "One of the intentions of issuing a PO," according to Russell (2012) "is to provide another option to criminal prosecution because of its immediate accessibility to victims and offers a broad range of protection to prevent victims from future physical abuse" (p. 532).

In a review of the literature on IPV, Russell (2012) identified 43 methodologically sound studies on the effectiveness of POs in keeping victims safe, victim satisfaction, characteristics of victims involved in PO cases, factors that predict whether POs are issued or denied, and enforcement of these POs. Because women are more likely than men to seek orders of protection, and because the vast majority of studies have focused on males as perpetrators rather than complainants, what we know about individuals seeking orders of protection is mostly limited to female victims. Russell's review demonstrated that women who seek and are granted these orders are relatively young (in their 20s and early 30s), and their representation among the major racial groups is roughly proportionate to the numbers in the population. They are as likely as not to be married and to be financially dependent on their partners, and are mostly unemployed or work only part time, with incomes of less than $15,000 per year.

Married victims do not seek long-term POs as often as unmarried victims do (Russell, 2012). Kaci (1992) also found that married women were less likely to follow through with a long-term PO (17.7%) compared to unmarried women (32.5%). Although the reasons for this are not entirely clear, one plausible explanation is that these women are reluctant to provoke the abuser out of fear that they will be revictimized or fear losing any financial support provided by their partner. Russell's (2012) review suggested that among married victims with children, those who seek POs are more likely to suffer from mental health disorders than those who do not seek POs. Also, women who are issued POs, regardless of whether or not they have children, tend to have more mental health issues, including PTSD and depression, and women from rural areas report more mental health issues than urban women. Russell found that in the few studies in which gender comparisons could be made, women were granted POs at significantly higher rates than men, even when controlling for abuse history, especially in cases involving lower level violence. However, no gender differences were found in the enforcement of POs, and no differences were evident in the rates of recidivism.

In her review, Russell (2012) found that victims of IPV generally reported feeling safer and having greater psychological well-being after obtaining a PO, so in this sense, POs do result in positive outcomes. However, feelings of safety appeared to be related to the amount of contact that is maintained by the victim with an abuser after separation, with those severing all ties feeling significantly safer than those who maintained some contact (which is problematic for women with children). Furthermore, most studies defined PO effectiveness by the extent to which they are violated and/or victims experience further abuse, and by this definition, success should be regarded as mixed (Russell, 2012). Although some studies found

POs to reduce violence against victims, with one large study of 2,700 women reporting a 70% reduction in violence reported to police (Holt, Kernic, Wolf, & Rivera, 2003), Russell found that POs are violated at a rate of between 44% to 70%, and 60% of women report having been stalked while a PO was in effect; thus, POs should not be regarded as fail-safe.

The majority of PO violations occur in the first 3 months of the order. The best predictors of subsequent violations after an order is issued are the severity of the criminal charges against the offender as well as previous violations (also see Volume 1, Chapter 3). Russell concluded that the effectiveness of POs would be substantially increased if scholars and legal actors could agree on what rates of PO violations and revictimization should define their effectiveness. She cited Dugan (2002), whose research found that PO violations are reduced when they are categorized as felonies, However, Russell (2012) also cited other research suggesting that PO effectiveness may also depend on more rigorous enforcement, as evidenced by Diviney, Parekh, and Olson (2009), who reported that in a mandatory arrest state, only half of PO violators were arrested. Russell concluded that policies should ensure that violations of POs are met with swift consequences, and law enforcement training should better equip officers with an understanding of IPV and PO orders. "In addition, at least data from the few studies examining female offenders suggest that males and females are treated differently within the PO process. Legal actors should examine the contextual reasons that underlie such differences" (Russell, 2012, p. 548).

Tertiary Prevention: Criminal Justice Sanctions

Since the 1980s, when IPV initially began to be regarded as a serious social problem, criminal sanctions have become increasingly more stringent and pervasive. Only a few states continue to allow police officers full discretion in making arrests in cases involving violent intimate relationships. Most states have enacted policies that encourage arrest and more vigorous "no-drop" prosecution (i.e., victims are no longer required to press charges), based on the premise that violence between intimate partners is a serious, progressive problem, and even the most minor assaults must be prosecuted before victims are exposed to even greater danger. Approximately one-third of reported domestic violence offenses and approximately three-fifths of arrests result in charges being filed against the perpetrator (Garner & Maxwell, 2009).

Impact on rates of recidivism.   Maxwell and Garner (2012) intended to provide an up-to-date account of the literature on the topic of criminal justice sanctions for IPV, focusing on the 31 most methodologically rigorous studies. Two causal mechanisms have been theorized to account for the effectiveness of arrest and prosecution: fear of sanctions and victim empowerment. However, because none of the reviewed studies adequately measured these variables, the authors assumed a general crime control effect that is neutral about causal mechanisms. Within this framework, a majority of findings showed no statistically significant effects for criminal justice sanctions on IPV recidivism rates. Among those studies that did find an effect, two thirds found sanctions to correlate with reductions in recidivism; however, the remaining one third found sanctions to correlate with an *increase* in recidivism. Aside from the inherently contradictory trends toward both greater and lesser recidivism, there was a wide range of methodological differences across studies. Due to the high variability in measures of repeat offending (e.g., the follow-up time frame), rates ranged from 3.1% to 65.5%. Many of the studies were unclear about the exact nature of the sentence imposed and what constitutes a "prosecution" or a "conviction." A diversity of analytic methods hindered analysis of the effect sizes, and none of the studies addressed the issue of sample selection bias (e.g., a number of studies had missing data, causing cases to be dropped, which in turn creates sample bias). After a careful consideration of the data, Maxwell and Garner determined that the research evidence is currently insufficient to make definite conclusions regarding the effectiveness of criminal sanctions.

Limitations of criminal sanctions.   Other studies of criminal justice sanctions have likewise yielded contradictory data, some of it quite discouraging. For instance, although there has been an increase in domestic violence convictions overall, arrests are

60% less likely to result in a conviction in pro-arrest states compared to those that allow police discretion (Hirschel, 2008). At the same time, these policies may not necessarily be in the best interests of victims, as evidenced by victims' tendency to not report repeat assaults to authorities in states where decisions to prosecute are reserved for the district attorney (Hotaling & Buzawa, 2003). Furthermore, a very small percentage of perpetrators, approximately 8%, represent the vast majority of subsequent arrests, which is estimated to be more than 80% (Maxwell, Garner, & Fagan, 2001).

In their recent review, Shernock and Russell (2012) examined the role of gender and racial/ethnic status on criminal justice responses to IPV in four broad areas: arrest (39 articles), prosecution (24 articles), POs (16 articles), and jury decision making (27 articles). All of the studies used either official data sources or interviews with victims and suspects, but rarely both. The authors found no conclusive evidence of discrimination against ethnic minority groups in either arrest, prosecution, or sentencing; however, several studies indicated a clear bias across gender and sexual orientation. For example, the studies indicated that women are more likely than men to be cited rather than to be taken into custody, although this discrepancy is not as pronounced when the decision is made on whether to file charges as misdemeanors or felonies, and men are more likely than women to be convicted and to be given harsher sentences. In studies using mock juries, blame and responsibility are assigned far more often to male than to female perpetrators (Shernock & Russell, 2012). Even after controlling for diverse variables (e.g., physical injuries), the literature clearly demonstrated that female perpetrators are treated more leniently than male perpetrators (Shernock & Russell, 2012). Finally, the proportion of dual arrests was far higher in same-sex couples compared to heterosexual couples, perhaps due to the incorrect assumption by police that same-sex couples only engage in mutual violence.

Effectiveness of Intervention Programs

Individuals who are affected by IPV seek help in a variety of settings, including mental health clinics, private therapy offices, shelters, and various social service agencies. In many cases, issues related to

IPV emerge in individual, couples, family, or group therapy after someone has sought help for other problems, such as depression or coping with difficult children (Stith, McCollum, & Rosen, 2011).

Perpetrator treatment.   Most research on IPV perpetrators has been conducted on programs that specifically target partner violence. Although these programs often accept voluntary clients, the majority of them work with individuals who have been convicted by the court and have been mandated for a specified number of treatment sessions. The most complete and up-to-date information on perpetration intervention programs, also known as batterer intervention programs (BIPs), was made available by Price and Rosenbaum (2009) in their national survey. Of the 1,850 U.S. programs they contacted, 1,400 agreed to participate. Approximately one in five operate as part of a women's shelter, the others operate in private practice or community mental health or other social service settings. Approximately 90% of the clients are male, and 10% are female. The mean number of sessions required across programs is 31 (although in some states, mandate clients are required to complete 52 weeks). More than 80% of clients are treated in the group modality, and almost exclusively in a same-sex format, with the mean length of each group at 90 min. Only 13% of the programs offer couples or family counseling.

Although some states mandate a specific IPV treatment approach, there is some diversity in the programs offered. A majority of the programs incorporate a psychoeducational component, and approximately half are based on some variation of a psychoeducational feminist model. Feminist models are based on a gendered view of IPV, in which men seek to dominate women with physical, sexual, and emotional abuse and other coercive tactics in order to maintain male privilege. Approximately half of the programs report using some variation of CBT techniques to help clients overcome irrational and aggressive impulses, and 26% identify their model as "therapeutic." Three in four programs have an anger management component, and 55% offer substance abuse treatment or information. Although not asked about in the Price and Rosenbaum (2009) survey, many programs that are categorized generally as CBT

include stress management, communication and conflict resolution skills, and empathy-building (Hamel, 2005). Building on research that found high levels of bidirectional abuse and similar motives across gender (Langhinrichsen-Rohling, McCullars, & Misra, 2012), the group perpetrator program that was offered by Hamel (2012) also helps participants identify and change the various mutual abuse dynamics.

Unfortunately, Price and Rosenbaum (2009) found that little effort is made across programs to assign clients to differential treatment based on assessment needs, as 90% of clients go into a "one-size-fits-all" treatment approach. Also, only 31% of the programs follow established ethical guidelines of mental health associations. The exact percentage of program counselors who are licensed mental health professionals is not known; however, only 15% of states have a licensure requirement in their state standards for BIPs (Maiuro & Eberle, 2008).

Eckhardt et al. (2013a) conducted a systematic investigation of the effectiveness of BIPs as part of the PASK series of manuscripts. The authors included in their review only studies that used either a randomized or quasi-experimental design. Twenty studies evaluated the effectiveness of traditional BIPs; that is, psychoeducational and or CBT delivered in a group setting; and an additional 10 looked at the effectiveness of alternative approaches and modalities. The authors found mixed evidence for the effectiveness of traditional perpetrator interventions on lowering rates of recidivism, with lesser effect sizes for the most rigorous, randomized studies, although Gondolf (2012) reported considerably higher overall effect sizes when analyzed by sophisticated (but controversial) statistical procedures (Gondolf, 2012).

More promising results were found for the 10 programs that included alternative content to the feminist or CBT model studies. One used a quasi-experimental design; the others used a randomized design. Only two studies relied strictly on self-reports for outcome data; the rest combined self-and partner reports, and two studies included criminal justice data. Nearly three in four participants sampled were court ordered. There were five studies that focused on interventions seeking to increase client motivation and strengthen the counselor–client alliance, based on the transtheoretical stages of change model. Some of the interventions were delivered in a separate session that was conducted prior to a client's participation in a BIP, and in others, the motivational component was delivered during the course of an entire program, usually 4–6 months in length. There were three studies that examined couples and couples group therapies, one that looked at a program that addressed both substance abuse and IPV, and another that reported on a case-management approach.

One study on in-group motivational enhancement, and three of the studies measuring the effects of pre-BIP motivational enhancement, found significantly lower rates of recidivism among the treatment groups compared to the control group (one involved the partner in a couples session). Recidivism rates were also found to be significantly lower for individuals who completed IPV intervention in a couples format compared to a traditional feminist-model group (Brannen & Rubin, 1996) or no treatment (Stith, Rosen, McCollum, & Thomsen, 2004), although Stith, Rosen, et al. (2004) also found the multicouples format superior to the traditional one-couple format. Eckhardt et al. (2013b) found no evidence in the available research for the superiority of any particular intervention over another. They therefore concluded that

> there is no empirical justification for agencies, state organizations, judges, mental health professionals, or others involved in improving the lives of those impacted by IPV to limit the type of services offered to clients, or to restrict the theoretical and ideological underpinnings of such methods. (Eckhardt et al., 2013b, p. 3)

Interventions with victims. Victims of IPV may find help in a variety of ways, through professional mental health counseling and law enforcement or informal support network, and from the more than 2,000 shelters operating in the United States (National Coalition Against Domestic Violence, 2008). Domestic violence shelters vary in the range of services that they provide, including crisis lines, short-term and transitional housing, peer support and professional counseling, job placement and legal services, and community outreach (Hines & Malley-Morrison, 2005).

Although half of the shelters surveyed in the national shelter study by Hines and Douglas (2011) indicated that their services are available to all populations, the authors expressed skepticism about the extent and quality of services available to male victims, citing previous accounts by men who were denied services, ridiculed, and sometimes told that they, and not their partner, was the real abuser (e.g., Hines et al., 2007). Furthermore, their study showed that "resources did not predict the availability of services to men. Rather, the overall political climate in which the agency was located seemed to be more important" (p. 22). For example, underserved populations are more likely to find services from shelters that receive federal funding, lesbians tend to be denied services in more conservative areas, and heterosexual men are least likely to find services in more liberal and affluent areas.

Eckhardt et al. (2013a) examined 28 studies that focused on the effectiveness of interventions for IPV victims and survivors. Of these, 13 were concerned with brief interventions (planned intervention consisting of ≤3 hr of contact with the victim). The majority of articles reported on data that had been collected from various health care services; for example, interventions that were conducted in prenatal care clinics, intended to encourage the use of safety plans, increase victim self-empowerment, and access community resources and support. Overall, the authors found only inconsistent effects for brief interventions. Within health care contexts, positive outcomes were consistently found only for the use of safety plans, and only one fourth of the studies found an increased use of community resources. Perhaps more disappointing, only two of seven articles reported a significant impact of the intervention on subsequent abuse revictimization compared to a control group. However, encouraging results were reported for legal advocacy interventions, in the increased use of safety behaviors, greater access to social support, and significant reductions in exposure to abuse relative to the control condition.

Among the 15 studies on longer, more traditional interventions in the Eckhardt et al. (2013a) review, evidence was found for the effectiveness of structured programs with a supportive advocacy component in reducing revictimization rates when compared to a no-treatment control. In particular,

CBT was deemed to be an effective intervention for helping victims overcome the psychological and emotional effects of abuse. Community advocacy from paraprofessionals can also lead to long-term improvements in social support and quality-of-life for survivors after their shelter experiences:

> In summary, the research literature on extended (as opposed to brief) counseling and advocacy interventions for IPV victims provides a number of encouraging findings. Several well-specified interventions have been associated with significant changes in outcome variables such as PTSD symptoms, depression, and quality-of-life. Post-shelter community advocacy and home visitation for new mothers have also been associated with significant reductions in IPV re-victimization. Although more limited, the research also indicates that supportive group interventions can have measurable impact on social support and emotional distress. (Eckhardt et al., 2013a, p. 219)

SUMMARY AND CONCLUSIONS

Largely reflecting the feminist movement and the early pioneering work of a handful of prolific social scientists (e.g., Straus et al., 1981/2006), IPV finally achieved recognition as a serious issue in the 1970s (Dutton, 1995). Early theoretical underpinnings and research (i.e., pre-1975; Straus & Gelles, 1999) primarily reflected research results that were drawn from highly specialized populations (e.g., women/couples coming to the attention of police, shelter samples). That research can be credited with garnering increasing public and scholarly attention to the plight of women who experience IPV; however, it was drastically limited in the extent to which it can be generalized to the larger population of female victims. For instance, Straus (1999b) reported that in the 1985 Family Violence Survey, an arrest was made in only 1% of the cases of female victimization, leading him to conclude that research on criminal justice and clinical samples (e.g., R.E. Dobash & Dobash, 1979) neglects to account for as much as 99% of all cases of IPV against women. The large gap between the

gendered perspective and the violence perspective has resulted in a longstanding and acrimonious debate that has been widely publicized in the IPV field (Corvo, Dutton, & Chen, 2009; Dekeseredy, 2011; Dutton & Nicholls, 2005; Straus, 1999a) and that remains to date (Corvo et al., 2008; Johnson, 2011).

The significance of the theoretical divide in the IPV field can scarcely be exaggerated, and the chasm that separates the two camps continues to prevent advancements in prevention and intervention. IPV has been a recognized epidemic and public health priority for as long as three decades. Yet, prevalence rates remain high (10% to 30% of the general population reports perpetrating IPV within the past 12 months; Black et al., 2011; Desmarais et al., 2012a, 2012b; Straus, 1999a; Whitaker et al., 2007). In addition, treatment programs have been weighed down by outdated theoretical perspectives that offer a single explanation (i.e., patriarchy) for a multidimensional and complex public health problem. Until very recently, simplistic, one-size-fits-all models (e.g., Duluth) have been *the only available treatment option* in many U.S. states (Maiuro & Eberle, 2008; Price & Rosenbaum, 2009). As further evidence, as recently as a decade ago, the APA published recommended teaching documents that reflected a single theoretical perspective (APA Intimate Partner Abuse and Relationship Violence Working Group, 2002).

To achieve progress in protecting children, women, and men, and to enhance public policy, is going to require a dramatic paradigm shift in the IPV field (Dutton & Nicholls, 2005; Hamel & Nicholls, 2007; Straus, 1999a). The prevention of violence is one of the highest priorities of psychologists (APA Intimate Partner Abuse and Relationship Violence Working Group, 1996, 2002; Finkelhor, 1986). "To have a significant impact upon the elimination of relationship violence, an organized effort in promotion of nonviolence is needed" (APA Intimate Partner Abuse and Relationship Violence Working Group, 2002, p. 54). A particularly important recent development is that the Violence Against Women Act reauthorization bill would extend protections and programs to same-sex couples, indigenous tribes, and undocumented immigrants, as well as improve the delivery of services to male victims (*The Washington Post*, 2012). The bill, which originally was enacted in

1994 to provide grant money for police departments and agencies to provide aid to IPV victims and to support the prosecution of domestic violence offenders, has received bipartisan support every time it has needed reauthorization. In 2012, it was proposed that the reauthorization of the Act should include LGBT domestic violence survivors and illegal immigrants. Visas would be extended to undocumented immigrants who experience domestic violence provided they meet all of the requirements in the bill. The bill would also provide funding for programs that serve those in the LGBT community who experience domestic violence and prohibit discrimination in funding based on gender.

As reflected by the approach that was taken in the present chapter, theoretical and empirical evidence strongly supports a consideration of both patriarchal pathways (e.g., misogynistic attitudes, male dominance, economic disparities between men and women) and gender-neutral pathways (e.g., unemployment, poor frustration tolerance, ineffective communication style) to IPV perpetration. To date, in excess of 200 studies have found that men and women inflict IPV at roughly equivalent rates (Archer, 2000, 2002; Fiebert, 2010, 2012; Stets & Straus, 1989; Whitaker et al., 2007; see Dutton & Nicholls, 2005; Straus, 2006, 2009, for reviews). Reciprocal IPV has been found to be the most common form of IPV across several large studies (Anderson, 2002; Capaldi & Owen, 2001; Gelles & Straus, 1988; Kessler et al., 2001; Medeiros & Straus, 2007; Moffitt et al., 2001; Stets & Straus, 1989; Straus et al., 1981/2006; Whitaker et al., 2007; Williams & Frieze, 2005). Women have been found to instigate nonreciprocal IPV (e.g., 71%, Whitaker et al., 2007) and to use one or more acts of physical aggression frequently (Archer, 2000). In addition, the NISVS indicated that women are as likely as men to commit diverse forms of IPV (Black et al., 2011) and to perpetrate high rates of severe or clinical-level violence (Black et al., 2011; e.g., 7% for women vs. 5% for men, Stets & Straus, 1992; Straus, 2011). Women, however, are consistently found to be the more likely victims of serious injury or homicide as a result of IPV (Archer, 2000; Straus, 2009, p. 246), although these gender differences are often noted to be small, particularly in dating couples (Straus, 2004; Whitaker et al., 2007).

More than 10 review articles (see Lawrence et al., 2012) and several meta-analyses (e.g., Archer, 2000; Straus, 2011) demonstrated two relatively consistent findings: First, psychological and physical abuse alike have important implications for the mental and physical health of victims of IPV. Second, female IPV victims generally suffer more severe outcomes than male victims, and/or male perpetrators of abuse are generally found to be more likely to inflict serious injury or death. Insufficient research has examined the psychological effects of IPV on men, but considerable evidence demonstrates elevated rates of diverse mental health problems and increased utilization of mental health services and medications among women who have experienced IPV (Lawrence et al., 2012).

It is well documented that physical violence that is perpetrated by women against their partners is less likely to result in physical injury than violence that is inflicted by men (Straus, 2004), and women suffer higher rates of serious injury than men (Lawrence et al., 2012; National Research Council, 1996; Rennison, 2003); however, the physical, psychological, and financial effects resulting from women's perpetration of physical IPV are neither infrequent nor inconsequential (e.g., Coker et al., 2002; Reid et al., 2008; Rennison, 2003; Zhang et al., 2012). In fact, when mild or moderate physical assaults are compared, there is little evidence of gender disparity in injuries (Lawrence et al., 2012). The NISVS (Black et al., 2011) found that 81% of women and 35% of men who experienced rape, physical violence, or stalking by an intimate partner reported at least one impact related to the IPV experiences, such as fear, concern for safety, injury, or having missed at least 1 day of work or school. Research clearly demonstrates that although women are injured more, men are far from immune to IPV. Although there is considerable room for continued prevention and intervention improvements, it is positive to see some evidence of recent declines in both lethal and nonlethal IPV since the early 1990s (Catalano, 2012; Dugan, Nagin, & Rosenfeld, 1999). Remaining gaps in the literature include research into the implications of IPV for male victims, IPV in LGBT couples, and further examination of gender and IPV that takes greater account of contextual considerations.

IPV interventions can be divided into three categories. *Primary prevention* is aimed at preventing IPV from ever occurring, *secondary prevention* identifies and intervenes when the early warning signs of IPV are present, and *tertiary prevention* is designed to address IPV perpetrators and/or victims (Hyman, Guruge, Stewart, & Ahmad, 2000). The sheer prevalence and pervasiveness of the problem magnified by the extent to which IPV cuts across societal, gender, and sexual boundaries suggests the need for prevention and intervention at all three levels within local, state, and national domains. These should address treatment and prevention for both sexes, implementation of gender-inclusive and gender-sensitive interventions, and inclusion of LGBT prevention and treatment programs. Thus far, unfortunately, only a minority of studies has found any statistically significant effect for reducing reabuse rates (Eckhardt et al., 2013b). Research documenting interventions for perpetrators is similarly disappointing. Contrary to widely employed practices (Price & Rosenbaum, 2009), systematic investigations of treatment clearly demonstrate that the theoretical foundation for interventions with perpetrators should not be restricted to a traditional feminist approach (Eckhardt et al., 2013b). It is concerning that the basic principles of ethical and effective treatment rarely appear to inform IPV treatment with perpetrators (e.g., just 15% of treatment providers are certified). In the larger criminal justice literature, there is extensive literature documenting the value of gearing the treatment to the individual risk factors and needs of the individual (see the risk–needs–responsivity model; Andrews, Bonta, & Wormith, 2010) and inadvertently escalating adverse outcomes when interventions are in excess of the needs of the offender (see Dvoskin, Skeem, Novaco, & Douglas, 2012). Unfortunately, these wisdoms have not been woven into the IPV literature, and we would encourage IPV service and treatment providers and decision makers alike to consider the relevance of the broader treatment literature in order to ensure that IPV victims and perpetrators are receiving evidence-informed interventions.

We have endeavored to offer some concrete suggestions for keeping victims safe (see Appendix 12.1; Nicholls et al., 2010). In particular, professionals should be mindful that many victims might not return after an initial visit; therefore, the opportunity to provide a basic safety plan should be seized at the earliest opportunity. In addition, we recommend that service providers remain open minded and support victims in implementing a plan that is best suited to the situation and reflects their individual preferences (see Nicholls et al., 2010).

APPENDIX 12.1. VICTIM SAFETY PLAN

PRECAUTIONS

1. Make sure you understand your partner's use of violence. Recognize situations when he/she is becoming increasingly agitated, and be aware of how the violence escalates over time. It is crucial to quickly determine when your partner is becoming dangerous, and when you are at risk for being harmed.
2. Prearrange a safe place to stay—with a trusted friend or family member. While your partner is out, remove any weapons that may be in the house. If you don't feel comfortable removing weapons, call the police and ask them to assist you. Then make your escape to the safe place and stay there. If you have children, bring them with you.
3. Train the eldest and most responsible child to be aware of your partner's cycle of violence and how to call the police in an emergency. Also see to it that the same safe place, or an alternative, is available for them. Make sure they understand the importance of secrecy. Very young children can inadvertently talk.
4. Inform anyone about your situation whom your partner might contact. Ask the people who are providing the safe place to not disclose your location. Alert your employer about the situation and ask that they not speak to your partner without your permission.
5. Inform children not to disclose your safe place to anyone.

What to do During a Violent Incident

1. Escape from the abuse at the earliest opportunity.
2. Take a survival kit with you.

A survival kit includes items you will need after leaving. These should be kept in an easily accessible location, such as the trunk of your car, or somewhere close at hand. You may have more than one kit in several locations. Your kit should include the following:

Money: If you don't have time to bring a checkbook and credit card with you, it is important to put aside cash, enough for you to pay for lodging and food for a few days. You will need cash even if you have a credit card because your partner could cancel your credit card. Cash may be necessary if you do not have a cell phone and need to use a pay phone.

Clothing: The kit should include a small, portable bag with enough clothes for you and your children, including warm clothes in case of cold weather.

Keys: You should have an extra set of keys to your vehicles, your house, or anything else you will need access to (e.g., place of business, safety deposit box).

Important phone numbers:

Police (911)
Local shelter
County victim/witness programs
County social services
County probation
Legal assistance
Your therapist, and the phone number of your partner's therapist
Any friends or family members who can help you

Vital Documents: Your kit should contain necessary documents. If you are unable to secure the originals in advance, then have copies available, or a plan on how to retrieve the originals when you need them. Important documents to have include the following:

- Driver's license (for both yourself and your partner, or copies)
- Bank account numbers and paperwork
- Social security numbers for you, your partner, and your children
- Birth certificates for you, your partner, and your children

- Recent pay stubs for you and your partner
- Mortgage papers and other documents for jointly owned properties
- Marriage license
- Various insurance policies

If time allows, after securing your physical safety, secure valuables, such as jewelry, and anything else that may be of importance to you (e.g., photos, heirlooms).

References

Achenbach, T. M., & Edelbrock, C. S. (1983). *Manual for the Child Behavior Checklist and Revised Child Behavior Profile*. Burlington: University of Vermont, Department of Psychiatry.

Achenbach, T. M., & Edelbrock, C. S. (1987). *Manual for the Youth Self-Report and Profile*. Burlington: University of Vermont, Department of Psychiatry.

Alhabib, S., Nur, U., & Jones, R. (2010). Domestic violence against women: Systematic review of prevalence studies. *Journal of Family Violence, 25,* 369–382. doi:10.1007/s10896-009-9298-4

American Psychological Association, Intimate Partner Abuse and Relationship Violence Working Group. (1996). *Intimate partner abuse and relationship violence*. Washington, DC: American Psychological Association.

American Psychological Association, Intimate Partner Abuse and Relationship Violence Working Group. (2002). *Intimate partner abuse and relationship violence*. Washington, DC: American Psychological Association. Retrieved from http://www.apa.org/about/division/activities/partner-abuse.pdf

Anderson, K. L. (2002). Perpetrator or victim? Relationships between intimate partner violence and well-being. *Journal of Marriage and Family, 64,* 851–863. doi:10.1111/j.1741-3737.2002.00851.x

Andrews, D. A., Bonta, J., & Wormith, J. S. (2010). The Level of Service (LS) Assessment of adults and older adolescents. In R. K. Otto & K. S. Douglas (Eds.), *Handbook of violence risk assessment* (pp. 199–225). New York, NY: Routledge/Taylor & Francis Group.

Archer, J. (2000). Sex differences in aggression between heterosexual partners: A meta-analytic review. *Psychological Bulletin, 126,* 651–680. doi:10.1037/0033-2909.126.5.651

Archer, J. (2002). Sex differences in physically aggressive acts between heterosexual partners: A meta-analytic review. *Aggression and Violent Behavior, 7,* 313–351. doi:10.1016/S1359-1789(01)00061-1

Archer, J. (2006). Cross-cultural differences in physical aggression between partners: A social-role analysis. *Personality and Social Psychology Review, 10,* 133–153. doi:10.1207/s15327957pspr1002_3

Babcock, J. C., Green, C. E., & Robie, C. (2004). Does batterers' treatment work? A meta-analytic review of domestic violence treatment. *Clinical Psychology Review, 23,* 1023–1053. doi:10.1016/j.cpr.2002.07.001

Bandura, A. (1971). *Social learning theory.* Morristown, NJ: General Learning Press.

Bandura, A. (1973). *Aggression: A social learning analysis.* Englewood Cliffs, NJ: Prentice-Hall.

Bell, M., Goodman, L., & Dutton, M. (2007). The dynamics of staying and leaving: Implications for battered women's emotional well-being and experiences of violence at the end of a year. *Journal of Family Violence, 22,* 413–428. doi:10.1007/s10896-007-9096-9

Besant, A. (2012, October 3). Canada's 77-year-old "black widow" charged with attempted murder. *Global Post.* Retrieved from http://www.globalpost.com/dispatch/news/regions/americas/canada/121003/canadas-77-year-old-black-widow-charged-attempted-murde

Black, M. C., Basile, K. C., Breiding, M. J., Smith, S. G., Walters, M. L., Merrick, M. T., . . . Stevens, M. R. (2011). *The National Intimate Partner and Sexual Violence Survey (NISVS): 2010 summary report.* Atlanta, GA: National Center for Injury Prevention and Control, Centers for Disease Control and Prevention. Retrieved from http://www.cdc.gov/violenceprevention/pdf/nisvs_report2010-a.pdf

Bograd, M. (1988). Feminist perspectives on wife assault: An introduction. In K. Yllo & M. Bograd (Eds.), *Feminist perspectives on wife abuse* (pp. 11–26). Newbury Park, CA: Sage.

Bookwala, J., Frieze, I. H., Smith, C., & Ryan, K. (1992). Predictors of dating violence: A multivariate analysis. *Violence and Victims, 7,* 297–311.

Brand, P. A., & Kidd, A. H. (1986). Frequency of physical aggression in heterosexual and female homosexual dyads. *Psychological Reports, 59,* 1307–1313. doi:10.2466/pr0.1986.59.3.1307

Brannen, S. J., & Rubin, A. (1996). Comparing the effectiveness of gender-specific and couples groups in a court-mandated spouse abuse treatment program. *Research on Social Work Practice, 6,* 405–424. doi:10.1177/104973159600600401

Browne, A. (1987). *When battered women kill.* New York, NY: Free Press.

Buttell, F., & Starr, E. (2013). Lifting the veil: Foundations for a gender-inclusive paradigm of intimate partner violence. In B. Russell (Ed.), *Perceptions of female offenders: How stereotypes and social norms affect criminal justice responses* (pp. 117–132). New York, NY: Springer. doi:10.1007/978-1-4614-5871-5_8

Buzawa, E. S., & Buzawa, C. G. (2002a). Defining and measuring domestic violence and its impact. In E. S. Buzawa & C. G. Buzawa (Eds.), *Domestic violence: The criminal justice response* (pp. 13–30). Thousand Oaks, CA: Sage. Retrieved from http://www.sagepub.com/upm-data/3241_Buzawa_Chp2Final.pdf

Buzawa, E. S., & Buzawa, C. G. (2002b). *Domestic violence: The criminal justice response.* Thousand Oaks, CA: Sage.

Campbell, J. C. (1986). Nursing assessment for risk of homicide with battered women. *ANS. Advances in Nursing Science, 8,* 36–51. doi:10.1097/00012272-198607000-00006

Campbell, J. C., Glass, N., Sharps, P. W., Laughon, K., & Bloom, T. (2007). Intimate partner homicide: Review and implications of research policy. *Trauma, Violence, & Abuse, 8,* 246–269. doi:10.1177/1524838007303505

Campbell, J. C., Webster, D. W., & Glass, N. (2009). The Danger Assessment: Validation of a lethality risk assessment instrument for intimate partner femicide. *Journal of Interpersonal Violence, 24,* 653–674. doi:10.1177/0886260508317180

Campbell, J. C., Webster, D., Koziol-McLain, J., Block, C., Campbell, D., Curry, M. A., & Laughon, K. (2003). Risk factors for femicide in abusive relationships: Results from a multisite case control study. *American Journal of Public Health, 93,* 1089–1097. doi:10.2105/AJPH.93.7.1089

Capaldi, D. M., Knoble, N. B., Shortt, J. W., & Kim, H. K. (2012). A systematic review of prevalence of physical violence in intimate relationships—Part 2: Rates of male and female perpetration. *Partner Abuse, 3,* 231–280. doi:10.1891/1946-6560.3.2.231

Capaldi, D. M., & Owen, L. D. (2001). Physical aggression in a community sample of at-risk young couples: Gender comparison for high frequency, injury, and fear. *Journal of Family Psychology, 15,* 425–440. doi:10.1037/0893-3200.15.3.425

Carlson, B. E. (1991). Outcomes of physical abuse and observation of marital violence among adolescents in placement. *Journal of Interpersonal Violence, 6,* 526–534. doi:10.1177/088626091006004011

Carney, M., & Barner, J. (2012). Prevalence of partner abuse: Rates of emotional abuse and control. *Partner Abuse, 3,* 286–335. doi:10.1891/1946-6560.3.3.286

Cascardi, M., & Vivian, D. (1995). Context for specific episodes of marital violence: Gender and severity of violence differences. *Journal of Family Violence, 10,* 265–293. doi:10.1007/BF02110993

Catalano, S. (2007). *Intimate partner violence in the US.* Washington, DC: Bureau of Justice Statistics.

Retrieved from http://bjs.ojp.usdoj.gov/content/pub/pdf/ipvus.pdf

Catalano, S. (2012). *Intimate partner violence, 1993–2010*. Washington, DC: Bureau of Justice Statistics. Retrieved from http://www.bjs.gov/index.cfm?ty=pbdetail&iid=4536

Celi, E. (2011). *Breaking the silence: A practical guide for male victims of domestic violence*. Victoria, Australia: Global.

Coker, A. L. (2007). Does physical intimate partner violence affect sexual health? A systematic review. *Trauma, Violence, & Abuse, 8*, 149–177. doi:10.1177/1524838007301162

Coker, A. L., Davis, K. E., Arias, I., Desai, S., Sanderson, M., Brandt, H. M., & Smith, P. H. (2002). Physical and mental health effects of intimate partner violence for men and women. *American Journal of Preventive Medicine, 23*, 260–268. doi:10.1016/S0749-3797(02)00514-7

Coleman, D. H., & Straus, M. (1986). Marital power, conflict, and violence in a nationally representative sample of American couples. *Violence and Victims, 1*, 141–157.

Connor-Smith, J. K., Henning, K., Moore, S., & Holdford, R. (2011). Risk assessments by female victims of intimate partner violence: Predictors of risk perceptions and comparison to an actual measure. *Journal of Interpersonal Violence, 26*, 2517–2550. doi:10.1177/0886260510383024

Cook, P. (1997). *Abused men: The hidden side of domestic violence*. Westport, CT: Praeger.

Cook, P. (2009). *Abused men: The hidden side of domestic violence* (2nd ed.). Westport, CT: Praeger.

Corvo, K., Dutton, D., & Chen, W. (2008). Toward evidence based practice with domestic violence perpetrators. *Journal of Aggression, Maltreatment & Trauma, 16*, 111–130. doi:10.1080/10926770801921246

Corvo, K., Dutton, D., & Chen, W. (2009). Do Duluth model interventions with perpetrators of domestic violence violate mental health professional ethics? *Ethics & Behavior, 19*, 323–340. doi:10.1080/10508420903035323

Crowell, N. A. & Burgess, A.W. (1996). *Understanding violence against women*. Washington, DC: National Academy Press.

Davies, J., Lyon, E., & Monti-Cantania, D. (1998). *Safety planning with battered women*. Thousand Oaks, CA: Sage.

Day, T. (1995). *The health-related costs of violence against women in Canada: The tip of the iceberg*. London, Ontario, Canada: Centre for Research on Violence Against Women and Children.

DeKeseredy, W. S. (2011). Feminist contributions to understanding woman abuse: Myths, controversies and realities. *Aggression and Violent Behavior, 16*, 297–302. doi:10.1016/j.avb.2011.04.002

DeMaris, A. (1992). Male versus female initiation of aggression: The case of courtship violence. In E. Viano (Ed.), *Intimate violence: Interdisciplinary perspectives* (pp. 111–120). Washington, DC: Taylor & Francis.

Desmarais, S. L., Reeves, K. A., Nicholls, T. L., Telford, R. P., & Fiebert, M. S. (2012a). Prevalence of physical violence in intimate relationships, Part 1: Rates of male and female victimization. *Partner Abuse, 3*, 140–169. doi:10.1891/1946-6560.3.2.140

Desmarais, S. L., Reeves, K. A., Nicholls, T. L., Telford, R. P., & Fiebert, M. S. (2012b). Prevalence of physical violence in intimate relationships, Part 2: Rates of male and female perpetration. *Partner Abuse, 3*, 170–198. doi:10.1891/1946-6560.3.2.170

Dienemann, J., Campbell, J., Landenburger, K., & Curry, M. (2002). The Domestic Violence Survivor Assessment: A tool for counseling women in intimate partner violence relationships. *Patient Education and Counseling, 46*, 221–228. doi:10.1016/S0738-3991(01)00216-6

Diviney, C. L., Parekh, A., & Olson, L. M. (2009). Outcomes of civil protective orders. *Journal of Interpersonal Violence, 24*, 1209–1221. doi:10.1177/0886260508322185

Dixon, L., Archer, J., & Graham-Kevan, N. (2012). Perpetrator programmes for partner violence: Are they based on ideology or evidence? *Legal and Criminological Psychology, 17*, 196–215. doi:10.1111/j.2044-8333.2011.02029.x

Dixon, L., & Graham-Kevan, N. (2011). Understanding the nature and etiology of intimate partner violence and implications for practice and policy. *Clinical Psychology Review, 31*, 1145–1155. doi:10.1016/j.cpr.2011.07.001

Dobash, R. E., & Dobash, R. P. (1979). *Violence against wives: A case against the patriarchy*. New York, NY: Free Press.

Dobash, R. P., & Dobash, R. E. (1995). Reflections on findings from the Violence Against Women Survey. *Canadian Journal of Criminology, 37*, 457–484.

Dobash, R. P., & Dobash, R. E. (2004). Women's violence to men in intimate relationships. *The British Journal of Criminology, 44*, 324–349. doi:10.1093/bjc/azh026

Douglas, E. M., & Hines, D. (2011). The helpseeking experiences of men who sustain intimate partner violence. *Journal of Family Violence, 26*, 473–485. doi:10.1007/s10896-011-9382-4

Dugan, L. (2002). *Domestic violence legislation: Exploring its impact on domestic violence and the likelihood that police are informed and arrest*. Washington, DC: U.S. Department of Justice. Retrieved from http://www.ncjrs.gov/pdffiles1/nij/grants/196853.pdf

Dugan, L., Nagin, D. S., & Rosenfeld, R. (1999). Explaining the decline in intimate partner homicide: The effects of changing domesticity, women's status, and domestic violence resources. *Homicide Studies, 3*, 187–214. doi:10.1177/1088767999003003001

Dutton, D., Corvo, K., & Hamel, J. (2009). The gender paradigm in domestic violence research and practice: Part II—The information website of the American Bar Association. *Aggression and Violent Behavior, 14*, 30–38. doi:10.1016/j.avb.2008.08.002

Dutton, D. G. (1995). *The domestic assault of women.* Vancouver, Canada: UBC Press.

Dutton, D. G. (2006). *Rethinking domestic violence.* Vancouver, Canada: UBC Press.

Dutton, D. G., & Nicholls, T. L. (2005). The gender paradigm in domestic violence research and theory: Part I—The conflict of theory and data. *Aggression and Violent Behavior, 10*, 680–714. doi:10.1016/j.avb.2005.02.001

Dvoskin, J. A., Skeem, J. L., Novaco, R. W., & Douglas, K. S. (2012). What if psychology redesigned the criminal justice system? In J. A. Dvoskin, J. L. Skeem, R. W. Novaco, & K. S. Douglas (Eds.), *Using social science to reduce violent offending* (pp. 291–302). New York, NY: Oxford University Press.

Eckhardt, C. I., Murphy, C. M., Whitaker, D. J., Sprunger, J., Dykstra, R., & Woodard, K. (2013a). The effectiveness of intervention programs for perpetrators and victims of intimate partner violence. *Partner Abuse, 4*, 196–231.

Eckhardt, C. I., Murphy, C. M., Whitaker, D. J., Sprunger, J., Dykstra, R., & Woodard, K. (2013b). *The effectiveness of intervention programs for perpetrators and victims of intimate partner violence* (online summary). Available at http://www.springerpub.com/content/journals/PA-KnowledgeBase-41410.pdf

English, D. J., Marshall, D. B., & Stewart, A. J. (2003). Effects of family violence on child behavior and health during early childhood. *Journal of Family Violence, 18*, 43–57. doi:10.1023/A:1021453431252

Esquivel-Santovena, E., Lambert, T., & Hamel, J. (2013). Partner abuse worldwide. *Partner Abuse, 4*, 1–8.

Federal Bureau of Investigation. (n.d.). *Federal Bureau of Investigation: Uniform crime reporting.* Retrieved from http://www.fbi.gov/about-us/cjis/ucr/ucr

Felson, R., & Messner, S. (1998). Disentangling the effects of gender and intimacy on victim precipitation in homicide. *Criminology, 36*, 405–424. doi:10.1111/j.1745-9125.1998.tb01253.x

Felson, R., & Outlaw, M. (2007). The control motive and marital violence. *Violence and Victims, 22*, 387–407. doi:10.1891/088667007781553964

Felson, R. B. (2002). *Violence and gender reexamined.* Washington, DC: American Psychological Association. doi:10.1037/10470-000

Felson, R. B. (2006). Is violence against women about women or about violence? *Contexts, 5*, 21–25. doi:10.1525/ctx.2006.5.2.21

Felson, R. B., & Lane, K. (2010). Does violence involving women and intimate partners have a special etiology? *Criminology, 48*, 321–338. doi:10.1111/j.1745-9125.2010.00186.x

Fergusson, D., Horwood, J., & Ridder, E. (2005). Partner violence and mental health outcomes in a New Zealand birth cohort. *Journal of Marriage and Family, 67*, 1103–1119. doi:10.1111/j.1741-3737.2005.00202.x

Fernández-Fuertes, A. A., & Fuertes, A. (2010). Physical and psychological aggression in dating relationships of Spanish adolescents: Motives and consequences. *Child Abuse & Neglect: The International Journal, 34*, 183–191. doi:10.1016/j.chiabu.2010.01.002

Fiebert, M. (2010). References examining assaults by women on their spouses or male partners: An annotated bibliography. *Sexuality & Culture, 14*, 49–91. doi:10.1007/s12119-009-9059-9

Fiebert, M. (2012). *References examining assaults by women on their spouses or male partners: An annotated bibliography.* Retrieved from http://www.csulb.edu/~mfiebert/assault.htm

Finkelhor, D. (1986). Prevention approaches to child sexual abuse. In L. Lystad (Ed.), *Violence in the home: Interdisciplinary perspectives* (pp. 296–308). New York, NY: Brunner/Mazel.

Follingstad, D. R., Bradley, R. G., Helff, C. M., & Laughlin, J. E. (2002). A model for predicting dating violence: Anxious attachment, angry temperament, and need for relationship control. *Violence and Victims, 17*, 35–47. doi:10.1891/vivi.17.1.35.33639

Follingstad, D. R., DeHart, D., & Green, E. (2004). Psychologists' judgments of psychologically aggressive actions when perpetrated by a husband versus a wife. *Violence and Victims, 19*, 435–452. doi:10.1891/vivi.19.4.435.64165

Follingstad, D. R., Hause, E., Rutledge, L., & Polek, D. (1992). Effects of battered women's early responses on later abuse patterns. *Violence and Victims, 7*, 109–128.

Follingstad, D. R., Wright, S., Lloyd, S., & Sebastian, J. A. (1991). Sex differences in motivations and effects in dating violence. *Family Relations: Interdisciplinary Journal of Applied Family Studies, 40*, 51–57. doi:10.2307/585658

Foshee, V. A., Bauman, K. E., Ennett, S. T., Suchindran, C., Benefield, T., & Linder, G. (2005). Assessing the effects of the dating violence prevention program "Safe Dates" using random coefficient regression modeling. *Prevention Science, 6,* 245–258. doi:10.1007/s11121-005-0007-0

Garcia-Moreno, C., Jansen, H., Ellsberg, M., Heise, L., & Watts, C. (2006). Prevalence of intimate partner violence: Findings from the WHO multi-country study on women's health and domestic violence. *The Lancet, 368,* 1260–1269. doi:10.1016/S0140-6736(06)69523-8

Garner, J., & Maxwell, C. (2009). Prosecution and conviction rates for intimate partner violence. *Criminal Justice Review, 34,* 44–79. doi:10.1177/0734016808324231

Geffner, R., & Pagelow, M. (1990). Victims of spouse abuse. In R. Ammerman & H. Hersen (Eds.), *Treatment of family violence: A sourcebook* (pp. 113–135). New York, NY: Wiley.

Gelles, R. J., & Straus, M. A. (1988). *Intimate violence: The causes and consequences of abuse in the American family.* New York, NY: Simon and Schuster.

Gelles, R. J., & Straus, M. A. (1999). The medical and psychological costs of family violence. In M. A. Straus & R. J. Gelles (Eds.), *Physical violence in American families: Risk factors and adaptations to violence in 8,145 families* (pp. 425–430). New Brunswick, NJ: Transaction.

Glass, N., Eden, K., Bloom, T., & Perrin, N. (2010). Computerized aid improves safety decision process for survivors of intimate partner violence. *Journal of Interpersonal Violence, 25,* 1947–1964. doi:10.1177/0886260509354508

Gondolf, E. (1996). *Characteristics of batterers in a multi-site evaluation of batterer intervention systems.* St. Paul: Minnesota Center Against Violence and Abuse. Retrieved from http://www.mincava.umn.edu/documents/gondolf/batchar.html

Gondolf, E. (2012). *The future of batterer programs: Reassessing evidence-based practice.* Lebanon, NH: Northeastern University Press.

Goodkind, J., Sullivan, C., & Bybee, D. (2004). A contextual analysis of battered women's safety planning. *Violence Against Women, 10,* 514–533. doi:10.1177/1077801204264368

Gordon, M. (2000). Definitional issues in violence against women: Surveillance and research from a violence research perspective. *Violence Against Women, 6,* 747–783. doi:10.1177/1077801200006007004

Greaves, L., Hankivsky, O., & Kingston-Riechers, J. (1995). *Selected estimates of the cost of violence against women.* London, Ontario, Canada: Centre for Research on Violence Against Women and Children.

Hahlweg, K., & Markman, H. J. (1988). Effectiveness of behavioral marital therapy: Empirical status of behavioral techniques in preventing and alleviating marital distress. *Journal of Consulting*

and Clinical Psychology, 56, 440–447. doi:10.1037/0022-006X.56.3.440

Hamel, J. (2005). *Gender inclusive treatment of intimate partner abuse.* New York, NY: Springer.

Hamel, J. (2007). Male victims of domestic violence and reasons why they stay with their abuser. In N. Jackson (Ed.), *Domestic violence encyclopedia* (pp. 457–459). New York, NY: Routledge.

Hamel, J. (2012). "But she's violent, too!": Holding domestic violence offenders accountable within a systemic approach to batterer intervention. *Journal of Aggression, Conflict, and Peace Research, 4,* 124–135. doi:10.1108/17596591211244139

Hamel, J. (2014). *Gender-inclusive treatment of intimate partner abuse: Evidence-based approaches* (2nd ed.). New York, NY: Springer.

Hamel, J., Desmarais, S. L., Nicholls, T. L., Malley-Morrison, K., & Aaronson, J. (2009). Domestic violence and child custody: Are family court professionals' decisions based on erroneous beliefs? *Journal of Aggression, Conflict and Peace Research, 1,* 37–52. doi:10.1108/17596599200900011

Hamel, J., & Nicholls, T. L. (Eds.). (2007). *Family interventions in domestic violence.* New York, NY: Springer.

Henton, J., Cate, R., Koval, J., Lloyd, S., & Christopher, S. (1983). Romance and violence in dating relationships. *Journal of Family Issues, 4,* 467–482. doi:10.1177/019251383004003004

Hines, D. (2014). Extent and implications of the presentation of false facts by domestic violence agencies in the United States. *Partner Abuse, 5,* 69–82.

Hines, D., & Douglas, E. (2011). The reported availability of U.S. domestic violence services to victims who vary by age, sexual orientation, and gender. *Partner Abuse, 2,* 3–30. doi:10.1891/1946-6560.2.1.3

Hines, D., & Malley-Morrison, K. (2005). *Family violence in the United States: Defining, understanding, and combating abuse.* Thousand Oaks, CA: Sage.

Hirschel, D. (2008). *Domestic violence cases: What research shows about arrest and dual arrest cases.* Retrieved from http://www.ojp.usdoj.gov/nij/publications/dv-dual-arrest-222679/dv-dual-arrest.pdf

Holt, V. L., Kernic, M., Wolf, M., & Rivera, F. (2003). Do protection orders affect the likelihood of future violence and injury? *American Journal of Preventive Medicine, 24,* 16–21. doi:10.1016/S0749-3797(02)00576-7

Holtzworth-Munroe, A., & Stuart, G. L. (1994). Typologies of male batterers: Three subtypes and the differences among them. *Psychological bulletin, 116,* 476.

Hotaling, G., & Buzawa, E. (2003). *Foregoing criminal justice assistance: The non-reporting of new incidents of abuse in a court sample of domestic violence victims.* Washington, DC: U.S. Department of Justice.

Hughes, H. M., Parkinson, D., & Vargo, M. (1989). Witnessing spouse abuse and experiencing physical abuse: A "double whammy"? *Journal of Family Violence, 4,* 197–209. doi:10.1007/BF01006629

Huth-Bocks, A. C., Levendosky, A. A., & Semel, M. A. (2001). The direct and indirect effects of domestic violence on young children's intellectual functioning. *Journal of Family Violence, 16,* 269–290. doi:10.1023/A:1011138332712

Hyman, I., Guruge, S., Stewart, D. E., & Ahmad, F. (2000). Primary prevention of violence against women. *Women's Health Issues, 10,* 288–293. doi:10.1016/S1049-3867(00)00066-9

Irwin, J. (2004). *Discounted stories: Domestic violence and lesbians* (Unpublished doctoral dissertation) University of Sydney, Syndey, Australia.

Irwin, J. (2008). (Dis)counted stories domestic violence and lesbians. *Qualitative Social Work: Research and Practice, 7,* 199–215. doi:10.1177/1473325008089630

Island, D., & Letellier, P. (1991). *Men who beat the men who love them: Battered gay men and domestic violence.* Binghamton, NY: Haworth.

Joachim, J. (2000). Shaping the human rights agenda: The case of violence against women. In M. K. Meyer & E. Prugl (Eds.), *Gender politics in global governance* (pp. 142–160). Lanham, MD: Rowman and Little Field.

Johnson, M. (2008). *A typology of domestic violence: Intimate terrorism, violence resistance, and situational couple violence.* Lebanon, NH: Northeastern University Press.

Johnson, M. (2011). Gender and types of intimate partner violence: A response to antifeminist literature review. *Aggression and Violent Behavior, 16,* 290–296

Johnson, M. P. (1995). Patriarchal terrorism and common couple violence: Two forms of violence against women. *Journal of Marriage and the Family, 57,* 283–294. doi:10.2307/353683

Kaci, J. H. (1992). A study of protective orders issued under California's Domestic Violence Prevention Act. *Criminal Justice Review, 17,* 61–76. doi:10.1177/073401689201700105

Kaslow, N. J., & Thompson, M. P. (2008). Associations of child maltreatment and intimate partner violence with psychological adjustment among low SES, African American children. *Child Abuse & Neglect: The International Journal, 32,* 888–896. doi:10.1016/j.chiabu.2007.09.012

Kelly, J. B., & Johnson, M. P. (2008). Differentiation among types of intimate partner violence: Research update and implications for interventions. *Family Court Review, 46,* 476–499. doi:10.1111/j.1744-1617.2008.00215.x

Kendall, J., Pelucio, M., Casaletto, J., Thompson, K., Barnes, S., Pettit, E., & Aldrich, M. (2009). Impact of emergency department intimate partner violence intervention. *Journal of Interpersonal Violence, 24,* 280–306. doi:10.1177/0886260508316480

Kernic, M. A., Wolf, M. E., Holt, V. L., McKnight, B., Huebner, C. E., & Rivara, F. P. (2003). Behavioral problems among children whose mothers are abused by an intimate partner. *Child Abuse & Neglect: The International Journal, 27,* 1231–1246. doi:10.1016/j.chiabu.2002.12.001

Kernsmith, P. (2005). Exerting power or striking back: A gendered comparison of motivations for domestic violence perpetration. *Violence and Victims, 20,* 173–185. doi:10.1891/0886-6708.2005.20.2.173

Kessler, R. C., & Molnar, B. E., Feurer, L. D., & Appelbaum, M. (2001). Patterns and mental health predictors of domestic violence in the United States: Results from the National Comorbidity Survey. *International Journal of Law and Psychiatry, 24,* 487–508. doi:10.1016/S0160-2527(01)00080-2

Knickerbocker, L., Heyman, R. E., Slep, A., Jouriles, E. N., & McDonald, R. (2007). Co-occurrence of child and partner maltreatment definitions, prevalence, theory, and implications for assessment. *European Psychologist, 12,* 36–44. doi:10.1027/1016-9040.12.1.36

Kropp, P. R., Hart, S. D., Webster, C. D., & Eaves, D. (2008). *Manual for the Spousal Assault Risk Assessment Guide–2nd Edition.* Vancouver, British Columbia, Canada: ProActive ReSolutions.

Krug, E. G., Dahlberg, L. L., Mercy, J. A., Zwi, A. B., & Lozano, R. (Eds.). (2002). *World report on violence and health.* Geneva, Switzerland: World Health Organization. Retrieved from http://whqlibdoc.who.int/publications/2002/9241545615_eng.pdf

Kwong, M. J., Bartholomew, K., & Dutton, D. (1999). Gender differences in patterns of relationship violence in Alberta. *Canadian Journal of Behavioural Science, 31,* 150–160. doi:10.1037/h0087083

Langhinrichsen-Rohling, J., Huss, M., & Ramsey, S. (2000). The clinical utility of batterer typologies. *Journal of Family Violence, 15,* 37–53. doi:10.1023/A:1007597319826

Langhinrichsen-Rohling, J., McCullars, A., & Misra, T. (2012). Motivations for men and women's intimate partner violence perpetration: A comprehensive review. *Partner Abuse, 3,* 429–468. doi:10.1891/1946-6560.3.4.429

Langhinrichsen-Rohling, J., Misra, T., Selwyn, C., & Rohling, M. (2012). Rates of bi-directional versus uni-directional intimate partner violence across samples, sexual orientation, and race/ethnicities: A comprehensive review. *Partner Abuse, 3,* 199–230. doi:10.1891/1946-6560.3.2.199

Laroche, D. (2005). *Aspects of the context and consequences of domestic violence: Situational couple violence and intimate terrorism in Canada in 1999*. Institut de la statistique du Quebec. Available at http://www.stat.gouv.qc.ca

Lawrence, E., Orengo-Aguayo, R., Langer, A., & Brock, R. L. (2012). The impact and consequences of partner abuse on partners. *Partner Abuse, 3*, 406–428. doi:10.1891/1946-6560.3.4.406

Lehmann, P., & Simmons, C. (2009). *Strengths-based batterer intervention: A new paradigm in ending family violence*. New York, NY: Springer.

LeJeune, C., & Follette, V. (1994). Taking responsibility: Sex differences in reporting dating violence. *Journal of Interpersonal Violence, 9*, 133–140. doi:10.1177/088626094009001009

Lie, G. Y., Schilit, R., Bush, J., Montagne, M., & Reyes, L. (1991). Lesbians in currently aggressive relationships: How frequently do they report aggressive past relationships? *Violence and Victims, 6*, 121–135.

MacDonell, K. (2012). The combined and independent impact of witnessed interparental violence and child maltreatment. *Partner Abuse, 3*, 358–378. doi:10.1891/1946-6560.3.3.358

Maiuro, R., & Eberle, J. (2008). State standards for domestic violence perpetrator treatment: Current status, trends and recommendations. *Violence and Victims, 23*, 133–155. doi:10.1891/0886-6708.23.2.133

Maxwell, C., & Garner, J. (2012). The crime control effects of criminal sanctions for intimate partner violence. *Partner Abuse, 3*, 469–500. doi:10.1891/1946-6560.3.4.469

Maxwell, C., Garner, J., & Fagan, J. (2001). *The effects of arrest on intimate partner violence: New evidence from the spouse assault replication program*. Washington, DC: National Institute of Justice.

McCarroll, J. E., Ursano, R. J., Fan, Z., & Newby, J. H. (2004). Patterns of mutual and nonmutual spouse abuse in the US Army (1998–2002). *Violence and Victims, 19*, 453–468. doi:10.1891/vivi.19.4.453.64171

Medeiros, R. A., & Straus, M. A. (2007). Risk factors for physical violence between dating partners: Implications for gender-inclusive prevention and treatment of family violence. In J. Hamel & T. Nicholls (Eds.), *Family interventions in domestic violence* (pp. 59–85). New York, NY: Springer.

Merrill, G. S., & Wolfe, V. (2000). Battered gay men: An exploration of abuse, help seeking, and why they stay. *Journal of Homosexuality, 39*, 1–30. doi:10.1300/J082v39n02_01

Mihalic, S. W., & Elliott, D. (1997). A social learning theory model of marital violence. *Journal of Family Violence, 12*, 21–47. doi:10.1023/A:1021941816102

Moffitt, T. E., Caspi, A., Rutter, M., & Silva, P. A. (2001). *Sex differences in antisocial behaviour: Conduct disorder, delinquency, and violence in the Dunedin Longitudinal Study*. Cambridge, England: Cambridge University Press. doi:10.1017/CBO9780511490057

Morse, B. J. (1995). Beyond the Conflict Tactics Scale: Assessing gender differences in partner violence. *Violence and Victims, 10*, 251–272.

National Center for Injury Prevention and Control. (2003). *Costs of intimate partner violence against women in the United States*. Atlanta, GA: Centers for Disease Control and Prevention.

National Coalition Against Domestic Violence. (2008). *National directory of domestic violence programs*. Denver, CO: Author.

Nicholls, T., Pritchard, M., Reeves, K., & Hilterman, E. (2013). Risk assessment in intimate partner violence: A review of contemporary approaches. *Partner Abuse, 4*, 76–168. doi:10.1891/1946-6560.4.1.76

Nicholls, T. L., & Dutton, D. G. (2001). Abuse committed by women against male intimates. *Journal of Couples Therapy, 10*, 41–57. doi:10.1300/J036v10n01_04

Nicholls, T. L., Hilterman, E., & Tengrstrom, A. (2010). *Decision-Making in Abusive Relationships Interview (DIARI). Consulation version 1.0*. Port Conquitlam, British Columbia, Canada: Forensic Psychiatric Services Commission.

Niolon, P., Whitaker, D., Feder, L., Campbell, J., Wallinder, J., & Self-Brown, S. (2009). A multicomponent intervention to prevent partner violence within an existing services intervention. *Professional Psychology: Research and Practice, 40*, 264–271. doi:10.1037/a0013422

O'Keefe, M. (1996). The differential effects of family violence on adolescent adjustment. *Child & Adolescent Social Work Journal, 13*, 51–68. doi:10.1007/BF01876595

O'Leary, K. D., Smith Slep, A. M., & O'Leary, S. G. (2007). Multivariate models of men's and women's partner aggression. *Journal of Consulting and Clinical Psychology, 75*, 752–764. doi:10.1037/0022-006X.75.5.752

Pagelow, M. D. (1984). *Family violence*. New York, NY: Praeger.

Price, B. J., & Rosenbaum, A. (2009). Batterer intervention programs: A report from the field. *Violence and Victims, 24*, 757–770. doi:10.1891/0886-6708.24.6.757

Reid, R. J., Bonomi, A. E., Rivara, F. P., Fishman, P. A., Carrell, D. S., & Thompson, R. S. (2008). Intimate partner violence among men. *American Journal of Preventive Medicine, 34*, 478–485. doi:10.1016/j.amepre.2008.01.029

Rennison, C. M. (2003). *Intimate partner violence, 1993–2001*. Washington, DC: U.S. Department of Justice, Bureau of Justice Statistics.

Renzetti, C. M. (1989). Building a second closet: Third-party responses to victims of lesbian partner abuse. *Family Relations: Interdisciplinary Journal of Applied Family Studies, 38*, 157–163. doi:10.2307/583669

Renzetti, C. M. (1992). *Violent betrayal: Partner abuse in lesbian relationships*. Newbury Park, CA: Sage. doi:10.4135/9781483325767

Roberts, A. (2006). Classification typology and assessment of five levels of woman battering. *Journal of Family Violence, 21*, 521–527. doi:10.1007/s10896-006-9044-0

Russell, B. (2012). Effectiveness, victim safety, characteristics and enforcement of protective orders. *Partner Abuse, 3*, 531–552. doi:10.1891/1946-6560.3.4.531

Seelau, S. M., & Seelau, E. P. (2005). Gender-role stereotypes and perceptions of heterosexual, gay and lesbian domestic violence. *Journal of Family Violence, 20*, 363–371. doi:10.1007/s10896-005-7798-4

Sellers, B., Desmarais, S., & Tirotti, M. (in press). He said, she said: Content and framing of male and female-perpetrated partner violence in print news. *Violence and Victims*.

Serbin, L. A., Stack, D. M., De Genna, N., Grunzeweig, N., Temcheff, C. E., Schwartzman, A. E., & Ledingham, J. (2004). When aggressive girls become mothers: Problems in parenting, health, and development across two generations. In M. Putallaz & K. L. Bierman (Eds.), *Aggression, antisocial behavior, and violence among girls* (pp. 262–285). New York, NY: Guilford Press.

Shernock, S., & Russell, B. (2012). Gender and racial/ethnic differences in criminal justice decision making in intimate partner violence cases. *Partner Abuse, 3*, 501–530. doi:10.1891/1946-6560.3.4.501

Shorey, R. C., Meltzer, C., & Cornelius, T. L. (2010). Motivations for self-defensive aggression in dating relationships. *Violence and Victims, 25*, 662–676. doi:10.1891/0886-6708.25.5.662

Shupe, A., Stacey, W., & Hazlewood, L. (1987). *Violent men, violent couples: The dynamics of domestic violence*. New York, NY: Wiley.

Simon, T. R., Anderson, M., Thompson, M. P., Crosby, A. E., Shelley, G., & Sacks, J. J. (2001). Attitudinal acceptance of intimate partner violence among U.S. adults. *Violence and Victims, 16*, 115–126.

Simpson, L. E., Doss, B. D., Wheeler, J., & Christensen, A. (2007). Relationship violence among couples seeking therapy: Common couple violence or battering?. *Journal of Marital and Family Therapy, 33*, 270–283.

Sinha, M. (2012). *Family violence in Canada: A statistical profile, 2010*. Ottawa, Ontario, Canada: Statistics Canada.

Sorenson, S., & Taylor, C. (2005). Female aggression toward male intimate partners: An examination of social norms in a community-based sample. *Psychology of Women Quarterly, 29*, 78–96. doi:10.1111/j.1471-6402.2005.00170.x

Statistics Canada. (2004). *The General Social Survey—Cycle 18 victimization*. Ottawa, Ontario, Canada: Author.

Statistics Canada. (2011). *Family violence in Canada: A statistical profile*. Ottawa, Ontario, Canada: Author.

Sternberg, K. J., Lamb, M. E., Guterman, E., & Abbott, C. B. (2006). Effects of early and later family violence on children's behavior problems and depression: A longitudinal, multi-informant perspective. *Child Abuse & Neglect: The International Journal, 30*, 283–306. doi:10.1016/j.chiabu.2005.10.008

Stets, J. E., & Hammons, S. A. (2002). Gender, control, and marital commitment. *Journal of Family Issues, 23*, 3–25. doi:10.1177/0192513X02023001001

Stets, J. E., & Straus, M. A. (1989). The marriage license as a hitting license: A comparison of assaults in dating, cohabiting, and married couples. *Journal of Marriage and the Family, 31*, 233–239.

Stets, J. E., & Straus, M. A. (1990). Gender differences in reporting marital violence and its medical and psychological consequences. In M. A. Straus & R. J. Gelles (Eds.), *Physical violence in American families: Risk factors and adaptations to violence in 8,145 families* (pp. 151–165). New Brunswick, NJ: Transaction.

Stets, J., & Straus, M. (1992). The marriage license as a hitting license. In M. A. Straus & R. J. Gelles (Eds.), *Physical violence in American families* (pp. 227–244). New Brunswick, NJ: Transaction.

Stith, S., McCollum, E., & Rosen, K. (2011). *Couples therapy for domestic violence: Finding safe solutions*. Washington, DC: American Psychological Association. doi:10.1037/12329-000

Stith, S. M., Rosen, K. H., McCollum, E. E., & Thomsen, C. J. (2004). Treating intimate partner violence within intact couple relationships: Outcomes of multi-couple versus individual couple therapy. *Journal of Marital and Family Therapy, 30*, 305–318. doi:10.1111/j.1752-0606.2004.tb01242.x

Stith, S. M., Smith, D. B., Penn, C. E., Ward, D. B., & Tritt, D. (2004). Intimate partner physical abuse perpetration and victimization risk factors: A meta-analytic review. *Aggression and Violent Behavior: A Review Journal, 10*, 65–98. doi:10.1016/j.avb.2003.09.001.

Straus, M. A. (1976). Sexual inequality, cultural norms, and wife-beating. In E. C. Viano (Ed.), *Victims and society* (pp. 543–559). Washington, DC: Visage Press.

Straus, M. A. (1990). *Manual for the conflict tactics scale*. Durham: University of New Hampshire, Family Research Laboratory.

Straus, M. A. (1991). Conceptualization and measurement of battering: Implications for public policy. In M. Steinman (Ed.), *Woman battering: Policy responses* (pp. 19–47). Cincinnati, OH: Anderson. Retrieved from http://pubpages.unh.edu/~mas2/VB30.pdf

Straus, M. A. (1999a). The controversy over domestic violence by women: A methodological, theoretical, and sociology of science analysis. In X. Arriaga & S. Oskamp (Eds.), *Violence in intimate relationships* (pp. 17–44). Thousand Oaks, CA: Sage. Retrieved from http://pubpages.unh.edu/~mas2/CTS21.pdf

Straus, M. A. (1999b). The National Family Violence Surveys. In M. A. Straus & R. J. Gelles (Eds.), *Physical violence in American families: Risk factors and adaptations to violence in 8,145 families* (pp. 3–16). New Brunswick, NJ: Transaction.

Straus, M. A. (2004). Prevalence of violence against dating partners by male and female university students worldwide. *Violence Against Women, 10,* 790–811. doi:10.1177/1077801204265552

Straus, M. A. (2006). Future research on gender symmetry in physical assaults on partners. *Violence Against Women, 12,* 1086–1097. doi:10.1177/1077801206293335

Straus, M. A. (2008). Dominance and symmetry in partner violence by male and female university students in 32 nations. *Children and Youth Services Review, 30,* 252–275. doi:10.1016/j.childyouth.2007.10.004

Straus, M. A. (2009). Gender symmetry in partner violence: Evidence and implications for prevention and treatment. In D. J. Whitaker & J. R. Lutzker (Eds.), *Preventing partner violence: Research and evidence-based intervention strategies* (pp. 245–271). Washington, DC: American Psychological Association. doi:10.1037/11873-011

Straus, M. A. (2010). Thirty years of denying the evidence on gender symmetry in partner violence: Implications for prevention and treatment. *Partner Abuse, 1,* 332–362. doi:10.1891/1946-6560.1.3.332

Straus, M. A. (2011). Gender symmetry and mutuality in perpetration of clinical-level partner violence: Empirical evidence and implications for prevention and treatment. *Aggression and Violent Behavior, 16,* 279–288. doi:10.1016/j.avb.2011.04.010

Straus, M. A., & Gelles, R. J. (Eds.). (1999). *Physical violence in American families: Risk factors and adaptations to violence in 8,145 families.* New Brunswick, NJ: Transaction.

Straus, M. A., Gelles, R. J., & Steinmetz, S. K. (2006). *Behind closed doors: Violence in the American family.* New York, NY: Doubleday/Anchor. (Original work published 1981)

Straus, M. A., Hamby, S. L., Boney-McCoy, S., & Sugarman, D. B. (1996). The revised Conflict Tactics Scales (CTS-2). *Journal of Family Issues, 17,* 283–316. doi:10.1177/019251396017003001

Straus, M. A., & Ramirez, I. L. (2007). Gender symmetry in prevalence, severity, and chronicity of physical aggression against dating partners by university students in Mexico and USA. *Aggressive Behavior, 33,* 281–290. doi:10.1002/ab.20199

Taft, A. J., Watson, L. F., & Lee, C. (2004). Violence against young Australian women and association with reproductive events: A cross-sectional analysis of a national population sample. *Australian and New Zealand Journal of Public Health, 28,* 324–329. doi:10.1111/j.1467-842X.2004.tb00438.x

Tetterton, S., & Farnsworth, E. (2011). Older women and intimate partner violence: Effective interventions. *Journal of Interpersonal Violence, 26,* 2929–2942. doi:10.1177/0886260510390962

Thurman v. City of Torrington, 595 F.Supp. 1521 (1984).

Tjaden, P., & Thoennes, N. (1998). *Prevalence, incidence, and consequences of violence against women: Findings from the National Violence Against Women Survey.* Washington, DC: US Department of Justice. Retrieved from www.ncjrs.gov/pdffiles/172837.pdf

Tjaden, P., & Thoennes, N. (2000). Prevalence and consequences of male-to-female and female-to-male intimate partner violence as measured by the National Violence Against Women Survey. *Violence Against Women, 6,* 142–161. doi:10.1177/10778010022181769

Tjaden, P., Thoennes, N., & Allison, C. J. (1999). Comparing violence over the life span in samples of same-sex and opposite-sex cohabitants. *Violence and Victims, 14,* 413–425.

Turell, S. T. (2000). A descriptive analysis of same-sex relationship violence for a diverse sample. *Journal of Family Violence, 15,* 281–293. doi:10.1023/A:1007505619577

Violence Against Women Act of 1994, Pl. 103-322, 103rd Cong. (1994).

Walby, S. (2004). *The cost of domestic violence: Research summary.* London, England: UK Department of Trade.

Waldner-Haugrud, L. K., Gratch, L., & Magruder, B. (1997). Victimization and perpetration rates of violence in gay and lesbian relationships: Gender issues explored. *Violence and Victims, 12,* 173–184.

Walker, L. (1979). *The battered woman.* New York, NY: Harper & Row.

Walker, L. (1983). *The battered woman syndrome.* New York, NY: Springer.

Walker, L. (2009). *The battered woman syndrome* (3rd ed.). New York, NY: Springer.

Walker, L. A. (1984). Battered women, psychology, and public policy. *American Psychologist, 39,* 1178–1182. doi:10.1037/0003-066X.39.10.1178

Washington Post. (2012, April). *Reauthorize the Violence Against Women Act.* Retrieved from http://articles.washingtonpost.com/2012-04-23/opinions/35453699_1_immigrant-women-violence-against-women-act-sexual-violence

Waters, H., Hyder, A., Rajkotia, Y., Basu, S., Rehwinkel, J. A., & Butchart, A. (2004). *The economic dimensions of interpersonal violence*. Geneva, Switzerland: Department of Injuries and Violence Prevention, World Health Organization.

Whitaker, D. J., Haileyesus, T., Swahn, M., & Saltzman, L. S. (2007). Differences in frequency of violence and reported injury between relationships with reciprocal and nonreciprocal intimate partner violence. *American Journal of Public Health, 97,* 941–947. doi:10.2105/AJPH.2005.079020

Whitaker, D. J., Murphy, C. M., Eckhardt, C. I., Hodges, A. E., & Cowart, M. (2013). Effectiveness of primary prevention efforts of intimate partner violence. *Partner Abuse, 4,* 175–195.

Williams, S., & Frieze, I. (2005). Patterns of violence relationships, psychological distress, and marital satisfaction in a national sample of men and women. *Sex Roles, 52,* 771–784. doi:10.1007/s11199-005-4198-4

Wilson, M., & Daly, M. (1992). Who kills whom in spouse killings? On the exceptional sex ratio of spousal homicides in the United States. *Criminology, 30,* 189–216. doi:10.1111/j.1745-9125.1992.tb01102.x

Wolfe, D. A., Wekerle, C., Scott, K., Straatman, A. L., Grasley, C., & Reitzel-Jaffe, D. (2003). Dating violence prevention with at-risk youth: A controlled outcome evaluation. *Journal of Consulting and Clinical Psychology, 71,* 279–291. doi:10.1037/0022-006X.71.2.279

World Health Organization. (1997). *Violence against women: A priority health issue*. Geneva, Switzerland: Author. Retrieved from http://www.who.int/gender/violence/prioreng/en/index.html

World Health Organization. (2005). *WHO multi-country study on women's health and domestic violence against women: Summary report of initial results on prevalence, health outcomes and women's responses*. Geneva, Switzerland: Author. Retrieved from http://www.who.int/gender/violence/who_multicountry_study/summary_report/summary_report_English2.pdf

World Health Organization. (2006). *WHO facts on intimate partner violence and alcohol*. Geneva, Switzerland: Author. Retrieved from http://www.who.int/violence_injury_prevention/violence/world_report/factsheets/fs_intimate.pdf

Wu, V., Huff, H., & Bhandari, M. (2010). Pattern of physical injury associated with intimate partner violence in women presenting to the emergency department: A systematic review and meta-analysis. *Trauma, Violence, & Abuse, 11,* 71–82. doi:10.1177/1524838010367503

Zhang, T., Hoddenbagh, J., McDonald, S., & Scrim, K. (2012). *An estimation of the economic impact of spousal violence in Canada, 2009*. Ottawa, Ontario, Canada: Department of Justice Canada.

Zink, T., Jacobson, C., Pabst, S., Regan, S., & Fisher, B. (2006). A lifetime of intimate partner violence: Coping strategies of older women. *Journal of Interpersonal Violence, 21,* 634–651. doi:10.1177/0886260506286878

APPLICATIONS OF FORENSIC PSYCHOLOGY IN CIVIL CASES

CHAPTER 13

CHILD CUSTODY AND ACCESS

Marc J. Ackerman and Jonathan W. Gould

This chapter is designed to introduce the reader to important concepts related to child custody evaluations. The chapter is not intended as an in-depth discussion of all relevant issues in the child custody arena. The chapter will, however, direct the reader to published peer-reviewed literature, research, and standards that will provide a greater in-depth discussion of the relevant topics.

IMPORTANCE OF THE PROBLEM

Fifty years ago, Thomas Kuhn (1962) wrote *The Structure of Scientific Revolution*, in which he defined and popularized the concept of a "paradigm shift" (p. 10). Kuhn argued that scientific advancement is not evolutionary but is a "series of peaceful interludes punctuated by intellectually violent revolutions," and in those revolutions, "one conceptual world view is replaced by another." A paradigm shift is a change from one way of thinking to another. It is a revolution, a transformation, a metamorphosis.

In normal periods of scientific exploration, a particular way of viewing the world dominates. This is called a paradigm. The function of a paradigm is to supply puzzles for scientists to solve and to provide tools for their solution. A crisis in science arises when confidence is lost in the ability of the paradigm to solve particularly worrying puzzles (Zalta, 2011).

Kuhn (1962) argued that a paradigm shift does not spontaneously happen; it results from the influence of agents of change. We believe that there has been a paradigm shift occurring in psychology and law over the past several decades. Custody evaluators are just becoming aware of the importance of this paradigm shift. The agents of change in this shift include changes in the admissibility of scientific evidence, changes in case law, changes in methodology, changes in content-specific areas of custody-related factors, and changes in interdisciplinary cooperation and understanding of child custody concerns.

The legal system has moved from a common law–based notion of blind acceptance of opinions offered by expert witnesses to a critical examination of the reliability of procedures that are used to generate the data on which expert opinions are based (Mnookin & Gross, 2003). Judges and attorneys struggle to understand the process of scientific investigation (Gatowski et al., 2001; R. F. Kelly & Ramsey, 2007), while rules of evidence, case law, and legal scholarship place increasing emphasis on the importance of scientifically informed expert opinions (Faigman, Saks, Sanders, & Cheng, 2008).

An important element of the paradigm shift is its focus on evidence-based practice and the concomitant awareness of the lack of usefulness of clinical intuition and judgment when it is offered as the basis for expert testimony (Faigman et al., 2008). *Ipse dixit* is dead.[1] Long live emphasis on scientifically informed expert opinions!

---

[1]*Ipse dixit* is Latin for "he himself said it," meaning that the only proof we have of the fact is that this person said it; an assertion made but not proved; an unsupported statement that rests solely on the authority of the individual who makes it.

http://dx.doi.org/10.1037/14461-013
APA Handbook of Forensic Psychology: Vol. 1. Individual and Situational Influences in Criminal and Civil Contexts,
B. L. Cutler and P. A. Zapf (Editors-in-Chief)

Science is "a set of systematic safeguards against confirmation bias, that is, the tendency to seek out evidence consistent with our hypotheses and to deny, dismiss, or distort evidence that runs counter to them" (Lilienfeld, 2010, p. 282). B. F. Skinner (1953) stated that science requires a "willingness to accept facts even when they are opposed to wishes" (p. 12). Other scholars have talked about the purpose of science as "bending over backwards to prove ourselves wrong" (Feynman, 1985, as cited in Lilienfeld, 2010, p. 282).

Chopra and Mlodinow (2011) expressed the tension between science and clinical intuition well, writing:

> Scientists are often guided by their intuition and subjective feelings, but they recognize the need for another step: verification. Science proceeds in a loop of observation, theory, and experiment. The loop is repeated until the theory and the empirical evidence are in harmony. But this method would fail if concepts were not precisely defined and experiments were not rigorously controlled. These elements of the scientific method are crucial, and it is they that determine the difference between good science and bad science, or between science and pseudoscience. (p. 14)

Gone are the days when experts may opine on issues for which there is no scientific foundation. Expert opinions must be based on information that is derived from reliable procedures.

RELEVANT PSYCHOLOGICAL THEORY AND PRINCIPLES

Increasingly, mental health professionals are being asked to base their written work products and oral testimony on rules governing "evidence-based practice" (Greeno, 2001). Whether one is providing clinical or forensic mental health services, there is an increasing expectation that mental health professionals base their methods and techniques on research that supports their efficacy (American Psychological Association [APA], 2010a; Tippins & Wittmann, 2005a, 2005b).

In *Daubert v. Merrell Dow Pharmaceuticals, Inc.* (1993), the U.S. Supreme Court declared,

> Unlike an ordinary witness, an expert is permitted wide latitude to offer opinions, including those that are not based on firsthand knowledge or observation. Presumably, this relaxation of the usual requirement of firsthand knowledge . . . is premised on an assumption that the expert's opinion will have a reliable basis in the knowledge and experience of his discipline. (p. 592)

The judge's responsibility under *Daubert* is to "determine nothing less than whether the experts' testimony reflects 'scientific knowledge,' whether their findings are 'derived by the scientific method' and whether their work product amounts to 'good science'" (pp. 1311, 1315).

R. F. Kelly and Ramsey (2007, 2009) argued that the jurisprudence of family law is increasingly influenced by social science research and empirical outcomes. We believe that both law[2] and psychology[3] require that expert testimony must rest on the use of reliable procedures that provide a foundation for trustworthy opinions that are relevant to the task at hand. Therefore, we posit that there is both an ethical requirement[4] and a literature-based argument that forensic mental health professionals (a) base their methods and procedures on research that supports their efficacy and (b) show a logical relationship between the data that are generated by the evaluation procedures and the opinions that are offered to the court (Heilbrun, Grisso, & Goldstein, 2009; R. F. Kelly & Ramsey, 2007).

---

[2]The *Daubert* Court declared, "[A]n expert's testimony both rests on a reliable foundation and is relevant to the task at hand" (p. 597).

[3]APA's (2010a) Ethical Standard 9.01a states: "Psychologists base the opinions contained in their recommendations, reports, and diagnostic or evaluative statements, including forensic testimony, on information and techniques sufficient to substantiate their findings" (p. 1,071).

[4]APA's (2010a) Ethical Standard 2.04 states: "Psychologists' work is based upon established scientific and professional knowledge of the discipline" (p. 1,064).

A careful reading of both psychologists' ethical responsibilities and best practice aspirations (APA, 2010a, 2010b, 2013; Association of Family and Conciliation Courts [AFCC], 2007) and documents reflecting the current state of the art in forensic mental health and law clearly indicate that child custody evaluators need to base their work products on scientifically informed methods and peer-reviewed, published behavioral science research (Ackerman & Kane, 2011; Amundson, Duda, & Gill, 2000; Austin, 2001; Bow & Quinnell, 2004; Galatzer-Levy, Kraus, & Galatzer-Levy, 2009; Gould & Martindale, 2007; Otto, Buffington-Vollum, & Edens, 2003; Rohrbaugh, 2008; Roseby, 1995; Stahl, 2010; Wingspread Conference, 2001).

Transparency Principle

Child custody evaluations are often conducted in an atmosphere of distrust and animosity (Martindale, 2004) that is characterized by high conflict between parents and, at times, between attorneys. "In order to be effective, evaluators must utilize procedures designed to avoid fueling suspicion and contributing to the acrimony" (Martindale, 2004, p. 33).

Everything that an evaluator does should reflect a fundamental commitment toward being *transparent*. This means that everything that an evaluator has in his or her file should be available to both attorneys and the court for review. An evaluator should be "an open book", and the guiding principle should be that the evaluator's file and the manner in which the evaluator formulated opinions are open to scrutiny. An evaluator needs to be prepared to discuss hypotheses that were considered and discarded as well as to discuss hypotheses that were considered and were included in the final opinion.

Martindale (2004) wrote that the term *transparency*

is intended to describe a philosophy from which a pattern of professional behavior logically follows. The philosophy guides us in our roles as evaluators and, subsequently, in our roles as testifying experts. (1) *As evaluators*, in order to gather information helpful to triers of fact and to the families being assessed, forensic examiners

must be unencumbered by personal or philosophical agendas; must be committed to a balanced approach in their work; and, must be alert to phenomena that adversely affect decision making. (2) *As testifying experts*, in order to be effective, forensic examiners must be credible; must recognize that credibility is earned and that complete openness is one means by which an expert establishes credibility; and, must respect the rights of those wishing to question an expert's opinions and the manner in which they were formulated. The pattern of behavior that flows from the stated philosophy includes (1) prior to commencing an evaluation, actively disclosing any prior or current relationships with the participants; (2) being diligent in the creation and maintenance of one's records; and, (3) producing, in response to a legally permissible request, the complete contents of one's file in the matter being litigated. (p. 33)

Increasing Consensus

There are fewer and fewer areas of professional disagreement in the literature addressing how to conduct a child custody assessment. In fact, there is an emerging consensus about how evaluations should be conducted (Ackerman, 2006; Ackerman & Kane, 2011; Galatzer-Levy et al., 2009; Gould, 2006; Gould & Martindale, 2007, 2013; Kirkpatrick, 2004; Rohrbaugh, 2008; Stahl, 2010). There is also an emerging consensus about the critical role of science and the scientific process in crafting child custody evaluations (Ackerman & Kane, 2011; Bow & Quinnell, 2004; Drozd, Olesen, & Siani, in press; Galatzer-Levy et al., 2009). There continues to be a strong research focus on factors that are associated with children's postdivorce adjustment (Amato & Gilbreth, 1999; Buchanan & Jahromi, 2008; Deutsch & Pruett, 2009; Pruett, Williams, Insabella, & Little, 2003) and the application of these factors to the development of parenting plans (Kuehnle & Drozd, 2012). Judges and attorneys have reported that the information that is drawn from a child custody evaluation can be a source of helpful information (Ackerman & Kane, 2011; Bow & Quinnell, 2004), often leading to an increased opportunity to settle a custody dispute. Recently, however, the view has been expressed that the more that attorneys and judges become aware of what a competently crafted child custody evaluation ought to include, there is an increased awareness of, and frustration about, the variability that exists in the quality of child custody evaluations (Feinberg & Gould, 2012).

Voices of Caution

Some scholars have questioned the usefulness of mental health professionals' participation in child custody evaluations (Emery, Otto, & O'Donahue, 2005), and others have questioned the scientific integrity of expert opinions that directly address the ultimate issue of legal and physical custody based on those evaluations (Tippins & Wittman, 2005a). Still other scholars are frustrated by the variable quality of child custody evaluations (Melton, Petrila, Poythress, & Slobogin, 1987, 1997, 2007; O'Donohue & Bradley, 1999; Weisz, 1999) and by the lack of sufficiency of research support for expert opinions about child custody determination (Melton et al., 2007; Tippins & Wittmann, 2005a, 2005b).

Importance of Scholarly Debate

Scholarly debate about differences in theory, interpretation of research findings, and alternate approaches to professional practice are part of the necessary tensions in an evolving field. Behavioral scientists and legal scholars within the child custody assessment arena need to participate in and encourage academic debates about alternate, rival conceptual models of theory and practice. In order to minimize advocacy over scholarship, individuals who are involved in scholarly debate need to practice systematic self-reflection (Westen & Weinberger, 2005) so as to minimize the potential effects of confirmatory bias on their thinking and on their teaching of others. As noted by Wood and Nezworski (2005),

> The history of science can be viewed as a constant and largely successful struggle to overcome confirmatory biases. The scientific method is a tool to help people

progress toward the truth despite their all-too-human susceptibility to confirmation bias and other errors. (p. 657)

Self-reflection and knowledge of the tricks that our minds can play on us are among the best known ways to lessen the effects that various biases have on our thinking (Westen & Weinberger, 2005).

Changes in the Child Custody Field

Our field of study continues to grow at a rapid pace. There continues to be an increasing consensus about the general methodology that is used in custody evaluations (Ackerman & Kane, 2011; Ackerman & Pritzl, 2011; Bow & Quinnell, 2002; Kirkpatrick, 2004). There is an increasingly vital integration of information from subdisciplines within psychology and an integration taken from disciplines outside of psychology into mainstream child custody literature (e.g., Galatzer-Levy et al., 2009; Gould & Martindale, 2007; Kuehnle & Drozd, 2012). There continues to be a healthy, dynamic tension between law and psychology as they are applied to child custody evaluations (R. F. Kelly & Ramsey, 2009; Ramsey & Kelly, 2007). Some scholars have provided useful ideas about how to teach attorneys and judges to be better consumers of mental health research (Drozd et al., in press; R. F. Kelly & Ramsey, 2009), and some attorneys have become involved in training mental health professionals how to better understand rules of evidence as they are applied to child custody work (Tippins, 2012).

Heilbrun et al. (2009) wrote that "a forensic assessment is guided by the specific legal question facing the legal decision maker. For every type of FMHA [forensic mental health assessment], there is a body of law controlling the legal decision to be made" (p. 12). Among the many challenges in child custody work is that the legal standard of the "best interests of the child" is poorly defined.

The Best Interests of the Child Standard

Each state legislature controls its own child custody law, and custody laws vary considerably from state to state. Some states have a set of statutory criteria that delineate specific factors to be considered when making a child custody decision, other states provide no statutory guidance defining the best interests of the child, and some states have case law that provides guidance in defining factors associated with the best interests of the child.

Forty states and the District of Columbia have statutes in which the factors to be considered in examining the best interests standard are identified.[5] In six states, there is case law in which factors to be considered are addressed.[6] In four states, the identification of the factors to be considered is left to the judge.[7]

Despite the lack of consistent guidance in defining the concept of the best interests of the child, each of the 50 states plus the District of Columbia has a law that indicates that judicial decisions are to be based on the best interests of the child (Cotter, 2006). The underlying idea is that judicial determinations need to be based on each child's unique present and future best interests (Elrod & Spector, 2004).

A frequently cited and as yet unsolved problem in the child custody area is the lack of uniform consensus about the meaning of the term *best interests of the child* (Elrod & Spector, 2004; Gould, 1998, 2006; Gould & Martindale, 2008). Emery et al. (2005) wrote,

> Individualized decision making is appealing on the surface, but we are deeply concerned that a standard vague enough to be interpreted differently for each family that comes before the court (a) encourages parents to enter into custody disputes (thereby increasing parental conflict), because the outcome of a court hearing is difficult to predict; and (b) allows for bias to intrude in the exercise of judicial discretion. (pp. 5–6)

Emery et al. (2005) argued that "the law has interpreted children's best interests to be primarily their best psychological interests (as opposed to other possibilities such as their economic, educational, or medical interests)" (p. 6). Given the lack of consensus in the behavioral science literature about the definition of the psychological best interests of the child, one cannot conduct a child custody assessment without operationally defining those areas of parent–child functioning that are of concern in each family that is under examination (Gould, 1998, 1999, 2006; Gould & Martindale, 2008). Defining the questions that guide the evaluator in his or her investigation is the lynchpin of a well-designed child custody evaluation (Gould & Martindale, 2008) and will be discussed in detail later in this chapter.

In the remainder of this section, we discuss the changes in rules of evidence as they pertain to expert witness testimony.

Changes in Rules of Evidence and Expert Testimony

Among the most important agents of change in the legal system that have triggered the paradigm shift in child custody evaluations are the Supreme Court's *Daubert* decision and its progeny as well as the concomitant changes to the Federal Rules of Evidence (FRE) that were adopted in 2000. These changes in the legal system focused greater attention on the need for reliable and valid methods and procedures to be employed when generating data that are relied on by expert witnesses in the development of their opinions (Gatowski et al., 2001). These changes in law and rules of evidence were also intended to rid the court of junk science (Faigman et al., 2008).

The changes to the FRE for qualification of an expert witness and the admissibility of expert testimony acknowledge the importance of reliable methodology; that is, an increased focus on the importance of the scientific process (Gould & Martindale, in press).

Expert witnesses need to be qualified by the court in a particular field. FRE 702 provides the court with direction about who is and who is not an expert.

---

[5]The information cited about how different states that addressed the best interests of the child standard was compiled by Milfred "Bud" Dale, PhD, JD, and was used with his permission (personal communication, October 20, 2011). Those states are Alabama, Alaska, Arizona, Colorado, Connecticut, Delaware, Florida, Georgia, Hawaii, Iowa, Idaho, Illinois, Indiana, Kansas, Kentucky, Louisiana, Maine, Michigan, Minnesota, Missouri, Montana, Nebraska, Nevada, New Hampshire, New Jersey, New Mexico, North Dakota, Ohio, Oklahoma, Oregon, Pennsylvania, Tennessee, Texas, Utah, Vermont, Virginia, Washington, West Virginia, Wisconsin, and Wyoming.

[6]Those states are Maryland, Mississippi, New York, Rhode Island, South Carolina, and South Dakota.

[7]Those states are Arkansas, California, Massachusetts, and North Carolina.

Helpfulness. Examination of the commentary regarding Rule 702 suggests that the language, "assist the trier of fact," means that the testimony needs to be helpful and relevant. That is, the information must be sufficiently tied to the facts of the case so that it will assist the judge in resolving a factual issue.

Valid scientific inquiry. FRE 702 "requires a valid scientific connection to the pertinent inquiry as a precondition to admissibility" (*Daubert*, 1993, pp. 591–592). Rule 702 requires that an expert be qualified and that the content of the expert's testimony be scientifically valid (Faigman et al., 2008). Notice the similarity in language between Rule 702 and the APA's (2010a) Ethical Standards 2.01 (a) and 9.01 (a).

FRE 702 contains two other requirements. The rule requires an examination of the qualifications of the witness. Courts have interpreted this qualifications requirement in a flexible manner so that the court can examine the expert's claimed expertise against the demands of the testimony (Faigman et al., 2008). The admissibility of expert testimony is challenged at times in court. The court will generally rule that the issue goes to the weight of the testimony and not to the admissibility.

The court also has responsibility to determine whether the expert testimony is reliable. The *Daubert* Court wrote,

> The trial judge must determine at the outset . . . whether the expert is proposing to testify to (1) scientific knowledge that (2) will assist the trier of fact to understand or determine a fact in issue. This entails a preliminary assessment of either the reasoning or methodology underlying the testimony as scientifically valid and/ or whether that reasoning or methodology properly can be applied to the facts in issue. (pp. 592–593)

Prior to the *Daubert* decision, expert witness testimony was admissible if its theory and methods were generally accepted within the relevant scientific community. In 1923, the U.S. District Court for the District of Columbia announced the *Frye* test (*Frye v. United States*, 1923), which required a proponent of scientific evidence to establish that the expert witness's theory and method were generally accepted within the relevant scientific community (Faigman et al., 2008; Hunt, 2010). In *Frye*, the Court declared,

> Just when a scientific principle or discovery crosses the line between the experimental and demonstrable stages is difficult to define. Somewhere in this twilight zone the evidential force of the principle must be recognized, and while courts will go a long way in admitting expert testimony deduced from a well-recognized scientific principle or discovery, the thing from which the deduction is made must be sufficiently established to have gained general acceptance in the particular field in which it belongs. (p. 1014)

The *Frye* test involves a two-step analysis: (1) defining the relevant scientific community, and (2) evaluating the testimony and publications to determine the existence of a general consensus. At its core, the purpose of the *Frye* test is to ensure that "the scientific theory or discovery from which an expert derives an opinion is reliable" (*Hildwin v. State*, 2006, p. 792).

The *Daubert* Court made several changes to the rule governing the admissibility of scientific evidence. First, *Daubert* changed who determined what were and what were not reliable scientific theories and methods. The *Frye* rule identified the professional community as the gatekeeper of reliable scientific theories and methods. Concerns had been raised by lower courts around the country about the lack of clarity surrounding the gatekeeping role of the professional community. *Daubert* changed the gatekeeper function to the court and included as one of its flexible criteria the community standard component of *Frye*.

A second change brought about by the *Daubert* Court was a nonexclusive set of criteria for trial courts to consider in assessing the reliability of scientific expert testimony. The Court made it quite clear that it did "not presume to set out a definitive checklist or test" and that "general observations" (Daubert, 1993, p. 593) were being offered. Those observations, which we believe are best conceptualized as criteria, are

- whether the expert's technique or theory can be or has been tested—that is, whether the expert's theory can be challenged in some objective sense, or whether it is instead simply a subjective, conclusory approach that cannot reasonably be assessed for reliability;
- whether the technique or theory has been subject to peer review and publication;
- the known or potential rate of error of the technique or theory when it is applied;
- the existence and maintenance of standards and controls; and
- whether the technique or theory has been generally accepted in the scientific community.

In *Kumho Tire Co. v. Carmichael* (1999), the Supreme Court held that these nonexclusive criteria might also be useful in assessing the reliability of nonscientific expert testimony, depending on "the particular circumstances of the particular case at issue" (p. 1175). The *Kumho* Court gave trial courts "considerable leeway in deciding in a particular case how to go about determining whether particular expert testimony is reliable" (pp. 1167, 1176). No single criterion is necessarily dispositive of the reliability of a particular expert's testimony.

In 1997, in *General Electric Co. v. Joiner* (1997), the Supreme Court declared,

> Conclusions and methodology are not entirely distinct from one another. Trained experts commonly extrapolate from existing data. But nothing in either *Daubert* or the Federal Rules of Evidence requires a district court to admit opinion evidence that is connected to the existing data only by the *ipse dixit* of the expert. A court may conclude that there is simply too great an analytical gap between the data and the opinions proffered. (p. 519)

Thus, expert testimony can no longer be admissible when the opinions are based on the clinical experience or intuition of the witness. Expert testimony must have its basis in peer-reviewed literature and/or data that have been drawn from scientific methods. We cannot emphasize enough that currently, testimony *must* be based on scientific research or scientific literature and not on the expert's personal opinion or unsupported professional interpretation of literature or research.

Another agent of change is the rule of evidence that governs the bases of expert testimony. Where Rule 702 addresses *who* is an expert, Rule 703 addresses the *bases of opinion* testimony by experts. Once an expert has been qualified to offer testimony, then the court turns its attention to the methods that were used by the expert to gather the data on which the expert opinions are based. Rule 703 declares:

> The facts or data in the particular case upon which an expert bases an opinion or inference may be those perceived by or made known to the expert at or before the hearing. If of a type reasonably relied upon by experts in the particular field in forming opinions or inferences upon the subject, the facts or data need not be admissible in evidence in order for the opinion or inference to be admitted. Facts or data that are otherwise inadmissible shall not be disclosed to the jury by the proponent of the opinion or inference unless the court determines that their probative value in assisting the jury to evaluate the expert's opinion substantially outweighs their prejudicial effect.

Expert opinions that are admissible at trial may be drawn from three possible sources. First, the expert may have firsthand observational experience. Second, expert testimony may be based on information that is presented in the form of a hypothesis or information that was obtained during the trial proceedings.

The third source identified by Rule 703 is the presentation of data to the expert outside of court and other than by his own perception. The child custody evaluation is an example of this third source. Custody evaluators often gather information from multiple independent sources prior to forming an opinion about the case. Rule 703 anticipates that the gathering of such information is part of the usual and customary practices among evaluators. Attention is directed to the reliability and general acceptance of the techniques employed rather than to less productive inquiries such as whether hearsay is involved. Only those data that are "of a type reasonably relied upon by experts in the particular field" are admitted into evidence.

Right tool for the right job.   Another legal agent of change that has affected child custody evaluation training and practice is drawn from case law regarding employment discrimination. In 1971, the U.S. Supreme Court handed down a decision in a matter that was only remotely related to custody evaluations (*Griggs v. Duke Power*), yet the ruling contained an admonition that custody evaluators would be wise to heed. The *Griggs* Court declared that evaluator assessment "devices and mechanisms" (p. 436) must be demonstrably reasonable measures of job performance. Individuals who employ psychological tests must "measure" and describe only those aspects of the person that relate directly to the job for which the person is being evaluated.

The lesson that custody evaluators can take from the *Griggs* decision is that our attempts to assess the characteristics that bear directly on parenting are more likely to meet with success if we conceptualize parenting as a job and focus our attention on those attributes, behaviors, attitudes, and skills that are reliably related to the demands of the job. Examining an attribute in the absence of evidence of its connection to parenting effectiveness leaves an evaluator open to criticism on several fronts (Gould & Martindale, in press).

The legal agents of change that have contributed to the paradigm shift in child custody assessment include:

■ the *Daubert* trilogy and its focus on expert testimony needing to be based on data that are obtained from the use of reliable methods and procedures;

■ the need for expert testimony to be logically connected to the data and to the professional literature;

■ the inadmissibility of expert testimony based on the ipse dixit ("because I said so") of the witness;

■ the qualification of experts who have specialized knowledge in the issues before the court; and

■ the use of psychological tests that measure and describe only those aspects of the person that relate directly to aspects of parenting behavior or parent-to-parent communication.

RESEARCH REVIEW

During the 1980s and early 1990s, the literature describing how to conduct child custody evaluations was in its infancy. Texts and peer-reviewed articles describing the evaluation process identified no particular underlying model that could be used to guide an evaluator's behavior or methodology. Some authors suggested that clinical evaluation models be applied to child custody assessment (Skafte, 1985; Stahl, 1994), and others introduced an evidence-based approach to child custody evaluations (Ackerman, 1995, 2006; Schutz, Dixon, Lindenberger, & Ruther, 1989). Through the 1990s and 2000s, authors encouraged evaluators to employ forensic methods and procedures (Ackerman, 2006; Ackerman & Kane, 2011; Gould, 1998, 2006) and urged evaluators to be guided by the forensic model as it is applied to child custody evaluations (Gould & Martindale, 2007; Martindale & Gould, 2004).

The need to use reliable procedures in conducting child custody evaluations was first described by Schutz et al. (1989). Schutz et al. emphasized the need for evaluation procedures to be tied to reliable procedures and for expert opinions to be based on peer-reviewed literature that was drawn from the behavioral sciences.

Grisso (1986, 2003) wrote that forensic evaluations should focus on functional abilities. Applying this concept to child custody evaluations, a custody evaluation should be an evaluation of functional parenting abilities.

Otto and Edens (2003) elaborated on Grisso's (1986, 2003) functional abilities model by including an analysis of functional components, causal components, and interactive components in a parenting evaluation. Functional components were defined as a parent's characteristics and abilities to care for children. The focus of a child custody evaluation was defined as an examination of the caretaker's child-rearing abilities. Otto and Edens wrote that "forensic assessments that describe only diagnoses, personality characteristics, or general intellectual capacities of parents and fail to assess the caretaker's child-rearing abilities are of little value" (p. 250).

The competency concept requires assessment of the caretaker's knowledge, understanding, beliefs, values, attitudes, and behaviors pertaining to parenting each child. Otto and Edens (2003) argued that in order to adequately complete a competency-based evaluation, the evaluator must be clear about the specific functional abilities being measured and how an assessment of those abilities relates to this particular parent's parenting competencies.

Many authors have extended the forensic assessment model that is used in other areas of criminal and civil forensic evaluation practice to child custody work (Ackerman, 2006; Ackerman & Kane, 2011; Galatzer-Levy et al., 2009; Gould, 1998, 2006; Gould & Martindale, 2007; Rohrbaugh, 2008; Schutz et al., 1989). Gould (1998, 2006) and Ackerman (2006) argued that the criteria articulated by the Supreme Court in *Daubert* were relevant and should be considered when crafting a child custody evaluation. Whether or not a particular state adopted the *Daubert* criteria or a *Frye* standard for expert testimony, these authors suggested that the *Daubert* criteria, which stress reliance on scientifically derived knowledge and crafting evaluation procedures that emphasize scientific process, would likely result in a more reliable, relevant, and helpful work product for the Court, thereby reflecting the usefulness of the psychological sciences as applied to child custody decision making.

Conceptual differences between a scientifically informed model and a clinical-judgment informed model of child custody assessment began to be examined. Gould and Stahl (2000) argued that child custody evaluations should employ the scientific process as articulated in the literature on forensic methods and procedures (e.g., Melton et al., 1987, 1997, 2007) and the application of empirically based research findings to the development of developmentally appropriate parenting plans. They also opined that science without context provides a meaningless report. Scientific process and empirical findings that have been drawn from peer-reviewed literature need to be integrated into an advisory report through the judicious use of clinical judgment.

> Although competent and well-intentioned practitioners may differ in how they conduct a proper child custody evaluation, it is necessary that each practitioner logically, coherently, and competently defend his or her approach to a child custody evaluation from within the framework of the behavioral science literature. (Gould & Stahl, 2000, p. 398)

Martindale and Gould (2004) integrated the components of a forensic model and applied them to child custody assessment, which addressed the relationship between psychological ethics and scientifically informed methodology that is critical to a competently crafted child custody advisory report. As applied to child custody evaluations, the essential components of the forensic model are as follows:

- The evaluator's role, the purpose of the evaluation, and the focus of the evaluation are defined by the court.
- Where possible, the evaluator obtains (at the outset) a list of specific psycholegal issues concerning which the court seeks advisory input.
- The evaluator conducts all professional activities in accordance with regulations and/or guidelines that have been promulgated by state regulatory boards.
- The procedures employed by the evaluator are informed by the psychologists' Code of Ethics (APA, 2010a), the *Specialty Guidelines for Forensic Psychology* (APA, 2013), APA's (2010b) *Guidelines for Child Custody Evaluations*, and similar documents that have been developed by organizations that conceptualize the child custody evaluation as an inherently forensic psychological activity.

■ The selection of assessment instruments is guided by the 1985 and 1999 editions of the *Standards for Educational and Psychological Testing* (American Educational Research Association, APA, & National Council on Measurement in Education, 1985, 1999), and particular attention is given to the established reliability and validity of instruments that are under consideration (Heilbrun, 1992, 1995; Otto, Edens, & Barcus, 2000).

■ Detailed records of all aspects of the evaluation are created and preserved and are made available in a timely manner to individuals with the legal authority to inspect or possess them.

■ All professional activities are performed with recognition of the investigative nature of the task:
   • an acknowledgment of the limitations that are inherent in our evaluative procedures;
   • an understanding of the distinction between psychological issues and the specific psycholegal questions before the court; and
   • an appreciation of the need not to engage in therapeutic endeavors before, during, or after the evaluation.

The forensic model, as applied to child custody evaluations, served as a foundation for the AFCC's (1994, 2007) *Model Standards of Practice for Child Custody Evaluations.* The forensic model is premised in part on the integration of legal and scientific principles in crafting a child custody evaluation. In their summary of changes in the child custody arena over the past 50 years, Elrod and Dale (2008) argued that the work product of child custody evaluators needs to meet the requirements of expert testimony.

> Many argue that if society and courts wish to use mental health evaluators as experts and to make child custody cases into truly interdisciplinary endeavors, then law and science should demand rigorous scrutiny so that courts are informed consumers of expert evidence. (Elrod & Dale, 2008, p. 417)

The forensic model is now the dominant model that is used by child custody evaluators across disciplines (Ackerman & Kane, 2010, 2011; Bow & Quinnell, 2001). Ackerman and Kane's (2010, 2011) summary of current research supports the view that custody evaluators across disciplines embrace the methodological elements that comprise the forensic model, although psychiatrists and social workers place less value on the role of psychological testing in the evaluation process than do psychologists. As of the writing of this chapter, no research has been published examining the degree to which psychologists who are conducting child custody evaluations follow the procedures that have been recommended by the APA (2010b) child custody guidelines or the AFCC (2007) *Model Standards.*

Kirkpatrick (2004) identified 26 evaluation-related custody evaluation practices that constituted a set of minimal practice standards that went beyond the aspirational goals of existing guidelines and parameters. He asserted that these 26 evaluation-related practice ideas constitute a floor rather than a ceiling for conducting child custody evaluations that reflect "a consensus about where the field is now" (p. 67). Today, there is a consensus in the mainstream child custody literature about which methods and procedures should be included in a competently conducted examination (Ackerman & Kane, 2010; Bow & Quinnell; 2002; Gould, 2006; Kirkland, 2002; Otto et al., 2003; Otto & Heilbrun, 2002; Rohrbaugh, 2008; Stahl, 2010).

Kirkpatrick's (2004) table has been adapted to current standards and guidelines, as shown in Appendix 13.1.

Professional Practice Guidelines, Ethical Standards, and Child Custody Assessment

A third agent of change is the ethical standards and professional practice guidelines that are used by child custody evaluators. APA's (2010a) Code of Ethics, APA's (2010b) *Guidelines for Child Custody Evaluations in Family Law Proceedings*, the child custody evaluation standards from the American Academy of Matrimonial Lawyers (2010), APA's (2013) *Specialty*

Guidelines for Forensic Psychologists, and the AAFC (2007) *Model Standards* all embrace the need for evaluators to employ reliable methods and procedures; offer opinions that are supported by data that are generated by those reliable procedures; and avoid offering opinions for which there is little, if any, support in the peer-reviewed professional literature.

State Laws and Statutes

Another agent of change includes state laws and statutes regarding conducting child custody evaluations, rules of evidence, and standards of professional conduct. At least 37 states have adopted *Daubert* or its state equivalent, and 15 states and the District of Columbia continue to use the *Frye* rule (Hunt, 2010).

Several states have incorporated APA's (2010b) child custody guidelines into their psychology licensing law statutes and have defined them as minimal practice standards. It is critical that evaluators determine if their jurisdiction has incorporated the APA child custody guidelines into state law or any other guidelines or codes.

Some states have defined by statute or case law specific elements that must be included in a child custody evaluation (e.g., California, Florida). Evaluators should determine if their state has a law that specifically identifies what should be included in a child custody evaluation.

Some states have defined by statute specific types of training that are needed before conducting a child custody evaluation. A rule of thumb is to always check the state laws in the state in which you intend to conduct an evaluation in order to determine what evaluators are and are not allowed to do.

Evaluators who are engaged to conduct interstate evaluations or who are retained to conduct an evaluation in a state in which they are not licensed should check with the state licensing board in the state in which the evaluation will take place. Evaluators should ascertain whether a nonresident psychologist who is licensed in another state is permitted to come into the state to conduct an evaluation. Similarly, if asked to provide testimony in a state in which an evaluator is not licensed, it is important to check with the licensing board about whether

a nonresident psychologist who is licensed in another state is permitted to come into the state and provide testimony.

Below is a list of questions about your state laws that you should consider before beginning a child custody evaluation.

Evolution of Mental Health Standard of Practice and Child Custody Assessment

Survey research has helped to identify the community standard among child custody evaluators. The first generation of survey research investigated methods and procedures that are used by evaluators in conducting child custody assessments. Keilin and Bloom (1986), Ackerman and Ackerman (1997), and Bow and Quinnell (2001) investigated the methods and procedures that are most commonly used by custody evaluators. By the middle 2000s, an emerging consensus was found among custody evaluators who supported the use of multiple interviews with parents and children, direct observation of parent–child interactions, psychological testing when necessary, collateral interviews, and record review (Bow, 2006).

The second generation of survey research has begun to examine the use of specific procedures. A series of survey studies examined the use of psychological tests in child custody evaluation (Bow, Flens, & Gould, 2010; Bow, Flens, Gould, & Greenhut, 2006; Bow, Gould, Flens, & Greenhut, 2006) and evaluators' understanding and use of custody-related concepts (e.g., Ackerman & Pritzl, 2011; Bow, Gould, & Flens, 2009).

Survey data have provided information about a variety of areas of practice. We summarized data from several studies in an effort to show the professional practice trends across several decades and studies. Table 13.1 shows the average amount of time that is spent in child custody evaluation activities.

One important trend in research and scholarship has been to emphasize the importance of evaluators' neutrality. Neutrality can be established through appointment by the court as its expert or through a consent order that is signed by both attorneys. Survey data support trends in the literature. Table 13.2

TABLE 13.1

Average Time Spent in Child Custody Evaluation Activities

Activity	Mean hours			
	A & P	B & Q	A & A	K & B
Observations	2.7	1.6	2.6	1.9
Reviewing materials	5.6	3.0	2.6	—
Collateral contacts	3.2	4.0	1.6	1.3
Psychological testing	6.1	3.0	5.2	5.2
Report writing	10.6	7.3	5.3	2.8
Interviewing parents	7.1	4.2	4.7	4.1
Interviewing children	3.6	1.8	2.7	1.6
Interviewing significant others	2.3	1.5	1.6	1.3
Consulting with attorneys	1.3	0.9	1.2	1.4
Testifying in court	2.6	—	2.2	2.3
Total	46.1	28.5	29.7	21.9

Note. A & P = Ackerman and Pritzl (2011), Psychologists; B & Q = Bow and Quinnell (2001), Psychologists; A & A = Ackerman and Ackerman (1997), Psychologists; K & B = Keilin and Bloom (1986), Mental Health Professionals.

presents survey data showing that judges and attorneys prefer child custody evaluators to be neutral appointments, either through court appointment or mutual agreement. Although a guardian ad litem appointed psychologist would be considered neutral, survey data reveal that judges and attorneys do not view them as court-appointed psychologists. Second-opinion experts and rebuttal witnesses remain the least favored of these groups.

Psychological testing has been a controversial issue in child custody assessment. Survey data reveal that testing is frequently used in child custody evaluations. When testing adults, the Minne-

sota Multiphasic Personality Inventory—2 has remained the gold standard, although we would not be surprised to find subsequent data to show increased use of the Minnesota Multiphasic Personality Inventory—2 Restructured Form (see Table 13.3). The Rorschach has remained a popular instrument over time, even though it has been heavily criticized (Wood, Nezworski, Lilienfeld, & Garb, 2003).

It is important to take note of the continued use of assessment techniques that have little, if any, psychometric integrity. Survey data show continued frequent use of projective techniques such as the Sentence

TABLE 13.2

Preferred Conditions of Retainment

Judges	Attorneys				
	A & S	A & D	A & K	A & H	Grand mean
Court-appointed	4.19	4.00	3.93	3.90	4.01
Mutually agreed	3.94	3.96	4.22	4.34	4.12
GAL-appointed	3.89	3.68	3.50	3.21	3.57
Second-opinion	2.94	2.86	2.89	2.91	2.90
Rebuttal witness	2.90	2.90	2.81	2.90	2.88

Note. A & S = Ackerman and Steffen (2000), Attorneys; A & D = Ackerman and Drosdeck (2009), Judges; A & K = Ackerman and Kelly-Poulos (2000), Attorneys; A & H = Ackerman and Hakes (2010), Attorneys; GAL = guardian ad litem.

TABLE 13.3

Preferred Tests With Adults

Test	A & A	B, G, F, & G	A & P
Minnesota Multiphasic Personality Inventory—2	91.5	90.6	97.2
Millon Clinical Multiaxial Inventory—III	34.3	58.0	71.3
Rorschach	47.8	—	51.9
Sentence Completion	22.4	25.3	40.6
Personality Assessment Inventory	—	17.9	28.0

Note. A & A = Ackerman and Ackerman (1997), Psychologists; B, G, F, & G = Bow, Gould, Flens, and Greenhut (2006), Psychologists; A & P = Ackerman and Pritzl (2011), Psychologists.

Completion Test and the Thematic Apperception Test (TAT), even though they do not fulfill *Daubert* criteria. The Personality Assessment Inventory has gained popularity over the years and is being used more frequently. Significant concerns have been expressed about the use of the Millon Clinical Multiaxial Inventory—III (Hynan, 2004).

Many of the same concerns that have been raised regarding the use of psychological tests in adult assessment are also concerns about the use of psychological tests in child assessment. The psychological assessment of children often involves the use of projective drawings and the Bricklin Perceptual Scales (BPS; Bricklin, 1994), which do not meet *Daubert* criteria. The Rorschach continues to remain in modest usage with children over time. Lastly, the use of checklists like the Child Behavior Checklist (Achenbach, 1991) and the Behavioral Assessment System for Children—2nd edition (BASC–2) are being used more frequently as a means of seeing

how accurately parents assess their children's development (see Table 13.4).

Survey research has helped to define how evaluations are conducted (Ackerman & Ackerman, 1997; Ackerman & Pritzl, 2011; Bow & Quinnell, 2001). Psychologists report that all children should be observed with parents, and psychological testing should be performed on all parties and significant others. The most recent data revealed that a majority of psychologists report that they do not participate in home visits (42%) or consult with the parties' attorneys (46.9%), though a significant minority does favor those practices (Ackerman & Pritzl, 2011).

Judges and attorneys were asked to identify what procedures they would expect psychologists to perform, would not expect psychologists to perform, or were neutral about. The standard of practice is empirically defined as activities that a majority of people would participate in within their profession. The bold numbers in Table 13.5 represent what a

TABLE 13.4

Preferred Tests With Children

Test	A & A	B, G, F, & G	A & P
Child Behavior Checklist	—	23.0	23.0
Minnesota Multiphasic Personality Inventory—Adolescent	19.9	38.8	58.1
Rorschach	27.4	—	39.5
Projective Drawings	24.4	17.9	57.5
Bricklin Perceptual Scales	34.4	12.8	39.3

Note. A & A = Ackerman and Ackerman (1997), Psychologists; B, G, F, & G = Bow, Gould, Flens, and Greenhut (2006), Psychologists; A & P = Ackerman and Pritzl (2011), Psychologists.

TABLE 13.5

Evaluation Procedures

Procedure	Do not expect		Neutral		Expect			
	Judges	Attorneys	Judges	Attorneys	Judges			Attorneys
	A & S (%)	A & K (%)	A & S (%)	A & K (%)	A & S (%)	A & D (%)	A & K (%)	A & H (%)
Observation of children under 6 with parent(s)	2.6	0.0	9.0	6.0	**88.4**	87.5	94.0	91.5
Observation of children 6–12 with parent(s)	1.9	0.8	11	6.5	**87.1**	84.4	92.7	96.9
Observation of children over 12 with parent(s)	7.7	5.5	23.2	26.0	**69.0**	70.8	69.0	84.5
Review mental health records	1.9	3.0	7.7	11.0	**90.3**	95.8	86.0	96.1
Review pleading of family law cases	27.1	38.0	42.6	21.0	30.3	42.7	41.0	**67.4**
Review legal records	32.9	46.6	44.5	26.7	22.6	30.2	26.7	45.7
Review criminal records	21.9	21.3	35.5	18.0	42.6	**54.7**	60.7	69.8
Review children's school records	3.9	1.6	18.7	19.5	**77.4**	79.2	78.9	84.4
Review children's medical records	5.2	5.7	24.7	27.6	**70.1**	—	66.7	65.9
Review parents' medical records	17.4	16.4	**52.2**	45.9	30.3	**53.1**	37.7	47.7
Contact collateral sources	15.5	13.8	40.6	30.9	43.9	**61.5**	55.3	89.1
Perform psychological testing on parents	3.2	3.2	19.9	16.9	**76.9**	72.6	79.8	82.8
Perform psychological testing on children	2.6	1.6	23.5	12.9	**73.9**	—	85.5	49.6
Perform psychological testing on significant others	13.7	14.5	35.9	31.5	**50.3**	36.2	54.0	35.7
Home visit	31.4	35.5	39.7	32.2	28.8	24.5	27.3	**50.4**
Consult with GAL	13.0	8.6	24.7	28.4	**62.3**	69.1	62.9	72.1
Consult with parties' attorneys	30.7	14.6	42.5	39.8	26.8	33.7	45.5	44.9
Interview parent	3.6	2.4	1.4	1.6	**95.0**	97.9	96.0	98.4
Interview children	0.0	0.8	1.8	1.6	**98.2**	92.6	97.6	97.7
Interview significant others	8.7	5.6	17.8	15.2	**73.5**	80.6	79.2	83.7
Write a report	0.6	0.0	7.2	4.0	**92.2**	90.6	96.0	94.6
Testify in court	3.9	2.5	29.6	13.4	**66.4**	68.4	84.1	84.4

Note. A & S = Ackerman and Steffen (2000), Attorneys; A & K = Ackerman and Kelly-Poulos (2000), Attorneys; A & D = Ackerman and Drosdeck (2009), Judges; A & H = Ackerman and Hakes (2010), Attorneys; GAL = guardian ad litem.

majority of attorneys and judges expect the standard of practice to be for psychologists.

It is surprising that judges and attorneys do not more strongly favor the interviewing and testing of significant others, particularly stepparents. These individuals can have a significant and perhaps profound influence on children's psychological development. Accordingly, we strongly recommend that significant others, and particularly stepparents, be assessed similarly to parents.

Survey research describing reasons that have been given by evaluators in decision making about recommendations for sole custody is found in Table 13.6 and for joint custody in Table 13.7. In an open-ended format, participants were asked to identify reasons that would be used to award sole custody in a case. Abuse-related issues and inability to cooperate and communicate remain major concerns. Substance abuse and geographic distance were also variables that were considered significant.

TABLE 13.6

Reasons for Sole Custody

Reason	Psychologists		Judges		Attorneys		
	A & A	A & P	A & S	A & D	A & K	A & H	Grand mean
Inability to communicate/cooperate	2	2	2	1	2	1	1.6
Physical/sexual abuse	3	1	1	3	1	3	2
Inability to care for children	—	—	—	—	—	2.2	
Parents mentally ill	1	4	3	—	3	5	3.2
Substance abuse	4	3	4	2	4	4	3.5
Domestic violence	6	—	5	4	5	—	5
Geographical distance	5	—	7	6	6	—	6
Alienation	—	5	—	—	—	—	
Criminal history	—	—	—	5	—	—	

Note. A & A = Ackerman and Ackerman (1997), Psychologists; A & P = Ackerman and Pritzl (2011), Psychologists; A & S = Ackerman and Steffen (2000), Attorneys; A & D = Ackerman and Drosdeck (2009), Judges; A & K = Ackerman and Kelly-Poulos (2000), Attorneys; A & H = Ackerman and Hakes (2010), Attorneys.

When participants were asked to identify reasons for awarding joint custody, cooperation/communication was number one across the board. This is consistent with research indicating that the quality of communication between the parents has a profound effect on the adjustment of the child(ren). Factors of attachment, psychological health, and best interest were obviously well represented in these studies.

Some scholars have argued that there is no scientifically informed basis for expert opinions about custodial placement, particularly with no research available on the efficacy of different parenting plans (Tippins & Wittmann, 2005a). As a result of these arguments, some jurisdictions across the country have discouraged evaluators from offering expert opinions about custodial placement (New York State Matrimonial Commission, 2006).

The present authors' experience is that there is now an increased emphasis on shared placement schedules. In these six studies, however, shared placement schedules were preferred approximately 18% of the time, whereas joint custody with primary

TABLE 13.7

Reasons for Joint Custody

Reason	Psychologists		Judges		Attorneys		
	A & A	A & P	A & S	A & D	A & K	A & H	Grand mean
Cooperation/communication	1	1	1	1	1	1	1
Attachment to both	2	4	2	—	2	4	2.8
Contact with both	4	5	2	2	2	2	2.8
Geographic proximity	6	—	3	3	3	—	3.75
Psychologically healthy	3	2	5	5	6	—	4.2
Desire of parents	5	—	4	—	5	5	4.75
Child's choice	7	—	6	—	4	—	5.6
Best interest	—	3	—	4	—	3	3.3

Note. A & A = Ackerman and Ackerman (1997), Psychologists; A & P = Ackerman and Pritzl (2011), Psychologists; A & S = Ackerman and Steffen (2000), Attorneys; A & D = Ackerman and Drosdeck (2009), Judges; A & K = Ackerman and Kelly-Poulos (2000), Attorneys; A & H = Ackerman and Hakes (2010), Attorneys.

TABLE 13.8

Conditions of Placement

Condition	Psychologists		Judges		Attorneys		
	A & A	A & P	A & S	A & D	A & K	A & H	Grand mean
Sole custody without visits	2.71	—	3.91	4.35	2.69	1.56	2.98
Sole custody with visits	32.35	—	36.33	21.49	33.02	18.86	29.42
Joint custody	46.38	—	45.00	49.53	52.40	46.60	47.79
Shared placement	17.52	—	12.27	20.24	16.10	24.92	17.81
Splitting children	6.41	4.40	4.45	3.71	3.78	1.64	4.27
Foster placement	2.90	2.60	2.17	1.57	0.71	—	2.11

Note. A & A = Ackerman and Ackerman (1997), Psychologists; A & P = Ackerman and Pritzl (2011), Psychologists; A & S = Ackerman and Steffen (2000), Attorneys; A & D = Ackerman and Drosdeck (2009), Judges; A & K = Ackerman and Kelly-Poulos (2000), Attorneys; A & H = Ackerman and Hakes (2010), Attorneys.

placement to one parent was preferred in nearly 50% of the cases (see Table 13.8). It is important to note that shared placement does not mean a 50/50 time share.

The survey data (see Table 13.9) reveal that when custody evaluators were asked to specifically identify preferred placement schedules, 50/50 schedules were not the most favored across the board. The 9/5 placement schedule remains a very popular choice. There still are a number of judges who prefer the traditional alternate weekend schedule.

Evaluators need to be mindful of the lack of empirical support for the efficacy of any parenting plan. There is a need for evaluators to be familiar with parenting plan research (i.e., Kuehnle &

Drozd, 2012) and, when asked, evaluators need to be able to defend their opinions about the lack of empirical support for parenting plans.

Table 13.10 describes information about the cost of child custody evaluations. Fees for evaluations vary considerably across the nation, and the information in Table 13.10 does not address the fee structure for various geographic areas. Psychologists in some jurisdictions charge as little as $125/hr (e.g., areas of North and South Carolina), whereas psychologists in other jurisdictions charge upward of $400/hr (e.g., California, New York).

Over the years, there has been a professional debate about whether psychologists should be

TABLE 13.9

Preferred Placement Schedule

Schedule	% Psychologists		% Judges		% Attorneys	
	A & A	A & P	A & S	A & D	A & K	A & H
12/2 without midweek dinner	—	39.2	14.0	>0.8	>13.3	>4.0
12/2 with midweek dinner	—	—	30.4	16.8	—	—
11/3	—	4.7	8.8	—	4.2	—
10/4	—	12.5	7.2	3.3	9.8	6.67
9/5	—	22.7	4.0	10.0	19.6	29.33
8/6	—	11.7	2.4	—	2.8	4.0
50/50	—	35.9	6.4	15.0	12.6	46.66
No favorite	—	11.7	20.0	58.0	21.0	4.0

Note. A & A = Ackerman and Ackerman (1997), Psychologists; A & P = Ackerman and Pritzl (2011), Psychologists; A & S = Ackerman and Steffen (2000), Attorneys; A & D = Ackerman and Drosdeck (2009), Judges; A & K = Ackerman and Kelly-Poulos (2000), Attorneys; A & H = Ackerman and Hakes (2010), Attorneys.

TABLE 13.10

Cost of Child Custody Evaluations

Psychologists	Per hour ($)	Per evaluation ($)
K & B	88	965
L & C	110	2109
A & A	121	2646
B & Q-1	144	3335
A & P	181	5653

Note. K & B = Keilin and Bloom (1986), Mental Health Professionals; L & C = LaFortune and Carpenter (1998), Psychologists; A & A = Ackerman and Ackerman (1997), Psychologists; B & Q-1 = Bow and Quinnell (2001), Psychologists; A & P = Ackerman and Pritzl (2011), Psychologists.

allowed or required to testify to the ultimate issue (custody/placement) in child custody cases (Melton et al., 2007; New York State Matrimonial Commission, 2006). A well-respected minority continue to say that psychologists should not testify to the ultimate issue (Tippins & Wittmann, 2005a). Survey data suggest that the percentage of psychologists who say that they should testify about the ultimate issue is decreasing over time (see Table 13.11). Attention needs to be paid to this issue as time progresses.

Research studies have begun to identify the age at which evaluators place weight on children's expressed preferences (see Table 13.12). Additional research needs to be performed in this area.

Survey data described in Table 13.12 show that virtually no weight is given to the expressed preference of a 5-year-old child, and little weight is given to the expressed preference of a 10-year-old child.

Children's expressed preferences are given significant weight when they reach the age of 15.

A final area discussed in survey research is the potential risk that is involved in conducting a child custody evaluation (see Table 13.13). Research has found that psychologists who are performing child custody evaluations are at significant risk for a board complaint (Kirkland & Kirkland, 2001). A check with most licensure boards and ethics committees demonstrates that complaints resulting from child custody evaluations have either the highest or second highest frequency.

PRACTICE AND POLICY ISSUES

In the preceding sections, we described how changes in case law, changes in rules of evidence for expert testimony, changes in professional practice guidelines

TABLE 13.11

Should Psychologists Testify About the Ultimate Issue?

Psychologists	Yes (%)
B & Q-1	94.0
B & Q-2	84.0
B & Q-3	86.0
A & P	58.8
A & D	67.7
A & H	57.6

Note. B & Q-1 = Bow and Quinnell (2001), Psychologists; B & Q-2 = Bow and Quinnell (2004), Attorneys; B & Q-3 = Bow and Quinnell (2004), Judges; A & P = Ackerman and Pritzl (2011), Psychologists; A & D = Ackerman and Drosdeck (2009), Judges; A & H = Ackerman and Hakes (2010), Attorneys.

TABLE 13.12

Importance of Children's Wishes in Custody Cases

Psychologists	Wishes of 15-year-old	Wishes of 10-year-old	Wishes of 5-year-old
A & P	16/40	33/40	39/40
A & D	18/40	31/40	37/40
A & H	17/40	30/40	39/40

Note. A & P = Ackerman and Pritzl (2011), Psychologists; A & D = Ackerman and Drosdeck (2009), Judges; A & H = Ackerman and Hakes (2010), Attorneys.

and ethical standards of behavior, and results drawn from survey research have shown a convergence on an assessment model that emphasizes the use of reliable and valid procedures; reliance on peer-reviewed, scientifically informed literature; attention to the analytic gap between the data that are obtained during the evaluation and the expert opinions that are expressed; and the importance of citing the limitations of one's forensic psychological work product. Next, we move to a discussion of issues that are relevant to practice and policy regarding child custody and access.

Procedures for Conducting a Child Custody Evaluation

In this section, we discuss the procedures that are used in a child custody evaluation that have been informed by the forensic model. A competently conducted child custody evaluation must be based on data that have been gathered by reliable methods and procedures (Ackerman, 2006; Gould & Bell, 2000). The obtained data must be gathered in a manner that complies with sound scientific methods, and the

techniques that are used to evaluate the data must be valid. Additionally, information about parental behavior, child behavior, or parent–child interaction should have a reasonable expectation of assisting the fact finder in determining a fact in issue.

A child custody evaluation should follow the scientific process, which, at its most elementary level, involves three steps: observation, inference, and hypothesis generation. *Observation* is the act of recognizing or noting a fact or an occurrence. *Inference* is a conclusion that is based on an observation. A *hypothesis* is a proposed explanation or interpretation of the conclusion that is derived from the observation; it can be tested through further investigation. We recommend using this three-step process when recording data that are obtained from face-to-face or telephonic interviews, parent–child interactions, and record review.

Standard 12.2 of the AFCC's (2007) *Model Standards* directs, "In their reports and in their testimony, evaluators shall be careful to differentiate among information gathered, observations made, data collected, inferences made, and opinions formulated" (p. 89).

TABLE 13.13

Risks in Conducting Child Custody Evaluations

Risk	B & Q-1 (%)	A & Do (%)	A & P (%)	B & M (%)
Malpractice suits	10	13.5	19	17
Board complaints	35	38	49.5	52
Ethics complaints	35	15	9	22
Threatened with violence	—	—	17	—
Property destroyed	—	—	11.1	—

Note. B & Q-1 = Bow and Quinnell (2001), Psychologists; A & Do = Ackerman and Dolezal (2006), Risks; A & P = Ackerman and Pritzl (2011), Psychologists; B & M = Bow and Martindale (2009), Risks.

The revised *Specialty Guidelines for Forensic Psychology* also direct us to clearly differentiate observations, inferences, and opinions (APA, 2013). Guideline 11.02 addresses the importance of differentiating observations, inferences, and conclusions. The guideline reads: "In their communications, forensic practitioners strive to distinguish observations, inferences, and conclusions. Forensic practitioners are encouraged to explain the relationship between their expert opinions and the legal issues and facts of the case at hand" (p. 16). We encourage evaluators to write their reports in ways that assist the reader to differentiate the observational data from the inferences that were made by the evaluator and to show how the data and inferences logically lead to the opinions.

A global assertion as to what is or is not in a child's best interests has little probative value unless empirical data indicate that the specifics on which that opinion is based have predictive value. Unlike commonly accepted methods that are used in a therapeutic context, forensic methods and procedures are designed to produce a trustworthy set of data that allows an expert to offer a reliable opinion.

The degree to which independent sources of information converge to support a hypothesis is a measure of the consistency of the data. When each of the four data-gathering sources leads to similar inferences about parenting practices, an increased probability exists that the opinions that are drawn from these data are accurate. Reliability decreases as fewer of the independent sources of information support a particular hypothesis.

Semistructured interview format.   Interview formats may be defined along a continuum from unstructured to structured. In the *unstructured* format, the interviewer asks open-ended questions, and the interviewee is permitted the freedom to respond in any way that the answer may take him or her. A *structured* interview is the polar opposite of the clinical interview. In a structured interview, a predefined set of questions is asked, and the interviewee is expected to provide specific answers to specific questions. Often, such interviews are used when attempting to gather data in an effort to rule out or rule in a specific psychiatric diagnosis. A *semistructured* interview is a hybrid of the unstructured and structured interview

formats. A semistructured interview format allows the same set of questions to be asked of each parent as would occur in a structured interview. The evaluator may inquire into additional areas specific to the parent or to the context of the particular evaluation, but the initial set of information that is obtained from both parents should be based on the same set of general questions (Gould, 1998, 2006).

Although no research findings have been reported in which the reliability of semistructured interviews has been examined using a population of parents who are undergoing child custody assessment, it has been generally reported in the forensic psychology literature that information that is gathered through semistructured interview formats has higher levels of reliability than information that is gathered through unstructured interview formats (Rogers, 2001). "The versatility of clinical interviews, which allow the full exploration of case-specific information, is achieved at the expense of standardization. Particularly when interviews are not coupled with structured interviews, the potential for biased evaluations increases" (Rogers & Shuman, 2000, pp. 151–152). Semistructured interview formats allow for the development of interview questions that are directly related to the content areas that have been identified by the court, the parties, or the attorneys as relevant areas of investigation. That is, questions can be asked of both parents regarding psycholegally relevant areas of parental or family functioning.

Too many child custody evaluators focus the attention of their parent interviews on historical information about adult relationships and marital behaviors. Too often, there is little information gathering about areas that are relevant to parenting, the parent–child relationship, parent-to-parent communication history, parent-to-parent cooperation, parent–child attachment, sibling relationships, and other child- and parenting-related issues.

In reviewing reports that have been prepared by evaluators, it becomes clear that an evaluator's focus is lost when there is extensive coverage of each litigant's strengths and deficiencies *as a spouse* rather than of each litigant's strengths and deficiencies *as a parent*. It is our experience that in the course of pretrial discovery, an evaluator's records are produced and reviewed, and it is not at all uncommon to encounter records that clearly reflect that more information was gathered about marital interactions than about parent–child dynamics and issues.

An evaluator can also lose focus when recommendations reflect attentiveness to the needs of one or both of the parents and relative inattentiveness to the best interests of the child(ren). In *Ford v. Ford* (1962), the U.S. Supreme Court, confirming an earlier opinion by the Supreme Court of Appeals in Virginia, declared "the rule that the welfare of the infant is the primary, paramount, and controlling consideration of the court in all controversies between parents over the custody of their minor children. All other matters are subordinate" (p. 193). In *Palmore v. Sidoti* (1984), the Supreme Court ruled that "the goal of granting custody based on the best interests of the child is indisputably a substantial governmental interest for purposes of the Equal Protection Clause" (p. 433). Both in *Ford v. Ford* and in *Palmore v. Sidoti*, the Court asserted that children's best interests are elevated above the interests of their parents.

Too often, we observe that evaluators provide little relevant information about how children experience life in their binuclear family units (Ahrons, 1987). Often, little if any information is provided in custody reports about each child's experiences with issues that are relevant to the investigative questions that are before the court. The writings of Smart (2002) provide a useful framework for developing a child-centered interview format that is aimed at gathering information about each child's experiences with each parent.

In a forensic context such as a child custody evaluation, it is critical that the interview data be checked against other sources of information such as data from psychological tests, collateral informants, and direct behavioral observations. It is virtually impossible for an evaluator to determine the forensic value of interview data without the support of information from independent sources (Ackerman, 2006; Gould, 2006; Martindale & Gould, 2004).

Courts are best served when evaluators focus their inquiries on issues that are relevant to the matters before the court. To do so means asking, "Were specific questions about particular areas of concern in this family asked in a direct manner?" For example, if there are concerns about domestic violence, did the interviewer use a peer-reviewed domestic violence interview protocol in conducting the interview? Was each family member interviewed about each event that is of concern to the court?

If there are concerns about parental discipline techniques, the evaluator must ask questions about parenting style, discipline style, parenting philosophy, religious affiliation and philosophy, corporal punishment, anger expression, impulsivity, alternative disciplinary strategies, and other relevant factors that contribute to an understanding of a parent's disciplinary style. Children should also be asked about these behaviors of concern. In addition, children should be interviewed more than once in order to examine the consistency of their responses over time. The evaluator should carefully note similarities and differences between children's statements after having been transported by one parent versus the other. Finally, interviewing children and parents together provides an opportunity to talk about allegations of concern.

Among the more recent changes reflected in the literature is an increasing awareness that some children are eager to participate in some ways in decision making about residential placement (Parkinson & Cashmore, 2008). There is a myth about children's reluctance to participate in legal proceedings regarding their custodial placement (Parkinson & Cashmore, 2008). Recent studies have shown that children want their opinions to be known and to be taken seriously; however, they do not want to be the decision makers. Research findings have shown that children's acceptance of the decisions that are made about their custody are better accepted when they perceive the decision-making process as fair, even if the outcome is not desirable. In other words, when children perceive that decision makers have taken time to listen and take their ideas seriously, children report higher levels of satisfaction with the residential placement outcome (Parkinson & Cashmore, 2008).

Child accounts of family life frequently are overshadowed by their parents' interpretation of family events (Smart, 2002). When evaluators interview children about their experiences in each family, child accounts of life in each parent's home often vastly differ from their parents' accounts (Smart & Neale, 2000). Smart (2002) stated,

> It is not that children's accounts obliterate or correct the parents' accounts; nor is it the other way around. Rather, it is to acknowledge that people stand in different relationships to one another, have access to different resources, and regard different things as important. (p. 309)

Taking children's stories seriously means giving legitimacy to their experiences on the same level as that given to the parents' experiences. One is not necessarily more important than the other. Each experience needs to be thoroughly understood (Gould & Martindale, 2009).

Psychological tests. The purpose of psychological testing in child custody evaluations is to provide a set of data that can be used to compare each parent's scores against those from a normative population. The construction of a psychological test is based on one or more theories that are held by test developers. The test manual should provide information about the test's underlying theory of science, established reliability and validity statistics, normative data, and other measurement-related criteria. Examination of the psychometric integrity (e.g., reliability and validity) of the measurement tools that are used in a child custody evaluation goes to the heart of the question of reliability. If the tools that are used to measure a factor do not have adequate reliability and validity, then the data on which the interpretations, conclusions, and recommendations will be based are seriously flawed.

Evaluators should consider the reliability and validity of the measurement tools that they use in a child custody evaluation. Child custody evaluators need to examine whether the measurement tool has an appropriate level of reliability and validity with regard to the specific issue in dispute (see Ackerman & Kane, 2011; Gould, Martindale, & Flens, 2009; Otto et al., 2000, for a discussion of criteria needed for a test to be used in a forensic context). Evaluators need to ask whether the test has context-specific normative data for male and female custody litigants. More and more, researchers have

reported data revealing how male and female custody litigants score on psychological tests that are commonly used in child custody assessment (Bathurst, Gottfried, & Gottfried, 1997; McCann et al., 2001). There is also an increasing awareness of the limitation of some psychological tests that are used in child custody evaluations (Hynan, 2004), particularly the significant limitations that are inherent in currently used measures of parent–child attachment (Hynan, 2012; Lamb, 2012; Ludolph, 2012) and the still-too-often administered projective techniques (Gould & Martindale, in press; Gould et al., 2009).

Interpretation of any psychological test requires an understanding of several variables that may affect the test data and their interpretation. It is important for custody evaluators to include a discussion of the interpretation of each parent's validity scales, addressing, at the very least, their possible effects on the certainty and usefulness of the test data (Gould et al., 2009).

The APA (2010a) Code of Ethics addresses the need for psychologists to be aware of threats to the reliability of test data and interpretations.

> When interpreting assessment results, including automated interpretations, psychologists take into account the purpose of the assessment as well as the various test factors, test-taking abilities, and other characteristics of the person being assessed, such as situational, personal, linguistic, and cultural differences, that might affect psychologists' judgments or reduce the accuracy of their interpretations. They indicate any significant limitations of their interpretations. (p. 24)

Among the more relevant situation variables in custody litigation is the stress that is placed on the parents by the divorce, litigation, personal living arrangements, and changes in the relationship with their children. Although responses to stress vary among individuals, the presence of stress is almost universal in divorce.

The stress that results from involvement in custody litigation can be enormous. Litigants often believe that the most important elements of their lives—their relationship to their children and their sense of self-worth—are at stake (Galatzer-Levy et al., 2009).

During the course of the legal dispute, many parents live under a microscope where day-to-day problems become the bases for emergency ex parte motions, or at least seem likely to become factors in litigation. The resulting intense pressure and scrutiny may affect how parents respond to questions on psychological tests (Gould et al., 2009).

Some parents react negatively to having their parenting abilities investigated. Other parents become angry over the idea that someone outside of the family may influence whether or when they may spend time with their children. Such negative reactions may affect how a parent responds to questions on psychological tests. Many parents' scores on psychological tests may reflect how they are responding to the context of the custodial dispute or to the pressures involved in custodial assessment. Psychological test scores may reflect the influence of situational or contextual variables. Interpretation of test data must include a discussion of how these situation or contextual variables may affect interpretation of the test scores (Gould et al., 2009).

Questionnaires and self-report inventories.

Custody evaluations often include questionnaires, self-report inventories, and other measures of parenting or parent–child behavior that appear relevant to the questions at hand (Dies, 2008). Self-report measures are a peculiar type of measurement tool. Some have well-established reliability and validity and have been supported for use in child custody evaluations. Some have well-established statistical properties but have no support in the literature for use in child custody evaluations. Others have no published reliability or validity information and have been used for years in child custody evaluations, despite the lack of a proper scientific foundation. Still others have no published statistical information, and no historical use in child custody evaluations, yet are included in an evaluation because of an evaluator's personal preference, which is unsupported by the literature. (See Gould, 1998, for a discussion of advantages and limitations of self-report measures that are used in child custody evaluations.)

How the evaluator uses the information that is obtained from self-report measures is critical in understanding the relative weight that is assigned to the information. One might use information that has been obtained from self-report measures in a manner similar to that obtained from interview data. Evaluators may choose to examine the degree to which information that is obtained from a self-report measure is consistent with information that is obtained from other independent data sources. Results from self-report measures should be treated like information that was obtained from face-to-face interviews.

Behavioral observations of parent and child.

The fourth area of data collection is the evaluator's behavioral observation of each parent with each minor child and, if appropriate, behavioral observation of each parent with all of the minor children (Lampl, 2009). When no restraining orders or other legal impediments to face-to-face contact would make such observations unwise or potentially dangerous, direct observation of parent-to-parent communication may also be an important source of information. When a restraining order exists, it is advantageous for the evaluator to seek the court's permission to modify the restraining order for a one-time exception in order to allow for this observation to occur.

Currently, there is no standard in the field of child custody evaluations that addresses how to conduct the observational component of the evaluation. The AFCC (2007) *Model Standards* direct evaluators who are engaged in observational tasks not to become participants in the observation. Model Standard 10.1, addressing the awareness of observer effects, states that "evaluators shall be mindful of the fact that their presence in the same physical environment as those being observed creates a risk that they will influence the very behaviors and interactions that they are endeavoring to observe" (p. 21). If the simple fact of their presence has a distorting effect, becoming an active participant increases the distortion exponentially and, most importantly, the "direction" of the distorting effect cannot be discerned, and therefore, cannot be factored or accounted for in some manner.

The evaluator should be minimally involved in any participation during the parent–child observations. During the parent–child observation, the evaluator should create a context that as closely as possible represents how the parent and child interact. The more the evaluator interacts during the parent–child observation, the less the observation is a measure of what the parent and child do when they are alone. It is a valid criticism that the act of observing during a home visit creates enough change for the parent–child interactions to be deemed unrepresentative. We suggest minimizing evaluator-imposed behaviors as much as possible.

Similar concerns apply to parent–child observations that occurr in the evaluator's office. The office is not an environment with which the child is familiar. Additionally, the office context is not representative of the child's natural environment.

Evaluators need to consider how the type of environment may affect the parent's behavior, the child's behavior, and their interaction. Upon completion of the parent–child observation, we encourage evaluators to speak with each parent and child about the ways in which the observed interaction was or was not similar to their typical means of interacting.

Evaluators are wise to set ground rules for the observation. One important ground rule is to advise the parent and child(ren) that the evaluator will not engage in conversations with them during the observation. Another important ground rule is that the evaluator will not accept documents or other materials that might otherwise be provided during an interview. It has been our experience that parents try to engage in conversation when ground rules are not clearly articulated. A third ground rule is that only parents and/or caretakers who are parties to the litigation can attend and participate in the observations. The ground rules should clearly indicate that the observation time is for observation and not for the exchange of documents or for the imparting of information about the other parent.

Knowing the degree of evaluator involvement in the observation may significantly alter how family members relate to each other. It is important that the evaluator describe how the observation was conducted and his or her degree of involvement with different family members during the observation. It is important to note that we are not suggesting that the evaluator describe the *impact* of his or her participation in the interactions.

Another important area of examination is what specific aspects of parent–child interaction are targeted for assessment and how they were assessed. It is essential for the evaluator to take contemporaneous notes or to make an audio recording of parent–child observations. These observational data should be descriptive rather than interpretative. For example, the data should reflect behavioral descriptions such as the following:

> The parent sat next to the child, looking at the child and smiling. The child responded by smiling and reaching toward the parent. The child hugged the parent and placed her head on mother's shoulder. The parent responded by hugging and kissing the child on her head. Both parent and child kissed each other on the cheek. The child let go of the parent and asked to be placed back on the floor. The parent placed the child on the floor and the child returned to the dolls.

By contrast, an interpretive statement is, "The parent was loving toward her child." Little useful information is conveyed to the reader when labels such as *loving* are provided. Different people have different definitions of what defines *loving*. Providing behavioral descriptions of observed interactions allows the reader to make independent judgments of the meaning of the behavior.

Collateral record review and collateral interviews. The acquisition of reliable and relevant collateral information is arguably among the most important components of a child custody evaluation (Ackerman & Kane, 2011; Austin & Kirkpatrick, 2004; Gould, 2006; Kirkland, McMillan, & Kirkland, 2006). A critical component of a child custody evaluation is obtaining information from third-party observers about parent–child interactions. The idea is to obtain information about parent–child interactions that are representative of day-to-day parent–child experiences from people who are outside of the immediate family (Austin, 2002; Gould, 2006; Kirkland, 2002; Kirkland et al., 2006). Any competently conducted custody evaluation must include information from third-party sources about how the parent and child have been observed in their daily lives outside of the artificial and contrived circumstances of the evaluator's office. Information from people who have observed the parent and child interact in different situations is often the most important data that are obtained in a child custody evaluation. Similarly, obtaining historical records may shed light on important aspects of parental cooperation and conflict; parenting challenges, difficulties, or triumphs; and historical components to the parent–child relationship. Several authors have described limitations and cautions associated with the use of collateral informants (Austin, 2002; Otto & Heilbrun, 2002).

Austin and Kirkpatrick (2004) pointed out that individuals who are the most emotionally distant from the custodial dispute are likely to be the most objective. Information that is obtained from them is therefore likely to be of greater accuracy than is information that is obtained from people such as relatives or close friends. This leads some evaluators to eliminate lists containing the names of people who are indisputably allied with one of the litigants from collateral sources. We believe this to be a mistake.

Gould and Martindale (2013) reminded us that the term *collateral source information* has an unintended and unfortunate consequence. Far too many evaluators conceptualize the input from collaterals only as *information* and fail to recognize its incalculable value as stimulus material in subsequent interviews with the litigants. Some of the most useful information that is obtained from the litigants emerges when they respond to statements that have been offered by collaterals.

Integrating Independent Sources of Information Collected During the Evaluation

The forensic model admonishes evaluators to employ a multimethod approach to gathering data. Using a forensic methodology that includes obtaining information from different sources such as interviews, test data, record review, and direct observation provides a means of examining the degree to which different, independent sources of information provide support for a particular hypothesis. There is a direct relationship between the number of independent data sources that converge on a conclusion and, therefore, support a hypothesis, and the confidence that the

evaluator holds in the certainty that the data support the hypothesis.

As a general rule, information from two different data sources provides less powerful support for a hypothesis than does information from three different data sources, which is less powerful than support from four different data sources. The nature and source of information also needs to be considered, with some types of data being assigned greater weight (meaning) than others.

Integrating Peer-Reviewed Research With Evaluation Findings

With only rare exceptions, the information that is imparted by custody experts in their reports and testimony is not information that they uncovered. Experts are, in reality, perpetual students. Good experts devour the professional literature, critically examine published research, and draw on the knowledge base of an entire profession each time they conduct an evaluation. The task of the skilled evaluator is to decide what research is applicable to the specific family who is the focus of the court's attention, to apply the research, and to explain how the cited research sheds light on the particular issues that are in dispute (Martindale & Gould, 2007).

The position of the AFCC, as reflected in its *Model Standards*, is seen in Model Standard 4.6 (b):

> Evaluators are strongly encouraged to utilize and make reference to pertinent peer-reviewed published research in the preparation of their reports. Where peer-reviewed published research has been alluded to, evaluators shall provide full and accurate references to the cited research. (2007, p. 78)

Our position concerning citations to scientifically informed research finds support in Standard 2.04 of APA's Code of Ethics (APA, 2010a), which directs psychologists to base their work "upon established scientific and professional knowledge of the discipline . . . [and] established scientific and professional knowledge" (p. 1064) found in peer-reviewed literature.

In this section, we provided a description of the procedures that are used in a child custody evaluation. We explained the relevance of each procedural step in developing a comprehensive data set, and we provided a list of questions to guide evaluators when examining the thoroughness of the work product. In the following section, we discuss several areas of child custody assessment that require specialized knowledge beyond that which is provided in general training programs that are aimed at teaching child custody methods and procedures.

Professional Practice and Assessing Complex Issues

How to assess the complex issues discussed in this section is under continuous reformulation as the custody field moves toward a more evidence-based model of assessment. One interesting development is the application of the concept of gatekeeping to include domestic violence, alienation, and relocation assessments. Austin, Pruett, Kirkpatrick, Gould, and Flens (2014) argued that gatekeeping is a powerful explanatory concept that can be applied to the analysis of many different kinds of parenting behavior that affects children's access to one or both parents.

Kuehnle and Drozd (2012) edited the most comprehensive book to date that summarizes the current, state-of-the art scholarship and research on parenting plans. Similarly, Kuehnle and Connell (2009) edited the most useful explanation of how to conduct assessments of allegations of child sexual abuse within the context of a child custody dispute. Lamb (2010) summarized the increasingly complex and extensive literature on the role of fathers, within both intact families and divorced families. Drozd et al. (in press) wrote about the importance of research in child custody assessment and the importance of knowing how to determine what is and is not good research on which to base expert opinions. R. F. Kelly and Ramsey (2007) addressed the need for judges and attorneys to learn how to determine good research from bad.

The trend in the peer-reviewed literature and conference presentations is on addressing the empirical foundation for many of the most relevant areas of concern that are investigated by child custody evaluators. In this section, we summarize some of those relevant areas, with particular focus on how to structure an evaluation when allegations of one or more of these factors arise.

Many of the complex issues that are examined in a child custody evaluation are related to allegations of child maltreatment and the potential risk that such behavior poses to a child. When there are allegations of child maltreatment, a rival hypothesis must be simultaneously considered: "Is the person who is alleging the maltreatment attempting to interfere with or thwart the child's relationship with the alleged perpetrator?" Similarly, when there is a request to relocate to a geographically distant community, a rival hypothesis that must be examined is: "Is the person who is requesting the court to allow the minor child to relocate attempting to interfere with or thwart the child's relationship with the nonmoving parent?"

Gatekeeping. Research findings have generally supported the proposition that children are best served when they have strong and healthy relationships with both parents (J. B. Kelly & Emery, 2003). These relationships develop through children's frequent and continuous contact with each parent, especially during the children's early years (J. B. Kelly & Lamb, 2000; Lamb & Kelly, 2001, 2009). In child custody disputes, among the most frequently occurring assessment issues is how to develop and maintain a child's unfettered access to each parent. Many child custody disputes concern the extent of paternal involvement in parenting children. The study of gatekeeping within a child custody context should provide useful ideas that can be applied in the development of parenting plans.

Over the past decade, several scholars have begun to examine a gatekeeping framework that has been applied to child custody matters (Austin, Flens, & Kirkpatrick, 2010; Austin, Gould, Kirkpatrick, & Eidman, 2006; Pruett, Arthur, & Ebling, 2007; Pruett et al., 2003). Gatekeeping includes one parent's attitudes and behaviors toward the other parent and his or her parenting abilities and the other parent's involvement with and access to their children (Adamson, 2010). It is a bidirectional or mutual-influence process that occurs both in intact families and in postseparation and never-married family systems (Adamson, 2010; Trinder, 2008).

A distinction must be drawn between caretaking and gatekeeping. *Caretaking* refers to those parental activities that address daily health, safety, security, and other similar functions. *Gatekeeping* refers to the process by which one parent controls the ability of the other to function as an effective caretaker. In particular, a restrictive gatekeeper limits access to the child, thereby preventing the other parent to participate in meaningful parenting activities. With limited access to the child, there can be no meaningful parenting activities that facilitate the development in the child of a perception of both parents as effective caretakers.

When conducting a child custody evaluation, it is important to investigate the role of parental gatekeeping from the child's birth forward. Examining the ways in which the primary caretaker provided access to the other parent of their newborn child may help to inform the evaluator about the role of gatekeeping during the marriage. The evaluator also needs to examine the degree to which the other parent took advantage of opportunities to engage in child care that were provided by the primary caretaker.

Investigating the historical and current role of gatekeeping in each family is an important component of a child custody evaluator's assessment of family functioning. Research findings have shown that the extent and quality of parental involvement are among the main factors in predicting children's adjustment and future development (Galatzer-Levy et al., 2009; J. B. Kelly & Emery, 2003).

Relocation analysis. Among the most difficult challenges facing divorcing families is the decision by one parent to relocate with the child(ren) to a geographically distant community, leaving the other parent behind. Nearly half of children of divorce relocate after the divorce is finalized. Some of these relocations entail residential changes within the former family community, whereas approximately one-third of relocations entail residential changes out of the geographic area within 2 years following separation (Braver & O'Connell, 1998).

Evaluators need to be familiar with jurisdiction-specific statutory requirements and case law decisions pertaining to relocation (Stahl, 2010). Many states have statutes that address factors to be considered by the court when determining whether a child may relocate with his or her parent (Elrod, 2006).

Several current child custody texts include extensive discussions about assessment of requests to relocate (Ackerman, 2006; Ackerman & Kane, 2005, 2010; Gould, 2006; Rohrbaugh, 2008; Stahl, 2010). Several models guiding the evaluation of requests to relocate are presented in the forensic psychological literature. Shear (1996) argued that evaluators must appreciate that a move within the context of divorce is one factor in a long line of events, experiences, and changes that may have a significant impact on a child. A request to move away must not be examined in isolation but rather as part of the larger story of a child's emerging life. How the child has coped with previous changes, that is, the manner in which the child adjusted to stressors and other change agents, informs us of the tolerance the child may have to another significant change.

A more contemporary perspective on relocation focuses attention on empirically determined risk factors to the child (Austin, 2000b, 2000c, 2000d; Austin & Gould, 2006). Relocation presents a significant number of risk factors for children (Austin, 2008a, 2008b).

- *Developmental age of the child.* The younger the child, the more likely the risk to the child's relationship with each parent (Austin, 2000c). Research has identified two groups of children who appear more likely to be harmed by relocation: children age 6 years and under and children age 12 years and older. The 6- to 12-year-old children appear to be the group to incur less detriment (Austin, 2008a). However, research also shows that relocation, in general, presents a risk to children of all ages, thereby increasing the likelihood of emotional and behavioral problems by approximately 25% (Austin, 2008b). Children relocating with intact families have a 25% increase in experiencing emotional and academic problems. Children relocating after divorce have about a 38% increase in experiencing emotional and academic problems, which is approximately 13% more than children in intact families (Austin & Gould, 2006).
- *The geographic distance of the move.* The farther the move, the more likely the risk to the child's relationship with the nonmoving parent (Austin, 2008a, 2008b).
- *The degree of prerelocation involvement of the noncustodial parent in the child's daily activities.*

The higher the degree of prerelocation involvement, the greater the risk to the child's relationship with the nonmoving parent as well as the greater the risk to the child's psychological well-being (Austin, 2000c, 2008b).

- *The history of parental conflict.* The higher the level of interparental conflict, the greater the risk to the child. Some moves tend to exacerbate parental conflict, which adversely affects the child's psychological well-being (Austin, 2000a, 2008a, 2008b), whereas other moves reduce parental conflict (Austin & Gould, 2006).

- *The sex of the child.* Boys have decreased opportunities to learn from their biological fathers about sex role identification. Girls have decreased opportunities to learn from their biological fathers about socializing behaviors (Austin, 2000c; Gould, 2006).

- *Prerelocation involvement of each parent in the child's extracurricular activities.* The greater the noncustodial parent's prerelocation involvement, the greater the risk to the child's psychological well-being (Austin, 2000c, 2008b).

- *The child's temperament.* The more difficulty that children have adjusting to change, the more difficult will be the child's adjustment to the move (Gould et al., 2010).

- *The relative contribution of each parent to each child's life.* Fathers and mothers tend to bring different parenting resources and opportunities to their children. Children are at greater risk when the unique contribution of one parent is diminished due to the relocation (Austin, 2008b; Austin & Gould, 2006).

- *Loss/gain of social capital resources.* Relocation may involve losing or gaining interpersonal, social, familial, and community resources that have an influence on a child's life (Austin et al., 2006, 2010). Among the factors to be examined are the loss of extended family involvement, loss of peer-group involvement, loss of community involvement, and so forth (Austin et al., 2010; Austin & Gould, 2006).

We recommend that when evaluators explain their evaluation results, they organize the data that were obtained during the evaluation around two criteria: the behavioral science model such as Austin's

factors, and the specific factors that are articulated in the state statute or case law decision from the state in which the evaluation is being conducted. If a parent moves away with a child, the evaluator must recognize that it will effectively end the relationship with the other parent as it currently exists.

Never-married parents and parents in short-lived relationships.   A significant minority of children are born to single parents (Emery et al., 2005). Increasingly, custody disputes between two never-married parents lead to a child custody evaluation. Although the evaluation methodology remains unchanged in the assessment of relevant variables, there may be unique factors to consider when making recommendations to the court about custodial placement and parental access in these situations.

Parents of short-lived relationships may differ from married parents in a number of ways (Raisner, 1997). Never-married parents often have not established a separate family unit, and they may not know each other very well, particularly if the pregnancy occurred during a short-term relationship.

A second difference is that often the child has had little or no contact with the nonresidential parent. Some of these children have been raised with a parent substitute. This often adds another important dimension. The parent substitute, or stepparent, may have been identified to the child as his or her biological father, or the child may have been taught that his or her biological father does not care and therefore has no legitimate right to visit.

Under such circumstances, visitation plans may be necessary in order to provide increased time for the child to learn about and to adjust to the concept of his or her biological parent. Time may also be necessary for the child to become accustomed to the participation of the biological parent in his or her life. Similar concerns are focused on the child's need to adjust to new siblings (stepsiblings and half-siblings), stepparent, grandparents, and other extended family members (Gould, 2006).

Children may also have significant emotional reactions to the knowledge and understanding of the role of the biological father. Some of these children may need to participate in counseling, family therapy, or some other form of intervention. The respective parents may need to attend counseling sessions or some type of mediation through which they can negotiate unresolved issues that may interfere with the healthy establishment of a parent–child relationship.

Never-married parents "have extra anger, resentment, suspicion, or fear if they are being forced—by a court—into renewing a relationship with the other parent" (Raisner, 1997, p. 92). An educational focus may be, in part, to assure them that they need not repair their former relationship but instead focus on ways to develop a working relationship through which their child can enjoy the support of each parent in encouraging the child's relationship with the other.

Besides concerns about how the child can learn to incorporate a new parent or extended family into his or her life, there is also the concern that some never-married parents have had their child reared by other relatives. Thus, the introduction of the biological father into the child's life may result in feelings of displacement on the part of those who raised the child. These people and their feelings also need to be addressed in some respectful way.

A final factor is unique to same-sex relationships. Gay and lesbian parents who never married but who lived within a structured, committed relationship in which parental roles were defined may struggle with their parental roles after the love relationship dissolves. There is seldom, if ever, any legal status for the nonbiological parent, homosexual partner who wishes to maintain an ongoing relationship with the child.

A similar situation occurs when the never-married parent eventually marries and then divorces the stepfather after many years. This is not unique to never-married parents, of course, as these issues are also problematic when birth parents have married, divorced, and remarried, and when biological mothers subsequently divorce the stepfather after many years.

The stepfather may have had significant influence in the child's life, and the continuing relationship with the stepfather may significantly affect the child's best psychological interests either positively or negatively. Often the legal status of the stepfather was never clarified through formal adoption. At some point, the biological father reenters the picture. The evaluator may need to consider not only the visitation issues related to the biological father, but also the child's need to maintain an ongoing relationship with the stepfather.

Useful parenting planning may include a focus on educational information about child development for the parent who has had little contact with the child. There is also a need to spend time helping the parents create a workable communications system. This may include a stepparent or the primary caretaker who may feel displaced. The intervention needs to focus more on problem-solving and conflict resolution skills than on the exploration of feelings and introspection. As Raisner (1997) stated, "Teach parents how to make and respond to a request, how to structure a discussion, and how to use solution-based decision making techniques" (p. 99).

Assessing Sexual Abuse Allegations Within the Context of a Child Custody Evaluation

Current myths about children and sexual abuse suggest that sexually abused children act in certain ways that make the identification of those who have been abused easy and reliable. Some states have case law that supports this unfounded notion.[8] The behavioral science literature provides little, if any, foundation on which to make clear, consistent statements about our ability to identify who has been abused, who has done the abusing, and when a child has been abused (Kuehnle, 1996; Kuehnle & Connell, 2009). Custody evaluators are often asked to offer opinions to the court about whether a child is at risk of sexual abuse within the context of custodial determinations.

There is some empirical support for the notion that professionals believe that allegations occurring within a custody context are less likely to be true. Evaluators have been found to view abuse as more likely when there are multiple-episode rather than single-episode reports. Reports in which there was a prior allegation

---

[8] See *State of North Carolina v. Ronnie Lane Stancil*, 559 S.E.2d, 788 (2002), in which the Supreme Court of North Carolina declared that "an expert witness may testify, upon a proper foundation, as to the profiles of sexually abused children and whether a particular complainant has symptoms or characteristics consistent therewith."

of abuse were seen as more likely to be real than those with no prior report (U.S. Department of Justice, 2000a, 2000b).

For many years, it was believed that certain statements or behaviors that were made by children enabled one to discriminate between abused and nonabused children. Among the most popular was the display of age-inappropriate sexual knowledge. The assumption was that sexually abused children would possess developmentally advanced concepts about sexuality and sexual behavior as a result of their exposure to sexually exploitive or abusive behavior. However, research has demonstrated that both abused and nonabused children display sexual behaviors, with sexually abused children revealing significantly higher frequency of sexual behaviors in certain categories (Friedrich, 2002; Friedrich, Fisher, Broughton, Houston, & Shafran, 1998). Making matters more difficult for evaluators is the fact that only a minority of sexually abused children exhibit sexual problem behavior, whereas some children who have not been sexually abused act out sexually (Friedrich, 2002). Another commonly held belief that is not supported by research is that sexually abused children are hesitant to talk about the experience of abuse. The assumption was that sexually abused children feel ashamed or will have been threatened or bribed not to disclose the abuse. It is just as likely that a child may tell adults who have been supportive and helpful, thus increasing the likelihood that the child will talk openly about the abuse (Ceci, Kulkofsky, Klemfuss, Sweeney, & Bruck, 2007; Ceci, Papierno, & Kulkofsky, 2007; Kuehnle & Connell, 2009; Pipe, Lamb, Orbach, & Cederborg, 2007).

Haskett, Weiland, Hutcheson, and Tavana (1995) demonstrated that the use of sexually anatomically correct dolls to confirm sexual abuse was widespread in the late 1980s. However, cases reviewed in their study showed a relatively low rate of use of the dolls but, as expected, a higher rate of use with younger children. The child's affect and behavior during the interview and disclosure were also important factors in decision making. However, the authors warned that using affect as an indicator to substantiate allegations of sexual abuse can be problematic (p. 19). Sexually anatomically correct dolls should be used today only after the entire interview process is completed, for clarification purposes alone. Any other use is not supported by research.

There are many different models that describe how to conduct an evaluation of alleged child sexual abuse within the context of a custody determination. We believe that the most comprehensive books guiding such evaluations are Kuehnle's (1996) book, *Assessing Allegations of Child Sexual Abuse*, and Kuehnle and Connell's (2009) book, *The Evaluation of Child Sexual Abuse Allegations*.

Among the most comprehensive models guiding the assessment of alleged sexual abuse is the American Professional Society on the Abuse of Children's (1990) *Practice Guidelines: Psychosocial Evaluation of Suspected Sexual Abuse in Children*. Another useful approach to the evaluation of child sexual abuse is offered by the American Academy of Child and Adolescent Psychiatry's (1988) *Guidelines for the Clinical Evaluation of Child and Adolescent Sexual Abuse*. APA's *Guidelines for Psychological Evaluations in Child Protection Matters* (APA Board of Professional Affairs, 1999) is a useful professional practice guideline for psychologists who are involved in conducting evaluations in child protection matters. A final resource is the suggestions of your state professional association. Different states have different laws surrounding the reporting of child sexual abuse during a custody evaluation.
It is wise to know your state laws and your ethical obligations under those laws.

The evaluator must be familiar with the considerable behavioral science literature involving directly relevant aspects of investigating allegations of child sexual abuse. We recommend that evaluators have the following references: Kuehnle and Connell (2009); Pipe et al. (2007); and Kuehnle and Drozd (2005). We also recommend that the evaluator become familiar with the multiple hypotheses framework that was articulated by Kuehnle (2006). We encourage evaluators to address in the body of their report the support for or against each of these hypotheses:

■ The child is a victim of sexual abuse, and the allegation is credible and accurate.
■ The child is a victim of sexual abuse, but due to age or cognitive deficits, does not have the verbal

skills to provide a credible description of his or her abuse.

- The child is a victim of sexual abuse, but due to fear, will not disclose his or her abuse.
- The child is a victim of sexual abuse, but due to misguided loyalty, will not disclose his or her abuse.
- The child is not a victim of sexual abuse and is credible but has misperceived an innocent interaction. (A variation of this hypothesis might be that the child is truthful but has misperceived an ambiguous or innocent situation, or has misidentified an alleged suspect.)
- The child is not a victim of sexual abuse but has been unintentionally contaminated by a concerned or hypervigilant caretaker or authority figure.
- The child is not a victim of sexual abuse but has been intentionally manipulated by a caretaker or authority figure into believing that he or she has been abused.
- The child is not a victim of sexual abuse but knowingly falsely accuses someone of sexual abuse because of pressure by caretakers or authority figures who believe that the child has been abused.
- The child is not a victim of sexual abuse but knowingly falsely accuses someone of sexual abuse for reasons of personal aggrandizement or revenge.[9]

Kuehnle (2006) reported that the most frequent child sexual abuse allegations come from a parent who truly believes that the abuse occurred as a function of misreading the data.

Child Alienation

Over the past 25 years, considerable discussion has focused on the dynamics and processes of child alienation. Several different models describe child alienation.

The first professional writings about child alienation were offered by Reich (1933/1949), who wrote about parents who seek "revenge on the partner through robbing him or her of the pleasure in the child" (p. 265). Wallerstein and Kelly (1980) were the first to identify, in a population of divorced families, a child's irrational rejection of a parent and her resistance or refusal to visit the parent. The initial formulation of an alienated child posited a pathological alignment between an angry parent and an older child or adolescent that sprang from the dynamics of the separation, including the child's reaction to the divorce (Wallerstein & Kelly, 1980). It was Gardner (1985) who developed a more elaborate and detailed description of this alienation process. He also offered a series of criteria for assessing this alienation process and described a continuum of alienating behaviors ranging from mild to severe. Parental alienation syndrome (PAS) was first defined by Gardner as a conscious or unconscious attempt by one parent to behave in such a way as to alienate the child or children from the other parent. In his initial writings, Gardner identified the mother as the parent who is most often engaged in systematic attempts to alienate a child from the other parent (Gardner, 1992). In his later writings, Gardner (2002) indicated that fathers were becoming as likely as mothers to engage in PAS.

According to Gardner (1985), the purpose of PAS is to align the child with one parent by forcing the other parent out of the child's life. PAS includes, but is not limited to, conscious, intentional programming techniques. Time is the alienating parent's most powerful ally. The longer the alienating parent has direct control over the child, the greater will be the alienating influence. As the alienating parent is able to dominate the child's time, the target parent is unable to spend time with the child. The result is a widening of the gap between the child's strengthening alliance with the alienating parent and the child's weakening alliance with the target parent. Eventually, the child adopts the malicious, intolerant, rejecting attitude of the alienating parent toward the target parent, resulting in a belief system in which the child views the target parent with hatred and fear (Gardner, 1992). Several authors have argued for the usefulness of the PAS concept, most notably, Dunne and Hedrick (1994), Rand (1997a, 1997b), and Warshak (2001, 2002,

---

[9]Although preadolescent and adolescent children may be capable of knowingly falsely accusing someone of sexual abuse for secondary gains (i.e., escape from the family, revenge, removal of an adult from the family, etc.), preschool and young school-age children are probably not cognitively sophisticated enough to initiate a false sexual abuse allegation.

2010). Another concern is what Cartwright (1993) termed *virtual allegations*:

> They refer to those cases in which the abuse is only hinted, its real purpose being to cast aspersions on the character of the noncustodial parent in a continuing program of denigration. For the alienator, virtual allegations avoid the need to fabricate incidents of alleged abuse with their attendant possibility of detection and probability of punishment of perjury. (pp. 208–209)

Bruch (2002) criticized Gardner's PAS, citing several areas of concern. She noted, "Gardner confounds a child's developmentally related reaction to divorce and high parental conflict (including violence) with psychosis. In doing so, he fails to recognize parents' and children's angry, often inappropriate, and totally unpredictable behavior following separation" (p. 530). She further criticized Gardner for positing that PAS occurs primarily in young children, suggesting that the current literature does not support the notion that young children are most vulnerable to alienation pressures. Another concern voiced by Bruch is how the use of PAS focuses attention away from potentially dangerous or abusive behavior on the part of the parent who is seeking custody to that of the custodial parent.

In 2001, J. B. Kelly and Johnston published a reformulation of alienation dynamics and proposed a continuum of child–parent relationships after separation and divorce. J. B. Kelly and Johnston provided a road map for evaluators to use in distinguishing the alienated child (who persistently refuses and rejects visitation because of unreasonable negative views and feelings) from other children who also resist contact with a parent after separation based on a variety of normal, realistic, and/or developmentally predictable reasons. At the healthiest end of the continuum are the majority of separated children who have positive relationships with both parents. They value both parents and wish to spend significant (often equal) amounts of time with each parent.

The next step along the continuum describes children who have an *affinity* for one parent while also desiring continuity and contact with both parents. Affinity for one parent is characterized by the ways in which children feel closer to one parent than the other. It may result from temperament, gender, age, shared interests, sibling preferences of parents, and parenting practices. Such affinities may shift over time with changing developmental needs and situations. "Although these children may occasionally express an overt preference for a parent, they still want substantial contact with and love from both parents" (J. B. Kelly & Johnston, 2001, p. 252).

The third step along the continuum describes children who have developed an *alliance* with one parent. During the marriage or separation, these children demonstrate or express a consistent preference for one parent over the other. They often want limited contact with the nonpreferred parent after the separation. Allied children generally do not fully reject the other parent nor do they seek to terminate all contact. They tend to express some ambivalence toward this parent, including anger, sadness, and love, as well as resistance to contact. J. B. Kelly and Johnston (2001) noted that such alliances might have their roots in family dysfunction that may have preceded the divorce insofar as children may have been encouraged to take sides or carry hostile messages between the parents. Alliances appear to occur more often in older schoolchildren in response to the dynamics of the marital breakup. Older children tend to make moral assessments and judgments about which parent caused the breakup, who is most hurt, who is most vulnerable, and who needs and/or deserves the child's unfettered help and support.

A fourth step along the continuum finds children who are realistically *estranged* from one of their parents as a consequence of that parent's history of family violence, abuse, or neglect, and they need to be clearly distinguished from alienated children. These children have taken sides in the family because of a fact-based history of violence or explosive outbursts of a parent during the marriage or after separation. Sometimes the children have been targets of violence and abusive behavior from this parent, and in some cases, from other family members. These children may find that the only time they can feel safe enough to reject the violent or abusive parent is after the separation, when the child is protected by the custodial parent.

These children do not have to be direct witnesses to violence. They may witness the aftermath of intimate partner violence or they may be traumatized by an act of violence that from an adult's perspective may not have been very serious or injurious. J. B. Kelly and Johnston (2001) stated, "The mix of intense anger towards the abusive parent, and phobic reactions to that parent caused by subconscious fear of retaliation looks like alienation. But unlike alienated children, the estranged children do not harbor *unreasonable* [emphasis added] anger and/or fear" (p. 253).

Children who have suffered exposure to abuse or who have been victims of abuse generally suffer from some type of traumatic stress reaction. Evaluators need to assess these children for trauma reactions. If no trauma reaction is found, then the evaluator might wish to consider alienation among other possible alternative hypotheses. Among the reasons that children may become estranged from a parent include,

- severe parental deficiencies including persistent immature and self-centered behaviors;
- chronic emotional abuse of the child or preferred parent;
- physical abuse that goes undetected;
- characterologically angry, rigid, and restrictive parenting styles; and/or
- psychiatric disturbance or substance abuse that grossly interferes with parenting capacities and family functioning.

J. B. Kelly and Johnston (2001) reminded us that,

> Unfortunately, the responses of these realistically estranged children following separation are commonly and incorrectly interpreted and played out in custody disputes as PAS cases. The deficient, abusive, or violent parent frequently accuses the other parent of alienating the child against him or her. They vigorously resist any suggestion that marital violence or severe parenting deficiencies have negatively impacted the parent–child relationship. (p. 254)

At the extreme end of the continuum are children who are *alienated* from a parent after separation and divorce. These children tend to express their rejection of that parent stridently and without apparent guilt or ambivalence. They also may strongly resist or completely refuse any contact with the rejected parent.

Often, the parent who has been rejected has been less involved in the child's life than the other parent or possesses somewhat less robust parenting competencies. The child's complaints and allegations about the rejected parent may reflect some true incident that has been grossly distorted and exaggerated, resulting in the child holding highly negative views and feelings. It is the gross distortion and exaggeration without a reality-based foundation that makes this a *pathological* response.

J. B. Kelly and Johnston (2001) reported that everybody contributes to the alienation process. Contributions of the alienating parent include the following:

- The alienating parent harbors a deep distrust and fear of the other parent.
- The alienating parent is absolutely convinced that the other parent is irrelevant and/or an evil influence on the child.
- The rejected parent's attempts to visit the child are viewed as harassment.
- The alienating parent does not pass along letters or phone messages from the other parent
- The alienating parent strongly supports the child's rights to make his or her own decisions about visiting the other parent.
- The alienating parent confirms for the child that the other parent is not worthy of the child's attention.
- The rejected parent is denigrated in the child's presence and the child is encouraged to point out the other parent's faults.
- The alienating parent fervently believes that the other parent is dangerous to the child.
- The alienating parent convinces the child that the other parent does not and has never loved or cared for the child.
- The alienating parent and child tell stories about the other parent's lack of care and lack of love, demonstrating the other parent's presumed lack of concern.

Contributions of the alienated child include the following:

- child's age and cognitive capacity;
- child's feelings of abandonment by the rejected parent;
- child's temperament and vulnerabilities;
- other parent–child relationship factors; and
- a lack of external support for child.

Contributions of the rejected parent include the following:

- passivity and withdrawal in the face of high conflict;
- counterrejection of the alienated child;
- harsh and rigid parenting style;
- self-centeredness and immaturity of the rejected parent;
- rejected parent has critical and demanding traits; and
- rejected parent has diminished empathy for the aligned child.

Drozd and Olesen (2004) proposed an assessment model to distinguish children who are abused from those who are alienated, arguing that a conceptual framework that organizes multiple hypotheses is needed when assessing allegations and counterallegations of abuse and alienation. They proposed several hypotheses that can be examined when a child resists visiting one or both parents. The first hypothesis examines the child's resistance to visit a parent as a normal developmental variation in his or her development and/or the result of normal variations in family dynamics. A second hypothesis is that the child has been exposed to intimate partner violence and/or substance abuse in the home and/or is the target of direct abuse or neglect. A third hypothesis is that the child's resistance to visit a parent is the result of poor parenting on the part of one or both parents. Included in this analysis is investigation of one parent's parenting behaviors that are alleged to undermine the child's relationship with the other parent (alienation) as well as investigation of allegations of rigid or insensitive parenting on the part of the rejected parent. Drozd and Olesen recently added an analysis of more complex interactions among four primary factors. These *hybrid* analyses include

examination of complex interactions among some combination of poor parenting, protective parenting, alienating behaviors, and/or abuse (Drozd & Olesen, 2010).

Domestic Violence

The forensic assessment of allegations of domestic violence remains one of the hot topics for research. It presents a unique challenge to evaluators not only because of the complexity of the psychological variables that are involved in a comprehensive assessment but also because of the political aspects of many issues that are involved in domestic violence (Gould & Martindale, 2007).

There are several reasons why a systematic exploration of allegations of domestic violence is critical in child custody evaluations. The first involves concerns about placing a child in a family context in which parental violence occurs. Children who are living in homes in which parental violence occurs are more likely to be targets of violence themselves (Jaffe, Crooks, & Poisson, 2003; Jaffe, Lemon, & Poisson, 2003). The second reason is that children who are living in a family context in which domestic violence occurs are psychologically affected by their exposure to parental violence (Bascoe, Davies, Sturge-Apple, & Cummings, 2009; Davies & Cummings, 2006; Davies & Sturge-Apple, 2007; Davies, Sturge-Apple, Cicchetti, & Cummings, 2007; Davies, Sturge-Apple, Winter, Cummings, & Farrell, 2006). A third concern is that parents who are involved in domestic violence tend to be poorer supervisors of their children's behavior.

Typically, the victim of the parental violence tends to be more depressed and is often focused on his or her safety issues rather than on the needs of the child (Gould & Martindale, 2007). Another concern is that children who are raised in homes in which domestic violence occurs often identify with the aggressor, resulting in children attributing less parenting legitimacy to the victimized parent (Bancroft & Silverman, 2002)

Recent research findings have strongly suggested that the population of individuals who allege domestic violence while undergoing custody evaluations is drawn from a different population than those who allege domestic violence and are living in domestic violence shelters (Dutton, 2006a, 2006b). Understanding differences between these populations on factors such as lethality risk, type of physical violence, frequency of physical violence, and intensity of domestic violence may be important for the evaluator to explore and the court to better understand (Dutton, Hamel, & Aaronson, 2010).

Assessing allegations of domestic violence   Drozd, Kleinman, and Olesen (2000) suggested that investigators of allegations of domestic violence within the context of a custody and visitation dispute need to recognize the larger family system context. When an allegation of domestic violence is raised, evaluators should also examine rival hypotheses that include, but are not limited to, the motivation of the reporting party. A comprehensive evaluation should include the following steps at a minimum:

- obtain civil and criminal complaints and judgments from police, courts, and other relevant venues;
- obtain work records;
- assess for weapons access;
- examine substance and alcohol use;
- evaluate risk assessment;
- investigate collateral contacts, including former romantic partners;
- examine power and control variables in the relationship;
- examine how the parents argued (type of interaction);
- examine how the parents resolved the argument (methods of resolution);
- examine triggers for creating fights;
- investigate the parents' understanding of the fight triggers and how to avoid them;
- assess psychological variables that may contribute to one's propensity toward violence, for example, impulsiveness, low frustration tolerance, rigid versus flexible thinking, authoritarian worldview, and sex role perspective;
- evaluate parental insight into their anger and its management;
- evaluate parental insight into the cycle of violence within their relationship; that is, how it starts and what attributions each parent makes about the other parent's motivation;

- examine psychological/emotional abuse variables;
- examine financial/economic abuse variables;
- examine sexual abuse variables;
- investigate the child's exposure to forms of violence and conflict;
- examine child disciplinary techniques (what is used); and
- examine deployment of child disciplinary techniques and assess the parents' awareness and use of multiple disciplinary strategies sans corporal punishment.

We note the work of others in the field and encourage evaluators to become informed about the more clinically oriented evaluation models such as that developed by Bancroft and Silverman (2002).

Attachment and Parenting Plans

Attachment theory is very popular today. The original notion was that mothers love their babies by protecting them from harm and by nurturing them to explore their environment. Mothers who protect their infants and toddlers from harm create an environment in which the child is able to fully explore his or her surroundings and grow up to be big and strong and securely attached. The problem with this romantic formulation is that little research supports it (Ludolph, 2012; Ludolph & Dale, 2012).

In the beginning of attachment research, it was believed that the early years of a child's life are critical to developing secure attachment, and once formed, a securely attached infant or toddler is prepared to handle the big, bad world. Over the past 10 years, however, we have learned that children's attachments are not necessarily stable over time (Thompson, 2000). Attachments may change over time, and there are predictable, acceptable reasons for that change, especially if the child's environment changes, as often happens, in separating and divorcing families.

It appears that the first 36 months of life are critically important, and a child is best served by safe, secure, and consistent caretaking from his or her parents during this period. The less disruption there is to the child's attachment to either caretaker, the better for the child. Your job as an evaluator is to craft a parenting plan that creates a stable, safe, and predictable environment for the child, no matter his or her age. Disrupted attachments can most often be rehabilitated. Children need to spend time with each parent in order to develop the view that each parent's home is safe. Children need to engage in a variety of activities with each parent, across different contexts.

There is little, if any, empirical research demonstrating which parenting plan is best for which children. For many years, child development specialists and child custody evaluators tried to develop common-sense parenting plans based on research. We present some of those ideas that have taken hold in the child custody literature over the past 10 years.

Infants and toddlers generally need time with each parent but are unable to tolerate a lot of time away from either parent. If there is a primary caretaker, then the noncustodial parent should spend time with the infant at least three to four times a week in a variety of different contexts. Infants' memories are limited, and infants have virtually no language expression. Frequent visits allow the infant to have multiple experiences over time with the noncustodial parent, which increases the likelihood that the infant will begin to remember who the noncustodial parent is. Depending on the early care-taking history, infants may tolerate one or more overnights with the noncustodial parent. Infants and early-stage toddlers may tolerate more overnights, depending on the care-taking history, the temperament of the child, the level of conflict between the parents, and other associated factors (Gould & Stahl, 2001).

Infant attachment is best facilitated when each parent is able to provide experiences in a variety of settings and across a broad range of parenting situations. An infant is well served when both parents are involved in bathing, feeding, clothing, playing, soothing, diapering, and other parent–child interactions (J. B. Kelly & Lamb, 2000).

As children grow, their memories and language skills improve. As memory and language improve, toddlers and preschoolers are able to spend more time away from each parent. The general rule of thumb is that an early-stage toddler can tolerate approximately 1 to 2 days away from one parent, whereas an older toddler might be able to spend 2 or 3 days away from a parent (J. B. Kelly & Lamb, 2000).

Preschool children often can tolerate 3 to 4 nights away, but parents need to be sensitive to children's feelings of homesickness and a need for contact with the other parent. A good rule of thumb is that both parents must be sensitive to their children's needs. Even when researchers recommend no more than 2 days away from a parent during toddlerhood, if the child reacts poorly to that separation, parents need to adjust the parenting plan. This is where things get dicey during custodial disputes. It is important to respond to the specific and unique needs of each child. If a child is homesick, parents need to place the needs of the child ahead of their own needs and allow the child to have access to the absent parent. The dicey part is when the parent is projecting the parent's own distress about being separated from the child and making it seem as if the child is distressed.

Most children in elementary school are able to handle alternate weeks with each parent. This does not mean that a 1-week-on/1-week-off parenting plan is appropriate for all children in elementary school. This means only that most elementary school-age children have the capacity to tolerate such parental separations. Whether such a plan makes sense for a particular child will depend on a variety of variables that are too extensive to discuss here.

Researchers have found no support for the notion that midweek overnights with the noncustodial parent interfere with a child's adjustment (J. B. Kelly & Lamb, 2000). On the other hand, clinical experience has taught us that some children are comfortable with midweek overnights, whereas others find them disruptive. Again, although research shows that midweek overnights do not adversely affect adjustment, some children are more comfortable throwing their book bags in one place for the week.

Many parents ask for *make-up* time when planned parenting time is missed for work or other reasons. If researchers have it right, make-up time creates more confusion for children because it interferes with the consistency of their schedules (Pruett, Ebling, & Insabella, 2004). Once again, a parent might need to sacrifice make-up parenting time in order to provide consistent scheduling for the children.

SUMMARY AND CONCLUSIONS

A paradigm shift has occurred in the practice of child custody evaluations to a more evidence-based approach as a result of *Daubert*. Recognizing the requirements of rules of evidence when preparing a child custody evaluation is important, leading evaluators to employ reliable and relevant assessment techniques. The use of reliable and relevant assessment techniques will lead to gathering information on which more trustworthy expert opinions can be based. Considerable survey research has been performed in the past two decades by Ackerman and his associates as well as Bow and his associates. Evaluators should be mindful of the results of these studies when performing custody or access evaluations. Survey data indicate that most evaluators use the forensic model when conducting child custody assessments. It is essential for evaluators to be familiar with the laws and statutes in their jurisdiction and be knowledgeable about the standards and guidelines promulgated by the various state and national professional organizations.

A child custody evaluation includes investigating specific questions that define the scope of the evaluation; observing parent–child interactions; talking with collateral contacts; reviewing records; administering, scoring, and interpreting psychological tests; and interviewing parents, children, and significant others. Integration of the obtained evaluation data with behavioral science research provides a more scientifically informed foundation for expert opinions.

In this chapter, we discussed consensus and controversies about several topics of current interest, including the use of psychological testing, attachment theory, domestic violence assessment, child maltreatment evaluation, relocation analyses, never-married parents, alienation dynamics and its assessment, and the development of parenting plans.

We encourage practitioners not to become complacent with the methods that they have used for decades. We encourage practitioners to embrace the changes in child custody scholarship, methodology, and professional practice by incorporating them into their evaluation practice while keeping an eye on the ever-changing demands of the legal system and the families we serve.

APPENDIX 13.1

CURRENT CHILD CUSTODY STANDARDS AND GUIDELINES

Standard	Foundation
1. Child custody evaluations are by definition *forensic* evaluations.	American Academy of Child and Adolescent Psychiatry (1997); American Academy of Matrimonial Lawyers (2010); Galatzer-Levy, Kraus, and Galatzer-Levy (2009); Gould (2006); Heilbrun (2001); Melton, Petrila, Poythress, and Slobogin (2007); Otto, Buffington-Vollum, and Edens (2003)
2. The purpose of the evaluation is to assess the psychological best interests of the child.	American Academy of Matrimonial Lawyers (2010); APA (2010b); Martindale (2001)
3. The court is the evaluator's primary client.	AFCC (2007); American Academy of Child and Adolescent Psychiatry (1997); Melton, Petrila, Poythress, and Slobogin (2007); North Carolina Psychological Association (1994)
4. The evaluator is either court-appointed or assigned by consent.	Ackerman (2006); American Academy of Child and Adolescent Psychiatry (1997); Committee on Ethical Guidelines for Forensic Psychology (2011); Gould (2006); Heilbrun (2001); Melton, Petrila, Poythress, and Slobogin (2007)
5. The scope of the evaluation is anchored to specific referral questions.	Ackerman (2006); American Academy of Matrimonial Lawyers (2010); APA (2010b); Gould (2006); Heilbrun (2001)
6. The evaluator obtains informed consent from all parties.	AFCC (2007); American Academy of Child and Adolescent Psychiatry (1997); American Academy of Matrimonial Lawyers (2010); APA (2010b); California Rules of Court (2003); Committee on Ethical Guidelines for Forensic Psychology (2011); Heilbrun (2001); Martindale (2001)

7. The skills, knowledge, and expertise needed to conduct a competent evaluation by the evaluator to gain specialized forensic competence.

Ackerman (2006); AFCC (2007); American Academy of Matrimonial Lawyers (2010); APA (2010b); Committee on Ethical Guidelines for Forensic Psychology (2011); Gould (2006); Heilbrun (2001)

8. Record keeping is of the highest standard and one's records should be retained.

American Academy of Matrimonial Lawyers (2010); Committee on Ethical Guidelines for Forensic Psychology (2011); Gould (2006); Martindale (2001)

9. The evaluator uses multiple avenues of data gathering.

Ackerman (2006); American Academy of Matrimonial Lawyers (2010b); California Rules of Court (2003); Galatzer-Levy, Kraus, and Galatzer-Levy (2009); Heilbrun (2001); Melton, Petrila, Poythress, and Slobogin (2007)

10. Opinions are not given about the psychological functioning of any individual who has not been personally evaluated.

AFCC (2007); American Academy of Matrimonial Lawyers (2010); American Academy of Psychiatry and Law (1995); APA (2010b); Committee on Ethical Guidelines for Forensic Psychologists (1991)

11. The evaluator clarifies with the parties in advance his or her contractual arrangements for conducting the evaluation.

Ackerman (2006); American Academy of Matrimonial Lawyers (2010); APA (2010b); California Rules of Court (2003); Committee on Ethical Guidelines for Forensic Psychology (2011); Martindale (2001); Melton, Petrila, Poythress, and Slobogin (2007); Stahl (1999); Strasburger, Guthiel, and Brodsky (1997)

12. The evaluator acknowledges any implicit or explicit limitations of psychological knowledge and techniques used in the evaluation.

APA (2010b); Melton, Petrila, Poythress, and Slobogin (2007); Otto and Heilbrun (2002)

13. The evaluator avoids ex parte communication with counsel or the judge.

AFCC (2007); American Academy of Matrimonial Lawyers (2010); California Rules of Court (2003); North Carolina Psychological Association (1994); Stahl (1999)

14. The evaluator avoids accepting allegations as facts.

American Academy of Matrimonial Lawyers (2010); Gould (2006); Melton, Petrila, Poythress, and Slobogin (2007); North Carolina Psychological Association (1994)

15. It is important to assess the family factors that affect the child(ren).

AFCC (2007); American Academy of Matrimonial Lawyers (2010); APA (2010b); Otto, Buffington-Vollum, and Edens (2003)

16. Evaluators shall have a minimum of a master's degree in a mental health field.

AFCC (2007); American Academy of Matrimonial Lawyers (2010); California Rules of Court (2003)

17. The evaluator shall be knowledgeable about the relevant statutes and case law governing child custody.

Ackerman (2006); American Academy of Matrimonial Lawyers (2010); Heilbrun (2001); Melton, Petrila, Poythress, and Slobogin (2007)

18. Comparable evaluation techniques should be used to evaluate each litigant.

Ackerman (2006); AFCC (1994); American Academy of Matrimonial Lawyers (2010); Gould (2006)

19. Appropriate and relevant collateral information is obtained.

Ackerman (2006); AFCC (2007); American Academy of Matrimonial Lawyers (2010); APA (2010b); Gould (2006); Heilbrun (2001); Melton, Petrila, Poythress, and Slobogin (2007); North Carolina Psychological Association (1994); Otto, Buffington-Vollum, and Edens (2003); Skafte (1985)

20. The quality of the relationship between parent/caretaker and child should be assessed.

Ackerman (2006); AFCC (2007); American Academy of Matrimonial Lawyers (2010); Galatzer-Levy, Kraus, and Galatzer-Levy (2009); Gould (2006); Stahl (1999)

21. Evaluators should adhere to the ethical principles in their own professions.

Ackerman (2006); AFCC (2007); American Academy of Child and Adolescent Psychiatry (1997); American Academy of Matrimonial Lawyers (2010); Galatzer-Levy, Kraus, and Galatzer-Levy (2009); Martindale (2001); Melton, Petrila, Poythress, and Slobogin (2007)

22. There are essential differences between traditional clinical practice and the performance of child custody evaluations.

American Academy of Child and Adolescent Psychiatry (1997); American Academy of Matrimonial Lawyers (2010); Galatzer-Levy, Kraus, and Galatzer-Levy (2009); Gould (2006); Melton, Petrila, Poythress, and Slobogin (2007)

23. Evaluators need to be aware of and knowledgeable about special considerations in child custody evaluations.

Ackerman (2006); American Academy of Child and Adolescent Psychiatry (1997); American Academy of Matrimonial Lawyers (2010); Gould (2006); Stahl (1999)

24. Evaluators must be aware of relevant law, local rules, and rules of discovery.

American Academy of Matrimonial Lawyers (2010); Committee on Ethical Guidelines for Forensic Psychology (2011); Heilbrun (2001); Melton, Petrila, Poythress, and Slobogin (2007)

References

Achenbach, T. M. (1991). *Manual for the Child Behavior Checklist/4–18, YSR, and TRF profiles*. Burlington: University of Vermont, Department of Psychiatry.

Ackerman, M. J. (1995). *Clinician's guide to child custody evaluations*. New York, NY: Wiley.

Ackerman, M. J. (2006). *Clinician's guide to child custody evaluations* (3rd ed.). New York, NY: Wiley.

Ackerman, M. J., & Ackerman, M. C. (1997). Child custody evaluation practices: A survey of experienced professionals (revisited). *Professional Psychology: Research and Practice, 28*, 137–145. doi:10.1037/0735-7028.28.2.137

Ackerman, M. J., & Dolezal, S. (2006). Experienced custody evaluators' views of controversial issues. *American Journal of Family Law, 15*, 200–205.

Ackerman, M. J., & Drosdeck, C. M. (2009). In the best interest of the child: A survey of family law judges. In M. J. Ackerman & A. W. Kane (Eds.), *Psychological experts in divorce actions* (5th ed., pp. 298–304). New York, NY: Aspen.

Ackerman, M. J., & Hakes, A. J. (2010). Family law attorneys' expectations of psychologists in child custody evaluations. In M. J. Ackerman & A. W. Kane (Eds.), *Psychological experts in divorce actions* (5th ed., pp. 299–304). New York, NY: Aspen.

Ackerman, M. J., & Kane, A. W. (1998). *Psychological experts in divorce actions* (3rd ed.). New York, NY: Aspen.

Ackerman, M. J., & Kane, A. W. (2005). *Psychological experts in divorce actions* (4th ed.). New York, NY: Aspen.

Ackerman, M. J., & Kane, A. W. (2010). *Psychological experts in divorce actions* (4th ed., 2010 cumulative supplement). New York, NY: Aspen.

Ackerman, M. J., & Kane, A. W. (2011). *Psychological experts in divorce actions* (5th ed.). New York, NY: Aspen.

Ackerman, M. J., & Kelly-Poulos, S. (2000). Expectations of psychologists performing child custody evaluations by family law attorneys. In M. J. Ackerman & A. W. Kane (Eds.), *Psychological experts in divorce actions* (5th ed., pp. 301–302). New York, NY: Aspen.

Ackerman, M. J., & Pritzl, T. B. (2011). Child custody evaluation practices: A 20-year follow up. *Family Court Review, 49*, 618–628. doi:10.1111/j.1744-1617.2011.01397.x

Ackerman, M. J., & Steffen, L. J. (2000). Family law judges' expectations of psychologists performing child custody evaluations. *American Journal of Family Law, 8*, 458–470.

Adamsons, K. (2010). Using identity theory to develop a midrange model of parental gatekeeping and parenting behavior. *Journal of Family Theory & Review, 2*, 137–148. doi:10.1111/j.1756-2589.2010.00047.x

Ahrons, C. R. (1987). The relationship between former spouses. In D. Perlman & S. Duck (Eds.), *Intimate relationships: Development, dynamics, and deterioration* (pp. 269–296). Newbury Park, CA: Sage.

Amato, P. R., & Gilbreth, J. G. (1999). Nonresistant fathers and children's well-being: A meta-analysis. *Journal of Marriage and the Family, 61*, 557–573. doi:10.2307/353560

American Academy of Child and Adolescent Psychiatry. (1997). Practice parameters for the forensic evaluation of children and adolescents who may have been physically or sexually abused. *Journal of the American Academy of Child and Adolescent Psychiatry, 36*, 37S–56S.

American Academy of Child and Adolescent Psychiatry, Committee on Rights and Legal Matters, Subcommittee on Guidelines for Evaluation of Child Sexual Abuse. (1988). Guidelines for the clinical evaluation of child and adolescent sexual abuse: Position statement of the American Academy of Child and Adolescent Psychiatry. *Journal of the American Academy of Child and Adolescent Psychiatry, 27*, 655–657. doi:10.1097/00004583-198809000-00025

American Academy of Matrimonial Lawyers. (2010). *Child custody standards*. Chicago, IL: Author.

American Educational Research Association, American Psychological Association, & National Council on Measurement in Education. (1985). *The standards for educational and psychological testing*. Washington, DC: American Psychological Association.

American Educational Research Association, American Psychological Association, & National Council on Measurement in Education. (1999). *The standards for educational and psychological testing*. Washington, DC: American Psychological Association.

American Professional Society on the Abuse of Children. (1977). *Practice guidelines: Psychosocial Evaluation of suspected sexual abuse in children*. New York, NY: Author.

American Psychological Association. (2010a). *Ethical principles of psychologists and code of conduct (2002, Amended June 1, 2010)*. Retrieved from http://www.apa.org/ethics/code/index.aspx

American Psychological Association. (2010b). Guidelines for child custody evaluations in family law proceedings. *American Psychologist, 65*, 863–867. doi:10.103.1037/a0021250

American Psychological Association. (2013). Specialty guidelines for forensic psychology. *American Psychologist, 68*, 7–19. doi:10.1037/a0029889

American Psychological Association Board of Professional Affairs, Committee on Professional Practice and Standards. (1999). Guidelines for psychological evaluations in child protection matters. *American Psychologist, 54*, 586–593. doi:10.1037/0003-066X.54.8.586

Amundson, J. K., Duda, R., & Gill, E. (2000). A minimalist approach to child custody evaluations. *American Journal of Forensic Psychology, 18*, 63–87.

Association of Family and Conciliation Courts. (1994). Model standards of practice for child custody evaluations. *Family Court Review, 32*, 504–513.

Association of Family and Conciliation Courts. (2007). Model standards of practice for child custody evaluations. *Family Court Review, 45*, 70–91. doi:10.1111/j.1744-1617.2007.129_3.x

Austin, W. G. (2000a). Assessing credibility in allegations of marital violence in the high-conflict child custody case. *Family Court Review, 38*, 462–477. doi:10.1111/j.174-1617.2000.tb00585.x

Austin, W. G. (2000b). A forensic psychology model of risk assessment for child custody relocation law. *Family Court Review, 38*, 192–207. doi:10.1111/j.174-1617.2000.tb00569.x

Austin, W. G. (2000c). Relocation law and the threshold of harm: Integrating legal and behavioral perspectives. *Family Law Quarterly, 34*, 63–82.

Austin, W. G. (2000d). Risk reduction interventions in the child custody relocation case. *Journal of Divorce & Remarriage, 33*, 65–73. doi:10.1300/J087v33n01_04

Austin, W. G. (2001). Partner violence and risk assessment in child custody evaluation. *Family Court Review, 39*, 483–496. doi:10.1111/j.174-1617.2001.tb00627.x

Austin, W. G. (2002). Guidelines for utilizing collateral sources of information in child custody evaluations. *Family Court Review, 40*, 177–184. doi:10.1111/j.174-1617.2002.tb00828.x

Austin, W. G. (2008a). Relocation, research and forensic evaluation, Part I: Effects of residential mobility on children of divorce. *Family Court Review, 46*, 136–149.

Austin, W. G. (2008b). Relocation, research and forensic evaluation: Part II. Research support for the relocation risk assessment model. *Family Court Review, 46*, 347–365. doi:10.1111/j.1744-1617.2008.00205.x

Austin, W. G., Flens, J. R., & Kirkpatrick, H. D. (2010, June). *Gatekeeping and child custody evaluation: Theory, measurement & applications.* Paper presented at the 47th Annual Conference of the Association of Family and Conciliation Courts, Denver, CO.

Austin, W. G., & Gould, J. W. (2006). Exploring three functions in child custody evaluation for the relocation case: Prediction, investigation, and making recommendations for a long-distance parenting plan. *Journal of Child Custody: Research, Issues, and Practices, 3*, 63–108. doi:10.1300/J190v03n03_04

Austin, W. G., Gould, J. W., Kirkpatrick, H. D., & Eidman, M. (2006, October). *Application of gatekeeping to child custody evaluations.* Paper presented at the 7th Association of Family & Conciliation Courts' International Symposium on Child Custody Evaluations, Atlanta, GA.

Austin, W. G., & Kirkpatrick, H. D. (2004). The investigation component in forensic mental health evaluations: Considerations for parenting time. *Journal of Child Custody: Research, Issues, and Practices, 1*, 23–46. doi:10.1300/J190v01n02_02

Austin, W. G., Pruett, M., Kirkpatrick, H. D., Gould, J. W., & Flens, J. R. (2014). *Parental gatekeeping and child custody: Child access evaluation: Part I.* Manuscript submitted for publication.

Bancroft, L., & Silverman, J. G. (2002). *The batterer as parent: The impact of domestic violence on family dynamics.* Thousand Oaks, CA: Sage.

Bascoe, S. M., Davies, P. T., Sturge-Apple, M. L., & Cummings, E. M. (2009). Children's insecure representations of the interparental relationship and their psychological maladjustment: Children's peer information processing as an explanatory mechanism. *Developmental Psychology, 45*, 1740–1751. doi:10.1037/a0016688

Bathurst, K., Gottfried, A. W., & Gottfried, A. E. (1997). Normative data for the MMPI-2 in child custody litigation. *Psychological Assessment, 9*, 205–211. doi:10.1037/1040-3590.9.3.205

Bow, J., Flens, J., Gould, J. W., & Greenhut, D. (2006). An analysis of administration, scoring, and interpretation of the MMPI–2 and MCMI–III in child custody evaluations. *Journal of Child Custody: Research, Issues, and Practices, 2*, 1–22. doi:10.1300/J190v02n04_01

Bow, J. N. (2006). Review of empirical research on child custody practice. *Journal of Child Custody: Research, Issues, and Practices, 3*, 23–50. doi:10.1300/J190v03n01_02

Bow, J. N., Flens, J. R., & Gould, J. W. (2010). Using the MMPI–2 and MCMI–III in forensic evaluations: A survey of psychologists. *Journal of Forensic Psychology Practice, 10*, 37–52.

Bow, J. N., Gould, J. W., & Flens, J. R. (2009). Examining parental alienation in child custody cases: A survey of mental health and legal professionals. *American Journal of Family Therapy, 37*, 127–145.

Bow, J. N., Gould, J. W., Flens, J. R., & Greenhut, D. (2006). Testing in child custody evaluations—Selection, usage, and Daubert admissibility: A survey of psychologists. *Journal of Forensic Psychology Practice 6*, 17–38. doi:10.1300/J158v06n02_02

Bow, J. N., & Martindale, D. A. (2009). Developing and managing a child custody practice. *Journal of Forensic Psychology Practice, 9*, 127–137. doi:10.1080/15228930802575482

Bow, J. N., & Quinnell, F. A. (2001). Psychologists' current practices and procedures in child custody evaluations: Five years after American Psychological Association guidelines. *Professional Psychology: Research and Practice, 32*, 261–268. doi:10.1037/0735-7028.32.3.261

Bow, J. N., & Quinnell, F. A. (2002). A critical review of child custody evaluation reports. *Family Court Review, 40*, 164–176. doi:10.1111/j.174-1617.2002.tb00827.x

Bow, J. N., & Quinnell, F. A. (2004). Critique of child custody evaluations by the legal profession. *Family Court Review, 42*, 115–127. doi:10.1177/1531244504421009

Braver, S. L., & O'Connell, D. (1998). *Divorced dads: Shattering the myths: The surprising truth about fathers, children, and divorce.* New York, NY: Tarcher Putnam.

Bricklin, B. (1984). *Bricklin Perceptual Scales.* Furlong, PA: Village.

Bruch, C. S. (2002). Parental alienation syndrome and parental alienation: Getting it wrong in child custody cases. *Family Law Quarterly, 35*, 527–552.

Buchanan, C. M., & Jahromi, P. L. (2008). A psychological perspective on shared custody arrangements. *Wake Forest University Law Review, 2*, 419–439.

Cartwright, G. F. (1993). Expanding the parameters of parental alienation syndrome. *The American Journal of Family Therapy, 21*, 205–215. doi:10.1080/01926189308250919

Ceci, S. J., Kulkofsky, S., Klemfuss, J. Z., Sweeney, C. D., & Bruck, M. (2007). Unwarranted assumptions about children's testimonial accuracy. *Annual Review of Clinical Psychology, 3*, 311–328. doi:10.1146/annurev.clinpsy.3.022806.091354

Ceci, S. J., Papierno, P. B., & Kulkofsky, S. (2007). Representational constraints on children's suggestibility. *Psychological Science, 18*, 503–509. doi:10.1111/j.1467-9280.2007.01930.x

Chopra, D., & Mlodinow, L. (2011). *War of the worldviews: Where science and spirituality meet—And do not.* New York, NY: Harmony.

Cotter, D. M. (2006). Relocation of the custodial parent: A state by state survey. *Divorce Litigation, 18*, 89–112.

Daubert v. Merrell Dow Pharmaceuticals, 113 S. Ct. 2786 (1993).

Davies, P. T., & Cummings, E. M. (2006). Interparental discord, family process, and developmental psychopathology. In D. Cicchetti & D. J. Cohen (Eds.), *Developmental psychopathology* (2nd ed., Vol. 3, pp. 86–128). New York, NY: Wiley.

Davies, P. T., & Sturge-Apple, M. L. (2007). Advances in the formulation of emotional security theory: An ethologically-based perspective. *Advances in Child Development and Behavior, 35*, 87–137. doi:10.1016/B978-0-12-009735-7.50008-6

Davies, P. T., Sturge-Apple, M. L., Cicchetti, D., & Cummings, E. M. (2007). The role of child adrenocortical functioning in pathways between forms of interparental conflict and child maladjustment. *Developmental Psychology, 43*, 918–930. doi:10.1037/0012-1649.43.4.918

Davies, P. T., Sturge-Apple, M. L., Winter, M. A., Cummings, E. M., & Farrell, D. (2006). Child adaptational development in contexts of interparental conflict over time. *Child Development, 77*, 218–233. doi:10.1111/j.1467-8624.2006.00866.x

Deutsch, R., & Pruett, M. K. (2009). Child adjustment and high conflict divorce. In R. M. Galatzer-Levy & L. Kraus (Eds.), *The scientific basis of custody decisions* (2nd ed., pp. 353–374). New York, NY: Wiley.

Dies, R. R. (2008). The use of questionnaires in child custody evaluations. *Journal of Child Custody: Research, Issues, and Practices, 4*, 103–122.

Drozd, L., Kleinman, T., & Olesen, N. (2000). Alienation or abuse? In *Proceedings of the Fourth International Symposium on Child Custody Evaluations* (pp. 169–181). Madison, WI: Association of Family and Conciliation Courts.

Drozd, L. M., & Olesen, N. W. (2004). Is it abuse, alienation, and/or estrangement? A decision tree. *Journal of Child Custody: Research, Issues, and Practices, 1*, 65–106. doi:10.1300/J190v01n03_05

Drozd, L. M., & Olesen, N. W. (2010). Abuse and alienation are each real: A response to a critique by Joan Meier. *Journal of Child Custody: Research, Issues, and Practices, 7*, 253–265. doi:10.1080/15379418.2010.521118

Drozd, L., Olesen, N., & Siani, M. (in press). *Road map for parenting plan evaluations: A systematic decision tree approach.* Sarasota, FL: Professional Resource Press.

Dunne, J., & Hedrick, M. (1994). The parental alienation syndrome: An analysis of sixteen selected cases. *Journal of Divorce & Remarriage, 21*, 21–38. doi:10.1300/J087v21n03_02

Dutton, D. G. (2006a). Domestic abuse assessment in child custody disputes: Beware the domestic violence research paradigm. *Journal of Child Custody: Research, Issues, and Practices, 2*, 23–42. doi:10.1300/J190v02n04_02

Dutton, D. G. (2006b). On comparing apples with apples deemed nonexistent: A reply to Johnson. *Journal of Child Custody: Research, Issues, and Practices, 2*, 53–63. doi:10.1300/J190v02n04_04

Dutton, D. G., Hamel, J., & Aaronson, J. (2010). The gender paradigm in family court processes:

Re-balancing the scales of justice from biased social science. *Journal of Child Custody: Research, Issues, and Practices, 7*, 1–31. doi:10.1080/15379410903554816

Elrod, L. D. (2006). A move in the right direction? Best interests of the child emerging as the standard for relocation cases. *Journal of Child Custody: Research, Issues, and Practices, 3*, 29–61. doi:10.1300/J190v03n03_03

Elrod, L. D., & Dale, M. D. (2008). Paradigm shifts and pendulum swings in child custody: The interests of children in the balance. *Family Law Quarterly, 42*, 381–418.

Elrod, L. D., & Spector, R. G. (2004). A review of the year in family law: Children's issues remain the focus. *Family Law Quarterly, 37*, 527–575.

Emery, R. E., Otto, R. K., & O'Donahue, W. T. (2005). A critical assessment of child custody evaluations: Limited science and a flawed system. *Psychological Science in the Public Interest, 6*(1), 1–29. doi:10.1111/j.1529-1006.2005.00020.x

Faigman, D. L., Saks, M. J., Sanders, J., & Cheng, E. K. (2008). *Modern scientific evidence: Standards, statistics, and research methods* (Student ed.). Eagan, MN: Thomson West.

Federal Rules of Evidence, 28 C.F.R. § 101–1103 (2010).

Feinberg, J., & Gould, J. W. (2012, June). *The credible and helpful child custody report.* Workshop presented at the 49th annual conference of the Association of Family & Conciliation Courts, Chicago, Il.

Ford v. Ford, 371 U.S. 187 (1962).

Friedrich, W. N. (2002). *Psychological assessment of sexually abused children and their families.* Thousand Oaks, CA: Sage.

Friedrich, W. N., Fisher, J., Broughton, D., Houston, M., & Shafran, C. R. (1998). Normative sexual behavior in children: A contemporary sample. *Pediatrics, 101*, e9. doi:10.1542/peds.101.4.e9

Frye v. United States, 293 F. 1013 (D.C. Cir. 1923).

Galatzer-Levy, R. M., Kraus, L., & Galatzer-Levy, J. (Eds.). (2009). *The scientific basis of child custody decisions* (2nd ed.). New York, NY: Wiley.

Gardner, R. A. (1985). Recent trends in divorce and custody litigation. *Academy Forum (A Publication of the American Academy of Psychoanalysis), 29*(2), 3–7.

Gardner, R. A. (1992). *The parental alienation syndrome: A guide for mental health and legal professionals.* Creskill, NJ: Creative Therapeutics.

Gardner, R. A. (2002). The empowerment of children in the development of parental alienation syndrome. *American Journal of Forensic Psychology, 20*, 5–29.

Gatowski, S. I., Dobbin, S. A., Richardson, J. T., Ginsburg, G. P., Merlino, M. L., & Dahr, V. (2001).

Asking the gatekeepers: A national survey of judges on judging expert evidence in a post-*Daubert* world. *Law and Human Behavior, 25*, 433–458. doi:10.1023/A:1012899030937

General Electric Co. v. Joiner, 522 U.S. 136 (1997).

Gould, J. W. (1998). *Conducting scientifically crafted child custody evaluations.* Thousand Oaks, CA: Sage.

Gould, J. W. (1999). Professional interdisciplinary collaboration and the development of psycholegal questions guiding court ordered child custody evaluations. *Juvenile & Family Court Journal, 50*(1), 43–52. doi:10.1111/j.1755-6988.1999.tb01277.x

Gould, J. W. (2006). *Conducting scientifically crafted child custody evaluations* (2nd ed.). Sarasota, FL: Professional Resource Press.

Gould, J. W., & Bell, L. C. (2000). Forensic methods and procedures applied to child custody evaluations: What judges need to know in determining a competent forensic workproduct. *Juvenile & Family Court Journal, 51*(3), 21–29. doi:10.1111/j.1755-6988.2000.tb00023.x

Gould, J. W., & Martindale, D. A. (2007). *The art and science of child custody evaluations.* New York, NY: Guilford Press.

Gould, J. W., & Martindale, D. A. (2008). Custody evaluation reports: The case for references to the peer-reviewed professional literature. *Journal of Child Custody: Research, Issues, and Practices, 5*, 217–227. doi:10.1080/15379410802583700

Gould, J. W., & Martindale, D. A. (2009). Specific-questions guide to child custody investigations. *The Matrimonial Strategist, 27*(5), 1–3.

Gould, J. W., & Martindale, D. A. (2013). Child custody evaluation. In R. K. Otto (Ed.), *Handbook of psychology: Vol. 11. Forensic psychology* (pp. 101–138). New York, NY: Wiley.

Gould, J. W., & Martindale, D. A. (in press). *Mental health professionals involved in child custody litigation: From court-appointed evaluators to retained experts.* Sarasota, FL: Professional Resource Press.

Gould, J. W., Martindale, D. A., & Flens, J. R. (2009). Responsible use of psychological tests in child custody assessment. In R. M. Galatzer-Levy, L. Kraus, & J. Galatzer-Levy (Eds.), *The scientific basis of child custody decisions* (2nd ed., pp. 85–124). New York, NY: Wiley.

Gould, J. W., & Stahl, P. M. (2000). The art and science of child custody evaluations: Integrating clinical and mental health models. *Family Court Review, 38*, 392–414. doi:10.1111/j.174-1617.2000.tb00581.x

Gould, J. W., & Stahl, P. M. (2001). Never paint by the numbers: A response to Kelly & Lamb (2000), Solomon (2001), and Lamb & Kelly (2001). *Family Court Review, 39*, 372–376. doi:10.1111/j.174-1617.2001.tb00619.x

Greeno, C. G. (2001). Introduction to the technical series: What is science, and how does it help us? *Family Process, 40,* 115–120. doi:10.1111/j.1545-5300.2001.4010100115.x

Griggs v. Duke Power, 401 U.S. 424 (1971).

Grisso, T. (1986). *Evaluating competencies: Forensic assessment and instruments. Perspectives in law and psychology.* New York, NY: Kluwer Academic/Plenum Press. doi:10.1007/978-1-4899-5046-8

Grisso, T. (2003). *Evaluating competencies: Forensic assessments and instruments* (2nd ed.). New York, NY: Kluwer Academic/Plenum Press.

Haskett, M., Weiland, K., Hutcheson, J., & Tavana, T. (1995). Substantiation of sexual abuse allegations: Factors involved in the decision-making process. *Journal of Child Sexual Abuse, 4,* 19–47. doi:10.1300/J070v04n02_02

Heilbrun, K. (1992). The role of psychological testing in forensic assessment. *Law and Human Behavior, 16,* 257–272. doi:10.1007/BF01044769

Heilbrun, K. (1995). Child custody evaluations: Critically assessing mental health experts and psychological tests. *Family Law Quarterly, 29,* 63–78.

Heilbrun, K. (2001). *Principles of forensic mental health assessment.* New York, NY: Kluwer Academic/Plenum Press.

Heilbrun, K., Grisso, T., & Goldstein, A. M. (2009). *Foundations of forensic mental health assessment. Best practices in forensic mental health assessment.* New York, NY: Oxford University Press.

Hildwin v. State, 951 So. 2d 784 (Fla. 2006).

Hunt, J. W. (2010). *Admissibility of expert testimony in state courts.* Retrieved from http://www.fitzhunt.com/sites/default/files/news/Admissibility%20of%20Expert%20Testimony%20in%20State%20Courts-Hunt.pdf

Hynan, D. J. (2004). Unsupported gender differences on some personality disorder scales of the Millon Clinical Multiaxial Inventory—III. *Professional Psychology: Research and Practice, 35,* 105–110. doi:10.1037/0735-7028.35.1.105

Hynan, D. J. (2012). Young children, attachment security, and parenting schedules. *Family Court Review, 50,* 471–480. doi:10.1111/j.1744-1617.2012.01462.x

Jaffe, P. G., Crooks, C. V., & Poisson, S. E. (2003). Common misconceptions in addressing domestic violence in child custody disputes. *Juvenile & Family Court Journal, 54*(4), 57–67. doi:10.1111/j.1755-6988.2003.tb00086.x

Jaffe, P. G., Lemon, N. K. D., & Poisson, S. E. (2003). *Child custody & domestic violence: A call for safety and accountability.* Thousand Oaks, CA: Sage.

Keilin, W. G., & Bloom, L. J. (1986). Child custody evaluation practices: A survey of experienced professionals. *Professional Psychology: Research and Practice, 17,* 338–346. doi:10.1037/0735-7028.17.4.338

Kelly, J. B., & Emery, R. E. (2003). Children's adjustment following divorce: Risk and resilience perspectives. *Family Relations: Interdisciplinary Journal of Applied Family Studies, 52,* 352–362. doi:10.1111/j.1741-3729.2003.00352.x

Kelly, J. B., & Johnston, J. R. (2001). The alienated child: A reformulation of parental alienation syndrome. *Family Court Review, 39,* 249–266. doi:10.1111/j.174-1617.2001.tb00609.x

Kelly, J. B., & Lamb, M. E. (2000). Using child development research to make appropriate custody and access decisions for young children. *Family Court Review, 38,* 297–311. doi:10.1111/j.174-1617.2000.tb00577.x

Kelly, R. F., & Ramsey, S. H. (2007). Perspectives on family law & social science research: Assessing and communicating social science information in family and child judicial settings: Standards for judges and allied professionals. *Family Court Review, 45,* 22–41. doi:10.1111/j.1744-1617.2007.00126.x

Kelly, R. F., & Ramsey, S. H. (2009). Child custody evaluations: The need for systems-level outcome assessments. *Family Court Review, 47,* 286–303. doi:10.1111/j.1744-1617.2009.01255.x

Kirkland, K. (2002). The epistemology of child custody evaluations. *Family Court Review, 40,* 185–189. doi:10.1111/j.174-1617.2002.tb00829.x

Kirkland, K., & Kirkland, K. L. (2001). Frequency of child custody evaluation complaints and related disciplinary action: A survey of the Association of State and Provincial Psychology Boards. *Professional Psychology: Research and Practice, 32,* 171–174. doi:10.1037/0735-7028.32.2.171

Kirkland, K., McMillan, E. L., & Kirkland, K. L. (2006). Use of collateral contacts in child custody evaluations. *Journal of Child Custody: Research, Issues, and Practices, 2,* 95–109. doi:10.1300/J190v02n04_08

Kirkpatrick, H. D. (2004). A floor, not a ceiling: Beyond guidelines: An argument for minimum standards of practice in conducting child custody and visitation evaluations. *Journal of Child Custody: Research, Issues, and Practices, 1,* 61–75. doi:10.1300/J190v01n01_05

Kuehnle, K. (1996). *Assessing allegations of child sexual abuse.* Sarasota, FL: Professional Resource Press.

Kuehnle, K. (2006, June). *Investigating sexual abuse allegations.* Paper presented at the annual conference of the American Academy of Forensic Psychology, San Juan, Puerto Rico.

Kuehnle, K., & Connell, M. (2009). *The evaluation of child sexual abuse allegations: A comprehensive guide to assessment and testimony.* New York, NY: Wiley.

Kuehnle, K., & Drozd, L. (Eds.). (2005). *Child custody litigation: Allegations of child sexual abuse.* New York, NY: Haworth Press.

Kuehnle, K., & Drozd, L. (Eds.). (2012). *Parenting plan evaluations: Applied research for the family court.* New York, NY: Oxford University Press.

Kuhn, T. S. (1962). *The structure of scientific revolutions* (3rd ed.). Chicago, IL: University of Chicago Press.

Kumho Tire Company Ltd. et al. v. Carmichael et al., 256 U.S. 137 (1999).

LaFortune, K. A., & Carpenter, B. N. (1998). Custody evaluations: A survey of mental health professionals. *Behavioral Sciences and the Law, 16,* 207–224.

Lamb, M. E. (2010). *The role of the father in child development* (5th ed.). New York, NY: Wiley.

Lamb, M. E. (2012). A wasted opportunity to engage with the literature on the implications of attachment research for family court professionals. *Family Court Review, 50,* 481–485. doi:10.1111/j.1744-1617.2012.01463.x

Lamb, M. E., & Kelly, J. B. (2001). Using empirical literature to guide the development of parenting plans for young children: A rejoinder to Solomon and Biringen. *Family Court Review, 39,* 365–371. doi:10.1111/j.174-1617.2001.tb00618.x

Lamb, M. E., & Kelly, J. B. (2009). Improving the quality of parent–child contact in separating families with infants and young children: Empirical research foundations. In R. M. Galatzer-Levy, L. Kraus, & J. Galatzer-Levy (Eds.), *The scientific basis of child custody decisions* (2nd ed., pp. 187–214). New York, NY: Wiley.

Lampl, A. (2009). Observations of parents, care takers, and children for child custody assessment. In R. M. Galatzer-Levy, L. Kraus, & J. Galatzer-Levy (Eds.), *The scientific basis of child custody decisions* (2nd ed., pp. 71–84). New York, NY: Wiley.

Lilienfeld, S. O. (2010). Can psychology become a science? *Personality and Individual Differences, 49,* 281–288. doi:10.1016/j.paid.2010.01.024

Ludolph, P. S. (2012). The special issue on attachment: Overreaching theory and data. *Family Court Review, 50,* 486–495. doi:10.1111/j.1744-1617.2012.01464.x

Ludolph, P. S., & Dale, M. D. (2012). Attachment in child custody: An additive factor not a determinative one. *Family Law Quarterly, 46,* 1–40.

Martindale, D. A. (2001). Cross-examining mental health experts in child custody litigation. *The Journal of Psychiatry & Law, 29,* 483–511.

Martindale, D. A. (2004). Integrity and transparency: A commentary on record keeping in child custody evaluations. *Journal of Child Custody: Research, Issues, and Practices, 1,* 31–40. doi:10.1300/J190v01n01_03

Martindale, D. A., & Gould, J. W. (2004). The forensic model: Ethics and scientific methodology applied to child custody evaluations. *Journal of Child Custody: Research, Issues, and Practices, 1,* 1–22. doi:10.1300/J190v01n02_01

Martindale, D. A., & Gould, J. W. (2007). Custody evaluation reports: The case for empirically-derived information. *Journal of Forensic Psychology Practice, 7,* 87–99. doi:10.1300/J158v07n03_06

McCann, J. T., Flens, J. R., Campagna, V., Colman, P., Lazzaro, T., & Connor, E. (2001). The MCMI–III in child evaluations: A normative study. *Journal of Forensic Psychology Practice, 1,* 27–44. doi:10.1300/J158v01n02_02

Melton, G. B., Petrila, J., Poythress, M. G., & Slobogin, C. (1987). *Psychological evaluations for the courts: A handbook for mental health professionals and lawyers.* New York, NY: Guilford Press.

Melton, G. B., Petrila, J., Poythress, M. G., & Slobogin, C. (1997). *Psychological evaluations for the courts: A handbook for mental health professionals and lawyers* (2nd ed.). New York, NY: Guilford Press.

Melton, G. B., Petrila, J., Poythress, M. G., & Slobogin, C. (2007). *Psychological evaluations for the courts: A handbook for mental health professionals and lawyers* (3rd ed.). New York, NY: Guilford Press.

Mnookin, J. L., & Gross, S. R. (2003). Expert information and expert evidence: A preliminary taxonomy. *Seton Hall Law Review, 34,* 141–189.

New York State Matrimonial Commission. (2006). *Report to the Chief Judge of the State of New York.* Retrieved from http://www.nycourts.gov/reports/matrimonialcommissionreport.pdf

North Carolina Psychological Association. (1994). *Child custody guidelines.* Raleigh, NC: Author.

O'Donohue, W., & Bradley, A. R. (1999). Conceptual and empirical issues in child custody evaluations. *Clinical Psychology: Science and Practice, 6,* 310–322. doi:10.1093/clipsy/6.3.310

Otto, R. K., Buffington-Vollum, J. K., & Edens, J. F. (2003). Child custody evaluations. In A. M. Goldstein & I. B. Weiner (Eds.), *Handbook of psychology: Vol. 11. Forensic psychology* (pp. 179–208). New York, NY: Wiley.

Otto, R. K., & Edens, J. F. (2003). Parenting capacity. In T. Grisso (Ed.), *Evaluating competencies: Forensic assessments and instruments* (2nd ed., pp. 229–307). New York, NY: Kluwer Academic/Plenum Press.

Otto, R. K., Edens, J. F., & Barcus, E. H. (2000). The use of psychological testing in child custody evaluations. *Family Court Review, 38,* 312–340. doi:10.1111/j.174-1617.2000.tb00578.x

Otto, R. K., & Heilbrun, K. (2002). The practice of forensic psychology: A look to the future in light of the past. *American Psychologist, 57,* 5–18. doi:10.1037/0003-066X.57.1.5

Palmore v. Sidoti, 466 U.S. 429 (1984).

Parkinson, P., & Cashmore, J. (2008). *The voice of a child in family law disputes.* Oxford, England: Oxford University Press. doi:10.1093/acprof: oso/9780199237791.001.0001

Pipe, M. E., Lamb, M. E., Orbach, Y., & Cederborg, A. C. (Eds.). (2007). *Child sexual abuse: Disclosure, delay, and denial.* Mahwah, NJ: Erlbaum.

Pruett, M. K., Arthur, L., & Ebling, R. (2007). The hand that rocks the cradle: Maternal gatekeeping after divorce. *Pace Law Review, 27,* 709–739.

Pruett, M. K., Ebling, R., & Insabella, G. (2004). Critical aspects of parenting plans for young children: Interjecting data into the debate about overnights. *Family Court Review, 42,* 39–59. doi:10.1177/1531244504421004

Pruett, M. K., Williams, T. Y., Insabella, G., & Little, T. D. (2003). Family and legal indicators of child adjustment to divorce among families with young children. *Journal of Family Psychology, 17,* 169–180. doi:10.1037/0893-3200.17.2.169

Raisner, J. K. (1997). Family mediation and never married parents. *Family Court Review, 35,* 90–101. doi:10.1111/j.174-1617.1997.tb00448.x

Ramsey, S. H., & Kelly, R. F. (2007). Law making through the adversarial process: The need for standards for social science briefs in family law cases. In L. Wardle & C. Williams (Eds.), *Family law: Balancing interests and pursuing priorities* (pp. 135–144). Buffalo, NY: Hein.

Rand, D. C. (1997a). The spectrum of parental alienation syndrome (Part I). *American Journal of Forensic Psychology, 15,* 23–52.

Rand, D. C. (1997b). The spectrum of parental alienation syndrome (Part II). *American Journal of Forensic Psychology, 15,* 39–92.

Reich, W. (1949). *Character analysis* (3rd ed.). (T. P. Wolfe, Trans.). New York, NY: Orgone Institute Press. (Original work published 1933)

Rogers, R. (2001). *The handbook of diagnostic and structured interviewing.* New York, NY: Guilford Press.

Rogers, R., & Shuman, D. W. (2000). *Conducting insanity evaluations* (2nd ed.). New York, NY: Guilford Press.

Rohrbaugh, J. B. (Ed.). (2008). *A comprehensive guide to child custody evaluations: Mental health and legal perspectives.* New York, NY: Springer. doi:10.1007/978-0-387-71894-1

Roseby, V. (1995). Uses of psychological testing in a child-focused approach to child custody evaluations. *Family Law Quarterly, 29,* 97–110.

Schutz, B. M., Dixon, E. B., Lindenberger, J. C., & Ruther, N. J. (1989). *Solomon's sword: A practical guide to conducting child custody evaluations.* San Francisco, CA: Jossey-Bass.

Shear, L. E. (1996). Life stories, doctrines and decision making: Three high courts confront the move-sway dilemma. *Family Court Review, 34,* 439–458. doi:10.1111/j.174-1617.1996.tb00435.x

Skafte, D. (1985). *Child custody evaluations: A practical guide.* Thousand Oaks, CA: Sage.

Skinner, B. F. (1953). *Science and human behavior.* New York, NY: Macmillan.

Smart, C. (2002). From children's shoes to children's voices. *Family Court Review, 40,* 307–319. doi:10.1111/j.174-1617.2002.tb00842.x

Smart, C., & Neale, B. (2000). "It's my life, too": Children's perspectives on post-divorce parenting. *Family Law, 30,* 163–169.

Stahl, P. M. (1994). *Conducting child custody evaluations: A comprehensive guide.* Thousand Oaks, CA: Sage.

Stahl, P. M. (1999). *Complex issues in child custody evaluations.* Los Angeles, CA: Sage.

Stahl, P. M. (2010). *Conducting child custody evaluations: From basic to complex issues.* Thousand Oaks, CA: Sage.

State of North Carolina v. Rannie Lane Stancil, 599 S.E.2d, 788 (2002).

Strasburger, L. H., Guthiel, T. G., & Brodsky, S. A. (1997). On wearing two hats: Role conflict in serving as both psychotherapist and expert witness. *American Journal of Psychiatry, 154,* 448–456.

Thompson, R. A. (2000). The legacy of early attachments. *Child Development, 71,* 145–152. doi:10.1111/1467-8624.00128

Tippins, T. M. (2012, December). *Evidence for forensic psychologists.* Workshop presented by the American Academy of Forensic Psychology, Sarasota, FL.

Tippins, T. M., & Wittmann, J. P. (2005a). Empirical and ethical problems with custody recommendations: A call for clinical humility and judicial vigilance. *Family Court Review, 43,* 193–222. doi:10.1111/j.1744-1617.2005.00019.x

Tippins, T. M., & Wittmann, J. P. (2005b). A third call: Restoring the noble empirical principles of two professionals. *Family Court Review, 43,* 270–282. doi:10.1111/j.1744-1617.2005.00028.x

Trinder, L. (2008). Maternal gate closing and gate opening in post divorce families. *Journal of Family Issues, 29,* 1298–1324. doi:10.1177/0192513X08315362

U.S. Department of Justice. (2000a). *Extent, nature, and consequences of intimate partner violence: Findings from the National Violence Against Women Survey* (NCJ Publication No. 181867). Washington, DC: Author.

U.S. Department of Justice. (2000b). *Full report of the prevalence, incidence, and consequences of intimate partner violence against women: Findings from the National Violence Against Women Survey* (NCJ Publication No. 183781). Washington, DC: Author.

Wallerstein, J. S., & Kelly, J. B. (1980). *Surviving the breakup: How children and parents cope with divorce.* New York, NY: Basic Books.

Warshak, R. A. (2001). Current controversies regarding parental alienation syndrome. *American Journal of Forensic Psychology, 19,* 29–59.

Warshak, R. A. (2002). Misdiagnosis of parental alienation syndrome. *American Journal of Forensic Psychology, 20,* 31–52.

Warshak, R. A. (2010). *Divorce poison: How to protect your family from bad-mouthing and brainwashing* (2nd ed.). New York, NY: HarperCollins.

Weisz, V. G. (1999). Commentary on "conceptual and empirical issues in child custody evaluations."

Clinical Psychology: Science and Practice, 6, 328–331. doi:10.1093/clipsy/6.3.328

Westen, D., & Weinberger, J. (2005). Clinical judgment in science: Reply. *American Psychologist, 60,* 659–661. doi:10.1037/0003-066X.60.6.659

Wingspread Conference. (2001). High conflict custody cases: Reforming the system for children. *Family Court Review, 39,* 146–157.

Wood, J. M., & Nezworski, M. T. (2005). Science as a history of corrected mistakes [Comment]. *American Psychologist, 60,* 657–658. doi:10.1037/0003-066X.60.6.657

Wood, J. M., Nezworski, T., Lilienfeld, S. O., & Garb, H. N. (2003). *What's wrong with the Rorschach: Science confronts the controversial inkblot test.* New York, NY: Jossey-Bass.

Zalta, E. N. (Ed.). (2011). *The Stanford encyclopedia of philosophy.* Retrieved from http://plato.stanford.edu/archives/win2003/entries/davidson

CHAPTER 14

PERSONAL INJURY AND OTHER TORT MATTERS

Eric Y. Drogin, Leigh D. Hagan, Thomas J. Guilmette, and Lisa Drago Piechowski

Personal injury and other tort matters present ample opportunity for employing the unique contributions of forensic psychologists. The injuries in question are by no means restricted to traditional medical afflictions, as mental pain and suffering are prominently featured in a broad array of cases that are based in the workplace, the home, and any other setting in which human beings may interact.

Tort cases are civil matters in which some individual or group had a duty, breached that duty, did so in a fashion that resulted in harm, and was ultimately determined to have a sufficiently causal role in the harm in question. Forensic psychologists are involved in gauging the nature and severity of such harm and in addressing the extent to which a particular defendant's actions—or lack thereof—were to blame.

Of central importance is the forensic psychologist's recognition that mental pain and suffering are multidimensional experiences that may result from a diverse array of potential influences. As in other areas of clinical investigation, the professional literature has repeatedly established that culture and psychosocial context are critical factors in understanding a litigant's disability and his or her contributing mental health symptomatology (Garg, Datillio, & Miazzo, 2011). The stress associated with protracted litigation itself cannot be overlooked as a potential causative factor.

Not surprisingly, in light of the personal desperation of some litigants—and the vast sums that may result from a successful lawsuit—the assessment of malingering is a key factor in tort-related forensic

evaluations; this task is further complicated by the limits of clinical judgment alone in detecting malingering without the use of specific symptom and performance validity measures.

The forensic evaluator must consider in each case what mental health disorders may be present, what legally relevant functional abilities may have been affected by an allegedly traumatic event, and what may be the nature and strength of any causal connection between such event and a litigant's resultant functional abilities. Posttraumatic stress disorder (PTSD) is an omnipresent focus of personal injury and other tort litigation; major depressive disorder and generalized anxiety disorder (GAD) are also prominently featured in such cases. However, it would be difficult to overemphasize the importance in these matters of conducting a functional assessment as opposed to focusing merely on the presence or absence of a particular psychiatric diagnosis.

Regarding assessment methodology, there is no uniform battery or selection of measures that forensic psychologists will employ in investigating a particular type of injury. As a general matter, evaluators in these cases will be expected to use a biopsychosocial model that benefits from standardized interview procedures, standardized tests, and reference to collateral sources. Forensic reports are prized for their brevity, comprehensiveness, transparency, and clarity.

As in other areas of forensic practice, personal injury and other tort evaluators are obligated to adhere diligently to ethical canons, standards of practice, and legal regulations. Role clarification,

http://dx.doi.org/10.1037/14461-014
APA Handbook of Forensic Psychology: Vol. 1. Individual and Situational Influences in Criminal and Civil Contexts,
B. L. Cutler and P. A. Zapf (Editors-in-Chief)

familiarity with specialized assessment issues, appropriate record keeping, and adherence to proper interstate practice boundaries are particularly relevant considerations in this context. The presence of third-party observers has emerged as a controversial topic in forensic psychology within the context of personal injury evaluations, and practitioners will need to be prepared to address the expectations of all parties when the issue surfaces in a given case.

This chapter addresses each of these notions and others from the perspective of relevant psychological theory and principles, the current state of scientific research, and practice and policy issues.

IMPORTANCE OF THE PROBLEM

Personal injury cases address a diverse collection of alleged wrongs, including those that are occasioned by "workplace violence or harassment, medical malpractice, toxic torts, or civil lawsuits filed in the wake of criminal acts" (L. Miller, Sadoff, & Dattilio, 2011, p. 278). These cases present considerable opportunity for forensic psychologists because the causes and manifestations of the injuries in question are not strictly medical by any means. As noted by Melton, Petrila, Poythress, and Slobogin (2007), "The plaintiff may claim that the defendant's negligence caused not only physical harm but mental pain and suffering as well, and may request an evaluation gauging the nature and extent of this pain and suffering" (p. 37).

Personal injury cases "are firmly anchored in doctrines, principles, and traditions of tort law" (Parry & Drogin, 2007, p. 414). Tort law "empowers those who suffer certain sorts of injuries or invasions to seek remedies from those who brought about those injuries or invasions" (Hershovitz, 2012, p. 99). In order for a plaintiff's attorney to prevail in asserting that a tort has actually occurred, he or she faces the burden of establishing that each of four basic elements is present.

- *Duty*: Did the defendant actually bear some affirmative responsibility to do something—or perhaps, not to do something? A fellow psychologist may have been obligated to conduct psychotherapy in an appropriate fashion. A teacher may

have been obligated to refrain from conducting an inappropriate relationship with a student. Note that although there might be criminal penalties associated with various kinds of failures to honor one's duties, the focus in tort law is a civil one.

- *Breach*: Perhaps the defendant had a duty—but did he or she actually fail to meet that obligation? It is not enough for plaintiffs to establish that someone was supposed to do (or not do) something. Failure must actually occur.

- *Harm*: If a defendant had a duty and breached it, something bad must still have happened to someone in order for a tort to have occurred. Plaintiffs who have not suffered some sort of identifiable injury, even if someone owed them something, will not be able to prevail legally under these circumstances.

- *Causality*: Even if there was a duty, and that duty was breached, and harm occurred, was the defendant's wrongful behavior truly the source of the injury in question? If so, to what extent was it the source?

This last notion of causality, which is specifically addressed by the concept of *proximate cause*, is one that has bedeviled British and American law students for centuries. Sperino (2013) correctly observed that proximate cause is "a notoriously flexible and theoretically inconsistent concept" (p. 1,200), and teasing apart its various definitions and practical implications could easily evolve into an exercise occupying most of the space allotted for this chapter. For our purposes, it suffices to establish that proximate cause amounts to "sufficient contribution to harm as to incur civil liability" (Drogin, Dattilio, Sadoff, & Gutheil, 2011, p. 739), with the key word here being *contribution*. This has two important ramifications. First, the defendant need not have been the only person or entity who caused the injury or injuries in question—multiple parties may have contributed. Second, the defendant's wrongdoing need not have been the only factor that contributed to the harm that was suffered by the plaintiff. Perhaps the defendant harmed the plaintiff in a way that was made worse by a failure to get the injury treated properly, or perhaps some other unforeseen event occurred, such as a natural disaster. Still, some degree of liability is likely to attach.

Nonlawyers might presume that the term *damages* refers to the harm that was allegedly suffered by a plaintiff, and indeed this is often the case. Damages also may refer, however, to the amount of money that is paid to a plaintiff on the negotiation of an advantageous settlement or at the conclusion of a successful civil trial (Eisenberg, 2013). These damages may reflect a host of different financially related considerations, such as lost wages, costs of treatment, and compensation for pain and suffering or emotional distress (Hunter & Amoroso, 2012).

Negligence is another term that is commonly encountered in forensic tort practice. It is closely linked to the notion of *standard of care*. As noted by Drogin and Meyer (2011),

> Negligence in common English usage means carelessness or recklessness. However, as a legal term of art, negligent conduct is conduct falling below the standard of care. Standard of care is also a legal term of art. While jurisdictional definitions may vary slightly, in general the standard of care is defined as the conduct of an average, prudent individual in similar circumstances. (p. 544)

A critical metric for gauging the importance of the problem of personal injury and other tort matters is financial impact. Although those in favor of robust tort options for plaintiffs argue that to this day, "consumers are not sufficiently protected," and "victims are not adequately compensated for injuries" (Shepherd, 2013, p. 258), such assertions are countered by others who maintain that "frivolous lawsuits are bankrupting businesses" (Graffam, 2012, p. 14) and that the current tort scheme "deters too much desirable behavior" while encouraging attorneys to sue entities who are "guilty of nothing more than having deep pockets" (DeLeon, 2012, p. 1,789). In the personal injury arena, for example, it has been suggested that "national enactment of draconian medical malpractice reforms would save the federal budget $54 billion over 10 years" (Rasmussen, 2013, p. 54). The *tort reform movement* reinforces such concerns with an insistence that

"doctors have responded to rising liability insurance rates by giving up high-risk practices, limiting their practices to minimal litigation risk areas, or moving to states that enforce caps on liability" (Lu, 2010, p. 316). Viewed from the perspective of the doctoral-level mental health professional, annual psychological malpractice rates have long approached or exceeded $3,000 in some jurisdictions (Wagner, 2002), and average annual psychiatric malpractice rates are currently more than $6,000 (Daly, 2010).

RELEVANT PSYCHOLOGICAL THEORY AND PRINCIPLES

The etiology of psychological injuries and harm emerging after a traumatic event, even without the prospect of litigation, is often multifactorial and the result of a complex interaction of pre-, peri-, and postinjury factors that may be psychological, personality related, biological, socially mediated, or some combination thereof (e.g., biopsychosocial and diathesis-stress models). The most common psychological injuries encountered in tort litigation are those that are associated with emotional distress/mental disorders such as depression, anxiety, or PTSD; cognitive impairments following traumatic brain injury (TBI), particularly from mild TBI or concussion; and pain and suffering, as evidenced most often in chronic pain syndromes or other medical symptoms.

Evidence for the complex interface of multiple factors being the genesis of psychological injuries following an event has been extant for years. For example, Shalev (1997) advocated an integrated multidimensional and biopsychosocial approach as the main explanatory model of PTSD. Many other authors have advanced similar perspectives (e.g., Young, 2008a). Among the evidence that has been cited for the multiplicity of causative factors include the contribution of childhood and adult cumulative trauma as a predictor of PTSD symptomatology (Cloitre et al., 2009), the role of premorbid personality (e.g., negative emotionality) and individual factors (Bowman, 2005; M. W. Miller, 2003), and even the potential role of neuropeptides and central nervous system inflammation as biomarkers of PTSD (Baker, Nievergelt, & O'Connor, 2012).

Mild brain injury or concussion is defined generally as occurring with a limited loss of consciousness (e.g., <30 min, if at all), a Glasgow Coma Scale (Barlow, 2012) score of between 13 and 15, and posttraumatic amnesia of less than 24 hr. Within these injury parameters, evidence strongly suggests that complete recovery should be expected in the vast majority of cases (Carroll et al., 2004; McCrea, 2008; McCrea et al., 2009; Meares et al., 2011). However, there remains a small minority of individuals who report persisting and disabling symptoms associated with concussion.

In cases where there is no history of multiple concussions or positive findings on neuroimaging, then other nonneurologic factors such as preinjury physical and psychiatric problems (e.g., anxiety, PTSD symptoms, and pain; Ponsford et al., 2012), as well as premorbid psychosocial issues, psychological comorbidities, postinjury stressors, and substance abuse (McCrea, 2008), are believed to be important in symptom maintenance. Carroll et al. (2004) also described the possible contributions of alcohol use, older age, severity of other associated injuries, and seizures as potentially contributing to long-term poorer outcomes in individuals with mild TBI.

The biopsychosocial model of symptom creation and maintenance is germane to chronic pain syndromes (Schultz et al., 2005; Young, 2008a), as it is generally accepted that pain is "a multidimensional experience produced by multiple influences" (Melzack & Katz, 2006, p. 144). Not only are the types of physical trauma and specific tissue damage important physiological considerations, but personality characteristics (Gatchel & Kishino, 2006) and a person's beliefs, expectations, attributions, and fear/avoidance (Pincus, 2006) also can contribute significantly to his or her pain perception.

The role of culture and psychosocial contexts are also known to contribute to an individual's physical symptoms and disability. A classic example is the phenomenon of mass psychogenic illness, or what was previously known as *mass hysteria*. In these types of cases, groups of people develop a constellation of symptoms that are suggestive of an organic illness but without a clearly identified etiology

(Jones et al., 2000). A predominant feature in mass psychogenic illness is the rapid emergence of symptoms often of members within a cohesive social unit (Bartholomew & Muniratnam, 2011) who are typically under physical or psychological stress who suddenly believe that they have been made ill by some external/environmental cause. Examples include the medical consequences of a water pollution accident in Camelford, England (David & Wessely, 1995), in the absence of objective evidence that the pollution could create such physical symptoms, and a purported case of a constellation of subjective physical symptoms that were attributed to toxic exposure at a high school in Tennessee (Jones et al., 2000). In most cases, symptoms tend to be transmitted within specific social networks, suggesting that the term *sociogenic illness* would also be appropriate (Ryan & Morrow, 1992).

Among the most common types of litigated personal injuries (e.g., PTSD, mild TBI, pain), there is often considerable overlap of symptomatology, which can further complicate conceptualization of the disorder and its assessment. For example, there appears to be significant comorbidity between PTSD and chronic pain (Asmundson & Taylor, 2006), to the point where they have been described as "mutually maintaining conditions" (Sharp & Harvey, 2001, p. 871, as cited in Boccaccini, Boothby, & Overduin, 2006). Complaints of cognitive deficits have also been associated with PTSD and chronic pain, and persons with a history of mild TBI also report a host of affective and physical symptoms. Iverson, King, Scott, and Adams (2001) reported that worker's compensation patients with pain complaints reported comparable or more cognitive symptoms than patients with head injuries who were not involved in litigation. Iverson and McCracken (1997) reported that 42% of 170 chronic pain patients who were not in litigation and were without a history of head injury reported at least one cognitive complaint. Thirty-nine percent of these pain patients reported three or more cognitive symptoms that could have met the criteria for a postconcussive syndrome even though they had not sustained any head trauma.

Pain (headache) is the most common physical complaint following mild TBI and is often a significant target of treatment by medical personnel (Packard, 2008). Affective symptoms are so common following mild brain injury that the research criteria for postconcussional disorder that are listed in the *Diagnostic and Statistical Manual of Mental Disorders, Fourth Edition, Text Revision* (*DSM–IV–TR*; American Psychiatric Association, 2000) include four psychological/emotional symptoms (e.g., irritability or aggression on little or no provocation; anxiety, depression, or affective liability; changes in personality; and apathy or lack of spontaneity) out of eight total. The general, nonspecific symptoms associated with postconcussional disorder are also reported by healthy adults as well as by nonbrain-injured persons with various medical and psychological disorders (Iverson, Lange, Brooks, & Rennison, 2010; McCrea, 2008), thereby complicating the issue of causality even more. The relevant forensic ramifications of a revamped diagnostic view of *Diagnostic and Statistical Manual of Mental Disorders, Fifth Edition* (*DSM–5*) neurocognitive disorders that no longer includes "postconcussional disorder" per se (American Psychiatric Association, 2013) have yet to be determined.

The descriptions of the events and details that may have led to an event resulting in a psychological injury can also be complicated and distorted by normal cognitive processes, even for individuals who are not involved in litigation. Human memory is not mechanical and thus does not record past events with 100% clarity and accuracy. Davis and Loftus (2007) described that "original perceptions and judgments as well as later memory and judgments include a mixture of actual features of the original information or event and altered, distorted, or added features" (p. 196). Misremembering an event can be a function of multiple factors, including beliefs and expectations about the events or people involved, the creation of a narrative or story to make sense of a chain of prior circumstances, and the introduction of postevent information, to name just a few (Davis & Loftus, 2007). The details of conversations, which are often relevant to litigation (e.g., who said what to whom and when), are also vulnerable to failures and distortions (Davis & Friedman, 2007).

In addition, the age of the witness can add error to the accurate recall of prior events and conversations. For example, younger children's memories are particularly vulnerable to suggestibility in comparison to older children (Melnyk, Crossman, & Scullin, 2007) and to the quality of the investigative interview that is used to obtain the information (Lamb, Orbach, Warren, Esplin, & Hershkowitz, 2007). On the other end of the age spectrum, older adults exhibit significant variability with regard to their recall of prior events. In general, evidence suggests that the recall of the elderly witness is generally less detailed and accurate when it is compared to that of younger adults (Mueller-Johnson & Ceci, 2007). There is also an increased susceptibility in the elderly witness to false recognition and false recall of novel information (LaVoie, Mertz, & Richmond, 2007).

Litigation Effects

There is a history in the fields of psychology and law of ascribing a litigating plaintiff's injuries and disabilities to the hope and expectation of financial reward rather than to the genuine deficits that are associated with legitimate trauma, especially when the etiology for the complaints is unclear. In years past, this phenomenon was described by various terms, most notably, *accident neurosis* or *compensation neurosis* (Mayou, 1996). Similarly, Bellamy (1997) attributed poor treatment outcome in patients with pending litigation to a host of factors, including suggestion, somatization, rationalization, a distorted sense of justice, victim status, and entitlement to further the exaggerated sick role. Although the influence of compensation as a motivator or as an additional variable that may influence the expression of symptoms and persisting disability cannot be ignored, its primary or central role in personal injury litigation has been challenged (Mayou, 1996). Studies have revealed that in most cases, litigants are not cured by a verdict (Bryant & Harvey, 2003; Mendelson, 1995). Evans (1994) summarized this issue with the following:

> Although it has been claimed that it is the process of litigation and the prospect of receiving financial remuneration that are the all-important factors in promoting continued disability in the

absence of an obvious physical cause, the research would suggest that it should also be borne in mind that there are very powerful psychological, cultural, and interpersonal factors which all operate to maintain disability and are all too frequently ignored in the evaluation and treatment of patients that are involved in compensable injury accidents. (pp. 29–30)

The potential for compensation, however, is a variable that still needs to be considered in personal injury litigation. For example, meta-analytic procedures that were used to assess the relationship between disability compensation and pain found that compensation was related to increased reports of pain and decreased treatment efficacy (Rohling, Binder, & Langhinrichsen-Rohling, 1995). A meta-analytic review of the effects of financial incentives on recovery after closed head injury revealed a moderate effect size of 0.47, with the effect being particularly strong for individuals with mild TBI (Binder & Rohling, 1996), resulting in the authors concluding that "the data showed more abnormality and disability in patients with financial incentives despite less severe injuries" (p. 7). A number of literature reviews of recovery from mild TBI have implicated litigation/compensation as important variables in persistent and disabling postconcussive symptoms (Carroll et al., 2004; Kashluba, Paniak, & Casey, 2008). However, in examining memory functioning among mild TBI patients who are involved in litigation, mild to moderate TBI patients not involved in litigation, severe TBI patients not in litigation, depressed patients, and patients with somatization disorders, Suhr, Tranel, Wefel, and Barrash (1997) found that nonneurological factors such as psychological status and medication use were related to memory impairment, and litigation status alone was not predictive of memory performance.

Litigation has been implicated in the response bias in plaintiffs' histories (Weissman, 1990). For example, Lees-Haley et al. (1997) compared the responses of 131 litigating and 315 nonlitigating adults on a questionnaire that asked them to report the degree to which specific symptoms and other aspects of life were problematic in the past and at the present. Results revealed that the plaintiffs rated their pre-injury functioning as superior to that of the nonplaintiffs, effectively describing themselves as "hypernormal" prior to their injury. A similar finding was reported in a comparison of a group of 90 patients with a concussion who were temporarily fully disabled with a group of 177 healthy controls on a postconcussion symptom inventory (Iverson et al., 2010). The patients were asked to rate the frequency and intensity of their symptoms and co-occurring life problems at the current time and retrospectively based on the month before they sustained their mild TBI; the healthy controls were asked to rate the same symptoms at the current time. The patients with a concussion reported fewer and less severe pre-injury symptoms than those reported by the controls, even though there was no reason to believe that the control group was any healthier than were the patients with concussions prior to their injuries. This suggests that people who sustain an injury may be biased toward underestimating or underreporting the frequency and severity of symptoms that they were experiencing prior to their trauma, reflecting what Iverson et al. (2010) described as "the good-old-days bias." Furthermore, individuals who failed effort testing (e.g., tests for malingering) tended to retrospectively report even fewer pre-injury symptoms compared to those individuals who passed effort testing.

Additional studies have described the effect that litigation might have on self-report. For example, Lees-Haley (1990) found that one-half of nonbrain-injured personal injury plaintiffs who were not seeking compensation for brain damage scored in the potentially impaired range on a neuropsychological test of mental processing speed. The author questioned whether (a) emotional personal injury could reduce neuropsychological scores in the absence of brain damage, (b) the sheer stress of litigation could contaminate neuropsychological assessment, or (c) voluntary manipulation could account for the decreased performance. Lees-Haley (1989) has described *litigation response syndrome* as potentially accounting for various symptoms of anxiety, depression, and stress that may resemble the complaints that are initially described by the plaintiff as an injury in his or her lawsuit, even though the symptoms are believed to be a temporary response to the stress that is associated with the process of litigation, which he described as being "a deeply frustrating and emotionally disturbing experience" (p. 110).

Lanyon (2001) conducted a principal components analysis of 15 self-report scales taken from the Balanced Inventory of Desirable Responding (Li & Li, 2008), the Minnesota Multiphasic Personality Inventory—2 (MMPI-2; Butcher, Graham, Ben-Porath, Tellegen, & Dahlstrom, 2001), and the Psychological Screening Inventory (Lanyon, 2007) that were administered to 101 general forensic clients, including those involved in child custody cases, personal injury cases, sex offenses, and criminal offenses, and found three distinct factors: exaggeration of psychiatric symptoms versus exaggeration of personal adjustment, exaggeration of virtue, and exaggeration of physical health difficulties.

A number of psychological inventories, such as the Millon Clinical Multiaxial Inventory—III (MCMI–III; Millon, Davis, & Millon, 1997) and the Personality Assessment Inventory (PAI; Morey, 2007), include scales that assess the validity of the respondent's self-report, and some measures have been developed specifically for that purpose (e.g., Structured Inventory of Malingered Symptomatology [Wisdom, Callahan, & Shaw, 2010], Miller Forensic Assessment of Symptoms Test [H. A. Miller, 2001], and Structured Inventory of Reported Symptoms [SIRS–2; Rogers, Sewell, & Gillard, 2010]). In an attempt to identify exaggerated symptom reporting and response bias, the MMPI-2 (Butcher et al., 2001, and its restructured form, the MMPI–2–RF; Ben-Porath & Tellegen, 2011) has become a cornerstone in the assessment of personal injury (Ackerman, 2010; Heilbronner & Henry, 2013; Otto, 2002; Pope, Butcher, & Seelen, 2006) given the numerous studies that have examined its validity scales (e.g., Infrequency Scale [F], Infrequency-Psychopathology Scale [Fp], Symptom Validity Scale [FBS], Henry-Heilbronner Index [HHI], and Response Bias Scale [RBS]) in forensic samples as well as its sensitivity to somati-

zation and overreporting of health concerns, for which personal injury litigants are at high risk (Lanyon & Almer, 2002; Young, 2008b; Youngjohn, Spector, & Mapou, 1997).

Malingering

The complex interaction of biological, psychological, and psychosocial factors that may influence a personal injury litigant's symptom presentation and maintenance must also include consideration of the potential for the intentional production of false or grossly exaggerated physical or psychological symptoms that are motivated by external incentives such as financial compensation or malingering (American Psychiatric Association, 2013). According to the *DSM–5* (American Psychiatric Association, 2013), the motivation for malingering is an external incentive (e.g., secondary gain), and symptoms are voluntarily produced. This differs conceptually from disorders of deception where the motivation is for primary gain, such as relief from psychological distress or other unpleasant emotional states, and where symptom production is believed to be nonvolitional or to stem from unconscious motives, as in the cases of conversion and somatoform disorders. Naturally, however, both primary and secondary gain as motivators for symptom exaggeration can coexist.

Much has been written in the last 25 years on the assessment and detection of malingering, beginning particularly with the publication in 1988 of *Clinical Assessment of Malingering and Deception* by Richard Rogers (Rogers, 1988). The nature and scope of the problem of malingering, particularly in medicolegal cases, has undergone some transformation over time, including an attempt to provide more specific diagnostic criteria, as evidenced by the publication of proposed criteria for malingered neurocognitive dysfunction (Slick, Sherman, & Iverson, 1999), which has been modified and updated as the criteria for malingered neuropsychological dysfunction (Slick & Sherman, 2013). Professional organizations such as the National Academy of Neuropsychology (NAN) and the American Academy of Clinical Neuropsychology (AACN) have each published position papers on the importance of the assessment of effort, response bias, and malingering in forensic neuropsychological evaluations (Bush et al., 2005; Heilbronner, Sweet, Morgan, Larrabee, & Millis, 2009, respectively).

The base rates of malingering can only be estimated. However, in a survey of the American Board of Clinical Neuropsychology membership, base rates of probable malingering and symptom exaggeration were estimated to occur in 29% of personal injury cases and in 30% of disability exams (Mittenberg, Patton, Canyock, & Condit, 2002). More specifically, clinicians estimated that malingering and excessive symptom exaggeration occurred in 39% of mild head injury cases, 31% of chronic pain cases, 27% of neurotoxic cases, and 22% of electrical injuries. In evaluations that were conducted for Social Security disability, Chafetz (2008) reported a probable malingering rate of between 46% and 60%. Among a group of 318 patients with chronic pain who were undergoing a psychological evaluation, 35% were classified as exhibiting evidence of probable or definite malingered pain-related disability (Greve, Bianchini, Etherton, Ord, & Curtis, 2009)

Much of the research on malingering detection has been conducted in the field of clinical neuropsychology, where a number of measures have been developed specifically for the assessment of feigned cognitive disorders (Boone, 2007; Larrabee, 2007) in multiple conditions, but particularly in mild TBI (Carone & Bush, 2013), although many of these procedures have also been studied in, and applied to, patients with chronic pain. These types of measures are known collectively as *performance validity tests* and may stand alone (e.g., developed and administered solely for the purpose of evaluating effort or malingering) or be embedded (i.e., included in a standardized neuropsychological test for which empirically derived cutoffs have been established to identify failure based on inadequate effort or malingering rather than genuine brain dysfunction). The sensitivity and specificity of a number of both standalone and embedded performance validity tests are well known (Boone, 2007; Heilbronner et al., 2009; Larrabee, 2007). The administration of these procedures in the assessment of reported neurocognitive dysfunction in personal injury cases is critical given the limitations of

clinical judgment alone in the detection of malingering (Guilmette, 2013).

Malingering assessment is further complicated by the lack of a standard pattern of results or test profiles that are evident in all cases of negative response bias. Research has not revealed a typical malingering test profile. For example, among eight measures of suspect effort that were used in a sample of 105 patients who were undergoing evaluation for litigation or disability compensation, only two measures shared more than 50% of the score variance (Nelson et al., 2003), reflecting the likelihood that patients may attempt to malinger using different strategies across different tests. Evidence further suggests that negative response bias may vary considerably within the course of a single exam (Boone, 2009). This heterogeneity in response validity was also shown among 122 participants who were evaluated in a compensation-seeking context in which factor-analytic evidence found four distinct cognitive and psychological constructs (e.g., underreporting of psychological symptoms, overreporting of neurotic symptoms, insufficient cognitive effort, and overreporting of psychotic/rarely endorsed symptoms), reflecting highly differential responding to measures of cognitive effort versus psychological (e.g., MMPI–2; Butcher et al., 2001) self-report (Nelson, Sweet, Berry, Bryant, & Granacher, 2007).

Impediments to Assessment

In the assessment of psychological harm in personal injury cases, clinicians are required to make difficult decisions that can have far-reaching consequences. One of the most difficult is the consideration of causality between an event and the resulting condition. Young (2008a) proposed five ways in which clinicians might consider formulating this relationship: (a) The event is the sole cause of the psychological condition as there were no latent signs before the injury; (b) the event is the preponderant factor with the disorder, which was present in latent or potential form but would not have been manifest without the event; (c) the event is a partial aggravating factor such that the disorder had been clinically evident premorbidly but the injury adversely affected the condition; (d) the event is a minor factor because the disorder had been well developed premorbidly, to which the injury contributed in only a small way; or (e) the injury is unrelated to the psychological disorder.

In making these types of decisions, it is often necessary for psychologists to wade through hundreds of pages of documents that include information about the plaintiff's premorbid history, parameters of the injury, assessments by other professionals, treatment effects, test results, and, in some cases, lengthy depositions. The capacity to integrate and distill this complex information from myriad sources is challenging and potentially exposes some of the limitations that are inherent in clinical judgment.

The clinical judgment literature has identified several areas that pose challenges for the expert witness to arrive at a scientifically based conclusion. Meehl (1954) cautioned against the blind acceptance of the accuracy of clinical judgment more than half a century ago. In comparison to actuarial or mechanical judgments regarding human behavior, clinical decisions are rarely superior (Grove, Zald, Lebow, Snitz, & Nelson, 2000). The reasons for this are likely manifold. For example, one impediment to complex decision making is the use of heuristics, which can both simplify but also add error to decisional strategies (Tversky & Kahneman, 1974). *Heuristics* are decisional strategies that are used most often to simplify or integrate data about which some decision needs to be made. However, the adoption of certain heuristics may result in the clinician focusing too heavily on some data that may be misleading and not taking into account other more important data, such as base rate information.

Clinicians are also vulnerable to confirmatory bias and limitations of configural interpretation. With the former, clinicians may draw some conclusions or impressions early in the decision-making process that they may then seek to confirm throughout the remainder of the record rather than searching for disconfirmatory information or conducting a more balanced search (Mendel et al., 2011). Consequently, it is critical that clinicians avoid drawing conclusions or forming impressions prematurely. With regard to configural interpretation, research has generally revealed that humans have limited capacity for complex configural analysis

(Wedding & Faust, 1989). Thus, the administration of multiple psychological tests, particularly those that measure similar constructs, may detract from rather than add to diagnostic accuracy.

Another limiting factor that adversely affects clinical decisions is the degree to which significant intersubtest variability exists, even in a nonclinical population. For example, Schretlen, Munro, Anthony, and Pearlson (2003) found as many as 6 *SD*s between the highest and lowest standard score among 15 tests that were administered to 197 healthy adults. A 9-point intersubtest scatter was noted in almost 30% of the Wechsler Adult Intelligence Scale—Fourth Edition normative sample (Wechsler, 2008a, 2008b). Clinicians who assume abnormality based on test scatter or test score variability rather than on test patterns are prone to making diagnostic errors.

Last, with regard to malingering assessment, the literature does not support that psychologists are able to detect the inaccurate or fabricated self-report of their patients. Relying solely on clinical judgment to make a determination about the veracity of a plaintiff's report or history is fraught with danger. The capacity for the vast majority of people to detect lies is barely above chance (Bond & DePaulo, 2006). In forensic cases, clinicians cannot function as they would in the context of being a treatment provider where, in most cases, the client's report is generally accepted without requiring verification and with the expectation that the client is always motivated to engage in treatment to improve his or her life situation.

Effects of Litigation on Treatment

The effects of litigation on treatment in personal injury cases, which is believed by many researchers to be ineffective due to the lack of motivation for improvement, is not well known because of the difficulty of studying patients prospectively and because patients cannot be randomly assigned to treatment groups based on their involvement with litigation. However, in a review of the literature, Evans (1994) summarized that the purported adverse effects of litigation and compensation on treatment outcome can be ameliorated by "early intervention and a well-planned and orchestrated treatment strategy, along with the appropriate psychological intervention and management" (p. 30). He opined that this type of intervention can be "extremely effective in reducing time lost from work" (p. 30) and the utilization of other medical services. Evans also asserted that disability insurance carriers shoulder some of the burden of lost work and increasing medical expenses when they fail to make timely payments for medical bills and to reimburse workers for lost wages.

Scarano and Jankovic (1998) found that patients with posttraumatic, neurologic, movement disorders who were treated at a movement disorders clinic and were involved with litigation seemed to have more severe and persistent disability than those patients who were not involved with litigation, although the authors could not definitively conclude that the legal system had adversely affected the outcome of the patients. Landers et al. (2007) compared two groups of neck pain patients, those with litigation/worker's compensation involvement and those without, at the start of physical therapy and then 12 weeks later. The authors found that the individuals who were involved with litigation/worker's compensation had greater neck disability and functional limitations after therapy, but they also had greater disability at initial presentation, again raising the question of whether the litigation group had more severe injuries before treatment.

In comparing a group of patients with chronic musculoskeletal pain who failed to complete a functional restoration program (noncompleters) to a group of patients who did, Proctor (2002) described a host of factors that separated the two groups. For example, unresolved litigation, a negative relationship with the employer, and other negative views of work were more common in the noncompleter group than in the completer group. In addition, there were a number of other pretreatment psychological and medical risk factors that were associated with failure to complete the treatment program and a poorer posttreatment outcome.

Maxwell (2001) investigated the relationship among secondary gain incentives, progress in therapy, and cognitive response sets related to the degree of cooperation among 69 patients who were undergoing physical therapy. Regressions revealed that the patients who exhibited a disability exaggeration cognitive response were more likely to have a secondary gain incentive than patients who did not, and angry negativity was a significant predictor of poor progress in therapy.

The relationship between treatment response and unresolved litigation with personal injury plaintiffs is complex and difficult to predict. Some studies have found that being in litigation is associated with poorer treatment outcome than not being in litigation, but the effect of litigation itself is not necessarily causative. Except in cases of malingering, other factors appear to also play an important role, which is consistent with the realization that complex behaviors are often the result of multiple interacting variables.

RESEARCH REVIEW

According to Heilbrun (2001), identifying the relevant forensic issues that are contained in the larger legal issues to be decided is the first step in any forensic mental health assessment. However, this is not always easy. Koch, Nader, and Haring (2009) noted that forensic assessment in personal injury claims is made more complex by the lack of fit between what the law needs to know and decide and what psychology is best suited to address. The legal elements of a tort were discussed earlier in this chapter; they define what the law needs to know and decide. Considering this legal definition in light of psychological knowledge, the forensic issues can be broken down into three questions or tasks for the forensic mental health expert to address:

- What mental health disorders are present?
- What legally relevant functional abilities were affected by the traumatic event?
- What is the nature and strength of any causal connection between the allegedly traumatic event(s) and the resultant functional abilities of the plaintiff? (Kane, Nelson, Dvoskin, & Pitt, 2013)

Mental Health Disorders

Although many diagnoses have been alleged in personal injury claims, some diagnoses are seen more frequently than others. Witt and Weitz (2007) reported that the most common symptoms seen following motor vehicle accidents include chronic pain, depression, and anxiety (including PTSD). Melton et al. (2007) reported that the condition variously known as traumatic neurosis/PTSD/acute stress disorder (ASD) is the most commonly observed mental injury in personal injury cases.

Koch, O'Neill, and Douglas (2005) listed PTSD, ASD, and major depressive episode as conditions that may be the subject of personal injury litigation. Kane et al. (2013) pointed to PTSD as the most common diagnosis in personal injury cases. Bryant et al. (2010) found, in a study of 1,084 patients who had experienced a traumatic injury, that 1 year following the injury, 31% of the patients reported having a psychiatric disorder, and 22% reported having a psychiatric disorder that they had never had before. The most common new disorders were GAD, PTSD, and agoraphobia.

PTSD has been studied extensively. According to the *DSM–5*, the diagnosis of PTSD requires exposure to a traumatic event in which the person was exposed to "actual or threatened death, serious injury, or sexual violence" by means of "experiencing," "witnessing," or "learning" of such phenomena in various ways (American Psychiatric Association, 2013, p. 271). It has been estimated that one-third of the population will be exposed to a trauma of this nature at some point in their lives (Brunello et al., 2001). Among those exposed to such events, most people will not develop PTSD. Brunello et al. (2001) noted that only 10% to 20% of people who are exposed to severe trauma develop PTSD. Bomyea, Risbrough, and Lang (2012) proposed that pre-trauma individual biological and cognitive differences may contribute to the risk of developing PTSD following a trauma. They suggested that biological factors, including the dysregulation of serotonin, catecholamines, and glucocorticoids, along with cognitive variables such as intelligence and neuropsychological functioning, created a vulnerability to developing PTSD following a trauma. The addition of more specific cognitive biases, such as negative attributions, rumination, and fear of emotion, were hypothesized to interact with the experience of trauma to predict the development of PTSD.

PTSD is twice as common among women as among men (Kessler, Sonnega, Bromet, Hughes, & Nelson, 1995). The traumas most commonly associated with PTSD are combat exposure among men and rape and sexual molestation among women (Kessler et al., 1995). Some differences have been noted in the symptom profiles of men and women with PTSD. Green (2003) found that men were significantly more likely than women to suffer with irritability and to use alcohol to excess. In terms of symptom frequency, more than 90% of the participants of both sexes with PTSD reported experiencing insomnia, anxiety when they were reminded of the trauma, intrusive thoughts, irritability, and poor concentration. Other frequently reported symptoms (reported by >75% of participants) included a loss of interest, recurrent dreams of the trauma, avoidance of places or activities associated with the trauma, and a foreshortened sense of the future. Only 18% of the participants reported that they were unable to recall parts of the trauma (Green, 2003). Based on a review of the literature, Koch et al. (2005) reported that approximately 50% of individuals who are suffering from PTSD have a spontaneous remission of symptoms in the first year, and as many as 10% of those with PTSD stay chronically distressed.

According to the National Institute of Mental Health (NIMH, 2001), major depression affects almost 10 million American adults each year, and approximately twice as many women as men. The average age of onset of depression is the mid-20s, but depression can develop at any age. Dysthymia affects approximately 5.4% of the U.S. adult population, with an age of onset from childhood through early adulthood (NIMH, 2001). The highest lifetime risk of major depression was among middle-aged adults (Hasin, Godwin, Stinson, & Grant, 2005). Half of individuals with major depression reported wanting to die, with one-third considering suicide and 9% having made a suicide attempt. Current and lifetime major depressive disorder was associated with other psychiatric disorders, especially substance dependence, anxiety disorders, and personality disorders (Hasin et al., 2005).

The U.S. Department of Health and Human Services (1999) estimated that as many as 80% of people with depression can be treated effectively, generally without missing much time from work or needing costly hospitalization. Effective treatments for depression include medication, psychotherapy, or a combination of both. Early intervention with antidepressant medication was significantly associated with a shortened disability episode (Dewa, Hoch, Lin, Paterson, & Goering, 2003).

Depression can have a significant impact on an individual's functioning. A longitudinal study comparing patients with depression to those with rheumatoid arthritis and to healthy individuals found that found that depression resulted in impairments in performing mental–interpersonal tasks, time management tasks, output tasks, and physical tasks. These functional deficits persisted even after an improvement in clinical symptoms such that clinical improvement did not result in full recovery of job performance (Adler et al., 2006). Mildly impaired executive functions including verbal fluency, inhibition, working memory, set-maintenance, and set-shifting were found in another study (Stordal et al., 2004). Depressed persons were found to spend more days in bed than people with chronic medical conditions such as hypertension, diabetes, and arthritis (Wells et al., 1989). Unfortunately, the use of anti-depressant medications (specifically selective serotonin reuptake inhibitors) was found to be associated with impaired episodic memory and poorer recognition memory (Wadsworth, Moss, Simpson, & Smith, 2005).

In addition to PTSD and depression, GAD and phobic avoidance can develop following a traumatic experience (Grant, Beck, Marquess, Palyo, & Clapp, 2008; Mayou, Bryant, & Ehlers, 2001). GAD has been estimated to have a lifetime prevalence rate of between 3% and 6% and is more common in women than in men (Kessler, Keller, & Wittchen, 2001). GAD has been associated with increased impairments in psychosocial functioning, role functioning, work productivity, and health (Revicki et al., 2012). One study found that individuals with GAD were almost twice as likely as others to miss more than 2 weeks from work or to exhibit impaired work performance (Plaisier et al., 2010).

Functional Assessment

A forensic evaluation differs from a clinical evaluation in important respects (Heilbrun, 2001; Heilbrun, DeMatteo, Marczyk, & Goldstein, 2008; Melton et al., 2007). A clinical evaluation provides information about an individual's diagnosis, symptoms, treatment, course, and prognosis. A forensic evaluation expands on and translates this information into data about an individual's *functional capacity*. Heilbrun, Grisso, and Goldstein (2009) reviewed and integrated various guidelines for forensic mental health assessment, noting that throughout these guidelines, there was an emphasis on conducting a functional assessment. This is accomplished by identifying the functional capacity that is directly relevant to the legal question, explaining the relationship between diagnosis and functional capacity, and not substituting diagnosis for an analysis of functional capacity. Although these authors were speaking of forensic practice more broadly, these comments directly apply to evaluations in personal injury cases.

As discussed earlier in this chapter, establishing harm is a required element of a tort. *Harm* refers not to the assignment of a specific diagnostic label but to a change in the plaintiff's ability to carry out important functions in his or her daily life as a result of the injury. Therefore, in tort cases, the legal criteria are functional and relate to impairment or capacity rather than to diagnosis. As such, tort cases require a functional analysis of the plaintiff in order to understand how, if at all, the defendant's actions have affected the plaintiff's life (S.A. Greenberg, Shuman, & Meyer, 2004).

Functional capacity was defined by Grisso (2003) as that which an individual can do or accomplish, as well as the knowledge, understanding, or beliefs that may be necessary for that accomplishment. Because functional capacity is distinct from diagnosis, it cannot be assumed that the presence of a particular condition is necessarily related to a specific level of functioning. Young (2010) differentiated among symptoms (i.e., subjective experiences of the plaintiff), functional impact (i.e., observable changes in the plaintiff's ability to carry out life activities), impairments (i.e., limitations resulting from a condition), and disabilities (i.e., inability to perform in a specific role or context), stressing that these terms should not be used interchangeably.

S.A. Greenberg et al. (2004) pointed out that a diagnosis is not an essential element of a legal claim or defense and warned that substituting a diagnosis for an analysis of functioning (a) can be misleading, (b) does not serve the purposes of the court, and (c) has the potential to distort an objective assessment of the plaintiff. In a further critique of the use of diagnoses in forensic practice, Mellsop, Fraser, Tapsell, and Menkes (2011) questioned the validity and reliability of psychiatric classification systems in general and especially as applied to legal issues. The authors pointed to the inconsistent application of diagnostic criteria and the proliferation of what they termed *dubious psychiatric categories.* Mellsop et al. suggested that given the current limitations of psychiatric classification systems, courts should regard diagnostic labels with skepticism.

A functional assessment in the context of tort litigation must be driven by the relevant legal issues of tort law, which include describing the harm that was suffered by the plaintiff and establishing the extent of a causal relationship between the actions of the defendant and the plaintiff's loss of function. As Grisso (2003) pointed out, functional capacity is shaped by the specific context or situational demands that are relevant to the individual being evaluated. In determining how the plaintiff has been harmed, it is important to consider how his or her functioning has changed in terms of the contextual demands of activities of daily living and functioning in various life roles, such as work, child care, social relationships, leisure, and education.

Piechowski (2011) proposed categorizing functional capacities that are related to mental health conditions in terms of three domains: *cognitive*, which includes concentration, memory, comprehension, expression, processing, and problem solving; *interpersonal*, which involves the ability to engage in appropriate interactions with others; and *emotional*, which focuses on areas such as stress tolerance, emotional control, mood stability, and judgment. Unfortunately, there are no specific psychological tests that can determine the important roles that an individual plays and how each aspect of these roles was affected by the events in question (Young, 2010).

Assessment Methodology

Heilbrun et al. (2008) noted that despite significant conceptual and empirical advances over the last two decades, there remains considerable inconsistency in the quality of forensic assessment practice. The lack of substantive or regulatory guidance for many forensic professional activities makes it difficult to determine what constitutes minimally satisfactory practice in forensic psychology. These comments are very applicable to evaluations in personal injury cases.

Specifically, little empirical research exists that addresses how best to conduct evaluations in personal injury cases. S.A. Greenberg (2003) described the challenges of investigating the assessment practices of psychologists who conduct such evaluations—a task that is complicated by the variety of conditions and circumstances that are seen in personal injury cases, making it difficult to identify a single methodology that would be appropriate across the board. The authors noted that "although we may be able to identify a general evaluation protocol or format for personal injury examinations, we should not expect to identify a uniform battery or selection of tests used in every personal injury evaluation" (p. 413).

Torres, Skidmore, and Gross (2012) described best practices for the forensic assessment of PTSD as including (a) the use of a biopsychosocial model, standardized procedures, and numerous information sources such as standardized tests and collateral sources; (b) comparisons of the examinee with relevant group data and base rates; (c) consideration of iatrogenic and litigation-related factors; (d) comparisons of current and premorbid levels of functioning; and (e) an assessment of response style and the possibility that the examinee may be exaggerating, feigning, or otherwise malingering. Unfortunately, the authors found that in general, psychologists' practices are not wholly consistent with these recommendations. Torres et al. surveyed 173 licensed psychologists who were either nonboard certified, board certified in clinical psychology, or board certified in forensic psychology. They found that board-certified forensic psychologists were more likely than psychologists in the other two groups to (a) use the *DSM-IV-TR* (American Psychiatric

Association, 2000) as their criterion reference when they were evaluating claims of PTSD, (b) make broader use of third-party data, and (c) more frequently assess for overreporting of symptoms. There were no differences between the groups, however, in terms of the number or types of assessment instruments that they used.

According to S.A. Greenberg (2003), there is no psychological test that can reliably assess what the plaintiff's functioning was like prior to the events in question or separate the effects of one trauma from another. Psychological testing, however, can be a valuable source of information that can be used to both formulate and confirm hypotheses about psychological constructs that are relevant to the legal issue as well as to disconfirm hypotheses (Heilbrun, 1992). Melton et al. (2007) described psychological testing as being more relevant in personal injury evaluations than in any other forensic context because many of the constructs that are measured by psychological tests are directly related to the assessment of distress and impairments in an individual's functional abilities.

Witt and Weitz (2007) suggested that psychological testing can be useful in forensic evaluations in three ways. First, testing may be helpful in identifying the presence of personality disorders that, if present, may have influenced the plaintiff's functioning and adjustment prior to the injury that is the subject of the litigation. Second, psychological testing provides a standardized method for assessing the plaintiff's current symptoms by comparing the plaintiff's symptom report to the reports of individuals in normal or clinical samples. Third, psychological testing can help in determining if the plaintiff is exaggerating symptoms or otherwise dissimulating through the use of standalone measures of response style as well as validity scales that are imbedded in multiscale inventories, such as those found in the MMPI–2 (Butcher et al., 2001).

Otto and Heilbrun (2002) distinguished among three types of psychological tests that are used in forensic evaluations: *Clinical assessment instruments* assess clinical constructs such as anxiety, depression, anger, and intelligence, and are designed to assist in assessment diagnosis and treatment planning with clinical populations; *forensically relevant instruments* assess clinical constructs that are typically of interest in forensic settings, such as measures of response style; and *forensic assessment instruments* directly assess psycholegal constructs such as trial competence. No forensic assessment instruments exist that directly assess emotional harm, leaving psychologists who are conducting tort evaluations to choose from clinical assessment instruments and forensically related instruments (S.A. Greenberg, 2003). Otto and Heilbrun noted that the use of clinical assessment instruments (e.g., MMPI [Butcher et al., 2001]; PAI [Morey, 2007]), which despite being well validated and having good normative databases, has substantial limitations in terms of their use in forensic applications. This stems from the fact that such measures were developed for the purpose of therapeutic evaluation and, therefore, assess and describe constructs that are not directly relevant to a particular legal standard or issue. Otto and Heilbrun warned that using clinical assessment instruments to draw conclusions about psycholegal issues is inherently problematic if their use is based on the erroneous assumption that there is a direct relationship between the clinical factor being assessed and the legal issue in question. Further, there has been little research addressing the ecological validity of clinical assessment instruments in forensic contexts (Koch et al., 2009).

Despite these concerns, surveys of psychologists who are performing forensic evaluations indicate that clinical assessment instruments are widely used in forensic evaluations (Archer, Buffington-Vollum, Stredney, & Handel, 2006; Boccaccini & Brodsky, 1999; Bow, Flens, & Gould, 2010; Lally, 2003; Torres et al., 2012). The MMPI (Butcher et al., 2001) was the most frequently named instrument in these surveys. Boccaccini and Brodsky (1999), for example, found that the MMPI was used in 89% of emotional injury cases by the psychologists who responded to their survey. More than a decade later, Bow et al. (2010) had similar results, with 87% of respondents reporting using the MMPI in forensic evaluations. Torres et al. (2012) reported that more than one-third of the psychologists they surveyed reported using the MMPI in more than 50% of their assessments. The MMPI is used extensively outside of forensic contexts as well. In surveys of clinical and neuropsychologists, Camara, Nathan, and Puente (2000) found that the MMPI was the most widely used psychological test. Other clinical assessment instruments mentioned in the surveys as being used in forensic evaluations included the PAI (Morey, 2007) and the MCMI (Millon et al., 1997).

Less information is available about the use of forensically related instruments in personal injury evaluations. In Boccaccini and Brodsky's (1999) survey, the SIRS (Rogers, Bagby, & Dickens, 1992) was the only forensically related instrument that was mentioned; it was used in 11% of emotional injury evaluations. S. A. Greenberg (2003) commented that this was a surprising finding in view of the fact that so few personal injury claims are based on psychotic symptoms. Slick, Tan, Strauss, and Hultsch (2004) surveyed neuropsychologists who performed evaluations in financial compensation or personal injury cases. The majority of their respondents (79%) reported using at least one specialized technique for detecting malingering in every evaluation. The Rey 15-Item Test (Rey-15; Morse, Douglas-Newman, Mandel, & Swirsky-Sacchetti, 2013) and the Test of Memory Malingering (TOMM; Tombaugh, 1996) were the most frequently mentioned instruments. Torres et al. (2012) reported that the TOMM (12.2%) and the SIRS (11.4%) were frequently used forensically related instruments among the respondents in their survey. Also mentioned by the respondents were the M-FAST (4.9%; H. A. Miller, 2001) and the Rey-15 (4.1%). Disturbingly, the respondents of this survey reported that clinical opinion was the most frequently used methodology for the detection of symptom overreporting (65.9%).

The assessment of PTSD has had more attention in the literature than other conditions, but many questions about assessment in forensic contexts remain unanswered. According to Koch et al. (2005), a careful assessment of PTSD following a trauma requires a systematic evaluation of the objective and subjective threat that was experienced by the plaintiff during the trauma as well as investigation of the presence of negative emotional arousal. The authors advocated a multitrait, multimethod approach to the assessment using structured interviews, multiscale inventories, symptom-specific inventories, and collateral source material. The authors noted that

although multiple reliable measures of PTSD exist, the efficacy of their use in personal injury evaluations is unknown because they have not been evaluated sufficiently within litigating samples and are infrequently used by forensic assessors.

A study by Shapinsky, Rapport, Henderson, and Axelrod (2005) found that PTSD scales that are intended for civilian (as opposed to military) populations had poor diagnostic specificity for nontraumatic stressors and were overly sensitive to everyday distress and trait characteristics. Specialized instruments for PTSD assessment include both structured interviews and self-report inventories. For example, the Clinician-Administered PTSD Scale (CAPS; Blake, Weathers, Nagy, & Kaloupek, 1995) is a structured interview with good psychometric properties, including high interrater reliability for PTSD symptoms (Koch et al., 2005). The CAPS has the disadvantage, however, of being very time consuming to administer (Foa & Tolin, 2000). Torres et al. (2012) indicated that only 14% of the respondents in their survey reported using the CAPS. The self-report inventory, the Trauma Symptom Inventory (TSI; Briere, 2001), was used more frequently (19.4%). In addition to scales assessing reported symptoms of PTSD, the TSI has three validity scales, including the Atypical Responding (ATR) scale, which is designed to detect symptom exaggeration. Unfortunately, most of the research to date supporting the effectiveness of the ATR scale in detecting feigning has used simulators, which is a significant limitation in determining the usefulness of the ATR scale in actual forensic evaluations (Rubenzer, 2009).

Psychological testing is but one source of data in a personal injury evaluation. Other sources include information that is obtained directly from the plaintiff through interview and observation and data that are obtained from collateral sources. Information that is obtained directly from the plaintiff can vary in accuracy for a variety of reasons, including the unreliability of memory and limitations in insight. Heilbrun (2001) noted that one of the more important distinctions between a forensic assessment and a therapeutic assessment is the presumed accuracy of the self-report of the individual being evaluated. Specifically, several authors have suggested that the accuracy of self-reported data appears to be influenced by situational factors such as involvement in litigation or compensation-seeking (Greiffenstein, Baker, & Johnson-Greene, 2002; Lees-Haley et al., 1997; Williams, Lees-Haley, & Djanogly, 1999), reporting that in compensation situations, examinees were more likely to report superior premorbid functioning and poorer current functioning, and they were more likely to exaggerate the number and severity of their symptoms, than examinees who were not seeking compensation. Rogers and Payne (2006) advised that overly broad questions about the plaintiff's condition, functioning, and impairment should be avoided, as such an approach may elicit efforts on the part of the plaintiff to prove his or her case rather than to respond frankly. The authors recommended that in order to minimize this possibility, the examiner should probe closely for descriptive details before asking general questions about the plaintiff's condition.

The use of collateral data in forensic evaluations is well established (Heilbrun, Rosenfeld, Warren, & Collins, 1994; Melton et al., 2007; Nicholson & Norwood, 2000). Third-party information can take the form of written records or data that are obtained through interviewing individuals who have direct knowledge of the plaintiff. As noted by Heilbrun, Warren, and Picarello (2003), third-party information can "potentially increase the accuracy of findings and conclusions through its integration with other sources of data, as part of a multitrait, multimethod approach to [forensic mental health assessment]" (p. 71). Lewis, Rubin, and Drake (2006) also emphasized the important role of third-party information: "Utilizing multiple sources of data whenever possible is critical in forming a forensic opinion." (p. 43). Heilbrun et al. noted that individuals who have had the greatest degree of contact with the plaintiff are potentially the most valuable collateral informants. However, the authors cautioned that it is important to be sensitive to the potential biases of each source. Potential collateral sources suggested by Heilbrun et al. include personal contacts (e.g., family members, neighbors, coworkers), professional contacts (e.g., medical or mental health professionals), personal documents (e.g., letters, journals), and professional documentation (e.g., financial records, employment records,

medical records). Kane (2007) emphasized the importance of obtaining and reviewing all records that are reasonably likely to address the pre- and posttrauma status of the plaintiff.

Communicating Results

Kane (2008) suggested that the task of a forensic psychologist is to educate the retaining attorney, judge, and jury about psychological concepts and information, including the evaluation process, diagnosis, and treatment of psychological disorders. In order to accomplish this effectively, it is important that both written reports and testimony focus on explicating findings in language that is understandable to a layperson and avoiding the use of unexplained professional terminology (Heilbrun, 2001; Kane, 2008; Melton et al., 2007; Weiner, 2006).

Melton et al. (2007) discussed ways in which forensic evaluation reports differ from clinical reports. First, the recipients of the report are likely to be judges and lawyers, not other mental health professionals. Because of this, it is important to ensure that relevant information is easy to identify and understand. This can be facilitated by using topical headings to organize the report and by avoiding unexplained jargon. Second, Melton et al. suggested that because the information in the report may end up in the public record, it is important to avoid unnecessarily infringing on the privacy rights of the individuals who are mentioned in the report. Third, Melton et al. emphasized the need to pay attention to detail and to ensure the accuracy of the information that is contained in the report. In addition, Melton et al. noted that although the substance and organization of reports may vary, regardless of context, it is important to separate facts from inferences, to stay within the scope of the referral question, and to avoid including either too much or too little information.

According to L. Miller et al. (2011), a good report in a personal injury case displays four qualities: brevity, comprehensiveness, transparency, and clarity. Brevity and comprehensiveness can be accomplished through careful organization. This allows the expert to convey his or her opinion without creating a report that is "bloated, rambling, redundant, and disorganized," while containing all of the points that contributed to the expert's conclusions (p. 297). Linking the data presented in the report to these conclusions contributes to its transparency. The authors suggested that conclusions that are not supported by clinical observations or test findings as described in the report should not be included. The use of plain language, as opposed to professional jargon, increases clarity. The authors warned that the use of unexplained technical or professional language risks confusing or alienating the reader.

In a similar vein, Gold and Stejskal (2011) recommended that forensic reports should provide enough information to support the expert's opinions, using nontechnical language. Although no one format was recommended, the authors proposed that the content of the report include information about the degree of psychological distress experienced by the examinee; relevant diagnoses (if any); the causation of the diagnosis; the associated degree of impairment evident in the examinee; and the examinee's prognosis, including expected course, likely chronicity, and expected duration of the impairment.

According to a 2005 survey of state courts that was conducted by the U.S. Bureau of Justice Statistics, the vast majority (97%) of civil cases are settled prior to trial (Langton & Cohen, 2008). This suggests that the majority of psychological examinations in tort cases will not result in courtroom testimony. Heilbrun (2001) noted that in many cases, the written report is the only product of the expert's evaluation. He stressed the importance of creating an organized report; cross-checking factual information; and clarifying the relationship among data, reasoning, and conclusions. He noted that testimony, if required, involves presenting what has already been documented in the written report; thus, a well-written report can be used to promote organized, well-supported testimony.

Standards for the admissibility of expert evidence are discussed elsewhere in this chapter. Challenges, when they do occur, often do not preclude the expert's entire testimony. LaDuke, DeMatteo, Heilbrun, and Swirsky-Sachetti (2012) surveyed 59 neuropsychologists about their experiences in forensic contexts. The survey participants indicated that

their courtroom testimony was infrequently challenged, and when challenged, the focus was on specific aspects of their testimony rather than their testimony as a whole. Simply because testimony is deemed admissible, however, does not mean that it is effective or persuasive. Boccaccini and Brodsky (2002) surveyed 488 jury-eligible adults about the believability of expert witnesses. The respondents indicated that they preferred local experts with practical experience over purely academic experts who conducted research but did not treat patients. This was especially relevant when the expert's opinion concerned a clinical issue.

Edens et al. (2012) found numerous examples in published cases in which mental health expert witnesses were accused of bias. Terms used in these cases included "hired gun," "junk science," "witch doctor," and "voodoo psychobabble." Welner, Mastellon, Stewart, Weinert, and Stratton (2012) warned against expert testimony based on opinions that are derived from the "self-serving account of the litigant or a battery of tests" that "incorporate only a fraction of relevant factual information" about the plaintiff (p. 5). However, these authors also opined that attorneys who are operating in an adversarial legal system are concerned less about obtaining objective, evidence-based testimony than they are about finding an expert who can provide an opinion that will lead to a favorable settlement or verdict.

Suggestions for Future Research

The professional literature addressing personal injury evaluations is heavily weighted toward theoretical rather than empirical studies. Empirical research is adequate in terms of describing the prevalence and course of various mental disorders and the impairments associated with these disorders, as well as in surveys regarding the frequency of test usage by psychologists in forensic evaluations. Other aspects of personal injury evaluation remain understudied. First, additional research is needed in terms of determining not just the frequency of test usage but also the efficacy of various combinations of assessment instruments in personal injury evaluations and the components of an appropriate test battery. Second, given the lack of forensic assessment instruments that are available to address relevant legal issues in tort cases, additional research is needed to establish the extent to which the clinical constructs being assessed by clinical instruments can be extrapolated to address legal issues. Third, there is a need for more research to establish the ecological validity of psychological assessment instruments in tort cases. This is particularly important in the application of embedded validity scales that are used to make assumptions about the veracity of the plaintiff's presentation. Most studies addressing the validity, reliability, specificity, and sensitivity of these scales have been based on simulation studies. Fourth, little research exists in terms of identifying and assessing an individual's relevant functional capacities in personal injury cases. Although some areas of forensic practice (e.g., competency to stand trial) have clearly defined functional abilities, evaluation in tort cases does not as easily lend itself to this. Finally, although evaluators are frequently asked to opine about causality (again, whether the harm claimed by the plaintiff was caused by the actions of the defendant), there is little research about the methodologies that are used to assess causality or the accuracy of experts' opinions about this critical element of tort law.

Suggestions for Practice

Despite the identified gaps in the research relating to evaluations in tort cases, some inferences can be drawn from the literature to guide psychologists who are performing these evaluations.

■ *Clearly identify the psycholegal questions that the evaluation is intended to address.* Before beginning the evaluation, it is critical to understand the legal issues related to the evaluation and the role that psychological data can play in informing these issues. The psycholegal questions provide the framework for the ensuing evaluation, ensure the collection of relevant data, and allow the evaluator to frame his or her opinions in a manner that addresses the key issues of tort litigation—the nature and extent of the harm that was incurred by the plaintiff and the strength of the causal relationship between this harm and the actions of the defendant.

■ *Use a multitrait, multimethod approach to assessment.* A comprehensive evaluation in this area of practice requires obtaining data from a variety of sources (e.g., the plaintiff, treatment providers, collaterals) using diverse methods (e.g., interviews, psychological testing, review of written records). This facilitates the collection of data that will allow the evaluator to more fully understand the plaintiff's condition both before and after the alleged injury. The multitrait, multimethod approach also allows for the cross-validation of data, which is essential in addressing any inconsistencies that may arise.

■ *Focus on identifying functional impairment rather than on determining a diagnosis.* The legal questions arising in tort litigation revolve around changes in the plaintiff's functional capacity, not in the assignment of a diagnostic label. A diagnosis does not describe what the plaintiff is and is not able to do, nor does it explain how the plaintiff's functioning has changed as a result of the alleged injury. The evaluator should consider the important roles in which the plaintiff is required to function and the extent to which the plaintiff is able to meet the cognitive, interpersonal, and emotional demands of these roles.

■ *Understand the scientific limits of psychological practice, especially in terms of establishing causality, offering predictions about future behavior, and determining pre-injury functioning.* The causal relationship between changes in the plaintiff's functioning and the defendant's actions has always been a core element of tort litigation. However, there are no psychological tests or methods of assessment that can directly address this question. Opinions regarding causality must be formed through extrapolation and require inferences on the part of the evaluator.

■ *Select psychological tests that are reliable and well validated, but be aware of the limitations when using clinical assessment instruments in a forensic context.* There are no forensic assessment instruments that assess constructs that are directly related to tort litigation. Evaluations in personal injury cases must rely on clinical assessment instruments and forensically related instruments. Evaluators should be familiar with the psychometric properties of the tests they employ and the extent (or lack) of research regarding the ecological validity of these instruments for use in personal injury evaluations.

- *Present findings objectively, using clear language and acknowledging contradictory findings and potential limitations of one's opinions.* Whether communicating opinions in the form of a written report or in courtroom testimony, it is important to present this information in a manner that is clear, unambiguous, and objective. The use of unexplained jargon should always be avoided. The material should be organized in a manner that facilitates the identification of relevant data and avoids confusion or misunderstandings.

PRACTICE AND POLICY ISSUES

Contemporary practice parameters obligate forensic psychologists to adhere diligently to ethical canons, standards of practice, and regulations when practicing in personal injury and other tort matters. As guests in the house of law, forensic psychologists must also familiarize themselves with the legal requirements that are relevant to the preparation and presentation of their findings and opinions. Psychologists who fail to adequately comport with ethical principles, practice standards, regulatory requirements, and legal construction attendant to tort practice put their efforts in some peril and risk substantially undermining the interests of the individuals they serve.

Ethical guidance includes broad principles and more specific codes for conducting practice that is germane to tort issues. For members of the American Psychological Association (APA), the *Ethical Principles of Psychologists and Code of Conduct* (APA, 2010) addresses conflicts between law and ethics, bases for scientific and professional judgment, disclosures of confidential information, documentation of professional work, bases for and interpretation of assessment data, and informed consent. Of particular interest is the admonition for psychologists to "uphold professional standards of conduct, clarify their professional roles and obligations, accept appropriate responsibility for their behavior, and

seek to manage conflicts of interest that could lead to exploitation or harm" (p. 1,062).

The profession also offers tort psychologists guidance with respect to record keeping (APA, 2007), test user qualifications (Turner, DeMers, Fox, & Reed, 2001), testing standards (American Educational Research Association [AERA], APA, & National Council on Measurement in Education, 2014), and special ethical considerations for the forensic practitioner (Committee on Ethical Guidelines for Forensic Psychologists, 2013). Boards of Psychology (BOP) promulgate regulatory requirements, typically in the form of standards of practice, and scholarly literature offers interpretations of standards for practical use in torts and other forensic applications (e.g., Heilbrun et al., 2008).

Ethical principles, standards of practice, and regulatory requirements are distinguishable in at least four respects, including their basis of authority, intent, applicability, and enforcement. On the one hand, because membership in a professional organization is entirely voluntary, the organizations' canons apply only to its members. The associations' *principles* aspire to elevate the level of professional practice, and their enforcement sanctions range from corrective educative measures to expulsion from membership.

Standards, on the other hand, refer to "a model accepted as correct by custom, consent, or authority" (Black, 2009, p. 1,535) and derive from two sources: customary ways of doing things in a particular field (i.e., industry standard) or practices that have been internally established and adopted by the field itself (Heilbrun et al., 2008). In this instance, the court, not a professional organization, determines whether the psychologist's efforts meet the relevant forensic standard. In the arena of personal injury and other torts, psychologists who practice below the prevailing benchmark face several potential challenges, including failing to qualify as an expert, having their testimony excluded as inadmissible, or earning little judicial deliberative weight.

Beyond ethical canons and practice standards lie certain *regulatory authorities*, most prominently in the form of administrative law in the domain of BOPs. Regulations have their authority in administrative law that is intended to protect consumers and is applicable to all licensees or individuals who are operating within the scope of practice as defined in the regulations. Enforcement power ranges from corrective educative measures, temporary supervised practice, and the exclusion of certain areas of practice to a permanent loss of one's license. Many BOPs specifically articulate standards below which the practitioner must not fall. Some BOPs incorporate the APA principles and code of conduct (APA, 2010), thereby elevating those aspirational and voluntary principles to absolute practice requirements. Other BOPs promulgate their own regulations without reference to any other entity's standards. Of particular importance to tort practice are the near-universal requirements for licensees to (a) confine their practice to areas of competence, (b) avoid misleading statements, (c) refrain from dual roles that are not limited to sexualized relationships, (d) execute an informed consent process that is inclusive of fees and information disclosure, (e) administer and report assessment services appropriately, and (f) maintain records for a term of years.

Tort psychologists who practice across state lines are well advised to familiarize themselves with the local regulations and standards. Some jurisdictions include court testimony within the definition of scope of practice of psychology; others do not. Almost all jurisdictions require that psychologists limit their practice to areas of competence, which is a burden that is borne by the practitioner. Whether psychologists may testify in a personal injury matter in a jurisdiction where they do not hold a license depends on that jurisdiction's definition of the scope of practice and other considerations. Information regarding multijurisdictional practice requirements is available through the Association of State and Provincial Psychology Boards (2010), the National Register of Health Service Providers in Psychology (2012), and scholarly literature (Drogin, 2008).

Beyond profession-centered guidance, psychologists who are practicing in tort controversies should look to the law and rules of evidence for instructive cautions. Herein lie several specifications that are broadly applicable to forensic practice but that have particular relevance in the tort practice contexts. It is essential for forensic psychologists to understand the parameters of *qualification as an expert* and *admissibility of opinion testimony*.

Roles and Responsibilities

Psychologists who take the witness stand in their capacity as therapists should prepare themselves for frequent challenges, including role duality, necessity of active practice, and predicates for the hearsay exception. Psychologists who function as therapists, usually on behalf of a plaintiff in a personal injury case, must remain diligent in their responsibility to avoid multiple conflicting roles. In an effort to help their patients, some psychologists feel justified in advocating in court, which is an inclination that is best reconsidered if not resisted altogether.

> Psychologists, psychiatrists, and other mental health professionals have given and received criticism about the use of expert witnesses whose partisanship appears to overwhelm their professionalism. Engaging in conflicting therapeutic and forensic relationships exacerbates the danger that experts will be more concerned with case outcome than the accuracy of their testimony. . . . What they do know, they know primarily, if not solely, from their patients' point of view. They are usually sympathetic to their patient's plight, and they usually want their patient to prevail. (S.A. Greenberg & Shuman, 1997, p. 56)

Other scholars caution against the slippery slope of multiple relations, inclusive of serving as therapist/advocate in the therapy office and testifying as a behavioral scientist with opinions that are held to a reasonable degree of reasonable certainty in support of a particular legal conclusion in a tort controversy (Gottlieb & Younggren, 2009; S.A. Greenberg & Shuman, 2007; Shuman, Greenberg, Heilbrun, & Foote, 1998).

Other scholars argue that not all dual roles constitute a conflict. Some scholars distinguish between impermissible boundary violations, which are always unethical and likely violate rules of court, as contrasted with occasional appropriate boundary crossings, which are part of a well-constructed treatment plan and do not cause impairment, exploitation, or harm (Lazarus & Zur, 2002). From this viewpoint, the overarching distinctions hinge on the preservation of the client's welfare and ultimate therapeutic effectiveness. Scholars who embrace this perspective view the comingled responsibilities of a treating expert as a compatible hybrid role with professionally defensible boundaries (L. Greenberg & Gould, 2001; Heltzel, 2007).

Psychologists who serve as treaters in a tort matter, whether by advanced knowledge of the pending lawsuit or by unanticipated unfolding circumstances, need to be aware of the boundary controversy in order to comply with obligations that are anchored in ethics, practice standards, regulations, and the rules of court. Appropriately informed treating psychologists who come to the tort dispute by advanced knowledge or in mid-course of treatment should document their adherence to their informed consent obligation by carefully thinking through the benefits and risks that are attendant to opening the door to therapy disclosure and assessment findings while considering the potential negative impact on the therapeutic advocacy relationship if the comingled role of expert fails to persuade the trier of fact about proximate cause, extent of harm, and prospects for therapeutic recovery. Disclosure, particularly under cross-examination, could damage the therapeutic alliance and undermine the patient's view of working with any therapist in the future.

Treatment record construction and maintenance can also cause discomfort for the patient and therapist when comingling roles. The patient might take umbrage on learning that statements that were made in the context of presumed treatment confidentiality have come to light through discovery in the course of tort or other personal injury litigation only to find those statements used by the defendant to prove a theory of causation that undermines the plaintiff's legal position or that substantially undercuts the extent of the damages that are recoverable from the claim.

When stepping into the tort arena, treating psychologists must remain alert to their obligations to several other audiences beyond their duty to their patients. Some researchers argue that limiting the construct of the client to a single person (usually the patient) causes a distraction that "obscures the fact that psychologists have ethical obligations to all parties in every case, regardless of the number or the

nature of the relationships" (Fisher, 2009, p. 1). Treating psychologists often find themselves obligated to their patient's legal adversary to produce information under the rules of discovery and to fairly acknowledge competing theories of causation and harm. Treaters might find themselves obligated to their patients' attorneys, whom the psychologists are advising about theories of causation and harm. Similarly, treaters might find themselves obligated to the court when they are granted the privilege of giving intellectually honest scientific opinion testimony. Beyond the courtroom, treaters find themselves compelled to comport with BOP regulatory requirements and codified practice standards and further bound to professional organizations' ethical canons by virtue of voluntary membership.

Even when treating psychologists are motivated by benign intent to help their patients, they might find themselves on the receiving end of a tort action that is brought by their patients in the context of a *friendly expert* lawsuit alleging acts of unauthorized release of information or omission of treatment, assessment, or referral to specialists or any other issue about which the patient might construe that the friendly psychologist breached a duty (*Marrogi v. Howard*, 2002). The claim might lack merit, but simply finding oneself named as a defendant creates profound distress and tremendous disruption to one's practice.

Beyond the roles of treater and evaluating expert, personal injury and other tort matters present other opportunities for psychologists to bring their specialized knowledge to the case. When serving in a nontestifying consulting capacity, forensic psychologists can properly represent the profession by bringing forward sound scientific information that is relevant and helpful to the tort issue. The consulting psychologist might assist the retaining attorney by informing him or her about a wide range of subject matter, including but not exclusive to practice standards, ethical principles, regulatory requirements, assessment methods, terms of art, generally accepted practices, and scientifically sound hypotheses that might bear on the alleged causation and claim of harm.

In their consulting capacity, forensic psychologists can also assist the retaining counsel with discovery requests that are informed by specialized knowledge of record-keeping guidelines (APA, 2007) and their practical implications (Drogin, Connell, Foote, & Sturm, 2010). Knowledge of BOP regulatory requirements for record construction and retention can also assist retaining counsel secure records from the reluctant expert for the opposing party.

In actual practice as consultants, psychologists can identify for retaining counsel the records to discover, including notes of interviews with a party and collateral informants, test data that are inclusive of answer sheets and graphic displays, release authorizations, correspondence and records from third parties, insurance reimbursement records inclusive of diagnoses and dates of service, and all documents in the other professionals' custody or control in hard copy and digital format not simply limited to documents in their possession. When discovered records indicate that a litigant made otherwise confidential statements directly to or in the presence of a third party, those statements might be discoverable to the extent that the litigant waived his or her expectation of privilege by voluntarily disclosing the information in an unprotected communication. Additionally, consulting psychologists might review answers to mental health questionnaires and inventories with an eye toward consistency or lack thereof with other statements that were made by the litigant. For almost all of these materials, litigants have likely waived privilege by virtue of putting their mental state at issue when claiming psychological harm.

Also from a practical perspective, consulting psychologists can advise retaining counsel when counsel is faced with impediments to discovery such as a neuropsychologist's objection to the release of test data and protocols based on professional standards (AACN, 2003; *Applied Innovations v. Regents of the University of Minnesota and National Computer Systems*, 1989; Kaufmann, 2009). Conversely, the consulting psychologist might advise the retaining defense counsel of the professional standards that are pertinent to plaintiff's counsel's effort to be present during the plaintiff's evaluation by the defense expert, as described in further detail in the next section. In some instances, a protective order can resolve objections to discovery demands,

sensitivities to test security, and concerns about unwarranted redistribution of discovery information. The court can bar the disclosure of records beyond the litigation personnel, seal the information in the court file, and require attestation that the psychologist shredded protected information in keeping with security practices or returned the materials to an officer of the court at the conclusion of the case.

Yet another role for a forensic psychologist in tort litigation is that of the academic—as subject matter or pure expert. Psychologists functioning in this capacity may appear on behalf of plaintiffs or defendants and may testify with foundational information that is relevant to the legal question and assist the jury in understanding subject matter that is likely beyond the ordinary grasp of a layperson, but without evaluating the plaintiff or particularizing opinions to any individual in the personal injury matter. For example, in response to the plaintiff's expert's testimony, a defense-retained subject matter expert might enlighten the jury about the cautions against unproctored or take-home MMPI–2 administrations (APA, 1994), critical issues surrounding effort testing with cognitive assessments, proper characterization of correlational findings, value of base-rate data, significant diagnostic limitations in torts, importance of multisource assessment methods (Strauss & Smith, 2009), and fundamental compromises to assessment methods (e.g., single-hypothesis testing, confirmatory bias, selective attention to data, premature closure, pull to affiliate, and other biases/prejudices).

Admissibility Cautions

The most relevant, helpful, learned, insightful and well-formulated opinions are of little value if they are inadmissible in court. Forensic psychologists in tort practice should be mindful of two frequent objections that might thwart their contribution to the proceedings: absence of an active practice and impermissible hearsay. With respect to the former, experts who anticipate testifying about a breach in the standard of care often have the burden to show that they have an active practice in the subject area about which they intend to opine. Although impeccable credentials might facilitate one's qualification as an expert, the court could rule the testimony inadmissible if the proponent does not currently practice in the subject matter area that is relevant to the lawsuit. A preeminent psychologist with an adult practice who does not treat or evaluate children might not be allowed to rebut the testimony of a child psychology specialist with respect to harm and treatment needs of an injured child. Similarly, the court might bar the testimony of the department chair of a well-known university if that person's duties for many years have been administrative in nature, without an active clinical practice.

A hearsay objection poses a challenge to defense and plaintiff experts alike. Hearsay is an out-of-court statement that is offered for the truth of the matter. Because hearsay constitutes the majority of what forensic psychologists rely on, they should familiarize themselves with the predicates that earn the expert hearsay exception.

Many jurisdictions follow the Federal Rules of Evidence (FRE) or a closely related construction that permits opinion testimony rather than mere factual recitation. FRE 702 states that "if scientific, technical, or other specialized knowledge will assist the trier of fact to understand the evidence or to determine a fact in issue, a witness qualified as an expert by knowledge, skill, experience, training, or education, may testify thereto in the form of an opinion or otherwise." However, the admissibility of expert testimony is conditioned on showing that "(1) the testimony is based upon sufficient facts or data, (2) the testimony is the product of reliable principles and methods, and (3) the witness has applied the principles and methods reliably to the facts of the case."

The FRE also grant an expert hearsay exception for psychologists who employ methods on which others in the field rely. FRE 703 states that "if of a type reasonably relied upon by experts in the particular field in forming opinions or inferences upon the subject, the facts or data need not be admissible in evidence in order for the opinion or inference to be admitted." Accordingly, experts will want to arm themselves with foreknowledge of the methods and procedures that other forensic psychologists employ when developing opinions on the relevant issues in tort litigation. The standard is not universal acceptance of methods for gathering,

combining, or interpreting data, but whether the reasonable psychologist employs such methods relating to personal injury claims. Procedures that are offered as new and exciting might, by definition, precipitate an inadmissibility ruling because experts in the same field do not employ those methods in the context pertinent to the tort controversy.

In anticipation of such an objection, psychologists should consider identifying the peer-reviewed scientific literature and other recognized sources in order to substantiate that reasonable psychologists rely on such methods when forming opinions and inference, bearing in mind that the underlying data or source materials need not be admissible. To meet the standard, psychologists could prepare a substantial compendium of literature that cites the methods in question. Online search engines such as the National Center for Biotechnology Information's PubMed, National Library of Medicine's MedLine, and APA's PsycINFO are helpful for showing the extent of a body of literature for the purpose at hand.

Closely related to the expert hearsay exception is the standard for the admissibility of scientific evidence. Because standards vary across jurisdictions, forensic psychologists should familiarize themselves with the controlling rule before entering the tort arena. The *Frye* rule requires that "the thing from which the deduction is made must be sufficiently established to have gained general acceptance in the particular field in which it belongs" (*Frye v. United States*, 1923). Assessment methods or means of combining data that have not gained standing and recognition among the scientific authorities would likely invite objection in *Frye* jurisdictions.

Other jurisdictions adhere to the multiprong *Daubert* standard, which holds that the factors of FRE 702, not *Frye's* general acceptance threshold, govern the admissibility of scientific testimony. In *Daubert* jurisdictions, the court "must make a preliminary assessment of whether the testimony's underlying reasoning or methodology is scientifically valid and properly can be applied to the facts at issue" (*Daubert v. Merrell Dow Pharmaceuticals, Inc.*, 1993). In formulating its assessment, the court considers several factors, including whether the theory or technique in question can be (and has been) tested, whether it has been subjected to peer review and publication, its known or potential error rate and the existence and maintenance of standards controlling its operation, and whether it has attracted widespread acceptance within a relevant scientific community. (*Daubert v. Merrell Dow Pharmaceuticals, Inc.*, 1993, p. 580)

Some state courts have adopted the federal rules in their whole cloth; others have established case-law variants (e.g., Maryland's standard based on *Frye* and *Reed v. State*, 1978), and others (e.g., Virginia) rely on case law and have no published rules of evidence. Because some personal injury cases hinge on the admissibility of scientific testimony, it is incumbent on forensic psychologists to inform themselves of the relevant rule.

Clearing the general acceptance hurdle or multifactor validity test is not sufficient. Psychologists in personal injury litigation might also bear the burden to show that their assessment methods closely approximate the facts and circumstances of the case at hand based on certain fundamental requirements.

Such testimony cannot be speculative or founded on assumptions that have an insufficient factual basis. Such testimony also is inadmissible if the expert has failed to consider all of the variables that bear on the inferences to be deduced from the facts observed. Further, where tests are involved, such testimony should be excluded unless there is proof that the conditions existing at the time of the tests and at the time relevant to the facts at issue are substantially similar. (*Tittsworth v. Robinson*, 1996)

In practical application, in a hypothetical claim of psychological harm based on trauma subsequent to a motor vehicle accident, when opining that the defendant's acts or omissions proximately caused the plaintiff's impairments, experts should sufficiently inform themselves about any prior claims of psychological harm stemming from prior unrelated traumatic events that might better explain the current claim.

When assessing harm, psychologists should consider all variables, inclusive of findings that potentially mitigate the alleged harm or that suggest symptom magnification. It is not enough to merely inventory harm, particularly by self-report. Under the previously noted *substantially similar* rule, psychologists must show that the assessment procedures accounted for the facts and circumstances particularized to the case. In practical application, an assessment of the plaintiff's damages that is based primarily on the evaluator's experience or published research citing a broadly inclusive cohort of other persons in motor vehicle accidents might fail the substantially similar test absent a showing of congruence between the conditions of the particular accident and the facts of the more generalized comparison groups that are cited in the research literature. For example, it is not likely that the psychologist could draw inferences about emotional damages stemming from a very minor accident that required only a brief medical examination and no medical or mental health treatment if the evaluator based his or her inferences on a comparison group of other persons who had experienced serious motor vehicle accidents with considerable physical injuries requiring extensive emergency medical care and substantial mental health treatment.

Forensic psychologists should remain equally attentive to other objectionable subject matter so they can avoid awkward moments on the stand. Although plaintiffs in torts and personal injury cases seek redress through the redistribution of wealth, there is one source of money that is potentially prohibited from mention in some jurisdictions: insurance. Appellate courts have held that, except where the insurance company is the named defendant in a direct action authorized by the insurance policy, "the mention of insurance constitutes reversible error requiring a new trial when the comment probably has misled or prejudiced the jury" (*Lombard v. Rohrbaugh*, 2001, p. 353). The rationale underpinning this policy is to make certain that the jury does not ignore the necessity of proof of fault simply to award damages that are payable by the third-party insurance company rather than by the defendant.

Although psychologists cannot testify about a party's insurance coverage, they might find themselves required to disclose their own financial relationship with the defendant's insurance carrier when the plaintiff intends to show bias in the experts' practice patterns. Several appellate courts have balanced the policy of barring testimony about the defendant's insurance coverage against the probative value of disclosure of the expert's substantial financial relationship with the defendant's insurance company, which pays the expert's fees.

> Testimony concerning liability insurance may be elicited for the purpose of showing bias or prejudice of a witness if there is a substantial connection between the witness and the liability carrier. If a substantial connection is demonstrated, its probative value concerning potential bias or prejudice outweighs any prejudice to the defendant resulting from the jury's knowledge that the defendant carries liability insurance. (*Lombard v. Rohrbaugh*, 2001, p. 356)

The practical applications for the forensic psychologist are twofold. First, the expert should seek advance clarification from retaining counsel about any prohibition against even passing reference to insurance applicable to either party. Second, psychologists who derive considerable income from expert services in torts and personal injury cases should anticipate the requirement to disclose their own financial relationship with insurance companies and the law firms that retain them. This disclosure is not limited to inventorying prior testimony history; it can also include the production of paid invoices and related tax documents.

Dealing With Diagnoses

The issues of diagnoses and diagnostic standards in torts and personal injury cases bear special attention whether the psychologist's role is that of a treater, evaluator, nontestifying consultant, or academic expert. Although many clinically focused practitioners reflexively assess for a formal diagnosis, there are several very good reasons for not formulating a traditional diagnosis. First, torts and personal injury cases do not require a diagnosis in order to prove liability or damages that were proximately caused by the defendant's acts or omissions. Second, ordinarily, direct evidence is the best evidence. Reference to the prevailing diagnostic nomenclature interposes an unnecessary filter through which the jury must view the psychological evidence. Third, diagnoses do not necessarily assist the jury in their deliberation as they apply the evidence to the law. In many instances, the battle of the experts plays out over the validity of a proposed diagnosis—a dispute that often generates more heat than light for the jury. Fourth, many of the current diagnostic criteria draw from self-report, which is a source that is subject to challenge. When the self-report of an interested party is draped in the cloak of scientific certainty and the seeming specificity of diagnostic nomenclature, there is risk that the jury might lose sight of the fact that the expert opinion relied, in large part, on the litigant's self-serving narrative. The risk of misattribution of probative value is in play for plaintiffs' experts who opine the presence of a condition that is reflective of harm (e.g., acute stress disorder, dissociative disorder, PTSD, major depression) just as it is when the defense expert counters with a competing diagnostic explanation (e.g., malingering or antisocial or borderline personality disorders).

Fifth, the *DSM*, in its various iterations, is not the only nomenclature for classifying psychological conditions. Psychologists who are practicing in a medical or neuropsychological setting often rely on the *International Statistical Classification of Diseases, 10th edition* (World Health Organization, 2010). Through a collaborative effort, the psychodynamic community propounded the *Psychodynamic Diagnostic Manual* (American Psychoanalytic Association, 2006) as a reaction to the narrowing scope of the traditional diagnostic taxonomy that inventories symptoms without fully accounting for the healthy mental processes and without inference to treatment strategies.

Sixth, although experts sometimes testify that the *DSM* is the diagnostic "bible," full disclosure requires acknowledgment of the more disquieting parallels to the bible. In particular, both have contested material (i.e., *DSM–5*'s "Conditions for

Further Study"; American Psychiatric Association, 2013). Decisions about what to include were made by committee votes. Scholarship over the last 60 years gives little basis for comfort in relying on clinical judgment when superior methods exist or when modesty suggests that psychologists should abandon their claim to reasonable certainty (Meehl, 1954).

When clinical judgments flow from the dynamic process of a committee, the forensic psychologist will find further cause for hesitancy to express opinions to the requisite degree of certainty on reflecting on Meehl's (1973) cautions about the compromises to group processes that are inherent in committee deliberations.

> In one respect, the clinical case conference is no different from other academic group phenomena such as committee meetings in that many intelligent, educated, sane, rational persons seem to undergo a kind of intellectual deterioration when they gather around a table in one room. The cognitive degradation and feckless vocalizations that are characteristic of committees are too well known to require comment. Somehow, the group situation brings out the worst in many people and results in an intellectual functioning that is at the lowest common denominator, which in clinical psychology and psychiatry is likely to be pretty low. (Meehl, 1973, pp. 227–228)

Per the *DSM–5*, "the relative severity and valence of individual criteria and their contribution to a diagnosis require clinical judgment" (American Psychiatric Association, 2013, p. 19). This endorsement of clinical judgment is at odds with other research showing the discouragingly low value of subject inference, which is a dubious metric (Underwager & Wakefield, 1992). Reliance on years of experience does not add validity either. "Our field is famous for supporting conclusions during testimony simply on the basis of 'accumulated clinical experience,' a phrase which may mean nothing more than accumulated personal bias" (Wittman, 1985, p. 78).

Further, the *DSM*'s dynamic evolution departs from comparison with the somewhat static nature of the bible. Presently, the *DSM* is now in its seventh iteration. What had its genesis in a World War II Army medical manual and first appeared in 1952 with 106 diagnoses spanning only 130 pages has now expanded to several hundred specified mental conditions requiring 947 pages.

Appreciating the importance of reliability as a sine qua non of validity, forensic psychologists who offer scientific opinions on tort matters would have understandable reservations about underpinning their conclusions on a diagnostic compendium that has demonstrated considerable inconsistency (i.e., changeability, variation) since its inception. What is a mental disorder one year is not the next (e.g., homosexuality and hysteria), and what was not a disorder one year becomes one the next (e.g., PTSD). Of the current *DSM*, criticism is due with respect to rater reliability, low specificity (i.e., overlap in diagnostic criteria), and reliance on self-report.

The *DSM–5*'s front-end cautions give forensic psychologists the most compelling reasons to omit formal diagnoses in torts and personal injury cases. Before iterating the diagnoses themselves, *DSM–5* cautions that this resource "was developed to meet the needs of clinicians, public health professionals, and research investigators rather than all of the technical needs of the courts and legal professionals," that there exists an "imperfect fit between the questions of ultimate concern to the law and the information contained in a clinical diagnosis," and that "assignment of a particular diagnosis does not imply a specific level of impairment or disability," with the final caveat that "even when diminished control over one's behavior is a feature of the disorder, having the diagnosis in itself does not demonstrate that the individual is (or was) unable to control his or her behavior at a particular time" (American Psychiatric Association, 2013, p. 25). Of particular relevance for tort evaluations is the *DSM–5*'s caution that "a diagnosis does not carry any necessary implications regarding the etiology or causes of the individual's mental disorder or the individual's degree of control over behaviors that may be associated with the disorder" (American Psychiatric Association, 2013, p. 25).

Assisting the Jury

When contemplating decisions about diagnoses or any other aspect of a tort matter, psychologists functioning in any capacity can bring value by remaining focused on the essential role of the expert: to assist the jury with evidence and testimony that is relevant to the legal question and is helpful in explaining issues that are beyond the ordinary knowledge of a layperson.

In practical terms, psychologists can assist retaining counsel and the jury by translating terms of art and technical parlance into language that is familiar to laypersons. For example, the professional's reference to signs and symptoms might imply an unwarranted clinical and scientific profundity to which the lay juror might accord undeserved weight. The psychologist can assist the retaining attorney in consultation or the jury through testimony by clarifying the critical distinction between a sign as an objective observation and a symptom as a self-report. This distinction is particularly relevant when addressing diagnoses, such as PTSD, that hinge almost exclusively on self-report, but which the jury might hear in the seemingly more powerful clinical vernacular as presenting symptoms.

Similarly, the psychologist might clarify for the jury the true nature of correlational testimony, which is often encountered in tort case testimony. For example, if the plaintiff's expert testifies that "there is a robust correlation between the traumatic event and permanent emotional damages," the defense psychologist can assist by clarifying that (a) correlation simply refers to a degree of relationship between two events without any causal implication of the type required to prove proximate cause in a tort; (b) robust is a subjective term, not a scientific designation; (c) a relatively low correlational value (e.g., .3) might have merit for exploratory research without rising to the reasonable certainty threshold; and (d) other events might have a correlation of equal or greater strength than the plaintiff's expert's causal theory (i.e., prior trauma, preexisting emotional impairment, or external incentives, including the prospect of compensation) taking into account the fact that a hypothetical correlation of .3 fails to account for 91% of the variance between the two observations.

In the same vein, the plaintiff's expert might assist the jury in understanding the nature of a damages assessment when challenged by defense counsel's cross-examination designed to undercut losses by illuminating the plaintiff's residual functional capacity. The plaintiff's expert can help the jury understand that a diligent damages assessment not only takes into account the injured person's current functional capacity but also considers the loss of functioning relative to the pre-injury baseline. Hypothetically, under cross-examination, the plaintiff's expert might (a) concede that the injured person's cognitive capacity falls within the average range; (b) advise that average can be as low as the 25th percentile (Wechsler, 2008b); (c) clarify that the convention within the field is to particularize the appraisal of current functioning to the individual's pre-injury baseline functioning; and (d) for the purpose of this hypothetical, explain that the plaintiff functioned in the high average range, which conceivably could equate with the 90th percentile, thereby reflecting a significant postinjury decrement.

Ultimate-Issue Opinions

The ultimate issue is the legal question that the jury must answer. Whether the forensic psychologist may give ultimate-issue testimony in a tort or personal injury case is a matter of some debate within the profession. Some in the field argue that such testimony is improper because it crosses the line between psychology and the law and invades the province of the jury (Shuman & Sales, 1998). Others contend that in civil matters, including torts, ultimate-issue testimony may be proper if the proponent clears the antecedent thresholds of relevance, helpfulness, and scientific foundation (Rogers & Ewing, 1989).

FRE 704 permits ultimate-issue testimony in some instances. With certain specifically articulated exceptions, "testimony in the form of an opinion or inference otherwise admissible is not objectionable because it embraces an ultimate issue to be decided by the trier of fact." Some states have adopted this rule or its close equivalent within their own evidentiary rules or by statute. In Maryland, for example, a psychologist who is "qualified as an expert witness may testify on ultimate issues, including insanity, competency to stand trial, and matters within the scope of that psychologist's special knowledge, in any case in any court in any administrative hearing" (Maryland Courts and Judicial Proceedings, 2013). Virginia takes a similar position but distinguishes between allowable ultimate-issue testimony and impermissible conclusions of law.

> In a civil proceeding . . . no expert or lay witness while testifying in a civil proceeding shall be prohibited from expressing an otherwise admissible opinion or conclusion as to any matter of fact solely because that fact is the ultimate issue or critical to the resolution of the case. However, in no event shall such witness be permitted to express any opinion which constitutes a conclusion of law. (Va. Code Ann., 1993)

Some scholars would further argue that failure to address the ultimate issue is a disservice to the parties and fails to assist the jury. The proponents of this view contend that the forensic psychologist is only offering scientific opinions and not drawing legal conclusions, legal opinions, or factual determinations, nor is the forensic psychologist depriving the jurors of the power to reach their own verdict.

The prudent psychologist who is functioning in a forensic capacity in a tort or personal injury matter will want to seek instruction from the retaining attorney about the permissibility of opinions that go to the heart of the legal question. The advice might range from including an opinion on the legal elements (causation and harm) that underlie the ultimate issue, to an opinion on the ultimate issue itself, or to offer no opinions that the court might construe as invading the jury's province. Whatever the opinions, the forensic psychologist must offer them to a reasonable degree of psychological certainty or risk the opposing party's motion to strike the testimony.

Psychological Testing: Necessity or Embellishment?

Psychometric assessment distinguishes the field of psychology from other mental health professions. Forensic psychologists can assist in torts and personal injury cases with specialized testing but should discern when testing is not necessary. When contemplating this decision, the psychologist would be wise to consider the ethics and standards of the profession as well as the rules that are applicable to guests in the house of law.

The necessity to possess competence to perform certain methods and procedures spans ethical obligations (e.g., APA, 2010) and BOP regulatory requirements. As an example, psychological generalists should not venture into the tort forum to offer opinions about the meaning and import of neuropsychological tests without sufficient education, training, and experience with these specialized assessments. Similarly, psychologists would be prudent to avoid offering opinions that require specialized medical knowledge, even if they have passing acquaintance with medical matters.

Forensic psychologists in torts who load up an evaluation with a litany of spurious tests will not find safe harbor in the rationalization that "this is my standard battery." Measures should be relevant to the issues that have been raised in the complaint and observed during the evaluation or are in response to previous findings in the records. Excessive testing that is not responsive to the case-specific issues might give the appearance of churning fees or opportunistic practice and would invite criticism under ethical and regulatory standards.

When deciding which tests, if any, to include, the informed psychologist must bear in mind the admissibility requirement that the evidence should be helpful; that is, probative and of assistance to the jury. The psychologist might want to reconsider employing instruments that do not contribute incremental utility above and beyond what more direct evidence (e.g., a party's statements or behavior) might tell the jury. More is not necessarily better. Administering additional tests of low reliability actually degrades their assessment utility because when combining data, the data cannot rise above their weakest contributor. Again, a party's own statements and behaviors can be most helpful because they provide direct evidence that does not require the additional layers and lenses of interpretation and does not interpose the straw man of distraction about test development, administration, scoring, and interpretation.

Psychological examiners might consider self-examination according to the following components before choosing tests in a tort or personal injury case.

- *Competence*: Will the examiner be able to prove the requisite knowledge and skill for the proposed evaluation procedures, including methods of combining and interpreting data?
- *Relevance*: Do the proposed evaluation procedures address the issues that are raised in the alleged tort?
- *Scientific*: Will the anticipated procedures form sufficient scientific bases to satisfy the legal standard for admissibility (e.g., *Frye*, *Daubert*, local variant)?
- *Probative value*: Will the anticipated procedures aid the jury in understanding the issues?
- *Incremental utility*: Do the proposed evaluation methods contribute new and reliable information and understanding that is not already available from existing data?
- *Parsimony*: Are other evaluative methods available that would yield equivalent utility and reliability more efficiently and with fewer intervening assumptions?
- *Direct evidence*: Is there sufficient prima facie information based on a party's statements or conduct that might obviate the need for evaluative procedures that interpose a layer of interpretation and inference?

Presence of Third-Party Observers

In the current sophisticated tort litigation environment, plaintiffs' attorneys are more likely than in the past to assert themselves into the defense experts' evaluations and interviews. This tactic raises important practice and policy concerns as well as personal discomfort and logistical complications for the evaluator. As with almost all issues in the litigation arena, there are two sides to the argument. The plaintiffs' attorneys will likely contend that they are entitled to be present in order to protect their clients' interests, to hear what their clients disclose, to observe their clients' demeanor, to raise objection to any procedure or inquiry that exceeds the agreed-on or court-ordered scope of the evaluation, or merely to put their clients at ease. Plaintiffs' attorneys might further argue that they are entitled to all discovery arising from the evaluation, including the interactions that are not reduced to writing, such as gestures, intonation, and undocumented statements.

Mental health professionals who have not experienced in-person scrutiny since early career supervision typically object to opposing counsel's presence, citing multiple concerns including departure from the usual and customary evaluation process (AERA et al., 2014), ethical cautions (e.g., APA, 2010; Duff & Fisher, 2005) risks of taint/contamination (Gavett, Lynch, & McCaffrey, 2005; Kehrer, Sanchez, Habif, Rosenbaum, & Townes, 2000), threats to test security (AERA et al., 2014; APA, 2010, EPCC § 9.11), copyright constraints (*Applied Innovations v. Regents of the University of Minnesota and National Computer Systems*, 1989; Committee on Ethical Guidelines for Forensic Psychologists, 2012), research from social psychology demonstrating behavior changes prompted by observer presence (Chekroun & Brauer 2002; Lynch, 2005), and unwarranted intrusion of litigation tension into the scientific data collection process (Lees-Haley, 1997).

Responsive to these objections, plaintiffs' attorneys often counter that (a) litigation is the raison d'être for the evaluation, and the attorneys' presence is only an honest acknowledgment of that fact; (b) psychologists-in-training typically conduct evaluations and interviews with third-party observers; (c) scrutiny of the examiner and examinee is even handed; (d) counsel is entitled to in vivo discovery of gestures, inflections, and pauses that are not available through record production; (e) third-party presence could sufficiently satisfy plaintiff's counsel, who might elect not to pursue certain trial tactics and expense on satisfaction with the evaluation process; (f) there is ample precedent for language interpreters as third parties present as a necessity without the evaluators' aforementioned objections; (g) passive reassurance of the plaintiff could actually facilitate more complete and valid data collection; and (h) some evaluators require a third-party presence to protect against complaints from high-conflict litigants.

Policy, ethics, standards, regulations, and law provide guidance to tort psychologists who must sort out the conflicts surrounding third-party presence. APA offers information to assist evaluators concerning the appropriateness of observers' presence but makes clear that it is not dispensing legal advice, setting standards, or establishing guidelines (Committee on Psychological Tests and Assessment, 2007). APA identifies, without endorsing the following options: Conduct the evaluation in the presence of an observer, minimize the intrusion, use assessment measures that are less affected by observation, recommend that the request for a third party be withdrawn, or decline to perform the assessment under observation. Ultimately, APA appears to leave the decision to the evaluator. "Psychologists will need to exercise their own professional judgment in choosing the appropriate course of action" (Committee on Psychological Tests and Assessment, 2007, p. 4).

Neuropsychologists have staked a claim on the issue of third-party observers during testing and have produced position papers on point. NAN takes the position that "neuropsychologists should strive to minimize all influences that may compromise accuracy of assessment and should make every effort to exclude observers from the evaluation" (The National Academy of Neuropsychology Policy and Planning Committee, 2000, p. 380), but does not state an absolute bar to third-party observers. In support of its position, NAN cites ethical canons, testing standards, test instruction manuals, test standardization processes, and implications from social psychology research.

AACN distinguishes between third-party observers who are either involved (financial, legal, personal stakeholders) or uninvolved (no stake in evaluation outcome, present for education purposes). AACN asserts a clearly exclusionary third-party observer policy declaring that

> it is not permissible for involved third parties to be physically or electronically present during the course of an evaluation assessment of a plaintiff patient with the exceptions of [toddlers who require caregiver present or older children or adults with extreme behavioral disturbances]. (AACN, 2001, p. 434)

Scholars have weighed in on both sides of the argument, with neuropsychologists standing in strongest opposition (e.g., Howe & McCaffrey, 2010).

Some appellate courts have held that the trier may fashion any means necessary to protect the plaintiff from intrusive or offensive probing by the evaluator (*Vinson v. Superior Court*, 1987). In *Toyota Motor Sales, U.S.A., Inc. v. Superior Court* (*Braun;* 2010), the appellate court ruled against plaintiff *Braun*'s counsel's presence during a mental health evaluation by a defense-retained expert. *Braun* then countered that his attorney would simply listen passively from an adjoining room, but the appellate court further ruled that the plaintiff had not shown that the attorney's presence was necessary to protect privacy, nor that any rare or exceptional circumstance was in play that might otherwise warrant the attorney's presence as a safeguard.

As a practical matter, forensic psychologists in tort and personal injury matters will want to inform themselves of the courts' precedents and policies with respect to the presence of third-party observers. Plaintiff-retained evaluators can assist by advising plaintiff's counsel and the court, when appropriate, of exceptional particularized circumstances warranting plaintiff's counsel's passive presence (e.g., audio/video recording, listening from adjoining room, in-room presence without communicating by sound/gesture). Defense-retained evaluators might assist by advising the retaining attorney of the cautions and concerns that are anchored in ethics, standards, and research with respect to the presence of third-party observers.

CONCLUSION

The most accurate, effective, and ethically supportable forensic psychological evaluations in personal injury and other tort matters will reflect a stepwise, scientifically informed approach to assessment and a straightforward, expressive, and appropriately restrained method of reporting. The questions addressed by the evaluation should be identified clearly, with a multimethod, multitrait approach to assessment. The proper focus should be on the identification of functional impairment rather than the mere assignation of diagnoses. Recognizing scientific limitations is critical in conveying results accurately and persuasively. Psychological tests must be reliable, well validated, and appropriate to the forensic evaluative context.

This growing area of forensic practice—with its substantial medical–psychological interface—will continue to contribute to the visibility and prominence of psychologists in integrated care settings. The establishment of such inroads should not be left solely to more traditional research and treatment modalities. Interdisciplinary assessment is an increasing fact of court-related service provision. The legal profession should not be allowed to resort to the often more familiar medical specialties due to a failure by psychologists to offer their unique forensic contributions in conjunction with related health care professions.

References

Ackerman, M. J. (2010). *Essentials of forensic psychological assessment* (2nd ed.). Hoboken, NJ: Wiley.

Adler, D. A., McLaughlin, T. J., Rogers, W. H., Chang, H., Lapitsky, L., & Lerner, D. (2006). Job performance deficits due to depression. *American Journal of Psychiatry, 163*, 1569–1576. doi:10.1176/appi.ajp.163.9.1569

American Academy of Clinical Neuropsychology. (2001). Policy statement on the presence of third party observers in neuropsychological assessments. *Clinical Neuropsychologist, 15*, 433–439. doi:10.1076/clin.15.4.433.1888

American Academy of Clinical Neuropsychology. (2003). Official position of the American Academy of Clinical Neuropsychology on ethical complaints made against clinical neuropsychologists during adversarial proceedings. *Clinical Neuropsychologist, 17*, 443–445. doi:10.1076/clin.17.4.443.27943

American Education Research Association, American Psychological Association, & National Council on Measurement in Education. (2014). *Standards for educational and psychological testing*. Washington, DC: American Educational Research Association.

American Psychiatric Association. (2000). *Diagnostic and statistical manual of mental disorders* (4th ed., text rev.). Washington, DC: Author.

American Psychiatric Association. (2013). *Diagnostic and statistical manual of mental disorders* (5th ed.). Washington, DC: Author.

American Psychoanalytic Association. (2006). *Psychodynamic diagnostic manual*. Bethesda, MD: Interdisciplinary Council on Developmental & Learning Disorders.

American Psychological Association. (1994). Report of the Ethics Committee, 1993. *American Psychologist, 49*, 659–666. doi:10.1037/0003-066X.49.7.659

American Psychological Association. (2007). Record keeping guidelines. *American Psychologist, 62*, 993–1004. doi:10.1037/0003-066X.62.9.993

American Psychological Association. (2010). *Ethical principles of psychologists and code of conduct (2002, Amended June 1, 2010)*. Retrieved from http://www.apa.org/ethics/code/index.aspx

Applied Innovations v. Regents of the University of Minnesota and National Computer Systems, Inc., 876 F.2d 626 (8th Cir. 1989) *aff'g* Regents of the University of Minnesota and National Computer Systems vs. Applied Innovations, Inc., 685 F. Supp. 698 (D. Minn. 1987).

Archer, R. P., Buffington-Vollum, J. K., Stredney, R. V., & Handel, R. W. (2006). A survey of psychological test use patterns among forensic psychologists. *Journal of Personality Assessment, 87*, 84–94.

Asmundson, G. J. G., & Taylor, S. (2006). PTSD and chronic pain: Cognitive–behavioral perspectives and practical implications. In G. Young, A. W. Kane, & K. Nicholson (Eds.), *Psychological knowledge in court: PTSD, pain, and TBI* (pp. 225–241). New York, NY: Springer Science + Business Media.

Association of State and Provincial Psychology Boards. (2010). ASPPB mobility program policy and procedures manual. Retrieved from www.asppb.net/files/public/Mobility/ASPPB_Mobility_ Program_Policies_and_Procedures.pdf

Baker, D. G., Nievergelt, C. M., & O'Connor, D. T. (2012). Biomarkers of PTSD: Neuropeptides and immune signaling. *Neuropharmacology, 62*, 663–673.

Barlow, P. (2012). A practical review of the Glasgow Coma Scale and score. *Surgeon, 10*, 114–119.

Bartholomew, R. E., & Muniratnam, M. C. S. (2011). How should mental health professionals respond to outbreaks of mass psychogenic illness? *Journal of Cognitive Psychotherapy, 25*, 235–239. doi:10.1891/0889-8391.25.4.235

Bellamy, R. (1997, March). Compensation neurosis: Financial reward for illness as a nocebo. *Clinical Orthopaedics and Related Research, 336*, 94–106. doi:10.1097/00003086-199703000-00013

Ben-Porath, Y. S., & Tellegen, A. (2011). *MMPI-2 RF: Manual for administration, scoring, and interpretation*. Minneapolis: University of Minnesota Press.

Binder, L. M., & Rohling, M. L. (1996). Money matters: Meta-analytic review of the effects of financial incentives on recovery after closed-head injury. *American Journal of Psychiatry, 153*, 7–10.

Black, H. C. (2009). *Black's law dictionary* (9th ed.). St. Paul, MN: West.

Blake, D. D., Weathers, F. W., Nagy, L. M., & Kaloupek, D. G. (1995). The development of a clinician-administered PTSD scale. *Journal of Traumatic Stress, 8,* 75–90. doi:10.1002/jts.2490080106

Boccaccini, M. T., Boothby, J. L., & Overduin, L. Y. (2006). Evaluating the validity of pain complaints in personal injury cases: Assessment approaches of forensic and pain specialists. *Journal of Forensic Psychology Practice, 6,* 51–62. doi:10.1300/J158v06n03_03

Boccaccini, M. T., & Brodsky, S. L. (1999). Diagnostic test usage by forensic psychologists in emotional injury cases. *Professional Psychology: Research and Practice, 30,* 253–259. doi:10.1037/0735-7028.30.3.253

Boccaccini, M. T., & Brodsky, S. L. (2002). Believability of expert and lay witnesses: Implications for trial consultation. *Professional Psychology: Research and Practice, 33,* 384–388. doi:10.1037/0735-7028.33.4.384

Bomyea, J., Risbrough, V., & Lang, A. J. (2012). A consideration of select pre-trauma factors as key vulnerabilities in PTSD. *Clinical Psychology Review, 32,* 630–641. doi:10.1016/j.cpr.2012.06.008

Bond, C. F., Jr., & DePaulo, B. M. (2006). Accuracy of deception judgments. *Personality and Social Psychology Review, 10,* 214–234. doi:10.1207/s15327957pspr1003_2

Boone, K. B. (Ed.). (2007). *Assessment of feigned cognitive impairment: A neuropsychological perspective.* New York, NY: Guilford Press.

Boone, K. B. (2009). The need for continuous and comprehensive sampling of effort/response bias during neuropsychological examinations. *Clinical Neuropsychologist, 23,* 729–741. doi:10.1080/13854040802427803

Bow, J. N., Flens, J. R., & Gould, J. W. (2010). MMPI–2 and MCMI–III in forensic evaluations: A survey of psychologists. *Journal of Forensic Psychology Practice, 10,* 37–52. doi:10.1080/15228930903173021

Bowman, M. L. (2005). The role of individual factors in predicting posttraumatic stress disorder. In I. Shultz & R. Gatchel (Eds.), *Handbook of complex occupational disability claims: Early risk identification, intervention, and prevention* (pp. 315–332). New York, NY: Springer Science + Business Media.

Briere, J. (2001). *Manual for the DAPS: Detailed Assessment of Posttraumatic Stress.* Odessa, FL: Psychological Assessment Resources.

Brunello, N., Davidson, J. R., Deahl, M., Kessler, R. C., Mendlewicz, J., Racagni, G., . . . Zohar, J. (2001). Posttraumatic stress disorder: Diagnosis and epidemiology, comorbidity and social consequences, biology and treatment. *Neuropsychobiology, 43,* 150–162. doi:10.1159/000054884

Bryant, R. A., & Harvey, A. G. (2003). The influence of litigation on maintenance of posttraumatic stress disorder. *Journal of Nervous and Mental Disease, 191,* 191–193. doi:10.1097/01.NMD.0000055080.96195.EE

Bryant, R. A., O'Donnell, M. L., Creamer, M., McFarlane, A. C., Clark, C. R., & Silove, D. (2010). The psychiatric sequelae of traumatic injury. *American Journal of Psychiatry, 167,* 312–320. doi:10.1176/appi.ajp.2009.09050617

Bush, S. S., Ruff, R. M., Tröster, A. I., Barth, J. T., Koffler, S. P., Pliskin, N. H., . . . Silver, C. H. (2005). Symptom validity assessment: Practice issues and medical necessity NAN policy and planning committee. *Archives of Clinical Neuropsychology, 20,* 419–426. doi:10.1016/j.acn.2005.02.002

Butcher, J. N., Graham, J. R., Ben-Porath, Y. S., Tellegen, A., & Dahlstrom, W. G. (2001). *MMPI-2: Manual for administration, scoring, and interpretation.* San Antonio, TX: Pearson Assessments.

Camara, W. J., Nathan, J. S., & Puente, A. E. (2000). Psychological test usage: Implications in professional psychology. *Professional Psychology: Research and Practice, 31,* 141–154. doi:10.1037/0735-7028.31.2.141

Carone, D. A., & Bush, S. S. (Eds.). (2013). *Mild traumatic brain injury: Symptom validity assessment and malingering.* New York, NY: Springer.

Carroll, L. J., Cassidy, J. D., Peloso, P. M., Borg, J., von Holst, H., Holm, L., . . . Pepin, M. (2004). Prognosis for mild traumatic brain injury: Results of the WHO Collaborating Centre Task Force on Mild Traumatic Brain Injury. *Journal of Rehabilitation Medicine, 43,* 84–105.

Chafetz, M. D. (2008). Malingering on the Social Security Disability Consultative Exam: Predictors and base rates. *Clinical Neuropsychologist, 22,* 529–546.

Chekroun, P., & Brauer, M. (2002). The bystander effect and social control behavior: The effect of the presence of others on people's reactions to norm violations. *European Journal of Social Psychology, 32,* 853–867. doi:10.1002/ejsp.126

Cloitre, M., Stolbach, B. C., Herman, J. L., van der Kolk, B., Pynoos, R., Wang, J., & Petkova, E. (2009). A developmental approach to complex PTSD: Childhood and adult cumulative trauma as predictors of symptom complexity. *Journal of Traumatic Stress, 22,* 399–408. doi:10.1002/jts.20444

Committee on Ethical Guidelines for Forensic Psychologists. (2013). Specialty guidelines for forensic psychology. *American Psychologist, 68,* 7–19. doi:10.1037/a0029889

Committee on Psychological Tests and Assessment. (2007). *Statement on third party observers in psychological testing and assessment: A framework for decision making*. Retrieved from www.apa.org/science/programs/testing/third-party-observers.pdf

Daly, R. (2010). Was vital component omitted from healthcare reform? *Psychiatric News, 45*, 5.

Daubert v. Merrell Dow Pharmaceuticals, Inc., 509 U.S. 579 (1993).

David, A. S., & Wessely, S. C. (1995). The legend of Camelford: Medical consequences of a water pollution accident. *Journal of Psychosomatic Research, 39*, 1–9. doi:10.1016/0022-3999(94)00085-J

Davis, D., & Friedman, R. D. (2007). Memory for conversation: The orphan child of witness memory researchers. In M. P, Toglia, J. D. Read, D. R. Ross, & R. C. L. Lindsay (Eds.), *Handbook of eyewitness psychology* (Vol. 1, pp. 33–52). Mahwah, NJ: Erlbaum.

Davis, D., & Loftus, E. F. (2007). Internal and external sources of misinformation in adult witness memory. In M. P, Toglia, J. D. Read, D. R. Ross, & R. C. L. Lindsay (Eds.), *Handbook of eyewitness psychology* (Vol. 1, pp. 195–237). Mahwah, NJ: Erlbaum.

DeLeon, M. H. (2012). Public choice theory, interest groups, and tort reform. *University of Illinois Law Review, 2012*, 1787–1809.

Dewa, C. S., Hoch, J. S., Lin, E., Paterson, M., & Goering, P. (2003). Pattern of antidepressant use and duration of depression-related absence from work. *British Journal of Psychiatry, 183*, 507–513. doi:10.1192/bjp.183.6.507

Drogin, E. Y. (2008). Interstate forensic mental health practice: A jurisprudent science perspective. *Journal of Psychiatry and Law, 36*, 345–351.

Drogin, E. Y., Connell, M., Foote, W., & Sturm, C. (2010). The American Psychological Association's revised "Record Keeping Guidelines": Implications for the practitioner. *Professional Psychology: Research and Practice, 41*, 236–243. doi:10.1037/a0019001

Drogin, E. Y., Dattilio, F. M., Sadoff, R. L., & Gutheil, T. G. (Eds.). (2011). *Handbook of forensic assessment: Psychological and psychiatric perspectives*. Hoboken, NJ: Wiley. doi:10.1002/9781118093399

Drogin, E. Y., & Meyer, D. J. (2011). Psychiatric and psychological malpractice. In E. Y. Drogin, F. M. Dattilio, R. L. Sadoff, & T. G. Gutheil (Eds.), *Handbook of forensic assessment: Psychological and psychiatric perspectives* (pp. 543–570). Hoboken, NJ: Wiley. doi:10.1002/9781118093399.ch24

Duff, K., & Fisher, J. M. (2005). Ethical dilemmas with third party observers. *Journal of Forensic Neuropsychology, 4*, 65–82. doi:10.1300/J151v04n02_06

Edens, J. F., Smith, S. T., Magyar, M. S., Mullen, K., Pitta, A., & Petrila, J. (2012). "Hired guns," "charlatans," and their "voodoo psychobabble": Case law references to

various forms of perceived bias among mental health expert witnesses. *Psychological Services, 9*, 259–271. doi:10.1037/a0028264

Eisenberg, M. A. (2013). Conflicting formulas for measuring expectation damages. *Arizona Law Review, 45*, 369–408.

Evans, R. W. (1994). The effects of litigation on treatment outcome with personal injury patients. *American Journal of Forensic Psychology, 12*, 19–34.

Fed. R. Ev. 702.

Fed. R. Ev. 703.

Fed. R. Ev. 704.

Fisher, M. A. (2009). Replacing "who is the client?" with a different ethical question. *Professional Psychology: Research and Practice, 40*, 1–7. doi:10.1037/a0014011

Foa, E. B., & Tolin, D. F. (2000). Comparison of the PTSD Symptom Scale—Interview Version and the Clinician-Administered PTSD Scale. *Journal of Traumatic Stress, 13*, 181–191. doi:10.1023/A:1007781909213

Frye v. United States, 293 F. 1013 (D.C. Cir. 1923).

Garg, S., Dattilio, F. M., & Miazzo, P. (2011). Transcultural considerations. In E. Y. Drogin, F. M. Dattilio, R. L. Sadoff, & T. G. Gutheil (Eds.), *Handbook of forensic assessment: Psychological and psychiatric perspectives* (pp. 679–696). Hoboken, NJ: Wiley.

Gatchel, R. J., & Kishino, N. (2006). The influence of personality characteristics on pain patients: Implications for causality in pain. In G. Young, A. Kane, & K. Nicholson (Eds.), *Psychological knowledge and evidence in court: PTSD, pain and TBI* (pp. 149–162). New York, NY: Springer.

Gavett, B. F., Lynch, J. K., & McCaffrey, R. J. (2005). Third party observers: The effect size is greater than you might think. *Journal of Forensic Neuropsychology, 4*, 49–64. doi:10.1300/J151v04n02_05

Gold, L. H., & Stejskal, W. J. (2011). *Employment discrimination and harassment*. Hoboken, NJ: Wiley.

Gottlieb, M. C., & Younggren, J. N. (2009). Is there a slippery slope? Considerations regarding multiple relationships and risk management. *Professional Psychology: Research and Practice, 40*, 564–571. doi:10.1037/a0017231

Graffam, M. H. (2012). The web of tort "reform." *Trial, 48*, 14–16.

Grant, D. M., Beck, J. G., Marques, L., Palyo, S. A., & Clapp, J. D. (2008). The structure of distress following trauma: Posttraumatic stress disorder, major depressive disorder, and generalized anxiety disorder. *Journal of Abnormal Psychology, 117*, 662–672. doi:10.1037/a0012591

Green, B. (2003). Post-traumatic stress disorder: Symptom profiles in men and women. *Current Medical Research and Opinion, 19*, 200–204. doi:10.1185/030079903125001604

Greenberg, L., & Gould, J. (2001). The treating expert: A hybrid role with firm boundaries. *Professional Psychology: Research and Practice, 32,* 469–478. doi:10.1037/0735-7028.32.5.469

Greenberg, S. A. (2003). Personal injury examinations in torts for emotional distress. In I. B. Weiner (Ed.), *Comprehensive handbook of psychology: Vol. 11. Forensic psychology* (pp. 233–257). Hoboken, NJ: Wiley.

Greenberg, S. A., & Shuman, D. W. (1997). Irreconcilable conflict between therapeutic and forensic roles. *Professional Psychology: Research and Practice, 28,* 50–57. doi:10.1037/0735-7028.28.1.50

Greenberg, S. A., & Shuman, D. W. (2007). When worlds collide: Therapeutic and forensic roles. *Professional Psychology: Research and Practice, 38,* 129–132. doi:10.1037/0735-7028.38.2.129

Greenberg, S. A., Shuman, D. W., & Meyer, R. G. (2004). Unmasking forensic diagnosis. *International Journal of Law and Psychiatry, 27,* 1–15. doi:10.1016/j.ijlp.2004.01.001

Greiffenstein, M. F., Baker, W. J., & Johnson-Greene, D. (2002). Actual versus self-reported scholastic achievement of litigating post-concussion and severe closed head injury claimants. *Psychological Assessment, 14,* 202–208. doi:10.1037/1040-3590.14.2.202

Greve, K. W., Bianchini, K. J., Etherton, J. L., Ord, J. S., & Curtis, K. L. (2009). Detecting malingered pain-related disability: Classification accuracy of the Portland Digit Recognition Test. *Clinical Neuropsychologist, 23,* 850–869. doi:10.1080/13854040802585055

Grisso, T. (2003). *Evaluating competencies: Forensic assessments and instruments* (2nd ed.). New York, NY: Kluwer Academic/Plenum.

Grove, W. M., Zald, D. H., Lebow, B. S., Snitz, B. E., & Nelson, C. (2000). Clinical versus mechanical prediction: A meta-analysis. *Psychological Assessment, 12,* 19–30. doi:10.1037/1040-3590.12.1.19

Guilmette, T. J. (2013). The role of clinical judgment in symptom validity assessment. In D. A. Carone & S. S. Bush (Eds.), *Mild traumatic brain injury: Symptom validity assessment and malingering* (pp. 31–43). New York, NY: Springer.

Hasin, D. S., Goodwin, R. D., Stinson, F. S., & Grant, B. F. (2005). Epidemiology of major depressive disorder: Results from the National Epidemiological Survey on Alcoholism and Related Conditions. *Archives of General Psychiatry, 62,* 1097–1106. doi:10.1001/archpsyc.62.10.1097

Heilbronner, R. L., & Henry, G. K. (2013). Psychological assessment of symptom magnification in mild traumatic brain injury cases. In D. A. Carone & S. S. Bush (Eds.), *Mild traumatic brain injury: Symptom validity assessment and malingering* (pp. 183–202). New York, NY: Springer.

Heilbronner, R. L., Sweet, J. J., Morgan, J. E., Larrabee, G. J., & Millis, S. (2009). American Academy of Clinical Neuropsychology consensus conference statement on the neuropsychological assessment of effort, response bias, and malingering. *Clinical Neuropsychologist, 23,* 1093–1129. doi:10.1080/13854040903155063

Heilbrun, K. (1992). The role of psychological testing in forensic assessment. *Law and Human Behavior, 16,* 257–272.

Heilbrun, K. (2001). *Principles of forensic mental health assessment.* New York, NY: Kluwer Academic/Plenum.

Heilbrun, K., DeMatteo, D., Marczyk, G., & Goldstein, A. M. (2008). Standards of practice and care in forensic mental health assessment: Legal, professional, and principles-based consideration. *Psychology, Public Policy, and Law, 14,* 1–26. doi:10.1037/1076-8971.14.1.1

Heilbrun, K., Grisso, T., & Goldstein, A. M. (2009). *Foundations of forensic mental health assessment.* New York, NY: Oxford University Press.

Heilbrun, K., Rosenfeld, B., Warren, J., & Collins, S. (1994). The use of third-party information in forensic assessments: A two-state comparison. *Bulletin of the American Academy of Psychiatry and the Law, 22,* 399–406.

Heilbrun, K., Warren, J., & Picarello, K. (2003). Third party information in forensic assessment. In I. B. Weiner (Ed.), *Comprehensive handbook of psychology: Vol. 11. Forensic psychology* (pp. 69–86). Hoboken, NJ: Wiley.

Heltzel, T. (2007). Compatibility of therapeutic and forensic roles. *Professional Psychology: Research and Practice, 38,* 122–128. doi:10.1037/0735-7028.38.2.122

Hershovitz, S. (2012). What does tort law do? What can it do? *Valparaiso University Law Review, 47,* 99–118.

Howe, L. L., & McCaffrey, R. J. (2010). Third party observation during neuropsychological evaluation: An update on the literature, practical advice for practitioners, and future direction. *Clinical Neuropsychologist, 24,* 518–537. doi:10.1080/13854041003775347

Hunter, R. J., Jr., & Amoroso, H. (2012). Damages for pain and suffering and emotional distress in products liability cases involving strict liability and negligence. *Faulkner Law Review, 3,* 277–302.

Iverson, G. L., King, R. J., Scott, J. G., & Adams, R. L. (2001). Cognitive complaints in litigating patients with head injuries or chronic pain. *Journal of*

Forensic Neuropsychology, 2, 19–30. doi:10.1300/J151v02n01_02

Iverson, G. L., Lange, R. T., Brooks, B. L., & Rennison, V. L. A. (2010). "Good old days" bias following mild traumatic brain injury. *Clinical Neuropsychologist, 24*, 17–37. doi:10.1080/13854040903190797

Iverson, G. L., & McCracken, L. M. (1997). "Postconcussive" symptoms in persons with chronic pain. *Brain Injury, 11*, 783–790. doi:10.1080/026990597122990

Jones, T. F., Craig, A. S., Hoy, D., Gunter, E. W., Ashley, D. L., Barr, D. B., . . . Schaffner, W. (2000). Mass psychogenic illness attributed to toxic exposure at a high school. *New England Journal of Medicine, 342*, 96–100. doi:10.1056/NEJM200001133420206

Kane, A. W. (2007). Conducting a psychological evaluation. In G. Young, A. W. Kane, & K. Nicholson (Eds.), *Causality of psychological injury: Presenting evidence in court* (pp. 293–323). New York, NY: Springer Science + Business Media.

Kane, A. W. (2008). Forensic psychology, psychological injuries, and the law. *Psychological Injury and Law, 1*, 36–58. doi:10.1007/s12207-007-9000-1

Kane, A. W., Nelson, E. M., Dvoskin, J. A., & Pitt, S. E. (2013). Evaluation for personal injury claims. In R. Roesch & P. A. Zapf (Eds.), *Forensic assessments in criminal and civil law: A handbook for lawyers* (pp. 148–160). New York, NY: Oxford University Press.

Kashluba, S., Paniak, C., & Casey, J. E. (2008). Persistent symptoms associated with factors identified by the WHO task force on mild traumatic brain injury. *Clinical Neuropsychologist, 22*, 195–208. doi:10.1080/13854040701263655

Kaufmann, P. M. (2009). Protecting raw data and psychological tests from wrongful disclosure: A primer on the law and other persuasive strategies. *Clinical Neuropsychologist, 23*, 1130–1159. doi:10.1080/13854040903107809

Kehrer, C. A., Sanchez, P., Habif, J., Rosenbaum, G., & Townes, B. (2000). Effects of a significant-other observer on neuropsychological test performance. *Clinical Neuropsychologist, 14*, 67–71. doi:10.1076/1385-4046(200002)14:1;1-8;FT067

Kessler, R. C., Keller, M. B., & Wittchen, H. (2001). The epidemiology of generalized anxiety disorder. In O. Brawman-Mintzer (Ed.), *The psychiatric clinics of North America: Generalized anxiety disorder* (pp. 19–40). Philadelphia, PA: W.B. Saunders.

Kessler, R. C., Sonnega, A., Bromet, E., Hughes, M., & Nelson, C. B. (1995). Posttraumatic stress disorder in the national comorbidity survey. *Archives of General Psychiatry, 52*, 1048–1060. doi:10.1001/archpsyc.1995.03950240066012

Koch, W. J., Nader, R., & Haring, M. (2009). The science and pseudoscience of assessing psychological injuries. In J. Skeem, K. Douglas, & S. Lilienfeld (Eds.), *Psychological science in the courtroom: Controversies and consensus* (pp. 263–283). New York, NY: Guilford Press.

Koch, W. J., O'Neill, M., & Douglas, K. S. (2005). Empirical limits for the forensic assessment of PTSD litigants. *Law and Human Behavior, 29*, 121–149. doi:10.1007/s10979-005-1401-7

LaDuke, C., DeMatteo, D., Heilbrun, K., & Swirsky-Sacchetti, T. (2012). Clinical neuropsychology in forensic contexts: Practitioners' experience, training, and practice. *Professional Psychology: Research and Practice, 43*, 503–509. doi:10.1037/a0028161

Lally, S. (2003). What tests are acceptable for use in forensic evaluation? A survey of experts. *Professional Psychology: Research and Practice, 34*, 491–498. doi:10.1037/0735-7028.34.5.491

Lamb, M. E., Orbach, Y., Warren, A. R., Esplin, P. W., & Hershkowitz, I. (2007). Enhancing performance: Factors affecting the informativeness of young witnesses. In M. P, Toglia, J. D. Read, D. R. Ross, & R. C. L. Lindsay (Eds.), *Handbook of eyewitness psychology* (Vol. 1, pp. 429–457). Mahwah, NJ: Erlbaum.

Landers, M. R., Cheung, W., Miller, D., Summons, T., Wallmann, H. W., McWhorter, J. W., & Druse, T. (2007). Workers' compensation and litigation status influence the functional outcome of patients with neck pain. *Clinical Journal of Pain, 23*, 676–682. doi:10.1097/AJP.0b013e31813d110e

Langton, L., & Cohen, T. H. (2008). *Bureau of Justice Statistics special report: Civil bench and jury trials in state courts, 2005*. Washington, DC: U.S. Department of Justice.

Lanyon, R. I. (2001). Dimensions of self-serving misrepresentations in forensic assessment. *Journal of Personality Assessment, 76*, 169–179. doi:10.1207/S15327752JPA7601_10

Lanyon, R. I. (2007). Utility of the Psychological Screening Inventory: A review. *Journal of Clinical Psychology, 63*, 283–307.

Lanyon, R. I., & Almer, E. R. (2002). Characteristics of compensable disability patients who choose to litigate. *Journal of the American Academy of Psychiatry and the Law, 30*, 400–404.

Larrabee, G. J. (Ed.). (2007). *Assessment of malingered neuropsychological deficits*. New York, NY: Oxford University Press.

LaVoie, D. J., Mertz, H. K., & Richmond, T. L. (2007). Implications for the elderly eyewitness. In M. P, Toglia, J. D. Read, D. R. Ross, & R. C. L. Lindsay (Eds.), *Handbook of eyewitness psychology* (Vol. 1, pp. 605–625). Mahwah, NJ: Erlbaum.

Lazarus, A. A., & Zur, O. (Eds.). (2002). *Dual relationships and psychotherapy*. New York, NY: Springer.

Lees-Haley, P. (1989). Litigation Response Syndrome: How the stress of litigation confuses the issues in personal injury, family and criminal ligation. *Defense Counsel Journal, 56*, 110–114.

Lees-Haley, P. (1990). Contamination of neuropsychological testing by litigation. *Forensic Reports, 3*, 421–426.

Lees-Haley, P. R. (1997). Attorneys influence expert evidence in forensic psychological and neuropsychological cases. *Assessment, 4*, 321–324.

Lees-Haley, P. R., Williams, C. W., Zasler, N. D., Marguilies, S., English, L. T., & Stevens, K. B. (1997). Response bias in plaintiffs' histories. *Brain Injury, 11*, 791–800. doi:10.1080/026990597123007

Lewis, D., Rubin, P., & Drake, C. (2006). Expanding the net: Suggestions for forensic mental health examiners on identifying and obtaining third-party information. *Journal of Forensic Psychology Practice, 6*, 39–51. doi:10.1300/J158v06n02_03

Li, F., & Li, Y. (2008). The Balanced Inventory of Desirable Responding: A factor analysis. *Psychological Reports, 103*, 727–731.

Lombard v. Rohrbaugh, 551 S.E.2d 353 (2001).

Lu, V. (2010). Using medical liability tort reform to improve patient care. *Annals of Health Law Advance Directive, 19*, 316–327.

Lynch, J. (2005). Effect of a third party observer on neuropsychological test performance following closed head injury. *Journal of Forensic Neuropsychology, 4*, 17–25. doi:10.1300/J151v04n02_02

Marrogi v. Howard, 805 So.2d 1118 (La. 2002).

Maryland Courts and Judicial Proceedings § 9-120 (2013).

Maxwell, B. M. (2001). Cognitive set, secondary gain, and progress in physical rehabilitation. *Dissertation Abstracts International: Section B, The Sciences and Engineering, 61*, AAI9990759.

Mayou, R. (1996). Accident neurosis revisited. *British Journal of Psychiatry, 168*, 399–403. doi:10.1192/bjp.168.4.399

Mayou, R., Bryant, B., & Ehlers, A. (2001). Prediction of psychological outcomes one year after a motor vehicle accident. *American Journal of Psychiatry, 158*, 1231–1238. doi:10.1176/appi.ajp.158.8.1231

McCrea, M., Iverson, G. L., McAllister, T. W., Hemmeke, T. A., Powell, M. R., Barr, W. B., & Kelly, J. P. (2009). An integrated review of recovery after mild traumatic brain injury (MTBI): Implications for clinical management. *Clinical Neuropsychologist, 23*, 1368–1390. doi:10.1080/13854040903074652

McCrea, M. A. (2008) *Mild traumatic brain injury and postconcussion syndrome: The new evidence base for diagnosis and treatment*. New York, NY: Oxford University Press.

Meares, S., Shores, E. A., Taylor, A. J., Batchelor, J., Bryant, R. A., Baguley, I. J., . . . Marosszeky, J. E. (2011). The prospective course of postconcussion syndrome: The role of mild traumatic brain injury. *Neuropsychology, 25*, 454–465. doi:10.1037/a0022580

Meehl, P. E. (1954). *Clinical versus statistical prediction: A theoretical analysis and a review of the evidence*. Minneapolis: University of Minnesota Press. doi:10.1037/11281-000

Meehl, P. E. (1973). Why I do not attend case conferences. In P. E. Meehl (Ed.), *Psychodiagnosis: Selected papers* (pp. 225–302). Minneapolis: University of Minnesota Press.

Mellsop, G. W., Fraser, D., Tapsell, R., & Menkes, D. B. (2011). Courts' misplaced confidence in psychiatric diagnoses. *International Journal of Law and Psychiatry, 34*, 331–335. doi:10.1016/j.ijlp.2011.08.005

Melnyk, L., Crossman, A. M., & Scullin, M. H. (2007). The suggestibility of children's memory. In M. P, Toglia, J. D. Read, D. R. Ross, & R. C. L. Lindsay (Eds.), *Handbook of eyewitness psychology* (Vol. 1, pp. 401–427). Mahwah, NJ: Erlbaum.

Melton, G., Petrila, J., Poythress, N., & Slobogin, C. (2007). *Psychological evaluations for the courts* (3rd ed.). New York, NY: Guilford Press.

Melzack, R., & Katz, J. (2006). Pain in the 21st century: The neuromatrix and beyond. In G. Young, A. W. Kane, & K. Nicholson (Eds.), *Psychological knowledge in court: PTSD, pain, and TBI* (pp. 129–148). New York, NY: Springer Science + Business Media.

Mendel, R., Traut-Mattausch, E., Jonas, E., Leucht, S., Kane, J. M., Maino, K., . . . Hamann, J. (2011). Confirmatory bias: Why psychiatrists stick to the wrong preliminary diagnosis. *Psychological Medicine, 41*, 2651–2659. doi:10.1017/S0033291711000808

Mendelson, G. (1995). "Compensation neurosis" revisited: Outcome studies of the effects of litigation. *Journal of Psychosomatic Research, 39*, 695–706. doi:10.1016/0022-3999(94)00154-W

Miller, H. A. (2001). *M-FAST professional manual*. Lutz, FL: Psychological Assessment Resources.

Miller, L., Sadoff, R. L., & Dattilio, F. M. (2011). Personal injury: The independent medical examination in psychology and psychiatry. In E. Y. Drogin, F. M. Dattilio, R. L. Sadoff, & T. G. Gutheil (Eds.), *Handbook of forensic assessment: Psychological and psychiatric perspectives* (pp. 277–302). Hoboken, NJ: Wiley. doi:10.1002/9781118093399.ch13

Miller, M. W. (2003). Personality and the etiology and expression of PTSD: A three-factor model perspective. *Clinical Psychology: Science and Practice, 10,* 373–393.

Millon, T., Davis, R., & Millon, C. (1997). *MCMI-III manual* (2nd ed.). Minneapolis, MN: National Computer Systems.

Mittenberg, W., Patton, C., Canyock, E. M., & Condit, D. C. (2002). Base rates of malingering and symptom exaggeration. *Journal of Clinical and Experimental Neuropsychology, 24,* 1094–1101.

Morey, L. C. (2007). *Personality Assessment Inventory professional manual* (2nd ed.). Lutz, FL: Psychological Assessment Resources.

Morse, C. L., Douglas-Newman, K., Mandel, S., & Swirsky-Sacchetti, T. (2013). The utility of the Rey-15 Recognition Trial to detect invalid performance in a forensic neuropsychological sample. *Clinical Neuropsychologist, 27,* 1395–1407.

Mueller-Johnson, K., & Ceci, S. J. (2007). The elderly eyewitness: A review and prospectus. In M. P, Toglia, J. D. Read, D. R. Ross, & R. C. L. Lindsay (Eds.), *Handbook of eyewitness psychology* (Vol. 1, pp. 577–603). Mahwah, NJ: Erlbaum.

National Academy of Neuropsychology Policy and Planning Committee. (2000). Presence of third party observers during neuropsychological testing: Official statement of the National Academy of Neuropsychology. *Archives of Clinical Neuropsychology, 15,* 379–380.

National Institute of Mental Health. (2001). *The numbers count: Mental disorders in America.* Retrieved from http://www.namigc.org/documents/numberscount.pdf

National Register of Health Service Providers in Psychology. (2012). *Licensure mobility.* Retrieved from http://www.nationalregister.org/licensure_mobility.html

Nelson, N. W., Boone, K., Dueck, A., Wagener, L., Lu, P., & Grills, C. (2003). Relationships between eight measures of suspect effort. *Clinical Neuropsychologist, 17,* 263–272. doi:10.1076/clin.17.2.263.16511

Nelson, N. W., Sweet, J. J., Berry, D. T. R., Bryant, F. B., & Granacher, R. P. (2007). Response validity in forensic neuropsychology: Exploratory factor analytic evidence of distinct cognitive and psychological constructs. *Journal of the International Neuropsychological Society, 13,* 440–449. doi:10.1017/S1355617707070373

Nicholson, R. A., & Norwood, S. (2000). The quality of forensic psychological assessments, reports, and testimony: Acknowledging the gap between promise and practice. *Law and Human Behavior, 24,* 9–44. doi:10.1023/A:1005422702678

Otto, R. K. (2002). Use of the MMPI–2 in forensic settings. *Journal of Forensic Psychology Practice, 2,* 71–91. doi:10.1300/J158v02n03_05

Otto, R. K., & Heilbrun, K. (2002). The practice of forensic psychology: A look toward the future in light of the past. *American Psychologist, 57,* 5–18. doi:10.1037/0003-066X.57.1.5

Packard, R. C. (2008). Chronic post-traumatic headache: Associations with mild brain injury, concussion, and post-concussive disorder. *Current Pain and Headache Reports, 12,* 67–73. doi:10.1007/s11916-008-0013-6

Parry, J., & Drogin, E. Y. (2007). *Mental disability law, evidence and testimony: A comprehensive reference manual for lawyers, judges and mental disability professionals.* Washington, DC: American Bar Association.

Piechowski, L. D. (2011). *Evaluation of workplace disability.* New York, NY: Oxford University Press.

Pincus, T. (2006). Effect of cognition on pain experience and pain behavior: Diathesis-stress and the causal conundrum. In G. Young, A. W. Kane, & K. Nicholson (Eds.), *Psychological knowledge in court: PTSD, pain, and TBI* (pp. 163–180). New York, NY: Springer Science + Business Media.

Plaisier, I., Beekman, A. T. F., de Graaf, R., Smit, J. H., van Dyck, R., & Penninx, B. W. J. H. (2010). Work functioning in persons with depressive and anxiety disorders: The role of specific psychopathological characteristics. *Journal of Affective Disorders, 125,* 198–206. doi:10.1016/j.jad.2010.01.072

Ponsford, J., Cameron, P., Fitzgerald, M., Grant, M., Mikocka-Walus, A., & Schonberger, M. (2012). Predictors of postconcussive symptoms 3 months after mild traumatic brain injury. *Neuropsychology, 26,* 304–313. doi:10.1037/a0027888

Pope, K. S., Butcher, J. N., & Seelen, J. (2006). *The courts' recognition, use, and restriction of MMPI-based testimony.* Washington, DC: American Psychological Association.

Proctor, T. J. (2002). A comprehensive biopsychosocial evaluation of functional restoration completion status in chronic musculoskeletal pain disability patients. *Dissertation Abstracts International: Section B, The Sciences and Engineering, 62,* AAI0802821.

Rasmussen, J. (2013). New types of med-mal "tort reform" surface. *Trial, 49,* 54.

Reed v. State, 283 Md. 374; 391 A.2d 364 (Md. 1978).

Revicki, D. A., Travers, K., Wyrwich, K. W., Svedsäter, H., Locklear, J., Mattera, M. S., . . . Montgomery, S. (2012). Humanistic and economic burden of generalized anxiety disorder in North America and Europe. *Journal of Affective Disorders, 140,* 103–112. doi:10.1016/j.jad.2011.11.014

Rogers, R. (Ed.). (1988). *Clinical assessment of malingering and deception*. New York, NY: Guilford Press.

Rogers, R., Bagby, R. M., & Dickens, S. E. (1992). *Structured Interview of Reported Symptoms: Professional manual*. Odessa, FL: Psychological Assessment Resources.

Rogers, R., & Ewing, C. P. (1989). Ultimate opinion proscriptions: A cosmetic fix and a plea for empiricism. *Law and Human Behavior, 13*, 357–374. doi:10.1007/BF01056408

Rogers, R., & Payne, J. (2006). Damages and rewards: Assessment of malingered disorders in compensation cases. *Behavioral Sciences and the Law, 24*, 645–658. doi:10.1002/bsl.687

Rogers, R., Sewell, K. W. & Gillard, N. D. (2010). *SIRS-2: Professional manual*. Lutz, FL: Psychological Assessment Resources.

Rohling, M. L., Binder, L. M., & Langhinrichsen-Rohling, J. (1995). Money matters: A meta-analytic review of the association between financial compensation and the experience and treatment of chronic pain. *Health Psychology, 14*, 537–547. doi:10.1037/0278-6133.14.6.537

Rubenzer, S. (2009). Posttraumatic stress disorder: Assessing response style and malingering. *Psychological Injury and Law, 2*, 114–142. doi:10.1007/s12207-009-9045-4

Ryan, C. M., & Morrow, L. A. (1992). Dysfunctional buildings or dysfunctional people: An examination of the sick building syndrome and allied disorders. *Journal of Consulting and Clinical Psychology, 60*, 220–224. doi:10.1037/0022-006X.60.2.220

Scarano, V. R., & Jankovic, J. (1998). Post-traumatic movement disorders: Effects of the legal system. *Journal of Forensic Sciences, 43*, 334–339.

Schretlen, D. J., Munro, C. A., Anthony, J. C., & Pearlson, G. D. (2003). Examining the range of normal intraindividual variability in neuropsychological test performance. *Journal of the International Neuropsychological Society, 9*, 864–870. doi:10.1017/S1355617703960061

Schultz, I. Z., Crook, J. M., Berkowitz, J., Meloche, G. R., Milner, R., & Zuberbier, O. A. (2005). Biopsychosocial multivariate predictive model of occupational low back disability. In I. Schultz & R. Gatchel (Eds.), *Handbook of complex occupational disability claims: Early risk identification, intervention, and prevention* (pp. 191–202). New York, NY: Springer Science + Business Media.

Shalev, A. Y. (1997). Acute to chronic: Etiology and pathophysiology of PTSD—a biopsychological approach. In C. S. Fullerton & R. J. Ursano (Eds.), *Posttraumatic stress disorder: Acute and long-term responses to trauma and disaster* (pp. 209–240). Washington, DC: American Psychiatric Press.

Shapinsky, A. C., Rapport, L. J., Henderson, M. J., & Axelrod, B. N. (2005). Civilian PTSD scales: Relationships with trait characteristics and everyday distress. *Assessment, 12*, 220–230. doi:10.1177/1073191104273130

Sharp, T. J., & Harvey, A. G. (2001). Chronic pain and posttraumatic disorder: Mutual maintenance? *Clinical Psychology Review, 21*, 857–877. doi:10.1016/S0272-7358(00)00071-4

Shepherd, J. (2013). Products liability and economic activity: An empirical analysis of tort reform's impact on businesses, employment, and production. *Vanderbilt Law Review, 66*, 257–321.

Shuman, D. W., Greenberg, S., Heilbrun, K., & Foote, W. E. (1998). An immodest proposal: Should treating mental health professionals be barred from testifying about their patients? *Behavioral Sciences and the Law, 16*, 509–523. doi:10.1002/(SICI)1099-0798(199823)16:4<509::AID-BSL324>3.0.CO;2-Y

Shuman, D. W., & Sales, B. D. (1998). The admissibility of expert testimony based upon clinical judgment and scientific research. *Psychology, Public Policy, and Law, 4*, 1226–1252. doi:10.1037/1076-8971.4.4.1226

Slick, D. J., & Sherman, E. M. S. (2013). Differential diagnosis of malingering. In D. A. Carone & S. S. Bush (Eds.), *Mild traumatic brain injury: Symptom validity assessment and malingering* (pp. 57–72). New York, NY: Springer.

Slick, D. J., Sherman, E. M., & Iverson, G. L. (1999). Diagnostic criteria for malingered neurocognitive dysfunction: Proposed standards for clinical practice and research. *Clinical Neuropsychologist, 13*, 545–561. doi:10.1076/1385-4046(199911)13:04;1-Y;FT545

Slick, D. J., Tan, J. E., Strauss, E. H., & Hultsch, D. F. (2004). Detecting malingering: A survey of experts' practices. *Archives of Clinical Neuropsychology, 19*, 465–473. doi:10.1016/j.acn.2003.04.001

Sperino, S. F. (2013). Statutory proximate cause. *Notre Dame Law Review, 88*, 1199–1247.

Stordal, K. I., Lundervold, A. J., Egeland, J., Mykletun, A., Asbjørnsen, A., Landrø, N. I., . . . Lund, A. (2004). Impairment across executive functions in recurrent major depression. *Nordic Journal of Psychiatry, 58*, 41–47. doi:10.1080/08039480310000789

Strauss, M. E., & Smith, G. T. (2009). Construct validity: Advances in theory and methodology. *Annual Review of Clinical Psychology, 5*, 1–25. doi:10.1146/annurev.clinpsy.032408.153639

Suhr, J., Tranel, D., Wefel, J., & Barrash, J. (1997). Memory performance after head injury: Contributions of malingering, litigation status, psychological factors, and medication use. *Journal of Clinical and Experimental Neuropsychology, 19*, 500–514. doi:10.1080/01688639708403740

Tittsworth v. Robinson 252 Va. 151; 475 S.E.2d 261 (Va. 1996).

Tombaugh, T. N. (1996). *TOMM: Test of Memory Malingering.* North Tonawanda, NY: Multi-Health Systems.

Torres, L., Skidmore, S., & Gross, N. (2012). Assessment of post-traumatic stress disorder: Differences in standards and practice between licensed and board-certified psychologists. *Psychological Injury and Law, 5,* 1–11. doi:10.1007/s12207-012-9118-7

Toyota Motor Sales, U.S.A., Inc. v. Superior Court (Braun), 189 Cal.App.4th 1391 (2010).

Turner, S. M., DeMers, S. T., Fox, H. R., & Reed, G. (2001). APA's guidelines for test user qualifications: An executive summary. *American Psychologist, 56,* 1099–1113. doi:10.1037/0003-066X.56.12.1099

Tversky, A., & Kahneman, D. (1974). Judgment under uncertainty: Heuristics and biases. *Science, 185,* 1124–1131. doi:10.1126/science.185.4157.1124

Underwager, R., & Wakefield, H. (1992). Poor psychology produces poor law. *Law and Human Behavior, 16,* 233–243. doi:10.1007/BF01044800

U.S. Department of Health and Human Services. (1999). *Mental health: A report of the Surgeon General.* Rockville, MD: Author.

Va. Code Ann. § 8.01-401.3 (1993).

Vinson v. Superior Court, 43 Cal.3d 833 (1987).

Wadsworth, E. J. K., Moss, S. C., Simpson, S. A., & Smith, A. P. (2005). SSRIs and cognitive performance in a working sample. *Human Psychopharmacology: Clinical and Experimental, 20,* 561–572. doi:10.1002/hup.725

Wagner, M. K. (2002). The high cost of prescription privileges. *Journal of Clinical Psychology, 58,* 677–680. doi:10.1002/jclp.10052

Wechsler, D. (2008a). *Wechsler Adult Intelligence Scale—Fourth Edition: Administration and scoring manual.* San Antonio, TX: Pearson.

Wechsler, D. (2008b). *Wechsler Adult Intelligence Scale—Fourth Edition: Technical and interpretive manual.* San Antonio, TX: Pearson.

Wedding, D., & Faust, D. (1989). Clinical judgment and decision making in neuropsychology. *Archives of Clinical Neuropsychology, 4,* 233–265. doi:10.1016/0887-6177(89)90016-4

Weiner, I. B. (2006). Writing forensic reports. In I. B. Weiner & A. K. Hess (Eds.), *Handbook of forensic psychology* (3rd ed., pp. 631–651). Hoboken, NJ: Wiley.

Weissman, H. N. (1990). Distortions and deceptions in self presentation: Effects of protracted litigation in personal injury cases. *Behavioral Sciences and the Law, 8,* 67–74. doi:10.1002/bsl.2370080108

Wells, K. B., Stewart, A., Hays, R. D., Burnam, M. A., Rogers, W., Daniels, M., . . . Ware, J. (1989). The functioning and well-being of depressed patients: Results from the medical outcomes study. *JAMA, 262,* 914–919. doi:10.1001/jama.1989.03430070062031

Welner, M., Mastellon, T., Stewart, J. J., Weinert, B., & Stratton, J. M. B. (2012). Peer-reviewed forensic consultation: Safeguarding expert testimony and protecting the uninformed court. *Journal of Forensic Psychology Practice, 12,* 1–34. doi:10.1080/15228932.2011.588526

Williams, C. W., Lees-Haley, P. R., & Djanogly, S. E. (1999). Clinical scrutiny of litigants' self-reports. *Professional Psychology: Research and Practice, 30,* 361–367. doi:10.1037/0735-7028.30.4.361

Wisdom, N. M., Callahan, J. L., & Shaw, T. G. (2010). Diagnostic utility of the Structured Inventory of Malingered Symptomatology to detect malingering in a forensic sample. *Archives of Clinical Neuropsychology, 25,* 118–125.

Witt, P. H., & Weitz, S. E. (2007). Personal injury evaluations in motor vehicle accident cases. *Journal of Psychiatry and Law, 35,* 3–24.

Wittman, J. S. (1985). Child advocacy and the scientific model and family court: A theory for pretrial self-assessment. *Journal of Psychiatry and Law, 13,* 61–82.

World Health Organization. (2010). *ICD–10: International statistical classification of diseases and related health problems.* New York, NY: Author.

Young, G. (2008a). Psychological injury and law: An integrative model. *Psychological Injury and Law, 1,* 150–160. doi:10.1007/s12207-008-9019-y

Young, G. (2008b). Somatization and medically unexplained symptoms in psychological injury: Diagnoses and dynamics. *Psychological Injury and Law, 1,* 224–242. doi:10.1007/s12207-008-9021-4

Young, G. (2010). Trends in psychological/psychiatric injury and law: Continuing education, practice comments, recommendations. *Psychological Injury and Law, 3,* 323–355. doi:10.1007/s12207-010-9092-x

Youngjohn, J. R., Spector, J., & Mapou, R. L. (1997). Neuropsychological findings in silicone breast-implant complainants: Brain damage, somatization, or compensation neuroses? *Clinical Neuropsychologist, 11,* 132–141. doi:10.1080/13854049708407041

CHAPTER 15

EMPLOYMENT DISCRIMINATION

Margaret S. Stockdale, Katherine A. Sliter, and Leslie Ashburn-Nardo

Gone are the days when job postings routinely read "Blacks or Women Need Not Apply," but discrimination continues to occur at all stages of employment, from hiring and promotion to pay and training opportunities. Moreover, modern discriminatory actions have become more difficult to detect because they can take different, subtler forms than in previous decades, and more demographic groups are being recognized as systematic targets of discrimination.

Psychologists have a vital role to play in the forensics of employment discrimination. First, as behavioral scientists, psychologists have a rich theoretical basis of knowledge that is backed by a wealth of empirical research examining how and why humans engage in or are the targets of prejudicial beliefs and discriminatory acts. Our science therefore not only informs courts in helping to shape decisions about culpability and credibility but also advances our own theory and research when it is grounded in the realities of the relevant legal landscape. Second, psychologists directly impact legal decision making by serving as expert witnesses. Third, we provide guidance to employers in order to help shape the policies and practices that seek to end unlawful discrimination and create healthy, productive, and inclusive organizational work environments.

What follows is a review of the relevant laws and legal frameworks for the major forms of employment discrimination—race, sex, and age—with a nod toward emerging areas of interest among psychological researchers and practitioners: weight/appearance, sexual orientation, religion, and national origin. Unless noted, our discussion is limited to discrimination issues within the United States. Next, we review major psychological theories and important research findings, with a particular focus on race and sex discrimination, including sexual harassment. In the final section, we focus on policies and practices that are informed by psychological theory and research that may help to abate discriminatory practices.

IMPORTANCE OF THE PROBLEM

Racism and sexism are certainly the most well-known and well-researched forms of employment discrimination. This is unsurprising given the historical repression of members of both groups in the United States. However, present-day discussions of race and sex discrimination are not merely recountings of bygone experiences. Even though both have been illegal since 1964, discrimination against racial minorities and discrimination against women continue to be the most commonly reported forms of discrimination (Puhl, Andreyeva, & Brownell, 2008). In 2012 alone, the Equal Employment Opportunity Commission (EEOC), the federal agency that is charged with enforcing employment discrimination law, processed 33,512 cases alleging race discrimination and 30,356 alleging sex discrimination, which together account for a majority of the cases that were filed (EEOC, 2013). Thousands more face discrimination on the basis of other characteristics, such as religion, age, and national

http://dx.doi.org/10.1037/14461-015
APA Handbook of Forensic Psychology: Vol. 1. Individual and Situational Influences in Criminal and Civil Contexts,
B. L. Cutler and P. A. Zapf (Editors-in-Chief)

origin. In fact, religious discrimination appears to be one of the fastest growing forms of workplace discrimination, with religious discrimination claims rising 82% between 1997 and 2009 (Blair, 2010). This increase was many times greater than that observed for either race (16%) or sex (15%), and was only rivaled by the 55% increase in age discrimination claims during this same time period. In terms of raw numbers, religious and national origin discrimination still make up a relatively small, though certainly not inconsequential, proportion of the overall discrimination charges that are reported to the EEOC (3,811 and 10,883 cases in 2012, respectively), but age discrimination comprises a larger proportion, with 22,857 reports in 2012 (EEOC, 2013).

Sexual orientation discrimination is another type of discrimination that is gaining recognition. In a review of more than 50 studies investigating incidences of sexual orientation discrimination, Badgett, Lau, Sears, and Ho (2007) demonstrated that for individuals who are lesbian, gay, bisexual, or transgendered (LGBT), employment discrimination is a pervasive and persistent problem. When LGBT individuals were asked to report on their own experiences in the workplace, as many as 68% reported having experienced employment discrimination due to their orientation. In states where sexual orientation discrimination is illegal, LGBT individuals file discrimination claims at approximately the same rates as women and racial minorities do. Furthermore, this trend does not appear to be simply a matter of perception, as this same review found that as many as 30% of heterosexual employees reported having witnessed discrimination against LGBT individuals (Badgett et al., 2007).

Weight-related discrimination is also a problem. Despite the fact that the majority of Americans are now overweight (Flegal, Carroll, Ogden, & Curtin, 2010), physical size remains one of the last characteristics for which it is considered socially acceptable to discriminate. Because of this, a significant portion of American adults face weight-related discrimination. When a large nationwide sample of adults was surveyed from 1995 to 1996, the rate of weight-related discrimination was relatively low (7.3%), but this value rose by approximately

two-thirds to 12.2% when a similar sample of adults was surveyed from 2004 to 2006 (Carr & Friedman, 2005). This, and other research, has also demonstrated that certain groups are at greater risk for weight-related discrimination, including women, those who are young, and those who could be categorized as obese (Carr & Friedman, 2005; Puhl et al., 2008).

Legal Overview

Given the wide variations in state and local antidiscrimination laws, the present chapter will focus on the federal policies and case law that are specific to the addressed forms of discrimination. The Civil Rights Act of 1964 (CRA) was sweeping, landmark legislation that sought to end racial, ethnic, sex, religious, and national origin discrimination and unfair treatment across a broad spectrum of public life. Title VII of the Act concerned employment discrimination and has been the primary legislative tool guiding legal activity and forensic psychology research and theory. Other important legislative structures include the Equal Pay Act of 1963 (EPA), the Age Discrimination in Employment Act of 1967 (ADEA), the Americans With Disabilities Act of 1990 (ADA), the Civil Rights Act of 1991 (CRA-1991), and the Lilly Ledbetter Fair Pay Act of 2009.

Title VII prohibits organizations that employ 15 or more persons for at least 20 calendar weeks in a month from not hiring, discharging, or in other ways discriminating against a person with respect to his or her essential conditions and privileges of employment on the basis of the individual's race, color, religion, sex, or national origin (Section 703a(1)), or from segregating employees on the basis of these classifications, which adversely affect employment opportunities or employment statuses (Section 703a(2)). Title VII also prohibits employers from retaliating against employees who oppose an unlawful employment practice or who make or assist with a charge of employment discrimination, including testifying or participating in an investigation (Section 704a), regardless of the merits of the charge. The EPA prohibits wage discrimination on the basis of sex for work in the same establishment that requires substantially equal skill, effort, and responsibility under similar working conditions. The ADEA prohibits employment discrimination against individuals who are over age 40 on the basis of age, and the ADA prohibits employers from discriminating against individuals who have a major life disability, or who are perceived to have such a disability, but who can perform the essential functions of the job with or without a reasonable accommodation. "Reasonable accommodations" are those that do not incur undue hardship on the employer. The Lilly Ledbetter Fair Pay Act codifies what had been the standard practice of recognizing that each pay period in which pay discrimination is evident violates the EPA and starts the 180-day statute of limitations under a continuing violation theory. *Ledbetter v. Goodyear Tire & Rubber Co.* (2007) had overturned this practice.

Disparate treatment and disparate impact. Two doctrines guide claims that can be made in Title VII cases: disparate treatment and disparate impact. *Disparate treatment* requires evidence of the intention to discriminate, but modern discriminatory acts are often subtle and difficult to identify. In recognition of this, the U.S. Supreme Court outlined the evidentiary burden for making a claim of disparate treatment discrimination, known as the *McDonnell Douglas/Burdine* standard: (a) Plaintiff must demonstrate that he or she is a member of a protected group and experienced a negative employment decision in which his or her protected-group status was a motivating factor; (b) defendant must present a nondiscriminatory reason for the decision; and (c) plaintiff demonstrates that this nondiscriminatory reason is not the true reason but rather is pretext for discrimination (*McDonnell Douglas Corp. v. Green*, 1973; *Texas Department of Community Affairs v. Joyce Ann Burdine*, 1981).

In a *disparate impact* analysis, a neutral employment practice (e.g., scores on a preemployment test, height/weight requirements) disproportionately adversely affects members of a protected group. *Griggs v. Duke Power* (1971) outlined the evidentiary framework: (a) The complaining party demonstrates that a neutral employment practice creates adverse impact (see Gutman, 2005, for a discussion of the various ways this can be established); then

(b) the employer must show that the practice is job related and a business necessity, and that there is not an equally or more acceptable practice that would have less adverse impact.

Special topics. Title VII provides strong protection against discrimination for many social groups, and the framework of the disparate treatment and disparate impact doctrines offers clear guidelines as to what actually constitutes legally recognized discrimination. However, gaining redress for several of the forms of discrimination included in this chapter requires different, and in some cases circuitous, legislative approaches.

Age Discrimination

The evidentiary burden for establishing disparate treatment age discrimination is generally consistent with the *McDonnell Douglas/Burdine* framework when direct evidence of intentional discrimination is unavailable or difficult to establish. The plaintiff may also provide statistical evidence of a *pattern and practice* of discriminatory treatment against older workers as well as a convincing argument that the employer's pattern and practice is not job related. The disparate impact doctrine for ADEA cases, however, is suspect after the Supreme Court ruling in *Hazen v. Biggins* (1993). Specifically, the *Hazen* Court held that ADEA was established to halt the use of stigmatizing age-related stereotypes in employment decisions. In *Hazen*, at issue was the termination of an older employee shortly before his pension would be vested. Because this practice was not based in stereotypes, albeit correlated with age, the Court found no ADEA violation (Friedman & Strickler, 2001).

There are other features of ADEA claims that are unique from Title VII claims. For example, age discrimination can be proven even if some of the comparators (employees treated more favorably) are 40 or older. Thus, it is unlawful for an employer to discriminate on the basis of age against an employee over age 40 in favor of a younger employee who is also over 40 (*O'Connor v. Consolidated Coin Caterers Corporation*, 1996). Interestingly, the Supreme Court ruled in a benefits case that it is lawful for older employees to receive a better benefit than younger employees who are 40 years old or older (*General Dynamics v. Cline*, 2004). Also, there are several exemptions in ADEA. Although an ADEA amendment lifted the mandatory retirement age, employers can still mandate an age-65 retirement clause for bona fide executives or those with executive power. Safety officers, such as police officers and firefighters, are exempt from ADEA claims, and commercial airline pilots are held to a mandatory retirement requirement at age 60 (see Sterns, Doverspike, & Lax, 2005, for a fuller discussion).

Sexual Harassment

Sexual harassment as a claim of discrimination has a unique history and supporting case law. "Sex" as a protected category was added late to the 1964 CRA, with no legislative history; therefore, there is no record of what acts of sex discrimination Congress intended to prohibit. Early cases (e.g., *Williams v. Saxbe*, 1976) failed to rule on whether sexual harassment (i.e., refusal to submit to a supervisor's sexual advances) violated Title VII. An accumulation of such cases, public outcry, and a convincing theory marshaled by legal scholar Catherine MacKinnon (1979) compelled the EEOC to establish guidelines to define and prohibit unlawful sexual harassment. The guidelines outline two major forms of harassing conduct: quid pro quo ("submission to or rejection of such conduct by an individual is used as the basis for employment decisions affecting such individual"; 29 C.F.R § 1604.11(a)(2)) and hostile environment ("submission to [unwelcome sexual conduct that] is made either explicitly or implicitly a term or condition of an individual's employment"; 29 C.F.R § 1604.11(a)(1)).

The major Supreme Court cases that have interpreted and shaped these guidelines include *Meritor Savings Bank v. Vinson* (1986), which established the legitimacy of a hostile environment claim of harassment; *Harris v. Forklift Systems, Inc.* (1993), which rejected the psychological damages requirement; *Faragher v. City of Boca Raton* (1998) and *Burlington Industries v. Ellerth* (1998), which clarified employer liability and provided an "affirmative defense" for claims in which tangible employment consequences were not conditioned on sexual cooperation; and *Oncale v. Sundowner Offshore Services* (1998), which

held that the sex composition of the harasser and target is irrelevant to a claim, allowing same-sex sexual harassment cases to be litigated.

A recent Supreme Court case considered a racial harassment case (*Vance v. Ball State University*, 2013) which furthered defined the meaning of the term *supervisor*. The Court ruled that for purposes of vicarious liability under Title VII, a supervisor is a person who is empowered by their employer to take tangible employment actions. Under the *Faragher/Ellerth* doctrine, employers are liable when their supervisors have harassed an employee, but lower courts differed on their definitions, with some holding that only individuals with the power to hire, fire, and transfer (as opposed to only guiding employees' day-to-day duties) are defined as supervisors. The Supreme Court's agreement with this interpretation results in a substantial narrowing of the scope of employers' liability. This outcome has important implications on organization policies and practices toward all forms of unlawful harassment.

Weight-Related

Although obesity is not an explicitly protected class under Title VII, discrimination on the basis of one's physical size may qualify for protection if this discrimination systematically and disproportionately affects individuals who are from a class that is protected. A key example of this is the case of *Frank v. United Airlines* (2000). United Airlines had strict height and weight limits for employees who were serving as flight attendants, and an issue arose when it was demonstrated that women were being systematically eliminated on the basis of these size restrictions at a greater rate than men were. Eliminating people on the basis of weight is legally allowable if excessive size would preclude effective performance of the job, but the height and weight charts that were used for men were based on a large body frame, whereas those used for women were based on a medium or small body frame, making the weight restrictions *more* restrictive for females, who are a protected class.

The ADA offers a little more room for coverage of obesity discrimination, although simply being obese is neither recognized as a disability under the

ADA nor protected without further criteria being met. One way in which obesity can be protected under the ADA is if a person's obesity can be directly attributed to a physiological illness or impairment. Alternately, physical health problems that are caused by, or exacerbated by, a person's obesity (e.g., diabetes, hypertension) may also be protected, leading to indirect protection against obesity-related discrimination. Obesity may also be covered under the ADA if an employer discriminates on the basis of a perceived disability. That is, although the obesity itself is not legally considered a disability, if an employer treats a person unfairly because the employer thinks that the person is disabled due to his or her obesity, then that may be grounds for ADA protection for the targeted individual.

Sexual Orientation

Although there is also no federal protection against employment discrimination on the basis of sexual orientation, some plaintiffs have sought to bring suit indirectly under Title VII. For example, in *Vickers v. Fairfield Medical Center* (2006), the male plaintiff claimed that he was discriminated against on the basis of sex (protected under Title VII) because he was perceived as too effeminate as a result of his sexual orientation. His claim was that the mannerisms and behaviors resulting from his sexual orientation were deemed undesirable, when they would have been acceptable in a woman, thereby resulting in sex discrimination. Unfortunately, in this case and others, the plaintiff's claims were denied specifically because the court did not want to circuitously extend Title VII to include sexual orientation as a protected class.

Common Defenses Against Employment Discrimination Claims and Miscellaneous Issues

Defenses against claims of employment discrimination generally rest on the employer's ability to demonstrate that the actions were job related and on the plaintiff's failure to demonstrate that the employer's explanation was pretext for discrimination (disparate treatment) or that the neutral employment practice was not substantially job related (disparate impact). In age discrimination claims, a bona fide

seniority system is a statutory defense. For several types of discrimination, employers can also use a *bona fide occupational qualification* defense, which claims that the class characteristic (e.g., sex, religious affiliation, age) is essential to a major aspect of the job. Bona fide occupational qualification defenses are not applicable to race discrimination claims.

There are other legal issues that are not reviewed here for space considerations but that nonetheless are important for forensic psychologists to be familiar with, depending on the nature of the issues in the case they may be asked to examine or for research questions. One is procedural requirements for making a claim of discrimination under one or more of the applicable laws. Landy (2005) summarized these requirements as well as an outline of the case litigation process. A second issue is the important distinction between single plaintiff, class action, and pattern and practice cases. In *single plaintiff cases*, the more common type, an individual brings suit against a person or entity. *Class action cases*—those in which a large number of similarly situated cases are coalesced into a single case—first go through a class certification phase in which plaintiffs have to demonstrate that they meet the definition of a class: (a) *commonality*, the major legal or factual issue(s) are common to all members of the class; (b) *adequacy*, the named plaintiffs adequately represent the interests of all members of the class; (c) *numerosity*, the class is large enough to justify consolidation; and (d) *typicality*, the major claims are typical of all of the plaintiffs or defendants (see Landy, 2005).

Pattern and practice cases focus on company-wide practices that result in discrimination against one or more protected classes by disparate treatment or disparate impact. In fact, disparate impact is a subtype of pattern and practice, but claims of other practices, such as a company culture that permits objectionable stereotypes or a chilly climate against a class of individuals that festers (e.g., stereotypes that women are sex objects), may also be litigated under a pattern and practice theory. The EEOC may intervene in any case in an effort to ferret out business practices that unlawfully discriminate against protected classes. The Supreme Court's ruling in the class certification appeal in *Wal-Mart Stores, Inc. v. Betty Dukes et al.* (2011), however, placed serious doubt that a pattern and practice claim based on "corporate culture" theory will succeed. Instead, the *Wal-Mart* Court required evidence of a specific, identifiable, widely implemented employment practice to satisfy the "commonality" class certification requirement.

To summarize, judgments regarding employment discrimination are guided primarily by Title VII of the CRA, including the disparate treatment and disparate impact doctrines. Employment discrimination on the basis of age is guided by the ADEA, which adheres closely to Title VII law, with some important distinctions, especially the dubiousness of disparate impact claims. Other forms of discrimination also have their own supporting legislation and case law. State laws on employment discrimination tend to closely follow federal law but often broaden the scope of the legal protections to include sexual orientation, and possibly soon, weight.

RELEVANT PSYCHOLOGICAL THEORY AND PRINCIPLES

One way in which psychologists have particularly enriched the understanding of employment discrimination is by studying and identifying its cognitive, social, and affective antecedents. The theories established as a result of study in these areas provide practitioners and researchers with rich knowledge of *why* individuals may engage in discriminatory behavior (see also Volume 2, Chapter 5, this handbook). In the following sections, we identify several of these key theories and principles.

Stereotyping and Implicit Bias

Given the many legal proscriptions that were outlined in the previous section, readers may wonder whether and why employment discrimination continues to be a problem. Although research has demonstrated that some people minimize the significance of discrimination today (e.g., Kaiser, Drury, Spalding, Cheryan, & O'Brien, 2009), contemporary studies indisputably demonstrate the pervasive and insidious influence of stereotypes in employment decisions (e.g., Moss-Racusin, Dovidio, Brescoll,

Graham, & Handelsman, 2012). Although a comprehensive review of the stereotyping literature is well beyond the scope of this chapter (for more on this topic, see Volume 2, Chapter 5, this handbook), we focus here on recent theories and research regarding stereotype content and application, including theories about the substance or content of stereotypes and when stereotypes are likely to affect employment practices.

People evaluate other people on two fundamental dimensions: warmth and competence. This idea is grounded in the classic work of Asch (1946) but also forms the basis of the more recent stereotype content model (SCM; Fiske, Cuddy, Glick, & Xu, 2002). SCM suggests that warmth and competence operate orthogonally such that some groups are stereotyped uniformly positively (e.g., middle-class Americans as *warm* and *competent*), some uniformly negatively (e.g., welfare recipients as *cold* and *incompetent*), and some ambivalently (e.g., Asians as *cold* and *competent*, the elderly as *warm* and *incompetent*). Moreover, stereotype content dictates our feelings toward these groups: We admire uniformly positive groups, envy competent but cold groups, pity incompetent but warm groups, and feel contempt toward uniformly negative groups.

Such stereotypes and affective reactions exist to justify the social order (Jost, 2001), helping us make sense of conditions that otherwise would seem unfair. We see rich people, for example, as having earned their position because they surely must be savvy (competent) yet cutthroat (cold). Welfare recipients must be not only unskilled (incompetent) but also willing to mooch off the government (cold). With regard to employment discrimination, employers likely justify why White men are overrepresented in higher status, influential positions; they must have characteristics that make them better suited than women and minorities. Conveniently, women and minorities are not uniformly negatively stereotyped; rather, their positive stereotypes (e.g., women as nurturing, Blacks as athletically or musically gifted) make them seen as suitable for positions of little influence (teachers) or probability of success (professional athletes, musicians).

Importantly, people often apply stereotypes spontaneously, making biased judgments with little intent or conscious awareness. Indeed, people often have stereotypic-implicit biases despite explicit motivations to be nonprejudiced and egalitarian (Dovidio, Kawakami, & Beach, 2001). These implicit biases are most likely to manifest themselves when people are cognitively taxed or pressed for time, or when they are not particularly motivated to individuate (e.g., Fazio & Towles-Schwen, 1999)—conditions that describe overworked employers who are evaluating people that they potentially may never meet. Aversive racism theory (Gaertner & Dovidio, 1986) further suggests that, because we are motivated not to think of ourselves as biased individuals, our stereotypes influence judgments most often in ambiguous circumstances that allow us to attribute our judgments to factors besides bias. Accordingly, a review of selection studies revealed that Black candidates were discriminated against only when their job qualifications were ambiguous, not when they were clearly weak or strong (Dovidio & Gaertner, 2000).

In summary, contemporary theories and research on stereotyping and implicit bias may help us understand why employment discrimination persists in the face of laws that aim to redress and prevent it. As this literature suggests, stereotypes need not be uniformly negative in order to lead to disparate treatment, and they can influence even well-intentioned individuals.

Gender Disparities

Although stereotyping and prejudice are relevant to class-based employment disparities such as pay gaps and selection and promotion differences, this section reviews the explanatory mechanisms that have been broadly discussed as sources of gender disparities: those that imply differences in the attributes of the class (e.g., supply-side or employee characteristics), those that imply differences in the way employers treat different classes of employees (e.g., demand-side, employer, or institutional characteristics), and those that imply broader cultural and social factors that shape the characteristics of the labor pool.

A supply-side perspective on gender-based employment disparities places the onus on differences in the characteristics in the suppliers of labor;

that is, potential employees. This is the primary assumption of the neoclassical economic perspective on employment patterns (e.g., Becker, 1957). Accordingly, women have different types and amounts of human capital that, on average, are less valuable to employers than men's. Historically, this referred to attributes such as level of education, type and length of experience, and likelihood of taking extended breaks from the labor market (e.g., Polachek, 1975). These differences were theorized to explain occupational sex segregation, or an imbalance in the percentage of women and men who occupy various broad categories of jobs. Gender distributions in human capital have by-and-large disappeared on most characteristics, such as level of education and amount of job experience (Lips, 2013), but differences in choice of college major or other forms of specialized training persist and account largely for differences in occupational choices (Shauman, 2006).

Women and men tend to be segregated not only by occupation, but also by hierarchical levels within occupational classes, such that men tend to occupy higher managerial levels in an organization than do women (Schäfer, Tucci, & Gottschall, 2012). This is sometimes characterized as a *glass ceiling* for women and a *glass elevator* for men. Common supply-side explanations for hierarchical segregation include gender differences in the tolerance for job attributes that attach to many higher ranking positions, such as full-time work schedules, overnight travel, relocation, and erratic work schedules (e.g., Bond, Thompson, Galinsky, & Prottas, 2002; Presser & Hermsen, 1996).

There are some jobs for which selection or promotion on the basis of a single or set of related traits may be common. For example, firefighters must pass physical ability tests, which tend to show fairly sizable gender differences, particularly for upper-body strength (Miller, MacDougall, Tarnopolsky, & Sale, 1993). The selection of weight-loss counselors, on the other hand, may be based largely on their ability to show emotional connections with clients, and women tend to have advantages over men on traits such as empathy, expressiveness, self-disclosure, and agreeableness (Hyde, 2005). In large-scale selection contexts, where traits of the selection pool may approximate a normal curve and the selection ratio is very high (few selected compared to many who apply), substantial gender differences in the pool that survives the cutoff may be observed. Often, this is the basis of disparate impact charges for which the employing organization must produce a viable, job-relevant reason for the use of tests that measure such traits.

Demand-side explanations for gender (and other class) employment disparities focus on the discriminatory acts of employers and their agents and their policies, practices, and other institutional structures that have discriminatory impact on protected groups. Employers' stereotypes and biases against women and other classes of individuals discussed previously are classic demand-side explanations for employment discrimination. Structural characteristics of organizations can also create barriers to women's equitable treatment in the workplace. Biased promotion ladders (e.g., extensive overseas travel), veterans' preferences, and sexualized work environments (e.g., environments with a high degree of sexual bantering; Gutek, 1993) exacerbate biased treatment and biased processing of information about female employees.

Heilman and Haynes (2008) theorized that a lack of fit between the perceived characteristics of an applicant/incumbent and the perceived requirements of the job exacerbate bias against women in several ways. First, factors that increase the salience of feminine stereotypes of the female job holder/applicant, such as when she holds a token position or is particularly attractive, increase lack-of-fit perceptions. Female employees who are perceived to violate the norms for feminine behavior also tend to be evaluated less positively (Eagly & Karau, 2002). Factors that increase the masculine attributes of the job, such as male domination in the gender composition of job holders and a focus on agentic job qualities, increase lack-of-fit perceptions. Third, ambiguity in the evaluation procedures increases subjectivity and concomitant reliance on stereotypes and biases (Heilman & Haynes, 2008). Fourth, bias is affected by motivational factors. Evaluators (e.g., supervisors) whose own performance is interdependent on the performance of their subordinates,

or who are held accountable for their evaluations (in particular, for the employment discrimination implications), are more motivated to avoid bias (Heilman & Haynes, 2008; Krieger, 2007).

Gender role socialization underlies other theories of gender disparities in employment statuses. The *social glass ceiling* refers to impediments to women's advancement that stem from social and cultural factors that are pervasive in our society. Women have long been socialized to adopt family-centered roles and men to adopt work-centered roles (Bielby & Bielby, 1989; Eagly, 1987). Marriage and having children tend to be associated with career setbacks for women, as they divert their time to nonwork tasks (i.e., raising children, housework), but to career advantages for men (Drobnič, Blossfeld, & Rohwer, 1999). These social role differences are changing toward egalitarianism but are still quite evident (Bond et al., 2002), and they can create gender disparities in work outcomes through either demand-side or supply-side mechanisms. On the demand side, employers may stereotypically believe that women, especially those with child care responsibilities, will be less reliable employees; thus, employees may behave in a discriminatory manner toward such women. On the supply side, female employees may decide that the demands of full-time employment, especially in highly competitive or demanding occupations, create excessive family–life demands; as a result, these employees may opt out of opportunities for career advancement.

Sexual Harassment

Broadly speaking, sexual harassment encompasses a wide variety of behaviors that are rooted in a patriarchal societal structure that privileges "men's dominance of economics, production, and sexuality" (Gruber & Morgan, 2005, p. x). To be legally actionable, the behaviors need to occur in the context of either a workplace (thus, covered by Title VII of the CRA) or an academic setting (covered by Title IX of the Education Amendments of 1982); therefore, organizational factors, such as workplace norms, power differences, gender composition of work groups, leadership practices, and organizational culture impact the form, frequency, and severity of sexually harassing experiences

(Fitzgerald, Drasgow, Hulin, Gelfand, & Magley, 1997; Ilies, Hauseman, Schwochau, & Stibal, 2003).

Person characteristics may compound volatile workplace or environment characteristics. Pryor's (1987) person X situation model posited that men with a propensity to sexually harass, as predicted by personality and attitudinal variables such as hostility (Lee, Gizzarone, & Ashton, 2003) and hostile sexism (Glick & Fiske, 1997), are more likely to harass when situational norms are permissive (Pryor, Giedd, & Williams, 1995). In Fitzgerald et al.'s (1997) integrated theory of sexual harassment, climate of the work environment with regard to tolerance for sexual harassment, defined by the dominance of men in a particular work group (the *job–gender context*), and the gender typicality of targets' jobs play important roles in affecting the frequency and severity of harassment within that organization. Similarly, a criminology theory, routine activities theory, has been invoked to explain organizational characteristics that predict sexual harassment (DeCoster, Estes, & Mueller, 1999): Sexually harassing work environments are those where potentially *vulnerable targets* (e.g., women) are at risk of encountering *motivated offenders* (e.g., men in male-dominated work environments), without the aid of *capable guardians* (e.g., trained supervisors, strong antiharassment policies and practices).

Target characteristics predict who may be particularly vulnerable to harassment, and although "blame-the-victim" conjectures are noxious to most scholars, theoretical understanding of victim vulnerability informs preventive and restorative antiharassment approaches for organizations. Young, unmarried women are typically more vulnerable to sexual harassment than are others (U.S. Merit Systems Protection Board, 1995), but so too are women who espouse feminist attitudes or personality traits (Berdahl, 2007b). Male targets are typically young and inexperienced and are perceived as less masculine (Stockdale, 2005). Victim vulnerability may be a function of different goals for perpetrators. Individuals who engage in sexually harassing conduct to gain sexual access to their target, such as when a supervisor conditions employment consequences on submission to sexual advances, may select as

their targets individuals who are in lower status positions. On the other hand, individuals who harass in order to protect their privileged status, such as when men in historically masculine occupations engage in gender-degrading behaviors, may choose as their targets female pioneers in those occupations who threaten the status quo, or other men who do not meet their internalized standards for masculinity (Berdahl, 2007a; Stockdale, 2005).

Theories Unique to Weight/Appearance, Age, Sexual Orientation, Religion, and National Origin Discrimination

Discrimination on the bases of factors other than race and sex can also be explained with several type-specific theories. With weight discrimination, for instance, individuals who make employment decisions often feel that this discrimination is rational. In a review of weight discrimination, Roehling (2002) addressed this issue by highlighting the fact that people tend to view weight as being controllable. Weight is not innate, and because of this, it tends to be perceived as something that an individual could change if he or she had the desire and willpower to do so. Thus, individuals who are overweight are often viewed as being at fault for their condition, and discrimination may be considered justified because people believe that these individuals "choose to be that way." Compounding this is the fact that people often make a host of other negative attributions toward individuals who are overweight or obese (e.g., that their job performance is not as good, they are less intelligent and motivated, they are not as socially skilled). Thus, weight-related discrimination may not occur because of conscious dislike but because of the distorted belief that the very appearance of overweight individuals is indicative of traits that would be undesirable for the organization.

Age discrimination, too, can occur as a result of preconceived notions about the job-related abilities of older individuals. Within Western cultures, there is a pervasive belief that older people are significantly less mentally and physically robust than younger people, and that they are increasingly reliant on younger individuals (Nelson, 2008). Therefore, older employees' skills may be viewed as diminished, and older applicants may be viewed as less qualified for desired jobs, even in the face of evidence to the contrary. Unfortunately, this bias tends to be automatic and unconscious, and as outlined in terror management theory, may represent younger individuals' attempts to psychologically distance themselves from the inevitability of old age (Solomon, Greenberg, & Pyszczynski, 1991). By shifting the blame of aging to older individuals and simultaneously ascribing negative characteristics to them, younger individuals can subconsciously deceive themselves that age is something that will not happen to them.

Sexual orientation discrimination, on the other hand, is less often motivated by any notions of fitness for the job. Rather, a more common motivation for employment discrimination against individuals who are LGBT, or at least are perceived to be LGBT, is sexual prejudice. Sexual prejudice, or negative attitudes about a person because of his or her sexuality, may be motivated by a variety of experiences or influences, such as prior negative interactions with LGBT individuals, discomfort with one's own sexual feelings or urges, or a belief that the "gay lifestyle" is in direct conflict with one's personal values (Herek, 2000). Regardless of the reason for the feelings, sexual prejudice may help to explain why so many LGBT individuals report discrimination: Although they may be seen as perfectly well qualified for a given position, personal negative beliefs about their sexuality may make others actively seek to avoid working with them.

Finally, both religious and national origin discrimination can be explained through the lens of assimilation bias in the workplace. Organizations naturally develop their own cultures, which are primarily determined by, and reinforced by, members of the social majority. Individuals who conform to this organizational culture—through their dress, mannerisms, and social interactions—tend to be welcomed, whereas those who do not assimilate are often viewed and treated as outsiders (Green, 2005). Characteristics and mannerisms that are related to religion and/or national origin (e.g., head and body coverings, piercings and tattoos, hairstyles, linguistic accents, or primary use of a non-English language) can automatically signal differences from the primary organizational culture, leading to an increased propensity for discrimination.

RESEARCH REVIEW

As a result of the numerous social and psychological forces that have been described thus far, the demographic groups identified are at particular risk for discrimination. For some of these groups, the discrimination faced is a long-recognized problem, whereas the plight of other groups has only been recently acknowledged. Regardless, each demographic group faces unique challenges, and these challenges will be illustrated in this section.

Race Discrimination

Although the United States has been characterized by some as *postracial* since the election of the nation's first African American President, data on employment discrimination suggest otherwise. A comprehensive review of race-based employment discrimination would easily comprise a chapter in itself; rather, we present some contemporary evidence in key areas of employment: selection, performance appraisal, compensation, and workplace climate.

Blacks are discriminated against in selection decisions largely as a function of stereotypes and implicit bias. For example, in one highly cited field experiment, résumés with stereotypically Black names (e.g., Jamal) were significantly less likely to lead to callbacks than were those with "White names" (e.g., Greg), regardless of industry or occupation (Bertrand & Mullainathan, 2004). Black raters who implicitly favor Whites may also demonstrate anti-Black selection tendencies, but only on tasks that are stereotypically associated with Whites' success (Ashburn-Nardo & Johnson, 2008; Ashburn-Nardo, Knowles, & Monteith, 2003). When Black applicants are reviewed by potential employers, they are still likely targets of discrimination, but only under particular circumstances. Consistent with aversive racism theory, Dovidio and Gaertner (2000) found evidence for race-based discrimination in selection only when an applicant's credentials were ambiguous. Additionally, Ziegert and Hanges (2005) found that evaluator-implicit racial bias predicted discrimination in hiring decisions, but only when the culture was one that tolerated discrimination rather than promoted equality. Thus, selection discrimination appears to occur when discriminatory judgments can be justified in some way.

For racial minorities who are hired, evidence of discrimination also exists in the domain of performance appraisal. For example, in both military and civilian samples, data suggest that Black supervisors evaluate Black and White employees similarly, but White supervisors evaluate Black employees significantly worse than they do White employees (Stauffer & Buckley, 2005). When the individuals being evaluated are in leadership positions, discrimination is perhaps more nuanced. For example, when organizations are succeeding, Blacks and White women in leadership roles are evaluated more negatively than White men are; however, when the organization's outlook is more negative, Black women leaders experience "double jeopardy" and are evaluated more negatively than Black men and White men and women (Rosette & Livingston, 2012). Some research suggests that this racial bias in performance appraisal serves to justify the status quo; that is, people tend to evaluate Black leaders and White subordinates negatively yet to positively evaluate Black subordinates and White leaders, thereby rewarding those who fit their stereotypic roles and punishing those who do not (Knight, Hebl, Foster, & Mannix, 2003).

According to a news release by the Bureau of Labor Statistics, even as recently as the fourth quarter of 2012, median weekly earnings for Black men in the United States were 76.0% that of White men; the disparity was somewhat smaller (83.4%) for Black versus White women (U.S. Department of Labor Bureau of Labor Statistics, 2013). Similar racial disparities exist in terms of leadership positions in organizations. According to Livingston and Pearce (2009), there were only four Black male chief executive officers in the Fortune 500 at the time of their study. The Fortune 500 saw its first Black woman chief executive officer in 2009 (Rosette & Livingston, 2012). Such disparities may be due in part to poor perceived fit between Black men and women and the leader prototype

(Rosette, Leonardelli, & Phillips, 2008). But even in domains in which Blacks are perceived as a stereotypic good fit (e.g., athletics), their salaries are penalized more than Whites for celebrating their successes (Hall & Livingston, 2012).

Finally, racial minorities report experiencing a chillier workplace climate than their White peers, suggesting the existence of what has been termed "everyday racism." Indeed, Cortina (2008) argued that in organizations that prohibit discriminatory behavior, employees who are racially biased may direct their hostilities toward minorities in subtle ways, such as via incivility. By definition, *incivility* is ambiguous in intent (Andersson & Pearson, 1999), making it difficult to regulate or even recognize. However, Blacks (Deitch et al., 2003) and Latinos (K. T. Schneider, Hitlan, & Radhakrishnan, 2000) report experiencing racial micro-aggressions in the workplace more than Whites do. Furthermore, to the extent that minorities perceive such discrimination at work, their job satisfaction and psychological well-being suffers (Deitch et al., 2003), and they report being less psychologically engaged (Plaut, Thomas, & Goren, 2009), which certainly can have implications for the organization's bottom line (e.g., Harter, Schmidt, & Hayes, 2002).

Gender Discrimination

Surveys of women and men in corporate business settings have demonstrated that female executives perceive discrimination to be an important barrier to women's career success, whereas male executives tend to minimize this source of bias (Catalyst Institute, 1996; Galinsky et al., 2003). A nationally representative sample of mature women (average age = 54) found that 12% of women who were employed between 1984 and 1989 perceived that they had been discriminated against at work on the basis of sex, race, age, marital status, nationality, or disability (Pavalko, Mossakowski, & Hamilton, 2003). A field study of performance appraisals in a single, large financial services firm found that, as expected, women were evaluated less positively in high-impact, male-dominated line positions but not in more female-dominated staff positions (Lyness & Heilman, 2006).

Experimental research on sex discrimination has generally followed the Goldberg paradigm (Goldberg, 1968) in which work-related stimuli (e.g., résumés) that vary only by gender of the target are randomly assigned to research participants who make judgments of the perceived qualifications and willingness to hire or promote the job candidate. An early meta-analysis of the research using this paradigm to test the role of gender stereotypes in job-related evaluations found a small pro-male bias (Swim, Borgida, Maruyama, & Myers, 1989). However, experimental research has continued to show that pro-male gender bias on employment-relevant criteria has persisted, particularly when the fit between gender stereotypes and job stereotypes is poor (e.g., Davison & Burke, 2000), or when women are perceived to violate prescriptive norms for feminine behavior (e.g., Rudman & Glick, 2001; Rudman, Moss-Racusin, Phelan, & Nauts, 2012). Extending this paradigm to a working sample, Moss-Racusin et al. (2012) had male and female science faculty review résumés of comparably qualified male and female recent college graduates who were seeking a laboratory-manager position in an academic science department. Male and female faculty showed a preference for the male applicant over the female applicant because they believed the male applicant to be more competent.

Related to the experimental research paradigm are audit tests in which researchers send matched confederates to apply for open positions or submit fictitious résumés for real, advertised job openings and evaluate whether one class of applicants (e.g., White males) is treated better than another class (women or minorities; e.g., Bertrand & Mullainathan, 2004). Riach and Rich (2002) reviewed employment discrimination studies using this paradigm and found consistent pro-White biases. Tests of sex discrimination using this paradigm found that men received preferential treatment compared to women in male-dominated jobs and high-prestige jobs, but that women may be preferred to men in female-dominated or low-prestige jobs (studies reviewed by Riach & Rich, 2002; see also Leslie, King, Bradley, & Hebl, 2008).

From a supply-side perspective, there is also research to show that women and men express preferences for different job attributes, which may account for differences in job assignments, occupational choices, and upward advancement decisions (e.g., Konrad, 2003). Moreover, women tend to be less likely than men to engage in negotiation, which may account for some differences in pay levels (Stuhlmacher & Walters, 1999), but research has also shown that women who do engage in assertive negotiation tactics are perceived as less likeable and less hirable than men who similarly negotiate (Bowles, Babcock, & Lai, 2007).

There has also been some speculation that women are deficient on certain cognitive skills, such as math and spatial reasoning, which explains the paucity of women in advanced careers in science, engineering, and mathematics (e.g., former Harvard President Lawrence Summer's remarks; see WISELI, 2005), but the scientific evidence for *innate* gender differences in cognitive abilities is extremely weak (Hill, Corbett, & St. Rose, 2010). Small gender differences on various traits do exist (Hyde, 2005), but most, such as mathematics abilities, are very small (and sometimes favor women) and would not account for large differences in occupational choices or success with the exception of occupations where single traits or trait clusters are largely responsible for job performance.

Sexual Harassment

Research on sexual harassment has confirmed that sexual harassment is prevalent in the workplace and that women are more likely than men to experience harassment (Ilies et al., 2003), but incidence rates for men are not trivial (Stockdale, Visio, & Batra, 1999). A recent meta-analysis (41 studies, 70,000 respondents) examining the antecedents and consequences of sexual harassment (Willness, Steel, & Lee, 2007) found that the most impactful antecedent was working in a unit of an organization that had a climate that was tolerant of sexual harassment. Working in a male-dominated work environment was also significantly associated with harassment experiences, particularly in non-military samples (a finding most likely due to the low variance in gender composition in military work settings). Among the most commonly reported consequences of sexual harassment are job dissatisfaction, particularly with coworkers and supervisors and for military respondents. Organizational commitment is also adversely affected, as is work or job withdrawal and workgroup productivity (Willness et al., 2007). Sexual harassment has also been associated with reductions in business unit–level productivity (Raver & Gelfand, 2005) as well as the job attitudes of coworkers of individuals who have been harassed (Glomb et al., 1997).

Willness et al.'s (2007) meta-analysis also confirmed several psychological and health-related outcomes of experiencing sexual harassment, including detriments to general mental health and physical symptoms, such as somatic complaints of nausea, headaches, shortness of breath, and exhaustion. Posttraumatic stress disorder has been associated with sexual harassment experiences in both military and nonmilitary samples. Posttraumatic stress disorder has also been shown to be associated with harassment experiences even when other sources of past trauma have been controlled (Stockdale, Logan, & Weston, 2009).

Other Forms of Discrimination: Weight, Sexual Orientation, Religious Affiliation, and National Origin

The study of weight and sexual orientation discrimination is quite a modern movement, with these forms of discrimination remaining largely underexamined prior to the 21st century. Recent research in this area has demonstrated consistent evidence of discrimination on the basis of both factors and has also highlighted subgroups that are at particular vulnerability for both forms of employment discrimination. In terms of weight discrimination, the overall estimated prevalence is approximately 5%–10%, but these values are many times higher for certain groups. Approximately 40% of individuals who are medically classifiable as obese (>20% above a healthy body weight), for example, report weight-related employment discrimination, and women and young individuals are many times more likely to report this form of discrimination than are comparably overweight older individuals and males (Puhl et al., 2008). Similarly, sexual orientation discrimination in the workplace is reported by as much as 68% of LGBT employees (Badgett et al.,

2007), but rates are higher for males, especially in occupations that are stereotypically strongly masculine (Pichler, Varma, & Bruce, 2010).

Research on employment discrimination relating to age, religion, and national origin has been regularly conducted for a longer period of time, and consistent issues have been demonstrated in all three areas. Age discrimination remains one of the forms of discrimination that is most often reported to the EEOC (2013), and some research indicates that its frequency is actually increasing. The aging of the American workforce, coupled with a rapidly changing and evermore technologically dependent work environment, are perhaps the most obvious antecedents of this trend. Demographic shifts may also help to explain why discrimination due to religion and discrimination due to national origin have been increasing at the same time (Blair, 2010). Today, a larger proportion of Americans either practice a non-Christian religion or are foreign born than in the past (Morgan, 2004), making the workplace a more religiously and ethnically diverse place. At the same time, persistent concerns about discrimination continue to simmer following the 9/11 attacks and more recent events in the Middle East, the debates over immigration and border control, and similar situations. These social forces may help to explain why discrimination on the bases of age, religion, and national origin has increased, despite long-standing and strong legal protections.

PRACTICE AND POLICY ISSUES

Strategies to combat employment discrimination and class-based disparities in employment outcomes are based on various frames that change-seekers use to comprehend the source of the problem. Ely and Meyerson (2000) presented an analysis that serves as a framework that is applicable to most forms of employment discrimination discussed in this chapter. Their analysis includes three traditional frames, each of which has produced a variety of practical approaches, and a fourth, nontraditional frame, for addressing discrimination and disparity.

The first frame, "fix the person" (or "fix the woman," in Ely and Meyerson's, 2000, discussion), claims that a deficiency in characteristics of the disparaged class is the source of inequity and that appropriate interventions help to rectify those deficiencies. These interventions may include negotiation training and mentoring programs to improve the ability to obtain employment outcomes (e.g., pay, desirable job assignments) commensurate with comparators (e.g., White men). Ely and Meyerson (2000) noted that although such strategies may shrink the gap in employment outcomes, they preserve the standards and status quo of the privileged class and perpetuate the view that the disparaged class is deficient. In a subsection that follows, we review (with meta-analytic findings, when available) interventions that are focused on the target group.

The second frame, "valuing diversity" (or "value the feminine" according to Ely and Meyerson, 2000), seeks to affirm the differences that women, and presumably other typically disparaged groups, bring to organizations, and to capitalize on those differences in an effort to increase organizational functioning. Examples include diversity training and awards for contributions to diversity. Although this approach lifts up and legitimizes other ways of being, Ely and Meyerson (2000) caution that it leaves stereotypes as well as the processes that produce differences intact.

The third frame, "create equal opportunities" (Ely & Meyerson, 2000), tackles the institutional structures, policies, and practices that have traditionally exacerbated class-based disparities and replaces them with new ones to remove or alter these structural barriers. Affirmative action programs are classic examples of this approach, as are work–family flexibility practices. Such approaches have arguably helped to lower the hurdles that many individuals face in gaining an economic foothold through employment equality. As noted by Ely and Meyerson and many others, such practices have faced rising criticism and backlash throughout society. We review structural-based equal employment opportunity programs, including affirmative action, in a subsequent section.

Ely and Meyerson's (2000) fourth frame, "frame 4," characterizes gender not as a static categorical distinction but as a "set of social relations through which the categories male and female, masculine and feminine, derive meaning and shape another"

(pp. 115–116). Informal practices with gendered consequences include the prevailing assumption that the model employee is one who has virtually no time-based or geographic-based limitations on his or her commitment to work, or that the model employee personality displays traits of ambition, personal striving, and competitiveness. By extension, frame 4 thinking would view heteronormativity, ablebodiedness, thinness, Anglo-Saxon cultural practices, and youthfulness as normative and admired by society. Interventions to address frame 4 thinking are in its infancy, so we provide only recommendations for practice and policy development.

Fix the Person (Individual-Centered Approaches)

Although "assertiveness training" programs were denounced as sexist because they sought to make women "act like men," various manifestations of these programs have survived. One is negotiation training. Although research has shown that negotiation training in general produces small but positive effects (Movius, 2008), research has also demonstrated a backlash against women who negotiate for better employment outcomes (Bowles et al., 2007) because negotiation in women is perceived to violate prescriptive gender norms. Individual-centered approaches to sexual harassment focus on empowering people to respond assertively to unwanted sexual attention and other gender harassment (e.g., Kihnley, 2000). Stockdale and Sagrestano (2010), however, noted that targets have paid costs, such as backlash and retaliation, for assertive responses to such conduct.

Another common "fix the person" strategy to combat employment discrimination is to offer special programs to benefit minorities. However, when executed improperly, these programs may be perceived by minorities as insincere, or worse, as suggesting that they are flawed or inferior. For example, although mentoring programs are often effective, power issues complicate race-unmatched mentor–mentee relationships (Ragins, 1997). Unsolicited help offered by majority-group members may inadvertently convey assumptions of incompetence (M. E. Schneider, Major, Luhtanen, & Crocker, 1996). Thus, it may be more effective to offer aid programs in general and encourage all organizational members to apply if they choose.

Valuing Diversity

The valuing diversity frame is based on the assumption that "individuals from nontraditional backgrounds, that is, cultural backgrounds that have been largely unrepresented in white collar businesses, bring unique perspectives to the workplace which add wisdom and insight to the collective knowledge of the firm" (Ellis & Sonnenfeld, 1994, p. 83). This approach involves strategies to increase awareness and appreciation of a diverse workforce, sending a message to all employees that diversity is valued. Like the other approaches to combating discrimination, this approach works for some but not all employees. Specifically, majority-group members tend to perceive such organizations as being fairer to minorities, even when it is clear that the effort is mere window dressing; consequently, such programs ironically desensitize majority-group members to discrimination and increase backlash toward minorities who claim discrimination (Kaiser et al., 2013). Perhaps more effective are subtle strategies that highlight minority groups' value. For example, displaying art depicting diverse individuals might increase minorities' sense of belonging in the organization (Cheryan, Plaut, Davies, & Steele, 2009).

Allport's (1954) classic intergroup contact approach of purposely creating opportunities for intergroup contact—potentially dispelling stereotypes and identifying common ground—falls under this category. Contact has proven effective in improving intergroup relations (Pettigrew & Tropp, 2006), but the caveat is that the benefits are largely for majority-group members. For minority group members, contact—especially via trivial means that does not necessarily promote long-term friendship—does less to improve outgroup attitudes (Tropp & Pettigrew, 2005).

Perhaps the opposite of the valuing diversity frame is colorblindness. *Colorblind* policies minimize the importance of social group memberships in organizational decisions, but they may unwittingly send the messages that minorities' personal identities do not matter and that minorities and women should assimilate to majority-group standards.

Thus, to the extent that majority-group members in an organization espouse a colorblind worldview, minorities perceive greater bias and are less engaged in the organization psychologically (Plaut et al., 2009). Indeed, a growing body of literature highlights the problems associated with colorblindness and instead advocates for multiculturalism—that is, seeing the organization as a salad bowl where each group adds unique and valued flavor rather than as a melting pot where the only identity that matters is that of the organization (Apfelbaum, Norton, & Sommers, 2012).

A comprehensive study of various diversity practices for increasing the proportion of female or Black managers in large, private businesses provides compelling evidence of their effectiveness (or lack thereof). Kalev, Dobbin, and Kelly (2006) examined records from more than 700 private-sector businesses, from 1971 to 2002, for associations between various diversity management programs and the gender and race composition of managerial employees. Their findings were not encouraging: Diversity training had no appreciable influence on the percentage of women or Black men in management positions and had a slightly negative effect for Black women. Similarly, programs to combat bias by including "diversity management" in employee evaluations had either no effect or a negative effect (for Black men) on the representation of women and minorities in management.

Create Equal Opportunities

This frame addresses the importance of reducing or removing institutional barriers to, or proactively creating opportunities for, the advancement of underrepresented social groups. Affirmative action programs are regarded as important proactive measures, but this is a large umbrella that encompasses many types of practices, some of which, like quota programs and parallel selection programs (i.e., top–down selection of candidates grouped by sex or race), have been explicitly outlawed. Kalev et al. (2006) assessed the impact of the presence of an affirmative action plan—having a committee charged with diversity oversight and having a professional staff of diversity officers— on the advancement of women and Blacks into management. All such efforts showed significant gains for both White women and Black men into management, and diversity committees and staff showed gains for Black women. Growth in the percentage of White and Black women in management accompanied work–family accommodations, but not the implementation of mentoring programs (except for Black women).

Monitoring practices in which organizations track equal employment opportunity–related statistics and related matters have been championed, especially when the results are made public. Krieger (2007) noted that such practices increase an organization's accountability and keep a check on the subtle influences of cognitive bias. Increasing feelings of personal responsibility may make employees more inclined to monitor their own and colleagues' behavior and confront prejudice when they see it. Interpersonal prejudice confrontation involves speaking out when one experiences or witnesses prejudice, and it has demonstrated success in curbing discriminatory behavior (see Czopp & Ashburn-Nardo, 2012). Ashburn-Nardo, Morris, and Goodwin (2008) offered some strategies that organizations might use to encourage confrontation without increasing backlash and resentment.

Frame 4

The issues addressed by frame 4 thinking are both radical and amorphous because they are woven into the very fabric of what we have been socialized to believe is normal, and there are no set strategies that directly target and change these beliefs. For example, people often assume that women are primarily responsible for the private spheres of life (i.e., the home, raising children) and men for the public spheres (i.e., work, politics; Ely & Meyerson, 2000), that a spouse is of the opposite sex, or that working requires the use of both hands. Frame 4 approaches instead require people to think outside the box and consider ways that the organization subtly reinforces the status quo. Interventions to disrupt these normative thoughts require constant attention to the underlying assumptions of formal policies and processes as well as to informal practices, norms, and patterns of work.

In a recent essay in *The Atlantic Magazine*, Ann-Marie Slaughter (2012) described her decision to leave her dream job as the director of policy planning at the U.S. State Department because she realized that she could not do everything her job demanded and be an adequate mother. To many, this sounded like either a cop out or a confession that career women should re-evaluate their priorities. But what she really said was that the standards and norms for paid work have been shaped and reinforced by male, particularly privileged, White-male, standards, and as long as these standards prevail, women as a whole have very little chance of making this work. Time-honored labor practices are exactly that—time, such as a reliance on valuing billable hours, utilization, hours spent in the office or in the laboratory, and set time spans to make tenure or partnership. Compensation and other reward systems are often based on time-related accomplishments, which privilege those whose time is not conflicted by other demands. A frame 4 intervention would be to challenge this assumption. Instead of time, results or impact could replace the norms we use to evaluate an individual's achievement and worth.

The assumptions of frame 4 thinking may be beyond the purview of forensic psychologists, but this approach to combating discrimination offers a glimpse into how we can help organizations conceptualize efforts to help them effectively change in ways that may have long-term benefits for employment equity.

SUMMARY AND CONCLUSIONS

In spite of significant social, legal, and organizational advancements, employment discrimination still exists in the United States. Individuals from a variety of demographic groups not only face difficulties in obtaining employment, but may also face harassment from coworkers and supervisors, may be overlooked for promotions, may receive lower salaries for comparable work, and may experience other forms of discrimination at all levels of employment. Because of the continued presence of discrimination in the workplace, it is important for both researchers and practitioners to understand which groups are at greatest risk, the antecedents of this mistreatment, and the ways in which organizations can prevent and respond to discrimination. This chapter has highlighted many key findings in this area, which have been drawn from years of research in the social and behavioral sciences, all of which can benefit those individuals who are seeking to understand and eliminate workplace discrimination.

One key finding illustrated in this chapter is that discrimination in the modern workplace has several characteristics that set it apart from the discrimination that has been observed in past decades. One way in which modern discrimination is unique is that it tends to be far less obvious than in the past. Overt discrimination certainly does still occur, but subtle forms of discrimination, such as microaggressions and incivility, are more common. This subtlety often makes modern discrimination more difficult to recognize and combat and, when combined with the gains achieved by women and minorities, may lead majority-group members today to reject the notion that employment discrimination continues to be a problem.

In a related vein, modern discrimination differs from its older instantiations by oftentimes being less intentional and being rooted in biases that exist outside of conscious awareness. Many people, including employers, consciously espouse egalitarian ideals and are genuinely unaware of practices that are culturally insensitive and that serve to perpetuate the status quo. Many social biases begin to form at an early age (e.g., through exposure to stereotypic images in the media) and are reinforced to the point that they seem like truisms. These socially ingrained perceptions are widely shared, often even by targets of discrimination. Consider, for example, gender stereotypes about male agency and female communality. Gender role socialization processes continue to align men with public spheres of work and economically rewarded accomplishments and women with private spheres of home and family, and these processes shape not only the work-related options that individuals believe are available to them but also employers' and their agents' beliefs about the appropriate roles of women and men. Under some conditions, the resulting employment disparities are the result of forces that are outside employers'

control, and in other cases, they are the result of employers' stereotypes and prejudicial opinions and actions. Forensic psychologists help jurists and triers of fact find the truth between these poles.

Another important finding highlighted in this chapter is that modern discrimination affects far more demographic groups than previously recognized. Discrimination on the bases of sex and race continues to occur, and therefore continues to be widely researched, but several other demographic groups are now identified as being particularly at risk for discrimination. Research has consistently demonstrated that age, weight, sexual orientation, religion, national origin, and disability (real or perceived) are all factors for which discrimination is likely. These forms of discrimination also may have unique predictors. For these demographic factors, as with race, the evidence tends to point more clearly to prejudicial attitudes as a motivator for discrimination, particularly for historically disdained or mistrusted groups, such as LGBTs, non-Christians, and overweight people. The legal landscape for some classifications is not yet settled; therefore, forensic psychologists have the opportunity to conduct research that may inform the shape that future laws may take as well as provide consultation to employers to develop best practices for minimizing inequitable disparities and ending discrimination.

Although discrimination persists, there is reason for optimism. Discrimination in the workplace is not inevitable, and organizations can take steps to ensure that all prospective and current employees are treated fairly. In this chapter, we reviewed strategies for organizational responses to create sustainable and impactful change. Of these, strategies that affect the underlying structures that create disparity, and those that involve keeping a check on individual bias, appear to be the most promising. The use of well-crafted policies for addressing mistreatment, explicit and nonbiased criteria in making decisions, and training in how to identify and reduce bias and prejudices are all examples of such approaches. There is still much work to be done in this area, though. Because of this, we urge forensic psychologists to continue research that informs legal decision making as well as research into effective organizational interventions that assure true equity for all. Indeed, we hope that this chapter, along with the others in this volume, highlights the importance of merging theory and empirical findings with best practices in organizations. Only when science and practice work collaboratively do we have a chance for success in understanding and finding solutions for social problems like employment discrimination.

References

Age Discrimination in Employment Act of 1967, Pub. L. No. 90-202 (1967).

Allport, G. W. (1954). *The nature of prejudice*. Reading, MA: Addison-Wesley.

Americans With Disabilities Act of 1990, Pub. L. No. 110-336 (1990).

Andersson, L. M., & Pearson, C. M. (1999). Tit for tat? The spiraling effect of incivility in the workplace. *Academy of Management Review, 24*, 452–471.

Apfelbaum, E. P., Norton, M. I., & Sommers, S. R. (2012). Racial color blindness emergence, practice, and implications. *Current Directions in Psychological Science, 21*, 205–209. doi:10.1177/0963721411434980

Asch, S. E. (1946). Forming impressions of personality. *The Journal of Abnormal and Social Psychology, 41*, 258–290. doi:10.1037/h0055756

Ashburn-Nardo, L., & Johnson, N. J. (2008). Implicit outgroup favoritism and intergroup judgment: The moderating role of stereotypic context. *Social Justice Research, 21*, 490–508. doi:10.1007/s11211-008-0078-8

Ashburn-Nardo, L., Knowles, M. L., & Monteith, M. J. (2003). Black Americans' implicit racial associations and their implications for intergroup judgment. *Social Cognition, 21*, 61–87. doi:10.1521/soco.21.1.61.21192

Ashburn-Nardo, L., Morris, K. A., & Goodwin, S. A. (2008). The confronting prejudiced responses (CPR) model: Applying CPR in organizations. *Academy of Management Learning and Education, 7*, 332–342. doi:10.5465/AMR.2007.24351879

Badgett, M. V. L., Lau, H., Sears, B., & Ho, D. (2007). Bias in the workplace: Consistent evidence of sexual orientation and gender identity discrimination 1998–2008. *Chicago-Kent Law Review, 84*, 559–596.

Becker, G. S. (1957). *The economics of discrimination*. Chicago, IL: University of Chicago Press.

Berdahl, J. L. (2007a). Harassment based on sex: Protecting social status in the context of gender hierarchy. *Academy of Management Review, 32*, 641–658. doi:10.5465/AMR.2007.24351879

Berdahl, J. L. (2007b). Sexual harassment of uppity women. *Journal of Applied Psychology, 92*, 425–437. doi:10.1037/0021-9010.92.2.425

Bertrand, M., & Mullainathan, S. (2004). Are Emily and Greg more employable than Lakisha and Jamal? A field experiment on labor market discrimination. *American Economic Review, 94*, 991–1013. doi:10.1257%2F0002828042002561

Bielby, W. T., & Bielby, D. D. (1989). Family ties: Balancing commitments to work and family in dual earner households. *American Sociological Review, 54*, 776–789. doi:10.2307/2117753

Blair, K. S. (2010). Better disabled than devout? Why Title VII has failed to provide adequate accommodations against workplace religious discrimination. *Arkansas Law Review, 63*, 515–557.

Bond, J. T., Thompson, C., Galinsky, E., & Prottas, D. (2002). *Highlights of the National Study of the Changing Workforce*. New York, NY: Families and Work Institute.

Bowles, H. R., Babcock, L., & Lai, L. (2007). Social incentives for gender differences in the propensity to initiate negotiations: Sometimes it does hurt to ask. *Organizational Behavior and Human Decision Processes, 103*, 84–103. doi:10.1016/j.obhdp.2006.09.001

Burlington Industries, Inc. v. Ellerth, 524 U.S. 742 (1998).

Carr, D., & Friedman, M. A. (2005). Is obesity stigmatizing? Body weight, perceived discrimination, and psychological well-being in the United States. *Journal of Health and Social Behavior, 46*, 244–259. doi:10.1177/002214650504600303

Catalyst Institute. (1996). *Women in corporate leadership: Progress and prospects*. New York, NY: Author.

Cheryan, S., Plaut, V. C., Davies, P. G., & Steele, C. M. (2009). Ambient belonging: How stereotypical cues impact gender participation in computer science. *Journal of Personality and Social Psychology, 97*, 1045–1060. doi:10.1037/a0016239

Civil Rights Act of 1964, Pub. L. No. 88-352 (1964).

Civil Rights Act of 1991, Pub. L. No. 102-166 (1991).

Cortina, L. M. (2008). Unseen injustice: Incivility as modern discrimination in organizations. *Academy of Management Review, 33*, 55–75. doi:10.5465/AMR.2008.27745097

Czopp, A. M., & Ashburn-Nardo, L. (2012). Interpersonal confrontations of prejudice. In D. W. Russell & C. A. Russell (Eds.), *The psychology of prejudice: Interdisciplinary perspectives on contemporary issues* (pp. 175–201). Hauppauge, NY: Nova Science.

Davison, H. K., & Burke, M. J. (2000). Sex discrimination in simulated employment contexts: A meta-analytic investigation. *Journal of Vocational Behavior, 56,* 225–248. doi:10.1006/jvbe.1999.1711

De Coster, S., Estes, S. B., & Mueller, C. W. (1999). Routine activities and sexual harassment in the workplace. *Work and Occupations, 26,* 21–49. doi:10.1177/0730888499026001003

Deitch, E. A., Barsky, A., Butz, R. M., Chan, S., Brief, A. P., & Bradley, J. C. (2003). Subtle yet significant: The existence and impact of everyday racial discrimination in the workplace. *Human Relations, 56,* 1299–1324. doi:10.1177/00187267035611002

Dovidio, J. F., & Gaertner, S. L. (2000). Aversive racism and selection decisions: 1989–1999. *Psychological Science, 11,* 315–319. doi:10.1111/1467-9280.00262

Dovidio, J. F., Kawakami, K., & Beach, K. R. (2001). Implicit and explicit attitudes: Examination of the relationship between measures of inter-group bias. In R. Brown, & S. L. Gaertner (Eds.), Blackwell handbook of social psychology: Intergroup processes (pp. 175–197). Malden, MA: Blackwell.

Drobnič, S., Blossfeld, H. P., & Rohwer, G. (1999). Dynamics of women's employment patterns over the family life course: A comparison of the United States and Germany. *Journal of Marriage and the Family, 61,* 133–146. doi:10.2307/353889

Eagly, A. H. (1987). *Sex differences in social behavior: A social-role interpretation.* Hillsdale, NJ: Erlbaum.

Eagly, A. H., & Karau, S. J. (2002). Role congruity theory of prejudice toward female leaders. *Psychological Review, 109,* 573–598. doi:10.1037/0033-295X.109.3.573

Ellis, C., & Sonnenfeld, J. A. (1994). Diverse approaches to managing diversity. *Human Resource Management, 33,* 79–109.

Ely, R. J., & Meyerson, D. E. (2000). Theories of gender in organizations: A new approach to organizational analysis and change. *Research in Organizational Behavior, 22,* 103–151. doi:10.1016/S0191-3085(00)22004-2

Equal Employment Opportunity Commission. (2013). *Enforcement and litigation statistics.* Retrieved from http://www.eeoc.gov/eeoc/statistics/enforcement/index.cfm

Equal Pay Act of 1963, Pub. L. No. 88-38 (1963).

Faragher v. City of Boca Raton, 524 U.S. 775 (1998).

Fazio, R. H., & Towles-Schwen, T. (1999). The MODE model of attitude–behavior processes. In S. Chaiken & Y. Trope (Eds.), *Dual-process theories in social psychology* (pp. 97–116). New York, NY: Guilford Press.

Fiske, S. T., Cuddy, A. C., Glick, P., & Xu, J. (2002). A model of (often mixed) stereotype content: Competence and warmth respectively follow from perceived status and competition. *Journal of Personality and Social Psychology, 82,* 878–902. doi:10.1037/0022-3514.82.6.878

Fitzgerald, L. F., Drasgow, F., Hulin, C. L., Gelfand, M. J., & Magley, V. J. (1997). Antecedents and consequences of sexual harassment in organizations: A test of an integrated model. *Journal of Applied Psychology, 82,* 578–589. doi:10.1037/0021-9010.82.4.578

Flegal, K. M., Carroll, M. D., Ogden, C. L., & Curtin, L. R. (2010). Prevalence and trends in obesity among U.S. adults, 1999–2008. *JAMA, 303,* 235–241. doi:10.1001/jama.2009.2014

Frank v. United Airlines, 216 F. 3d. 845 (2000).

Friedman, J. W., & Strickler, G. M. (2001). *The law of employment discrimination: Cases and materials* (5th ed.). New York, NY: Foundation Press.

Gaertner, S. L., & Dovidio, J. F. (1986). The aversive form of racism. In J. F. Dovidio & S. L. Gaertner (Eds.), *Prejudice, discrimination, and racism* (pp. 61–89). Orlando, FL: Academic Press.

Galinisky, E., Salmon, K., Bond, J. T., Kropf, M. B., Moore, M., & Harrington, B. (2003). *Leaders in a global economy: A study of executive women and men.* Retrieved from http://www.catalyst.org/knowledge/leaders-global-economy-study-executive-women-and-men

General Dynamics v. Cline, 540 U.S. 581 (2004).

Glick, P., & Fiske, S. T. (1997). Hostile and benevolent sexism: Measuring ambivalent sexist attitudes toward women. *Psychology of Women Quarterly, 21,* 119–135. doi:10.1111/j.1471-6402.1997.tb00104.x

Glomb, T. M., Richman, W. L., Hulin, C. L., Drasgow, F., Schneider, K. T., & Fitzgerald, L. F. (1997). Ambient sexual harassment: An integrated model of antecedents and consequences. *Organizational Behavior and Human Decision Processes, 71,* 309–328. doi:10.1006/obhd.1997.2728

Goldberg, P. (1968). Are women prejudiced against women? *Trans-Action, 5,* 28–30.

Green, T. (2005). Work culture and discrimination. *California Law Review, 93,* 623–666.

Griggs v. Duke Power, 401 U.S. 424 (1971).

Gruber, J., & Morgan, P. (Eds.). (2005). *In the company of men: Male dominance and sexual harassment.* Boston, MA: Northeastern University Press.

Gutek, B. A. (1993). Changing the status of women in management. *Applied Psychology: An International Review, 42,* 301–311. doi:10.1111/j.1464-0597.1993.tb00746.x

Gutman, A. (2005). Adverse impact: Judicial, regulatory, and statutory authority. In F. J. Landy (Ed.), *Employment discrimination: Behavioral, quantitative, and legal perspectives* (pp. 20–46). San Francisco, CA: Jossey-Bass.

Hall, E. V., & Livingston, R. W. (2012). The hubris penalty: Biased responses to "celebration" displays of black football players. *Journal of Experimental Social Psychology*, 48, 899–904. doi:doi.org/10.1016/j.jesp.2012.02.004.

Harris v. Forklift Systems, Inc., 510 U.S. 17 (1993).

Harter, J. K., Schmidt, F. L., & Hayes, T. L. (2002). Business-unit-level relationship between employee satisfaction, employee engagement, and business outcomes: A meta-analysis. *Journal of Applied Psychology*, 87, 268–279. doi:10.1037/0021-9010.87.2.268

Hazen v. Biggins, 507 U.S. 604 (1993).

Heilman, M. E., & Haynes, M. C. (2008). Subjectivity in the appraisal process: A facilitator of gender bias in work settings. In E. Borgida & S. T. Fiske (Eds.), *Beyond common sense: Psychological science in the courtroom* (pp. 127–155). Malden, MA: Blackwell.

Herek, G. M. (2000). The psychology of sexual prejudice. *Current Directions in Psychological Science*, 9, 19–22. doi:10.1111/1467-8721.00051

Hill, C., Corbett, C., & St. Rose, A. (2010). *Why so few? Women in science, technology, engineering, and mathematics.* Washington, DC: AAUW. Retrieved from http://www.aauw.org/learn/research/upload/whysofew.pdf

Hyde, J. S. (2005). The gender similarities hypothesis. *American Psychologist*, 60, 581–592. doi:10.1037/0003-066X.60.6.581

Ilies, R., Hauseman, N., Schwochau, S., & Stibal, J. (2003). Reported incidence rates of work-related sexual harassment in the United States: Using meta-analysis to explain reported rate disparities. *Personnel Psychology*, 56, 607–631. doi:10.1111/j.1744-6570.2003.tb00752.x

Jost, J. T. (2001). Outgroup favoritism and the theory of system justification: A paradigm for investigating the effects of socioeconomic success on stereotype content. In G. Moskowitz (Ed.), *Cognitive social psychology: The Princeton Symposium on the Legacy and Future of Social Cognition* (pp. 89–102). Hillsdale, NJ: Erlbaum.

Kaiser, C. R., Drury, B. J., Spalding, K. E., Cheryan, S., & O'Brien, L. T. (2009). The ironic consequences of Obama's election: Decreased support for social justice. *Journal of Experimental Social Psychology*, 45, 556–559. doi:10.1016/j.jesp.2009.01.006

Kaiser, C. R., Major, B., Jurcevic, I., Dover, T. L., Brady, L. M., & Shapiro, J. R. (2013). Presumed fair: Ironic effects of organizational diversity structures. *Journal of Personality and Social Psychology*, 104, 504–519. doi:10.1037/a0030838.

Kalev, A., Dobbin, F., & Kelly, E. (2006). Best practices or best guesses? Assessing the efficacy of corporate affirmative action and diversity policies. *American Sociological Review*, 71, 589–617. doi:10.1177/000312240607100404

Kihnley, J. (2000). Unraveling the ivory fabric: Institutional obstacles to the handling of sexual harassment complaints. *Law & Social Inquiry*, 25, 69–90. doi:10.1111/j.1747-4469.2000.tb00151.x

Knight, J. L., Hebl, M. R., Foster, J. B., & Mannix, L. M. (2003). Out of role? Out of luck: The influence of race and leadership status on performance appraisals. *Journal of Leadership & Organizational Studies*, 9, 85–93. doi:10.1177/107179190300900308

Konrad, A. M. (2003). Family demands and job attribute preferences: A 4-year longitudinal study of women and men. *Sex Roles*, 49, 35–46. doi:10.1023/A:1023957502570

Krieger, L. H. (2007). The watched variable improves: On eliminating sex discrimination in employment. In F. J. Crosby, M. S. Stockdale, & S. A. Ropp (Eds.), *Sex discrimination in the workplace* (pp. 295–329). Malden, MA: Blackwell.

Landy, F. J. (2005). Phases of employment litigation. In F. J. Landy (Ed.), *Employment discrimination litigation: Behavioral, quantitative, and legal perspectives* (pp. 3–19). San Francisco, CA: Jossey-Bass.

Ledbetter v. Goodyear Tire & Rubber Co., 55 U.S. 618 (2007).

Lee, K., Gizzarone, M., & Ashton, M. C. (2003). Personality and the likelihood to sexually harass. *Sex Roles*, 49, 59–69. doi:10.1023/A:1023961603479

Leslie, L. M., King, E. B., Bradley, J. C., & Hebl, M. R. (2008). Triangulation across methodologies: All signs point to persistent stereotyping and discrimination in organizations. *Industrial and Organizational Psychology: Perspectives on Science and Practice*, 1, 399–404. doi:10.1111/j.1754-9434.2008.00073.x

Lilly Ledbetter Fair Pay Act of 2009, Pub. L. No. 111-2 (2009).

Lips, H. M. (2013). The gender pay gap: Challenging the rationalizations, perceived equity, discrimination, and the limits of human capital models. *Sex Roles*, 68, 169–185. doi:10.1007/s11199-012-0165-z

Livingston, R. W., & Pearce, N. A. (2009). The teddy-bear effect. Does having a baby face benefit Black chief executive officers? *Psychological Science*, 20, 1229–1236. doi:10.1111/j.1467-9280.2009.02431.x

Lyness, K. S., & Heilman, M. E. (2006). When fit is fundamental: Performance evaluations and promotions of upper-level female and male managers. *Journal of Applied Psychology*, 91, 777–785. doi:10.1037/0021-9010.91.4.777

MacKinnon, C. A. (1979). *Sexual harassment of working women: A case of sex discrimination.* New Haven, CT: Yale University Press.

McDonnell Douglas Corp. v. Green, 414 U.S. 811 (1973).

Meritor Savings Bank v. Vinson, 477 U.S. 57 (1986).

Miller, A. E. J., MacDougall, J. D., Tarnopolsky, M. A., & Sale, D. G. (1993). Gender differences in strength and muscle fiber characteristics. *European Journal of Applied Physiology and Occupational Physiology*, *66*, 254–262. doi:10.1007/BF00235103

Morgan, J. F. (2004). How should business respond to a more religious workplace? *SAM Advanced Management Journal*, *69*(4), 11–19.

Moss-Racusin, C. A., Dovidio, J. F., Brescoll, V. L., Graham, M. J., & Handelsman, J. (2012). Science faculty's subtle gender biases favor male students. *Proceedings of the National Academy of Sciences, USA*, *109*, 16474–16479. doi:10.1073/pnas.1211286109

Movius, H. (2008). The effectiveness of negotiation training. *Negotiation Journal*, *24*, 509–531. doi:10.1111/j.1571-9979.2008.00201.x

Nelson, T. D. (2008). The young science of prejudice against older adults: Established answers and open questions about ageism. In E. Borgida & S. T. Fiske (Eds.), *Beyond common sense: Psychological science in the courtroom* (pp. 45–61). Malden, MA: Blackwell.

O'Connor v. Consolidated Coin Caterers Corp., 517 U.S. 308 (1996).

Oncale v. Sundowner Offshore Services, 523 U.S. 75 (1998).

Pavalko, E. K., Mossakowski, K. N., & Hamilton, V. J. (2003). Does perceived discrimination affect health? Longitudinal relationships between work discrimination and women's physical and emotional health. *Journal of Health and Social Behavior*, *44*, 18–33. doi:10.2307/1519813

Pettigrew, T. F., & Tropp, L. R. (2006). A meta-analytic test of intergroup contact theory. *Journal of Personality and Social Psychology*, *90*, 751–783. doi:10.1037/0022-3514.90.5.751

Pichler, S., Varma, A., & Bruce, T. (2010). Heterosexism in employment decisions: The role of job misfit. *Journal of Applied Social Psychology*, *40*, 2527–2555. doi:10.1111/j.1559-1816.2010.00669.x

Plaut, V. C., Thomas, K. M., & Goren, M. J. (2009). Is multiculturalism or color blindness better for minorities? *Psychological Science*, *20*, 444–446. doi:10.1111/j.1467-9280.2009.02318.x

Polachek, S. W. (1975). Differences in expected post-school investment as a determinant of market wage differentials. *International Economic Review*, *16*, 451–470. doi:10.2307/2525825

Presser, H. B., & Hermsen, J. M. (1996). Gender differences in the determinants of over-night work-related travel among employed Americans. *Work and Occupations*, *23*, 87–115. doi:10.1177/0730888496023001005

Pryor, J. B. (1987). Sexual harassment proclivities in men. *Sex Roles*, *17*, 269–290. doi:10.1007/BF00288453

Pryor, J. B., Giedd, J. L., & Williams, K. B. (1995). A social psychological model for predicting sexual harassment. *Journal of Social Issues*, *51*, 69–84. doi:10.1111/j.1540-4560.1995.tb01309.x

Puhl, R. M., Andreyeva, T., & Brownell, K. D. (2008). Perceptions of weight discrimination: Prevalence and comparison to race and gender discrimination in America. *International Journal of Obesity*, *32*, 992–1000. doi:10.1038/ijo.2008.22

Ragins, B. R. (1997). Diversified mentoring relationships in organizations: A power perspective. *Academy of Management Review*, *22*, 482–521.

Raver, J. L., & Gelfand, M. J. (2005). Beyond the individual victim: Linking sexual harassment, team processes, and team performance. *Academy of Management Journal*, *48*, 387–400. doi:10.5465/AMJ.2005.17407904

Riach, P. A., & Rich, J. (2002). Field experiments of discrimination in the market place. *The Economic Journal*, *112*, F480–F518. doi:10.1111/1468-0297.00080

Roehling, M. V. (2002). Weight discrimination in the American workplace: Ethical issues and analysis. *Journal of Business Ethics*, *40*, 177–189. doi:10.1023/A:1020347305736

Rosette, A. S., Leonardelli, G. J., & Phillips, K. W. (2008). The White standard: Racial bias in leader categorization. *Journal of Applied Psychology*, *93*, 758–777. doi:10.1037/0021-9010.93.4.758

Rosette, A. S., & Livingston, R. W. (2012). Failure is not an option for Black women: Effects of organizational performance on leaders with single versus dual-subordinate identities. *Journal of Experimental Social Psychology*, *48*, 1162–1167. doi:10.1016/j.jesp.2012.05.002

Rudman, L. A., & Glick, P. (2001). Prescriptive gender stereotypes and backlash toward agentic women. *Journal of Social Issues*, *57*, 743–762. doi:10.1111/0022-4537.00239

Rudman, L. A., Moss-Racusin, C. A., Phelan, J. E., & Nauts, S. (2012). Status incongruity and backlash effects: Defending the gender hierarchy motivates prejudice against female leaders. *Journal of Experimental Social Psychology*, *48*, 165–179. doi:10.1016/j.jesp.2011.10.008

Schäfer, A., Tucci, I., & Gottschall, K. (2012). *Top down or bottom up? A cross-national study of vertical occupational sex segregation in 12 European countries.* Retrieved from http://hdl.handle.net/10419/52137

Schneider, K. T., Hitlan, R. T., & Radhakrishnan, P. (2000). An examination of the nature and correlates of ethnic harassment experiences in multiple contexts. *Journal of Applied Social Psychology, 85,* 3–12. doi:10.1037/0021-9010.85.1.3

Schneider, M. E., Major, B., Luhtanen, R., & Crocker, J. (1996). Social stigma and the potential costs of assumptive help. *Personality and Social Psychology Bulletin, 22,* 201–209. doi:10.1177/0146167296222009

Shauman, K. A. (2006). Occupational sex segregation and the earnings of occupations: What causes the link among college-educated workers? *Social Science Research, 35,* 577–619. doi:10.1016/j.ssresearch.2004.12.001.

Slaughter, A. (2012, July/August). Why women still can't have it all. *Atlantic Magazine.* Retrieved from http://www.theatlantic.com/magazine/archive/2012/07/why-women-still-cant-have-it-all/309020

Solomon, S., Greenberg, J., & Pyszczynski, T. (1991). *A terror management theory of social behavior: The psychological functions of self-esteem and world-views, 24,* 93–159. *Advances in Experimental Social Psychology.* doi:10.1016/S0065-2601(08)60328-7

Stauffer, J. M., & Buckley, M. R. (2005). The existence and nature of racial bias in supervisory ratings. *Journal of Applied Psychology, 90,* 586–591. doi:10.1037/0021-9010.90.3.586

Sterns, H. L., Doverspike, D., & Lax, G. (2005). The age discrimination in employment act. In F. Landy (Ed.), *Employment discrimination: Litigation: Behavioral, quantitative, and legal perspectives* (pp. 256–293). San Francisco, CA: Jossey-Bass.

Stockdale, M. S. (2005). The sexual harassment of men: Articulating the approach–rejection theory of sexual harassment. In J. Gruber & P. Morgan (Eds.), *In the company of men: Male dominance and sexual harassment* (pp. 117–142). Boston, MA: Northeastern University Press.

Stockdale, M. S., Logan, T. K., & Weston, R. (2009). Sexual harassment and posttraumatic stress disorder: Damages beyond prior abuse. *Law and Human Behavior, 33,* 405–418. doi:10.1007/s10979-008-9162-8

Stockdale, M. S., & Sagrestano, L. M. (2010). Strategies and resources for institutions and targets of sexual harassment in employment and education. In M. Paludi & F. L. Denmark (Eds.), *Victims of sexual assault and abuse: Resources and responses for individuals and families* (pp. 211–239). San Francisco, CA: Praeger.

Stockdale, M. S., Visio, M., & Batra, L. (1999). The sexual harassment of men: Evidence for a broader theory of sexual harassment and sex discrimination. *Psychology, Public Policy, and Law, 5,* 630–664. doi:10.1037/1076-8971.5.3.630

Stuhlmacher, A. F., & Walters, A. E. (1999). Gender differences in negotiation outcome: A meta-analysis. *Personnel Psychology, 52,* 653–677. doi:10.1111/j.1744-6570.1999.tb00175.x

Swim, J., Borgida, E., Maruyama, G., & Myers, D. G. (1989). Joan McKay versus John McKay: Do gender stereotypes bias evaluations? *Psychological Bulletin, 105,* 409–429. doi:10.1037/0033-2909.105.3.409

Texas Department of Community Affairs v. Joyce Ann Burdine, 450 U.S. 248 (1981).

Title IX of the Education Amendments of 1982, 20 U.S.C. § 1681 (1982).

Tropp, L. R., & Pettigrew, T. F. (2005). Relationships between intergroup contact and prejudice among minority and majority status groups. *Psychological Science, 16,* 951–957. doi:10.1111/j.1467-9280.2005.01643.x

U.S. Department of Labor Bureau of Labor Statistics. (2013). *Usual weekly earnings of wage and salary workers: Fourth quarter 2012.* Retrieved from http://www.bls.gov/schedule/archives/wkyeng_nr.htm

U.S. Merit Systems Protection Board. (1995). *Sexual harassment in the federal workplace: Trends, progress, and continuing challenges.* Washington, DC: U.S. Government Printing Office.

Vance v. Ball State University, 570 U.S. (2013).

Vickers v. Fairfield Medical Center, 453 F. 3d 757 (2006).

Wal-Mart Stores, Inc. v. Betty Dukes et al., 113 S. Ct. 2541 (2011).

Williams v. Saxbe, 413 F. Supp. 6544—Dist. Court, Dist. of Columbia (1976).

Willness, C. R., Steel, P., & Lee, K. (2007). A meta-analysis of the antecedents and consequences of workplace sexual harassment. *Personnel Psychology, 60,* 127–162. doi:10.1111/j.1744-6570.2007.00067.x

WISELI. (2005). *Response to Lawrence Summers' remarks on women in science.* Retrieved from http://wiseli.engr.wisc.edu/archives/summers.php#conference-info

Ziegert, J. C., & Hanges, P. J. (2005). Employment discrimination: The role of implicit attitudes, motivation, and a climate for racial bias. *Journal of Applied Psychology, 90,* 553–562. doi:10.1037/0021-9010.90.3.553

CHAPTER 16

CIVIL COMPETENCIES

Douglas Mossman and Helen M. Farrell

This chapter reviews the legal, empirical, and clinical literatures on civil competencies. We begin by describing the overarching rationales for civil competencies and the psychological theories that apply to all civil competencies. We then describe the research and practice implications for three specific competencies: to refuse or accept treatment, to make a will, and to manage personal affairs. We conclude by summarizing the principles that apply to evaluations of all types of civil competencies.

IMPORTANCE OF THE PROBLEM

Competence is a general legal term that points to a key feature of intelligent human functioning: the capacity to obtain and use information to make rational decisions about important aspects of one's life. References to insanity in the Hebrew Bible (see, for example, I Samuel 21:10–15) and in classical Greek and Latin sources (R. S. Smith & Trzaskoma, 2007) tell us that ancient societies knew that certain conditions rendered people mentally unsound. Modern legal rules concerning decisional incapacity have lineages dating back centuries (Blackstone, 1775; *Frith's case*, 1790).

Traditionally, the legal categorization of a person as *non compos mentis* (Latin for not having mastery of one's mind) assumed that someone who had a mental *disease* or cognitive *defect* suffered from global incapacity in most or all aspects of functioning (Stock, 1839). Until relatively recently, persons who were hospitalized because of a mental impairment lost many of their legal rights—including the right to vote, to drive an automobile, and to enter into binding legal arrangements—without any formal inquiry into their actual competence in specific areas (*Gillis v. Cameron*, 1963). Courts typically regarded persons with mental illnesses as incompetent for all legal purposes, including management of their financial and personal affairs (Meisel, 2005).

For the last few decades, however, civil commitment statutes have expressly preserved hospitalized persons' customary civil rights, including their rights to make personal decisions (e.g., Civil Rights of Patients, 1989). The recognition that individuals may be competent for some purposes despite focal areas of decisional incompetence has led courts to make competence adjudications concerning specific incapacities—such as incompetence to make treatment decisions or to stand trial (see Chapter 5, this volume for more on criminal competencies)—rather than global, plenary adjudications about all legal capacities (Meisel, 2005). Thus, for example, courts recognize that someone who has been adjudicated incompetent to manage his or her financial affairs is not necessarily incompetent to make personal decisions to obtain a divorce (Mossman & Shoemaker, 2010), and a court's order stating that an individual is incompetent for several discrete purposes preserves the person's rights in other areas of decision making (Berg, Appelbaum, Lidz, & Parker, 2001).

Questions about an individual's competence arise in connection with many major life events, including getting married or divorced, making a will, consenting to or refusing treatment, participating in research, having sex, handling personal affairs, managing finances, buying or selling a house, and entering into a business contract. Decisions about an individual's competence related to any of these areas require distinct legal determinations by courts and, in many cases, specially focused mental health evaluations.

Experienced forensic clinicians therefore expect that requests for their opinions on an individual's competence will address the evaluated individual's mental capacity for a specific activity. Yet as a general matter, all forensic evaluations of specific competencies investigate how well the evaluee can (a) make choices based on an adequate understanding and appreciation of the nature and consequences of a specific task, and (b) identify and use relevant information logically and rationally. Understanding, appreciation, and reasoning, in turn, require diverse types and dimensions of intellectual functioning, including accurate perception and assimilation of sensory impressions, memory, data interpretation, language and other executive functions, grasp of reality, and affect regulation.

Social Values

Legal requirements of competence affirm several cherished social values related to human functioning, including the preservation of individual dignity and autonomy. As the following paragraphs explain, these values may create conflicts with a third social concern: the protection of vulnerable individuals.

Preservation of dignity. When someone refuses psychotropic drugs in a hospital, executes a will, files for divorce, or engages in any of the other decisional tasks mentioned earlier, the legal requirement of competence ensures and promotes respect for the dignity of the individuals involved. Usually, courts assume that adults are competent, but forensic clinicians may be consulted when the presumption of competence is challenged either by one of the parties to a legal proceeding or by the court itself.

Features of legal proceedings (including opportunities for adversarial challenges) and the ethical obligations of legal and mental health professionals serve as vehicles for preserving the dignity of the

involved individuals and for expressing the social values underlying those proceedings. Ethical guidelines for forensic psychologists and psychiatrists (American Academy of Psychiatry and the Law, 2005; American Psychological Association, 2013) direct evaluators to reach opinions only after they have considered and balanced the factors that support both positions in an adversarial proceeding. Attorneys are accountable to the standards that are set forth in the American Bar Association's (2013) *Model Rules of Professional Conduct*. The official Comment 6 to Rule 1.14 advises attorneys:

> In determining the extent of the client's diminished capacity . . . consider and balance such factors as: the client's ability to articulate reasoning leading to a decision, variability of state of mind and ability to appreciate a decision with the known long-term commitments and values of the client.

The presumption of competence is overcome only when a court concludes that the person is or (for retrospective assessments) was not mentally or physically capable at the time of the legally relevant action in question. In reaching conclusions, courts examine factors in light of their jurisdiction's applicable standard of proof. Proof beyond a reasonable doubt—the strictest standard—is required for findings of guilt in adult criminal and juvenile delinquency proceedings. This level of proof falls just short of absolute certainty and is usually not the standard for civil cases. Instead, the legal standard typically applied in civil matters requires only that a preponderance of the evidence favor one side or the other; that is, the fact-finder needs to determine only whether the evidence for one side "is of greater weight or more convincing than the evidence which is offered in opposition to it; that is, evidence which as a whole shows that the fact sought to be proved is more probable than not" (*Braud v. Kinchen*, 1975, p. 659). In resolving matters involving civil competencies, however, courts often must find clear and convincing proof—an intermediate standard— regarding the key propositions in the case. Such proof requires that the fact-finder be in "reasonable certainty of the truth of the ultimate fact in controversy" (*Lepre v. Caputo*, 1974, p. 124). "Clear and convincing proof will be shown where the truth of the facts asserted is highly probable" (*In re Estate of Lobe*, 1984, p. 414).

Autonomy. Competence is necessary for the exercise of autonomy. As the word's Ancient Greek origins (αύτο, "self," and νόμος, "law") suggest, exercising autonomy involves being a law to oneself; that is, autonomous persons are self-governing agents (Buss, 2008). Autonomy is a key concept in many areas of philosophy, where the term directs our attention toward an agent's commitments to acting and toward whether the agent can rightfully regard his or her own judgments and decisions about how he or she should act as authoritative. Beginning with Kant (1785/2002), philosophers have often used autonomy to point to the ability to impose objective moral law on oneself. Kant was concerned with how and under what circumstances a free, rational individual could exercise autonomy by choosing actions solely out of respect for moral duty; that is, deciding to act simply for the sake of doing what is morally correct, without regard to other incentives. On Kant's view, the capacity to comply with moral law is an essential aspect of human dignity and a key feature of autonomous action.

In the contexts that are considered in this chapter, however, autonomy has a more prosaic meaning: The term refers to a rational individual's capacity to make informed, unforced decisions based on those beliefs and desires that the individual deems relevant. Understood this way, autonomy is a predicate for the process of shared decision making that is embodied in current notions of informed consent for medical treatment, which, over the last half-century, have become a core precept of medical ethics. Rather than looking toward the ideal or best outcome as determined by a physician, Americans now accept as an established principle that respecting patients' competent choices is a paramount desideratum (i.e., something that is needed or wanted) of appropriate medical care.

Protection. Among the longstanding historical justifications for requiring competence is the social duty to identify and protect individuals whose mental maladies prevent them from looking out for themselves (*Penington v. Thompson*, 1880). One of the earliest mentions of the government's protective duty is the statute *De Prerogativa Regis* (1324), which codified already-established law on the King's fiduciary duty to act on behalf of the property interests of "lunatics."

Legal requirements that social commitments, sales agreements, and contracts be enforceable only against individuals who possess a threshold level of mental capacity reflect concern about protecting the integrity of important social processes from impaired participants, as well as concern about protecting impaired persons from neglect or exploitation. The state exercises its protective duties through two avenues that are traditionally labeled the *parens patriae* and police power authority. *Parens patriae* (Latin for parent of the nation) refers to the state's obligation to intervene on behalf of individuals who need protection (Custer, 1978). Originally applied to mentally incapacitated adults, the *parens patriae* doctrine was gradually applied to children in the 17th and 18th centuries. It has evolved from a legal principle granting the sovereign absolute protective rights to a set of rules that are associated with the rights and obligations of the state and courts toward children and incapacitated adults. The doctrine of *parens patriae* was an accepted feature of early American law and received the U.S. Supreme Court's official approval in an 1890 case: "This prerogative of parens patriae . . . is a most beneficent function, and often necessary to be exercised in the interests of humanity, and for the prevention of injury to those who cannot protect themselves" (*Mormon Church v. United States*, 1890, p. 57). The legitimate use of *police powers* allows the state to exercise its responsibility to protect the populace from the harmful conduct of the individual. Thus, early laws governing the disposition of individuals who were deemed non compos mentis included provisions for their confinement, "as it was dangerous to leave them at large, from the furious nature of their malady" (Stock, 1839, p. 75).

As noted earlier, legal and mental health professionals now recognize many species of competencies. Often, context is a significant variable in determining which of these sometimes-competing values achieves primacy. Legal opinions often reflect compromises among the individual-focused concerns about autonomy, privacy, beneficence, and paternalism, along with socially focused concerns about economic efficiency, tolerance of differences, and protection from harm. In this chapter, we consider three representative civil competencies concerning which the law recognizes the need for a minimal standard of functioning:

- competence to refuse/accept treatment,
- competence to make a will (often called "testamentary capacity"), and
- competence to manage one's personal affairs and estate.

In each of these areas, an assurance of legal competence vindicates two ideals that play key roles in American jurisprudence and social ethics. On one hand, Americans prize individuals' exercise of their freedom and loathe interference with personal decisions—even stupid ones. Yet, our respect for and legal protection of individual freedom are tempered by recognition of a societal obligation to protect persons whose compromised decision-making capacity leaves them vulnerable. True exercise of autonomy requires rationality, and assuring that parties are competent when making major decisions recognizes that genuine human freedom belongs only to persons who can meaningfully perceive consequences and pursue reasonable goals.

RELEVANT PSYCHOLOGICAL THEORY AND PRINCIPLES

Although modern legal rulings now address specific competencies, Appelbaum and Grisso (1988) and Saks (2002) developed general frameworks that identify key aspects of competence in general. These frameworks have proven useful in helping forensic clinicians to address the legal criteria for a broad variety of competencies, including those required to stand trial (Poythress, Monahan, Bonnie, Otto, & Hoge, 2002), to consent to treatment (Grisso & Appelbaum, 1998a), to maintain a divorce action (Mossman & Shoemaker, 2010), to consent to research (Appelbaum & Roth, 1982;

Kim, Caine, Currier, Leibovici, & Ryan, 2001), and to appoint a proxy decision maker (Kim et al., 2011).

Grisso and Appelbaum (1998a; see also Appelbaum, 2007; Berg, Appelbaum, & Grisso, 1996) describe four themes that recur in most jurisdictions' rules about an individual's competence to consent to treatment and that apply to other competencies as well (see Exhibit 16.1). Their four-item rubric addresses individuals' abilities

- to express or communicate their choices,
- to understand information that is relevant to their choices,
- to appreciate their situations and the consequences of their choices, and
- to think rationally about their choices.

These aspects of competence are especially relevant in contexts such as having to defend oneself against a criminal charge, making a decision about medical treatment, or participating in medical research—activities that require individuals to assimilate information relevant to some new situation in which they find themselves, consider that information in light of their personal circumstances and preferences, and express decisions about courses of future action that others find reasonable.

In her writing, Saks (1999) focused on individuals (often, persons who suffer from psychoses) who express choices unambiguously but who fail to take key information into account because they do not acknowledge that they are ill or because they hold "patently false beliefs" (p. 71). On one hand, Saks argued that respect for persons' autonomy requires that a competence standard should not require persons simply to "believe what most people would believe . . . . [W]e should try . . . to characterize the standard in a way that does not refer essentially to majorities" (p. 71). But when people base their decisions on "beliefs that obviously distort reality[, or] are based on little evidence[, or] are indisputably false[, or] are patently delusional" (p. 71), they show clear indications of incompetence in decision making.

A second quality that is relevant to competence in general is the optimal characteristics of a

Exhibit 16.1
Four Dimensions to Evaluating the Quality of a Patient's Decision

■ Choice

Ability to communicate a choice and to express a consistent preference

■ Understanding

Ability to grasp relevant information; that is, the major features of information disclosed:
Proposed treatment, treatment alternatives, risks, benefits
Consequences of no treatment

■ Appreciation

Appreciating the illness and its consequences
Recognition that one is ill and how the information applies to one's own situation

■ Reasoning

Rational manipulation of information
Explains decision making and reasoning
Applies information in light of rational beliefs and desires

Note. Data from Grisso and Appelbaum, 1998a.

competence assessment. Fifty years ago, clinical judgments about competence consisted of little more than an unreflective response to an evaluee's legal psychopathology. Now, however, evaluators increasingly recognize that a systematic approach to gathering and considering data is a requirement of any conscientious evaluation.

An important reason for this recognition is the accumulation of findings over the last decade showing the clear superiority of structured approaches to a broad array of assessment activities. One reason for this is that, when questions arise concerning a patient's capacity to make treatment decisions, many physicians do not know what judgment standard to apply, and they may fail to mention relevant criteria or to apply those criteria specifically to treatment decisions (McKinnon, Cournos, & Stanley, 1989). Physicians may also reach conclusions about capacity based solely on a diagnosis—for example, assuming that dementia categorically implies incompetence (Markson, Kern, Annas, & Glantz,

1994). Not surprisingly, then, unstructured capacities assessments have very limited reliability, if any (Marson, Hawkins, McIntruff, Bartolucci, & Harrell, 1997). Evidence suggests, however, that mechanisms that simply direct evaluators' attention to applicable criteria (e.g., by providing a list of legal standards to guide judgments) improve capacity evaluations (Marson, Earnst, Jamil, Barolucci, & Harrell, 2000; Marson et al., 1997), and the use of systematic assessment approaches (e.g., providing a set of assessment questions) generates even further improvement (Etchells et al., 1999).

RESEARCH REVIEW AND PRACTICE AND POLICY ISSUES

In the following pages, we review the relevant research and discuss the practice and policy issues for three types of civil competence: competence to accept or refuse treatment, testamentary capacity, and competence to manage own's personal affairs.

Competence to Refuse or Accept Treatment

Competent individuals have a right to refuse unwanted treatment; this right endures even after they have undergone civil commitment for psychiatric care. Broadly speaking, this right stems from general informed consent doctrine and from state and federal constitutional rights (Appelbaum, 1988).

In involuntary psychiatric treatment contexts, various authors have offered four potential constitutional bases for a right to refuse treatment:

■ If one views psychotropic medications as mind-altering substances that change an individual's thinking and beliefs, then forcing medications on an individual implicates that person's First Amendment guarantee of free speech (Winick, 1997).

■ Because psychiatric hospitalization involves confinement that is similar to criminal incarceration, some authors suggest that the potential dangers of psychotropic medication make its forced administration a violation of Eighth Amendment protections against cruel and unusual punishment (McCarron, 1990; Symonds, 1980).

- The Fourteenth Amendment guarantees of due process and equal protection are violated if non-psychiatric patients have a right to refuse medication but psychiatric patients do not.
- Forcing medication is intrusive and violates a general right to privacy that is derivable from the First, Fourth, Fifth, and Ninth Amendments, in a manner similar to Supreme Court holdings in matters involving procreation and the family (Ciccone, Tokoli, Clements, & Gift, 1990).

Although the U.S. Supreme Court has never issued a decision regarding civilly committed patients' right to refuse treatment, state court decisions in the 1980s established that involuntary hospitalization does not necessarily clear the way for forced treatment with antipsychotic drugs. In various states, courts have ruled that persons who are hospitalized for psychiatric care can be forcibly medicated only (a) if they are adjudicated incompetent to make treatment decisions and would have wanted medications had they been competent (*Rogers v. Commissioner of Mental Health*, 1982), (b) if forced medication passes an independent psychiatric review of treatment appropriateness (e.g., *Rennie v. Klein*, 1983), or (c) if a judicial finding of the patient's incompetence is coupled with the determination that forced administration of psychotropic drugs will serve the patient's best interests (e.g., *Rivers v. Katz*, 1986).

A voluntarily hospitalized psychiatric patient must, like medical and surgical patients, give informed consent for treatment, except in emergency circumstances or if the patient has been declared legally incompetent. From a legal perspective, informed consent encompasses three rather distinct elements:

- receipt of relevant knowledge about proposed treatment and its alternatives;
- adequate capacity to assimilate, reason about, and make decisions using that information; and
- absence of coercion such that the consent is voluntary.

According to Appelbaum (2007) "legal standards for decision-making capacity for consent to treatment vary somewhat across jurisdictions," but, as is the case with many other competencies, the standards follow the four-item rubric discussed earlier, *viz.*, "the abilities to communicate a choice, to understand the relevant information, to appreciate the medical consequences of the situation, and to reason about treatment choices" (p. 1835).

Research.   Investigators have attempted to understand involuntary psychiatric patients' refusals to receive treatment by studying the circumstances surrounding medication refusals. An examination of 432 refusals that led to override requests in Oregon hospitals found that the refusals came mainly from seriously ill, unemployed, single persons who had previously undergone psychiatric hospitalization and who refused treatment because of denial of their mental illness or their delusional ideas about the medications. The majority of refusals were eventually overridden through Oregon's informal review proceedings (Godard, Bloom, Williams, & Faulkner, 1986). A small, 31-patient study that compared potential refusing to nonrefusing patients at a Los Angeles Veterans Affairs hospital found that refusers had more severe psychosis, higher mood elevation, and less positive attitudes toward treatment than nonrefusers did (Marder et al., 1984). A chart review of patients who were medicated under the New Jersey *Rennie* procedure found that these patients had more often needed extended emergent forcible medication; were more likely to have schizophrenia; and were significantly more likely to have histories of assault, threats, and property damage (Greenberg & Attia, 1993).

Individuals who are likely to be found incompetent to make decisions regarding their medical treatment are commonly found in the medical and surgical inpatient units of hospitals. Impaired decision making in hospitalized patients often goes undetected (Cohen, McCue, & Green, 1993; Etchells et al., 1997, 1999; Fitten & Waite, 1990), even when patients decline recommended treatment (Raymont et al., 2004). Any medical condition or treatment that adversely affects an individual's mental processing may be associated with incompetence, but because a range of severity is associated with most diagnoses, no medical condition in which consciousness is retained invariably leads to decisional incapacity (Cohen et al., 1993). Certain medical conditions (including unstable angina, diabetes mellitus, and HIV) are generally not associated with an incapacity for decision making in the absence of accompanying cognitive impairment; however, stroke and dementia do adversely affect an individual's decisional capacity (Appelbaum & Grisso, 1997; Moser et al., 2002; Palmer et al., 2005). Intensive care units and nursing homes include substantial proportions of incompetent patients (Goodwin, Smyer, & Lair, 1995; Pruchno, Smyer, Rose, & Hartman-Stein, 1995). Persons with Alzheimer's disease and other dementias have high rates of decisional incompetence; most patients with mild-to-moderate dementia may have significant impairment, and among patients with more severe dementia, incompetence is universal (Kim, Karlawish, & Caine, 2002).

Psychoses often impair an individual's competency. Schizophrenia has a stronger association with impaired capacity than does depression (Grisso & Appelbaum, 1995; Palmer, Dunn, Depp, Eyler, & Jeste, 2007; Vollmann, Bauer, Danker-Hoipfe, & Helmchen, 2003). The strongest predictors of incompetence for psychiatric patients are their lack of awareness of their illness and the need for treatment (Cairns et al., 2005).

Research has established some potentially helpful relationships between frequently used clinical assessment tools and an individual's capacity for making medical treatment decisions. Evaluees' scores on the Mini-Mental Status Examination (MMSE; Folstein, Folstein, & McHugh, 1975) correspond to clinicians' judgments about the evaluee's capacity. MMSE scores range from 0 to 30, with lower scores indicating decreasing cognitive function. Although no single cutoff score yields both high sensitivity and high specificity, scores less than 19 imply a strong likelihood of incompetence, and scores in the mid-20s or greater are highly suggestive of competence (Etchells et al., 1997).

Instruments that have been developed specifically to standardize assessment appear to achieve respectable levels of reliability and validity (Dunn, Nowrangi, Palmer, Jeste, & Saks, 2006; Sturman, 2005). The levels of interrater reliability that have been reported for the MacArthur Competence Assessment Tool for Treatment (Grisso & Appelbaum, 1998b) appear consistently higher than those that have been achieved through simple structuring of assessment practices (Cairns et al., 2005; Dunn et al., 2006; Raymont et al., 2004, 2007).

Practice and policy issues. Evaluations of treatment-refusing patients typically occur in hospitals. When initiating such evaluations, consulting examiners should apply the behavioral principles that are applicable to hospital-based mental health consultations in general. These include asking the treating clinicians about the circumstances of the refusal and the types of information they have provided to their patients. The primary treating clinicians' observations about their own interactions and impressions of the patient's reasons, patterns, or style of refusing may provide important clues about whether a refusal stems from psychopathology or from doctor–patient interaction problems that have arisen during the course of care. Consulting examiners should also review the patient's treatment records in order to develop a thorough grasp of the patient's condition as viewed by the treating clinicians. When the consulting examiner's own training and experience are insufficient to understand or learn about key features of the patient's illness, proposed treatment(s), treatment alternatives, and consequences of no treatment, the examiner should seek such information and/or reference materials from the treating clinicians or from colleagues with sufficient expertise to provide educational advice.

Treating clinicians typically do not request independent assessments of a patient's competence to refuse treatment unless the refusal may have serious consequences. Under these circumstances, consulting examiners who assess treatment-refusing patients take on a grave responsibility when they evaluate a patient's decisional capacity. Developing a clear understanding of the clinical context is a crucial step in preparing for the in-person examination of the patient. Information from family members and nursing staff may also be helpful.

During the initial portion of the examination, the consulting examiner should inform the patient of the nature and purpose of the proposed interview. Often, evaluees whose decisional capacity is questioned cannot provide informed consent for the examination, and their medical needs at the time of assessment override the examiner's customary obligation to obtain explicit consent for the assessment (Grisso & Appelbaum, 1998a). In some patients, fluctuations in mental state affect capacity, and where this clinical presentation is expected, consultants should try to conduct at least two evaluations at some interval apart.

Particularly in hospital settings, evaluations of medical decision-making competence often focus on the exercise of capacity in the context of the specific treatment(s) under consideration (Drane, 1985). Several authors (e.g., Appelbaum, 2007; Dastidar & Odden, 2011; Searight, 1992) have provided tables of sample questions that examiners can easily adapt and apply to specific treatment settings and evaluation circumstances.

Data collection also can be facilitated by the use of standardized instruments or structured interviews. As noted earlier, the MMSE is an easily administered instrument that helps to identify cognitively impaired patients at the high and low ends of the range of capacity. Although no cognitive screen's results directly translate into a judgment about an individual's capacity for a specific treatment decision, the use of such instruments may help examiners discover unrecognized areas of impairment (e.g., a still-conversational elderly person who cannot draw a clock or write a sentence) and may facilitate functional comparisons to large groups of individuals.

Over the past two decades, researchers' desires to better standardize, evaluate, and increase the reliability and validity of competence evaluations have led to the development of formal assessment instruments for treatment competence. The best known and most widely used of these instruments is the McArthur Competence Assessment Tool for Treatment (MacCAT–T; Grisso, Appelbaum, & Hill-Fotouhi, 1997), which is a structured interview

that, unlike many other assessment instruments, incorporates information that is specific to a given patient's decision-making situation (Dunn et al., 2006; Sturman, 2005). The MacCAT–T takes approximately 20 min to administer and score, assuming that the person who administers and scores the test has experience with the format and scoring criteria.

The MacCAT–T's quantitative scores concerning the four-item competence rubric discussed earlier provide numerical reference points that are particularly suited to research and making comparisons. In individual evaluation contexts, these numbers are to be integrated with other data when reaching judgments about an individual's competence. The MacCAT–T authors emphasized that their instrument does not give an overall competence rating and should be used to make a judgment about an individual's capacity in conjunction with one's clinical assessment (Grisso et al., 1997).

The MacCAT–T has been evaluated in several diagnostic groups, including persons with mood and thought disorders and persons with heart disease (Carpenter et al., 2000; Grisso & Appelbaum, 1995; Grisso et al., 1997; Palmer, Dunn, Appelbaum, & Jeste, 2004; Vollmann et al., 2003). This extensive research base for the MacCAT–T may have particular value when an assessment is challenging and is likely to be resolved in court. In a reliability study using transcribed interviews based on the MacCAT–T, Raymont et al. (2007) "found a strong level of agreement between individual raters' assessments in our subsample (mean kappa = 0.76)" (p. 114).

Other instruments that can be used to assess an individual's treatment decisional competency include the Hopkins Competency Assessment Test (HCAT; Janofsky, McCarthy, & Folstein, 1992), the Capacity to Consent to Treatment Instrument (CCTI; Marson, Ingram, Cody, & Harrell, 1995), and the Hopemont Capacity Assessment Interview (HCAI; Edelstein, 1999). Moye, Karel, Azar, and Guerra (2004) and Dastidar and Odden (2011) provided comparisons of key features of the MacCAT–T, HCAI, and CCTI that can prove helpful in selecting instruments. Two recent studies supported the usefulness of the CCTI in evaluating capacity in persons with neurological disorders and brain injuries (Dreer, DeVivo, Novack, Krzywanski, & Marson, 2008; Triebel, Martin, Nabors, & Marson, 2009).

Competence to Make a Will

The term *testamentary capacity* refers to a person's mental ability to make or alter a will, which is the legal instrument by which an individual, or *testator*, expresses his or her wishes regarding the dispersal of property after his or her death. In ancient and medieval societies, inheritance of a father's estate (chiefly real property) was often governed by laws regarding primogeniture, which prevented the weakening of holdings through division (A. Smith, 1776/1904). In Anglo-American legal tradition, laws regarding the disposal of property through wills and requirements that a testator be of "sound mind" extend back to the sixteenth century (Hall, Hall, Myers, & Champman, 2009).

In modern Anglo-American law, a testator needs to satisfy a rather modest legal standard of competence that derives from Lord Cockburn's holding in the 1870 English case, *Banks v. Goodfellow*. Cockburn's criteria are as follows:

> A testator shall understand the nature of the act and its effects; shall understand the extent of the property of which he is disposing; shall be able to comprehend and appreciate the claims to which he ought to give effect; and with a view to the latter object, that no disorder of the mind shall poison his affections, pervert his sense of right, or prevent the exercise of his natural faculties—that no insane delusion shall influence his will in disposing of his property and bring about a disposal of it which, if the mind had been sound, would not been made. (*Banks v. Goodfellow*, 1870, p. 565)

The *Banks* criteria have been accepted in the United States through case law (e.g., *Gilmer v. Brown*, 1947; *In re Honigman's Will*, 1960), although in the United States, the doctrine of insane delusion is conceptualized as being distinct from the cognitive features of testamentary capacity. That is,

a testator can meet the cognitive requirements for testamentary capacity—knowing that one is making a will, the identity of one's typical heirs, and the impact of one's act on the inheritors—yet suffer from a form of psychosis that makes the will invalid (American Law Institute, 2003).

Adults are presumed to be of sound mind and to have the ability to make a will. Litigation about testamentary capacity usually arises when one or more of the following *suspicious circumstances* occurs (Shulman, Cohen, Kirsh, Hull, & Champine, 2007; Spenceley, 2009):

- Desires expressed in the will reflect a striking alteration of the testator's previously and consistently expressed wishes;
- The testator had a mental or neurologic disorder that could impair his or her thinking, judgment, or reality testing;
- The testator was dependent on others and particularly vulnerable to their influence or suggestion; and/or
- The testator changed his will several times, apparently to control the actions of persons who are critical to the testator's well-being.

Most writers on this topic expect that challenges to testamentary capacity will increase in future years, for several reasons.

- The number of older adults who have mental infirmity will rise, and rising per capita wealth will make large estates (i.e., estates that are potentially enviable and worth fighting over) more common.
- Rising rates of divorce, remarriage, and nonmarriage have created more complex family structures; these make asset disposition more complicated and increase the possible circumstances in which potential heirs may feel unfairly treated or neglected (Hall et al., 2009; Kennedy, 2012; Shulman et al., 2007).
- Advances in medical care have lowered the mortality of many medical problems that might impair persons' testamentary capacity, including chronic and progressive medical disorders such as cancer, cardiovascular disease, vascular disease, strokes, dementias, kidney failure, liver

failure, lung disease, and diabetes, as well as primary psychiatric disorders (particularly psychoses). This means that persons live far longer with these conditions and are more likely to be suffering from a major medical problem when they prepare their wills.

Many of the infirmities that give rise to questions about testamentary capacity may also raise questions about a testator's susceptibility to undue influence at the time that a will is prepared or revised. Yet undue influence is a distinct legal issue that requires a differently focused psycholegal inquiry. *Undue influence* occurs when someone improperly induces a possibly competent but vulnerable testator to secure changes in a will such that its provisions reflect ends that are different from what the testator would otherwise have wanted. Situations ripe for undue influence can develop when a power imbalance or a dependency relationship exists between a weaker testator and the influencer. Although the case law criteria for undue influence vary from state to state, the typical legal indicia include the following:

- a susceptible party;
- another's opportunity to influence the susceptible party;
- the actual or attempted imposition of improper influence; and
- an outcome showing the effect of the improper influence. (*Ingle v. Ingle*, 2006)

Among the potential wielders of undue influence are family members, friends, caregivers (e.g., doctors, nurses, or home health aides), and other professionals (e.g., attorneys or spiritual leaders). Whereas cases involving questions about an individual's testamentary capacity focus primarily on the mental state of the testator, courts examining claims of undue influence look for evidence of attempts to control, deceive, pressure, or coerce the testator, combined with the testator's isolation from others and his or her vulnerability to inappropriate persuasion (see Exhibit 16.2).

Research. Testamentary capacity has been the subject of just a few empirical studies. To our knowledge, just one instrument, the Legal Capacity Questionnaire

---

Exhibit 16.2
Factors Indicative of Undue Influence

- Mental or physical disabilities render the testator particularly vulnerable.
- Influencer increases the testator's perceived helplessness.
- Influencer isolates the testator from other persons (family and friends).
- Influencer procured the attorney, brought the testator to the attorney, and was present when the will was prepared.
- Influencer actively misled the testator about the motives or behavior of other potential beneficiaries.
- The undue influence altered disposition of the property or caused an unusual disposition.

Note. Data from M. J. Quinn, Nerenberg, Goldman, and Piazza, 2010.

(LCQ; Walsh, Brown, Kaye, & Grigsby, 1994), has been designed specifically for assessing an individual's competence to make a will, and it is intended for attorneys to use in interviewing potential testators. The LCQ is a six-page downloadable form that contains multiple-choice, true–false, and short-answer questions about simple financial transactions, basic legal matters, and specific items (e.g., family members' names) relevant to the legal criteria for testamentary capacity. The LCQ has scoring instructions, with the highest score, 30, being most indicative of capacity.

To our knowledge, the LCQ has not been the subject of independent empirical study, but the instrument's creators collected some data regarding the instrument from 65 persons (age range 60–99 years) who lived in community settings, retirement homes, and skilled nursing facilities. They found a strong correlation between scores on the LCQ and scores on the MMSE and the Behavioral Dyscontrol Scale (Grigsby & Kaye, 1996), which is a brief measure that was originally designed to assess geriatric patients' ability to function independently. Walsh et al. (1994) suggested that when clients score 24 or greater on the LCQ, their attorneys can proceed confidently with estate planning despite their clients' mild impairments; scores of 20 or less imply that the attorney should exercise "extreme caution" and contact a mental health professional (Walsh et al., 1994). Limitations of the LCQ include its rather modest empirical grounding; the absence of independent, peer-reviewed research; and a failure to address directly whether a client is understanding a will or is experiencing potentially invalidating psychotic symptoms.

Very little empirical research exists on the relationship between measures of psychopathology and testamentary capacity. Reasons for this include the individualized nature of testamentary capacity assessments and the fact that in many cases, testamentary capacity is assessed retrospectively, following the testator's death. A few European investigators have explored the relationship between standardized instruments and issues that are relevant to will-making competence.

Roked and Patel (2008) used the MMSE and the Revised Cambridge Examination for Mental Disorders of the Elderly (CAMDEX–R; Roth, Huppert, Mountjoy, & Tym, 1999) to evaluate 74 elderly nursing-home residents (median age = 80 years) who had *DSM–IV* diagnoses of Alzheimer's disease; then, they arranged for an independent assessment of the subjects' testamentary capacity. The independent assessment determined that 34 (46%) of the 74 participants lacked testamentary capacity, and the MMSE and CAMDEX–R classified 87% of the cases correctly. Of those participants who had MMSE scores of 20 to 26, 92% had capacity; 95% of those with scores of 10 or less lacked capacity. Roked and Patel concluded that in retrospective assessments of testamentary capacity, medical notes containing information about an individual's cognitive testing could aid mental health professionals in formulating opinions.

Fontana, Dagnino, Cocito, and Balestrino (2008) developed a semiquantitative scoring system for evaluating the quality of an individual's handwriting. They then investigated the relationship between handwriting scores and performance on the Milan Overall Dementia Assessment (MODA; Brazzelli, Capitani, Della Sala, Spinnler, & Zuffi, 1994) and the MMSE in 25 consecutive patients who had been referred to an Italian academic neuropsychology service for the evaluation of mental deterioration.

Fontana et al. found that their handwriting scoring system had good interrater reliability and correlated significantly with both MODA and MMSE scores. The authors concluded that if further investigation supported their initial findings, "analysis of handwriting may be a useful addition to the methods available for the posthumous evaluation of testamentary capacity" of deceased persons who have left handwritten wills (Fontana et al., 2008, p. 257).

Jovanović, Jovović, Milovanović, and Jašović-Gašić (2008) investigated the morbidity structure of 156 testators whose will challenges were the subject of consecutive retrospective assessments of testamentary capacity by the Belgrade Forensic Psychiatry Centre in 1965–2005. The testators were mostly men over the age of 65 years who executed holograph wills and died within a year afterward. The Serbian criteria for testamentary capacity are that "the testator must be capable of reasoning, his will must be serious, real and free, and his intent must be clear and unconditional" (Jovanović et al., 2008, p. 486). The authors found that two diagnostic categories strongly predicted a lack of capacity: organic mental disorders (94% of cases) and substance-induced mental disorders (83% of cases).

Finally, a few investigators have examined the relationship between professionals' views and the legal components of testamentary capacity. Spar, Hankin, and Stodden (1995) surveyed 300 members of the National College of Probate Judges for their views on mental capacity and the factors that influence it. Out of 119 responding judges, 52% viewed a testator's recognition of property from a list as sufficient demonstration of knowing the nature and extent of one's bounty. Although 56% of the respondents said that a mental illness was necessary to a finding of incompetence, one-fourth disagreed with the statement that a "lack of capacity requires mental illness." A positive finding (from the standpoint of mental health professionals' self-esteem) was that 51% of judicial "respondents found expert testimony to be 'extremely influential'" in cases involving testamentary capacity (Spar et al., 1995, p. 397).

In her doctoral dissertation, Finello (2009) described a vignette-response study whose participants were "332 doctoral-level psychologists selected for their experience in forensic psychology or aging" (p. x). The study manipulated variables that were related to knowing that a will transfers property, knowing one's assets, naming one's potential heirs, and providing a nondelusional rationale for how one's estate will be distributed. Finello found that most of the respondents did not know the specifics of their states' legal criteria for testamentary capacity, but all four variables were positively related to professionals' conclusions that an individual had capacity—evidencing a professional consensus on what constitutes an individual's competence to make a will.

Practice and policy issues. Despite the paucity of empirical research on an individual's competence to make a will, authors who have written recently about assessing testamentary capacity (Dastidar & Odden, 2011; Hall et al., 2009; Jacoby & Steer, 2007; Kennedy, 2012; Shulman et al., 2007; Shulman, Peisah, Jacoby, Heinik, & Finkel, 2009) display substantial agreement about the proper foci and components of an evaluation, as described next.

Contemporaneous assessment of a still-living testator. Courts and attorneys may ask a mental health professional to evaluate a still-living testator when the testator's behavior, peculiar or unusual disposition preferences, or family discord either suggest a lack of testator competence or create suspicion that the will might be challenged later. In these situations, evaluations of testamentary capacity proceed in ways that are similar to other forensic mental health assessments—but with some unique or distinctive features.

Background information. Matters to address at the outset include determining whether the lawyer or client is requesting the evaluation, establishing fees and who is responsible for payment, and determining the expected outcome of the assessment (e.g., preliminary verbal report only vs. written report and possible testimony). Having established these matters, the examiner should find out what circumstances (e.g., family acrimony or intent to exclude a usual heir) or concerns (e.g., the client's odd statements or mental status) have generated the referral. Typically, this information will come from the attorney who was asked to prepare the

---

> **Exhibit 16.3**
> **Important Documents in Evaluating Testamentary Capacity**
>
> ---
>
> - The specific will or wills in question
> - Any previous wills
> - Other legal documents with likely relevance
> - Financial records or other description of the testator's assets (for corroboration)
> - Records and reports from health care providers, including:
>   - mental health professionals
>   - other inpatient and outpatient caregivers
>   - residential centers, home health care agencies, or nursing homes
>   - pharmacy or other medication records
> - Records documenting academic and employment history
>
> *Note.* Data from Hall et al., 2009; Roof, 2012; Shulman et al., 2009.

---

will, who should also provide or assist the examiner with obtaining the records and documents listed in Exhibit 16.3.

Collateral informants. Interviews with the still-living testator provide the examiner's principal interview data. Speaking with other persons can prove helpful, however, particularly in preparing for the evaluation of the prospective testator, and particularly if the other persons (e.g., neighbors) are relatively unbiased. Individuals who know the testator may help the examiner learn things that are helpful in scheduling (e.g., the time of day when the testator's mental functioning is at its best), in planning the evaluation (e.g., making arrangements so that the impact of a hearing impairment will not interfere with conversation), and in knowing about unexpected topics to explore (e.g., "Mr. Stein told me he speaks Hebrew to his cat Moses because that's the language Moses speaks").

Interview: General matters. The clinical forensic interview should take place in a setting that allows comfort, privacy, and freedom from interruption. Arranging for video recording of the interview is now relatively easy and will help to document the testator's mental state if litigation arises later.

The interview should begin with efforts to engage the evaluee's cooperation and informed consent, followed shortly by an assessment of the evaluee's understanding of why the evaluation was arranged ("My lawyer says we better do this because otherwise, my children will spend years in court fighting over this") and the evaluee's feelings about being evaluated ("If your cat was a prophet, you'd leave him money, too"). The evaluator should also complete an assessment of the testator's mental status, with particular awareness about the potential impact of the following mental problems:

- *Dementias.* When dementias (e.g., Alzheimer's disease) are severe, attorneys are likely to recognize and understand their impact on an individual's testamentary capacity. The conversational and social functioning of individuals with mild or even moderate dementia is sometimes good enough that their deficits can go unrecognized without careful probing. Looking for the presence and impact of dementia is therefore important (especially with elderly evaluees). If dementia is detected, careful documentation of the testator's reasons for his or her dispositional choices is important, particularly if, despite his or her condition, the testator appears to have retained capacity. On the other hand, dementia can impair an individual's insight, perception, and judgment, and testators may develop suspiciousness or paranoia about the reasons things are missing or did not happen.

- *Alcohol, drugs, and medications.* Elderly persons are especially vulnerable to the effects of drugs and alcohol on thinking and judgment. Over-the-counter medications (e.g., antihistamines) and prescription drugs (e.g., benzodiazepines) that have modest mental effects in young people have longer half-lives in elderly individuals and can have big effects on their alertness, perception, and memory. Intoxication may cloud an individual's perception and judgment, and persistent heavy use of drugs or alcohol can lead to mental problems that are similar to those caused by dementias.

- *Mood disorders.* Depressive and manic episodes often are accompanied by delusional beliefs, impaired judgment, irritability, and impulsiveness, which may compromise the testator's perceptions of family members and decision making related to making a will.

- *Delusions.* Many conditions are associated with paranoid thinking—the disorders discussed above, as well as several neurological diseases, psychoses, brain lesions, brain injuries, and delirium. Because the testator must be free of "insane delusions" that affect decisions regarding the disposition of property, delusional beliefs may render a potential testator incompetent to make a will. When delusions are present, the examiner should evaluate them carefully to gauge their impact on the testator's decisions about his or her disposition of property.

Testing.   As noted earlier, individuals' scores on basic tests of cognitive ability are correlated with evaluators' conclusions about his or her testamentary capacity. Although examiners should not treat findings from these tests as dispositive, using the MMSE, the Montreal Cognitive Assessment (MoCA; Nasreddine et al., 2005), or similar instruments during the evaluation can help the examiner quickly survey areas of cognitive capacity that may not be otherwise tapped in a conversational interview or mental status exam. Cognitive tests may also contribute to a diagnostic formulation and may help the examiner detect the presence and extent of cognitive deficits in (for example) a demented evaluee who has retained good social and conversational skills. The MMSE, MoCA, and similar instruments allow comparison with other individuals and may provide vivid examples of ways in which evaluees retain or have lost their cognitive capacity.

Questions specific to testamentary capacity. Although no one has developed a forensic assessment instrument that is specific to testamentary capacity, several writers on this topic have developed lists of questions that can help an examiner address the criteria set out in *Banks.* Exhibit 16.4 offers examples of questions, and additional examples are available in several of the sources we cited.

Deceased testator.   Forensic clinicians may receive requests to evaluate an individual's testamentary capacity after the testator has died. The evaluator should review the will in question and clarify with

---

Exhibit 16.4
Sample Questions Regarding Testamentary Capacity

Assets
- Would you describe your financial assets for me and tell me about their value?
- What other property do you own? Do you have any other valuable possession that you should mention in your will?
- What about your bank accounts? How much do they contain?

Relatives
- Tell me about all your relatives. How do you get along with them? Have any of them treated you unfairly? (If yes:) Please tell me about what happened.
- Who are the important people in your life now? How are they important to you?

Making a will
- If someone didn't know what a will is, how would you explain what a will is?
- Have you made a will before?
- Have you changed your will? (If yes:) What changes did you make? What was your reason for that?

Recipients
- Tell me about how you decided to choose the people who will inherit from you. Why did you leave [recipient A] that amount?
- Did you exclude any relatives, or give them lower amounts than others? Why was that? How do you think they'll feel about that? How will your decision affect them?
- Are you leaving anything to people outside your family? (If yes:) Tell me about your relationship with them. How did you decide to make them a beneficiary?
- Does anyone disagree with your will? Do you think people might fight [or "dispute" or "contest"] your will after your death? (If yes:) Why would they do that?

Note. Data from Hall et al., 2009; Roof, 2012; Shulman et al., 2007.

---

the retaining attorney the terms of the bequest being probated, the beneficiaries and the objectors, their relationships with the testator and each other, the bases of the objection(s) to probating the will, the terms of prior wills and codicils, and any other information the attorney has. Through either the executor's signed authorization or the probate judge's subpoena, the evaluator should receive access to the decedent's confidential medical records. The evaluator may

also interview the testator's former caregivers (e.g., physicians and nurses) regarding their observations beyond those that appear in chart notes. Evaluators should consider speaking with friends, business associates, family members, witnesses to the will, and others who are likely to have relevant knowledge. Information about the testator's ability to perform basic activities of daily living (ADLs) and more complex activities (e.g., managing money, taking medications as directed, or driving) may be helpful (Gutheil, 2007).

The evaluator's goal is to address the legal criteria using information that is contained in medical and other records listed in Exhibit 16.3 plus recollections of other persons who were in contact with the testator around the time the will was made. Retrospective assessments can be difficult, but a forensic evaluator often can assemble enough reliable information about the testator's clinical condition and thinking to allow formulation of an opinion with reasonable medical or scientific certainty. Although the competency assessment should address the testator's mental state on the day the will was signed, observations of good cognitive and emotional functioning after the will's execution are more relevant than later observations of impairment. Nonetheless, the evaluator must relate any clinical or collateral data to the testator's mental state at the time of the will's creation (Gutheil, 2007; Koson, 1982).

Report preparation. Broadly, the mental health evaluator tries to explain the testator's intentions and whether any mental conditions distorted the expression of the intent. The evaluator should relate any diagnoses and disabilities to the jurisdiction's criteria for testamentary capacity. Although a lack of capacity invalidates the entire will, the evaluator should also consider whether the testator's limitations affected all of the terms of the will or only certain portions (Gorman, 1996; Royall et al., 2002; Shulman, Hull, & Cohen, 2003). Exhibit 16.5 lists a set of topics that the examiner should attempt to address in a written report.

Competence to Manage Personal Affairs
Black's Law Dictionary (Black, 1983) and the legal codes of many states define *guardian* as

---

Exhibit 16.5
Topics to Address in a Forensic Report on Testamentary Capacity

---

- Whether findings support the presence of a clinical disorder that could impair decision-making or impulse control.
- Findings showing whether the testator experienced behavioral disturbances (e.g., impulsiveness) or symptoms of a mental illness (particularly evidence of a psychosis) when the will was executed and, if so, a description of those disturbances or symptoms.
- Explanation(s) for big changes from any previous plans for the disposition of assets (e.g., in previous wills) or from previously and consistently expressed wishes about the disposition of assets.
- Level of appreciation of the consequences of making a particular asset distribution, especially if it deviates from or will exclude "natural" beneficiaries (family members or a spouse).
- A description of interpersonal and intrafamilial conflicts, along with the testator's response(s) to understanding of these conflicts.
- Evidence of inconsistency or problems with expressing clear, consistent wishes about the disposition of assets.

Note. Data from Shulman et al., 2007.

---

a person lawfully invested with the power, and charged with the duty, of taking care of the person and managing the property and rights of another person, who, for some peculiarity of status, or defect of age, understanding, or self-control, is considered incapable of administering his own affairs. (p. 361)

Guardianships create a form of surrogate decision making such that the choices of the former decision maker (variously called the *ward* or the *incapacitated person*) are replaced by those of a substitute decision maker—the *guardian* (or, in some jurisdictions, the *conservator* or *curator*) of the person in question. Guardianships are the primary method of implementing substituted decision making internationally where, in contrast to recent trends in the United States, intellectual or psychosocial disabilities still create a presumption that the afflicted persons cannot participate independently and need pity and protection from their own failings (Dinerstein, 2012).

Guardianship was one of the earliest foci of mental health law (Melton, Petrila, Poythress, & Slobogin, 2007). Needs for guardianship were recognized in Ancient Roman law (Appelbaum, 1982). Fourteenth-century English court records describe in detail proceedings that led to the guardianship of Emma de Beston, who was "not of sound mind, having neither sense nor memory nor sufficient intelligence to manage herself, her lands, or her goods" (Roffe & Roffe, 1995, p. 1708). Neugebauer (1989) noted that between the 13th and 17th centuries, guardianship evolved from a legal protective mechanism that was primarily for individuals with large estates to a "social welfare" institution that also looked after "agricultural workers, artisans, and tradesmen—individuals with little or no land and only modest personal property [facilitated by] the court's creation of an informal system of monitored guardianship" (p. 1582).

In the United States, each jurisdiction has a statutory scheme for establishing guardianships of adults who cannot manage to meet their personal needs (i.e., physical health, food, clothing, or shelter), handle their finances, or both (Berg et al., 1996). The specific criteria that set the standards for determining a potential ward's level of incapacitation vary between jurisdictions (Slovenko, 2004). Statutes in several states incorporate the language and procedures that are set out in the Uniform Guardianship and Protective Proceedings Act (UGPPA; National Conference of Commissioners on Uniform State Laws, 1997), which, in section 102(5), defines an incapacitated person as someone who cannot "receive and evaluate information or make or communicate decisions to such an extent that the individual lacks the ability to meet essential requirements for physical health, safety or self-care even with appropriate technological assistance" (National Conference of Commissioners on Uniform State Laws, 1997, p. 1).

Guardianships have traditionally bestowed plenary authority over wards' persons and property. Recently, however, many U.S. jurisdictions have enacted statutory provisions for *partial* or *limited* guardianships. In describing Arizona's 2003 guardianship statute, for example, Watkins (2007) noted that the law "created a mechanism for individuals who were incapable of managing certain affairs of their lives" to retain the ability to handle other matters. "Limited guardianships were designed to promote self-determination and autonomy; the expressed intent of such guardianships was that wards retain those rights and decision-making authorities not granted to the guardian" (p. 35). An important implication for mental health practitioners is that in jurisdictions with statutory provisions for limited guardianships, "blanket pronouncements on competency" will be "particularly suspect where the controlling statute calls for determinations" regarding the prospective ward's specific limitations, abilities, and disabilities" (Drogin & Gutheil, 2011, p. 538).

Mental health professionals' reports often provide most of the clinical evidence that is considered by courts during guardianship proceedings. In an ideal world, clinicians' reports would contain nuanced descriptions of prospective wards' mental conditions and functional capabilities, thus laying a detailed basis for courts to order necessary protections while permitting wards to manage those matters for which they have retained adequate functioning. Yet research on guardianship evaluations from the 1970s onward suggests that mental health professionals' efforts often fall short of this ideal.

Research. The earliest reports on guardianship (Alexander & Lewin, 1972; Blenkner, Bloom, Nielson, & Weber, 1974) pointed out that guardianships seem to provide little benefit for wards and raised questions about their vulnerability to elder abuse. Reports from the 1970s and 1980s noted the dearth of empirical studies about guardianship (Keith & Wacker, 1994). A 1990s multistate study (Lisi, Burns, & Lussenden, 1994) that examined hundreds of guardianship hearings and legal files found that most wards had no legal representation, medical evaluation rarely occurred absent a statutory requirement, medical testimony was rarely taken during actual hearings, most hearings lasted less than 15 min, and plenary (unlimited) guardianships result in 87% of cases.

Responding to reforms recommended by national organizations that represent the elderly person's interest, several states have changed their guardianship statutes substantially since the 1990s. Often guided by the UGPPA (National Conference of Commissioners on Uniform State Laws, 1997), state legislatures have required that clinical evaluators assess an individual's functional strengths and weaknesses and be professionally qualified to evaluate the individual alleged impairments. These statutes also direct courts to explore and potentially impose limited guardianship orders that reflect the ward's retained capacities. The results of these legislative changes are mixed. One of earliest studies suggested that in Iowa and Missouri, the introduction of statutory language on limited guardianship made little practical difference in outcomes: A request for a full guardianship was tantamount to receiving one, limited guardianships were seldom used, and few guardianship petitions were denied either before or after legislative reform (Keith & Wacker, 1993).

Research also suggests that guardianship evaluations are suboptimal. A study of Ohio and Washington state case files from the late 1980s found that clinicians' evaluations were often "sketchy" and "conclusory" (Bulcroft, Kielkopf, & Tripp, 1991). A study that examined West Virginia and Pennsylvania cases from the late 1990s found that overall, "evaluation thoroughness was substandard"—most clinical reports did not usually describe the individual's emotional functioning or ADLs (Dudley & Goins, 2003).

One of the more recent studies on guardianship compared the quality of clinical assessments for guardianship and courts' imposition of limited guardianship orders from three states that had implemented varying levels of statutory reform along the lines of the UGPPA. Moye et al. (2007) examined nearly 300 reports from Colorado (major reform), Pennsylvania (intermediate reform), and Massachusetts (limited reform) that had been submitted in the years 2002 through 2005. The authors assigned a "quality score" to the reports based on six indicators that were drawn from recommendations by the American Bar Association–American

Psychological Association judicial handbook on capacity determinations (American Bar Association Commission on Law and Aging and American Psychological Association, 2006). Among their findings:

- Most reports described diagnoses, mental symptoms, and illness severity, although illness duration and medications appeared less often.
- ADLs appeared in one-third of the Colorado cases, one-fifth of the Pennsylvania cases, and fewer than one-tenth of the Massachusetts cases.
- More than one-fourth of the reports provided general conclusions about the prospective ward's decision-making abilities without describing specific symptoms of mental impairment.
- Nearly two-thirds of the reports included statements about the prospective ward's capacity for self-care without describing specific functional symptoms.
- Oral testimony was more complete than written reports: Testifying clinicians provided information about a prospective ward's diagnosis, symptoms, prognosis, and functional deficits much more frequently.
- Limited guardianship orders were issued in one-third of Colorado cases but only rarely in Massachusetts and Pennsylvania cases. More complete clinical reports (based on the presence or absence of the six indicators) were more likely to result in limited guardianships.

Moye et al. (2007) concluded that "clinical and juridical practice is improved in states with more progressive statutory guidance" but that "even in Colorado, . . . clinical evidence" in mental health professionals' reports "was often incomplete" (p. 611).

Research on assessment tools. Writing in 1996 about the availability of guardianship-specific tests for psychologists, Mary Joy Quinn lamented, "Clearly they are needed. Just as clearly they do not exist" (p. 139). Matters are very different now, however, and mental health professionals who undertake guardianship evaluations can choose from an abundance of instruments that have been designed to aid in their assessments. The Center for Reducing Risks in Vulnerable Populations (CRRVP) at the

University of Illinois at Chicago has compiled a list of more than 70 published instruments that might aid in the functional assessment of potential wards (CRRVP, 2009). Here, we provide brief descriptions of a few instruments with features that might be especially relevant to the evaluation of older adults who are undergoing evaluations for guardianship.

The Assessment of Capacity for Everyday Decision-Making (ACED; Lai et al., 2008) is intended to help evaluators gauge how well cognitively impaired persons can solve functional problems. Using a semistructured interview format, the interviewer collects information from caregivers about the individual's functional deficits, which allows the content to be tailored to an individual evaluee. For standardized content, evaluees receive information about a functional problem along with options to address it and the risks and benefits of these options, which minimizes the impact of short-term memory limitations. The ACED is organized along the four-item competence rubric (i.e., choice, understanding, appreciation, and reasoning) and includes a scoring system that allows for research on the instrument's reliability. Intraclass correlation coefficients reported by Lai et al. (2008) implied good interrater reliability for understanding, appreciation, and reasoning and 93% agreement for choice. Internal consistency for ACED abilities was also good, with Cronbach alpha values of at least 0.84. The ACED thus appears to provide a reliable, patient-specific tool for evaluating the decision-making capacity of individuals who have problems with instrumental activities of daily living (IADLs) and deficits in cognitive ability.

The Aid to Capacity Evaluation (ACE; Etchells et al., 1999) is one of several semistructured tools that can be used to examine an evaluee's decision-making capacity concerning a medical decision that the evaluee is actually facing. It examines the evaluee's understanding of the problem, proposed treatment, treatment alternatives, and refusing treatment; the evaluee's perception of the consequences of accepting or refusing treatment; and whether the decision is influenced by hallucinations, delusions, or depression. The ACE has scoring guidelines for rating evaluees as *definitely incapable, probably incapable, probably capable,* or *definitely capable*. Using expert assessments and an adjudication panel as a "gold standard" for incapacity, the ACE had a receiver operating characteristic curve the area under which was 0.90. The ACE often takes less than 10 min to administer and is freely available on the Internet—features that make it a potentially attractive tool in primary care settings (Tunzi, 2001).

The Capacity Assessment Tool (CAT; Carney, Neugroschl, Morrison, Marin, & Siu, 2001) is another instrument that is well suited to primary care settings, with properties that support its usefulness in guardianship evaluations. Like the ACED, the CAT evaluates decision making regarding choices that an evaluee actually faces. It follows the four-item competence rubric and allows calculation of an overall capacity score relative to the evaluee's particular situation and decision. The only published evaluation of the CAT (Carney et al., 2001) indicated high agreement with independent psychiatric assessments of each individual's ability and overall competence, but as of this writing, the instrument has not undergone other evaluation.

The Direct Assessment of Functional Status (DAFS; Loewenstein et al., 1989) is one of the better studied instruments that is available for in situ assessment of IADLs. The DAFS has 85 items that evaluate a variety of behaviors within several functional domains (e.g., communication, using transportation, handling financial issues, and shopping) and is designed for administration in an outpatient setting. The original study reported that the DAFS had "high interrater and test–retest reliabilities," with "significant correlations between the scale and established measures of functional status" (Loewenstein et al., 1989, p. 114). A subsequent study by the same authors found that the "many subtests of the DAFS were sensitive to functional decline," so that "the scale has utility in objectively establishing longitudinal patterns of deterioration" (Loewenstein et al., 1995, p. 495). A recent revision of the DAFS (DAFS–R; McDougall, Becker, Vaughan, Acee, & Delville, 2010) has 55 items; easier items have been removed, and more difficult questions related to medication management have been added. The DAFS–R is therefore more sensitive to the early decrements in IADLs that may signal

initial cognitive impairment in community-dwelling individuals, and it appears to have acceptable reliability features.

Willis, Marsiske, and colleagues designed the Everyday Problems Test (EPT; Willis & Marsiske, 1993) to evaluate older persons' ability to meet the cognitive demands that are involved in using printed materials in seven domains of daily living: food preparation, medication and health behaviors, phone calls, shopping, financial matters, housekeeping, and transportation. The EPT has 12 items on each of the scales. The items related to printed stimuli (e.g., a prescription label) ask the evaluee to solve two related practical problems (e.g., calculating the number of pills to take). Marsiske and Willis (1995) reported that standardized alpha reliabilities of the scales ranged from 0.62 to 0.74, and the alpha reliability of the total measure is 0.94; 1-year test–retest reliability for the full measure is 0.91. The instruction manuals and alternative versions of the EPT (offering open-ended and multiple-choice formats) are available online from the Department of Psychiatry at the University of Washington (http://www.uwpsychiatry.org/sls/researchers/ept/ept.htm). The manuals provide detailed instructions for giving the test and describe the process for obtaining certification in administration of the EPT.

A related assessment measure is the Revised Observed Tasks of Daily Living (OTDL–R; Diehl et al., 2005), which is a performance-based test that is used to evaluate how well persons can perform nine tasks: three tasks relate to medication use (i.e., following label directions, understanding a leaflet, and completing a patient form), three tasks concern using a telephone (i.e., looking up and dialing a number, and using a rate discount in a phone book), and three tasks concern financial management (i.e., making change, balancing a checkbook, and writing and mailing a check for a utility bill). Evaluees are assigned scores on 28 subtasks. The initial report for the ODTL–R described ratings in a heterogeneous 126-member sample. Cronbach's α was 0.71 for medication use, 0.66 for telephone use, 0.71 for financial management, and 0.82 for the full measure (Diehl et al., 2005). The range of difficulty of the OTDL–R items allowed the authors to find correlations in expectable directions with age, education, general health, verbal ability, memory, inductive reasoning, and perceptual speed, suggesting that the instrument is a valid and relevant measure of older adults' functional status. One can download materials and manuals for the OTDL–R from the University of Florida at http://marsiskelab. phhp.ufl.edu/otdl/otdl.html.

Practice and policy issues. In 2004, the American Psychological Association published guidelines for psychological practice that state that examiners should "strive to be familiar with the theory, research, and practice of various methods of intervention with older adults, particularly with current research evidence about their efficacy with this age group" (p. 237). But dozens of appropriate assessment instruments are available, and this poses some problems for capacity evaluators.

- The existence of so many tools makes it hard for an evaluator to be familiar with most of them—let alone become comfortable, "knowledgeable," and competent in using them.
- Although many of these instruments have undergone evaluations that yielded peer-reviewed publications, few of the instruments have been the subject of more than a handful of publications, which makes it difficult to feel a high level of confidence in many of them.
- Most of the instruments have not received broad (or general) acceptance as tools for evaluating the need for guardianship.
- The few generally accepted instruments for assessing cognitive status—for example, the MMSE and the MoCA—provide indices of capabilities that, although relevant to community functioning, are different from the practical skills and functioning that are needed to manage one's personal and financial affairs.

Evaluators can effectuate practical solutions to these problems by remembering that no structured instrument is a "capacimeter" that somehow measures an individual's competence (Kapp & Mossman, 1996). Rather, the value of structured assessment instruments inheres chiefly in their assuring a systematic and consistent approach to looking at the types of behavior and performance capacities that are relevant to the evaluation. That is, having used a previously tested instrument allows the examiner to describe an evaluee's behavioral responses to specific practical tasks (e.g., how the evaluee handled the task of making change or writing a check). The use of previously published instruments also gives the fact-finder some assurance that the examiner's judgments are reasonably reliable and do not arise from idiosyncratic interpretations of what is needed to function competently and independently.

As Skelton, Kunik, Regev, and Naik (2010) noted, "Capacity determination is a complex, cross-disciplinary process that ideally involves a range of professionals" (pp. 300–301) who can contribute to a full understanding of an individual's ability to (a) meet personal needs and hygiene, (b) take care of one's home, (c) manage ADLs (such as shopping, cooking, and cleaning), (d) handle medical self-care, and (e) handle financial matters. Skelton et al. suggested that a geriatrics team is often in the best position to implement a standardized, thorough process of assessing an older adult's capacity to live safely and independently.

Ideally, an assessment of the five areas noted in the preceding paragraph would take place where the evaluee lives, followed by an interdisciplinary meeting of caregivers and specialists who can make recommendations for intervention. In addition to community-based observation of the evaluee, the team develops and contributes information based on background research (e.g., history gathering, talking with the evaluee's family members), a thorough evaluation of medical status, and a comprehensive mental status evaluation that might include administration of one or more assessment instruments such as those described earlier.

Of course, individual evaluators can often gather this type of information through examination of available medical records and discussions with caregivers. But in recognition of the multiple assessment skills that are involved in a guardianship evaluation, some jurisdictions (e.g., Kentucky) require that the evaluation be completed by a multidisciplinary team whose members have skills and expertise that are relevant to the prospective ward's disability. Concerning the capacity to handle one's medical affairs, Skelton et al. (2010) provided a helpful list of sample questions for evaluees about medications and medical needs (modeled after Grisso and Appelbaum's [1998a] four-item competence rubric mentioned earlier) that clinicians can tailor to an evaluee's specific clinical situation.

Skelton et al. (2010) also noted that appointing a legal guardian is just one possible outcome of a capacity assessment and may not be the most effective way to optimize an evaluee's welfare. When guardianship is needed, however, the evaluation approach described earlier allows clinicians to provide the fact-finder with detailed, relevant information about an individual's decision-making capacity, ability to live independently, and behavior that might endanger others, as well as any dangers faced by a prospective ward.

The American Psychological Association publication, "What Practitioners Should Know About Working With Older Adults" (Abeles, 1998), provides an excellent review of developmental, psychological, and medical factors that are relevant to guardianship evaluations of elderly individuals. This advisory also provides a helpful summary of accommodations that are useful in optimizing the performance of older persons, and these are summarized in Exhibit 16.6.

An understanding of the jurisdiction's scheme for guardianship is important to ensuring that the evaluation and report meet the fact-finder's needs and address the applicable statutory definitions that are relevant to guardianship (Berg et al., 1996). In some cases, jurisdictions have explicit, detailed requirements for guardianship reports. Kentucky provides one example (see Kentucky Revised Statutes, 2012, § 387.540(4)), and its detailed statutory outline of information that is required in reports by court-appointed examiners (see Exhibit 16.7) may be useful to forensic clinicians in other jurisdictions where statutory guidelines are less specific.

SUMMARY AND CONCLUSIONS

Although this chapter has addressed the forensic evaluation of just a few civil competencies, we hope that these specific examples will help readers grasp general concepts that arise in most assessments of

---

Exhibit 16.6
Helpful Accommodations When Testing Older Evaluees

- Older adults (particularly persons who have had little formal education) may be unfamiliar with testing procedures generally. Explaining the purpose of testing and how it works may help older adults overcome their reticence to participate.
- To promote optimal performance, give advance notice that the evaluee should bring assistive devices (e.g., hearing aids, eyeglasses) to the evaluation. If needed, use large print materials.
- Conduct the evaluation in a well-lit, quiet room that has space to comfortably accommodate a wheelchair or other mobility devices.
- Try to use evaluation tools and tests that are designed for assessing older adults.
- If the evaluee is experiencing pain or discomfort, try to reduce it.
- Find out what medication the evaluee is taking and consider its potential impact on the evaluee performance.
- Make sure the evaluee has heard and understands the test instructions.
- Speak clearly, using simple language, without shouting.
- Choose testing times and durations to optimize the evaluee's function and minimize the impact of fatigue. Also, using multiple testing sessions helps in gauging how the evaluee performs across sessions and at different times of the day.

Note. Data from Abeles, 1998.

---

decisional competence. Forensic evaluators who engage in such assessments entertain a complex amalgam of facts that fall along several intersecting conceptual dimensions. Legal decisions ultimately rise and fall on determining the presence or absence of specific elements that courts should consider in making a determination of competency. The forensic clinician's general role is to make clinical findings and describe their impact on legal constructs. The forensic examiner begins with a clearly identified set of psycholegal questions, then applies the relevant clinical instruments and assessment techniques to gather data that will provide a neutral, unbiased, scientifically grounded answer to those questions.

Exhibit 16.7
Contents of an Interdisciplinary Guardianship Report

(a) A description of the nature and extent of the respondent's disabilities, if any;

(b) Current evaluations of the respondent's social, intellectual, physical, and educational condition, adaptive behavior, and social skills;

(c) An opinion as to whether guardianship or conservatorship is needed, the type of guardianship or conservatorship needed, if any, and the reasons therefor;

(d) An opinion as to the length of time guardianship or conservatorship will be needed by the respondent, if at all, and the reasons therefor;

(e) If limited guardianship or conservatorship is recommended, a further recommendation as to the scope of the guardianship or conservatorship, specifying particularly the rights to be limited and the corresponding powers and duties of the limited guardian or limited conservator;

(f) A description of the social, educational, medical, and rehabilitative services currently being utilized by the respondent, if any;

(g) A determination whether alternatives to guardianship or conservatorship are available;

(h) A recommendation as to the most appropriate treatment or rehabilitation plan and living arrangement for the respondent and the reasons therefor;

(i) A listing of all medications the respondent is receiving, the dosage, and a description of the impact of the medication upon the respondent's mental and physical condition and behavior;

(j) An opinion whether attending a hearing on a petition filed under KRS 387.530 would subject the respondent to serious risk of harm;

(k) The names and addresses of all individuals who examined or interviewed the respondent or otherwise participated in the evaluation; and

(l) Any dissenting opinions or other comments by the evaluators.

Note. From Kentucky Revised Statutes, 2012, § 387.540(4).

References

Abeles, N. (1998). What practitioners should know about working with older adults. *Professional Psychology: Research and Practice, 29,* 413–427. doi:10.1037/0735-7028.29.5.413

Alexander, G., & Lewin, T. (1972). *The aged and the need for surrogate management.* Syracuse, NY: Syracuse University.

American Academy of Psychiatry and the Law. (2005). *Ethics guidelines for the practice of forensic psychiatry.* Retrieved from http://www.aapl.org/ethics.htm

American Bar Association. (2013). *Model rules of professional conduct.* Retrieved from http://www.americanbar.org/groups/professional_responsibility/publications/model_rules_of_professional_conduct

American Bar Association Commission on Law and Aging, American Psychological Association, and National College of Probatic Judges. (2006). *Judicial determination of capacity of older adults in guardianship proceedings: A handbook for judges.* Washington, DC: American Bar Association and American Psychological Association.

American Law Institute. (2003). *Restatement of the Law Third, Property (Wills and Other Donative Transfers).* Philadelphia, PA: Author.

American Psychological Association. (2004). Guidelines for psychological practice with older adults. *American Psychologist, 59,* 236–260. doi:10.1037/0003-066X.59.4.236

American Psychological Association. (2013). Specialty guidelines for forensic psychology. *American Psychologist, 68,* 7–19. doi:10.1037/a0029889

Appelbaum, P. S. (1982). Limitations on guardianship of the mentally disabled. *Hospital and Community Psychiatry, 33,* 183–184.

Appelbaum, P. S. (1988). The right to refuse treatment with antipsychotic medications: Retrospect and prospect. *American Journal of Psychiatry, 145,* 413–419.

Appelbaum, P. S. (2007). Assessment of patients' competence to consent to treatment. *New England Journal of Medicine, 357,* 1834–1840. doi:10.1056/NEJMcp074045

Appelbaum, P. S., & Grisso, T. (1988). Assessing patients' capacities to consent to treatment. *New England Journal of Medicine, 319,* 1635–1638. doi:10.1056/NEJM198812223192504

Appelbaum, P. S., & Grisso, T. (1997). Capacities of hospitalized, medically ill patients to consent to treatment. *Psychosomatics: Journal of Consultation and Liaison Psychiatry, 38,* 119–125. doi:10.1016/S0033-3182(97)71480-4

Appelbaum, P. S., & Roth, L. H. (1982). Competency to consent to research. A psychiatric overview. *Archives of General Psychiatry, 39,* 951–958. doi:10.1001/archpsyc.1982.04290080061009

Banks v. Goodfellow, LR5 QB 549 (1870).

Berg, J. W., Appelbaum, P. S., & Grisso, T. (1996). Constructing competence: Formulating standards of legal competence to make medical decisions. *Rutgers Law Review, 48,* 345–371.

Berg, J. W., Appelbaum, P. S., Lidz, C. W., & Parker, L. (2001). *Informed consent: Legal theory and clinical practice* (2nd ed.). New York, NY: Oxford University Press. doi:10.1007/978-1-4757-3405-8_2

Black, H. C. (1983). *Black's law dictionary: Abridged* (5th ed.). St. Paul, MN: West.

Blackstone, W. (1775). *Commentaries on the laws of England* (7th ed., Vol. 2). Oxford, England: Clarendon Press.

Blenkner, B., Bloom, M., Nielson, M., & Weber, R. (1974). *Final report: Protective services for older people: Findings from the Benjamin Rose Institute study*. Cleveland, OH: Benjamin Rose Institute.

Braud v. Kinchen, 310 So. 2d 657 (La. App. 1st Cir., 1975).

Brazzelli, M., Capitani, E., Della Sala, S., Spinnler, H., & Zuffi, M. (1994). A neuropsychological instrument adding to the description of patients with suspected cortical dementia: The Milan Overall Dementia Assessment. *Journal of Neurology, Neurosurgery, and Psychiatry, 57*, 1510–1517. doi:10.1136/jnnp.57.12.1510

Bulcroft, K., Kielkopf, M. R., & Tripp, K. (1991). Elderly wards and their legal guardians: Analysis of country probate records in Ohio and Washington. *Gerontologist, 31*, 156–164. doi:10.1093/geront/31.2.156

Buss, S. (2008). Personal autonomy. In E. N. Zalta (Ed.), *Stanford encyclopedia of philosophy*. Retrieved from http://plato.stanford.edu/entries/personal-autonomy

Cairns, R., Maddock, C., Buchanan, A., David, A. S., Hayward, P., Richardson, G., . . . Hotopf, M. (2005). Prevalence and predictors of mental incapacity in psychiatric in-patients. *British Journal of Psychiatry, 187*, 379–385. doi:10.1192/bjp.187.4.379

Carney, M. T., Neugroschl, J., Morrison, R. S., Marin, D., & Siu, A. L. (2001). The development and piloting of a capacity assessment tool. *Journal of Clinical Ethics, 12*, 17–23.

Carpenter, W. T., Gold, M. J., Lahti, A. C., Queern, C. A., Conley, R. R., Bartko, J. J., . . . Appelbaum, P. S. (2000). Decisional capacity for informed consent in schizophrenia research. *Archives of General Psychiatry, 57*, 533–538. doi:10.1001/archpsyc.57.6.533

Center for Reducing Risks in Vulnerable Populations. (2009). *Instrument bank table* (current to June 29, 2009). Retrieved from http://www.nursing.uic.edu/sites/default/files/Alphabetical_Variable_Listing.pdf

Ciccone, J. R., Tokoli, J. F., Clements, C. D., & Gift, T. E. (1990). Right to refuse treatment: Impact of *Rivers v. Katz. Bulletin of the American Academy of Psychiatry and the Law, 18*, 203–215.

Civil Rights of Patients, Ohio Revised Code § 5122.301 (1989).

Cohen, L. M., McCue, J. D., & Green, G. M. (1993). Do clinical and formal assessments of the capacity of patients in the intensive care unit to make decisions agree? *Archives of Internal Medicine, 153*, 2481–2485. doi:10.1001/archinte.1993.00410210109012

Custer, L. B. (1978). The origins of the doctrine of parens patriae. *Emory Law Journal, 27*, 195–244.

Dastidar, J. G., & Odden, A. (2011). How do I determine if my patient has decision-making capacity? *Hospitalist, 15*(8), 24–31.

De Prerogativa Regis, 17 Edward 2 c.9 (1324).

Diehl, M., Marsiske, M., Horgas, A. L., Rosenberg, A., Saczynski, J. S., & Willis, S. L. (2005). The Revised Observed Tasks of Daily Living: A performance-based assessment of everyday problem solving in older adults. *Journal of Applied Gerontology, 24*, 211–230. doi:10.1177/0733464804273772

Dinerstein, R. D. (2012). Implementing legal capacity under Article 12 of the UN Convention on the Rights of Persons With Disabilities: The difficult road from guardianship to supported decision-making. *Human Rights Brief, 19*(2), 8–12.

Drane, J. F. (1985). The many faces of competency. *Hastings Center Report, 15*, 17–21. doi:10.2307/3560639

Dreer, L. E., DeVivo, M. J., Novack, T. A., Krzywanski, S., & Marson, D. C. (2008). Cognitive predictors of medical decision-making capacity in traumatic brain injury. *Rehabilitation Psychology, 53*, 486–497. doi:10.1037/a0013798

Drogin, E. Y., & Gutheil, T. G. (2011). Guardianship. In E. Y. Drogin, F. M. Dattilio, R. L. Sadoff, & T. G. Gutheil (Eds.), *Handbook of forensic assessment: Psychological and psychiatric perspectives* (pp. 521–542). Hoboken, NJ: Wiley.

Dudley, K. C., & Goins, R. T. (2003). Guardianship capacity evaluations of older adults: Comparing current practice to legal standards in two states. *Journal of Aging and Social Policy, 15*, 97–115. doi:10.1300/J031v15n01_06

Dunn, L. B., Nowrangi, M. A., Palmer, B. W., Jeste, D. V., & Saks, E. R. (2006). Assessing decisional capacity for clinical research or treatment; a review of instruments. *American Journal of Psychiatry, 163*, 1323–1334. doi:10.1176/appi.ajp.163.8.1323

Edelstein, B. (1999). *Hopemont Capacity Assessment Interview manual and scoring guide*. Morgantown: West Virginia University.

Etchells, E., Darzins, P., Silberfeld, M., Singer, P. A., McKenny, J., Naglie, G., . . . Strang, D. (1999). Assessment of patients' capacity to consent to treatment. *Journal of General Internal Medicine, 14*, 27–34. doi:10.1046/j.1525-1497.1999.00277.x

Etchells, E., Katz, M. R., Shuchman, M., Wong, G., Workman, S., Choudhry, N. K., . . . Singer, P. A. (1997). Accuracy of clinical impressions and Mini-Mental State Exam scores for assessing capacity to consent to major medical treatment. *Psychosomatics: Journal of Consultation and Liaison Psychiatry, 38,* 239–245. doi:10.1016/S0033-3182(97)71460-9

Finello, C. M. (2009). *Testamentary competence: Defining functional abilities* (Doctoral dissertation). Philadelphia, PA: Drexel University. Retrieved from http://idea.library.drexel.edu/bitstream/1860/3033/1/Finello_Christina.pdf

Fitten, L. J., & Waite, M. S. (1990). Impact of medical hospitalization on treatment decision-making capacity in the elderly. *Archives of Internal Medicine, 150,* 1717–1721. doi:10.1001/archinte.1990.00040031717022

Folstein, M. F., Folstein, S. E., & McHugh, P. R. (1975). Mini-Mental State: A practical method for grading the cognitive state of patients for the clinician. *Journal of Psychiatric Research, 12,* 189–198. doi:10.1016/0022-3956(75)90026-6

Fontana, P., Dagnino, F., Cocito, L., & Balestrino, M. (2008). Handwriting as a gauge of cognitive status: A novel forensic tool for posthumous evaluation of testamentary capacity. *Neurological Sciences, 29,* 257–261. doi:10.1007/s10072-008-0977-3

Frith's Case, 22 How. St. Tr. 307 (1790).

Gillis v. Cameron, 324 F.2d 419 (D.C. Cir. 1963).

Gilmer v. Brown, 44 S.E.2d 16 (Va. 1947).

Godard, S. L., Bloom, J. D., Williams, M. H., & Faulkner, L. R. (1986). The right to refuse treatment in Oregon: A two-year statewide experience. *Behavioral Sciences and the Law, 4,* 293–304. doi:10.1002/bsl.2370040305

Goodwin, P. E., Smyer, M. A., & Lair, T. (1995). Decision-making incapacity among nursing home residents: Results from the 1987 NMES survey. *Behavioral Sciences and the Law, 13,* 405–414. doi:10.1002/bsl.2370130308

Gorman, W. F. (1996). Testamentary capacity in Alzheimer's disease. *Elder Law Journal, 4,* 225–246.

Greenberg, W. M., & Attia, S. (1993). Nonemergent forcible medication in an acute hospital. *Bulletin of the American Academy of Psychiatry and the Law, 21,* 465–473.

Grigsby, J., & Kaye, K. (1996). *The Behavioral Dyscontrol Scale: Manual* (2nd ed.). Denver, CO: Authors.

Grisso, T., & Appelbaum, P. S. (1995). The MacArthur Treatment Competence Study. III. Abilities of patients to consent to psychiatric and medical treatments. *Law and Human Behavior, 19,* 149–174. doi:10.1007/BF01499323

Grisso, T., & Appelbaum, P. S. (1998a). *Assessing competence to consent to treatment: A guide for physicians and other health professionals.* New York, NY: Oxford University Press.

Grisso, T., & Appelbaum, P. S. (1998b). *The MacArthur Competence Assessment Tool for Treatment (MacCAT–T).* Sarasota, FL: Professional Resources Press.

Grisso, T., Appelbaum, P. S., & Hill-Fotouhi, C. (1997). The MacCAT–T: A clinical tool to assess patients' capacities to make treatment decisions. *Psychiatric Services, 48,* 1415–1419.

Gutheil, T. G. (2007). Common pitfalls in the evaluation of testamentary capacity. *Journal of the American Academy of Psychiatry and the Law, 35,* 514–517.

Hall, R. C. W., Hall, R. C. W., Myers, W. C., & Chapman, M. J. (2009). Testamentary capacity: History, physicians' role, requirements, and why wills are challenged. *Clinical Geriatrics, 17*(6), 18–24.

In re Estate of Lobe, 348 N.W.2d 413 (Minn. App. 1984).

In re Honigman's Will, 168 N.E.2d 676 (N.Y. 1960).

Ingle v. Ingle, 2006-Ohio-3749 (Greene Co., 2006).

Jacoby, R., & Steer, P. (2007). How to assess capacity to make a will. *British Medical Journal, 335,* 155–157. doi:10.1136/bmj.39232.706840.AD

Janofsky, J. S., McCarthy, R. J., & Folstein, M. F. (1992). The Hopkins Competency Assessment Test: A brief method for evaluating patients' capacity to give informed consent. *Hospital and Community Psychiatry, 43,* 132–136.

Jovanović, A. A., Jovović, S., Milovanović, S., & Jašović-Gašić, M. (2008). Medical reasons for retrospective challenges of testamentary capacity. *Psychiatria Danubina, 20,* 485–493.

Kant, I. (2002). *Groundwork for the metaphysics of morals* (A. W. Wood, Trans.). Binghamton, NY: Vail-Ballou Press. (Original work published 1785)

Kapp, M. B., & Mossman, D. (1996). Measuring decisional capacity: Cautions on the construction of a "capacimeter." *Psychology, Public Policy, and Law, 2,* 73–95. doi:10.1037/1076-8971.2.1.73

Keith, P. M., & Wacker, R. R. (1993). Guardianship reform: Does revised legislation make a difference in outcomes for proposed wards? *Journal of Aging and Social Policy, 4,* 139–155. doi:10.1300/J031v04n03_10

Keith, P. M., & Wacker, R. R. (1994). *Older wards and their guardians.* Westport, CT: Praeger.

Kennedy, K. M. (2012). Testamentary capacity: A practical guide to assessment of ability to make a valid will. *Journal of Forensic and Legal Medicine, 19,* 191–195. doi:10.1016/j.jflm.2011.12.029

Kentucky Revised Statutes § 387.540(4) (2012).

Kim, S. Y. H., Caine, E. D., Currier, G. W., Leibovici, A., & Ryan, J. M. (2001). Assessing the competence of persons with Alzheimer's disease in providing informed consent for participation in research. *American Journal of Psychiatry, 158*, 712–717. doi:10.1176/appi.ajp.158.5.712

Kim, S. Y. H., Karlawish, J. H., Kim, H. M., Wall, I. F., Bozoki, A. C., & Appelbaum, P. S. (2011). Preservation of the capacity to appoint a proxy decision maker: Implications for dementia research. *Archives of General Psychiatry, 68*, 214–219. doi:10.1001/archgenpsychiatry.2010.191

Kim, S. Y. H., Karlawish, J. H. T., & Caine, E. D. (2002). Current state of research on decision-making competence of cognitively impaired elderly persons. *American Journal of Geriatric Psychiatry, 10*, 151–165. doi:10.1097/00019442-200203000-00006

Koson, D. F. (1982). Forensic psychiatric examinations: Competency. *Journal of Forensic Sciences, 27*, 119–124.

Lai, J. M., Gill, T. M., Cooney, L. M., Bradley, E. H., Hawkins, K. A., & Karlawish, J. H. (2008). Everyday decision-making ability in older persons with cognitive impairment. *American Journal of Geriatric Psychiatry, 16*, 693–696. doi:10.1097/JGP.0b013e31816c7b54

Lepre v. Caputo, 131 N.J. Super. 118, 328 A. 2d 650 (1974).

Lisi, L., Burns, A., & Lussenden, K. (1994). *National study of guardianship systems: Findings and recommendations.* Ann Arbor, MI: The Center for Social Gerontology.

Loewenstein, D. A., Amigo, E., Duara, R., Guterman, A., Hurwitz, D., Berkowitz, N., . . . Eisdorfer, C. (1989). A new scale for the assessment of functional status in Alzheimer's disease and related disorders. *Journal of Gerontology, 44*, 114–121. doi:10.1093/geronj/44.4.P114

Loewenstein, D. A., Duara, R., Rubert, M. P., Arguelles, T., Lapinski, K. J., & Eisdorfer, C. (1995). Deterioration of functional capacities in Alzheimer's disease after a 1-year period. *International Psychogeriatrics, 7*, 495–503. doi:10.1017/S1041610295002237

Marder, S. R., Swann, E., Winslade, W. J., Van Putten, T., Chien, C. P., & Wilkins, J. N. (1984). A study of medication refusal by involuntary psychiatric patients. *Hospital and Community Psychiatry, 35*, 724–726.

Markson, L. J., Kern, D. C., Annas, G. J., & Glantz, L. H. (1994). Physician assessment of patient competence. *Journal of the American Geriatrics Society, 42*, 1074–1080.

Marsiske, M., & Willis, S. L. (1995). Dimensionality of everyday problem solving in older adults. *Psychology and Aging, 10*, 269–283. doi:10.1037/0882-7974.10.2.269

Marson, D. C., Earnst, K. S., Jamil, F., Barolucci, A., & Harrell, L. (2000). Consistency of physicians' legal standard and personal judgments of competency in patients with Alzheimer's disease. *Journal of the American Geriatrics Society, 48*, 911–918.

Marson, D. C., Hawkins, L., McIntruff, B., Bartolucci, A., & Harrell, L. E. (1997). Cognitive models that predict physician judgments of capacity to consent in mild Alzheimer's disease. *Journal of the American Geriatrics Society, 45*, 458–464.

Marson, D. C., Ingram, K. K., Cody, H. A., & Harrell, L. E. (1995). Assessing the competency of patients with Alzheimer's disease under different legal standards. *Archives of Neurology, 52*, 949–954. doi:10.1001/archneur.1995.00540340029010

McCarron, M. C. (1990). Comment, the right to refuse antipsychotic drugs: Safeguarding the mentally incompetent patient's right to procedural due process. *Marquette Law Review, 73*, 477–512.

McDougall, G. J., Becker, H., Vaughan, P. W., Acee, T. W., & Delville, C. L. (2010). The revised direct assessment of functional status for independent older adults. *Gerontologist, 50*, 363–370. doi:10.1093/geront/gnp139

McKinnon, K., Cournos, F., & Stanley, B. (1989). *Rivers in practice: Clinicians' assessments of patients' decision-making capacity.* Hospital and Community Psychiatry, 40, 1159–1162.

Meisel, A. (2005). Ethics and law: Physician-assisted dying. *Journal of Palliative Medicine, 8*, 609–623. doi:10.1089/jpm.2005.8.609

Melton, G. B., Petrila, J., Poythress, N. G., & Slobogin, C. (2007). *Psychological evaluations for the courts: A handbook for mental health professionals and lawyers* (3rd ed.). New York, NY: Guilford Press.

Mormon Church v. United States, 136 U.S. 1 (1890).

Moser, D. J., Schultz, S. K., Arndt, S., Benjamin, M. L., Fleming, F. W., Brems, C. S., . . . Andreasen, N. C. (2002). Capacity to provide informed consent for participation in schizophrenia and HIV research. *American Journal of Psychiatry, 159*, 1201–1207. doi:10.1176/appi.ajp.159.7.1201

Mossman, D., & Shoemaker, A. N. (2010). Incompetence to maintain a divorce action: When breaking up is odd to do. *St. John's Law Review, 84*, 117–197.

Moye, J., Karel, M. J., Azar, A. R., & Guerra, R. J. (2004). Capacity to consent to treatment: Empirical comparisons of three instruments in older adults with and without dementia. *Gerontologist, 44,* 166–175. doi:10.1093/geront/44.2.166

Moye, J., Wood, S., Edelstein, B., Armesto, J. C., Bower, E. H., Harrison, J. A., & Wood, E. (2007). Clinical evidence in guardianship of older adults is inadequate: Findings from a tri-state study. *Gerontologist, 47,* 604–612. doi:10.1093/geront/47.5.604

Nasreddine, Z. S., Phillips, N. A., Bédirian, V., Charbonneau, S., Whitehead, V., Collin, I., . . . Chertkow, H. (2005). The Montreal Cognitive Assessment (MoCA): A brief screening tool for mild cognitive impairment. *Journal of the American Geriatrics Society, 53,* 695–699. doi:10.1111/j.1532-5415.2005.53221.x

National Conference of Commissioners on Uniform State Laws. (1997). *Uniform Guardianship and Protective Proceedings Act (1997).* Chicago, IL: Author. Retrieved from http://www.azcourts.gov/Portals/83/pdf/UniformProbateCode1997.pdf

Neugebauer, R. (1989). Diagnosis, guardianship, and residential care of the mentally ill in medieval and early modern England. *American Journal of Psychiatry, 146,* 1580–1584.

Palmer, B. W., Dunn, L. B., Appelbaum, P. S., & Jeste, D. V. (2004). Correlates of treatment-related decision-making capacity among middle-aged and older patients with schizophrenia. *Archives of General Psychiatry, 61,* 230–236.

Palmer, B. W., Dunn, L. B., Appelbaum, P. S., Mudaliar, S., Thal, L., Henry, R., . . . Jeste, D. V. (2005). Assessment of capacity to consent to research among older persons with schizophrenia, Alzheimer disease, or diabetes mellitus. *Archives of General Psychiatry, 62,* 726–733. doi:10.1001/archpsyc.62.7.726

Palmer, B. W., Dunn, L. B., Depp, C. A., Eyler, L. T., & Jeste, D. V. (2007). Decisional capacity to consent to research among patients with bipolar disorder: Comparison with schizophrenia patients and healthy subjects. *Journal of Clinical Psychiatry, 68,* 689–696.

Penington v. Thompson, 5 Del. Ch. 328 (Del. Ch. 1880).

Poythress, N., Monahan, J., Bonnie, R., Otto, R. K., & Hoge, S. K. (2002). *Adjudicative competence: The MacArthur Studies.* New York, NY: Kluwer Academic/Plenum. doi:10.1007/978-1-4419-8493-7

Pruchno, R. A., Smyer, M. A., Rose, M. S., & Hartman-Stein, P. E. (1995). Competence of long-term care residents to participate in decisions about their medical care: A brief, objective assessment. *Gerontologist, 35,* 622–629. doi:10.1093/geront/35.5.622

Quinn, M. J. (1996). Commentary—Everyday competencies and guardianship: Refinements and realities. In M. Smyer, K. W. Schaie, & M. B. Kapp (Eds.), *Older adults' decision-making and the law* (pp. 128–141). New York, NY: Springer.

Quinn, M. J., Nerenberg, L., Goldman, E., & Piazza, D. (2010). *Undue influence: Definitions and applications. Final Report to Borchard Foundation Center on Law and Aging.* San Francisco: California Superior Court, County of San Francisco.

Raymont, V., Bingley, W., Buchanan, A., David, A. S., Hayward, P., Wessely, S., & Hotopf, M. (2004). The prevalence and associations of mental incapacity in medical in-patients. *Lancet, 364,* 1421–1427. doi:10.1016/S0140-6736(04)17224-3

Raymont, V., Buchanan, A., David, A. S., Hayward, P., Wessely, S., & Hotopf, M. (2007). The inter-rater reliability of mental capacity assessments. *International Journal of Law and Psychiatry, 30,* 112–117. doi:10.1016/j.ijlp.2005.09.006

Rennie v. Klein, 720 F.2d 266 (3d Cir. 1983).

Rivers v. Katz, 495 N.E. 2d 337 (N.Y., 1986).

Roffe, D., & Roffe, C. (1995). Madness and care in the community: A medieval perspective. *BMJ (Clinical Research Ed.), 311,* 1708–1712. doi:10.1136/bmj.311.7021.1708

Rogers v. Commissioner of Mental Health, 458 N.E. 2d 308 (Mass. 1982).

Roked, F., & Patel, A. (2008). Which aspects of cognitive function are best associated with testamentary capacity in patients with Alzheimer's disease? *International Journal of Geriatric Psychiatry, 23,* 552–553. doi:10.1002/gps.1947

Roof, J. G. (2012). Testamentary capacity and guardianship assessments. *Psychiatric Clinics of North America, 35,* 915–927. doi:10.1016/j.psc.2012.08.011

Roth, M., Huppert, F. A., Mountjoy, C. Q., & Tym, E. (1999). *CAMDEX–R: The Revised Cambridge Examination for Mental Disorders of the Elderly* (2nd ed.). Cambridge, England: Cambridge University Press.

Royall, D. R., Lauterbach, E. C., Cummings, J. L., Reeve, A. Rummans, T. A., Kaufer, D. I., . . . Coffey, C. E. (2002). Executive control function: A review of its promise and challenges for clinical research. *Journal of Neuropsychiatry and Clinical Neurosciences, 14,* 377–405. doi:10.1176/appi.neuropsych.14.4.377

Saks, E. R. (1999). *Research involving persons with mental disorders that may affect decisionmaking capacity.* Rockville, MD: National Bioethics Advisory Commission. Retrieved from http://bioethics.georgetown.edu/nbac/capacity/volumeii.pdf

Saks, E. R. (2002). *Refusing care: Forced treatment and the rights of the mentally ill.* Chicago, IL: University of Chicago Press. doi:10.7208/chicago/9780226733999.001.0001

Searight, H. R. (1992). Assessing patient competence for medical decision making. *American Family Physician, 45,* 751–759.

Shulman, K. I., Cohen, C. A., Kirsh, F. C., Hull, I. M., & Champine, P. R. (2007). Assessment of testamentary capacity and vulnerability to undue influence. *American Journal of Psychiatry, 164,* 722–727. doi:10.1176/appi.ajp.164.5.722

Shulman, K. I., Hull, I. M., & Cohen, C. A. (2003). Testamentary capacity and suicide: An overview of legal and psychiatric issues. *International Journal of Law and Psychiatry, 26,* 403–415. doi:10.1016/S0160-2527(03)00044-X

Shulman, K. I., Peisah, C., Jacoby, R., Heinik, J., & Finkel, S. (2009). Contemporaneous assessment of testamentary capacity. *International Psychogeriatrics, 21,* 433–439. doi:10.1017/S1041610209008874

Skelton, F., Kunik, M. E., Regev, T., & Naik, A. D. (2010). Determining if an older adult can make and execute decisions to live safely at home: A capacity assessment and intervention model. *Archives of Gerontology and Geriatrics, 50,* 300–305. doi:10.1016/j.archger.2009.04.016

Slovenko, R. J. (2004). Civil competency. In R. I. Simon & L. H. Gold (Eds.), *The American Psychiatric Publishing textbook of forensic psychiatry: The clinician's guide* (pp. 205–230). Arlington, VA: American Psychiatric.

Smith, A. (1904). *An inquiry into the nature and causes of the wealth of nations.* London, England: Methuen & Co. (Original work published 1776)

Smith, R. S., & Trzaskoma, S. M. (2007). *Apollodorus' library and Hyginus' Fabulae: Two handbooks of Greek mythology.* Indianapolis, IN: Hackett.

Spar, J. E., Hankin, M., & Stodden, A. B. (1995). Assessing mental capacity and susceptibility to undue influence. *Behavioral Sciences and the Law, 13,* 391–403. doi:10.1002/bsl.2370130307

Spenceley, R. H. W. (2009). *The estate planner's handbook* (3rd ed.). Toronto, Ontario, Canada: CCH Canadian.

Stock, J. S. (1839). *A practical treatise on the law of non compotes mentis, or persons of unsound mind.* New York, NY: Halsted & Voorhies.

Sturman, E. D. (2005). The capacity to consent to treatment and research: A review of standardized assessment tools. *Clinical Psychology Review, 25,* 954–974. doi:10.1016/j.cpr.2005.04.010

Symonds, E. (1980). Mental patients' rights to refuse drugs: Involuntary medication as cruel and unusual punishment. *Hastings Constitutional Law Quarterly, 7,* 701–738.

Triebel, K. L., Martin, R. C., Nabors, L. B., & Marson, D. C. (2009). Medical decision-making capacity in patients with malignant glioma. *Neurology, 73,* 2086–2092. doi:10.1212/WNL.0b013e3181c67bce

Tunzi, M. (2001). Can the patient decide? Evaluating patient capacity in practice. *American Family Physician, 64,* 299–306.

Vollmann, J., Bauer, A., Danker-Hoipfe, H., & Helmchen, H. (2003). Competence of mentally ill patients: A comparative empirical study. *Psychological Medicine, 33,* 1463–1471. doi:10.1017/S0033291703008389

Walsh, A., Brown, B., Kaye, K., & Grigsby, J. (1994). *Mental capacity: Legal and medical aspects of assessment and treatment* (2nd ed.). Colorado Springs, CO: Shepard's/McGraw-Hill.

Watkins, H. G. (2007, November). The right to vote of persons under guardianship—limited or otherwise. *Arizona Attorney, 29,* 34–45.

Willis, S. L., & Marsiske, M. (1993). *Manual for the Everyday Problems Test.* University Park: Pennsylvania State University.

Winick, B. J. (1997). *The right to refuse mental health treatment.* Washington, DC: American Psychological Association. doi:10.1037/10264-000

Index